THE QUR'AN

With a Phrase-by-Phrase
English Translation
6th Edition

Translated by

Ali Quli Qarai

Sixth (Fifth Revised) Edition 2018
Fifth (Fourth Revised) Edition 2018 Fourth
(Third Revised) Edition 2015 Third (Revised)
Edition 2009
Second (Revised) Edition 2005
First Edition 2003

ISBN: 978-1-955725-05-7   Hardcover

ISBN: 978-1-955725-29-3   Paperback

ISBN: 9781955725040 epub

© Ali Quli Qarai, 2018

All rights reserved

Contents

Translator's Preface		vi
Preface to the Fourth Edition		xv
Transliteration of Arabic Words		xvii
Prayer for Recitation on Commencing a Reading of the Qur'ān		xviii

THE QUR'AN

No.	Sūrah Name	Order	Place/Period of Revelation	Page
1	The Opening (al-Fātiḥah)	1	Makkah	1
2	The Heifer (al-Baqarah)	87	Madīnah	2
3	The House of Imran (Āl-i 'Imrān)	89	Madīnah	59
4	Women (al-Nisā')	92	Madīnah	92
5	The Table (al-Mā'idah)	113	Madīnah	127
6	Cattle (al-An'ām)	55	Makkah	152
7	The Elevations (al-A'rāf)	39	Makkah	179
8	The Spoils (al-Anfāl)	88	Madīnah	210
9	Repentance (al-Tawbah)	114	Madīnah	222
10	Jonah (Yūnus)	51	Makkah	245
11	Hūd (Hūd)	52	Makkah	262
12	Joseph (Yūsuf)	53	Makkah	280
13	Thunder (al-Ra'd)	96	Madīnah	297
14	Abraham (Ibrāhīm)	72	Makkah	305
15	Hijr (al-Ḥijr)	54	Makkah	313
16	The Bee (al-Naḥl)	70	Makkah	320
17	The Night Journey (al-Isrā')	50	Makkah	337
18	The Cave (al-Kahf)	69	Makkah	352
19	Mary (Maryam)	44	Makkah	367
20	Ta Ha (Ṭā Hā)	45	Makkah	377
21	The Prophets (al-Anbiyā')	73	Makkah	390
22	The Pilgrimage (al-Ḥajj)	104	Madīnah	401
23	The Faithful (al-Mu'minūn)	74	Makkah	413
24	The Light (al-Nūr)	103	Madīnah	423
25	The Criterion (al-Furqān)	42	Makkah	436
26	The Poets (al-Shu'arā')	47	Makkah	445
27	The Ant (al-Naml)	48	Makkah	458
28	The Story (al-Qaṣaṣ)	49	Makkah	469
29	The Spider (al-'Ankabūt)	85	Makkah	482
30	The Byzantines (al-Rūm)	84	Makkah	492
31	Luqmān (Luqmān)	57	Makkah	500
32	Prostration (al-Sajdah)	75	Makkah	505
33	The Confederates (al-Aḥzāb)	90	Madīnah	509
34	Sheba (Saba')	58	Makkah	522
35	The Originator (al-Fāṭir)	43	Makkah	530
36	Ya Sin (Yā Sīn)	41	Makkah	537

37	The Ranged Ones (*al-Ṣaffāt*)	56	*Makkah*	545
38	Sad (*Ṣād*)	38	*Makkah*	555
39	Throngs (*al-Zumar*)	59	*Makkah*	563
40	The Forgiver (*al-Ghāfir*)	60	*Makkah*	574
41	Elaborated (*Fuṣṣilat*)	61	*Makkah*	586
42	Counsel (*al-Shūrā*)	62	*Makkah*	594
43	Ornaments (*al-Zukhruf*)	63	*Makkah*	602
44	Smoke (*al-Dukhān*)	64	*Makkah*	611
45	Fallen on Knees (*al-Jāthiyah*)	65	*Makkah*	614
46	al-Ahqaf (*al-Aḥqāf*)	66	*Makkah*	619
47	Muḥammad	95	*Madīnah*	625
48	Victory (*al-Fatḥ*)	112	*Madīnah*	630
49	Apartments (*al-Ḥujurāt*)	107	*Madīnah*	636
50	Qaf (*Qāf*)	34	*Makkah*	639
51	The Scatterers (*al-Dhāriyāt*)	67	*Makkah*	643
52	The Mount (*al-Ṭūr*)	76	*Makkah*	647
53	The Star (*al-Najm*)	23	*Makkah*	650
54	The Moon (*al-Qamar*)	37	*Makkah*	654
55	The All-beneficent (*al-Raḥmān*)	97	*Madīnah*	658
56	The Imminent (*al-Wāqiʿah*)	46	*Makkah*	662
57	Iron (*al-Ḥadīd*)	94	*Madīnah*	666
58	The Pleader (*al-Mujādilah*)	106	*Madīnah*	672
59	The Banishment (*al-Ḥashr*)	101	*Madīnah*	676
60	The Woman Tested (*al-Mumtaḥanah*)	91	*Madīnah*	681
61	Ranks (*al-Ṣaff*)	109	*Madīnah*	684
62	Friday (*al-Jumuʿah*)	110	*Madīnah*	687
63	The Hypocrites (*al-Munāfiqūn*)	105	*Madīnah*	688
64	Privation (*al-Taghābun*)	111	*Madīnah*	690
65	Divorce (*al-Ṭalāq*)	99	*Madīnah*	693
66	The Disallowing (*al-Taḥrīm*)	108	*Madīnah*	696
67	Sovereignty (*al-Mulk*)	77	*Makkah*	698
68	The Pen (*al-Qalam*)	3	*Makkah*	701
69	The Besieger (*al-Ḥāqqah*)	78	*Makkah*	705
70	Lofty Stations (*al-Maʿārij*)	79	*Makkah*	707
71	Noah (*Nūḥ*)	71	*Makkah*	710
72	The Jinn (*al-Jinn*)	40	*Makkah*	712
73	Enwrapped (*al-Muzzammil*)	4	*Makkah*	715
74	Shrouded (*al-Muddaththir*)	5	*Makkah*	717
75	Resurrection (*al-Qiyāmah*)	31	*Makkah*	720
76	The Human Being (*al-Insān*)	98	*Madīnah*	722
77	The Emissaries (*al-Mursalāt*)	33	*Makkah*	724
78	The Tiding (*al-Nabaʾ*)	80	*Makkah*	727
79	The Wresters (*al-Nāziʿāt*)	81	*Makkah*	729
80	He Frowned (*ʿAbasa*)	24	*Makkah*	731
81	The Winding Up (*al-Takwīr*)	7	*Makkah*	732
82	The Rending (*al-Infiṭār*)	82	*Makkah*	734
83	The Defrauders (*al-Muṭaffifīn*)	86	*Madīnah*	735
84	The Splitting (*al-Inshiqāq*)	83	*Makkah*	737

85	The Houses (*al-Burūj*)	27	*Makkah*	738
86	The Nightly Visitor (*al-Ṭāriq*)	36	*Makkah*	739
87	The Most Exalted (*al-Aʿlā*)	8	*Makkah*	740
88	The Enveloper (*al-Ghāshiyah*)	68	*Makkah*	741
89	The Dawn (*al-Fajr*)	10	*Makkah*	742
90	The Town (*al-Balad*)	35	*Makkah*	744
91	The Sun (*al-Shams*)	26	*Makkah*	745
92	The Night (*al-Layl*)	9	*Makkah*	746
93	Morning Brightness (*al-Ḍuḥā*)	11	*Makkah*	747
94	Opening (*al-Sharḥ*)	12	*Makkah*	747
95	The Fig (*al-Tīn*)	28	*Makkah*	748
96	The Clinging Tissue (*al-ʿAlaq*)	2	*Makkah*	748
97	The Ordainment (*al-Qadr*)	25	*Makkah*	749
98	The Proof (*al-Bayyinah*)	100	*Madīnah*	750
99	The Quake (*al-Zalzalah*)	93	*Madīnah*	751
100	The Chargers (*al-ʿĀdiyāt*)	14	*Makkah*	751
101	The Catastrophe (*al-Qāriʿah*)	30	*Makkah*	752
102	Rivalry (*al-Takāthur*)	16	*Makkah*	752
103	Time (al-ʿAṣr)	13	*Makkah*	753
104	The Scandal-monger (*al-Humazah*)	32	*Makkah*	753
105	The Elephant (*al-Fīl*)	19	*Makkah*	754
106	Quraysh (*Quraysh*)	29	*Makkah*	754
107	Vital Aid (*al-Māʿūn*)	17	*Makkah*	755
108	Abundance (*al-Kawthar*)	15	*Makkah*	755
109	The Faithless (*al-Kāfirūn*)	18	*Makkah*	755
110	Help (*al-Naṣr*)	102	*Madīnah*	756
111	Palm Fibre (*al-Masad*)	6	*Makkah*	756
112	Pure Monotheism (*al-Ikhlāṣ*)	22	*Makkah*	757
113	Daybreak (*al-Falaq*)	20	*Makkah*	757
114	Humans (*al-Nās*)	21	*Makkah*	757

Sources Consulted	756
Index of Subjects, Names and Terms	758

(The chronological order and place of revelation of the *sūrahs* given here is based on a close tally of parallel sequences found in more than a score of various versions of related reports narrated by Saʿīd b. Musayyab, from Imam ʿAlī, and from Ibn ʿAbbās by ʿAṭā, Abū Ṣāliḥ, ʿIkrimah and Ḥasan al-Baṣrī, Kurayb (or Abū Kurayb), Zuhrī, Ḍaḥḥāk, Jābir b. Zayd, Mujāhid and Ḥusayn b. Wāqid, and cited by Muqātil b. Sulaymān, Yaʿqūbī, Ibn al-Ḍurays, Nayshābūrī, ʿĀṣimī, Ibn al-Nadīm, Abū ʿAmr al-Dānī, Bayhaqī, Wāḥdī, Ḥaskānī, Ibn al-ʿArabī, Ṭabrisī, Shahristānī, Zarkashī, and Suyūṭī in their works. However, a close scrutiny suggests that the order given above presents only an approximate picture of the actual chronological order.)

Translator's Preface

The Qur'ān as such does not need an introduction. Rather it is *we*, human beings, who need the Qur'ān to be introduced to ourselves, to be provided with an initial knowledge of as to *who* we are, *what* we are, *whence* we come, *where* we stand, and *whither* we are bound. Without such a knowledge, we are lost, living as losers regardless of whatever we may imagine to be our achievements. The Qur'ān is, in its own words, "light,"[1] which means that it is self-manifesting, with no need of an external agent to be made manifest; other things need light to become visible and manifest. *With it Allah guides those who pursue His pleasure to the ways of peace, and brings them out from darkness into light by His will, and guides them to a straight path* (5:16).

In this respect it is like its Author and Speaker, who is the *Light of the heavens and the earth* (24:35). Existence being light, all contingent beings stand in need of the Source of Being for their existence, whereas the Source itself is self-subsisting and self-manifesting. All existents exist through Allah and are known through Him, not that He is known through them.

Also, like the Qur'ān and its Author, its communicator, the Seal of the Prophets (ṣ), is a source of light,[2] who brings people out of the darkness of ignorance and ingratitude, unfaith and unreason, into the blessed light of knowledge, faith, gratitude and intellect: *[This is] a Book We have sent down to you that you may bring mankind out from darkness into light, by the command of their Lord, to the path of the All-mighty, the All-laudable* (14:1).

Of course, the Qur'ān is not an exception among revealed scriptures in that it is a source of light and guidance. So were the Torah and the Gospel, scriptures that were given to Moses[3] and Jesus.[4] All scriptures of Divine origin that were brought by various prophets were a source of light and guidance.[5] Nor is the Prophet of Islam (ṣ) an exception among God-sent emissaries.[6] He (ṣ) is the ultimate link in a long chain of prophetic missions whose history began with Adam himself.

Nevertheless, the Qur'ān is a unique document, not only in the realm of religious literature but also in the domain of language. It is unique among revealed scriptures not only because it is the latest and the last, and, therefore, the most up-to-date of them, but also because it is the only one which has been preserved in the original form that it was revealed to its prophet. Therefore, it serves as the ultimate criterion and standard against which the contents of all other religious literature, irrespective of their origin, are to be evaluated and judged. It is a work of inimitable literary beauty and excellence. But unlike other literary works produced by inspired human genius, such as the literary masterpieces in prose and poetry in various languages of the world whose charm and appeal are limited to particular cultures and periods beyond which they have little general relevance or appeal, the language and discourse of the Qur'ān and their relevance are universal and everlasting.

---

[1] The Qur'ān, 4:174; 5:15; 7:157; 42:52; 64:8.
[2] *O Prophet! Indeed We have sent you as a witness, as a bearer of good news and as a warner and as a summoner to Allah by His permission, and as a radiant lamp.* (33:45-46)
[3] 5:44; 6:91; 37:117.
[4] 5:46.
[5] 3:184; 35:25.
[6] *Say, 'I am not a novelty among the apostles....'* (46:9)

This is not meant to belittle human genius and achievement. After all, the human being is himself one of the greatest masterpieces of Divine creativity, and, at his best, "God's vicegerent on the earth," and his capacities are literally boundless.

The Prophet (ṣ) himself was the most eloquent of speakers, whose eloquence has never been equalled by any poet or sage. An Apostle *sent to the unlettered to recite to them His signs, to purify them, and to teach them the Book and wisdom*, even the most learned confess to be "unlettered" before him. The Prophet (ṣ) surpassed all Arabs in eloquence. Yet the beauty and splendour of the Qur'ān far exceeds even the best specimens of the sayings of the Seal of the Prophets (ṣ). The stupendous miracle of the Qur'ān has to be *experienced* in order to be acknowledged as such. The sun, so it is said, is its own evidence. Of course, this applies only to those who can see.

Human speech is a human creation, whereas, the Qur'ān is literally a Divine discourse. No wonder that it is inimitable, for even the humblest of living beings in the realm of Divine creation surpasses all human contrivance: *O mankind! Listen to a parable that is being drawn: indeed those whom you invoke besides Allah will never create even a fly, even if they all rallied for it!* (22:73). No wonder, then, that the Qur'ān should be such as described by its own words: *Say, 'Should all humans and jinn rally to bring the like of this Qur'ān, they will not bring the like of it, even if they assisted one another* (17:88).

Every moment of our life, day and night, we are immersed in God's bounteous gifts: *If you enumerate Allah's blessings, you will not be able to count them* (14:34). Yet the Qur'ān is one of the greatest of all gifts to humanity. It is the living Book of life, which addresses itself to "the living": *This is just a reminder and a manifest Qur'ān, so that anyone who is alive may be warned* (36:69-70). Those who are alive to the summons of their being are also alive to its call, receptive to its good news and warnings, a summons that is perpetual, answering which brings further life, a life on the top of life: *O you who have faith! Answer Allah and the Apostle when he summons you to that which will give you life* (8:22). *Whoever acts righteously, [whether] male or female, should he be faithful, We shall revive him with a good life and pay them their reward by the best of what they used to do* (16:97).

This promise of a new life is, of course, fulfilled in this very life for those who answer its summons, but there is also the promise of a greater and more splendid life in the Hereafter, in comparison with which the life of this world is no more than diversion and play: *The life of this world is nothing but diversion and play, while the abode of the Hereafter is indeed Life, had they known!* (29:64). There is no death for the pupils of the Qur'ān; for them every 'death' is a birth into a higher realm of existence and entry into a world more vast and expansive than the earlier one: *Take the lead towards forgiveness from your Lord and a paradise as vast as the heavens and the earth, prepared for those who have faith in Allah and His apostles. That is Allah's grace, which He grants to whomever He wishes, and Allah is dispenser of a great grace* (57:21).

This call to a higher life is a summons to a higher knowledge and a higher effort: *Allah will raise those of you who have faith and those who have been given knowledge in rank, and Allah is well aware of what you do* (58:11). *Say, 'Are those who know equal to those who do not know?'* (39:9). It preaches that one's higher efforts and endeavours are the ultimate fruits of one's life: *Nothing belongs to man except what he strives for* (53:39). The life of the Hereafter is only a 'celestial' counterpart of the terrestrial life we live here.

Nothing is more important for man than the knowledge of the very Source of reality. Any knowledge that is not informed with this awareness is just a kind of ignorance. All effort and endeavour that does not derive from this knowledge is ultimately fruitless and fated to end in futility and failure.[1] The Qur'ān is the most reliable source of this knowledge and the best guide for human effort and endeavour. It teaches that the Source of being is also the Source of guidance.

To a humanity wailing under the burden of injustice, the Qur'ān offers a creed of deliverance: *Certainly We sent Our apostles with manifest signs, and We sent down with them the Book and the Balance, so that mankind may maintain justice; and We sent down iron, in which there is a great might and uses for mankind, and so that Allah may know those who help Him and His apostles in [their] absence* (57:25).

To human beings lacking a sense of divinely ordained purpose and direction in life, like seafarers on an uncharted sea without compass or guidance, the Qur'ān offers a delivering vision of life and human destiny, helping them rediscover their destiny and dignity as human beings and recover their true orientation as wayfarers on the Godward path of infinite perfection: *Certainly, We have honoured the Children of Adam, and carried them over land and sea, and provided them with all the good things, and given them advantage over many of those We have created with a complete preference* (17:70).

From the viewpoint of the Qur'ān, establishment and maintenance of justice is one of the chief purposes of all religions and revealed scriptures. This is a mission that has always been neglected by mankind, a neglect that has allowed injustice to assume almost cosmic proportions in the present-day world. Being the last of God-sent scriptures, there is no wonder then that it should lay so much stress upon justice, an emphasis unequalled by any other book, sacred or secular.

The Qur'ān preaches an order based on justice. There is no injustice in the realm of creation; it is man who engenders injustice by his wrongdoing, by yielding to misdirected motives in violation of the Divine norms: *Indeed Allah does not wrong people in the least; rather it is people who wrong themselves* (10:44). However, justice remains merely a mirage in a world where inner purity is neglected and where inner spiritual disorder rules unheeded. The call of the Qur'ān is one of constant struggle, purification and *jihād*, inward and outward, against the inner satanic forces of disoriented desires and their external manifestations in the form of social and political agents and institutions of corruption. It views human history as a continuous struggle against unfaith and untruth, injustice and corruption, and holds out the promise of the ultimate victory of righteousness: *'Indeed My righteous servants shall inherit the earth'* (21:105).

If worldly life is short and its enjoyments and sufferings transitory for all mortals, what is a better life than a life spent for the purpose approved by the very Source of life? If death is inevitable for every mortal, tyrant or victim, faithful or faithless, well-provided or deprived, powerful or powerless, what is a better 'death' than one which is the threshold of an everlasting life of fulfillment?

All religions have a high regard for martyrdom, but no scripture describes so vividly the higher life attained by the martyrs, thus giving martyrdom its true appeal: *Do not suppose those who were slain in the way of Allah to be dead; rather they are living and provided for near their Lord, exulting in what Allah has given them out of His grace, and rejoicing for those who have not yet joined them from*

---

[1] *Say, 'Shall we inform you about the biggest losers in regard to works? Those whose endeavour goes awry in the life of the world, while they suppose they are doing good.' They are the ones who deny the signs of their Lord and the encounter with Him. So their works have failed. On the Day of Resurrection We will not set for them any weight.* (18:103-105)

[those left] behind them that they will have no fear, nor will they grieve. They rejoice in Allah's blessing and grace, and that Allah does not waste the reward of the faithful (3:169-171).

To a youth languishing on the plane of animal existence, captive of materialistic values and rendered spiritually impotent by sensual pursuits and indifferent to struggle against oppression and injustice, the Qur'ān suggests a spiritual diet and a programme of spiritual rehabilitation, self-purification, and *jihād*. To a world bewildered by the din of the communication media orchestrated by Satanic forces bent on the deception of thinking minds, the Qur'ān gives *a light to walk by*, enabling the faithful human being to see facts through the apparently impenetrable curtains of deceit and disinformation: *O you who have faith! Be wary of Allah and have faith in His Apostle. He will grant you a double share of His mercy and give you a light to walk by, and forgive you* (57:28).

For communities which have lost their moral and spiritual bearings, the Qur'ān holds out the great promise of restoration of their spiritual and moral equilibrium through its high spirituality and ethics.

About this Translation:

The Qur'ān is, paradoxically, both untranslatable and 'translation-friendly.' It is a celestial symphony with splendid rhythms and rhymes whose melodious grandeur is rarely captured fully even by the best of the grand masters of *qirā'ah*, the art of Qur'ānic recitation. As such and as a text of matchless literary elegance and eloquence, no translation can ever hope to capture even fleeting flashes of its splendour. At the same time, despite its wonderful aesthetic complexities, the Qur'ānic text is astonishingly clear, simple and straightforward in its style. The simplicity comes firstly from the economy and simplicity of Qur'ānic vocabulary and diction.[1] A second factor is its strikingly uniform phraseology. A third factor is its characteristic syntactical structure made up either of short sentences, as in the brief Makkan *sūrah*s placed at the end of the Book, or of longer sentences wherein clauses and phrases are arranged in a serial logical sequential order. Were it not for this last characteristic of the Qur'ānic text, the approach adopted in the present translation would not have been possible.

The translation of a literary text is expected to meet the following four requirements: it should (1) be able to convey the meanings of the source text in an intelligible manner; (2) have a natural and easy form of expression; (3) convey the spirit and the manner of the original; (4) produce a similar response in the reader. While a translation of the Qur'ān can be expected to succeed in meeting the first two of these requirements in varying degrees, depending on the translator's competence, there appear to be insurmountable barriers in the way of meeting, even partially, the last two requirements.

First, there are visible limits to the extent the translator can convey fully the meanings of the source text. Here the primary problem encountered by the translator is absence in the English language of semantically equivalent terms for certain Arabic words, some of which play a key role in the Qur'ānic message, such as *taqwā, kufr, īmān, shirk, ḥaqq, bāṭil, ma'rūf, munkar, fitnah, ghayb, sunnah, tawbah, walī,* and *ẓulm*. In such cases, the translator has to suffice with approximations which fall short of conveying the full semantic scope and richness of the original terms, giving a truncated or lopsided sense to the message communicated.[2]

---

[1] A comparison between the diction of the Arabic poetry of the period and that of the Qur'ān will make this fact evident.

[2] There are other terms which pose problems in varying degrees, such as *amr, āyah, 'azm, baghy, barā'ah, ba's, birr, ḍalālah, dhanb, dhikr, faḍl, faḥshā', fasād, fisq, fujūr, ghāwī, ḥanīf, haraj, ḥasanah, ḥarām, hawā, ḥayā', hidāyah, ḥijāb, ḥikmah, ḥisāb, ḥukm, iḥsān, is-*

As to the second requirement, that the translation have an easy and natural form of expression, that depends mainly on the translator's understanding of the nature, meaning and purpose of translation and his approach.

Translations in general have been divided into two broad categories, (1) translations which aim at formal equivalence, and the so-called (2) dynamic (or functional) equivalence translations. Formal equivalence translations attempt to reproduce the formal elements of the source text including grammatical units, seek consistency of word usage, and reproduce meanings in terms of the source context. That is, they do not normally attempt to make adjustments in idiom, but rather try to reproduce such expressions more or less literally, so that the reader may be able to perceive something of the way in which the original document employed local cultural elements to convey meanings. A dynamic-equivalence translation has been defined as "the closest natural equivalent to the source language message."[1]

The second approach has an obvious advantage over the first one in that it is better suited to meet the very goal of discourse, which is communication. But it assumes that the translator can fully comprehend and fathom the intents and meanings of the original source text and that the only task that remains for him to accomplish is to find and produce the closest natural equivalent of the source language message. Such an assumption is not always warranted and it takes a simplistic view of the nature and character of discourse and meaning. There are often cases where, firstly, the *real* intent and meaning of the source text may be either indeterminate or it may elude the translator, and, secondly, at times there may be simply no easy and natural equivalent in the target language. However, in many cases the requirement of an easy and natural form of expression obliges the translator to make adjustments of various kinds to produce a stylistically satisfactory equivalent.

The aware reader of translated literary texts is conscious of the approximations or rather the inherent inadequacies involved in the process of translation. This inadequacy is quite evident in the case of Qur'ān translations. The best purpose a translation may serve is as a means of access to the Arabic Qur'ān itself.

Interlinear translations abound in Persian and Urdu. In fact, the interlinear approach has been the dominant practice in translations of the Qur'ān published in these languages during the last two hundred years. Recent translations in Persian show a trend away from this practice, while it is still dominant in Urdu. As these languages are written from right to left like Arabic, the interlinear format—with the Arabic text and its translation appearing in alternating lines—has been a convenient and popular way of presenting the meanings of the Qur'ānic text. This format has been very helpful for readers who do not read the Arabic Qur'ān merely for the sake of the *thawāb* of reciting its text, but are also eager to obtain the additional and higher benefit of understanding its meanings and reflecting

lām, ikhlāṣ, 'iṣyān, istikbār, isrāf, 'izzah, jahl, jannah, karīm, khabīth, khashyah, mala', mann, mujrim, munīb, muṭaffif, nabī, nifāq, ni'mah, qiyām, raḥmah, rijs, rushd, ṣalāḥ, sayyi'ah, takdhīb, taskhīr, ṭayyib, ṭughyān, ummah, wakīl, zaygh. Their exact and complete meanings should be sought and elicited from the contexts in which they are employed in the Arabic text. Moreover, there are some common words, such as *abb* (father), *akhkh* (brother), and *ukht* (sister), which have a semantic field different from that of the corresponding terms in English. *Abb* may refer to an uncle (as with reference to Ishmael in 2:133, and also in 6:74, 9:114; 19:42-44, 26:69-70 with reference to Āzar) or an ancestor, *akhkh* may at times mean a compatriot (as in 7:65, 7:73, 7:85 with reference to the prophets Hūd, Ṣāliḥ and Shu'ayb), and *ukht* may refer to a woman's clan or lineage (as in 19:28 with reference to Mary). In these and similar cases, I have retained the Qur'ānic diction, leaving determination of the meaning to the commentaries.

[1] Nida, Eugene A., *Toward a Science of Translating*, pp. 165-166.

upon its verses. There are many Persian- and Urdu-speaking Muslims who have quite an impressive working grasp of the meanings of the Qur'ān without having undergone any formal training in Arabic grammar and without possessing any extensive vocabulary.

Some of these interlinear translations, especially the older versions, are word-for-word renderings. They are in fact dictionaries of the Qur'ān in that they mention the meaning of each Arabic word and phrase in the line below. Although useful as dictionaries, they often fail to make the meanings of the Qur'ānic text intelligible, as the prose of the translated text turns out to be awkward, unnatural and at times inscrutable.

An interlinear English translation of the Qur'ān, similar to those in Urdu and Persian, is obviously of little benefit, as the two languages are written in opposite directions. The phrase-for-phrase approach adopted in this translation is intended to bring some of the advantage of the interlinear translations to English-speaking readers of the Holy Qur'ān. "Mirror-paraphrasing" is a new approach to translation of sacred Islamic texts, mainly the Qur'ān and *ḥadīth*. In this approach, the translation of the source text develops phrase by phrase, with the translation appearing opposite the corresponding phrase in Arabic. Each phrase in the target or receptor language *mirrors* the semantic import of the phrase in the source text.

At first when such an approach was suggested to my mind, it was not at all clear whether it would be feasible. It seemed that it would result in an unnatural and warped style. But as I worked through the translation, it was a surprise to find that it did seem to work (with few exceptions, such as in verse 2:105, where the verb *yawaddu* comes at the beginning of the sentence). In any case, the results were not as dismal as might be expected. However, one had to deal with two constant constraints, firstly, of having to cover the complete meaning of each phrase of the source text in a corresponding phrase of the target text, and, secondly, of connecting the successive phrases in such a manner as to generate, so far as possible, a fluent, clear, intelligible, natural and stylistically acceptable prose.

The utility of such an approach will be evident to the reader who wants to understand the Arabic text by referring to the translation of each phrase and verse. All that he needs for following the meaning of the Arabic text of the Qur'ān is an elementary knowledge of Arabic, which means an elemental knowledge of Arabic vocabulary and morphology. However, a reader who already possesses such an elementary knowledge of Arabic will not find much difficulty in following the Arabic text with the help of the translation provided here. After several readings, it is hoped, the reader will be able to follow the Arabic without needing to refer to the translation.

The main features of the method and approach followed in this translation may be described as follows:

1. As my principal aim was to provide a translation affording direct access to the Arabic Qur'ān, I have tried, so far as possible, to maintain a formal equivalence between the phrases and clauses of the source and the target text, but I have not hesitated to make adjustments when required by the need for intelligibility, clarity and naturalness of expression, so far as permitted by the constraint imposed by the method of "mirror-paraphrasing." These adjustments are of various kinds and it is not possible to describe all of them here. They involve: making grammatical changes, such as those of tense, aspect, voice, person and number; substitution of nouns by verbs and vice versa;[1]

---

[1] E.g., *We delivered those who had faith and were Godwary.* (27:53)

making obligatory omissions[1] and additions; and making explicit what is implicit in the source text.[2] At times they involve adjustments of idiom and syntactical changes. The reader should be aware about the presence of these changes when collating the Arabic text with the translation.

2. Translation has been carried out according to what appeared to be the most probable among the interpretations mentioned by the commentators. Occasionally I have mentioned alternate interpretations in the footnotes when they appeared to be significant. Throughout the course of this translation extensive reference was made to various classical commentaries of the Qur'ān, such as those of Ṭabarī, Rāzī, Zamakhsharī, and Suyūṭī among Sunnī works, and Ṭabāṭabā'ī's *al-Mīzān*, Ṭabrisī's *Majmaʿ al-Bayān*, and Baḥrānī's *Tafsīr al-Burhān* among Shī'ī works. Some of the other works consulted are mentioned in the bibliography given in the appendices.

Exegetical traditions of the Imams of the Prophet's family have been given special attention due to their unparalleled importance for Qur'ānic hermeneutics. Their importance and weight will be evident to anyone who undertakes an unbiased study of their traditions and teachings. In fact, a large part of the early Sunnī hermeneutic tradition, as represented by Ibn ʿAbbās, his pupils and the succeeding generations of commentators, also derives from Imam ʿAlī b. Abī Ṭālib, with whom Ibn ʿAbbās was closely associated and from whom he had acquired his Qur'ānic learning, being a boy in his early teens at the time of the Prophet's demise.

3. The treatment of Qur'ānic idioms is an important part of the policy followed in translation. Broadly speaking, they fall into three categories. There are some Arabic idioms which though unfamiliar to the English-speaking audience are not difficult to understand when translated literally. These have been rendered literally. Examples are:

نَبَذَ فَرِيقٌ مِنَ ٱلَّذِينَ أُوتُوا۟ ٱلْكِتَٰبَ كِتَٰبَ ٱللَّهِ وَرَآءَ ظُهُورِهِمْ

a part of those who were given the Book cast the Book of Allah behind their backs.[3] *(2:101);*

أَلَآ إِنَّهُمْ يَثْنُونَ صُدُورَهُمْ لِيَسْتَخْفُوا۟ مِنْهُ

Behold, they fold up their breasts to hide [their secret feelings] from him[4] *(11:5);*

ٱشْدُدْ بِهِۦٓ أَزْرِى

Strengthen my back through him[5] *(20:31);*

وَلَا تُصَعِّرْ خَدَّكَ لِلنَّاسِ

Do not turn your cheek disdainfully from the people (31:18);

تَتَجَافَىٰ جُنُوبُهُمْ عَنِ ٱلْمَضَاجِعِ

their sides vacate their beds (32:16);

حَتَّىٰ تَضَعَ ٱلْحَرْبُ أَوْزَارَهَا

till the war lays down its burdens (47:4).

Some idioms are unintelligible when translated literally. These have to be paraphrased appropriately in order to be understood. Examples are:

وَتَوَدُّونَ أَنَّ غَيْرَ ذَاتِ ٱلشَّوْكَةِ تَكُونُ لَكُمْ

you were eager that it should be the one that was unarmed[6] *(8:7);*

فَرَدُّوٓا۟ أَيْدِيَهُمْ فِىٓ أَفْوَٰهِهِمْ

but they did not respond to them[7] *(14:9);*

فَضَرَبْنَا عَلَىٰٓ ءَاذَانِهِمْ فِى ٱلْكَهْفِ سِنِينَ عَدَدًا

so We put them to sleep[8] *in the Cave for several years (18:11);*

وَنَحْشُرُ ٱلْمُجْرِمِينَ يَوْمَئِذٍ زُرْقًا

on that day We shall muster the guilty with blind eyes[9] *(20:102);*

---

[1] E.g., *whether you advise us or not.* (26:136)
[2] E.g., *Everyone of them will return to Us.* (21:93)
[3] The same idiom occurs several times in the Bible (1Kings 14:9, Isaiah 38:17, Ezekiel 23:35, and Nehemiah 9:26).
[4] That is, to conceal one's spite within one's heart.
[5] That is, reinforce my strength through him.
[6] Lit., 'one that was free of thorns.' That is, one which was unarmed and, therefore, easy to defeat.
[7] Lit., 'they thrust their hands into their mouths.'
[8] Lit., 'We struck on their ears.'
[9] Lit., 'with blued eyes.'

Translator's Preface

قُرَّتُ عَيْنٍ لِّى وَلَكَ

a [source of] comfort to me and you [1] (28:9);

وَمَن يُسْلِمْ وَجْهَهُ إِلَى ٱللَّهِ

Whoever surrenders his heart to Allah [2] (31:22);

وَتُقَطِّعُوٓا۟ أَرْحَامَكُمْ

and ill-treat your blood relations [3] (47:22);

وَلَا يَأْتِينَ بِبُهْتَـٰنٍ يَفْتَرِينَهُۥ بَيْنَ أَيْدِيهِنَّ وَأَرْجُلِهِنَّ

nor produce a lie they may have hatched between their hands and feet, [4] (60:12);

يَوْمَ يُكْشَفُ عَن سَاقٍ

—the day when the catastrophe occurs [5] (68:42).

In certain cases it may be possible to substitute an English idiom, as in the following:

فَإِنَّ ذَٰلِكَ مِنْ عَزْمِ ٱلْأُمُورِ

that is indeed the steadiest of courses [6] (3:186);

نُوَلِّهِۦ مَا تَوَلَّىٰ

We shall abandon him to his devices [7] (4:115);

إِنَّ قَوْمِى ٱتَّخَذُوا۟ هَـٰذَا ٱلْقُرْءَانَ مَهْجُورًا

Indeed my people consigned this Qur'ān to oblivion [8] (25:30);

فَأَبَىٰٓ أَكْثَرُ ٱلنَّاسِ إِلَّا كُفُورًا

But most people are only intent on ingratitude [9] (25:50);

فَسَوْفَ يَكُونُ لِزَامًۢا

so that will continue to haunt you; or (and soon it will be inextricable) [10] (25:77);

قَبْلَ أَن يَرْتَدَّ إِلَيْكَ طَرْفُكَ

in the twinkling of an eye [11] (27:40);

فَلَا تَذْهَبْ نَفْسُكَ عَلَيْهِمْ حَسَرَٰتٍ

so do not fret yourself to death regretting for them [12] (35:8);

كُلُوا۟ وَٱشْرَبُوا۟ هَنِيٓـًٔۢا

enjoy your food and drink [13] (52:19).

4. The translation is based on Ḥafṣ' version of the reading of 'Āṣim, which is the most popular of the readings of the Holy Qur'ān throughout the Muslim world. Some of the alternate readings, where they appeared significant to this translator, have been noted in the footnotes with their translation.

5. Instances of ellipsis in the Qur'ān—which in the context of English means "omission of a word or phrase necessary for a complete syntactical construction but not necessary for understanding"—often go beyond such a description and are not always so evident. These have been indicated in the footnotes.

6. Cross references have been mentioned under verses in some cases, but a relatively extensive index of subjects, names and terms has been placed in the appendix. Entries which are not mentioned expressly in the text but involve an implicit reference, as mentioned in commentaries and exegetical traditions, are marked with an asterisk.

As the works consulted for preparing the index[14] had made use of copies of the

---

[1] Lit., 'a refreshment of the eye to me and you.'
[2] Lit., 'submits his face toward Allah.'
[3] Lit., 'sever your wombs (or ties of kinship).'
[4] Lit., 'nor bring any slander which they had forged themselves between their hands and their feet.'
[5] Lit., 'the day that the shin shall be laid bare,' or 'the day the shank shall be uncovered.'
[6] Mir Ahmed Ali: 'that is a result of firm determination of affairs.'
[7] Lit., 'We will turn him to that to which he has himself turned.'
[8] Lit., 'my people have taken this Qur'ān as a forsaken thing.'
[9] Pickthall: 'but most of mankind begrudge aught save ingratitude.'
[10] Lit., 'so it will be inseparable (or ineluctable).'
[11] Pickthall: 'before thy gaze returneth unto thee.'
[12] Mir Ahmed Ali: 'so let not thy self go (in vain) in grief for them.'
[13] Pickthall: 'Eat and drink in health [(as reward) for what ye used to do].'
[14] These are: (1) K. Fani and B. Khorramshahi, Farhang-e Mawḍū'ī-ye Qur'ān-e Majīd (A Subject Index to the Glorious Qur'ān), Tehran: Intishārāt-e al-Hudā, 1369 H. Sh., 2nd impression; (2) Muḥammad Fāris Barakāt, al-Jāmi' li Mawāḍi' Āyāt al-Qur'ān al-Karīm, Qum: Dār al-Hijrah, 1404 H.; (3) al-Sayyid Sharaf al-Dīn 'Alī al-Ḥusaynī al-Astarābādī al-Gharawī, Ta'wīl al-Āyāt al-Ẓāhirah fī Faḍā'il al-'Itrat al-Ṭāhirah, Qum: Mu'assasat al-Nashr al-Islāmī

Qur'ān with different systems of numbering the verses, there might be a discrepancy of one or two between the number of a verse as given in the index and its corresponding number in the Arabic text.

The verses are numbered in accordance with the now most prevalent system followed by the so-called Madīnah codex, despite its serious defect of excluding from the count the *Basmalah*, which is the first verse of every *sūrah* excepting Sūrat al-Tawbah, the ninth *sūrah*. The *Basmalah* at the head of the 113 *sūrah*s is regarded as part of the Qur'ān by many Sunnī authorities and unanimously so by the Shī'ah.

I am grateful to the Centre for Translation of the Holy Qur'ān for entrusting me with the task of working on the English translation of the Qur'ān, in particular to its Director, Ḥujjatulislām Muḥammad Naqdī, for his unflagging support and assistance. During the course of my work I have benefited greatly from the generous encouragement and assistance provided by Dr Muḥammad Legenhausen, who patiently read the entire manuscript and suggested useful changes and corrections. His suggestions have been very helpful in formulating the policy to be followed in this translation.

My thanks are also due to Brother Shujā' 'Alī Mīrzā, who has read the entire manuscript and with his suggestions and corrections contributed to the soundness of the final manuscript. However, the responsibility is entirely mine for any lapses and errors that may have remained, and I humbly request the honoured readers to convey their remarks and suggestions by corresponding on the e-mail address provided below.

I am most grateful to my friend Muḥammad Riḍā Parvez for procuring for the Centre the needed software for generating the Arabic text.[1] My thanks are also due to brothers Mahdī Ṣayf and Mahdī Allāhyārī of the Centre for their assistance in type work and providing the graphics, and to my sons, Sayyid Muḥammad Riḍā and Sayyid Ḥasan Riḍā, for their assistance in preparing the subject index. I am also grateful to Sayyid Muḥammad Riḍā for making a thorough check of the Arabic text in the final print of the manuscript.

It has been my prayer to Allah to divest my motives of all traces of the desire for worldly gain, and to make His good pleasure the sole goal of my intentions and efforts. With the hope that this effort has been made for the sake of His pleasure—a hope that is not altogether free from trepidation—I dedicate the reward for it to the noble spirit of my late eldest sister, Martyr Sayyidah Mahliqā Qarā'ī, and to the spirits of more than 290 innocent souls aboard the Iranian passenger Airbus plane (Iran Air Flight 655), shot down in Iranian waters in the Persian Gulf on July 3, 1988 by the U.S. warship, the Vincennes.

Ali Quli Qarai
Email: altawhid@gmail.com

---

al-Ṭābi'ah li Jamā'at al-Mudarrisīn, 3rd impression, 1421 H. Sh.

[1] The Arabic text used in the present edition comes from a different source.

Preface to the Fourth Edition

In my preface to the first edition, I had written that the Qur'ān as such does not need an introduction. That was, of course, a hyperbole aimed to make a certain point. In fact, a serious reader of the Qur'ān, in addition to some background in the early history of Islam, needs constant assistance while reading in order to acquire an adequate grasp of its contents and to avoid misunderstanding many passages.

Probably, no other sacred book is as demanding as the Qur'ān with respect to the prerequisites for an adequate understanding of a substantial part of its contents. As most readers are unable to invest sufficient time and effort for its understanding, it remains—notwithstanding the clarity of the text itself—probably also the most misunderstood of scriptures among Muslims and non-Muslim alike.

The problem largely arises due to the common reader's unawareness of relevant context. As many passages of the Qur'ān are embedded in their historical settings, the unaware reader is sometimes like one reading a century-old editorial of a newspaper without any clear idea of its historical context. The message carried may not be time-bound, but a correct interpretation can only be possible in the light of the historical context.

Knowledge of the Prophet's *sīrah*, or the 23-year history of his mission, is certainly necessary to be able to place the various Qur'ānic texts—especially the Madanī *sūrahs*, but also many pertaining to the Makkan period—in their original setting. This is particularly difficult in view of the fact that the *sūrahs* do not follow a chronological order in the existing arrangement, and neither most copies of the Arabic Qur'ān nor most translations—including the present one—carry sufficient preparatory material aimed to equip the reader with an overall view of the original context, related events and other accompanying referents, granting that there may be significant evidence within some *sūrahs* to guide someone with an in-depth knowledge of the *sīrah* to make an educated guess of the settings.

A related problem, among several crucial to understanding, lies in interpreting the actual referents of certain nouns preceded by the definite article 'the.'[1]

Another similar issue relates to pronouns.[2] A careful, critical study of reliable commentaries may not help clarify every ambiguity, but is essential for an adequate

---

[1] As in *al-nās, al-mu'minūn, al-ṣāliḥūn, al-ṣādiqūn, al-kāfirūn, al-mushrikūn, al-munāfiqūn, al-Yahūd, al-Naṣārā*, etc. These terms may refer, respectively, either to 'people' (or mankind) in general, to persons who are faithful, righteous, truthful, faithless, idolaters, Jews or Christians in general, or to *specific* groups of them. As in English, the definite article *'al'* is often used to specify a group or category of persons 'previously specified by context or by circumstance.' Some cases of the resulting ambiguity are such texts as: "When the sacred months have passed, kill *the* polytheists wherever *you* find *them*, capture *them* and besiege *them*, and lie in wait for *them* at every ambush (9:5); "*The* Jews and *the* Christians say, 'We are Allah's children and His beloved ones' " (5:18); "*The* Jews say, 'Ezra is the son of Allah.' " The reader should be aware of possible ambiguities involved in such cases.

[2] Such as the pronoun 'you' (used independently or suffixed), and such phrases as *'Yā ayyuhal ladhīna āmanū,'* which may refer to contemporary Muslims or to Muslims in general. Similar ambiguities arise from pronouns 'they' and 'them.' Some significant instances of this are: "Woe to *them* who write the Book with *their* hands and then say, 'This is from Allah,' that *they* may sell it for a paltry gain" (2:79); "And kill *them* wherever *you* confront *them*, and expel *them* from where they expelled *you*," (2:191); "seize *them* and kill *them* wherever *you* find *them*," (4:89, 91); and "*They* will not cease fighting *you* until *they* turn *you* away from *your* religion, if *they* can. (2:217)

understanding of relevant passages.

Muslim scholars have written hundreds of commentaries on the Qurʾān in Arabic, Persian, Urdu, Turkish, and other languages, reflecting not only different standpoints pertaining to grammar and etymology, but also the various theological and legal viewpoints of their schools and sects. These may be useful in various degrees for the studious eager to invest sufficient time and effort to delve into the often voluminous texts. However, what a common intelligent reader needs is some sort of companions to the Qurʾān, succinct commentaries that guide the reader from beginning to end, to illuminate the context sufficiently for an adequate understanding, without entering the maze of elaborate theological, legal, historical, etymological and grammatical details and debates.

Because of the lack of such handy support material, the Qurʾān has been a victim of ignorance and misunderstanding among Muslims and non-Muslims alike. Perhaps this is one of the reasons why a generation of young Muslim zealots, or psychopaths, with a flimsy understanding of the Qurʾān, or some of its verses, has fallen under the spell of a bigoted, murderous and self-righteous cult with iconoclastic pretensions. Its votaries, who have been proliferating since the last three decades with the impetus of petrodollars, have brought unprecedented discredit to Islam and the Qurʾān in the popular mind.

Due to being free from the baggage of compound ignorance piled up through centuries, many non-Muslims are perhaps better placed than many a Muslim to appreciate the truth, elegance and promise of the Qurʾān. Yet many of them are cornered into cavalier antagonism and trivial accusations resulting not only from a skewed understanding of the Qurʾān, but also by the bigotry, intolerance, violence and atrocities that mark some of its self-styled adherents.

That the Qurʾān itself stands in perpetual need of an authoritative interpretor by celestial design was declared by its Prophet, as recorded in the famous Thaqalayn Tradition, narrated widely in Sunni and Shīʿī sources. The sorry state of things visible throughout the world and many Muslim countries is no doubt a consequence of forsaking either or both of these twin sources of guidance.

Ali Quli Qarai
April 14, 2015

Transliteration of Arabic Text

The following table shows the system followed in transliterating the Arabic text.

ا	alif	a		ع	ʿayn	ʿ	
		ā	(long vowel)	غ	ghayn	gh	
		â	(with madd)	ف	fā	f	
ب	bā	b		ق	qāf	q	
ت	tā	t		ك	kāf	k	
ث	thā	th		ل	lām	l	
ج	jīm	j		م	mīm	m	
ح	ḥā	ḥ		ن	nūn	n	
خ	khā	kh				ṇ	(for nazal nūn)
د	dāl	d		ه	hā	h	
ذ	dhāl	dh		و	wāw	w	(consonantal)
ر	rā	r				ū	(long vowel)
ز	zāy	z				û	(with madd)
س	sīn	s		ى	yā	y	(consonantal)
ش	shīn	sh				ī	(long vowel)
ص	ṣād	ṣ				î	(with madd)
ض	ḍād	ḍ		ء	hamzah	ʾ	ʾa, ʾi, ʾu
ط	ṭā	ṭ					depending on the vowel
ظ	ẓā	ẓ					

Short vowels   ´ (fatḥah) = a

_ (kasrah) = i   ُ (ḍammah) = u

(ṣ)—stands for ṣallallāhu ʿalayhi wa ālihī, an invocation of blessings for the Prophet, meaning 'May God bless him and his Family.'
(ʿa)—stands for ʿalayhis/ʿalayhas salām, meaning 'May peace be upon him/her.'
(r)—stands for riḍwānullāh ʿalayhi/ʿalayhā, meaning 'May God be pleased with him/her.'

A Supplication for Recitation on Commencing a Reading of the Qur'an[1]

اَللَّهُمَّ إِنِّي أَشْهَدُ أَنَّ هَذَا كِتَابُكَ الْمُنْزَلُ مِنْ عِنْدِكَ عَلَى رَسُولِكَ مُحَمَّدِ بْنِ عَبْدِ اللَّهِ، وَ كَلَامُكَ النَّاطِقُ عَلَى لِسَانِ نَبِيِّكَ، جَعَلْتَهُ هَادِياً مِنْكَ إِلَى خَلْقِكَ وَ حَبْلًا مُتَّصِلًا فِيمَا بَيْنَكَ وَ بَيْنَ عِبَادِكَ.

O God, I bear witness that this is Your scripture revealed by You to Muhammad, son of 'Abdullah, Your Apostle. It is Your Word, annunciated on the tongue of Your Prophet, which You made Your guide for Your creatures and a connecting cord between Yourself and Your servants.

اللَّهُمَّ إِنِّي نَشَرْتُ عَهْدَكَ وَ كِتَابَكَ، اللَّهُمَّ فَاجْعَلْ نَظَرِي فِيهِ عِبَادَةً، وَ قِرَاءَتِي فِيهِ فِكْراً، وَ فِكْرِي فِيهِ اعْتِبَاراً، وَ اجْعَلْنِي مِمَّنِ اتَّعَظَ بِبَيَانِ مَوَاعِظِكَ فِيهِ وَ اجْتَنَبَ مَعَاصِيَكَ.

O God, I have opened this scripture and covenant of Yours, so let my gaze in it be an act of worship, my reading of it accompanied with thought and make my thinking instructive; place me among those who accept Your advices set forth in it and refrain from disobeying You.

وَ لَا تَطْبَعْ عِنْدَ قِرَاءَتِي عَلَى سَمْعِي، وَ لَا تَجْعَلْ عَلَى بَصَرِي غِشَاوَةً، وَ لَا تَجْعَلْ قِرَاءَتِي قِرَاءَةً لَا تَدَبُّرَ فِيهَا، بَلِ اجْعَلْنِي أَتَدَبَّرُ آيَاتِهِ وَ أَحْكَامَهُ، آخِذاً بِشَرَائِعِ دِينِكَ، وَ لَا تَجْعَلْ نَظَرِي فِيهِ غَفْلَةً وَ لَا قِرَاءَتِي هَذَراً.

During my reading, do not seal off my hearing, nor let my sight be blocked by a veil, and don't let it be a reading devoid of reflection. Rather, enable me to reflect over its verses and edicts, and to adhere to the ordinances of Your religion. Do not make my gaze in it one of inattention and my reading of it mere babbling.

إِنَّكَ أَنْتَ الرَّءُوفُ الرَّحِيمُ فِي الدُّعَاءِ عِنْدَ الْفَرَاغِ مِنْ قِرَاءَةِ الْقُرْآنِ، اللَّهُمَّ إِنِّي قَدْ قَرَأْتُ مَا قَضَيْتَ مِنْ كِتَابِكَ الَّذِي أَنْزَلْتَ فِيهِ عَلَى نَبِيِّكَ الصَّادِقِ ص، فَلَكَ الْحَمْدُ رَبَّنَا. اللَّهُمَّ اجْعَلْنِي مِمَّنْ يُحِلُّ حَلَالَهُ وَ يُحَرِّمُ حَرَامَهُ، وَ يُؤْمِنُ بِمُحْكَمِهِ وَ مُتَشَابِهِهِ، وَ اجْعَلْهُ لِي أُنْساً فِي قَبْرِي، وَ أُنْساً فِي حَشْرِي، وَ اجْعَلْنِي مِمَّنْ تُرَقِّيهِ بِكُلِّ آيَةٍ قَرَأَهَا دَرَجَةً فِي أَعْلَى عِلِّيِّينَ، آمِينَ رَبَّ الْعَالَمِينَ.

Indeed, You are most kind and merciful towards prayers made at the conclusion of a reading of the Qur'an. O God, I have read the scripture revealed by You to Your veracious Prophet, for which You, O Lord, are to be thanked. O God, make me one of those who allow what it permits and disallow what it forbids, and believe in its explicit and ambiguous verses. Make the Qur'an my friend and companion in my grave and at my resurrection and make me one of those who soar by a degree with every verse they recite, rising to the loftiest reaches of the highest heaven. Amen, O Lord of all the worlds!

---

[1] Biḥār al-Anwār, lxxxix, 206-207, from Miṣbāḥ al-Anwār. Makārim al-Akhlāq, 343; al-Ikhtiṣāṣ, 141.

1. The Opening[1]
al-Fātiḥah

سُورَةُ الْفَاتِحَةِ

1 بِسْمِ اللَّهِ الرَّحْمَٰنِ الرَّحِيمِ ۝ In the Name of God, the All-beneficent, the All-merciful.

2 الْحَمْدُ لِلَّهِ رَبِّ الْعَالَمِينَ ۝ All praise belongs to God,[2] Lord of all the worlds,

3 الرَّحْمَٰنِ الرَّحِيمِ ۝ the All-beneficent, the All-merciful,

4 مَالِكِ يَوْمِ الدِّينِ ۝ Master[3] of the Day of Retribution.

5 إِيَّاكَ نَعْبُدُ وَإِيَّاكَ نَسْتَعِينُ ۝ You alone do we worship, and to You alone do we turn for help.

6 اهْدِنَا الصِّرَاطَ الْمُسْتَقِيمَ ۝ Guide us on the straight path,

7 صِرَاطَ الَّذِينَ أَنْعَمْتَ عَلَيْهِمْ غَيْرِ الْمَغْضُوبِ عَلَيْهِمْ وَلَا الضَّالِّينَ ۝ the path of those whom You have blessed[4] —such as[5] have not incurred Your wrath,[6] nor are astray.[7]

---

[1] That is, 'the opening' *sūrah*. Another common name of the *sūrah* is 'Sūrat al-Ḥamd,' that is, the *sūrah* of the Lord's praise. According to some reports, it is the first *sūrah* to be revealed to the Prophet (ṣ).

[2] In Muslim parlance the phrase *al-ḥamdu lillāh* also signifies 'thanks to God.'

[3] This is in accordance with the reading *māliki yawm al-dīn*, adopted by 'Āṣim, al-Kisā'ī, Ya'qūb al-Ḥaḍramī, and Khalaf. Other authorities of *qirā'ah* (the science of the text of the Qur'ān) have read '*maliki yawm al-dīn*,' meaning 'Sovereign of the Day of Retribution' (see *Mu'jam al-Qirā'āt al-Qur'āniyyah*). Traditions ascribe both readings to Imam Ja'far al-Ṣādiq ('a). See al-Qummī, al-'Ayyāshī, *Tafsīr al-Imām al-'Askarī*.

[4] For further Qur'ānic references to 'those whom God has blessed,' see 4:69 and 19:58; see also 5:23, 110; 12:6; 27:19; 28:17; 43:59; 48:2.

[5] This is in accordance with the *qirā'ah* of 'Āṣim, *ghayril-maghḍūbi*, which appears in the Arabic text above. However, in accordance with an alternative, and perhaps preferable, reading *ghayral-maghḍūbi* (attributed to Imam 'Alī b. Abī Ṭālib ('a) as well as to Ibn Mas'ūd and Ubayy b. Ka'b among the Companions, and to Ibn Kathīr al-Makkī, among the seven authorities of *qirā'ah*), the translation will be: 'not of those who have incurred Your wrath, nor those who are astray.' (see *Mu'jam al-Qirā'āt al-Qur'āniyyah*)

[6] For further references to 'those who incur God's wrath,' see 4:93; 5:60; 7:71, 152; 8:16; 16:106; 20:81; 42:16; 48:6; 58:14; 60:13.

[7] For further references to 'those who are astray,' see 2:108, 175; 3:90; 4:116, 136, 167; 5:12, 60, 77; 6:74, 77, 125, 140; 7:30, 179; 14:3, 18, 27; 15:56; 17:72, 97; 19:38; 22:4, 12; 23:106; 25:44; 28:50; 31:11; 33:36, 67; 34:8; 36:47; 38:26; 39:22; 40: 34; 41:52; 42:18; 45:23; 46:5, 32; 60:1.

2. The Heifer[1]
al-Baqarah

In the Name of God,
the All-beneficent, the All-merciful.

1 Alif, Lām, Mīm.

2 This is the Book,[2] there is no doubt in it,
a guidance to the Godwary,[3]

3 who believe in the Unseen,
maintain the prayer,
and spend[4] out of what We have provided for them;

4 and who believe in what has been sent down to *you*[5]
and what was sent down before *you*,
and are certain of the Hereafter.

5 Those follow their Lord's guidance,
and it is they who are the felicitous.

6 As for the faithless, it is the same to them
whether *you* warn them or do not warn them,
they will not have faith.

7 God has set a seal on their hearts and their hearing,[6]
and there is a blindfold on their sight,
and there is a great punishment for them.

---

[1] The *sūrah* takes its name from the story of the heifer (*baqarah*) mentioned in verses 67-73. One of the earliest Madanī *sūrah*s, preceded probably only by Sūrat al-Muṭaffifīn (83) and Sūrat al-Ḥajj (22).

[2] The term 'the Book' in the Qur'ān, in such contexts, means a Divine scripture.

[3] Or 'This Book, in which there is no doubt, is guidance to the Godwary.' Or 'This Book is no doubt a guidance to the Godwary.'

[4] The expression 'to spend' is used in the Qur'ān elliptically to mean spending in the way of God and for the sake of His pleasure. Cf. **2**:195, 261-262, 272; **8**:60; **9**:34; **47**:38; **57**:10.

[5] That is, the Prophet, may God bless him and his Family. Throughout this translation whenever the pronoun '*you*' refers to the second person singular in the Arabic and is meant as an address to the Prophet, it has been italicized (for similar reasons, also the related verbs) in order to distinguish it from cases where it stands for the second person plural. This is to avoid the use of 'thee' and 'thou.'

[6] The hearing and sight, often mentioned in the Qur'ān, refer to the inner spiritual hearing and vision by the means of which the faithful apprehend spiritual truths. Cf. **2**:17, 20; **3**:13; **6**:46, 50, 104, 110; **7**:179, 198; **10**:43; **11**:20, 24; **13**:16; **16**:108; **19**:38; **22**:46; **24**:44; **32**:12; **35**:19; **36**:66; **40**:58; **45**:23; **46**:26; **47**:23; **50**:22; **59**:2.

8 Among the people are those who say,
    'We have faith in God and the Last Day,'
    but they have no faith.
9 They seek to deceive God and those who have faith,
    yet they deceive no one but themselves,
    but they are not aware.
10 There is a sickness in their hearts;
    then God increased their sickness,
    and there is a painful punishment for them
    because of the lies they used to tell.
11 When they are told,
    'Do not cause corruption on the earth,'
    they say, 'We are only reformers!'
12 Behold! They are themselves the agents of corruption,
    but they are not aware.
13 And when they are told,
    'Believe like the people who have believed,'
    they say, 'Shall we believe like the fools who have believed?'
    Behold! They are themselves the fools,
    but they do not know.
14 When they meet the faithful, they say, 'We believe,'
    but when they are alone with their devils,
    they say, 'We are with you;
    we were only deriding them.'
15 It is God who derides them,[1]
    and leaves them bewildered in their rebellion.
16 They are the ones who bought error for guidance,
    so their trade did not profit them,
    nor were they guided.

---

[1] That is, by letting them imagine that they are mocking the faithful.

17 Their parable is that of one who lighted a torch,
   and when it had lit up all around him,
   God took away their light,
   and left them sightless in a manifold darkness.[1]
18 Deaf, dumb, and blind, they will not come back.
19 Or that of a rainstorm from the sky,
   wherein is darkness, thunder, and lightning:
   they put their fingers in their ears
   due to the thunderclaps, apprehensive of death;
   and God besieges the faithless.[2]
20 The lightning almost snatches away their sight:
   whenever it shines for them, they walk in it,
   and when the darkness falls upon them, they stand.
   Had God willed,
   He would have taken away their hearing and sight.
   Indeed, God has power over all things.

21 O mankind! Worship your Lord,
   who created you and those who were before you,
   so that you may be Godwary.
22 —He who made the earth a place of repose for you,
   and the sky a canopy,
   and He sends down water from the sky,
   and with it brings forth crops for your sustenance.
   So do not set up equals to God, while you know.
23 And if you are in doubt
   concerning what We have sent down to Our servant,

---

[1] The one who lights the torch in the parable is the Prophet (ṣ), who illuminated the spiritual horizons of the Arabia of those days with the message of Islam. But the hypocrites, with their inward blindness, did not benefit from its light and continued to remain in the darkness of their faithlessness.

[2] This is another parable for the condition of the hypocrites. In it the Prophet's mission, with its downpour of Divine knowledge, the accompanying light of guidance, along with the hardships of struggle against polytheism and injustice, is likened to a rainstorm.

then bring a *surah* like it,
and invoke your helpers besides God,
if you are truthful.

24 But if you do not—and you will not—
then beware of the Fire whose fuel will be humans
and stones, prepared for the faithless.

25 And give good news to those who have faith
and do righteous deeds,
that for them shall be
gardens with streams running in them:
whenever they are provided with their fruit for nourishment,
they will say, 'This is what we were provided before,'
and they were given something resembling it.
There will be chaste mates for them,
and they will remain therein.

26 Indeed, God is not ashamed to draw a parable
whether it is that of a gnat or something above it.
As for those who have faith,
they know it is the truth from their Lord;
and as for the faithless, they say,
'What did God mean by this parable?'
Thereby He leads many astray, and guides many thereby;
and leads no one astray thereby except the transgressors

27 —those who break the covenant made with God
after having pledged it solemnly,
and sever what God has commanded to be joined,
and cause corruption on the earth—
it is they who are the losers.

28 How can you be unfaithful to God,

[seeing that] you were lifeless and He gave you life,
then He will make you die, and then bring you to life,
and then you will be brought back to Him?
29 It is He who created for you
    all that is in the earth,
then He turned to the heaven,
    and fashioned it into seven heavens,
and He has knowledge of all things.

30 When your Lord said to the angels,
    'I am indeed going to set a viceroy on the earth,'
they said, 'Will You set in it
someone who will cause corruption in it and shed blood,
while we celebrate Your praise and proclaim Your sanctity?'
He said, 'Indeed, I know what you do not know.'
31 And He taught Adam the Names, all of them;
    then presented them[1] to the angels
and said, 'Tell me the names of these,
    if you are truthful.'
32 They said, 'Immaculate are You!
We have no knowledge except what You have taught us.
Indeed, You are the All-knowing, the All-wise.'
33 He said, 'O Adam, inform them[2] of their names,'
    and when he had informed them of their names,
He said, 'Did I not tell you
that I know the Unseen of the heavens and the earth,
    and that I know whatever you disclose
    and whatever you conceal?'

---

[1] The pronoun in the phrase 'He presented them' (*'araḍahum*) is masculine, indicating that it does not refer to the 'Names' but to their referents.

[2] That is, the angels, about the names of those referents.

وَإِذْ قُلْنَا لِلْمَلَائِكَةِ اسْجُدُوا لِآدَمَ	34 And when We said to the angels, 'Prostrate before Adam,'
فَسَجَدُوا إِلَّا إِبْلِيسَ	they prostrated, but not Iblis:
أَبَىٰ وَاسْتَكْبَرَ	he refused and acted arrogantly,
وَكَانَ مِنَ الْكَافِرِينَ ۩	and he was one of the faithless.
وَقُلْنَا يَا آدَمُ اسْكُنْ أَنْتَ وَزَوْجُكَ الْجَنَّةَ	35 We said, 'O Adam, dwell with your mate in paradise,
وَكُلَا مِنْهَا رَغَدًا حَيْثُ شِئْتُمَا	and eat thereof freely whencesoever you wish,
وَلَا تَقْرَبَا هَٰذِهِ الشَّجَرَةَ	but do not approach this tree,
فَتَكُونَا مِنَ الظَّالِمِينَ ۩	lest you should be among the wrongdoers.'
فَأَزَلَّهُمَا الشَّيْطَانُ عَنْهَا	36 Then Satan caused them to stumble from it,
فَأَخْرَجَهُمَا مِمَّا كَانَا فِيهِ	and he dislodged them from what state they were in;
وَقُلْنَا اهْبِطُوا بَعْضُكُمْ لِبَعْضٍ عَدُوٌّ	and We said, 'Get down, being enemies of one another!
وَلَكُمْ فِي الْأَرْضِ مُسْتَقَرٌّ	On the earth shall be your abode
وَمَتَاعٌ إِلَىٰ حِينٍ ۩	and sustenance for a time.'
فَتَلَقَّىٰ آدَمُ مِنْ رَبِّهِ كَلِمَاتٍ	37 Then Adam received certain words from his Lord,
فَتَابَ عَلَيْهِ	and He turned to him clemently.
إِنَّهُ هُوَ التَّوَّابُ الرَّحِيمُ ۩	Indeed, He is the All-clement, the All-merciful.
قُلْنَا اهْبِطُوا مِنْهَا جَمِيعًا	38 We said, 'Get down from it, all together!
فَإِمَّا يَأْتِيَنَّكُمْ مِنِّي هُدًى	Yet, should any guidance come to you from Me,
فَمَنْ تَبِعَ هُدَايَ	those who follow My guidance
فَلَا خَوْفٌ عَلَيْهِمْ وَلَا هُمْ يَحْزَنُونَ ۩	shall have no fear, nor shall they grieve.
وَالَّذِينَ كَفَرُوا وَكَذَّبُوا بِآيَاتِنَا	39 But those who are faithless and deny Our signs,
أُولَٰئِكَ أَصْحَابُ النَّارِ	they shall be the inmates of the Fire
هُمْ فِيهَا خَالِدُونَ ۩	and they shall remain in it.
يَا بَنِي إِسْرَائِيلَ اذْكُرُوا نِعْمَتِيَ الَّتِي أَنْعَمْتُ عَلَيْكُمْ	40 O Children of Israel, remember My blessing which I bestowed upon you,
وَأَوْفُوا بِعَهْدِي أُوفِ بِعَهْدِكُمْ	and fulfill My covenant that I may fulfill your covenant,
وَإِيَّايَ فَارْهَبُونِ ۩	and be in awe of Me alone.
وَآمِنُوا بِمَا أَنْزَلْتُ	41 And believe in that which I have sent down
مُصَدِّقًا لِمَا مَعَكُمْ	confirming that which is with you,

     and do not be the first ones to deny it,
     and do not sell My signs for a paltry gain,
     and be wary of Me alone.

42 Do not mix the truth with falsehood,
   nor conceal the truth while you know.

43 And maintain the prayer, and give the *zakāt*,
   and bow along with those who bow in prayer.

44 Will you bid others to piety and forget yourselves,
   while you recite the Book?
   Do you not exercise your reason?

45 And take recourse in patience and prayer,
   and it[1] is indeed hard except for the humble

46 —those who are certain
   that they will encounter their Lord,
   and that they will return to Him.

47 O Children of Israel,
   remember My blessing which I bestowed upon you,
   and that I gave you an advantage over all the nations.

48 Beware of the day when
   no soul will compensate for another,
   neither any intercession shall be accepted from it,
   nor any ransom shall be received from it,
   nor will they be helped.

49 [Recall] when We delivered you from Pharaoh's clan
   who inflicted a terrible torment on you,
   and slaughtered your sons
   and spared your women,
   and in that there was a great test from your Lord.

50 And when We parted the sea with you,[2]

---

[1] The pronoun, being feminine, refers to prayer, rather than to patience or to the seeking of recourse.
[2] That is, through your entering it.

and We delivered you and drowned Pharaoh's clan
as you looked on.

51 And when We made an appointment with Moses
for forty nights,
you took up the Calf for worship in his absence,
and you were wrongdoers.

52 Then We excused you after that
so that you might give thanks.

53 And when We gave Moses the Book and the Criterion[1]
so that you might be guided.

54 And [recall] when Moses said to his people,
'O my people! You have indeed wronged yourselves
by taking up the Calf for worship.
Now turn penitently to your Maker,
and slay [the guilty among] your folks.
That will be better for you with your Maker.'
Then He turned to you clemently.
Indeed, He is the All-clement, the All-merciful.

55 And when you said, 'O Moses, we will not believe you
until we see God visibly,'
a thunderbolt seized you as you looked on.

56 Then We raised you up after your death
so that you might give thanks.

57 We shaded you with clouds,
and sent down to you manna and quails [saying]:
'Eat of the good things We have provided for you.'
And they did not wrong Us,
but they used to wrong only themselves.

---

[1] That is, that by means of which truth and falsehood are distinguished from each other (cf. 21:48). Elsewhere (3:4; 25:1) the Qur'ān is also called al-Furqān.

58 And when We said, 'Enter this town,[1]
and eat thereof freely whencesoever you wish,
and enter while prostrating at the gate,
and say, "Relieve us of the burden of our sins,"[2]
so that We may forgive your iniquities,
and soon We will enhance the virtuous.'

59 But the wrongdoers changed the saying
with other than what they were told.
So We sent down on those who were wrongdoers
a plague from the sky
because of the transgressions they used to commit.

60 And when Moses prayed for water for his people,
We said, 'Strike the rock with your staff.'
Thereat twelve fountains gushed forth from it;
every tribe came to know its drinking-place.
'Eat and drink of God's provision,
and do not act wickedly on the earth, causing corruption.'

61 And when you said, 'O Moses,
'We will not put up with one kind of food.
So invoke your Lord for us,
that He may bring forth for us of that which the earth grows
—its greens and cucumbers,
its garlic, lentils, and onions.'
He said, 'Do you seek to replace
what is superior with that which is inferior?
Go down to any town

---

[1] This city, according to tradition (see *Tafsīr al-Imām al-'Askarī*), was Arīḥā' or Jericho (or Jerusalem, according to some commentators), an ancient city of Palestine near the northwest shore of the Dead Sea. A stronghold commanding the valley of the lower Jordan River, it was captured and destroyed by Joshua forty years later.

[2] Or '[We beseech] forgiveness [for our sins].'

and you will indeed get what you ask for!'
So they were struck with abasement and poverty,
and they earned God's wrath.
That, because they would deny the signs of God
and kill the prophets unjustly.
That, because they would disobey
and commit transgressions.

62 Indeed, the faithful, the Jews,
the Christians, and the Sabaeans
—those who have faith in God and the Last Day
and act righteously—
they shall have their reward near their Lord,
and they will have no fear, nor will they grieve.

63 And when We took a pledge from you,
and raised the Mount above you [declaring],
'Hold on with power to what We have given you
and remember that which is in it
so that you may be Godwary.'

64 Again, you turned away after that;
and were it not for God's grace on you and His mercy,
you would have surely been among the losers.

65 And certainly you know
those of you who violated the Sabbath,
whereupon We said to them, 'Be you spurned apes.'

66 So We made it an exemplary punishment
for the present and the succeeding generations,
and an advice to the Godwary.

67 And when Moses said to his people,
   'God commands you to slaughter a cow,'
   they said, 'Are you mocking us?'
   He said, 'I seek God's protection
      lest I should be one of the ignorant!'

68 They said, 'Invoke your Lord for us,
      that He may clarify for us what she may be.'
   He said, 'He says, She is a cow,
      neither old nor young, of a middle age.
   Now do what you are commanded.'

69 They said, 'Invoke your Lord for us,
      that He may clarify for us what her colour may be.'
   He said, 'He says, She is a cow that is yellow,
      of a bright hue, pleasing to the onlookers.'

70 They said, 'Invoke your Lord for us,
      that He may clarify for us what she may be.
   Indeed, all cows are much alike to us,
      and, if God wishes, we will surely be guided.'

71 He said, 'He says, She is a cow
      not broken to till the earth or water the tillage,
      sound and without blemish.'
   They said, 'Now have you come up with the truth!'
   And they slaughtered it,
      though they were about not to do it.

72 And when you killed a soul,
   and accused one another about it
   —and God was to expose what you were concealing—

73 We said, 'Strike him with a piece of it.'
   thus does God revive the dead,
   and He shows you His signs

　　　　　　　　　　　　so that you may exercise your reason.

لَعَلَّكُمْ تَعْقِلُونَ ۝

74　Then your hearts hardened after that;
　　　so they are like stones, or even harder.
　　For there are indeed some stones
　　　from which streams gush forth,
　　and there are some of them that split
　　　and water issues from them,
　　and there are some that fall for the fear of God.
　　And God is not oblivious of what you do.

75　Are you then eager that they should believe you,[1]
　　though a part of them would hear the word of God
　　and then they would distort it,[2]
　　after they had understood it
　　and they knew what they were doing?

76　When they meet the faithful, they say, 'We believe,'
　　and when they are alone with one another,
　　they say, 'Do you recount to them
　　what God has revealed to you,
　　that they may argue with you therewith before your Lord?
　　Do you not exercise your reason?'

77　Do they not know that God knows
　　whatever they hide and whatever they disclose?

78　And among them are the illiterate
　　who know nothing of the Book except hearsay,[3]
　　and they only make conjectures.

79　So woe to them who write the Book with their hands

---

[1] This is an address to the Muslims who were eager that the Jews should embrace Islam and follow the Prophhet's teachings.
[2] Cf. 4:46; 5:13, 41, for this characteristic of the Jews.
[3] That is, what they learnt through word of mouth from their scribes and priests, rather than from a direct knowledge of the scriptures. Or 'hopes,' or 'lies.'

and then say, 'This is from God,'
that they may sell it for a paltry gain.
So woe to them for what their hands have written,
and woe to them for what they earn!

80 And they say, 'The Fire shall not touch us
except for a number of days.'
Say, 'Have you taken a promise from God?
If so, God will never break His promise.
Or do you ascribe to God what you do not know?'

81 Certainly whoever commits misdeeds
and is besieged by his iniquity
—such shall be the inmates of the Fire,
and they will remain in it.

82 And those who have faith and do righteous deeds,
—they shall be the inhabitants of paradise;
they shall remain in it.

83 When We took a pledge from the Children of Israel,
[saying]: 'Worship no one but God,
do good to your parents, relatives,
orphans and the needy,
speak kindly to people,
maintain the prayer, and give the *zakāt*,'
you turned away, except a few of you,
and you were disregardful.

84 And when We took a pledge from you, [saying]:
'You shall not shed your own people's blood,
and you shall not expel your folks from your homes,'
you pledged,

and you testify[1] [to this pledge of your ancestors].
85 Then there you were, killing your folks
    and expelling a part of your folks from their homes,
    backing one another against them in sin and aggression!
If they came to you as captives, you would ransom them,
    though their expulsion itself was forbidden you.
What! Do you believe in part of the Book
    and deny another part?
So what is the requital of those of you who do that
    except disgrace in the life of this world?
And on the Day of Resurrection,
    they shall be consigned to the severest punishment.
And God is not oblivious of what you do.
86 They are the ones who
    bought the life of this world for the Hereafter;
    so their punishment shall not be lightened,
    nor will they be helped.
87 Certainly We gave Moses the Book,
    and followed him with the apostles,
    and We gave Jesus, the son of Mary, clear proofs,
    and confirmed him with the Holy Spirit.
Is it not that whenever an apostle brought you[2]
    that which was not to your liking,
    you would act arrogantly;
    so you would impugn a group of them,
    and slay another group?
88 And they say, 'Our hearts are uncircumcised.'[3]

---

[1] Or 'and you testified.'
[2] That is, the Jews.
[3] Uncircumcised: unconverted, heathen, faithless; cf. **4:155**. In Leviticus 26.41, it is said of the Israelites, 'Then when their uncircumcised hearts are humbled and they pay for their sin, I will remember my covenant with Jacob,' and in Jeremiah 9.26: 'Even the whole house of Israel is uncircumcised in heart.' There are other similar expressions and phrases in the Bible: "uncircumcised lips" (Exodus 6.12 and 6.30); "their ear

Rather, God has cursed them for their unfaith, بَلْ لَعَنَهُمُ اللَّهُ بِكُفْرِهِمْ
so few of them have faith. فَقَلِيلًا مَا يُؤْمِنُونَ ۝

89 And when there came to them a Book from God, وَلَمَّا جَاءَهُمْ كِتَابٌ مِنْ عِنْدِ اللَّهِ
 confirming that which is with them مُصَدِّقٌ لِمَا مَعَهُمْ
—and earlier they would pray for victory وَكَانُوا مِنْ قَبْلُ يَسْتَفْتِحُونَ
 over the pagans— عَلَى الَّذِينَ كَفَرُوا
so when there came to them what they recognized, فَلَمَّا جَاءَهُمْ مَا عَرَفُوا
 they denied it. كَفَرُوا بِهِ ۚ
So may the curse of God be on the faithless! فَلَعْنَةُ اللَّهِ عَلَى الْكَافِرِينَ ۝

90 Evil is that for which they have sold their souls, بِئْسَمَا اشْتَرَوْا بِهِ أَنْفُسَهُمْ
 by defying what God has sent down, أَنْ يَكْفُرُوا بِمَا أَنْزَلَ اللَّهُ
 out of envy, that God should bestow His grace بَغْيًا أَنْ يُنَزِّلَ اللَّهُ مِنْ فَضْلِهِ
 on any of His servants that He wishes. عَلَى مَنْ يَشَاءُ مِنْ عِبَادِهِ ۖ
Thus they earned wrath upon wrath, فَبَاءُوا بِغَضَبٍ عَلَى غَضَبٍ ۚ
and there is a humiliating punishment for the faithless. وَلِلْكَافِرِينَ عَذَابٌ مُهِينٌ ۝

91 When they are told, 'Believe in what God has sent down,' وَإِذَا قِيلَ لَهُمْ آمِنُوا بِمَا أَنْزَلَ اللَّهُ
 they say, 'We believe in what was sent down to us,' قَالُوا نُؤْمِنُ بِمَا أُنْزِلَ عَلَيْنَا
 and they disbelieve what is besides it, وَيَكْفُرُونَ بِمَا وَرَاءَهُ
 though it is the truth confirming what is with them. وَهُوَ الْحَقُّ مُصَدِّقًا لِمَا مَعَهُمْ ۗ
Say, 'Then why would you kill the prophets of God formerly, قُلْ فَلِمَ تَقْتُلُونَ أَنْبِيَاءَ اللَّهِ مِنْ قَبْلُ
 should you be faithful?' إِنْ كُنْتُمْ مُؤْمِنِينَ ۝

92 Certainly Moses brought you manifest proofs, وَلَقَدْ جَاءَكُمْ مُوسَىٰ بِالْبَيِّنَاتِ
 but then you took up the Calf in his absence, ثُمَّ اتَّخَذْتُمُ الْعِجْلَ مِنْ بَعْدِهِ
 and you were wrongdoers. وَأَنْتُمْ ظَالِمُونَ ۝

93 And when We took covenant with you وَإِذْ أَخَذْنَا مِيثَاقَكُمْ
 and raised the Mount above you [declaring], وَرَفَعْنَا فَوْقَكُمُ الطُّورَ
 'Hold on with power to what We have given you, خُذُوا مَا آتَيْنَاكُمْ بِقُوَّةٍ
 and do listen!' وَاسْمَعُوا ۖ

---

is uncircumcised and they cannot hearken" (Jeremiah 6.10); "uncircumcised in heart, and uncircumcised in flesh" (Ezekiel 44.7, 9); "uncircumcised in heart and ears" (Acts 7.51), "putting off the body of the sins of the flesh by the circumcision of Christ" (Colossians 2.11).

قَالُوا سَمِعْنَا وَعَصَيْنَا	They said, 'We hear, and disobey,'
وَأُشْرِبُوا فِي قُلُوبِهِمُ	and their hearts had been imbued
الْعِجْلَ بِكُفْرِهِمْ ۚ	with the love of the Calf, due to their unfaith.
قُلْ بِئْسَمَا يَأْمُرُكُم بِهِ إِيمَانُكُمْ	Say, 'Evil is that to which your faith prompts you,
إِن كُنتُم مُّؤْمِنِينَ ۝	should you be faithful!'
۹۴ قُلْ إِن كَانَتْ لَكُمُ الدَّارُ الْآخِرَةُ	94 Say, 'If the abode of the Hereafter
عِندَ اللَّهِ خَالِصَةً مِّن دُونِ النَّاسِ	were exclusively for you with God and not for other people,
فَتَمَنَّوُا الْمَوْتَ إِن كُنتُمْ صَادِقِينَ ۝	then long for death, should you be truthful.
۹۵ وَلَن يَتَمَنَّوْهُ أَبَدًا	95 But they will not long for it ever
بِمَا قَدَّمَتْ أَيْدِيهِمْ ۚ	because of what their hands have sent ahead,[1]
وَاللَّهُ عَلِيمٌ بِالظَّالِمِينَ ۝	and God knows best the wrongdoers.
۹۶ وَلَتَجِدَنَّهُمْ	96 Surely, you will find them
أَحْرَصَ النَّاسِ عَلَىٰ حَيَاةٍ	the greediest of all people for life
وَمِنَ الَّذِينَ أَشْرَكُوا ۚ	—even the idolaters.
يَوَدُّ أَحَدُهُمْ لَوْ يُعَمَّرُ أَلْفَ سَنَةٍ	Each of them is eager to live a thousand years,
وَمَا هُوَ بِمُزَحْزِحِهِ مِنَ الْعَذَابِ	though it would not deliver him from the punishment,
أَن يُعَمَّرَ ۗ	were he to live that long.
وَاللَّهُ بَصِيرٌ بِمَا يَعْمَلُونَ ۝	And God sees best what they do.
۹۷ قُلْ مَن كَانَ عَدُوًّا لِّجِبْرِيلَ	97 Say, 'Whoever is an enemy of Gabriel [should know that]
فَإِنَّهُ نَزَّلَهُ عَلَىٰ قَلْبِكَ	it is he who has brought it down on *your* heart
بِإِذْنِ اللَّهِ	with the will of God,
مُصَدِّقًا لِّمَا بَيْنَ يَدَيْهِ	confirming what has been revealed before it,
وَهُدًى وَبُشْرَىٰ لِلْمُؤْمِنِينَ ۝	and as a guidance and good news for the faithful.'
۹۸ مَن كَانَ عَدُوًّا لِّلَّهِ	98 [Say,] 'Whoever is an enemy of God,
وَمَلَائِكَتِهِ وَرُسُلِهِ	His apostles and His angels,
وَجِبْرِيلَ وَمِيكَالَ	and Gabriel and Michael, [let him know that]
فَإِنَّ اللَّهَ عَدُوٌّ لِّلْكَافِرِينَ ۝	God is indeed the enemy of the faithless.'
۹۹ وَلَقَدْ أَنزَلْنَا إِلَيْكَ آيَاتٍ بَيِّنَاتٍ ۖ	99 We have certainly sent down manifest signs to *you*,

---

[1] That is, to the scene of judgement and retribution on the Day of Resurrection. Or 'prepared,' 'made ready,' or 'committed,' 'perpetrated.'

وَمَا يَكْفُرُ بِهَا إِلَّا الْفَاسِقُونَ ۝

and no one denies them except transgressors.

100 Is it not that whenever they made a covenant,
    a part of them would cast it away?
    Rather, the majority of them do not have faith.

101 And when there came to them an apostle from God,
    confirming that which is with them,
    a part of those who were given the Book cast
    the Book of God behind their back,
    as if they did not know that it is God's Book.

102 And they followed what the devils pursued
    during Solomon's reign[1]
    —and Solomon was not faithless,
    but it was the devils who were faithless—
    teaching the people magic
    and what was sent down to the two angels at Babylon,
    Hārūt and Mārūt,
    who would not teach anyone without telling him,
    'We are only a test,[2] so do not be faithless.'
    But they would learn from those two
    that with which they would cause a split
    between man and his wife
    —though they could not harm anyone with it
    except with God's leave.
    They would learn that which would harm them
    and bring them no benefit;
    though they certainly knew that anyone who buys it
    has no share in the Hereafter.

---

[1] Or 'they followed what the devils recited during Solomon's reign.' Or 'they followed the lies the devils uttered against Solomon's reign.'

[2] Or 'temptation.'

وَلَبِئْسَ مَا شَرَوْا بِهِ أَنْفُسَهُمْ Surely, evil is that for which they sold their souls,
لَوْ كَانُوا يَعْلَمُونَ ۝ had they known!

وَلَوْ أَنَّهُمْ آمَنُوا وَاتَّقَوْا 103 Had they been faithful and Godwary,
لَمَثُوبَةٌ مِنْ عِنْدِ اللَّهِ خَيْرٌ the reward from God would have surely been better,
لَوْ كَانُوا يَعْلَمُونَ ۝ had they known!

يَا أَيُّهَا الَّذِينَ آمَنُوا 104 O you who have faith!
لَا تَقُولُوا رَاعِنَا وَقُولُوا انْظُرْنَا وَاسْمَعُوا Do not say Ra'inā, but say *Unẓurnā*, and listen![1]
وَلِلْكَافِرِينَ عَذَابٌ أَلِيمٌ ۝ And there is a painful punishment for the faithless.

مَا يَوَدُّ الَّذِينَ كَفَرُوا 105 Neither the faithless
مِنْ أَهْلِ الْكِتَابِ from among the People of the Book like,
وَلَا الْمُشْرِكِينَ nor the idolaters,
أَنْ يُنَزَّلَ عَلَيْكُمْ مِنْ خَيْرٍ مِنْ رَبِّكُمْ that any good be showered on you from your Lord;
وَاللَّهُ يَخْتَصُّ بِرَحْمَتِهِ مَنْ يَشَاءُ but God singles out for His mercy whomever He wishes,
وَاللَّهُ ذُو الْفَضْلِ الْعَظِيمِ ۝ and God is dispenser of a mighty grace.

مَا نَنْسَخْ مِنْ آيَةٍ أَوْ نُنْسِهَا 106 For any verse [or command] that We abrogate or defer,
نَأْتِ بِخَيْرٍ مِنْهَا أَوْ مِثْلِهَا We bring another, better than it or similar to it.
أَلَمْ تَعْلَمْ أَنَّ اللَّهَ عَلَى كُلِّ شَيْءٍ قَدِيرٌ ۝ Do you not know that God has power over all things?

أَلَمْ تَعْلَمْ أَنَّ اللَّهَ لَهُ 107 Do you not know that to God belongs
مُلْكُ السَّمَاوَاتِ وَالْأَرْضِ the kingdom of the heavens and the earth?
وَمَا لَكُمْ مِنْ دُونِ اللَّهِ مِنْ وَلِيٍّ And besides God you do not have any friend
وَلَا نَصِيرٍ ۝ or helper.

أَمْ تُرِيدُونَ أَنْ تَسْأَلُوا رَسُولَكُمْ 108 Would you make such demands of your Apostle
كَمَا سُئِلَ مُوسَى مِنْ قَبْلُ as were formerly made of Moses?
وَمَنْ يَتَبَدَّلِ الْكُفْرَ بِالْإِيمَانِ Whoever changes faith for unfaith
فَقَدْ ضَلَّ سَوَاءَ السَّبِيلِ ۝ certainly strays from the right way.

---

[1] The Jews in ridiculing the Prophet would say *rā'inā* (meaning, 'have regard for us') with a change of accent turning it into another word which made it a term of reproach. The Muslims are told to say *unẓurnā* (meaning, 'give us a little respite') instead while addressing the Prophet (ṣ), as there is no room in this term for such a distortion.

109 وَدَّ كَثِيرٌ مِنْ أَهْلِ الْكِتَابِ لَوْ يَرُدُّونَكُمْ مِنْ بَعْدِ إِيمَانِكُمْ كُفَّارًا حَسَدًا مِنْ عِنْدِ أَنْفُسِهِمْ مِنْ بَعْدِ مَا تَبَيَّنَ لَهُمُ الْحَقُّ ۖ فَاعْفُوا وَاصْفَحُوا حَتَّىٰ يَأْتِيَ اللَّهُ بِأَمْرِهِ ۗ إِنَّ اللَّهَ عَلَىٰ كُلِّ شَيْءٍ قَدِيرٌ ۝

110 وَأَقِيمُوا الصَّلَاةَ وَآتُوا الزَّكَاةَ ۚ وَمَا تُقَدِّمُوا لِأَنْفُسِكُمْ مِنْ خَيْرٍ تَجِدُوهُ عِنْدَ اللَّهِ ۗ إِنَّ اللَّهَ بِمَا تَعْمَلُونَ بَصِيرٌ ۝

111 وَقَالُوا لَنْ يَدْخُلَ الْجَنَّةَ إِلَّا مَنْ كَانَ هُودًا أَوْ نَصَارَىٰ ۗ تِلْكَ أَمَانِيُّهُمْ ۗ قُلْ هَاتُوا بُرْهَانَكُمْ إِنْ كُنْتُمْ صَادِقِينَ ۝

112 بَلَىٰ مَنْ أَسْلَمَ وَجْهَهُ لِلَّهِ وَهُوَ مُحْسِنٌ فَلَهُ أَجْرُهُ عِنْدَ رَبِّهِ وَلَا خَوْفٌ عَلَيْهِمْ وَلَا هُمْ يَحْزَنُونَ ۝

113 وَقَالَتِ الْيَهُودُ لَيْسَتِ النَّصَارَىٰ عَلَىٰ شَيْءٍ وَقَالَتِ النَّصَارَىٰ لَيْسَتِ الْيَهُودُ عَلَىٰ شَيْءٍ وَهُمْ يَتْلُونَ الْكِتَابَ ۗ كَذَٰلِكَ قَالَ الَّذِينَ لَا يَعْلَمُونَ مِثْلَ قَوْلِهِمْ ۚ فَاللَّهُ يَحْكُمُ بَيْنَهُمْ يَوْمَ الْقِيَامَةِ فِيمَا كَانُوا فِيهِ يَخْتَلِفُونَ ۝

114 وَمَنْ أَظْلَمُ مِمَّنْ مَنَعَ مَسَاجِدَ اللَّهِ أَنْ يُذْكَرَ فِيهَا اسْمُهُ

---

109 Many of the People of the Book are eager
  to turn you into unbelievers after your faith,
    out of their inner envy,
  and after the truth had become manifest to them.
  Yet excuse them and forbear
    until God issues His edict.
  Indeed, God has power over all things.

110 And maintain the prayer and give the *zakāt*.
  Any good that you send ahead for your own souls,
    you shall find it with God.
  God indeed watches what you do.

111 And they say, 'No one will enter paradise
    except one who is a Jew or Christian.'
  Those are their [false] hopes!
  Say, 'Produce your evidence, should you be truthful.'

112 Certainly whoever submits his will to God
    and is virtuous,
  he shall have his reward with his Lord,
    and they will have no fear, nor shall they grieve.

113 The Jews say, 'The Christians stand on nothing,'
    and the Christians say, 'The Jews stand on nothing,'
  though they follow the same Book.
  So said those who had no knowledge,
    words similar to what they say.
  God will judge between them on the Day of Resurrection
    concerning that about which they used to differ.

114 Who is a greater wrongdoer than those who
    deny access to the mosques of God
  lest His Name be celebrated therein,

and try to ruin them?
Such ones may not enter them,
except in fear.
There is disgrace for them in this world,
and a great punishment in the Hereafter.[1]

115 To God belong the east and the west:
so whichever way you turn, there is the face of God!
God is indeed all-bounteous, all-knowing.

116 And they say, 'God has offspring.' Immaculate is He!
No, to Him belongs whatever there is in the heavens
and the earth. All are obedient to Him,

117 the Originator of the heavens and the earth.
When He decides on a matter,
He just says to it, 'Be!' and it is.

118 Those who have no knowledge say,
'Why does not God speak to us, or come to us a sign?'
So said those who were before them,
words similar to what they say.
Alike are their hearts.
We have certainly made the signs clear
for a people who have certainty.

119 Indeed, We have sent you with the truth,
as a bearer of good news and as a warner,
and you will not be questioned
concerning the inmates of hell.

120 Never will the Jews be pleased with you,
nor the Christians,

---

[1] This refers to the Quraysh, who did not allow the Muslims to perform the ḥajj or ʿumrah pilgrimage after their migration to Madīnah. Only after the treaty of Hudaybiyyah (6 H.) did they concede their right to visit Makkah.

unless you followed their creed.
Say, 'Indeed, it is the guidance of God
which is the true guidance.'
And should you follow their base desires
after the knowledge that has come to you,
you will not have against God any friend
or helper.

121 Those to whom We have given the Book
follow it as it ought to be followed:
they have faith in it.
As for those who deny it
—it is they who are the losers.

122 O Children of Israel,
remember My blessing which I bestowed upon you,
and that I gave you an advantage over all the nations.

123 Beware of the Day
when no soul shall compensate for another,
neither will any ransom be accepted from it,
nor will any intercession benefit it,
nor will they be helped.

124 When his Lord tested Abraham with certain words,
and he fulfilled them,
He said, 'I am making you the Imam[1] of mankind.'
Said he, 'And from among my descendants?'
He said, 'My pledge does not extend to the unjust.'

125 And [remember] when We made the House
a place of reward[2] for mankind and a sanctuary, [declaring],

---

[1] That is, the spiritual and temporal guide and leader of mankind. For other Qurʾānic occurrences of this term, see 17:71; 25:74; 28:5; 32:24; 36:12.

[2] Or 'confluence,' or 'resort,' depending on whether the term *mathābah* is taken to mean a place of spiritual reward, a place of gathering, or a place to which one frequently returns.

'Take the venue of prayer from Abraham's Station.'[1]
We charged Abraham and Ishmael with its upkeep,
  saying, 'Purify My House
for those who go around it, those who make it a retreat
  and those who bow and prostrate.'

126 When Abraham said,
  'My Lord, make this a secure town,
  and provide its people with fruits
—such of them as have faith in God and the Last Day,'
He said, 'As for him who is faithless,
I will provide for him too for a short time,
then I will shove him toward the punishment of the Fire,
  and it is an evil destination.'

127 As Abraham raised the foundations of the House
  with Ishmael, they prayed: 'Our Lord, accept it from us!
  Indeed, You are the All-hearing, the All-knowing.

128 'Our Lord, make us submissive to You,
  and raise a nation submissive to You from our progeny,
  show us our rites, and turn to us clemently.
  Indeed, You are the All-clement, the All-merciful.'

129 'Our Lord, raise amongst them
  an apostle from among them,
  who will recite to them Your signs
and teach them the Book and wisdom, and purify them.
  Indeed, You are the All-mighty, the All-wise.'

130 And who will ever forsake Abraham's creed
  except one who debases himself?
We certainly chose him in the present world,
and in the Hereafter he will indeed be among the Righteous.

---

[1] Abraham's Station (*maqām Ibrāhīm*) is a spot at a few meters' distance from the Ka'bah where a stone relic is kept that bears the footprint of Abraham, behind which the pilgrims offer the prayer of the *ṭawāf*.

131 When his Lord said to him, 'Submit,'
he said, 'I submit to the Lord of all the worlds.'

132 Abraham enjoined this creed upon his children,
and so did Jacob, [saying], 'My children!
God has indeed chosen this religion for you;
so do not die except in complete surrender to God.'

133 Were you witnesses when death approached Jacob,
when he asked his children,
'What will you worship after me?'
They said, 'We will worship your God,
and the God of your fathers, Abraham, Ishmael, and Isaac,
the One God, and to Him do we submit.'

134 That was a nation that has passed:
for it there will be what it has earned,
and for you there will be what you have earned,
and you will not be questioned about what they used to do.

135 They say, 'Be either Jews or Christians
so that you may be rightly guided.'
Say, 'No, rather we will follow the creed of Abraham,
a *ḥanīf*, and he was not one of the polytheists.'

136 Say, 'We have faith in God,
and that which has been sent down to us,
and that which was sent down to Abraham,
Ishmael, Isaac, Jacob and the Tribes,[1]
and that which Moses and Jesus were given,
and what the prophets were given from their Lord;
we make no distinction between any of them
and to Him do we submit.'

---

[1] That is, the twelve tribes of the Israelites, who received the revelations through the prophets that were sent to them. Cf. **2:140; 3:84; 4:163.**

137 فَإِنْ آمَنُوا بِمِثْلِ مَا آمَنْتُم بِهِ فَقَدِ اهْتَدَوا ۖ So if they believe in the like of what you believe in, then they are surely guided;

وَإِن تَوَلَّوْا but if they turn away,

فَإِنَّمَا هُمْ فِي شِقَاقٍ ۖ then know that they are only steeped in defiance.

فَسَيَكْفِيكَهُمُ اللَّهُ ۚ God shall suffice you against them,

وَهُوَ السَّمِيعُ الْعَلِيمُ ۝ and He is the All-hearing, the All-knowing.

138 صِبْغَةَ اللَّهِ ۖ 'The baptism of God,

وَمَنْ أَحْسَنُ مِنَ اللَّهِ صِبْغَةً ۖ and who baptizes better than God?

وَنَحْنُ لَهُ عَابِدُونَ ۝ And Him do we worship.'

139 قُلْ أَتُحَاجُّونَنَا فِي اللَّهِ Say, 'Will you argue with us concerning God,

وَهُوَ رَبُّنَا وَرَبُّكُمْ while He is our Lord and your Lord,

وَلَنَا أَعْمَالُنَا and to us our deeds belong,

وَلَكُمْ أَعْمَالُكُمْ and to you your deeds belong,

وَنَحْنُ لَهُ مُخْلِصُونَ ۝ and we worship Him dedicatedly?'

140 أَمْ تَقُولُونَ إِنَّ إِبْرَاهِيمَ [Ask them,] 'Do you say that Abraham,

وَإِسْمَاعِيلَ وَإِسْحَاقَ وَيَعْقُوبَ وَالْأَسْبَاطَ Ishmael, Isaac, Jacob, and the Tribes

كَانُوا هُودًا أَوْ نَصَارَىٰ ۗ were Jews or Christians?'

قُلْ أَأَنتُمْ أَعْلَمُ أَمِ اللَّهُ ۗ Say, 'Is it you who know better, or God?'

وَمَنْ أَظْلَمُ مِمَّن And who is a greater wrongdoer than someone who

كَتَمَ شَهَادَةً عِندَهُ مِنَ اللَّهِ ۗ conceals a testimony that is with him from God?

وَمَا اللَّهُ بِغَافِلٍ عَمَّا تَعْمَلُونَ ۝ And God is not oblivious of what you do.

141 تِلْكَ أُمَّةٌ قَدْ خَلَتْ ۖ That was a nation that has passed:

لَهَا مَا كَسَبَتْ for it there will be what it has earned,

وَلَكُم مَّا كَسَبْتُمْ ۖ and for you there will be what you have earned,

وَلَا تُسْأَلُونَ عَمَّا كَانُوا يَعْمَلُونَ ۝ and you will not be questioned about what they used to do.

الجزء الثاني [PART 2]

142 سَيَقُولُ السُّفَهَاءُ مِنَ النَّاسِ The foolish among the people[1] will say,

مَا وَلَّاهُمْ 'What has turned them away

عَن قِبْلَتِهِمُ الَّتِي كَانُوا عَلَيْهَا ۚ from the *qiblah* they were following?'[2]

---

[1] That is, the Jews or the hypocrites amongst Muslims, or both.
[2] The Muslims first used to pray facing in the direction of Bayt al-Maqdis. This and the verses that follow

Say, 'To God belong the east and the west.
   He guides whomever He wishes to a straight path.'

143 Thus We have made you a middle nation
   that you may be witnesses to the people,
   and that the Apostle may be a witness to you.
   We did not appoint the *qiblah* you were following
   but that We may ascertain those who follow the Apostle
      from those who turn back on their heels.
   It was indeed a hard thing
      except for those whom God has guided.
   And God would not let your prayers go to waste.[1]
   God is indeed most kind and merciful to mankind.

144 We certainly see *you* turning *your* face about in the sky.
   We will surely turn *you* to a *qiblah* of your liking:
      so turn *your* face towards the Holy Mosque,
   and wherever you may be, turn your faces towards it!
   Indeed, those who were given the Book
      surely know that it is the truth from their Lord.
   And God is not oblivious of what they do.

145 Even if *you* bring those who were given the Book
      every kind of sign,[2]
   they will not follow *your qiblah*.
   Nor shall *you* follow their *qiblah*,
      nor will any of them follow the *qiblah* of the other.
   And if *you* follow their base desires,

---

pertain to the change of the *qiblah*, or the direction faced during prayer, from Quds to the Ka'bah, in Makkah, on the 15th of Sha'bān, 2 H.

[1] '*Īmān*' here means prayers. God reassures the faithful that the prayers they have offered earlier facing towards Quds will not be wasted by the change of *qiblah*.

[2] That is, every kind of miracle.

after the knowledge that has come to you,
you will be one of the wrongdoers.

146 Those whom We have given the Book
recognize him just as they recognize their sons,[1]
but a part of them indeed conceal the truth
while they know.

147 This is the truth from *your* Lord;
so do not be among the sceptics.

148 Everyone has a cynosure to which he turns;
so take the lead in all good works.
Wherever you may be,
God will bring you all together.
Indeed, God has power over all things.

149 Whencesoever you may go out,
turn *your* face towards the Holy Mosque.
It is indeed the truth from *your* Lord,
and God is not oblivious of what you do.

150 And whencesoever you may go out,
turn *your* face towards the Holy Mosque,
and wherever you may be, turn your faces towards it,
so that the people may have no allegation against you,
neither those of them who are wrongdoers.[2]
So do not fear them, but fear Me,
that I may complete My blessing on you
and so that you may be guided.

151 Even as We sent to you an Apostle
from among yourselves,
who recites to you Our signs, and purifies you,
and teaches you the Book and wisdom,

---
[1] Cf. **6:20**.
[2] As suggested by the *Tafsīr al-Qummī*, *illā* here stands for *wa lā*, and does not imply exclusion.

and teaches you what you did not know.

152 Remember Me and I will remember you,
and thank Me and do not be ungrateful to Me.

153 O you who have faith!
Take recourse in patience and prayer;
indeed God is with the patient.

154 Do not call those who were slain in God's way 'dead.'
No, they are living, but you are not aware.

155 We will surely test you
    with a measure of fear and hunger
and a loss of wealth, lives, and fruits;
and give good news to the patient

156 —those who, when an affliction visits them,
say, 'Indeed, we belong to God,
and to Him do we indeed return.'

157 It is they who receive the blessings of their Lord
    and mercy,
and it is they who are the rightly guided.

158 Safā and Marwah are indeed
    among God's sacraments.
 So whoever makes *hajj* to the House,
    or performs the '*umrah*,
there is no sin upon him to circuit between them.
Should anyone do good of his own accord,
then God is indeed appreciative, all-knowing.

159 Indeed, those who conceal what We have sent down
    of manifest proofs and guidance,
after We have clarified it in the Book for mankind,
—they shall be cursed by God

and cursed by all the cursers,

160 except such as repent, make amends, and clarify
—those I shall pardon,
and I am the All-clement, the All-merciful.

161 Indeed, those who turn faithless, and die faithless,
—it is they on whom shall be the curse of God,
the angels and all mankind.

162 They will remain in it
and their punishment shall not be lightened,
nor will they be granted any respite.

163 Your god is the One God, there is no god except Him,
the All-beneficent, the All-merciful.

164 Indeed, in the creation of the heavens and the earth,
and the alternation of night and day,
and the ships that sail at sea
with profit to men,
and the water that God sends down from the sky
—with which He revives the earth after its death,
and scatters therein every kind of animal—
and the changing of the winds,
and the clouds disposed between the sky
and the earth,
there are signs for a people who exercise their reason.

165 Among the people are those who set up
compeers besides God,
loving them as if loving God
—but the faithful have a more ardent love for God—
though the wrongdoers will see,
when they sight the punishment,

that power, altogether, belongs to God,
and that God is severe in punishment.

166 When those who were followed will disown the followers,
and they will sight the punishment
while all their means of recourse will be cut off,

167 and when the followers will say,
'Had there been another turn for us,
we would disown them as they disown us now!'
Thus shall God show them their deeds
as regrets for themselves,
and they shall not leave the Fire.

168 O mankind!
Eat of what is lawful and pure in the earth,
and do not follow in Satan's steps.
He is indeed your manifest enemy.

169 He only prompts you to commit evil and indecent acts,
and that you attribute to God what you do not know.

170 When they are told, 'Follow what God has sent down,'
they say, 'No, we will follow
what we have found our fathers following.'
What, even if their fathers neither exercised their reason
nor were guided?!

171 The parable of the faithless
is that of someone who shouts after that which
does not hear anything except a call and cry:
deaf, dumb, and blind, they do not exercise their reason.

172 O you who have faith!
Eat of the good things We have provided you,
and thank God, if it is Him that you worship.

173 He has forbidden you only carrion,
blood, the flesh of the swine,
and that which has been offered to other than God.
But should someone be compelled,
without being rebellious or transgressive,[1]
there shall be no sin upon him.
God is indeed all-forgiving, all-merciful.
174 Indeed, those who conceal
what God has sent down of the Book
and sell it for a paltry gain
—they do not ingest into their bellies
except fire,
and God shall not speak to them
on the Day of Resurrection,
nor shall He purify them,
and there is a painful punishment for them.
175 They are the ones who bought error for guidance,
and punishment for pardon:
how patient of them to face the Fire![2]
176 That is so because God has sent down the Book
with the truth,
and those who differ about the Book
are surely in extreme defiance.

177 Piety is not to turn your faces
to the east or the west;
rather, piety is [personified by] those who have faith
in God and the Last Day, the angels,

---

[1] According to some exegetical traditions, *bāghī* refers to one who rebels against a just ruler (or, to a hunter), and *'ādī* to a thief or highwayman (see Ṭabarī, Rāzī, *al-Tafsīr al-Burhān*). Cf. **6:145**; **16:115**.

[2] Or 'what has made them tolerant of the Fire?'

the Book, and the prophets, وَالْكِتَابِ وَالنَّبِيِّينَ

and who give their wealth, for the love of Him,[1] وَآتَى الْمَالَ عَلَىٰ حُبِّهِ

to relatives, orphans, the needy, ذَوِي الْقُرْبَىٰ وَالْيَتَامَىٰ وَالْمَسَاكِينَ

the traveler and the beggar, وَابْنَ السَّبِيلِ وَالسَّائِلِينَ

and for the freeing of the slaves, وَفِي الرِّقَابِ

and maintain the prayer and give the zakāt, وَأَقَامَ الصَّلَاةَ وَآتَى الزَّكَاةَ

and those who fulfill their covenants, وَالْمُوفُونَ بِعَهْدِهِمْ

when they pledge themselves, إِذَا عَاهَدُوا

and those who are patient in stress and distress,[2] وَالصَّابِرِينَ فِي الْبَأْسَاءِ وَالضَّرَّاءِ

and in the heat of battle. وَحِينَ الْبَأْسِ

They are the ones who are true to their covenant, أُولَٰئِكَ الَّذِينَ صَدَقُوا

and it is they who are the Godwary. وَأُولَٰئِكَ هُمُ الْمُتَّقُونَ ۝

178 O you who have faith! يَا أَيُّهَا الَّذِينَ آمَنُوا

Retribution is prescribed for you regarding the slain: كُتِبَ عَلَيْكُمُ الْقِصَاصُ فِي الْقَتْلَى

freeman for freeman, slave for slave, الْحُرُّ بِالْحُرِّ وَالْعَبْدُ بِالْعَبْدِ

and female for female. وَالْأُنْثَىٰ بِالْأُنْثَىٰ

But if one is granted any extenuation by his brother,[3] فَمَنْ عُفِيَ لَهُ مِنْ أَخِيهِ شَيْءٌ

let the follow up [for the blood-money] be honourable, فَاتِّبَاعٌ بِالْمَعْرُوفِ

and let the payment to him be with kindness. وَأَدَاءٌ إِلَيْهِ بِإِحْسَانٍ

That is a remission from your Lord and a mercy; ذَٰلِكَ تَخْفِيفٌ مِنْ رَبِّكُمْ وَرَحْمَةٌ

and should anyone transgress after that, فَمَنِ اعْتَدَىٰ بَعْدَ ذَٰلِكَ

there shall be a painful punishment for him. فَلَهُ عَذَابٌ أَلِيمٌ ۝

179 There is life for you in retribution, وَلَكُمْ فِي الْقِصَاصِ حَيَاةٌ

O you who possess intellects! يَا أُولِي الْأَلْبَابِ

Maybe you will be Godwary! لَعَلَّكُمْ تَتَّقُونَ ۝

180 Prescribed for you, كُتِبَ عَلَيْكُمْ

when death approaches any of you إِذَا حَضَرَ أَحَدَكُمُ الْمَوْتُ

and he leaves behind any property, إِنْ تَرَكَ خَيْرًا

---

[1] Or 'despite their love of it.' Cf. **76**:8.
[2] That is, in poverty and sickness.
[3] That is, by the heir of the victim.

is that he make a bequest for his parents and relatives, الْوَصِيَّةُ لِلْوَالِدَيْنِ وَالْأَقْرَبِينَ
in an honourable manner, بِالْمَعْرُوفِ
—an obligation on the Godwary. حَقًّا عَلَى الْمُتَّقِينَ ۝

181 And should anyone alter it after hearing it, فَمَنْ بَدَّلَهُ بَعْدَ مَا سَمِعَهُ
its sin shall indeed lie on those who alter it. فَإِنَّمَا إِثْمُهُ عَلَى الَّذِينَ يُبَدِّلُونَهُ
God is indeed all-hearing, all-knowing. إِنَّ اللَّهَ سَمِيعٌ عَلِيمٌ ۝

182 But should someone, fearing فَمَنْ خَافَ
deviance or sin on the testator's behalf, مِنْ مُوصٍ جَنَفًا أَوْ إِثْمًا
set things right between them, فَأَصْلَحَ بَيْنَهُمْ
there is no sin upon him. فَلَا إِثْمَ عَلَيْهِ
God indeed is all-forgiving, all-merciful. إِنَّ اللَّهَ غَفُورٌ رَحِيمٌ ۝

183 O you who have faith! يَا أَيُّهَا الَّذِينَ آمَنُوا
Prescribed for you is fasting كُتِبَ عَلَيْكُمُ الصِّيَامُ
as was prescribed for those who were before you, كَمَا كُتِبَ عَلَى الَّذِينَ مِنْ قَبْلِكُمْ
so that you may be Godwary. لَعَلَّكُمْ تَتَّقُونَ ۝

184 That for known days. أَيَّامًا مَعْدُودَاتٍ
But should any of you be sick or on a journey, فَمَنْ كَانَ مِنْكُمْ مَرِيضًا أَوْ عَلَى سَفَرٍ
let it be a similar number of other days. فَعِدَّةٌ مِنْ أَيَّامٍ أُخَرَ
Those who find it straining shall be liable وَعَلَى الَّذِينَ يُطِيقُونَهُ
to atonement by feeding a needy person. فِدْيَةٌ طَعَامُ مِسْكِينٍ
Should anyone do good of his own accord, فَمَنْ تَطَوَّعَ خَيْرًا
that is better for him, فَهُوَ خَيْرٌ لَهُ
and to fast is better for you, should you know. وَأَنْ تَصُومُوا خَيْرٌ لَكُمْ إِنْ كُنْتُمْ تَعْلَمُونَ ۝

185 The month of Ramaḍān شَهْرُ رَمَضَانَ
is one in which the Qur'ān was sent down الَّذِي أُنْزِلَ فِيهِ الْقُرْآنُ
as guidance for mankind, هُدًى لِلنَّاسِ
with manifest proofs of guidance and the Criterion.[1] وَبَيِّنَاتٍ مِنَ الْهُدَى وَالْفُرْقَانِ
So let those of you who witness it fast in it, فَمَنْ شَهِدَ مِنْكُمُ الشَّهْرَ فَلْيَصُمْهُ

---

[1] See footnote at 2:53.

and as for someone who is sick or on a journey,
    let it be a similar number of other days.
God desires ease for you,
    and He does not desire hardship for you,
    and so that you may complete the number,
    and magnify God for guiding you,
    and that you may give thanks.

186 When My servants ask you about Me,
    tell them that I am indeed nearmost.
I answer the supplicant's call when he calls Me.
So let them respond to Me and have faith in Me,
    so that they may fare rightly.

187 You are permitted on the night of the fast
    to go into your wives:
they are a garment for you,
    and you are a garment for them.
God knew that you would betray yourselves,
    so He pardoned you and excused you.
So now consort with them,
    and seek what God has ordained for you,
    and eat and drink
until the white streak becomes manifest to you
    from the dark streak at the crack of dawn.[1]
Then complete the fast until nightfall,
    and do not consort with them
    while you dwell in confinement in the mosques.
These are God's bounds, so do not approach them.
Thus does God clarify His signs for mankind
    so that they may be Godwary.

---

[1] That is, until the first appearance of the dawn.

188 Do not eat up your wealth among yourselves wrongfully, nor proffer it to the judges in order to eat up a part of the people's wealth sinfully, while you know [that it is immoral to do so].

189 They question *you* concerning the new moons. *Say,* 'They are timekeeping signs for the people and [for the sake of] hajj.' It is not piety that you enter the houses from their rear; rather piety is [personified by] one who is Godwary, and enter the houses from their doors, and be wary of God, so that you may be felicitous.

190 Fight in the way of God those who fight you, but do not transgress. Indeed, God does not like transgressors.

191 And kill them wherever you confront them, and expel them from where they expelled you, for persecution[1] is graver than killing. But do not fight them near the Holy Mosque unless they fight you therein; but if they fight you, kill them; such is the requital of the faithless.[2]

192 But if they desist, God is indeed all-forgiving, all-merciful.

193 Fight them until persecution[3] is no more, and religion becomes exclusively for God.

---

[1] Or 'polytheism.'

[2] This refers to the polytheists of Makkah, who, after oppressing the Muslims for more than a decade, had continued their belligerence by depriving them of the right to perform the ḥajj or ʿumrah. These verses for the first time command all Muslims to engage in armed struggle against their oppressors.

[3] Or 'polytheism,' as narrated from Imam Muḥammad al-Bāqir (Ṭabrisī), Mujāhid, Qatādah, Rabīʿ, and Ḍaḥḥāk (Ṭabarī).

Then if they desist, there shall be no reprisal
　　except against the wrongdoers.
194 A sacred month for a sacred month,
　　and all sanctities require retribution.
　So should anyone aggress against you,
　　assail him in the manner he assailed you,[1]
　and be wary of God,
　　and know that God is with the Godwary.

195 Spend in the way of God,
　and do not cast yourselves with your own hands
　　into destruction; and be virtuous.
　Indeed, God loves the virtuous.
196 Complete the *hajj* and the *'umrah* for God's sake,
　　and if you are prevented,
　then make such sacrificial offering as is feasible.
　And do not shave your heads
　　until the offering reaches its assigned place.
　But should any of you be sick,
　　or have a hurt in his head,[2]
　let the atonement be by fasting, or charity, or sacrifice.
　And when you have security
　—for those who enjoy [release from the restrictions]
　　by virtue of their *'umrah* until the *hajj*—
　　let the offering be such as is feasible.
　As for someone who cannot afford the offering,
　　let him fast three days during the hajj
　　and seven when you return;
　　that is a period of ten complete days.

[1] Cf. **16**:126.
[2] Such as a wound on the scalp.

ذَٰلِكَ لِمَنْ لَمْ يَكُنْ أَهْلُهُ	That is for someone whose family does not
حَاضِرِي الْمَسْجِدِ الْحَرَامِ	dwell by the Holy Mosque.
وَاتَّقُوا اللَّهَ	And be wary of God,
وَاعْلَمُوا أَنَّ اللَّهَ شَدِيدُ الْعِقَابِ ۝	and know that God is severe in retribution.
الْحَجُّ أَشْهُرٌ مَعْلُومَاتٌ	197 The *hajj* season is in months well-known;
فَمَنْ فَرَضَ فِيهِنَّ الْحَجَّ	so whoever decides on *hajj* pilgrimage therein,
فَلَا رَفَثَ	should know that there is to be no sexual contact,
وَلَا فُسُوقَ وَلَا جِدَالَ فِي الْحَجِّ	vicious talk, or disputing during the *hajj*.
وَمَا تَفْعَلُوا مِنْ خَيْرٍ يَعْلَمْهُ اللَّهُ	Whatever good you do, God knows it.
وَتَزَوَّدُوا فَإِنَّ خَيْرَ الزَّادِ التَّقْوَىٰ	And take provision, for Godwariness is the best provision.
وَاتَّقُونِ يَا أُولِي الْأَلْبَابِ ۝	Be wary of Me, O you who possess intellects!
لَيْسَ عَلَيْكُمْ جُنَاحٌ	198 There is no sin upon you
أَنْ تَبْتَغُوا فَضْلًا مِنْ رَبِّكُمْ	in seeking your Lord's bounty [during *hajj* season].
فَإِذَا أَفَضْتُمْ مِنْ عَرَفَاتٍ	Then when you stream out of 'Arafāt
فَاذْكُرُوا اللَّهَ عِنْدَ الْمَشْعَرِ الْحَرَامِ	remember God at the Holy Mash'ar,
وَاذْكُرُوهُ كَمَا هَدَاكُمْ	and remember Him as He has guided you,
وَإِنْ كُنْتُمْ مِنْ قَبْلِهِ لَمِنَ الضَّالِّينَ ۝	and earlier you were indeed among the astray.
ثُمَّ أَفِيضُوا مِنْ حَيْثُ أَفَاضَ النَّاسُ	199 Then stream out from where the people stream out,
وَاسْتَغْفِرُوا اللَّهَ	and plead to God for forgiveness;
إِنَّ اللَّهَ غَفُورٌ رَحِيمٌ ۝	indeed God is all-forgiving, all-merciful.
فَإِذَا قَضَيْتُمْ مَنَاسِكَكُمْ	200 And when you finish your rites,
فَاذْكُرُوا اللَّهَ كَذِكْرِكُمْ آبَاءَكُمْ	remember God as you would remember your fathers,
أَوْ أَشَدَّ ذِكْرًا	or with a more ardent remembrance.
فَمِنَ النَّاسِ مَنْ يَقُولُ	Among the people there are those who say,
رَبَّنَا آتِنَا فِي الدُّنْيَا	'Our Lord, give us in this world,'
وَمَا لَهُ فِي الْآخِرَةِ مِنْ خَلَاقٍ ۝	but for such there is no share in the Hereafter.
وَمِنْهُمْ مَنْ يَقُولُ	201 And among them there are those who say,
رَبَّنَا آتِنَا فِي الدُّنْيَا حَسَنَةً	'Our Lord, give us good in this world
وَفِي الْآخِرَةِ حَسَنَةً	and good in the Hereafter,

            and save us from the punishment of the Fire.'
202 Such shall partake of what they have earned,
            and God is swift at reckoning.

203 Remember God in the appointed days.
            Then whoever hastens off in a couple of days,
               there is no sin upon him,
            and whoever delays, there is no sin upon him
            —that for one who has been Godwary—
            and be wary of God,
            and know that toward Him you will be gathered.

204 Among the people
            is he whose talk about worldly life impresses you,
            and he holds God witness to what is in his heart,
            though he is the staunchest of enemies.

205 If he were to wield authority,
            he would try to cause corruption in the land
               and to ruin the crop and the stock,
            and God does not like corruption.

206 When he is told, 'Be wary of God,'
               conceit seizes him sinfully;
so let hell suffice him, and it is surely an evil resting place!

207 And among the people is he who sells his soul[1]
            seeking the pleasure of God,
            and God is most kind to His servants.

208 O you who have faith! Enter into submission,
            all together,
            and do not follow in Satan's steps;
            he is indeed your manifest enemy.

---

[1] Or 'his life.'

209 And should you stumble
   after the manifest proofs that have come to you,
   know that God is all-mighty, all-wise.
210 Do they await anything but
   that God's command should come to them
   in the shades of the clouds, with the angels,
   and the matter be decided once for all?
   To God all matters are returned.
211 Ask the Children of Israel
   how many a manifest sign We had given them.
   Whoever changes God's blessing after it has come to him,
   indeed God is severe in retribution.
212 Worldly life has been glamorized for the faithless,
   and they ridicule the faithful.
   But those who are Godwary
   shall be above them on the Day of Resurrection,
   and God provides for whomever He wishes
   without any reckoning.
213 Mankind were a single community;
   then God sent the prophets
   as bearers of good news and warners,
   and He sent down with them the Book with the truth,
   that it[1] may judge between the people
   concerning that about which they differed,
   and none differed in it except those who were given it,
   after manifest proofs had come to them,
   out of envy among themselves.
   Then God guided those who had faith
   to the truth of what they differed in, by His will,

---

[1] That is the Book.

and God guides whomever He wishes
   to a straight path.
214 Do you suppose that you will enter paradise
   though there has not yet come to you
   the like of what befell those who went before you?
   Stress and distress befell them
   and they were convulsed until
   the apostle and the faithful who were with him said,
   'When will God's help come?'
   Behold! God's help is indeed near!
215 They ask you as to what they should spend.
   Say, 'Whatever wealth you spend,
   let it be for parents, relatives, orphans,
   the needy, and the traveler.'
   And whatever good that you may do,
   God indeed knows it.

216 Warfare has been prescribed for you,
   though it is repulsive to you.
   Yet it may be that you dislike something
   which is good for you,
   and it may be that you love something
   which is bad for you,
   and God knows and you do not know.
217 They ask you concerning warfare in the holy month.
   Say, 'It is an outrageous thing to fight in it,
   but to keep people from God's way,
   and to be unfaithful to Him,
   and to keep people from the Holy Mosque,
   and to expel its people from it

are more outrageous with God.
And persecution is graver than killing.
And they will not cease fighting you
until they turn you away from your religion, if they can.
And whoever of you turns away from his religion
and dies faithless
—they are the ones whose works have failed
in this world and the Hereafter.
They shall be the inmates of the Fire,
and they shall remain in it.

218 Indeed, those who are faithful
and those who have migrated
and waged *jihād* in the way of God
—it is they who expect God's mercy,
and God is all-forgiving, all-merciful.

219 They ask *you* concerning wine and gambling.
Say, 'There is a great sin in both of them,
and some profits for the people,
but their sinfulness outweighs their profit.'
And they ask you as to what they should spend.
Say, 'All that is surplus.'
Thus does God clarify His signs for you
so that you may reflect
220 about the world and the Hereafter.
And they ask *you* concerning the orphans.
Say, 'It is better to set right their affairs,[1]
and if you intermingle with them,
they are, of course, your brothers:

---

[1] That is, it is better to manage their affairs than to stand aloof due to the fear of mishandling them. Cf. 4:2.

God knows those who cause corruption
from those who set things right,
and had God wished,
He would have put you to hardship.'
God is indeed all-mighty, all-wise.

221 Do not marry idolatresses until they embrace faith.
A faithful slave girl is better than an idolatress,
though she should impress you.
And do not marry your women to idolaters
until they embrace faith.
A faithful slave is better than an idolater,
though he should impress you.
Those invite others to the Fire,
but God invites to paradise and pardon, by His will,
and He clarifies His signs for the people
so that they may take admonition.

222 They ask you concerning intercourse during menses.
Say, 'It is hurtful.'[1]
So keep away from wives during the menses,[2]
and do not approach them till they are clean.
And when they become clean,
go into them as God has commanded you.
God indeed loves the penitent
and He loves those who keep clean.

223 Your women are a tillage for you,
so come to your tillage whenever you like,
and send ahead for your souls, and be Godwary,
and know that you will encounter Him;

---

[1] Or 'offensive.'
[2] That is, 'refrain from sexual intercourse.'

and give good news to the faithful.

224 Do not make God an obstacle, through your oaths,
to being pious and Godwary,
and to bringing about concord between people.
And God is all-hearing, all-knowing.

225 God will not take you to task
for what is unconsidered in your oaths,
but He will take you to task
for what your hearts have incurred,
and God is all-forgiving, all-forbearing.

226 For those who forswear their wives[1]
there shall be a waiting period of four months.
And if they recant,
God is indeed all-forgiving, all-merciful.

227 But if they resolve on divorce,
God is indeed all-hearing, all-knowing.

228 Divorced women shall wait by themselves
for three periods of purity after menses,
and it is not lawful for them to conceal
what God has created in their wombs
if they believe in God and the Last Day;
and their husbands have a greater right to restore them
during this duration, if they desire reconcilement.
The wives have rights similar to the obligations upon them,
in accordance with honourable norms;
and men have a degree above them,
and God is all-mighty and all-wise.

229 [Revocable] divorce may be only twice;

---

[1] That is, by pronouncing *īlā*, a pre-Islamic practice which allowed the husband to take an oath to refrain from sexual relations with his wife, which left the wife in a state of uncertainty for an indefinite period. According to this verse, the husband must decide within four months either to restore the marriage or to divorce her.

فَإِمْسَاكٌ بِمَعْرُوفٍ	then let there be either an honourable retention,
أَوْ تَسْرِيحٌ بِإِحْسَانٍ	or a kindly release.
وَلَا يَحِلُّ لَكُمْ أَنْ تَأْخُذُوا	It is not lawful for you to take back
مِمَّا آتَيْتُمُوهُنَّ شَيْئًا	anything from what you have given them,[1]
إِلَّا أَنْ يَخَافَا	unless the couple fear
أَلَّا يُقِيمَا حُدُودَ اللَّهِ	that they may not maintain God's bounds.
فَإِنْ خِفْتُمْ أَلَّا يُقِيمَا حُدُودَ اللَّهِ	But if you fear they would not maintain God's bounds,
فَلَا جُنَاحَ عَلَيْهِمَا	there is no sin upon them[2]
فِيمَا افْتَدَتْ بِهِ	in what she may give to secure her own release.
تِلْكَ حُدُودُ اللَّهِ فَلَا تَعْتَدُوهَا	These are God's bounds, so do not transgress them,
وَمَنْ يَتَعَدَّ حُدُودَ اللَّهِ	and whoever transgresses the bounds of God
فَأُولَٰئِكَ هُمُ الظَّالِمُونَ ۝	—it is they who are the wrongdoers.
فَإِنْ طَلَّقَهَا	230 And if he divorces her,
فَلَا تَحِلُّ لَهُ مِنْ بَعْدُ	she will not be lawful for him thereafter
حَتَّىٰ تَنْكِحَ زَوْجًا غَيْرَهُ	until she marries a husband other than him;
فَإِنْ طَلَّقَهَا	then if he divorces her,
فَلَا جُنَاحَ عَلَيْهِمَا أَنْ يَتَرَاجَعَا	there is no sin upon them to remarry
إِنْ ظَنَّا أَنْ يُقِيمَا حُدُودَ اللَّهِ	if they think that they can maintain God's bounds.
وَتِلْكَ حُدُودُ اللَّهِ يُبَيِّنُهَا	These are God's bounds, which He clarifies
لِقَوْمٍ يَعْلَمُونَ ۝	for a people who have knowledge.
وَإِذَا طَلَّقْتُمُ النِّسَاءَ فَبَلَغْنَ أَجَلَهُنَّ	231 When you divorce women and they complete their term,
فَأَمْسِكُوهُنَّ بِمَعْرُوفٍ	then either retain them honourably
أَوْ سَرِّحُوهُنَّ بِمَعْرُوفٍ	or release them honourably,
وَلَا تُمْسِكُوهُنَّ ضِرَارًا	and do not retain them maliciously
لِتَعْتَدُوا	in order that you may transgress;
وَمَنْ يَفْعَلْ ذَٰلِكَ فَقَدْ ظَلَمَ نَفْسَهُ	and whoever does that certainly wrongs himself.
وَلَا تَتَّخِذُوا آيَاتِ اللَّهِ هُزُوًا	Do not take the signs of God in derision,
وَاذْكُرُوا نِعْمَتَ اللَّهِ عَلَيْكُمْ	and remember God's blessing upon you,
وَمَا أَنْزَلَ عَلَيْكُمْ	and what He has sent down to you

---

[1] That is, to the wives.
[2] That is, the husband and wife.

of the Book and wisdom, to advise you therewith.
Be wary of God,
and know that God has knowledge of all things.

232 When you divorce women
and they complete their term of waiting,
do not hinder them from remarrying their husbands,
when they honourably reach mutual consent.
Herewith are advised
those of you who believe in God
and the Last Day.
That will be more decent and purer for you,
and God knows and you do not know.

233 Mothers shall suckle their children
for two full years,
—that for such as desire to complete the suckling—
and on the father shall be their maintenance and clothing,
in accordance with honourable norms.
No soul is to be tasked except according to its capacity:
neither the mother shall be made to suffer harm
on her child's account,
nor the father on account of his child,
and on the heir devolve [duties and rights] similar to that.
And if the couple desire to wean,
with mutual consent and consultation,
there will be no sin upon them.
And if you want to have your children wet-nursed,
there will be no sin upon you
so long as you pay what you give
in accordance with honourable norms,
and be wary of God,

and know that God watches what you do.

234 As for those of you who die leaving wives,
  they shall wait by themselves four months and ten days,
  and when they complete their term,
    there will be no sin upon you
      in respect of what they may do with themselves
      in accordance with honourable norms.
  And God is well aware of what you do.

235 There is no sin upon you in what you may hint
    in proposing to [recently widowed] women,
  or what you may secretly cherish within your hearts.
  God knows that you will be thinking of them,
    but do not make troth with them secretly,
    unless you say honourable words,
  and do not resolve on a marriage tie
    until the prescribed term is complete.[1]
  Know that God knows what is in your hearts,
    so beware of Him;
    and know that God is all-forgiving, all-forbearing.

236 There is no sin upon you if you divorce women
    while you have not yet touched them
    or settled a dowry for them.
  Yet provide for them
    —the well-off according to his capacity,
    and the poorly-off according to his capacity—
  with a sustenance that is honourable,
    an obligation on the virtuous.

237 And if you divorce them before you touch them,
    and you have already settled a dowry for them,

---

[1] That is, until the waiting period of four months and ten days prescribed for the widow is complete.

فَنِصْفُ مَا فَرَضْتُمْ	then pay them half of what you have settled,
إِلَّا أَن يَعْفُونَ	unless they forgo it,
أَوْ يَعْفُوَ الَّذِي بِيَدِهِ عُقْدَةُ النِّكَاحِ ۚ	or someone in whose hand is the marriage tie forgoes it.[1]
وَأَن تَعْفُوا أَقْرَبُ لِلتَّقْوَىٰ ۚ	And to forgo is nearer to Godwariness;
وَلَا تَنسَوُا الْفَضْلَ بَيْنَكُمْ ۚ	so do not forget graciousness among yourselves.
إِنَّ اللَّهَ بِمَا تَعْمَلُونَ بَصِيرٌ ۝	God indeed watches what you do.

238 Be watchful of your prayers,
and especially the middle prayer,[2]
and stand in obedience[3] to God;

239 and should you fear a danger,
then pray on foot or mounted,
and when you are safe, remember God,
as He taught you what you did not know.

240 Those of you who die leaving wives
shall bequeath for their wives
providing for a year, without turning them out;
but if they leave, there is no sin upon you
in respect of what they may do with themselves
in accordance with honourable norms.
And God is all-mighty, all-wise.

241 For the divorced women there shall be a provision,
in accordance with honourable norms
—an obligation on the Godwary.

242 Thus does God clarify His signs to you
so that you may exercise your reason.

243 Have you not regarded those who left their homes

---

[1] That is, the wife's guardian or the husband. The bride's guardian may forgo the half of the dowry which is her right to receive, or the husband may refrain from demanding half of the dowry he has already paid.
[2] That is, the *ẓuhr* (noon) prayer, according to several traditions narrated from the Imams of the Prophet's Household, as well as many traditions narrated in the Sunnī sources (see *al-Tafsīr al-Burhān*, al-Ṭabarī's *Jāmiʿ al-Bayān*). According to other interpretations, the phrase 'the middle prayer' refers to the *ʿaṣr* (afternoon), *maghrib* (sunset) or *fajr* (dawn) prayer.
[3] Or 'stand humbly' (or 'prayerfully,' 'devoutly') before God.

in thousands, apprehensive of death,
whereupon God said to them, 'Die,'
then He revived them?
God is indeed gracious to mankind,
but most people do not give thanks.

244 Fight in the way of God,
and know that God is all-hearing, all-knowing.

245 Who is it that will lend God a good loan
that He may multiply it for him severalfold?
And God tightens and expands the means of life,
and to Him you shall be brought back.

246 Have you not regarded the elite of the Israelites
after Moses, when they said to their prophet,
'Appoint for us a king,
that we may fight in the way of God.'
He said, 'May it not be that
you will not fight if fighting were prescribed for you?'
They said, 'Why should we not fight in the way of God,
when we have been expelled from our homes
and separated from our children?'
So when fighting was prescribed for them,
they turned away except a few of them,
and God knows well the wrongdoers.

247 Their prophet said to them,
'God has appointed Saul as king for you.'
They said, 'How can he have kingship over us,
when we have a greater right to kingship than him,
as he has not been given ample wealth?'
He said, 'God has indeed chosen him over you,
and enhanced him vastly in knowledge and physique,

وَاللَّهُ يُؤْتِي مُلْكَهُ مَن يَشَاءُ ۗ   and God gives His kingdom to whomever He wishes,
وَاللَّهُ وَاسِعٌ عَلِيمٌ ۝   and God is all-bounteous, all-knowing.'

وَقَالَ لَهُمْ نَبِيُّهُمْ   248 Their prophet said to them,
إِنَّ آيَةَ مُلْكِهِ   'Indeed, the sign of his kingship shall be
أَن يَأْتِيَكُمُ التَّابُوتُ   that the Ark will come to you,
فِيهِ سَكِينَةٌ مِّن رَّبِّكُمْ   bearing tranquillity from your Lord
وَبَقِيَّةٌ مِّمَّا تَرَكَ آلُ مُوسَىٰ   and the relics left behind by the House of Moses
وَآلُ هَارُونَ تَحْمِلُهُ الْمَلَائِكَةُ ۚ   and the House of Aaron, borne by the angels.
إِنَّ فِي ذَٰلِكَ لَآيَةً لَّكُمْ   There is indeed a sign in that for you,
إِن كُنتُم مُّؤْمِنِينَ ۝   should you be faithful.'

فَلَمَّا فَصَلَ طَالُوتُ بِالْجُنُودِ   249 As Saul set out with the troops,
قَالَ إِنَّ اللَّهَ مُبْتَلِيكُم بِنَهَرٍ   he said, 'God will test you with a stream:
فَمَن شَرِبَ مِنْهُ فَلَيْسَ مِنِّي   anyone who drinks from it will not belong to me,
وَمَن لَّمْ يَطْعَمْهُ فَإِنَّهُ مِنِّي   but those who do not drink from it will belong to me,
إِلَّا مَنِ اغْتَرَفَ غُرْفَةً بِيَدِهِ ۚ   barring someone who draws a scoop with his hand.'
فَشَرِبُوا مِنْهُ إِلَّا قَلِيلًا مِّنْهُمْ ۚ   But they drank from it, all except a few of them.
فَلَمَّا جَاوَزَهُ   So when he crossed it
هُوَ وَالَّذِينَ آمَنُوا مَعَهُ   along with the faithful who were with him,
قَالُوا لَا طَاقَةَ لَنَا الْيَوْمَ   they said, 'We have no strength today
بِجَالُوتَ وَجُنُودِهِ ۚ   against Goliath and his troops.'
قَالَ الَّذِينَ يَظُنُّونَ أَنَّهُم مُّلَاقُو اللَّهِ   Those who were certain they will encounter God said,
كَم مِّن فِئَةٍ قَلِيلَةٍ   'How many a small party
غَلَبَتْ فِئَةً كَثِيرَةً   has overcome a larger party
بِإِذْنِ اللَّهِ ۗ   by God's will!
وَاللَّهُ مَعَ الصَّابِرِينَ ۝   And God is with the patient.'

وَلَمَّا بَرَزُوا   250 So when they marched out
لِجَالُوتَ وَجُنُودِهِ   for encounter with Goliath and his troops,
قَالُوا رَبَّنَا أَفْرِغْ عَلَيْنَا صَبْرًا   they said, 'Our Lord, pour patience upon us,
وَثَبِّتْ أَقْدَامَنَا   make our feet steady,
وَانصُرْنَا عَلَى الْقَوْمِ الْكَافِرِينَ ۝   and assist us against the faithless lot.'

251 Thus they routed them with God's will,
  and David killed Goliath,
  and God gave him kingdom and wisdom,
  and taught him whatever He liked.
  Were it not for God's repelling the people
    by means of one another,
  the earth would surely have been corrupted;
  but God is gracious to the world's people.

252 These are the signs of God
  which We recite for you in truth,
  and you are indeed one of the apostles.

[PART 3]

253 These are the apostles,
  some of whom We gave an advantage over others:
  of them are those to whom God spoke,
  and some of them He raised in rank,
  and We gave Jesus, son of Mary, manifest proofs
    and strengthened him with the Holy Spirit.
  Had God wished
  those who succeeded them wouldn't have fought one another
    after the manifest proofs had come to them.
  But they differed.
  There were among them those who had faith
  and there were those who were faithless.
  Had God wished, they would have not fought one another;
  but God does whatever He desires.

254 O you who have faith!
  Spend out of what We have provided you
  before there comes a day
  on which there will be no bargaining,

neither friendship, nor intercession.
And the faithless—they are the wrongdoers.

255 God—there is no god except Him—
    is the Living One, the All-sustainer.
Neither drowsiness befalls Him nor sleep.
To Him belongs whatever is in the heavens
    and whatever is on the earth.
Who is it that may intercede with Him
    except with His permission?
He knows what is before them and what is behind them,
    and they do not comprehend anything of His knowledge
    except what He wishes.
His seat embraces the heavens and the earth,
    and He is not wearied by their preservation,
    and He is the All-exalted, the All-supreme.

256 There is no compulsion in religion:
    rectitude has become distinct from error.
So one who disavows satanic entities[1]
    and has faith in God
has held fast to the firmest handle
    for which there is no breaking;
    and God is all-hearing, all-knowing.

257 God is the master of the faithful:
    He brings them out of darkness into light.
As for the faithless, their masters are satanic entities,
    who drive them out of light into darkness.
They shall be the inmates of the Fire,
    and they will remain in it.

---

[1] The word *ṭāghūt* has been said to refer to Satan (also called the 'rebel angel' and 'rebel against God'), idols, soothsayers, magicians, rebellious humans and jinn, and the carnal soul. In short, anything that install itself in a commanding role that belongs to God is *ṭāghūt* or a fake deity. Cf. **4:**51, 60, 76; **5:**60; **16:**36.

258 Have you not regarded him[1]
who argued with Abraham about his Lord,
only because God had given him kingdom?
When Abraham said,
'My Lord is He who gives life and brings death,'
he replied, 'I too give life and bring death.'
Abraham said,
'God indeed brings the sun from the east;
    now you bring it from the west.'
Thereat the faithless one was dumbfounded.
And God does not guide the wrongdoing lot.

259 Or him[2] who came upon a township
    as it lay desolate, its walls fallen on its roofs.
He said, 'How will God revive this after its death?!'
So God made him die for a hundred years,
    then He resurrected him.
He said, 'How long did you remain?'
Said he, 'I have remained a day or part of a day.'
He said, 'No, you have remained a hundred years.
Now look at your food and drink which have not rotted!
Then look at your ass!
This, that We may make you a sign for mankind.
And look at the bones, how We raise them up
    and then clothe them with flesh!'
When it became evident to him, he said,
    'I know that God has power over all things.'

260 And when Abraham said, 'My Lord!
Show me how You revive the dead,'
He said, 'Do you not believe?'

---

[1] That is, Nimrod.
[2] That is, Ezra ('Uzayr).

He said, 'Yes indeed,
but in order that my heart may be at rest.'
He said,
'Catch four of the birds and cut them into pieces,
    and place a part of them on every mountain,
    then call them; they will come to you hastening.
And know that God is all-mighty and all-wise.'

261 The parable of those who spend their wealth
    in God's way
is that of a grain which grows seven ears,
    in every ear a hundred grains.
God enhances severalfold for whomever He wishes,
and God is all-bounteous, all-knowing.

262 Those who spend their wealth in the way of God
and then do not follow up what they have spent
    with reproaches[1] and affronts,
they shall have their reward near their Lord,
and they will have no fear, nor will they grieve.

263 A polite reply and forgiving [their annoyance]
is better than a charity followed by affront.
God is all-sufficient, most forbearing.

264 O you who have faith!
Do not render your charities void
    by reproaches and affronts,
like those who spend their wealth to be seen by people
    and have no faith in God and the Last Day.
Their parable[2] is that of a rock covered with soil:
a downpour strikes it, leaving it bare.

---

[1] More exactly, with reproachful reminders of past favours. Cf. 2:264 below.
[2] Or 'example.'

They have no power over anything they have earned,
and God does not guide the faithless lot.

265 The parable of those who spend their wealth
  seeking God's pleasure
    and to confirm themselves in their faith,
  is that of a garden on a hillside:
  the downpour strikes it,
    whereupon it brings forth its fruit twofold;
  and if it is not a downpour that strikes it, then a shower,
  and God watches what you do.

266 Would any of you like to have
  a garden of palm trees and vines,
  with streams running in it,
    with all kinds of fruit for him therein,
  and old age were to strike him while he had weakly offspring;
    whereupon a fiery hurricane were to hit it,
      whereat it lies burnt?
  Thus does God clarify His signs for you
    so that you may reflect.

267 O you who have faith!
  Spend of the good things you have earned
    and of what We bring forth for you from the earth,
  and do not be of the mind to give the bad part of it,
  for you yourselves would not take it, unless you ignore it.
  And know that God is all-sufficient, all-laudable.

268 Satan frightens you of poverty
    and prompts you to commit indecent acts.
  But God promises you His forgiveness and grace,
    and God is all-bounteous, all-knowing.

269 He grants wisdom to whomever He wishes,

وَمَنْ يُؤْتَ الْحِكْمَةَ and he who is given wisdom
فَقَدْ أُوتِيَ خَيْرًا كَثِيرًا is certainly given an abundant good,
وَمَا يَذَّكَّرُ إِلَّا أُولُو الْأَلْبَابِ ۝ and none takes admonition except those who possess intellect.
وَمَا أَنْفَقْتُمْ مِنْ نَفَقَةٍ 270 Whatever charity you may give
أَوْ نَذَرْتُمْ مِنْ نَذْرٍ or vows that you may vow,
فَإِنَّ اللَّهَ يَعْلَمُهُ God indeed knows it,
وَمَا لِلظَّالِمِينَ مِنْ أَنْصَارٍ ۝ and the wrongdoers have no helpers.
إِنْ تُبْدُوا الصَّدَقَاتِ فَنِعِمَّا هِيَ 271 If you disclose your charities, that is well,
وَإِنْ تُخْفُوهَا وَتُؤْتُوهَا الْفُقَرَاءَ but if you hide them and give them to the poor,
فَهُوَ خَيْرٌ لَكُمْ that is better for you,
وَيُكَفِّرُ عَنْكُمْ مِنْ سَيِّئَاتِكُمْ and it will atone for some of your misdeeds,
وَاللَّهُ بِمَا تَعْمَلُونَ خَبِيرٌ ۝ and God is well aware of what you do.
لَيْسَ عَلَيْكَ هُدَاهُمْ 272 It is not up to you to guide them;
وَلَكِنَّ اللَّهَ يَهْدِي مَنْ يَشَاءُ rather, it is God who guides whomever He wishes.
وَمَا تُنْفِقُوا مِنْ خَيْرٍ فَلِأَنْفُسِكُمْ Whatever wealth you spend, it is for your own benefit,
وَمَا تُنْفِقُونَ إِلَّا ابْتِغَاءَ وَجْهِ اللَّهِ as you do not spend but to seek God's pleasure,
وَمَا تُنْفِقُوا مِنْ خَيْرٍ and whatever wealth you spend
يُوَفَّ إِلَيْكُمْ وَأَنْتُمْ لَا تُظْلَمُونَ ۝ will be repaid to you in full, and you will not be wronged.
لِلْفُقَرَاءِ الَّذِينَ أُحْصِرُوا 273 The charities are for the poor who are straitened
فِي سَبِيلِ اللَّهِ in the way of God,[1]
لَا يَسْتَطِيعُونَ ضَرْبًا فِي الْأَرْضِ not capable of moving about in the land [for trade].
يَحْسَبُهُمُ الْجَاهِلُ أَغْنِيَاءَ The unaware suppose them to be well-off
مِنَ التَّعَفُّفِ because of their reserve.
تَعْرِفُهُمْ بِسِيمَاهُمْ You recognize them by their mark;
لَا يَسْأَلُونَ النَّاسَ إِلْحَافًا they do not ask the people importunately.
وَمَا تُنْفِقُوا مِنْ خَيْرٍ And whatever wealth you may spend,
فَإِنَّ اللَّهَ بِهِ عَلِيمٌ ۝ God indeed knows it.
الَّذِينَ يُنْفِقُونَ أَمْوَالَهُمْ بِاللَّيْلِ وَالنَّهَارِ 274 Those who give their wealth by night and day,
سِرًّا وَعَلَانِيَةً secretly and openly,

---

[1] That is, due to their engagement in *jihād* or in learning and teaching Islamic sciences or martial arts, or due to the rigours of spiritual wayfaring.

they shall have their reward near their Lord,
and they will have no fear, nor will they grieve.
275 Those who exact usury will not stand
but like one
deranged by the Devil's touch.
That is because they say,
'Trade is just like usury.'
While God has allowed trade and forbidden usury.
Whoever, on receiving advice from his Lord,
relinquishes usury,
shall keep the gains of what is past,
and his matter will rest with God.
As for those who resume,
they shall be the inmates of the Fire
and they will remain in it.
276 God brings usury to naught, but makes charities flourish.
God does not like any sinful ingrate.
277 Indeed, those who have faith, do righteous deeds,
maintain the prayer and give the *zakāt*,
they shall have their reward near their Lord,
and they will have no fear, nor will they grieve.
278 O you who have faith! Be wary of God,
and abandon all claims to what remains of usury,
should you be faithful.
279 And if you do not, then be informed of a war
from God and His apostle.
And if you repent, then you will have your principal,
neither harming others, nor suffering harm.
280 If the debtor is in straits,
let there be a respite until the time of ease;

and if you remit the debt as charity,
  it will be better for you, should you know.
281 And beware of a day
  in which you will be brought back to God.
  Then every soul shall be recompensed fully
    for what it has earned,
  and they will not be wronged.
282 O you who have faith!
  When you contract a loan for a specified term,
    write it down.
  Let a writer write with honesty between you,
    and let not the writer refuse to write
      as God has taught him.
  So let him write,
    and let the one who incurs the debt dictate,
      and let him be wary of God, his Lord,
    and not diminish anything from it.
  But if the debtor be feeble-minded, or weak,
    or incapable of dictating himself,
  then let his guardian dictate with honesty,
    and take as witness two witnesses from your men,
  and if there are not two men, then a man and two women
    —from those whom you approve as witnesses—
    so that if one of the two defaults
    the other will remind her.
  The witnesses must not refuse when they are called,
    and do not consider it wearisome to write it down,
      whether it be a big or small sum,
      as a loan lent until its term.
  That is more just with God

and more upright in respect to testimony,
and the likeliest way to avoid doubt,
unless it is an on the spot deal
you transact between yourselves,
in which case there is no sin upon you not to write it.
Take witnesses when you make a deal,
and let no harm be done to the writer or witness,
and if you did that, it would be sinful of you.
Be wary of God and God will teach you,
and God has knowledge of all things.

283 If you are on a journey and cannot find a writer,
then a retained pledge shall suffice.
And if one of you entrusts to another,
let him who is trusted deliver his trust,
and let him be wary of God, his Lord.
And do not conceal your testimony;
anyone who conceals it, his heart will indeed be sinful.
And God knows well what you do.

284 To God belongs whatever is in the heavens
and whatever is in the earth.
Whether you disclose what is in your hearts or hide it,
God will bring you to account for it.
Then He will forgive whomever He wishes
and punish whomever He wishes,
and God has power over all things.

285 The Apostle has faith
in what has been sent down to him from his Lord,
and all the faithful.
Each of them has faith in God,

His angels, His scriptures and His apostles.
[They declare,] 'We make no distinction
between any of His apostles.'
And they say, 'We hear and obey.
Our Lord, forgive us, and toward You is the return.'
286 God does not task any soul beyond its capacity.
Whatever good it earns is to its own benefit,
and whatever evil it incurs is to its own harm.

'Our Lord!
Do not take us to task if we forget or make mistakes!
Our Lord! Do not place upon us a burden
   as You placed on those who were before us!
Our Lord!
Do not lay upon us what we have no strength to bear!
Excuse us, forgive us, and be merciful to us!
You are our Master,
   so help us against the faithless lot!'

3. THE PROGENY OF IMRAN[1]
Āl-i 'Imrān

In the Name of God,
the All-beneficent, the All-merciful.

1 *Alif, Lām, Mīm.*
2 God—there is no god except Him—
   is the Living One, the All-sustainer.
3 He has sent down to you the Book with the truth
   confirming what was revealed before it,
   and He had sent down the Torah and the Evangel

---

[1] This Madanī sūrah is named after the expression 'the House of 'Imrān' (*āl-i 'Imrān*) mentioned in verse 33. As indicated by verses 121 ff. and 138 ff., its latter half was revealed following the Battle of Uḥud in Shawwāl, 3 H.

4 before as guidance for mankind,
and He has sent down the Criterion.[1]
Indeed, those who deny the signs of God,
there is a severe punishment for them;
and God is all-mighty, avenger.
5 Nothing is indeed hidden from God
in the earth or in the sky.
6 It is He who forms you in the wombs of your mothers
however He wishes.
There is no god except Him, the All-mighty, the All-wise.
7 It is He who has sent down to you the Book.
Parts of it are definitive verses,
which are the mother of the Book,
while others are ambiguous.[2]
As for those in whose hearts is deviance,
they pursue what is ambiguous in it,
pursuing misguidance and aiming at its misinterpretation.
But no one knows its interpretation except God
and those firmly grounded in knowledge;
they say, 'We believe in it;
all of it[3] is from our Lord.'
Only those who possess intellect take admonition.
8 [They say,] 'Our Lord! Do not make our hearts swerve
after You have guided us,
and bestow Your mercy on us.
Indeed, You are the All-munificent.
9 Our Lord! You will indeed gather mankind
on a day in which there is no doubt.
God indeed does not break His promise.'

---

[1] Cf. 2:53.
[2] Or 'metaphorical.'
[3] I.e., the revealed text and its interpretation, or the definitive and the ambiguous verses.

10 As for the faithless,
neither their wealth nor their children shall avail them
anything against God;
it is they who will be fuel for the Fire;

11 as in the case of Pharaoh's clan
and those who were before them, who denied Our signs.
So God seized them for their sins,
and God is severe in retribution.

12 Say to the faithless,
'You shall be overcome and gathered toward hell,
and it is an evil resting place.'

13 There was certainly a sign for you
    in the two hosts that met:[1]
one host fighting in the way of God
and the other faithless,
who saw them as visibly twice as many.
God strengthens whomever He wishes with His help.
There is indeed a moral in that for those who have insight.

14 To mankind has been made to seem decorous
    the love of worldly allures,
    including women and children,
    accumulated piles of gold and silver,
    horses of mark, livestock and farms.
Those are the wares of the life of this world;
but goodness of one's destination lies with God.

15 Say, 'Shall I inform you of something better than that?
    For those who are Godway
    there will be gardens near their Lord,

---

[1] A reference to the Battle of Badr (17th Ramaḍān 2 H.) during which the Makkan troops, thrice as strong as the Muslim force, faced a humiliating defeat and many of their leaders were killed.

with streams running in them,
to remain in them,
and chaste mates, and God's pleasure.'
And God watches His servants.

16 Those who say, 'Our Lord! Indeed, we have faith.
So forgive us our sins,
and save us from the punishment of the Fire.'

17 They are patient and truthful,
obedient and charitable,
and plead for God's forgiveness at dawns.

18 God bears witness that there is no god except Him —
and so do the angels and those who possess knowledge
— maintainer of justice,
there is no god except Him, the Almighty, the All-wise.

19 Indeed, with God religion is Islām,[1]
and those who were given the Book did not differ
except after knowledge had come to them,
out of envy among themselves.
And whoever denies God's signs
should know that God is swift at reckoning.

20 If they argue with you,
say, 'I have submitted my will to God,
and so has he who follows me.'
And say to those who were given the Book
and the uninstructed ones,[2] 'Do you submit?'
If they submit, they will certainly be guided;
but if they turn away, your duty is only to communicate,
and God watches His servants.

---

[1] Or 'religion is submission to God.'
[2] That is, the Arabs, who, unlike the Jews and the Christians, did not possessed any scripture.

21 Those who deny God's signs
and kill the prophets unjustly,[1]
and kill those who call for justice
from among the people,
inform them of a painful punishment.

22 They are the ones whose works have failed
in this world and the Hereafter,
and they will have no helpers.

23 Have you not regarded those
who were given a share of the Book,
who are summoned to the Book of God
in order that it may judge between them,
whereat a part of them turn away
and they are disregardful?

24 That is because they say,
'The Fire shall not touch us
except for numbered days,'
and they have been misled in their religion
by what they used to fabricate.

25 But how will it be with them when We gather them
on a day in which there is no doubt,
and every soul shall be recompensed fully
for what it has earned,
and they will not be wronged?

26 Say, 'O God, Master of all sovereignty!
You give sovereignty to whomever You wish,
and strip of sovereignty whomever You wish;
You make mighty whomever You wish,
and You degrade whomever You wish;

---

[1] That is, the Jews. Verses 21-25 relate to them.

   all choice is in Your hand.
   Indeed, You have power over all things.

27 You make the night pass into the day
   and You make the day pass into the night.
   You bring forth the living from the dead
   and You bring forth the dead from the living,
   and provide for whomever You wish without reckoning.'

28 The faithful should not take the faithless
   for protectors and allies
   instead of the faithful,
   and whoever does that
   God will have nothing to do with him,
   except out of caution, when you are wary of them.
   God warns you to beware of disobeying Him,
   and toward God is the return.

29 Say, 'Whether you hide what is in your hearts, or disclose it,
   God knows it,
   and He knows whatever there is in the heavens
   and whatever there is in the earth;
   and God has power over all things.'

30 The day when every soul will find
   present whatever good it has done;
   and as for the evil it has done,
   it will wish there were a far distance between it and itself.
   God warns you to beware of disobeying Him,
   and God is most kind to His servants.

31 Say, 'If you love God, then follow me;
   God will love you and forgive you your sins,
   and God is all-forgiving, all-merciful.'

Āl-i 'Imrān

32 *Say, 'Obey God and the Apostle.'*
But if they turn away,
indeed God does not like the faithless.

33 Indeed, God chose Adam and Noah,
and the progeny of Abraham and the progeny of Imran
above all the nations;

34 some of them are descendants of the others,
and God is all-hearing, all-knowing.

35 When the wife of Imran said,
'My Lord, I dedicate to You what is in my belly,
in consecration.
Accept it from me;
indeed You are the All-hearing, the All-knowing.'

36 When she bore her, she said,
'My Lord, I have borne a female child'
—and God knew better what she had borne,
and the male was no match for the female[1]—
'and I have named her Mary,
and I commend her and her offspring to Your care
against the evil of the outcast Satan.'

37 Thereupon her Lord accepted her
with a gracious acceptance,
and made her grow up in a worthy fashion,
and He charged Zechariah with her care.
Whenever Zechariah visited her in the sanctuary,
he would find provisions with her.
He said, 'O Mary, from where does this come for you?'
She said, 'It comes from God.

---

[1] I.e. the male child she expected was no match for Mary, whom she had borne.

38 Thereat Zechariah supplicated his Lord.
He said, 'My Lord!
Grant me a good offspring from You!
You indeed hear all supplications.'

39 Then the angels called out to him,
as he stood praying in the sanctuary:
'God gives you the good news of John,
as a confirmer of a Word of God,[1]
eminent and chaste,
a prophet and one of the righteous.'

40 He said, 'My Lord, how shall I have a son
while old age has overtaken me
and my wife is barren?'
Said He, 'So it is that God does whatever He wishes.'

41 He said, 'My Lord, grant me a sign.'
Said He, 'Your sign
is that you will not speak to people for three days
except in gestures.
Remember your Lord much often,
and glorify Him morning and evening.'

42 And when the angels said,
'O Mary, God has chosen you and purified you,
and He has chosen you above the world's women.

43 O Mary, be obedient to your Lord,
and prostrate and bow down
with those who bow in worship.'

44 These accounts are from the Unseen,
which We reveal to you,

God provides whomever He wishes without reckoning.'

---

[1] That is, Jesus ('a).

وَمَا كُنتَ لَدَيْهِمْ إِذْ يُلْقُونَ أَقْلَامَهُمْ أَيُّهُمْ يَكْفُلُ مَرْيَمَ وَمَا كُنتَ لَدَيْهِمْ إِذْ يَخْتَصِمُونَ ۝

and you were not with them when they were casting lots
to see which of them would take charge of Mary's care,
nor were you with them when they were contending.

إِذْ قَالَتِ الْمَلَائِكَةُ يَا مَرْيَمُ إِنَّ اللَّهَ يُبَشِّرُكِ بِكَلِمَةٍ مِنْهُ اسْمُهُ الْمَسِيحُ عِيسَى ابْنُ مَرْيَمَ وَجِيهًا فِي الدُّنْيَا وَالْآخِرَةِ وَمِنَ الْمُقَرَّبِينَ ۝

45 When the angels said, 'O Mary,
God gives you the good news of a Word from Him
whose name is Messiah, Jesus, son of Mary,
distinguished in the world and the Hereafter,
and one of those brought near to God.

وَيُكَلِّمُ النَّاسَ فِي الْمَهْدِ وَكَهْلًا وَمِنَ الصَّالِحِينَ ۝

46 He will speak to the people in the cradle
and in adulthood,
and will be one of the righteous.'

قَالَتْ رَبِّ أَنَّىٰ يَكُونُ لِي وَلَدٌ وَلَمْ يَمْسَسْنِي بَشَرٌ ۖ قَالَ كَذَٰلِكِ اللَّهُ يَخْلُقُ مَا يَشَاءُ ۚ إِذَا قَضَىٰ أَمْرًا فَإِنَّمَا يَقُولُ لَهُ كُنْ فَيَكُونُ ۝

47 She said, 'My Lord, how shall I have a child
seeing that no human has ever touched me?'
He said, 'So it is that God creates whatever He wishes.
When He decides on a matter
He just says to it "Be!" and it is.

وَيُعَلِّمُهُ الْكِتَابَ وَالْحِكْمَةَ وَالتَّوْرَاةَ وَالْإِنْجِيلَ ۝

48 He will teach him the Book and wisdom,
the Torah and the Evangel,

وَرَسُولًا إِلَىٰ بَنِي إِسْرَائِيلَ أَنِّي قَدْ جِئْتُكُمْ بِآيَةٍ مِنْ رَبِّكُمْ ۖ أَنِّي أَخْلُقُ لَكُمْ مِنَ الطِّينِ كَهَيْئَةِ الطَّيْرِ فَأَنفُخُ فِيهِ فَيَكُونُ طَيْرًا بِإِذْنِ اللَّهِ ۖ وَأُبْرِئُ الْأَكْمَهَ وَالْأَبْرَصَ وَأُحْيِي الْمَوْتَىٰ بِإِذْنِ اللَّهِ ۖ وَأُنَبِّئُكُم بِمَا تَأْكُلُونَ وَمَا تَدَّخِرُونَ فِي بُيُوتِكُمْ ۚ إِنَّ فِي ذَٰلِكَ لَآيَةً لَّكُمْ

49 and he will be an apostle to the Children of Israel,
[and he will declare,] 'I have certainly brought you
a sign from your Lord:
I will create for you out of clay
the form of a bird,
then I will breathe into it,
and it will become a bird by God's leave.
I heal the blind and the leper
and I revive the dead by God's leave.
I will tell you what you have eaten
and what you have stored in your houses.
There is indeed a sign in that for you,

إِن كُنتُم مُّؤْمِنِينَ ۝	should you be faithful.
وَمُصَدِّقًا	50 [I come] to confirm the truth of
لِّمَا بَيْنَ يَدَيَّ مِنَ التَّوْرَاةِ	that which is before me of the Torah,
وَلِأُحِلَّ لَكُم	and to make lawful for you
بَعْضَ الَّذِي حُرِّمَ عَلَيْكُمْ	some of the things that were forbidden you.
وَجِئْتُكُم بِآيَةٍ مِّن رَّبِّكُمْ	I have brought you a sign from your Lord;
فَاتَّقُوا اللَّهَ وَأَطِيعُونِ ۝	so be wary of God and obey me.
إِنَّ اللَّهَ رَبِّي وَرَبُّكُمْ	51 God is indeed my Lord and your Lord;
فَاعْبُدُوهُ ۚ هَٰذَا صِرَاطٌ مُّسْتَقِيمٌ ۝	so worship Him. This is a straight path.'
فَلَمَّا أَحَسَّ عِيسَىٰ مِنْهُمُ الْكُفْرَ	52 When Jesus sensed their faithlessness,
قَالَ مَنْ أَنصَارِي إِلَى اللَّهِ	he said, 'Who will be my helpers in God's way?'
قَالَ الْحَوَارِيُّونَ نَحْنُ أَنصَارُ اللَّهِ	The Disciples said, 'We will be helpers of God.
آمَنَّا بِاللَّهِ	We have faith in God,
وَاشْهَدْ بِأَنَّا مُسْلِمُونَ ۝	and you be witness that we have submitted to Him.
رَبَّنَا آمَنَّا بِمَا أَنزَلْتَ	53 Our Lord, we believe in what You have sent down,
وَاتَّبَعْنَا الرَّسُولَ	and we follow the apostle,
فَاكْتُبْنَا مَعَ الشَّاهِدِينَ ۝	so write us among the witnesses.'
وَمَكَرُوا	54 Then they[1] plotted [against Jesus],
وَمَكَرَ اللَّهُ	and God also devised,
وَاللَّهُ خَيْرُ الْمَاكِرِينَ ۝	and God is the best of devisers.
إِذْ قَالَ اللَّهُ يَا عِيسَىٰ إِنِّي مُتَوَفِّيكَ	55 When God said, 'O Jesus, I shall take your soul,[2]
وَرَافِعُكَ إِلَيَّ	and I shall raise you up toward Myself,
وَمُطَهِّرُكَ مِنَ الَّذِينَ كَفَرُوا	and I shall clear you of the calumnies of the faithless,

---

[1] That is, the opponents of Jesus among the Jews.
[2] *Tawaffā* means 'to exact fully' something, 'to receive in full,' 'to take one's full share,' and in the present Qur'ānic context it is used in the sense of taking away of the soul, either temporarily, as during sleep (as in 6:60), or permanently, as at the time of death (as in 3:193; 4:97; 6:61; 7:37,126; 8:50; 10:46; 12:101; 13:40; 16:28; 22:5; 32:11; 40:67, 77; 47:27). In verse 39:42, it is used to refer to the taking of the soul both during sleep and death: *'It is God who takes (yatawaffā) the souls at death, and those that have not died during their sleep. He retains those for whom He has decreed death, but releases the rest for a specified term.'* The passive form of the verb, *tuwuffiya* means 'to die,' 'to expire,' and to 'pass away.' It occurs in 2:234, 240. In a tradition, Imam 'Alī ibn Mūsā al-Riḍā ('a) explains that Jesus Christ ('a) "was raised alive from the earth to the heaven. Then his soul was taken away between the earth and the heaven. After he was raised to the heaven his soul was restored to his body, and hence the words of God, the Almighty and the Glorious, *'When God said: 'O Jesus, I shall take your soul, and I shall raise you up to Myself...'"* (*'Uyūn akhbār al-Riḍā*, Tehran: Intishārāt-e Jahān, n.d., ed. Sayyid Mahdī al-Ḥusaynī al-Lājwardī, vol. 1, p. 215; cf. *Biḥār al-anwār*, vol. 14, p. 338).

and I shall set those who follow you
above the faithless until the Day of Resurrection.
Then to Me will be your return,
whereat I will judge between you
concerning that about which you used to differ.

56 As for the faithless,
I will punish them with a severe punishment
in the world and the Hereafter;
and they will have no helpers.'

57 But as for those who have faith and do righteous deeds,
He will pay them in full their rewards,
and God does not like the wrongdoers.

58 These that We recite to you
are from the signs and the Wise Reminder.[1]

59 Indeed, the case of Jesus with God
is like the case of Adam: He created him from dust,
then said to him, 'Be,' and he was.

60 This is the truth from your Lord,
so do not be among the skeptics.

61 Should anyone argue with you concerning him,
after the knowledge that has come to you,
say, 'Come! Let us call our sons and your sons,
our women and your women, our souls and your souls,
then let us pray earnestly
and call down God's curse upon the liars.'

62 This is indeed the true account, for sure.
There is no god but God,
and indeed God is the All-mighty, the All-wise.

63 But if they turn away,

---

[1] Or 'the Definitive Reminder.' This is yet another name of the Holy Qur'ān

indeed God knows best the agents of corruption.

64 Say, 'O People of the Book!
    Come to a common word between us and you:
        that we will worship no one but God,
        that we will not ascribe any partner to Him,
        and that some of us will not take some others as lords besides God.'
    But if they turn away,
        say, 'Be witnesses that we have submitted to God.'

65 O People of the Book!
    Why do you argue concerning Abraham?
    Neither the Torah nor the Evangel were sent down until long after him.
    Do you not exercise your reason?

66 Ah! You are the ones who argue
        about that of which you have knowledge.
    But why do you argue
        about that of which you have no knowledge?
    And God knows and you do not know.

67 Abraham was neither a Jew nor a Christian.
        Rather he was a *ḥanif*, a *muslim*,[1]
        and he was not one of the polytheists.

68 Indeed, the nearest of all people to Abraham
        are those who follow him,
        and this prophet and those who have faith,
        and God is the friend of the faithful.

69 A group of the People of the Book were eager
        to lead you astray;
        yet they lead no one astray except themselves,

---

[1] That is, one who has submitted to God.

but they are not aware.

70 O People of the Book!
Why do you deny God's signs
while you testify to their truth?

71 O People of the Book!
Why do you mix the truth with falsehood,
and conceal the truth while you know it?

72 A group of the People of the Book say,
'Believe in what has been sent down to the faithful
at the beginning of the day,
and disbelieve at its end,
so that they may turn back from their religion.'

73 [They say] 'Do not believe anyone
except him who follows your religion.'
Say, 'Guidance is indeed the guidance of God.'
[They say] ['Do not believe] that anyone may be given
the like of what you were given,
or that he may argue with you before your Lord.'[1]
Say, 'All grace is indeed in God's hand;
He grants it to whomever He wishes,
and God is all-bounteous, all-knowing.

74 He singles out for His mercy whomever He wishes,
and God is dispenser of a mighty grace.'

75 Among the People of the Book is he who,
if you entrust him with a quintal,[2] will repay it to you,
and among them is he who,

---

[1] This is in accordance with 2:76 where the Jews are described as making a similar statement. Alternatively, it may be understood as being part of the reply the Prophet is asked to give to the Jews, in which case the translation will be as follows: 'Say, "Guidance is indeed the guidance of God, so that anyone may be given the like of what you were given, or that he may argue with you before your Lord."'

[2] Quintal: hundredweight. The American Heritage Dictionary gives the following history of the English 'quintal': Middle English, a unit of weight, from Old French, from Medieval Latin *quintāle*, from Arabic *qinṭar*, from Late Greek *kentēnarion*, from Late Latin *centēnārium* (*pondus*), hundred(weight), from Latin *centēnārius*, of a hundred.

إِنْ تَأْمَنْهُ بِدِينَارٍ لَا يُؤَدِّهِ إِلَيْكَ
    إِلَّا مَا دُمْتَ عَلَيْهِ قَائِمًا
ذَٰلِكَ بِأَنَّهُمْ قَالُوا
لَيْسَ عَلَيْنَا فِي الْأُمِّيِّينَ سَبِيلٌ
وَيَقُولُونَ عَلَى اللَّهِ الْكَذِبَ
    وَهُمْ يَعْلَمُونَ ۝

if you entrust him with a *dinar*, will not repay it to you
    unless you stand persistently over him.
That is because they say,
'We have no obligation to the non-Jews.'
But they attribute lies to God,
    and they know it.

بَلَىٰ مَنْ أَوْفَىٰ بِعَهْدِهِ وَاتَّقَىٰ
فَإِنَّ اللَّهَ يُحِبُّ الْمُتَّقِينَ ۝

76 Yes, whoever fulfills his commitments and is wary of God
—God indeed loves the Godwary.

إِنَّ الَّذِينَ يَشْتَرُونَ بِعَهْدِ اللَّهِ
    وَأَيْمَانِهِمْ ثَمَنًا قَلِيلًا
أُولَٰئِكَ لَا خَلَاقَ لَهُمْ فِي الْآخِرَةِ
وَلَا يُكَلِّمُهُمُ اللَّهُ
وَلَا يَنظُرُ إِلَيْهِمْ يَوْمَ الْقِيَامَةِ
وَلَا يُزَكِّيهِمْ
وَلَهُمْ عَذَابٌ أَلِيمٌ ۝

77 Those who sell God's covenant
    and their oaths for a paltry gain—
there shall be no share for them in the Hereafter
    and God will not speak to them,
nor will He look at them on the Day of Resurrection,
    nor will He purify them,
and there is a painful punishment for them.

وَإِنَّ مِنْهُمْ لَفَرِيقًا
يَلْوُونَ أَلْسِنَتَهُم بِالْكِتَابِ
لِتَحْسَبُوهُ مِنَ الْكِتَابِ
وَمَا هُوَ مِنَ الْكِتَابِ
وَيَقُولُونَ هُوَ مِنْ عِنْدِ اللَّهِ
وَمَا هُوَ مِنْ عِنْدِ اللَّهِ
وَيَقُولُونَ عَلَى اللَّهِ الْكَذِبَ
وَهُمْ يَعْلَمُونَ ۝

78 There is indeed a group of them
    who alter their tone while reading out some text,
so that you may suppose it to be from the Book,
    though it is not from the Book,
and they say, 'It is from God,'
    though it is not from God,
and they attribute lies to God,
    and they know it.

مَا كَانَ لِبَشَرٍ
أَن يُؤْتِيَهُ اللَّهُ الْكِتَابَ
وَالْحُكْمَ وَالنُّبُوَّةَ
ثُمَّ يَقُولَ لِلنَّاسِ
كُونُوا عِبَادًا لِي مِنْ دُونِ اللَّهِ
وَلَٰكِن كُونُوا رَبَّانِيِّينَ
بِمَا كُنتُمْ تُعَلِّمُونَ الْكِتَابَ

79 It does not behoove any human
    that God should give him the Book,
    judgement and prophethood,
    and then he should say to the people,
'Be my servants instead of God.'
Rather he would say, 'Be a godly people,
    by virtue of your teaching the Book

and by virtue of your studying it.'

80 And he would not command you to take the angels and the prophets for lords. Would he call you to unfaith after you have submitted to God?

81 When God took a compact with the prophets, [He said,] 'Inasmuch as I have given you [the knowledge] of the Book and wisdom,[1] should an apostle come to you thereafter confirming what is with you, you shall believe in him and help him.' Said He, 'Do you pledge and accept My covenant on this condition?' They said, 'We pledge.' He said, 'Then be witnesses, and I, too, am among witnesses along with you.'

82 Then whoever turns away after that —it is they who are the transgressors.

83 Do they seek a religion other than that of God, while to Him submits whoever there is in the heavens and the earth, willingly or unwillingly, and to Him they will be brought back?

84 Say, 'We have faith in God, and in what has been sent down to us, and what was sent down to Abraham, Ishmael, Isaac, Jacob and the Tribes, and what Moses, Jesus and the prophets were given by their Lord.

---

[1] Or, in accordance with an alternate reading (with *lammā*, instead of *lamā*), 'Since I have given you of the Book and wisdom,' or 'As I have given you . . .'

We make no distinction between any of them,
and to Him do we submit.'

85 Should anyone pursue a religion other than Islam,
it shall never be accepted from him,
and he will be among the losers in the Hereafter.

86 How shall God guide a people
who have disbelieved after their faith
and after bearing witness that the Apostle is true,
and after manifest proofs had come to them?
God does not guide the wrongdoing lot.

87 Their requital is that there shall be upon them
the curse of God, the angels, and all mankind.

88 They will remain in it,
and their punishment will not be lightened,
nor will they be granted any respite,

89 except such as repent after that and make amends,
for God is all-forgiving, all-merciful.

90 Indeed, those who turn faithless after their faith,
and then advance in faithlessness,
their repentance will never be accepted,
and it is they who are the astray.

91 Indeed, those who turn faithless, and die faithless,
a world of gold will not be accepted from any of them
should he offer it for ransom.
For such there will be a painful punishment,
and they will have no helpers.

92 You will never attain piety
until you spend out of what you hold dear,
and whatever you may spend of anything,

God indeed knows it.

[PART 4]

93. All food was lawful to the Children of Israel
except what Israel[1] had forbidden himself
before the Torah was sent down.
Say, 'Bring the Torah and read it,
if you are truthful.'

94. So whoever fabricates lies against God
after that
—it is they who are the wrongdoers.

95. Say, 'God has spoken the truth;
so follow the creed of Abraham, a *ḥanīf*,
and he was not one of the polytheists.

96. Indeed, the first house to be set up for mankind
is the one at Bakkah,[2]
blessed and a guidance for all nations.

97. In it are manifest signs and Abraham's Station,
and whoever enters it shall be secure.
And it is the duty of mankind toward God
to make pilgrimage to the House
—for those who can afford the journey to it—
and should anyone renege on his obligation,
God is indeed without need of the creatures.

98. Say, 'O People of the Book!
Why do you deny the signs of God,
while God is witness to what you do?'

99. Say, 'O People of the Book!
why do you bar the faithful from the way of God,

---

[1] That is Jacob ('a).
[2] The Holy Mosque or the city of Makkah, or the territory where they stand.

seeking to make it crooked,
while you are witnesses to its truthfulness?
And God is not oblivious of what you do.'

100 O you who have faith,
if you obey a part of those who were given the Book,
they will turn you back, after your faith,
into faithless ones.

101 And how would you be faithless
while the signs of God are recited to you
and His Apostle is in your midst?
Whoever takes recourse in God
is certainly guided to a straight path.

102 O you who have faith!
Be wary of God with the wariness due to Him
and do not die except in the state of submission.

103 Hold fast, all together, to God's cord,
and do not be divided into sects.
Remember God's blessing upon you
when you were enemies,
then He brought your hearts together,
so you became brothers with His blessing.
And you were on the brink of a pit of Fire,
whereat He saved you from it.
Thus does God clarify His signs for you
so that you may be guided.

104 There has to be a nation among you
summoning to all that is good,
bidding what is right, and forbidding what is wrong.
It is they who are the felicitous.

105 Do not be like those who became divided into sects

وَاخْتَلَفُوا مِنْ بَعْدِ مَا جَاءَهُمُ الْبَيِّنَاتُ ۚ
وَأُولَٰئِكَ لَهُمْ عَذَابٌ عَظِيمٌ ۝

and differed after manifest signs had come to them.
For such there will be a great punishment

يَوْمَ تَبْيَضُّ وُجُوهٌ
وَتَسْوَدُّ وُجُوهٌ ۚ

106 on the day when some faces will turn bright
and some faces will turn dark.

فَأَمَّا الَّذِينَ اسْوَدَّتْ وُجُوهُهُمْ
أَكَفَرْتُمْ بَعْدَ إِيمَانِكُمْ
فَذُوقُوا الْعَذَابَ
بِمَا كُنْتُمْ تَكْفُرُونَ ۝

As for those whose faces turn black
[they will be told], 'Did you disbelieve after your faith?
So taste the punishment
because of what you used to disbelieve.'

وَأَمَّا الَّذِينَ ابْيَضَّتْ وُجُوهُهُمْ
فَفِي رَحْمَةِ اللَّهِ
هُمْ فِيهَا خَالِدُونَ ۝

107 But as for those whose faces become white,
they shall dwell in God's mercy,
and they will remain in it.

تِلْكَ آيَاتُ اللَّهِ
نَتْلُوهَا عَلَيْكَ بِالْحَقِّ ۗ
وَمَا اللَّهُ يُرِيدُ ظُلْمًا لِلْعَالَمِينَ ۝

108 These are the signs of God
which We recite to you in truth,
and God does not desire any wrong for the creatures.

وَلِلَّهِ مَا فِي السَّمَاوَاتِ
وَمَا فِي الْأَرْضِ ۚ
وَإِلَى اللَّهِ تُرْجَعُ الْأُمُورُ ۝

109 To God belongs whatever is in the heavens
and whatever is in the earth,
and to God all matters are returned.

كُنْتُمْ خَيْرَ أُمَّةٍ أُخْرِجَتْ
لِلنَّاسِ
تَأْمُرُونَ بِالْمَعْرُوفِ وَتَنْهَوْنَ عَنِ الْمُنْكَرِ
وَتُؤْمِنُونَ بِاللَّهِ ۗ
وَلَوْ آمَنَ أَهْلُ الْكِتَابِ
لَكَانَ خَيْرًا لَهُمْ ۚ
مِنْهُمُ الْمُؤْمِنُونَ
وَأَكْثَرُهُمُ الْفَاسِقُونَ ۝

110 You are the best nation ever brought forth
for mankind:
you bid what is right and forbid what is wrong,
and have faith in God.
And if the People of the Book had believed,
it would have been better for them.
Among them some are faithful,
but most of them are transgressors.

لَنْ يَضُرُّوكُمْ إِلَّا أَذًى ۖ
وَإِنْ يُقَاتِلُوكُمْ يُوَلُّوكُمُ الْأَدْبَارَ
ثُمَّ لَا يُنْصَرُونَ ۝

111 They[1] will never do you any harm, except for some hurt;
and if they fight you, they will turn their backs to flee,
then they will not be helped.

ضُرِبَتْ عَلَيْهِمُ الذِّلَّةُ

112 Abasement is stamped upon them

---

[1] That is, the Jews.

wherever they are found, أَيْنَ مَا ثُقِفُوا
except for an asylum from God إِلَّا بِحَبْلٍ مِنَ اللَّهِ
and an asylum from the people. وَحَبْلٍ مِنَ النَّاسِ
They earned the wrath of God, وَبَاءُوا بِغَضَبٍ مِنَ اللَّهِ
and poverty has been stamped upon them. وَضُرِبَتْ عَلَيْهِمُ الْمَسْكَنَةُ
That, because they would deny the signs of God ذَٰلِكَ بِأَنَّهُمْ كَانُوا يَكْفُرُونَ بِآيَاتِ اللَّهِ
and kill the prophets unjustly. وَيَقْتُلُونَ الْأَنْبِيَاءَ بِغَيْرِ حَقٍّ
That, because they would disobey ذَٰلِكَ بِمَا عَصَوْا
and commit transgression. وَكَانُوا يَعْتَدُونَ ﴿١١٢﴾

113 Yet they are not all alike. لَيْسُوا سَوَاءً
Among the People of the Book is an upright nation; مِنْ أَهْلِ الْكِتَابِ أُمَّةٌ قَائِمَةٌ
they recite God's signs in the watches of the night يَتْلُونَ آيَاتِ اللَّهِ آنَاءَ اللَّيْلِ
and prostrate. وَهُمْ يَسْجُدُونَ ﴿١١٣﴾

114 They have faith in God and the Last Day, يُؤْمِنُونَ بِاللَّهِ وَالْيَوْمِ الْآخِرِ
and bid what is right وَيَأْمُرُونَ بِالْمَعْرُوفِ
and forbid what is wrong, وَيَنْهَوْنَ عَنِ الْمُنْكَرِ
and they are active in performing good deeds. وَيُسَارِعُونَ فِي الْخَيْرَاتِ
Those are among the righteous. وَأُولَٰئِكَ مِنَ الصَّالِحِينَ ﴿١١٤﴾

115 Whatever good they do, وَمَا يَفْعَلُوا مِنْ خَيْرٍ
they will not go unappreciated for it, فَلَنْ يُكْفَرُوهُ
and God knows well the Godwary. وَاللَّهُ عَلِيمٌ بِالْمُتَّقِينَ ﴿١١٥﴾

116 As for the faithless, إِنَّ الَّذِينَ كَفَرُوا
neither their wealth nor their children will avail them لَنْ تُغْنِيَ عَنْهُمْ أَمْوَالُهُمْ وَلَا أَوْلَادُهُمْ
anything against God. مِنَ اللَّهِ شَيْئًا
They shall be the inmates of the Fire, وَأُولَٰئِكَ أَصْحَابُ النَّارِ
and they will remain in it. هُمْ فِيهَا خَالِدُونَ ﴿١١٦﴾

117 The parable of what they spend in the life of this world مَثَلُ مَا يُنْفِقُونَ فِي هَٰذِهِ الْحَيَاةِ الدُّنْيَا
is that of a cold wind كَمَثَلِ رِيحٍ فِيهَا صِرٌّ
that strikes the tillage of a people who wronged themselves, أَصَابَتْ حَرْثَ قَوْمٍ ظَلَمُوا أَنْفُسَهُمْ

destroying it.
فَأَهْلَكَتْهُ

God does not wrong them,
وَمَا ظَلَمَهُمُ اللَّهُ

but they wrong themselves.
وَلَـٰكِنْ أَنْفُسَهُمْ يَظْلِمُونَ ۝

118 O you who have faith!
يَا أَيُّهَا الَّذِينَ آمَنُوا

Do not take your confidants from others than yourselves;
لَا تَتَّخِذُوا بِطَانَةً مِنْ دُونِكُمْ

they will spare nothing to ruin you.
لَا يَأْلُونَكُمْ خَبَالًا

They are eager to see you in distress.
وَدُّوا مَا عَنِتُّمْ

Hatred has already shown itself from their mouths,
قَدْ بَدَتِ الْبَغْضَاءُ مِنْ أَفْوَاهِهِمْ

and what their breasts hide within is yet worse.
وَمَا تُخْفِي صُدُورُهُمْ أَكْبَرُ

We have certainly made the signs clear for you,
قَدْ بَيَّنَّا لَكُمُ الْآيَاتِ

should you exercise your reason.
إِنْ كُنْتُمْ تَعْقِلُونَ ۝

119 Ah! You are the ones who bear love towards them,
هَا أَنْتُمْ أُولَاءِ تُحِبُّونَهُمْ

while they do not love you,
وَلَا يُحِبُّونَكُمْ

though you believe in all the Books.
وَتُؤْمِنُونَ بِالْكِتَابِ كُلِّهِ

When they meet you, they say, 'We believe,'
وَإِذَا لَقُوكُمْ قَالُوا آمَنَّا

but when they are alone,
وَإِذَا خَلَوْا

they bite their fingertips at you out of rage.
عَضُّوا عَلَيْكُمُ الْأَنَامِلَ مِنَ الْغَيْظِ

Say, 'Die of your rage!'
قُلْ مُوتُوا بِغَيْظِكُمْ

God indeed knows well what is in the breasts.
إِنَّ اللَّهَ عَلِيمٌ بِذَاتِ الصُّدُورِ ۝

120 If some good befalls you, it upsets them,
إِنْ تَمْسَسْكُمْ حَسَنَةٌ تَسُؤْهُمْ

but if some ill befalls you, they rejoice at it.
وَإِنْ تُصِبْكُمْ سَيِّئَةٌ يَفْرَحُوا بِهَا

Yet if you are patient and Godwary,
وَإِنْ تَصْبِرُوا وَتَتَّقُوا

their guile will not harm you in any way.
لَا يَضُرُّكُمْ كَيْدُهُمْ شَيْئًا

God indeed encompasses what they do.
إِنَّ اللَّهَ بِمَا يَعْمَلُونَ مُحِيطٌ ۝

121 When you left your family at dawn
وَإِذْ غَدَوْتَ مِنْ أَهْلِكَ

to settle the faithful in their positions for battle
تُبَوِّئُ الْمُؤْمِنِينَ مَقَاعِدَ لِلْقِتَالِ

—and God is all-hearing, all-knowing.
وَاللَّهُ سَمِيعٌ عَلِيمٌ ۝

122 When two groups among you were about
إِذْ هَمَّتْ طَائِفَتَانِ مِنْكُمْ

to lose courage
أَنْ تَفْشَلَا

—though God is their protector,
and in God alone let all the faithful put their trust.

123 Certainly God helped you at Badr,
when you were weak [in the enemy's eyes].
So be wary of God so that you may give thanks.

124 When you were saying to the faithful,
'Is it not enough for you
that your Lord should aid you
with three thousand angels sent down?'

125 Yes, if you are steadfast and Godwary,
and should they come at you suddenly,
your Lord will aid you
with five thousand angels sent in [to the scene of battle].

126 God did not appoint it but as a good news for you,
and to reassure with it your hearts,
and victory[1] comes only from God,
the All-mighty, the All-wise,

127 that He may cut down a section of the faithless,
or subdue them,
so that they retreat disappointed.

128 You have no hand in the matter,
whether He accepts their repentance or punishes them,
for they are indeed wrongdoers.

129 To God belongs whatever there is in the heavens
and whatever there is in the earth:
He forgives whomever He wishes
and punishes whomever He wishes,
and God is all-forgiving, all-merciful.

130 O you who have faith!

---

[1] Or 'help.'

لَا تَأْكُلُوا الرِّبَا أَضْعَافًا مُضَاعَفَةً ۖ وَاتَّقُوا اللَّهَ لَعَلَّكُمْ تُفْلِحُونَ ۝

Do not exact usury, twofold and severalfold, and be wary of God so that you may be felicitous.

وَاتَّقُوا النَّارَ الَّتِي أُعِدَّتْ لِلْكَافِرِينَ ۝

131 Beware of the Fire which has been prepared for the faithless,

وَأَطِيعُوا اللَّهَ وَالرَّسُولَ لَعَلَّكُمْ تُرْحَمُونَ ۝

132 and obey God and the Apostle so that you may be granted His mercy.

وَسَارِعُوا إِلَىٰ مَغْفِرَةٍ مِنْ رَبِّكُمْ وَجَنَّةٍ عَرْضُهَا السَّمَاوَاتُ وَالْأَرْضُ أُعِدَّتْ لِلْمُتَّقِينَ ۝

133 Hasten towards your Lord's forgiveness and a paradise as vast as the heavens and the earth, prepared for the Godwary

الَّذِينَ يُنْفِقُونَ فِي السَّرَّاءِ وَالضَّرَّاءِ وَالْكَاظِمِينَ الْغَيْظَ وَالْعَافِينَ عَنِ النَّاسِ ۗ وَاللَّهُ يُحِبُّ الْمُحْسِنِينَ ۝

134 —those who spend in ease and adversity, and suppress their anger, and excuse the faults of the people, and God loves the virtuous;

وَالَّذِينَ إِذَا فَعَلُوا فَاحِشَةً أَوْ ظَلَمُوا أَنْفُسَهُمْ ذَكَرُوا اللَّهَ فَاسْتَغْفَرُوا لِذُنُوبِهِمْ وَمَنْ يَغْفِرُ الذُّنُوبَ إِلَّا اللَّهُ وَلَمْ يُصِرُّوا عَلَىٰ مَا فَعَلُوا وَهُمْ يَعْلَمُونَ ۝

135 and those who, when they commit an indecent act or wrong themselves, remember God, and plead to God seeking forgiveness for their sins —and who forgives sins except God?— and who do not persist in what they have committed while they know.

أُولَٰئِكَ جَزَاؤُهُمْ مَغْفِرَةٌ مِنْ رَبِّهِمْ وَجَنَّاتٌ تَجْرِي مِنْ تَحْتِهَا الْأَنْهَارُ خَالِدِينَ فِيهَا ۚ وَنِعْمَ أَجْرُ الْعَامِلِينَ ۝

136 Their reward is forgiveness from their Lord, and gardens with streams running in them, to remain in them. How excellent is the reward of the workers!

قَدْ خَلَتْ مِنْ قَبْلِكُمْ سُنَنٌ فَسِيرُوا فِي الْأَرْضِ فَانْظُرُوا كَيْفَ كَانَ عَاقِبَةُ الْمُكَذِّبِينَ ۝

137 Certain Divine precedents have passed before you. So travel through the land and observe how was the fate of the deniers.

هَٰذَا بَيَانٌ لِلنَّاسِ وَهُدًى وَمَوْعِظَةٌ لِلْمُتَّقِينَ ۝

138 This is an explanation for mankind, and a guidance and advice for the Godwary.

وَلَا تَهِنُوا وَلَا تَحْزَنُوا

139 Do not weaken or grieve:

3:140   The Progeny of Imran   82

وَأَنْتُمُ الْأَعْلَوْنَ إِنْ كُنْتُمْ مُؤْمِنِينَ ۝

you shall have the upper hand, should you be faithful.

إِنْ يَمْسَسْكُمْ قَرْحٌ

140 If wounds afflict you,

فَقَدْ مَسَّ الْقَوْمَ قَرْحٌ مِثْلُهُ

    like wounds have already afflicted those people;

وَتِلْكَ الْأَيَّامُ نُدَاوِلُهَا بَيْنَ النَّاسِ

and We make such vicissitudes rotate among mankind,

وَلِيَعْلَمَ اللَّهُ الَّذِينَ آمَنُوا

    so that God may ascertain those who have faith,

وَيَتَّخِذَ مِنْكُمْ شُهَدَاءَ

    and that He may take martyrs[1] from among you,

وَاللَّهُ لَا يُحِبُّ الظَّالِمِينَ ۝

    and God does not like the wrongdoers.

وَلِيُمَحِّصَ اللَّهُ الَّذِينَ آمَنُوا

141 And so that God may purge those who have faith

وَيَمْحَقَ الْكَافِرِينَ ۝

    and that He may wipe out the faithless.

أَمْ حَسِبْتُمْ أَنْ تَدْخُلُوا الْجَنَّةَ

142 Do you suppose that you would enter paradise,

وَلَمَّا يَعْلَمِ اللَّهُ

    while God has not yet ascertained

الَّذِينَ جَاهَدُوا مِنْكُمْ

      those of you who have waged *jihād*

وَيَعْلَمَ الصَّابِرِينَ ۝

    and He has not ascertained the steadfast?

وَلَقَدْ كُنْتُمْ تَمَنَّوْنَ الْمَوْتَ

143 Certainly you were longing for death

مِنْ قَبْلِ أَنْ تَلْقَوْهُ

    before you had encountered it.

فَقَدْ رَأَيْتُمُوهُ وَأَنْتُمْ تَنْظُرُونَ ۝

    Then certainly you saw it, as you were looking on.

وَمَا مُحَمَّدٌ إِلَّا رَسُولٌ

144 Muḥammad is but an apostle;

قَدْ خَلَتْ مِنْ قَبْلِهِ الرُّسُلُ

    other apostles have passed before him.

أَفَإِنْ مَاتَ أَوْ قُتِلَ

    If he dies or is slain,

انْقَلَبْتُمْ عَلَىٰ أَعْقَابِكُمْ

      will you turn back on your heels?

وَمَنْ يَنْقَلِبْ عَلَىٰ عَقِبَيْهِ

    Anyone who turns back on his heels

فَلَنْ يَضُرَّ اللَّهَ شَيْئًا

      will not harm God in the least,

وَسَيَجْزِي اللَّهُ الشَّاكِرِينَ ۝

    and soon God will reward the grateful.

وَمَا كَانَ لِنَفْسٍ أَنْ تَمُوتَ إِلَّا بِإِذْنِ اللَّهِ

145 No soul may die except by God's leave,

كِتَابًا مُؤَجَّلًا

    at an appointed time.

وَمَنْ يُرِدْ ثَوَابَ الدُّنْيَا

    Whoever desires the reward of this world,

نُؤْتِهِ مِنْهَا

      We will give him of it;

وَمَنْ يُرِدْ ثَوَابَ الْآخِرَةِ

    and whoever desires the reward of the Hereafter,

نُؤْتِهِ مِنْهَا

      We will give him of it;

---

[1] Or 'witnesses.'

وَسَنَجْزِي الشَّاكِرِينَ ﴿١٤٥﴾ and soon We will reward the grateful.

146 How many a prophet there has been
وَكَأَيِّنْ مِنْ نَبِيٍّ
قَاتَلَ مَعَهُ رِبِّيُّونَ كَثِيرٌ   with whom a multitude of godly men fought.
فَمَا وَهَنُوا لِمَا أَصَابَهُمْ   They did not falter for what befell them
فِي سَبِيلِ اللَّهِ   in the way of God,
وَمَا ضَعُفُوا وَمَا اسْتَكَانُوا   neither did they weaken, nor did they abase themselves;
وَاللَّهُ يُحِبُّ الصَّابِرِينَ ﴿١٤٦﴾   and God loves the steadfast.

147 All that they said was,
وَمَا كَانَ قَوْلَهُمْ إِلَّا أَنْ قَالُوا
رَبَّنَا اغْفِرْ لَنَا ذُنُوبَنَا   'Our Lord, forgive our sins
وَإِسْرَافَنَا فِي أَمْرِنَا   and our excesses in our affairs,
وَثَبِّتْ أَقْدَامَنَا   make our feet steady,
وَانْصُرْنَا عَلَى الْقَوْمِ الْكَافِرِينَ ﴿١٤٧﴾   and help us against the faithless lot.'

148 So God gave them the reward of this world
فَآتَاهُمُ اللَّهُ ثَوَابَ الدُّنْيَا
وَحُسْنَ ثَوَابِ الْآخِرَةِ   and the fair reward of the Hereafter;
وَاللَّهُ يُحِبُّ الْمُحْسِنِينَ ﴿١٤٨﴾   and God loves the virtuous.

149 O you who have faith!
يَا أَيُّهَا الَّذِينَ آمَنُوا
إِنْ تُطِيعُوا الَّذِينَ كَفَرُوا   If you obey the faithless,
يَرُدُّوكُمْ عَلَى أَعْقَابِكُمْ   they will turn you back on your heels,
فَتَنْقَلِبُوا خَاسِرِينَ ﴿١٤٩﴾   and you will become losers.

150 Rather, God alone is your Master,
بَلِ اللَّهُ مَوْلَاكُمْ
وَهُوَ خَيْرُ النَّاصِرِينَ ﴿١٥٠﴾   and He is the best of helpers.

151 We shall cast terror into the hearts of the faithless
سَنُلْقِي فِي قُلُوبِ الَّذِينَ كَفَرُوا الرُّعْبَ
بِمَا أَشْرَكُوا بِاللَّهِ   because of their ascribing partners to God,
مَا لَمْ يُنَزِّلْ بِهِ سُلْطَانًا   for which He has not sent down any authority,
وَمَأْوَاهُمُ النَّارُ   and their refuge shall be the Fire,
وَبِئْسَ مَثْوَى الظَّالِمِينَ ﴿١٥١﴾   and evil is the final abode of the wrongdoers.

152 God certainly fulfilled His promise to you
وَلَقَدْ صَدَقَكُمُ اللَّهُ وَعْدَهُ
إِذْ تَحُسُّونَهُمْ بِإِذْنِهِ   when you were slaying them with His leave,
حَتَّى إِذَا فَشِلْتُمْ وَتَنَازَعْتُمْ فِي الْأَمْرِ   until you lost courage, disputed about the matter,
وَعَصَيْتُمْ   and disobeyed

after He showed you what you loved.[1]
Some among you desire this world,
and some among you desire the Hereafter.
Then He turned you away from them
so that He might test you.
Certainly He has excused you,
for God is gracious to the faithful.

153 When you were fleeing
without paying any attention to anyone,
while the Apostle was calling you from your rear,
He requited you with grief upon grief,
so that you may not grieve for what you lose
nor for what befalls you,
and God is well aware of what you do.

154 Then He sent down to you safety after grief
—a drowsiness that came over a group of you—
while another group, anxious only about themselves,
entertained false notions about God,
notions of pagan ignorance.
They say, 'Do we have any role in the matter?'
Say, ' The matter indeed belongs totally to God.'
They hide in their hearts
what they do not disclose to you.
They say, 'Had we any role in the matter,
we would not have been slain here.'
Say, 'Even if you had remained in your houses,
those destined to be slain would have set out
toward the places where they were laid to rest,
so that God may test what is in your breasts,

---

[1] That is, the spoils of war.

and that He may purge what is in your hearts,
and God knows well what is in the breasts.'

155 Those of you who fled
   on the day when the two hosts met,
only Satan had made them stumble
   because of some of their deeds.
Certainly God has excused them,
   for God is all-forgiving, all-forbearing.

156 O you who have faith!
Do not be like the faithless
   who say of their brethren,
     when they travel in the land or go into battle,
'Had they stayed with us they would not have died
   or been killed,'
so that God may make it a regret in their hearts.
But God gives life and brings death,
   and God watches what you do.

157 Whether you are slain in the way of God or die,
   forgiveness and mercy from God are surely
   better than what they amass.

158 If you die or are slain,
   you will surely be gathered toward God.

159 It is by God's mercy that *you* are gentle to them;
and had *you* been harsh and hardhearted,
   they would have surely scattered from around *you*.
So *excuse* them and *plead* for forgiveness for them,
   and *consult* them in the affairs,
   and once *you* are resolved, put *your* trust in God.
Indeed, God loves those who trust in Him.

160 If God helps you, no one can overcome you,

وَإِنْ يَخْذُلْكُمْ but if He forsakes you,
فَمَنْ ذَا الَّذِى يَنْصُرُكُمْ مِنْ بَعْدِهِ who will help you after Him?
وَعَلَى اللَّهِ فَلْيَتَوَكَّلِ الْمُؤْمِنُونَ ۝ So in God alone let all the faithful put their trust.

161 وَمَا كَانَ لِنَبِيٍّ أَنْ يَغُلَّ A prophet may not breach his trust,
وَمَنْ يَغْلُلْ and whoever breaches his trust
يَأْتِ بِمَا غَلَّ يَوْمَ الْقِيَامَةِ will bring his breaches on the Day of Resurrection;
ثُمَّ تُوَفَّىٰ كُلُّ نَفْسٍ then every soul shall be recompensed fully
مَا كَسَبَتْ for what it has earned,
وَهُمْ لَا يُظْلَمُونَ ۝ and they will not be wronged.

162 أَفَمَنِ اتَّبَعَ رِضْوَانَ اللَّهِ Is he who follows the course of God's pleasure
كَمَنْ بَاءَ بِسَخَطٍ مِنَ اللَّهِ like him who earns God's displeasure
وَمَأْوَاهُ جَهَنَّمُ وَبِئْسَ الْمَصِيرُ ۝ and whose refuge is hell, an evil destination?

163 هُمْ دَرَجَاتٌ عِنْدَ اللَّهِ They have ranks with God,
وَاللَّهُ بَصِيرٌ بِمَا يَعْمَلُونَ ۝ and God watches what they do.

164 لَقَدْ مَنَّ اللَّهُ عَلَى الْمُؤْمِنِينَ God certainly favoured the faithful
إِذْ بَعَثَ فِيهِمْ رَسُولًا when He raised up among them an apostle
مِنْ أَنْفُسِهِمْ from among themselves
يَتْلُو عَلَيْهِمْ آيَاتِهِ وَيُزَكِّيهِمْ to recite to them His signs, and to purify them
وَيُعَلِّمُهُمُ الْكِتَابَ وَالْحِكْمَةَ and teach them the Book and wisdom,
وَإِنْ كَانُوا مِنْ قَبْلُ لَفِى ضَلَالٍ مُبِينٍ ۝ and earlier they had indeed been in manifest error.

165 أَوَلَمَّا أَصَابَتْكُمْ مُصِيبَةٌ What, when an affliction visits you
قَدْ أَصَبْتُمْ مِثْلَيْهَا —while you have inflicted twice as much—
قُلْتُمْ أَنَّىٰ هَٰذَا do you say, 'How is this?'!
قُلْ هُوَ مِنْ عِنْدِ أَنْفُسِكُمْ Say, 'This is from your own souls.'
إِنَّ اللَّهَ عَلَىٰ كُلِّ شَىْءٍ قَدِيرٌ ۝ Indeed, God has power over all things.

166 وَمَا أَصَابَكُمْ يَوْمَ الْتَقَى الْجَمْعَانِ What befell you on the day when the two hosts met,
فَبِإِذْنِ اللَّهِ was by God's permission,
وَلِيَعْلَمَ الْمُؤْمِنِينَ ۝ so that He may ascertain the faithful,

167 وَلِيَعْلَمَ الَّذِينَ نَافَقُوا and ascertain the hypocrites.
وَقِيلَ لَهُمْ تَعَالَوْا When they were told: 'Come,

fight in the way of God, or defend yourselves,
they said, 'If we knew any fighting,
   we would have surely followed you.'
That day they were nearer to unfaith than to faith.
They say with their mouths what is not in their hearts,
and God knows well whatever they conceal.

168 Those who said of their brethren,
   while they themselves sat back:
'Had they obeyed us, they would not have been killed.'
Say, 'Then keep death off from yourselves,
   if you are truthful.'

169 Do not suppose
those who were slain in the way of God
   to be dead;
no, they are living and provided for near their Lord,

170 exulting in what God has given them out of His grace,
and rejoicing for those who have not yet joined them
from those left behind them
that they will have no fear,
   nor will they grieve.

171 They rejoice in God's blessing and grace,
   and that God does not waste the reward of the faithful.

172 Those who responded to God and the Apostle
   even after they had been wounded
—for those of them who have been virtuous and Godwary
   there shall be a great reward.

173 —Those to whom the people said,
'All the people have gathered against you, so fear them.'
   That only increased them in faith,
   and they said, 'God is sufficient for us,

and He is an excellent trustee.'

174 So they returned with God's blessing and grace,
untouched by any harm.
They pursued the pleasure of God,
and God is dispenser of a great grace.

175 That is only Satan, frightening you of his followers!
Fear them not, and fear Me,
should you be faithful.

176 Do not grieve for those who are active in unfaith;
they will not hurt God in the least:
God desires to give them no share in the Hereafter,
and there is a great punishment for them.

177 Those who have bought unfaith for faith
will not hurt God in the least,
and there is a painful punishment for them.

178 Let the faithless not suppose
that the respite We grant them is good for their souls:
We give them respite only that they may increase in sin,
and there is a humiliating punishment for them.

179 God will not leave the faithful
in your present state,
until He has separated the bad ones from the good.
God will not acquaint you with the Unseen,
but God chooses from His apostles
whomever He wishes.
So have faith in God and His apostles;
and if you are faithful and Godwary,
there shall be a great reward for you.

180 Let the stingy not suppose that their grudging
what God has given them out of His bounty

is good for them; no, it is bad for them.
They will be collared with what they grudge
   on the Day of Resurrection.
To God belongs the heritage of the heavens
       and the earth,
   and God is well aware of what you do.

181 God has certainly heard the remark of those
   who said, 'God is poor and we are rich.'
   We will record what they have said,
   and their killing of the prophets unjustly,[1]
   and We shall say, 'Taste the punishment of the burning.
182 That is because of what your hands have sent ahead,
       and because God is not tyrannical to His servants.'
183 To those who say,
   'God has pledged us not to believe in any apostle
   unless he brings us an offering consumed by fire,'
   say, 'Apostles before me certainly did bring you
       manifest signs and what you speak of.
       Then why did you kill them, if you are truthful?'
184 But if they deny you,
   apostles have been denied before you,
   who came with manifest signs, holy writs,
       and an illuminating scripture.

185 Every soul shall taste death,
   and you will indeed be paid your full rewards
       on the Day of Resurrection.
   Whoever is delivered from the Fire

---

[1] Verses 181-184 are addressed to the Jews. Cf. 2:61, 91; 3:21, 112; 4:155; 5:70, where the Jews are accused of killing the prophets.

and admitted to paradise
has certainly succeeded.
The life of this world is nothing but the wares of delusion.

186 You will surely be tested in your possessions
and your souls,
and you will surely hear
from those who were given the Book before you
and from the polytheists much affront;
but if you are patient and Godwary,
that is indeed the steadiest of courses.

187 When God took
a covenant with those who were given the Book:
'You shall explain it for the people,
and you shall not conceal it,'
they cast it behind their backs
and sold it for a paltry gain.
How evil is what they buy!

188 Do not suppose those
who brag about what they have done
and love to be praised for what they have not done
—do not suppose them saved from punishment,
and there is a painful punishment for them.

189 To God belongs the kingdom of the heavens
and the earth,
and God has power over all things.

190 Indeed, in the creation of the heavens and the earth
and the alternation of night and day,
there are signs for those who possess intellect.

191 Those who remember God

standing, sitting, and lying on their sides,
and reflect on the creation of the heavens and the earth
[and say], 'Our Lord, You have not created this in vain!
Immaculate are You!
Save us from the punishment of the Fire.

192 Our Lord, whoever that You make enter the Fire
will surely have been disgraced by You,
and the wrongdoers will have no helpers.

193 Our Lord, we have indeed heard a summoner
calling to faith, declaring, "Have faith in your Lord!"
So we believed.
Our Lord, forgive us our sins
and absolve us of our misdeeds,
and make us die with the pious.

194 Our Lord, give us what You have promised us
through Your apostles,
and do not disgrace us on the Day of Resurrection.
Indeed, You do not break Your promise.'

195 Then their Lord answered them,
'I do not waste the work of any worker among you,
whether male or female;
you are all on the same footing.
So those who migrated
and were expelled from their homes,
and were tormented in My way,
and who fought and were killed
—I will surely absolve them of their misdeeds
and I will admit them into gardens
with streams running in them,
as a reward from God,

and God—with Him is the best of rewards.'
196 Never be misled by the bustle of the faithless in the towns.
197 It is a trivial enjoyment; then their refuge is hell, and it is an evil resting place.
198 But those who are wary of their Lord
—for them shall be gardens with streams running in them,
to remain in them,
a hospitality from God;
and what is with God is better for the pious.
199 Among the People of the Book there are indeed
those who have faith in God,
and in what has been sent down to you,
and in what has been sent down to them.
Humble toward God,
they do not sell the signs of God for a paltry gain.
They shall have their reward near their Lord;
God is indeed swift at reckoning.
200 O you who have faith!
Be patient, stand firm, and close your ranks,
and be wary of God, so that you may be felicitous.

4. WOMEN[1]
al-Nisā'

In the Name of God,
the All-beneficent, the All-merciful.

1 O mankind! Be wary of your Lord
who created you from a single soul,

---

[1] This Madanī *sūrah* makes frequent reference to matters concerning women (*nisā'*), hence its name. Revealed after the *sūrah*s Āl-i 'Imrān and al-Aḥzāb.

and created its mate from it, وَخَلَقَ مِنْهَا زَوْجَهَا
and, from the two of them, scattered numerous men وَبَثَّ مِنْهُمَا رِجَالًا كَثِيرًا
and women. وَنِسَاءً
Be wary of God, in whose Name you adjure one another, وَاتَّقُوا اللَّهَ الَّذِي تَسَاءَلُونَ بِهِ
and of [severing the ties with] blood relations. وَالْأَرْحَامَ

2 Give the orphans their property, إِنَّ اللَّهَ كَانَ عَلَيْكُمْ رَقِيبًا ۞
and do not replace the good with the bad, وَآتُوا الْيَتَامَى أَمْوَالَهُمْ
and do not eat up their property وَلَا تَتَبَدَّلُوا الْخَبِيثَ بِالطَّيِّبِ
by mingling it with your own property, وَلَا تَأْكُلُوا أَمْوَالَهُمْ
for that is indeed a great sin.[1] إِلَىٰ أَمْوَالِكُمْ

3 If you fear that you may not deal justly with the orphans,[2] إِنَّهُ كَانَ حُوبًا كَبِيرًا ۞
then marry other women that you like, وَإِنْ خِفْتُمْ أَلَّا تُقْسِطُوا فِي الْيَتَامَى
two, three, or four. فَانْكِحُوا مَا طَابَ لَكُمْ مِنَ النِّسَاءِ
But if you fear that you may not treat them fairly, مَثْنَى وَثُلَاثَ وَرُبَاعَ
then [marry only] one, فَإِنْ خِفْتُمْ أَلَّا تَعْدِلُوا
or [marry from among] your slave-women. فَوَاحِدَةً
That makes it likelier that you will not be unfair. أَوْ مَا مَلَكَتْ أَيْمَانُكُمْ

4 Give women their dowries, handing it over to them;[3] ذَٰلِكَ أَدْنَىٰ أَلَّا تَعُولُوا ۞
but if they remit anything of it of their own accord, وَآتُوا النِّسَاءَ صَدُقَاتِهِنَّ نِحْلَةً
then consume it as something lawful and wholesome. فَإِنْ طِبْنَ لَكُمْ عَنْ شَيْءٍ مِنْهُ نَفْسًا

5 Do not give the feeble-minded your property فَكُلُوهُ هَنِيئًا مَرِيئًا ۞
which God has assigned you to manage: وَلَا تُؤْتُوا السُّفَهَاءَ أَمْوَالَكُمُ
provide for them out of it, and clothe them, الَّتِي جَعَلَ اللَّهُ لَكُمْ قِيَامًا
and speak to them honourable words. وَارْزُقُوهُمْ فِيهَا وَاكْسُوهُمْ

6 Test the orphans when they reach the age of marriage. وَقُولُوا لَهُمْ قَوْلًا مَعْرُوفًا ۞
Then if you discern in them maturity, وَابْتَلُوا الْيَتَامَى حَتَّى إِذَا بَلَغُوا النِّكَاحَ
deliver to them their property. فَإِنْ آنَسْتُمْ مِنْهُمْ رُشْدًا
And do not consume it lavishly and hastily فَادْفَعُوا إِلَيْهِمْ أَمْوَالَهُمْ

---

[1] See verse **2:220** and the footnote.
[2] That is, girl orphans.
[3] That is, the dowry is to be given to the wife herself and into her possession, not to her father, guardian or tribal chief, as was customary in pre-Islamic Arabia.

    lest they should grow up.
As for him who is well-off, let him be abstemious,
    and as for him who is poor,
        let him eat in an honourable manner.
And when you deliver to them their property,
    take witnesses over them,
    and God suffices as reckoner.

7 Men have a share in the heritage left by parents
    and near relatives,
and women have a share in the heritage left by parents
    and near relatives,
      whether it be little or much,
    a share ordained by God.

8 And when the division is attended by relatives,
    the orphans and the needy,
    provide for them out of it,
    and speak to them honourable words.

9 Let those fear [the result of mistreating orphans who,
    were they to leave behind weak offspring,
    would be concerned on their account.
    So let them be wary of God,
    and let them speak upright words.

10 Those who consume the property of orphans wrongfully,
    only ingest fire into their bellies,
    and soon they will enter the Blaze.

11 God enjoins you concerning your children:
    for the male shall be the like of the share of two females,
    and if there be [two or] more than two females,
    then for them shall be two-thirds of what he[1] leaves;

---

[1] That is, the deceased person.

but if she be alone, then for her shall be a half; وَإِنْ كَانَتْ وَاحِدَةً فَلَهَا النِّصْفُ
and for each of his parents وَلِأَبَوَيْهِ لِكُلِّ وَاحِدٍ مِنْهُمَا
   a sixth of what he leaves, السُّدُسُ مِمَّا تَرَكَ
   if he has children; إِن كَانَ لَهُ وَلَدٌ
but if he has no children, فَإِن لَّمْ يَكُن لَّهُ وَلَدٌ
   and his parents are his sole heirs, وَوَرِثَهُ أَبَوَاهُ
   then it shall be a third for his mother; فَلِأُمِّهِ الثُّلُثُ
but if he has brothers, then a sixth for his mother, فَإِن كَانَ لَهُ إِخْوَةٌ فَلِأُمِّهِ السُّدُسُ
   after paying off any bequest he may have made مِن بَعْدِ وَصِيَّةٍ يُوصِى بِهَا
   or any debt he may have incurred. أَوْ دَيْنٍ
Your parents and your children آبَاؤُكُمْ وَأَبْنَاؤُكُمْ
   —you do not know which of them لَا تَدْرُونَ أَيُّهُمْ
   is likelier to be beneficial for you. أَقْرَبُ لَكُمْ نَفْعًا
This is an ordinance from God. فَرِيضَةً مِّنَ اللَّهِ
God is indeed all-knowing, all-wise. إِنَّ اللَّهَ كَانَ عَلِيمًا حَكِيمًا ۝

12 For you shall be a half of what your wives leave, وَلَكُمْ نِصْفُ مَا تَرَكَ أَزْوَاجُكُمْ
   if they have no children; إِن لَّمْ يَكُن لَّهُنَّ وَلَدٌ
but if they have children, فَإِن كَانَ لَهُنَّ وَلَدٌ
   then for you shall be a fourth of what they leave, فَلَكُمُ الرُّبُعُ مِمَّا تَرَكْنَ
   after paying off any bequest they may have made مِن بَعْدِ وَصِيَّةٍ يُوصِينَ بِهَا
   or any debt they may have incurred. أَوْ دَيْنٍ
And for them it shall be a fourth of what you leave, وَلَهُنَّ الرُّبُعُ مِمَّا تَرَكْتُم
   if you have no children; إِن لَّمْ يَكُن لَّكُمْ وَلَدٌ
but if you have children, فَإِن كَانَ لَكُمْ وَلَدٌ
   then for them shall be an eighth of what you leave, فَلَهُنَّ الثُّمُنُ مِمَّا تَرَكْتُم
   after paying off any bequest you may have made مِّن بَعْدِ وَصِيَّةٍ تُوصُونَ بِهَا
   or any debt you may have incurred. أَوْ دَيْنٍ
If a man or woman is inherited by siblings[1] وَإِن كَانَ رَجُلٌ يُورَثُ كَلَالَةً أَوِ امْرَأَةٌ
   and has a brother or a sister, وَلَهُ أَخٌ أَوْ أُخْتٌ

---

[1] *Kalālah* means the siblings of a deceased person without a first-degree heir. See verse **4:176** below.

then each of them shall receive a sixth;
but if they are more than that,
then they shall share in one third,
after paying off any bequest he may have made
　　or any debt he may have incurred
without prejudice.[1]
This is an enjoinment from God,
and God is all-knowing, all-forbearing.

13 These are God's bounds,
and whoever obeys God and His Apostle,
He shall admit him to gardens
with streams running in them,
　　to remain in them.
That is the great success.

14 But whoever disobeys God and His Apostle,
and transgresses the bounds set by God,
He shall make him enter a Fire, to remain in it,
and there will be a humiliating punishment for him.

15 Should any of your women commit an indecent act,[2]
　　produce against them four witnesses from yourselves,
and if they testify,
detain them[3] in their houses
　　until death finishes them,
or God decrees a course for them.[4]

16 Should two among you commit it,
　　chastise them both;[5]

---

[1] That is, the will should not encroach on the rights of the heirs, for instance by acknowledging a nonexistent debt.
[2] That is, adultery.
[3] That is, the women against whom testimony has been given.
[4] Superseded by the punishment by stoning for adultery and by verse **24**:2, which prescribes the punishment for fornication.
[5] That is, fornication (or sodomy, according to some exegetes).

but if they repent and reform, let them alone.
God is indeed all-clement, all-merciful.

17 Acceptance of repentance by God is only for those
who commit evil out of ignorance,
and then repent promptly.
It is such whose repentance God will accept,
and God is all-knowing, all-wise.

18 But acceptance of repentance is not for those
who go on committing misdeeds:
when death approaches any of them,
he says, 'I repent now.'
Nor is it for those who die while they are faithless.
For such We have prepared a painful punishment.

19 O you who have faith!
It is not lawful for you to inherit women forcibly,
and do not press them
to take away part of what you have given them,
unless they commit a gross indecency.[1]
Consort with them in an honourable manner;
and should you dislike them,
maybe you dislike something
while God invests it with an abundant good.

20 If you desire to take a wife in place of another,
and you have given one of them a quintal of gold,
do not take anything away from it.
Would you take it by way of calumny and flagrant sin?!

21 How could you take it back,
when you have known[2] each other,
and they have taken from you a solemn covenant?

---

[1] That is, adultery.
[2] Know: To have sexual intercourse with (archaic).

22 Do not marry
any of the women whom your fathers had married,
excluding what is already past.
That is indeed an indecency,
an outrage and an evil course.

23 Forbidden to you are your mothers,
your daughters and your sisters,
your paternal aunts and your maternal aunts,
your brother's daughters and your sister's daughters,
your foster-mothers who have suckled you
and your sisters through wet-nursing,
your wives' mothers,
and your stepdaughters who are under your care
born of the wives whom you have gone into
—but if you have not gone into them
there is no sin upon you—
and the wives of your sons
who are from your own loins,
and that you should marry two sisters at one time
—excluding what is already past;
indeed God is all-forgiving, all-merciful—

[PART 5]

24 and married women
excepting your slave-women.
This is God's ordinance for you.
As to others than these, it is lawful for you
to seek [temporary union with them] with your wealth,
in wedlock, not in license.
For the enjoyment you have had from them thereby,
give them their dowries, by way of settlement,

and there is no sin upon you
in what you may agree upon after the settlement.
God is indeed all-knowing, all-wise.

25 As for those of you who cannot afford
to marry faithful free women,
then let them marry from what you own,
from among your faithful slave-women.
Your faith is best known only to God;
you are all on a similar footing.
So marry them with their masters' permission,
and give them their dowries in an honourable manner
—such of them as are chaste women,
not licentious ones or those who take paramours.
But should they commit an indecent act on marrying,
there shall be for them
only half the punishment for free women.
This is for those of you who fear falling into fornication;
but it is better that you be continent,[1]
and God is all-forgiving, all-merciful.

26 God desires to explain [the laws] to you and guide you
to the customs of those who were before you,[2]
and to turn toward you clemently,
and God is all-knowing, all-wise.

27 God desires to turn toward you clemently,
but those who pursue their base appetites desire
that you fall into gross waywardness.

28 God desires to lighten your burden,
for man was created weak.

29 O you who have faith! Do not eat up your wealth

---

[1] That is, by refraining from marriage with slave-women.
[2] That is, to the customs of the prophets of the past and their communities.

بَيْنَكُمْ بِالْبَاطِلِ   among yourselves unrightfully,[1]
إِلَّا أَن تَكُونَ تِجَارَةً عَن تَرَاضٍ مِّنكُمْ   but it should be trade by mutual consent.
وَلَا تَقْتُلُوا أَنفُسَكُمْ   And do not kill yourselves.[2]
إِنَّ اللَّهَ كَانَ بِكُمْ رَحِيمًا ۩   Indeed, God is most merciful to you.
وَمَن يَفْعَلْ ذَٰلِكَ عُدْوَانًا وَظُلْمًا 30 And whoever does that in aggression and injustice,
فَسَوْفَ نُصْلِيهِ نَارًا   We will soon make him enter the Fire,
وَكَانَ ذَٰلِكَ عَلَى اللَّهِ يَسِيرًا ۩   and that is easy for God.
إِن تَجْتَنِبُوا كَبَائِرَ مَا تُنْهَوْنَ عَنْهُ 31 If you avoid the major sins that you are forbidden,
نُكَفِّرْ عَنكُمْ سَيِّئَاتِكُمْ   We will absolve you of your misdeeds
وَنُدْخِلْكُم مُّدْخَلًا كَرِيمًا ۩   and admit you to a noble abode.
وَلَا تَتَمَنَّوْا مَا فَضَّلَ اللَّهُ بِهِ 32 Do not covet the advantage which God has given
بَعْضَكُمْ عَلَىٰ بَعْضٍ   some of you over others.
لِّلرِّجَالِ نَصِيبٌ مِّمَّا اكْتَسَبُوا   To men belongs a share of what they have earned,
وَلِلنِّسَاءِ نَصِيبٌ مِّمَّا اكْتَسَبْنَ   and to women a share of what they have earned.
وَاسْأَلُوا اللَّهَ مِن فَضْلِهِ   And ask God for His bounty.
إِنَّ اللَّهَ كَانَ بِكُلِّ شَيْءٍ عَلِيمًا ۩   Indeed, God has knowledge of all things.
وَلِكُلٍّ جَعَلْنَا مَوَالِيَ 33 For everyone We have appointed heirs
مِمَّا تَرَكَ الْوَالِدَانِ وَالْأَقْرَبُونَ   to what the parents and near relatives leave,
وَالَّذِينَ عَقَدَتْ أَيْمَانُكُمْ   as well as those with whom you have made a compact;
فَآتُوهُمْ نَصِيبَهُمْ   so give them their share of the heritage.
إِنَّ اللَّهَ كَانَ عَلَىٰ كُلِّ شَيْءٍ شَهِيدًا ۩   Indeed, God is witness to all things.
الرِّجَالُ قَوَّامُونَ عَلَى النِّسَاءِ 34 Men are the managers of women,
بِمَا فَضَّلَ اللَّهُ   because of the advantage God has granted
بَعْضَهُمْ عَلَىٰ بَعْضٍ   some of them over others,
وَبِمَا أَنفَقُوا مِنْ أَمْوَالِهِمْ   and by virtue of their spending out of their wealth.
فَالصَّالِحَاتُ قَانِتَاتٌ   Righteous women are obedient
حَافِظَاتٌ لِّلْغَيْبِ   and watchful in the absence of their husbands
بِمَا حَفِظَ اللَّهُ   of what God has enjoined them to guard.

---

[1] That is, by way of usury, gambling, usurpation, false claim, or any other illegitimate means.
[2] That is, do not destroy yourselves by consuming wealth acquired through illegitimate means, such as usury, gambling, fraud, theft, bribery, usurpation and so on; or it means, do not commit suicide, or murder, or, do not expose yourselves recklessly to mortal danger.

وَاللَّاتِي تَخَافُونَ نُشُوزَهُنَّ	As for those wives whose misconduct you fear,
فَعِظُوهُنَّ	first advise them,
وَاهْجُرُوهُنَّ فِي الْمَضَاجِعِ	and [if ineffective] keep away from them in the bed,
وَاضْرِبُوهُنَّ	and [as the last resort] beat them.
فَإِنْ أَطَعْنَكُمْ	Then if they obey you,
فَلَا تَبْغُوا عَلَيْهِنَّ سَبِيلًا	do not seek any course of action against them.
إِنَّ اللَّهَ كَانَ عَلِيًّا كَبِيرًا ۝	Indeed, God is all-exalted, all-great.

35 If you fear a split between the two of them,
then appoint an arbiter from his relatives
and an arbiter from her relatives.
If they desire reconcilement, God shall reconcile them.[1]
God is indeed all-knowing, all-aware.

36 Worship God and do not ascribe any partners to Him,
and be good to parents,
the relatives, the orphans, the needy,
the near neighbour and the distant neighbour,
the companion at your side,
the traveler, and your slaves.
God indeed does not like
those who are arrogant and boastful.

37 Those who are themselves stingy
and bid other people to be stingy, too,
and conceal what God has given them out of His bounty—
We have prepared a humiliating punishment for the faithless

38 and those who spend their wealth to be seen by people,
and believe neither in God nor in the Last Day.
As for him who has Satan for his companion
—an evil companion is he!

39 What harm would it have done them

---

[1] That is, if the arbiters consider it advisable for the couple to remain united in wedlock, God will bring about a conciliation between them.

had they believed in God and the Last Day,
and spent out of what God has provided them?
God knows them well.

40 Indeed, God does not wrong anyone
even to the extent of an atom's weight,
and if it be a good deed He doubles its reward,
and gives from Himself a great reward.

41 So how shall it be,
when We bring a witness from every nation
and We bring you as a witness to them?

42 On that day, those who were faithless and disobeyed
the Apostle, will wish the earth were levelled with them,
and they will not conceal any matter from God.

43 O you who have faith!
Do not approach prayer when you are intoxicated,
not until you know what you are saying,
nor enter mosques in the state of ritual impurity
—except while passing through—
until you have washed yourselves.
But if you are sick or on a journey,
or any of you has come from the toilet,
or you have touched women,[1]
and you cannot find water,
then make your ablution on clean ground
and wipe a part of your faces and your hands.
God is indeed all-excusing, all-forgiving.

44 Have you not regarded those who were given
a share of the Book,

---

[1] That is, if you have performed sexual intercourse.

who purchase error

and desire that you too should lose the way? يَشْتَرُونَ الضَّلَالَةَ وَيُرِيدُونَ أَنْ تَضِلُّوا السَّبِيلَ ۞

45 But God knows your enemies better,

and God suffices as friend, and God suffices as helper.

46 Among the Jews are those who

    pervert words from their meanings

and say, 'We hear and disobey'

    and 'Hear without listening!' and '*Rāʿinā*,'

twisting their tongues and reviling the faith.

But had they said, 'We hear and obey'

    and 'Listen' and '*Unẓurnā*,'

it would have been better for them, and more upright.[1]

But God has cursed them for their faithlessness,

so they will not believe except a few.

47 O you who were given the Book!

Believe in what We have sent down

confirming what is with you,

before We blot out the faces

    and turn them backwards, or curse them

    as We cursed the People of the Sabbath,

and God's command is bound to be fulfilled.

48 Indeed, God does not forgive

    that a partner should be ascribed to Him,

but He forgives anything besides that

    to whomever He wishes.

Whoever ascribes partners to God

has indeed fabricated a lie in great sinfulness.

49 Have you not regarded those who style themselves as pure?

---

[1] See 2:104 and the related footnote.

Indeed, it is God who purifies whomever He wishes, بَلِ اللَّهُ يُزَكِّي مَن يَشَاءُ
and they will not be wronged وَلَا يُظْلَمُونَ
so much as a single date-thread. فَتِيلًا ۝
50 Look, how they fabricate lies against God! انظُرْ كَيْفَ يَفْتَرُونَ عَلَى اللَّهِ الْكَذِبَ
That suffices for a flagrant sin. وَكَفَىٰ بِهِ إِثْمًا مُّبِينًا ۝
51 Have you not regarded those أَلَمْ تَرَ إِلَى الَّذِينَ
who were given a share of the Book,[1] أُوتُوا نَصِيبًا مِّنَ الْكِتَابِ
believing in idols and satanic entities يُؤْمِنُونَ بِالْجِبْتِ وَالطَّاغُوتِ
and saying of the pagans: وَيَقُولُونَ لِلَّذِينَ كَفَرُوا
'These are better guided on the way than the faithful'? هَٰؤُلَاءِ أَهْدَىٰ مِنَ الَّذِينَ آمَنُوا سَبِيلًا ۝
52 They are the ones whom God has cursed, أُولَٰئِكَ الَّذِينَ لَعَنَهُمُ اللَّهُ
and whomever God curses, وَمَن يَلْعَنِ اللَّهُ
you will never find any helper for him. فَلَن تَجِدَ لَهُ نَصِيرًا ۝
53 Do they have a share in sovereignty?[2] أَمْ لَهُمْ نَصِيبٌ مِّنَ الْمُلْكِ
If so, they will not give the people فَإِذًا لَّا يُؤْتُونَ النَّاسَ
so much as a speck on a date-stone! نَقِيرًا ۝
54 Or do they envy those people أَمْ يَحْسُدُونَ النَّاسَ
for what God has given them out of His bounty? عَلَىٰ مَا آتَاهُمُ اللَّهُ مِن فَضْلِهِ
We have certainly given the progeny of Abraham فَقَدْ آتَيْنَا آلَ إِبْرَاهِيمَ
the Book and wisdom, الْكِتَابَ وَالْحِكْمَةَ
and We have given them a great sovereignty.[3] وَآتَيْنَاهُم مُّلْكًا عَظِيمًا ۝
55 Of them[4] are some who believe in *him*, فَمِنْهُم مَّنْ آمَنَ بِهِ
and of them are some who deter others from *him*; وَمِنْهُم مَّن صَدَّ عَنْهُ
and hell suffices for a blaze! وَكَفَىٰ بِجَهَنَّمَ سَعِيرًا ۝
56 Indeed, those who deny Our signs, إِنَّ الَّذِينَ كَفَرُوا بِآيَاتِنَا
We shall soon make them enter a Fire: سَوْفَ نُصْلِيهِمْ نَارًا

---

[1] A reference to the Jews, or the hypocrites amongst the Muslims.
[2] Or 'in the kingdom.'
[3] A reference to the Imamate, as mentioned in 2:124. According to the traditions of the Imams of the Prophet's descent (who represent Abraham's progeny, through Ishmael), by the 'great sovereignty' is meant the office of the Imamate, because to obey the Imam is to obey God and to disobey him is to disobey God. See the commentaries of Furāt al-Kūfī, 'Ayyāshī, Qummī and Ḥibrī.
[4] That is, from among the Jews there are some who believe in the Prophet (ṣ).

as often as their skins become scorched, كُلَّمَا نَضِجَتْ جُلُودُهُمْ
We shall replace them with other skins, بَدَّلْنَاهُمْ جُلُودًا غَيْرَهَا
so that they may taste the punishment. لِيَذُوقُوا الْعَذَابَ
God is indeed all-mighty, all-wise. إِنَّ اللَّهَ كَانَ عَزِيزًا حَكِيمًا ۝

57 As for those who have faith and do righteous deeds, وَالَّذِينَ آمَنُوا وَعَمِلُوا الصَّالِحَاتِ
We shall admit them into gardens سَنُدْخِلُهُمْ جَنَّاتٍ
with streams running in them, تَجْرِي مِنْ تَحْتِهَا الْأَنْهَارُ
to remain in them forever. خَالِدِينَ فِيهَا أَبَدًا
In it there will be chaste mates for them, لَهُمْ فِيهَا أَزْوَاجٌ مُطَهَّرَةٌ
and We shall admit them into a deep shade.[1] وَنُدْخِلُهُمْ ظِلًّا ظَلِيلًا ۝

58 Indeed, God commands you to deliver the trusts إِنَّ اللَّهَ يَأْمُرُكُمْ أَنْ تُؤَدُّوا الْأَمَانَاتِ
to their rightful owners, إِلَىٰ أَهْلِهَا
and, when you judge between people, وَإِذَا حَكَمْتُمْ بَيْنَ النَّاسِ
to judge with fairness. أَنْ تَحْكُمُوا بِالْعَدْلِ
Excellent indeed is what God advises you. إِنَّ اللَّهَ نِعِمَّا يَعِظُكُمْ بِهِ
God is indeed all-hearing, all-seeing. إِنَّ اللَّهَ كَانَ سَمِيعًا بَصِيرًا ۝

59 O you who have faith! يَا أَيُّهَا الَّذِينَ آمَنُوا
Obey God and obey the Apostle أَطِيعُوا اللَّهَ وَأَطِيعُوا الرَّسُولَ
and those vested with authority among you.[2] وَأُولِي الْأَمْرِ مِنْكُمْ
And if you dispute concerning anything, فَإِنْ تَنَازَعْتُمْ فِي شَيْءٍ
refer it to God and the Apostle, فَرُدُّوهُ إِلَى اللَّهِ وَالرَّسُولِ
if you have faith in God and the Last Day. إِنْ كُنْتُمْ تُؤْمِنُونَ بِاللَّهِ وَالْيَوْمِ الْآخِرِ
That is better and more favourable in outcome. ذَٰلِكَ خَيْرٌ وَأَحْسَنُ تَأْوِيلًا ۝

60 Have you not regarded those who claim أَلَمْ تَرَ إِلَى الَّذِينَ يَزْعُمُونَ
that they believe in what has been sent down to you أَنَّهُمْ آمَنُوا بِمَا أُنْزِلَ إِلَيْكَ
and what was sent down before you? وَمَا أُنْزِلَ مِنْ قَبْلِكَ
They desire to seek the judgment of satanic entities, يُرِيدُونَ أَنْ يَتَحَاكَمُوا إِلَى الطَّاغُوتِ
though they were commanded to reject them, وَقَدْ أُمِرُوا أَنْ يَكْفُرُوا بِهِ

---

[1] Or 'into a shady twilight;' see the footnote at **25:45**.
[2] Cf. verse **4:54** above.

and Satan desires to lead them astray into far error. وَيُرِيدُ الشَّيْطَانُ أَن يُضِلَّهُمْ ضَلَالًا بَعِيدًا ۝

61 When they are told, 'Come to what God has sent down
and come to the Apostle,'
you see the hypocrites keep away from you aversely.

62 But how will it be when an affliction visits them
because of what their hands have sent ahead?
Then they will come to you, swearing by God,
'We desired nothing but goodwill and comity.'

63 They are the ones whom God knows
as to what is in their hearts.
So let them alone, and advise them and speak to them
far-reaching words concerning themselves.

64 We did not send any apostle
but to be obeyed by God's leave.
Had they, when they wronged themselves,
come to you and pleaded to God for forgiveness,
and the Apostle had pleaded forgiveness for them,
they would have surely found God clement and merciful.

65 But no, by your Lord! They will not believe
until they make you a judge in their disputes,
then do not find within their hearts any dissent
to your verdict and submit in full submission.

66 Had We prescribed for them, commanding:
'Slay [the guilty among] your folks[1]
or leave your habitations,'
they would not have done it except a few of them.
And if they had done as they were advised,
it would have been better for them
and stronger in confirming their faith.

---

[1] As in the case of the Israelites who were ordered to kill those who were guilty among them of the worship of the Calf. See 2:54.

⁶⁷ Then We would have given them from Us a great reward,

⁶⁸ and We would have surely guided them to a straight path.

⁶⁹ Whoever obeys God and the Apostle
—they are with those whom God has blessed,
including the prophets and the truthful,
the martyrs and the righteous,
and excellent companions are they!

⁷⁰ That is the grace of God,
and God suffices as knower of His creatures.

⁷¹ O you who have faith! Take your precautions,
then go forth in companies, or go forth en masse.

⁷² Among you is indeed he who drags his feet,
and should an affliction visit you, he says,
'It was certainly God's blessing
that I did not accompany them!'

⁷³ But should a bounty from God come to you,
he will surely say,
as if there were no affection between you and him,
'I wish I were with them
so that I had achieved a great success!'

⁷⁴ Let those fight in the way of God
who sell the life of this world for the Hereafter;
and whoever fights in the way of God,
and is then slain, or he subdues the enemy,
We shall soon give him a great reward.

⁷⁵ Why should you not fight in the way of God
and the oppressed men, women,
and children, who say, 'Our Lord,
bring us out of this town whose people are oppressors,

and appoint for us a protector from Yourself,
and appoint for us a helper from Yourself'?
76 Those who have faith fight in the way of God,
and those who are faithless
fight in the way of satanic entities.
So fight the allies of Satan;
indeed the stratagems of Satan are always flimsy.
77 Have you not regarded those who were told,
'Keep your hands off from warfare,
and maintain the prayer and give the *zakāt*'?
But when fighting was prescribed for them,
behold, a part of them feared those people
as if fearing God, or were even more afraid,
and they said, 'Our Lord!
Why did You prescribe fighting for us?
Why did You not respite us for a short time?!'[1]
Say, 'The enjoyments of this world are trifle
and the Hereafter is better for the Godwary,
and you will not be wronged so much as a single date-thread.
78 Wherever you may be, death will overtake you,
even if you were in fortified towers.'
If any good befalls them,
they say, 'This is from God;'
and when an ill befalls them,
they say, 'This is from *you*.'
Say, 'All is from God.'
What is the matter with these people
that they would not understand any matter?
79 Whatever good befalls *you* is from God;

---

[1] Or 'until an imminent time;' that is, until the time of natural death, which is not far in any case. Cf. **14**:44; **63**:10-11.

and whatever ill befalls *you* is from *yourself*.
We sent *you* as an apostle to mankind,
and God suffices as witness.

80 Whoever obeys the Apostle certainly obeys God;
and as for those who turn their backs on *you*,
We have not sent *you* to keep watch over them.

81 They profess obedience to *you*,
but when they go out from *your* presence,
a group of them conspire overnight
to do something other than what *you* say.
But God records what they conspire overnight.
So *disregard* them and *put your* trust in God,
for God suffices as trustee.

82 Do they not contemplate the Qurʾān?
Had it been from someone other than God,
they would have surely found much discrepancy in it.

83 When a report of safety or alarm comes to them,
they immediately broadcast it;
but had they referred it to the Apostle
or to those vested with authority among them,
those of them who investigate would have ascertained it.
And were it not for God's grace upon you and His mercy,
you would have surely followed Satan, all except a few.

84 So *fight* in the way of God:
you are responsible only for *yourself*,
but *urge* on the faithful to fight.
Maybe God will curb
the might of the faithless,
for God is greatest in might and severest in punishment.

85 Whoever intercedes for a good cause

shall receive a share of it,
and whoever intercedes for an evil cause
   shall share its burden,
and God has supreme authority over all things.

86 When you are greeted with a salute,
   greet with a better one than it, or return it;
   indeed God takes account of all things.

87 God—there is no god except Him—
   will surely gather you on the Day of Resurrection,
      in which there is no doubt;
   and who is more truthful in speech than God?

88 Why should you be two groups concerning the hypocrites,[1]
   while God has made them relapse into unfaith
      because of their deeds?
   Do you desire to guide someone God has led astray?
   Whomever God leads astray,
      you will never find any way for him.

89 They are eager that you should disbelieve
   just as they have disbelieved, so that you all become alike.
   So do not make friends with anyone from among them,
      until they migrate in the way of God.
   But if they turn their backs, seize them and kill them
      wherever you find them,
   and do not take from among them allies
      or helpers,

90 excepting those who join a people
   between whom and you there is a treaty,
   or such as come to you

---

[1] A reference to the hypocrites of Makkah who feigned sympathy for the Muslims while remaining in Makkah and continuing to work for their enemies.

al-Nisā' 4:92

  with hearts reluctant to fight you
   or to fight their own people.
  Had God wished, He would have imposed them upon you,
   and then they would have surely fought you.
  So if they keep out of your way
   and do not fight you and offer you peace,
  then God does not allow you
   any course of action against them.

91 You will find others desiring to be secure from you
   and from their own people;
  yet whenever they are called back to polytheism,
   they relapse into it.
  So if they do not keep out of your way, nor offer you peace,
   nor keep their hands off from fighting,
  then seize them and kill them wherever you confront them,
   and it is such against whom We have given you
    a clear sanction.

92 A believer may not kill another believer,
   unless it is by mistake.
  Anyone who kills a believer by mistake
   should set free a believing slave
   and pay blood-money to his family,[1]
   unless they remit it in charity.
  If he[2] belongs to a people who are hostile to you
   but is a believer,
  then a believing slave is to be set free.
  If he belongs to a people with whom you have a treaty,
   the blood-money is to be paid to his family

---

[1] That is, to the family of the victim.
[2] That is, the victim.

and a believing slave is to be set free.
He who does not afford [freeing a slave],
must fast for two successive months as a penance from God,
and God is all-knowing, all-wise.

93 Should anyone kill a believer intentionally,
his requital shall be hell, to remain in it;
God shall be wrathful at him and curse him
and He will prepare for him a great punishment.

94 O you who have faith!
When you issue forth in the way of God, try to ascertain:
do not say to someone who offers you peace,
'You are not a believer,'
seeking the transitory wares of the life of this world.
But with God are plenteous gains.
You too were such earlier, but God did you a favour.
Therefore, do ascertain.
God is indeed well aware of what you do.

95 Not equal are those of the faithful who sit back
—excepting those who suffer from some disability—
and those who wage *jihād* in the way of God
with their possession and persons.
God has graced those who wage *jihād*
with their possessions and persons
by a degree over those who sit back;
yet to each God has promised the best reward,
and God has graced those who wage *jihād*
over those who sit back with a great reward:

96 ranks from Him, forgiveness and mercy,
and God is all-forgiving, all-merciful.

97 إِنَّ الَّذِينَ تَوَفَّاهُمُ الْمَلَائِكَةُ ظَالِمِي أَنْفُسِهِمْ قَالُوا فِيمَ كُنْتُمْ ۖ قَالُوا كُنَّا مُسْتَضْعَفِينَ فِي الْأَرْضِ ۚ قَالُوا أَلَمْ تَكُنْ أَرْضُ اللَّهِ وَاسِعَةً فَتُهَاجِرُوا فِيهَا ۚ فَأُولَٰئِكَ مَأْوَاهُمْ جَهَنَّمُ ۖ وَسَاءَتْ مَصِيرًا ۝

98 إِلَّا الْمُسْتَضْعَفِينَ مِنَ الرِّجَالِ وَالنِّسَاءِ وَالْوِلْدَانِ لَا يَسْتَطِيعُونَ حِيلَةً وَلَا يَهْتَدُونَ سَبِيلًا ۝

99 فَأُولَٰئِكَ عَسَى اللَّهُ أَنْ يَعْفُوَ عَنْهُمْ ۚ وَكَانَ اللَّهُ عَفُوًّا غَفُورًا ۝

100 وَمَنْ يُهَاجِرْ فِي سَبِيلِ اللَّهِ يَجِدْ فِي الْأَرْضِ مُرَاغَمًا كَثِيرًا وَسَعَةً ۚ وَمَنْ يَخْرُجْ مِنْ بَيْتِهِ مُهَاجِرًا إِلَى اللَّهِ وَرَسُولِهِ ثُمَّ يُدْرِكْهُ الْمَوْتُ فَقَدْ وَقَعَ أَجْرُهُ عَلَى اللَّهِ ۗ وَكَانَ اللَّهُ غَفُورًا رَحِيمًا ۝

101 وَإِذَا ضَرَبْتُمْ فِي الْأَرْضِ فَلَيْسَ عَلَيْكُمْ جُنَاحٌ أَنْ تَقْصُرُوا مِنَ الصَّلَاةِ إِنْ خِفْتُمْ أَنْ يَفْتِنَكُمُ الَّذِينَ كَفَرُوا ۚ إِنَّ الْكَافِرِينَ كَانُوا لَكُمْ عَدُوًّا مُبِينًا ۝

102 وَإِذَا كُنْتَ فِيهِمْ فَأَقَمْتَ لَهُمُ الصَّلَاةَ فَلْتَقُمْ طَائِفَةٌ مِنْهُمْ مَعَكَ وَلْيَأْخُذُوا أَسْلِحَتَهُمْ فَإِذَا سَجَدُوا

97 Indeed, those whom the angels take away
while they are wronging themselves,
they[1] ask, 'What state were you in?'
They reply, 'We were oppressed in the land.'
They say, 'Was not God's earth vast enough
so that you might migrate in it?'
The refuge of such shall be hell,
and it is an evil destination.

98 Except those oppressed among men,
women and children,
who have neither access to any means
nor are guided to any way.

99 Maybe God will excuse them,
for God is all-excusing, all-forgiving.

100 Whoever migrates in the way of God
will find many havens and plenitude in the earth.
And whoever leaves his home
migrating toward God and His Apostle,
and is then overtaken by death,
his reward shall certainly fall on God,
and God is all-forgiving, all-merciful.

101 When you journey in the land,
there is no sin upon you in shortening the prayers
if you fear that the faithless may trouble you;
indeed the faithless are your manifest enemies.

102 When you are among them, leading them in prayers,
let a group of them stand with you,
carrying their weapons.
And when they have done the prostrations,

---

[1] That is, the angels.

let them withdraw to the rear,
then let the other group which has not prayed come
    and pray with *you*,
    taking their precautions and bearing their weapons.
The faithless are eager that *you* should be oblivious
    of your weapons and your baggage,
    so that they could assault you all at once.
But there is no sin upon you,
    if you are troubled by rain or are sick,
    to set aside your weapons;
    but take your precautions.
God has indeed prepared
    a humiliating punishment for the faithless.

103 When you have finished the prayers, remember God,
    standing, sitting and lying down;
and when you feel secure, perform the complete prayers,
    for the prayer is indeed
    a timed prescription for the faithful.

104 Do not slacken in the pursuit of those people.[1]
    If you are suffering,
    they are also suffering like you,
    but you expect from God what they do not expect,
    and God is all-knowing, all-wise.

105 Indeed, We have sent down to *you* the Book
    with the truth,
    so that *you* may judge between the people
    by what God has shown *you*;
    do not be an advocate for the traitors,

106   and *plead* to God for forgiveness;

---

[1] That is, the retreating troops of the Makkan aggressors after the Battle of Uḥud.

indeed God is all-forgiving, all-merciful.

107 And *do not plead* for those who betray themselves; indeed God does not like those who are treacherous and sinful.

108 They try to hide their real character from people, but they do not try to hide from God, though He is with them when they conspire overnight with a discourse that He does not approve of. And God encompasses whatever they do.

109 Aha! There you are, pleading for them in the life of this world! But who will plead for them with God on the Day of Resurrection, or will be their defender?

110 Whoever commits evil or wrongs himself and then pleads to God for forgiveness, will find God all-forgiving, all-merciful.

111 Whoever commits a sin, commits it only against himself; and God is all-knowing, all-wise.

112 Whoever commits an iniquity or sin and then accuses an innocent person of it, is indeed guilty of calumny and a flagrant sin.

113 Were it not for God's grace and His mercy on you, a group of them were bent on leading you astray; but they do not mislead anyone except themselves and they cannot do you any harm. God has sent down to you the Book and wisdom, and He has taught you what you did not know, and great is God's grace upon you.

114 There is no good in much of their secret talks,
  excepting someone who enjoins charity or what is right
     or reconciliation between people,
  and whoever does that, seeking God's pleasure,
     soon We shall give him a great reward.

115 Whoever defies the Apostle,
  after the guidance has become clear to him,
     and follows a way other than that of the faithful,
  We shall abandon him to his devices
     and We will make him enter hell, and it is an evil destination.

116 Indeed, God does not forgive
     that any partner should be ascribed to Him,
  but He forgives anything besides that to whomever He wishes.
  And whoever ascribes partners to God
     has certainly strayed into far error.

117 They invoke none but females besides Him,
     and invoke none but some froward Satan,[1]

118   whom God has cursed,
  and who said, 'I will surely take of Your servants
     a settled share,

119 and I will lead them astray and give them [false] hopes,
  and prompt them to slit the ears of cattle,[2]
     and I will prompt them to alter God's creation.'
  Whoever takes Satan as master instead of God
     has certainly incurred a manifest loss.

120 He makes them promises and gives them [false] hopes,
  yet Satan does not promise them anything but delusion.

121 The refuge of such shall be hell,
     and they will not find any escape from it.

---

[1] Most of the idols and deities worshiped by Arab pagans had female names, e.g. Lāt, Manāt, 'Uzzā, Nā'ilah, etc.
[2] This refers to the pagan practice of slitting the ears of camels as a sign of their dedication to pagan deities.

122 As for those who have faith and do righteous deeds,
We will admit them into gardens
with streams running in them,
to remain in them forever
—a true promise of God,
and who is truer in speech than God?

123 It will be neither after your hopes
nor the hopes of the People of the Book:
whoever commits evil shall be requited for it,
and he will not find for himself besides God
any friend or helper.

124 And whoever does righteous deeds,
whether male or female, should he be faithful
—such shall enter paradise
and they will not be wronged
so much as the speck on a date-stone.

125 Who has a better religion than him
who submits his will to God, being virtuous,
and follows the creed of Abraham, a *ḥanīf*?
And God took Abraham for a dedicated friend.

126 To God belongs whatever is in the heavens
and whatever is on the earth,
and God encompasses all things.

127 They seek *your* ruling concerning women.
Say, 'God gives you a ruling concerning them
and what is announced to you in the Book
concerning girl orphans
—whom you do not give what has been prescribed for them,

and yet you desire to marry them—
and about the weak among children:
that you should maintain the orphans with justice,
and whatever good you do,
indeed God knows it well.

128 If a woman fears from her husband
    misconduct or desertion,
there is no sin upon the couple
    if they reach a reconciliation between themselves;
and reconcilement is better.
The souls are prone to greed;
    but if you are virtuous and Godwary,
God is indeed well aware of what you do.

129 You will not be able to be fair between wives,
    even if you are eager to do so.
Yet do not turn away from one altogether,
    leaving her as if in a suspense.
But if you are conciliatory and Godwary,
    God is indeed all-forgiving, all-merciful.

130 But if they separate,
God will suffice each of them out of His bounty,
    and God is all-bounteous, all-wise.

131 To God belongs whatever is in the heavens
    and whatever is on the earth.
We have certainly enjoined those who were given the Book
    before you, and you, that you should be wary of God.
But if you are faithless, [you should know that]
    to God belongs whatever is in the heavens
and whatever is on the earth,

and God is all-sufficient, all-laudable.

132 To God belongs whatever is in the heavens
and whatever is on the earth,
and God suffices as trustee.

133 If He wishes, He will take you away, O mankind,
and bring others in your place;
God has the power to do that.

134 Whoever desires the reward of this world,
should know that with God
is the reward of this world and the Hereafter,
and God is all-hearing, all-seeing.

135 O you who have faith!
Be maintainers of justice
and honest witnesses for the sake of God,
even if it should be against yourselves
or your parents and near relatives,
and whether it be someone rich or poor,
for God has a greater right over them.
So do not follow your base desires, lest you should be unfair,
and if you distort the testimony or disregard it,
God is indeed well aware of what you do.

136 O you who have faith!
Have faith in God and His Apostle
and the Book that He has sent down to His Apostle
and the Book He had sent down earlier.
Whoever disbelieves in God and His angels,
His Books and His apostles and the Last Day,
has certainly strayed into far error.

137 As for those who believe and then disbelieve,
then believe again and then disbelieve

    and then increase in disbelief,
God will never forgive them,
    nor will He guide them to any right way.

138 Inform the hypocrites
    that there is a painful punishment for them
139 —those who take the faithless for allies
    instead of the faithful.
Do they seek honour with them?
If so, all honour belongs to God.

140 Certainly He has sent down to you in the Book
that when you hear God's signs being disbelieved
    and derided,
do not sit with them
    until they engage in some other discourse,
or else you too will be like them.
God will indeed gather the hypocrites
    and the faithless in hell all together

141 —those who lie in wait for you:
    if there is a victory for you from God,
    they say, 'Were we not with you?'
But if the faithless get a share of victory,
    they say, 'Did we not prevail upon you
    and defend you against the faithful?'
God will judge between you on the Day of Resurrection,
and God will never provide the faithless
    any way to prevail over the faithful.

142 The hypocrites seek to deceive God,
    but it is He who outwits them.
When they stand up for prayer,
    they stand up lazily, showing off to the people,

وَلَا يَذْكُرُونَ اللَّهَ إِلَّا قَلِيلًا ۝

and not remembering God except a little,

١٤٣ مُذَبْذَبِينَ بَيْنَ ذَٰلِكَ

wavering in between:

لَا إِلَىٰ هَٰؤُلَاءِ وَلَا إِلَىٰ هَٰؤُلَاءِ ۚ

neither with these, nor with those.

وَمَنْ يُضْلِلِ اللَّهُ

And whomever God leads astray,

فَلَنْ تَجِدَ لَهُ سَبِيلًا ۝

you will never find any way for him.

١٤٤ يَا أَيُّهَا الَّذِينَ آمَنُوا

O you who have faith!

لَا تَتَّخِذُوا الْكَافِرِينَ أَوْلِيَاءَ

Do not take the faithless for allies

مِنْ دُونِ الْمُؤْمِنِينَ ۚ

instead of the faithful.

أَتُرِيدُونَ أَنْ تَجْعَلُوا لِلَّهِ

Do you wish to give God

عَلَيْكُمْ سُلْطَانًا مُبِينًا ۝

a clear sanction against yourselves?

١٤٥ إِنَّ الْمُنَافِقِينَ

Indeed, the hypocrites will be

فِي الدَّرْكِ الْأَسْفَلِ مِنَ النَّارِ

in the lowest reach of the Fire,

وَلَنْ تَجِدَ لَهُمْ نَصِيرًا ۝

and you will never find any helper for them,

١٤٦ إِلَّا الَّذِينَ تَابُوا وَأَصْلَحُوا

except for those who repent and reform

وَاعْتَصَمُوا بِاللَّهِ

and hold fast to God

وَأَخْلَصُوا دِينَهُمْ لِلَّهِ

and dedicate their religion exclusively to God.

فَأُولَٰئِكَ مَعَ الْمُؤْمِنِينَ ۖ

Those are with the faithful,

وَسَوْفَ يُؤْتِ اللَّهُ الْمُؤْمِنِينَ أَجْرًا عَظِيمًا ۝

and soon God will give the faithful a great reward.

١٤٧ مَا يَفْعَلُ اللَّهُ بِعَذَابِكُمْ

Why should God punish you

إِنْ شَكَرْتُمْ وَآمَنْتُمْ ۚ

if you give thanks and be faithful?

وَكَانَ اللَّهُ شَاكِرًا عَلِيمًا ۝

And God is appreciative, all-knowing.

الجزء السادس

[PART 6]

١٤٨ لَا يُحِبُّ اللَّهُ

God does not like

الْجَهْرَ بِالسُّوءِ مِنَ الْقَوْلِ

the disclosure of anyone's evil conduct in speech,

إِلَّا مَنْ ظُلِمَ ۚ

except by someone who has been wronged,

وَكَانَ اللَّهُ سَمِيعًا عَلِيمًا ۝

and God is all-hearing, all-knowing.

١٤٩ إِنْ تُبْدُوا خَيْرًا

Whether you disclose a good deed that you do

أَوْ تُخْفُوهُ أَوْ تَعْفُوا عَنْ سُوءٍ

or hide it, or excuse an evil deed,

فَإِنَّ اللَّهَ كَانَ عَفُوًّا قَدِيرًا ۝

God is indeed all-excusing, all-powerful.

١٥٠ إِنَّ الَّذِينَ يَكْفُرُونَ بِاللَّهِ وَرُسُلِهِ

Those who disbelieve in God and His apostles

and seek to separate God from His apostles,
and say, 'We believe in some and disbelieve in some'
and seek to take a way in between

151 —it is they who are truly faithless,
and We have prepared for the faithless
a humiliating punishment.

152 But those who have faith in God and His apostles
and make no distinction between any of them
—them He will soon give their rewards,
and God is all-forgiving, all-merciful.

153 The People of the Book ask you
to bring down for them a Book from the heaven.
Certainly they asked Moses for something greater than that,
for they said, 'Show us God visibly,'
whereat a thunderbolt seized them for their wrongdoing.
Then they took up the Calf for worship,
after all the clear proofs that had come to them.
Yet We excused that,
and We gave Moses a manifest authority.

154 We raised the Mount above them
for the sake of their covenant,
and We said to them, 'Enter while prostrating at the gate'
and We said to them, 'Do not violate the Sabbath,'
and We took a solemn covenant from them.

155 Then because of their breaking their covenant,
their denial of God's signs,
their killing of the prophets unjustly,
and for their saying, 'Our hearts are uncircumcised.'[1]
Indeed, God has set a seal on them[2] for their unfaith,

---

[1] Ellipsis. The phrase omitted is: 'We cursed them.' Cf. **2:88; 5:13**.
[2] That is, on their hearts.

so they do not have faith except a few.
156 And for their faithlessness,
and their uttering a monstrous calumny against Mary,
157 and for their saying, 'We killed the Messiah,
Jesus son of Mary, the apostle of God'
—though they did not kill him, nor crucify him,
but so it was made to appear to them.
Indeed, those who differ concerning him[1]
are in doubt about him:[2]
they do not have any knowledge of that
beyond following conjectures,
and certainly they did not kill him.
158 Indeed, God raised him up toward Himself,
and God is all-mighty, all-wise.[3]
159 There is none among the People of the Book
but will surely believe in him before his death;
and on the Day of Resurrection
he will be a witness against them.[4]
160 Due to the wrongdoing of the Jews,
We prohibited them certain good things
that were permitted to them earlier,
and for their barring many people from the way of God,
161 and for their taking usury
—though they had been forbidden from it—
and for eating up the wealth of the people wrongfully.
And We have prepared for the faithless among them
a painful punishment.

---

[1] Or 'it.'
[2] Or 'it.'
[3] See verse 3:55 and the related footnote.
[4] That is, every Jew or Christian, before dying, will believe in the Prophet Muḥammad (ṣ), or, according to another interpretation, in Jesus ('a).

162 But as for those who are firmly grounded in knowledge from among them and faithful,
they believe in what has been sent down to you,
and what was sent down before you
—those who maintain the prayer, give the *zakāt*,
and believe in God and the Last Day
—them We shall give a great reward.

163 We have indeed revealed to you
as We revealed to Noah and the prophets after him,
and as We revealed to Abraham and Ishmael,
Isaac, Jacob, and the Tribes, Jesus,
Job, Jonah, Aaron and Solomon
—and We gave David the Psalms—

164 and apostles that We have recounted to you earlier
and apostles We have not recounted to you,
—and to Moses God spoke directly—

165 apostles, as bearers of good news and warners,
so that mankind may not have any argument against God,
after the sending of the apostles,
and God is all-mighty, all-wise.

166 But God bears witness to what He has sent down to you
—He sent it down with His knowledge—
and the angels bear witness too,
and God quite suffices as witness.

167 Indeed, those who are faithless
and bar others from the way of God,
have certainly strayed into far error.

168 Indeed, those who are faithless and do wrong,
God will never forgive them,
nor will He guide them to any way,

169 except the way to hell, to remain in it forever, and that is easy for God.

170 O mankind! The Apostle has certainly brought you the truth from your Lord.
So have faith! That is better for you.
And if you are faithless, [you should know that] to God belongs whatever is in the heavens and the earth, and God is all-knowing, all-wise.

171 O People of the Book!
Do not exceed the bounds in your religion, and do not attribute anything to God except the truth.
The Messiah, Jesus son of Mary, was only an apostle of God, and His Word that He cast toward Mary and a spirit from Him.
So have faith in God and His apostles, and do not say, 'God is a trinity.'
Relinquish such a creed! That is better for you.
God is but the One God.
He is far too immaculate to have any son.
To Him belongs whatever is in the heavens and whatever is on the earth, and God suffices as trustee.

172 The Messiah would never disdain being a servant of God, nor would the angels brought near to Him.
And whoever disdains His worship and is arrogant, He will gather them all toward Him.

173 As for those who have faith and do righteous deeds, He will pay them in full their rewards, and He will enhance them out of His grace.

But those who are disdainful and arrogant,
  He will punish them with a painful punishment,
  and they will not find besides God
  any friend or helper.

174 O mankind!
  Certainly a proof[1] has come to you from your Lord,
  and We have sent down to you a manifest light.[2]

175 As for those who have faith in God, and hold fast to Him,
  He will admit them to His mercy and grace,
  and He will guide them on a straight path to Him.

176 They ask you for a ruling.
  Say, 'God gives you a ruling concerning the *kalālah*:[3]
  If a man dies and has no children [or parents],
  but has a sister,
  for her shall be a half of what he leaves,
  and he shall inherit from her if she has no children.
  If there be two sisters,
  they shall receive two-thirds of what he leaves.
  But if there be several brothers and sisters,
  for the male shall be like the share of two females.
  God explains [the laws] for you
  lest you should go astray,
  and God has knowledge of all things.'

---

[1] That is, the Prophet Muḥammad (ṣ), or the Qur'ān.
[2] The Qur'ān, according to Mujāhid, Qatādah and Suddī. The *wilāyah* of Imām 'Alī b. Abī Ṭālib ('a) according to traditions from Imām Ja'far b. Muḥammad al-Ṣādiq ('a) and Imām Muḥammad al-Bāqir ('a). See the commentaries of Furāt al-Kūfī and al-'Ayyāshī under this verse.
[3] See the footnote at verse 4:12 above.

5. The Table[1]
al-Mā'idah

In the Name of God,
the All-beneficent, the All-merciful.

1 O you who have faith! Keep your agreements.
You are permitted animals of grazing livestock,
except for what is now announced to you,
disallowing game while you are in pilgrim sanctity.[2]
Indeed, God decrees whatever He desires.

2 O you who have faith!
Do not violate God's sacraments,
neither the sacred month,[3]
nor the offering,[4] nor the necklaces,
nor those bound[5] for the Sacred House
who seek their Lord's bounty and His pleasure.
But when you emerge from pilgrim sanctity
you may hunt for game.
Ill feeling for a people should not lead you,
because they barred you from the Sacred Mosque,
to transgress.
Cooperate in piety and Godwariness,
but do not cooperate in sin and aggression,
and be wary of God.
Indeed, God is severe in retribution.

3 You are prohibited carrion,
blood, the flesh of swine,

---

[1] Last of the Madanī *sūrah*s, it takes its name from 'the table' (*al-mā'idah*) mentioned in verses 112-115.
[2] That is, while you are in a state of *iḥrām*, while performing *ḥajj* or *'umrah*.
[3] That is, the month of Dhū al-Ḥijjah, during which the *ḥajj* is performed.
[4] That is, the sheep, camel or cow brought for the sacrifice. The 'necklaces' mean the token objects hung around the neck of the sacrificial animal.
[5] That is, the pilgrims heading for *ḥajj* or *'umrah*.

and what has been offered to other than God,
and the animal strangled or beaten to death,
and that which dies by falling or is gored to death,
and that which is mangled by a beast of prey
    —barring that which you may purify[1]—
and what is sacrificed on stone altars to idols,
and that you should divide by raffling with arrows.
All that is transgression.
Today the faithless have despaired of your religion.
So do not fear them, but fear Me.
Today I have perfected your religion for you,
    and I have completed My blessing upon you,
    and I have approved Islam as your religion.

But should anyone be compelled by hunger,
    without inclining to sin,
    then God is indeed all-forgiving, all-merciful.

4 They ask you as to what is lawful for them.
Say, 'All the good things are lawful for you.'
As for what you have taught hunting dogs to catch,
    teaching them by what God has taught you,
eat of what they catch for you
and mention God's Name over it, and be wary of God.
God is indeed swift at reckoning.

5 Today all the good things have been made lawful for you:
—the food of those who were given the Book
    is lawful for you, and your food is lawful for them—
and the chaste ones from among faithful women,
and chaste women

---

[1] That is, by duly slaughtering the animal wounded by the beast of prey.

of those who were given the Book before you,
when you have given them their dowries, in wedlock,
not in license, nor taking paramours.
Should anyone renounce his faith, his works shall fail
and he will be among the losers in the Hereafter.

6 O you who have faith! When you stand up for prayer,
    wash your faces,
       and your hands up to the elbows,
    and wipe a part of your heads
    and your feet up to the ankles.
If you are *junub*,[1] purify yourselves.
But if you are sick, or on a journey,
    or any of you has come from the toilet,
or you have touched women,[2] and you cannot find water,
    then make *tayammum* with clean ground
    and wipe a part of your faces and your hands with it.
God does not desire to put you to hardship,
    but He desires to purify you
    and to complete His blessing upon you
    so that you may give thanks.

7 Remember God's blessing upon you
and His covenant with which He has bound you,
    when you said, 'We hear and obey.'
And be wary of God.
Indeed, God knows well what is in the breasts.

8 O you who have faith!
Be maintainers of justice, as witnesses for God's sake,
    and ill feeling for a people should never lead you
    to be unfair.

---
[1] That is, in a state of ritual impurity.
[2] That is, if you have had sexual intercourse.

Be fair; that is nearer to Godwariness, and be wary of God. God is indeed well aware of what you do.

9 God has promised those who have faith
    and do righteous deeds
forgiveness and a great reward.

10 As for those who are faithless and deny Our signs,
they shall be the inmates of hell.

11 O you who have faith!
Remember God's blessing upon you
when a people set out to extend their hands against you,
    but He withheld their hands from you,
and be wary of God,
and in God alone let all the faithful put their trust.

12 Certainly God took a pledge from the Children of Israel,
and We raised among them twelve chiefs.
And God said, 'I am with you!
Surely, if you maintain the prayer and give the *zakāt*
and have faith in My apostles and support them
and lend God a good loan,
I will surely absolve you of your misdeeds,
    and I will surely admit you into gardens
    with streams running in them.
But whoever of you disbelieves after that
has certainly strayed from the right way.'

13 Then, because of their breaking their covenant
We cursed them and made their hearts hard:
they pervert words from their meanings,
and have forgotten a part of what they were reminded.
You will not cease to learn of some of their treachery,
excepting a few of them.

فَاعْفُ عَنْهُمْ وَاصْفَحْ ۚ

Yet *excuse* them and *forbear*.

إِنَّ اللَّهَ يُحِبُّ الْمُحْسِنِينَ ۝

Indeed, God loves the virtuous.

وَمِنَ الَّذِينَ قَالُوا إِنَّا نَصَارَىٰ

14 Also from those who say, 'We are Christians,'

أَخَذْنَا مِيثَاقَهُمْ

We took their pledge;

فَنَسُوا حَظًّا مِمَّا ذُكِّرُوا بِهِ

but they forgot a part of what they were reminded.

فَأَغْرَيْنَا بَيْنَهُمُ الْعَدَاوَةَ وَالْبَغْضَاءَ

So We stirred up enmity and hatred among them

إِلَىٰ يَوْمِ الْقِيَامَةِ ۚ

until the Day of Resurrection,

وَسَوْفَ يُنَبِّئُهُمُ اللَّهُ

and God will soon inform them

بِمَا كَانُوا يَصْنَعُونَ ۝

concerning what they had been doing.

يَا أَهْلَ الْكِتَابِ

15 O People of the Book!

قَدْ جَاءَكُمْ رَسُولُنَا يُبَيِّنُ لَكُمْ

Certainly Our Apostle has come to you, clarifying for you

كَثِيرًا مِمَّا كُنْتُمْ تُخْفُونَ مِنَ الْكِتَابِ

much of what you used to hide of the Book,

وَيَعْفُو عَنْ كَثِيرٍ ۚ

and excusing many an offense of yours.

قَدْ جَاءَكُمْ مِنَ اللَّهِ نُورٌ

Certainly there has come to you a light from God

وَكِتَابٌ مُبِينٌ ۝

and a manifest Book.

يَهْدِي بِهِ اللَّهُ مَنِ اتَّبَعَ رِضْوَانَهُ

16 With it God guides those who pursue His pleasure

سُبُلَ السَّلَامِ

to the ways of peace,

وَيُخْرِجُهُمْ مِنَ الظُّلُمَاتِ إِلَى النُّورِ بِإِذْنِهِ

and brings them out from darkness into light by His will,

وَيَهْدِيهِمْ إِلَىٰ صِرَاطٍ مُسْتَقِيمٍ ۝

and guides them to a straight path.

لَقَدْ كَفَرَ الَّذِينَ قَالُوا

17 They are certainly faithless who say,

إِنَّ اللَّهَ هُوَ الْمَسِيحُ ابْنُ مَرْيَمَ ۚ

'God is the Messiah, son of Mary.'

قُلْ فَمَنْ يَمْلِكُ مِنَ اللَّهِ شَيْئًا

Say, 'Who can avail anything against God

إِنْ أَرَادَ أَنْ يُهْلِكَ الْمَسِيحَ ابْنَ مَرْيَمَ

should He wish to destroy the Messiah, son of Mary,

وَأُمَّهُ وَمَنْ فِي الْأَرْضِ جَمِيعًا ۗ

and his mother, and everyone upon the earth?'

وَلِلَّهِ مُلْكُ السَّمَاوَاتِ

To God belongs the kingdom of the heavens

وَالْأَرْضِ وَمَا بَيْنَهُمَا ۚ

and the earth, and whatever is between them.

يَخْلُقُ مَا يَشَاءُ ۚ

He creates whatever He wishes,

وَاللَّهُ عَلَىٰ كُلِّ شَيْءٍ قَدِيرٌ ۝

and God has power over all things.

وَقَالَتِ الْيَهُودُ وَالنَّصَارَىٰ

18 The Jews and the Christians say,

'We are God's children and His beloved ones.'
Say, 'Then why does He punish you for your sins?'
No, you are humans from among His creatures.
He forgives whomever He wishes
   and punishes whomever He wishes,
and to God belongs the kingdom of the heavens
   and the earth and whatever is between them,
and toward Him is your return.

19 O People of the Book!
Certainly Our Apostle has come to you,
   clarifying [the Divine teachings] for you
     after a gap in the appearance of the apostles,
lest you should say,
'There did not come to us any bearer of good news
   nor any warner.'
Certainly there has come to you
   a bearer of good news and warner.
And God has power over all things.

20 When Moses said to his people,
'O my people, remember God's blessing upon you
when He appointed prophets among you
   and made you kings,
   and gave you what none of the nations were given.

21 O my people, enter the Holy Land
   which God has ordained for you,
   and do not turn your backs,
   or you will turn losers.'

22 They said, 'O Moses, there are a tyrannical people in it.
   We will not enter it until they leave it.

But once they leave it, we will go in.'
23 Said two men from among those who were Godfearing and whom God had blessed:
'Go at them by the gate!
For once you have entered it, you will be the victors.
Put your trust in God alone, should you be faithful.'
24 They said, 'O Moses,
we will never enter it so long as they remain in it.
Go ahead, you and your Lord, and fight!
We will be sitting right here.'
25 He said, 'My Lord!
I have no power over anyone except myself and my brother,
so part us from the transgressing lot.'
26 He said, 'It shall be forbidden them for forty years: they shall wander about in the land.
So do not grieve for the transgressing lot.'

27 *Relate* to them truly the account of Adam's two sons.
When the two of them offered an offering,
it was accepted from one of them
and not accepted from the other.
One of them said, 'Surely I will kill you.'
The other one said, 'God accepts only from the Godwary.
28 Even if you extend your hand toward me to kill me,
I will not extend my hand toward you to kill you.
Indeed, I fear God, the Lord of all the worlds.
29 I desire that you earn the burden of my sin[1] and your sin,
to become one of the inmates of the Fire,
and such is the requital of the wrongdoers.'

---

[1] That is, 'the sin of murdering me.'

30 فَطَوَّعَتْ لَهُ نَفْسُهُ قَتْلَ أَخِيهِ فَقَتَلَهُ فَأَصْبَحَ مِنَ الْخَاسِرِينَ ۝

So his soul prompted him to kill his brother and he killed him, and thus became one of the losers.

31 فَبَعَثَ اللَّهُ غُرَابًا يَبْحَثُ فِي الْأَرْضِ لِيُرِيَهُ كَيْفَ يُوَارِي سَوْءَةَ أَخِيهِ ۚ قَالَ يَا وَيْلَتَا أَعَجَزْتُ أَنْ أَكُونَ مِثْلَ هَٰذَا الْغُرَابِ فَأُوَارِيَ سَوْءَةَ أَخِي ۖ فَأَصْبَحَ مِنَ النَّادِمِينَ ۝

Then God sent a crow, exploring in the ground, to show him how to bury the corpse of his brother. He said, 'Woe to me! Am I unable to be even like this crow and bury my brother's corpse?' Thus he became regretful.

32 مِنْ أَجْلِ ذَٰلِكَ كَتَبْنَا عَلَىٰ بَنِي إِسْرَائِيلَ أَنَّهُ مَنْ قَتَلَ نَفْسًا بِغَيْرِ نَفْسٍ أَوْ فَسَادٍ فِي الْأَرْضِ فَكَأَنَّمَا قَتَلَ النَّاسَ جَمِيعًا وَمَنْ أَحْيَاهَا فَكَأَنَّمَا أَحْيَا النَّاسَ جَمِيعًا ۚ وَلَقَدْ جَاءَتْهُمْ رُسُلُنَا بِالْبَيِّنَاتِ ثُمَّ إِنَّ كَثِيرًا مِنْهُمْ بَعْدَ ذَٰلِكَ فِي الْأَرْضِ لَمُسْرِفُونَ ۝

That is why We decreed for the Children of Israel that whoever kills a soul,[1] without the guilt of manslaughter or corruption on the earth, is as though he had killed all mankind, and whoever saves a life is as though he had saved all mankind. Our apostles certainly brought them clear signs, yet even after that many of them commit excesses on the earth.

33 إِنَّمَا جَزَاءُ الَّذِينَ يُحَارِبُونَ اللَّهَ وَرَسُولَهُ وَيَسْعَوْنَ فِي الْأَرْضِ فَسَادًا أَنْ يُقَتَّلُوا أَوْ يُصَلَّبُوا أَوْ تُقَطَّعَ أَيْدِيهِمْ وَأَرْجُلُهُمْ مِنْ خِلَافٍ أَوْ يُنْفَوْا مِنَ الْأَرْضِ ۚ ذَٰلِكَ لَهُمْ خِزْيٌ فِي الدُّنْيَا ۖ وَلَهُمْ فِي الْآخِرَةِ عَذَابٌ عَظِيمٌ ۝

Indeed, the requital of those who wage war against God and His Apostle and try to cause corruption on the earth, is that they shall be slain or crucified, or shall have their hands and feet cut off on opposite sides, or be banished from the land. That is a disgrace for them in this world, and in the Hereafter there is a great punishment for them,

34 إِلَّا الَّذِينَ تَابُوا مِنْ قَبْلِ أَنْ تَقْدِرُوا عَلَيْهِمْ ۖ

excepting those who repent before you capture them,

---

[1] Or 'takes a life.'

and know that God is all-forgiving, all-merciful. فَاعْلَمُوا أَنَّ اللَّهَ غَفُورٌ رَحِيمٌ ۝

35 O you who have faith! Be wary of God,
and seek the means of recourse to Him,
and wage *jihād* in His way, so that you may be felicitous.

36 If the faithless possessed
all that is on the earth, and as much of it besides,
to redeem themselves with it
from the punishment of the Day of Resurrection,
it shall not be accepted from them,[1]
and there is a painful punishment for them.

37 They would long to leave the Fire,
but they shall never leave it,
and there is a lasting punishment for them.

38 As for the thief, man or woman, cut off their hands
as a requital for what they have earned.
That is an exemplary punishment from God,
and God is all-mighty, all-wise.

39 But whoever repents after his wrongdoing, and reforms,
God shall accept his repentance.
God is indeed all-forgiving, all-merciful.

40 Do you not know that to God belongs
the kingdom of the heavens and the earth?
He punishes whomever He wishes,
and forgives whomever He wishes,
and God has power over all things.

41 O Apostle! *Do not grieve*
for those who are active in promoting unfaith,
such as those who say, 'We believe' with their mouths,
but whose hearts have no faith,

---

[1] Cf. **13**:18 and **39**:47.

وَمِنَ الَّذِينَ هَادُواْ and the Jews
سَمَّاعُونَ لِلْكَذِبِ who eavesdrop with the aim of telling lies [against you]
سَمَّاعُونَ لِقَوْمٍ آخَرِينَ لَمْ يَأْتُوكَ and eavesdrop for other people who do not come to you.
يُحَرِّفُونَ الْكَلِمَ مِنْ بَعْدِ مَوَاضِعِهِ They pervert words from their meanings,
يَقُولُونَ إِنْ أُوتِيتُمْ هَذَا فَخُذُوهُ and say, 'If you are given this, take it,
وَإِنْ لَمْ تُؤْتَوْهُ فَاحْذَرُوا but if you are not given this, beware!'
وَمَنْ يُرِدِ اللَّهُ فِتْنَتَهُ Yet whomever God wishes to mislead,[1]
فَلَنْ تَمْلِكَ لَهُ مِنَ اللَّهِ شَيْئًا you cannot avail him anything against God.
أُولَئِكَ الَّذِينَ They are the ones
لَمْ يُرِدِ اللَّهُ أَنْ يُطَهِّرَ قُلُوبَهُمْ whose hearts God did not desire to purify.
لَهُمْ فِي الدُّنْيَا خِزْيٌ There is disgrace for them in this world,
وَلَهُمْ فِي الْآخِرَةِ عَذَابٌ عَظِيمٌ ﴿٤١﴾ and there is a great punishment for them in the Hereafter.

سَمَّاعُونَ لِلْكَذِبِ 42 Eavesdroppers with the aim of telling lies,
أَكَّالُونَ لِلسُّحْتِ consumers of illicit gains!
فَإِنْ جَاءُوكَ فَاحْكُمْ بَيْنَهُمْ —if they come to you, judge between them,
أَوْ أَعْرِضْ عَنْهُمْ or disregard them.
وَإِنْ تُعْرِضْ عَنْهُمْ فَلَنْ يَضُرُّوكَ شَيْئًا If you disregard them, they will not harm you in any way.
وَإِنْ حَكَمْتَ فَاحْكُمْ بَيْنَهُمْ بِالْقِسْطِ But if you do judge, judge between them with justice.
إِنَّ اللَّهَ يُحِبُّ الْمُقْسِطِينَ ﴿٤٢﴾ Indeed, God loves the just.

وَكَيْفَ يُحَكِّمُونَكَ 43 And how should they make you a judge,
وَعِنْدَهُمُ التَّوْرَاةُ while with them is the Torah,
فِيهَا حُكْمُ اللَّهِ in which is God's judgement?
ثُمَّ يَتَوَلَّوْنَ مِنْ بَعْدِ ذَلِكَ Yet in spite of that they turn their backs on Him
وَمَا أُولَئِكَ بِالْمُؤْمِنِينَ ﴿٤٣﴾ and they are not believers.

إِنَّا أَنْزَلْنَا التَّوْرَاةَ فِيهَا هُدًى وَنُورٌ 44 We sent down the Torah containing guidance and light.
يَحْكُمُ بِهَا النَّبِيُّونَ الَّذِينَ أَسْلَمُوا The prophets, who had submitted,[2] judged by it
لِلَّذِينَ هَادُوا وَالرَّبَّانِيُّونَ وَالْأَحْبَارُ for the Jews, and so did the rabbis and the scribes,
بِمَا اسْتُحْفِظُوا مِنْ كِتَابِ اللَّهِ as they were charged to preserve the Book of God
وَكَانُوا عَلَيْهِ شُهَدَاءَ and were witnesses to it.

---

[1] Or 'to punish.'
[2] That is, to God's commandments as revealed to Moses.

So do not fear the people, but fear Me,
and do not sell My signs for a paltry gain.
Those who do not judge by what God has sent down
—it is they who are the faithless.

45 In it We prescribed for them: a life for a life,
an eye for an eye, a nose for a nose,
and an ear for an ear, a tooth for a tooth,
and retaliation for wounds.
Yet whoever remits it out of charity,
that shall be an atonement for him.
Those who do not judge by what God has sent down
—it is they who are the wrongdoers.

46 We followed them with Jesus son of Mary
to confirm that which was before him of the Torah,
and We gave him the Evangel
containing guidance and light,
confirming what was before it of the Torah,
and as guidance and advice for the Godwary.

47 Let the people of the Evangel judge
by what God has sent down in it.
Those who do not judge by what God has sent down
—it is they who are the transgressors.

48 We have sent down to you the Book with the truth,
confirming what is before it of the Book
and as a guardian over it.
So *judge* between them by what God has sent down,
and *do not follow* their base desires
against the truth that has come to you.
For each community among you We had appointed

a code of law and a path,[1]
and had God wished
He would have made you one community,
but His purposes required that He should test you
with respect to what He has given you.
So take the lead in all good works.
To God shall be the return of you all,
whereat He will inform you
concerning that about which you used to differ.

49 *Judge* between them by what God has sent down,
and *do not follow* their base desires.
Beware of them lest they should beguile *you*
from part of what God has sent down to *you*.
But if they turn their backs on *you*,
then *know* that God desires to punish them
for some of their sins,
and indeed many of those people are transgressors.

50 Do they seek the judgement of pagan ignorance?
But who is better than God in judgement
for a people who have certainty?

51 O you who have faith!
Do not take the Jews and the Christians for allies:
they are allies of each other.
Any of you who allies with them is indeed one of them.
Indeed, God does not guide the wrongdoing lot.

52 Yet *you* see those in whose hearts is a sickness
rushing to them,
saying, 'We fear lest a turn of fortune should visit us.'
Maybe God will bring about a victory

---

[1] Or, 'For everyone of you We have appointed a way of approach, whereby he comes' (reading *minhā jā'a*, instead of *minhāja*).

or a command from Him,
and then they will be
regretful for what they kept secret in their hearts,
53 and the faithful will say,
'Are these the ones who swore by God
with solemn oaths that they were with you?!'
Their works have failed, and they have become losers.
54 O you who have faith!
Should any of you desert his religion,
God will soon bring a people whom He loves
and who love Him,
who will be humble towards the faithful,
stern towards the faithless,
waging *jihād* in the way of God,
not fearing the blame of any blamer.
That is God's grace
which He grants to whomever He wishes,
and God is all-bounteous, all-knowing.
55 Your guardian is only God, His Apostle,
and the faithful who maintain the prayer
and give the *zakāt* while bowing down.
56 Whoever takes for his guardians God,
His Apostle and the faithful [should know that]
the confederates of God are indeed victorious.
57 O you who have faith! Do not take
those who take your religion in derision and play,
from among those who were given the Book before you,
and the infidels, as allies,
and be wary of God, should you be faithful.
58 When you call to prayer,

they take it in derision and play.
That is because they are a people who do not reason.

59 Say, 'O People of the Book!
Are you vindictive toward us[1] for any reason except
that we have faith in God
and in what has been sent down to us
and in what was sent down before,
and that most of you are transgressors?'

60 Say, 'Shall I inform you
concerning something worse than that
as requital from God?
Those whom God has cursed
and with whom He is wrathful,
and turned some of whom into apes and swine,
and worshipers[2] of satanic entities!
Such are in a worse situation and more astray
from the right way.'

61 When they come to you, they say, 'We believe.'
Certainly they enter with disbelief and leave with it,
and God knows best what they have been concealing.

62 You see many of them actively engaged
in sin and aggression and consuming illicit gains.
Surely, evil is what they have been doing.

63 Why do not the rabbis and the scribes forbid them
from sinful speech and consuming illicit gains?
Surely, evil is what they have been working.

64 The Jews say, 'God's hand is tied up.'
Tied up be their hands,
and cursed be they for what they say!

---

[1] Or 'Do you find fault with us....'
[2] Or 'servants.'

No, His hands are wide open: He bestows as He wishes.
Surely many of them will be increased
  by what has been sent to you from your Lord
    in rebellion and unfaith,
and We have cast enmity and hatred amongst them
until the Day of Resurrection.
Every time they ignite the flames of war,
God puts them out.
They seek to cause corruption on the earth,
  and God does not like the agents of corruption.
65 Had the People of the Book believed and been Godwary,
  We would have absolved them of their misdeeds
  and admitted them into gardens of bliss.
66 Had they observed the Torah and the Evangel,
  and what was sent down to them from their Lord,
they would have drawn nourishment from above them
    and from beneath their feet.
There is an upright group among them,
  but what many of them do is evil.

67 O Apostle!
  Communicate that which has been sent down to you
    from your Lord,
  and if you do not,
    you will not have communicated His message,
  and God will protect you from those people.
  Indeed, God does not guide the faithless lot.

68 Say, 'O People of the Book! You do not stand on anything
  until you observe the Torah and the Evangel

and what has been sent down to you from your Lord.'
Surely many of them will be increased
by what has been sent down to you from your Lord
in rebellion and unfaith.
So *do not grieve* for the faithless lot.

69 Indeed, the faithful,
the Jews, the Sabaeans, and the Christians
—those who have faith in God and the Last Day
and act righteously—
they will have no fear, nor will they grieve.

70 Certainly We took a pledge from the Children of Israel
and We sent apostles to them.
Whenever an apostle brought them
that which was not to their liking,
they would impugn a part of them and a part they would slay.

71 They supposed there would be no testing,
so they became blind and deaf.
Thereafter God accepted their repentance,
yet again many of them became blind and deaf,
and God watches what they do.

72 They are certainly faithless who say,
'God is the Messiah, son of Mary.'
But the Messiah had said, 'O Children of Israel!
Worship God, my Lord and your Lord.
Indeed, whoever ascribes partners to God,
God will forbid him entry into paradise,
and his refuge will be the Fire,
and the wrongdoers will not have any helpers.'

73 They are certainly faithless who say,
'God is the third person of a trinity,'
while there is no god except the One God.
If they do not desist from what they say,
there shall befall the faithless among them
a painful punishment.

74 Will they not repent to God
and plead to Him for forgiveness?
Yet God is all-forgiving, all-merciful.

75 The Messiah, son of Mary, is but an apostle.
Certainly other apostles have passed before him,
and his mother was a truthful one.
Both of them would eat food.
Look how We clarify the signs for them,
and yet, *look*, how they go astray!

76 *Say,* 'Do you worship, besides God,
what has no power to bring you any benefit or harm,
while God—He is the All-hearing, the All-knowing?!'

77 *Say,* 'O People of the Book!
Do not unduly exceed the bounds in your religion
and do not follow the base desires of a people
who went astray in the past and led many astray,
and themselves strayed from the right path.'

78 The faithless among the Children of Israel were cursed
on the tongue of David and Jesus son of Mary.
That, because they would disobey
and commit transgressions.

79 They would not forbid one another
from the wrongs that they committed.
Surely, evil is what they had been doing.

80 You see many of them allying with the faithless.
Surely, evil is what they have sent ahead for their own souls,
　　as God is displeased with them
　　and they shall remain in punishment.

81 Had they believed in God and the Prophet
　　and what has been sent down to him,
　　they would not have taken them for allies.
　　But most of them are transgressors.

[PART 7]

82 Surely, you will find
　　the most hostile of all people towards the faithful
　　　to be the Jews and the polytheists,
　　and surely you will find
　　the nearest of them in affection for the faithful
　　　to be those who say 'We are Christians.'
　That is because there are priests and monks among them,
　　and because they are not arrogant.

83 When they hear what has been revealed to the Apostle,
　　you see their eyes fill with tears
　　because of the truth that they recognize.
　They say, 'Our Lord, we believe;
　　so write us down among the witnesses.

84 Why should we not believe in God
　　and the truth that has come to us,
　　eager as we are that our Lord should admit us
　　among the righteous people?'

85 So, for what they said, God requited them
　　with gardens with streams running in them,
　　　to remain in them,
　　and that is the reward of the virtuous.

86 But as for those who are faithless and deny Our signs
—they shall be the inmates of hell.

87 O you who have faith! Do not prohibit the good things
that God has made lawful for you,
and do not transgress.
Indeed, God does not like the transgressors.

88 Eat the lawful and good things that God has provided you,
and be wary of God in whom you have faith.

89 God will not take you to task
for what is frivolous in your oaths;
but He will take you to task for what you pledge in earnest.
The atonement for it is to feed ten needy persons
with the average food you give to your families,
or their clothing, or the freeing of a slave.
He who cannot afford any of these shall fast for three days.
That is the atonement for your oaths when you vow.
But keep your oaths.
Thus does God clarify His signs for you
so that you may give thanks.

90 O you who have faith!
Indeed, wine, gambling, idols and the divining arrows
are abominations of Satan's doing,
so avoid them, so that you may be felicitous.

91 Indeed, Satan seeks
to cast enmity and hatred among you
through wine and gambling,
and to hinder you from the remembrance of God
and from prayer.
Will you, then, relinquish?

92 Obey God and obey the Apostle, and beware;

      but if you turn your backs,
          then know that Our Apostle's duty is only
              to communicate in clear terms.

93 There will be no sin upon those who have faith
          and do righteous deeds
      in regard to what they have eaten in the past
          so long as they are Godwary and faithful
            and do righteous deeds,
      and are further Godwary and faithful,
      and are further Godwary and virtuous.
      And God loves the virtuous.

94 O you who have faith!
      God will surely test you with some of the game
          within the reach of your hands and spears,
      so that God may know those who fear Him in secret.
      So whoever transgresses after that,
          there is a painful punishment for him.

95 O you who have faith!
      Do not kill any game when you are in pilgrim sanctity.
      Should any of you kill it intentionally,
          its atonement will be
              the counterpart from cattle of what he has killed,
          as judged by two just men among you,
      brought to the Ka'bah as an offering,
      or an atonement by feeding needy persons,
          or its equivalent in fasting,
      that he may taste the untoward consequence of his conduct.
      God has excused what is already past;
      but should anyone resume, God will take vengeance on him,
          for God is all-mighty, avenger.

96 You are permitted the game of the sea and its food,
a provision for you and for the caravans,
but you are forbidden the game of the land
so long as you remain in pilgrim sanctity,
and be wary of God toward whom you will be gathered.

97 God has made the Ka'bah, the Sacred House,
a means of sustentation for mankind,
and also the sacred month, the offering and the garlands,
so that you may know
that God knows whatever there is in the heavens
and whatever there is in the earth,
and that God has knowledge of all things.

98 Know that God is severe in retribution,
and that God is all-forgiving, all-merciful.

99 The Apostle's duty is only to communicate
and God knows whatever you disclose
and whatever you conceal.

100 Say, 'The good and the bad are not equal,
though the abundance of the bad should amaze you.'
So be wary of God, O you who possess intellect,
so that you may be felicitous!

101 O you who have faith! Do not ask about things
which, if they are disclosed for you, will upset you.
Yet if you ask about them
while the Qur'ān is being sent down,
they shall be disclosed to you.
God has excused it,
and God is all-forgiving, all-forbearing.

102 Certainly some people asked about them before you
and then came to disbelieve in them.

103 God has not prescribed any such thing as *Baḥīrah*, *Sā'ibah*, *Waṣīlah*, or *Ḥām*;[1] but those who are faithless fabricate lies against God, and most of them do not exercise their reason.

104 When they are told, 'Come to what God has sent down and come to the Apostle,' they say, 'Sufficient for us is what we have found our fathers following.' What, even if their fathers did not know anything and were not guided?!

105 O you who have faith! Take care of your own souls. Those who are astray cannot harm you if you are guided. To God will be the return of you all, whereat He will inform you concerning what you have been doing.

106 O you who have faith! The witness between you, when death approaches any of you, while making a bequest, shall be two just men from among yourselves, or two from among others[2] if you are journeying in the land and the affliction of death visits you. You shall detain the two of them after the prayer, and, if you have any doubt, they shall vow by God, 'We will not sell it for any gain, even if it were a relative,

---

[1] The pre-Islamic Arabs used these terms for individual camels and sheep, which were subject to such practices as the slitting of ears, the forbidding of their use for burden, their dedication to idols, and restriction of their flesh to males. The commentators give different descriptions of these primitive customs and their significance, reflecting probably their varying practice among pre-Islamic Arabs.

[2] That is, from among non-Muslims, on non-availability of Muslim witnesses during journey.

nor will we conceal the testimony of God,
for then we would be among the sinners.'

107 But if it is found that both of them were guilty of sin,[1]
then two others shall stand up in their place
from among those nearest in kinship to the claimants
and swear by God:
'Our testimony is truer than their testimony,
and we have not transgressed,
for then we would be among the wrongdoers.'

108 That makes it likelier that they give the testimony
in its genuine form,
or fear that other oaths will be taken after their oaths.
Be wary of God and listen,
and God does not guide the transgressing lot.

109 The day God will gather the apostles
and say, 'What was the response given to you?'
They will say, 'We have no knowledge.
You know best indeed all that is Unseen.'

110 When God will say, O Jesus son of Mary,
remember My blessing upon you and upon your mother,
when I strengthened you with the Holy Spirit,
so you would speak to the people in the cradle
and in adulthood,
and when I taught you the Book and wisdom,
the Torah and the Evangel,
and when you would create from clay
the form of a bird with My leave,
and you would breathe into it
and it would become a bird with My leave,

---

[1] That is, of the sin of perjury.

    and you would heal the blind and the leper with My leave,
        and you would raise the dead with My leave;
    and when I held back the Children of Israel from you
        when you brought them manifest proofs,
        whereat the faithless among them said,
        'This is nothing but plain magic.'

111 And when I inspired the Disciples,
    saying, 'Have faith in Me and My apostle,'
    they said, 'We have faith.
    Be witness that we have submitted to God.'

112 When the Disciples said, 'O Jesus son of Mary!
    Can your Lord send down to us
        a table[1] from the sky?'
    Said he, 'Be wary of God, if you be faithful.'

113 They said, 'We desire to eat from it,
    and our hearts will be at rest:
    we shall know that you have told us the truth,
    and we will be among witnesses to it.'

114 Said Jesus son of Mary, 'O God! Our Lord!
    Send down to us a table from the heaven,
        to be a festival for us,
    for the first ones among us and the last ones
        and as a sign from You,
    and provide for us; for You are the best of providers.'

115 God said, 'I will indeed send it down to you.
    But should any of you disbelieve after this,
    I will indeed punish him with a punishment
    such as I do not punish anyone in all creation.'

116 And when God will say, 'O Jesus son of Mary!

---

[1] Table: The food and drink served at meals.

أَأَنتَ قُلتَ لِلنَّاسِ	Was it you who said to the people,
اتَّخِذُونِي وَأُمِّيَ إِلَٰهَيْنِ مِن دُونِ اللَّهِ	"Take me and my mother for gods besides God"?
قَالَ سُبْحَانَكَ	He will say, 'Immaculate are You!
مَا يَكُونُ لِي أَنْ أَقُولَ مَا لَيْسَ لِي بِحَقٍّ	It does not behoove me to say what I have no right to.
إِن كُنتُ قُلْتُهُ فَقَدْ عَلِمْتَهُ	Had I said it, You would certainly have known it:
تَعْلَمُ مَا فِي نَفْسِي	You know whatever is in my self,
وَلَا أَعْلَمُ مَا فِي نَفْسِكَ	and I do not know what is in Your Self.
إِنَّكَ أَنتَ عَلَّامُ الْغُيُوبِ ۝	Indeed, You know best all that is Unseen.
مَا قُلْتُ لَهُمْ	117 I did not say to them anything
إِلَّا مَا أَمَرْتَنِي بِهِ	except what You had commanded me to say:
أَنِ اعْبُدُوا اللَّهَ رَبِّي وَرَبَّكُمْ	"Worship God, my Lord and your Lord."
وَكُنتُ عَلَيْهِمْ شَهِيدًا	And I was a witness to them
مَا دُمْتُ فِيهِمْ	so long as I was among them.
فَلَمَّا تَوَفَّيْتَنِي	But when You had taken me away,
كُنتَ أَنتَ الرَّقِيبَ عَلَيْهِمْ	You Yourself were watchful over them,
وَأَنتَ عَلَىٰ كُلِّ شَيْءٍ شَهِيدٌ ۝	and You are witness to all things.
إِن تُعَذِّبْهُمْ فَإِنَّهُمْ عِبَادُكَ	118 If You punish them, they are indeed Your servants;
وَإِن تَغْفِرْ لَهُمْ	but if You forgive them,
فَإِنَّكَ أَنتَ الْعَزِيزُ الْحَكِيمُ ۝	You are indeed the All-mighty, the All-wise.'
قَالَ اللَّهُ هَٰذَا يَوْمُ	119 God will say, 'This day
يَنفَعُ الصَّادِقِينَ صِدْقُهُمْ	truthfulness shall benefit the truthful.
لَهُمْ جَنَّاتٌ	For them there will be gardens
تَجْرِي مِن تَحْتِهَا الْأَنْهَارُ	with streams running in them,
خَالِدِينَ فِيهَا أَبَدًا	to remain in them forever.
رَضِيَ اللَّهُ عَنْهُمْ وَرَضُوا عَنْهُ	God is pleased with them and they are pleased with Him.
ذَٰلِكَ الْفَوْزُ الْعَظِيمُ ۝	That is a great success.'
لِلَّهِ مُلْكُ السَّمَاوَاتِ	120 To God belongs the kingdom of the heavens
وَالْأَرْضِ وَمَا فِيهِنَّ	and the earth and whatever there is in them,
وَهُوَ عَلَىٰ كُلِّ شَيْءٍ قَدِيرٌ ۝	and He has power over all things.

6. The Cattle[1]
al-Anʿām

In the Name of God,
the All-beneficent, the All-merciful.

1 All praise belongs to God who created the heavens and the earth
and made darkness and light.
Yet the faithless equate others with their Lord.

2 It is He who created you from clay,
then ordained the term of your life
—the specified term is with Him—
and yet you are in doubt.

3 He is God in the heavens and on the earth:
He knows your secret and your overt matters,
and He knows what you earn.

4 There did not come to them any sign
from among the signs of their Lord,
but that they have been disregarding it.

5 They certainly denied the truth when it came to them,
but soon there will come to them the news
of what they have been deriding.

6 Have they not regarded
how many a generation We have destroyed before them
whom We had granted power in the land
in respects that We did not grant you,
and We sent abundant rains for them from the sky
and made streams run for them.
Then We destroyed them for their sins,

---

[1] This Makkī sūrah takes its name from 'the cattle' (al-anʿām) mentioned in verses 136-146 which deal with pagan superstitions and regulations related to cattle.

and brought forth another generation after them. وَأَنشَأْنَا مِن بَعْدِهِمْ قَرْنًا آخَرِينَ ۝

7 Had We sent down to you a Book on paper وَلَوْ نَزَّلْنَا عَلَيْكَ كِتَابًا فِي قِرْطَاسٍ
so they could touch it with their own hands, فَلَمَسُوهُ بِأَيْدِيهِمْ
still the faithless would have said, لَقَالَ الَّذِينَ كَفَرُوا
'This is nothing but plain magic.' إِنْ هَٰذَا إِلَّا سِحْرٌ مُبِينٌ ۝

8 They say, 'Why has not an angel been sent down to him?' وَقَالُوا لَوْلَا أُنزِلَ عَلَيْهِ مَلَكٌ
Were We to send down an angel, وَلَوْ أَنزَلْنَا مَلَكًا
the matter would surely be decided, لَقُضِيَ الْأَمْرُ
and then they would not be granted any respite. ثُمَّ لَا يُنظَرُونَ ۝

9 Had We made him an angel, وَلَوْ جَعَلْنَاهُ مَلَكًا
We would have surely made him a man, لَجَعَلْنَاهُ رَجُلًا
and We would have still confounded them وَلَلَبَسْنَا عَلَيْهِم
just as they confound the truth now. مَا يَلْبِسُونَ ۝

10 Apostles were certainly derided before you. وَلَقَدِ اسْتُهْزِئَ بِرُسُلٍ مِن قَبْلِكَ
Then those who ridiculed them were besieged فَحَاقَ بِالَّذِينَ سَخِرُوا مِنْهُم
by what they used to deride. مَا كَانُوا بِهِ يَسْتَهْزِئُونَ ۝

11 Say, 'Travel through the land, قُلْ سِيرُوا فِي الْأَرْضِ
and see how was the fate of the deniers.' ثُمَّ انظُرُوا كَيْفَ كَانَ عَاقِبَةُ الْمُكَذِّبِينَ ۝

12 Say, 'To whom belongs whatever there is in the heavens قُل لِّمَن مَّا فِي السَّمَاوَاتِ
and the earth?' وَالْأَرْضِ
Say, 'To God. He has made mercy binding for Himself. قُل لِّلَّهِ كَتَبَ عَلَىٰ نَفْسِهِ الرَّحْمَةَ
He will surely gather you on the Day of Resurrection, لَيَجْمَعَنَّكُمْ إِلَىٰ يَوْمِ الْقِيَامَةِ
in which there is no doubt. لَا رَيْبَ فِيهِ
Those who have ruined their souls will not have faith.' الَّذِينَ خَسِرُوا أَنفُسَهُمْ فَهُمْ لَا يُؤْمِنُونَ ۝

13 To Him belongs whatever abides in the night and the day, وَلَهُ مَا سَكَنَ فِي اللَّيْلِ وَالنَّهَارِ
and He is the All-hearing, the All-knowing. وَهُوَ السَّمِيعُ الْعَلِيمُ ۝

14 Say, 'Shall I take for guardian anyone other than God, قُلْ أَغَيْرَ اللَّهِ أَتَّخِذُ وَلِيًّا
the originator of the heavens and the earth, فَاطِرِ السَّمَاوَاتِ وَالْأَرْضِ
who feeds and is not fed?' وَهُوَ يُطْعِمُ وَلَا يُطْعَمُ
Say, 'I have been commanded قُلْ إِنِّي أُمِرْتُ

to be the foremost of those who submit to God,'
and [told,] "Never *be* one of the polytheists." '

15 *Say,* 'Indeed, should I disobey my Lord, I fear
the punishment of a tremendous day.'

16 Whoever is spared of it on that day,
He will have certainly been merciful to him,
and that is a manifest success.

17 Should God visit you with some distress
there is no one to remove it except Him;
and should He bring you some good,
then He has power over all things.

18 And He is the All-dominant over His servants,
and He is the All-wise, the All-aware.

19 *Say,* 'What thing is greatest as witness?'
Say, 'God! He is witness between me and you,
and this Qur'ān has been revealed to me
in order that I may warn you thereby
and whomever it may reach.'
'Do you indeed bear witness
that there are other gods besides God?'
Say, 'I do not bear witness to any such thing.'
Say, 'Indeed, He is the One God,
and I disown whatever you associate with Him.'

20 Those whom We have given the Book recognize *him*
just as they recognize their own sons.[1]
Those who have ruined their souls will not have faith.

21 Who is a greater wrongdoer than him
who fabricates lies against God or denies His signs?

---

[1] That is, the Prophet's genuineness was quite evident to the Jews and the Christians because of the prophesies concerning the Prophet's advent and his description in their scriptures.

Indeed, the wrongdoers will not be felicitous. إِنَّهُ لَا يُفْلِحُ الظَّالِمُونَ ۞

22 On the day when We gather them all together, وَيَوْمَ نَحْشُرُهُمْ جَمِيعًا
We shall say to those who ascribed partners to God, ثُمَّ نَقُولُ لِلَّذِينَ أَشْرَكُوا
'Where are your partners that you used to claim?' أَيْنَ شُرَكَاؤُكُمُ الَّذِينَ كُنتُمْ تَزْعُمُونَ ۞

23 Then their only excuse will be to say, ثُمَّ لَمْ تَكُن فِتْنَتُهُمْ إِلَّا أَن قَالُوا
'By God, our Lord, we were not polytheists.' وَاللَّهِ رَبِّنَا مَا كُنَّا مُشْرِكِينَ ۞

24 *Look*, how they forswear themselves, انظُرْ كَيْفَ كَذَبُوا عَلَىٰ أَنفُسِهِمْ
and what they used to fabricate has forsaken them! وَضَلَّ عَنْهُم مَّا كَانُوا يَفْتَرُونَ ۞

25 There are some of them who prick up their ears at *you*, وَمِنْهُم مَّن يَسْتَمِعُ إِلَيْكَ
but We have cast veils on their hearts وَجَعَلْنَا عَلَىٰ قُلُوبِهِمْ أَكِنَّةً
lest they should understand it, أَن يَفْقَهُوهُ
and a deafness into their ears; وَفِي آذَانِهِمْ وَقْرًا
and though they see every sign, they will not believe in it. وَإِن يَرَوْا كُلَّ آيَةٍ لَّا يُؤْمِنُوا بِهَا
When they come to *you*, to dispute with *you*, حَتَّىٰ إِذَا جَاءُوكَ يُجَادِلُونَكَ
the faithless say, يَقُولُ الَّذِينَ كَفَرُوا
'These are nothing but myths of the ancients.' إِنْ هَٰذَا إِلَّا أَسَاطِيرُ الْأَوَّلِينَ ۞

26 They dissuade others from following *him*, وَهُمْ يَنْهَوْنَ عَنْهُ
and themselves avoid *him*; وَيَنْأَوْنَ عَنْهُ
yet they destroy no one but themselves, وَإِن يُهْلِكُونَ إِلَّا أَنفُسَهُمْ
but they are not aware. وَمَا يَشْعُرُونَ ۞

27 Were *you* to see when they are brought to a halt by the Fire, وَلَوْ تَرَىٰ إِذْ وُقِفُوا عَلَى النَّارِ
whereupon they will say, فَقَالُوا
'Alas, were we to be sent back into the world يَا لَيْتَنَا نُرَدُّ
we would not deny the signs of our Lord, وَلَا نُكَذِّبَ بِآيَاتِ رَبِّنَا
and we would be among the faithful!' وَنَكُونَ مِنَ الْمُؤْمِنِينَ ۞

28 Indeed, now has become evident to them بَلْ بَدَا لَهُم
what they used to hide before. مَّا كَانُوا يُخْفُونَ مِن قَبْلُ
But were they to be sent back وَلَوْ رُدُّوا
they would revert to what they were forbidden, لَعَادُوا لِمَا نُهُوا عَنْهُ
and they are indeed liars. وَإِنَّهُمْ لَكَاذِبُونَ ۞

29 They say, 'There is nothing but our life of this world,
and we will not be resurrected.'
30 Were you to see
when they are brought to a halt before their Lord.
He will say, 'Is this not a fact?'
They will say, 'Yes, by our Lord!'
He will say, 'So taste the punishment
because of what you used to deny.'
31 They are certainly losers who deny the encounter with God.
When the Hour overtakes them suddenly,
they will say, 'Alas for us, for what we neglected in it!'
And they will bear their burdens on their backs.
Behold, evil is what they bear!
32 The life of the world is nothing but play and diversion,
and the abode of the Hereafter is surely better
for those who are Godwary.
Will you not exercise your reason?
33 We certainly know that what they say grieves you.
Yet it is not you that they deny,
but it is God's signs that the wrongdoers impugn.
34 Apostles were certainly denied before you,
yet they patiently bore being denied and tormented
until Our help came to them.
Nothing can change the words of God,
and there have certainly come to you
some of the accounts of the apostles.
35 And should their aversion be hard on you,
find, if you can, a tunnel into the ground,
or a ladder into the heaven, that you may bring them a sign.
Had God wished,

He would have brought them together on guidance. لَجَمَعَهُمْ عَلَى الْهُدَىٰ
So *do not be* one of the ignorant. فَلَا تَكُونَنَّ مِنَ الْجَاهِلِينَ ۝

36 Only those who listen will respond to *you*. إِنَّمَا يَسْتَجِيبُ الَّذِينَ يَسْمَعُونَ
As for the dead, God will resurrect them, وَالْمَوْتَىٰ يَبْعَثُهُمُ اللَّهُ
then they will be brought back to Him. ثُمَّ إِلَيْهِ يُرْجَعُونَ ۝

37 They say, 'Why has not وَقَالُوا لَوْلَا
a sign been sent down to him from his Lord?' نُزِّلَ عَلَيْهِ آيَةٌ مِنْ رَبِّهِ
Say, 'God is indeed able to send down a sign,' قُلْ إِنَّ اللَّهَ قَادِرٌ عَلَىٰ أَنْ يُنَزِّلَ آيَةً
but most of them do not know. وَلَٰكِنَّ أَكْثَرَهُمْ لَا يَعْلَمُونَ ۝

38 There is no animal on land وَمَا مِنْ دَابَّةٍ فِي الْأَرْضِ
nor bird that flies with its wings, وَلَا طَائِرٍ يَطِيرُ بِجَنَاحَيْهِ
but they are communities like yourselves. إِلَّا أُمَمٌ أَمْثَالُكُمْ
We have not omitted anything from the Book. مَا فَرَّطْنَا فِي الْكِتَابِ مِنْ شَيْءٍ
Then they will be gathered toward their Lord. ثُمَّ إِلَىٰ رَبِّهِمْ يُحْشَرُونَ ۝

39 Those who deny Our signs are deaf and dumb, وَالَّذِينَ كَذَّبُوا بِآيَاتِنَا صُمٌّ وَبُكْمٌ
in a manifold darkness. فِي الظُّلُمَاتِ
God leads astray whomever He wishes, مَنْ يَشَإِ اللَّهُ يُضْلِلْهُ
and whomever He wishes He puts him on a straight path. وَمَنْ يَشَأْ يَجْعَلْهُ عَلَىٰ صِرَاطٍ مُسْتَقِيمٍ ۝

40 *Say*, 'Tell me, should God's punishment overtake you, قُلْ أَرَأَيْتَكُمْ إِنْ أَتَاكُمْ عَذَابُ اللَّهِ
or should the Hour overtake you, أَوْ أَتَتْكُمُ السَّاعَةُ
will you supplicate anyone other than God, أَغَيْرَ اللَّهِ تَدْعُونَ
if you are truthful? إِنْ كُنْتُمْ صَادِقِينَ ۝

41 No, Him you will supplicate, and He will remove بَلْ إِيَّاهُ تَدْعُونَ فَيَكْشِفُ
that for which you supplicated Him, if He wishes, مَا تَدْعُونَ إِلَيْهِ إِنْ شَاءَ
and you will forget what you ascribe to Him as partners.' وَتَنْسَوْنَ مَا تُشْرِكُونَ ۝

42 We have certainly sent apostles to nations before *you*, وَلَقَدْ أَرْسَلْنَا إِلَىٰ أُمَمٍ مِنْ قَبْلِكَ
then We seized them with hardship and distress فَأَخَذْنَاهُمْ بِالْبَأْسَاءِ وَالضَّرَّاءِ
so that they might entreat Us. لَعَلَّهُمْ يَتَضَرَّعُونَ ۝

43 Then why did they not فَلَوْلَا
entreat when Our punishment overtook them! إِذْ جَاءَهُمْ بَأْسُنَا تَضَرَّعُوا

وَلَـٰكِن قَسَتْ قُلُوبُهُمْ
But their hearts had hardened,
وَزَيَّنَ لَهُمُ ٱلشَّيْطَـٰنُ
and Satan had made to seem decorous to them
مَا كَانُوا۟ يَعْمَلُونَ ۝
what they had been doing.

فَلَمَّا نَسُوا۟ مَا ذُكِّرُوا۟ بِهِ 44 So when they forgot what they had been admonished of,
فَتَحْنَا عَلَيْهِمْ أَبْوَٰبَ كُلِّ شَىْءٍ
We opened for them the gates of all good things.
حَتَّىٰٓ إِذَا فَرِحُوا۟ بِمَآ أُوتُوٓا۟
When they became proud of what they were given,
أَخَذْنَـٰهُم بَغْتَةً
We seized them suddenly,
فَإِذَا هُم مُّبْلِسُونَ ۝
whereat they became despondent.

فَقُطِعَ دَابِرُ ٱلْقَوْمِ ٱلَّذِينَ ظَلَمُوا۟ 45 Thus the wrongdoing lot were rooted out,
وَٱلْحَمْدُ لِلَّهِ رَبِّ ٱلْعَـٰلَمِينَ ۝
and all praise belongs to God, the Lord of all the worlds.

قُلْ أَرَءَيْتُمْ إِنْ أَخَذَ ٱللَّهُ سَمْعَكُمْ 46 Say, 'Tell me, should God take away your hearing
وَأَبْصَـٰرَكُمْ
and your sight
وَخَتَمَ عَلَىٰ قُلُوبِكُم
and set a seal on your hearts,
مَّنْ إِلَـٰهٌ غَيْرُ ٱللَّهِ يَأْتِيكُم بِهِ
which god other than God can restore it for you?'
ٱنظُرْ كَيْفَ نُصَرِّفُ ٱلْـَٔايَـٰتِ
Look, how We paraphrase the signs variously;
ثُمَّ هُمْ يَصْدِفُونَ ۝
nevertheless they turn away.

قُلْ أَرَءَيْتَكُمْ إِنْ أَتَىٰكُمْ عَذَابُ ٱللَّهِ 47 Say, 'Tell me, should God's punishment overtake you
بَغْتَةً أَوْ جَهْرَةً
suddenly or visibly,
هَلْ يُهْلَكُ إِلَّا ٱلْقَوْمُ ٱلظَّـٰلِمُونَ ۝
will anyone be destroyed except the wrongdoing lot?'

وَمَا نُرْسِلُ ٱلْمُرْسَلِينَ 48 We do not send the apostles
إِلَّا مُبَشِّرِينَ وَمُنذِرِينَ
except as bearers of good news and warners.
فَمَنْ ءَامَنَ وَأَصْلَحَ
As for those who are faithful and righteous,
فَلَا خَوْفٌ عَلَيْهِمْ وَلَا هُمْ يَحْزَنُونَ ۝
they will have no fear, nor will they grieve.

وَٱلَّذِينَ كَذَّبُوا۟ بِـَٔايَـٰتِنَا 49 But as for those who deny Our signs,
يَمَسُّهُمُ ٱلْعَذَابُ
the punishment shall befall them
بِمَا كَانُوا۟ يَفْسُقُونَ ۝
because of the transgressions they used to commit.

قُل لَّآ أَقُولُ لَكُمْ 50 Say, 'I do not say to you
عِندِى خَزَآئِنُ ٱللَّهِ
that I possess the treasuries of God,
وَلَآ أَعْلَمُ ٱلْغَيْبَ
nor do I know the Unseen,
وَلَآ أَقُولُ لَكُمْ إِنِّى مَلَكٌ
nor do I say to you that I am an angel.

I follow only what is revealed to me.'
Say, 'Are the blind one and the seer equal?
So will you not reflect?'

51 And *warn* by its[1] means those who fear
    being gathered toward their Lord,
besides whom they will have neither friend nor intercessor,
    so that they may be Godwary.

52 *Do not drive away* those who supplicate their Lord
    morning and evening, desiring His face.[2]
Neither are you accountable for them in any way,
    nor are they accountable for you in any way,
so that you should drive them away
    and thus become one of the wrongdoers.

53 Thus do We test them by means of one another
    so that they should say,
'Are these the ones whom God has favoured
    from among us?!'
Does not God know best the grateful?!

54 When those who have faith in Our signs come to *you*,
    say, 'Peace to you!
Your Lord has made mercy incumbent upon Himself:
whoever of you commits an evil deed out of ignorance
    and then repents after that and reforms,
then He is indeed all-forgiving, all-merciful.'

55 Thus do We elaborate[3] the signs,
    so that the way of the guilty may be brought to light.

56 *Say*, 'I have been forbidden to worship

---

[1] That is, the Qur'ān, referred to in the preceding verse: 'I follow only what is revealed to me.'
[2] Or 'desiring only Him.' The phrase *yurīdūna wajha* has been interpreted variously as meaning 'seeking His nearness,' 'seeking His presence,' 'desiring His reward,' 'seeking His pleasure,' and 'pursuing His path.' Cf. **18:28**.
[3] Or 'articulate.' Cf. **6:**97, 98, 126, 154; **7:**32, 52, 145, 174; **9:11**; **10:**5, 24, 37; **11:1**; **13:2**; **30:28**; **41:**3, 44.

those whom you invoke besides God.'
Say, 'I do not follow your base desires, for then I will go astray,
and I will not be among the rightly guided.'

57 Say, 'I indeed stand on a manifest proof from my Lord
and you have denied it.
What you seek to hasten is not up to me.
Judgement belongs only to God;
He expounds the truth[1] and He is the best of judges.'

58 Say, 'If what you seek to hasten were with me,
the matter would have been decided between you and me,
and God knows best the wrongdoers.'

59 With Him are the treasures of the Unseen;[2]
no one knows them except Him.
He knows whatever there is in land and sea.
No leaf falls without His knowing it,
nor is there a grain in the darkness of the earth,
nor anything fresh or withered
but it is in a manifest Book.

60 It is He who takes your souls by night,
and He knows what you do by day,
then He reanimates you therein
so that a specified term may be completed.
Then to Him will be your return,
whereat He will inform you concerning what you used to do.

61 He is the All-dominant over His servants,
and He sends guards to protect you.
When death approaches anyone of you,
Our messengers take him away,
and they do not neglect their duty.

---

[1] Or 'He judges by the truth,' after a variant reading (*yaqḍī* instead of *yaquṣṣu*).
[2] Or 'the keys of the Unseen.'

62 Then they are returned to God, their real Master.
Behold, all judgement belongs to Him
and He is the swiftest of reckoners.
63 Say, 'Who delivers you from the darkness
of land and sea,
when you invoke Him suppliantly and secretly:
"If He delivers us from this,
we will surely be among the grateful"?'
64 Say, 'It is God who delivers you from them
and from every distress,
but then you ascribe partners to Him.'
65 Say, 'He is able to send you
a punishment from above you
or from under your feet,
or confound you as [hostile] factions,
and make you taste one another's violence.'
Look, how We paraphrase the signs variously
so that they may understand!
66 Your people have denied it, though it is the truth.
Say, 'It is not my business to watch over you.'
67 For every prophecy there is a preordained setting,
and soon you will know.
68 When you see those who gossip impiously about Our signs,
avoid them until they engage
in some other discourse;
but if Satan makes you forget, do not sit,
after remembering, with the wrongdoing lot.
69 Those who are Godwary
are in no way accountable for them,[1]

---

[1] That is, for those who deride God's signs.

      but this is merely for admonition's sake,
        so that they may beware.[1]

70 *Leave alone* those who take their religion
     for play and diversion
     and whom the life of this world has deceived,
     and admonish with it,
lest any soul should perish because of what it has earned:
It shall not have any friend besides God
     nor any intercessor;
and though it should offer every kind of ransom,
     it will not be accepted from it.
They are the ones who perish
     because of what they have earned;
they shall have boiling water for drink
and a painful punishment for what they used to deny.

71 *Say,* 'Shall we invoke besides God
     that which can neither benefit us nor harm us,
and turn back on our heels after God has guided us,
     like someone seduced by the devils
     and bewildered in the land,
who has companions that invite him to guidance,
     [saying,] "Come to us!"?'
Say, 'It is God's guidance which is true guidance.
     and we have been commanded to submit
     to the Lord of all the worlds,

72 and told, "Maintain the prayer and be wary of Him;
     it is He toward whom you will be gathered."'

73 It is He who created the heavens and the earth
     with consummate wisdom,

---

[1] That is, of the company of those who deride God's signs.

and the day He says to something, 'Be!' it is.
His word is the truth, and to Him belongs all sovereignty
   on the day when the Trumpet will be blown.
Knower of the sensible and the Unseen,
He is the All-wise, the All-aware.

74 When Abraham said to Azar, his father,
   'Do you take idols for gods?
   Indeed, I see you and your people to be in clear error.'
75 Thus did We show Abraham
      the dominions of the heavens and the earth,
      that he might be of those who possess certitude.
76 When night darkened over him, he saw a star
   and said, 'This is my Lord!'
   But when it set, he said, 'I do not like those who set.'
77 Then, when he saw the moon rising,
   he said, 'This is my Lord!'
   But when it set, he said, 'Had my Lord not guided me,
      I would surely have been among the astray lot.'
78 Then, when he saw the sun rising,
   he said, 'This is my Lord! This is bigger!'
   But when it set, he said, 'O my people,
   I indeed disown what you take as His partners.'
79 Indeed, I have turned my face
   toward Him who originated the heavens and the earth,
      as a *ḥanīf*,
   and I am not one of the polytheists.'
80 His people argued with him.
   He said, 'Do you argue with me concerning God,
      while He has guided me for certain?

I do not fear what you ascribe to Him as His partners,
excepting anything that my Lord may wish.
My Lord embraces all things in His knowledge.
Will you not then take admonition?

81 How could I fear what you ascribe to Him as partners,
when you do not fear ascribing partners to God
for which He has not sent down any authority to you?
So tell me, which of the two sides
has a greater right to safety, if you know?

82 Those who have faith
and do not taint their faith with wrongdoing
—it is they for whom there will be safety,
and they are the rightly guided.'

83 This was Our argument
that We gave to Abraham against his people.
We raise in rank whomever We wish.
Your Lord is indeed all-wise, all-knowing.

84 And We gave him Isaac and Jacob
and guided each of them.
And Noah We had guided before,
and from his offspring, David and Solomon,
Job, Joseph, Moses and Aaron
—thus do We reward the virtuous—

85 and Zechariah, John, Jesus and Ilyās
—each of them among the righteous—

86 and Ishmael, Elisha, Jonah and Lot
—each We preferred over all the nations—

87 and from among their fathers, descendants and brethren
—We chose them
and guided them to a straight path.

88 That is God's guidance:
  with it He guides whomever He wishes of His servants.
  But were they to ascribe any partners to God,
  what they used to do would not avail them.
89 They are the ones whom We gave the Book,
       judgement and prophethood.
   So if these disbelieve in them,
       We have certainly entrusted them to a people
       who will never disbelieve in them.
90 They are the ones whom God has guided.
       So *follow* their guidance.
   Say, 'I do not ask you any recompense for it.
       It is just an admonition for all the nations.'
91 They did not regard God with the regard due to Him
   when they said,
       'God has not sent down anything to any human.'
   Say, 'Who had sent down the Book
       that was brought by Moses
       as a light and guidance for the people,
       which you make into parchments that you display,
          while you conceal much of it,
       and [by means of which] you were taught
       what you did not know, neither you nor your fathers?'
   Say, 'God!'
       Then leave them to play around in their impious gossip.
92 Blessed is this Book that We have sent down,
       confirming what was revealed before it,
       so that you may warn the Mother of Cities
       and those around it.[1]

---

[1] That is, the people of Makkah, known at the time as 'the Mother of the Cities.'

Those who believe in the Hereafter believe in it,
    and they are watchful of their prayers.

93 Who is a greater wrongdoer than him
    who lies against God, or says, 'It has been revealed to me,'
        while nothing was revealed to him,
and says, 'I will bring the like of what God has sent down?'
Were you to see when the wrongdoers
    are in the throes of death,
and the angels extend their hands [saying]:
    'Give up your souls!
Today you will be requited with a humiliating punishment
    because of what you used to attribute to God untruly,
    and for your being disdainful towards His signs.'

94 'Certainly you have come to Us alone,
    just as We created you the first time,
and left behind whatever We had bestowed on you.
We do not see your intercessors with you
    —those whom you claimed
        to be Our partners in deciding your fate.
Certainly all links between you have been cut,
and what you used to claim has forsaken you!'

95 God is indeed the splitter of the grain and the pit.[1]
    He brings forth the living from the dead
        and He brings forth the dead from the living.
That is God! Then where do you stray?

96 Splitter of the dawn, He has made the night for rest,
    and the sun and the moon for calculation.[2]
That is the ordaining of the All-mighty, the All-knowing.

---

[1] That is, the single, central kernel or stone of certain fruits, such as a date, peach or cherry.
[2] That is, of time: days, months and years.

97 It is He who made the stars for you,
so that you may be guided by them in the darkness
of land and sea.
We have certainly elaborated the signs
for a people who have knowledge.

98 It is He who created you from a single soul,
then there is the enduring abode
and the place of temporary lodging.[1]
We have certainly elaborated the signs
for a people who understand.

99 It is He who sends down water from the sky,
and brings forth with it every kind of growing thing.
Then, from it We bring forth vegetation
from which We produce the grain in clusters
and from the palm-tree, from its blossoms,
low-hanging clusters [of dates],
and gardens of grapes, olives and pomegranates,
similar and dissimilar.
Look at its fruit as it fructifies and ripens.
There are indeed signs in that for a people who have faith.

100 They make the jinn partners of God,
though He has created them,
and carve out sons and daughters for Him,
without any knowledge.
Immaculate is He
and far above what they allege concerning Him!

---

[1] The terms *mustaqarr* and *mustawda'* (alternatively read as *mustaqirr* and *mustawdi'*) have been interpreted variously. According to one interpretation, they refer to the mother's womb (*raḥm*) and the father's loins (*ṣulb*) respectively. 'Ayyāshī cites several traditions under this verse from the Imams Muḥammad al-Bāqir, Ja'far al-Ṣādiq, Mūsā al-Kāẓim and 'Alī al-Hādī, which interpret *mustaqarr* (or *mustaqirr*) as the heart of someone whose faith is constant and permanent, and *mustawda'* as that of one whose faith is temporary, passing away at or before death. (Cf. *al-Tafsīr al-Burhān* and *al-Tafsīr al-Ṣāfī*)

101 The originator of the heavens and the earth
—how could He have a child
when He has had no spouse?
He created all things
and has knowledge of all things.

102 That is God, your Lord,
there is no god except Him, the creator of all things;
so worship Him.
He watches over all things.

103 The eyesights do not perceive Him,
yet He apprehends the eyesights,
and He is the All-attentive,[1] the All-aware.

104 [Say,] 'Insights have already come to you from your Lord.
So whoever sees, it is to the benefit of his own soul,
and whoever remains blind, it is to its detriment,
and I am not a keeper over you.'

105 Thus do We paraphrase the signs variously,
lest they should say, 'You have received instruction,'
and so that We may make it clear for
people who have knowledge.

106 *Follow that which has been revealed to you from your Lord,*
there is no god except Him,
and *turn away* from the polytheists.

107 Had God wished
they would not have ascribed partners to Him.
We have not made you a caretaker for them,
nor is it your duty to watch over them.

108 Do not abuse those whom they invoke besides God,

---

[1] Or 'All-gracious.' Cf. **22**:63; **31**:16; **33**:34; **67**:14.

lest they should abuse God out of hostility,[1] فَيَسُبُّوا اللَّهَ عَدْوًا

without any knowledge. بِغَيْرِ عِلْمٍ

That is how كَذَٰلِكَ

to every people We have made their conduct seem decorous. زَيَّنَّا لِكُلِّ أُمَّةٍ عَمَلَهُمْ

Then their return will be to their Lord ثُمَّ إِلَىٰ رَبِّهِم مَّرْجِعُهُمْ

and He will inform them concerning what they used to do. فَيُنَبِّئُهُم بِمَا كَانُوا يَعْمَلُونَ

109 They swear by God with solemn oaths وَأَقْسَمُوا بِاللَّهِ جَهْدَ أَيْمَانِهِمْ

that were a sign to come to them they would believe in it. لَئِن جَاءَتْهُمْ آيَةٌ لَّيُؤْمِنُنَّ بِهَا

Say, 'The signs are only with God,' قُلْ إِنَّمَا الْآيَاتُ عِندَ اللَّهِ

and what will bring home to you[2] وَمَا يُشْعِرُكُمْ

that they will not believe even if they came? أَنَّهَا إِذَا جَاءَتْ لَا يُؤْمِنُونَ

110 We transform their hearts and their visions وَنُقَلِّبُ أَفْئِدَتَهُمْ وَأَبْصَارَهُمْ

as they did not believe in it the first time, كَمَا لَمْ يُؤْمِنُوا بِهِ أَوَّلَ مَرَّةٍ

and We leave them bewildered in their rebellion. وَنَذَرُهُمْ فِي طُغْيَانِهِمْ يَعْمَهُونَ

[PART 8]

111 Even if We had sent down angels to them, وَلَوْ أَنَّنَا نَزَّلْنَا إِلَيْهِمُ الْمَلَائِكَةَ

and the dead had spoken to them, وَكَلَّمَهُمُ الْمَوْتَىٰ

and We had gathered all things before them manifestly,[3] وَحَشَرْنَا عَلَيْهِمْ كُلَّ شَيْءٍ قُبُلًا

they would still not believe unless God wished, مَّا كَانُوا لِيُؤْمِنُوا إِلَّا أَن يَشَاءَ اللَّهُ

but most of them are ignorant. وَلَٰكِنَّ أَكْثَرَهُمْ يَجْهَلُونَ

112 That is how for every prophet We have assigned وَكَذَٰلِكَ جَعَلْنَا لِكُلِّ نَبِيٍّ

as enemies the devils from among humans and jinn, عَدُوًّا شَيَاطِينَ الْإِنسِ وَالْجِنِّ

who inspire each other يُوحِي بَعْضُهُمْ إِلَىٰ بَعْضٍ

with seductive statements to deceive the people. زُخْرُفَ الْقَوْلِ غُرُورًا

Had *your* Lord wished, they would not have done it. وَلَوْ شَاءَ رَبُّكَ مَا فَعَلُوهُ

So *leave* them with what they fabricate, فَذَرْهُمْ وَمَا يَفْتَرُونَ

113 so that toward it may incline the hearts وَلِتَصْغَىٰ إِلَيْهِ أَفْئِدَةُ

of those who do not believe in the Hereafter, الَّذِينَ لَا يُؤْمِنُونَ بِالْآخِرَةِ

and so that they may be pleased with it وَلِيَرْضَوْهُ

---

[1] Or 'out of transgression,' or 'wrongfully.'
[2] That is, to the faithful.
[3] Or, 'in their diversity.'

and commit what they commit.

114 [*Say*,] 'Shall I seek a judge other than God,
   while it is He who has sent down to you the Book
   whose contents have been well-elaborated?'
   Those We have given the Book
   know that it has been sent down from *your* Lord
      with the truth;
      so do not be one of the skeptics.

115 The word of *your* Lord has been fulfilled
      in truth and justice.
   Nothing can change His words,
      and He is the All-hearing, the All-knowing.

116 If you obey most of those on the earth,
   they will lead you astray from the way of God.
   They follow nothing but conjectures
   and they do nothing but make surmises.

117 Your Lord knows best those who stray from His way,
      and He knows best those who are guided.

118 Eat from that
      over which God's Name has been mentioned,
   if you are believers in His signs.

119 Why should you not eat
      that over which God's Name has been mentioned,
      while He has already elaborated for you
      whatever He has forbidden you,
   excepting what you may be compelled to eat?
   Indeed, many mislead others by their base desires,
      without possessing any knowledge.
   Indeed, *your* Lord knows best the transgressors.

120 Renounce outward sins and the inward ones.

Indeed, those who commit sins
shall be requited for what they used to commit.
121 Do not eat anything of that
over which God's Name has not been mentioned,
and that is indeed transgression.
Indeed, the satans inspire their friends
to dispute with you,
and if you obey them, you will indeed be polytheists.
122 Is he who was lifeless, then We gave him life
and provided him with a light
by which he walks among the people,
like one who dwells in a manifold darkness
which he cannot leave?
To the faithless is thus presented as decorous
what they have been doing.
123 Thus have We installed in every town
its major criminals, so that they may plot therein.
Yet they do not plot except against themselves,
but they are not aware.
124 When a sign comes to them, they say,
'We will not believe until we are given
the like of what was given to God's apostles.'
God knows best where to place His apostleship!
Soon the guilty will be visited by
a degradation from God and a severe punishment
because of the plots they used to devise.
125 Whomever God desires to guide,
He opens his breast to Islam,
and whomever He desires to lead astray,
He makes his breast narrow and straitened

as if he were climbing to a height.[1]
Thus does God lay [spiritual] defilement
on those who do not have faith.

126 This is the straight path of your Lord.
We have already elaborated the signs
for a people who take admonition.

127 For them shall be the abode of peace near their Lord
and He will be their friend because of what they used to do.

128 On the day that He will gather them all together,
[He will say], 'O community of the jinn!
You made many followers among humans.'
Their friends from among the humans will say,
'Our Lord, we took advantage of each other,
and we completed our term You had appointed for us.'
He will say, 'The Fire is your abode,
to remain in it, except what God may wish.'
Your Lord is indeed all-wise, all-knowing.

129 That is how We make wrongdoers one another's friends
because of what they used to perpetrate.

130 'O community of the jinn and humans!
Did there not come to you apostles from yourselves,
recounting to you My signs
and warning you of the encounter of this Day?'
They will say, 'We do bear witness against ourselves.'
The life of this world had deceived them,
and they will testify against themselves
that they had been faithless.

131 This is because your Lord would never
destroy the towns unjustly

---

[1] That is, makes his spiritual and intellectual capacities shrink.

while their people were unaware.

132 For everyone there are ranks
in accordance with what they have done,
and your Lord is not oblivious of what they do.

133 Your Lord is the All-sufficient dispenser of mercy.
If He wishes, He will take you away
and make whomever He wishes succeed you,
just as He produced you
from the descendants of another people.

134 Indeed, what you are promised will surely come
and you will not be able to thwart it.

135 Say, 'O my people, act according to your ability;
I too am acting.
Soon you will know
in whose favour will be the outcome of that abode.
Indeed, the wrongdoers will not prosper.'

136 They dedicate to God
a portion of the crops and cattle He has created
and say, 'This is for God,' so do they maintain,
'and this is for our partners.'
But what is for their partners does not reach God,
and what belongs to God reaches their partners.
Evil is the judgement that they make.

137 That is how
to many of the polytheists is presented as decorous
the slaying of their children
by those whom they ascribe as partners to God
that they may ruin them
and confound their religion for them.
Had God wished, they would not have done it.

So *leave* them with what they fabricate.

138 They say, 'These cattle and tillage are a taboo:
none may eat them except whom we wish,' they maintain,
and there are cattle whose backs are forbidden
and cattle over which they do not mention God's Name,
  fabricating a lie against Him.
Soon He will requite them for what they used to fabricate.

139 And they say, 'That which is in the bellies of these cattle
  is exclusively for our males and forbidden to our wives.
But if it be still-born, they will all share it.'
Soon He will requite them for their allegations.
He is indeed all-wise, all-knowing.

140 They are certainly losers
  who slay their children foolishly without knowledge,
  and forbid what God has provided them,
    fabricating lies against God.
They have certainly gone astray and are not guided.

141 It is He who produces gardens
    trellised and without trellises,
    and palm-trees and crops of diverse produce,
    olives and pomegranates, similar and dissimilar.
Eat of its fruits when it fructifies,
and give its due on the harvest day, and be not wasteful;
  indeed He does not like the wasteful.

142 Of the cattle some are for burden and some for slaughter.
Eat of what God has provided you
  and do not follow in Satan's footsteps;
  he is indeed your manifest enemy.

143 Eight pairs:[1] two of sheep

---

[1] Cf. **39**:6.

and two of goats.

Say, 'Is it the two males that He has forbidden
   or the two females,
   or what is contained in the wombs of the two females?
   Inform me with knowledge, should you be truthful.'

144 And two of camels and two of oxen.
Say, 'Has He forbidden the two males or the females,
   or what is contained in the wombs of the two females?
Were you witnesses when God enjoined this upon you?'
So who is a greater wrongdoer
   than him who fabricates lies against God
   to mislead the people without any knowledge?
Indeed, God does not guide the wrongdoing lot.

145 Say, 'I do not find in what has been revealed to me
   that anyone should be forbidden to eat anything
   except carrion or spilt blood,
   or the flesh of swine—for that is indeed unclean—
   or an impiety offered to other than God.'
But should someone be compelled,
   without being rebellious or aggressive,
   indeed your Lord is all-forgiving, all-merciful.

146 To the Jews We forbade
   every animal having an undivided hoof,
   and of oxen and sheep We forbade them their fat,
   except what is borne by their backs, or the entrails
   or what is attached to the bones.
We requited them with that for their rebelliousness,
   and We indeed speak the truth.

147 But if they impugn you, say,
   'Your Lord is dispenser of an all-embracing mercy,

                    but His punishment will not be averted

                        from the guilty lot.'

148 The polytheists will say, 'Had God wished

      we would not have ascribed any partner to Him,

                      nor our fathers,

        nor we would have forbidden anything.'

    Those who were before them had impugned[1] likewise

            until they tasted Our punishment.

Say, 'Do you have any revealed knowledge

           that you can produce for us?

         You follow nothing but conjectures,

     and you do nothing but make surmises.'

149 Say, 'To God belongs the conclusive argument.

  Had He wished, He would have surely guided you all.'

150 Say, 'Bring your witnesses

    who may testify that God has forbidden this.'

    So if they testify, do not testify with them,

  and do not follow the base desires of those

           who deny Our signs,

  and those who do not believe in the Hereafter

    and equate others with their Lord.

151 Say, 'Come, I will recount

  what your Lord has forbidden you.

That you shall not ascribe any partners to Him,

  and you shall be good to the parents,

you shall not kill your children due to penury

  —We will provide for you and for them—

  you shall not approach indecencies,

  the outward among them and the inward ones,

---

[1] Or 'those who were before them had lied likewise,' in accordance with an alternate reading. (see al-Zamakhsharī, al-Rāzī, and al-Ṭabrisī)

and you shall not kill a soul whose life
God has made inviolable, except with due cause.
This is what He has enjoined upon you
so that you may exercise your reason.

152 Do not approach the orphan's property,
except in the best manner, until he comes of age.
Observe fully the measure and the balance[1] with justice.'
We task no soul except according to its capacity.
'And when you speak, be just, even if it were a relative;
and fulfill God's covenants.
This is what He enjoins upon you
so that you may take admonition.'

153 'This indeed is my straight path, so follow it,
and do not follow other ways,
for they will separate you from His way.
This is what He enjoins upon you
so that you may be Godwary.'

154 Then We gave Moses the Book,
completing Our blessing on him who is virtuous,
and as an elaboration[2] of all things,
and as guidance and mercy,
so that they may believe in the encounter with their Lord.

155 And this Book We have sent down is a blessed one;
so follow it and be Godwary,
so that you may receive His mercy.

156 Lest you should say, 'The Book was sent down only
to two communities before us,[3]

---

[1] That is, weights and measures.
[2] Or 'articulation.'
[3] That is, Jews and Christians.

and we were indeed unaware of their studies,'
157 or say, 'If the Book had been sent down to us,
we would have surely been better-guided than them.'
There has already come to you a manifest proof
from your Lord, and guidance and mercy.
So who is a greater wrongdoer
than him who denies the signs of God
and turns away from them?
Soon We shall requite those who turn away from Our signs
with a terrible punishment
because of what they used to evade.

158 Do they await anything but
that the angels should come to them,
or *your* Lord should come,
or some of *your* Lord's signs should come?
The day when some of *your* Lord's signs do come,
faith will not benefit any soul
that had not believed beforehand
and had not earned some goodness in its faith.
Say, 'Wait! We too are waiting!'

159 Indeed, those who split up their religion and became sects,
you will not have anything to do with them.
Their matter rests only with God;
then He will inform them concerning what they used to do.

160 Whoever brings virtue
will receive a reward ten times its like;
but whoever brings vice
will not be requited except with its like,
and they will not be wronged.[1]

---

[1] Cf. **27**:89; **28**:84.

161 Say, 'My Lord has indeed guided me to a straight path,
the upright religion, the creed of Abraham, a *ḥanīf*,
and he was not one of the polytheists.'

162 Say, 'Indeed, my prayer and my worship,
my life and my death,
are for the sake of God, the Lord of all the worlds.

163 He has no partner,
and I have been commanded to follow this creed,
and I am the first of those who submit to God.'

164 Say, 'Shall I seek a Lord other than God,
while He is the Lord of all things?'
No soul does evil except against itself,
and no bearer shall bear another's burden;
then your return will be to your Lord,
whereat He will inform you
concerning that about which you used to differ.

165 It is He who has made you successors on the earth,
and raised some of you in rank above others
so that He may test you with respect to what He has given you.
Your Lord is indeed swift in retribution,
and He is indeed all-forgiving, all-merciful.

7. The Elevations[1]

al-A'rāf

In the Name of God,
the All-beneficent, the All-merciful.

1 *Alif, Lām, Mīm, Ṣād.*

2 This is a Book that has been sent down to *you*
—so let there be no disquiet in *your* heart on its account

---

[1] This Makkī *sūrah* is named after 'the Elevations' (*al-A'rāf*) mentioned in verses 46-8.

لِتُنذِرَ بِهِ   that you may warn thereby—
وَذِكْرَىٰ لِلْمُؤْمِنِينَ ۝   and as admonition for the faithful.

3 Follow what has been sent down to you from your Lord,
   and do not follow any masters besides Him.
   Little is the admonition that you take!

4 How many a town We have destroyed!
   Our punishment came to it at night,
   or while they were taking a midday nap.

5 Their cry, when Our punishment overtook them,
   was only that they said,
      'We have indeed been wrongdoers!'

6 We will surely question those
   to whom the apostles were sent,
   and We will surely question the apostles.

7 Then We will surely recount to them with knowledge,
   for We had not been absent.

8 The weighing of deeds on that Day is a truth.
   As for those whose deeds weigh heavy in the scales
   —it is they who are the felicitous.

9 As for those whose deeds weigh light in the scales,
   —it is they who have ruined their souls,
   because they used to wrong Our signs.

10 Certainly We have established you on the earth,
   and made in it various means of livelihood for you.
   Little do you thank.

11 Certainly We created you, then We formed you,
   then We said to the angels, 'Prostrate before Adam.'
   So they all prostrated, but not Iblis:
   he was not among those who prostrated.

12 Said He, 'What prevented you from prostrating,

when I commanded you?'	إِذْ أَمَرْتُكَ
'I am better than him,' he said.	قَالَ أَنَا خَيْرٌ مِنْهُ
'You created me from fire and You created him from clay.'	خَلَقْتَنِي مِن نَّارٍ وَخَلَقْتَهُ مِن طِينٍ ۝
13 'Get down from it!' He said.	قَالَ فَاهْبِطْ مِنْهَا
'It is not for you to be arrogant therein.	فَمَا يَكُونُ لَكَ أَن تَتَكَبَّرَ فِيهَا
Begone! You are indeed among the degraded ones.'	فَاخْرُجْ إِنَّكَ مِنَ الصَّاغِرِينَ ۝
14 He said, 'Respite me till the day they will be resurrected.'	قَالَ أَنظِرْنِي إِلَىٰ يَوْمِ يُبْعَثُونَ ۝
15 Said He, 'You are indeed among the reprieved.'	قَالَ إِنَّكَ مِنَ الْمُنظَرِينَ ۝
16 'As You have consigned me to perversity,' he said,	قَالَ فَبِمَا أَغْوَيْتَنِي
'I will surely lie in wait for them on Your straight path.	لَأَقْعُدَنَّ لَهُمْ صِرَاطَكَ الْمُسْتَقِيمَ ۝
17 Then I will come at them from their front and rear,	ثُمَّ لَآتِيَنَّهُم مِّن بَيْنِ أَيْدِيهِمْ وَمِنْ خَلْفِهِمْ
and from their right and left,	وَعَنْ أَيْمَانِهِمْ وَعَن شَمَائِلِهِمْ
and You will not find most of them to be grateful.'	وَلَا تَجِدُ أَكْثَرَهُمْ شَاكِرِينَ ۝
18 Said He, 'Begone hence, blameful and banished!	قَالَ اخْرُجْ مِنْهَا مَذْءُومًا مَّدْحُورًا
Whoever of them follows you,	لَّمَن تَبِعَكَ مِنْهُمْ
I will surely fill hell with you all.'	لَأَمْلَأَنَّ جَهَنَّمَ مِنكُمْ أَجْمَعِينَ ۝
19 [Then He said to Adam,] 'O Adam,	وَيَا آدَمُ
dwell with your mate in paradise,	اسْكُنْ أَنتَ وَزَوْجُكَ الْجَنَّةَ
and eat thereof whence you wish;	فَكُلَا مِنْ حَيْثُ شِئْتُمَا
but do not approach this tree,	وَلَا تَقْرَبَا هَٰذِهِ الشَّجَرَةَ
lest you should be among the wrongdoers.'	فَتَكُونَا مِنَ الظَّالِمِينَ ۝
20 Then Satan tempted them, to expose to them	فَوَسْوَسَ لَهُمَا الشَّيْطَانُ لِيُبْدِيَ لَهُمَا
what was hidden from them of their nakedness,	مَا وُورِيَ عَنْهُمَا مِن سَوْآتِهِمَا
and he said, 'Your Lord has only forbidden you	وَقَالَ مَا نَهَاكُمَا رَبُّكُمَا
from this tree	عَنْ هَٰذِهِ الشَّجَرَةِ
lest you should become angels,	إِلَّا أَن تَكُونَا مَلَكَيْنِ
or lest you become immortals.'	أَوْ تَكُونَا مِنَ الْخَالِدِينَ ۝
21 And he swore to them, 'I am indeed your well-wisher.'	وَقَاسَمَهُمَا إِنِّي لَكُمَا لَمِنَ النَّاصِحِينَ ۝
22 Thus he brought about their fall by deception.	فَدَلَّاهُمَا بِغُرُورٍ
So when they tasted of the tree,	فَلَمَّا ذَاقَا الشَّجَرَةَ

their nakedness became apparent to them,
and they began to stitch over themselves
　　with the leaves of paradise.
Their Lord called out to them,
　'Did I not forbid you from that tree,
　and tell you, "Satan is indeed your manifest enemy?" '

23 They said, 'Our Lord, we have wronged ourselves!
　If You do not forgive us and have mercy upon us,
　we will surely be among the losers.'

24 He said, 'Get down, being enemies of one another!
　On the earth shall be your abode
　　and sustenance for a time.'

25 He said, 'In it you will live, and in it you will die,
　and from it you will be raised from the dead.'

26 'O Children of Adam!
　We have certainly sent down to you garments
　to cover your nakedness, and for adornment.
　Yet the garment of Godwariness—that is the best.'
　That is one of God's signs,
　so that they may take admonition.

27 'O Children of Adam! Do not let Satan tempt you,
　like he expelled your parents from paradise,
　stripping them of their garments
　to show them their nakedness.
　Indeed, he sees you—he and his hosts—
　whence you do not see them.
　We have indeed made the devils friends
　of those who have no faith.'

28 When they commit an indecency, they say,
　'We found our fathers practising it

وَاللَّهُ أَمَرَنَا بِهَا ۗ and God has enjoined it upon us.'
قُلْ إِنَّ اللَّهَ لَا يَأْمُرُ بِالْفَحْشَاءِ ۖ Say, 'Indeed, God does not enjoin indecencies.
أَتَقُولُونَ عَلَى اللَّهِ مَا لَا تَعْلَمُونَ ۝ Do you attribute to God what you do not know?'

قُلْ أَمَرَ رَبِّي بِالْقِسْطِ ۖ 29 Say, 'My Lord has enjoined justice,'
وَأَقِيمُوا وُجُوهَكُمْ and [He has enjoined,] 'Set your heart on Him
عِنْدَ كُلِّ مَسْجِدٍ at every occasion of prayer,
وَادْعُوهُ مُخْلِصِينَ لَهُ الدِّينَ ۚ and invoke Him, putting your exclusive faith in Him.
كَمَا بَدَأَكُمْ Even as He brought you forth in the beginning,
تَعُودُونَ ۝ so will you return.'

فَرِيقًا هَدَىٰ 30 He has guided a part [of mankind]
وَفَرِيقًا حَقَّ عَلَيْهِمُ الضَّلَالَةُ ۗ and a part has deserved to be consigned to error,
إِنَّهُمُ اتَّخَذُوا الشَّيَاطِينَ أَوْلِيَاءَ مِنْ دُونِ اللَّهِ for they took the devils for masters instead of God,
وَيَحْسَبُونَ أَنَّهُمْ مُهْتَدُونَ ۝ and supposed that they were guided.

يَا بَنِي آدَمَ 31 O Children of Adam!
خُذُوا زِينَتَكُمْ عِنْدَ كُلِّ مَسْجِدٍ Put on your adornment on every occasion of prayer,
وَكُلُوا وَاشْرَبُوا وَلَا تُسْرِفُوا ۚ and eat and drink, but do not waste;
إِنَّهُ لَا يُحِبُّ الْمُسْرِفِينَ ۝ indeed He does not like the wasteful.

قُلْ مَنْ حَرَّمَ زِينَةَ اللَّهِ 32 Say, 'Who has forbidden the adornment of God
الَّتِي أَخْرَجَ لِعِبَادِهِ which He has brought forth for His servants,
وَالطَّيِّبَاتِ مِنَ الرِّزْقِ ۚ and the good things of His provision?'
قُلْ هِيَ لِلَّذِينَ آمَنُوا فِي الْحَيَاةِ الدُّنْيَا Say, 'These are for the faithful in the life of this world,
خَالِصَةً يَوْمَ الْقِيَامَةِ ۗ and exclusively for them on the Day of Resurrection.'
كَذَٰلِكَ نُفَصِّلُ الْآيَاتِ Thus do We elaborate the signs
لِقَوْمٍ يَعْلَمُونَ ۝ for a people who have knowledge.

قُلْ إِنَّمَا حَرَّمَ رَبِّيَ الْفَوَاحِشَ 33 Say, 'My Lord has only forbidden indecencies,
مَا ظَهَرَ مِنْهَا وَمَا بَطَنَ the outward among them and the inward ones,
وَالْإِثْمَ وَالْبَغْيَ بِغَيْرِ الْحَقِّ and sin and undue aggression,
وَأَنْ تُشْرِكُوا بِاللَّهِ and that you should ascribe to God partners
مَا لَمْ يُنَزِّلْ بِهِ سُلْطَانًا for which He has not sent down any authority,
وَأَنْ تَقُولُوا عَلَى اللَّهِ and that you should attribute to God

what you do not know.

34 There is a preordained time for every nation:
    when their time comes,
they shall not defer it by a single hour
    nor shall they advance it.

35 O Children of Adam!
If there come to you apostles from yourselves,
    recounting to you My signs,
then those who are Godwary and righteous
will have no fear, nor will they grieve.

36 But those who deny Our signs and disdain them,
    they shall be the inmates of the Fire
        and they shall remain in it.

37 So who is a greater wrongdoer than him
    who fabricates lies against God, or denies His signs?
Their share, as decreed in the Book, shall reach them.
When Our messengers[1] come to take them away,
they will say, 'Where is that which you used to invoke
        besides God?'
They will say, 'They have forsaken us,'
and will testify against themselves that they were faithless.

38 He will say, 'Enter, along with the nations
    of jinn and humans, who passed before you,
    into the Fire!'
Every time that a nation enters hell,
    it will curse its sister nation.
When they all join in it,

---

[1] That is, the angels of death.

the last of them will say about the first of them, قَالَتْ أُخْرَاهُمْ لِأُولَاهُمْ
   'Our Lord, it was they who led us astray; رَبَّنَا هَٰؤُلَاءِ أَضَلُّونَا
   so give them a double punishment of the Fire.' فَآتِهِمْ عَذَابًا ضِعْفًا مِنَ النَّارِ
He will say, 'It is double for each of you, قَالَ لِكُلٍّ ضِعْفٌ
   but you do not know.' وَلَٰكِنْ لَا تَعْلَمُونَ ۝

39 And the first of them will say to the last of them, وَقَالَتْ أُولَاهُمْ لِأُخْرَاهُمْ
   'You have no merit over us! فَمَا كَانَ لَكُمْ عَلَيْنَا مِنْ فَضْلٍ
   So taste the punishment فَذُوقُوا الْعَذَابَ
   because of what you used to perpetrate.' بِمَا كُنْتُمْ تَكْسِبُونَ ۝

40 Indeed, those who deny Our signs and disdain them— إِنَّ الَّذِينَ كَذَّبُوا بِآيَاتِنَا وَاسْتَكْبَرُوا عَنْهَا
   the gates of the heaven will not be opened for them, لَا تُفَتَّحُ لَهُمْ أَبْوَابُ السَّمَاءِ
   nor shall they enter paradise وَلَا يَدْخُلُونَ الْجَنَّةَ
   until the camel passes through the needle's eye,[1] حَتَّىٰ يَلِجَ الْجَمَلُ فِي سَمِّ الْخِيَاطِ
   and thus do We requite the guilty. وَكَذَٰلِكَ نَجْزِي الْمُجْرِمِينَ ۝

41 They shall have hell for their resting place, لَهُمْ مِنْ جَهَنَّمَ مِهَادٌ
   and over them shall be sheets of fire, وَمِنْ فَوْقِهِمْ غَوَاشٍ
   and thus do We requite the wrongdoers. وَكَذَٰلِكَ نَجْزِي الظَّالِمِينَ ۝

42 As for those who have faith and do righteous deeds وَالَّذِينَ آمَنُوا وَعَمِلُوا الصَّالِحَاتِ
   —We task no soul except according to its capacity— لَا نُكَلِّفُ نَفْسًا إِلَّا وُسْعَهَا
   they shall be the inhabitants of paradise أُولَٰئِكَ أَصْحَابُ الْجَنَّةِ
   and they shall remain in it. هُمْ فِيهَا خَالِدُونَ ۝

43 We will remove whatever rancour there is in their breasts, وَنَزَعْنَا مَا فِي صُدُورِهِمْ مِنْ غِلٍّ
   and streams will run for them. تَجْرِي مِنْ تَحْتِهِمُ الْأَنْهَارُ
   They will say, 'All praise belongs to God, وَقَالُوا الْحَمْدُ لِلَّهِ
   who guided us to this. الَّذِي هَدَانَا لِهَٰذَا
We would have never been guided had not God guided us. وَمَا كُنَّا لِنَهْتَدِيَ لَوْلَا أَنْ هَدَانَا اللَّهُ
   Our Lord's apostles had certainly brought the truth.' لَقَدْ جَاءَتْ رُسُلُ رَبِّنَا بِالْحَقِّ
The call will be made to them: وَنُودُوا
   'This is paradise, which you have been given to inherit أَنْ تِلْكُمُ الْجَنَّةُ أُورِثْتُمُوهَا

---

[1] Or, 'until the cable passes through the needle's eye.'

because of what you used to do!'

44 The inhabitants of paradise will call out
to the inmates of the Fire,
'We found what our Lord promised us to be true;
did you find what your Lord promised you to be true?'
'Yes,' they will say.
Then a caller will announce in their midst,
'May God's curse be on the wrongdoers!'

45 —Those who bar others from the way of God,
and seek to make it crooked,
and disbelieve in the Hereafter.

46 There will be a veil between them.
And on the Elevations will be certain men
who recognize each of them by their mark.
They will call out to the inhabitants of paradise,
'Peace be to you!'
(They[1] will not have entered it,
though they would be eager to do so.

47 When their look is turned
toward the inmates of the Fire,
they will say, 'Our Lord,
do not put us among the wrongdoing lot!')

48 The occupants of the Elevations will call out
to certain men whom they recognize by their marks,
'Your rallying[2] did not avail you,
nor what you used to disdain.

49 Are these[3] the ones concerning whom you swore
that God will not extend them any mercy?'

---

[1] That is, the people of paradise.
[2] Or 'your amassing.'
[3] That is, the people who will be about to enter paradise.

ادْخُلُوا الْجَنَّةَ 'Enter paradise![1]
لَا خَوْفٌ عَلَيْكُمْ وَلَا أَنْتُمْ تَحْزَنُونَ ۝ You shall have no fear, nor shall you grieve.'
وَنَادَىٰ أَصْحَابُ النَّارِ 50 The inmates of the Fire will call out
أَصْحَابَ الْجَنَّةِ   to the inhabitants of paradise,
أَنْ أَفِيضُوا عَلَيْنَا مِنَ الْمَاءِ 'Pour on us some water,
أَوْ مِمَّا رَزَقَكُمُ اللَّهُ   or something of what God has provided you.'
قَالُوا إِنَّ اللَّهَ حَرَّمَهُمَا They will say, 'God has forbidden these two
عَلَى الْكَافِرِينَ ۝   to the faithless!'
الَّذِينَ اتَّخَذُوا دِينَهُمْ لَهْوًا وَلَعِبًا 51 Those who took their religion for diversion and play
وَغَرَّتْهُمُ الْحَيَاةُ الدُّنْيَا   and whom the life of the world had deceived.
فَالْيَوْمَ نَنْسَاهُمْ So today We will forget them
كَمَا نَسُوا لِقَاءَ يَوْمِهِمْ هَٰذَا   as they forgot the encounter of this day of theirs,
وَمَا كَانُوا بِآيَاتِنَا يَجْحَدُونَ ۝   and used to impugn Our signs.

وَلَقَدْ جِئْنَاهُمْ بِكِتَابٍ 52 Certainly We have brought them a Book
فَصَّلْنَاهُ عَلَىٰ عِلْمٍ   which We have elaborated with knowledge,
هُدًى وَرَحْمَةً لِقَوْمٍ يُؤْمِنُونَ ۝   as guidance and mercy for a people who have faith.
هَلْ يَنْظُرُونَ إِلَّا تَأْوِيلَهُ 53 Do they await anything but its fulfillment?
يَوْمَ يَأْتِي تَأْوِيلُهُ The day when its fulfillment comes,
يَقُولُ الَّذِينَ نَسُوهُ مِنْ قَبْلُ   those who had forgotten it before will say,
قَدْ جَاءَتْ رُسُلُ رَبِّنَا بِالْحَقِّ 'Our Lord's apostles had certainly brought the truth.
فَهَلْ لَنَا مِنْ شُفَعَاءَ فَيَشْفَعُوا لَنَا Do we have any intercessors to intercede for us,
أَوْ نُرَدُّ   or could we be returned to the world,
فَنَعْمَلَ غَيْرَ الَّذِي كُنَّا نَعْمَلُ so that we may act differently from what we used to?'
قَدْ خَسِرُوا أَنْفُسَهُمْ They have already ruined their souls,
وَضَلَّ عَنْهُمْ مَا كَانُوا يَفْتَرُونَ ۝   and what they used to fabricate has forsaken them.

إِنَّ رَبَّكُمُ اللَّهُ الَّذِي خَلَقَ 54 Your Lord is indeed God, who created
السَّمَاوَاتِ وَالْأَرْضَ فِي سِتَّةِ أَيَّامٍ   the heavens and the earth in six days,

---

[1] Addressed to the people about to enter paradise.

and then settled on the Throne.
He draws the night's cover over the day,
   which pursues it swiftly,
and [He created] the sun, the moon, and the stars,
   [all of them] disposed by His command.
Lo! All creation and command belong to Him.
Blessed is God, the Lord of all the worlds.

55 Supplicate your Lord, beseechingly and secretly.
Indeed, He does not like the transgressors.

56 Do not cause corruption on the earth after its restoration,
   and supplicate Him with fear and hope:
   indeed God's mercy is close to the virtuous.

57 It is He who sends forth the winds
   as harbingers of His mercy.
When they bear rain-laden clouds,
We drive them toward a dead land and send down water on it,
   and with it We bring forth all kinds of crops.
Thus shall We raise the dead;
   maybe you will take admonition.

58 The good land—its vegetation comes out
   by the permission of its Lord,
   and as for that which is bad,
   it does not come out except sparsely.
Thus do We paraphrase the signs variously
   for a people who give thanks.

59 Certainly We sent Noah to his people.
He said, 'O my people, worship God!
   You have no other god besides Him.
   I indeed fear for you the punishment

    of a tremendous day.'   يَوْمٍ عَظِيمٍ ﴿٥٩﴾

60 The elite of his people said,   قَالَ الْمَلَأُ مِنْ قَوْمِهِ

    'Indeed, we see you to be in manifest error.'   إِنَّا لَنَرَاكَ فِي ضَلَالٍ مُبِينٍ ﴿٦٠﴾

61 He said, 'O my people, I am not in error.   قَالَ يَا قَوْمِ لَيْسَ بِي ضَلَالَةٌ

    Rather, I am an apostle from the Lord of all the worlds.   وَلَكِنِّي رَسُولٌ مِنْ رَبِّ الْعَالَمِينَ ﴿٦١﴾

62 I communicate the messages of my Lord to you,   أُبَلِّغُكُمْ رِسَالَاتِ رَبِّي

    and I am your well-wisher,   وَأَنْصَحُ لَكُمْ

    and I know from God what you do not know.   وَأَعْلَمُ مِنَ اللَّهِ مَا لَا تَعْلَمُونَ ﴿٦٢﴾

63 Do you consider it odd   أَوَعَجِبْتُمْ

    that a reminder from your Lord should come to you   أَنْ جَاءَكُمْ ذِكْرٌ مِنْ رَبِّكُمْ

    through a man from yourselves,   عَلَىٰ رَجُلٍ مِنْكُمْ

    to warn you and so that you may be Godwary   لِيُنْذِرَكُمْ وَلِتَتَّقُوا

    and so that you may receive His mercy?'   وَلَعَلَّكُمْ تُرْحَمُونَ ﴿٦٣﴾

64 But they impugned him.   فَكَذَّبُوهُ

    So We delivered him   فَأَنْجَيْنَاهُ

    and those who were with him in the ark,   وَالَّذِينَ مَعَهُ فِي الْفُلْكِ

    and We drowned those who impugned Our signs.   وَأَغْرَقْنَا الَّذِينَ كَذَّبُوا بِآيَاتِنَا

    They were indeed a blind lot.   إِنَّهُمْ كَانُوا قَوْمًا عَمِينَ ﴿٦٤﴾

65 To the people of 'Ād We sent Hūd, their compatriot.   وَإِلَىٰ عَادٍ أَخَاهُمْ هُودًا

    He said, 'O my people, worship God!   قَالَ يَا قَوْمِ اعْبُدُوا اللَّهَ

    You have no other god besides Him.   مَا لَكُمْ مِنْ إِلَٰهٍ غَيْرُهُ

    Will you not then be wary of Him?'   أَفَلَا تَتَّقُونَ ﴿٦٥﴾

66 The elite of his people who were faithless said,   قَالَ الْمَلَأُ الَّذِينَ كَفَرُوا مِنْ قَوْمِهِ

    'Indeed, we see you to be in folly,   إِنَّا لَنَرَاكَ فِي سَفَاهَةٍ

    and indeed we consider you to be a liar.'   وَإِنَّا لَنَظُنُّكَ مِنَ الْكَاذِبِينَ ﴿٦٦﴾

67 He said, 'O my people, I am not in folly.   قَالَ يَا قَوْمِ لَيْسَ بِي سَفَاهَةٌ

    Rather, I am an apostle from the Lord of all the worlds.   وَلَكِنِّي رَسُولٌ مِنْ رَبِّ الْعَالَمِينَ ﴿٦٧﴾

68 I communicate to you the messages of my Lord   أُبَلِّغُكُمْ رِسَالَاتِ رَبِّي

    and I am a trustworthy well-wisher for you.   وَأَنَا لَكُمْ نَاصِحٌ أَمِينٌ ﴿٦٨﴾

69 Do you consider it odd that   أَوَعَجِبْتُمْ

that a reminder from your Lord should come to you
through a man from yourselves, to warn you?
Remember when He made you successors
after the people of Noah,
and increased you vastly in creation.
So remember God's bounties so that you may be felicitous.'

70 They said, 'Have you come to tell us
that we should worship God alone
and abandon what our fathers have been worshiping?
Bring us what you threaten us with, if you are truthful.'

71 He said, 'There has become due against you
a punishment and wrath from your Lord.
Do you dispute with me regarding names
which you have named—you and your fathers—
for which God has not sent down any authority?
So wait! I too am waiting along with you.'

72 Then We delivered him and those who were with him
by a mercy from Us,
and We rooted out those who impugned Our signs
and were not faithful.

73 To the people of Thamūd We sent Ṣāliḥ, their compatriot.
He said, 'O my people, worship God!
You have no other god besides Him.
There has come to you a clear proof from your Lord:
This she-camel of God is a sign for you.
Let her alone to graze freely in God's land,
and do not cause her any harm,[1]
for then you shall be seized by a painful punishment.

---

[1] Or 'do not touch her with malice.'

74 Remember when He made you successors
after the people of 'Ād,
and settled you in the land:
you build palaces in its plains,
and carve out dwellings from mountains.
So remember God's bounties,
and do not act wickedly on the earth, causing corruption.'

75 The elite of his people who were oppressors said
to those who were oppressed
—to those among them who had faith—
'Do you know that Ṣāliḥ has been sent by his Lord?'
They said, 'We believe in what he has been sent with.'

76 Those who were oppressors said,
'We indeed disbelieve in what you have believed.'

77 So they hamstrung the She-camel
and defied the command of their Lord,
and they said, 'O Ṣāliḥ, bring us what you threaten us with,
if you are one of the apostles.'

78 Thereupon the earthquake seized them
and they lay lifeless prostrate in their homes.

79 So he abandoned them to their fate, and said,
'O my people! Certainly I communicated to you
the message of my Lord,
and I was your well-wisher,
but you did not like well-wishers.'

80 And Lot, when he said to his people,
'What! Do you commit an outrage
none in the world ever committed before you?!

81 Indeed, you come to men with desire

مِنْ دُونِ النِّسَاءِ ۚ   instead of women!
بَلْ أَنْتُمْ قَوْمٌ مُسْرِفُونَ ۝   You are indeed a dissolute lot.'

وَمَا كَانَ جَوَابَ قَوْمِهِ إِلَّا أَنْ قَالُوا   82 But the only answer of his people was that they said,
أَخْرِجُوهُمْ مِنْ قَرْيَتِكُمْ ۖ   'Expel them from your town!
إِنَّهُمْ أُنَاسٌ يَتَطَهَّرُونَ ۝   They are indeed a puritanical lot.'

فَأَنْجَيْنَاهُ وَأَهْلَهُ   83 Thereupon We delivered him and his family,
إِلَّا امْرَأَتَهُ   except his wife;
كَانَتْ مِنَ الْغَابِرِينَ ۝   she was one of those who remained behind.

وَأَمْطَرْنَا عَلَيْهِمْ مَطَرًا ۖ   84 Then We poured down upon them a rain of stones.
فَانْظُرْ كَيْفَ كَانَ عَاقِبَةُ الْمُجْرِمِينَ ۝   So *observe* how was the fate of the guilty!

وَإِلَىٰ مَدْيَنَ   85 To the people of Midian,
أَخَاهُمْ شُعَيْبًا ۗ   We sent Shu'ayb, their compatriot.
قَالَ يَا قَوْمِ اعْبُدُوا اللَّهَ   He said, 'O my people, worship God!
مَا لَكُمْ مِنْ إِلَٰهٍ غَيْرُهُ ۖ   You have no other god besides Him.
قَدْ جَاءَتْكُمْ بَيِّنَةٌ مِنْ رَبِّكُمْ ۖ   There has come to you a clear proof from your Lord.
فَأَوْفُوا الْكَيْلَ وَالْمِيزَانَ   Observe fully the measure and the balance,
وَلَا تَبْخَسُوا النَّاسَ أَشْيَاءَهُمْ   do not cheat the people of their goods,[1]
وَلَا تُفْسِدُوا فِي الْأَرْضِ بَعْدَ إِصْلَاحِهَا ۚ   and do not cause corruption in the land after its restoration.
ذَٰلِكُمْ خَيْرٌ لَكُمْ إِنْ كُنْتُمْ مُؤْمِنِينَ ۝   That is better for you, if you are faithful.

وَلَا تَقْعُدُوا بِكُلِّ صِرَاطٍ   86 And do not lie in wait on every road
تُوعِدُونَ وَتَصُدُّونَ عَنْ سَبِيلِ اللَّهِ   to threaten and bar from the way of God
مَنْ آمَنَ بِهِ وَتَبْغُونَهَا عِوَجًا ۚ   those who have faith in Him, seeking to make it crooked.
وَاذْكُرُوا إِذْ كُنْتُمْ قَلِيلًا فَكَثَّرَكُمْ ۖ   Remember when you were few and He multiplied you,
وَانْظُرُوا كَيْفَ كَانَ عَاقِبَةُ الْمُفْسِدِينَ ۝   and see how was the fate of the agents of corruption.

وَإِنْ كَانَ طَائِفَةٌ مِنْكُمْ آمَنُوا   87 If a group of you have believed
بِالَّذِي أُرْسِلْتُ بِهِ   in what I have been sent with,
وَطَائِفَةٌ لَمْ يُؤْمِنُوا   and a group have not believed,
فَاصْبِرُوا حَتَّىٰ يَحْكُمَ اللَّهُ بَيْنَنَا ۚ   be patient until God judges between us,

---

[1] That is, by employing short weights and measures.

and He is the best of judges.'

[PART 9]

88 The elite of his people who were oppressors said,
'O Shu'ayb, we will surely expel you
and the faithful who are with you from our town,
or else you shall revert to our creed.'
He said, 'What! Even if we should be unwilling?!

89 We would be fabricating a lie against God
if we revert to your creed
after God had delivered us from it.
It does not behoove us to return to it,
unless God, our Lord, should wish so.
Our Lord embraces all things in His knowledge.
In God alone we have put our trust.'
'Our Lord! Judge justly between us and our people,
and You are the best of judges!'

90 The elite of his people who were faithless said,
'If you follow Shu'ayb, you will indeed be losers.'

91 So the earthquake seized them
and they lay lifeless prostrate in their homes.

92 Those who impugned Shu'ayb
became as if they had never lived there.
Those who impugned Shu'ayb
were themselves the losers.

93 So he abandoned them to their fate and said,
'O my people!
Certainly, I communicated to you the messages of my Lord,
and I was your well-wisher.
So how should I grieve for a faithless lot?'

94 وَمَا أَرْسَلْنَا فِي قَرْيَةٍ مِنْ نَبِيٍّ إِلَّا أَخَذْنَا أَهْلَهَا بِالْبَأْسَاءِ وَالضَّرَّاءِ لَعَلَّهُمْ يَضَّرَّعُونَ ۝

94 We did not send a prophet to any town
without visiting its people with stress and distress
so that they might entreat for God's forgiveness.

ثُمَّ بَدَّلْنَا مَكَانَ السَّيِّئَةِ الْحَسَنَةَ حَتَّىٰ عَفَوْا وَقَالُوا قَدْ مَسَّ آبَاءَنَا الضَّرَّاءُ وَالسَّرَّاءُ فَأَخَذْنَاهُمْ بَغْتَةً وَهُمْ لَا يَشْعُرُونَ ۝

95 Then We changed their ill conditions to good,
until they multiplied in numbers and said,
'Adversity and ease certainly befell our fathers.'
Then We seized them suddenly while they were unaware.

وَلَوْ أَنَّ أَهْلَ الْقُرَىٰ آمَنُوا وَاتَّقَوْا لَفَتَحْنَا عَلَيْهِمْ بَرَكَاتٍ مِنَ السَّمَاءِ وَالْأَرْضِ وَلَٰكِنْ كَذَّبُوا فَأَخَذْنَاهُمْ بِمَا كَانُوا يَكْسِبُونَ ۝

96 If the people of the towns had been faithful and Godwary,
We would have opened to them blessings
from the heaven and the earth.
But they impugned Our apostles;
so We seized them because of what they used to perpetrate.

أَفَأَمِنَ أَهْلُ الْقُرَىٰ أَنْ يَأْتِيَهُمْ بَأْسُنَا بَيَاتًا وَهُمْ نَائِمُونَ ۝

97 Do the people of the towns feel secure
from Our punishment overtaking them at night
while they are asleep?

أَوَأَمِنَ أَهْلُ الْقُرَىٰ أَنْ يَأْتِيَهُمْ بَأْسُنَا ضُحًى وَهُمْ يَلْعَبُونَ ۝

98 Do the people of the towns feel secure
from Our punishment overtaking them at midday
while they are playing around?

أَفَأَمِنُوا مَكْرَ اللَّهِ فَلَا يَأْمَنُ مَكْرَ اللَّهِ إِلَّا الْقَوْمُ الْخَاسِرُونَ ۝

99 Do they feel secure from God's devising?
No one feels secure from God's devising
except the people who are losers.

أَوَلَمْ يَهْدِ لِلَّذِينَ يَرِثُونَ الْأَرْضَ مِنْ بَعْدِ أَهْلِهَا أَنْ لَوْ نَشَاءُ أَصَبْنَاهُمْ بِذُنُوبِهِمْ وَنَطْبَعُ عَلَىٰ قُلُوبِهِمْ فَهُمْ لَا يَسْمَعُونَ ۝

100 Does it not dawn upon those who inherited the earth
after its former inhabitants
that if We wish We will punish them for their sins
and set a seal on their hearts so they would not hear?

تِلْكَ الْقُرَىٰ نَقُصُّ عَلَيْكَ مِنْ أَنْبَائِهَا وَلَقَدْ جَاءَتْهُمْ رُسُلُهُمْ بِالْبَيِّنَاتِ فَمَا كَانُوا لِيُؤْمِنُوا بِمَا كَذَّبُوا مِنْ قَبْلُ

101 These are the towns
some of whose accounts We recount to you.
Their apostles certainly brought them clear proofs,
but they were not the ones to believe
in what they had impugned earlier.

Thus does God put a seal on the hearts of the faithless.

102 We did not find in most of them
    any loyalty to covenants.
Indeed, We found most of them to be transgressors.

103 Then We sent Moses after them with Our signs
    to Pharaoh and his elite, but they wronged them.
So *observe* how was the fate of the agents of corruption!

104 And Moses said, 'O Pharaoh,
    I am indeed an apostle from the Lord of all the worlds.

105 It behooves me to say nothing about God
    except the truth.
I certainly bring you a clear proof from your Lord.
So let the Children of Israel go with me.'

106 He said, 'If you have brought a sign, produce it,
    if you are truthful.'

107 Thereat he threw down his staff,
    and behold, it became a manifest python.

108 Then he drew out his hand,
    and behold, it was bright to the onlookers.

109 The elite of Pharaoh's people said,
    'This is indeed an expert magician;

110   he seeks to expel you from your land.'
    'So what do you advise?'

111 They said, 'Put him and his brother off for a while,
    and send heralds to the cities

112 to bring you every expert magician.'

113 And the magicians came to Pharaoh.
    They said, 'We shall indeed have a reward

إِنْ كُنَّا نَحْنُ الْغَالِبِينَ ۝

if we were to be the victors?'[1]

قَالَ نَعَمْ 114 He said, 'Of course!

وَإِنَّكُمْ لَمِنَ الْمُقَرَّبِينَ ۝   And you shall indeed be among those near to me.'

قَالُوا يَا مُوسَىٰ إِمَّا أَنْ تُلْقِيَ 115 They said, 'O Moses, will you throw first,

وَإِمَّا أَنْ نَكُونَ نَحْنُ الْمُلْقِينَ ۝   or shall we throw?'

قَالَ أَلْقُوا ۖ 116 He said, 'Throw yours.'

فَلَمَّا أَلْقَوْا سَحَرُوا أَعْيُنَ النَّاسِ   So when they threw, they bewitched the people's eyes

وَاسْتَرْهَبُوهُمْ   and overawed them,

وَجَاءُوا بِسِحْرٍ عَظِيمٍ ۝   producing a tremendous magic.

وَأَوْحَيْنَا إِلَىٰ مُوسَىٰ أَنْ أَلْقِ عَصَاكَ ۖ 117 And We signalled to Moses: 'Throw down your staff.'

فَإِذَا هِيَ تَلْقَفُ مَا يَأْفِكُونَ ۝   And behold, it was swallowing what they had faked.

فَوَقَعَ الْحَقُّ 118 So the truth came out,

وَبَطَلَ مَا كَانُوا يَعْمَلُونَ ۝   and what they had wrought was reduced to naught.

فَغُلِبُوا هُنَالِكَ وَانْقَلَبُوا صَاغِرِينَ ۝ 119 Thereat they were vanquished, and retreated, humiliated.

وَأُلْقِيَ السَّحَرَةُ سَاجِدِينَ ۝ 120 And the magicians fell down in prostration.

قَالُوا آمَنَّا بِرَبِّ الْعَالَمِينَ ۝ 121 They said, 'We have believed in the Lord of all the worlds,

رَبِّ مُوسَىٰ وَهَارُونَ ۝ 122   the Lord of Moses and Aaron.'

قَالَ فِرْعَوْنُ 123 Pharaoh said,

آمَنْتُمْ بِهِ قَبْلَ أَنْ آذَنَ لَكُمْ ۖ   'Do you profess faith in Him before I may permit you?

إِنَّ هَٰذَا لَمَكْرٌ مَكَرْتُمُوهُ فِي الْمَدِينَةِ   It is indeed a plot you have devised in the city

لِتُخْرِجُوا مِنْهَا أَهْلَهَا ۖ   to expel its people from it.

فَسَوْفَ تَعْلَمُونَ ۝   Soon you will know the consequences!

لَأُقَطِّعَنَّ أَيْدِيَكُمْ وَأَرْجُلَكُمْ 124 Surely I will cut off your hands and feet

مِنْ خِلَافٍ   on opposite sides,

ثُمَّ لَأُصَلِّبَنَّكُمْ أَجْمَعِينَ ۝   and then I will crucify all of you.'

قَالُوا إِنَّا إِلَىٰ رَبِّنَا مُنْقَلِبُونَ ۝ 125 They said, 'We will indeed return to our Lord.

وَمَا تَنْقِمُ مِنَّا إِلَّا أَنْ 126 You are vindictive toward us only because

آمَنَّا بِآيَاتِ رَبِّنَا لَمَّا جَاءَتْنَا ۚ   we believed in the signs of our Lord when they came to us.'

---

[1] This is in accordance with the reading of Ḥafṣ and that of the Ḥijāzī qāris. However, in accordance with an alternate reading (with an interrogative hamzah before inna, exactly as in 26:41, a parallel verse) the translation will be, 'Shall we indeed have a reward if we were to be the victors?' (see Mu'jam al-Qirā'āt al-Qur'āniyyah, ii, pp. 388-389).

      'Our Lord! Pour patience upon us,
         and grant us to die as *muslims*.'

127 The elite of Pharaoh's people said,
    'Will you leave Moses and his people
         to cause corruption in the land,
         and to abandon you and your gods?'
He said, 'We will kill their sons and spare their women,
         and indeed we are dominant over them.'

128 Moses said to his people,
    'Turn to God for help and be patient.
    The earth indeed belongs to God;
He makes whomever of His servants He wishes to inherit it,
    and the outcome will be in favour of the Godwary.'

129 They said, 'We were tormented before you came to us
        and also after you came.'
He said, 'Maybe your Lord will destroy your enemy
        and make you successors in the land,
        and then He will see how you act.'

130 Certainly We afflicted Pharaoh's clan
    with droughts and loss of produce,
    so that they may take admonition.

131 But whenever any good came to them,
    they would say, 'This is our due.'
But if any ill visited them,
    they took it for ill omens attending Moses
    and those who were with him.
(Behold! The cause of their ill omens is indeed from God,
    but most of them do not know.)

132 And they said,
    'Whatever sign you may bring us, to bewitch us,

فَمَا نَحْنُ لَكَ بِمُؤْمِنِينَ ۝

we are not going to believe you.'

فَأَرْسَلْنَا عَلَيْهِمُ الطُّوفَانَ وَالْجَرَادَ

133 So We sent against them a flood and locusts,

وَالْقُمَّلَ وَالضَّفَادِعَ وَالدَّمَ

    lice, frogs and blood,

آيَاتٍ مُفَصَّلَاتٍ

    as distinct signs.

فَاسْتَكْبَرُوا وَكَانُوا قَوْمًا مُجْرِمِينَ ۝

But they acted arrogantly, and they were a guilty lot.

وَلَمَّا وَقَعَ عَلَيْهِمُ الرِّجْزُ قَالُوا

134 Whenever a plague fell upon them, they would say,

يَا مُوسَى ادْعُ لَنَا رَبَّكَ

    'O Moses, invoke your Lord for us

بِمَا عَهِدَ عِندَكَ

    by the covenant He has made with you.

لَئِن كَشَفْتَ عَنَّا الرِّجْزَ

    If you remove the plague from us,

لَنُؤْمِنَنَّ لَكَ

    we will certainly believe in you

وَلَنُرْسِلَنَّ مَعَكَ بَنِي إِسْرَائِيلَ ۝

    and let the Children of Israel go along with you.'

فَلَمَّا كَشَفْنَا عَنْهُمُ الرِّجْزَ

135 But when We had removed the plague from them

إِلَىٰ أَجَلٍ هُم بَالِغُوهُ

    until a term that they should have completed,

إِذَا هُمْ يَنكُثُونَ ۝

    behold, they broke their promise.

فَانتَقَمْنَا مِنْهُمْ

136 So We took vengeance on them

فَأَغْرَقْنَاهُمْ فِي الْيَمِّ

    and drowned them in the sea,

بِأَنَّهُمْ كَذَّبُوا بِآيَاتِنَا وَكَانُوا عَنْهَا غَافِلِينَ ۝

for they impugned Our signs and were oblivious to them.

وَأَوْرَثْنَا الْقَوْمَ الَّذِينَ كَانُوا يُسْتَضْعَفُونَ

137 We made the people who were oppressed heirs

مَشَارِقَ الْأَرْضِ وَمَغَارِبَهَا الَّتِي بَارَكْنَا فِيهَا

    to the east and west of the land which We had blessed,

وَتَمَّتْ كَلِمَتُ رَبِّكَ الْحُسْنَىٰ

    and your Lord's best word of promise was fulfilled

عَلَىٰ بَنِي إِسْرَائِيلَ بِمَا صَبَرُوا

    for the Children of Israel because of their patience,

وَدَمَّرْنَا مَا كَانَ يَصْنَعُ فِرْعَوْنُ وَقَوْمُهُ

and We destroyed what Pharaoh and his people had built

وَمَا كَانُوا يَعْرِشُونَ ۝

    and whatever they used to erect.

وَجَاوَزْنَا بِبَنِي إِسْرَائِيلَ الْبَحْرَ

138 We carried the Children of Israel across the sea,

فَأَتَوْا عَلَىٰ قَوْمٍ

    whereat they came upon a people

يَعْكُفُونَ عَلَىٰ أَصْنَامٍ لَهُمْ

    attending to certain idols that they had.

قَالُوا يَا مُوسَى اجْعَل لَّنَا إِلَٰهًا

They said, 'O Moses, make for us a god

كَمَا لَهُمْ آلِهَةٌ

    like the gods that they have.'

قَالَ إِنَّكُمْ قَوْمٌ تَجْهَلُونَ ۝

He said, 'You are indeed an ignorant lot.

إِنَّ هَٰؤُلَاءِ مُتَبَّرٌ مَا هُمْ فِيهِ

139 What they are engaged in is indeed bound to perish,

and what they have been doing shall come to naught.'

140 He said, 'Shall I find you a god other than God, while He has graced you over all the nations?'

141 And when We delivered you from Pharaoh's clan who inflicted on you a terrible torment, slaughtering your sons and sparing your women, and there was a great test in that from your Lord.

142 We made an appointment with Moses for thirty nights, and completed them with ten more; thus the tryst of his Lord was completed in forty nights. And Moses said to Aaron, his brother, 'Be my successor among my people, and set things right and do not follow the way of the agents of corruption.'

143 When Moses arrived at Our tryst and his Lord spoke to him, he said, 'Lord, show Yourself to me, that I may look at You!' He said, 'You shall not see Me. But look at the mountain: if it abides in its place, then you will see Me.' So when his Lord disclosed Himself to the mountain, He levelled it,[1] and Moses fell down swooning. When he recovered, he said, 'Immaculate are You! I turn to You in penitence, and I am the first of the faithful.'

144 He said, 'O Moses, I have chosen you over the people with My messages and My speech. So take what I give you and be among the grateful.'

145 We wrote for him in the Tablets

---

[1] Or 'He made it crumble.'

advice concerning all things
   and an elaboration of all things, [and We said],
'Hold on to them with power, and bid your people
   to hold on to the best of what is in them.
Soon I shall show you the abode of the transgressors.

146 Soon I shall turn away from My signs
   those who are unduly arrogant in the earth:
though they should see every sign, they will not believe in it,
and if they see the way of rectitude they will not follow it,
and if they see the way of error they will follow it.
That is because they impugn Our signs
   and are oblivious to them.'

147 Those who deny Our signs
      and the encounter of the Hereafter,
   their works have failed.
Shall they be requited except for what they used to do?

148 The people of Moses took up in his absence
   a calf cast from their ornaments
   —a body that gave out a lowing sound.
Did they not regard that it did not speak to them,
   nor did it guide them to any way?
They took it up for worship and they were wrongdoers.

149 But when they became remorseful
   and realised they had gone astray,
they said, 'Should our Lord have no mercy on us,
and forgive us, we will be surely among the losers.'

150 When Moses returned to his people, angry and indignant,
he said, 'Evil has been your conduct in my absence!
   Would you hasten on the edict of your Lord?'
He threw down the tablets

وَأَخَذَ بِرَأْسِ أَخِيهِ   and seized his brother by the head,
يَجُرُّهُ إِلَيْهِ   pulling him towards himself.
قَالَ ابْنَ أُمَّ   He said, 'Son of my mother,
إِنَّ الْقَوْمَ اسْتَضْعَفُونِي   indeed this people thought me to be weak,
وَكَادُوا يَقْتُلُونَنِي   and they were about to kill me.
فَلَا تُشْمِتْ بِيَ الْأَعْدَاءَ   So do not let the enemies gloat over me,
وَلَا تَجْعَلْنِي مَعَ الْقَوْمِ الظَّالِمِينَ ۝   and do not take me with the wrongdoing lot.'

151 قَالَ رَبِّ اغْفِرْ لِي وَلِأَخِي   He said, 'My Lord, forgive me and my brother
وَأَدْخِلْنَا فِي رَحْمَتِكَ   and admit us into Your mercy,
وَأَنتَ أَرْحَمُ الرَّاحِمِينَ ۝   for You are the most merciful of the merciful.

152 إِنَّ الَّذِينَ اتَّخَذُوا الْعِجْلَ   Indeed, those who took up the calf for worship
سَيَنَالُهُمْ غَضَبٌ مِّن رَّبِّهِمْ   shall be overtaken by their Lord's wrath
وَذِلَّةٌ فِي الْحَيَاةِ الدُّنْيَا   and abasement in the life of the world.'
وَكَذَٰلِكَ نَجْزِي الْمُفْتَرِينَ ۝   Thus do We requite the fabricators of lies.

153 وَالَّذِينَ عَمِلُوا السَّيِّئَاتِ   Yet to those who commit misdeeds,
ثُمَّ تَابُوا مِن بَعْدِهَا وَآمَنُوا   but repent after that and believe,
إِنَّ رَبَّكَ مِن بَعْدِهَا   —indeed, after that, your Lord
لَغَفُورٌ رَّحِيمٌ ۝   shall surely be all-forgiving, all-merciful.

154 وَلَمَّا سَكَتَ عَن مُّوسَى الْغَضَبُ   When Moses' indignation abated,
أَخَذَ الْأَلْوَاحَ   he picked up the tablets
وَفِي نُسْخَتِهَا هُدًى وَرَحْمَةٌ   whose inscriptions contained guidance and mercy
لِّلَّذِينَ هُمْ لِرَبِّهِمْ يَرْهَبُونَ ۝   for those who are in awe of their Lord.

155 وَاخْتَارَ مُوسَىٰ قَوْمَهُ سَبْعِينَ رَجُلًا   Moses chose seventy men from his people
لِّمِيقَاتِنَا   for Our tryst,
فَلَمَّا أَخَذَتْهُمُ الرَّجْفَةُ   and when the earthquake seized them,
قَالَ رَبِّ لَوْ شِئْتَ   he said, 'My Lord, had You wished,
أَهْلَكْتَهُم مِّن قَبْلُ وَإِيَّايَ   You would have destroyed them and me before.
أَتُهْلِكُنَا بِمَا فَعَلَ السُّفَهَاءُ مِنَّا   Will You destroy us for what fools amongst us have done?
إِنْ هِيَ إِلَّا فِتْنَتُكَ   It is only Your test
تُضِلُّ بِهَا مَن تَشَاءُ   by which You lead astray whomever You wish

  and guide whomever You wish.
  You are our master, so forgive us and have mercy on us,
   for You are the best of those who forgive.
156 And appoint goodness for us in this world
   and the Hereafter,
  for indeed we have come back to You.'
  Said He, 'I visit My punishment on whomever I wish,
   but My mercy embraces all things.[1]
  Soon I shall appoint it for those who are Godwary
   and give the *zakāt*
  and those who believe in Our signs
157 —those who follow the Apostle, the untaught prophet,
  whose mention they find written with them
   in the Torah and the Evangel,
  who bids them to do what is right
  and forbids them from what is wrong,
  makes lawful to them all the good things
  and forbids them from all vicious things,
  and relieves them of their burdens
  and the shackles that were upon them
  —those who believe in him, honour him, and help him
  and follow the light that has been sent down with him,[2]
  they are the felicitous.'
158 Say, 'O mankind!
  I am the Apostle of God to you all, of Him
  to whom belongs the kingdom of the heavens and the earth.
   There is no god except Him.
   He gives life and brings death.'
  So have faith in God and His Apostle, the untaught prophet,

---

[1] Cf. **6:12**.
[2] Cf. **4:174**.

who has faith in God and His words,
and follow him, so that you may be guided.

159 Among the people of Moses is a nation
who guide the people by the truth
and do justice thereby.

160 We split them up into twelve tribal communities,
and We revealed to Moses,
when his people asked him for water,
saying, 'Strike the rock with your staff,'
whereat twelve fountains gushed forth from it.
Every tribe came to know its drinking-place.
We shaded them with clouds,
and We sent down to them manna and quails:
'Eat of the good things We have provided you.'
And they did not wrong Us,
but they used to wrong only themselves.

161 When they were told, 'Settle in this town
and eat thereof whence you wish,
and say, "Relieve [us of the burden of our sins],"
and enter while prostrating at the gate,
that We may forgive your iniquities,
and soon We shall enhance the virtuous,'[1]

162 the wrongdoers changed that saying
with other than what they had been told.
So We sent against them a plague from the sky
because of the wrongs they used to commit.

163 Ask them[2] about the town that
was situated on the seaside,
when they violated the Sabbath,

---

[1] Cf. 2:58.
[2] That is, the Jews, to whom the following passages relate, up to verse 171.

when their fish would come to them on the Sabbath day,
visibly on the shore,
but on days when they were not keeping Sabbath
they would not come to them.
Thus did We test them
because of the transgressions they used to commit.

164 When a group of them said,
'Why do you advise a people whom God will destroy
or punish with a severe punishment?'
They said, 'As an excuse before your Lord
and with the hope that they may be Godwary.'

165 So when they forgot what they had been reminded of
We delivered those who forbade evil conduct
and seized the wrongdoers with a terrible punishment
because of the transgressions they used to commit.

166 When they defied [the command pertaining to]
what they were forbidden from,
We said to them, 'Be you spurned apes.'[1]

167 And when your Lord proclaimed
that He would surely send against them,[2]
until the Day of Resurrection,
those who would inflict a terrible punishment on them.
Your Lord is indeed swift in retribution,
and indeed He is all-forgiving, all-merciful.

168 We dispersed them into communities around the earth:
some of them were righteous,
and some of them otherwise,
and We tested them with good and bad times
so that they may come back.

---

[1] Cf. 2:65.
[2] That is, the Jews.

169 Then they were succeeded by an evil posterity
which inherited the Book:
they grab the transitory gains of this lower world
and say, 'It will be forgiven us.'
And if similar transitory gains were to come their way,
they would grab them too.
Was not the covenant of the Book taken with them
that they shall not attribute anything to God except truth
—and they have studied what is in it?
The abode of the Hereafter is better
for those who are Godwary.
Do you not exercise your reason?

170 As for those who hold fast to the Book
and maintain the prayer
—We do not waste
the reward of those who set things right.

171 When We plucked the mountain
and held it above them as if it were a canopy
(and they thought it was about to fall on them):
'Hold on with power to what We have given you
and remember that which is in it,
so that you may be Godwary.'

172 When your Lord took from the Children of Adam
their descendants from their loins,
and made them bear witness over themselves,
[He said to them,] 'Am I not your Lord?'
They said, 'Yes indeed! We bear witness.'
This, lest you should say on the Day of Resurrection,
'We were indeed unaware of this,'

173 or lest you should say,
'Our fathers ascribed partners to God before us
and we were descendants after them.
Will You then destroy us because of what the falsifiers did?'
174 Thus do We elaborate the signs,
so that they may come back.

175 *Relate* to them an account of him
to whom We gave Our signs, but he cast them off.
Thereupon Satan pursued him,
and he became one of the perverse.
176 Had We wished,
We would have surely raised him by their means,
but he clung to the earth
and followed his base desires.
So his parable is that of a dog:
if you make for it, it lolls out its tongue,
and if you let it alone, it lolls out its tongue.
Such is the parable of the people who impugn Our signs.
So *recount* these narratives, so that they may reflect.
177 Evil is the parable of the people who deny Our signs
and used to wrong themselves.
178 Whomever God guides is rightly guided,
and whomever He leads astray
—it is they who are the losers.
179 Certainly We have winnowed out for hell
many of the jinn and humans:
they have hearts with which they do not understand,
they have eyes with which they do not see,
they have ears with which they do not hear.

They are like cattle; rather, they are more astray.
It is they who are the heedless.[1]

180 To God belong the Best Names,
so supplicate Him by them,
and abandon those who commit sacrilege in His names.
Soon they shall be requited for what they used to do.

181 Among those We have created are a nation
who guide by the truth and do justice thereby.

182 As for those who impugn Our signs,
We will draw them imperceptibly into ruin,
whence they do not know.

183 And I will grant them respite,
for My devising is indeed sure.

184 Have they not reflected
that there is no madness in their companion,
and that he is just a manifest warner?

185 Have they not contemplated
the dominions of the heavens and the earth,
and whatever things God has created,
and that maybe their time[2] has already drawn near?
So what discourse will they believe after this?!

186 Whomever God leads astray has no guide,
and He leaves them bewildered in their rebellion.

187 They question you concerning the Hour, when will it set in?
Say, 'Its knowledge is only with my Lord:
none except Him shall manifest it at its time.
It will weigh heavy on the heavens and the earth.
It will not overtake you but suddenly.'
They ask you as if you were in the know of it.

---
[1] Cf. **8**:21-24, 55; **25**:44.
[2] That is, death.

Say, 'Its knowledge is only with God,
    but most people do not know.'

188 Say, 'I have no control over any benefit for myself,
    nor over any harm, except what God may wish.
    Had I known the Unseen,
    I would have acquired much good,
    and no ill would have befallen me.
I am only a warner and bearer of good news
    to a people who have faith.'

189 It is He who created you from a single soul,
    and made from it its mate,
    so that he might find comfort with her.
    So when he had covered[1] her, she bore a light burden
    and passed some time with it.
When she had grown heavy,
    they both invoked God, their Lord:
    'If You give us a healthy child,
    we will be surely grateful.'

190 Then when He gave them a healthy child,
    they ascribed partners to Him in what He had given them.
Far is God above having
    any partners that they ascribe to Him!

191 Do they ascribe to Him partners that create nothing
    and have been created themselves,
192 and who can neither help them,
    nor help themselves?
193 If you call them to guidance, they will not follow you:
    it is the same to you whether you call them

---

[1] Cover: to copulate with.

or whether you are silent.

194 Indeed, those whom you invoke besides God
are creatures like you.
So invoke them: they should answer you,
if you are truthful.

195 Do they have any feet to walk with?
Do they have any hands to grasp with?
Do they have any eyes to see with?
Do they have any ears to hear with?
Say, 'Invoke your partners that you ascribe to God
and try out your stratagems[1] against me
without granting me any respite.

196 My protector is indeed God
who has sent down the Book,
and He takes care of the righteous.

197 Those whom you invoke besides Him
can neither help you,
nor help themselves.'

198 If you call them to guidance, they will not hear.
You see them observing you, but they do not perceive.

199 *Adopt* a policy of excusing the faults of people,
bid what is right, and *turn away* from the ignorant.

200 Should a temptation from Satan disturb *you*,
invoke the protection of God;
indeed He is all-hearing, all-knowing.

201 When those who are Godwary are touched
by a visitation[2] of Satan,
they remember God and, behold, they perceive.

---

[1] Or 'try out your guile against me.' Cf. **11:55**.
[2] Or 'insinuation.'

202 But their brethren,[1] they draw them into perversity,
and then they do not spare any harm.

203 When *you* do not bring them a sign,
they say, 'Why do you not improvise one?'
Say, 'I only follow what is revealed to me from my Lord;
these are insights from your Lord,
and guidance and mercy for people who have faith.'

204 When the Qur'ān is recited, listen to it and be silent,
maybe you will receive God's mercy.

205 And remember *your* Lord within your heart,
beseechingly and reverentially, without being loud,
morning and evening,
and *do not be* among the heedless.

206 Indeed, those who are stationed near *your* Lord
do not disdain to worship Him.
They glorify Him and prostrate to Him.

8. The Spoils[2]
al-Anfāl

In the Name of God,
the All-beneficent, the All-merciful.

1 They ask *you* concerning the *anfāl*.[3]
Say, 'The *anfāl* belong to God and the Apostle.'
So be wary of God and settle your differences,
and obey God and His Apostle,
if you are faithful.

2 The faithful are only those

---

[1] That is, the polytheists, who are referred to as brethren of Satans.
[2] This Madanī *sūrah* takes its name from the term *al-anfāl* mentioned in verse 1.
[3] Or, 'They ask you for the *anfāl*,' according to an alternate reading (*yas'alūnaka al-anfāl*). In the present Qur'ānic context, the term *anfāl* refers to the spoils of war.

إِذَا ذُكِرَ اللَّهُ وَجِلَتْ قُلُوبُهُمْ	whose hearts tremble with awe when God is mentioned,
وَإِذَا تُلِيَتْ عَلَيْهِمْ آيَاتُهُ	and when His signs are recited to them,
زَادَتْهُمْ إِيمَانًا	they[1] increase their faith,
وَعَلَىٰ رَبِّهِمْ يَتَوَكَّلُونَ ۝	and who put their trust in their Lord,
٣ الَّذِينَ يُقِيمُونَ الصَّلَاةَ	3 maintain the prayer
وَمِمَّا رَزَقْنَاهُمْ يُنْفِقُونَ ۝	and spend out of what We have provided them.
٤ أُولَٰئِكَ هُمُ الْمُؤْمِنُونَ حَقًّا	4 It is they who are truly faithful.
لَهُمْ دَرَجَاتٌ عِنْدَ رَبِّهِمْ	They shall have ranks near their Lord,
وَمَغْفِرَةٌ وَرِزْقٌ كَرِيمٌ ۝	forgiveness and a noble provision.
٥ كَمَا أَخْرَجَكَ رَبُّكَ مِنْ بَيْتِكَ	5 As your Lord brought you out from your home
بِالْحَقِّ	with a judicious purpose,
وَإِنَّ فَرِيقًا مِنَ الْمُؤْمِنِينَ لَكَارِهُونَ ۝	a part of the faithful were indeed reluctant.
٦ يُجَادِلُونَكَ فِي الْحَقِّ	6 They disputed with you concerning the truth
بَعْدَمَا تَبَيَّنَ	after it had become clear,
كَأَنَّمَا يُسَاقُونَ إِلَى الْمَوْتِ	as if they were being driven towards death
وَهُمْ يَنْظُرُونَ ۝	while they looked on.
٧ وَإِذْ يَعِدُكُمُ اللَّهُ	7 When God promised you victory over
إِحْدَى الطَّائِفَتَيْنِ أَنَّهَا لَكُمْ	one of the two companies, [saying], 'It is for you,'
وَتَوَدُّونَ	you were eager
أَنَّ غَيْرَ ذَاتِ الشَّوْكَةِ تَكُونُ لَكُمْ	that it should be the one that was unarmed.[2]
وَيُرِيدُ اللَّهُ أَنْ يُحِقَّ الْحَقَّ بِكَلِمَاتِهِ	But God desires to confirm the truth with His words
وَيَقْطَعَ دَابِرَ الْكَافِرِينَ ۝	and to root out the faithless,
٨ لِيُحِقَّ الْحَقَّ	8 so that He may confirm the truth
وَيُبْطِلَ الْبَاطِلَ	and bring falsehood to naught,
وَلَوْ كَرِهَ الْمُجْرِمُونَ ۝	though the guilty should be averse.
٩ إِذْ تَسْتَغِيثُونَ رَبَّكُمْ	9 When you appealed to your Lord for help,
فَاسْتَجَابَ لَكُمْ أَنِّي مُمِدُّكُمْ	He answered you: 'I will aid you
بِأَلْفٍ مِنَ الْمَلَائِكَةِ مُرْدِفِينَ ۝	with a thousand angels in a file.'
وَمَا جَعَلَهُ اللَّهُ إِلَّا بُشْرَىٰ	10 God did not appoint it but as a good news,

---

[1] That is, the signs of God, when they are recited to the faithful.
[2] Literally, 'one that was free of thorns.' That is, one which was unarmed and, therefore, easy to encounter.

and to reassure your hearts.
Victory[1] comes only from God.
God is indeed all-mighty, all-wise.

11 When He covered you with drowsiness
  as a sense of security from Him,
and sent down water from the sky
  to purify you with it,
and to repel from you the defilement of Satan,
and to fortify your hearts,
and to make your feet steady with it.

12 Then your Lord signalled to the angels:
  'I am indeed with you; so steady the faithful.
I will cast terror into the hearts of the faithless.
So strike their necks,
  and strike their every limb joint!'

13 That, because they defied God and His Apostle.
And whoever defies God and His Apostle,
God is indeed severe in retribution.

14 'Taste this, and know that
  for the faithless is the punishment of the Fire.'

15 O you who have faith! When you encounter
  the faithless advancing for battle,
do not turn your backs to flee from them.

16 Whoever turns his back to flee from them that day
  —unless he is diverting to fight
    or retiring towards another troop—
he shall certainly earn God's wrath,
and his refuge shall be hell, an evil destination.

17 You did not kill them; rather it was God who killed them;

---

[1] Or 'help.'

and you did not throw when you threw,[1] وَمَا رَمَيْتَ إِذْ رَمَيْتَ
rather it was God who threw, وَلَـٰكِنَّ اللَّهَ رَمَىٰ
that He might test the faithful وَلِيُبْلِيَ الْمُؤْمِنِينَ
with a good test from Himself.[2] مِنْهُ بَلَاءً حَسَنًا
God is indeed all-hearing, all-knowing. إِنَّ اللَّهَ سَمِيعٌ عَلِيمٌ ۝

18 Such is the case, and know that ذَٰلِكُمْ وَأَنَّ
God undermines the stratagems of the faithless. اللَّهَ مُوهِنُ كَيْدِ الْكَافِرِينَ ۝

19 If you sought a verdict, إِنْ تَسْتَفْتِحُوا
the verdict has already come to you;[3] فَقَدْ جَاءَكُمُ الْفَتْحُ
and if you cease your belligerence, it is better for you; وَإِنْ تَنْتَهُوا فَهُوَ خَيْرٌ لَكُمْ
but if you resume, We too shall return وَإِنْ تَعُودُوا نَعُدْ
and your troops will never avail you وَلَنْ تُغْنِيَ عَنْكُمْ فِئَتُكُمْ شَيْئًا
though they should be ever so many, وَلَوْ كَثُرَتْ
and know that God is with the faithful. وَأَنَّ اللَّهَ مَعَ الْمُؤْمِنِينَ ۝

20 O you who have faith! يَا أَيُّهَا الَّذِينَ آمَنُوا
Obey God and His Apostle, أَطِيعُوا اللَّهَ وَرَسُولَهُ
and do not turn away from him while you hear him. وَلَا تَوَلَّوْا عَنْهُ وَأَنْتُمْ تَسْمَعُونَ ۝

21 Do not be like those who say, وَلَا تَكُونُوا كَالَّذِينَ قَالُوا
'We hear,' though they do not hear. سَمِعْنَا وَهُمْ لَا يَسْمَعُونَ ۝

22 Indeed, the worst of beasts in God's sight إِنَّ شَرَّ الدَّوَابِّ عِنْدَ اللَّهِ
are the deaf and dumb who do not exercise reason. الصُّمُّ الْبُكْمُ الَّذِينَ لَا يَعْقِلُونَ ۝

23 Had God known any good in them, وَلَوْ عَلِمَ اللَّهُ فِيهِمْ خَيْرًا
He would have surely made them hear, لَأَسْمَعَهُمْ
and were He to make them hear, وَلَوْ أَسْمَعَهُمْ
they would turn away, being disregardful. لَتَوَلَّوْا وَهُمْ مُعْرِضُونَ ۝

24 O you who have faith! يَا أَيُّهَا الَّذِينَ آمَنُوا

---

[1] According to tradition, at the outset of the battle of Badr, the Prophet (ṣ) took a handful of dust, containing sand and pebbles, and threw it at the enemy troops. It struck in the face every warrior of the enemy, entering their eyes, noses and mouths, disconcerting them, resulting ultimately in their being routed by the small Muslim force.
[2] Or 'that He might grant the faithful a splendid award from Himself.'
[3] Addressed to the faithless.

Answer God and the Apostle
when he summons you to that which will give you life.
Know that God intervenes between a man and his heart
and that you will be gathered toward Him.

25 And beware of a punishment
which shall not visit the wrongdoers among you
exclusively,
and know that God is severe in retribution.

26 Remember when you were few,
abased in the land,
and feared lest the people should despoil you,
and He gave you refuge,
and strengthened you with His help,
and provided you with all the good things
so that you may give thanks.

27 O you who have faith!
Do not betray God and the Apostle,
and do not betray your trusts knowingly.

28 Know that your possessions and children are only a test,
and that God—with Him is a great reward.

29 O you who have faith! If you are wary of God,
He will appoint a criterion[1] for you,
and absolve you of your misdeeds and forgive you,
for God is dispenser of a mighty grace.

30 When the faithless plotted against you
to take you captive, or to kill or expel you
—they plotted and God devised,
and God is the best of devisers.

---

[1] That is, a knowledge which will enable you to distinguish between truth and falsehood.

31 When Our signs are recited to them,
    they say, 'We have heard already.
    If we want, we too can say like this.
    These are nothing but myths of the ancients.'

32 And when they said, 'O God,
    if this be the truth from You,
    rain down upon us stones from the sky,
    or bring us a painful punishment.'

33 But God will not punish them while you are in their midst,
    nor will God punish them
    while they plead for forgiveness.

34 What excuse have they
    that God should not punish them,
    when they bar the faithful from the Holy Mosque,
    and they are not its custodians?
    Its custodians are only the Godwary,
    but most of them do not know.

35 Their prayer at the House is nothing
    but whistling and clapping.
    So taste the punishment because of what you used to deny.

36 Indeed, the faithless spend their wealth
    to bar from the way of God.
    Soon they will have spent it,
    then it will be a cause of regret to them,
    then they will be overcome,
    and the faithless will be gathered toward Hell,

37 so that God may separate the bad ones from the good,
    and place the bad on one another
    and pile them up together, and cast them into hell.
    It is they who are the losers.

38 Say to the faithless,
if they cease [their belligerence against the Muslims],
what is already past shall be forgiven them.
But if they resume their hostilities,
the precedent of the former peoples has already come to pass.
39 Fight them until persecution[1] is no more,
and religion becomes exclusively for God.
So if they desist, God indeed watches what they do.
40 But if they turn away, then know that God is your Master:
an excellent master and an excellent helper!

[PART 10]

41 Know that whatever thing you may come by,
a fifth of it is for God and the Apostle,
for the relatives and the orphans,
for the needy and the traveler,
if you have faith in God
and what We sent down to Our servant
on the Day of Separation,[2] the day when the two hosts met;
and God has power over all things.
42 When you were on the nearer side,[3]
and they[4] on the farther side,
while the caravan was below you,
and had you agreed together on an encounter,
you would have certainly failed to keep the tryst,[5]
but it was in order that God may carry through
a matter that was bound to be fulfilled,
so that he who perishes might perish by a clear proof,

---

[1] Or 'faithlessness,' or 'polytheism.' Cf. 2:193.
[2] That is, the day on which the Battle of Badr took place.
[3] That is, on the side of the valley nearer to Madinah.
[4] That is, the army of the polytheists of Makkah.
[5] Or 'you would not have kept the tryst.'

and he who lives may live on by a clear proof,
and God is indeed all-hearing, all-knowing.

43 When God showed them[1] to you as few in your dream,
and had He shown them as many, you would have lost heart,
and disputed about the matter.
But God spared you.
He knows well indeed what is in the breasts.

44 And when He showed them to you
—when you met them on the battlefield—
as few in your eyes,
and He made you appear few in their eyes
it was in order that God may carry through
a matter that was bound to be fulfilled,
and to God all matters are returned.

45 O you who have faith! When you meet a host in battle,
stand firm and remember God much
so that you may prosper.

46 Obey God and His Apostle and do not dispute,
or you will lose heart and your power will be gone.
And be patient; indeed God is with the patient.

47 Do not be like those who left their homes
vainly and to show off to the people,
and to bar other people from the way of God,
and God encompasses what they do.

48 When Satan made their deeds seem decorous to them,
and said [to the faithless], 'None will defeat you today
from among those people,
and I will stand by you.'
But when the two hosts sighted each other,

---

[1] That is, the enemy troops.

he took to his heels, saying,
'Indeed, I am quit of you. I see what you do not see.
Indeed, I fear God and God is severe in retribution.'

49 When the hypocrites said,
   and also those in whose hearts is a sickness,
      'Their religion has deceived them.'
   But whoever puts his trust in God,
   then God is indeed all-mighty, all-wise.

50 Were you to see
   when the angels take away the faithless,
      striking their faces and their backs,
   [saying], 'Taste the punishment of the burning.

51 That is because of what your hands have sent ahead,
   and God is not tyrannical to His servants.'

52 Like the precedent of Pharaoh's clan
      and those who were before them,
         who denied God's signs,
      so God seized them for their sins.
   God is indeed all-strong, severe in retribution.

53 That is because God never changes a blessing
      that He has bestowed on a people
   unless they change what is in their own souls,
   and God is all-hearing, all-knowing:

54 Like the precedent of Pharaoh's clan
      and those who were before them,
         who impugned the signs of their Lord;
      so We destroyed them for their sins,
   and We drowned Pharaoh's clan,
   and they were all wrongdoers.

55 Indeed, the worst of beasts in God's sight

are those who are faithless;

so they will not have faith.

56 —Those with whom you made a treaty

and who violated their treaty every time,

and who are not Godwary.

57 So if you confront them in battle,

treat them in such a wise as to disperse

those who are behind them,

so that they may take admonition.

58 And if you fear treachery from a people,

break off the treaty with them in a like manner.

Indeed, God does not like the treacherous.

59 Let the faithless not suppose

that they have outmaneuvered God.

Indeed, they cannot frustrate His power.

60 Prepare against them whatever you can

of military power and war-horses,

awing thereby the enemy of God,

and your enemy, and others besides them,

whom you do not know, but God knows them.

And whatever you spend in the way of God

will be repaid to you in full, and you will not be wronged.

61 If they incline toward peace,

you too incline toward it and *put your trust in God*.

Indeed, He is the All-hearing, the All-knowing.

62 But if they desire to deceive *you*,

God is indeed sufficient for *you*.

It is He who strengthened *you* with His help

and with the means of the faithful,

63 and united their hearts.

Had you spent all wealth that is on the earth,
you could not have united their hearts,
but God united them together.
He is indeed all-mighty, all-wise.

64 O Prophet! Sufficient for you is God
and those of the faithful who follow you.

65 O Prophet! *Urge* on the faithful to fight:
If there be twenty steadfast men among you,
they will overcome two hundred;
and if there be a hundred of you,
they will overcome a thousand of the faithless,
for they are a lot who do not understand.

66 Now God has lightened your burden,
knowing that there is weakness in you.
So if there be a hundred steadfast men among you,
they will overcome two hundred;
and if there be a thousand,
they will overcome two thousand, by God's leave,
and God is with the steadfast.

67 A prophet may not take captives
until he has thoroughly decimated the enemy in the land.
You desire the transitory gains of this world,
while God desires for you the reward of the Hereafter,
and God is all-mighty, all-wise.

68 Had it not been for a prior decree of God,
there would have surely befallen you
a great punishment for what you took.

69 Avail yourselves of the spoils you have taken,
as lawful and good,
and be wary of God.

God is indeed all-forgiving, all-merciful.

70 O Prophet!
Say to the captives who are in your hands,
'If God finds any good in your hearts,
He will give you something which is better
than what has been taken away from you,
and He will forgive you,
and God is all-forgiving, all-merciful.'

71 But if they seek to betray *you*,
then they have already betrayed God earlier,
and He gave *you* power over them,
and God is all-knowing, all-wise.

72 Indeed, those who have believed and migrated
and waged *jihād* with their possessions and persons
in the way of God,
and those who gave them shelter and help
—they are heirs of one another.
As for those who have believed but did not migrate,
you have no heirship in relation to them whatsoever
until they migrate.
Yet if they ask your help for the sake of religion,
it is incumbent on you to help them,
excepting against a people with whom you have a treaty,
and God watches what you do.

73 As for the faithless, they are allies of one another.
Unless you do the same, there will be strife in the land
and great corruption.

74 Those who have believed, migrated,
and waged *jihād* in the way of God,

وَالَّذِينَ آوَوْا وَنَصَرُوا
and those who gave them shelter and help,
أُولَٰئِكَ هُمُ الْمُؤْمِنُونَ حَقًّا
it is they who are truly faithful.
لَهُم مَّغْفِرَةٌ وَرِزْقٌ كَرِيمٌ ۝
For them shall be forgiveness and a noble provision.
وَالَّذِينَ آمَنُوا مِن بَعْدُ وَهَاجَرُوا
75 Those who believed afterwards,
وَجَاهَدُوا مَعَكُمْ
and migrated and waged *jihād* along with you,
فَأُولَٰئِكَ مِنكُمْ
they belong with you;
وَأُولُو الْأَرْحَامِ
but the blood relatives
بَعْضُهُمْ أَوْلَىٰ بِبَعْضٍ
are more entitled to inherit from one another
فِي كِتَابِ اللَّهِ
in the Book of God.[1]
إِنَّ اللَّهَ بِكُلِّ شَيْءٍ عَلِيمٌ ۝
Indeed, God has knowledge of all things.

سُورَةُ التَّوْبَةِ

9. Repentance[2]

al-Tawbah

بَرَاءَةٌ مِّنَ اللَّهِ 1 This is a declaration of repudiation by God
وَرَسُولِهِ and His Apostle addressed
إِلَى الَّذِينَ عَاهَدتُّم مِّنَ الْمُشْرِكِينَ ۝ to the polytheists with whom you had made a treaty:
فَسِيحُوا فِي الْأَرْضِ أَرْبَعَةَ أَشْهُرٍ 2 Travel unmolested in the land for four months,
وَاعْلَمُوا أَنَّكُمْ غَيْرُ مُعْجِزِي اللَّهِ but know that you cannot frustrate God,
وَأَنَّ اللَّهَ مُخْزِي الْكَافِرِينَ ۝ and that God will disgrace the faithless.
وَأَذَانٌ مِّنَ اللَّهِ وَرَسُولِهِ 3 This is an announcement from God and His Apostle
إِلَى النَّاسِ يَوْمَ الْحَجِّ الْأَكْبَرِ to all the people on the day of the greater *ḥajj*:[3]
أَنَّ اللَّهَ بَرِيءٌ مِّنَ الْمُشْرِكِينَ وَرَسُولُهُ that God and His Apostle repudiate the polytheists:
فَإِن تُبْتُمْ فَهُوَ خَيْرٌ لَّكُمْ If you repent[4] that is better for you;
وَإِن تَوَلَّيْتُمْ but if you turn your backs on God,
فَاعْلَمُوا أَنَّكُمْ غَيْرُ مُعْجِزِي اللَّهِ know that you cannot frustrate God,
وَبَشِّرِ الَّذِينَ كَفَرُوا بِعَذَابٍ أَلِيمٍ ۝ and *inform* the faithless of a painful punishment—
إِلَّا الَّذِينَ عَاهَدتُّم مِّنَ الْمُشْرِكِينَ 4 excluding the polytheists with whom you have made a treaty,

---

[1] Cf. 33:6.
[2] This late Madanī *sūrah* is named after 'repentance,' mentioned in verses 3 & 5.
[3] That is, the tenth of Dhū al-Ḥijjah, the day on which the pilgrims perform some of the major rites of the *ḥajj* in Minā.
[4] That is, abandon idolatry.

ثُمَّ لَمْ يَنقُصُوكُمْ شَيْئًا   and who did not violate any of its terms with you,
وَلَمْ يُظَاهِرُوا عَلَيْكُمْ أَحَدًا   nor backed anyone against you.
فَأَتِمُّوا إِلَيْهِمْ عَهْدَهُمْ إِلَىٰ مُدَّتِهِمْ   So fulfill the treaty with them until the end of its term.
إِنَّ اللَّهَ يُحِبُّ الْمُتَّقِينَ ۝   Indeed, God loves the Godwary.

5 فَإِذَا انسَلَخَ الْأَشْهُرُ الْحُرُمُ   Then, when the sacred months have passed,
فَاقْتُلُوا الْمُشْرِكِينَ حَيْثُ وَجَدتُّمُوهُمْ   kill the polytheists wherever you find them,
وَخُذُوهُمْ وَاحْصُرُوهُمْ   capture them and besiege them,
وَاقْعُدُوا لَهُمْ كُلَّ مَرْصَدٍ   and lie in wait for them at every ambush.
فَإِن تَابُوا وَأَقَامُوا الصَّلَاةَ وَآتَوُا الزَّكَاةَ   But if they repent, maintain the prayer and give the *zakāt*,
فَخَلُّوا سَبِيلَهُمْ   then let them alone.
إِنَّ اللَّهَ غَفُورٌ رَّحِيمٌ ۝   God is indeed all-forgiving, all-merciful.

6 وَإِنْ أَحَدٌ مِّنَ الْمُشْرِكِينَ اسْتَجَارَكَ   If any of the polytheists seeks asylum from *you*,
فَأَجِرْهُ حَتَّىٰ يَسْمَعَ كَلَامَ اللَّهِ   *grant* him asylum until he hears the Word of God.
ثُمَّ أَبْلِغْهُ مَأْمَنَهُ   Then convey him to his place of safety.
ذَٰلِكَ بِأَنَّهُمْ قَوْمٌ لَّا يَعْلَمُونَ ۝   That is because they are a people who do not know.

7 كَيْفَ يَكُونُ لِلْمُشْرِكِينَ عَهْدٌ   How shall the polytheists have any valid treaty
عِندَ اللَّهِ وَعِندَ رَسُولِهِ   with God and His Apostle?!
إِلَّا الَّذِينَ عَاهَدتُّمْ   (Excluding those with whom you made a treaty
عِندَ الْمَسْجِدِ الْحَرَامِ   at the Holy Mosque;
فَمَا اسْتَقَامُوا لَكُمْ   so long as they are steadfast with you,
فَاسْتَقِيمُوا لَهُمْ   be steadfast with them.
إِنَّ اللَّهَ يُحِبُّ الْمُتَّقِينَ ۝   Indeed, God loves the Godwary.)

8 كَيْفَ وَإِن يَظْهَرُوا عَلَيْكُمْ   How? For if they get the better of you,
لَا يَرْقُبُوا فِيكُمْ إِلًّا وَلَا ذِمَّةً   they will observe toward you neither kinship nor covenant.
يُرْضُونَكُم بِأَفْوَاهِهِمْ   They please you with their mouths
وَتَأْبَىٰ قُلُوبُهُمْ   while their hearts spurn you,
وَأَكْثَرُهُمْ فَاسِقُونَ ۝   and most of them are transgressors.

9 اشْتَرَوْا بِآيَاتِ اللَّهِ ثَمَنًا قَلِيلًا   They have sold the signs of God for a paltry gain,
فَصَدُّوا عَن سَبِيلِهِ   and have barred the people from His way.
إِنَّهُمْ سَاءَ مَا كَانُوا يَعْمَلُونَ ۝   Evil indeed is what they have been doing.

10 They observe toward a believer
neither kinship nor covenant,
and it is they who are the transgressors.

11 Yet if they repent
and maintain the prayer and give the *zakāt*,
then they are your brethren in faith.
We elaborate the signs for a people who have knowledge.

12 But if they break their pledges
after their having made a treaty
and revile your religion,
then fight the leaders of unfaith
—indeed they have no commitment to pledges—
maybe they will desist.

13 Will you not make war on a people who broke their pledges
and resolved to expel the Apostle,
and opened hostilities against you initially?
Do you fear them?
But God is worthier of being feared by you,
should you be faithful.

14 Make war on them,
so that God may punish them by your hands
and humiliate them and help you against them,
and heal the hearts of a faithful folk

15 and remove rage from their hearts,
and God turns clemently to whomever He wishes,
and God is all-knowing, all-wise.

16 Do you suppose that you will be let off
while God has not yet ascertained
those of you who wage *jihād*
and those who do not take,

besides God and His Apostle and the faithful,
anyone as their confidant?
God is well aware of what you do.

17 The polytheists may not maintain
   God's mosques
   while they are witness to their own unfaith.
   Their works have failed
   and they shall remain in the Fire.

18 Only those shall maintain God's mosques
   who believe in God and the Last Day,
   and maintain the prayer and give the *zakāt*,
   and fear no one except God.
   They, hopefully, will be among the guided.

19 Do you regard the providing of water to *ḥajj* pilgrims
   and the maintenance of the Holy Mosque
   as similar in worth to someone who has faith in God
       and believes in the Last Day
   and wages *jihād* in the way of God?
   They are not equal with God,
   and God does not guide the wrongdoing lot.

20 Those who have believed and migrated,
   and waged *jihād* in the way of God
       with their possessions and persons
   have a greater rank near God,
   and it is they who are the triumphant.

21 Their Lord gives them the good news of His mercy
       and His pleasure,
   and for them there will be gardens with lasting bliss,

22   to remain in them forever.
   With God indeed is a great reward.

23 O you who have faith!
Do not befriend your fathers and brothers[1]
if they prefer unfaith to faith.
Those of you who befriend them
—it is they who are the wrongdoers.

24 Say, 'If your fathers and your sons,
your brethren, your spouses, and your kinsfolk,
the possessions that you have acquired,
the business you fear may suffer,
and the dwellings you are fond of,
are dearer to you than God and His Apostle
and to waging *jihād* in His way,
then wait until God issues His edict,
and God does not guide the transgressing lot.

25 God has already helped you in many situations,
and on the Day of Ḥunayn,
when your great number impressed you,
but it did not avail you in any way,
and the earth became narrow for you with all its expanse,[2]
whereupon you turned your backs to flee.

26 Then God sent down His composure
upon His Apostle and upon the faithful,
and He sent down hosts you did not see,
and He punished the faithless,
and that is the requital of the faithless.

27 Then God will turn clemently after that
to whomever He wishes.
God is indeed all-forgiving, all-merciful.

28 O you who have faith!

---

[1] Or 'Do not take your fathers and brothers for intimates.'
[2] That is, you were at a complete loss and at the end of your wits.

The polytheists are indeed unclean:
so let them not approach the Holy Mosque
    after this year.
Should you fear poverty,
God will enrich you out of His bounty, if He wishes.
God is indeed all-knowing, all-wise.

29 Fight those who do not have faith in God
    nor believe in the Last Day,
    nor forbid what God and His Apostle have forbidden,
    nor practise the true religion,
    from among those who were given the Book,
    until they pay the tribute out of hand, degraded.

30 The Jews say, 'Ezra is the son of God,'
    and the Christians say, 'Christ is the son of God.'
    That is an opinion that they mouth,
    imitating the opinions of the faithless of former times.
    May God assail them, where do they stray?!

31 They have taken their scribes and their monks
        as lords besides God,
        and also Christ, Mary's son;
    though they were not commanded
        except to worship only the One God,
        there is no god except Him;
        He is far too immaculate
        to have any partners that they ascribe to Him!

32 They desire to put out
        the light of God with their mouths,
        but God is intent on perfecting His light
        though the faithless should be averse.

33 It is He who has sent His Apostle with guidance
and the religion of truth,
that He may make it prevail over all religions,
though the polytheists should be averse.

34 O you who have faith!
Indeed, many of the scribes and monks
wrongfully eat up the people's wealth,
and bar them from the way of God.
Those who treasure up gold and silver,
and do not spend it in the way of God,
inform them of a painful punishment

35 on the day when these shall be heated in hellfire
and therewith branded on their foreheads,
their sides and their backs [and told]:
'This is what you treasured up for yourselves!
So taste what you have treasured!'

36 Indeed, the number of months with God
is twelve months in God's Book,
the day when He created the heavens and the earth.
Of these, four are sacred.
That is the upright religion.
So do not wrong yourselves during them.[1]
Fight all the polytheists,
just as they fight you together,
and know that God is with the Godwary.

37 *Nasī*[2] is indeed an increase in unfaith,
whereby the faithless are led further astray.
They allow it in one year and forbid it another year,
so as to fit in with the number

---

[1] The sacred months are Muḥarram, Rajab, Dhū al-Qaʻdah and Dhū al-Ḥijjah.
[2] A pre-Islamic practice of intercalation. Its exact character is somewhat uncertain.

which God has made inviolable, مَا حَرَّمَ اللَّهُ
thus permitting what God has forbidden. فَيُحِلُّوا مَا حَرَّمَ اللَّهُ
Their evil deeds appear to them as decorous, زُيِّنَ لَهُمْ سُوءُ أَعْمَالِهِمْ
and God does not guide the faithless lot. وَاللَّهُ لَا يَهْدِي الْقَوْمَ الْكَافِرِينَ ۝

38 O you who have faith! What is the matter with you يَا أَيُّهَا الَّذِينَ آمَنُوا مَا لَكُمْ
that when you are told: 'Go forth in the way of God,' إِذَا قِيلَ لَكُمُ انْفِرُوا فِي سَبِيلِ اللَّهِ
you sink heavily to the ground? اثَّاقَلْتُمْ إِلَى الْأَرْضِ
Are you pleased with the life of this world أَرَضِيتُمْ بِالْحَيَاةِ الدُّنْيَا
instead of the Hereafter? مِنَ الْآخِرَةِ
But the wares of the life of this world فَمَا مَتَاعُ الْحَيَاةِ الدُّنْيَا
are insignificant compared with the Hereafter. فِي الْآخِرَةِ إِلَّا قَلِيلٌ ۝

39 If you do not go forth, إِلَّا تَنْفِرُوا
He will punish you with a painful punishment يُعَذِّبْكُمْ عَذَابًا أَلِيمًا
and replace you with another people, وَيَسْتَبْدِلْ قَوْمًا غَيْرَكُمْ
and you will not hurt Him in the least, وَلَا تَضُرُّوهُ شَيْئًا
and God has power over all things. وَاللَّهُ عَلَىٰ كُلِّ شَيْءٍ قَدِيرٌ ۝

40 If you do not help him,[1] إِلَّا تَنْصُرُوهُ
then God has certainly helped him فَقَدْ نَصَرَهُ اللَّهُ
when the faithless expelled him as one of two [refugees], إِذْ أَخْرَجَهُ الَّذِينَ كَفَرُوا ثَانِيَ اثْنَيْنِ
when the two of them were in the cave إِذْ هُمَا فِي الْغَارِ
and he said to his companion, إِذْ يَقُولُ لِصَاحِبِهِ
'Do not grieve; God is indeed with us.' لَا تَحْزَنْ إِنَّ اللَّهَ مَعَنَا
Then God sent down His composure upon him فَأَنْزَلَ اللَّهُ سَكِينَتَهُ عَلَيْهِ
and strengthened him with hosts you did not see, وَأَيَّدَهُ بِجُنُودٍ لَمْ تَرَوْهَا
and He made the word of the faithless the lowest; وَجَعَلَ كَلِمَةَ الَّذِينَ كَفَرُوا السُّفْلَىٰ
and the word of God is the highest; وَكَلِمَةُ اللَّهِ هِيَ الْعُلْيَا
and God is all-mighty, all-wise. وَاللَّهُ عَزِيزٌ حَكِيمٌ ۝

41 Go forth, whether armed lightly or heavily, انْفِرُوا خِفَافًا وَثِقَالًا

---

[1] That is, the Prophet (ṣ).

and wage *jihād* with your possessions and persons
in the way of God.
That is better for you, should you know.

42 Were it an accessible gain or a short journey,
they would have surely followed *you*;
but the distance seemed too far to them.
Yet they will swear by God:
'If we could, we would have surely gone forth with you.'
They merely destroy themselves,
and God knows that they are indeed liars.

43 May God excuse *you*!
Why did *you* grant them leave [to stay behind]
before those who told the truth were evident to *you*
and *you* had ascertained the liars?

44 Those who believe in God
and the Last Day do not ask *your* leave [exempting them]
from waging *jihād* with their possessions and their persons,
and God knows best the Godwary.

45 Only those seek a leave of exemption from *you*
who do not believe in God and the Last Day
and whose hearts are in doubt,
so they waver in their doubt.

46 Had they desired to go forth,
they would have surely made some preparations for it;
but God was averse to arouse them,
so He held them back, and it was said to them,
'Be seated with those who sit back.'

47 Had they gone forth with you,
they would have only added to your troubles,
and they would have spread rumours in your midst,

يَبْغُونَكُمُ الْفِتْنَةَ seeking to cause sedition among you.
وَفِيكُمْ سَمَّاعُونَ لَهُمْ ۗ They have some spies among you,
وَاللَّهُ عَلِيمٌ بِالظَّالِمِينَ ۝ and God knows best the wrongdoers.
لَقَدِ ابْتَغَوُا الْفِتْنَةَ مِن قَبْلُ 48 They certainly sought to cause sedition earlier
وَقَلَّبُوا لَكَ الْأُمُورَ and upset the matters for you,
حَتَّىٰ جَاءَ الْحَقُّ وَظَهَرَ أَمْرُ اللَّهِ until the truth came and God's command prevailed,
وَهُمْ كَارِهُونَ ۝ much as they were averse.
وَمِنْهُم مَّن يَقُولُ 49 Among them there are some who say,
ائْذَن لِّي وَلَا تَفْتِنِّي ۚ 'Give me leave, and do not put me to temptation.'[1]
أَلَا فِي الْفِتْنَةِ سَقَطُوا ۗ Behold, they have already fallen into temptation[2]
وَإِنَّ جَهَنَّمَ لَمُحِيطَةٌ بِالْكَافِرِينَ ۝ and indeed hell besieges the faithless.
إِن تُصِبْكَ حَسَنَةٌ تَسُؤْهُمْ ۖ 50 If some good should befall you, it upsets them;
وَإِن تُصِبْكَ مُصِيبَةٌ but if an adversity befalls you,
يَقُولُوا قَدْ أَخَذْنَا أَمْرَنَا مِن قَبْلُ they say, 'We had already taken our precautions in advance,'
وَيَتَوَلَّوا وَّهُمْ فَرِحُونَ ۝ and they go away rejoicing.
قُل لَّن يُصِيبَنَا 51 Say, 'Nothing will befall us
إِلَّا مَا كَتَبَ اللَّهُ لَنَا except what God has ordained for us.
هُوَ مَوْلَانَا ۚ He is our Master,
وَعَلَى اللَّهِ فَلْيَتَوَكَّلِ الْمُؤْمِنُونَ ۝ and in God alone let all the faithful put their trust.'
قُلْ هَلْ تَرَبَّصُونَ بِنَا 52 Say, 'Do you await anything to befall us
إِلَّا إِحْدَى الْحُسْنَيَيْنِ ۖ except one of the two excellent things?[3]
وَنَحْنُ نَتَرَبَّصُ بِكُمْ أَن يُصِيبَكُمُ اللَّهُ But we await that God will visit on you
بِعَذَابٍ مِّنْ عِندِهِ أَوْ بِأَيْدِينَا ۖ a punishment, from Him, or by our hands.
فَتَرَبَّصُوا إِنَّا مَعَكُم مُّتَرَبِّصُونَ ۝ So wait! We too are waiting along with you.'
قُلْ أَنفِقُوا طَوْعًا أَوْ كَرْهًا 53 Say, 'Spend willingly or unwillingly,
لَّن يُتَقَبَّلَ مِنكُمْ ۖ it shall never be accepted from you;
إِنَّكُمْ كُنتُمْ قَوْمًا فَاسِقِينَ ۝ for you are indeed a transgressing lot.'
وَمَا مَنَعَهُمْ أَن تُقْبَلَ مِنْهُمْ نَفَقَاتُهُمْ 54 Nothing stops their charities from being accepted

---

[1] Or 'do not push me into sinfulness (or unfaith),' or 'do not put me in a predicament.' Cf. Ṭabarī and Ṭūsī.
[2] Or 'sinfulness (or unfaith),' or 'a predicament,' based on how the word '*fitnah*' is interpreted in the preceding sentence.
[3] That is, victory or martyrdom.

except that they have no faith in God and His Apostle
and do not perform the prayer except lazily,
and do not spend but reluctantly.

55 So let not their wealth and children impress you:
God only desires to punish them with these
  in the life of this world,
and that their souls may depart while they are faithless.

56 They swear by God that they belong with you,[1]
but they do not belong with you.
Rather they are a frightened lot.

57 If they could find a refuge,
  a hideout or a hole to creep into,
they would turn to it in frantic haste.

58 There are some of them who blame you
  regarding the distribution of the charities:
if they are given from them, they are pleased,
but if they are not given from them,
  behold, they are displeased.

59 [It would have been better] if they had been pleased
with what God and His Apostle gave them,
  and had said, 'God is sufficient for us;
God and His Apostle will give us out of His grace.
Indeed, we beseech God.'

60 The charities are only for the poor and the needy,
  and those employed to collect them,
and those whose hearts are to be reconciled,
and for the freedom of the slaves and the debtors,
and to be spent in the way of God, and for the traveler.
This is an ordinance from God,

---

[1] That is, with the faithful.

and God is all-knowing, all-wise.

61 Among them are those who torment the Prophet,
and say, 'He is an ear.'[1]
Say, 'An ear that is good for you.
He has faith in God and trusts the faithful,
and is a mercy for those of you who have faith.'
As for those who torment the Apostle of God,
there is a painful punishment for them.

62 They swear to you by God to please you;
but God and His Apostle are worthier
that they should please Him, should they be faithful.

63 Do they not know that whoever opposes God
and His Apostle,
there awaits him the Fire of hell, to remain in it?
That is a great disgrace.

64 The hypocrites are apprehensive
lest a *sūrah* should be sent down against them,
informing them about what is in their hearts.
Say, 'Go on deriding.
God will indeed bring out what you are apprehensive of.'

65 If you question them [regarding their conduct],
they will surely say,
'We were just gossiping and amusing ourselves.'
Say,
'Were you deriding God, His signs, and His apostles?

66 Do not make excuses.
You have disbelieved after your faith.'
If We do forgive a group among you,
We will punish another group,

---

[1] That is, easily persuadable, unquestioning and naive.

for they have been guilty.

67 The hypocrites, men and women, are all alike:
they bid what is wrong and forbid what is right,
and are tight-fisted.[1]
They have forgotten God, so He has forgotten them.
The hypocrites are indeed the transgressors.

68 God has promised the hypocrites, men and women,
and the faithless,
the Fire of hell, to remain in it.
That suffices them.
God has cursed them,
and there is a lasting punishment for them.

69 [Hypocrites! Your case is] similar to those who were
before you,
who were more powerful than you
and more abounding in wealth and children:
they enjoyed their share [of worldly existence];
you too enjoy your share,
just like those who were before you enjoyed their share,
and you have gossiped impiously as they gossiped.
They are the ones whose works have failed
in this world and the Hereafter,
and it is they who are the losers.

70 Has there not come to them
the account of those who were before them
—the people of Noah, 'Ād, and Thamūd,
and the people of Abraham, the inhabitants of Midian,
and the towns that were overturned?[2]
Their apostles brought them manifest proofs.

---

[1] That is, they are reluctant to spend in the way of God.
[2] That is, the towns of the people of Lot. Cf. **53**:53; **69**:9.

So it was not God who wronged them, فَمَا كَانَ اللَّهُ لِيَظْلِمَهُمْ
but it was they who used to wrong themselves. وَلَـٰكِن كَانُوا أَنفُسَهُمْ يَظْلِمُونَ ۝

71 But the faithful, men and women, وَالْمُؤْمِنُونَ وَالْمُؤْمِنَاتُ
    are friends of one another: بَعْضُهُمْ أَوْلِيَاءُ بَعْضٍ ۚ
they bid what is right and forbid what is wrong يَأْمُرُونَ بِالْمَعْرُوفِ وَيَنْهَوْنَ عَنِ الْمُنكَرِ
    and maintain the prayer, give the *zakāt*, وَيُقِيمُونَ الصَّلَاةَ وَيُؤْتُونَ الزَّكَاةَ
    and obey God and His Apostle. وَيُطِيعُونَ اللَّهَ وَرَسُولَهُ ۚ
It is they to whom God will soon grant His mercy. أُولَـٰئِكَ سَيَرْحَمُهُمُ اللَّهُ ۗ
God is indeed all-mighty, all-wise. إِنَّ اللَّهَ عَزِيزٌ حَكِيمٌ ۝

72 God has promised the faithful, men and women, وَعَدَ اللَّهُ الْمُؤْمِنِينَ وَالْمُؤْمِنَاتِ
    gardens with streams running in them, جَنَّاتٍ تَجْرِي مِن تَحْتِهَا الْأَنْهَارُ
    to remain in them, خَالِدِينَ فِيهَا
and good dwellings in the Gardens of Eden.[1] وَمَسَاكِنَ طَيِّبَةً فِي جَنَّاتِ عَدْنٍ ۚ
Yet God's pleasure is greater [than all these]; وَرِضْوَانٌ مِّنَ اللَّهِ أَكْبَرُ ۚ
    that is the great success. ذَٰلِكَ هُوَ الْفَوْزُ الْعَظِيمُ ۝

73 O Prophet! يَا أَيُّهَا النَّبِيُّ
Wage jihād against the faithless and the hypocrites, جَاهِدِ الْكُفَّارَ وَالْمُنَافِقِينَ
    and *be* severe with them. وَاغْلُظْ عَلَيْهِمْ ۚ
Their refuge shall be hell, and it is an evil destination. وَمَأْوَاهُمْ جَهَنَّمُ ۖ وَبِئْسَ الْمَصِيرُ ۝

74 They swear by God that they did not say it. يَحْلِفُونَ بِاللَّهِ مَا قَالُوا
But they certainly did utter the word of unfaith وَلَقَدْ قَالُوا كَلِمَةَ الْكُفْرِ
    and renounced faith after their *islām*. وَكَفَرُوا بَعْدَ إِسْلَامِهِمْ
They contemplated what they could not achieve, وَهَمُّوا بِمَا لَمْ يَنَالُوا ۚ
    and they were vindictive only وَمَا نَقَمُوا إِلَّا
        because God and His Apostle had enriched them أَنْ أَغْنَاهُمُ اللَّهُ وَرَسُولُهُ
            out of His grace. مِن فَضْلِهِ ۚ
Yet if they repent, it will be better for them; فَإِن يَتُوبُوا يَكُ خَيْرًا لَّهُمْ ۖ
    but if they turn away, وَإِن يَتَوَلَّوْا
God will punish them with a painful punishment يُعَذِّبْهُمُ اللَّهُ عَذَابًا أَلِيمًا

---

[1] Or 'eternal [or everlasting] gardens.' Cf. **13**:23; **16**:31; **18**:31; **19**:61; **20**:76; **35**:33; **38**:50; **40**:8; **61**:12; **98**:8.

فِى الدُّنْيَا وَالْآخِرَةِ ۖ in this world and the Hereafter,
وَمَا لَهُمْ فِى الْأَرْضِ مِنْ وَلِىٍّ وَلَا نَصِيرٍ ۝ and they will not find in this land any friend or helper.

وَمِنْهُمْ مَنْ عَاهَدَ اللَّهَ 75 Among them are those who made a pledge with God:
لَئِنْ آتَانَا مِنْ فَضْلِهِ 'If He gives us out of His bounty,
لَنَصَّدَّقَنَّ we will surely give the *zakāt*
وَلَنَكُونَنَّ مِنَ الصَّالِحِينَ ۝ and we will be among the righteous.'

فَلَمَّا آتَاهُمْ مِنْ فَضْلِهِ 76 But when He gave them out of His bounty,
بَخِلُوا بِهِ وَتَوَلَّوْا وَهُمْ مُعْرِضُونَ ۝ they begrudged it and turned away, being disregardful.

فَأَعْقَبَهُمْ نِفَاقًا فِى قُلُوبِهِمْ 77 So He caused hypocrisy to ensue in their hearts
إِلَىٰ يَوْمِ يَلْقَوْنَهُ until the day they will encounter Him,
بِمَا أَخْلَفُوا اللَّهَ because of their going back
مَا وَعَدُوهُ on what they had promised God
وَبِمَا كَانُوا يَكْذِبُونَ ۝ and because of the lies they used to tell.

أَلَمْ يَعْلَمُوا أَنَّ اللَّهَ يَعْلَمُ 78 Do they not know that God knows
سِرَّهُمْ وَنَجْوَاهُمْ their secret thoughts and hears their secret talks
وَأَنَّ اللَّهَ عَلَّامُ الْغُيُوبِ ۝ and that God is knower of all that is Unseen?

الَّذِينَ يَلْمِزُونَ الْمُطَّوِّعِينَ 79 Those who blame the voluntary donors
مِنَ الْمُؤْمِنِينَ from among the faithful
فِى الصَّدَقَاتِ concerning the charities
وَالَّذِينَ لَا يَجِدُونَ — and as for those who do not find
إِلَّا جُهْدَهُمْ anything except what their means permit,
فَيَسْخَرُونَ مِنْهُمْ they ridicule them—
سَخِرَ اللَّهُ مِنْهُمْ God will put them to ridicule,
وَلَهُمْ عَذَابٌ أَلِيمٌ ۝ and there is a painful punishment for them.

اسْتَغْفِرْ لَهُمْ 80 Whether you plead forgiveness for them
أَوْ لَا تَسْتَغْفِرْ لَهُمْ or do not plead forgiveness for them,
إِنْ تَسْتَغْفِرْ لَهُمْ سَبْعِينَ مَرَّةً even if you plead forgiveness for them seventy times,
فَلَنْ يَغْفِرَ اللَّهُ لَهُمْ ۚ God will never forgive them
ذَٰلِكَ بِأَنَّهُمْ كَفَرُوا بِاللَّهِ وَرَسُولِهِ ۗ because they defied God and His Apostle;
وَاللَّهُ لَا يَهْدِى الْقَوْمَ الْفَاسِقِينَ ۝ and God does not guide the transgressing lot.

81 Those who were left behind[1] rejoiced for sitting back against [the command of] the Apostle of God,[2]
and were reluctant to wage *jihād*
with their possessions and persons in the way of God,
and they said, 'Do not go forth in this heat.'
Say, The fire of hell is severer in heat,
should they understand.

82 So let them laugh a little; much will they weep
as a requital for what they used to perpetrate.

83 If God brings *you* back [from the battlefront]
   to a group of them
   and they seek *your* permission to go forth,
say, 'You shall never go forth with me,
and you shall not fight with me against any enemy.
You were indeed pleased to sit back the first time,
so sit back with those who stay behind.'

84 And never *pray* over any of them when he dies,
   nor *stand* at his graveside.
They indeed defied God and His Apostle
   and died as transgressors.

85 Let not their possessions or their children impress *you.*
God only desires to punish them with these in this world,
and that their souls may depart while they are faithless.

86 When a *sūrah* is sent down declaring: 'Have faith in God,
   and wage *jihād* along with His Apostle,
the affluent among them ask *you* for leave,
and say, 'Let us remain with those who sit back.'

87 They are pleased to be with those who stay back,[3]

---

[1] That is, those who refrained from participating in *jihād* with the Prophet (ṣ). Cf. verse 46.
[2] Or 'for their staying away from [the expedition of] the Apostle of God.'
[3] That is, along with women and children, the invalid and the decrepit.

and their hearts have been sealed.
So they do not understand.

88 But the Apostle and the faithful who are with him
wage *jihād* with their possessions and persons,
and to such belong all the blessings,
and it is they who are the felicitous.

89 God has prepared for them gardens
with streams running in them, to remain in them.
That is the great success.

90 Some of the Bedouins who sought to be excused came
so that they may be granted leave to stay back;
while those who lied to God and His Apostle sat back.
Soon there will visit the faithless among them
a painful punishment.

91 There is no blame on the weak,
nor on the sick, nor on those
who do not find anything to spend,
so long as they are sincere to God and His Apostle.
There is no cause for blaming the virtuous,
and God is all-forgiving, all-merciful.

92 Nor is there any blame on those to whom,
when they came to you to provide them with a mount,
you said, 'I do not find any mount for you,'
and they turned back, their eyes flowing with tears,
grieved because they did not find any means to spend.

[PART 11]

93 The blame lies only on those who ask *your* leave
[to stay behind] though they are well-off.
They are pleased to be with those who stay back;
God has set a seal on their hearts,

so they do not know [the outcome of their conduct].

94 They will offer you excuses when you return to them.
Say, 'Do not make excuses; we will never believe you.
God has informed us of your state of affairs.
God and His Apostle will observe your conduct,
then you will be returned
to the Knower of the sensible and the Unseen,
and He will inform you concerning what you used to do.'

95 They will swear to you by God, when you return to them,
so that you may leave them alone.
So leave them alone. They are indeed filth,
and their refuge shall be hell,
a requital for what they used to perpetrate.

96 They swear to you that you may be reconciled to them.
But even if you are reconciled to them
God will not be reconciled to the transgressing lot.

97 The Bedouins are more obdurate in unfaith and hypocrisy,
and more apt to be ignorant of the precepts
that God has sent down to His Apostle,
and God is all-knowing, all-wise.

98 Among the Bedouins are those who regard
what they spend as a loss,
and they watch for a reversal of your fortunes.
Theirs shall be an adverse turn of fortune,
and God is all-hearing, all-knowing.

99 Yet among the Bedouins are also
those who believe in God and the Last Day,
and regard what they spend
as a means of attaining nearness to God
and the blessings of the Apostle.

أَلَا إِنَّهَا قُرْبَةٌ لَهُمْ
Now, it shall indeed bring them nearness,
سَيُدْخِلُهُمُ اللَّهُ فِي رَحْمَتِهِ
and God will admit them into His mercy.
إِنَّ اللَّهَ غَفُورٌ رَحِيمٌ ۝
God is indeed all-forgiving, all-merciful.

100 وَالسَّابِقُونَ الْأَوَّلُونَ
100 The early vanguard
مِنَ الْمُهَاجِرِينَ وَالْأَنْصَارِ
of the Emigrants and the Helpers
وَالَّذِينَ اتَّبَعُوهُم بِإِحْسَانٍ
and those who followed them in virtue
رَضِيَ اللَّهُ عَنْهُمْ وَرَضُوا عَنْهُ
—God is pleased with them and they are pleased with Him,
وَأَعَدَّ لَهُمْ جَنَّاتٍ
and He has prepared for them gardens
تَجْرِي تَحْتَهَا الْأَنْهَارُ خَالِدِينَ فِيهَا أَبَدًا
with streams running in them, to remain in them forever.
ذَٰلِكَ الْفَوْزُ الْعَظِيمُ ۝
That is the great success.

101 وَمِمَّنْ حَوْلَكُم مِّنَ الْأَعْرَابِ مُنَافِقُونَ
101 There are hypocrites among the Bedouins around you
وَمِنْ أَهْلِ الْمَدِينَةِ مَرَدُوا عَلَى النِّفَاقِ
and among the people of Madīnah, steeped in hypocrisy.
لَا تَعْلَمُهُمْ نَحْنُ نَعْلَمُهُمْ
You do not know them; We know them,
سَنُعَذِّبُهُم مَّرَّتَيْنِ
and We will punish them twice,
ثُمَّ يُرَدُّونَ إِلَىٰ عَذَابٍ عَظِيمٍ ۝
then they shall be consigned to a great punishment.

102 وَآخَرُونَ اعْتَرَفُوا بِذُنُوبِهِمْ
102 There are others who have confessed to their sins,
خَلَطُوا عَمَلًا صَالِحًا وَآخَرَ سَيِّئًا
having mixed up righteous conduct with other that was evil.
عَسَى اللَّهُ أَن يَتُوبَ عَلَيْهِمْ
Maybe God will accept their repentance.
إِنَّ اللَّهَ غَفُورٌ رَحِيمٌ ۝
God is indeed all-forgiving, all-merciful.

103 خُذْ مِنْ أَمْوَالِهِمْ صَدَقَةً
103 *Take* charity from their possessions
تُطَهِّرُهُمْ وَتُزَكِّيهِم بِهَا وَصَلِّ عَلَيْهِمْ
to cleanse them and purify them thereby, and bless them.
إِنَّ صَلَاتَكَ سَكَنٌ لَّهُمْ
Your blessing is indeed a comfort to them,
وَاللَّهُ سَمِيعٌ عَلِيمٌ ۝
and God is all-hearing, all-knowing.

104 أَلَمْ يَعْلَمُوا
104 Do they not know
أَنَّ اللَّهَ هُوَ يَقْبَلُ التَّوْبَةَ عَنْ عِبَادِهِ
that it is God who accepts the repentance of His servants
وَيَأْخُذُ الصَّدَقَاتِ
and receives the charities,
وَأَنَّ اللَّهَ هُوَ التَّوَّابُ الرَّحِيمُ ۝
and that it is God who is the All-clement, the All-merciful?

105 وَقُلِ اعْمَلُوا فَسَيَرَى اللَّهُ عَمَلَكُمْ
105 *Say*, 'Go on working: God will see your conduct,
وَرَسُولُهُ وَالْمُؤْمِنُونَ
and His Apostle and the faithful as well,

وَسَتُرَدُّونَ	and you will be returned
إِلَىٰ عَالِمِ الْغَيْبِ وَالشَّهَادَةِ	to the Knower of the sensible and the Unseen,
فَيُنَبِّئُكُم بِمَا كُنتُمْ تَعْمَلُونَ ۝	and He will inform you concerning what you used to do.'
وَآخَرُونَ مُرْجَوْنَ لِأَمْرِ اللَّهِ	106 There are others waiting God's edict:
إِمَّا يُعَذِّبُهُمْ وَإِمَّا يَتُوبُ عَلَيْهِمْ	either He will punish them, or turn to them clemently,
وَاللَّهُ عَلِيمٌ حَكِيمٌ ۝	and God is all-knowing, all-wise.
وَالَّذِينَ اتَّخَذُوا مَسْجِدًا ضِرَارًا	107 As for those who took to a mosque for sabotage
وَكُفْرًا وَتَفْرِيقًا بَيْنَ الْمُؤْمِنِينَ	and defiance, and to cause division among the faithful,
وَإِرْصَادًا	and for the purpose of ambush to be used
لِّمَنْ حَارَبَ اللَّهَ وَرَسُولَهُ مِن قَبْلُ	by those who have fought God and His Apostle before
وَلَيَحْلِفُنَّ إِنْ أَرَدْنَا إِلَّا الْحُسْنَىٰ	—they will surely swear, 'We desired nothing but good,'
وَاللَّهُ يَشْهَدُ إِنَّهُمْ لَكَاذِبُونَ ۝	and God bears witness that they are indeed liars.
لَا تَقُمْ فِيهِ أَبَدًا	108 *Do not stand* in it ever!
لَّمَسْجِدٌ أُسِّسَ عَلَى التَّقْوَىٰ	A mosque founded on Godwariness
مِنْ أَوَّلِ يَوْمٍ	from the very first day
أَحَقُّ أَن تَقُومَ فِيهِ	is worthier that you stand in it for prayer.
فِيهِ رِجَالٌ يُحِبُّونَ أَن يَتَطَهَّرُوا	Therein are men who love to keep pure,
وَاللَّهُ يُحِبُّ الْمُطَّهِّرِينَ ۝	and God loves those who keep pure.
أَفَمَنْ أَسَّسَ بُنْيَانَهُ	109 Is he who founds his building
عَلَىٰ تَقْوَىٰ مِنَ اللَّهِ وَرِضْوَانٍ	on Godwariness and the pursuit of God's pleasure
خَيْرٌ أَم مَّنْ أَسَّسَ بُنْيَانَهُ	better-off or someone who founds his building
عَلَىٰ شَفَا جُرُفٍ هَارٍ	on the brink of a collapsing bank
فَانْهَارَ بِهِ فِي نَارِ جَهَنَّمَ	which collapses with him into the fire of hell?
وَاللَّهُ لَا يَهْدِي الْقَوْمَ الظَّالِمِينَ ۝	God does not guide the wrongdoing lot.
لَا يَزَالُ بُنْيَانُهُمُ الَّذِي بَنَوْا	110 The building they have built will never cease
رِيبَةً فِي قُلُوبِهِمْ	to be a source of disquiet in their hearts
إِلَّا أَن تَقَطَّعَ قُلُوبُهُمْ	until their hearts are cut into pieces,
وَاللَّهُ عَلِيمٌ حَكِيمٌ ۝	and God is all-knowing, all-wise.
إِنَّ اللَّهَ اشْتَرَىٰ مِنَ الْمُؤْمِنِينَ	111 Indeed, God has bought from the faithful

their souls and their possessions
for paradise to be theirs:
they fight in the way of God,
kill and are killed.
A promise binding upon Him
in the Torah and the Evangel and the Qur'ān.
And who is truer to his promise than God?
So rejoice in the bargain you have made with Him,
and that is the great success.

112 [The faithful are] penitent, devout,
celebrators of God's praise, wayfarers,[1] who bow
and prostrate in prayer,
bid what is right
and forbid what is wrong,
and keep God's bounds
—and *give* good news to the faithful.

113 The Prophet and the faithful may not
plead for the forgiveness of the polytheists,
even if they should be their relatives,
after it has become clear to them
that they will be the inmates of hell.

114 Abraham's pleading forgiveness for his father
was only to fulfill a promise he had made him.[2]
So when it became clear to him
that he was an enemy of God,
he repudiated him.
Indeed, Abraham was most plaintive and forbearing.

---

[1] Or 'those who fast.'
[2] Cf. **19**:47, **60**:4.

115 God does not lead any people astray
   after He has guided them, until He has made clear for them
   what they should beware of.
   Indeed, God has knowledge of all things.

116 Indeed, to God belongs the kingdom of the heavens
   and the earth. He gives life and brings death.
   And besides God you do not have
   any friend or helper.

117 Certainly God turned clemently to the Prophet
   and the Emigrants and the Helpers,
   who followed him in the hour of difficulty,
   after the hearts of a part of them were about to swerve.
   Then He turned clemently to them
   —indeed He is most kind and merciful to them—

118 and to the three who were left behind.
   When the land became narrow for them
   with all its expanse,
   and their own souls weighed heavily on them,[1]
   and they knew that there was no refuge from God
   except in Him,
   then He turned clemently toward them
   so that they might be penitent.
   Indeed, God is the All-clement, the All-merciful.

119 O you who have faith!
   Be wary of God, and be with the Truthful.

120 It is not fitting for the people of Madīnah
   and the Bedouins around them

---

[1] That is, they were at a complete loss and were oppressed by a feeling of guilt.

to hang back behind the Apostle of God[1]
and prefer their own lives to his life.
That is because they neither experience any thirst,
nor fatigue, nor hunger, in the way of God,
nor do they tread any ground enraging the faithless,
nor do they gain any ground against an enemy
but a righteous deed is written for them on its account.
Indeed, God does not waste the reward of the virtuous.

121 And neither do they incur any expense, big or small,
nor do they cross any valley,
but it is written to their account,
so that God may reward them
by the best of what they used to do.

122 Yet it is not for the faithful to go forth en masse.[2]
But why should not there go forth
a group from each of their sections
to become learned in religion and to warn their people
when they return to them,
so that they may beware?

123 O you who have faith!
Fight the faithless who are in your vicinity,
and let them find severity in you,
and know that God is with the Godwary.

124 Whenever a *sūrah* is sent down,
there are some of them[3] who say,
'Which of you did it increase in faith?'
As for those who have faith, it increases them in faith,

---

[1] That is, by failing to accompany the Apostle of God during his campaign.
[2] That is, it is not feasible, or reasonable, for all the faithful to set out for Madīnah, the Prophet's city, for the study of Islamic doctrines and laws.
[3] That is, the hypocrites.

and they rejoice.
125 But as for those in whose heart is a sickness,
it only adds defilement to their defilement,
and they die while they are faithless.
126 Do they not see that they
are tried once or twice every year?
Yet they neither repent, nor do they take admonition.
127 Whenever a *sūrah* is sent down,
they look at one another:
'Is anybody observing you?'
Then they slip away.
God has turned their hearts away from the truth
for they are a people who do not understand.
128 There has certainly come to you an apostle
from among yourselves.
Grievous to him is your distress;
he has deep concern for you
and is most kind and merciful to the faithful.
129 But if they turn their backs on *you*,
say, 'God is sufficient for me.
There is no god except Him.
In Him alone I have put my trust
and He is the Lord of the Great Throne.'

10. JONAH[1]
Yūnus

In the Name of God,
the All-beneficent, the All-merciful.

1 *Alif, Lām, Rā.*

---

[1] 'Yūnus' (Jonah) is the prophet whose account appears in this Makkī *sūrah*.

These are the signs of the Wise[1] Book.
2 Does it seem odd to these people
that We have revealed to a man from among themselves,
declaring, 'Warn mankind
 and give good news to the faithful
that they are in good standing with their Lord'?
The faithless say, 'This is indeed a plain magician.'
3 Your Lord is indeed God, who created the heavens
 and the earth in six days,
and then settled on the Throne, directing the command.[2]
There is no intercessor, except after His leave.
That is God, your Lord! So worship Him.
Will you not then take admonition?
4 To Him will be the return of you all;
that is God's true promise.
Indeed, He originates the creation, then He will bring it back
 so that He may reward those who have faith
 and do righteous deeds with justice.
As for the faithless, they shall have boiling water for drink,
 and a painful punishment
because of what they used to deny.
5 It is He who made the sun a radiance
 and the moon a light,
 and ordained its phases
that you might know the number of years
 and the calculation of time.
God did not create all that except with consummate wisdom.
He elaborates the signs for a people who have knowledge.
6 Indeed, in the alternation of night and day,

---

[1] Or 'Definitive.'
[2] Cf. **13:2**; **32:5**.

وَمَا خَلَقَ اللَّهُ فِي السَّمَاوَاتِ وَالْأَرْضِ
لَآيَاتٍ لِقَوْمٍ يَتَّقُونَ ۝
and whatever God has created in the heavens and the earth,
there are surely signs for a people who are Godwary.

7 إِنَّ الَّذِينَ لَا يَرْجُونَ لِقَاءَنَا
وَرَضُوا بِالْحَيَاةِ الدُّنْيَا
وَاطْمَأَنُّوا بِهَا
وَالَّذِينَ هُمْ عَنْ آيَاتِنَا غَافِلُونَ ۝

7 Indeed, those who do not expect to encounter Us
and who are pleased with the life of this world
and satisfied with it,
and those who are oblivious of Our signs

8 أُولَٰئِكَ مَأْوَاهُمُ النَّارُ
بِمَا كَانُوا يَكْسِبُونَ ۝

—it is they whose refuge shall be the Fire
because of what they used to do.

9 إِنَّ الَّذِينَ آمَنُوا وَعَمِلُوا الصَّالِحَاتِ
يَهْدِيهِمْ رَبُّهُمْ بِإِيمَانِهِمْ
تَجْرِي مِنْ تَحْتِهِمُ الْأَنْهَارُ
فِي جَنَّاتِ النَّعِيمِ ۝

9 Indeed, those who have faith and do righteous deeds,
their Lord guides them by the means of their faith.
Streams will run for them
in gardens of bliss.

10 دَعْوَاهُمْ فِيهَا سُبْحَانَكَ اللَّهُمَّ
وَتَحِيَّتُهُمْ فِيهَا سَلَامٌ
وَآخِرُ دَعْوَاهُمْ أَنِ الْحَمْدُ لِلَّهِ
رَبِّ الْعَالَمِينَ ۝

10 Their call therein will be, 'O God! Immaculate are You!'
and their greeting therein will be, 'Peace!'
and their concluding call, 'All praise belongs to God,
the Lord of all the worlds.'

11 وَلَوْ يُعَجِّلُ اللَّهُ لِلنَّاسِ الشَّرَّ
اسْتِعْجَالَهُمْ بِالْخَيْرِ
لَقُضِيَ إِلَيْهِمْ أَجَلُهُمْ
فَنَذَرُ الَّذِينَ لَا يَرْجُونَ لِقَاءَنَا
فِي طُغْيَانِهِمْ يَعْمَهُونَ ۝

11 Were God to hasten ill[1] for mankind
with their haste for good,
their term would have been over.
But We leave those who do not expect to encounter Us
bewildered in their rebellion.

12 وَإِذَا مَسَّ الْإِنْسَانَ الضُّرُّ
دَعَانَا لِجَنْبِهِ أَوْ قَاعِدًا أَوْ قَائِمًا
فَلَمَّا كَشَفْنَا عَنْهُ ضُرَّهُ
مَرَّ كَأَنْ لَمْ يَدْعُنَا
إِلَىٰ ضُرٍّ مَسَّهُ
كَذَٰلِكَ زُيِّنَ لِلْمُسْرِفِينَ
مَا كَانُوا يَعْمَلُونَ ۝

12 When distress befalls man
he supplicates Us, lying on his side, sitting, or standing;
but when We remove his distress,
he passes on as if he had never supplicated Us
concerning the distress that had befallen him.
To the transgressors is thus presented as decorous
what they have been doing.

13 وَلَقَدْ أَهْلَكْنَا الْقُرُونَ

13 Certainly We destroyed the generations

---

[1] That is, punishment.

that have passed before you
when they perpetrated wrongs:
their apostles brought them manifest proofs,
but they would not have faith.
Thus do We requite the guilty lot.

14 Then We made you successors on the earth
    after them
    so that We may observe how you will act.

15 When Our manifest signs are recited to them,
    those who do not expect to encounter Us say,
    'Bring a Qur'ān other than this, or alter it.'
Say, 'I may not alter it
    of my own accord.
I follow only what is revealed to me.
Indeed, should I disobey my Lord, I fear
    the punishment of a tremendous day.'

16 Say, 'Had God so wished,
    I would not have recited it to you,
    nor would He have made it known to you,
for I have dwelled among you for a lifetime before it.
Do you not exercise your reason?'

17 So who is a greater wrongdoer than him
who fabricates lies against God, or denies His signs?
Indeed, the guilty will not prosper.

18 They worship besides God
    that which neither causes them any harm,
    nor brings them any benefit,
and they say, 'These are our intercessors with God.'
Say, 'Will you inform God
    about something He does not know

فِى السَّمَاوَاتِ وَلَا فِى الْأَرْضِ ۚ in the heavens or on the earth?'

سُبْحَانَهُ وَتَعَالَىٰ Immaculate is He and far above having

عَمَّا يُشْرِكُونَ ۝ any partners that they ascribe to Him!

وَمَا كَانَ النَّاسُ إِلَّا أُمَّةً وَاحِدَةً 19 Mankind were but a single religious community;

فَاخْتَلَفُوا ۚ then they differed.

وَلَوْلَا كَلِمَةٌ سَبَقَتْ مِن رَّبِّكَ And were it not for a prior decree of *your* Lord,

لَقُضِىَ بَيْنَهُمْ decision would have been made between them

فِيمَا فِيهِ يَخْتَلِفُونَ ۝ concerning that about which they differ.

وَيَقُولُونَ لَوْلَا أُنزِلَ عَلَيْهِ آيَةٌ 20 They say, 'Why has not some sign[1] been sent down to him

مِّن رَّبِّهِ ۖ from his Lord?'

فَقُلْ إِنَّمَا الْغَيْبُ لِلَّهِ Say, 'The knowledge of the Unseen belongs only to God.

فَانتَظِرُوا إِنِّى مَعَكُم مِّنَ الْمُنتَظِرِينَ ۝ So wait. I too am waiting along with you.'

وَإِذَا أَذَقْنَا النَّاسَ رَحْمَةً 21 When We let people taste Our mercy

مِّن بَعْدِ ضَرَّاءَ مَسَّتْهُمْ after a distress that has befallen them,

إِذَا لَهُم مَّكْرٌ فِى آيَاتِنَا ۚ behold, they scheme against Our signs!

قُلِ اللَّهُ أَسْرَعُ مَكْرًا ۚ Say, 'God is more swift at devising.'

إِنَّ رُسُلَنَا يَكْتُبُونَ مَا تَمْكُرُونَ ۝ Indeed, Our messengers write down what you scheme.

هُوَ الَّذِى يُسَيِّرُكُمْ فِى الْبَرِّ وَالْبَحْرِ ۖ 22 It is He who carries you across land and sea.

حَتَّىٰ إِذَا كُنتُمْ فِى الْفُلْكِ When you are in the ships,

وَجَرَيْنَ بِهِم بِرِيحٍ طَيِّبَةٍ and they sail along with them with a favourable wind,

وَفَرِحُوا بِهَا being joyful on its account,

جَاءَتْهَا رِيحٌ عَاصِفٌ there comes upon them a tempestuous wind

وَجَاءَهُمُ الْمَوْجُ مِن كُلِّ مَكَانٍ and waves assail them from every side,

وَظَنُّوا أَنَّهُمْ أُحِيطَ بِهِمْ ۙ and they think that they are besieged,

دَعَوُا اللَّهَ مُخْلِصِينَ لَهُ الدِّينَ they invoke God putting exclusive faith in Him,

لَئِنْ أَنجَيْتَنَا مِنْ هَٰذِهِ 'If You deliver us from this,

لَنَكُونَنَّ مِنَ الشَّاكِرِينَ ۝ we will surely be among the grateful.'

فَلَمَّا أَنجَاهُمْ 23 But when He delivers them,

إِذَا هُمْ يَبْغُونَ فِى الْأَرْضِ بِغَيْرِ الْحَقِّ ۗ behold, they commit violations on the earth unduly!

---

[1] That is, miracle.

O mankind!
Your violations are only to your own detriment.
   These are the wares of the life of this world;
   then to Us will be your return,
whereat We will inform you concerning what you used to do.
24 The parable of the life of this world is that of water
   which We send down from the sky.
   It mingles with the earth's vegetation
   from which humans and cattle eat.
When the earth puts on its luster and is adorned,
   and its inhabitants think they have power over it,
   Our edict comes to it, by night or day,
   whereat We turn it into a mown field,
   as if it did not flourish the day before.
Thus do We elaborate the signs for a people who reflect.
25 God invites to the abode of peace,
and He guides whomever He wishes to a straight path.
26 Those who are virtuous shall receive the best reward
   and an enhancement.
Neither dust nor abasement shall overcast their faces.
They shall be the inhabitants of paradise,
   and they shall remain in it.
27 For those who have committed misdeeds,
   the requital of a misdeed shall be its like,
   and they shall be overcast by abasement.
They shall have no one to protect them from God.
They will be as if their faces were covered
   with dark patches of the night.
They shall be the inmates of the Fire,
   and they shall remain in it.

28 On the day when We gather them all together,
We shall say to those who ascribe partners to God,
'Stay where you are—you and your partners!'
Then We shall set them apart from one another,
and their partners[1] will say,
'It was not us that you worshiped.

29 God suffices as a witness between you and us.
We were indeed unaware of your worship.'

30 There every soul will examine what it has sent in advance,
and they will be returned to God, their real Master,
and what they used to fabricate will forsake them.

31 Say, 'Who provides for you out of the heaven and the earth?
Who controls your hearing and sight,
and who brings forth the living from the dead
and brings forth the dead from the living,
and who directs the command?'
They will say, 'God.'
Say, 'Will you not then be wary of Him?'

32 That, then, is God, your true Lord.
So what is there after the truth except error?
Then where are you being led away?

33 Thus the word of your Lord became due
against those who transgress:
that they shall not have faith.

34 Say, 'Is there anyone among your partners
who originates the creation and then brings it back?'
Say, 'God originates the creation, then He will bring it back.'
Then where do you stray?

---

[1] That is, the false gods whom the polytheists associated with God.

35 Say, 'Is there anyone among your partners
who may guide to the truth?'
Say, 'God guides to the truth.
Is He who guides to the truth worthier to be followed,
or he who is not guided unless he is shown the way?
What is the matter with you? How do you judge?'
36 Most of them just follow conjectures;
indeed, conjecture is no substitute for the truth.
God indeed knows best what they do.
37 This Qur'ān could not have been fabricated
by anyone besides God;
rather, it is a confirmation of what was revealed before it,
and an elaboration of the Book,
there is no doubt in it,
from the Lord of all the worlds.
38 Do they say, 'He has fabricated it?'
Say, 'Then bring a *sūrah* like it,
and invoke whomever you can, besides God,
if you are truthful.'
39 They indeed impugn
something whose knowledge they do not comprehend,
and whose explanation has not yet come to them.
Those who were before them impugned likewise.
So *observe* how was the fate of the wrongdoers!
40 Some of them believe in it,
and some of them do not believe in it,
and *your* Lord best knows the agents of corruption.
41 If they impugn *you*, say, 'My deeds belong to me
and your deeds belong to you:
you are absolved of what I do

وَأَنَا بَرِيءٌ مِمَّا تَعْمَلُونَ ۝
and I am absolved of what you do.'

وَمِنْهُم مَّن يَسْتَمِعُونَ إِلَيْكَ ۚ 42 There are some of them who prick up their ears at you.
أَفَأَنتَ تُسْمِعُ الصُّمَّ But can you make the deaf hear
وَلَوْ كَانُوا لَا يَعْقِلُونَ ۝ even if they do not exercise their reason?

وَمِنْهُم مَّن يَنظُرُ إِلَيْكَ ۚ 43 There are some of them who observe you.
أَفَأَنتَ تَهْدِي الْعُمْيَ But can you guide the blind
وَلَوْ كَانُوا لَا يُبْصِرُونَ ۝ even if they do not see?

إِنَّ اللَّهَ لَا يَظْلِمُ النَّاسَ شَيْئًا 44 Indeed, God does not wrong people in the least;
وَلَٰكِنَّ النَّاسَ أَنفُسَهُمْ يَظْلِمُونَ ۝ rather, it is people who wrong themselves.

وَيَوْمَ يَحْشُرُهُمْ 45 On the day He will gather them
كَأَن لَّمْ يَلْبَثُوا it will be as if they had not remained in the world
إِلَّا سَاعَةً مِّنَ النَّهَارِ except for an hour of the day,
يَتَعَارَفُونَ بَيْنَهُمْ ۚ getting acquainted with one another.
قَدْ خَسِرَ الَّذِينَ كَذَّبُوا بِلِقَاءِ اللَّهِ They are certainly losers who deny the encounter with God,
وَمَا كَانُوا مُهْتَدِينَ ۝ and they are not guided.

وَإِمَّا نُرِيَنَّكَ بَعْضَ الَّذِي نَعِدُهُمْ 46 Whether We show you a part of what We promise them,
أَوْ نَتَوَفَّيَنَّكَ or take you away [before that],
فَإِلَيْنَا مَرْجِعُهُمْ in any case their return will be to Us,
ثُمَّ اللَّهُ شَهِيدٌ عَلَىٰ مَا يَفْعَلُونَ ۝ and God is witness to what they do.

وَلِكُلِّ أُمَّةٍ رَّسُولٌ ۖ 47 There is an apostle[1] for every nation;
فَإِذَا جَاءَ رَسُولُهُمْ so when their apostle comes,
قُضِيَ بَيْنَهُم بِالْقِسْطِ judgement is made between them with justice,
وَهُمْ لَا يُظْلَمُونَ ۝ and they are not wronged.

وَيَقُولُونَ مَتَىٰ هَٰذَا الْوَعْدُ 48 They say, 'When will this promise be fulfilled,
إِن كُنتُمْ صَادِقِينَ ۝ should you be truthful?'

قُل لَّا أَمْلِكُ لِنَفْسِي ضَرًّا 49 Say, 'I have no control over any harm for myself
وَلَا نَفْعًا nor over any benefit
إِلَّا مَا شَاءَ اللَّهُ ۗ except what God may wish.
لِكُلِّ أُمَّةٍ أَجَلٌ ۚ There is a time for every nation:

---

[1] Or 'There is a messenger.'

when their time comes, إِذَا جَاءَ أَجَلُهُمْ
they shall not defer it by a single hour فَلَا يَسْتَأْخِرُونَ سَاعَةً
nor shall they advance it.' وَلَا يَسْتَقْدِمُونَ ۝

50 Say, 'Tell me, should His punishment overtake you قُلْ أَرَأَيْتُمْ إِنْ أَتَاكُمْ عَذَابُهُ
by night or day, [you will not be able to avert it]; بَيَاتًا أَوْ نَهَارًا
so what part of it do the guilty seek to hasten?' مَاذَا يَسْتَعْجِلُ مِنْهُ الْمُجْرِمُونَ ۝

51 'What! Do you believe it when it has befallen? Now? أَثُمَّ إِذَا مَا وَقَعَ آمَنْتُمْ بِهِ آلْآنَ
While you would seek to hasten it earlier?!' وَقَدْ كُنْتُمْ بِهِ تَسْتَعْجِلُونَ ۝

52 Then it will be said to those who were wrongdoers, ثُمَّ قِيلَ لِلَّذِينَ ظَلَمُوا
'Taste the everlasting punishment. ذُوقُوا عَذَابَ الْخُلْدِ
Shall you be requited except for what you used to earn?' هَلْ تُجْزَوْنَ إِلَّا بِمَا كُنْتُمْ تَكْسِبُونَ ۝

53 They inquire of you, 'Is it true?' وَيَسْتَنْبِئُونَكَ أَحَقٌّ هُوَ
Say, 'Yes! By my Lord, it is true, قُلْ إِي وَرَبِّي إِنَّهُ لَحَقٌّ
and you cannot frustrate Him.' وَمَا أَنْتُمْ بِمُعْجِزِينَ ۝

54 Were any soul that has done wrong to possess وَلَوْ أَنَّ لِكُلِّ نَفْسٍ ظَلَمَتْ
whatever there is on the earth, مَا فِي الْأَرْضِ
it would surely offer it for ransom. لَافْتَدَتْ بِهِ
They will hide their remorse وَأَسَرُّوا النَّدَامَةَ
when they sight the punishment لَمَّا رَأَوُا الْعَذَابَ
and judgement will be made between them with justice وَقُضِيَ بَيْنَهُمْ بِالْقِسْطِ
and they will not be wronged. وَهُمْ لَا يُظْلَمُونَ ۝

55 Behold, to God indeed belongs أَلَا إِنَّ لِلَّهِ
whatever is in the heavens and the earth. مَا فِي السَّمَاوَاتِ وَالْأَرْضِ
Behold, God's promise is indeed true, أَلَا إِنَّ وَعْدَ اللَّهِ حَقٌّ
but most of them do not know. وَلَكِنَّ أَكْثَرَهُمْ لَا يَعْلَمُونَ ۝

56 It is He who gives life and brings death, هُوَ يُحْيِي وَيُمِيتُ
and to Him you shall be brought back. وَإِلَيْهِ تُرْجَعُونَ ۝

57 O mankind! There has certainly come to you يَا أَيُّهَا النَّاسُ قَدْ جَاءَتْكُمْ
an advice from your Lord, مَوْعِظَةٌ مِنْ رَبِّكُمْ
and cure for what is in the breasts, وَشِفَاءٌ لِمَا فِي الصُّدُورِ

and guidance and mercy for the faithful.

58 Say, 'In God's grace and His mercy—
let them rejoice in that!
It is better than what they amass.'

59 Say, 'Have you regarded what God has sent down
for you of His provision,
whereupon you have made some of it unlawful
and some lawful?'
Say, 'Did God give you the sanction to do so,
or do you fabricate lies against God?'

60 What is the idea of those
who fabricate lies against God [concerning
their own situation on the Day of Resurrection?
God is indeed gracious to mankind,
but most of them do not give thanks.

61 You do not engage in any work,
neither do you recite any part of the Qur'ān,
nor do you perform any deed
without Our being witness over you
when you are engaged therein.
Not an atom's weight escapes your Lord
in the earth or in the heaven,
nor is there anything smaller than that nor bigger,
but it is in a manifest Book.

62 Behold! The friends of God will indeed have no fear
nor will they grieve
63 —those who have faith and are Godwary.
64 For them is good news in the life of this world
and in the Hereafter.
(There is no altering the words of God.)

That is the great success.

65 *Do not grieve* at their remarks;
 indeed all might belongs to God;
 He is the All-hearing, the All-knowing.

66 Behold, to God indeed belongs whoever is in the heavens
 and whoever is on the earth.
 What do they pursue who invoke
 partners besides God?
 They merely follow conjectures
 and they only make surmises.

67 It is He who made the night for you,
 that you may rest in it,
 and the day to provide visibility.
 There are indeed signs in that for people who listen.

68 They say, 'God has offspring!' Immaculate is He!
 He is the All-sufficient.
 To Him belongs whatever is in the heavens
 and whatever is in the earth.
 You have no authority for this statement.
 Do you attribute to God what you do not know?

69 *Say*, 'Indeed, those who fabricate lies against God
 will not prosper.'

70 Their life will be a brief enjoyment in this world;
 then to Us shall be their return,
 then We shall make them taste the severe punishment
 because of what they used to deny.

71 *Relate* to them the account of Noah
 when he said to his people,
 'O my people! If my stay among you be hard on you

and also my reminding you of God's signs, وَتَذْكِيرِى بِآيَاتِ اللَّهِ
for my part I have put my trust in God alone. فَعَلَى اللَّهِ تَوَكَّلْتُ
So conspire together, along with your partners,[1] فَأَجْمِعُوا أَمْرَكُمْ وَشُرَكَاءَكُمْ
leaving nothing vague in your plan; ثُمَّ لَا يَكُنْ أَمْرُكُمْ عَلَيْكُمْ غُمَّةً
then carry it out against me without giving me any respite. ثُمَّ اقْضُوا إِلَيَّ وَلَا تُنْظِرُونِ ۝

72 If you turn your back on me, فَإِنْ تَوَلَّيْتُمْ
I do not ask any reward from you; فَمَا سَأَلْتُكُمْ مِنْ أَجْرٍ
my reward lies only with God إِنْ أَجْرِيَ إِلَّا عَلَى اللَّهِ
and I have been commanded وَأُمِرْتُ
to be of those who submit to Him.' أَنْ أَكُونَ مِنَ الْمُسْلِمِينَ ۝

73 But they impugned him. فَكَذَّبُوهُ
So We delivered him فَنَجَّيْنَاهُ
and those who were with him in the ark وَمَنْ مَعَهُ فِي الْفُلْكِ
and We made them the successors,[2] وَجَعَلْنَاهُمْ خَلَائِفَ
and We drowned those who impugned Our signs. وَأَغْرَقْنَا الَّذِينَ كَذَّبُوا بِآيَاتِنَا
So *observe* how was the fate of those who were warned! فَانْظُرْ كَيْفَ كَانَ عَاقِبَةُ الْمُنْذَرِينَ ۝

74 Then after him We sent other apostles to their people. ثُمَّ بَعَثْنَا مِنْ بَعْدِهِ رُسُلًا إِلَى قَوْمِهِمْ
They brought them clear proofs, فَجَاءُوهُمْ بِالْبَيِّنَاتِ
but they would not believe فَمَا كَانُوا لِيُؤْمِنُوا
something they had impugned before. بِمَا كَذَّبُوا بِهِ مِنْ قَبْلُ
Thus do We seal the hearts of the transgressors. كَذَلِكَ نَطْبَعُ عَلَى قُلُوبِ الْمُعْتَدِينَ ۝

75 Then, after them, We sent ثُمَّ بَعَثْنَا مِنْ بَعْدِهِمْ
Moses and Aaron to Pharaoh and his elite مُوسَى وَهَارُونَ إِلَى فِرْعَوْنَ وَمَلَئِهِ
with Our signs, بِآيَاتِنَا
but they acted arrogantly and they were a guilty lot. فَاسْتَكْبَرُوا وَكَانُوا قَوْمًا مُجْرِمِينَ ۝

76 When the truth came to them from Us, فَلَمَّا جَاءَهُمُ الْحَقُّ مِنْ عِنْدِنَا
they said, 'This is indeed plain magic!' قَالُوا إِنَّ هَذَا لَسِحْرٌ مُبِينٌ ۝

77 Moses said, 'Do you say of the truth قَالَ مُوسَى أَتَقُولُونَ لِلْحَقِّ
when it comes to you [that it is magic]? لَمَّا جَاءَكُمْ

---

[1] That is, the false deities whom you worship besides God.
[2] That is, of those who perished in the Flood.

أَسِحْرٌ هَٰذَا وَلَا يُفْلِحُ السَّاحِرُونَ ۝	Is this magic? Magicians do not prosper.'
78 قَالُوا أَجِئْتَنَا لِتَلْفِتَنَا	78 They said, 'Have you come to us to turn us away
عَمَّا وَجَدْنَا عَلَيْهِ آبَاءَنَا	from what we found our fathers following,
وَتَكُونَ لَكُمَا الْكِبْرِيَاءُ فِي الْأَرْضِ	so that supremacy may be yours in the land?
وَمَا نَحْنُ لَكُمَا بِمُؤْمِنِينَ ۝	We will not believe in the two of you.'[1]
79 وَقَالَ فِرْعَوْنُ ائْتُونِي بِكُلِّ سَاحِرٍ عَلِيمٍ ۝	79 Pharaoh said, 'Bring me every expert magician.'
80 فَلَمَّا جَاءَ السَّحَرَةُ	80 So when the magicians came,
قَالَ لَهُمْ مُوسَىٰ	Moses said to them,
أَلْقُوا مَا أَنْتُمْ مُلْقُونَ ۝	'Throw down what you have to throw.'
81 فَلَمَّا أَلْقَوْا	81 So when they threw down [their sticks and ropes],
قَالَ مُوسَىٰ مَا جِئْتُمْ بِهِ السِّحْرُ	Moses said, 'What you have produced is magic.
إِنَّ اللَّهَ سَيُبْطِلُهُ	Presently, God will indeed bring it to naught.
إِنَّ اللَّهَ لَا يُصْلِحُ عَمَلَ	Indeed, God does not foster the efforts
الْمُفْسِدِينَ ۝	of those who cause corruption.
82 وَيُحِقُّ اللَّهُ الْحَقَّ بِكَلِمَاتِهِ	82 God will confirm the truth with His words,
وَلَوْ كَرِهَ الْمُجْرِمُونَ ۝	though the guilty should be averse.'
83 فَمَا آمَنَ لِمُوسَىٰ	83 But none believed in Moses
إِلَّا ذُرِّيَّةٌ مِنْ قَوْمِهِ	except some youths from among his people
عَلَىٰ خَوْفٍ مِنْ فِرْعَوْنَ وَمَلَئِهِمْ	for the fear of Pharaoh and their own elders
أَنْ يَفْتِنَهُمْ	that he would persecute them.
وَإِنَّ فِرْعَوْنَ لَعَالٍ فِي الْأَرْضِ	For Pharaoh was indeed a tyrant in the land,
وَإِنَّهُ لَمِنَ الْمُسْرِفِينَ ۝	and indeed he was an unrestrained despot.
84 وَقَالَ مُوسَىٰ يَا قَوْمِ	84 And Moses said, 'O my people!
إِنْ كُنْتُمْ آمَنْتُمْ بِاللَّهِ فَعَلَيْهِ تَوَكَّلُوا	If you have faith in God, put your trust in Him,
إِنْ كُنْتُمْ مُسْلِمِينَ ۝	if you have submitted to Him.'
85 فَقَالُوا عَلَى اللَّهِ تَوَكَّلْنَا	85 Whereat they said, 'In God alone we have put our trust.'
رَبَّنَا لَا تَجْعَلْنَا فِتْنَةً	'Our Lord! Do not make us a means of test
لِلْقَوْمِ الظَّالِمِينَ ۝	for the wrongdoing lot,
86 وَنَجِّنَا بِرَحْمَتِكَ مِنَ الْقَوْمِ الْكَافِرِينَ ۝	86 and deliver us by Your mercy from the faithless lot.'

---

[1] That is, Moses and Aaron ('a).

87 We revealed to Moses and his brother وَأَوْحَيْنَا إِلَىٰ مُوسَىٰ وَأَخِيهِ
saying, 'Settle your people in the city,[1] أَن تَبَوَّآ لِقَوْمِكُمَا بِمِصْرَ بُيُوتًا
and let your houses face each other,[2] وَاجْعَلُوا بُيُوتَكُمْ قِبْلَةً
and maintain the prayer, وَأَقِيمُوا الصَّلَاةَ
and give good news to the faithful.' وَبَشِّرِ الْمُؤْمِنِينَ ۝

88 Moses said, 'Our Lord! وَقَالَ مُوسَىٰ رَبَّنَا
You have given Pharaoh and his elite إِنَّكَ آتَيْتَ فِرْعَوْنَ وَمَلَأَهُ
glamour and wealth in the life of this world, زِينَةً وَأَمْوَالًا فِي الْحَيَاةِ الدُّنْيَا
our Lord, that they may lead people astray from Your way! رَبَّنَا لِيُضِلُّوا عَن سَبِيلِكَ
Our Lord! Blot out their wealth رَبَّنَا اطْمِسْ عَلَىٰ أَمْوَالِهِمْ
and harden their hearts, وَاشْدُدْ عَلَىٰ قُلُوبِهِمْ
so that they do not believe فَلَا يُؤْمِنُوا
until they sight the painful punishment.' حَتَّىٰ يَرَوُا الْعَذَابَ الْأَلِيمَ ۝

89 Said He, 'Your[3] supplication has already been granted. قَالَ قَدْ أُجِيبَت دَّعْوَتُكُمَا
So be steadfast فَاسْتَقِيمَا
and do not follow the way of those who do not know.' وَلَا تَتَّبِعَانِّ سَبِيلَ الَّذِينَ لَا يَعْلَمُونَ ۝

90 We carried the Children of Israel across the sea, وَجَاوَزْنَا بِبَنِي إِسْرَائِيلَ الْبَحْرَ
whereat Pharaoh and his troops pursued them فَأَتْبَعَهُمْ فِرْعَوْنُ وَجُنُودُهُ
out of defiance and aggression. بَغْيًا وَعَدْوًا
When overtaken by drowning, he called out, حَتَّىٰ إِذَا أَدْرَكَهُ الْغَرَقُ قَالَ
'I do believe that there is no god except Him آمَنتُ أَنَّهُ لَا إِلَٰهَ إِلَّا الَّذِي
in whom the Children of Israel believe, آمَنَتْ بِهِ بَنُو إِسْرَائِيلَ
and I am one of those who submit to Him!' وَأَنَا مِنَ الْمُسْلِمِينَ ۝

91 [He was told,] 'What! Now? آلْآنَ
When you have been disobedient heretofore وَقَدْ عَصَيْتَ قَبْلُ
and were among the agents of corruption?! وَكُنتَ مِنَ الْمُفْسِدِينَ ۝

92 So today We shall deliver your body فَالْيَوْمَ نُنَجِّيكَ بِبَدَنِكَ
so that you may be a sign for those who come after you.' لِتَكُونَ لِمَنْ خَلْفَكَ آيَةً

---

[1] That is, Bayt al-Maqdis, in accordance with a tradition of Imam al-Ṣādiq ('a) (*Tafsīr al-Qummī*). Alternatively, 'Provide houses for your people in Egypt.'
[2] Or 'Make your homes places of worship.'
[3] That is, of Moses and Aaron ('a).

Many of the people are indeed
oblivious to Our signs.

93 Certainly We settled the Children of Israel
   in a worthy settlement
and We provided them with all the good things,
and they did not differ
until after the knowledge had come to them.
Your Lord will indeed judge between them
   on the Day of Resurrection
   concerning that about which they used to differ.

94 If you are in doubt
   about what We have sent down to you,
ask those who read the Book revealed before you.
The truth has certainly come to you from your Lord;
   so do not be among skeptics.

95 And do not be of those who impugn the signs of God,
   for then you shall be among the losers.

96 Indeed, those
against whom *your* Lord's judgement has become due
   will not have faith,

97 even though every sign were to come to them,
   until they sight the painful punishment.

98 Why there has not been any town that might believe,
so that its belief might benefit it,
   except the people of Jonah?
When they believed,
We removed from them the punishment of disgrace
   in the life of this world
and We provided for them for a time.

99   Had your Lord wished,
       all those who are on earth would have believed.
       Would you then force people
       until they become faithful?

100 No soul may have faith except by God's leave,
       and He lays defilement
       on those who do not exercise their reason.

101 Say, 'Observe what is in the heavens and the earth.'
       But neither signs nor warnings avail
       a people who have no faith.

102 Do they await anything except the like of the days
       of those who passed away before them?
       Say, 'Then wait!
       I too am waiting along with you.'

103 Then We will deliver Our apostles
       and those who have faith.
       Thus it is a must for Us to deliver the faithful.

104 Say, 'O people! If you are in doubt
       about my religion,
       then [know that] I do not worship those whom
       you worship besides God.
       Rather, I worship only God, who causes you to die,
       and I have been commanded to be among the faithful,

105 and that: "Dedicate *yourself* to the religion, as a *ḥanīf*,
       and *never be* one of the polytheists.

106 Nor *invoke* besides God
       that which neither benefits *you* nor can do *you* any harm.
       For if *you* do so,
       you will indeed be among the wrongdoers."'

107 Should God visit you with some distress,
there is no one to remove it except Him;
and should He desire any good for you,
none can stand in the way of His grace:
He grants it to whomever He wishes of His servants,
and He is the All-forgiving, the All-merciful.

108 Say, 'O mankind!
The truth has already come to you from your Lord.
Whoever is guided,
is guided only for the good of his own soul,
and whoever goes astray, goes astray only to its detriment,
and it is not my business to watch over you.'

109 *Follow that which is revealed to you,
and be patient* until God issues His judgement,
and He is the best of judges.

11. Hud[1]
Hūd

In the Name of God,
the All-beneficent, the All-merciful.

1 *Alif, Lām Rā.* This is a Book,
whose signs have been made definitive[2]
and then elaborated,
from One who is all-wise, all-aware,

2 declaring: 'Worship no one but God.
I am indeed a warner to you from Him
and a bearer of good news.

3 Plead with your Lord for forgiveness,
then turn to Him penitently.

---

[1] This Makkī *sūrah* is named after Hūd ('a), the prophet whose account is given in verses 50-60.
[2] Cf. 3:7.

He will provide you with a good provision
    for a specified term
and grant His grace to every meritorious person.
But if you turn your backs on Him,
indeed I fear for you the punishment of a terrible day.

4 To God will be your return,
    and He has power over all things.'

5 Behold, they fold up their breasts[1]
    to hide their secret feelings from Him.
Behold, when they draw their cloaks over their heads,[2]
He knows whatever they keep secret
    and whatever they disclose.
He knows well indeed whatever is in the breasts.

[PART 12]

6 There is no animal on the earth,
    but that its sustenance lies with God,
and He knows its enduring abode
    and its temporary place of lodging.
Everything is in a manifest Book.

7 It is He who created the heavens and the earth
    in six days
—and His Throne was then upon the waters—
that He may test you to see
    which of you is best in conduct.
Yet if you say, 'You will indeed be raised up after death,'
    the faithless will surely say,
    'This is nothing but plain magic.'

8 And if We defer their punishment until a certain time,
    they will surely say, 'What holds it back?'

---

[1] 'To fold up one's breast' is an idiomatic phrase, meaning to conceal one's spite within one's heart.
[2] So that they may not be recognized. Cf. 71:7.

Behold, on the day that it overtakes them
it shall not be turned away from them,
and they will be besieged by what they used to deride.

9 If We let man taste a [breath of] mercy from Us
and then withdraw it from him,
he becomes despondent and ungrateful.

10 And if We let him have a taste of Our blessings
after adversities have befallen him,
he will surely say, 'All ills have left me,'
indeed being joyful and vain,

11 excepting those who are patient and do righteous deeds.
For such there will be forgiveness and a great reward.

12 Look out lest you should disregard
aught of what has been revealed to you,
and be upset because they say,
'Why has not a treasure been sent down to him,
or why does not an angel accompany him?'
You are only a warner,
and God watches over all things.

13 Do they say, 'He has fabricated it?'
Say, 'Then bring ten *surah*s like it, fabricated,
and invoke whomever you can, besides God,
if you are truthful.'

14 But if they do not respond to you,
know that it has been sent down by God's knowledge,
and that there is no god except Him.
Will you, then, submit to God?

15 As for those who desire the life of this world and its glitter,
We will recompense them fully for their works therein,
and they will not be underpaid in it.

16 They are the ones for whom there will be nothing
in the Hereafter except Fire:
what they had accomplished in the world has failed,
and their works have come to naught.

17 Is he who stands on a clear proof from his Lord
and whom a witness of his own family follows?[1]
And before him[2] there was the Book of Moses,
a guide and mercy.
It is they who have faith in it,
and whoever denies him from among the factions,
the Fire is their tryst.
So do not be in doubt about it;
it is the truth from your Lord,
but most people do not have faith.

18 Who is a greater wrongdoer than him
who fabricates lies against God?
Such shall be presented before their Lord
and the witnesses will say,
'It is these who lied against their Lord.'
Behold! The curse of God is upon the wrongdoers

19 —those who bar others from the way of God
and seek to make it crooked,
and disbelieve in the Hereafter.

20 They cannot frustrate God on the earth,
nor do they have any protectors besides God.
For them the punishment shall be doubled,
for they could neither listen,
nor did they use to see.

---

[1] Ellipsis. That is, is such a person like someone who is not such? Or, can such a one be deterred by the denial of the ignorant?

[2] Or 'before it,' that is, the Qur'ān.

21 **They are the ones who have ruined their souls,**
   and what they used to fabricate has forsaken them.

22 **Undoubtedly, they are the ones**
   who will be the biggest losers in the Hereafter.

23 **Indeed, those who have faith and do righteous deeds**
   and are humble before their Lord
   —they shall be the inhabitants of paradise,
   and they shall remain in it.

24 **The parable of the two parties**
   is that of those who are blind and deaf
   and those who see and hear.
   Are they equal in comparison?
   Will you not then take admonition?

25 **Certainly We sent Noah to his people [to declare]:**
   'I am indeed a manifest warner to you:

26 **worship none but God.**
   Indeed, I fear for you the punishment of a painful day.'

27 **But the elite of the faithless from among his people said,**
   'We do not see you to be
   anything but a human being like ourselves,
   and we do not see anyone following you
   except the simpleminded riffraff from our midst.
   Nor do we see that you have any merit over us.
   Indeed, we consider you to be liars.'

28 **He said, 'O my people! Tell me,**
   should I stand on a clear proof from my Lord,
   and He has granted me His own mercy
   —though it should be lost on you—
   shall we force it upon you while you are averse to it?

29 O my people! I do not ask you any material reward for it.
My reward lies only with God.
But I will not drive away those who have faith.
They will indeed encounter their Lord.
But I see that you are an ignorant lot.

30 O my people! Who would come to my help against God
were I to drive them away?
Will you not then take admonition?

31 I do not say to you that I possess the treasuries of God,
neither do I know the Unseen.
I do not claim to be an angel,
neither do I say of those who are despicable in your eyes
that God will not grant them any good
—God knows best what is in their hearts—
for then I would indeed be a wrongdoer.'

32 They said, 'O Noah, you have disputed with us already,
and you have disputed much with us.
Now bring us what you threaten us with,
if you are truthful.

33 He said, 'God will indeed bring it on you if He wishes,
and you cannot frustrate Him.

34 My exhorting will not benefit you,
much as I may seek to exhort you,
if God desires to consign you to perversity.
He is your Lord, and to Him you will be returned.'

35 Do they say, 'He has fabricated it?'
Say, 'Should I have fabricated it,
then my guilt will lie upon me,
and I am absolved of your guilty conduct.'

36 It was revealed to Noah:
   'None of your people will believe
   except those who already have faith;
   so do not sorrow for what they used to do.

37 Build the ark before Our eyes and by Our revelation,
   and do not plead with Me for those who are wrongdoers:
   they shall indeed be drowned.'

38 As he was building the ark,
   whenever the elders of his people passed by him,
   they would ridicule him.
   He said, 'If you ridicule us [today],
   we will ridicule you [tomorrow] just as you ridicule us now.

39 Soon you will know who will be overtaken by
       a punishment that will disgrace him,
   and on whom a lasting punishment will descend.'

40 When Our edict came
   and the oven gushed a stream of water,
   We said, 'Carry in it a pair[1] of every kind of animal,
   along with your family—except those of them
   against whom the edict has already been given—
   and those who have faith.'
   And none believed with him except a few.

41 He said, 'Board it:
   In the Name of God it shall set sail and cast anchor.
   My Lord is indeed all-forgiving, all-merciful.'

42 And it sailed along with them amid waves
       rising like mountains.
   Noah called out to his son, who stood aloof,
   'O my son! 'Board with us,

---

[1] That is, male and female. Cf. **23**:27.

وَلَا تَكُن مَّعَ الْكَافِرِينَ ۝

and do not be with the faithless!'

قَالَ سَآوِي إِلَىٰ جَبَلٍ

43 He said, 'I will take refuge on a mountain;

يَعْصِمُنِي مِنَ الْمَاءِ

it will protect me from the flood.'

قَالَ

He said,

لَا عَاصِمَ الْيَوْمَ مِنْ أَمْرِ اللَّهِ

'There is none today who can protect from God's edict,

إِلَّا مَن رَّحِمَ

except someone upon whom He has mercy.'

وَحَالَ بَيْنَهُمَا الْمَوْجُ

Then the waves came between them,

فَكَانَ مِنَ الْمُغْرَقِينَ ۝

and he was among those who were drowned.

وَقِيلَ يَا أَرْضُ ابْلَعِي مَاءَكِ

44 Then it was said, 'O earth, swallow your water!

وَيَا سَمَاءُ أَقْلِعِي وَغِيضَ الْمَاءُ

O sky, leave off!' The waters receded;

وَقُضِيَ الْأَمْرُ وَاسْتَوَتْ عَلَى الْجُودِيِّ

the edict was carried out, and it[1] settled on Mount Judi.

وَقِيلَ بُعْدًا لِّلْقَوْمِ الظَّالِمِينَ ۝

Then it was said, 'Away with the wrongdoing lot!'

وَنَادَىٰ نُوحٌ رَّبَّهُ فَقَالَ رَبِّ

45 Noah called out to his Lord and said, 'My Lord!

إِنَّ ابْنِي مِنْ أَهْلِي

My son is indeed from my family,

وَإِنَّ وَعْدَكَ الْحَقُّ

and Your promise is indeed true,

وَأَنتَ أَحْكَمُ الْحَاكِمِينَ ۝

and You are the fairest of all judges.'

قَالَ يَا نُوحُ إِنَّهُ لَيْسَ مِنْ أَهْلِكَ

46 Said He, 'O Noah! He is indeed not of your family.

إِنَّهُ عَمَلٌ غَيْرُ صَالِحٍ

He is indeed a personification of unrighteous conduct.

فَلَا تَسْأَلْنِ

So do not ask Me

مَا لَيْسَ لَكَ بِهِ عِلْمٌ

something of which you have no knowledge.

إِنِّي أَعِظُكَ أَن تَكُونَ مِنَ الْجَاهِلِينَ ۝

I advise you, lest you should be among the ignorant.'

قَالَ رَبِّ إِنِّي أَعُوذُ بِكَ

47 He said, 'My Lord! I seek Your protection

أَنْ أَسْأَلَكَ

lest I should ask You

مَا لَيْسَ لِي بِهِ عِلْمٌ

something of which I have no knowledge.

وَإِلَّا تَغْفِرْ لِي وَتَرْحَمْنِي

If You do not forgive me and have mercy upon me

أَكُن مِّنَ الْخَاسِرِينَ ۝

I will be among the losers.'

قِيلَ يَا نُوحُ

48 It was said, 'O Noah!

اهْبِطْ بِسَلَامٍ مِّنَّا وَبَرَكَاتٍ

Disembark in peace from Us and with Our blessings

عَلَيْكَ وَعَلَىٰ أُمَمٍ

upon you and upon nations

---

[1] That is, the Ark of Noah.

to descend from those who are with you,
and nations whom We shall provide for,
then a painful punishment from Us shall befall them.'

49 These are accounts of the Unseen which We reveal to you.
Neither *you*, nor *your* people used to know them
before this.
So *be patient*.
The outcome will indeed be in favour of the Godwary.

50 And to 'Ād We sent Hūd, their compatriot.
He said, 'O my people! Worship God.
You have no other god besides Him:
you have merely fabricated [the deities that you worship].

51 'O my people! I do not ask you any reward for it.
My reward lies only with Him who originated me.
Do you not exercise your reason?

52 'O my people! Plead with your Lord for forgiveness,
then turn to Him penitently:
He will send copious rains for you from the sky,
and add power to your present power.
So do not turn your backs on Him as guilty ones.'

53 They said,
'O Hūd, you have not brought us any clear proof.
We are not going to abandon our gods for what you say,
and we are not going to believe you.

54 All we say is that some of our gods have visited you
with some evil.'
He said, 'I call God to witness
—and you too be my witnesses—
that I repudiate what you take as His partners

besides Him. مِنْ دُونِهِ

Now try out your stratagems against me, together, فَكِيدُونِي جَمِيعًا

without granting me any respite. ثُمَّ لَا تُنظِرُونِ ۝

56 Indeed, I have put my trust in God, إِنِّي تَوَكَّلْتُ عَلَى اللَّهِ

my Lord and your Lord. رَبِّي وَرَبِّكُم

There is no living being but He holds it by its forelock. مَّا مِن دَابَّةٍ إِلَّا هُوَ آخِذٌ بِنَاصِيَتِهَا

My Lord is indeed on a straight path. إِنَّ رَبِّي عَلَىٰ صِرَاطٍ مُّسْتَقِيمٍ ۝

57 But if you turn your backs on me, فَإِن تَوَلَّوْا

then [know that] I have communicated to you فَقَدْ أَبْلَغْتُكُم

whatever I was sent to you with. مَّا أُرْسِلْتُ بِهِ إِلَيْكُمْ

My Lord will make another people succeed you, وَيَسْتَخْلِفُ رَبِّي قَوْمًا غَيْرَكُمْ

and you will not hurt Him in the least. وَلَا تَضُرُّونَهُ شَيْئًا

My Lord is indeed watchful over all things.' إِنَّ رَبِّي عَلَىٰ كُلِّ شَيْءٍ حَفِيظٌ ۝

58 When Our edict came, وَلَمَّا جَاءَ أَمْرُنَا

We delivered Hūd and the faithful who were with him, نَجَّيْنَا هُودًا وَالَّذِينَ آمَنُوا مَعَهُ

by mercy from Us, بِرَحْمَةٍ مِّنَّا

and We delivered them from a harsh punishment. وَنَجَّيْنَاهُم مِّنْ عَذَابٍ غَلِيظٍ ۝

59 Such were the people of 'Ād: وَتِلْكَ عَادٌ

they disputed the signs of their Lord جَحَدُوا بِآيَاتِ رَبِّهِمْ

and disobeyed His apostles, وَعَصَوْا رُسُلَهُ

and followed the dictates of every stubborn tyrant. وَاتَّبَعُوا أَمْرَ كُلِّ جَبَّارٍ عَنِيدٍ ۝

60 So they were pursued by a curse in this world وَأُتْبِعُوا فِي هَٰذِهِ الدُّنْيَا لَعْنَةً

and on the Day of Resurrection. وَيَوْمَ الْقِيَامَةِ

Behold! 'Ād indeed defied their Lord. أَلَا إِنَّ عَادًا كَفَرُوا رَبَّهُمْ

Now, away with 'Ād, the people of Hud! أَلَا بُعْدًا لِّعَادٍ قَوْمِ هُودٍ ۝

61 And to Thamūd We sent Ṣāliḥ, their compatriot. وَإِلَىٰ ثَمُودَ أَخَاهُمْ صَالِحًا

He said, 'O my people! Worship God. قَالَ يَا قَوْمِ اعْبُدُوا اللَّهَ

You have no other god besides Him. مَا لَكُم مِّنْ إِلَٰهٍ غَيْرُهُ

He brought you forth from the earth هُوَ أَنشَأَكُم مِّنَ الْأَرْضِ

وَاسْتَعْمَرَكُمْ فِيهَا and made it your habitation.
فَاسْتَغْفِرُوهُ So plead with Him for forgiveness,
ثُمَّ تُوبُوا إِلَيْهِ then turn to Him penitently.
إِنَّ رَبِّي قَرِيبٌ مُّجِيبٌ ۝ My Lord is indeed nearmost and responsive.'

قَالُوا يَا صَالِحُ 62 They said, 'O Ṣāliḥ!
قَدْ كُنتَ فِينَا مَرْجُوًّا قَبْلَ هَٰذَا You were a source of hope to us before this.
أَتَنْهَانَا أَن نَّعْبُدَ Do you forbid us to worship
مَا يَعْبُدُ آبَاؤُنَا what our fathers have been worshiping?
وَإِنَّنَا لَفِي شَكٍّ مِّمَّا We have indeed grave doubts concerning
تَدْعُونَا إِلَيْهِ مُرِيبٍ ۝ that to which you invite us.'

قَالَ يَا قَوْمِ أَرَأَيْتُمْ 63 He said, 'O my people! Tell me,
إِن كُنتُ عَلَىٰ بَيِّنَةٍ مِّن رَّبِّي should I stand on a clear proof from my Lord,
وَآتَانِي مِنْهُ رَحْمَةً and He has granted me His own mercy,
فَمَن يَنصُرُنِي مِنَ اللَّهِ إِنْ عَصَيْتُهُ who will protect me from God should I disobey Him?
فَمَا تَزِيدُونَنِي غَيْرَ تَخْسِيرٍ ۝ For then you will increase me in nothing but loss.

وَيَا قَوْمِ هَٰذِهِ نَاقَةُ اللَّهِ لَكُمْ آيَةً 64 O my people! This she-camel of God is a sign for you.
فَذَرُوهَا تَأْكُلْ فِي أَرْضِ اللَّهِ Let her graze freely in God's land,
وَلَا تَمَسُّوهَا بِسُوءٍ and do not cause her any harm,
فَيَأْخُذَكُمْ عَذَابٌ قَرِيبٌ ۝ for then you will be seized by a prompt punishment.'

فَعَقَرُوهَا فَقَالَ 65 But they hamstrung her, whereupon he said,
تَمَتَّعُوا فِي دَارِكُمْ ثَلَاثَةَ أَيَّامٍ 'Enjoy yourselves in your homes for three days:
ذَٰلِكَ وَعْدٌ غَيْرُ مَكْذُوبٍ ۝ that is a promise not to be belied!'

فَلَمَّا جَاءَ أَمْرُنَا 66 So when Our edict came,
نَجَّيْنَا صَالِحًا وَالَّذِينَ آمَنُوا مَعَهُ We delivered Ṣāliḥ and the faithful who were with him
بِرَحْمَةٍ مِّنَّا by mercy from Us,
وَمِنْ خِزْيِ يَوْمِئِذٍ and from the [punishment and] disgrace of that day.
إِنَّ رَبَّكَ هُوَ الْقَوِيُّ الْعَزِيزُ ۝ Your Lord is indeed the All-strong, the All-mighty.

وَأَخَذَ الَّذِينَ ظَلَمُوا الصَّيْحَةُ 67 The Cry seized those who were wrongdoers,
فَأَصْبَحُوا فِي دِيَارِهِمْ جَاثِمِينَ ۝ and they lay lifeless prostrate in their homes,
كَأَن لَّمْ يَغْنَوْا فِيهَا 68 as if they had never lived there.

Behold! Thamūd indeed defied their Lord.
Now, away with Thamūd!

69 Certainly Our messengers came to Abraham
    with the good news, and said, 'Peace!'
    'Peace!' He replied.
    Presently he brought for them a roasted calf.
70 But when he saw their hands not reaching out for it,
    he took them amiss and felt a fear of them.
    They said, 'Do not be afraid.
    We have been sent to the people of Lot.'
71 His wife, standing by, laughed[1]
    as We gave her the good news of the birth of Isaac,
    and of Jacob after Isaac.
72 She said, 'Oh, my! Shall I, an old woman, bear children,
    and while this husband of mine is an old man?!
    That is indeed an odd thing!'
73 They said, 'Are you amazed at God's dispensation?
    That is God's mercy and His blessings upon you,
    members of the household.
    He is indeed all-laudable, all-glorious.'
74 So when the awe had left Abraham
    and the good news had reached him,
    he pleaded with Us concerning the people of Lot.
75 Abraham was indeed most forbearing,
    plaintive and penitent.
76 'O Abraham, let this matter alone!
    Your Lord's edict has already come,
    and an irrevocable punishment shall overtake them.'

---

[1] Or 'underwent menstruation.'

77 وَلَمَّا جَاءَتْ رُسُلُنَا لُوطًا
    سِيءَ بِهِمْ
    وَضَاقَ بِهِمْ ذَرْعًا
    وَقَالَ هَـٰذَا يَوْمٌ عَصِيبٌ ۝

77 When Our messengers came to Lot,
    he was distressed on their account
    and in a predicament for their sake,
    and he said, 'This is a terrible day!'

78 وَجَاءَهُ قَوْمُهُ يُهْرَعُونَ إِلَيْهِ
    وَمِن قَبْلُ كَانُوا يَعْمَلُونَ السَّيِّئَاتِ
    قَالَ يَا قَوْمِ هَـٰؤُلَاءِ بَنَاتِي
    هُنَّ أَطْهَرُ لَكُمْ
    فَاتَّقُوا اللَّهَ
    وَلَا تُخْزُونِ فِي ضَيْفِي
    أَلَيْسَ مِنكُمْ رَجُلٌ رَشِيدٌ ۝

78 Then his people came running toward him,
    and they had been committing vices heretofore.
    He said, 'O my people, these are my daughters:
    they are purer for you.[1]
    Be wary of God
    and do not humiliate me with regard to my guests.
    Isn't there a right-minded man among you?'

79 قَالُوا لَقَدْ عَلِمْتَ
    مَا لَنَا فِي بَنَاتِكَ مِنْ حَقٍّ
    وَإِنَّكَ لَتَعْلَمُ مَا نُرِيدُ ۝

79 They said, 'You already know
    that we have no interest in your daughters,
    and you surely know what we want.'

80 قَالَ لَوْ أَنَّ لِي بِكُمْ قُوَّةً
    أَوْ آوِي إِلَىٰ رُكْنٍ شَدِيدٍ ۝

80 He said, 'If only I had the power to deter you,
    or could take refuge in a mighty support!'

81 قَالُوا يَا لُوطُ إِنَّا رُسُلُ رَبِّكَ
    لَن يَصِلُوا إِلَيْكَ
    فَأَسْرِ بِأَهْلِكَ بِقِطْعٍ مِنَ اللَّيْلِ
    وَلَا يَلْتَفِتْ مِنكُمْ أَحَدٌ إِلَّا امْرَأَتَكَ
    إِنَّهُ مُصِيبُهَا مَا أَصَابَهُمْ
    إِنَّ مَوْعِدَهُمُ الصُّبْحُ
    أَلَيْسَ الصُّبْحُ بِقَرِيبٍ ۝

81 They said, 'O Lot, we are messengers of your Lord.
    They will never get at you.
    Set out with your family in a watch of the night,
    and none of you shall turn round, except your wife;
    indeed she will be struck by what strikes them.
    Indeed, their tryst is the dawn.
    Is not the dawn already near?'

82 فَلَمَّا جَاءَ أَمْرُنَا
    جَعَلْنَا عَالِيَهَا سَافِلَهَا
    وَأَمْطَرْنَا عَلَيْهَا حِجَارَةً
    مِن سِجِّيلٍ مَنضُودٍ ۝

82 So when Our edict came,
    We made its[2] topmost part its nethermost,
    and We rained on it stones
    of laminar shale,

83 مُسَوَّمَةً عِندَ رَبِّكَ
    وَمَا هِيَ مِنَ الظَّالِمِينَ بِبَعِيدٍ ۝

83 sent from your Lord [for the transgressors],[3]
    never far from the wrongdoers.

---

[1] That is, it would be purer for you to get married to them.
[2] That is, of the city of Sodom.
[3] Cf. **51**:34.

84 And to Midian We sent Shu'ayb, their compatriot.
He said, 'O my people! Worship God.
You have no other god besides Him.
Do not diminish the measure or the balance.
I indeed see that you are faring well,
but I fear for you
the punishment of a besieging day.'

85 'O my people!
Observe fully the measure and the balance with justice,
and do not cheat the people of their goods,[1]
and do not act wickedly on the earth, causing corruption.'

86 'What remains of God's provision[2] is better for you,
should you be faithful,
and I am not a keeper over you.'

87 They said, 'O Shu'ayb,
does your worship require that we abandon
what our fathers have been worshiping,
or that we should not do with our wealth whatever we wish?
You are indeed a gentle and sensible person.'

88 He said, 'O my people! Have you considered,
should I stand on a clear proof from my Lord,
who has provided me a good provision from Himself?[3]
I do not wish to oppose you
by what I forbid you.
I only desire to put things in order, as far as I can,
and my success lies only with God:
in Him alone I have put my trust,
and to Him I turn penitently.

---

[1] That is, by employing short weights and measures.
[2] That is, of your lawful earnings.
[3] That is, 'If I stand on a clear proof from my Lord, who has provided me with lawful means of livelihood, is it right for you to reject my call to faith in God and fair dealing?'

89 وَيَا قَوْمِ لَا يَجْرِمَنَّكُمْ شِقَاقِي أَنْ يُصِيبَكُمْ مِثْلُ مَا أَصَابَ قَوْمَ نُوحٍ أَوْ قَوْمَ هُودٍ أَوْ قَوْمَ صَالِحٍ ۚ وَمَا قَوْمُ لُوطٍ مِنْكُمْ بِبَعِيدٍ ۝ 89 O my people, do not let your defiance toward me lead you to be visited by the like of what was visited on the people of Noah, or the people of Hūd, or the people of Ṣāliḥ; and the people of Lot are not far from you.

90 وَاسْتَغْفِرُوا رَبَّكُمْ ثُمَّ تُوبُوا إِلَيْهِ ۚ إِنَّ رَبِّي رَحِيمٌ وَدُودٌ ۝ 90 Plead with your Lord for forgiveness, then turn to Him penitently. My Lord is indeed all-merciful, all-affectionate.'

91 قَالُوا يَا شُعَيْبُ مَا نَفْقَهُ كَثِيرًا مِمَّا تَقُولُ وَإِنَّا لَنَرَاكَ فِينَا ضَعِيفًا ۖ وَلَوْلَا رَهْطُكَ لَرَجَمْنَاكَ ۖ وَمَا أَنْتَ عَلَيْنَا بِعَزِيزٍ ۝ 91 They said, 'O Shu'ayb, we do not understand much of what you say. We indeed see that you are weak amongst us, and were it not for your tribe, we would have stoned you, and you are not a formidable hindrance for us.'

92 قَالَ يَا قَوْمِ أَرَهْطِي أَعَزُّ عَلَيْكُمْ مِنَ اللَّهِ وَاتَّخَذْتُمُوهُ وَرَاءَكُمْ ظِهْرِيًّا ۖ إِنَّ رَبِّي بِمَا تَعْمَلُونَ مُحِيطٌ ۝ 92 He said, 'O my people! Is my tribe more formidable in your sight than God, to whom you pay no regard? My Lord indeed encompasses whatever you are doing.

93 وَيَا قَوْمِ اعْمَلُوا عَلَىٰ مَكَانَتِكُمْ إِنِّي عَامِلٌ ۖ سَوْفَ تَعْلَمُونَ مَنْ يَأْتِيهِ عَذَابٌ يُخْزِيهِ وَمَنْ هُوَ كَاذِبٌ ۖ وَارْتَقِبُوا إِنِّي مَعَكُمْ رَقِيبٌ ۝ 93 O my people! Act according to your ability; I too am acting. Soon you will know who will be overtaken by a punishment that will disgrace him, and who is a liar. So be on the watch; I too will be watching along with you.'

94 وَلَمَّا جَاءَ أَمْرُنَا نَجَّيْنَا شُعَيْبًا وَالَّذِينَ آمَنُوا مَعَهُ بِرَحْمَةٍ مِنَّا وَأَخَذَتِ الَّذِينَ ظَلَمُوا الصَّيْحَةُ فَأَصْبَحُوا فِي دِيَارِهِمْ جَاثِمِينَ ۝ 94 When Our edict came, We delivered Shu'ayb and the faithful who were with him by mercy from Us. And the Cry seized those who were wrongdoers, whereat they lay lifeless prostrate in their homes,

95 كَأَنْ لَمْ يَغْنَوْا فِيهَا ۗ أَلَا بُعْدًا لِمَدْيَنَ 95 as if they had never lived there. Now, away with Midian!

—just as Thamūd was done away with! كَمَا بَعِدَتْ ثَمُودُ ۝

96 Certainly We sent Moses with Our signs
and a clear authority
97 to Pharaoh and his elite,
but they followed Pharaoh's dictates,
and Pharaoh's dictates were not right-minded.
98 On the Day of Resurrection he will lead his people
and conduct them into the Fire:
an evil goal for the incoming![1]
99 They are pursued by a curse in this world,
as well as on the Day of Resurrection;
evil is the award conferred upon them!

100 These are from the accounts of the townships
which We recount to you.
Of them there are some that still stand,
and some that have been mown down.
101 We did not wrong them, but they wronged themselves.
Of no avail to them were their gods whom
they would invoke besides God, in any wise,
when your Lord's edict came,
and they[2] did not increase them in anything but ruin.
102 Such is the seizing of your Lord
when He seizes the townships that are wrongdoing.
His seizing is indeed painful and severe.
103 There is indeed a sign in that
for those who fear the punishment of the Hereafter.
That is a day on which all mankind will be gathered,

---

[1] Or 'an evil watering place for the thirsty.'
[2] That is, their false gods.

and it is a day witnessed by all creatures.
104 We do not defer it but for a determinate term.
105 The day it comes, no one shall speak except by His leave.
On that day, some of them will be wretched
and some felicitous.
106 As for the wretched, they shall be in the Fire:
their lot therein will be groaning and wailing.
107 They will remain in it
for as long as the heavens and the earth endure
—except what *your* Lord may wish;
indeed *your* Lord does whatever He desires.
108 As for the felicitous, they will be in paradise.
They will remain in it
for as long as the heavens and the earth endure
—except what *your* Lord may wish—
an endless bounty.
109 So *do not be* in doubt about what these[1] worship:
they worship just as their fathers worshiped before,
and We shall surely pay them their full share,
undiminished.

110 Certainly We gave Moses the Book,
but differences arose about it,
and were it not for a prior decree of *your* Lord,
a decision would have been made between them;
indeed they are in grave doubt concerning it.
111 *Your* Lord will indeed recompense everyone fully
for their works.
He is indeed well aware of what they do.
112 So *be steadfast*, just as you have been commanded—

---
[1] That is, the idolaters of Arabia.

    you and whoever has turned to God with *you*—

    and do not overstep the bounds.

    Indeed, He watches what you do.

113 Do not incline toward the wrongdoers,

    lest the Fire should touch you,

    and you will not have any protector besides God;

    then you will not be helped.

114 *Maintain* the prayer at the two ends of the day,[1]

    and during the early hours of the night.

    Indeed, good deeds efface misdeeds.[2]

    That is an admonition for the mindful.

115 And *be* patient;

    indeed God does not waste the reward of the virtuous.

116 Why were there not among the generations before you a remnant of the wise

    who might forbid corruption in the land, except a few of those whom We delivered from among them?

    Those who were wrongdoers pursued [gratification]

    in the means of affluence they had been granted,

    and they were a guilty lot.

117 *Your* Lord would never destroy the townships unjustly

    while their inhabitants were bringing about reform.

118 Had *your* Lord wished, He would have made mankind one community;

    but they continue to differ,

119 except those on whom *your* Lord has mercy

    —and that is why He created them—

    and the word of *your* Lord has been fulfilled:

---

[1] That is, at dawn and sunset.
[2] Or 'Indeed, good deeds remove ills,' or 'Indeed, virtues efface vices.'

'I will surely fill hell with jinn and humans,
all together!'[1]

120 Whatever that We relate to you
of the accounts of the apostles
are those by which We strengthen *your* heart,
and there has come to *you* in this *sūrah* the truth
and an advice and admonition for the faithful.

121 *Say* to those who do not have faith,
'Act according to your ability; we too are acting.

122 And wait! We too are waiting.'

123 To God belongs the Unseen of the heavens and the earth,
and to Him all matters are returned.
So *worship* Him and trust in Him.
Your Lord is not oblivious of what you do.

12. JOSEPH[2]
Yūsuf

In the Name of God,
the All-beneficent, the All-merciful.

1 *Alif, Lām, Rā.* These are the signs of the Manifest Book.

2 Indeed, We have sent it down as an Arabic Qur'ān
so that you may exercise your reason.

3 We will recount to *you* the best of narratives[3]
in what We have revealed to *you* of this Qur'ān,
and prior to it *you* were indeed
among those who are unaware of it.

4 When Joseph said to his father,
'Father! I saw eleven planets,[4]

---

[1] That is, all of those who are followers of Satan. See **38**:85.
[2] 'Yūsuf' is Arabic for 'Joseph,' whose well-known story is told in this Makkī *sūrah*.
[3] Or 'We will tell you a story in the best style of narration.'
[4] Or 'stars.'

وَالشَّمْسَ وَالْقَمَرَ and the sun and the moon:
رَأَيْتُهُمْ لِي سَاجِدِينَ ۝ I saw them prostrating themselves before me,'

قَالَ يَا بُنَيَّ 5 he said, 'My son,
لَا تَقْصُصْ رُؤْيَاكَ عَلَىٰ إِخْوَتِكَ do not recount your dream to your brothers,
فَيَكِيدُوا لَكَ كَيْدًا ۚ lest they should devise schemes against you.
إِنَّ الشَّيْطَانَ لِلْإِنسَانِ عَدُوٌّ مُّبِينٌ ۝ Satan is indeed man's manifest enemy.

وَكَذَٰلِكَ يَجْتَبِيكَ رَبُّكَ 6 That is how your Lord will choose you
وَيُعَلِّمُكَ مِن تَأْوِيلِ الْأَحَادِيثِ and teach you the interpretation of dreams,[1]
وَيُتِمُّ نِعْمَتَهُ عَلَيْكَ and complete His blessing upon you
وَعَلَىٰ آلِ يَعْقُوبَ and upon the house of Jacob,
كَمَا أَتَمَّهَا عَلَىٰ أَبَوَيْكَ مِن قَبْلُ just as He completed it earlier for your fathers,
إِبْرَاهِيمَ وَإِسْحَاقَ ۚ Abraham and Isaac.
إِنَّ رَبَّكَ عَلِيمٌ حَكِيمٌ ۝ Your Lord is indeed all-knowing and all-wise.'

لَّقَدْ كَانَ فِي يُوسُفَ وَإِخْوَتِهِ 7 In Joseph and his brothers there are certainly
آيَاتٌ لِّلسَّائِلِينَ ۝ signs for the seekers.

إِذْ قَالُوا لَيُوسُفُ وَأَخُوهُ 8 When they[2] said, 'Surely Joseph and his brother[3]
أَحَبُّ إِلَىٰ أَبِينَا مِنَّا are dearer to our father than the rest of us,
وَنَحْنُ عُصْبَةٌ though we are a hardy band.
إِنَّ أَبَانَا لَفِي ضَلَالٍ مُّبِينٍ ۝ Our father is indeed in plain error.'

اقْتُلُوا يُوسُفَ أَوِ اطْرَحُوهُ أَرْضًا 9 'Kill Joseph or cast him away into some distant land,
يَخْلُ لَكُمْ وَجْهُ أَبِيكُمْ so that your father's attention may be exclusively towards you,
وَتَكُونُوا مِن بَعْدِهِ قَوْمًا صَالِحِينَ ۝ and you may thereafter become a righteous lot.'

قَالَ قَائِلٌ مِّنْهُمْ لَا تَقْتُلُوا يُوسُفَ 10 One of them said, 'Do not kill Joseph,
وَأَلْقُوهُ فِي غَيَابَتِ الْجُبِّ but throw him into the recess of a well
يَلْتَقِطْهُ بَعْضُ السَّيَّارَةِ so that some caravan may pick him up,
إِن كُنتُمْ فَاعِلِينَ ۝ if you are to do anything.'

قَالُوا يَا أَبَانَا 11 They said, 'Father!
مَا لَكَ لَا تَأْمَنَّا عَلَىٰ يُوسُفَ Why is it that you do not trust us with Joseph?

---

[1] Or 'the interpretation of visions.'
[2] That is, the brothers of Joseph ('a).
[3] That is, Benjamin.

We are indeed his well-wishers. وَإِنَّا لَهُ لَنَاصِحُونَ ۝

12 Let him go with us tomorrow
  so that he may eat lots of fruits and play,
  and we will indeed take good care of him.'

13 He said, 'It really upsets me that you should take him away,
  and I fear the wolf may eat him
  while you are oblivious of him.'

14 They said, 'Should the wolf eat him
  while we are a hardy band,
  then we will indeed be losers!'

15 So when they took him away
  and conspired to put him into the recess of a well,
  We revealed to him, '[A day will come when]
  you will surely inform them about this affair of theirs
  while they are not aware of your identity.'

16 In the evening, they came weeping to their father.

17 They said, 'Father! We had gone racing
  and left Joseph with our things,
  whereat the wolf ate him.
  But you will not believe us even if we spoke truly.'

18 And they produced sham blood on his shirt.
  He said,
  'No, your souls have made a matter seem decorous to you.
  Yet patience is graceful,
  and God is my resort against what you allege.'

19 There came a caravan, and they sent their water-drawer,
  who let down his bucket.
  'Good news!' he said. 'This is a young boy!'
  So they hid him as a piece of merchandise,
  and God knew best what they were doing.

20 And they sold him for a cheap price, a few dirhams,
    for they set small store by him.
21 The man from Egypt who had bought him said to his wife,
    'Give him an honourable place in the household.[1]
    Maybe he will be useful to us,
    or we may adopt him as a son.'

Thus did We establish Joseph in the land
and that We might teach him the interpretation of dreams.
God has full command of His affairs,
but most people do not know.

22 When he came of age,
    We gave him judgement and sacred knowledge,
    and thus do We reward the virtuous.
23 The woman in whose house he was, solicited him.
    She closed the doors and said, 'Come!!'
    He said, 'God forbid! He is indeed my Lord;
    He has given me a good abode.[2]
    Indeed, the wrongdoers do not prosper.'
24 She certainly made for him;
    and he would have made for her too
    had he not beheld the proof of his Lord.
    So it was, that We might turn away from him
    all evil and indecency.
    He was indeed one of Our dedicated servants.
25 They raced to the door,
    and she tore his shirt from behind,
    and they ran into her husband at the door.

---

[1] Or 'Keep him in a respectable manner.'
[2] Or 'He is indeed my master; he has kept me in a nice manner.'

She said, 'What is to be the requital of him
who has evil intentions for your wife
except imprisonment or a painful punishment?'

26 He said, 'It was she who solicited me.'
A witness of her own household testified [saying]:
'If his shirt is torn from the front,
she tells the truth and he lies.

27 But if his shirt is torn from behind,
then she lies and he tells the truth.'

28 So when he saw that his shirt was torn from behind,
he said, 'This is a case of you women's guile!
Your guile is great indeed!

29 Joseph, let this matter alone,
and you, woman, plead for forgiveness for your sin,
for you have indeed been erring.'

30 Some of the townswomen said,
'The chieftain's wife
has solicited her slave boy!
He has captivated her love.
Indeed, we see her to be in plain error.'

31 When she heard of their machinations,
she sent for them and arranged a repast,
and gave each of them a knife,
and said [to Joseph], 'Come out before them.'
So when they saw him, they marvelled at him
and cut their hands [absent-mindedly],
and they said, 'Good heavens!
This is not a human being!
This is but a noble angel!'

32 She said, 'He is the one on whose account you blamed me.

Certainly I did solicit him,
but he was continent,
and if he does not do what I bid him,
he will surely be imprisoned and humbled.'

33 He said, 'My Lord! The prison is dearer to me
than to what they invite me.
If You do not turn away their schemes from me,
I will incline towards them
and become one of the ignorant.'

34 So his Lord answered him
and turned away their stratagems from him.
Indeed, He is the All-hearing, the All-knowing.

35 Then it appeared to them,[1]
after they had seen all the signs [of his innocence],
that they should confine him for some time.

36 There entered the prison two youths along with him.
One of them said, 'I dreamed that I am pressing grapes.'
The other said, 'I dreamed that I am carrying
bread on my head, from which the birds are eating.'
'Inform us of its interpretation,' [they said],
'for indeed we see you to be a virtuous man.'

37 He said, 'Before the meals you are served come to you
I will inform you of its interpretation.
That is among things my Lord has taught me.
Indeed, I renounce the creed of the people
who have no faith in God
and who also disbelieve in the Hereafter.

38 I follow the creed of my fathers,
Abraham, Isaac and Jacob.

---

[1] That is, the menfolk.

مَا كَانَ لَنَا أَنْ نُشْرِكَ بِاللَّهِ مِنْ شَيْءٍ

It is not for us to ascribe any partner to God.

ذَٰلِكَ مِنْ فَضْلِ اللَّهِ عَلَيْنَا

That is by virtue of God's grace upon us

وَعَلَى النَّاسِ

and upon all mankind,

وَلَٰكِنَّ أَكْثَرَ النَّاسِ لَا يَشْكُرُونَ ۝

but most people do not give thanks.

يَا صَاحِبَيِ السِّجْنِ

39 O my prison mates!

أَأَرْبَابٌ مُتَفَرِّقُونَ خَيْرٌ

Are different masters better,

أَمِ اللَّهُ الْوَاحِدُ الْقَهَّارُ ۝

or God, the One, the All-paramount?

مَا تَعْبُدُونَ مِنْ دُونِهِ إِلَّا أَسْمَاءً

40 You do not worship besides Him but mere names

سَمَّيْتُمُوهَا أَنْتُمْ وَآبَاؤُكُمْ

that you and your fathers have coined,

مَا أَنْزَلَ اللَّهُ بِهَا مِنْ سُلْطَانٍ

for which God has not sent down any authority.

إِنِ الْحُكْمُ إِلَّا لِلَّهِ

Dispensation belongs only to God.

أَمَرَ أَلَّا تَعْبُدُوا إِلَّا إِيَّاهُ

He has commanded you to worship none except Him.

ذَٰلِكَ الدِّينُ الْقَيِّمُ

That is the upright religion,

وَلَٰكِنَّ أَكْثَرَ النَّاسِ لَا يَعْلَمُونَ ۝

but most people do not know.

يَا صَاحِبَيِ السِّجْنِ

41 O my prison mates!

أَمَّا أَحَدُكُمَا فَيَسْقِي رَبَّهُ خَمْرًا

As for one of you, he will serve wine to his master,

وَأَمَّا الْآخَرُ فَيُصْلَبُ

and as for the other, he will be crucified,

فَتَأْكُلُ الطَّيْرُ مِنْ رَأْسِهِ

and vultures will eat from his head.

قُضِيَ الْأَمْرُ الَّذِي فِيهِ تَسْتَفْتِيَانِ ۝

The matter about which you inquire has been decided.'

وَقَالَ لِلَّذِي ظَنَّ

42 Then he said to the one whom he knew

أَنَّهُ نَاجٍ مِنْهُمَا

would be delivered from among the two:

اذْكُرْنِي عِنْدَ رَبِّكَ

'Mention me to your master.'

فَأَنْسَاهُ الشَّيْطَانُ

But Satan caused him to forget

ذِكْرَ رَبِّهِ

mentioning it to his master.

فَلَبِثَ فِي السِّجْنِ بِضْعَ سِنِينَ ۝

So he remained in the prison for several years.

وَقَالَ الْمَلِكُ

43 [One day] the king said,

إِنِّي أَرَىٰ سَبْعَ بَقَرَاتٍ سِمَانٍ

'I saw in a dream seven fat cows

يَأْكُلُهُنَّ سَبْعٌ عِجَافٌ

being devoured by seven lean ones,

وَسَبْعَ سُنْبُلَاتٍ خُضْرٍ

and seven green ears

وَأُخَرَ يَابِسَاتٍ   and [seven] others that were dry.
يَا أَيُّهَا الْمَلَأُ أَفْتُونِي فِي رُؤْيَايَ   O courtiers, give me your opinion about my dream,
إِنْ كُنْتُمْ لِلرُّؤْيَا تَعْبُرُونَ ۝   if you can interpret dreams.'

44 قَالُوا أَضْغَاثُ أَحْلَامٍ   They said, 'These are muddled dreams,
وَمَا نَحْنُ بِتَأْوِيلِ الْأَحْلَامِ بِعَالِمِينَ ۝   and we do not know the interpretation of such dreams.'

45 وَقَالَ الَّذِي نَجَا مِنْهُمَا   Said the one of the two who had been released [from
وَادَّكَرَ بَعْدَ أُمَّةٍ   the prison, remembering [Joseph] after a long time:
أَنَا أُنَبِّئُكُمْ بِتَأْوِيلِهِ   'I will inform you of its interpretation;
فَأَرْسِلُونِ ۝   so let me go [to meet Joseph in the prison].'

46 يُوسُفُ أَيُّهَا الصِّدِّيقُ   'Joseph,' [he said], 'O truthful one,
أَفْتِنَا فِي سَبْعِ بَقَرَاتٍ سِمَانٍ   give us your opinion concerning seven fat cows
يَأْكُلُهُنَّ سَبْعٌ عِجَافٌ   who are eaten by seven lean ones,
وَسَبْعِ سُنْبُلَاتٍ خُضْرٍ وَأُخَرَ يَابِسَاتٍ   and seven green ears and [seven] others dry,
لَعَلِّي أَرْجِعُ إِلَى النَّاسِ   that I may return to these people
لَعَلَّهُمْ يَعْلَمُونَ ۝   so that they may know [the truth of the matter].'

47 قَالَ تَزْرَعُونَ سَبْعَ سِنِينَ دَأَبًا   He said, 'You will sow for seven consecutive years.
فَمَا حَصَدْتُمْ فَذَرُوهُ فِي سُنْبُلِهِ   Then leave in the ear whatever grain you harvest,
إِلَّا قَلِيلًا مِمَّا تَأْكُلُونَ ۝   except a little that you eat.

48 ثُمَّ يَأْتِي مِنْ بَعْدِ ذَلِكَ سَبْعٌ شِدَادٌ   Then after that there will come seven hard years
يَأْكُلْنَ مَا قَدَّمْتُمْ لَهُنَّ   which will eat up whatever you have set aside for them
إِلَّا قَلِيلًا مِمَّا تُحْصِنُونَ ۝   —all except a little which you preserve for seed.

49 ثُمَّ يَأْتِي مِنْ بَعْدِ ذَلِكَ عَامٌ   Then after that there will come a year
فِيهِ يُغَاثُ النَّاسُ   wherein the people will be granted relief
وَفِيهِ يَعْصِرُونَ ۝   and provided with rains therein.'[1]

50 وَقَالَ الْمَلِكُ ائْتُونِي بِهِ   The king said, 'Bring him to me!'
فَلَمَّا جَاءَهُ الرَّسُولُ   When the messenger came to him,[2]
قَالَ ارْجِعْ إِلَى رَبِّكَ   he said, 'Go back to your master,

---

[1] The translation given here is in accordance with the reading *yuṣarūn* narrated from al-Imam al-Ṣādiq; see *Majmaʿ al-Bayān* and *Tafsīr al-Qummī*; see also *Lisān al-ʿArab*, under *ʿaṣr*. The same reading is attributed to al-Aʿraj and ʿĪsā al-Baṣrī (*Muʿjam al-Qirāʾāt al-Qurʾāniyyah*). However, in accordance with the reading *yaʿṣirūn*, the meaning will be 'they will press [i.e. grapes or oil seeds, for juice and oil] therein.'

[2] That is, to Joseph (ʿa).

and ask him about the affair of the women
who cut their hands.
My Lord is indeed well aware of their stratagems.'
51 The king said, 'What was your business, women,
when you solicited Joseph?'
They said, 'Heaven be praised!
We know of no evil in him.'
The prince's wife said,
'Now the truth has come to light!
It was I who solicited him,
and he is indeed telling the truth.'
52 [Joseph said], 'I initiated this inquiry,
that he[1] may know that I did not betray him in his absence,
and that God does not further
the schemes of the treacherous.

[PART 13]

53 Yet I do not absolve my [own carnal] soul,
for the [carnal] soul indeed prompts humans to evil,
except inasmuch as my Lord has mercy.
My Lord is indeed all-forgiving, all-merciful.'
54 The king said, 'Bring him to me,
I will make him my favourite.'
Then, when he had spoken with him, he said,
'Indeed, today you will be honoured and trustworthy with us.'
55 He said, 'Put me in charge of the country's granaries.
I am indeed fastidious and well-informed.'
56 That is how We established Joseph in the land
that he may settle in it wherever he wished.
We confer Our mercy on whomever We wish,

---

[1] That is, the Egyptian nobleman in whose house Joseph ('a) was living.

and We do not waste the reward of the virtuous. وَلَا نُضِيعُ أَجْرَ الْمُحْسِنِينَ ۝

57 And the reward of the Hereafter is surely better وَلَأَجْرُ الْآخِرَةِ خَيْرٌ
for those who have faith and are Godwary. لِلَّذِينَ آمَنُوا وَكَانُوا يَتَّقُونَ ۝

58 [After some years] the brothers of Joseph came وَجَاءَ إِخْوَةُ يُوسُفَ
and entered his presence. فَدَخَلُوا عَلَيْهِ
He recognized them, but they did not recognize him. فَعَرَفَهُمْ وَهُمْ لَهُ مُنكِرُونَ ۝

59 When he had furnished them with their provision, وَلَمَّا جَهَّزَهُم بِجَهَازِهِمْ
he said, 'Bring me a brother that you have قَالَ ائْتُونِي بِأَخٍ لَكُم
through your father. مِّنْ أَبِيكُمْ
Do you not see that I give the full measure أَلَا تَرَوْنَ أَنِّي أُوفِي الْكَيْلَ
and that I am the best of hosts? وَأَنَا خَيْرُ الْمُنزِلِينَ ۝

60 But if you do not bring him to me, فَإِن لَّمْ تَأْتُونِي بِهِ
then there will be no rations for you with me, فَلَا كَيْلَ لَكُمْ عِندِي
and don't ever approach me.' وَلَا تَقْرَبُونِ ۝

61 They said, 'We will solicit him from his father. قَالُوا سَنُرَاوِدُ عَنْهُ أَبَاهُ
That we will surely do.' وَإِنَّا لَفَاعِلُونَ ۝

62 He said to his servants, وَقَالَ لِفِتْيَانِهِ
'Put their money back into their saddlebags. اجْعَلُوا بِضَاعَتَهُمْ فِي رِحَالِهِمْ
Maybe they will recognize it لَعَلَّهُمْ يَعْرِفُونَهَا
when they return to their folks, إِذَا انقَلَبُوا إِلَىٰ أَهْلِهِمْ
and maybe they will come back again.' لَعَلَّهُمْ يَرْجِعُونَ ۝

63 So when they returned to their father, they said, فَلَمَّا رَجَعُوا إِلَىٰ أَبِيهِمْ قَالُوا
'Father, the measure has been withheld from us, يَا أَبَانَا مُنِعَ مِنَّا الْكَيْلُ
so let our brother go with us فَأَرْسِلْ مَعَنَا أَخَانَا
so that we may obtain the measure, نَكْتَلْ
and we will indeed take good care of him.' وَإِنَّا لَهُ لَحَافِظُونَ ۝

64 He said, 'Should I trust you with him قَالَ هَلْ آمَنُكُمْ عَلَيْهِ
just as I trusted you with his brother before? إِلَّا كَمَا أَمِنتُكُمْ عَلَىٰ أَخِيهِ مِن قَبْلُ
Yet God is the best of protectors, فَاللَّهُ خَيْرٌ حَافِظًا

and He is the most merciful of merciful ones.'

65 And when they opened their baggage,
    they found their money restored to them.
    They said, 'Father, what more do we want?!
    This is our money, restored to us!
    We will get provisions for our family
    and take care of our brother,
    and add another camel-load of rations.
    These are meagre rations.'

66 He said, 'I will not let him go with you
    until you give me a solemn pledge by God
    that you will surely bring him back to me,
    unless you are made to perish.'
    When they had given him their solemn pledge,
    he said, 'God is witness over what we say.'

67 And he said, 'My sons, do not enter by one gate,
    but enter by separate gates,
    though I cannot avail you anything against God.
    Sovereignty belongs only to God.
    In Him alone I have put my trust;
    and in Him alone let all the trusting put their trust.'

68 When they entered whence their father had bidden them,
    it did not avail them anything against God,
    but only fulfilled a wish in Jacob's heart.
    He had indeed the knowledge of what We had taught him,
    but most people do not know.

69 When they entered into the presence of Joseph,
    he set his brother close to himself,
    and said, 'I am indeed your brother,
    so do not sorrow for what they used to do.'

70 When he had furnished them with their provisions,
he put the drinking-cup into his brother's saddlebag.
Then a herald shouted: 'O men of the caravan!
You are indeed thieves!'

71 They said, as they turned towards them,
'What are you missing?'

72 They said, 'We miss the king's goblet.'
'Whoever brings it shall have a camel-load of grain,'
[said the steward], 'I will guarantee that.'

73 They said, 'By God!
You certainly know that we did not come
to make trouble in this country, and we are not thieves.'

74 They said, 'What shall be its requital
if you prove to be lying?'

75 They said, 'The requital for it
shall be that he in whose saddlebag it is found
shall give himself over as its requital.
Thus do we requite the wrongdoers.'

76 Then he began with their sacks,
before opening his brother's sack.
Then he took it out from his brother's sack.
Thus did We devise for Joseph's sake.
He could not have held his brother under the king's law
unless God willed otherwise.
We raise in rank whomever We please,
and above every man of knowledge
is One who knows best.[1]

77 They said, 'If he has stolen [there is no wonder];
a brother of his had stolen before.'

---

[1] Or 'above every man of knowledge is one who knows better.'

فَأَسَرَّهَا يُوسُفُ فِي نَفْسِهِ

Thereupon Joseph kept the matter to himself

وَلَمْ يُبْدِهَا لَهُمْ

and he did not disclose it to them.

قَالَ أَنْتُمْ شَرٌّ مَكَانًا

He said, 'You are in a worse state!

وَاللَّهُ أَعْلَمُ بِمَا تَصِفُونَ ۝

And God knows best what you allege.'

قَالُوا يَا أَيُّهَا الْعَزِيزُ 78

They said, 'O emir!

إِنَّ لَهُ أَبًا شَيْخًا كَبِيرًا

Indeed, he has a father, a very old man;

فَخُذْ أَحَدَنَا مَكَانَهُ

so take one of us in his place.

إِنَّا نَرَاكَ مِنَ الْمُحْسِنِينَ ۝

Indeed, we see that you are a virtuous man.'

قَالَ مَعَاذَ اللَّهِ أَنْ نَأْخُذَ 79

He said, 'God forbid that we should detain

إِلَّا مَنْ وَجَدْنَا مَتَاعَنَا عِنْدَهُ

anyone except him with whom we found our wares,

إِنَّا إِذًا لَظَالِمُونَ ۝

for then we would indeed be wrongdoers.'

فَلَمَّا اسْتَيْأَسُوا مِنْهُ 80

When they had despaired of moving him,

خَلَصُوا نَجِيًّا

they withdrew to confer privately.

قَالَ كَبِيرُهُمْ أَلَمْ تَعْلَمُوا أَنَّ أَبَاكُمْ

The eldest of them said, 'Don't you know that your father

قَدْ أَخَذَ عَلَيْكُمْ مَوْثِقًا مِنَ اللَّهِ

has taken a solemn pledge from you by God,

وَمِنْ قَبْلُ مَا فَرَّطْتُمْ فِي يُوسُفَ

and earlier you have neglected your duty in regard to Joseph?

فَلَنْ أَبْرَحَ الْأَرْضَ حَتَّى يَأْذَنَ لِي أَبِي

So I will never leave this land until my father permits me,

أَوْ يَحْكُمَ اللَّهُ لِي

or God passes a judgement for me

وَهُوَ خَيْرُ الْحَاكِمِينَ ۝

and He is the best of judges.

ارْجِعُوا إِلَى أَبِيكُمْ فَقُولُوا يَا أَبَانَا 81

Go back to your father, and say, "Father!

إِنَّ ابْنَكَ سَرَقَ

Your son has indeed committed theft,

وَمَا شَهِدْنَا إِلَّا بِمَا عَلِمْنَا

and we testified only to what we knew,[1]

وَمَا كُنَّا لِلْغَيْبِ حَافِظِينَ ۝

and we could not have forestalled the unseen.

وَاسْأَلِ الْقَرْيَةَ الَّتِي كُنَّا فِيهَا 82

Ask the people of the town we were in

وَالْعِيرَ الَّتِي أَقْبَلْنَا فِيهَا

and the caravan with which we came.

وَإِنَّا لَصَادِقُونَ ۝

We indeed speak the truth."'

قَالَ بَلْ 83

He[2] said, 'No,

سَوَّلَتْ لَكُمْ أَنْفُسُكُمْ أَمْرًا

your souls have made a matter seem decorous to you.

فَصَبْرٌ جَمِيلٌ

Yet patience is graceful.

---

[1] That is, concerning the penalty for theft according to the custom of the Canaanites.
[2] That is, Jacob ('a), after hearing what his sons had told him.

Maybe God will bring them all back to me. عَسَى اللَّهُ أَن يَأْتِيَنِي بِهِمْ جَمِيعًا
Indeed, He is the All-knowing, the All-wise.' إِنَّهُ هُوَ الْعَلِيمُ الْحَكِيمُ ۝

84 He turned away from them and said, 'Alas for Joseph!' وَتَوَلَّىٰ عَنْهُمْ وَقَالَ يَا أَسَفَىٰ عَلَىٰ يُوسُفَ
    His eyes had turned white with grief, وَابْيَضَّتْ عَيْنَاهُ مِنَ الْحُزْنِ
    and he choked with suppressed agony. فَهُوَ كَظِيمٌ ۝

85 They said, 'By God! You will go on remembering Joseph قَالُوا تَاللَّهِ تَفْتَأُ تَذْكُرُ يُوسُفَ
    until you wreck your health حَتَّىٰ تَكُونَ حَرَضًا
    or perish.' أَوْ تَكُونَ مِنَ الْهَالِكِينَ ۝

86 He said, 'I complain of my anguish and grief only to God. قَالَ إِنَّمَا أَشْكُو بَثِّي وَحُزْنِي إِلَى اللَّهِ
    I know from God what you do not know.' وَأَعْلَمُ مِنَ اللَّهِ مَا لَا تَعْلَمُونَ ۝

87 'Go, my sons, and look for Joseph and his brother, يَا بَنِيَّ اذْهَبُوا فَتَحَسَّسُوا مِنْ يُوسُفَ وَأَخِيهِ
    and do not despair of God's mercy. وَلَا تَيْأَسُوا مِنْ رَوْحِ اللَّهِ
    Indeed, no one despairs of God's mercy إِنَّهُ لَا يَيْأَسُ مِنْ رَوْحِ اللَّهِ
    except the faithless lot.' إِلَّا الْقَوْمُ الْكَافِرُونَ ۝

88 Then, when they entered into his presence, فَلَمَّا دَخَلُوا عَلَيْهِ
    they said, 'O emir! Distress has befallen us and our family, قَالُوا يَا أَيُّهَا الْعَزِيزُ مَسَّنَا وَأَهْلَنَا الضُّرُّ
    and we have brought just a meager sum. وَجِئْنَا بِبِضَاعَةٍ مُزْجَاةٍ
    Yet grant us the full measure and be charitable to us! فَأَوْفِ لَنَا الْكَيْلَ وَتَصَدَّقْ عَلَيْنَا
    God indeed rewards the charitable.' إِنَّ اللَّهَ يَجْزِي الْمُتَصَدِّقِينَ ۝

89 He said, 'Have you realized what you did to Joseph قَالَ هَلْ عَلِمْتُمْ مَا فَعَلْتُمْ بِيُوسُفَ
    and his brother, وَأَخِيهِ
    when you were ignorant?' إِذْ أَنْتُمْ جَاهِلُونَ ۝

90 They said, 'Are you really Joseph?!' قَالُوا أَإِنَّكَ لَأَنْتَ يُوسُفُ
    He said, 'I am Joseph, and this is my brother. قَالَ أَنَا يُوسُفُ وَهَٰذَا أَخِي
    Certainly God has shown us favour. قَدْ مَنَّ اللَّهُ عَلَيْنَا
    Indeed, if one is Godwary and patient, إِنَّهُ مَنْ يَتَّقِ وَيَصْبِرْ
    God does not waste the reward of the virtuous.' فَإِنَّ اللَّهَ لَا يُضِيعُ أَجْرَ الْمُحْسِنِينَ ۝

91 They said, 'By God, قَالُوا تَاللَّهِ
    God has certainly preferred you over us, لَقَدْ آثَرَكَ اللَّهُ عَلَيْنَا
    and we have indeed been erring.' وَإِنْ كُنَّا لَخَاطِئِينَ ۝

92 He said, 'There shall be no reproach on you today.
   God will forgive you,
      and He is the most merciful of the merciful.
93 Take this shirt of mine,
   and cast it upon my father's face; he will regain his sight,
      and bring me all your folks.'
94 As the caravan set off, their father said,
   'I sense the scent of Joseph,
      if you will not consider me a dotard.'
95 They said, 'By God, you persist in your inveterate error.'
96 When the bearer of good news arrived,
      he cast it[1] on his face, and he regained his sight.
   He said, 'Did I not tell you,
      "I indeeed know from God what you do not know?" '
97 They said, 'Father!
      Plead with God for forgiveness of our sins!
      We have indeed been erring.'
98 He said, 'I shall plead with my Lord to forgive you;
      indeed He is the All-forgiving, the All-merciful.'
99 When they entered into the presence of Joseph,
      he set his parents close to himself,
      and said, 'Welcome to Egypt, in safety, God willing!'
100 And he seated his parents high upon the throne,
      and they fell down prostrate before him.
   He said, 'Father!
   This is the fulfillment of my dream of long ago,
      which my Lord has made come true.
   He was certainly gracious to me
      when He brought me out of the prison
      and brought you over from the desert

---

[1] That is, the shirt of Joseph ('a).

مِنْ بَعْدِ أَنْ نَزَغَ الشَّيْطَانُ
بَيْنِي وَبَيْنَ إِخْوَتِي ۚ
after that Satan had incited ill feeling
between me and my brothers.

إِنَّ رَبِّي لَطِيفٌ
لِّمَا يَشَاءُ ۚ
My Lord is indeed all-attentive
in bringing about what He wishes.

إِنَّهُ هُوَ الْعَلِيمُ الْحَكِيمُ ۝
Indeed, He is the All-knowing, the All-wise.'

101 رَبِّ قَدْ آتَيْتَنِي مِنَ الْمُلْكِ
وَعَلَّمْتَنِي مِن تَأْوِيلِ الْأَحَادِيثِ ۚ
فَاطِرَ السَّمَاوَاتِ وَالْأَرْضِ
أَنتَ وَلِيِّي فِي الدُّنْيَا وَالْآخِرَةِ ۖ
تَوَفَّنِي مُسْلِمًا
وَأَلْحِقْنِي بِالصَّالِحِينَ ۝

101 'My Lord! You have granted me a share in the kingdom,
and taught me the interpretation of dreams.
Originator of the heavens and earth!
You are my guardian in this world and the Hereafter!
Let my death be in submission to You,
and unite me with the Righteous.'

102 ذَٰلِكَ مِنْ أَنبَاءِ الْغَيْبِ
نُوحِيهِ إِلَيْكَ ۖ
وَمَا كُنتَ لَدَيْهِمْ
إِذْ أَجْمَعُوا أَمْرَهُمْ وَهُمْ يَمْكُرُونَ ۝

102 These are accounts from the Unseen
which We reveal to *you*,
and *you* were not with them
when they conspired together and schemed.

103 وَمَا أَكْثَرُ النَّاسِ
وَلَوْ حَرَصْتَ بِمُؤْمِنِينَ ۝

103 Yet most people
will not have faith, however eager *you* should be.

104 وَمَا تَسْأَلُهُمْ عَلَيْهِ مِنْ أَجْرٍ ۚ
إِنْ هُوَ إِلَّا ذِكْرٌ لِّلْعَالَمِينَ ۝

104 *You* do not ask them any reward for it:
it is just a reminder for all the nations.

105 وَكَأَيِّن مِّنْ آيَةٍ فِي السَّمَاوَاتِ وَالْأَرْضِ
يَمُرُّونَ عَلَيْهَا
وَهُمْ عَنْهَا مُعْرِضُونَ ۝

105 How many a sign there is in the heavens and the earth
that they pass by
while they are disregardful of it!

106 وَمَا يُؤْمِنُ أَكْثَرُهُم بِاللَّهِ
إِلَّا وَهُم مُّشْرِكُونَ ۝

106 And most of them do not believe in God
without ascribing partners to Him.

107 أَفَأَمِنُوا أَن تَأْتِيَهُمْ
غَاشِيَةٌ مِّنْ عَذَابِ اللَّهِ
أَوْ تَأْتِيَهُمُ السَّاعَةُ بَغْتَةً
وَهُمْ لَا يَشْعُرُونَ ۝

107 Do they feel secure from being overtaken
by a blanket punishment from God,
or being overtaken suddenly by the Hour,
while they are unaware?

108 قُلْ هَٰذِهِ سَبِيلِي
أَدْعُو إِلَى اللَّهِ ۚ عَلَىٰ بَصِيرَةٍ

108 Say, 'This is my way.
I summon to God with insight

—I and he who follows me.
Immaculate is God,
and I am not one of the polytheists.'

109 We did not send any apostles before you
except as men to whom We revealed
from among the people of the towns.
Have they not traveled through the land
so that they may observe
how was the fate of those who were before them?
And the abode of the Hereafter is surely better
for those who are Godwary.
Do you not exercise your reason?

110 When the apostles lost hope[1]
and they thought that they had been told lies,[2]
Our help came to them,
and We delivered whomever We wished,
and Our punishment will not be averted from the guilty lot.

111 There is certainly a moral in their accounts
for those who possess intellect.
This [Qur'ān] is not a fabricated discourse;
rather, it is a confirmation of what was revealed before it,
and an elaboration[3] of all things,
and a guidance and mercy for people who have faith.

---

[1] That is, when the apostles lost hopes of bringing their people to the right path.
[2] That is, the people to whom the apostles had been sent thought that the apostles had been told lies concerning the impending punishment of the faithless.
[3] Or 'unraveling.'

13. Thunder[1]
al-Ra'd

In the Name of God,
the All-beneficent, the All-merciful.

1 *Alif, Lām, Mīm, Rā.* These are the signs of the Book.
That which has been sent down to you from your Lord
   is the truth,
but most people do not believe in it.

2 It is God who raised the heavens
   without any pillars that you see,
   and then presided over the Throne.
He disposed the sun and the moon,
   each moving for a specified term.[2]
He directs the command, and elaborates the signs
   that you may be certain of encountering your Lord.

3 It is He who has spread out the earth
   and set in it firm mountains and streams,
   and of every fruit
   He has made in it two kinds.[3]
   He draws the night's cover over the day.
   There are indeed signs in that for people who reflect.

4 In the earth are neighbouring terrains of diverse kinds
   and vineyards, farms, and date palms
   growing from the same root and from diverse roots,
   all irrigated by the same water,
   and We give some of them an advantage over others
   in flavour.

---

[1] This Makkī *sūrah* takes its name from thunder (*al-ra'd*), mentioned in verse 13.
[2] Or 'until a specified time.'
[3] Or 'a pair,' or 'two mates.'

There are indeed signs in that
    for a people who exercise their reason.

5 If you are to wonder, then wonderful[1] is their remark,
    'When we have become dust,
        shall we be ushered into a new creation?'
They are the ones who defy their Lord;
    they shall have iron collars around their necks,
    they shall be the inhabitants of the Fire,
        and they will remain in it.

6 They would press you for evil sooner than for good,[2]
    though there have already gone by before them
        exemplary punishments.
Your Lord is indeed forgiving to mankind
    despite their wrongdoing,
and your Lord is indeed severe in retribution.

7 The faithless say,
    'Why has not some sign been sent down to him
        from his Lord?'
You are only a warner,
    and there is a guide for every people.

8 God knows what every female carries in her womb,
    and what the wombs reduce and what they increase,[3]
    and everything is by precise measure with Him,

9 the Knower of the sensible and the Unseen,
    the All-great, the All-sublime.

10 It is the same to Him whether any of you speaks secretly,
    or does so loudly,
    or whether he lurks in the night,

---

[1] That is, odd, astonishing.

[2] That is, they ask you to bring about the Divine punishment with which you have threatened them, instead of pleading for Divine mercy and forgiveness.

[3] That is, what the wombs reduce or increase of the embryo or the foetus or the time of gestation.

or is open to view in daytime.¹

وَسَارِبٌ بِالنَّهَارِ ۝

11 He has guardian angels, at his front and rear,
who guard him by God's command.
Indeed, God does not change a people's lot,
unless they change what is in their souls.
And when God wishes to visit ill on a people,
there is nothing that can avert it,
and they have no protector besides Him.

12 It is He who shows you the lightning,
inspiring fear and hope,
and He produces the clouds heavy with rain.

13 The Thunder celebrates His praise,
and the angels, too, in awe of Him,
and He releases the thunderbolts
and strikes with them whomever He wishes.
Yet they dispute concerning God,
though He is great in might.²

14 Only to Him belongs the true invocation;³
and those whom they invoke besides Him
do not answer them in any wise—
like someone who stretches his hands towards water
desiring that it should reach his mouth,
but it does not reach it—
and the invocations of the faithless only go awry.

15 To God prostrates whoever there is in the heavens
and the earth,
willingly or unwillingly,
and their shadows at sunrise and sunset.

---

¹ Or 'marches in daytime.'
² Or 'though He is severe in punishment.'
³ Or 'His is the invitation to the truth,' or 'His is the true invitation.'

16 Say, 'Who is the Lord of the heavens and the earth?'
    Say, 'God!'
   Say, 'Have you, then, taken others besides Him for protectors,
       who have no control over their own benefit or harm?'
   Say, 'Are the blind one and the seer equal?
       Or, are darkness and light equal?'
    Have they set up for God partners
       who have created like His creation,
       so that the creations seemed confusable to them?
   Say, 'God is the creator of all things,
       and He is the One, the All-paramount.'

17 He sends down water from the sky
    whereat the valleys are flooded to their capacity,
    and the flood carries along a swelling scum.
    And from what they smelt in the fire
       for the purpose of making ornaments or wares,
       there arises a similar scum.
That is how God compares truth and falsehood.
    As for the scum, it leaves as dross,
       and that which profits the people
       stays in the earth.
That is how God draws comparisons.

18 For those who answer the summons of their Lord
       there shall be the best of rewards.
    But as for those who do not answer Him,
       even if they possessed all that is on the earth
       and as much of it besides,
       they would surely offer it to redeem themselves with it.[1]
    For such there shall be an adverse reckoning,

[1] Cf. **5**:36 & **39**:47.

وَمَأْوَاهُمْ جَهَنَّمُ وَبِئْسَ الْمِهَادُ ۩ and their refuge shall be hell, and it is an evil resting place.

19 أَفَمَنْ يَعْلَمُ Is someone who knows

أَنَّمَا أُنْزِلَ إِلَيْكَ مِنْ رَبِّكَ that what has been sent down to you from your Lord

الْحَقُّ is the truth,

كَمَنْ هُوَ أَعْمَىٰ like someone who is blind?

إِنَّمَا يَتَذَكَّرُ أُولُو الْأَلْبَابِ ۩ Only those who possess intellect take admonition

20 الَّذِينَ يُوفُونَ بِعَهْدِ اللَّهِ —those who fulfill God's covenant

وَلَا يَنْقُضُونَ الْمِيثَاقَ ۩ and do not break the pledge solemnly made,

21 وَالَّذِينَ يَصِلُونَ مَا أَمَرَ اللَّهُ بِهِ and those who join what God has commanded

أَنْ يُوصَلَ to be joined,

وَيَخْشَوْنَ رَبَّهُمْ fear their Lord,

وَيَخَافُونَ سُوءَ الْحِسَابِ ۩ and are afraid of an adverse reckoning

22 وَالَّذِينَ صَبَرُوا —those who are patient

ابْتِغَاءَ وَجْهِ رَبِّهِمْ for the sake of their Lord's pleasure,

وَأَقَامُوا الصَّلَاةَ maintain the prayer,

وَأَنْفَقُوا مِمَّا رَزَقْنَاهُمْ and spend out of what We have provided them,

سِرًّا وَعَلَانِيَةً secretly and openly,

وَيَدْرَءُونَ بِالْحَسَنَةِ السَّيِّئَةَ and repel others' evil conduct with good.

أُولَٰئِكَ لَهُمْ عُقْبَى الدَّارِ ۩ For such will be the reward of the ultimate abode:

23 جَنَّاتُ عَدْنٍ the Gardens of Eden,

يَدْخُلُونَهَا وَمَنْ صَلَحَ which they will enter along with whoever is righteous

مِنْ آبَائِهِمْ وَأَزْوَاجِهِمْ وَذُرِّيَّاتِهِمْ from among their forebears, spouses and descendants,

وَالْمَلَائِكَةُ يَدْخُلُونَ عَلَيْهِمْ and the angels will call on them

مِنْ كُلِّ بَابٍ ۩ from every door:

24 سَلَامٌ عَلَيْكُمْ بِمَا صَبَرْتُمْ 'Peace be to you, for your patience.'

فَنِعْمَ عُقْبَى الدَّارِ ۩ How excellent is the reward of the ultimate abode!

25 وَالَّذِينَ يَنْقُضُونَ عَهْدَ اللَّهِ But as for those who break God's compact

مِنْ بَعْدِ مِيثَاقِهِ after having pledged it solemnly,

وَيَقْطَعُونَ مَا أَمَرَ اللَّهُ بِهِ أَنْ يُوصَلَ and sever what God has commanded to be joined,

وَيُفْسِدُونَ فِي الْأَرْضِ and cause corruption on the earth

—it is such on whom the curse will lie,
and for them will be the ills of the ultimate abode.

26 God expands the provision for whomever He wishes
and tightens it.
They rejoice in the life of this world,
but compared with the Hereafter the life of this world
is but a trifling enjoyment.

27 The faithless say,
'Why has not some sign been sent down to him
from his Lord?'
Say, 'Indeed, God leads astray whomever He wishes,
and guides to Himself those who turn penitently to Him

28 —those who have faith,
and whose hearts find rest in the remembrance of God.'
Behold! The hearts find rest solely in God's remembrance!

29 Those who have faith and do righteous deeds
—happy are they and good is their ultimate destination.

30 Thus have We sent you to a nation
before which many nations have passed away,
so that *you* may recite to them what We have revealed to you.
Yet they defy the All-beneficent.
Say, 'He is my Lord; there is no god except Him;
in Him alone I have put my trust,
and to Him alone will be my return.'

31 If only it were a Qur'ān[1]
whereby the mountains could be moved,
or the earth could be toured,[2]
or the dead could be spoken to . . . .[3]

---

[1] Or 'Even if it were a Qur'ān.'
[2] Or 'the ground could be split,' i.e., for making springs and wells.
[3] Ellipsis. The phrase omitted is 'all unbelievers would have embraced the faith.' Or 'still they would not have embraced the faith.' Cf. 6:111.

Indeed, all dispensation belongs to God. بَل لِلَّهِ الْأَمْرُ جَمِيعًا

Have not the faithful yet realised أَفَلَمْ يَيْأَسِ الَّذِينَ آمَنُوا

   that had God wished أَن لَّوْ يَشَاءُ اللَّهُ

He would have guided mankind all together? لَهَدَى النَّاسَ جَمِيعًا

The faithless will continue to be visited وَلَا يَزَالُ الَّذِينَ كَفَرُوا تُصِيبُهُم

   by catastrophes because of their doings, بِمَا صَنَعُوا قَارِعَةٌ

or they[1] will land near their habitations, أَوْ تَحُلُّ قَرِيبًا مِّن دَارِهِمْ

   until God's promise comes to pass. حَتَّىٰ يَأْتِيَ وَعْدُ اللَّهِ

Indeed, God does not break His promise. إِنَّ اللَّهَ لَا يُخْلِفُ الْمِيعَادَ ۞

32 Apostles were certainly derided before you. وَلَقَدِ اسْتُهْزِئَ بِرُسُلٍ مِّن قَبْلِكَ

But then I gave respite to those who were faithless, فَأَمْلَيْتُ لِلَّذِينَ كَفَرُوا

   then I seized them; ثُمَّ أَخَذْتُهُمْ

so how was My retribution? فَكَيْفَ كَانَ عِقَابِ ۞

33 Is He who sustains every soul[2] أَفَمَنْ هُوَ قَائِمٌ عَلَىٰ كُلِّ نَفْسٍ

   in spite of what it earns [comparable to the idols]? بِمَا كَسَبَتْ

Yet they ascribe partners to God! وَجَعَلُوا لِلَّهِ شُرَكَاءَ

Say, 'Name them!' قُلْ سَمُّوهُمْ

   Will you inform Him concerning أَمْ تُنَبِّئُونَهُ

something He does not know about on the earth, بِمَا لَا يَعْلَمُ فِي الْأَرْضِ

   or concerning what are mere words? أَم بِظَاهِرٍ مِّنَ الْقَوْلِ

Indeed, their scheming is presented as decorous to the faithless, بَلْ زُيِّنَ لِلَّذِينَ كَفَرُوا مَكْرُهُمْ

   and they have been barred from the right way; وَصُدُّوا عَنِ السَّبِيلِ

and whomever God leads astray, has no guide. وَمَن يُضْلِلِ اللَّهُ فَمَا لَهُ مِنْ هَادٍ ۞

34 There is a punishment for them in the life of this world, لَّهُمْ عَذَابٌ فِي الْحَيَاةِ الدُّنْيَا

and the punishment of the Hereafter will surely be harder, وَلَعَذَابُ الْآخِرَةِ أَشَقُّ

and they have no defender against God. وَمَا لَهُم مِّنَ اللَّهِ مِن وَاقٍ ۞

35 A description of the paradise promised to the Godwary: مَّثَلُ الْجَنَّةِ الَّتِي وُعِدَ الْمُتَّقُونَ

   streams run in it, تَجْرِي مِن تَحْتِهَا الْأَنْهَارُ

---

[1] That is, the disasters.
[2] Or 'Is He who maintains every soul in spite of what it earns.' Or 'Is He who is vigilant over every soul as to what it earns.' See 9:25, where *bimā* is also used in the sense of 'in spite of.'

its fruits and shade are everlasting.
Such is the requital of those who are Godwary,
and the requital of the faithless is the Fire.

36 Those whom We have given the Book[1]
rejoice in what has been sent down to you,
and some of the factions[2] deny a part of it.
Say, 'I have indeed been commanded to worship God
and not to ascribe any partner to Him.
To Him do I summon [all mankind]
and to Him will be my return.'

37 Thus We have sent it down
as a dispensation in Arabic;
and should you follow their base desires
after the knowledge that has come to you,
you shall have against God neither
any friend nor defender.[3]

38 Certainly We have sent apostles before you,
and We appointed for them wives and descendants;
and an apostle may not bring a sign
except by God's leave.
There is a written ordinance for every time:

39 God effaces and confirms whatever He wishes
and with Him is the Mother Book.[4]

40 Whether We show you some of what We promise them,[5]
or take you away [before that],
your duty is only to communicate,

---

[1] That is, the Jews and the Christians, or the faithful who followed the Prophet (ṣ).
[2] That is, Jewish and Christian sects.
[3] Cf. **2**:120, 145; **5**:48, 49; **23**:71; **42**:15.
[4] Cf. **43**:4.
[5] That is, the punishment.

and it is for Us to do the reckoning. وَعَلَيْنَا الْحِسَابُ ۝

41 Have they not seen how We visit the land أَوَلَمْ يَرَوْا أَنَّا نَأْتِي الْأَرْضَ
diminishing it at its edges? نَنْقُصُهَا مِنْ أَطْرَافِهَا
God judges, وَاللَّهُ يَحْكُمُ
and there is none who may repeal His judgement, لَا مُعَقِّبَ لِحُكْمِهِ
and He is swift at reckoning. وَهُوَ سَرِيعُ الْحِسَابِ ۝

42 Those who were before them also schemed;[1] وَقَدْ مَكَرَ الَّذِينَ مِنْ قَبْلِهِمْ
yet all devising belongs to God. فَلِلَّهِ الْمَكْرُ جَمِيعًا
He knows what every soul earns. يَعْلَمُ مَا تَكْسِبُ كُلُّ نَفْسٍ
Soon the faithless will know وَسَيَعْلَمُ الْكُفَّارُ
in whose favour the outcome of that abode will be. لِمَنْ عُقْبَى الدَّارِ ۝

43 The faithless say, 'You have not been sent by God.' وَيَقُولُ الَّذِينَ كَفَرُوا لَسْتَ مُرْسَلًا
Say, 'God suffices as a witness between me and you, قُلْ كَفَى بِاللَّهِ شَهِيدًا بَيْنِي وَبَيْنَكُمْ
and he who possesses the knowledge of the Boo وَمَنْ عِنْدَهُ عِلْمُ الْكِتَابِ ۝

14. ABRAHAM[2]
Ibrāhīm

In the Name of God, بِسْمِ اللَّهِ
the All-beneficent, the All-merciful. الرَّحْمَٰنِ الرَّحِيمِ

1 *Alif, Lām, Rā.* This is a Book We have sent down to you الر كِتَابٌ أَنْزَلْنَاهُ إِلَيْكَ
so that you may bring mankind out لِتُخْرِجَ النَّاسَ
from darkness into light, مِنَ الظُّلُمَاتِ إِلَى النُّورِ
by the command of their Lord, بِإِذْنِ رَبِّهِمْ
to the path of the All-mighty, the All-laudable إِلَىٰ صِرَاطِ الْعَزِيزِ الْحَمِيدِ ۝

2 —God, to whom belongs whatever is in the heavens اللَّهِ الَّذِي لَهُ مَا فِي السَّمَاوَاتِ
and whatever is on the earth. وَمَا فِي الْأَرْضِ
And woe to the faithless for a severe punishment وَوَيْلٌ لِلْكَافِرِينَ مِنْ عَذَابٍ شَدِيدٍ ۝

3 —those who prefer the life of this world الَّذِينَ يَسْتَحِبُّونَ الْحَيَاةَ الدُّنْيَا
to the Hereafter, عَلَى الْآخِرَةِ

---

[1] Ellipsis. The omitted phrase is 'but their plotting was of no avail to them.'
[2] This Makkī *sūrah* is named after Abraham, whose prayer appears in verses 35-41.

bar others from the way of God,
and seek to make it crooked.
They are in extreme error.

4 We did not send any apostle
except with the language of his people,
so that he might make Our messages clear to them.
Then God leads astray whomever He wishes,
and He guides whomsoever He wishes,
and He is the All-mighty, the All-wise.

5 Certainly We sent Moses with Our signs:
'Bring your people out from darkness into light
and remind them of God's holy days.'
There are indeed signs in that
for every patient and grateful servant.

6 When Moses said to his people,
'Remember God's blessing upon you
when He delivered you from Pharaoh's clan
who inflicted a terrible torment on you,
and slaughtered your sons
and spared your women,
and in that there was a great test from your Lord.

7 And remember when your Lord declared,
"If you are grateful, I will surely enhance you in blessing,
but if you are ungrateful, My punishment is indeed severe."'

8 And Moses said, 'Should you be faithless
—you and everyone on the earth, all together—
indeed God is all-sufficient, all-laudable.'

9 Has there not come to you the account
of those who were before you

—the people of Noah, 'Ād and Thamūd,
and those who were after them,
whom no one knows well except God?
Their apostles brought them clear proofs,
but they did not respond to them,[1]
and said, 'We disbelieve in what you have been sent with.
We have indeed grave doubts concerning
that to which you invite us.'

10 Their apostles said, 'Is there any doubt about God,
the originator of the heavens and the earth?!
He calls you to forgive you a part of your sins,
and grants you respite until a specified time.'[2]
They said, 'You are nothing but humans like us
who desire to bar us
from what our fathers used to worship.
So bring us a clear authority.'

11 Their apostles said to them,
'We are indeed just human beings like yourselves;
but God favours
whomever of His servants that He wishes.
We may not bring you an authority
except by God's leave,
and in God alone let all the faithful put their trust.

12 And why should we not put our trust in God,
seeing that He has guided us in our ways?
Surely, we will put up patiently
with whatever torment you may inflict upon us,
and in God alone let all the trusting put their trust.'

---

[1] Literally, 'they put their hands into their mouths,' an idiomatic expression that has been interpreted variously. See Ṭabrisī and Ṭabarī.
[2] Or 'for a specified term.'

13 But the faithless said to their apostles,
  'Surely, we will expel you from our land,
    or you shall revert to our creed.'
  Thereat their Lord revealed to them:
    'We will surely destroy the wrongdoers,
14 and We will surely settle you in the land after them.
    This promise is for someone
    who is awed to stand before Me and fears My threat.'
15 They[1] prayed for victory[2] [against the infidels],
    and every stubborn tyrant was defeated,
16 with hell lying ahead of him,[3]
    where he shall be given to drink of a purulent fluid,
17   gulping it down, but hardly swallowing it:
    death will assail him from every side,
      but he will not die,
    and there is a harsh punishment ahead of him.
18 A parable of those who defy their Lord:
    their deeds are like ashes
  over which the wind blows hard on a tempestuous day:
    they have no power over anything they have earned.
    That is extreme error.
19 Have you not regarded that God created the heavens
        and the earth
      with consummate wisdom?
    If He wishes, He will take you away
      and bring about a new creation,
20 and that is not a formidable thing for God.
21 Together, they will be presented before God.

---

[1] That is, the apostles.
[2] Or 'verdict;' that is, the verdict of God against the faithless.
[3] That is, with hell waiting for him.

Then, those who were oppressed will say to the oppressors,
    'We were indeed your followers.
So will you avail us against God's punishment
    in any wise?'
They will say, 'Had God guided us,
    we would have surely guided you.
It is the same to us whether we are restless or patient:
    there is no escape for us.'

22 When the matter is all over, Satan will say,
    'Indeed, God made you a promise that was true
    and I too made you a promise, but I failed you.
I had no authority over you,
    except that I called you and you responded to me.
So do not blame me, but blame yourselves.
I cannot respond to your distress calls,
    neither can you respond to my distress calls.
I indeed disavow your taking me for God's partner
    heretofore.
There is indeed a painful punishment for the wrongdoers.'

23 Those who have faith and do righteous deeds will be admitted
    into gardens with streams running in them,
    to remain in them,
    by the leave of their Lord.
Their greeting therein will be 'Peace!'

24 Have you not regarded how God has drawn a parable?
    A good principle[1] is like a good tree:
    its roots are steady and its branches are on high.
25 It gives its fruit every season by the leave of its Lord.

---

[1] Lit., 'a good word.'

God draws these parables for mankind
so that they may take admonition.

26 And the parable of a bad principle is that of a bad tree:
uprooted from the ground,
it has no stability.

27 God fortifies those who have faith
with a constant creed
in the life of this world and in the Hereafter,
and God leads astray the wrongdoers,
and God does whatever He wishes.

28 Have you not regarded those who have changed
God's blessing with ingratitude
and landed their people in the house of ruin?

29 —hell, which they shall enter, and it is an evil abode!

30 They have set up equals to God
to lead people astray from His way.
Say, 'Enjoy, for indeed your destination is hellfire!'

31 *Tell* My servants who have faith
to maintain the prayer
and to spend from what We have provided them
secretly and openly
before there comes a day
on which there will be neither any bargaining nor friendship.

32 It is God who created the heavens and the earth,
and He sends down water from the sky
and brings forth with it crops for your sustenance.
And He disposed the ships for your benefit
so that they may sail at sea by His command,

and He disposed the rivers for you.

33 He disposed the sun and the moon for you,
  constant in their courses,
  and He disposed the night and the day,

34 and gave you all that you had asked Him.[1]
  If you enumerate God's blessings,
  you will not be able to count them.
  The human being is indeed most unfair and ungrateful!

35 When Abraham said, 'My Lord!
  Make this city a sanctuary,
  and save me and my children from worshiping idols.

36 My Lord! They have indeed misled many people.
  So whoever follows me indeed belongs with me,
  and as for those who disobey me,
  well, You are indeed all-forgiving, all-merciful.

37 Our Lord! I have settled part of my descendants
  in a barren valley, by Your sacred House,
  our Lord, that they may maintain the prayer.
  So make the hearts of a part of the people fond of them,
  and provide them with fruits,
  so that they may give thanks.

38 Our Lord! You indeed know whatever we hide
  and whatever we disclose,
  and nothing is hidden from God
  on the earth or in the heaven.

39 All praise belongs to God, who,
  despite my old age, gave me
  Ishmael and Isaac.

---

[1] That is, He provided you with everything demanded by your nature and your innate capacities.

My Lord indeed hears all supplications.

40 My Lord! Make me a maintainer of prayer,
　　and my descendants as well.
　　Our Lord, accept my supplication.

41 Our Lord! Forgive me, my parents, and all the faithful,
　　on the day when the reckoning is held.'

42 Do not suppose that God is oblivious
　　of what the wrongdoers are doing.
　　He is only granting them respite
　　until the day when the eyes will be glazed.

43 Scrambling with their heads upturned,
　　there will be a fixed gaze in their eyes
　　and their hearts will be vacant.

44 *Warn the people of the day*
　　when the punishment will overtake them,
　　whereat the wrongdoers will say,
　　'Our Lord! Respite us for a short time
　　so that we may respond to Your call and follow the apostles.'[1]
　　[They will be told,] 'Did you not use to swear earlier
　　that there would be no reverse for you,

45 while you dwelt in the dwellings
　　of those who had wronged themselves [before]
　　and it had been made clear to you
　　how We had dealt with them [before you],
　　and We had also cited examples for you?'

46 They certainly devised their plots,
　　but their plots are known to God,
　　and their plots are not such

---

[1] The appeal for respite made by the wrongdoers indicates that the punishment mentioned here is one that will befall them in the life of this world.

as to dislodge the mountains.[1]

47 So do not suppose that God
will break His promise to His apostles.
Indeed, God is all-mighty, avenger.

48 The day when the earth is turned into another earth
and the heavens as well,
and they are presented before God,
the One, the All-paramount

49 —on that day *you* will see the guilty
bound together in chains,

50 their garments made of pitch[2]
and the Fire covering their faces,

51 so that God may reward every soul for what it has earned.[3]
God is indeed swift at reckoning.

52 This is a proclamation for mankind,
so that they may be warned thereby
and know that He is indeed the One God,
and those who possess intellect may take admonition.

[PART 14]

15. HIJR[4]

al-Ḥijr

In the Name of God,
the All-beneficent, the All-merciful.

1 *Alif, Lām, Rā.*
These are the signs of the Book and a manifest Qurʾān.

2 Much will the faithless wish that they had been *muslims*.[5]

---

[1] According to an alternate reading (with *la-tazūlu*), the meaning will be 'their plots are indeed such as to dislodge (or annihilate) [even] the mountains.'

[2] Or 'of molten copper.'

[3] Or, perhaps preferably, 'so that God may requite every soul with what it has earned,' which implies that deeds are identical with their recompense, or that deeds are their own recompense.

[4] This Makkī *sūrah* takes its name from Ḥijr (mentioned in verse 80), a place or region said to be inhabited by the people of Thamūd.

[5] That is, among those who have submitted to God.

3 *Leave* them to eat and enjoy
    and to be diverted by longings.
    Soon they will know.
4 We did not destroy any town
    but that it had a known term.
5 No nation can advance its time
    nor can it defer it.
6 They said,
    'O you, to whom the Reminder has been sent down,
    you are indeed crazy.[1]
7 Why do you not bring us the angels
    if you are truthful?!'
8 We do not send down the angels except with due reason,
    and then they will not be granted any respite.
9 Indeed, We have sent down the Reminder,[2]
    and indeed We will preserve it.
10 Certainly We sent apostles before you
    to former communities,
11 and there did not come to them any apostle
    but that they used to deride him.
12 That is how We let it pass
    through the hearts of the guilty:
13 they do not believe in it,
    and the precedent of the former peoples has already passed.
14 Were We to open for them a gate of the heaven,
    so that they could go on ascending through it,
15 they would surely say,
    'A spell has indeed been cast on our eyes;

---

[1] Or 'possessed,' that is by a demon or jinn. Cf. 7:184, 23:25, 70, 26:27, 34:8, 46, 37:36, 44:14, 51:39, 52, 52:29, 54:9, 68:51.

[2] That is, the Qur'ān.

rather, we are a bewitched lot.'

16 Certainly We have appointed houses[1] in the heaven and adorned them for the onlookers,

17 and We have guarded them from every outcast Satan,

18 except someone who may eavesdrop, whereat there pursues him a manifest flame.[2]

19 We spread out the earth, and cast in it firm mountains, and We grew in it every kind of balanced thing,

20 and made in it various means of livelihood for you and for those whom you do not provide for.

21 There is not a thing but that its sources are with Us, and We do not send it down except in a known measure.

22 And We send the fertilizing winds and send down water from the sky providing it for you to drink and you are not maintainers of its resources.

23 Indeed, it is We who give life and bring death and We are the inheritors.

24 Certainly We know the predecessors among you and certainly We know the successors,

25 and indeed it is *your* Lord who will resurrect them. He is indeed all-wise, all-knowing.

26 Certainly We created man out of a dry clay[3] drawn from an aging mud,

27 and We created the jinn earlier out of a piercing fire.

28 When your Lord said to the angels,

---

[1] House: One of the 12 parts into which the heavens are divided in astrology. Cf. **25:61**; **85:1**.
[2] Or 'meteor.'
[3] Or 'clinking clay,' that is, giving a clinking sound due to being hard and dry. Cf. **15:28**

إِنِّى خَالِقٌ بَشَرًا
'Indeed, I am going to create a human
مِن صَلْصَالٍ مِّنْ حَمَإٍ مَّسْنُونٍ ۝
out of a dry clay drawn from an aging mud.

فَإِذَا سَوَّيْتُهُ 29 So when I have proportioned him
وَنَفَخْتُ فِيهِ مِن رُّوحِى
and breathed into him of My spirit,
فَقَعُوا لَهُ سَاجِدِينَ ۝
then fall down in prostration before him.'

فَسَجَدَ الْمَلَائِكَةُ كُلُّهُمْ أَجْمَعُونَ ۝ 30 Thereat the angels prostrated, all of them together,

إِلَّا إِبْلِيسَ 31 but not Iblis:
أَبَىٰ أَن يَكُونَ مَعَ السَّاجِدِينَ ۝
he refused to be among those who prostrated.

قَالَ يَا إِبْلِيسُ مَا لَكَ أَلَّا تَكُونَ 32 He said, 'O Iblis! What kept you from being
مَعَ السَّاجِدِينَ ۝
among those who have prostrated?'

قَالَ لَمْ أَكُن لِّأَسْجُدَ لِبَشَرٍ 33 Said he, 'I will not prostrate before a human
خَلَقْتَهُ
whom You have created
مِن صَلْصَالٍ مِّنْ حَمَإٍ مَّسْنُونٍ ۝
out of a dry clay drawn from an aging mud.'

قَالَ فَاخْرُجْ مِنْهَا فَإِنَّكَ رَجِيمٌ ۝ 34 He said, 'Begone hence, for you are indeed an outcast,
وَإِنَّ عَلَيْكَ اللَّعْنَةَ 35 and indeed the curse shall lie on you
إِلَىٰ يَوْمِ الدِّينِ ۝
until the Day of Retribution.'[1]

قَالَ رَبِّ 36 He said, 'My Lord!
فَأَنظِرْنِى إِلَىٰ يَوْمِ يُبْعَثُونَ ۝
Respite me till the day they will be resurrected.'

قَالَ فَإِنَّكَ مِنَ الْمُنظَرِينَ ۝ 37 Said He, 'You are indeed among the reprieved
إِلَىٰ يَوْمِ الْوَقْتِ الْمَعْلُومِ ۝ 38 until the day of the known time.'

قَالَ رَبِّ بِمَا أَغْوَيْتَنِى 39 He said, 'My Lord! As You have consigned me to perversity,
لَأُزَيِّنَنَّ لَهُمْ فِى الْأَرْضِ
I will surely glamorize evil for them on the earth,
وَلَأُغْوِيَنَّهُمْ أَجْمَعِينَ ۝
and I will surely pervert them, all

إِلَّا عِبَادَكَ مِنْهُمُ الْمُخْلَصِينَ ۝ 40 except Your dedicated servants among them.'

قَالَ هَـٰذَا صِرَاطٌ عَلَىَّ مُسْتَقِيمٌ ۝ 41 He said, 'This is the path leading straight to Me.[2]
إِنَّ عِبَادِى لَيْسَ لَكَ عَلَيْهِمْ سُلْطَانٌ 42 Indeed, you do not have any authority over My servants,
إِلَّا مَنِ اتَّبَعَكَ مِنَ الْغَاوِينَ ۝
except the perverse who follow you,
وَإِنَّ جَهَنَّمَ لَمَوْعِدُهُمْ أَجْمَعِينَ ۝ 43 and indeed hell is the tryst of them all.'

---

[1] Or 'the Day of Judgement.'
[2] Read alternatively as *hādhā ṣirāṭun ʿalīyyun mustaqīm*, meaning 'this is an exalted straight path.' This reading is narrated from al-Imam al-Ṣādiq (*Majmaʿ al-Bayān*) and from thirteen other authorities, including Yaʿqūb, al-Ḍaḥḥāk, Mujāhid, Qatādah, and Ibn Sīrīn. (See *Muʿjam al-Qirāʾāt al-Qurʾāniyyah*)

لَهَا سَبْعَةُ أَبْوَابٍ ٤٤ It has seven gates,

لِكُلِّ بَابٍ مِنْهُمْ جُزْءٌ مَقْسُومٌ ۝ and to each gate belongs a separate portion of them.'

إِنَّ الْمُتَّقِينَ فِي جَنَّاتٍ وَعُيُونٍ ۝ ٤٥ Indeed, the Godwary will be amid gardens and springs.

ادْخُلُوهَا بِسَلَامٍ آمِنِينَ ۝ ٤٦ [They will be told,] "Enter it in peace and safety!"

وَنَزَعْنَا مَا فِي صُدُورِهِمْ مِنْ غِلٍّ ٤٧ We will remove whatever rancour there is in their breasts;

إِخْوَانًا intimate like brothers, [they will be reclining]

عَلَىٰ سُرُرٍ مُتَقَابِلِينَ ۝ on couches, facing one another.

لَا يَمَسُّهُمْ فِيهَا نَصَبٌ ٤٨ Therein neither weariness shall touch them,

وَمَا هُمْ مِنْهَا بِمُخْرَجِينَ ۝ nor will they ever be expelled from it.

نَبِّئْ عِبَادِي ٤٩ *Inform* my servants

أَنِّي أَنَا الْغَفُورُ الرَّحِيمُ ۝ that I am indeed the All-forgiving, the All-merciful,

وَأَنَّ عَذَابِي هُوَ الْعَذَابُ الْأَلِيمُ ۝ ٥٠ and that My punishment is a painful punishment.

وَنَبِّئْهُمْ عَنْ ضَيْفِ إِبْرَاهِيمَ ۝ ٥١ And *inform* them about the guests of Abraham,

إِذْ دَخَلُوا عَلَيْهِ فَقَالُوا سَلَامًا ٥٢ when they entered into his presence and said, 'Peace!'

قَالَ إِنَّا مِنْكُمْ وَجِلُونَ ۝ He said, 'We are indeed afraid of you.'

قَالُوا لَا تَوْجَلْ ٥٣ They said, 'Don't be afraid.

إِنَّا نُبَشِّرُكَ بِغُلَامٍ عَلِيمٍ ۝ Indeed, we give you the good news of a wise son.'

قَالَ أَبَشَّرْتُمُونِي ٥٤ He said, 'Do you give me good news,

عَلَىٰ أَنْ مَسَّنِيَ الْكِبَرُ though old age has befallen me?

فَبِمَ تُبَشِّرُونَ ۝ What is the good news that you bring me!?'

قَالُوا بَشَّرْنَاكَ بِالْحَقِّ ٥٥ They said, 'We bring you good news in truth;

فَلَا تَكُنْ مِنَ الْقَانِطِينَ ۝ so do not be despondent.'

قَالَ وَمَنْ يَقْنَطُ مِنْ رَحْمَةِ رَبِّهِ ٥٦ He said, 'Who despairs of his Lord's mercy

إِلَّا الضَّالُّونَ ۝ except the astray?!'

قَالَ فَمَا خَطْبُكُمْ أَيُّهَا الْمُرْسَلُونَ ۝ ٥٧ He said, 'O messengers, what is now your errand?'

قَالُوا إِنَّا أُرْسِلْنَا إِلَىٰ قَوْمٍ مُجْرِمِينَ ۝ ٥٨ They said, 'We have been sent toward a guilty people,

إِلَّا آلَ لُوطٍ ٥٩ [who will all perish] except the family of Lot.

إِنَّا لَمُنَجُّوهُمْ أَجْمَعِينَ ۝ We will indeed deliver all of them,

إِلَّا امْرَأَتَهُ قَدَّرْنَا ٦٠ except his wife, who,

We have ordained, will be among those who remain behind.'

إِنَّهَا لَمِنَ الْغَابِرِينَ ۝

61 So when the messengers came to Lot's family,

فَلَمَّا جَاءَ آلَ لُوطٍ الْمُرْسَلُونَ ۝

62 he said, 'You are strangers to me.'

قَالَ إِنَّكُمْ قَوْمٌ مُنْكَرُونَ ۝

63 They said, 'Indeed, we bring you
    what they used to doubt.

قَالُوا بَلْ جِئْنَاكَ بِمَا كَانُوا فِيهِ يَمْتَرُونَ ۝

64 We bring you the truth, and indeed we speak truly.

وَأَتَيْنَاكَ بِالْحَقِّ وَإِنَّا لَصَادِقُونَ ۝

65 Take your family in a watch of the night
    and follow in their rear,
    and none of you should turn around,
    and proceed as you are bidden.'

فَأَسْرِ بِأَهْلِكَ بِقِطْعٍ مِنَ اللَّيْلِ وَاتَّبِعْ أَدْبَارَهُمْ وَلَا يَلْتَفِتْ مِنْكُمْ أَحَدٌ وَامْضُوا حَيْثُ تُؤْمَرُونَ ۝

66 We apprised him of the matter
    that these[1] will be rooted out by dawn.

وَقَضَيْنَا إِلَيْهِ ذَٰلِكَ الْأَمْرَ أَنَّ دَابِرَ هَٰؤُلَاءِ مَقْطُوعٌ مُصْبِحِينَ ۝

67 The people of the city came, rejoicing.

وَجَاءَ أَهْلُ الْمَدِينَةِ يَسْتَبْشِرُونَ ۝

68 He said, 'These are indeed my guests.
    Do not bring dishonour on me.

قَالَ إِنَّ هَٰؤُلَاءِ ضَيْفِي فَلَا تَفْضَحُونِ ۝

69 Be wary of God and do not humiliate me.'

وَاتَّقُوا اللَّهَ وَلَا تُخْزُونِ ۝

70 They said, 'Did we not forbid you
    from defending[2] strangers?'

قَالُوا أَوَلَمْ نَنْهَكَ عَنِ الْعَالَمِينَ ۝

71 He said, 'These are my daughters, [marry them]
    if you should do anything.'

قَالَ هَٰؤُلَاءِ بَنَاتِي إِنْ كُنْتُمْ فَاعِلِينَ ۝

72 By your life, they were bewildered in their drunkenness.

لَعَمْرُكَ إِنَّهُمْ لَفِي سَكْرَتِهِمْ يَعْمَهُونَ ۝

73 So the Cry seized them at sunrise,

فَأَخَذَتْهُمُ الصَّيْحَةُ مُشْرِقِينَ ۝

74 and We made its[3] topmost part its nethermost,
    and rained on them stones of shale.

فَجَعَلْنَا عَالِيَهَا سَافِلَهَا وَأَمْطَرْنَا عَلَيْهِمْ حِجَارَةً مِنْ سِجِّيلٍ ۝

75 There are indeed signs in that for the percipient.

إِنَّ فِي ذَٰلِكَ لَآيَاتٍ لِلْمُتَوَسِّمِينَ ۝

76 Indeed, it is on a standing road,

وَإِنَّهَا لَبِسَبِيلٍ مُقِيمٍ ۝

77 and there is indeed a sign in that for the faithful.

إِنَّ فِي ذَٰلِكَ لَآيَةً لِلْمُؤْمِنِينَ ۝

78 Indeed, the inhabitants of Aykah[4] were wrongdoers.

وَإِنْ كَانَ أَصْحَابُ الْأَيْكَةِ لَظَالِمِينَ ۝

---

[1] That is, the people of Sodom.
[2] Or, from entertaining.
[3] That is, of the city of Sodom.
[4] Name of a town to which the prophet Shuʿayb (ʿa) was sent, or a land with dense growth of trees. Cf.

فَانْتَقَمْنَا مِنْهُمْ	79 So We took vengeance on them,
وَإِنَّهُمَا لَبِإِمَامٍ مُبِينٍ ۝	and indeed the two of them[1] are on an open highway.
وَلَقَدْ كَذَّبَ أَصْحَابُ الْحِجْرِ الْمُرْسَلِينَ ۝	80 Certainly the inhabitants of Ḥijr denied the apostles.
وَآتَيْنَاهُمْ آيَاتِنَا	81 We had given them Our signs
فَكَانُوا عَنْهَا مُعْرِضِينَ ۝	but they disregarded them.
وَكَانُوا يَنْحِتُونَ مِنَ الْجِبَالِ بُيُوتًا	82 They used to carve out dwellings from mountains
آمِنِينَ ۝	feeling secure.
فَأَخَذَتْهُمُ الصَّيْحَةُ مُصْبِحِينَ ۝	83 So the Cry seized them at dawn,
فَمَا أَغْنَىٰ عَنْهُمْ مَا كَانُوا يَكْسِبُونَ ۝	84 and what they used to earn did not avail them.
وَمَا خَلَقْنَا السَّمَاوَاتِ وَالْأَرْضَ	85 We did not create the heavens and the earth
وَمَا بَيْنَهُمَا	and whatever is between them
إِلَّا بِالْحَقِّ	except with consummate wisdom,
وَإِنَّ السَّاعَةَ لَآتِيَةٌ	and indeed the Hour is bound to come.
فَاصْفَحِ الصَّفْحَ الْجَمِيلَ ۝	So *forbear* with a graceful forbearance.
إِنَّ رَبَّكَ هُوَ الْخَلَّاقُ الْعَلِيمُ ۝	86 Indeed, *your* Lord is the All-creator, the All-knowing.
وَلَقَدْ آتَيْنَاكَ	87 Certainly We have given *you* [the *sūrah* of]
سَبْعًا مِنَ الْمَثَانِي وَالْقُرْآنَ الْعَظِيمَ ۝	the seven oft-repeated verses[2] and the great Qur'ān.
لَا تَمُدَّنَّ عَيْنَيْكَ	88 Do not extend *your* glance toward
إِلَىٰ مَا مَتَّعْنَا بِهِ أَزْوَاجًا مِنْهُمْ	what We have provided to certain groups of them,
وَلَا تَحْزَنْ عَلَيْهِمْ	and do not grieve for them.
وَاخْفِضْ جَنَاحَكَ لِلْمُؤْمِنِينَ ۝	Lower your wing to the faithful,[3]
وَقُلْ إِنِّي أَنَا النَّذِيرُ الْمُبِينُ ۝	89 and say, 'I am a manifest warner [of punishment]'
كَمَا أَنْزَلْنَا عَلَى الْمُقْتَسِمِينَ ۝	90 like what We sent down on those who split into bands,[4]
الَّذِينَ جَعَلُوا الْقُرْآنَ عِضِينَ ۝	91 who represented the Qur'ān as magic.

26:176; **38**:13; **50**:14.
[1] That is, Sodom and Aykah.
[2] That is, the Sūrat al-Fātiḥah, the opening *sūrah* of the Qur'ān.
[3] That is, be humble and gracious towards them. Cf. **17**:24; **26**:215.
[4] During the *ḥajj* season, bands of the idolaters of Quraysh, under the direction of al-Walīd b. al-Mughīrah, stationed themselves in the passes leading to Makkah to meet the arriving pilgrims with the object of reviling the Prophet (ṣ), representing him as a magician and the Qur'ān as a sorcery

92 By *your* Lord, We will question them all
93 concerning what they used to do.
94 So *proclaim* what *you* have been commanded,
and *turn* away from the polytheists.
95 We will indeed suffice *you* against the deriders
96 —those who set up besides God another deity.
Soon they will know!
97 Certainly We know that *you* become upset
because of what they say.
98 So *celebrate* the praise of *your* Lord
and *be* among those who prostrate,
99 and *worship your* Lord until certainty[1] comes to *you*.

16. THE BEE[2]
al-Naḥl

In the Name of God,
the All-beneficent, the All-merciful.

1 God's edict is coming! So do not seek to hasten it.
Immaculate is He and far above
having any partners that they ascribe to Him.
2 He sends down the angels with the Spirit of His command[3]
to whomever He wishes of His servants:
'Warn the people that there is no god except Me;
so be wary of Me.'
3 He created the heavens and the earth
with consummate wisdom.
He is far above having any partners that they ascribe to Him.
4 He created man from a drop of seminal fluid,[4]

---
[1] That is, death.
[2] A Makkī *sūrah*, named after the honey bee (*al-naḥl*) mentioned in verses 68-69.
[3] Or 'Law.'
[4] Or 'from a drop of semen;' cf. **18**:37; **22**:5; **23**:13-14; **35**:11; **36**:77; **40**:67; **53**:46; **75**:37; **76**:2; **80**:19.

and, behold, he is an open contender![1] فَإِذَا هُوَ خَصِيمٌ مُبِينٌ ۝

5 He created the cattle, وَالْأَنْعَامَ خَلَقَهَا

in which there is warmth[2] for you and other uses لَكُمْ فِيهَا دِفْءٌ وَمَنَافِعُ

and some of them you eat. وَمِنْهَا تَأْكُلُونَ ۝

6 There is in them a beauty for you وَلَكُمْ فِيهَا جَمَالٌ

when you bring them home for rest حِينَ تُرِيحُونَ

and when you drive them forth to pasture. وَحِينَ تَسْرَحُونَ ۝

7 And they bear your burdens to towns وَتَحْمِلُ أَثْقَالَكُمْ إِلَىٰ بَلَدٍ

which you could not reach except by straining yourselves. لَمْ تَكُونُوا بَالِغِيهِ إِلَّا بِشِقِّ الْأَنْفُسِ

Your Lord is indeed most kind and merciful. إِنَّ رَبَّكُمْ لَرَءُوفٌ رَحِيمٌ ۝

8 And horses, mules and asses, وَالْخَيْلَ وَالْبِغَالَ وَالْحَمِيرَ

for you to ride them, and for pomp, لِتَرْكَبُوهَا وَزِينَةً

and He creates what you do not know. وَيَخْلُقُ مَا لَا تَعْلَمُونَ ۝

9 With God rests guidance to the straight path,[3] وَعَلَى اللَّهِ قَصْدُ السَّبِيلِ

and some of them[4] are devious, وَمِنْهَا جَائِرٌ

and had He wished He would have guided you all. وَلَوْ شَاءَ لَهَدَاكُمْ أَجْمَعِينَ ۝

10 It is He who sends down water from the sky: هُوَ الَّذِي أَنْزَلَ مِنَ السَّمَاءِ مَاءً

from it you get your drink لَكُمْ مِنْهُ شَرَابٌ

and with it are sustained the plants وَمِنْهُ شَجَرٌ

wherein you pasture your herds. فِيهِ تُسِيمُونَ ۝

11 With it He makes the crops grow for you يُنْبِتُ لَكُمْ بِهِ الزَّرْعَ

and olives, date palms, vines, وَالزَّيْتُونَ وَالنَّخِيلَ وَالْأَعْنَابَ

and fruits of all kinds. وَمِنْ كُلِّ الثَّمَرَاتِ

There is indeed a sign in that for people who reflect. إِنَّ فِي ذَٰلِكَ لَآيَةً لِقَوْمٍ يَتَفَكَّرُونَ ۝

12 He disposed the night and the day for you, وَسَخَّرَ لَكُمُ اللَّيْلَ وَالنَّهَارَ

and the sun, the moon and the stars وَالشَّمْسَ وَالْقَمَرَ وَالنُّجُومُ

are disposed by His command. مُسَخَّرَاتٌ بِأَمْرِهِ

There are indeed signs in that إِنَّ فِي ذَٰلِكَ لَآيَاتٍ

---

[1] Or 'a lucid debater,' or 'an open adversary;' cf. **36:77**.
[2] That is, in the garments made from wool and leather.
[3] Cf. **20:50**; **76:3**; **92:12**.
[4] That is, some of the paths. Cf. **6:153**

for people who exercise their reason.

13 And whatever He has created for you in the earth of diverse hues
—there is indeed a sign in that for people who take admonition.

14 It is He who disposed the sea [for your benefit]
that you may eat from it fresh meat,
and obtain from it ornaments which you wear,
and you see the ships plowing through it,
so that you may seek of His bounty
and that you may give thanks.

15 He cast firm mountains in the earth
lest it should shake with you,
and made streams and ways so that you may be guided

16 —and the landmarks as well—
and by the stars they are guided.

17 Is He who creates like one who does not create?
Will you not then take admonition?

18 If you enumerate God's blessings,
you will not be able to count them.
God is indeed all-forgiving, all-merciful,

19 and God knows whatever you hide
and whatever you disclose.

20 Those whom they invoke besides God
do not create anything and are themselves created.

21 They are dead and lifeless
and are not aware when they will be resurrected.

22 Your God is the One God.
Those who do not believe in the Hereafter,
their hearts are in denial of the truth and they are arrogant.

23 Undoubtedly, God knows whatever they hide

وَمَا يُعْلِنُونَ ۚ and whatever they disclose.
إِنَّهُ لَا يُحِبُّ الْمُسْتَكْبِرِينَ ۝ Indeed, He does not like the arrogant.
وَإِذَا قِيلَ لَهُم 24 When they are asked,
مَّاذَا أَنزَلَ رَبُّكُمْ ۙ 'What is it that your Lord has sent down?,'
قَالُوا أَسَاطِيرُ الْأَوَّلِينَ ۝ they say, 'Myths of the ancients,' [with the result]
لِيَحْمِلُوا أَوْزَارَهُمْ كَامِلَةً 25 that they will bear the full weight of their own burden
يَوْمَ الْقِيَامَةِ ۙ on the Day of Resurrection,
وَمِنْ أَوْزَارِ الَّذِينَ along with part of the burden of those
يُضِلُّونَهُم بِغَيْرِ عِلْمٍ ۗ whom they mislead without any knowledge.
أَلَا سَاءَ مَا يَزِرُونَ ۝ Behold! Evil is what they bear!
قَدْ مَكَرَ الَّذِينَ مِن قَبْلِهِمْ 26 Those who were before them had also schemed.
فَأَتَى اللَّهُ بُنْيَانَهُم مِّنَ الْقَوَاعِدِ Then God came at their edifice from the foundations
فَخَرَّ عَلَيْهِمُ السَّقْفُ مِن فَوْقِهِمْ and the roof fell down upon them from above
وَأَتَاهُمُ الْعَذَابُ and the punishment overtook them
مِنْ حَيْثُ لَا يَشْعُرُونَ ۝ whence they were not aware.
ثُمَّ يَوْمَ الْقِيَامَةِ يُخْزِيهِمْ 27 Then, on the Day of Resurrection He will disgrace them
وَيَقُولُ أَيْنَ شُرَكَائِيَ الَّذِينَ and say, 'Where are My "partners"
كُنتُمْ تُشَاقُّونَ فِيهِمْ ۚ for whose sake you used to defy God?'
قَالَ الَّذِينَ أُوتُوا الْعِلْمَ Those who were given knowledge will say,
إِنَّ الْخِزْيَ الْيَوْمَ وَالسُّوءَ عَلَى الْكَافِرِينَ ۝ 'Indeed, disgrace and distress pursue the faithless today.'
الَّذِينَ تَتَوَفَّاهُمُ الْمَلَائِكَةُ 28 —Those whom the angels take away
ظَالِمِي أَنفُسِهِمْ ۖ while they were wronging themselves.
فَأَلْقَوُا السَّلَمَ مَا كُنَّا نَعْمَلُ مِن سُوءٍ ۚ Thereat they submit: 'We were not doing any evil!'
بَلَىٰ إِنَّ اللَّهَ عَلِيمٌ 'Yes,' [the angels reply,] 'God indeed knows well
بِمَا كُنتُمْ تَعْمَلُونَ ۝ what you used to do!
فَادْخُلُوا أَبْوَابَ جَهَنَّمَ خَالِدِينَ فِيهَا ۖ 29 Enter the gates of hell to remain in it.
فَلَبِئْسَ مَثْوَى الْمُتَكَبِّرِينَ ۝ Evil is the final abode of the arrogant.'
وَقِيلَ لِلَّذِينَ اتَّقَوْا 30 But to those who were Godwary it will be said,
مَاذَا أَنزَلَ رَبُّكُمْ ۚ 'What is it that your Lord has sent down?'
قَالُوا خَيْرًا ۗ They will say, 'Good.'

For those who do good in this world
  there will be a good reward,
    and the abode of the Hereafter is better,
    and the abode of the Godwary is surely excellent:
31 the Gardens of Eden, which they will enter,
    with streams running in them.
  There they will have whatever they wish,
    and thus does God reward the Godwary
32 —those whom the angels take away while they are pure.
  They say to them, 'Peace be to you!
    Enter paradise because of what you used to do.'
33 Do they await
  aught except that the angels should come to them,
    or your Lord's edict should come?
  Those who were before them had acted likewise;
    God did not wrong them,
    but they used to wrong themselves.
34 So the evils of what they had earned visited them,
    and they were besieged by what they used to deride.
35 The polytheists say, 'Had God wished,
    we would not have worshiped anything besides Him
      —neither we, nor our fathers—
    nor forbidden anything without His sanction.'
  Those who were before them had acted likewise.
  Is the apostles' duty
    anything but to communicate in clear terms?
36 Certainly We raised an apostle in every nation
    to preach: 'Worship God, and shun satanic entities.'
  Among them were some whom God guided,
    and among them were some who deserved to be in error.

فَسِيرُوا فِي الْأَرْضِ فَانْظُرُوا
كَيْفَ كَانَ عَاقِبَةُ الْمُكَذِّبِينَ ۝

So travel through the land and observe
how was the fate of the deniers.

إِنْ تَحْرِصْ عَلَىٰ هُدَاهُمْ
فَإِنَّ اللَّهَ لَا يَهْدِي مَنْ يُضِلُّ
وَمَا لَهُمْ مِنْ نَاصِرِينَ ۝

37 Even if you are eager for them to be guided,
indeed God does not guide those who mislead others,
and they will have no helpers.

وَأَقْسَمُوا بِاللَّهِ جَهْدَ أَيْمَانِهِمْ
لَا يَبْعَثُ اللَّهُ مَنْ يَمُوتُ
بَلَىٰ وَعْدًا عَلَيْهِ حَقًّا
وَلَٰكِنَّ أَكْثَرَ النَّاسِ لَا يَعْلَمُونَ ۝

38 They swear by God with solemn oaths
that God will not resurrect those who die.
Yes indeed, He will, it is a promise binding upon Him,
but most people do not know,

لِيُبَيِّنَ لَهُمُ الَّذِي يَخْتَلِفُونَ فِيهِ
وَلِيَعْلَمَ الَّذِينَ كَفَرُوا
أَنَّهُمْ كَانُوا كَاذِبِينَ ۝

39 so that He may clarify for them what they differ about,
and that the faithless may know
that they were liars.

إِنَّمَا قَوْلُنَا لِشَيْءٍ إِذَا أَرَدْنَاهُ
أَنْ نَقُولَ لَهُ كُنْ فَيَكُونُ ۝

40 All that We say to a thing, when We will it,
is to say to it 'Be!' and it is.

وَالَّذِينَ هَاجَرُوا فِي اللَّهِ
مِنْ بَعْدِ مَا ظُلِمُوا
لَنُبَوِّئَنَّهُمْ فِي الدُّنْيَا حَسَنَةً
وَلَأَجْرُ الْآخِرَةِ أَكْبَرُ
لَوْ كَانُوا يَعْلَمُونَ ۝

41 Those who migrate for the sake of God
after they have been wronged,
We will surely settle them in a good place in the world,
and the reward of the Hereafter is surely greater,
had they known.

الَّذِينَ صَبَرُوا وَعَلَىٰ رَبِّهِمْ يَتَوَكَّلُونَ ۝

42 —Those who are patient and put their trust in their Lord.

وَمَا أَرْسَلْنَا مِنْ قَبْلِكَ
إِلَّا رِجَالًا نُوحِي إِلَيْهِمْ
فَاسْأَلُوا أَهْلَ الذِّكْرِ
إِنْ كُنْتُمْ لَا تَعْلَمُونَ ۝

43 We did not send any apostles before you
except as men to whom We revealed.
Ask the People of the Reminder
if you do not know.

بِالْبَيِّنَاتِ وَالزُّبُرِ
وَأَنْزَلْنَا إِلَيْكَ الذِّكْرَ
لِتُبَيِّنَ لِلنَّاسِ
مَا نُزِّلَ إِلَيْهِمْ
وَلَعَلَّهُمْ يَتَفَكَّرُونَ ۝

44 We sent them with clear proofs and scriptures.
We have sent down the Reminder to you
so that you may clarify for these people
that which has been sent down to them,
so that they may reflect.

45 Do those who devise evil schemes feel secure
that God will not make the earth swallow them,
or the punishment will not overtake them
whence they are not aware?

46 Or that He will not seize them in the midst of their bustle,
whereupon they will not be able to frustrate Him?

47 Or that He will not visit them with attrition?[1]
Your Lord is indeed most kind and merciful.

48 Have they not regarded
that whatever thing God has created
casts its shadow to the right and the left,
prostrating to God in utter humility?

49 To God prostrates whatever is in the heavens
and whatever is on the earth, including animals and angels,
and they are not arrogant.

50 They fear their Lord above them,
and do what they are commanded.

51 God has said, 'Do not worship two gods.
Indeed, He is the One God, so be in awe of Me alone.'

52 To Him belongs whatever is in the heavens and the earth,
and to Him belongs the enduring religion.
Will you, then, be wary of other than God?

53 Whatever blessing you have is from God,
and when a distress befalls you,
you make entreaties to Him.

54 Then, when He removes the distress from you,
behold, a part of them ascribe partners to their Lord,

55 being unthankful for what We have given them.

---

[1] Or 'that He will not seize them amid panic.'

فَتَمَتَّعُوا۟ فَسَوْفَ تَعْلَمُونَ ۝

So let them enjoy. Soon they will know!

56 وَيَجْعَلُونَ لِمَا لَا يَعْلَمُونَ نَصِيبًا مِّمَّا رَزَقْنَاهُمْ ۗ تَاللَّهِ لَتُسْـَٔلُنَّ عَمَّا كُنتُمْ تَفْتَرُونَ ۝

56 To what they do not know, they attribute
    a share in what We have provided them.
    By God, you will surely be questioned
        concerning what you used to fabricate.

57 وَيَجْعَلُونَ لِلَّهِ الْبَنَاتِ سُبْحَانَهُۥ ۙ وَلَهُم مَّا يَشْتَهُونَ ۝

57 And they attribute daughters to God—immaculate is He—
    while they will have what they desire!

58 وَإِذَا بُشِّرَ أَحَدُهُم بِٱلْأُنثَىٰ ظَلَّ وَجْهُهُۥ مُسْوَدًّا وَهُوَ كَظِيمٌ ۝

58 When one of them is brought the news
    of a female newborn,
    his face becomes darkened
    and he chokes with suppressed agony.

59 يَتَوَارَىٰ مِنَ ٱلْقَوْمِ مِن سُوٓءِ مَا بُشِّرَ بِهِۦٓ ۚ أَيُمْسِكُهُۥ عَلَىٰ هُونٍ أَمْ يَدُسُّهُۥ فِى ٱلتُّرَابِ ۗ أَلَا سَآءَ مَا يَحْكُمُونَ ۝

59 He hides from the people
    out of distress at the news he has been brought:
    shall he retain it in humiliation,
    or bury it in the ground![1]
    Behold! Evil is the judgement that they make.

60 لِلَّذِينَ لَا يُؤْمِنُونَ بِٱلْـَٔاخِرَةِ مَثَلُ ٱلسَّوْءِ ۖ وَلِلَّهِ ٱلْمَثَلُ ٱلْأَعْلَىٰ ۚ وَهُوَ ٱلْعَزِيزُ ٱلْحَكِيمُ ۝

60 Of those who do not believe in the Hereafter
    there is an evil description,
    and the loftiest description belongs to God,
    and He is the All-mighty, the All-wise.

61 وَلَوْ يُؤَاخِذُ ٱللَّهُ ٱلنَّاسَ بِظُلْمِهِم مَّا تَرَكَ عَلَيْهَا مِن دَآبَّةٍ وَلَٰكِن يُؤَخِّرُهُمْ إِلَىٰٓ أَجَلٍ مُّسَمًّى ۖ فَإِذَا جَآءَ أَجَلُهُمْ لَا يَسْتَـْٔخِرُونَ سَاعَةً ۖ وَلَا يَسْتَقْدِمُونَ ۝

61 Were God to take mankind to task for their wrongdoing,
    He would not leave any living being upon it.[2]
    But He respites them until a specified time;
    so when their time comes
    they shall not defer it by a single hour
    nor shall they advance it.

62 وَيَجْعَلُونَ لِلَّهِ مَا يَكْرَهُونَ وَتَصِفُ أَلْسِنَتُهُمُ ٱلْكَذِبَ

62 They attribute to God what they dislike for themselves,
    and their tongues assert the lie

---

[1] This refers to the practice of pre-Islamic Arabs of burying their newborn daughters alive.
[2] That is, on the surface of the earth.

    that the best reward [in the Hereafter] will be theirs.[1]

    Undoubtedly, the Fire shall be their lot

    and they will be foremost in entering it.[2]

63 By God,

    We have certainly sent apostles to nations before you.

    But Satan made their deeds seem decorous to them.

    So he is their master today

    and there is a painful punishment for them.

64 We did not send down the Book to you

    except for the purpose that you may clarify for them

    what they differ about,

    and as guidance and mercy for people who have faith.

65 God sends down water from the sky

    with which He revives the earth after its death.

    There is indeed a sign in that for people who listen.

66 There is indeed a lesson for you in the cattle:

    We give you to drink from what is in their bellies,

    from between intestinal waste and blood,

    pure milk, pleasant to those who drink.

67 And from the fruits of date palms and vines,

    you draw wine and goodly provision.

    There are indeed signs in that

    for people who exercise their reason.

68 And your Lord inspired the bee

    saying: 'Make your home in the mountains,

    and on trees and the trellises that they erect.

69 Then eat from every kind of fruit

    and follow meekly the ways of your Lord.'

---

[1] That is, supposing that there is a hereafter. Cf. **18:36, 41:50**.
[2] Or 'they will be left to languish in it.'

There issues from its belly a juice of diverse hues يَخْرُجُ مِنْ بُطُونِهَا شَرَابٌ مُخْتَلِفٌ أَلْوَانُهُ
in which there is cure for the people. فِيهِ شِفَاءٌ لِلنَّاسِ
There is indeed a sign in that for a people who reflect. إِنَّ فِي ذَٰلِكَ لَآيَةً لِقَوْمٍ يَتَفَكَّرُونَ ۝

70 God has created you, then He takes you away, وَاللَّهُ خَلَقَكُمْ ثُمَّ يَتَوَفَّاكُمْ
and there are some among you وَمِنْكُمْ
who are relegated to the nethermost age مَنْ يُرَدُّ إِلَىٰ أَرْذَلِ الْعُمُرِ
so that they know nothing after some knowledge. لِكَيْ لَا يَعْلَمَ بَعْدَ عِلْمٍ شَيْئًا
God is indeed all-knowing, all-powerful. إِنَّ اللَّهَ عَلِيمٌ قَدِيرٌ ۝

71 God has granted some of you an advantage over others وَاللَّهُ فَضَّلَ بَعْضَكُمْ عَلَىٰ بَعْضٍ
in respect of provision. فِي الرِّزْقِ
Those who have been granted an advantage do not فَمَا الَّذِينَ فُضِّلُوا
give over their provision to their slaves بِرَادِّي رِزْقِهِمْ عَلَىٰ مَا مَلَكَتْ أَيْمَانُهُمْ
so that they become equal in its respect. فَهُمْ فِيهِ سَوَاءٌ
What, do they dispute the blessing of God? أَفَبِنِعْمَةِ اللَّهِ يَجْحَدُونَ ۝

72 God made for you mates from your own selves وَاللَّهُ جَعَلَ لَكُمْ مِنْ أَنْفُسِكُمْ أَزْوَاجًا
and appointed for you, from your mates, وَجَعَلَ لَكُمْ مِنْ أَزْوَاجِكُمْ
children and grandchildren, بَنِينَ وَحَفَدَةً
and We provided you with all the good things. وَرَزَقَكُمْ مِنَ الطَّيِّبَاتِ
What, do they believe in falsehood أَفَبِالْبَاطِلِ يُؤْمِنُونَ
while they deny the blessing of God? وَبِنِعْمَتِ اللَّهِ هُمْ يَكْفُرُونَ ۝

73 They worship besides God وَيَعْبُدُونَ مِنْ دُونِ اللَّهِ
what has no power to provide them مَا لَا يَمْلِكُ لَهُمْ رِزْقًا
with anything from the heavens and the earth, مِنَ السَّمَاوَاتِ وَالْأَرْضِ شَيْئًا
nor are they capable of doing that. وَلَا يَسْتَطِيعُونَ ۝

74 So do not draw comparisons for God: فَلَا تَضْرِبُوا لِلَّهِ الْأَمْثَالَ
indeed God knows and you do not know. إِنَّ اللَّهَ يَعْلَمُ وَأَنْتُمْ لَا تَعْلَمُونَ ۝

75 God draws a parable: a slave owned by a master, ضَرَبَ اللَّهُ مَثَلًا عَبْدًا مَمْلُوكًا
having no power over anything, لَا يَقْدِرُ عَلَىٰ شَيْءٍ
and someone, [a free man], whom We have provided وَمَنْ رَزَقْنَاهُ مِنَّا
with a goodly provision and he spends out of it رِزْقًا حَسَنًا فَهُوَ يُنْفِقُ مِنْهُ

سِرًّا وَجَهْرًا ۚ secretly and openly.

هَلْ يَسْتَوُونَ ۚ Are they equal?

الْحَمْدُ لِلَّهِ ۚ All praise belongs to God.

بَلْ أَكْثَرُهُمْ لَا يَعْلَمُونَ ۝ But most of them do not know.

76 وَضَرَبَ اللَّهُ مَثَلًا God draws another parable:

رَجُلَيْنِ أَحَدُهُمَا أَبْكَمُ Two men, one of whom is dumb,

لَا يَقْدِرُ عَلَىٰ شَيْءٍ   having no power over anything

وَهُوَ كَلٌّ عَلَىٰ مَوْلَاهُ   and who is a liability to his master:

أَيْنَمَا يُوَجِّههُّ لَا يَأْتِ بِخَيْرٍ ۖ wherever he directs him, he does not bring any good.

هَلْ يَسْتَوِي هُوَ وَمَنْ يَأْمُرُ بِالْعَدْلِ ۙ Is he equal to someone who enjoins justice

وَهُوَ عَلَىٰ صِرَاطٍ مُسْتَقِيمٍ ۝   and is steady on a straight path?

77 وَلِلَّهِ غَيْبُ السَّمَاوَاتِ وَالْأَرْضِ ۚ To God belongs the Unseen of the heavens and the earth.

وَمَا أَمْرُ السَّاعَةِ إِلَّا The matter of the Hour[1] is just

كَلَمْحِ الْبَصَرِ أَوْ هُوَ أَقْرَبُ ۚ   like the twinkling of an eye, or even shorter.

إِنَّ اللَّهَ عَلَىٰ كُلِّ شَيْءٍ قَدِيرٌ ۝ Indeed, God has power over all things.

78 وَاللَّهُ أَخْرَجَكُمْ God has brought you forth

مِنْ بُطُونِ أُمَّهَاتِكُمْ   from the bellies of your mothers

لَا تَعْلَمُونَ شَيْئًا   while you did not know anything.

وَجَعَلَ لَكُمُ السَّمْعَ وَالْأَبْصَارَ He invested you with hearing, sight,

وَالْأَفْئِدَةَ ۙ   and the hearts

لَعَلَّكُمْ تَشْكُرُونَ ۝   so that you may give thanks.

79 أَلَمْ يَرَوْا إِلَى الطَّيْرِ Have they not regarded the birds

مُسَخَّرَاتٍ فِي جَوِّ السَّمَاءِ   disposed in the air of the sky:

مَا يُمْسِكُهُنَّ إِلَّا اللَّهُ ۗ   no one sustains them except God.

إِنَّ فِي ذَٰلِكَ لَآيَاتٍ لِقَوْمٍ يُؤْمِنُونَ ۝ There are indeed signs in that for people who have faith.

80 وَاللَّهُ جَعَلَ لَكُمْ مِنْ بُيُوتِكُمْ It is God who has made your homes for you

سَكَنًا   a place of rest,

وَجَعَلَ لَكُمْ مِنْ جُلُودِ الْأَنْعَامِ بُيُوتًا and He made for you homes out of the skins of the cattle

تَسْتَخِفُّونَهَا   which you find light and portable

---

[1] Or 'The command of the Hour.'

on the day of your shifting and on the day of your halt, يَوْمَ ظَعْنِكُمْ وَيَوْمَ إِقَامَتِكُمْ
and out of their wool, fur and hair [He has appointed] وَمِنْ أَصْوَافِهَا وَأَوْبَارِهَا وَأَشْعَارِهَا
furniture and wares enduring for a while. أَثَاثًا وَمَتَاعًا إِلَىٰ حِينٍ ۝

81 It is God وَاللَّهُ
who made for you the shade from what He has created, جَعَلَ لَكُم مِّمَّا خَلَقَ ظِلَالًا
and made for you retreats in the mountains, وَجَعَلَ لَكُم مِّنَ الْجِبَالِ أَكْنَانًا
and made for you garments that protect you from heat, وَجَعَلَ لَكُمْ سَرَابِيلَ تَقِيكُمُ الْحَرَّ
and garments that protect you from your mutual violence. وَسَرَابِيلَ تَقِيكُم بَأْسَكُمْ
That is how He completes His blessing upon you كَذَٰلِكَ يُتِمُّ نِعْمَتَهُ عَلَيْكُمْ
so that you may submit to Him. لَعَلَّكُمْ تُسْلِمُونَ ۝

82 But if they turn their backs on you, فَإِن تَوَلَّوْا
your duty is only to communicate in clear terms. فَإِنَّمَا عَلَيْكَ الْبَلَاغُ الْمُبِينُ ۝

83 They recognize the blessing of God and then deny it, يَعْرِفُونَ نِعْمَتَ اللَّهِ ثُمَّ يُنكِرُونَهَا
and most of them are faithless. وَأَكْثَرُهُمُ الْكَافِرُونَ ۝

84 The day We shall raise up a witness from every nation, وَيَوْمَ نَبْعَثُ مِن كُلِّ أُمَّةٍ شَهِيدًا
the faithless will not be permitted to speak,[1] ثُمَّ لَا يُؤْذَنُ لِلَّذِينَ كَفَرُوا
nor will they be asked to propitiate God. وَلَا هُمْ يُسْتَعْتَبُونَ ۝

85 And when the wrongdoers sight the punishment, وَإِذَا رَأَى الَّذِينَ ظَلَمُوا الْعَذَابَ
it shall not be lightened for them, فَلَا يُخَفَّفُ عَنْهُمْ
nor will they be granted any respite. وَلَا هُمْ يُنظَرُونَ ۝

86 When the polytheists sight their partners, وَإِذَا رَأَى الَّذِينَ أَشْرَكُوا شُرَكَاءَهُمْ
they will say, 'Our Lord! قَالُوا رَبَّنَا
These are our partners هَٰؤُلَاءِ شُرَكَاؤُنَا
whom we used to invoke besides You.' الَّذِينَ كُنَّا نَدْعُو مِن دُونِكَ
But they will retort to them, 'You are indeed liars!' فَأَلْقَوْا إِلَيْهِمُ الْقَوْلَ إِنَّكُمْ لَكَاذِبُونَ ۝

87 They will submit to God on that day, وَأَلْقَوْا إِلَى اللَّهِ يَوْمَئِذٍ السَّلَمَ
and what they used to fabricate will forsake them. وَضَلَّ عَنْهُم مَّا كَانُوا يَفْتَرُونَ ۝

88 Those who are faithless and bar from the way of God الَّذِينَ كَفَرُوا وَصَدُّوا عَن سَبِيلِ اللَّهِ
—We shall add punishment to their punishment زِدْنَاهُمْ عَذَابًا فَوْقَ الْعَذَابِ

---

[1] Cf. **11**:105; **23**:108; **36**:65; **78**:38.

because of the corruption they used to cause.

89 The day We raise in every nation
a witness against them from among themselves,
We shall bring you as a witness against these.
We have sent down the Book to you
as a clarification of all things and as guidance, mercy
and good news for those who submit to God.

90 Indeed, God enjoins justice and kindness,
and generosity towards relatives,
and He forbids indecency, wrongdoing, and aggression.
He advises you so that you may take admonition.

91 Fulfill God's covenant when you pledge,
and do not break your oaths after pledging them solemnly
and having made God a witness over yourselves.
God indeed knows what you do.

92 Do not be like her who would undo her yarn,
breaking it up after spinning it to strength,
by making your oaths
a means of mutual deceit among yourselves,
so that one community may become more affluent
than another community.[1]
God only tests you thereby,
and He will clarify for you on the Day of Resurrection
what you used to differ about.

93 Had God wished,
He would have surely made you one community,
but He leads astray whomever He wishes
and guides whomever He wishes,
and you will surely be questioned

---

[1] Or 'for one community may be more numerous (or more affluent) than another community.'

عَمَّا كُنتُمْ تَعْمَلُونَ ۝ concerning what you used to do.

94 Do not make your oaths
وَلَا تَتَّخِذُوا أَيْمَانَكُمْ   a means of mutual deceit among yourselves,
دَخَلًا بَيْنَكُمْ
فَتَزِلَّ قَدَمٌ بَعْدَ ثُبُوتِهَا   lest feet should stumble after being steady
وَتَذُوقُوا السُّوءَ   and lest you suffer ill
بِمَا صَدَدتُّمْ عَن سَبِيلِ اللَّهِ   for barring from the way of God
وَلَكُمْ عَذَابٌ عَظِيمٌ ۝   and face a great punishment.

95 وَلَا تَشْتَرُوا بِعَهْدِ اللَّهِ ثَمَنًا قَلِيلًا Do not sell God's covenants for a paltry gain.
إِنَّمَا عِندَ اللَّهِ هُوَ خَيْرٌ لَّكُمْ   What is with God is indeed better for you,
إِن كُنتُمْ تَعْلَمُونَ ۝   should you know.

96 مَا عِندَكُمْ يَنفَدُ That which is with you will be spent and gone,
وَمَا عِندَ اللَّهِ بَاقٍ   but what is with God shall last forever,
وَلَنَجْزِيَنَّ الَّذِينَ صَبَرُوا أَجْرَهُم   and We will surely pay the patient their reward
بِأَحْسَنِ مَا كَانُوا يَعْمَلُونَ ۝   by the best of what they used to do.

97 مَنْ عَمِلَ صَالِحًا Whoever acts righteously,
مِّن ذَكَرٍ أَوْ أُنثَىٰ وَهُوَ مُؤْمِنٌ   whether male or female, should he be faithful,
فَلَنُحْيِيَنَّهُ حَيَاةً طَيِّبَةً   We shall revive him with a good life
وَلَنَجْزِيَنَّهُمْ أَجْرَهُم   and pay them their reward
بِأَحْسَنِ مَا كَانُوا يَعْمَلُونَ ۝   by the best of what they used to do.

98 فَإِذَا قَرَأْتَ الْقُرْآنَ فَاسْتَعِذْ بِاللَّهِ When you recite the Qur'ān, *seek the protection of God*
مِنَ الشَّيْطَانِ الرَّجِيمِ ۝   *against the outcast Satan.*

99 إِنَّهُ لَيْسَ لَهُ سُلْطَانٌ Indeed, he does not have any authority
عَلَى الَّذِينَ آمَنُوا   over those who have faith
وَعَلَىٰ رَبِّهِمْ يَتَوَكَّلُونَ ۝   and put their trust in their Lord.

100 إِنَّمَا سُلْطَانُهُ عَلَى الَّذِينَ يَتَوَلَّوْنَهُ His authority is only over those who befriend him
وَالَّذِينَ هُم بِهِ مُشْرِكُونَ ۝   and those who make him a partner of God.

101 وَإِذَا بَدَّلْنَا آيَةً مَّكَانَ آيَةٍ When We change a sign for another in its place
وَاللَّهُ أَعْلَمُ بِمَا يُنَزِّلُ   —and God knows best what He sends down—
قَالُوا إِنَّمَا أَنتَ مُفْتَرٍ   they say, 'You are only a fabricator.'

Indeed, most of them do not know.

102 Say,
the Holy Spirit has brought it down duly from your Lord
to fortify those who have faith
and as guidance and good news for those who submit.

103 We certainly know that they say,
'It is only a human that instructs him.'
The language of him to whom they refer is non-Arabic,
while this is a clear Arabic language.

104 Indeed, those who do not believe in the signs of God
—God shall not guide them
and there is a painful punishment for them.

105 Only those fabricate lies
who do not believe in the signs of God,
and it is they who are the liars.

106 Those who disbelieve in God after affirming their faith
—excepting someone who is compelled to recant
while his heart is at rest in faith—
but those who open up their breasts to unfaith,
God's wrath shall be upon them
and there is a great punishment for them.

107 That, because they preferred the life of the world
to the Hereafter
and that God does not guide the faithless lot.

108 They are the ones God has set a seal on their hearts
and on their hearing and sight,
and it is they who are the heedless.

109 Undoubtedly,
they are the ones who will be the losers in the Hereafter.

110 Thereafter your Lord will indeed be

to those who migrated after they were persecuted,
  waged *jihād* and remained steadfast
—indeed, after that, your Lord
  will surely be forgiving and merciful to them.

111 The day when every soul will come pleading for itself
  and every soul will be recompensed fully
    for what it has done,
  and they will not be wronged.

112 God draws a parable:
  There was a town secure and peaceful,
  its provision coming abundantly from every place.
  But it was ungrateful toward God's blessings.
  So God made it taste hunger and fear
  because of what they used to do.

113 There had already come to them
  an apostle from among themselves,
    but they impugned him.
  So the punishment seized them while they were wrongdoers.

114 Eat out of what God has provided you
    as lawful and good,
    and give thanks for God's blessing,
    if it is Him that you worship.

115 He has forbidden you only carrion,
    blood, the flesh of the swine,
    and that which has been offered to other than God.
    But if someone is compelled to eat any of that
      without being rebellious or aggressive,
    indeed God is all-forgiving, all-merciful.[1]

116 Do not say,

---

[1] Cf. 2:173; 5:3; 6:145.

asserting falsely with your tongues,
'This is lawful, and that is unlawful,'
attributing lies to God.
Indeed, those who attribute lies to God
will not prosper.

117 [Their share of the present life is a trifling enjoyment,
and there will be a painful punishment for them.

118 We forbade to the Jews
what We have recounted to you earlier,
and We did not wrong them,
but they used to wrong themselves.

119 Moreover, indeed your Lord,
to those who commit evil out of ignorance
and then repent after that and reform themselves
—indeed, after that, your Lord
will surely be forgiving and merciful to them.

120 Indeed, Abraham was a nation all by himself
obedient to God, a ḥanīf,
and he was not a polytheist.

121 Grateful as he was for His blessings,
He chose him and guided him to a straight path.

122 We gave him good in this world,
and in the Hereafter he will
indeed be among the Righteous.

123 Thereafter, We revealed to you,
saying, 'Follow the creed of Abraham, a ḥanīf,
who was not a polytheist.'

124 The Sabbath was only prescribed
for those who differed about it.
Your Lord will indeed judge between them

on the Day of Resurrection
concerning that about which they used to differ.

125 *Invite* to the way of *your Lord*
with wisdom and good advice
and *dispute* with them in a manner that is best.
Indeed, *your* Lord knows best
those who stray from His way,
and He knows best those who are guided.

126 If you retaliate, retaliate with the like of
what you have been made to suffer,
but if you are patient,
that is surely better for the steadfast.

127 So *be patient*,
and *you* cannot be patient except with God's help.
And *do not grieve* for them,
nor be upset by their guile.

128 Indeed, God is with those who are Godwary
and those who are virtuous.

[PART 15]

17. THE NIGHT JOURNEY[1]
al-Isrā'

In the Name of God,
the All-beneficent, the All-merciful.

1 Immaculate is He who
carried His servant on a journey by night
from the Sacred Mosque
to the Farthest Mosque whose environs We have blessed,
so that We might show him some of Our signs.

---

[1] This Makkī *sūrah* takes its name from the subject of verse 1, *isrā'* (lit. 'taking s.o. on a night journey'), relating to the celestial journey (*mi'rāj*) of the Prophet (ṣ).

Indeed, He is the All-hearing, the All-seeing.

2 We gave Moses the Book,
and made it a guide for the Children of Israel,
saying, 'Do not take any trustee besides Me'

3 —descendants of those whom We carried
[in the ark] with Noah.
He was indeed a grateful servant.

4 We revealed to the Children of Israel in the Book:
'Twice you will cause corruption on the earth
and you will perpetrate great tyranny.'

5 So when the first occasion of the two prophecies came,
We aroused against you Our servants
possessing great might,
and they ransacked your habitations,
and the promise was bound to be fulfilled.

6 Then We gave you back the turn to prevail over them,
and We aided you with children and wealth,
and made you greater in number,

7 saying, 'If you do good, you will do good to your own souls,
and if you do evil, it will be evil for them.'
So when the occasion for the other prophecy comes,
they will make your faces[1] wretched,
and enter the Mosque just as they entered it the first time,
and destroy utterly whatever they come upon.

8 Maybe your Lord will have mercy on you,
but if you revert, We too will revert,
and We have made hell a prison for the faithless.

---

[1] Or 'notables.'

9 إِنَّ هَذَا الْقُرْآنَ يَهْدِي لِلَّتِي هِيَ أَقْوَمُ وَيُبَشِّرُ الْمُؤْمِنِينَ الَّذِينَ يَعْمَلُونَ الصَّالِحَاتِ أَنَّ لَهُمْ أَجْرًا كَبِيرًا ۝ This Qurʾān indeed guides to what is most upright, and gives the good news to the faithful who do righteous deeds, that there is a great reward for them.

10 وَأَنَّ الَّذِينَ لَا يُؤْمِنُونَ بِالْآخِرَةِ أَعْتَدْنَا لَهُمْ عَذَابًا أَلِيمًا ۝ As for those who do not believe in the Hereafter, We have prepared a painful punishment for them.

11 وَيَدْعُ الْإِنْسَانُ بِالشَّرِّ دُعَاءَهُ بِالْخَيْرِ وَكَانَ الْإِنْسَانُ عَجُولًا ۝ Man prays for ill as avidly as he prays for good, and man is overhasty.

12 وَجَعَلْنَا اللَّيْلَ وَالنَّهَارَ آيَتَيْنِ فَمَحَوْنَا آيَةَ اللَّيْلِ وَجَعَلْنَا آيَةَ النَّهَارِ مُبْصِرَةً لِتَبْتَغُوا فَضْلًا مِنْ رَبِّكُمْ وَلِتَعْلَمُوا عَدَدَ السِّنِينَ وَالْحِسَابَ وَكُلَّ شَيْءٍ فَصَّلْنَاهُ تَفْصِيلًا ۝ We made the night and the day two signs. We effaced the sign of the night and made the sign of the day lightsome, so that you may seek from your Lord's bounty and that you may know the number of years and calculation of time, and We have elaborated everything in detail.[1]

13 وَكُلَّ إِنْسَانٍ أَلْزَمْنَاهُ طَائِرَهُ فِي عُنُقِهِ وَنُخْرِجُ لَهُ يَوْمَ الْقِيَامَةِ كِتَابًا يَلْقَاهُ مَنْشُورًا ۝ We have strapped every person's karma to his neck, and We shall bring it out for him on the Day of Resurrection as a book that he will find wide open.

14 اقْرَأْ كِتَابَكَ كَفَى بِنَفْسِكَ الْيَوْمَ عَلَيْكَ حَسِيبًا ۝ 'Read your book! Today your soul suffices as your own reckoner.'[2]

15 مَنِ اهْتَدَى فَإِنَّمَا يَهْتَدِي لِنَفْسِهِ وَمَنْ ضَلَّ فَإِنَّمَا يَضِلُّ عَلَيْهَا وَلَا تَزِرُ وَازِرَةٌ وِزْرَ أُخْرَى وَمَا كُنَّا مُعَذِّبِينَ حَتَّى نَبْعَثَ رَسُولًا ۝ Whoever is guided, is guided only for the good of his own soul, and whoever goes astray, goes astray only to its detriment. No bearer shall bear another's burden. We do not punish any community until We have sent an apostle.

16 وَإِذَا أَرَدْنَا أَنْ نُهْلِكَ قَرْيَةً أَمَرْنَا مُتْرَفِيهَا And when We desire to destroy a town We command its affluent ones [to obey God].

---

[1] Or 'articulated everything distinctly.'
[2] Or 'today you suffice as your own reckoner.'

> But they commit transgression in it, فَفَسَقُوا فِيهَا
> and so the word becomes due against it, فَحَقَّ عَلَيْهَا الْقَوْلُ
> and We destroy it utterly. فَدَمَّرْنَاهَا تَدْمِيرًا ۝

17 How many generations We have destroyed since Noah! وَكَمْ أَهْلَكْنَا مِنَ الْقُرُونِ مِنْ بَعْدِ نُوحٍ
> Your Lord is sufficient as [a witness who is] وَكَفَىٰ بِرَبِّكَ
> a well-informed observer of His servants' sins. بِذُنُوبِ عِبَادِهِ خَبِيرًا بَصِيرًا ۝

18 Whoever desires this transitory life, مَنْ كَانَ يُرِيدُ الْعَاجِلَةَ
> We expedite for him therein whatever We wish, عَجَّلْنَا لَهُ فِيهَا مَا نَشَاءُ
> for whomever We desire. لِمَنْ نُرِيدُ
> Then We appoint hell for him, ثُمَّ جَعَلْنَا لَهُ جَهَنَّمَ
> to enter it, blameful and spurned. يَصْلَاهَا مَذْمُومًا مَدْحُورًا ۝

19 Whoever desires the Hereafter وَمَنْ أَرَادَ الْآخِرَةَ
> and strives for it with an endeavour worthy of it, وَسَعَىٰ لَهَا سَعْيَهَا
> should he be faithful وَهُوَ مُؤْمِنٌ
> —the endeavour of such will be well-appreciated. فَأُولَٰئِكَ كَانَ سَعْيُهُمْ مَشْكُورًا ۝

20 To these and to those—to all We extend كُلًّا نُمِدُّ هَٰؤُلَاءِ وَهَٰؤُلَاءِ
> from the bounty of your Lord, مِنْ عَطَاءِ رَبِّكَ
> and the bounty of your Lord is not confined. وَمَا كَانَ عَطَاءُ رَبِّكَ مَحْظُورًا ۝

21 *Observe* how We have given some of them an advantage انْظُرْ كَيْفَ فَضَّلْنَا بَعْضَهُمْ
> over some others; عَلَىٰ بَعْضٍ
> yet the Hereafter is surely greater in respect of ranks وَلَلْآخِرَةُ أَكْبَرُ دَرَجَاتٍ
> and greater in respect of relative merit.[1] وَأَكْبَرُ تَفْضِيلًا ۝

22 Do not set up another god besides God, لَا تَجْعَلْ مَعَ اللَّهِ إِلَٰهًا آخَرَ
> or you will sit blameworthy, forsaken. فَتَقْعُدَ مَذْمُومًا مَخْذُولًا ۝

23 Your Lord has decreed وَقَضَىٰ رَبُّكَ
> that you shall not worship anyone except Him, أَلَّا تَعْبُدُوا إِلَّا إِيَّاهُ
> and He has enjoined kindness to parents. وَبِالْوَالِدَيْنِ إِحْسَانًا

---

[1] Or 'greater in respect of preference.'

Should they reach old age at your side
—any of them or both—
do not say to them, 'Fie!'[1]
And do not chide them, but speak to them noble words.

24 Lower the wing of humility to them mercifully,
and say, 'My Lord! Have mercy on them,
just as they reared me when I was a small child!'

25 Your Lord knows best what is in your hearts.
Should you be righteous,
He is indeed most forgiving toward penitents.

26 *Give* the relatives their due right,
and the needy and the traveler as well,
but do not squander wastefully.

27 The wasteful are indeed brothers of satans,
and Satan is ungrateful to his Lord.

28 And if you have to hold off assisting them for now,
seeking your Lord's mercy which you expect in the future,
speak to them gentle words.

29 Do not keep your hand chained to your neck,
nor open it altogether,[2]
or you will sit being blameworthy and regretful.

30 Indeed, your Lord expands the provision
for whomever He wishes,
and tightens it.
He is indeed a well-informed observer of His servants.

31 Do not kill your children for the fear of penury:
We will provide for them and for you.

---

[1] That is, do not grumble or speak to them in an ill-tempered manner. Uff is an interjection expressing displeasure and exasperation, indicating that one has been put out of patience.

[2] That is, neither be tight-fisted and miserly, nor be a spendthrift.

Killing them is indeed a great iniquity.

32 Do not approach fornication.
It is indeed an indecency and an evil way.

33 Do not kill a soul whose life
God has made inviolable,
    except with due cause,
and whoever is killed wrongfully,
    We have certainly given his heir an authority.
But let him not commit any excess in killing,[1]
    for he enjoys the support [of law].

34 Do not approach the orphan's property
    except in the best manner,
    until he comes of age.
Fulfill your covenants;
    indeed, all covenants are accountable.

35 When you measure, observe fully the measure,
    and weigh with an even balance.
That is better and more favourable in outcome.

36 Do not pursue
    anything that has not come to your knowledge.
Indeed, hearing, eyesight and the heart
    —all these are accountable.

37 Do not walk exultantly on the earth.
Indeed, you will neither pierce the earth,
    nor reach the mountains in height.

38 The evil of all these is detestable to your Lord.

39 These are among precepts that
    your Lord has revealed to you of wisdom.
Do not set up another god besides God,

---

[1] Such as mutilating the body of the murderer, or killing someone other than the guilty person for the sake of vengeance.

or you will be cast into hell,
being blameworthy and banished from His mercy.

40 Did your Lord prefer you for sons,
and Himself adopt females from among the angels?[1]
You indeed make a monstrous statement!

41 Certainly We have variously paraphrased
[the principles of guidance] in this Qur'ān
so that they may take admonition,
but it increases them only in aversion.

42 Say, 'Were there other gods besides Him, as they say,
they would have encroached on the Lord of the Throne.

43 Immaculate is He
and preeminently far above what they say!'

44 The seven heavens glorify Him and the earth, too,
and whoever is in them.
There is not a thing but celebrates His praise,
but you do not understand their glorification.
He is indeed all-forbearing, all-forgiving.

45 When you recite the Qur'ān,
We draw between you
and those who do not believe in the Hereafter
a hidden curtain,

46 and We cast veils on their hearts,
lest they should understand it,
and a deafness into their ears.
When you mention your Lord alone in the Qur'ān,
they turn their backs in aversion.

---

[1] Cf. 4:117; 37:150; 43:19; 53:21, 27.

47 We know best what they listen for
    when they listen to *you*,
    and when they hold secret talks,
    when the wrongdoers say,
    '[If you follow him,] you will be following just
    a bewitched man.'

48 *Look*, how they coin epithets for *you*;
    so they go astray, and cannot find a way.

49 They say, 'What, when we have become bones and dust,
    shall we really be raised in a new creation?'

50 Say, 'Yes, even if you should become stones or iron,

51 or a creature more fantastic to your minds!'
    They will say, 'Who will bring us back?'
    Say, 'He who originated you the first time.'
    They will nod their heads at you
    and say, 'When will that be?'
    Say, 'Maybe it is near!

52 The day He calls you,
    you will respond to Him, praising Him,
    and you will think you remained only for a little while.'

53 *Tell* My servants to speak in a manner which is the best.
    Indeed, Satan incites ill feeling between them,
    and Satan is indeed man's open enemy.

54 Your Lord knows you best.
    He will have mercy on you, if He wishes,
    or punish you, if He wishes,
    and We did not send you to watch over them.

55 *Your* Lord knows best whoever is in the heavens

وَالْأَرْضُ ۗ and the earth.

وَلَقَدْ فَضَّلْنَا بَعْضَ النَّبِيِّينَ Certainly We gave some prophets an advantage

عَلَىٰ بَعْضٍ ۖ over some others,

وَآتَيْنَا دَاوُودَ زَبُورًا ۝ and We gave David the Psalms.

56 Say, 'Invoke those whom you claim besides Him. قُلِ ادْعُوا الَّذِينَ زَعَمْتُم مِّن دُونِهِ

فَلَا يَمْلِكُونَ كَشْفَ الضُّرِّ عَنكُمْ They have no power to remove your distress,

وَلَا تَحْوِيلًا ۝ nor to bring about any change in your state.

57 They themselves are the ones who supplicate, أُولَـٰئِكَ الَّذِينَ يَدْعُونَ

يَبْتَغُونَ إِلَىٰ رَبِّهِمُ الْوَسِيلَةَ seeking a recourse to their Lord,[1]

أَيُّهُمْ أَقْرَبُ whoever is nearer to Him,

وَيَرْجُونَ رَحْمَتَهُ وَيَخَافُونَ عَذَابَهُ ۚ expecting His mercy and fearing His punishment.'

إِنَّ عَذَابَ رَبِّكَ كَانَ مَحْذُورًا ۝ Your Lord's punishment is indeed a thing to beware of.

58 There is not a town but We will destroy it وَإِن مِّن قَرْيَةٍ إِلَّا نَحْنُ مُهْلِكُوهَا

قَبْلَ يَوْمِ الْقِيَامَةِ before the Day of Resurrection,

أَوْ مُعَذِّبُوهَا عَذَابًا شَدِيدًا ۚ or punish it with a severe punishment.

كَانَ ذَٰلِكَ فِي الْكِتَابِ مَسْطُورًا ۝ That has been written in the Book.

59 Nothing keeps Us from sending signs وَمَا مَنَعَنَا أَن نُّرْسِلَ بِالْآيَاتِ

إِلَّا أَن كَذَّبَ بِهَا الْأَوَّلُونَ ۚ except that the former peoples denied them.

وَآتَيْنَا ثَمُودَ النَّاقَةَ مُبْصِرَةً We gave Thamūd the she-camel as an eye-opener,

فَظَلَمُوا بِهَا ۚ but they wronged her.

وَمَا نُرْسِلُ بِالْآيَاتِ إِلَّا تَخْوِيفًا ۝ We do not send the signs except for warning.

60 When We said to you, وَإِذْ قُلْنَا لَكَ

إِنَّ رَبَّكَ أَحَاطَ بِالنَّاسِ ۚ 'Your Lord indeed encompasses those people,'

وَمَا جَعَلْنَا الرُّؤْيَا الَّتِي أَرَيْنَاكَ We did not appoint the vision that We showed you

إِلَّا فِتْنَةً لِّلنَّاسِ except as a tribulation for the people

وَالشَّجَرَةَ الْمَلْعُونَةَ فِي الْقُرْآنِ ۚ and the tree cursed in the Qur'ān.

وَنُخَوِّفُهُمْ We warn them,

فَمَا يَزِيدُهُمْ إِلَّا طُغْيَانًا كَبِيرًا ۝ but it only increases them in their outrageous rebellion.

---

[1] Or 'Those whom they (i.e., the polytheists) invoke, themselves seek a recourse to their Lord....'

61 When We said to the angels, 'Prostrate before Adam,'
   they all prostrated, but not Iblis:
   he said, 'Shall I prostrate before someone
      whom You have created from clay?'

62 Said he, 'Do You see this one whom
   You have honoured above me?
   If You respite me until the Day of Resurrection,
   I will surely lay my yoke on his progeny, all except a few.'

63 Said He, 'Begone! Whoever of them follows you,
   the hell shall indeed be your requital, an ample reward.

64 Instigate whomever of them you can with your voice;[1]
   and rally against them your cavalry and infantry,
   and share with them in wealth and children,
   and make promises to them!'
   But Satan promises them nothing but delusion.

65 'As for My servants,
      you will have no authority over them.'
   And your Lord suffices as trustee.

66 Your Lord is He who drives for you the ships in the sea,
      so that you may seek His bounty.
   He is indeed most merciful to you.

67 When distress befalls you at sea,
   those whom you invoke besides Him are forsaken.
   But when He delivers you to land,
      you are disregardful of Him.
   Man is very ungrateful.

68 Do you feel secure
   that He will not make the coastland swallow you,

---

[1] Or 'Tempt whomever....'

أَوْ يُرْسِلَ عَلَيْكُمْ حَاصِبًا	or He will not unleash upon you a rain of stones?
ثُمَّ لَا تَجِدُوا لَكُمْ وَكِيلًا ۝	Then you will not find any defender for yourselves.
أَمْ أَمِنتُمْ	69 Do you feel secure
أَن يُعِيدَكُمْ فِيهِ تَارَةً أُخْرَىٰ	that He will not send you back into it another time
فَيُرْسِلَ عَلَيْكُمْ قَاصِفًا مِّنَ الرِّيحِ	and unleash against you a shattering gale
فَيُغْرِقَكُم بِمَا كَفَرْتُمْ	and drown you because of your unfaith?
ثُمَّ لَا تَجِدُوا لَكُمْ	Then you will not find for yourselves
عَلَيْنَا بِهِ تَبِيعًا ۝	any redresser against Us.
وَلَقَدْ كَرَّمْنَا بَنِي آدَمَ	70 Certainly We have honoured the Children of Adam
وَحَمَلْنَاهُمْ فِي الْبَرِّ وَالْبَحْرِ	and carried them over land and sea,
وَرَزَقْنَاهُم مِّنَ الطَّيِّبَاتِ	and provided them with all the good things,
وَفَضَّلْنَاهُمْ عَلَىٰ كَثِيرٍ مِّمَّنْ خَلَقْنَا تَفْضِيلًا ۝	and preferred them over many of those We have created with a complete preference.
يَوْمَ نَدْعُو كُلَّ أُنَاسٍ	71 The day We shall summon every group of people
بِإِمَامِهِمْ	along with their *imam*,[1]
فَمَنْ أُوتِيَ كِتَابَهُ بِيَمِينِهِ	then whoever is given his book in his right hand
فَأُولَٰئِكَ يَقْرَءُونَ كِتَابَهُمْ	—they will read their book,
وَلَا يُظْلَمُونَ	and they will not be wronged
فَتِيلًا ۝	so much as a single date-thread.
وَمَن كَانَ فِي هَٰذِهِ أَعْمَىٰ	72 But whoever has been blind in this world,
فَهُوَ فِي الْآخِرَةِ أَعْمَىٰ	will be blind in the Hereafter,
وَأَضَلُّ سَبِيلًا ۝	and even more astray from the right way.
وَإِن كَادُوا لَيَفْتِنُونَكَ	73 They were about to beguile you
عَنِ الَّذِي أَوْحَيْنَا إِلَيْكَ	from what God has revealed to *you*
لِتَفْتَرِيَ عَلَيْنَا	so that *you* may fabricate against Us
غَيْرَهُ	something other than that,
وَإِذًا لَّاتَّخَذُوكَ خَلِيلًا ۝	whereat they would have befriended *you*.
وَلَوْلَا أَن ثَبَّتْنَاكَ	74 Had We not fortified *you*,

---

[1] That is, leader. Cf. 4:41, 16:89.

certainly you might have inclined toward them a bit. لَقَدْ كِدتَّ تَرْكَنُ إِلَيْهِمْ شَيْئًا قَلِيلًا ۝

75 Then We would have surely made you taste إِذًا لَّأَذَقْنَاكَ
a double punishment in this life ضِعْفَ الْحَيَاةِ
and a double punishment after death, وَضِعْفَ الْمَمَاتِ
and then you would have not found for yourself ثُمَّ لَا تَجِدُ لَكَ
any helper against Us. عَلَيْنَا نَصِيرًا ۝

76 They were about to hound you out of the land, وَإِن كَادُوا لَيَسْتَفِزُّونَكَ مِنَ الْأَرْضِ
to expel you from it, لِيُخْرِجُوكَ مِنْهَا
but, then, they would not have stayed after you but a little. وَإِذًا لَّا يَلْبَثُونَ خِلَافَكَ إِلَّا قَلِيلًا ۝

77 A precedent touching those We have sent سُنَّةَ مَن قَدْ أَرْسَلْنَا
before you from among Our apostles, قَبْلَكَ مِن رُّسُلِنَا
and you will not find any change in Our precedent. وَلَا تَجِدُ لِسُنَّتِنَا تَحْوِيلًا ۝

78 *Maintain* the prayer from the sun's decline[1] أَقِمِ الصَّلَاةَ لِدُلُوكِ الشَّمْسِ
till the darkness of the night, إِلَىٰ غَسَقِ اللَّيْلِ
and *observe* particularly the dawn recital. وَقُرْآنَ الْفَجْرِ
The dawn recital is indeed attended by angels. إِنَّ قُرْآنَ الْفَجْرِ كَانَ مَشْهُودًا ۝

79 And *keep vigil* for a part of the night, وَمِنَ اللَّيْلِ فَتَهَجَّدْ بِهِ
as a supererogatory devotion for *you*. نَافِلَةً لَّكَ
It may be that *your* Lord will raise *you* عَسَىٰ أَن يَبْعَثَكَ رَبُّكَ
to a praiseworthy station. مَقَامًا مَّحْمُودًا ۝

80 And *say*, 'My Lord! 'Admit me with a worthy entrance, وَقُل رَّبِّ أَدْخِلْنِي مُدْخَلَ صِدْقٍ
and bring me out with a worthy departure, وَأَخْرِجْنِي مُخْرَجَ صِدْقٍ
and render me a favourable authority from Yourself.' وَاجْعَل لِّي مِن لَّدُنكَ سُلْطَانًا نَّصِيرًا ۝

81 And *say*, 'The truth has come, and falsehood has vanished. وَقُلْ جَاءَ الْحَقُّ وَزَهَقَ الْبَاطِلُ
Falsehood is indeed bound to vanish.' إِنَّ الْبَاطِلَ كَانَ زَهُوقًا ۝

82 We send down in the Qur'ān وَنُنَزِّلُ مِنَ الْقُرْآنِ
that which is a cure and mercy for the faithful, مَا هُوَ شِفَاءٌ وَرَحْمَةٌ لِّلْمُؤْمِنِينَ
and it increases the wrongdoers only in loss. وَلَا يَزِيدُ الظَّالِمِينَ إِلَّا خَسَارًا ۝

---

[1] That is, from noon onwards, when the sun crosses the meridian.

وَإِذَا أَنْعَمْنَا عَلَى الْإِنْسَانِ 83 When We bless man,
أَعْرَضَ وَنَأَىٰ بِجَانِبِهِ   he is disregardful and turns aside;
وَإِذَا مَسَّهُ الشَّرُّ كَانَ يَـُٔوسًا ۝ but when an ill befalls him, he is despondent.
قُلْ كُلٌّ يَعْمَلُ عَلَىٰ شَاكِلَتِهِ 84 Say, 'Everyone acts according to his character.
فَرَبُّكُمْ أَعْلَمُ   Your Lord knows best
بِمَنْ هُوَ أَهْدَىٰ سَبِيلًا ۝   who is better guided with regard to the way.'
وَيَسْـَٔلُونَكَ عَنِ الرُّوحِ 85 They question *you* concerning the Spirit.
قُلِ الرُّوحُ مِنْ أَمْرِ رَبِّي   Say, 'The Spirit is of the command of my Lord,[1]
وَمَا أُوتِيتُمْ مِنَ الْعِلْمِ   and you have not been given of the knowledge
إِلَّا قَلِيلًا ۝   except a few.'[2]
وَلَئِنْ شِئْنَا 86 If We wish,
لَنَذْهَبَنَّ بِالَّذِي أَوْحَيْنَا إِلَيْكَ   We would take away what We have revealed to you.
ثُمَّ لَا تَجِدُ لَكَ بِهِ عَلَيْنَا وَكِيلًا ۝   Then you would not find for *yourself* any defender against Us,
إِلَّا رَحْمَةً مِنْ رَبِّكَ 87 except a mercy from *your* Lord.
إِنَّ فَضْلَهُ كَانَ عَلَيْكَ كَبِيرًا ۝   His grace has indeed been great upon you.
قُلْ لَئِنِ اجْتَمَعَتِ الْإِنْسُ وَالْجِنُّ 88 Say, 'Should all humans and jinn rally
عَلَىٰ أَنْ يَأْتُوا بِمِثْلِ هَٰذَا الْقُرْآنِ   to bring the like of this Qur'ān,
لَا يَأْتُونَ بِمِثْلِهِ   they will not bring its like,
وَلَوْ كَانَ بَعْضُهُمْ لِبَعْضٍ ظَهِيرًا ۝   even if they assisted one another.'
وَلَقَدْ صَرَّفْنَا لِلنَّاسِ 89 We have certainly interspersed for the people
فِي هَٰذَا الْقُرْآنِ مِنْ كُلِّ مَثَلٍ   this Qur'ān with every kind of parable,
فَأَبَىٰ أَكْثَرُ النَّاسِ إِلَّا كُفُورًا ۝   but most of these people are only bent on ingratitude.[3]
وَقَالُوا لَنْ نُؤْمِنَ لَكَ حَتَّىٰ 90 They say, 'We will not believe you until
تَفْجُرَ لَنَا مِنَ الْأَرْضِ يَنْبُوعًا ۝   you make a spring gush forth for us from the ground.
أَوْ تَكُونَ لَكَ جَنَّةٌ مِنْ نَخِيلٍ وَعِنَبٍ 91 Or until you have a garden of date palms and vines
فَتُفَجِّرَ الْأَنْهَارَ خِلَالَهَا تَفْجِيرًا ۝   and you make streams gush through it.
أَوْ تُسْقِطَ السَّمَاءَ 92 Or until you cause the sky to fall
كَمَا زَعَمْتَ عَلَيْنَا كِسَفًا   in fragments upon us, just as you have averred.

---

[1] Or 'the Spirit relates to the command of my Lord.' Or 'the Spirit proceeds from the command of my Lord.'
[2] Or 'you have not been given of the knowledge except a little.'
[3] Or 'faithlessness.' Cf. **17**:99 below and **25**:50.

أَوْ تَأْتِيَ بِاللَّهِ وَالْمَلَائِكَةِ قَبِيلًا ۝ Or until you bring God and the angels right in front of us.

93 أَوْ يَكُونَ لَكَ بَيْتٌ مِنْ زُخْرُفٍ Or until you have a house of gold,

أَوْ تَرْقَىٰ فِي السَّمَاءِ or you ascend into the sky.

وَلَنْ نُؤْمِنَ لِرُقِيِّكَ And we will not believe your ascension

حَتَّىٰ تُنَزِّلَ عَلَيْنَا كِتَابًا نَقْرَؤُهُ until you bring down for us a book that we may read.'

قُلْ سُبْحَانَ رَبِّي Say, 'Immaculate is my Lord!

هَلْ كُنْتُ إِلَّا بَشَرًا رَسُولًا ۝ Am I anything but a human apostle?!'

94 وَمَا مَنَعَ النَّاسَ أَنْ يُؤْمِنُوا Nothing has kept these people from believing

إِذْ جَاءَهُمُ الْهُدَىٰ when guidance came to them,

إِلَّا أَنْ قَالُوا but their saying,

أَبَعَثَ اللَّهُ بَشَرًا رَسُولًا ۝ 'Has God sent a human as an apostle?!'

95 قُلْ لَوْ كَانَ فِي الْأَرْضِ مَلَائِكَةٌ Say, 'Had there been angels in the earth,

يَمْشُونَ مُطْمَئِنِّينَ walking around and residing [in it like humans do],

لَنَزَّلْنَا عَلَيْهِمْ مِنَ السَّمَاءِ We would have sent down to them from the heaven

مَلَكًا رَسُولًا ۝ an angel as apostle.'

96 قُلْ كَفَىٰ بِاللَّهِ شَهِيدًا بَيْنِي وَبَيْنَكُمْ Say, 'God suffices as witness between me and you.

إِنَّهُ كَانَ بِعِبَادِهِ خَبِيرًا بَصِيرًا ۝ He is indeed a well-informed observer of His servants.'

97 وَمَنْ يَهْدِ اللَّهُ فَهُوَ الْمُهْتَدِ Whomever God guides is rightly guided,

وَمَنْ يُضْلِلْ and whomever He leads astray

فَلَنْ تَجِدَ لَهُمْ أَوْلِيَاءَ مِنْ دُونِهِ you will never find for them any protector besides Him.

وَنَحْشُرُهُمْ يَوْمَ الْقِيَامَةِ On the Day of Resurrection, We will gather them

عَلَىٰ وُجُوهِهِمْ scrambling on their faces,[1]

عُمْيًا وَبُكْمًا وَصُمًّا ۖ مَأْوَاهُمْ جَهَنَّمُ blind, dumb, and deaf. Their refuge shall be hell.

كُلَّمَا خَبَتْ زِدْنَاهُمْ سَعِيرًا ۝ Whenever it subsides, We will intensify the blaze for them.

98 ذَٰلِكَ جَزَاؤُهُمْ بِأَنَّهُمْ كَفَرُوا بِآيَاتِنَا That is their requital because they denied Our signs

وَقَالُوا أَإِذَا كُنَّا عِظَامًا وَرُفَاتًا and said, 'What, when we have become bones and dust,

أَإِنَّا لَمَبْعُوثُونَ خَلْقًا جَدِيدًا ۝ shall we really be raised in a new creation?'

99 أَوَلَمْ يَرَوْا أَنَّ اللَّهَ Do they not see that God,

الَّذِي خَلَقَ السَّمَاوَاتِ وَالْأَرْضَ who created the heavens and the earth,

---

[1] Cf. 25:34; 54:48.

is able to create the like of them? قَادِرٌ عَلَىٰ أَن يَخْلُقَ مِثْلَهُمْ
He has appointed for them a term, in which there is no doubt; وَجَعَلَ لَهُمْ أَجَلًا لَّا رَيْبَ فِيهِ
yet the wrongdoers are only bent on ingratitude.[1] فَأَبَى الظَّالِمُونَ إِلَّا كُفُورًا ۝
100 Say, 'Even if you possessed قُل لَّوْ أَنتُمْ تَمْلِكُونَ
 the treasuries of my Lord's mercy, خَزَائِنَ رَحْمَةِ رَبِّي
 you would withhold them for the fear of being spent, إِذًا لَّأَمْسَكْتُمْ خَشْيَةَ الْإِنفَاقِ
 and man is very niggardly.' وَكَانَ الْإِنسَانُ قَتُورًا ۝

101 Certainly We gave Moses nine manifest signs. وَلَقَدْ آتَيْنَا مُوسَىٰ تِسْعَ آيَاتٍ بَيِّنَاتٍ
 So ask the Children of Israel. فَاسْأَلْ بَنِي إِسْرَائِيلَ
 When he came to them, Pharaoh said to him, إِذْ جَاءَهُمْ فَقَالَ لَهُ فِرْعَوْنُ
 'O Moses, indeed I think you are bewitched.' إِنِّي لَأَظُنُّكَ يَا مُوسَىٰ مَسْحُورًا ۝
102 He said, 'You certainly know that none has sent these signs قَالَ لَقَدْ عَلِمْتَ مَا أَنزَلَ هَٰؤُلَاءِ
 except the Lord of the heavens and the earth, إِلَّا رَبُّ السَّمَاوَاتِ وَالْأَرْضِ
 as eye-openers, بَصَائِرَ
 and I, O Pharaoh, indeed think you are doomed.' وَإِنِّي لَأَظُنُّكَ يَا فِرْعَوْنُ مَثْبُورًا ۝
103 He desired to exterminate them from the land, فَأَرَادَ أَن يَسْتَفِزَّهُم مِّنَ الْأَرْضِ
 so We drowned him and all those who were with him. فَأَغْرَقْنَاهُ وَمَن مَّعَهُ جَمِيعًا ۝
104 After him, We said to the Children of Israel, وَقُلْنَا مِن بَعْدِهِ لِبَنِي إِسْرَائِيلَ
 'Take up residence in the land, اسْكُنُوا الْأَرْضَ
 and when the occasion of the other promise comes,[2] فَإِذَا جَاءَ وَعْدُ الْآخِرَةِ
 We will gather you in mixed company.'[3] جِئْنَا بِكُمْ لَفِيفًا ۝
105 With the truth did We send it down, وَبِالْحَقِّ أَنزَلْنَاهُ
 and with the truth did it descend, وَبِالْحَقِّ نَزَلَ
 and We did not send you except as a bearer of good news وَمَا أَرْسَلْنَاكَ إِلَّا مُبَشِّرًا
 and warner. وَنَذِيرًا ۝
106 We have sent the Qur'ān in discrete parts, وَقُرْآنًا فَرَقْنَاهُ
 so that you may recite it for the people, a little at a time, لِتَقْرَأَهُ عَلَى النَّاسِ عَلَىٰ مُكْثٍ

---

[1] Or 'faithlessness.'
[2] Or 'when the promise of the Hereafter comes.'
[3] Or 'We shall bring you all together.' Or 'We shall bring you from all places.'

and We have sent it down piecemeal.

107 Say, 'Whether you believe in it or do not believe,
indeed, those who were given knowledge before it,
when it is recited to them,
fall down in prostration on their faces,

108 and say, "Immaculate is our Lord!
Our Lord's promise is indeed bound to be fulfilled."

109 Weeping, they fall down on their faces,
and it increases them in humility.'

110 Say, 'Invoke "God" or invoke "the All-beneficent."
Whichever of His Names you may invoke,
to Him belong the Best Names.'
Be neither loud in *your* prayer, nor murmur it,
but *follow* a middle course between these,

111 and *say*, 'All praise belongs to God,
who has neither any offspring,
nor has He any partner in sovereignty,
nor has He made any friend out of weakness,'
and *magnify* Him with a magnification worthy of Him.

18. THE CAVE[1]
al-Kahf

In the Name of God,
the All-beneficent, the All-merciful.

1 All praise belongs to God,
who has sent down the Book to His servant
and did not let any crookedness be in it,

2 a Book upright, to warn of a severe punishment from Him,
and to give good news to the faithful

---

[1] This Makkī *sūrah* derives its name from the story of the Companions of the Cave (*aṣḥāb al-kahf*) told at its beginning.

who do righteous deeds, الَّذِينَ يَعْمَلُونَ الصَّالِحَاتِ

that there shall be for them a good reward, أَنَّ لَهُمْ أَجْرًا حَسَنًا ۝

3 to abide in it forever, مَاكِثِينَ فِيهِ أَبَدًا ۝

4 and to warn those who say, 'God has offspring.' وَيُنْذِرَ الَّذِينَ قَالُوا اتَّخَذَ اللَّهُ وَلَدًا ۝

5 They do not have any knowledge of that, مَا لَهُمْ بِهِ مِنْ عِلْمٍ

nor did their fathers. وَلَا لِآبَائِهِمْ

Monstrous is the utterance that comes out of their mouths, كَبُرَتْ كَلِمَةً تَخْرُجُ مِنْ أَفْوَاهِهِمْ

and they say nothing but a lie. إِنْ يَقُولُونَ إِلَّا كَذِبًا ۝

6 You are liable to imperil your life for their sake, فَلَعَلَّكَ بَاخِعٌ نَفْسَكَ عَلَى آثَارِهِمْ

if they do not believe this discourse,[1] out of grief. إِنْ لَمْ يُؤْمِنُوا بِهَذَا الْحَدِيثِ أَسَفًا ۝

7 Indeed, We have made whatever is on the earth إِنَّا جَعَلْنَا مَا عَلَى الْأَرْضِ

an adornment for it that We may test them زِينَةً لَهَا لِنَبْلُوَهُمْ

to see which of them is best in conduct. أَيُّهُمْ أَحْسَنُ عَمَلًا ۝

8 And, indeed, We will surely turn وَإِنَّا لَجَاعِلُونَ

whatever is on it into a barren plain. مَا عَلَيْهَا صَعِيدًا جُرُزًا ۝

9 Do you suppose that the Companions of the Cave أَمْ حَسِبْتَ أَنَّ أَصْحَابَ الْكَهْفِ

and the Inscription وَالرَّقِيمِ

were among Our wonderful signs? كَانُوا مِنْ آيَاتِنَا عَجَبًا ۝

10 When the youths took refuge in the Cave, إِذْ أَوَى الْفِتْيَةُ إِلَى الْكَهْفِ

they said, 'Our Lord! Grant us a mercy from Yourself, فَقَالُوا رَبَّنَا آتِنَا مِنْ لَدُنْكَ رَحْمَةً

and help us on to rectitude in our affair.' وَهَيِّئْ لَنَا مِنْ أَمْرِنَا رَشَدًا ۝

11 So We put them to sleep[2] in the Cave فَضَرَبْنَا عَلَى آذَانِهِمْ فِي الْكَهْفِ

for several years. سِنِينَ عَدَدًا ۝

12 Then We aroused them that We might know ثُمَّ بَعَثْنَاهُمْ لِنَعْلَمَ

which of the two groups better reckoned أَيُّ الْحِزْبَيْنِ أَحْصَى

the period they had stayed. لِمَا لَبِثُوا أَمَدًا ۝

13 We relate to you their account in truth. نَحْنُ نَقُصُّ عَلَيْكَ نَبَأَهُمْ بِالْحَقِّ

They were indeed youths who had faith in their Lord, إِنَّهُمْ فِتْيَةٌ آمَنُوا بِرَبِّهِمْ

---

[1] That is, the Qur'ān. Or 'that they did not believe this discourse.'
[2] Literally: 'struck on their ears,' or 'drew a curtain (or veil) on their ears.'

وَزِدْنَاهُمْ هُدًى ۝	and We had enhanced them in guidance
وَرَبَطْنَا عَلَىٰ قُلُوبِهِمْ	14 and fortified their hearts
إِذْ قَامُوا فَقَالُوا	when they stood up and said,
رَبُّنَا رَبُّ السَّمَاوَاتِ وَالْأَرْضِ	'Our Lord is the Lord of the heavens and the earth.
لَنْ نَدْعُوَ مِنْ دُونِهِ إِلَٰهًا	We will never invoke any god besides Him,
لَقَدْ قُلْنَا إِذًا شَطَطًا ۝	for then we shall certainly have said an atrocious lie.
هَٰؤُلَاءِ قَوْمُنَا اتَّخَذُوا مِنْ دُونِهِ آلِهَةً	15 These—our people—have taken gods besides Him.
لَوْلَا يَأْتُونَ عَلَيْهِمْ بِسُلْطَانٍ بَيِّنٍ	Why do they not bring any clear authority touching them?
فَمَنْ أَظْلَمُ	So who is a greater wrongdoer
مِمَّنِ افْتَرَىٰ عَلَى اللَّهِ كَذِبًا ۝	than he who fabricates lies against God?
وَإِذِ اعْتَزَلْتُمُوهُمْ	16 When you have dissociated yourselves from them
وَمَا يَعْبُدُونَ إِلَّا اللَّهَ	and from what they worship except God,
فَأْوُوا إِلَى الْكَهْفِ	take refuge in the Cave.
يَنْشُرْ لَكُمْ رَبُّكُمْ مِنْ رَحْمَتِهِ	Your Lord will unfold His mercy for you,
وَيُهَيِّئْ لَكُمْ مِنْ أَمْرِكُمْ مِرْفَقًا ۝	and He will help you on to ease in your affair.'
وَتَرَى الشَّمْسَ إِذَا طَلَعَتْ	17 You may see the sun, when it rises,
تَزَاوَرُ عَنْ كَهْفِهِمْ ذَاتَ الْيَمِينِ	slanting toward the right of their cave,
وَإِذَا غَرَبَتْ تَقْرِضُهُمْ ذَاتَ الشِّمَالِ	and, when it sets, cut across them towards the left,
وَهُمْ فِي فَجْوَةٍ مِنْهُ	and they are in a cavern within it.
ذَٰلِكَ مِنْ آيَاتِ اللَّهِ	That is one of God's signs.
مَنْ يَهْدِ اللَّهُ فَهُوَ الْمُهْتَدِ	Whomever God guides is rightly guided,
وَمَنْ يُضْلِلْ	and whomever He leads astray,
فَلَنْ تَجِدَ لَهُ وَلِيًّا مُرْشِدًا ۝	you will never find for him any friend who can guide.
وَتَحْسَبُهُمْ أَيْقَاظًا وَهُمْ رُقُودٌ	18 You will suppose them to be awake, though they are asleep.
وَنُقَلِّبُهُمْ ذَاتَ الْيَمِينِ وَذَاتَ الشِّمَالِ	We turn them to the right and to the left,
وَكَلْبُهُمْ بَاسِطٌ ذِرَاعَيْهِ بِالْوَصِيدِ	and their dog lies stretching its forelegs at the threshold.
لَوِ اطَّلَعْتَ عَلَيْهِمْ	If you come upon them,
لَوَلَّيْتَ مِنْهُمْ فِرَارًا	you will surely turn to flee from them
وَلَمُلِئْتَ مِنْهُمْ رُعْبًا ۝	and will be filled with a terror of them.
وَكَذَٰلِكَ بَعَثْنَاهُمْ	19 So it was that We aroused them from sleep

لِيَتَسَاءَلُوا بَيْنَهُمْ	so that they might question one another.
قَالَ قَائِلٌ مِنْهُمْ كَمْ لَبِثْتُمْ	One of them said, 'How long have you stayed here?'
قَالُوا لَبِثْنَا يَوْمًا أَوْ بَعْضَ يَوْمٍ	They said, 'We have stayed for a day, or part of a day.'
قَالُوا رَبُّكُمْ أَعْلَمُ بِمَا لَبِثْتُمْ	They said, 'Your Lord knows best how long you have stayed.
فَابْعَثُوا أَحَدَكُمْ بِوَرِقِكُمْ هَـٰذِهِ	Send one of you with this money
إِلَى الْمَدِينَةِ	to the city.
فَلْيَنْظُرْ أَيُّهَا أَزْكَىٰ طَعَامًا	Let him observe which of them has the purest food
فَلْيَأْتِكُمْ بِرِزْقٍ مِنْهُ	and bring you provisions from there.
وَلْيَتَلَطَّفْ	Let him be careful,
وَلَا يُشْعِرَنَّ بِكُمْ أَحَدًا ۝	and let him not make anyone aware about you.
إِنَّهُمْ إِنْ يَظْهَرُوا عَلَيْكُمْ	20 Indeed, should they prevail over you,
يَرْجُمُوكُمْ	they will either stone you to death
أَوْ يُعِيدُوكُمْ فِي مِلَّتِهِمْ	or force you back into their creed,
وَلَنْ تُفْلِحُوا إِذًا أَبَدًا ۝	and then you will never prosper.'
وَكَذَٰلِكَ أَعْثَرْنَا عَلَيْهِمْ	21 So it was that We let them come upon them,[1]
لِيَعْلَمُوا أَنَّ وَعْدَ اللَّهِ حَقٌّ	so that they might know that God's promise is indeed true,
وَأَنَّ السَّاعَةَ لَا رَيْبَ فِيهَا	and that there is no doubt in the Hour.
إِذْ يَتَنَازَعُونَ بَيْنَهُمْ أَمْرَهُمْ	As they disputed among themselves about their matter,
فَقَالُوا ابْنُوا عَلَيْهِمْ بُنْيَانًا	they said, 'Build a building over them.
رَبُّهُمْ أَعْلَمُ بِهِمْ	Their Lord knows them best.'
قَالَ الَّذِينَ غَلَبُوا عَلَىٰ أَمْرِهِمْ	Those who had the say in their matter said,
لَنَتَّخِذَنَّ عَلَيْهِمْ مَسْجِدًا ۝	'We will set up a place of worship over them.'
سَيَقُولُونَ ثَلَاثَةٌ	22 They will say, 'They are three;
رَابِعُهُمْ كَلْبُهُمْ	their dog is the fourth of them,'
وَيَقُولُونَ خَمْسَةٌ	and they will say, 'They are five,
سَادِسُهُمْ كَلْبُهُمْ	their dog is the sixth of them,'
رَجْمًا بِالْغَيْبِ	taking a shot at the invisible.[2]
وَيَقُولُونَ سَبْعَةٌ	They will say, 'They are seven,
وَثَامِنُهُمْ كَلْبُهُمْ	their dog is the eighth of them.'

---

[1] That is, We let the people discover the cave where the Men of the Cave were.
[2] That is, making a wild guess.

قُل رَّبِّي أَعْلَمُ بِعِدَّتِهِم
Say, 'My Lord knows best their number,
مَّا يَعْلَمُهُمْ إِلَّا قَلِيلٌ
and none knows them except a few.'
فَلَا تُمَارِ فِيهِمْ
So do not dispute concerning them,
إِلَّا مِرَاءً ظَاهِرًا
except for a seeming dispute,
وَلَا تَسْتَفْتِ فِيهِم مِّنْهُمْ أَحَدًا ۝
and do not question about them any of them.

وَلَا تَقُولَنَّ لِشَيْءٍ 23 *Do not say* about anything,
إِنِّي فَاعِلٌ ذَٰلِكَ غَدًا ۝ 'I will surely do it tomorrow'
إِلَّا أَن يَشَاءَ اللَّهُ 24 without adding, 'God willing.'
وَاذْكُر رَّبَّكَ إِذَا نَسِيتَ And when you forget, remember your Lord
وَقُلْ عَسَىٰ أَن يَهْدِيَنِ رَبِّي and say, 'Maybe my Lord will guide me
لِأَقْرَبَ مِنْ هَٰذَا رَشَدًا ۝ to something more akin to rectitude than this.'

وَلَبِثُوا فِي كَهْفِهِمْ ثَلَاثَ مِائَةٍ سِنِينَ 25 They remained in the Cave for three hundred years,
وَازْدَادُوا تِسْعًا ۝ and added nine more to that number.
قُلِ اللَّهُ أَعْلَمُ بِمَا لَبِثُوا 26 Say, 'God knows best how long they remained.
لَهُ غَيْبُ السَّمَاوَاتِ وَالْأَرْضِ To Him belongs the Unseen of the heavens and the earth.
أَبْصِرْ بِهِ وَأَسْمِعْ How well does He see! How well does He hear!
مَا لَهُم مِّن دُونِهِ مِن وَلِيٍّ They have no guardian besides Him,
وَلَا يُشْرِكُ فِي حُكْمِهِ أَحَدًا ۝ and none shares with Him in His judgement.'

وَاتْلُ مَا أُوحِيَ إِلَيْكَ 27 *Recite* what has been revealed to you
مِن كِتَابِ رَبِّكَ from the Book of your Lord.
لَا مُبَدِّلَ لِكَلِمَاتِهِ Nothing can change His words,
وَلَن تَجِدَ مِن دُونِهِ مُلْتَحَدًا ۝ and you will never find any refuge besides Him.
وَاصْبِرْ نَفْسَكَ مَعَ الَّذِينَ 28 *Content yourself* with the company of those who
يَدْعُونَ رَبَّهُم بِالْغَدَاةِ وَالْعَشِيِّ supplicate their Lord morning and evening,
يُرِيدُونَ وَجْهَهُ desiring His Face,
وَلَا تَعْدُ عَيْنَاكَ عَنْهُمْ and *do not loose sight* of them,

تُرِيدُ زِينَةَ الْحَيَاةِ الدُّنْيَا ۖ	desiring the glitter of the life of this world.[1]
وَلَا تُطِعْ مَنْ أَغْفَلْنَا قَلْبَهُ	And *do not obey* him whose heart We have made oblivious
عَنْ ذِكْرِنَا	to Our remembrance
وَاتَّبَعَ هَوَاهُ	and who follows his base desires,
وَكَانَ أَمْرُهُ فُرُطًا ۞	and whose conduct is mere profligacy.
وَقُلِ الْحَقُّ مِنْ رَبِّكُمْ ۖ	29 And say, 'This is the truth from your Lord:
فَمَنْ شَاءَ فَلْيُؤْمِنْ	let anyone who wishes believe it,
وَمَنْ شَاءَ فَلْيَكْفُرْ ۚ	and let anyone who wishes disbelieve it.'
إِنَّا أَعْتَدْنَا لِلظَّالِمِينَ نَارًا	We have indeed prepared for the wrongdoers a Fire
أَحَاطَ بِهِمْ سُرَادِقُهَا ۚ	whose curtains will surround them on all sides.
وَإِنْ يَسْتَغِيثُوا	If they cry out for help,
يُغَاثُوا بِمَاءٍ كَالْمُهْلِ	they will be helped with a water like molten copper,
يَشْوِي الْوُجُوهَ ۚ	which will scald their faces.
بِئْسَ الشَّرَابُ وَسَاءَتْ مُرْتَفَقًا ۞	What an evil drink, and how ill a resting place!
إِنَّ الَّذِينَ آمَنُوا وَعَمِلُوا الصَّالِحَاتِ	30 As for those who have faith and do righteous deeds
إِنَّا لَا نُضِيعُ أَجْرَ	—indeed, We do not waste the reward
مَنْ أَحْسَنَ عَمَلًا ۞	of those who are good in deeds.
أُولَٰئِكَ لَهُمْ جَنَّاتُ عَدْنٍ	31 For such there will be the Gardens of Eden
تَجْرِي مِنْ تَحْتِهِمُ الْأَنْهَارُ	with streams running in them.
يُحَلَّوْنَ فِيهَا مِنْ أَسَاوِرَ مِنْ ذَهَبٍ	They will be adorned therein with bracelets of gold
وَيَلْبَسُونَ ثِيَابًا خُضْرًا	and wear green garments
مِنْ سُنْدُسٍ وَإِسْتَبْرَقٍ	of fine and heavy silk,
مُتَّكِئِينَ فِيهَا عَلَى الْأَرَائِكِ ۚ	reclining therein on couches.
نِعْمَ الثَّوَابُ وَحَسُنَتْ مُرْتَفَقًا ۞	How excellent a reward and how good a resting place!
وَاضْرِبْ لَهُمْ مَثَلًا رَجُلَيْنِ	32 *Draw* for them the parable of two men
جَعَلْنَا لِأَحَدِهِمَا جَنَّتَيْنِ مِنْ أَعْنَابٍ	for each of whom We had made two gardens of vines
وَحَفَفْنَاهُمَا بِنَخْلٍ	and We had surrounded them with date palms
وَجَعَلْنَا بَيْنَهُمَا زَرْعًا ۞	and placed crops between them.

---

[1] Cf. 6:52.

33 Both gardens yielded their produce
without stinting anything of it.
And We had set a stream gushing through them.

34 He had abundant fruits,
so he said to his companion as he conversed with him:
'I have more wealth than you,
and am stronger with respect to numbers.'[1]

35 He entered his garden while he wronged himself.
He said, 'I do not think that this will ever perish,

36 and I do not think that the Hour will ever set in.
And even if I am returned to my Lord,
I will surely find a resort better than this.'

37 His companion said to him as he conversed with him:
'Do you disbelieve in Him who created you from dust,
then from a drop of seminal fluid,
then fashioned you as a man?

38 But I say, "He is God, my Lord"
and I do not ascribe any partner to my Lord.

39 Why did you not say when you entered your garden,
"This is as God has willed!
There is no power except by God!"
If you see that I have lesser wealth than you and children,

40 maybe my Lord will give me
something better than your garden
and He will unleash upon it bolts from the sky,
so that it becomes a bare plain.

41 Or its water will sink down,
so that you will never be able to obtain it.'

42 And ruin closed in on his produce,

---

[1] That is, with respect to the number of servants and attendants and the size of family and clan.

فَأَصْبَحَ يُقَلِّبُ كَفَّيْهِ	and he began to wring his hands
عَلَىٰ مَا أَنفَقَ فِيهَا	for what he had spent on it,
وَهِيَ خَاوِيَةٌ عَلَىٰ عُرُوشِهَا	as it lay fallen on its trellises.
وَيَقُولُ	He was saying,
يَا لَيْتَنِي لَمْ أُشْرِكْ بِرَبِّي أَحَدًا ۝	'I wish I had not ascribed any partner to my Lord.'
وَلَمْ تَكُن لَّهُ فِئَةٌ	43 He had no party
يَنصُرُونَهُ مِن دُونِ اللَّهِ	to help him besides God,
وَمَا كَانَ مُنتَصِرًا ۝	nor could he help himself.
هُنَالِكَ الْوَلَايَةُ لِلَّهِ الْحَقِّ	44 There, all authority belongs to God, the Real.
هُوَ خَيْرٌ ثَوَابًا وَخَيْرٌ عُقْبًا ۝	He is best in rewarding and best in requiting.
وَاضْرِبْ لَهُم مَّثَلَ الْحَيَاةِ الدُّنْيَا	45 *Draw* for them the parable of the life of this world:
كَمَاءٍ أَنزَلْنَاهُ مِنَ السَّمَاءِ	It is like the water We send down from the sky.
فَاخْتَلَطَ بِهِ نَبَاتُ الْأَرْضِ	Then the earth's vegetation mingles with it.
فَأَصْبَحَ هَشِيمًا تَذْرُوهُ الرِّيَاحُ	Then it becomes chaff, scattered by the wind.
وَكَانَ اللَّهُ عَلَىٰ كُلِّ شَيْءٍ مُّقْتَدِرًا ۝	And God has power over all things.
الْمَالُ وَالْبَنُونَ	46 Wealth and children
زِينَةُ الْحَيَاةِ الدُّنْيَا	are an adornment of the life of the world,
وَالْبَاقِيَاتُ الصَّالِحَاتُ	but lasting righteous deeds
خَيْرٌ عِندَ رَبِّكَ ثَوَابًا وَخَيْرٌ أَمَلًا ۝	are better with your Lord in reward and better in hope.
وَيَوْمَ نُسَيِّرُ الْجِبَالَ	47 The day We shall set the mountains moving
وَتَرَى الْأَرْضَ بَارِزَةً	and you will see the earth in full view,
وَحَشَرْنَاهُمْ	We will gather them,
فَلَمْ نُغَادِرْ مِنْهُمْ أَحَدًا ۝	and We will not leave out anyone of them.
وَعُرِضُوا عَلَىٰ رَبِّكَ صَفًّا	48 They will be presented before *your* Lord in ranks,
لَّقَدْ جِئْتُمُونَا	[and told:] 'Certainly you have come to Us
كَمَا خَلَقْنَاكُمْ أَوَّلَ مَرَّةٍ	just as We created you the first time.
بَلْ زَعَمْتُمْ	But you maintained
أَلَّن نَّجْعَلَ لَكُم مَّوْعِدًا ۝	that We will not appoint a tryst for you.'
وَوُضِعَ الْكِتَابُ	49 The Book will be set up.

فَتَرَى الْمُجْرِمِينَ مُشْفِقِينَ مِمَّا فِيهِ
Then you will see the guilty apprehensive of what is in it.
وَيَقُولُونَ يَا وَيْلَتَنَا مَالِ هَذَا الْكِتَابِ
They will say, 'Woe to us! What a book is this!
لَا يُغَادِرُ صَغِيرَةً وَلَا كَبِيرَةً
It omits nothing, big or small,
إِلَّا أَحْصَاهَا
without enumerating it.'
وَوَجَدُوا مَا عَمِلُوا حَاضِرًا
They will find present whatever they had done,
وَلَا يَظْلِمُ رَبُّكَ أَحَدًا ۝
and your Lord does not wrong anyone.

وَإِذْ قُلْنَا لِلْمَلَائِكَةِ اسْجُدُوا لِآدَمَ
50 When We said to the angels, 'Prostrate before Adam,'
فَسَجَدُوا إِلَّا إِبْلِيسَ
they prostrated, but not Iblis.
كَانَ مِنَ الْجِنِّ
He was one of the jinn,
فَفَسَقَ عَنْ أَمْرِ رَبِّهِ
so he transgressed against his Lord's command.
أَفَتَتَّخِذُونَهُ وَذُرِّيَّتَهُ أَوْلِيَاءَ
Will you then take him and his offspring for masters
مِنْ دُونِي
in My stead,
وَهُمْ لَكُمْ عَدُوٌّ
though they are your enemies?
بِئْسَ لِلظَّالِمِينَ بَدَلًا ۝
How evil a substitute for the wrongdoers!

مَا أَشْهَدْتُهُمْ خَلْقَ
51 I did not make them witness to the creation
السَّمَاوَاتِ وَالْأَرْضِ
of the heavens and the earth,
وَلَا خَلْقَ أَنْفُسِهِمْ
nor to their own creation,
وَمَا كُنْتُ مُتَّخِذَ الْمُضِلِّينَ عَضُدًا ۝
nor do I take as assistants those who mislead others.

وَيَوْمَ يَقُولُ
52 The day He will say [to the polytheists],
نَادُوا شُرَكَائِيَ الَّذِينَ زَعَمْتُمْ
'Call those whom you maintained to be My partners,'
فَدَعَوْهُمْ فَلَمْ يَسْتَجِيبُوا لَهُمْ
they will call them, but they will not respond to them,
وَجَعَلْنَا بَيْنَهُمْ مَوْبِقًا ۝
for We shall set an abyss between them.

وَرَأَى الْمُجْرِمُونَ النَّارَ
53 The guilty will sight the Fire
فَظَنُّوا أَنَّهُمْ مُوَاقِعُوهَا
and know that they are about to fall into it,
وَلَمْ يَجِدُوا عَنْهَا مَصْرِفًا ۝
for they will find no way to escape it.

وَلَقَدْ صَرَّفْنَا فِي هَذَا الْقُرْآنِ
54 We have certainly interspersed this Qur'ān
لِلنَّاسِ مِنْ كُلِّ مَثَلٍ
with every kind of parable for the people.
وَكَانَ الْإِنْسَانُ أَكْثَرَ شَيْءٍ جَدَلًا ۝
But man is the most disputatious of creatures.

وَمَا مَنَعَ النَّاسَ أَنْ يُؤْمِنُوا
55 Nothing has kept these people from believing,

إِذْ جَاءَهُمُ الْهُدَىٰ   when guidance comes to them,

وَيَسْتَغْفِرُوا رَبَّهُمْ   and pleading to their Lord for forgiveness,

إِلَّا أَن تَأْتِيَهُمْ   except their demand that there come to pass for them

سُنَّةُ الْأَوَّلِينَ   the precedent of the former peoples,

أَوْ يَأْتِيَهُمُ الْعَذَابُ قُبُلًا ۝   or that the punishment come to them, face to face.[1]

وَمَا نُرْسِلُ الْمُرْسَلِينَ   56 We do not send the apostles

إِلَّا مُبَشِّرِينَ وَمُنذِرِينَ   except as bearers of good news and warners,

وَيُجَادِلُ الَّذِينَ كَفَرُوا بِالْبَاطِلِ   but those who are faithless dispute fallaciously

لِيُدْحِضُوا بِهِ الْحَقَّ ۖ   to refute thereby the truth,

وَاتَّخَذُوا آيَاتِي وَمَا أُنذِرُوا   having taken My signs and what they are warned of

هُزُوًا ۝   in derision.

وَمَنْ أَظْلَمُ مِمَّن ذُكِّرَ   57 Who is a greater wrongdoer than he who is reminded

بِآيَاتِ رَبِّهِ   of the signs of his Lord,

فَأَعْرَضَ عَنْهَا   whereat he disregards them

وَنَسِيَ مَا قَدَّمَتْ يَدَاهُ   and forgets what his hands have sent ahead?

إِنَّا جَعَلْنَا عَلَىٰ قُلُوبِهِمْ أَكِنَّةً   We have indeed cast veils on their hearts,

أَن يَفْقَهُوهُ   lest they should understand it,

وَفِي آذَانِهِمْ وَقْرًا ۖ   and a deafness into their ears;

وَإِن تَدْعُهُمْ إِلَى الْهُدَىٰ   and if you invite them to guidance,

فَلَن يَهْتَدُوا إِذًا أَبَدًا ۝   they will never let themselves be guided.

وَرَبُّكَ الْغَفُورُ ذُو الرَّحْمَةِ ۖ   58 Your Lord is the All-forgiving dispenser of mercy.

لَوْ يُؤَاخِذُهُم   Were He to take them to task

بِمَا كَسَبُوا   because of what they have committed,

لَعَجَّلَ لَهُمُ الْعَذَابَ ۚ   He would have surely hastened their punishment.

بَل لَّهُم مَّوْعِدٌ   But they have a tryst,

لَّن يَجِدُوا مِن دُونِهِ مَوْئِلًا ۝   when they will not find a refuge besides Him.[2]

وَتِلْكَ الْقُرَىٰ   59 Those are the towns

أَهْلَكْنَاهُمْ لَمَّا ظَلَمُوا   that We destroyed when they were wrongdoers,

وَجَعَلْنَا لِمَهْلِكِهِم مَّوْعِدًا ۝   and We appointed a tryst for their destruction.

---

[1] Or, 'visibly,' or 'in its different forms.'
[2] Or 'from which they will not find any refuge.'

60 When Moses said to his lad, 'I will go on journeying
until I have reached the confluence of the two seas,
or have spent a long time [traveling].'

61 So when they reached the confluence between them,
they forgot their fish,
which found its way into the sea, sneaking away.

62 So when they had passed on,
he said to his lad, 'Bring us our meal.
We have certainly met with much fatigue on this trip of ours.'

63 He said, 'Did you see?!
When we took shelter at the rock,
indeed I forgot about the fish
—and none but Satan made me forget to mention it!—
and it made its way into the sea in an amazing manner!'

64 He said, 'That is what we were after!'
So they returned, retracing their footsteps.

65 There they found one of Our servants
whom We had granted mercy from Ourselves,
and taught him knowledge from Our own.

66 Moses said to him, 'May I follow you
for the purpose that you teach me
some of the probity you have been taught?'

67 He said, 'Indeed, you cannot have patience with me!

68 And how can you have patience
about something you do not comprehend?'

69 He said, 'You will find me to be patient, God willing,
and I will not disobey you in any matter.'

70 He said, 'If you follow me,
do not question me concerning anything
until I myself first mention it for you.'

71	So they went on.
	When they boarded the boat, he made a hole in it. فَانْطَلَقَا حَتَّىٰ إِذَا رَكِبَا فِى السَّفِينَةِ خَرَقَهَا
	He said, 'Did you make a hole in it to drown its people? قَالَ أَخَرَقْتَهَا لِتُغْرِقَ أَهْلَهَا
	You have certainly done a monstrous thing!' لَقَدْ جِئْتَ شَيْئًا إِمْرًا ۝
72	He said, 'Did I not say قَالَ أَلَمْ أَقُلْ
	that you cannot have patience with me?' إِنَّكَ لَنْ تَسْتَطِيعَ مَعِىَ صَبْرًا ۝
73	He said, 'Do not take me to task for my forgetting, قَالَ لَا تُؤَاخِذْنِى بِمَا نَسِيتُ
	and do not be hard upon me.' وَلَا تُرْهِقْنِى مِنْ أَمْرِى عُسْرًا ۝
74	So they went on until they came upon a boy, فَانْطَلَقَا حَتَّىٰ إِذَا لَقِيَا غُلَامًا
	whereupon he slew him. فَقَتَلَهُ
	He said, 'Did you slay an innocent soul قَالَ أَقَتَلْتَ نَفْسًا زَكِيَّةً
	without his having slain anyone? بِغَيْرِ نَفْسٍ
	You have certainly done a dire thing!' لَقَدْ جِئْتَ شَيْئًا نُكْرًا ۝ ۞

[PART 16]

75	He said, 'Did I not tell you قَالَ أَلَمْ أَقُلْ لَكَ
	that you cannot have patience with me?' إِنَّكَ لَنْ تَسْتَطِيعَ مَعِىَ صَبْرًا ۝
76	He said, 'If I question you about anything after this, قَالَ إِنْ سَأَلْتُكَ عَنْ شَىْءٍ بَعْدَهَا
	do not keep me in your company. فَلَا تُصَاحِبْنِى
	You already have enough excuse on my part.' قَدْ بَلَغْتَ مِنْ لَدُنِّى عُذْرًا ۝
77	So they went on until they came to the people of a town. فَانْطَلَقَا حَتَّىٰ إِذَا أَتَيَا أَهْلَ قَرْيَةٍ
	They asked its people for food, اسْتَطْعَمَا أَهْلَهَا
	but they refused to extend them any hospitality. فَأَبَوْا أَنْ يُضَيِّفُوهُمَا
	There they found a wall which was about to collapse, فَوَجَدَا فِيهَا جِدَارًا يُرِيدُ أَنْ يَنْقَضَّ
	so he erected it. فَأَقَامَهُ
	He said, 'Had you wished, قَالَ لَوْ شِئْتَ
	you could have surely taken a wage for it.' لَاتَّخَذْتَ عَلَيْهِ أَجْرًا ۝
78	He said, 'This is where you and I shall part. قَالَ هَٰذَا فِرَاقُ بَيْنِى وَبَيْنِكَ
	I will inform you about the interpretation سَأُنَبِّئُكَ بِتَأْوِيلِ
	of that over which you could not maintain patience. مَا لَمْ تَسْتَطِعْ عَلَيْهِ صَبْرًا ۝
79	As for the boat, it belonged to some poor people أَمَّا السَّفِينَةُ فَكَانَتْ لِمَسَاكِينَ

يَعْمَلُونَ فِي الْبَحْرِ ۖ   who work on the sea.
فَأَرَدتُّ أَنْ أَعِيبَهَا   I wanted to make it defective,
وَكَانَ وَرَاءَهُم مَّلِكٌ   for behind them was a king
يَأْخُذُ كُلَّ سَفِينَةٍ غَصْبًا ۝   seizing every ship usurpingly.

وَأَمَّا الْغُلَامُ فَكَانَ أَبَوَاهُ مُؤْمِنَيْنِ   80 As for the boy, his parents were faithful persons,
فَخَشِينَا أَن يُرْهِقَهُمَا   and We feared he would overwhelm them
طُغْيَانًا وَكُفْرًا ۝   with rebellion and unfaith.

فَأَرَدْنَا أَن يُبْدِلَهُمَا رَبُّهُمَا   81 So We desired that their Lord should give them in exchange
خَيْرًا مِّنْهُ زَكَاةً وَأَقْرَبَ رُحْمًا ۝   one better than him in respect of purity and closer in mercy.

وَأَمَّا الْجِدَارُ فَكَانَ لِغُلَامَيْنِ يَتِيمَيْنِ   82 As for the wall, it belonged to two boy orphans
فِي الْمَدِينَةِ   in the city.
وَكَانَ تَحْتَهُ كَنزٌ لَّهُمَا   There was a treasure under it belonging to them.
وَكَانَ أَبُوهُمَا صَالِحًا   Their father had been a righteous man.
فَأَرَادَ رَبُّكَ أَن يَبْلُغَا أَشُدَّهُمَا   So your Lord desired that they should come of age
وَيَسْتَخْرِجَا كَنزَهُمَا رَحْمَةً مِّن رَّبِّكَ ۚ   and take out their treasure—as mercy from your Lord.
وَمَا فَعَلْتُهُ عَنْ أَمْرِي ۚ   I did not do that out of my own accord.
ذَٰلِكَ تَأْوِيلُ   This is the interpretation
مَا لَمْ تَسْطِع عَّلَيْهِ صَبْرًا ۝   of that over which you could not maintain patience.'

وَيَسْأَلُونَكَ عَن ذِي الْقَرْنَيْنِ ۖ   83 They question you concerning Dhul Qarnayn.
قُلْ سَأَتْلُو عَلَيْكُم مِّنْهُ ذِكْرًا ۝   Say, 'I will relate to you an account of him.'
إِنَّا مَكَّنَّا لَهُ فِي الْأَرْضِ   84 We had indeed granted him power in the land
وَآتَيْنَاهُ مِن كُلِّ شَيْءٍ سَبَبًا ۝   and given him the means to all things.
فَأَتْبَعَ سَبَبًا ۝   85 So he directed a means.[1]
حَتَّىٰ إِذَا بَلَغَ مَغْرِبَ الشَّمْسِ   86 When he reached the place where the sun sets,
وَجَدَهَا تَغْرُبُ فِي عَيْنٍ حَمِئَةٍ   he found it setting over a warm sea,
وَوَجَدَ عِندَهَا قَوْمًا ۗ   and by it he found a people.
قُلْنَا يَا ذَا الْقَرْنَيْنِ   We said, 'O Dhul Qarnayn!
إِمَّا أَن تُعَذِّبَ   You will either punish them,

---

[1] That is, made it take him towards a certain goal. Or 'followed.'

or treat them with kindness.'

87 He said, 'As for him who is a wrongdoer,
we will punish him.
Then he shall be returned to his Lord
and He will punish him with a dire punishment.

88 But as for him who has faith and acts righteously,
he shall have the best reward,
and we will assign him easy tasks under our command.'

89 Then he directed another means.

90 When he reached the place where the sun rises,
he found it rising on a people
for whom We had not provided any shield against it.

91 So it was,
and We were fully aware of whatever means he had.

92 Thereafter he directed another means.

93 When he reached the place between the two barriers,
he found between them a people
who could hardly understand a word [of his language].

94 They said, 'O Dhul Qarnayn!
Gog and Magog are indeed causing disaster in this land.
Shall we pay you a tribute
on condition that you build
a barrier between them and us?'

95 He said, 'What my Lord has furnished me is better.
Yet help me with some power,
and I will make a bulwark between you and them.

96 Bring me pieces of iron!'
When he had levelled up between the flanks,
he said, 'Blow!'
When he had turned it into fire,

قَالَ آتُونِى أُفْرِغْ عَلَيْهِ قِطْرًا ۝   he said, 'Bring me molten copper to pour over it.'

فَمَا اسْطَاعُوا أَن يَظْهَرُوهُ   97 So they could neither scale it,
وَمَا اسْتَطَاعُوا لَهُ نَقْبًا ۝   nor could they make a hole in it.

قَالَ هَذَا رَحْمَةٌ مِّن رَّبِّى ۖ   98 He said, 'This is a a gift of mercy from my Lord.
فَإِذَا جَاءَ وَعْدُ رَبِّى   But when the promise of my Lord is fulfilled,
جَعَلَهُ دَكَّاءَ ۖ   He will level it,[1]
وَكَانَ وَعْدُ رَبِّى حَقًّا ۝   and my Lord's promise is true.'

وَتَرَكْنَا بَعْضَهُمْ يَوْمَئِذٍ يَمُوجُ فِى بَعْضٍ ۖ   99 That day We will let them surge over one another,
وَنُفِخَ فِى الصُّورِ   and the Trumpet will be blown,
فَجَمَعْنَاهُمْ جَمْعًا ۝   and We will gather them all,

وَعَرَضْنَا جَهَنَّمَ يَوْمَئِذٍ   100 and on that day We will bring hell into view
لِّلْكَافِرِينَ عَرْضًا ۝   visibly for the faithless

الَّذِينَ كَانَتْ أَعْيُنُهُمْ فِى غِطَاءٍ عَن ذِكْرِى   101 —those whose eyes were blind to My remembrance
وَكَانُوا لَا يَسْتَطِيعُونَ سَمْعًا ۝   and who could not hear.

أَفَحَسِبَ الَّذِينَ كَفَرُوا   102 Do the faithless suppose
أَن يَتَّخِذُوا عِبَادِى مِن دُونِى أَوْلِيَاءَ ۚ   that they have taken My servants for protectors in My stead?
إِنَّا أَعْتَدْنَا جَهَنَّمَ   Indeed, We have prepared hell
لِلْكَافِرِينَ نُزُلًا ۝   for the hospitality of the faithless.

قُلْ هَلْ نُنَبِّئُكُم   103 Say, 'Shall we inform you
بِالْأَخْسَرِينَ أَعْمَالًا ۝   about the biggest losers in their works?

الَّذِينَ ضَلَّ سَعْيُهُمْ فِى الْحَيَاةِ الدُّنْيَا   104 Those whose efforts go awry in the life of the world,
وَهُمْ يَحْسَبُونَ أَنَّهُمْ يُحْسِنُونَ صُنْعًا ۝   while they suppose they are doing good.'

أُولَٰئِكَ الَّذِينَ كَفَرُوا بِآيَاتِ رَبِّهِمْ   105 They are the ones who deny the signs of their Lord
وَلِقَائِهِ   and encounter with Him.
فَحَبِطَتْ أَعْمَالُهُمْ   So their works have failed.
فَلَا نُقِيمُ لَهُمْ يَوْمَ الْقِيَامَةِ   On the Day of Resurrection We will not give them
وَزْنًا ۝   any weight.

ذَٰلِكَ جَزَاؤُهُمْ جَهَنَّمُ بِمَا كَفَرُوا   106 That is their requital—hell—because of their unfaith
وَاتَّخَذُوا آيَاتِى وَرُسُلِى هُزُوًا ۝   and their deriding My signs and My apostles.

---

[1] Or, 'He will make it crumble.'

107 As for those who have faith and do righteous deeds,
they will have the gardens of Firdaws[1] for abode,[2]

108 to remain in them;
they will not seek to leave them for another place.

109 Say, 'If the sea were ink for the words of my Lord,
the sea would be spent
before the words of my Lord are finished,
though We replenish it with another like it.'

110 Say, 'I am just a human being like you.
It has been revealed to me that your God is the One God.
So whoever expects to encounter his Lord,
let him act righteously,
and not associate anyone with the worship of his Lord.'

19. MARY[3]

Maryam

In the Name of God,
the All-beneficent, the All-merciful.

1 *Kāf, Hā, Yā, ʿAyn, Ṣād.*

2 This is an account[4] of your Lord's mercy
on Zechariah, His servant,

3 when he called out to his Lord with a secret cry.

4 He said, 'My Lord!
Indeed, my bones have become feeble,
and my head has turned white with age,
yet never have I,
my Lord, been unblessed in my supplications to You!

5 Indeed, I fear my kinsmen, after me,

---

[1] Said to be the highest and choicest part of paradise. Cf. Ṭabarī, Baḥrānī and Qummī.
[2] Or 'hospitality.'
[3] This Makkī *sūrah* takes its name from the story of Mary (ʿa) told in verses 16-34.
[4] Or 'a mention,' 'a reminder,' or 'a recollection.'

and my wife is barren. وَكَانَتِ امْرَأَتِي عَاقِرًا

So grant me from Yourself an heir فَهَبْ لِي مِن لَّدُنكَ وَلِيًّا ۞

6 who may inherit from me يَرِثُنِي

and inherit from the House of Jacob, وَيَرِثُ مِنْ آلِ يَعْقُوبَ ۖ

and make him, my Lord, pleasing to You!' وَاجْعَلْهُ رَبِّ رَضِيًّا ۞

7 'O Zechariah! Indeed, We give you the good news of a son, يَا زَكَرِيَّا إِنَّا نُبَشِّرُكَ بِغُلَامٍ

whose name is "John." اسْمُهُ يَحْيَىٰ

Never before have We made anyone his namesake.' لَمْ نَجْعَل لَّهُ مِن قَبْلُ سَمِيًّا ۞

8 He said, 'My Lord! How shall I have a son, قَالَ رَبِّ أَنَّىٰ يَكُونُ لِي غُلَامٌ

when my wife is barren وَكَانَتِ امْرَأَتِي عَاقِرًا

and I am already advanced in age?' وَقَدْ بَلَغْتُ مِنَ الْكِبَرِ عِتِيًّا ۞

9 He said, 'So shall it be. قَالَ كَذَٰلِكَ

Your Lord has said, "It is simple for Me." قَالَ رَبُّكَ هُوَ عَلَيَّ هَيِّنٌ

Certainly I created you before وَقَدْ خَلَقْتُكَ مِن قَبْلُ

when you were nothing.' وَلَمْ تَكُ شَيْئًا ۞

10 He said, 'My Lord! Appoint a sign for me.' قَالَ رَبِّ اجْعَل لِّي آيَةً ۚ

He said, 'Your sign is that قَالَ آيَتُكَ

you will not speak to the people for three complete nights.' أَلَّا تُكَلِّمَ النَّاسَ ثَلَاثَ لَيَالٍ سَوِيًّا ۞

11 So he emerged before his people from the Temple فَخَرَجَ عَلَىٰ قَوْمِهِ مِنَ الْمِحْرَابِ

and signalled to them that they should glorify God فَأَوْحَىٰ إِلَيْهِمْ أَن سَبِّحُوا

morning and evening. بُكْرَةً وَعَشِيًّا ۞

12 'O John!' [We said,] 'Hold on with power to the Book!' يَا يَحْيَىٰ خُذِ الْكِتَابَ بِقُوَّةٍ ۖ

And We gave him judgement while still a child, وَآتَيْنَاهُ الْحُكْمَ صَبِيًّا ۞

13 and compassion and purity from Us. وَحَنَانًا مِّن لَّدُنَّا وَزَكَاةً ۖ

He was Godwary, وَكَانَ تَقِيًّا ۞

14 and good to his parents, وَبَرًّا بِوَالِدَيْهِ

not self-willed or disobedient. وَلَمْ يَكُن جَبَّارًا عَصِيًّا ۞

15 Peace be to him the day he was born, the day he dies, وَسَلَامٌ عَلَيْهِ يَوْمَ وُلِدَ وَيَوْمَ يَمُوتُ

and the day he is raised alive! وَيَوْمَ يُبْعَثُ حَيًّا ۞

16 And *mention* in the Book Mary, وَاذْكُرْ فِي الْكِتَابِ مَرْيَمَ

إِذِ انتَبَذَتْ مِنْ أَهْلِهَا مَكَانًا شَرْقِيًّا ⑯   when she withdrew from her family to an easterly place.

17 فَاتَّخَذَتْ مِن دُونِهِمْ حِجَابًا   Thus did she seclude herself from them,

فَأَرْسَلْنَا إِلَيْهَا رُوحَنَا   whereupon We sent to her Our Spirit[1]

فَتَمَثَّلَ لَهَا بَشَرًا سَوِيًّا ⑰   and he became incarnate for her as a perfect human.

18 قَالَتْ   She said,

إِنِّي أَعُوذُ بِالرَّحْمَٰنِ مِنكَ   'I seek the protection of the All-beneficent from you,

إِن كُنتَ تَقِيًّا ⑱   should you be Godwary!'

19 قَالَ إِنَّمَا أَنَا رَسُولُ رَبِّكِ   He said, 'I am only a messenger of your Lord

لِأَهَبَ لَكِ غُلَامًا زَكِيًّا ⑲   that I may give you a pure son.'

20 قَالَتْ أَنَّىٰ يَكُونُ لِي غُلَامٌ   She said, 'How shall I have a child

وَلَمْ يَمْسَسْنِي بَشَرٌ   seeing that no human being has ever touched me,

وَلَمْ أَكُ بَغِيًّا ⑳   nor have I been unchaste?'

21 قَالَ كَذَٰلِكِ   He said, 'So shall it be.

قَالَ رَبُّكِ هُوَ عَلَيَّ هَيِّنٌ   Your Lord says, "It is simple for Me,

وَلِنَجْعَلَهُ آيَةً لِّلنَّاسِ   and so that We may make him a sign for mankind

وَرَحْمَةً مِّنَّا   and mercy from Us,

وَكَانَ أَمْرًا مَّقْضِيًّا ㉑ ✵   and it is a matter already decided."

22 فَحَمَلَتْهُ   Thus she conceived him,

فَانتَبَذَتْ بِهِ مَكَانًا قَصِيًّا ㉒   then withdrew with him to a distant place.

23 فَأَجَاءَهَا الْمَخَاضُ إِلَىٰ جِذْعِ النَّخْلَةِ   The birth pangs brought her to the trunk of a date palm.

قَالَتْ يَا لَيْتَنِي مِتُّ قَبْلَ هَٰذَا   She said, 'I wish I had died before this

وَكُنتُ نَسْيًا مَّنسِيًّا ㉓   and become a forgotten thing, beyond recall.'

24 فَنَادَاهَا مِن تَحْتِهَا   Thereupon he[2] called her from below her,

أَلَّا تَحْزَنِي   saying, 'Do not grieve!

قَدْ جَعَلَ رَبُّكِ تَحْتَكِ سَرِيًّا ㉔   Your Lord has made a spring to flow at your feet.

25 وَهُزِّي إِلَيْكِ بِجِذْعِ النَّخْلَةِ   Shake the trunk of the palm tree,

تُسَاقِطْ عَلَيْكِ رُطَبًا جَنِيًّا ㉕   freshly picked dates will drop upon you.

26 فَكُلِي وَاشْرَبِي وَقَرِّي عَيْنًا   Eat, drink and be comforted.

فَإِمَّا تَرَيِنَّ مِنَ الْبَشَرِ أَحَدًا   Then if you see any human,

---

[1] That is, Gabriel ('a).
[2] That is, the angel Gabriel, or the baby Jesus, whom she was carrying in her belly.

say, "I have indeed vowed a fast to the All-beneficent,
so I will not speak to any human today."'

27 Then, carrying him, she brought him to her people.
They said, 'O Mary,
you have certainly come up with an odd thing!

28 O kinswoman of the Aaronites!
Your father was not an evil man,
nor was your mother unchaste.'

29 Thereat she pointed to him.
They said, 'How can we speak
to one who is yet a baby in the cradle?'

30 He said, 'I am indeed a servant of God!
He has given me the Book and made me a prophet.

31 He has made me blessed, wherever I may be,
and He has enjoined me to maintain the prayer
and to pay the *zakāt*
as long as I live,

32 and to be good to my mother,
and He has not made me self-willed and wretched.

33 Peace to me the day I was born, the day I die,
and the day I am raised alive.'

34 That is Jesus, son of Mary,
a Word of the Real concerning whom they are in doubt.

35 It is not for God to take a son.
Immaculate is He!
When He decides on a matter,
He just says to it, 'Be!' and it is.

36 [Jesus said,] 'God is indeed my Lord and your Lord.
So worship Him.
This is a straight path.'

37 But the factions differed among themselves.
So woe to the faithless
   at the scene of a tremendous day.
38 How well they will hear and how well they will see
   on the day when they come to Us!
But today the wrongdoers are in plain error.
39 *Warn* them of the Day of Regret[1]
   when the matter will have been decided,
   while they are yet heedless and do not believe.
40 Indeed, We shall inherit the earth
   and whoever there is on it,
   and to Us they will be brought back.

41 And *mention* in the Book Abraham.
   He was indeed a truthful man and a prophet.
42 When he said to his father, 'Father!
   Why do you worship that which neither hears nor sees
   and is of no avail to you in any way?
43 Father! Indeed, a knowledge has already come to me
   which has not come to you.
   So follow me that I may guide you to a right path.
44 Father! Do not worship Satan.
   Satan is indeed disobedient to the All-beneficent.
45 Father! I am indeed afraid
   that a punishment from the All-beneficent will befall you,
   and you will become Satan's accomplice.'
46 He said, 'Abraham! Are you renouncing my gods?
   If you do not desist, I will stone you.
   Get away from me for a long while.'[2]

---

[1] Another name for the Day of Judgement.
[2] That is, 'Go away for good. Stop annoying me.'

47 He said, 'Peace be to you!
    I shall plead with my Lord to forgive you.
    He is indeed gracious to me.
48 I dissociate myself from you
    and whatever you invoke besides God.
    I will supplicate my Lord.
    Hopefully, I will not be unblessed in supplicating my Lord.'
49 So when he had left them
    and what they worshiped besides God,
    We gave him Isaac and Jacob,
    and each We made a prophet.
50 And We gave them out of Our mercy,
    and conferred on them a worthy and lofty repute.

51 And *mention* in the Book Moses.
    Indeed, he was exclusively dedicated to God,
    and was an apostle and prophet.
52 We called him from the right side of the Mount
    and We drew him near for confidential discourse.
53 And We gave him out of Our mercy
    his brother Aaron, a prophet.

54 And *mention* in the Book Ishmael.
    He was indeed true to his promise
    and an apostle and prophet.
55 He used to bid his family to maintain the prayer
    and to pay the *zakāt*,
    and was pleasing to his Lord.
56 And *mention* in the Book Idrīs.
    He was indeed a truthful man and a prophet,

57 وَرَفَعْنَاهُ مَكَانًا عَلِيًّا ۝ and We raised him to an exalted station.

58 أُولَٰئِكَ الَّذِينَ أَنْعَمَ اللَّهُ عَلَيْهِمْ They are the ones whom God has blessed
مِنَ النَّبِيِّينَ مِنْ ذُرِّيَّةِ آدَمَ from among the prophets of Adam's progeny,
وَمِمَّنْ حَمَلْنَا مَعَ نُوحٍ and from the progeny of those We carried with Noah,
وَمِنْ ذُرِّيَّةِ إِبْرَاهِيمَ وَإِسْرَائِيلَ and from among the progeny of Abraham and Israel,
وَمِمَّنْ هَدَيْنَا وَاجْتَبَيْنَا and from among those that We guided and chose.
إِذَا تُتْلَىٰ عَلَيْهِمْ آيَاتُ الرَّحْمَٰنِ When the signs of the All-beneficent were recited to them,
خَرُّوا سُجَّدًا وَبُكِيًّا ۩ ۝ they would fall down weeping in prostration.

59 فَخَلَفَ مِنْ بَعْدِهِمْ خَلْفٌ But they were succeeded by an evil posterity
أَضَاعُوا الصَّلَاةَ who neglected the prayer
وَاتَّبَعُوا الشَّهَوَاتِ and followed base appetites.
فَسَوْفَ يَلْقَوْنَ غَيًّا ۝ So they will soon encounter the reward of perversity,

60 إِلَّا مَنْ تَابَ وَآمَنَ وَعَمِلَ صَالِحًا barring those who repent, believe and act righteously.
فَأُولَٰئِكَ يَدْخُلُونَ الْجَنَّةَ Such will enter paradise
وَلَا يُظْلَمُونَ شَيْئًا ۝ and they will not be wronged in the least.

61 جَنَّاتِ عَدْنٍ الَّتِي وَعَدَ الرَّحْمَٰنُ Gardens of Eden promised by the All-beneficent
عِبَادَهُ بِالْغَيْبِ to His servants, while they were still unseen.
إِنَّهُ كَانَ وَعْدُهُ مَأْتِيًّا ۝ His promise is indeed bound to come to pass.

62 لَا يَسْمَعُونَ فِيهَا لَغْوًا إِلَّا سَلَامًا Therein they will not hear vain talk, but only 'Peace!'
وَلَهُمْ رِزْقُهُمْ فِيهَا بُكْرَةً Therein they will have their provision morning
وَعَشِيًّا ۝ and evening.

63 تِلْكَ الْجَنَّةُ الَّتِي نُورِثُ This is the paradise that We will give as inheritance
مِنْ عِبَادِنَا مَنْ كَانَ تَقِيًّا ۝ to those of Our servants who are Godwary.

64 وَمَا نَتَنَزَّلُ [O Gabriel, tell the Prophet,] 'We do not descend
إِلَّا بِأَمْرِ رَبِّكَ except by the command of *your* Lord.
لَهُ مَا بَيْنَ أَيْدِينَا To Him belongs whatever is before us
وَمَا خَلْفَنَا and whatever is behind us
وَمَا بَيْنَ ذَٰلِكَ and whatever is in between that,
وَمَا كَانَ رَبُّكَ نَسِيًّا ۝ and your Lord does not forget

65 —the Lord of the heavens and the earth
and whatever is between them.
So *worship* Him and *be steadfast* in His worship.
Do you know anyone who might be His namesake?'

66 Man says, 'What! Shall I, when I have been dead,
be brought forth alive?'
67 Does not man remember
that We created him before
when he was nothing?
68 By your Lord, We will surely gather them with the devils;
then We will surely bring them up around hell
scrambling on their knees.[1]
69 Then from every group We shall draw
whichever of them was more defiant toward the All-beneficent.
70 Then surely We will know best
those who deserve most to enter it.
71 There is none of you but will come to it:[2]
a matter that is a decided certainty with *your* Lord.
72 Then We will deliver those who are Godwary
and leave the wrongdoers in it, fallen on their knees.

73 When Our clear signs are recited to them,
the faithless say to the faithful,
'Which of the two groups is superior in station[3]
and better with respect to company?'[4]
74 How many a generation We have destroyed before them
who were superior in furnishings and appearance!

---

[1] Or 'in groups.'
[2] That is, they will approach it, without entering it.
[3] Or 'superior with respect to dwellings.'
[4] Or 'better with respect to gatherings.'

75 Say, 'Whoever abides in error,
   the All-beneficent shall prolong his respite
   until they sight what they have been promised:
   either punishment or the Hour.'
   Then they will know whose position is worse,
   and whose host is weaker.

76 God enhances in guidance those who are rightly guided,
   and lasting righteous deeds
   are better with your Lord in reward,
   and better at the return to God.

77 Have you not regarded him who denies Our signs
   and says, 'I will surely be given wealth and children'?

78 Has he come to know the Unseen,
   or taken a promise from the All-beneficent?

79 No indeed! We will write down what he says,
   and We will prolong his punishment endlessly.

80 We shall take over what he talks about from him[1]
   and he will come to Us alone.

81 They have taken gods besides God
   so that they may be a source of might to them.

82 No Indeed! Soon they will disown their worship,
   and they will be their opponents.

83 Have you not regarded
   that We unleash the devils upon the faithless
   to urge them vigorously?

84 So *do not make haste* against them;
   indeed We are counting[2] for them, a counting down.

85 The day We shall gather the Godwary

---

[1] That is, 'He will depart unaccompanied from the world, leaving in Our possession the wealth and children that he talks about.'
[2] That is, the number of their breaths.

إِلَى الرَّحْمَٰنِ وَفْدًا ۝ toward the All-beneficent, arriving on mounts,[1]

86 وَنَسُوقُ الْمُجْرِمِينَ إِلَىٰ جَهَنَّمَ وِرْدًا ۝ and drive the guilty as a thirsty herd towards hell,

87 لَا يَمْلِكُونَ الشَّفَاعَةَ no one will have the power to intercede with God,

إِلَّا مَنِ اتَّخَذَ عِندَ الرَّحْمَٰنِ عَهْدًا ۝ except him who has taken a covenant with the All-beneficent.

88 وَقَالُوا اتَّخَذَ الرَّحْمَٰنُ وَلَدًا ۝ They say, 'The All-beneficent has offspring!'

89 لَقَدْ جِئْتُمْ شَيْئًا إِدًّا ۝ You have certainly advanced something hideous!

90 تَكَادُ السَّمَاوَاتُ يَتَفَطَّرْنَ مِنْهُ The heavens are about to be rent apart at it,

وَتَنشَقُّ الْأَرْضُ   the earth to split open,

وَتَخِرُّ الْجِبَالُ هَدًّا ۝   and the mountains to collapse into bits,

91 أَن دَعَوْا لِلرَّحْمَٰنِ وَلَدًا ۝ that they should ascribe offspring to the All-beneficent!

92 وَمَا يَنبَغِي لِلرَّحْمَٰنِ أَن يَتَّخِذَ وَلَدًا ۝ It does not behoove the All-beneficent to have offspring.

93 إِن كُلُّ مَن فِي السَّمَاوَاتِ وَالْأَرْضِ There is none in the heavens and the earth

إِلَّا آتِي الرَّحْمَٰنِ عَبْدًا ۝   but he comes to the All-beneficent as a servant.

94 لَقَدْ أَحْصَاهُمْ Certainly He has counted them all

وَعَدَّهُمْ عَدًّا ۝   and numbered them precisely,

95 وَكُلُّهُمْ آتِيهِ and each of them will come to Him

يَوْمَ الْقِيَامَةِ فَرْدًا ۝   alone on the Day of Resurrection.

96 إِنَّ الَّذِينَ آمَنُوا وَعَمِلُوا الصَّالِحَاتِ Indeed, those who have faith and do righteous deeds

سَيَجْعَلُ لَهُمُ الرَّحْمَٰنُ وُدًّا ۝ —the All-beneficent will endear them to His creation.

97 فَإِنَّمَا يَسَّرْنَاهُ بِلِسَانِكَ We have indeed made it simple in your language

لِتُبَشِّرَ بِهِ الْمُتَّقِينَ   so that you may give good news thereby to the Godwary

وَتُنذِرَ بِهِ قَوْمًا لُّدًّا ۝   and *warn* with it a disputatious lot.

98 وَكَمْ أَهْلَكْنَا قَبْلَهُم مِّن قَرْنٍ How many a generation We have destroyed before them!

هَلْ تُحِسُّ مِنْهُم مِّنْ أَحَدٍ Can you descry any one of them,

أَوْ تَسْمَعُ لَهُمْ رِكْزًا ۝ or hear from them so much as a murmur?

---

[1] Or 'as incoming guests.'

20. TA HA[1]

Ṭā Hā

In the Name of God,
the All-beneficent, the All-merciful.

1 *Ṭā Hā!*
2 We did not send down the Qurʾān to you
   that you should be miserable,
3 but only as an admonition to him who fears his Lord.
4 A sending down of the Revelation from Him
   who created the earth and the lofty heavens
5 —the All-beneficent, settled on the Throne.
6 To Him belongs whatever is in the heavens
   and whatever is on the earth,
   and whatever is between them
   and whatever is under the ground.
7 Whether you speak loudly [or in secret tones]
   He indeed knows the secret and what is still more hidden.
8 God—there is no god except Him—
   to Him belong the Best Names.

9 Did the story of Moses come to *you*?
10 When he sighted a fire,
   he said to his family, 'Wait! Indeed, I descry a fire!
   Maybe I will bring you a brand from it,
   or find some guidance at the fire.'
11 So when he came to it, he was called, 'O Moses!
12 I am indeed your Lord!
   So take off your sandals.

---

[1] A Makkī *sūrah*. Like *Yā Sīn*, *Ṭā Hā* is said to be one of the names of the Prophet (ṣ). *Maʿānī al-akhbār*, p. 22.

إِنَّكَ بِالْوَادِ الْمُقَدَّسِ طُوًى ۝ You are indeed in the sacred valley of Ṭuwā.

وَأَنَا اخْتَرْتُكَ فَاسْتَمِعْ لِمَا يُوحَىٰ ۝ 13 I have chosen you, so listen to what is revealed.

إِنَّنِي أَنَا اللَّهُ لَا إِلَٰهَ إِلَّا أَنَا 14 I am indeed God—there is no god except Me.

فَاعْبُدْنِي   So worship Me

وَأَقِمِ الصَّلَاةَ لِذِكْرِي ۝   and maintain the prayer for My remembrance.

إِنَّ السَّاعَةَ آتِيَةٌ 15 Indeed, the Hour is bound to come:

أَكَادُ أُخْفِيهَا   I will have it hidden,

لِتُجْزَىٰ كُلُّ نَفْسٍ بِمَا تَسْعَىٰ ۝ so that every soul may be rewarded for its endeavour.

فَلَا يَصُدَّنَّكَ عَنْهَا 16 So do not let yourself be distracted from it

مَنْ لَا يُؤْمِنُ بِهَا   by those who do not believe in it

وَاتَّبَعَ هَوَاهُ   and follow their base desires,

فَتَرْدَىٰ ۝   or you will perish.'

وَمَا تِلْكَ بِيَمِينِكَ يَا مُوسَىٰ ۝ 17 'Moses, what is that in your right hand?'

قَالَ هِيَ عَصَايَ أَتَوَكَّأُ عَلَيْهَا 18 He said, 'It is my staff. I lean on it

وَأَهُشُّ بِهَا عَلَىٰ غَنَمِي   and with it I beat down leaves for my sheep,

وَلِيَ فِيهَا مَآرِبُ أُخْرَىٰ ۝   and I have other uses for it.'

قَالَ أَلْقِهَا يَا مُوسَىٰ ۝ 19 He said, 'Moses, throw it down.'

فَأَلْقَاهَا فَإِذَا هِيَ حَيَّةٌ تَسْعَىٰ ۝ 20 So he threw it down, and lo! it was a snake, moving swiftly.

قَالَ خُذْهَا وَلَا تَخَفْ 21 He said, 'Take hold of it, and do not fear.

سَنُعِيدُهَا سِيرَتَهَا الْأُولَىٰ ۝   We will restore it to its former state.

وَاضْمُمْ يَدَكَ إِلَىٰ جَنَاحِكَ 22 Now clasp your hand to your armpit:

تَخْرُجْ بَيْضَاءَ مِنْ غَيْرِ سُوءٍ   it will emerge bright, without any harm

آيَةً أُخْرَىٰ ۝   —this is yet another sign,

لِنُرِيَكَ مِنْ آيَاتِنَا الْكُبْرَى ۝ 23 that We may show you some of Our great signs.

اذْهَبْ إِلَىٰ فِرْعَوْنَ إِنَّهُ طَغَىٰ ۝ 24 Go to Pharaoh. He has indeed rebelled.'

قَالَ رَبِّ اشْرَحْ لِي صَدْرِي ۝ 25 He said, 'My Lord! Open my breast for me.

وَيَسِّرْ لِي أَمْرِي ۝ 26 Make my task easy for me.

وَاحْلُلْ عُقْدَةً مِنْ لِسَانِي ۝ 27 Remove the hitch from my tongue,[1]

يَفْقَهُوا قَوْلِي ۝ 28 so that they may understand my speech.

---

[1] That is, 'Grant me clarity of speech.'

29	Appoint for me a minister from my family,
30	Aaron, my brother.
31	Strengthen my back through him[1]
32	and make him my associate in my task,
33	so that we may glorify You greatly,
34	and remember You much.
35	You are indeed watching us.'
36	He said, 'Moses, your request has been granted!
37	Certainly We have done you a favour another time,
38	when We revealed to your mother whatever was to be revealed:
39	"Put him in the casket and cast it into the river. Then the river will cast it on the bank, and he shall be picked up by an enemy of Mine and an enemy of his." And I made you endearing to the people, and that you might be reared under My watchful eyes.
40	When your sister walked up [to Pharaoh's palace], saying, "Shall I show you someone who will take care of him?" Then We restored you to your mother, so that she might not grieve and be comforted. Then you slew a soul, whereupon We delivered you from anguish, and We tried you with various ordeals. Then you stayed several years among the people of Midian. Then you turned up as ordained, O Moses!
41	And I chose you for Myself.'
42	'Go ahead, you and your brother, with My signs,

---

[1] That is, 'reinforce my strength through him.'

and do not flag in My remembrance.

43 Both of you go to Pharaoh, for he has indeed rebelled.

44 Speak to him in a soft manner;
    maybe he will take admonition or fear.'

45 They said, 'Our Lord!
We are indeed afraid that he will forestall us
    or will exceed all bounds.'

46 He said, 'Do not be afraid,
    for I will be with the two of you,
    hearing and seeing [whatever happens].

47 So approach him and say,
    "We are the apostles of your Lord.
    Let the Children of Israel go with us
    and do not torture them!
We certainly bring you a sign from your Lord,
    and may peace be upon him who follows guidance!

48 Indeed, it has been revealed to us
    that punishment shall befall
those who impugn us and turn their backs on us."'

49 He said, 'Who is your Lord, Moses?'

50 He said, 'Our Lord is He who gave everything its creation
    and then guided it.'

51 He said, 'What about the former generations?'

52 He said, 'Their knowledge is with my Lord, in a Book.
My Lord neither makes any error nor forgets.'

53 He, who made the earth for you a cradle
    and threaded for you therein ways,
    and sent down water from the sky,
and We brought forth with it
    various kinds of vegetation,

54 ‘Eat and pasture your cattle. كُلُوا وَارْعَوْا أَنْعَامَكُمْ

There are indeed signs in that for those who have sense.’ إِنَّ فِي ذَٰلِكَ لَآيَاتٍ لِأُولِي النُّهَىٰ ۝

55 From it did We create you, into it shall We return you, مِنْهَا خَلَقْنَاكُمْ وَفِيهَا نُعِيدُكُمْ

and from it shall We bring you forth another time. وَمِنْهَا نُخْرِجُكُمْ تَارَةً أُخْرَىٰ ۝

56 Certainly We showed him all Our signs. وَلَقَدْ أَرَيْنَاهُ آيَاتِنَا كُلَّهَا

But he impugned them and refused to believe them. فَكَذَّبَ وَأَبَىٰ ۝

57 He said, ‘Have you come to us, قَالَ أَجِئْتَنَا

Moses, to expel us from our land with your magic? لِتُخْرِجَنَا مِنْ أَرْضِنَا بِسِحْرِكَ يَا مُوسَىٰ ۝

58 Yet we too will bring you a magic like it! فَلَنَأْتِيَنَّكَ بِسِحْرٍ مِثْلِهِ

So fix a tryst between us and you, فَاجْعَلْ بَيْنَنَا وَبَيْنَكَ مَوْعِدًا

which neither we shall fail nor you, at a middle place.’[1] لَا نُخْلِفُهُ نَحْنُ وَلَا أَنْتَ مَكَانًا سُوًى ۝

59 He said, ‘Your tryst shall be the Day of Adornment, قَالَ مَوْعِدُكُمْ يَوْمُ الزِّينَةِ

and let the people be assembled in early forenoon.’ وَأَنْ يُحْشَرَ النَّاسُ ضُحًى ۝

60 Then Pharaoh withdrew [to consult privately], فَتَوَلَّىٰ فِرْعَوْنُ

summoned up his guile, فَجَمَعَ كَيْدَهُ

and then arrived [at the scene of the contest]. ثُمَّ أَتَىٰ ۝

61 Moses said to them, ‘Woe to you! قَالَ لَهُمْ مُوسَىٰ وَيْلَكُمْ

Do not fabricate lies against God, لَا تَفْتَرُوا عَلَى اللَّهِ كَذِبًا

or He will obliterate you with a punishment. فَيُسْحِتَكُمْ بِعَذَابٍ

Whoever fabricates lies certainly fails.’ وَقَدْ خَابَ مَنِ افْتَرَىٰ ۝

62 So they disputed their matter among themselves, فَتَنَازَعُوا أَمْرَهُمْ بَيْنَهُمْ

and kept their confidential talks secret. وَأَسَرُّوا النَّجْوَىٰ ۝

63 They said, ‘These two are indeed magicians قَالُوا إِنْ هَٰذَانِ لَسَاحِرَانِ

who intend to expel you from your land يُرِيدَانِ أَنْ يُخْرِجَاكُمْ مِنْ أَرْضِكُمْ

with their magic بِسِحْرِهِمَا

and to abolish your excellent tradition![2] وَيَذْهَبَا بِطَرِيقَتِكُمُ الْمُثْلَىٰ ۝

64 So summon up your ingenuity, and come in orderly ranks. فَأَجْمِعُوا كَيْدَكُمْ ثُمَّ ائْتُوا صَفًّا

Today those who have the upper hand will triumph!’ وَقَدْ أَفْلَحَ الْيَوْمَ مَنِ اسْتَعْلَىٰ ۝

65 They said, ‘O Moses! Will you throw, قَالُوا يَا مُوسَىٰ إِمَّا أَنْ تُلْقِيَ

---

[1] Or ‘on a level ground,’ or ‘at a place of mutual consent.’
[2] Cf. **40:26**.

وَإِمَّا أَن نَّكُونَ أَوَّلَ مَنْ أَلْقَىٰ ۝	or shall we be the first to throw?'
قَالَ بَلْ أَلْقُوا ۖ	66 He said, 'No, you throw down first.'
فَإِذَا حِبَالُهُمْ وَعِصِيُّهُمْ يُخَيَّلُ إِلَيْهِ	Thereupon, behold, their ropes and staffs appeared to him
مِن سِحْرِهِمْ أَنَّهَا تَسْعَىٰ ۝	to wriggle swiftly, by their magic.
فَأَوْجَسَ فِي نَفْسِهِ خِيفَةً مُّوسَىٰ ۝	67 Then Moses felt a certain fear within his heart.
قُلْنَا لَا تَخَفْ	68 We said, 'Do not be afraid.
إِنَّكَ أَنتَ الْأَعْلَىٰ ۝	Indeed, you will have the upper hand.
وَأَلْقِ مَا فِي يَمِينِكَ	69 Throw down what is in your right hand,
تَلْقَفْ مَا صَنَعُوا ۖ	and it will swallow what they have conjured.
إِنَّمَا صَنَعُوا كَيْدُ سَاحِرٍ ۖ	What they have conjured is only a magician's trick,
وَلَا يُفْلِحُ السَّاحِرُ	and the magician does not fare well
حَيْثُ أَتَىٰ ۝	wherever he may show up.'
فَأُلْقِيَ السَّحَرَةُ سُجَّدًا	70 Thereat the magicians fell down prostrating.
قَالُوا	They said,
آمَنَّا بِرَبِّ هَارُونَ وَمُوسَىٰ ۝	'We have believed in the Lord of Aaron and Moses!'
قَالَ آمَنتُمْ لَهُ قَبْلَ أَنْ آذَنَ لَكُمْ ۖ	71 He said, 'Did you believe him before I should permit you?
إِنَّهُ لَكَبِيرُكُمُ الَّذِي عَلَّمَكُمُ السِّحْرَ ۖ	He is indeed your chief who has taught you magic!
فَلَأُقَطِّعَنَّ أَيْدِيَكُمْ وَأَرْجُلَكُم	Surely, I will cut off your hands and feet
مِّنْ خِلَافٍ	from opposite sides,
وَلَأُصَلِّبَنَّكُمْ فِي جُذُوعِ النَّخْلِ	and I will crucify you on the trunks of palm trees,
وَلَتَعْلَمُنَّ	and you will know
أَيُّنَا أَشَدُّ عَذَابًا	which of us can inflict a punishment severer
وَأَبْقَىٰ ۝	and more lasting.'
قَالُوا لَن نُّؤْثِرَكَ	72 They said, 'We will never prefer you
عَلَىٰ مَا جَاءَنَا مِنَ الْبَيِّنَاتِ	to the clear proofs which have come to us
وَالَّذِي فَطَرَنَا ۖ	and to Him who originated us.
فَاقْضِ مَا أَنتَ قَاضٍ ۖ	Decide whatever you want to decide.
إِنَّمَا تَقْضِي هَٰذِهِ الْحَيَاةَ الدُّنْيَا ۝	You can only decide about the life of this world.
إِنَّا آمَنَّا بِرَبِّنَا	73 We have indeed believed in our Lord
لِيَغْفِرَ لَنَا خَطَايَانَا	that He may forgive us our offences

and the magic you compelled us to perform.
God is better and more lasting.'

74 Whoever comes to his Lord laden with guilt,
for him shall be hell,
where he will neither live nor die.

75 But whoever comes to Him with faith
and he has done righteous deeds,
for such shall be the highest ranks

76 —the Gardens of Eden, with streams running in them,
to abide in them,
and that is the reward of him who keeps pure.

77 We revealed to Moses,
saying, 'Set out with My servants at night
and strike out for them a dry path through the sea.
Do not be afraid of being overtaken,
and have no fear [of getting drowned].

78 Then Pharaoh pursued them with his troops,
whereat they were engulfed
by what engulfed them of the sea.

79 Pharaoh led his people astray and did not guide them.

80 O Children of Israel!
We delivered you from your enemy,
and We appointed with you a tryst
on the right side of the Mount
and We sent down to you manna and quails:

81 'Eat of the good things We have provided you,
but do not overstep the bounds therein,
lest My wrath should descend on you.
And he on whom My wrath descends certainly perishes.[1]

---

[1] Or 'falls' (that is, into hell).

82 I indeed forgive those who repent,
become faithful, act righteously,
and thereafter follow guidance.'

83 'What prompted you to hasten ahead of your people,
O Moses?' [God said.]

84 He said, 'They are close upon my heels,
and I hurried on to You, my Lord,
so that You may be pleased.'

85 He said, 'We indeed tried your people in your absence,
and the Sāmirī[1] has led them astray.'

86 Thereupon Moses returned to his people,
indignant and grieved.

He said, 'O my people!
Did your Lord not give you a true promise?
Did the period of my absence seem too long to you?
Or did you desire
   that your Lord's wrath should descend on you
   and so you failed your tryst with me?'

87 They said, 'We did not fail our tryst with you
   of our own accord,
but we were laden
with the weight of those people's ornaments,
and we cast them [into the fire]
and so did the Samiri throw.'

88 Then he produced for them a calf
—a lifeless body with a low—
and they said, This is your god and the god of Moses,
so he[2] forgot!

---

[1] Apparently, one of the Israelites accompanying Moses ('a).
[2] The pronoun may be taken to refer either to the Sāmirī, concerning whom God says that he forgot Moses' teaching about the worship of the true God, or to Moses, who was said by the Sāmirī to have forgotten and left behind the Golden Calf and gone out in search of him.

⁸⁹ Did they not see that it did not answer them,
  nor could it bring them any benefit or harm?
⁹⁰ Aaron had certainly told them earlier,
  'O my people! You are only being tested by it.
  Indeed, your Lord is the All-beneficent.
  So follow me and obey my command!'
⁹¹ They had said, 'We will keep on attending to it
  until Moses returns to us.'
⁹² He said, 'O Aaron! What kept you,
  when you saw them going astray,
⁹³ from following me?
  Did you disobey my command?'
⁹⁴ He said, 'O son of my mother!
  Do not grab my beard or my head!
  I feared lest you should say,
  "You have caused a rift among the Children of Israel,
  and did not heed my word of advice."'
⁹⁵ He said, 'What is your business, O Samiri?'
⁹⁶ He said, 'I saw what they did not see.
  I took a handful of dust from the messenger's trail
  and threw it.
  That is how my soul prompted me.'
⁹⁷ He said, 'Begone!
  It shall be your lot throughout life to say,
  "Do not touch me!"
  There is indeed a tryst for you
  which you will not fail to keep!
  Now look at your god
  to whom you kept on attending.
  We will burn it down and then scatter its ashes into the sea.

98 Your God is indeed God. إِنَّمَا إِلَٰهُكُمُ اللَّهُ
There is no god except Him. الَّذِي لَا إِلَٰهَ إِلَّا هُوَ
He embraces all things in His knowledge.' وَسِعَ كُلَّ شَيْءٍ عِلْمًا ۝

99 Thus do We relate to you كَذَٰلِكَ نَقُصُّ عَلَيْكَ
 some accounts of what is past. مِنْ أَنْبَاءِ مَا قَدْ سَبَقَ
Certainly We have given you a Reminder from Ourselves. وَقَدْ آتَيْنَاكَ مِنْ لَدُنَّا ذِكْرًا ۝

100 Whoever disregards it shall bear on مَنْ أَعْرَضَ عَنْهُ فَإِنَّهُ يَحْمِلُ
the Day of Resurrection, the burden [of his denial], يَوْمَ الْقِيَامَةِ وِزْرًا ۝

101 remaining in it. خَالِدِينَ فِيهِ
Evil is their burden on the Day of Resurrection وَسَاءَ لَهُمْ يَوْمَ الْقِيَامَةِ حِمْلًا ۝

102 —the day the Trumpet will be blown; يَوْمَ يُنْفَخُ فِي الصُّورِ
on that day We will gather the guilty with blind eyes.[1] وَنَحْشُرُ الْمُجْرِمِينَ يَوْمَئِذٍ زُرْقًا ۝

103 They will whisper to one another: يَتَخَافَتُونَ بَيْنَهُمْ
 'You have stayed only for ten days.' إِنْ لَبِثْتُمْ إِلَّا عَشْرًا ۝

104 We know best what they will say, نَحْنُ أَعْلَمُ بِمَا يَقُولُونَ
 when the smartest of them in approach will say, إِذْ يَقُولُ أَمْثَلُهُمْ طَرِيقَةً
 'You stayed only a day!' إِنْ لَبِثْتُمْ إِلَّا يَوْمًا ۝

105 They question you concerning the mountains. وَيَسْأَلُونَكَ عَنِ الْجِبَالِ
Say, 'My Lord will scatter them like dust.' فَقُلْ يَنْسِفُهَا رَبِّي نَسْفًا ۝

106 Then He will leave it[2] as a level plain. فَيَذَرُهَا قَاعًا صَفْصَفًا ۝

107 You will not see any crookedness or unevenness in it. لَا تَرَىٰ فِيهَا عِوَجًا وَلَا أَمْتًا ۝

108 On that day يَوْمَئِذٍ
 they will follow the summoner without meandering. يَتَّبِعُونَ الدَّاعِيَ لَا عِوَجَ لَهُ
 Their voices will be muted before the All-beneficent, وَخَشَعَتِ الْأَصْوَاتُ لِلرَّحْمَٰنِ
 and you will hear nothing but a murmur. فَلَا تَسْمَعُ إِلَّا هَمْسًا ۝

109 Intercession will not avail that day يَوْمَئِذٍ لَا تَنْفَعُ الشَّفَاعَةُ
 except from him whom the All-beneficent allows إِلَّا مَنْ أَذِنَ لَهُ الرَّحْمَٰنُ
 and approves of his word. وَرَضِيَ لَهُ قَوْلًا ۝

---

[1] Literally, 'with blued eyes.' Cf. **17**:72, 97; **20**:124-125.
[2] That is, the earth.

110 He knows what is before them and behind them,
but they do not comprehend Him in their knowledge.

111 All faces shall be humbled before the Living One,
the All-sustainer,
and those will fail who bear the burden of wrongdoing.

112 But whoever does righteous deeds,
should he be faithful,
will fear neither injustice nor disparagement.

113 Thus We have sent it down as an Arabic Qurʾān
and We have paraphrased the warnings in it variously,
so that they may be Godwary,
or it may prompt them to remembrance of God.

114 So, exalted is God, the True Sovereign.
Do not hasten with the Qurʾān
before its revelation is completed for you,
and say, 'My Lord! Increase me in knowledge.'

115 Certainly We had enjoined Adam earlier,
but he forgot,
and We did not find any resoluteness in him.

116 When We said to the angels, 'Prostrate before Adam,'
they prostrated, but not Iblis: he refused.

117 We said, 'O Adam!
This is indeed an enemy of yours and your mate's.
So do not let him expel you from paradise,
or you will be miserable.

118 You will neither be hungry in it nor naked.

119 You will neither be thirsty in it,
nor suffer from the heat of the sun.'

120 Then Satan tempted him.
He said, 'O Adam! Shall I show you the tree of immortality,
and an imperishable kingdom?'

121 So they both ate of it,
and their nakedness became evident to them,
and they began to stitch over themselves
with the leaves of paradise.
Adam disobeyed his Lord and went amiss.

122 Then his Lord chose him
and turned to him clemently, and guided him.

123 He said, 'Get down from it both of you,[1] all together,
being enemies of one another!
Yet, should any guidance come to you from Me,
those who follow My guidance
will not go astray, nor will they be miserable.

124 But whoever disregards My remembrance
will have a wretched life,
and on the Day of Resurrection We shall raise him blind.'

125 He will say, 'My Lord! Why have You raised me blind,
though I used to see?'

126 He will say: 'So it is.
Our signs came to you, but you forgot them,
and so you will be forgotten today.'

127 Thus do We requite those who transgress
and do not believe in the signs of their Lord,
and the punishment of the Hereafter is severer
and more lasting.

128 Does it not dawn upon them
how many generations We have destroyed before them,

---

[1] That is, Adam and Eve, or Adam and Iblīs.

amid [the ruins of] whose dwellings they walk?
يَمْشُونَ فِي مَسَاكِنِهِمْ
There are indeed signs in that
إِنَّ فِي ذَٰلِكَ لَآيَاتٍ
for those who have good sense.
لِأُولِي النُّهَىٰ ۝

129 Were it not for a prior decree of *your* Lord and
وَلَوْلَا كَلِمَةٌ سَبَقَتْ مِنْ رَبِّكَ
a stated time, their doom would have been immediate.
لَكَانَ لِزَامًا وَأَجَلٌ مُسَمًّى ۝

130 So *be patient* with what they say,
فَاصْبِرْ عَلَىٰ مَا يَقُولُونَ
and *celebrate* the praise of *your* Lord
وَسَبِّحْ بِحَمْدِ رَبِّكَ
before the rising of the sun and before the sunset,
قَبْلَ طُلُوعِ الشَّمْسِ وَقَبْلَ غُرُوبِهَا
and *glorify* Him in watches of the night
وَمِنْ آنَاءِ اللَّيْلِ فَسَبِّحْ
and at the day's ends,
وَأَطْرَافَ النَّهَارِ
so that *you* may be pleased.
لَعَلَّكَ تَرْضَىٰ ۝

131 *Do not extend your* glance
وَلَا تَمُدَّنَّ عَيْنَيْكَ
toward what We have provided certain groups of them
إِلَىٰ مَا مَتَّعْنَا بِهِ أَزْوَاجًا مِنْهُمْ
as a glitter of the life of this world,
زَهْرَةَ الْحَيَاةِ الدُّنْيَا
in order that We may test them thereby.
لِنَفْتِنَهُمْ فِيهِ
The provision of *your* Lord is better and more lasting.
وَرِزْقُ رَبِّكَ خَيْرٌ وَأَبْقَىٰ ۝

132 And bid *your* family to prayer
وَأْمُرْ أَهْلَكَ بِالصَّلَاةِ
and *be* steadfast in maintaining it.
وَاصْطَبِرْ عَلَيْهَا
We do not ask any provision of *you*:
لَا نَسْأَلُكَ رِزْقًا
it is We who provide for *you*,
نَحْنُ نَرْزُقُكَ
and the ultimate outcome belongs to Godwariness.
وَالْعَاقِبَةُ لِلتَّقْوَىٰ ۝

133 They say, 'Why does he not bring us a sign from his Lord?'
وَقَالُوا لَوْلَا يَأْتِينَا بِآيَةٍ مِنْ رَبِّهِ
Has there not come to them a clear proof
أَوَلَمْ تَأْتِهِمْ بَيِّنَةُ
in that which is in the former scriptures?
مَا فِي الصُّحُفِ الْأُولَىٰ ۝

134 Had We destroyed them with a punishment before it,[1]
وَلَوْ أَنَّا أَهْلَكْنَاهُمْ بِعَذَابٍ مِنْ قَبْلِهِ
they would have surely said, 'Our Lord!
لَقَالُوا رَبَّنَا
Why did You not send us an apostle
لَوْلَا أَرْسَلْتَ إِلَيْنَا رَسُولًا
so that we might have followed Your signs
فَنَتَّبِعَ آيَاتِكَ
before we were abased and disgraced?'
مِنْ قَبْلِ أَنْ نَذِلَّ وَنَخْزَىٰ ۝

---

[1] That is, before the revelation of the Qur'ān.

135 Say, 'Everyone of us is waiting. So wait!
Soon you will know
who are the people of the right path,
and who is rightly guided.'

[PART 17]

21. THE PROPHETS[1]
al-Anbiyā'

In the Name of God,
the All-beneficent, the All-merciful.

1 Mankind's reckoning has drawn near to them,
yet they are disregardful in their obliviousness.

2 There does not come to them
any new reminder from their Lord
but they listen to it as they play around,

3 their hearts set on diversions.
The wrongdoers secretly whisper together, [saying],
'Is this not just a human being like yourselves?
Will you give in to magic with open eyes?'

4 He said, 'My Lord knows
every word spoken in the heaven and on the earth,
and He is the All-hearing, the All-knowing.'

5 But they said, 'They are muddled dreams!'
'He has indeed fabricated it!' 'He is indeed a poet!'
'Let him bring us a sign
like those sent to the former peoples.'

6 No town that We destroyed before them believed.[2]
Will these then have faith [if they are sent signs]?

7 We did not send any apostles before you
except as men, to whom We revealed.

---

[1] Accounts of several prophets (anbiyā') appear in this Makkī sūrah, hence its name.
[2] That is, they did not believe even after miracles were shown to them.

فَاسْأَلُوا أَهْلَ الذِّكْرِ Ask the People of the Reminder[1]
إِنْ كُنْتُمْ لَا تَعْلَمُونَ ۝ if you do not know.
8 وَمَا جَعَلْنَاهُمْ جَسَدًا We did not make them bodies
لَا يَأْكُلُونَ الطَّعَامَ that did not eat food,
وَمَا كَانُوا خَالِدِينَ ۝ nor were they immortal.
9 ثُمَّ صَدَقْنَاهُمُ الْوَعْدَ Then We fulfilled Our promise to them
فَأَنْجَيْنَاهُمْ وَمَنْ نَشَاءُ and We delivered them and whomever We wished,
وَأَهْلَكْنَا الْمُسْرِفِينَ ۝ and We destroyed the transgressors.
10 لَقَدْ أَنْزَلْنَا إِلَيْكُمْ كِتَابًا Certainly We have sent down to you a Book
فِيهِ ذِكْرُكُمْ in which there is an admonition for you.
أَفَلَا تَعْقِلُونَ ۝ Do you not exercise your reason?
11 وَكَمْ قَصَمْنَا مِنْ قَرْيَةٍ How many a town We have smashed
كَانَتْ ظَالِمَةً that had been wrongdoing,
وَأَنْشَأْنَا بَعْدَهَا قَوْمًا آخَرِينَ ۝ and We brought forth another people after it.
12 فَلَمَّا أَحَسُّوا بَأْسَنَا So when they sighted Our punishment,
إِذَا هُمْ مِنْهَا يَرْكُضُونَ ۝ behold, they ran away from it.
13 لَا تَرْكُضُوا 'Do not run away!
وَارْجِعُوا إِلَى مَا أُتْرِفْتُمْ فِيهِ Return to the opulence you were given to enjoy
وَمَسَاكِنِكُمْ and to your dwellings
لَعَلَّكُمْ تُسْأَلُونَ ۝ so that you may be questioned!'
14 قَالُوا يَا وَيْلَنَا إِنَّا كُنَّا ظَالِمِينَ ۝ They said, 'Woe to us! We have indeed been wrongdoers!'
15 فَمَا زَالَتْ تِلْكَ دَعْوَاهُمْ That remained their cry
حَتَّى جَعَلْنَاهُمْ حَصِيدًا until We turned them into a mown field,
خَامِدِينَ ۝ stilled like burnt ashes.
16 وَمَا خَلَقْنَا السَّمَاءَ وَالْأَرْضَ We did not create the heaven and the earth
وَمَا بَيْنَهُمَا لَاعِبِينَ ۝ and whatever is between them for play.
17 لَوْ أَرَدْنَا أَنْ نَتَّخِذَ لَهْوًا Had We desired to take up some diversion
لَاتَّخَذْنَاهُ مِنْ لَدُنَّا We would have taken it up with Ourselves,
إِنْ كُنَّا فَاعِلِينَ ۝ were We to do so.

---

[1] Cf. **16**:43.

18 بَلْ نَقْذِفُ بِالْحَقِّ عَلَى الْبَاطِلِ Indeed, We hurl the truth against falsehood,
فَيَدْمَغُهُ and it crushes its head,
فَإِذَا هُوَ زَاهِقٌ and behold, falsehood vanishes!
وَلَكُمُ الْوَيْلُ مِمَّا تَصِفُونَ ۝ And woe to you for what you allege about God.

19 وَلَهُ مَنْ فِي السَّمَاوَاتِ وَالْأَرْضِ To Him belongs whatever is in the heavens and the earth,
وَمَنْ عِنْدَهُ and those who are near Him
لَا يَسْتَكْبِرُونَ عَنْ عِبَادَتِهِ do not disdain to worship Him,
وَلَا يَسْتَحْسِرُونَ ۝ nor do they become weary.

20 يُسَبِّحُونَ اللَّيْلَ وَالنَّهَارَ لَا يَفْتُرُونَ ۝ They glorify Him night and day, without flagging.

21 أَمِ اتَّخَذُوا آلِهَةً مِنَ الْأَرْضِ Have they taken gods from the earth
هُمْ يُنْشِرُونَ ۝ who raise the dead?

22 لَوْ كَانَ فِيهِمَا آلِهَةٌ إِلَّا اللَّهُ Had there been any gods in them[1] other than God,
لَفَسَدَتَا they would surely have fallen apart.
فَسُبْحَانَ اللَّهِ رَبِّ الْعَرْشِ Clear is God, the Lord of the Throne,
عَمَّا يَصِفُونَ ۝ of what they allege concerning Him.

23 لَا يُسْأَلُ عَمَّا يَفْعَلُ He is not questioned concerning what He does,
وَهُمْ يُسْأَلُونَ ۝ but they are questioned.

24 أَمِ اتَّخَذُوا مِنْ دُونِهِ آلِهَةً Have they taken gods besides Him?
قُلْ هَاتُوا بُرْهَانَكُمْ Say, 'Produce your evidence!
هَذَا ذِكْرُ مَنْ مَعِيَ This is a precept of those who are with me
وَذِكْرُ مَنْ قَبْلِي and a precept of those who went before me.'
بَلْ أَكْثَرُهُمْ لَا يَعْلَمُونَ الْحَقَّ But most of them do not know the truth
فَهُمْ مُعْرِضُونَ ۝ and so they are disregardful.

25 وَمَا أَرْسَلْنَا مِنْ قَبْلِكَ مِنْ رَسُولٍ We did not send any apostle before you
إِلَّا نُوحِي إِلَيْهِ but that We revealed to him
أَنَّهُ لَا إِلَهَ إِلَّا أَنَا فَاعْبُدُونِ ۝ that 'There is no god except Me; so worship Me.'

26 وَقَالُوا اتَّخَذَ الرَّحْمَنُ وَلَدًا They say, 'The All-beneficent has offspring.'
سُبْحَانَهُ Immaculate is He!
بَلْ عِبَادٌ مُكْرَمُونَ ۝ Indeed, they are His honoured servants.

---

[1] That is, in the heavens and the earth.

لَا يَسْبِقُونَهُ بِالْقَوْلِ	27 They do not venture to speak ahead of Him,
وَهُم بِأَمْرِهِ يَعْمَلُونَ ۞	and they act by His command.
يَعْلَمُ مَا بَيْنَ أَيْدِيهِمْ وَمَا خَلْفَهُمْ	28 He knows what is before them and what is behind them,
وَلَا يَشْفَعُونَ	and they do not intercede
إِلَّا لِمَنِ ارْتَضَىٰ	except for someone He approves of,
وَهُم مِّنْ خَشْيَتِهِ مُشْفِقُونَ ۞	and they are apprehensive for the fear of Him.
وَمَن يَقُلْ مِنْهُمْ إِنِّي إِلَٰهٌ مِّن دُونِهِ	29 Should any of them say, 'I am a god besides Him,'
فَذَٰلِكَ نَجْزِيهِ جَهَنَّمَ	We will requite him with hell.
كَذَٰلِكَ نَجْزِي الظَّالِمِينَ ۞	Thus do We requite the wrongdoers.
أَوَلَمْ يَرَ الَّذِينَ كَفَرُوا	30 Have the faithless not regarded
أَنَّ السَّمَاوَاتِ وَالْأَرْضَ كَانَتَا رَتْقًا	that the heavens and the earth were interwoven
فَفَتَقْنَاهُمَا	and We unravelled them,
وَجَعَلْنَا مِنَ الْمَاءِ كُلَّ شَيْءٍ حَيٍّ	and We made every living thing out of water?
أَفَلَا يُؤْمِنُونَ ۞	Will they not then have faith?
وَجَعَلْنَا فِي الْأَرْضِ رَوَاسِيَ	31 We set firm mountains in the earth
أَن تَمِيدَ بِهِمْ	lest it should shake with them,
وَجَعَلْنَا فِيهَا فِجَاجًا سُبُلًا	and We made in them broad ways
لَعَلَّهُمْ يَهْتَدُونَ ۞	so that they may be guided to their destinations.
وَجَعَلْنَا السَّمَاءَ سَقْفًا مَّحْفُوظًا	32 We made the sky a preserved roof
وَهُمْ عَنْ آيَاتِهَا مُعْرِضُونَ ۞	and yet they are disregardful of its signs.
وَهُوَ الَّذِي خَلَقَ اللَّيْلَ وَالنَّهَارَ	33 It is He who created the night and the day,
وَالشَّمْسَ وَالْقَمَرَ	the sun and the moon,
كُلٌّ فِي فَلَكٍ يَسْبَحُونَ ۞	each swimming in an orbit.
وَمَا جَعَلْنَا لِبَشَرٍ مِّن قَبْلِكَ الْخُلْدَ	34 We did not give immortality to any human before you.
أَفَإِن مِّتَّ فَهُمُ الْخَالِدُونَ ۞	If you are fated to die, will they live on forever?
كُلُّ نَفْسٍ ذَائِقَةُ الْمَوْتِ	35 Every soul shall taste death,
وَنَبْلُوكُم بِالشَّرِّ وَالْخَيْرِ فِتْنَةً	and We will test you with good and ill by way of test,
وَإِلَيْنَا تُرْجَعُونَ ۞	and to Us you will be brought back.
وَإِذَا رَآكَ الَّذِينَ كَفَرُوا	36 Whenever the faithless see you
إِن يَتَّخِذُونَكَ إِلَّا هُزُوًا	they only take you in derision:

'Is this the one who speaks ill of your gods?'
And they dismiss the remembrance of the All-beneficent.

37 Man is a creature of haste.
Soon I will show you My signs.
So do not ask Me to hasten.

38 And they say, 'When will this promise be fulfilled,
if you are truthful?'

39 If only the faithless knew about the time when
they will not be able to keep the Fire off their faces
and their backs,
nor will they be helped![1]

40 Indeed, it will overtake them suddenly,
dumbfounding them.
So they will neither be able to avert it,
nor will they be granted any respite.

41 Apostles were certainly derided before you;
but those who ridiculed them were besieged
by what they had been deriding.

42 Say, 'Who can guard you, day and night,
against the punishment of the All-beneficent?'
They are indeed disregardful of their Lord's remembrance.

43 Do they have gods besides Us to defend them?
Neither can they help themselves,
nor can they shield [the idolaters] from Us.

44 We have indeed provided for them and their fathers
until they lived on for long years.
Do they not see how We visit the land
diminishing it at its edges?[2]
Are they the ones who will prevail?

---

[1] That is, had the faithless known their state in hell, they would not ask for the punishment to be hastened.
[2] Cf. **13:41**.

45 قُلْ إِنَّمَا أُنْذِرُكُمْ بِالْوَحْيِ ۚ وَلَا يَسْمَعُ الصُّمُّ الدُّعَاءَ إِذَا مَا يُنْذَرُونَ ۝

45 *Say, 'I indeed warn you by the means of revelation.'*
But the deaf do not hear the call
when they are warned.

46 وَلَئِنْ مَسَّتْهُمْ نَفْحَةٌ مِنْ عَذَابِ رَبِّكَ لَيَقُولُنَّ يَا وَيْلَنَا إِنَّا كُنَّا ظَالِمِينَ ۝

46 Should a whiff of your Lord's punishment touch them,
they will surely say, 'Woe to us!
We have indeed been wrongdoers!'

47 وَنَضَعُ الْمَوَازِينَ الْقِسْطَ لِيَوْمِ الْقِيَامَةِ فَلَا تُظْلَمُ نَفْسٌ شَيْئًا ۖ وَإِنْ كَانَ مِثْقَالَ حَبَّةٍ مِنْ خَرْدَلٍ أَتَيْنَا بِهَا ۗ وَكَفَىٰ بِنَا حَاسِبِينَ ۝

47 We shall set up just scales on the Day of Resurrection,
and no soul will be wronged in the least.
Even if it be the weight of a mustard seed
We will produce it and We suffice as reckoners.

48 وَلَقَدْ آتَيْنَا مُوسَىٰ وَهَارُونَ الْفُرْقَانَ وَضِيَاءً وَذِكْرًا لِلْمُتَّقِينَ ۝

48 Certainly We gave Moses and Aaron the Criterion,
a light and reminder for the Godwary.

49 الَّذِينَ يَخْشَوْنَ رَبَّهُمْ بِالْغَيْبِ وَهُمْ مِنَ السَّاعَةِ مُشْفِقُونَ ۝

49 —those who fear their Lord in secret
and are apprehensive of the Hour.

50 وَهَٰذَا ذِكْرٌ مُبَارَكٌ أَنْزَلْنَاهُ ۚ أَفَأَنْتُمْ لَهُ مُنْكِرُونَ ۝

50 This is a blessed reminder which We have sent down.
Will you then deny it?

51 وَلَقَدْ آتَيْنَا إِبْرَاهِيمَ رُشْدَهُ مِنْ قَبْلُ وَكُنَّا بِهِ عَالِمِينَ ۝

51 Certainly We gave Abraham his rectitude formerly,
and We knew him

52 إِذْ قَالَ لِأَبِيهِ وَقَوْمِهِ مَا هَٰذِهِ التَّمَاثِيلُ الَّتِي أَنْتُمْ لَهَا عَاكِفُونَ ۝

52 when he said to his father and his people,
'What are these images
to which you keep on attending?'

53 قَالُوا وَجَدْنَا آبَاءَنَا لَهَا عَابِدِينَ ۝

53 They said, 'We found our fathers worshiping them.'

54 قَالَ لَقَدْ كُنْتُمْ أَنْتُمْ وَآبَاؤُكُمْ فِي ضَلَالٍ مُبِينٍ ۝

54 He said, 'Certainly you and your fathers have been
in plain error.'

55 قَالُوا أَجِئْتَنَا بِالْحَقِّ أَمْ أَنْتَ مِنَ اللَّاعِبِينَ ۝

55 They said, 'Are you telling the truth,[1]
or are you just kidding?'

56 قَالَ بَلْ رَبُّكُمْ رَبُّ السَّمَاوَاتِ وَالْأَرْضِ

56 He said, 'Your Lord is indeed
the Lord of the heavens and the earth,

---

[1] Or 'Are you speaking seriously.'

الَّذِي فَطَرَهُنَّ	who originated them,
وَأَنَا عَلَىٰ ذَٰلِكُم مِّنَ الشَّاهِدِينَ ۝	and I bear witness to this.
وَتَاللَّهِ لَأَكِيدَنَّ أَصْنَامَكُم 57	57 By God, I will devise a stratagem against your idols
بَعْدَ أَن تُوَلُّوا مُدْبِرِينَ ۝	after you have gone away.'
فَجَعَلَهُمْ جُذَاذًا 58	58 So he broke them into pieces,
إِلَّا كَبِيرًا لَّهُمْ	all except the biggest of them,
لَعَلَّهُمْ إِلَيْهِ يَرْجِعُونَ ۝	so that they might come back to it.
قَالُوا مَن فَعَلَ هَٰذَا بِآلِهَتِنَا 59	59 They said, 'Whoever has done this to Our gods?!
إِنَّهُ لَمِنَ الظَّالِمِينَ ۝	He is indeed a wrongdoer!'
قَالُوا سَمِعْنَا فَتًى يَذْكُرُهُمْ 60	60 They said, 'We heard a young man speaking ill of them.
يُقَالُ لَهُ إِبْرَاهِيمُ ۝	He is called "Abraham."'
قَالُوا فَأْتُوا بِهِ عَلَىٰ أَعْيُنِ النَّاسِ 61	61 They said, 'Bring him before the people's eyes
لَعَلَّهُمْ يَشْهَدُونَ ۝	so that they may bear witness against him.'
قَالُوا أَأَنتَ فَعَلْتَ هَٰذَا بِآلِهَتِنَا 62	62 They said, 'Was it you who did this to our gods,
يَا إِبْرَاهِيمُ ۝	O Abraham?'
قَالَ بَلْ فَعَلَهُ كَبِيرُهُمْ هَٰذَا 63	63 He said, 'No, it was this biggest one of them who did it!
فَاسْأَلُوهُمْ إِن كَانُوا يَنطِقُونَ ۝	Ask them, if they can speak.'
فَرَجَعُوا إِلَىٰ أَنفُسِهِمْ فَقَالُوا 64	64 Thereat they came to themselves and said to one another,
إِنَّكُمْ أَنتُمُ الظَّالِمُونَ ۝	'It is you indeed who are the wrongdoers!'
ثُمَّ نُكِسُوا عَلَىٰ رُءُوسِهِمْ 65	65 Then they hung their heads.
لَقَدْ عَلِمْتَ	[However, they said], 'You certainly know
مَا هَٰؤُلَاءِ يَنطِقُونَ ۝	that they cannot speak.'
قَالَ أَفَتَعْبُدُونَ مِن دُونِ اللَّهِ 66	66 He said, 'Then, do you worship besides God
مَا لَا يَنفَعُكُمْ شَيْئًا وَلَا يَضُرُّكُمْ ۝	that which cannot cause you any benefit or harm?
أُفٍّ لَّكُمْ وَلِمَا تَعْبُدُونَ مِن دُونِ اللَّهِ 67	67 Fie on you and what you worship besides God!
أَفَلَا تَعْقِلُونَ ۝	Do you not exercise your reason?'
قَالُوا حَرِّقُوهُ وَانصُرُوا آلِهَتَكُمْ 68	68 They said, 'Burn him and help your gods,
إِن كُنتُمْ فَاعِلِينَ ۝	if you are to do anything!'
قُلْنَا يَا نَارُ كُونِي بَرْدًا وَسَلَامًا 69	69 We said, 'O fire!
عَلَىٰ إِبْرَاهِيمَ ۝	Be cool and safe for Abraham!'

70 وَأَرَادُوا بِهِ كَيْدًا They plotted to harm him,
فَجَعَلْنَاهُمُ الْأَخْسَرِينَ ۝ but We made them the biggest losers.
71 وَنَجَّيْنَاهُ وَلُوطًا إِلَى الْأَرْضِ We delivered him and Lot toward the land
الَّتِي بَارَكْنَا فِيهَا لِلْعَالَمِينَ ۝ which We have blessed for all nations.[1]
72 وَوَهَبْنَا لَهُ إِسْحَاقَ وَيَعْقُوبَ نَافِلَةً And We gave him Isaac, and Jacob as well for a grandson,[2]
وَكُلًّا جَعَلْنَا صَالِحِينَ ۝ and each of them We made righteous.
73 وَجَعَلْنَاهُمْ أَئِمَّةً يَهْدُونَ بِأَمْرِنَا We made them *imams*, guiding by Our command,
وَأَوْحَيْنَا إِلَيْهِمْ and We inspired them
فِعْلَ الْخَيْرَاتِ concerning the performance of good deeds,
وَإِقَامَ الصَّلَاةِ وَإِيتَاءَ الزَّكَاةِ the maintenance of prayers, and the giving of *zakāt*,
وَكَانُوا لَنَا عَابِدِينَ ۝ and they used to worship Us.

74 وَلُوطًا آتَيْنَاهُ حُكْمًا وَعِلْمًا We gave judgement and knowledge to Lot,
وَنَجَّيْنَاهُ مِنَ الْقَرْيَةِ and We delivered him from the town
الَّتِي كَانَتْ تَعْمَلُ الْخَبَائِثَ which used to commit vicious acts.
إِنَّهُمْ كَانُوا قَوْمَ سَوْءٍ فَاسِقِينَ ۝ They were indeed an evil and depraved lot.
75 وَأَدْخَلْنَاهُ فِي رَحْمَتِنَا And We admitted him into Our mercy.
إِنَّهُ مِنَ الصَّالِحِينَ ۝ He was indeed one of the righteous.

76 وَنُوحًا إِذْ نَادَىٰ مِنْ قَبْلُ And before that Noah; when he called out,
فَاسْتَجَبْنَا لَهُ We responded to him
فَنَجَّيْنَاهُ وَأَهْلَهُ مِنَ الْكَرْبِ الْعَظِيمِ ۝ and delivered him and his family from the great agony.
77 وَنَصَرْنَاهُ We rescued him
مِنَ الْقَوْمِ الَّذِينَ كَذَّبُوا بِآيَاتِنَا from the people who impugned Our signs.
إِنَّهُمْ كَانُوا قَوْمَ سَوْءٍ They were indeed an evil lot;
فَأَغْرَقْنَاهُمْ أَجْمَعِينَ ۝ so We drowned them all.

78 وَدَاوُودَ وَسُلَيْمَانَ And [remember] David and Solomon

---

[1] That is, Canaan.
[2] In a tradition of al-Imam al-Ṣādiq ('a), *nāfilatan* here is interpreted as meaning *walad al-walad nāfilatan*. Cf. *Ma'ānī al-akhbār*, p. 225.

when they gave judgement concerning the tillage
when the sheep of some people strayed into it by night,
and We were witness to their judgement.

79 We gave its understanding to Solomon,
and to each We gave judgement and knowledge.
We disposed
the mountains and the birds to glorify Us with David,
and We have been the doer of these things.

80 We taught him the making of coats of mail for you,
to protect you from your own violence.
Will you then be grateful?

81 And [We disposed] for Solomon the tempestuous wind
which blew by his command
toward the land which We have blessed,
and We have knowledge of all things.

82 Among the devils were some who dived for him
and performed tasks other than that,
and We were watchful over them.

83 And [remember] Job, when he called out to his Lord,
'Distress has indeed befallen me,
and You are the most merciful of the merciful.'

84 So We answered his prayer and removed his distress,
and We gave him back his family
along with others like them,
as a mercy from Us, and an admonition for the devout.

85 And [remember] Ishmael, Idris, and Dhul-Kifl
—each of them was among the patient.

86 We admitted them into Our mercy.

They were indeed among the righteous. إِنَّهُمْ مِنَ الصَّالِحِينَ ۝

87 And [remember] Jonah, when he left in a rage وَذَا النُّونِ إِذْ ذَهَبَ مُغَاضِبًا
thinking that We would not put him to hardship. فَظَنَّ أَنْ لَنْ نَقْدِرَ عَلَيْهِ
Then he cried out in the darkness, فَنَادَىٰ فِي الظُّلُمَاتِ
'There is no god except You! You are immaculate! أَنْ لَا إِلَٰهَ إِلَّا أَنْتَ سُبْحَانَكَ
I have indeed been among the wrongdoers!' إِنِّي كُنْتُ مِنَ الظَّالِمِينَ ۝

88 So We answered his prayer فَاسْتَجَبْنَا لَهُ
and delivered him from the agony, وَنَجَّيْنَاهُ مِنَ الْغَمِّ
and thus do We deliver the faithful. وَكَذَٰلِكَ نُنْجِي الْمُؤْمِنِينَ ۝

89 And [remember] Zechariah, when he cried out to his Lord, وَزَكَرِيَّا إِذْ نَادَىٰ رَبَّهُ
'My Lord! Do not leave me without an heir رَبِّ لَا تَذَرْنِي فَرْدًا
and You are the best of inheritors.' وَأَنْتَ خَيْرُ الْوَارِثِينَ ۝

90 So We answered his prayer and gave him John, فَاسْتَجَبْنَا لَهُ وَوَهَبْنَا لَهُ يَحْيَىٰ
and cured for him his wife of infertility. وَأَصْلَحْنَا لَهُ زَوْجَهُ
They were indeed active in performing good works, إِنَّهُمْ كَانُوا يُسَارِعُونَ فِي الْخَيْرَاتِ
and they would supplicate Us with eagerness and awe وَيَدْعُونَنَا رَغَبًا وَرَهَبًا
and were humble before Us. وَكَانُوا لَنَا خَاشِعِينَ ۝

91 And [remember] her who guarded her chastity, وَالَّتِي أَحْصَنَتْ فَرْجَهَا
so We breathed into her of Our spirit, فَنَفَخْنَا فِيهَا مِنْ رُوحِنَا
and made her and her son a sign for all the nations. وَجَعَلْنَاهَا وَابْنَهَا آيَةً لِلْعَالَمِينَ ۝

92 This community of yours is indeed one community, إِنَّ هَٰذِهِ أُمَّتُكُمْ أُمَّةً وَاحِدَةً
and I am your Lord. So worship Me. وَأَنَا رَبُّكُمْ فَاعْبُدُونِ ۝

93 They[1] have fragmented their religion among themselves, وَتَقَطَّعُوا أَمْرَهُمْ بَيْنَهُمْ
but everyone of them will return to Us: كُلٌّ إِلَيْنَا رَاجِعُونَ ۝

94 Whoever does righteous deeds, فَمَنْ يَعْمَلْ مِنَ الصَّالِحَاتِ
should he be faithful, وَهُوَ مُؤْمِنٌ
his endeavour shall not go unappreciated, فَلَا كُفْرَانَ لِسَعْيِهِ

---

[1] That is, the earlier religious communities, such as Jews and Christians. Cf. **23**:53

وَإِنَّا لَهُ كَاتِبُونَ ۝

and We will indeed record it for him.

95 It is forbidden for the people of any town
that We have destroyed [to return to the world]:
they shall not return

وَحَرَامٌ عَلَىٰ قَرْيَةٍ أَهْلَكْنَاهَا أَنَّهُمْ لَا يَرْجِعُونَ ۝

96 until when Gog and Magog are let loose
and they race down from every slope,[1]

حَتَّىٰ إِذَا فُتِحَتْ يَأْجُوجُ وَمَأْجُوجُ وَهُم مِّن كُلِّ حَدَبٍ يَنسِلُونَ ۝

97 and the true promise draws near to its fulfillment,
behold, the faithless will look on with a fixed gaze:
'Woe to us! We have certainly been oblivious of this!
We have indeed been wrongdoers!'

وَاقْتَرَبَ الْوَعْدُ الْحَقُّ فَإِذَا هِيَ شَاخِصَةٌ أَبْصَارُ الَّذِينَ كَفَرُوا يَا وَيْلَنَا قَدْ كُنَّا فِي غَفْلَةٍ مِّنْ هَٰذَا بَلْ كُنَّا ظَالِمِينَ ۝

98 Indeed, you and what [idols] you worship besides God
will be fuel for hell,
and you will enter it.

إِنَّكُمْ وَمَا تَعْبُدُونَ مِن دُونِ اللَّهِ حَصَبُ جَهَنَّمَ أَنتُمْ لَهَا وَارِدُونَ ۝

99 Had they been gods, they would not have entered it,
and they will all remain in it.

لَوْ كَانَ هَٰؤُلَاءِ آلِهَةً مَّا وَرَدُوهَا وَكُلٌّ فِيهَا خَالِدُونَ ۝

100 Their lot therein will be groaning,
and they will not hear anything in it.

لَهُمْ فِيهَا زَفِيرٌ وَهُمْ فِيهَا لَا يَسْمَعُونَ ۝

101 Indeed, those to whom there has gone beforehand
the promise of the best reward from Us
will be kept away from it.

إِنَّ الَّذِينَ سَبَقَتْ لَهُم مِّنَّا الْحُسْنَىٰ أُولَٰئِكَ عَنْهَا مُبْعَدُونَ ۝

102 They will not hear even its faint sound
and they will abide in what their souls desire.

لَا يَسْمَعُونَ حَسِيسَهَا وَهُمْ فِي مَا اشْتَهَتْ أَنفُسُهُمْ خَالِدُونَ ۝

103 The Great Terror will not upset them,
and the angels will receive them [saying]:
'This is your day which you were promised'

لَا يَحْزُنُهُمُ الْفَزَعُ الْأَكْبَرُ وَتَتَلَقَّاهُمُ الْمَلَائِكَةُ هَٰذَا يَوْمُكُمُ الَّذِي كُنتُمْ تُوعَدُونَ ۝

104 —the day We shall roll up the heaven
like rolling of the scrolls meant for writings.
We will bring it back just as We began the first creation
—a promise binding on Us.

يَوْمَ نَطْوِي السَّمَاءَ كَطَيِّ السِّجِلِّ لِلْكُتُبِ كَمَا بَدَأْنَا أَوَّلَ خَلْقٍ نُّعِيدُهُ وَعْدًا عَلَيْنَا

---

[1] Or, according to a less familiar reading (*jadath*, for *ḥadab*), 'they will be scrambling out of every grave.' Cf. 36:51.

That indeed We will do.

105 Certainly We wrote in the Psalms, after the Torah:
'My righteous servants shall indeed inherit the earth.'

106 There is indeed in this a proclamation
for a devout people.

107 We did not send you but as mercy to all the nations.[1]

108 Say, 'It has been revealed to me
that your God is the One God.
So will you submit?'

109 But if they turn away,
say, 'I have proclaimed to you all alike,
and I do not know
whether what you have been promised is far or near.

110 He indeed knows whatever is spoken aloud
and He knows whatever you conceal.

111 I do not know—maybe it is a test for you
and an enjoyment for a while.'

112 He said,[2] 'My Lord! Judge with justice.'
'Our Lord is the All-beneficent;
He is our resort against what you allege.'

22. THE PILGRIMAGE[3]
al-Ḥajj

In the Name of God,
the All-beneficent, the All-merciful.

1 O mankind! Be wary of your Lord!
The quake of the Hour is indeed a terrible thing.

2 The day that you will see it,

---

[1] Or 'to all the worlds.'
[2] Or 'Say,' according to an alternate reading (*qul* instead of *qāla*).
[3] Verses 26-37 of this *sūrah*, probably the first to be revealed at Madīnah, relate to the *ḥajj* pilgrimage, after which it is named.

every suckling female will be unmindful of what she suckled,
and every pregnant female will deliver her burden,
and you will see the people drunk,
yet they will not be drunken,
but God's punishment is severe.

3 Among the people are those who dispute about God
   without any knowledge
and follow every froward devil,

4 about whom it has been decreed
   that he will mislead those who take him for a friend
   and conduct them toward the punishment of the Blaze.

5 O people!
If you are in doubt about the resurrection,
   consider that We created you from dust,
   then from a drop of seminal fluid,
   then from a clinging tissue,[1] then from a fleshy tissue,[2]
      partly formed and partly unformed,
   so that We may manifest Our power to you.
We lodge in the wombs whatever We wish
   for a specified term,
   then We bring you forth as infants,
   then [We rear you] so that you may come of age.
Then there are some of you who are taken away,
and there are some of you who are relegated
   to the nethermost age,
   such that he knows nothing
      after having possessed some knowledge.
And you see the earth torpid,
yet when We send down water upon it, it stirs and swells

---

[1] That is, an embryo; cf. 23:13-14; 40:67; 75:38.
[2] That is, the fetus in the early stages of its development; cf. 23:13.

and grows every delightful kind of plant. وَأَنبَتَتْ مِن كُلِّ زَوْجٍ بَهِيجٍ ۝

6 All that is because God is the Reality ذَٰلِكَ بِأَنَّ اللَّهَ هُوَ الْحَقُّ
and it is He who revives the dead, وَأَنَّهُ يُحْيِي الْمَوْتَىٰ
and He has power over all things, وَأَنَّهُ عَلَىٰ كُلِّ شَيْءٍ قَدِيرٌ ۝

7 and because the Hour is bound to come, وَأَنَّ السَّاعَةَ آتِيَةٌ
there is no doubt in it, لَا رَيْبَ فِيهَا
and God will resurrect those who are in the graves. وَأَنَّ اللَّهَ يَبْعَثُ مَن فِي الْقُبُورِ ۝

8 Among the people are those who dispute concerning God وَمِنَ النَّاسِ مَن يُجَادِلُ فِي اللَّهِ
without knowledge or guidance, بِغَيْرِ عِلْمٍ وَلَا هُدًى
or an enlightening scripture, وَلَا كِتَابٍ مُّنِيرٍ ۝

9 turning aside disdainfully ثَانِيَ عِطْفِهِ
to lead others astray from the way of God. لِيُضِلَّ عَن سَبِيلِ اللَّهِ
For such there is disgrace in this world, لَهُ فِي الدُّنْيَا خِزْيٌ
and on the Day of Resurrection We will make him taste وَنُذِيقُهُ يَوْمَ الْقِيَامَةِ
the punishment of the burning: عَذَابَ الْحَرِيقِ ۝

10 'That is because of what your hands have sent ahead,[1] ذَٰلِكَ بِمَا قَدَّمَتْ يَدَاكَ
and because God is not tyrannical to the servants.' وَأَنَّ اللَّهَ لَيْسَ بِظَلَّامٍ لِّلْعَبِيدِ ۝

11 And among the people are those who worship God وَمِنَ النَّاسِ مَن يَعْبُدُ اللَّهَ
on the very fringe: عَلَىٰ حَرْفٍ
if good fortune befalls him, he is content with it; فَإِنْ أَصَابَهُ خَيْرٌ اطْمَأَنَّ بِهِ
but if an ordeal visits him he makes a turnabout, وَإِنْ أَصَابَتْهُ فِتْنَةٌ انقَلَبَ عَلَىٰ وَجْهِهِ
to become a loser in the world and the Hereafter. خَسِرَ الدُّنْيَا وَالْآخِرَةَ
That is clear loss. ذَٰلِكَ هُوَ الْخُسْرَانُ الْمُبِينُ ۝

12 He invokes besides God يَدْعُو مِن دُونِ اللَّهِ
that which can bring him neither benefit nor harm. مَا لَا يَضُرُّهُ وَمَا لَا يَنفَعُهُ
That is extreme error. ذَٰلِكَ هُوَ الضَّلَالُ الْبَعِيدُ ۝

13 He invokes someone whose harm is surely يَدْعُو لَمَن ضَرُّهُ
likelier than his benefit. أَقْرَبُ مِن نَّفْعِهِ
An evil master indeed and an evil companion! لَبِئْسَ الْمَوْلَىٰ وَلَبِئْسَ الْعَشِيرُ ۝

---

[1] Or 'prepared,' or 'committed.'

14 إِنَّ اللَّهَ يُدْخِلُ الَّذِينَ آمَنُوا
وَعَمِلُوا الصَّالِحَاتِ
جَنَّاتٍ تَجْرِي مِنْ تَحْتِهَا الْأَنْهَارُ
إِنَّ اللَّهَ يَفْعَلُ مَا يُرِيدُ ﴿١٤﴾
15 مَنْ كَانَ يَظُنُّ أَنْ لَنْ يَنْصُرَهُ اللَّهُ
فِي الدُّنْيَا وَالْآخِرَةِ
فَلْيَمْدُدْ بِسَبَبٍ إِلَى السَّمَاءِ
ثُمَّ لِيَقْطَعْ
فَلْيَنْظُرْ هَلْ يُذْهِبَنَّ كَيْدُهُ مَا يَغِيظُ ﴿١٥﴾
16 وَكَذَٰلِكَ أَنْزَلْنَاهُ آيَاتٍ بَيِّنَاتٍ
وَأَنَّ اللَّهَ يَهْدِي مَنْ يُرِيدُ ﴿١٦﴾
17 إِنَّ الَّذِينَ آمَنُوا وَالَّذِينَ هَادُوا وَالصَّابِئِينَ
وَالنَّصَارَىٰ وَالْمَجُوسَ وَالَّذِينَ أَشْرَكُوا
إِنَّ اللَّهَ يَفْصِلُ بَيْنَهُمْ
يَوْمَ الْقِيَامَةِ
إِنَّ اللَّهَ عَلَىٰ كُلِّ شَيْءٍ شَهِيدٌ ﴿١٧﴾

14 God will indeed admit those who have faith
and do righteous deeds
into gardens with streams running in them.
Indeed, God does whatever He desires.
15 Whoever thinks that God will not help *him*
in this world and the Hereafter,
let him stretch a rope to the ceiling
and hang himself,
and see if his artifice would remove his rage.
16 Thus have We sent it down as clear signs,
and indeed God guides whomever He desires.
17 The faithful, the Jews, the Sabaeans,
the Christians, the Magians and the polytheists
—God will indeed judge between them
on the Day of Resurrection.
God is indeed witness to all things.

18 أَلَمْ تَرَ أَنَّ اللَّهَ يَسْجُدُ لَهُ
مَنْ فِي السَّمَاوَاتِ وَمَنْ فِي الْأَرْضِ
وَالشَّمْسُ وَالْقَمَرُ وَالنُّجُومُ
وَالْجِبَالُ وَالشَّجَرُ وَالدَّوَابُّ
وَكَثِيرٌ مِنَ النَّاسِ
وَكَثِيرٌ حَقَّ عَلَيْهِ الْعَذَابُ
وَمَنْ يُهِنِ اللَّهُ
فَمَا لَهُ مِنْ مُكْرِمٍ
إِنَّ اللَّهَ يَفْعَلُ مَا يَشَاءُ ۩ ﴿١٨﴾

18 Have you not regarded that to God prostrates
whoever is in the heavens and whoever is on the earth,
and the sun, the moon, and the stars,
the mountains, the trees, and the animals
and many humans?
And many have come to deserve the punishment.
Whomever God humiliates
will find none who may bring him honour.
Indeed, God does whatever He wishes.

19 هَٰذَانِ خَصْمَانِ اخْتَصَمُوا فِي رَبِّهِمْ
فَالَّذِينَ كَفَرُوا
قُطِّعَتْ لَهُمْ ثِيَابٌ مِنْ نَارٍ

19 These two contending groups contend about their Lord.
As for those who are faithless,
cloaks of fire will be cut out for them,

and boiling water will be poured on their heads, يُصَبُّ مِنْ فَوْقِ رُءُوسِهِمُ الْحَمِيمُ ۝

20 with which their skins and entrails will fuse, يُصْهَرُ بِهِ مَا فِي بُطُونِهِمْ وَالْجُلُودُ ۝

21 and there will be clubs of iron for them. وَلَهُمْ مَقَامِعُ مِنْ حَدِيدٍ ۝

22 Whenever they desire to leave it out of anguish, كُلَّمَا أَرَادُوا أَنْ يَخْرُجُوا مِنْهَا مِنْ غَمٍّ
they will be turned back into it أُعِيدُوا فِيهَا
[and told]: 'Taste the punishment of the burning!' وَذُوقُوا عَذَابَ الْحَرِيقِ ۝

23 God will indeed admit those who have faith إِنَّ اللَّهَ يُدْخِلُ الَّذِينَ آمَنُوا
and do righteous deeds وَعَمِلُوا الصَّالِحَاتِ
into gardens with streams running in them, جَنَّاتٍ تَجْرِي مِنْ تَحْتِهَا الْأَنْهَارُ
adorned therein with bracelets of gold and pearl, يُحَلَّوْنَ فِيهَا مِنْ أَسَاوِرَ مِنْ ذَهَبٍ وَلُؤْلُؤًا
and their dress therein will be silk. وَلِبَاسُهُمْ فِيهَا حَرِيرٌ ۝

24 They have been guided to chaste speech, وَهُدُوا إِلَى الطَّيِّبِ مِنَ الْقَوْلِ
and guided to the path of the All-laudable. وَهُدُوا إِلَى صِرَاطِ الْحَمِيدِ ۝

25 Indeed, those who are faithless إِنَّ الَّذِينَ كَفَرُوا
and who bar from the way of God وَيَصُدُّونَ عَنْ سَبِيلِ اللَّهِ
and the Sacred Mosque, وَالْمَسْجِدِ الْحَرَامِ
which We have assigned for all people, الَّذِي جَعَلْنَاهُ لِلنَّاسِ
the native and the visitor being equal therein سَوَاءً الْعَاكِفُ فِيهِ وَالْبَادِ
—whoever tries to commit violation in it wrongfully, وَمَنْ يُرِدْ فِيهِ بِإِلْحَادٍ بِظُلْمٍ
We shall make him taste a painful punishment. نُذِقْهُ مِنْ عَذَابٍ أَلِيمٍ ۝

26 When We settled for Abraham the site of the House, وَإِذْ بَوَّأْنَا لِإِبْرَاهِيمَ مَكَانَ الْبَيْتِ
saying, Do not ascribe any partners to Me, أَنْ لَا تُشْرِكْ بِي شَيْئًا
and purify My House for those who circle around it وَطَهِّرْ بَيْتِيَ لِلطَّائِفِينَ
and those who stand in it for prayer وَالْقَائِمِينَ
and those who bow and prostrate themselves. وَالرُّكَّعِ السُّجُودِ ۝

27 And proclaim the ḥajj to all the people: وَأَذِّنْ فِي النَّاسِ بِالْحَجِّ
they will come to you on foot and on lean camels, يَأْتُوكَ رِجَالًا وَعَلَى كُلِّ ضَامِرٍ
coming from distant places, يَأْتِينَ مِنْ كُلِّ فَجٍّ عَمِيقٍ ۝

28 that they may witness the benefits for them, لِيَشْهَدُوا مَنَافِعَ لَهُمْ

وَيَذْكُرُوا اسْمَ اللَّهِ فِي أَيَّامٍ مَعْلُومَاتٍ
and mention God's Name during the known days

عَلَىٰ مَا رَزَقَهُم مِّن بَهِيمَةِ الْأَنْعَامِ ۖ
over the livestock He has provided them.

فَكُلُوا مِنْهَا وَأَطْعِمُوا الْبَائِسَ الْفَقِيرَ ۝
So eat thereof, and feed the destitute and the needy.

ثُمَّ لْيَقْضُوا تَفَثَهُمْ
29 Then let them do away with their untidiness,[1]

وَلْيُوفُوا نُذُورَهُمْ
 fulfill their vows,

وَلْيَطَّوَّفُوا بِالْبَيْتِ الْعَتِيقِ ۝
 and circle around the Ancient House.[2]

ذَٰلِكَ وَمَن يُعَظِّمْ حُرُمَاتِ اللَّهِ
30 That, and whoever venerates the sacraments of God,

فَهُوَ خَيْرٌ لَّهُ عِندَ رَبِّهِ ۗ
 that is better for him with his Lord.

وَأُحِلَّتْ لَكُمُ الْأَنْعَامُ
 You are permitted animals of grazing livestock,

إِلَّا مَا يُتْلَىٰ عَلَيْكُمْ ۖ
 except for what will be recited to you.

فَاجْتَنِبُوا الرِّجْسَ مِنَ الْأَوْثَانِ
 So avoid the abomination of idols,

وَاجْتَنِبُوا قَوْلَ الزُّورِ ۝
 and avoid false speech,

حُنَفَاءَ لِلَّهِ
31 as persons having pure faith in God,

غَيْرَ مُشْرِكِينَ بِهِ ۚ
 not ascribing partners to Him.

وَمَن يُشْرِكْ بِاللَّهِ
 Whoever ascribes partners to God

فَكَأَنَّمَا خَرَّ مِنَ السَّمَاءِ
 is as though he had fallen from a height,

فَتَخْطَفُهُ الطَّيْرُ
 then [his corpse] were devoured by vultures,

أَوْ تَهْوِي بِهِ الرِّيحُ فِي مَكَانٍ سَحِيقٍ ۝
 or his remains were blown away by the wind, far and wide.

ذَٰلِكَ وَمَن يُعَظِّمْ شَعَائِرَ اللَّهِ
32 That, and whoever venerates the sacraments of God

فَإِنَّهَا مِن تَقْوَى الْقُلُوبِ ۝
 —indeed that arises from the Godwariness of hearts.

لَكُمْ فِيهَا مَنَافِعُ إِلَىٰ أَجَلٍ مُّسَمًّى
33 You may benefit from them until a specified time,[3]

ثُمَّ مَحِلُّهَا إِلَى الْبَيْتِ الْعَتِيقِ ۝
 then their place of sacrifice is by the Ancient House.

وَلِكُلِّ أُمَّةٍ جَعَلْنَا مَنسَكًا
34 For every nation We have appointed a rite

لِيَذْكُرُوا اسْمَ اللَّهِ
 so that they might mention God's Name

عَلَىٰ مَا رَزَقَهُم مِّن بَهِيمَةِ الْأَنْعَامِ ۗ
 over the livestock He has provided them.

فَإِلَٰهُكُمْ إِلَٰهٌ وَاحِدٌ فَلَهُ أَسْلِمُوا ۗ
 Your God is the One God, so submit to Him.

وَبَشِّرِ الْمُخْبِتِينَ ۝
 And *give* good news to the humble

---

[1] According to the commentators, the phrase *li yaqḍū tafathahum* implies egress from the state of *iḥrām* (after the shortening of the hair or the nails, and the bath), and relief from its restrictions. Or it means 'let them perform their rites.'

[2] Or, 'the Free House,' that is, free from bondage of anyone's ownership.

[3] That is, you may benefit from the sacrificial animals, such as by using them as mounts or milking them, until they arrive at the place where they are to be sacrificed.

35 الَّذِينَ —those
إِذَا ذُكِرَ اللَّهُ وَجِلَتْ قُلُوبُهُمْ whose hearts tremble with awe when God is mentioned
وَالصَّابِرِينَ عَلَىٰ مَا أَصَابَهُمْ and who are patient through whatever visits them,
وَالْمُقِيمِي الصَّلَاةِ and who maintain the prayer
وَمِمَّا رَزَقْنَاهُمْ يُنفِقُونَ ۝ and spend out of what We have provided them.

36 وَالْبُدْنَ جَعَلْنَاهَا لَكُم We have appointed for you the sacrificial camels
مِّن شَعَائِرِ اللَّهِ as part of God's sacraments.
لَكُمْ فِيهَا خَيْرٌ There is good for you in them.
فَاذْكُرُوا اسْمَ اللَّهِ عَلَيْهَا صَوَافَّ So mention the Name of God over them as they stand,
فَإِذَا وَجَبَتْ جُنُوبُهَا فَكُلُوا مِنْهَا and when they have fallen on their flanks, eat from them
وَأَطْعِمُوا الْقَانِعَ وَالْمُعْتَرَّ and feed the self-contained needy and the mendicant.
كَذَٰلِكَ سَخَّرْنَاهَا لَكُمْ Thus have We disposed them for your benefit
لَعَلَّكُمْ تَشْكُرُونَ ۝ so that you may give thanks.

37 لَن يَنَالَ اللَّهَ لُحُومُهَا وَلَا دِمَاؤُهَا It is not their flesh or blood that reaches God;
وَلَـٰكِن يَنَالُهُ التَّقْوَىٰ مِنكُمْ rather, it is your piety that reaches Him.
كَذَٰلِكَ سَخَّرَهَا لَكُمْ Thus has He disposed them for your benefit
لِتُكَبِّرُوا اللَّهَ عَلَىٰ مَا هَدَاكُمْ so that you may magnify God for His guiding you.
وَبَشِّرِ الْمُحْسِنِينَ ۝ And *give* good news to the virtuous.

38 إِنَّ اللَّهَ يُدَافِعُ عَنِ الَّذِينَ آمَنُوا God will indeed defend those who have faith.
إِنَّ اللَّهَ لَا يُحِبُّ كُلَّ خَوَّانٍ كَفُورٍ ۝ Indeed, God does not like any ingrate traitor.

39 أُذِنَ لِلَّذِينَ يُقَاتَلُونَ Those who are fought against are permitted to fight
بِأَنَّهُمْ ظُلِمُوا because they have been wronged,
وَإِنَّ اللَّهَ عَلَىٰ نَصْرِهِمْ لَقَدِيرٌ ۝ and God is indeed able to help them

40 الَّذِينَ أُخْرِجُوا مِن دِيَارِهِم بِغَيْرِ حَقٍّ —those who were expelled from their homes unjustly
إِلَّا أَن يَقُولُوا رَبُّنَا اللَّهُ only because they said, 'God is our Lord.'
وَلَوْلَا دَفْعُ اللَّهِ النَّاسَ بَعْضَهُم بِبَعْضٍ Had not God repulsed the people from one another,
لَّهُدِّمَتْ صَوَامِعُ وَبِيَعٌ ruin would have befallen the monasteries, churches,
وَصَلَوَاتٌ وَمَسَاجِدُ synagogues and mosques
يُذْكَرُ فِيهَا اسْمُ اللَّهِ كَثِيرًا in which God's Name is much invoked.

وَلَيَنصُرَنَّ ٱللَّهُ مَن يَنصُرُهُۥٓ

God will surely help those who help Him.

إِنَّ ٱللَّهَ لَقَوِىٌّ عَزِيزٌ ۝

God is indeed all-strong, all-mighty.

ٱلَّذِينَ إِن مَّكَّنَّـٰهُمْ فِى ٱلْأَرْضِ 41 Those who, if We granted them power in the land,

أَقَامُوا۟ ٱلصَّلَوٰةَ وَءَاتَوُا۟ ٱلزَّكَوٰةَ

will maintain the prayer, give the *zakāt*,

وَأَمَرُوا۟ بِٱلْمَعْرُوفِ وَنَهَوْا۟ عَنِ ٱلْمُنكَرِ

bid what is right and forbid what is wrong,

وَلِلَّهِ عَـٰقِبَةُ ٱلْأُمُورِ ۝

and with God rests the outcome of all matters.

وَإِن يُكَذِّبُوكَ 42 If they impugn *you*,

فَقَدْ كَذَّبَتْ قَبْلَهُمْ قَوْمُ نُوحٍ

the people of Noah have impugned before them

وَعَادٌ وَثَمُودُ ۝

and ʿĀd and Thamūd,

وَقَوْمُ إِبْرَٰهِيمَ وَقَوْمُ لُوطٍ ۝ 43 as well as the people of Abraham, the people of Lot,

وَأَصْحَـٰبُ مَدْيَنَ 44 and the inhabitants of Midian,

وَكُذِّبَ مُوسَىٰ

and Moses was also impugned.

فَأَمْلَيْتُ لِلْكَـٰفِرِينَ ثُمَّ أَخَذْتُهُمْ

But I gave the faithless a respite, then I seized them,

فَكَيْفَ كَانَ نَكِيرِ ۝

and how was My rebuttal!

فَكَأَيِّن مِّن قَرْيَةٍ أَهْلَكْنَـٰهَا 45 How many towns We have destroyed

وَهِىَ ظَالِمَةٌ

when they had been wrongdoers!

فَهِىَ خَاوِيَةٌ عَلَىٰ عُرُوشِهَا

So they lie fallen on their trellises,

وَبِئْرٍ مُّعَطَّلَةٍ وَقَصْرٍ مَّشِيدٍ ۝

their wells neglected and their palaces in ruins!

أَفَلَمْ يَسِيرُوا۟ فِى ٱلْأَرْضِ 46 Have they not traveled through the land

فَتَكُونَ لَهُمْ قُلُوبٌ

so that they may have hearts

يَعْقِلُونَ بِهَا

with which they may exercise their reason,

أَوْ ءَاذَانٌ يَسْمَعُونَ بِهَا

or ears by which they may hear?

فَإِنَّهَا لَا تَعْمَى ٱلْأَبْصَـٰرُ

Indeed, it is not the eyes that turn blind,

وَلَـٰكِن تَعْمَى ٱلْقُلُوبُ

but it is the hearts that turn blind

ٱلَّتِى فِى ٱلصُّدُورِ ۝

—those which are in the breasts!

وَيَسْتَعْجِلُونَكَ بِٱلْعَذَابِ 47 They ask you to hasten the punishment,

وَلَن يُخْلِفَ ٱللَّهُ وَعْدَهُۥ

though God will never break His promise.

وَإِنَّ يَوْمًا عِندَ رَبِّكَ

Indeed, a day with *your* Lord

كَأَلْفِ سَنَةٍ مِّمَّا تَعُدُّونَ ۝

is like a thousand years by your reckoning.

48 To how many a town did I give respite
while it was doing wrong!
Then I seized it, and toward Me is the destination.

49 *Say, 'O mankind!*
I am only a manifest warner to you!'
50 As for those who have faith and do righteous deeds,
for them will be forgiveness and a noble provision.
51 But as for those who contend with Our signs,
seeking to frustrate their purpose,
they shall be the inmates of hell.
52 We did not send before you
any apostle or prophet
but that when he recited the scripture
Satan interjected something in his recitation.
Thereat God nullifies whatever Satan has interjected,
and then God confirms His signs,
and God is All-knowing, All-wise.
53 That He may make what Satan has thrown in
a test for those in whose hearts is a sickness
and those whose hearts have hardened.
The wrongdoers are indeed steeped in extreme defiance.
54 And so that those who have been given knowledge may know
that it is the truth from your Lord,
and so that they may have faith in it,
and their hearts may be humbled before Him.
God indeed guides those who have faith
to a straight path.
55 Those who are faithless will persist
in their doubt about it

حَتَّىٰ تَأْتِيَهُمُ السَّاعَةُ بَغْتَةً
أَوْ يَأْتِيَهُمْ عَذَابُ
يَوْمٍ عَقِيمٍ ۝

until the Hour will overtake them suddenly,
or they are overtaken by the punishment
of an inauspicious day.

ٱلْمُلْكُ يَوْمَئِذٍ لِلَّهِ
يَحْكُمُ بَيْنَهُمْ
فَٱلَّذِينَ آمَنُوا
وَعَمِلُوا ٱلصَّالِحَاتِ
فِي جَنَّاتِ ٱلنَّعِيمِ ۝

56 On that day all sovereignty will belong to God:
He will judge between them.
Then those who have faith
and do righteous deeds
will be in gardens of bliss,

وَٱلَّذِينَ كَفَرُوا وَكَذَّبُوا بِآيَاتِنَا
فَأُولَـٰٓئِكَ لَهُمْ عَذَابٌ مُّهِينٌ ۝

57 and those who are faithless and deny Our signs
—for such there will be a humiliating punishment.

وَٱلَّذِينَ هَاجَرُوا فِي سَبِيلِ ٱللَّهِ
ثُمَّ قُتِلُوا أَوْ مَاتُوا
لَيَرْزُقَنَّهُمُ ٱللَّهُ رِزْقًا حَسَنًا
وَإِنَّ ٱللَّهَ لَهُوَ خَيْرُ ٱلرَّازِقِينَ ۝

58 Those who migrate in the way of God
and then are slain, or die,
God will surely provide them with a good provision.
God is indeed the best of providers.

لَيُدْخِلَنَّهُم مُّدْخَلًا يَرْضَوْنَهُ
وَإِنَّ ٱللَّهَ لَعَلِيمٌ حَلِيمٌ ۝

59 He will admit them into an abode they are pleased with.
God is indeed all-knowing, all-forbearing.

ذَٰلِكَ وَمَنْ عَاقَبَ
بِمِثْلِ مَا عُوقِبَ بِهِ
ثُمَّ بُغِيَ عَلَيْهِ
لَيَنصُرَنَّهُ ٱللَّهُ
إِنَّ ٱللَّهَ لَعَفُوٌّ غَفُورٌ ۝

60 So will it be; and whoever retaliates
with the like of what he has been made to suffer,
and is aggressed against again thereafter,
God will surely help him.
God is indeed all-excusing, all-forgiving.

ذَٰلِكَ
بِأَنَّ ٱللَّهَ يُولِجُ ٱلَّيْلَ فِي ٱلنَّهَارِ
وَيُولِجُ ٱلنَّهَارَ فِي ٱلَّيْلِ
وَأَنَّ ٱللَّهَ سَمِيعٌ بَصِيرٌ ۝

61 So will it be,
because God makes the night pass into the day
and makes the day pass into the night,
and because God is all-hearing, all-seeing.

ذَٰلِكَ بِأَنَّ ٱللَّهَ هُوَ ٱلْحَقُّ
وَأَنَّ مَا يَدْعُونَ مِن دُونِهِ هُوَ ٱلْبَاطِلُ
وَأَنَّ ٱللَّهَ هُوَ ٱلْعَلِيُّ ٱلْكَبِيرُ ۝

62 So will it be, because God is the Reality,
and what they invoke besides Him is nullity,
and because God is the All-exalted, the All-great.

أَلَمْ تَرَ أَنَّ ٱللَّهَ أَنزَلَ

63 Have you not regarded that God sends down

water from the sky,
whereupon the earth turns green?
God is indeed all-attentive, all-aware.

64 To Him belongs whatever is in the heavens
and whatever is in the earth.
Indeed, God is the All-sufficient, the All-laudable.

65 Have you not regarded that God has disposed for you
whatever there is in the earth,
and that the ships sail at sea by His command,
and He sustains the heaven lest it should fall on the earth,
excepting when it does so by His leave?
God is indeed most kind and merciful to mankind.

66 It is He who gave you life,
then He makes you die, then He brings you to life.
Indeed, man is very ungrateful.

67 For every nation We have appointed rites of worship
which they observe;
so let them not dispute with *you* about your religion.[1]
And *invite* to your Lord.
You are indeed on a straight guidance.

68 But if they dispute with *you*,
say, 'God knows best what you are doing.

69 God will judge between you on the Day of Resurrection
concerning that about which you used to differ.'

70 Do you not know that God knows
whatever there is in the heaven and the earth?
All that is indeed in a Book.
That is indeed easy for God.

---

[1] Or 'the Law.'

71 They worship besides God
that for which He has not sent down any authority,
and of which they have no knowledge.
The wrongdoers will have no helper.

72 When Our manifest signs are recited to them,
you perceive denial on the faces of the faithless:
they would almost pounce
upon those who recite Our signs to them.
Say, 'Shall I inform you about something worse than that?
The Fire, which God has promised the faithless,
and it is an evil destination.'

73 O people! Listen to a parable that is being drawn:
Indeed, those whom you invoke besides God
will never create even a fly even if they all rallied to do so!
And if a fly should take away something from them,
they can not recover that from it.
Feeble is the pursuer and the pursued!

74 They do not regard God with the regard due to Him.
God is indeed all-strong, all-mighty.

75 God chooses messengers from angels
and from humans.
God is indeed all-hearing, all-seeing.

76 He knows that which is before them
and that which is behind them,
and to God all matters are returned.

77 O you who have faith!
Bow down and prostrate yourselves,
and worship your Lord, and do good,

                        so that you may be felicitous.

78 And wage *jihād* for the sake of God,
      a *jihād* which is worthy of Him.
    He has chosen you and has not placed for you
      any obstacle in the religion,
    the faith of your father, Abraham.
    He named you '*muslims*' before,
      and in this,[1]
    so that the Apostle may be a witness to you,
      and that you may be witnesses to mankind.
    So maintain the prayer, give the *zakāt*,
      and hold fast to God.
    He is your Master
    —an excellent master and an excellent helper.

[PART 18]

23. THE FAITHFUL[2]
al-Mu'minūn

In the Name of God,
the All-beneficent, the All-merciful.

1 Certainly the faithful have attained salvation
2 —those who are humble in their prayers,
3 who avoid vain talk,
4 who carry out their duty of *zakāt*,
5 who guard their private parts[3]
6 (except from their spouses or their slave women,
    for then they are not blameworthy;
7 but whoever seeks anything beyond that
    —it is they who are transgressors)

---

[1] That is, in the former scriptures and in the present one, that is, the Qur'ān.
[2] This Makkī *sūrah* is named after the faithful (*mu'minūn*) mentioned in verse 1.
[3] That is, those who refrain from unlawful sexual relations and cover their private parts properly, except in the state of privacy with their spouses.

وَالَّذِينَ هُمْ لِأَمَانَاتِهِمْ وَعَهْدِهِمْ رَاعُونَ ۝	8 and those who keep their trusts and covenants,
وَالَّذِينَ هُمْ عَلَىٰ صَلَوَاتِهِمْ يُحَافِظُونَ ۝	9 and who are watchful of their prayers.
أُولَٰئِكَ هُمُ الْوَارِثُونَ ۝	10 It is they who will be the inheritors,
الَّذِينَ يَرِثُونَ الْفِرْدَوْسَ	11 who shall inherit paradise,
هُمْ فِيهَا خَالِدُونَ ۝	and will remain in it.[1]
وَلَقَدْ خَلَقْنَا الْإِنسَانَ	12 Certainly We created man
مِن سُلَالَةٍ مِّن طِينٍ ۝	from an extract of clay.
ثُمَّ جَعَلْنَاهُ نُطْفَةً	13 Then We made him a drop of seminal fluid
فِي قَرَارٍ مَّكِينٍ ۝	lodged in a secure abode.
ثُمَّ خَلَقْنَا النُّطْفَةَ عَلَقَةً	14 Then We created the drop of fluid as a clinging tissue.
فَخَلَقْنَا الْعَلَقَةَ مُضْغَةً	Then We created the clinging tissue as a fleshy tissue.
فَخَلَقْنَا الْمُضْغَةَ عِظَامًا	Then We created the fleshy tissue as bones.
فَكَسَوْنَا الْعِظَامَ لَحْمًا	Then We clothed the bones with flesh.
ثُمَّ أَنشَأْنَاهُ خَلْقًا آخَرَ	Then We produced him as yet another creature.
فَتَبَارَكَ اللَّهُ أَحْسَنُ الْخَالِقِينَ ۝	So blessed is God, the best of creators!
ثُمَّ إِنَّكُم بَعْدَ ذَٰلِكَ لَمَيِّتُونَ ۝	15 Then, of course, you die after that.
ثُمَّ إِنَّكُمْ يَوْمَ الْقِيَامَةِ تُبْعَثُونَ ۝	16 Then you will indeed be raised on the Day of Resurrection.
وَلَقَدْ خَلَقْنَا فَوْقَكُمْ سَبْعَ طَرَائِقَ	17 Certainly We created above you the seven levels[2]
وَمَا كُنَّا عَنِ الْخَلْقِ غَافِلِينَ ۝	and We have not been oblivious of creation.
وَأَنزَلْنَا مِنَ السَّمَاءِ مَاءً بِقَدَرٍ	18 We sent down water from the sky in a measured manner,
فَأَسْكَنَّاهُ فِي الْأَرْضِ ۖ	and We lodged it within the ground,
وَإِنَّا عَلَىٰ ذَهَابٍ بِهِ لَقَادِرُونَ ۝	and We are indeed able to take it away.
فَأَنشَأْنَا لَكُم بِهِ	19 Then, with it We produced for you
جَنَّاتٍ مِّن نَّخِيلٍ وَأَعْنَابٍ	gardens of date palms and vines.
لَّكُمْ فِيهَا فَوَاكِهُ كَثِيرَةٌ	There are abundant fruits in them for you,
وَمِنْهَا تَأْكُلُونَ ۝	and you eat from them.
وَشَجَرَةً تَخْرُجُ مِن طُورِ سَيْنَاءَ	20 And a tree that grows on Mount Sinai
تَنبُتُ بِالدُّهْنِ وَصِبْغٍ لِّلْآكِلِينَ ۝	which produces oil and a seasoning for those who eat.

[1] Cf. 70:22-35
[2] Apparently, a reference to the seven heavens. Or, 'seven tracks.'

21 There is indeed a moral for you in the cattle:
   We give you to drink of that which is in their bellies,
      and you have many uses in them,
      and you eat some of them,
22 and you are carried on them and on ships.

23 Certainly We sent Noah to his people,
   and he said, 'O my people! Worship God!
      You have no other god besides Him.
      Will you not then be wary of Him?'
24 But the elite of the faithless from among his people said,
   'This is just a human being like you,
      who seeks to dominate you.
   Had God wished, He would have sent down angels.
   We never heard of such a thing among our forefathers.
25 He is just a man possessed by madness.
   So bear with him for a while.'
26 He said, 'My Lord! Help me, for they impugn me.'
27 So We revealed to him:
   'Build the ark before Our eyes and by Our revelation.
   When Our edict comes and the oven gushes,
      bring into it a pair of every kind[1] of animal,
      and your family, except
   those of them against whom the decree has gone beforehand,
   and do not plead with Me for those who are wrongdoers:
      they shall indeed be drowned.'
28 'When you, and those who are with you, are settled
      in the ark,
   say, "All praise belongs to God,

---

[1] Or 'bring into it two mates of every kind [of animal].'

الَّذِي نَجَّانَا مِنَ الْقَوْمِ الظَّالِمِينَ ۝

who has delivered us from the wrongdoing lot."

29 وَقُل رَّبِّ أَنزِلْنِي مُنزَلًا مُّبَارَكًا وَأَنتَ خَيْرُ الْمُنزِلِينَ ۝

And say, "My Lord! Land me with a blessed landing, for You are the best of those who bring ashore." '

30 إِنَّ فِي ذَٰلِكَ لَآيَاتٍ وَإِن كُنَّا لَمُبْتَلِينَ ۝

There are indeed signs in this; and indeed We have been testing.

31 ثُمَّ أَنشَأْنَا مِن بَعْدِهِمْ قَرْنًا آخَرِينَ ۝

Then after them We brought forth another generation,

32 فَأَرْسَلْنَا فِيهِمْ رَسُولًا مِّنْهُمْ أَنِ اعْبُدُوا اللَّهَ مَا لَكُم مِّنْ إِلَٰهٍ غَيْرُهُ ۚ أَفَلَا تَتَّقُونَ ۝

and We sent them an apostle from among themselves, saying, 'Worship God! You have no other god besides Him. Will you not then be wary of Him?'

33 وَقَالَ الْمَلَأُ مِن قَوْمِهِ الَّذِينَ كَفَرُوا وَكَذَّبُوا بِلِقَاءِ الْآخِرَةِ وَأَتْرَفْنَاهُمْ فِي الْحَيَاةِ الدُّنْيَا مَا هَٰذَا إِلَّا بَشَرٌ مِّثْلُكُمْ يَأْكُلُ مِمَّا تَأْكُلُونَ مِنْهُ وَيَشْرَبُ مِمَّا تَشْرَبُونَ ۝

Said the elite of his people, who were faithless, and who denied the encounter of the Hereafter and whom We had given affluence in the life of the world: 'This is just a human being like yourselves: he eats what you eat, and drinks what you drink.

34 وَلَئِنْ أَطَعْتُم بَشَرًا مِّثْلَكُمْ إِنَّكُمْ إِذًا لَّخَاسِرُونَ ۝

If you obey a human being like yourselves, you will indeed be losers.

35 أَيَعِدُكُمْ أَنَّكُمْ إِذَا مِتُّمْ وَكُنتُمْ تُرَابًا وَعِظَامًا أَنَّكُم مُّخْرَجُونَ ۝ ۞

Does he promise you that when you have died and become bones and dust you will indeed be raised from the dead?

36 هَيْهَاتَ هَيْهَاتَ لِمَا تُوعَدُونَ ۝

Far-fetched, far-fetched is what you are promised!

37 إِنْ هِيَ إِلَّا حَيَاتُنَا الدُّنْيَا نَمُوتُ وَنَحْيَا وَمَا نَحْنُ بِمَبْعُوثِينَ ۝

There is nothing but the life of this world: we live and die, and we will not be resurrected.

38 إِنْ هُوَ إِلَّا رَجُلٌ افْتَرَىٰ عَلَى اللَّهِ كَذِبًا وَمَا نَحْنُ لَهُ بِمُؤْمِنِينَ ۝

He is just a man who has fabricated a lie against God, and we will not believe in him.'

39 قَالَ رَبِّ انصُرْنِي بِمَا كَذَّبُونِ ۝

He said, 'My Lord! Help me, for they impugn me.'

40 قَالَ عَمَّا قَلِيلٍ لَّيُصْبِحُنَّ نَادِمِينَ ۝

Said He, 'In a little while they will become regretful.'

41 فَأَخَذَتْهُمُ الصَّيْحَةُ بِالْحَقِّ

So the Cry seized them justly

فَجَعَلْنَاهُمْ غُثَاءً ۚ and We turned them into a scum.
فَبُعْدًا لِلْقَوْمِ الظَّالِمِينَ ۝ So away with the wrongdoing lot!

42 ثُمَّ أَنْشَأْنَا مِنْ بَعْدِهِمْ قُرُونًا آخَرِينَ ۝ Then after them We brought forth other generations.

43 مَا تَسْبِقُ مِنْ أُمَّةٍ أَجَلَهَا No nation can advance its time
وَمَا يَسْتَأْخِرُونَ ۝ nor can it defer it.

44 ثُمَّ أَرْسَلْنَا رُسُلَنَا تَتْرَىٰ ۖ Then We sent Our apostles successively.
كُلَّ مَا جَاءَ أُمَّةً رَسُولُهَا Whenever there came to a nation its apostle,
كَذَّبُوهُ ۚ they impugned him,
فَأَتْبَعْنَا بَعْضَهُمْ بَعْضًا so We made them follow one another to extinction
وَجَعَلْنَاهُمْ أَحَادِيثَ ۚ and We turned them into folktales.
فَبُعْدًا لِقَوْمٍ لَا يُؤْمِنُونَ ۝ So away with the faithless lot!

45 ثُمَّ أَرْسَلْنَا مُوسَىٰ وَأَخَاهُ هَارُونَ Then We sent Moses and Aaron, his brother,
بِآيَاتِنَا وَسُلْطَانٍ مُبِينٍ ۝ with Our signs and a manifest authority,

46 إِلَىٰ فِرْعَوْنَ وَمَلَئِهِ to Pharaoh and his elites;
فَاسْتَكْبَرُوا وَكَانُوا قَوْمًا عَالِينَ ۝ but they acted arrogantly and they were a tyrannical lot.

47 فَقَالُوا أَنُؤْمِنُ لِبَشَرَيْنِ مِثْلِنَا They said, 'Shall we believe two humans like ourselves,
وَقَوْمُهُمَا لَنَا عَابِدُونَ ۝ while their people are our slaves?'

48 فَكَذَّبُوهُمَا So they impugned the two of them,
فَكَانُوا مِنَ الْمُهْلَكِينَ ۝ whereat they were among those who were destroyed.

49 وَلَقَدْ آتَيْنَا مُوسَى الْكِتَابَ Certainly We gave Moses the Book
لَعَلَّهُمْ يَهْتَدُونَ ۝ so that they might be guided,

50 وَجَعَلْنَا ابْنَ مَرْيَمَ وَأُمَّهُ آيَةً and We made the son of Mary and his mother a sign
وَآوَيْنَاهُمَا إِلَىٰ رَبْوَةٍ and sheltered them in a level highland
ذَاتِ قَرَارٍ وَمَعِينٍ ۝ with flowing water.

51 يَا أَيُّهَا الرُّسُلُ كُلُوا مِنَ الطَّيِّبَاتِ O apostles! Eat of the good things
وَاعْمَلُوا صَالِحًا ۖ and act righteously.
إِنِّي بِمَا تَعْمَلُونَ عَلِيمٌ ۝ I indeed know well what you do.

52 وَإِنَّ هَٰذِهِ أُمَّتُكُمْ أُمَّةً وَاحِدَةً This community of yours is indeed one community
وَأَنَا رَبُّكُمْ فَاتَّقُونِ ۝ and I am your Lord, so be wary of Me.

53 فَتَقَطَّعُوا أَمْرَهُمْ بَيْنَهُمْ زُبُرًا ۖ But they fragmented their religion among themselves,

each party rejoicing in what it had.

54 So *leave* them in their stupor for a while.

55 Do they suppose that whatever aid We provide them
in regard to wealth and children is because

56 We are eager to bring them good?
No, they are not aware!

57 Indeed, those who are
apprehensive for the fear of their Lord,

58 and who believe in the signs of their Lord,

59 and who do not ascribe partners to their Lord;

60 and who give whatever they give
while their hearts tremble with awe
that they are going to return to their Lord

61 —it is they who are zealous in performing good works,
and take the lead in them.

62 We task no soul except according to its capacity,
and with Us is a book that speaks the truth,
and they will not be wronged.

63 Their hearts are indeed in a stupor in regard to this,
and there are other deeds besides,
which they perpetrate.

64 When We seize their affluent ones with punishment,
behold, they make entreaties to Us.

65 'Do not make entreaties today!
Indeed, you will not receive any help from Us.

66 Certainly My signs used to be recited to you,
but you used to take to your heels,

67 being disdainful of it,[1]
talking nonsense in your nightly sessions.'

---

[1] That is, the Qurʾān. Or, 'him,' that is of the Prophet.

68 Have they not contemplated this discourse,[1] أَفَلَمْ يَدَّبَّرُوا الْقَوْلَ
or has anything come to them in it أَمْ جَاءَهُم
that did not come to their forefathers? مَا لَمْ يَأْتِ آبَاءَهُمُ الْأَوَّلِينَ ۝

69 Is it that they do not recognize their apostle,[2] أَمْ لَمْ يَعْرِفُوا رَسُولَهُمْ
and so they deny him?[3] فَهُمْ لَهُ مُنْكِرُونَ ۝

70 Do they say, 'There is madness in him'? أَمْ يَقُولُونَ بِهِ جِنَّةٌ
No, he has brought them the truth, بَلْ جَاءَهُم بِالْحَقِّ
and most of them are averse to the truth. وَأَكْثَرُهُمْ لِلْحَقِّ كَارِهُونَ ۝

71 Had the truth followed their base desires, وَلَوِ اتَّبَعَ الْحَقُّ أَهْوَاءَهُمْ
the heavens and the earth would have surely fallen apart لَفَسَدَتِ السَّمَاوَاتُ وَالْأَرْضُ
along with those who are in them. وَمَن فِيهِنَّ
We have indeed brought them their reminder, بَلْ أَتَيْنَاهُم بِذِكْرِهِمْ
but they are disregardful of their reminder. فَهُمْ عَن ذِكْرِهِم مُّعْرِضُونَ ۝

72 Do you ask a recompense from them? أَمْ تَسْأَلُهُمْ خَرْجًا
Yet your Lord's recompense is better فَخَرَاجُ رَبِّكَ خَيْرٌ
and He is the best of providers. وَهُوَ خَيْرُ الرَّازِقِينَ ۝

73 You indeed invite them to a straight path, وَإِنَّكَ لَتَدْعُوهُمْ إِلَىٰ صِرَاطٍ مُّسْتَقِيمٍ ۝

74 and those who do not believe in the Hereafter وَإِنَّ الَّذِينَ لَا يُؤْمِنُونَ بِالْآخِرَةِ
surely deviate from the path. عَنِ الصِّرَاطِ لَنَاكِبُونَ ۝

75 Should We have mercy upon them وَلَوْ رَحِمْنَاهُمْ
and remove their distress, وَكَشَفْنَا مَا بِهِم مِّن ضُرٍّ
they would surely persist, bewildered in their rebellion. لَلَجُّوا فِي طُغْيَانِهِمْ يَعْمَهُونَ ۝

76 We have already seized them with punishment, وَلَقَدْ أَخَذْنَاهُم بِالْعَذَابِ
yet they did not humble themselves before their Lord, فَمَا اسْتَكَانُوا لِرَبِّهِمْ
nor will they entreat Him for mercy, وَمَا يَتَضَرَّعُونَ ۝

77 until We open on them the gate حَتَّىٰ إِذَا فَتَحْنَا عَلَيْهِم بَابًا
of a severe punishment, ذَا عَذَابٍ شَدِيدٍ
whereupon they will be despondent in it. إِذَا هُمْ فِيهِ مُبْلِسُونَ ۝

---

[1] That is, the Qur'ān. Cf. **4:82, 47:24**.
[2] That is, 'Is the Apostle a stranger of an unknown background and a person unknown to them?'
[3] Or 'and so they are not at home with him.'

78 وَهُوَ الَّذِى أَنشَأَ لَكُمُ السَّمْعَ وَالْأَبْصَارَ وَالْأَفْئِدَةَ ۚ قَلِيلًا مَا تَشْكُرُونَ ۝

78 It is He who has created for you your hearing, sight and hearts. Little do you thank.

79 وَهُوَ الَّذِى ذَرَأَكُمْ فِى الْأَرْضِ وَإِلَيْهِ تُحْشَرُونَ ۝

79 It is He who created you on the earth, and you will be gathered toward Him.

80 وَهُوَ الَّذِى يُحْيِى وَيُمِيتُ وَلَهُ اخْتِلَافُ اللَّيْلِ وَالنَّهَارِ ۚ أَفَلَا تَعْقِلُونَ ۝

80 And it is He who gives life and brings death and due to Him is the alternation of day and night. Do you not exercise your reason?

81 بَلْ قَالُوا مِثْلَ مَا قَالَ الْأَوَّلُونَ ۝

81 Indeed, they say just like what the former peoples said.

82 قَالُوا أَإِذَا مِتْنَا وَكُنَّا تُرَابًا وَعِظَامًا أَإِنَّا لَمَبْعُوثُونَ ۝

82 They said, 'What, when we are dead and become dust and bones, shall we be resurrected?'

83 لَقَدْ وُعِدْنَا نَحْنُ وَآبَاؤُنَا هَٰذَا مِنْ قَبْلُ إِنْ هَٰذَا إِلَّا أَسَاطِيرُ الْأَوَّلِينَ ۝

83 'Certainly we and our fathers were promised this before. But these are nothing but myths of the ancients.'

84 قُلْ لِمَنِ الْأَرْضُ وَمَنْ فِيهَا إِنْ كُنْتُمْ تَعْلَمُونَ ۝

84 Say, 'To whom does the earth belong and whoever it contains, if you know?'

85 سَيَقُولُونَ لِلَّهِ ۚ قُلْ أَفَلَا تَذَكَّرُونَ ۝

85 They will say, 'To God.' Say, 'Will you not then take admonition?'

86 قُلْ مَنْ رَبُّ السَّمَاوَاتِ السَّبْعِ وَرَبُّ الْعَرْشِ الْعَظِيمِ ۝

86 Say, 'Who is the Lord of the seven heavens and the Lord of the Great Throne?'

87 سَيَقُولُونَ لِلَّهِ ۚ قُلْ أَفَلَا تَتَّقُونَ ۝

87 They will say, 'They belong to God.' Say, 'Will you not then be wary of Him?'

88 قُلْ مَنْ بِيَدِهِ مَلَكُوتُ كُلِّ شَىْءٍ وَهُوَ يُجِيرُ وَلَا يُجَارُ عَلَيْهِ إِنْ كُنْتُمْ تَعْلَمُونَ ۝

88 Say, 'In whose hand is the dominion of all things, and who gives shelter and no shelter can be provided from Him, if you know?'

89 سَيَقُولُونَ لِلَّهِ ۚ قُلْ فَأَنَّىٰ تُسْحَرُونَ ۝

89 They will say, 'They all belong to God.' Say, 'Then how are you being deluded?'[1]

---

[1] Or 'How are you being misled,' or 'How are you being rendered blind.'

90 We have indeed brought them the truth, بَلْ أَتَيْنَاهُم بِالْحَقِّ
    and they are surely liars. وَإِنَّهُمْ لَكَاذِبُونَ ۝

91 God has not taken any offspring, مَا اتَّخَذَ اللَّهُ مِن وَلَدٍ
    neither is there any god besides Him, وَمَا كَانَ مَعَهُ مِنْ إِلَٰهٍ
    for then each god would take away what he created, إِذًا لَّذَهَبَ كُلُّ إِلَٰهٍ بِمَا خَلَقَ
    and some of them would surely rise up against others. وَلَعَلَا بَعْضُهُمْ عَلَىٰ بَعْضٍ
    Clear is God of what they allege! سُبْحَانَ اللَّهِ عَمَّا يَصِفُونَ ۝

92 The Knower of the sensible and the Unseen, عَالِمِ الْغَيْبِ وَالشَّهَادَةِ
    He is above having any partners that they ascribe to Him. فَتَعَالَىٰ عَمَّا يُشْرِكُونَ ۝

93 *Say, 'My Lord! If You should show me* قُل رَّبِّ إِمَّا تُرِيَنِّي
    what they are promised, مَا يُوعَدُونَ ۝

94 then, Lord, do not put me, among the wrongdoing lot.' رَبِّ فَلَا تَجْعَلْنِي فِي الْقَوْمِ الظَّالِمِينَ ۝

95 We are indeed able to show you what We promise them. وَإِنَّا عَلَىٰ أَن نُّرِيَكَ مَا نَعِدُهُمْ لَقَادِرُونَ ۝

96 *Repel* ill conduct with that which is the best. ادْفَعْ بِالَّتِي هِيَ أَحْسَنُ السَّيِّئَةَ
    We know best whatever they allege. نَحْنُ أَعْلَمُ بِمَا يَصِفُونَ ۝

97 *Say, 'My Lord! I seek Your protection* وَقُل رَّبِّ أَعُوذُ بِكَ
    from the promptings of devils; مِنْ هَمَزَاتِ الشَّيَاطِينِ ۝

98 and I seek Your protection, my Lord, وَأَعُوذُ بِكَ رَبِّ
    from their presence near me.' أَن يَحْضُرُونِ ۝

99 When death comes to one of them, حَتَّىٰ إِذَا جَاءَ أَحَدَهُمُ الْمَوْتُ
    he says, 'My Lord! Take me back, قَالَ رَبِّ ارْجِعُونِ ۝

100 so that I may act righteously in what I have left behind.' لَعَلِّي أَعْمَلُ صَالِحًا فِيمَا تَرَكْتُ
    'By no means! These are mere words that he says.' كَلَّا إِنَّهَا كَلِمَةٌ هُوَ قَائِلُهَا
    And before them is a barrier وَمِن وَرَائِهِم بَرْزَخٌ
    until the day they will be resurrected. إِلَىٰ يَوْمِ يُبْعَثُونَ ۝

101 When the Trumpet is blown, فَإِذَا نُفِخَ فِي الصُّورِ
    there will be no ties between them on that day, فَلَا أَنسَابَ بَيْنَهُمْ يَوْمَئِذٍ
    nor will they ask about each other.[1] وَلَا يَتَسَاءَلُونَ ۝

---

[1] Cf. 70:10.

102 Then those whose deeds weigh heavy in the scales
—it is they who are the felicitous.

103 As for those whose deeds weigh light in the scales,
—they will be the ones who have ruined their souls,
and they will remain in hell.

104 The Fire will scorch their faces,
while they snarl, baring their teeth.

105 'Was it not that My signs were recited to you
but you would deny them?'

106 They will say, 'Our Lord! Our wretchedness overcame us,
and we were an astray lot.

107 Our Lord! Bring us out of this!
Then, if we revert, we will indeed be wrongdoers.'

108 He will say, 'Get lost in it, and do not speak to Me!

109 Indeed, there was a part of My servants
who would say, "Our Lord! We have believed.
So forgive us and have mercy on us,
and You are the best of the merciful."

110 But you took them by ridicule
until they made you forget My remembrance,[1]
and you used to laugh at them.

111 Indeed, I have rewarded them today for their patience.
They are indeed the triumphant.'

112 He will say,
'How many years did you remain on earth?'

113 They will say, 'We remained for a day, or part of a day;
yet ask those who keep the count.'

114 He will say, 'You only remained a little;
if only you had known.

---

[1] That is, 'your contemptuous attitude towards them made you oblivious of Me and My reminders and warnings.'

115 Did you suppose that We created you aimlessly,
and that you will not be brought back to Us?'

116 So exalted is God, the True Sovereign,
there is no god except Him,
the Lord of the Noble Throne.

117 Whoever invokes another god besides God
of which he has no proof,
his reckoning will indeed rest with his Lord.
The faithless will indeed not prosper.

118 Say, 'My Lord, forgive and have mercy,
and You are the best of the merciful.'

24. THE LIGHT[1]
al-Nūr

In the Name of God,
the All-beneficent, the All-merciful.

1 This is a *sūrah* which We have sent down and prescribed,
and We have sent down in it manifest signs
so that you may take admonition.

2 As for the fornicatress and the fornicator,
strike each of them a hundred lashes,
and let not pity for them overcome you in God's law,
if you believe in God and the Last Day,
and let their punishment be witnessed
by a group of the faithful.

3 The fornicator will not marry
anyone but a fornicatress or an idolatress,
and the fornicatress will be married by none
except a fornicator or an idolater,

---

[1] A Madanī *sūrah*, it is named after the 'Light Verse' (*nūr*=light) at **24:35**.

وَحَرَّمَ ذَٰلِكَ عَلَى الْمُؤْمِنِينَ ۩ and that is forbidden to the faithful.

4 وَالَّذِينَ يَرْمُونَ الْمُحْصَنَاتِ As for those who accuse chaste women
ثُمَّ لَمْ يَأْتُوا بِأَرْبَعَةِ شُهَدَاءَ   and do not bring four witnesses,
فَاجْلِدُوهُمْ ثَمَانِينَ جَلْدَةً   strike them eighty lashes,
وَلَا تَقْبَلُوا لَهُمْ شَهَادَةً أَبَدًا   and never accept any testimony from them after that,
وَأُولَٰئِكَ هُمُ الْفَاسِقُونَ ۩   and they are transgressors,

5 إِلَّا الَّذِينَ تَابُوا مِنْ بَعْدِ ذَٰلِكَ وَأَصْلَحُوا   excepting those who repent after that and reform,
فَإِنَّ اللَّهَ غَفُورٌ رَحِيمٌ ۩   for God is indeed all-forgiving, all-merciful.

6 وَالَّذِينَ يَرْمُونَ أَزْوَاجَهُمْ   As for those who accuse their wives [of adultery],
وَلَمْ يَكُنْ لَهُمْ شُهَدَاءُ إِلَّا أَنْفُسُهُمْ   but have no witnesses except themselves,
فَشَهَادَةُ أَحَدِهِمْ   the testimony of such a man
أَرْبَعُ شَهَادَاتٍ بِاللَّهِ   shall be a fourfold testimony sworn by God
إِنَّهُ لَمِنَ الصَّادِقِينَ ۩   that he is indeed stating the truth

7 وَالْخَامِسَةُ أَنَّ لَعْنَتَ اللَّهِ عَلَيْهِ   and a fifth oath that God's wrath shall be upon him
إِنْ كَانَ مِنَ الْكَاذِبِينَ ۩   if he were lying.

8 وَيَدْرَأُ عَنْهَا الْعَذَابَ   The punishment shall be averted from her
أَنْ تَشْهَدَ أَرْبَعَ شَهَادَاتٍ بِاللَّهِ   by her testifying with four oaths sworn by God
إِنَّهُ لَمِنَ الْكَاذِبِينَ ۩   that he is indeed lying,

9 وَالْخَامِسَةَ أَنَّ غَضَبَ اللَّهِ عَلَيْهَا   and a fifth oath that God's wrath shall be upon her
إِنْ كَانَ مِنَ الصَّادِقِينَ ۩   if he were stating the truth.

10 وَلَوْلَا فَضْلُ اللَّهِ عَلَيْكُمْ وَرَحْمَتُهُ   Were it not for God's grace and His mercy upon you,
وَأَنَّ اللَّهَ تَوَّابٌ حَكِيمٌ ۩   and that God is all-clement, all-wise.... [1]

11 إِنَّ الَّذِينَ جَاءُوا بِالْإِفْكِ   Indeed, those who initiated the calumny
عُصْبَةٌ مِنْكُمْ   are a group from among yourselves.
لَا تَحْسَبُوهُ شَرًّا لَكُمْ   Do not suppose it is a bad thing for you.
بَلْ هُوَ خَيْرٌ لَكُمْ   No, it is for your good.
لِكُلِّ امْرِئٍ مِنْهُمْ   Each man among them bears the onus for
مَا اكْتَسَبَ مِنَ الْإِثْمِ   his part in the sin,

---

[1] Ellipsis. For the omitted part of the sentence see verses 14 & 21 below.

وَالَّذِى تَوَلَّىٰ كِبْرَهُ and as for him who assumed its major burden
مِنْهُمْ from among them
لَهُ عَذَابٌ عَظِيمٌ ۝ there is a great punishment for him.

لَوْلَا إِذْ سَمِعْتُمُوهُ 12 When you first heard about it, why did not
ظَنَّ الْمُؤْمِنُونَ وَالْمُؤْمِنَاتُ بِأَنْفُسِهِمْ خَيْرًا the faithful, men and women, think well of their folks,
وَقَالُوا هَٰذَا إِفْكٌ مُبِينٌ ۝ and say, 'This is an obvious calumny'?

لَوْلَا جَاءُوا عَلَيْهِ بِأَرْبَعَةِ شُهَدَاءَ 13 Why did they[1] not bring four witnesses to it?
فَإِذْ لَمْ يَأْتُوا بِالشُّهَدَاءِ So when they could not bring the witnesses,
فَأُولَٰئِكَ عِنْدَ اللَّهِ هُمُ الْكَاذِبُونَ ۝ they are liars in God's sight.

وَلَوْلَا فَضْلُ اللَّهِ عَلَيْكُمْ وَرَحْمَتُهُ 14 Were it not for God's grace and His mercy upon you
فِي الدُّنْيَا وَالْآخِرَةِ in this world and the Hereafter,
لَمَسَّكُمْ there would have befallen you
فِي مَا أَفَضْتُمْ فِيهِ عَذَابٌ عَظِيمٌ ۝ a great punishment for what you ventured into,

إِذْ تَلَقَّوْنَهُ بِأَلْسِنَتِكُمْ 15 when you were receiving it on your tongues
وَتَقُولُونَ بِأَفْوَاهِكُمْ and were mouthing
مَا لَيْسَ لَكُمْ بِهِ عِلْمٌ something of which you had no knowledge,
وَتَحْسَبُونَهُ هَيِّنًا supposing it to be a light matter,
وَهُوَ عِنْدَ اللَّهِ عَظِيمٌ ۝ while it was a grave matter with God.

وَلَوْلَا إِذْ سَمِعْتُمُوهُ قُلْتُمْ 16 And why did you not, when you heard it, say,
مَا يَكُونُ لَنَا أَنْ نَتَكَلَّمَ بِهَٰذَا 'It is not for us to say such a thing.
سُبْحَانَكَ O God! You are immaculate!
هَٰذَا بُهْتَانٌ عَظِيمٌ ۝ This is a monstrous calumny!'

يَعِظُكُمُ اللَّهُ 17 God advises you
أَنْ تَعُودُوا لِمِثْلِهِ أَبَدًا lest you should ever repeat the like of it,
إِنْ كُنْتُمْ مُؤْمِنِينَ ۝ if you are faithful.

وَيُبَيِّنُ اللَّهُ لَكُمُ الْآيَاتِ 18 God clarifies the signs for you,
وَاللَّهُ عَلِيمٌ حَكِيمٌ ۝ and God is all-knowing, all-wise.

إِنَّ الَّذِينَ يُحِبُّونَ أَنْ تَشِيعَ الْفَاحِشَةُ 19 Indeed, those who want indecency to spread
فِي الَّذِينَ آمَنُوا among the faithful

---

[1] That is, those who had spread the slander accusing the Prophet's wife and one of the Companions.

—there is a painful punishment for them
in the world and the Hereafter,
and God knows and you do not know.

20 Were it not for God's grace and His mercy upon you
and that God is all-kind, all-merciful...

21 O you who have faith!
Do not follow in Satan's steps.
Whoever follows in Satan's steps [should know that]
he indeed prompts you to indecent and wrongful acts.
Were it not for God's grace and His mercy upon you,
not one of you would ever become pure.
But God purifies whomever He wishes,
and God is all-hearing, all-knowing.

22 The well-off and opulent among you should not vow[1]
that they will give no more to the relatives, the needy,
and those who have migrated in the way of God;
let them excuse and forbear.
Do you not love that God should forgive you?
God is all-forgiving, all-merciful.

23 Indeed, those who slander
chaste and unwary faithful women
shall be cursed in this world and the Hereafter,
and there shall be a great punishment for them

24 on the day when witness shall be given against them
by their tongues, their hands and their feet
concerning what they used to do.

25 On that day, God will pay them in full
their due recompense,

---

[1] Or 'Let the well-to-do and the opulent among you not fail to give....'

and they shall know that God is the Manifest Reality.

26 Vicious women are for vicious men,
    and vicious men for vicious women.
    Good women are for good men,
    and good men for good women.[1]
    These are absolved of what they say about them.[2]
    For them is forgiveness and a noble provision.

27 O you who have faith!
    Do not enter houses other than your own
      until you have announced [your arrival]
    and greeted their occupants.
    That is better for you.
    Maybe you will take admonition.

28 But if you do not find anyone in them,
    do not enter them until you are given permission.
    And if you are told: 'Turn back,' then do turn back.
    That will be more decent on your part.
    God knows best what you do.

29 There will be no sin upon you
    in entering [without announcing] uninhabited houses
      wherein you have goods belonging to you.
    God knows whatever you disclose
      and whatever you conceal.

30 *Tell* the faithful men to cast down their looks

---

[1] Or, 'Vicious words (or deeds) come from vicious persons, and vicious persons are worthy of vicious words (or deeds). Good words (or deeds) come from good people, and good people are worthy of good words (or deeds).' According to this interpretation, this verse is similar in meaning to 17:84. This interpretation is also supported by the last part of the verse: 'They are absolved of what they say about them].' However in accordance with the translation given above, the meaning of the verse will be similar to verse 24:3, at the beginning of this *sūrah*.

[2] That is, persons of good repute among the faithful stand legally absolved of any kind of allegations against them unless there is valid evidence to the contrary.

and to guard their private parts.
That is more decent for them.
God is indeed well aware of what they do.

31 And *tell* the faithful women to cast down their looks
and to guard their private parts,
and not to display their charms,
    beyond what is acceptably visible,
and let them draw their scarfs over their bosoms,
and not display their charms except to their husbands,
   or their fathers, or their husband's fathers,
   or their sons, or their husband's sons,
   or their brothers, or their brothers' sons,
   or their sisters' sons, or their women,[1]
   or their slave girls,
    or male dependents lacking [sexual] desire,
    or children uninitiated
    to women's intimate parts.[2]
And let them not thump their feet
   to make known their hidden ornaments.
Rally to God in repentance, O faithful,
   so that you may be felicitous.

32 Marry off those who are single among you,
   and the upright[3] among your male and female slaves.
   If they are poor,
   God will enrich them out of His bounty,
   and God is all-bounteous, all-knowing.

33 Those who cannot afford marriage should be continent

---

[1] That is, Muslim women. Hence it is not lawful for Muslim women to expose their charms before non-Muslim women, who may possibly describe what they see to their men.
[2] That is, boys who have not reached the age of virility.
[3] That is, those who are faithful, or honest and chaste.

until God enriches them out of His bounty.
As for those who seek an emancipation deal
    from among your slaves,
make such a deal with them
    if you know any good in them,
    and give them out of the wealth of God
    which He has given you.
Do not compel your female slaves to prostitution
    when they desire to be chaste,
seeking the transitory wares of the life of this world.
Should anyone compel them,
    God will indeed be, following their compulsion,
    forgiving and merciful to them.
34 Certainly We have sent down to you manifest signs
    and a description of those who passed before you,
    and an advice for the Godwary.

35 God is the Light of the heavens and the earth.
The parable of His Light is a niche wherein is a lamp
    —the lamp is in a glass,
    the glass as it were a glittering star—
    lit from a blessed olive tree,
        neither eastern nor western,
whose oil almost lights up,
    though fire should not touch it.
    Light upon light.
God guides to His Light whomever He wishes.
God draws parables for mankind,
    and God has knowledge of all things.
36 In houses God has allowed to be raised

وَيُذْكَرَ فِيهَا اسْمُهُ   and wherein His Name is celebrated,
يُسَبِّحُ لَهُ فِيهَا بِالْغُدُوِّ وَالْآصَالِ ۞   He is glorified therein, morning and evening,
37 رِجَالٌ لَا تُلْهِيهِمْ تِجَارَةٌ وَلَا بَيْعٌ   37 by men whom neither trade nor bargaining distracts
عَنْ ذِكْرِ اللَّهِ   from the remembrance of God,
وَإِقَامِ الصَّلَاةِ   and the maintenance of prayer
وَإِيتَاءِ الزَّكَاةِ   and the giving of *zakāt*.
يَخَافُونَ يَوْمًا   They are fearful of a day
تَتَقَلَّبُ فِيهِ الْقُلُوبُ وَالْأَبْصَارُ ۞   wherein the hearts and the sights will be transformed,
38 لِيَجْزِيَهُمُ اللَّهُ   38 so that God may reward them
أَحْسَنَ مَا عَمِلُوا   by the best of what they have done,
وَيَزِيدَهُمْ مِنْ فَضْلِهِ   and enhance them out of His grace,
وَاللَّهُ يَرْزُقُ مَنْ يَشَاءُ   and God provides for whomever He wishes
بِغَيْرِ حِسَابٍ ۞   without any reckoning.
39 وَالَّذِينَ كَفَرُوا   39 As for the faithless,
أَعْمَالُهُمْ كَسَرَابٍ بِقِيعَةٍ   their works are like a mirage in a plain,
يَحْسَبُهُ الظَّمْآنُ مَاءً   which the thirsty man supposes to be water.
حَتَّى إِذَا جَاءَهُ لَمْ يَجِدْهُ شَيْئًا   When he comes to it, he finds it to be nothing;
وَوَجَدَ اللَّهَ عِنْدَهُ   but there he finds God,
فَوَفَّاهُ حِسَابَهُ   who will pay him his full account,
وَاللَّهُ سَرِيعُ الْحِسَابِ ۞   and God is swift at reckoning.
40 أَوْ كَظُلُمَاتٍ فِي بَحْرٍ لُجِّيٍّ   40 Or like the manifold darkness in a deep sea,
يَغْشَاهُ مَوْجٌ مِنْ فَوْقِهِ مَوْجٌ   covered by billow upon billow,
مِنْ فَوْقِهِ سَحَابٌ   overcast by clouds;
ظُلُمَاتٌ بَعْضُهَا فَوْقَ بَعْضٍ   manifold layers of darkness, one on top of another:
إِذَا أَخْرَجَ يَدَهُ لَمْ يَكَدْ يَرَاهَا   when he brings out his hand, he can hardly see it.
وَمَنْ لَمْ يَجْعَلِ اللَّهُ لَهُ نُورًا   One whom God has not granted any light
فَمَا لَهُ مِنْ نُورٍ ۞   has no light.
41 أَلَمْ تَرَ أَنَّ   41 Have you not regarded that
اللَّهَ يُسَبِّحُ لَهُ مَنْ فِي السَّمَاوَاتِ   God is glorified by everyone in the heavens
وَالْأَرْضِ   and the earth,

and the birds spreading their wings.
Each knows his prayer and glorification,
and God knows best what they do.

46 To God belongs the kingdom of the heavens
and the earth,
and toward God is the destination.

43 Have you not regarded that God drives the clouds,
then He composes them, then He piles them up,
whereat you see the rain issuing from their midst?
And He sends down from the sky
hail, out of the mountains[1] that are in it,
and He strikes with it whomever He wishes
and turns it away from whomever He wishes.
The brilliance of its flashes almost takes away the sight.

44 God alternates the night and the day.
There is indeed a lesson in that for those who have insight.

45 God created every animal from water.
Among them are some that creep upon their bellies,
and among them are some that walk on two feet,
and among them are some that walk on four.
God creates whatever He wishes.
Indeed, God has power over all things.

46 Certainly We have sent down illuminating signs,
and God guides whomever He wishes
to a straight path.

47 They say, 'We have faith in God and His Apostle
and we obey.'
Then after that a part of them turn away,

---

[1] A metaphorical reference to the clouds.

and they do not have faith.

48 When they are summoned to God and His Apostle
that He may judge between them,
behold, a part of them turn aside.

49 But if justice be on their side,
they come compliantly to him.

50 Is there a sickness in their hearts?
Do they have doubts or fear
that God and His Apostle will be unjust to them?
Rather, it is they who are the wrongdoers.

51 All the response of the faithful,
when they are summoned to God and His Apostle
that He may judge between them,
is to say, 'We hear and obey.'
It is they who will be felicitous.

52 Whoever obeys God and His Apostle
and fears God and is wary of Him
—it is they who will be triumphant.

53 They swear by God with solemn oaths
that if *you* order them they will surely march out.
Say, 'Do not swear!
Honourable obedience [is all that is expected of you].
God is indeed well aware of what you do.'

54 Say, 'Obey God and obey the Apostle.'
But if you turn your backs, [you should know that]
he is only responsible for *his* burden
and you are responsible for your own burden,
and if you obey *him*, you will be guided,
and the Apostle's duty is only
to communicate in clear terms.

55 God has promised those of you who have faith
       and do righteous deeds
    that He will surely make them successors in the earth,
    just as He made those who were before them successors,
       and He will surely establish for them
          their religion which He has approved for them,
       and that He will surely change their state
          to security, after their fear,
    while they worship Me, not ascribing any partners to Me.
    Whoever is ungrateful after that
       —it is they who are the transgressors.

56 Maintain the prayer and give the *zakāt*,
       and obey the Apostle
       so that you may receive God's mercy.

57 Do not suppose that those who are faithless
       can frustrate God on the earth.
    Their refuge shall be the Fire,
       and it is surely an evil destination.

58 O you who have faith!
    Let your permission be sought by your slaves
       and those of you who have not yet reached puberty
          at three times:
       before the dawn prayer,
       and when you put off your garments at noon,
       and after the night prayer.
    These are three times of privacy for you.
    Apart from these, it is not sinful of you or them
       to frequent one another freely.
    Thus does God clarify the signs for you,

and God is all-knowing, all-wise.

59 When your children reach puberty,
let them ask for permission [at all times], just as those
[who matured] before them asked for permission.
Thus does God clarify His signs for you,
and God is all-knowing, all-wise.

60 As for women advanced in years
who do not expect to marry,
there will be no sin upon them
if they put off their cloaks,
without displaying their adornment.
But it is better for them to be modest,
and God is all-hearing, all-knowing.

61 There is no blame upon the blind,
nor any blame upon the lame,
nor any blame upon the sick,
nor upon yourselves
if you eat from your own houses,
or your fathers' houses, or your mothers' houses,
or your brothers' houses, or your sisters' houses,
or the houses of your paternal uncles,
or the houses of your paternal aunts,
or the houses of your maternal uncles,
or the houses of your maternal aunts,
or those whose keys are in your possession,
or those of your friends.
There will be no blame on you
whether you eat together or separately.
So when you enter houses, greet yourselves[1]

---

[1] Or 'greet your folks.'

تَحِيَّةً مِنْ عِندِ اللَّهِ مُبَارَكَةً طَيِّبَةً ۚ with a salutation from God, blessed and good.
كَذَٰلِكَ يُبَيِّنُ اللَّهُ لَكُمُ الْآيَاتِ Thus does God clarify His signs for you
لَعَلَّكُمْ تَعْقِلُونَ ۝ so that you may exercise your reason.

إِنَّمَا الْمُؤْمِنُونَ 62 Indeed, the faithful are
الَّذِينَ آمَنُوا بِاللَّهِ وَرَسُولِهِ those who have faith in God and His Apostle,
وَإِذَا كَانُوا مَعَهُ عَلَىٰ أَمْرٍ جَامِعٍ and when they are with him in a collective undertaking,
لَّمْ يَذْهَبُوا حَتَّىٰ يَسْتَأْذِنُوهُ ۚ they do not leave until they have sought his permission.
إِنَّ الَّذِينَ يَسْتَأْذِنُونَكَ Indeed, those who seek *your* permission
أُولَٰئِكَ الَّذِينَ يُؤْمِنُونَ بِاللَّهِ are those who have faith in God
وَرَسُولِهِ ۚ and His Apostle.
فَإِذَا اسْتَأْذَنُوكَ So when they seek *your* permission
لِبَعْضِ شَأْنِهِمْ for some of their [private] work,
فَأْذَن لِّمَن شِئْتَ مِنْهُمْ give permission to whomever of them *you* wish
وَاسْتَغْفِرْ لَهُمُ اللَّهَ ۚ and *plead* with God to forgive them.
إِنَّ اللَّهَ غَفُورٌ رَّحِيمٌ ۝ God is indeed all-forgiving, all-merciful.

لَّا تَجْعَلُوا دُعَاءَ الرَّسُولِ بَيْنَكُمْ 63 Do not consider the Apostle's summons amongst you
كَدُعَاءِ بَعْضِكُم بَعْضًا ۚ to be like your summoning one another.
قَدْ يَعْلَمُ اللَّهُ الَّذِينَ God certainly knows those of you who slip away
يَتَسَلَّلُونَ مِنكُمْ لِوَاذًا ۚ shielding one another from being noticed.
فَلْيَحْذَرِ الَّذِينَ يُخَالِفُونَ عَنْ أَمْرِهِ Those who disobey his orders should beware
أَن تُصِيبَهُمْ فِتْنَةٌ lest an affliction should visit them
أَوْ يُصِيبَهُمْ عَذَابٌ أَلِيمٌ ۝ or a painful punishment should befall them.

أَلَا 64 Behold!
إِنَّ لِلَّهِ مَا فِي السَّمَاوَاتِ To God indeed belongs whatever is in the heavens
وَالْأَرْضِ ۖ and the earth.
قَدْ يَعْلَمُ مَا أَنتُمْ عَلَيْهِ He certainly knows your state of affairs,
وَيَوْمَ يُرْجَعُونَ إِلَيْهِ and the day they are brought back to Him,
فَيُنَبِّئُهُم بِمَا عَمِلُوا ۗ He will inform them about what they have done,
وَاللَّهُ بِكُلِّ شَيْءٍ عَلِيمٌ ۝ and God has knowledge of all things.

25. The Criterion[1]
al-Furqān

In the Name of God,
the All-beneficent, the All-merciful.

1 Blessed is He who sent down the Criterion to His servant that he may be a warner to all the nations.

2 He, to whom belongs the sovereignty of the heavens and the earth, and who did not take up any offspring, nor has He any partner in sovereignty, and He created everything and determined it in a precise measure.

3 Yet they have taken gods besides Him who create nothing and have themselves been created, and who have no control over their own harm or benefit and have neither any control over their own death, nor life, nor resurrection.

4 The faithless say, 'This is nothing but a lie that he has fabricated and other people have abetted him in it.' Thus they have certainly come out with wrongdoing and falsehood.

5 They say, 'He has taken down myths of the ancients and they are dictated to him morning and evening.'

6 Say, 'It has been sent down by Him who knows the hidden in the heavens and the earth. He is indeed all-forgiving, all-merciful.'

---

[1] This Makkī *sūrah* takes its name from verse 1, which refers to the Qur'ān as '*al-Furqān*' (lit. 'the Distinguisher,' or 'the Separator,' i.e. a criterion for distinguishing between truth and falsehood).

7 And they say, 'What sort of apostle is this
  who eats food and walks in the marketplaces?
  Why has not an angel been sent down to him
  so as to be a warner along with him?'

8 Or, 'Why is not a treasure thrown to him,
  or why does he not have a garden from which he may eat?'
  And the wrongdoers say,
  'You are just following a bewitched man.'

9 *Look*, how they coin epithets for *you*;
  so they go astray and cannot find the way.

10 Blessed is He,
  who will grant *you* better than that if He wishes
  —gardens with streams running in them,
  and He will make for *you* palaces.

11 Indeed, they deny the Hour,
  and We have prepared
  a Blaze for those who deny the Hour.

12 When it[1] sights them from a distant place,
  they will hear it raging and roaring.

13 And when they are cast into a narrow place in it,
  bound together in chains,
  they will pray for their own annihilation.[2]

14 [They will be told:] 'Do not pray
  for a single annihilation today,
  but pray for many annihilations!'

15 *Say*, 'Is that better,
  or the everlasting paradise promised to the Godwary,
  which will be their reward and destination?'

16 There they will have whatever they wish, abiding therein,

---

[1] That is, hell.
[2] Cf. **43**:77; **78**:40.

a promise much besought, binding on your Lord.[1]

17 On the day that He will gather them
and those whom they worship besides God,
He will say,
'Was it you who led astray these servants of Mine,
or did they themselves stray from the way?'

18 They will say, 'Immaculate are You!
It does not behoove us
to take any master in Your stead!
But You provided for them and their fathers
until they forgot the Reminder,
and they were a ruined lot.'

19 So they will certainly impugn you in what you say,
and you will neither be able to circumvent punishment,
nor find help,
and whoever of you does wrong,
We shall make him taste a terrible punishment.

20 We did not send any apostles before you
but that they ate food
and walked in marketplaces.
We have made you a means of test for one another
to see if you will be patient and steadfast,
and your Lord is all-seeing.

[PART 19]

21 Those who do not expect to encounter Us say,
'Why have angels not been sent down to us,
or why do we not see our Lord?'
Certainly they are full of arrogance within their souls
and have become terribly defiant.

22 The day they will see the angels,

---

[1] Cf. 3:194: 'Our Lord, grant us what You have promised us through Your apostles.'

there will be no good news for the guilty on that day,
and they[1] will say, 'Keep off!'

23 Then We shall attend to the works they have done
and turn them into scattered dust.

24 On that day the inhabitants of paradise
will be in the best abode
and an excellent resting place.

25 The day when the sky with its clouds will be split open
and the angels will be sent down
in a majestic descent,

26 on that day, true sovereignty
will belong to the All-beneficent,
and it will be a hard day for the faithless.[2]

27 It will be a day when the wrongdoer will bite his hands,
saying,
'I wish I had followed the Apostle's way!

28 Woe to me!
I wish I had not taken so and so as a friend!

29 Certainly he led me astray from the Reminder
after it had come to me,
and Satan is a deserter of man.'

30 And the Apostle will say, 'O my Lord!
Indeed, my people
consigned this Qur'ān to oblivion.'

31 That is how for every prophet We assigned an enemy
from among the guilty,
and your Lord suffices as helper and guide.

---

[1] According to one interpretation, during pre-Islamic days, whenever during one of the holy months, in which warfare was prohibited by custom, an Arab felt threatened by someone belonging to a belligerent tribe, he would say, *Ḥijran mahjūrā*, thus telling the member of the hostile tribe to keep distance by appealing to the sanctity of the holy month. On this basis, it is the faithless who ask the angels to keep off and spare them of punishment.

[2] Cf. **74:9**.

32 The faithless say,
'Why has not the Qur'ān been sent down to him all at once?'
So it was, that We may strengthen *your* heart with it,
and We have recited it to *you* in a measured tone.

33 They do not bring *you* any representation
but that We bring *you* the truth [in reply to them]
and the best exposition.

34 Those who will be gathered, scrambling on their faces toward hell,
they are the worse situated and further astray from the way.

35 Certainly We gave Moses the Book
and We made Aaron, his brother, accompany him as minister.

36 Then We said, 'Let the two of you go
to the people who have impugned Our signs.'
Then We destroyed them utterly.

37 And Noah's people,
We drowned them when they impugned the apostles,
and We made them a sign for mankind,
and We have prepared for the wrongdoers
a painful punishment.

38 And 'Ād and Thamūd, and the people of Rass,
and many generations between them.

39 For each of them We drew examples,
and each We destroyed utterly.

40 Certainly they must have passed by
the town on which an evil shower was rained.
Have they not seen it?
Rather, they did not expect resurrection to happen.

41 When they see *you* they just take *you* in derision:

أَهَٰذَا الَّذِى بَعَثَ اللَّهُ رَسُولًا ۝	'Is this the one whom God has sent as an apostle!?
42 إِنْ كَادَ لَيُضِلُّنَا عَنْ آلِهَتِنَا	42 He was indeed about to lead us astray from our gods,
لَوْلَا أَنْ صَبَرْنَا عَلَيْهَا ۚ	had we not stood firm by them.'
وَسَوْفَ يَعْلَمُونَ حِينَ يَرَوْنَ الْعَذَابَ	Soon they will know, when they sight the punishment,
مَنْ أَضَلُّ سَبِيلًا ۝	who is further astray from the right way.
43 أَرَأَيْتَ مَنِ اتَّخَذَ	43 Have you seen him who has taken
إِلَٰهَهُ هَوَاهُ	his base desire to be his god?
أَفَأَنْتَ تَكُونُ عَلَيْهِ وَكِيلًا ۝	Is it your duty to watch over him?
44 أَمْ تَحْسَبُ	44 Do you suppose
أَنَّ أَكْثَرَهُمْ يَسْمَعُونَ أَوْ يَعْقِلُونَ ۚ	that most of them listen or exercise their reason?
إِنْ هُمْ إِلَّا كَالْأَنْعَامِ ۖ	They are just like cattle;
بَلْ هُمْ أَضَلُّ سَبِيلًا ۝	no, they are further astray from the way.
45 أَلَمْ تَرَ	45 Have you not regarded
إِلَىٰ رَبِّكَ كَيْفَ مَدَّ الظِّلَّ	how your Lord spreads the twilight?[1]
وَلَوْ شَاءَ لَجَعَلَهُ سَاكِنًا	(Had He wished He would have made it stand still.)
ثُمَّ جَعَلْنَا الشَّمْسَ عَلَيْهِ دَلِيلًا ۝	Then We made the sun a beacon for it.
46 ثُمَّ قَبَضْنَاهُ إِلَيْنَا	46 Then We retract it toward Ourselves,
قَبْضًا يَسِيرًا ۝	with a gentle retracting.
47 وَهُوَ الَّذِى جَعَلَ لَكُمُ اللَّيْلَ لِبَاسًا	47 It is He who made for you the night as a covering
وَالنَّوْمَ سُبَاتًا	and sleep for rest
وَجَعَلَ النَّهَارَ نُشُورًا ۝	and He made the day a recall to life.
48 وَهُوَ الَّذِى أَرْسَلَ الرِّيَاحَ	48 And it is He who sends the winds
بُشْرًا بَيْنَ يَدَىْ رَحْمَتِهِ ۚ	as harbingers of His mercy,
وَأَنْزَلْنَا مِنَ السَّمَاءِ مَاءً طَهُورًا ۝	and We send down from the sky purifying water,
49 لِنُحْيِىَ بِهِ بَلْدَةً مَيْتًا وَنُسْقِيَهُ	49 with which We revive a dead country and provide water to
مِمَّا خَلَقْنَا أَنْعَامًا وَأَنَاسِىَّ كَثِيرًا ۝	many of the cattle and humans We have created.
50 وَلَقَدْ صَرَّفْنَاهُ بَيْنَهُمْ	50 Certainly We distribute it among them
لِيَذَّكَّرُوا	so that they may take admonition.
فَأَبَىٰ أَكْثَرُ النَّاسِ إِلَّا كُفُورًا ۝	But most people are only bent on ingratitude.

---

[1] This is in accordance with a tradition of al-Imam al-Bāqir ('a) in which *ẓill* is explained as the twilight during the hours between daybreak and sunrise (see *Tafsīr al-Qummī*). Or 'extends the shadow.'

51 Had We wished,
We would have sent a warner to every town.

52 So *do not obey* the faithless,
but *wage* with it[1] a great *jihād* against them.

53 It is He who merged the two seas:
this one sweet and agreeable, and that one briny and bitter,
and between the two He set a barrier
and a forbidding hindrance.

54 It is He who created the human being from water,
then invested him with ties of blood and marriage,
and *your* Lord is all-powerful.

55 They worship besides God
that which neither brings them any benefit
nor causes them any harm,
and the faithless one is ever an abettor against his Lord.

56 We did not send you except as a bearer of good news
and warner.

57 Say, 'I do not ask you any reward for it,
except that anyone who wishes should take
the way leading to his Lord.'

58 Put *your* trust in the Living One, who does not die,
and *celebrate* His praise.
He suffices as one all-aware of the sins of His servants.

59 He, who created the heavens and the earth
and whatever is between them in six days,
and then settled on the Throne,
the All-beneficent;
so ask someone who is well aware about Him.[2]

---

[1] That is, with the help of the Qur'ān.
[2] Or, 'about it,' that is, about the creation of the heavens and the earth, or the meaning of the Throne.

60 When they are told:
 'Prostrate yourselves before the All-beneficent,'
 they say, 'What is "the All-beneficent"?
 Shall we prostrate ourselves before whatever you bid us?'
 And it increases their aversion.

وَإِذَا قِيلَ لَهُمُ
اسْجُدُوا لِلرَّحْمَٰنِ
قَالُوا وَمَا الرَّحْمَٰنُ
أَنَسْجُدُ لِمَا تَأْمُرُنَا
وَزَادَهُمْ نُفُورًا ۩

61 Blessed is He who appointed houses in the heavens
 and set in it a lamp and a shining moon.

تَبَارَكَ الَّذِي جَعَلَ فِي السَّمَاءِ بُرُوجًا
وَجَعَلَ فِيهَا سِرَاجًا وَقَمَرًا مُنِيرًا

62 It is He who made the night and the day alternate
 for someone who desires to take admonition,
 or desires to give thanks.

وَهُوَ الَّذِي جَعَلَ اللَّيْلَ وَالنَّهَارَ خِلْفَةً
لِمَنْ أَرَادَ أَنْ يَذَّكَّرَ
أَوْ أَرَادَ شُكُورًا

63 The servants of the All-beneficent are those who
 walk humbly on the earth,
 and, when the ignorant address them, say, 'Peace!'

وَعِبَادُ الرَّحْمَٰنِ الَّذِينَ
يَمْشُونَ عَلَى الْأَرْضِ هَوْنًا
وَإِذَا خَاطَبَهُمُ الْجَاهِلُونَ قَالُوا سَلَامًا

64 Those who spend the night for their Lord,
 prostrating and standing in worship.

وَالَّذِينَ يَبِيتُونَ لِرَبِّهِمْ
سُجَّدًا وَقِيَامًا

65 Those who say, 'Our Lord!
 Turn away from us the punishment of hell.
 Its punishment is indeed enduring.

وَالَّذِينَ يَقُولُونَ رَبَّنَا
اصْرِفْ عَنَّا عَذَابَ جَهَنَّمَ
إِنَّ عَذَابَهَا كَانَ غَرَامًا

66 It is indeed an evil station and abode.'

إِنَّهَا سَاءَتْ مُسْتَقَرًّا وَمُقَامًا

67 Those who, when spending,
 are neither wasteful nor tightfisted,
 but balanced between these two extremes.

وَالَّذِينَ إِذَا أَنْفَقُوا
لَمْ يُسْرِفُوا وَلَمْ يَقْتُرُوا
وَكَانَ بَيْنَ ذَٰلِكَ قَوَامًا

68 Those who do not invoke another deity besides God,
 and do not kill a soul whose life
  God has made inviolable, except with due cause,
 and do not commit fornication.
 (Whoever does that shall encounter its retribution,

69 the punishment being doubled for him

وَالَّذِينَ لَا يَدْعُونَ مَعَ اللَّهِ إِلَٰهًا آخَرَ
وَلَا يَقْتُلُونَ النَّفْسَ الَّتِي
حَرَّمَ اللَّهُ إِلَّا بِالْحَقِّ
وَلَا يَزْنُونَ
وَمَنْ يَفْعَلْ ذَٰلِكَ يَلْقَ أَثَامًا
يُضَاعَفْ لَهُ الْعَذَابُ

on the Day of Resurrection.
In it he will abide in humiliation forever,
70 except those who repent,
attain faith, and act righteously.
For such, God will replace their misdeeds
with good deeds,[1]
and God is all-forgiving, all-merciful.
71 And whoever repents and acts righteously
indeed turns to God with due penitence).
72 Those who do not give false testimony,[2]
and when they come upon frivolity,
pass by with dignity.
73 Those who, when reminded of the signs of their Lord,
do not turn a deaf ear and a blind eye to them.
74 And those who say, 'Our Lord!
Give us joy and comfort in our spouses and offspring,
and make us *imams* of the Godwary.'
75 Those shall be rewarded with sublime abodes
for their patience and steadfastness,
and they shall be met there with greetings and 'Peace,'
76 to abide in them,
an excellent station and abode.
77 Say, 'What store my Lord would set by you
were it not the sake of summoning you [to faith]?[3]
But you impugned me and my summons,
and it[4] will be inextricable from you.'

---

[1] Or 'their vices with virtues.'
[2] Or, 'those who do not take part in frivolities.' That is, those who do not attend music parties or take part in senseless and sinful gatherings and amusements. (See *Tafsīr al-Qummī*, *Manhaj al-Ṣādiqīn*)
[3] Or 'were it not for your supplications.'
[4] That is, the denial of the faithless, which will continue to haunt them; or its inextricable consequences (interpreted as an allusion to the punishment of the Quraysh, most of whose leaders were killed at Badr, ultimately as a consequence of impugning the Prophet (ṣ).

26. THE POETS[1]
al-Shuʿarāʾ

In the Name of God,
the All-beneficent, the All-merciful.

1 Ṭā, Sīn, Mīm.

2 These are the signs of the Manifest Book.

3 You are liable to imperil *your* life out of distress
that they will not have faith.

4 If We wish, We will send down to them
a sign from the heavens
before which their heads will remain bowed in humility.

5 There does not come to them
any new reminder from the All-beneficent
but that they disregard it.

6 They have already denied the truth,
but soon there will come to them the news
of what they have been deriding.

7 Have they not regarded the earth,
how many We have caused to grow in it
of every splendid kind of vegetation?

8 There is indeed a sign in that;
but most of them do not have faith.

9 Indeed, *your* Lord is the All-mighty, the All-merciful.

10 When *your* Lord called out to Moses:
saying, 'Go to those wrongdoing people,
11 the people of Pharaoh.
Will they not be wary of God?'

---

[1] This Makkī *sūrah* takes its name from verses 224-227 about 'the poets' (*shuʿarāʾ*).

قَالَ رَبِّ إِنِّي أَخَافُ أَن يُكَذِّبُونِ ۝	12 He said, 'My Lord! I fear they will impugn me,
وَيَضِيقُ صَدْرِي وَلَا يَنطَلِقُ لِسَانِي	13 and I will become upset, and my tongue will fail me.
فَأَرْسِلْ إِلَىٰ هَارُونَ ۝	So send for Aaron to join me.
وَلَهُمْ عَلَيَّ ذَنبٌ	14 Besides, they have a charge against me,
فَأَخَافُ أَن يَقْتُلُونِ ۝	and I fear they will kill me.'
قَالَ كَلَّا ۖ	15 He said, 'Certainly not!
فَاذْهَبَا بِآيَاتِنَا ۖ	Let both of you go with Our signs:
إِنَّا مَعَكُم مُّسْتَمِعُونَ ۝	We will indeed be with you, hearing everything.
فَأْتِيَا فِرْعَوْنَ فَقُولَا	16 So approach Pharaoh and say,
إِنَّا رَسُولُ رَبِّ الْعَالَمِينَ ۝	"We are indeed envoys of the Lord of all the worlds
أَنْ أَرْسِلْ مَعَنَا بَنِي إِسْرَائِيلَ ۝	17 that you let the Children of Israel leave with us."'
قَالَ أَلَمْ نُرَبِّكَ فِينَا وَلِيدًا	18 He said, 'Did we not rear you as a child among us,
وَلَبِثْتَ فِينَا مِنْ عُمُرِكَ سِنِينَ ۝	and did you not stay with us for years of your life?
وَفَعَلْتَ فَعْلَتَكَ الَّتِي فَعَلْتَ	19 Then you committed that deed of yours,
وَأَنتَ مِنَ الْكَافِرِينَ ۝	and you are an ingrate.'
قَالَ فَعَلْتُهَا إِذًا وَأَنَا مِنَ الضَّالِّينَ ۝	20 He said, 'I did that when I was astray.
فَفَرَرْتُ مِنكُمْ لَمَّا خِفْتُكُمْ	21 So I fled from you, as I was afraid of you.
فَوَهَبَ لِي رَبِّي حُكْمًا	Then my Lord gave me sound judgement
وَجَعَلَنِي مِنَ الْمُرْسَلِينَ ۝	and made me one of the apostles.
وَتِلْكَ نِعْمَةٌ تَمُنُّهَا عَلَيَّ	22 Is that a favour with which you reproach me
أَنْ عَبَّدتَّ بَنِي إِسْرَائِيلَ ۝	—that you have enslaved the Children of Israel?'
قَالَ فِرْعَوْنُ وَمَا رَبُّ الْعَالَمِينَ ۝	23 He said, 'And what is "the Lord of all the worlds?"'
قَالَ رَبُّ السَّمَاوَاتِ وَالْأَرْضِ	24 He said, 'The Lord of the heavens and the earth
وَمَا بَيْنَهُمَا ۖ	and whatever is between them
إِن كُنتُم مُّوقِنِينَ ۝	—should you have conviction.'
قَالَ لِمَنْ حَوْلَهُ	25 He said to those who were around him,
أَلَا تَسْتَمِعُونَ ۝	'Are you not listening?!'
قَالَ رَبُّكُمْ	26 He said, 'Your Lord
وَرَبُّ آبَائِكُمُ الْأَوَّلِينَ ۝	and the Lord of your forefathers!'
قَالَ إِنَّ رَسُولَكُمُ	27 He said, 'Indeed, your messenger,

الَّذِى أُرْسِلَ إِلَيْكُمْ لَمَجْنُونٌ ۝	who has been sent to you, is surely crazy!'
28 قَالَ رَبُّ الْمَشْرِقِ وَالْمَغْرِبِ	28 He said, 'The Lord of the east and the west
وَمَا بَيْنَهُمَا ۖ	and whatever is between them
إِن كُنتُمْ تَعْقِلُونَ ۝	—should you exercise your reason.'
29 قَالَ لَئِنِ اتَّخَذْتَ إِلَٰهًا غَيْرِى	29 He said, 'If you take up any god other than me,
لَأَجْعَلَنَّكَ مِنَ الْمَسْجُونِينَ ۝	I will surely make you a prisoner!'
30 قَالَ	30 He said,
أَوَلَوْ جِئْتُكَ بِشَىْءٍ مُّبِينٍ ۝	'What if I bring you something as an unmistakable proof?'
31 قَالَ فَأْتِ بِهِ	31 He said, 'Then bring it,
إِن كُنتَ مِنَ الصَّادِقِينَ ۝	if you are truthful.'
32 فَأَلْقَىٰ عَصَاهُ	32 Thereat he threw down his staff,
فَإِذَا هِىَ ثُعْبَانٌ مُّبِينٌ ۝	and behold, it was a manifest python.
33 وَنَزَعَ يَدَهُ	33 Then he drew out his hand,
فَإِذَا هِىَ بَيْضَاءُ لِلنَّاظِرِينَ ۝	and behold, it was bright to the onlookers.
34 قَالَ لِلْمَلَإِ حَوْلَهُ	34 He said to the elite who stood around him,
إِنَّ هَٰذَا لَسَاحِرٌ عَلِيمٌ ۝	'This is indeed an expert magician
35 يُرِيدُ أَن يُخْرِجَكُم مِّنْ أَرْضِكُم	35 who seeks to expel you from your land
بِسِحْرِهِ	with his magic.
فَمَاذَا تَأْمُرُونَ ۝	So what do you advise?'
36 قَالُوا أَرْجِهْ وَأَخَاهُ	36 They said, 'Put him and his brother off for a while,
وَابْعَثْ فِى الْمَدَائِنِ حَاشِرِينَ ۝	and send heralds to the cities
37 يَأْتُوكَ بِكُلِّ سَحَّارٍ عَلِيمٍ ۝	37 to bring you every expert magician.'
38 فَجُمِعَ السَّحَرَةُ	38 So the magicians were gathered
لِمِيقَاتِ يَوْمٍ مَّعْلُومٍ ۝	for the tryst of a known day,
39 وَقِيلَ لِلنَّاسِ هَلْ أَنتُم مُّجْتَمِعُونَ ۝	39 and the people were told: 'Will you all gather?!'
40 لَعَلَّنَا نَتَّبِعُ السَّحَرَةَ	40 'Maybe we will follow the magicians,
إِن كَانُوا هُمُ الْغَالِبِينَ ۝	if they are the victors!'
41 فَلَمَّا جَاءَ السَّحَرَةُ	41 So when the magicians came,
قَالُوا لِفِرْعَوْنَ	they said to Pharaoh,
أَئِنَّ لَنَا لَأَجْرًا إِن كُنَّا نَحْنُ الْغَالِبِينَ ۝	'Shall we have a reward if we were to be the victors?'

42 He said, 'Of course,
and you will be among members of my inner circle.'

43 Moses said to them,
'Throw down whatever you have to throw!'

44 So they threw down their sticks and ropes,
and said, 'By the might of Pharaoh,
we shall surely be victorious!'

45 Thereat Moses threw down his staff,
and behold, it was swallowing what they had faked.

46 Thereat the magicians fell down prostrating.

47 They said, 'We believe in the Lord of all the worlds,

48 the Lord of Moses and Aaron.'

49 He said, 'Did you believe him
before I should permit you?
He is indeed your chief
who has taught you magic!
Soon you will know!
I will cut off your hands and feet
from opposite sides,
and I will crucify you all.'

50 They said, 'There is no harm in that!
We shall indeed return to our Lord.

51 We indeed hope our Lord will forgive us our offences
for being the first to believe.'

52 Then We revealed to Moses,
saying, 'Set out with My servants at night,
for you will be pursued.'

53 Then Pharaoh sent heralds to the cities,

54 [proclaiming:] 'These[1] are indeed a small band.

---

[1] That is, the Israelites.

وَإِنَّهُمْ لَنَا لَغَائِظُونَ ۝	55	They have aroused our wrath,
وَإِنَّا لَجَمِيعٌ حَاذِرُونَ ۝	56	and we are alert and fully prepared.'[1]
فَأَخْرَجْنَاهُم مِّن جَنَّاتٍ وَعُيُونٍ ۝	57	So We took them out of gardens and springs,
وَكُنُوزٍ	58	and [made them leave behind] treasures
وَمَقَامٍ كَرِيمٍ ۝		and stately homes.
كَذَٰلِكَ	59	So it was,
وَأَوْرَثْنَاهَا بَنِي إِسْرَائِيلَ ۝		and We bequeathed them to the Children of Israel.
فَأَتْبَعُوهُم مُّشْرِقِينَ ۝	60	Then they pursued them at sunrise.
فَلَمَّا تَرَاءَى الْجَمْعَانِ	61	When the two hosts sighted each other,
قَالَ أَصْحَابُ مُوسَىٰ		the companions of Moses said,
إِنَّا لَمُدْرَكُونَ ۝		'We have indeed been caught up.'
قَالَ كَلَّا	62	He said, 'Of course, not!
إِنَّ مَعِيَ رَبِّي سَيَهْدِينِ ۝		Indeed, my Lord is with me. He will guide me.'
فَأَوْحَيْنَا إِلَىٰ مُوسَىٰ	63	Thereupon, We revealed to Moses:
أَنِ اضْرِب بِّعَصَاكَ الْبَحْرَ		'Strike the sea with your staff!'
فَانفَلَقَ		Whereupon it parted,
فَكَانَ كُلُّ فِرْقٍ كَالطَّوْدِ الْعَظِيمِ ۝		and each part was as if it were a great mountain.
وَأَزْلَفْنَا ثَمَّ الْآخَرِينَ ۝	64	There, We brought the others near,
وَأَنجَيْنَا مُوسَىٰ وَمَن مَّعَهُ أَجْمَعِينَ ۝	65	and We delivered Moses and all those who were with him.
ثُمَّ أَغْرَقْنَا الْآخَرِينَ ۝	66	Then We drowned the rest.
إِنَّ فِي ذَٰلِكَ لَآيَةً	67	There is indeed a sign in that,
وَمَا كَانَ أَكْثَرُهُم مُّؤْمِنِينَ ۝		but most of them do not have faith.
وَإِنَّ رَبَّكَ لَهُوَ الْعَزِيزُ الرَّحِيمُ ۝	68	Indeed, your Lord is the All-mighty, the All-merciful.
وَاتْلُ عَلَيْهِمْ نَبَأَ إِبْرَاهِيمَ ۝	69	*Relate* to them the account of Abraham
إِذْ قَالَ لِأَبِيهِ وَقَوْمِهِ	70	when he said to his father and his people,
مَا تَعْبُدُونَ ۝		'What is it that you are worshiping?!'
قَالُوا نَعْبُدُ أَصْنَامًا	71	They said, 'We worship idols,
فَنَظَلُّ لَهَا عَاكِفِينَ ۝		and we keep on attending to them.'

---

[1] Or, 'Surely we are all a well-armed host.'

72 He said, 'Do they hear you when you call them? قَالَ هَلْ يَسْمَعُونَكُمْ إِذْ تَدْعُونَ
73 Or do they bring you any benefit, or cause you any harm?' أَوْ يَنفَعُونَكُمْ أَوْ يَضُرُّونَ
74 They said, قَالُوا
    'Indeed, we found our fathers doing likewise.' بَلْ وَجَدْنَا آبَاءَنَا كَذَلِكَ يَفْعَلُونَ
75 He said, قَالَ
    'Have you regarded what you have been worshiping, أَفَرَأَيْتُم مَّا كُنتُمْ تَعْبُدُونَ
76 you and your ancestors? أَنتُمْ وَآبَاؤُكُمُ الْأَقْدَمُونَ
77 They are indeed enemies to me, فَإِنَّهُمْ عَدُوٌّ لِّي
    but the Lord of all the worlds, إِلَّا رَبَّ الْعَالَمِينَ
78 who created me, it is He who guides me, الَّذِي خَلَقَنِي فَهُوَ يَهْدِينِ
79 and provides me with food and drink, وَالَّذِي هُوَ يُطْعِمُنِي وَيَسْقِينِ
80 and when I get sick it is He who cures me, وَإِذَا مَرِضْتُ فَهُوَ يَشْفِينِ
81 who will make me die, then He will bring me to life, وَالَّذِي يُمِيتُنِي ثُمَّ يُحْيِينِ
82 and who, I hope, will forgive me my faults وَالَّذِي أَطْمَعُ أَن يَغْفِرَ لِي خَطِيئَتِي
    on the Day of Retribution.'[1] يَوْمَ الدِّينِ
83 'My Lord! Grant me [unerring] judgement رَبِّ هَبْ لِي حُكْمًا
    and unite me with the Righteous. وَأَلْحِقْنِي بِالصَّالِحِينَ
84 Confer on me a worthy repute among the posterity, وَاجْعَل لِّي لِسَانَ صِدْقٍ فِي الْآخِرِينَ
85 and make me one of the heirs to the paradise of bliss. وَاجْعَلْنِي مِن وَرَثَةِ جَنَّةِ النَّعِيمِ
86 Forgive my father, for he is one of those who are astray. وَاغْفِرْ لِأَبِي إِنَّهُ كَانَ مِنَ الضَّالِّينَ
87 Disgrace me not on the day that they will be resurrected, وَلَا تُخْزِنِي يَوْمَ يُبْعَثُونَ
88 the day when neither wealth nor children will avail, يَوْمَ لَا يَنفَعُ مَالٌ وَلَا بَنُونَ
89 except him who comes to God with a sound heart,'[2] إِلَّا مَنْ أَتَى اللَّهَ بِقَلْبٍ سَلِيمٍ
90 and paradise will be brought near for the Godwary, وَأُزْلِفَتِ الْجَنَّةُ لِلْمُتَّقِينَ
91 and hell will be brought into view for the perverse, وَبُرِّزَتِ الْجَحِيمُ لِلْغَاوِينَ
92 and they shall be told: وَقِيلَ لَهُمْ
    'Where is that which you used to worship أَيْنَ مَا كُنتُمْ تَعْبُدُونَ
93 besides God? مِن دُونِ اللَّهِ
    Do they help you, or do they help each other?' هَلْ يَنصُرُونَكُمْ أَوْ يَنتَصِرُونَ

---

[1] Or 'the Day of Judgement.'
[2] That is, a heart that is free from the love of the world.

فَكُبْكِبُوا فِيهَا	94	Then they will be cast into it on their faces
هُمْ وَالْغَاوُونَ ۞		—they and the perverse,
وَجُنُودُ إِبْلِيسَ أَجْمَعُونَ ۞	95	and the hosts of Iblis all together.
قَالُوا وَهُمْ فِيهَا يَخْتَصِمُونَ ۞	96	They will say, as they wrangle in it together,
تَاللَّهِ إِنْ كُنَّا لَفِي ضَلَالٍ مُبِينٍ ۞	97	'By God, we had indeed been in plain error,
إِذْ نُسَوِّيكُمْ بِرَبِّ الْعَالَمِينَ ۞	98	when we equated you with the Lord of all the worlds!
وَمَا أَضَلَّنَا إِلَّا الْمُجْرِمُونَ ۞	99	No one led us astray except the guilty.
فَمَا لَنَا مِنْ شَافِعِينَ ۞	100	Now we have no intercessors,
وَلَا صَدِيقٍ حَمِيمٍ ۞	101	nor do we have any sympathetic friend.
فَلَوْ أَنَّ لَنَا كَرَّةً	102	Had there been another turn for us,
فَنَكُونَ مِنَ الْمُؤْمِنِينَ ۞		we would be among the faithful.'
إِنَّ فِي ذَٰلِكَ لَآيَةً	103	There is indeed a sign in that;
وَمَا كَانَ أَكْثَرُهُمْ مُؤْمِنِينَ ۞		but most of them do not have faith.
وَإِنَّ رَبَّكَ لَهُوَ الْعَزِيزُ الرَّحِيمُ ۞	104	Indeed, *your* Lord is the All-mighty, the All-merciful.
كَذَّبَتْ قَوْمُ نُوحٍ الْمُرْسَلِينَ ۞	105	The people of Noah impugned the apostles,
إِذْ قَالَ لَهُمْ أَخُوهُمْ نُوحٌ	106	when Noah, their compatriot, said to them,
أَلَا تَتَّقُونَ ۞		'Will you not be wary of God?
إِنِّي لَكُمْ رَسُولٌ أَمِينٌ ۞	107	I am indeed a trusted apostle sent to you.
فَاتَّقُوا اللَّهَ وَأَطِيعُونِ ۞	108	So be wary of God and obey me.
وَمَا أَسْأَلُكُمْ عَلَيْهِ مِنْ أَجْرٍ	109	I do not ask you any reward for it;
إِنْ أَجْرِيَ إِلَّا عَلَىٰ رَبِّ الْعَالَمِينَ ۞		my reward lies only with the Lord of all the worlds.
فَاتَّقُوا اللَّهَ وَأَطِيعُونِ ۞	110	So be wary of God and obey me.'
قَالُوا أَنُؤْمِنُ لَكَ	111	They said, 'Shall we believe in you,
وَاتَّبَعَكَ الْأَرْذَلُونَ ۞		when it is the riffraff who follow you?'
قَالَ وَمَا عِلْمِي بِمَا كَانُوا يَعْمَلُونَ ۞	112	He said, 'What do I know as to what they used to do?
إِنْ حِسَابُهُمْ إِلَّا عَلَىٰ رَبِّي	113	Their reckoning is only with my Lord,
لَوْ تَشْعُرُونَ ۞		should you be aware.
وَمَا أَنَا بِطَارِدِ الْمُؤْمِنِينَ ۞	114	I will not drive away the faithful.
إِنْ أَنَا إِلَّا نَذِيرٌ مُبِينٌ ۞	115	I am just a manifest warner.'

116 They said, 'Noah, if you do not desist,
you will certainly be stoned to death.'

117 He said, 'My Lord!
My people have indeed impugned me.

118 So judge conclusively between me and them,
and deliver me and the faithful who are with me.'

119 Thereupon We delivered him
and those who were with him in the laden ark.

120 Then We drowned the rest.

121 There is indeed a sign in that;
but most of them do not have faith.

122 Indeed, your Lord is the All-mighty, the All-merciful.

123 The people of 'Ād impugned the apostles,

124 when Hūd, their compatriot, said to them,
'Will you not be wary of God?

125 I am indeed a trusted apostle sent to you.

126 So be wary of God and obey me.

127 I do not ask you any reward for it;
my reward lies only with the Lord of all the worlds.

128 Do you build an absurd sign on every prominence?

129 You set up structures as if you will be immortal,

130 and when you seize someone for punishment,
you seize him like tyrants.

131 So be wary of God and obey me.

132 Be wary of Him who has provided you
with whatever you know,

133 and aided you with sons and with cattle,

134 gardens and springs.

135 I indeed fear for you the punishment

of a tremendous day.' عَذَابَ يَوْمٍ عَظِيمٍ ۝

136 They said, 'It is the same to us
whether you lecture us or not.

137 These are nothing but the traditions of the ancients,[1]

138 and we will not be punished.'

139 So they impugned him, whereupon We destroyed them.
There is indeed a sign in that;
but most of them do not have faith.

140 Indeed, your Lord is the All-mighty, the All-merciful.

141 The people of Thamūd impugned the apostles,

142 when Ṣāliḥ, their compatriot, said to them,
'Will you not be wary of God?

143 I am indeed a trusted apostle sent to you.

144 So be wary of God and obey me.

145 I do not ask you any reward for it;
my reward lies only with the Lord of all the worlds.

146 Will you be left secure in that which is here

147 —amid gardens and springs,

148 farms and date palms with dainty blossoms

149 and dwellings you skillfully[2] carve out from mountains.

150 So be wary of God and obey me,

151 and do not obey the dictates of the transgressors

152 who cause corruption in the land
and do not set things right.'

153 They said, 'You are indeed one of the bewitched.

154 You are just a human being like us.
So bring us a sign, if you are truthful.'

155 He said, 'This is a she-camel;

---

[1] Or, 'This [i.e. their religion and custom] is nothing but the custom of our predecessors.' Or 'This [i.e. Hūd's teaching] is nothing but the fabrications of the ancients,' according to an alternate reading (*khaluq*, instead of *khuluq*).
[2] Or, 'vainly.'

لَهَا شِرْبٌ وَلَكُمْ شِرْبُ يَوْمٍ مَعْلُومٍ ۝

she shall drink and you shall drink on known days.

وَلَا تَمَسُّوهَا بِسُوءٍ

156 Do not cause her any harm,

فَيَأْخُذَكُمْ عَذَابُ

for then you shall be seized by the punishment

يَوْمٍ عَظِيمٍ ۝

of a terrible day.'

فَعَقَرُوهَا

157 But they hamstrung her,

فَأَصْبَحُوا نَادِمِينَ ۝

and consequently became regretful.

فَأَخَذَهُمُ الْعَذَابُ

158 So the punishment seized them.

إِنَّ فِي ذَٰلِكَ لَآيَةً ۖ

There is indeed a sign in that;

وَمَا كَانَ أَكْثَرُهُمْ مُؤْمِنِينَ ۝

but most of them do not have faith.

وَإِنَّ رَبَّكَ لَهُوَ الْعَزِيزُ الرَّحِيمُ ۝

159 Indeed, *your* Lord is the All-mighty, the All-merciful.

كَذَّبَتْ قَوْمُ لُوطٍ الْمُرْسَلِينَ ۝

160 The people of Lot impugned the apostles,

إِذْ قَالَ لَهُمْ أَخُوهُمْ لُوطٌ

161 when Lot, their compatriot, said to them,

أَلَا تَتَّقُونَ ۝

'Will you not be wary of God?

إِنِّي لَكُمْ رَسُولٌ أَمِينٌ ۝

162 I am indeed a trusted apostle sent to you.

فَاتَّقُوا اللَّهَ وَأَطِيعُونِ ۝

163 So be wary of God and obey me.

وَمَا أَسْأَلُكُمْ عَلَيْهِ مِنْ أَجْرٍ ۖ

164 I do not ask you any reward for it;

إِنْ أَجْرِيَ إِلَّا عَلَىٰ رَبِّ الْعَالَمِينَ ۝

my reward lies only with the Lord of all the worlds.

أَتَأْتُونَ الذُّكْرَانَ مِنَ الْعَالَمِينَ ۝

165 What! Of all people do you come to males,

وَتَذَرُونَ

166   abandoning

مَا خَلَقَ لَكُمْ رَبُّكُمْ مِنْ أَزْوَاجِكُمْ ۚ

your wives your Lord has created for you?

بَلْ أَنْتُمْ قَوْمٌ عَادُونَ ۝

You are indeed a transgressing lot.'

قَالُوا لَئِنْ لَمْ تَنْتَهِ يَا لُوطُ

167 They said, 'Lot, if you do not desist,

لَتَكُونَنَّ مِنَ الْمُخْرَجِينَ ۝

you will surely be banished.'

قَالَ إِنِّي لِعَمَلِكُمْ مِنَ الْقَالِينَ ۝

168 He said, 'I indeed detest your conduct.'

رَبِّ نَجِّنِي وَأَهْلِي مِمَّا يَعْمَلُونَ ۝

169 'My Lord! Deliver me and my family from what they do.'

فَنَجَّيْنَاهُ وَأَهْلَهُ أَجْمَعِينَ ۝

170 So We delivered him and all his family,

إِلَّا عَجُوزًا فِي الْغَابِرِينَ ۝

171 except an old woman who remained behind.

ثُمَّ دَمَّرْنَا الْآخَرِينَ ۝

172 Then We destroyed all the rest

وَأَمْطَرْنَا عَلَيْهِمْ مَطَرًا ۖ

173   and rained down upon them a rain [of stones].

فَسَاءَ مَطَرُ الْمُنْذَرِينَ ۝

Evil was the rain of those who were warned!

¹⁷⁴ There is indeed a sign in that;
but most of them do not have faith.

¹⁷⁵ Indeed, your Lord is the All-mighty, the All-merciful.

¹⁷⁶ The inhabitants of Aykah impugned the apostles,

¹⁷⁷ when Shu'ayb said to them,
'Will you not be wary of God?

¹⁷⁸ I am indeed a trusted apostle sent to you.

¹⁷⁹ So be wary of God and obey me.

¹⁸⁰ I do not ask you any reward for it;
my reward lies only with the Lord of all the worlds.

¹⁸¹ Observe the full measure,
and do not be of those who give short measure.

¹⁸² Weigh with an even balance,

¹⁸³ and do not cheat the people of their goods.
Do not act wickedly on the earth, causing corruption.

¹⁸⁴ Be wary of Him who created you
and the former generations.'

¹⁸⁵ They said, 'You are indeed one of the bewitched.

¹⁸⁶ You are just a human being like us,
and we indeed consider you to be a liar.

¹⁸⁷ Make a fragment from the sky fall upon us,
if you are truthful.'

¹⁸⁸ He said, 'My Lord knows best what you are doing.'

¹⁸⁹ So they impugned him, and then they were overtaken
by the punishment of the day of the overshadowing cloud.
It was indeed the punishment of a terrible day.

¹⁹⁰ There is indeed a sign in that;
but most of them do not have faith.

¹⁹¹ Indeed, your Lord is the All-mighty, the All-merciful.

وَإِنَّهُ لَتَنزِيلُ ﴿١٩٢﴾	192 This is indeed a Book sent down
رَبِّ الْعَالَمِينَ ﴿١٩٢﴾	by the Lord of all the worlds,
نَزَلَ بِهِ الرُّوحُ الْأَمِينُ ﴿١٩٣﴾	193 brought down by the Trustworthy Spirit
عَلَىٰ قَلْبِكَ	194 upon your heart
لِتَكُونَ مِنَ الْمُنذِرِينَ ﴿١٩٤﴾	(so that you may be one of the warners),
بِلِسَانٍ عَرَبِيٍّ مُبِينٍ ﴿١٩٥﴾	195 in a clear Arabic language.
وَإِنَّهُ لَفِي زُبُرِ الْأَوَّلِينَ ﴿١٩٦﴾	196 It is indeed foretold in the scriptures of the former peoples.
أَوَلَمْ يَكُن لَّهُمْ آيَةً	197 Is it not a sign for them
أَن يَعْلَمَهُ عُلَمَاءُ بَنِي إِسْرَائِيلَ ﴿١٩٧﴾	that the learned of the Children of Israel recognize it?
وَلَوْ نَزَّلْنَاهُ عَلَىٰ بَعْضِ الْأَعْجَمِينَ ﴿١٩٨﴾	198 Had We sent it down upon some non-Arab
فَقَرَأَهُ عَلَيْهِم	199 and had he recited it to them,
مَّا كَانُوا بِهِ مُؤْمِنِينَ ﴿١٩٩﴾	they would not have believed in it.
كَذَٰلِكَ سَلَكْنَاهُ	200 This is how We let it pass
فِي قُلُوبِ الْمُجْرِمِينَ ﴿٢٠٠﴾	through the hearts of the guilty:
لَا يُؤْمِنُونَ بِهِ	201 they do not believe in it
حَتَّىٰ يَرَوُا الْعَذَابَ الْأَلِيمَ ﴿٢٠١﴾	until they sight the painful punishment.
فَيَأْتِيَهُم بَغْتَةً وَهُمْ لَا يَشْعُرُونَ ﴿٢٠٢﴾	202 It will overtake them suddenly while they are unaware.
فَيَقُولُوا هَلْ نَحْنُ مُنظَرُونَ ﴿٢٠٣﴾	203 Thereupon they will say, 'Shall we be granted any respite?'
أَفَبِعَذَابِنَا يَسْتَعْجِلُونَ ﴿٢٠٤﴾	204 So do they seek to hasten on Our punishment?
أَفَرَأَيْتَ إِن مَّتَّعْنَاهُمْ سِنِينَ ﴿٢٠٥﴾	205 Tell me, should We let them enjoy for some years,
ثُمَّ جَاءَهُم مَّا كَانُوا يُوعَدُونَ ﴿٢٠٦﴾	206 then there comes to them what they have been promised,
مَا أَغْنَىٰ عَنْهُم	207 of what avail to them will be
مَّا كَانُوا يُمَتَّعُونَ ﴿٢٠٧﴾	that which they were given to enjoy?
وَمَا أَهْلَكْنَا مِن قَرْيَةٍ	208 We have not destroyed any town
إِلَّا لَهَا مُنذِرُونَ ﴿٢٠٨﴾	without its having warners
ذِكْرَىٰ	209 for the sake of admonition,
وَمَا كُنَّا ظَالِمِينَ ﴿٢٠٩﴾	and We were not unjust.
وَمَا تَنَزَّلَتْ بِهِ الشَّيَاطِينُ ﴿٢١٠﴾	210 It[1] has not been brought down by the devils.

---

[1] That is, the Qur'ān.

211 Neither does it behoove them,
nor are they capable of doing that.
212 They are indeed kept at bay even from hearing it.
213 So *do not invoke* any god besides God,
lest you should be among the punished.

214 *Warn* the nearest of your kinsfolk,
215 and lower *your* wing
to the faithful who follow *you*.
216 But if they disobey *you*,
say, 'I am absolved of what you do.'
217 And put *your* trust in the All-mighty, the All-merciful,
218 who sees *you* when *you* stand for prayer,
219 and your going about among those who prostrate.
220 Indeed, He is the All-hearing, the All-knowing.

221 Shall I inform you
on whom the devils descend?
222 They descend on every sinful liar.
223 They eavesdrop and most of them are liars.
224 As for the poets, only the perverse follow them.
225 Have you not regarded that they rove in every valley,
226 and that they say what they do not do?
227 Barring those who have faith, do righteous deeds,
and remember God much,
and vindicate themselves after they have been wronged.
And the wrongdoers will soon know
at what goal they will end up.

27. The Ant[1]
al-Naml

In the Name of God,
the All-beneficent, the All-merciful.

1 Ṭā, Sīn.
These are the signs of the Qur'ān and a manifest Book,
2 a guidance and good news for the faithful
3 —those who maintain the prayer and pay the *zakāt*,
and who are certain of the Hereafter.
4 As for those who do not believe in the Hereafter,
We have made their deeds seem decorous to them,
and so they are bewildered.
5 They are the ones for whom there is a terrible punishment,
and they are
the ones who will be the biggest losers in the Hereafter.

6 You indeed receive the Qur'ān
from One who is all-wise, all-knowing.

7 When Moses said to his family,
'Indeed, I descry a fire!
I will bring you some news from it,
or bring you a firebrand
so that you may warm yourselves.'
8 When he came to it,
he was called: 'Blessed is He who is in the fire
and who is as well around it,
and immaculate is God, the Lord of all the worlds!'

---

[1] This Makkī *sūrah* takes its name from the story of Solomon and the ant *(naml)*, mentioned in verses 15-19

9 'O Moses! I am indeed God, يَا مُوسَىٰ إِنَّهُ أَنَا اللَّهُ
    the All-mighty, the All-wise.' الْعَزِيزُ الْحَكِيمُ ۝

10 'Throw down your staff!' وَأَلْقِ عَصَاكَ
    When he saw it wriggling, as if it were a snake, فَلَمَّا رَآهَا تَهْتَزُّ كَأَنَّهَا جَانٌّ
    he turned his back to flee, without looking back. وَلَّىٰ مُدْبِرًا وَلَمْ يُعَقِّبْ
    'O Moses! 'Do not be afraid. يَا مُوسَىٰ لَا تَخَفْ
    Indeed, the apostles are not afraid before Me, إِنِّي لَا يَخَافُ لَدَيَّ الْمُرْسَلُونَ ۝

11 nor those who do wrong إِلَّا مَنْ ظَلَمَ
    and then make up for their fault with goodness, ثُمَّ بَدَّلَ حُسْنًا بَعْدَ سُوءٍ
    for indeed I am all-forgiving, all-merciful.' فَإِنِّي غَفُورٌ رَحِيمٌ ۝

12 'Insert your hand into your shirt. وَأَدْخِلْ يَدَكَ فِي جَيْبِكَ
    It will emerge bright without any fault, تَخْرُجْ بَيْضَاءَ مِنْ غَيْرِ سُوءٍ
    —among nine signs meant for Pharaoh and his people. فِي تِسْعِ آيَاتٍ إِلَىٰ فِرْعَوْنَ وَقَوْمِهِ
    They are indeed a transgressing lot.' إِنَّهُمْ كَانُوا قَوْمًا فَاسِقِينَ ۝

13 But when Our signs came to them, as eye-openers, فَلَمَّا جَاءَتْهُمْ آيَاتُنَا مُبْصِرَةً
    they said, 'This is plain magic.' قَالُوا هَٰذَا سِحْرٌ مُبِينٌ ۝

14 They impugned them وَجَحَدُوا بِهَا
    —though they were convinced in their hearts— وَاسْتَيْقَنَتْهَا أَنْفُسُهُمْ
    wrongfully and out of arrogance. ظُلْمًا وَعُلُوًّا
    So *observe* how was the fate of the agents of corruption! فَانْظُرْ كَيْفَ كَانَ عَاقِبَةُ الْمُفْسِدِينَ ۝

15 Certainly We gave knowledge to David and Solomon, وَلَقَدْ آتَيْنَا دَاوُودَ وَسُلَيْمَانَ عِلْمًا
    and they said, 'All praise belongs to God, وَقَالَا الْحَمْدُ لِلَّهِ
    who granted us an advantage الَّذِي فَضَّلَنَا
    over many of His faithful servants.' عَلَىٰ كَثِيرٍ مِنْ عِبَادِهِ الْمُؤْمِنِينَ ۝

16 Solomon inherited from David, وَوَرِثَ سُلَيْمَانُ دَاوُودَ
    and he said, 'O people! وَقَالَ يَا أَيُّهَا النَّاسُ
    We have been taught the speech of the birds, عُلِّمْنَا مَنْطِقَ الطَّيْرِ
    and we have been given out of everything. وَأُوتِينَا مِنْ كُلِّ شَيْءٍ
    This is indeed a clear advantage.' إِنَّ هَٰذَا لَهُوَ الْفَضْلُ الْمُبِينُ ۝

17 [Once] Solomon's hosts were marched out for him,
comprising jinn, humans and birds,
and they were held in check.

18 When they came to the Valley of Ants,
an ant said, 'O ants!
Enter your dwellings,
lest Solomon and his hosts should trample on you
while they are unaware.'

19 Whereat he smiled, amused at its words,
and he said, 'My Lord!
Inspire me to give thanks for Your blessing
with which You have blessed me and my parents,
and that I may do righteous deeds which please You,
and admit me, by Your mercy,
among Your righteous servants.'

20 [One day] he reviewed the birds,
and said, 'Why do I not see the hoopoe?
Or is he absent?'

21 'I will punish him with a severe punishment,
or I will behead him,
unless he brings me a credible excuse.'

22 He did not stay for long [before he turned up]
and said, 'I have alighted on something
which you have not alighted on,
and I have brought you from Sheba a definite report.

23 I found a woman ruling over them,
and she has been given everything,
and she has a great throne.

24 I found her and her people prostrating to the sun
instead of God,

وَزَيَّنَ لَهُمُ الشَّيْطَانُ أَعْمَالَهُمْ فَصَدَّهُمْ عَنِ السَّبِيلِ فَهُمْ لَا يَهْتَدُونَ ۝

and Satan has made their deeds seem decorous to them
—thus he has barred them from the way of God,
so they are not guided—

25 أَلَّا يَسْجُدُوا لِلَّهِ الَّذِي يُخْرِجُ الْخَبْءَ فِي السَّمَاوَاتِ وَالْأَرْضِ وَيَعْلَمُ مَا تُخْفُونَ وَمَا تُعْلِنُونَ ۝

so that they do not prostrate themselves to God,
who brings forth what is hidden in the heavens
and the earth,
and He knows whatever you hide
and whatever you disclose.

26 اللَّهُ لَا إِلَٰهَ إِلَّا هُوَ رَبُّ الْعَرْشِ الْعَظِيمِ ۩ ۝

God—there is no god except Him—
is the Lord of the Great Throne.'

27 قَالَ سَنَنظُرُ أَصَدَقْتَ أَمْ كُنتَ مِنَ الْكَاذِبِينَ ۝

He said, 'We shall presently see whether you are truthful,
or if you are one of the liars.'

28 اذْهَب بِّكِتَابِي هَٰذَا فَأَلْقِهْ إِلَيْهِمْ ثُمَّ تَوَلَّ عَنْهُمْ فَانظُرْ مَاذَا يَرْجِعُونَ ۝

Take this letter of mine and deliver it to them.
Then draw away from them
and observe what response they return.'

29 قَالَتْ يَا أَيُّهَا الْمَلَأُ إِنِّي أُلْقِيَ إِلَيَّ كِتَابٌ كَرِيمٌ ۝

She said, 'O members of the elite!
A noble letter has indeed been delivered to me.

30 إِنَّهُ مِن سُلَيْمَانَ وَإِنَّهُ بِسْمِ اللَّهِ الرَّحْمَٰنِ الرَّحِيمِ ۝

It is from Solomon, and it begins in the name of God,
the All-beneficent, the All-merciful.

31 أَلَّا تَعْلُوا عَلَيَّ وَأْتُونِي مُسْلِمِينَ ۝

It states, "Do not defy me,
and come to me in submission."'

32 قَالَتْ يَا أَيُّهَا الْمَلَأُ أَفْتُونِي فِي أَمْرِي مَا كُنتُ قَاطِعَةً أَمْرًا حَتَّىٰ تَشْهَدُونِ ۝

She said, 'O members of the elite!
Give me your opinion concerning my matter.
I do not decide any matter until you are present.'

33 قَالُوا نَحْنُ أُولُو قُوَّةٍ وَأُولُو بَأْسٍ شَدِيدٍ وَالْأَمْرُ إِلَيْكِ فَانظُرِي مَاذَا تَأْمُرِينَ ۝

They said, 'We are powerful and possess great might.
But it is up to you to command.
So consider what orders you will give.'

34 قَالَتْ إِنَّ الْمُلُوكَ إِذَا دَخَلُوا قَرْيَةً أَفْسَدُوهَا وَجَعَلُوا أَعِزَّةَ أَهْلِهَا أَذِلَّةً

She said, 'Indeed, when kings enter a town,
they devastate it
and make the mightiest of its people the weakest.

That is how they act.

35 I will send them a gift,
and then see what the envoys bring back.'

36 So when he[1] came to Solomon,
he said, 'Are you aiding me with wealth?
What God has given me
is better than what He has given you.
You are indeed proud of your gift!

37 Go back to them, for we will come at them with hosts
which they cannot face,
and we will expel them from it, abased and degraded.'

38 He said, 'O members of the elite!
Which of you will bring me her throne
before they come to me in submission?'

39 An afreet[2] from among the jinn said,
'I will bring it to you before you rise from your place.
I have the power to do it and am trustworthy.'

40 The one who had knowledge of the Book[3] said,
'I will bring it to you in the twinkling of an eye.'
So when he saw it set near him,
he said, 'This is by the grace of my Lord,
to test me if I will give thanks or be ungrateful.
Whoever gives thanks, gives thanks only for his own sake.
And whoever is ungrateful [should know that]
my Lord is indeed all-sufficient, all-generous.'

41 He said, 'Disguise her throne for her,
so that we may see whether she is discerning
or if she is one of the undiscerning ones.'

---

[1] That is, the envoy.

[2] *Ifrīt* (noun): devil, demon, giant, rebel; (adj.) cunning, sly, wily, smart, mischievous, rebellious, defiant.

[3] He is said to have been Solomon's vizier and successor, Āṣif ibn Barkhiyā.

42 So when she came, it was said to her,
'Is your throne like this one?'
She said, 'It seems to be the same,
and we were informed before it,[1]
and we had submitted.'

43 She had been barred from the way of God
by what she used to worship besides God,
for she belonged to a faithless people.

44 It was said to her, 'Enter the palace.'
So when she saw it, she supposed it to be a pool of water,
and she bared her shanks.
He said, 'It is a palace paved with crystal.'
She said, 'My Lord! Indeed, I have wronged myself,
and I submit with Solomon to God,
the Lord of all the worlds.'

45 Certainly We sent to Thamūd Ṣāliḥ, their compatriot,
with the summons: 'Worship God!'
But thereat they became two groups
contending with each other.

46 He said, 'O My people!
Why do you press for evil sooner than for good?
Why do you not plead to God for forgiveness
so that you may receive His mercy?'

47 They said, 'We take for a bad omen you
and those who are with you.'
He said, 'Your bad omens are from God.
You are indeed a people being tested.'

48 There were nine persons[2] in the city

---

[1] That is, 'we had knowledge of Solomon's extraordinary authority even before we saw such feats and we had submitted to him.'
[2] Or 'nine families' (or gangs).

who caused corruption in the land,
and did not set things right.

49 They said, 'Swear by God
that we will attack him and his family by night.
Then we will tell his heir
that we were not present at the murder of his family
and that we indeed speak the truth.'

50 They devised a plot, and We too devised a plan,
but they were not aware.

51 So *observe* how was the outcome of their plotting,
as We destroyed them and all their people.

52 So there lay their houses, fallen in ruin,
because of their wrongdoing.
There is indeed a sign in that
for a people who have knowledge.

53 And We delivered those who had faith
and were Godwary.

54 We also sent Lot, when he said to his people,
'What! Do you commit this indecency while you look on?
55 Do you approach men with [sexual] desire
instead of women?!
You are indeed an ignorant lot!'

[PART 20]

56 But the only answer of his people was that they said,
'Expel Lot's family from your town!
They are indeed a puritanical lot.'

57 So We delivered him and his family, except his wife.
We ordained her to be among those who remained behind.

58 Then We poured down upon them a rain [of stones].

فَسَاءَ مَطَرُ الْمُنْذَرِينَ ۝

Evil was that rain for those who had been warned!

قُلِ الْحَمْدُ لِلَّهِ 59 Say, 'All praise belongs to God,
وَسَلَامٌ عَلَىٰ عِبَادِهِ الَّذِينَ اصْطَفَىٰ and Peace be to His chosen servants..'
آللَّهُ خَيْرٌ أَمَّا يُشْرِكُونَ ۝ Is God better, or the partners they ascribe to Him?
أَمَّنْ خَلَقَ السَّمَاوَاتِ وَالْأَرْضَ 60 Is He who created the heavens and the earth,
وَأَنْزَلَ لَكُمْ مِنَ السَّمَاءِ مَاءً and sends down for you water from the sky,
فَأَنْبَتْنَا بِهِ حَدَائِقَ ذَاتَ بَهْجَةٍ whereby We grow delightful gardens,
مَا كَانَ لَكُمْ أَنْ تُنْبِتُوا شَجَرَهَا whose trees you could never cause to grow…?[1]
أَإِلَٰهٌ مَعَ اللَّهِ What! Is there a god besides God?
بَلْ هُمْ قَوْمٌ يَعْدِلُونَ ۝ They are indeed a lot who equate others with God.
أَمَّنْ جَعَلَ الْأَرْضَ قَرَارًا 61 Is He who made the earth an abode for you,
وَجَعَلَ خِلَالَهَا أَنْهَارًا and made rivers flowing through it,
وَجَعَلَ لَهَا رَوَاسِيَ and set firm mountains for its stability,
وَجَعَلَ بَيْنَ الْبَحْرَيْنِ حَاجِزًا and set a barrier between the two seas…?
أَإِلَٰهٌ مَعَ اللَّهِ What! Is there a god besides God?
بَلْ أَكْثَرُهُمْ لَا يَعْلَمُونَ ۝ Indeed, most of them do not know.
أَمَّنْ يُجِيبُ الْمُضْطَرَّ 62 Is He who answers the call of the distressed person
إِذَا دَعَاهُ وَيَكْشِفُ السُّوءَ when he invokes Him and removes his distress,
وَيَجْعَلُكُمْ خُلَفَاءَ الْأَرْضِ and makes you successors on the earth…?
أَإِلَٰهٌ مَعَ اللَّهِ What! Is there a god besides God?
قَلِيلًا مَا تَذَكَّرُونَ ۝ Little is the admonition that you take.

أَمَّنْ يَهْدِيكُمْ فِي ظُلُمَاتِ 63 Is He who guides you in the darkness
الْبَرِّ وَالْبَحْرِ of land and sea
وَمَنْ يُرْسِلُ الرِّيَاحَ and who sends the winds
بُشْرًا بَيْنَ يَدَيْ رَحْمَتِهِ as harbingers of His mercy…?
أَإِلَٰهٌ مَعَ اللَّهِ What! Is there a god besides God?
تَعَالَى اللَّهُ Far is God above having

---

[1] Ellipsis. The omitted phrase here and in the following verses (61-64) is 'better or the partners they ascribe to Him.'

any partners that they ascribe to Him. عَمَّا يُشْرِكُونَ ۞

64 Is He who originates the creation,
   then He will bring it back,
 and who provides for you from the heavens
   and the earth...?
 What! Is there a god besides God?
 Say, 'Produce your evidence,
   if you are truthful.'

65 Say,
 'No one in the heavens or the earth knows
   the Unseen except God,
 nor are they aware when they will be resurrected.'

66 Is their knowledge complete concerning the Hereafter?
   No, they are in doubt about it.
   Indeed, they are blind to it.

67 The faithless say,
 'What! When we and our fathers have become dust
   will we be raised from the dead?

68 We and our fathers were certainly promised this before.
   But these are just myths of the ancients.'

69 Say, 'Travel through the land
   and observe how was the fate of the guilty.'

70 *Do not grieve* for them,
   and *do not be upset* by their guile.

71 They say, 'When will this promise be fulfilled,
   if you are truthful?'

72 Say, 'Perhaps there is right behind you
   some of what you seek to hasten.'

73 Your Lord is indeed gracious to mankind,

but most of them do not give thanks.

74 Your Lord indeed knows whatever their breasts conceal and whatever they disclose.

75 There is no invisible thing in the heaven and the earth but it is in a manifest Book.[1]

76 This Qurʾān indeed recounts for the Children of Israel most of what they differ about,

77 and it is indeed a guidance and mercy for the faithful.

78 Your Lord will decide between them by His judgement, and He is the All-mighty, the All-knowing.

79 So put your trust in God, for you indeed stand on the manifest truth.

80 You cannot make the dead hear, nor can you make the deaf hear your call when they turn their backs upon you,

81 nor can you lead the blind out of their error. You can make only those hear you who believe in Our signs and have submitted.

82 When the word of judgement falls upon them, We will bring out for them an Animal[2] from the earth who will tell them that the people had no faith in Our signs.

83 On that day, We will resurrect[3] from every nation a group of those who denied Our signs, and they will be held in check.

84 When they come, He will say, 'Did you deny My signs without comprehending them in knowledge? What was it that you used to do?'

---

[1] That is, in 'the Preserved Tablet.'
[2] Or 'a beast.'
[3] See 20:124-125 where ḥashr is used in the sense of resurrection.

85 And the word of judgement shall fall upon them
　　　for their wrongdoing,
　　　and they will not speak.

86 Do they not see that We made the night
　　　that they may rest in it,
　　　and the day to provide visibility.
　　　There are indeed signs in that for people who have faith.

87 The day when the trumpet is blown,
　　　whoever is in the heavens will be terrified
　　　and whoever is on the earth,
　　　except such as God wishes,
　　　and all will come to Him in utter humility.

88 You see the mountains,
　　　which you suppose to be stationary,
　　　while they drift like passing clouds
　　　—the handiwork of God who has made everything faultless.
　　　He is indeed well aware of what you do.

89 Whoever brings virtue
　　　shall receive a reward better than it;
　　　and on that day they shall be secure from terror.

90 But whoever brings vice
　　　—they shall be cast on their faces into the Fire
　　　[and told:] 'Will you be requited
　　　with anything except what you used to do?'

91 [Say,] 'I have been commanded
　　　to worship the Lord of this city[1]
　　　who has made it inviolable[2]
　　　and to whom all things belong,

---

[1] That is, the holy city of Makkah.
[2] Or 'sacred.'

and I have been commanded
to be among those who submit,
92 and to recite the Qurʾān.'
Whoever is guided is guided only for his own good,
and as for him who goes astray,
say, 'I am just one of the warners.'
93 And say, 'All praise belongs to God.
Soon He will show you His signs,
and you will recognize them.'
Your Lord is not oblivious of what you do.

28. THE STORY[1]
al-Qaṣaṣ

In the Name of God,
the All-beneficent, the All-merciful.

1 Ṭā, Sīn, Mīm.
2 These are the signs of the Manifest Book.
3 We relate to you
truly some of the account of Moses and Pharaoh
for a people who have faith.
4 Pharaoh indeed tyrannized over the land,
reducing its people to factions,
abasing one group of them,
slaughtering their sons and sparing their women.
He was indeed one of the agents of corruption.
5 And We desired to show favour
to those who were oppressed in the land,
and to make them *imams* and to make them the heirs,
6 and to establish them in the land

---

[1] This Makkī *sūrah* is named after verse 25 wherein the word *qaṣaṣ* (story) occurs.

and to show Pharaoh and Hāmān and their hosts
that of which they were apprehensive from them.[1]

7 We revealed to Moses' mother, saying, 'Nurse him;
then, when you fear for him, cast him into the river,
and do not fear or grieve,
for We will restore him to you
and make him one of the apostles.'

8 Then Pharaoh's kinsmen picked him up
that he might be an enemy to them and a cause of grief.
Indeed, Pharaoh and Hāmān and their hosts
were iniquitous.

9 Pharaoh's wife said to him,
'[This infant will be] a source of comfort to me and you.
Do not kill him.
Maybe he will benefit us, or we will adopt him as a son.'
But they were not aware.

10 The heart of Moses' mother became desolate,
and indeed she was about to divulge it
had We not fortified her heart
so that she might have faith in God's promise.

11 She said to his sister, 'Follow him.'
So she watched him from a distance,
while they were not aware.

12 We had forbidden him to be suckled by any nurse
since before.
So she[2] said, 'Shall I show you a household
that will take care of him for you
and who will be his well-wishers?'

13 That is how We restored him to his mother

---

[1] That is, from the Israelites.
[2] That is, Moses' sister.

al-Qaṣaṣ 28:19

كَىۡ تَقَرَّ عَيۡنُهَا وَلَا تَحۡزَنَ	so that she might be comforted and not grieve,
وَلِتَعۡلَمَ أَنَّ وَعۡدَ ٱللَّهِ حَقٌّ	and that she might know that God's promise is true,
وَلَٰكِنَّ أَكۡثَرَهُمۡ لَا يَعۡلَمُونَ ۝	but most of them do not know.

14 وَلَمَّا بَلَغَ أَشُدَّهُۥ وَٱسۡتَوَىٰٓ   When he came of age and became fully matured,
آتَيۡنَٰهُ حُكۡمًا وَعِلۡمًا   We gave him judgement and knowledge,
وَكَذَٰلِكَ نَجۡزِى ٱلۡمُحۡسِنِينَ ۝   and thus do We reward the virtuous.

15 وَدَخَلَ ٱلۡمَدِينَةَ   [One day] he entered the city at a time when
عَلَىٰ حِينِ غَفۡلَةٍ مِّنۡ أَهۡلِهَا   its people were not likely to take notice.
فَوَجَدَ فِيهَا رَجُلَيۡنِ يَقۡتَتِلَانِ   He found there two men fighting,
هَٰذَا مِن شِيعَتِهِۦ   this one from among his followers
وَهَٰذَا مِنۡ عَدُوِّهِۦ   and that one from his enemies.
فَٱسۡتَغَٰثَهُ ٱلَّذِى مِن شِيعَتِهِۦ   The one who was from his followers sought his help
عَلَى ٱلَّذِى مِنۡ عَدُوِّهِۦ   against him who was from his enemies.
فَوَكَزَهُۥ مُوسَىٰ فَقَضَىٰ عَلَيۡهِ   So Moses hit him with his fist, whereupon he expired.
قَالَ هَٰذَا مِنۡ عَمَلِ ٱلشَّيۡطَٰنِ   He said, 'This is of Satan's doing.
إِنَّهُۥ عَدُوٌّ مُّضِلٌّ مُّبِينٌ ۝   He is indeed clearly a misleading enemy.'

16 قَالَ رَبِّ إِنِّى ظَلَمۡتُ نَفۡسِى فَٱغۡفِرۡ لِى   He said, 'My Lord! I have wronged myself. Forgive me!'
فَغَفَرَ لَهُۥٓ   So He forgave him.
إِنَّهُۥ هُوَ ٱلۡغَفُورُ ٱلرَّحِيمُ ۝   Indeed, He is the All-forgiving, the All-merciful.

17 قَالَ رَبِّ بِمَآ أَنۡعَمۡتَ عَلَىَّ   He said, 'My Lord! As You have blessed me,
فَلَنۡ أَكُونَ ظَهِيرًا لِّلۡمُجۡرِمِينَ ۝   I will never be a supporter of the guilty.'

18 فَأَصۡبَحَ فِى ٱلۡمَدِينَةِ   He rose at dawn in the city,
خَآئِفًا يَتَرَقَّبُ   fearful and vigilant,
فَإِذَا ٱلَّذِى ٱسۡتَنصَرَهُۥ بِٱلۡأَمۡسِ يَسۡتَصۡرِخُهُۥ   when, lo, the one who had sought his help the day before, shouted for his help once again.
قَالَ لَهُۥ مُوسَىٰٓ إِنَّكَ لَغَوِىٌّ مُّبِينٌ ۝   Moses said to him, 'You are indeed clearly perverse!'

19 فَلَمَّآ أَنۡ أَرَادَ أَن يَبۡطِشَ بِٱلَّذِى   But when he wanted to strike him
هُوَ عَدُوٌّ لَّهُمَا   who was an enemy of both of them,
قَالَ يَٰمُوسَىٰٓ أَتُرِيدُ أَن تَقۡتُلَنِى   he said, 'Moses, do you want to kill me,
كَمَا قَتَلۡتَ نَفۡسًۢا بِٱلۡأَمۡسِ   just like the one you killed yesterday?

You only want to be a tyrant in this land,
and you do not desire to be one who sets things right.'[1]

20 There came a man from the city outskirts, hurrying.
He said, 'Moses!
The elite are indeed conspiring to kill you.
So leave this place. I am indeed your well-wisher.'

21 So he left the city, fearful and vigilant.
He said, 'My Lord! Deliver me from the wrongdoing lot.'

22 And when he turned his face toward Midian,
he said, 'Maybe my Lord
will show me the right way.'

23 When he arrived at the well of Midian,
he found there a throng of people watering their flocks,
and he found, besides them,
two women holding back their flock.
He said, 'What is your business?'
They said, 'We do not water our flock
until the shepherds have driven out their flocks
and our father is an aged man.'

24 So he watered their flock for them.
Then he withdrew toward the shade and said, 'My Lord!
I am indeed in need of any good You may send down to me!'

25 Then one of the two women approached him,
walking bashfully.
She said, 'My father invites you
to pay you the wages for watering our flock for us.'
So when he came to him and recounted the story to him,
he said, 'Do not be afraid.

---

[1] Although Moses wanted to help him again, much against his own inclination, the Israelite thought that Moses was going to attack him.

You have been delivered from the wrongdoing lot.' نَجَوْتَ مِنَ الْقَوْمِ الظَّالِمِينَ ۝

26 One of the two women said, 'Father, hire him. قَالَتْ إِحْدَاهُمَا يَا أَبَتِ اسْتَأْجِرْهُ
The best you can indeed hire إِنَّ خَيْرَ مَنِ اسْتَأْجَرْتَ
is a powerful and trustworthy man.' الْقَوِيُّ الْأَمِينُ ۝

27 He said, 'Indeed, I desire to marry you قَالَ إِنِّي أُرِيدُ أَنْ أُنْكِحَكَ
to one of these two daughters of mine, إِحْدَى ابْنَتَيَّ هَاتَيْنِ
on condition that you hire yourself to me for eight years. عَلَىٰ أَنْ تَأْجُرَنِي ثَمَانِيَ حِجَجٍ
And if you complete ten, that will be up to you, فَإِنْ أَتْمَمْتَ عَشْرًا فَمِنْ عِنْدِكَ
and I do not want to be hard on you. وَمَا أُرِيدُ أَنْ أَشُقَّ عَلَيْكَ
You will find me, God willing, سَتَجِدُنِي إِنْ شَاءَ اللَّهُ
to be a righteous man.' مِنَ الصَّالِحِينَ ۝

28 He said, 'This will be by consent between you and me. قَالَ ذَٰلِكَ بَيْنِي وَبَيْنَكَ
Whichever of the two terms I complete, أَيَّمَا الْأَجَلَيْنِ قَضَيْتُ
there shall be no imposition upon me,[1] فَلَا عُدْوَانَ عَلَيَّ
and God is witness over what we say.' وَاللَّهُ عَلَىٰ مَا نَقُولُ وَكِيلٌ ۝

29 So when Moses completed the term فَلَمَّا قَضَىٰ مُوسَى الْأَجَلَ
and set out with his family, وَسَارَ بِأَهْلِهِ
he descried a fire on the side of the mountain. آنَسَ مِنْ جَانِبِ الطُّورِ نَارًا
He said to his family, 'Wait! Indeed, I descry a fire! قَالَ لِأَهْلِهِ امْكُثُوا إِنِّي آنَسْتُ نَارًا
Maybe I will bring you some news from it, لَعَلِّي آتِيكُمْ مِنْهَا بِخَبَرٍ
or a brand of fire أَوْ جَذْوَةٍ مِنَ النَّارِ
so that you may warm yourselves.' لَعَلَّكُمْ تَصْطَلُونَ ۝

30 When he approached it, فَلَمَّا أَتَاهَا
he was called from the right bank of the valley نُودِيَ مِنْ شَاطِئِ الْوَادِ الْأَيْمَنِ
in that blessed spot from the tree: فِي الْبُقْعَةِ الْمُبَارَكَةِ مِنَ الشَّجَرَةِ
'Moses! Indeed, I am God, أَنْ يَا مُوسَىٰ إِنِّي أَنَا اللَّهُ
the Lord of all the worlds!' رَبُّ الْعَالَمِينَ ۝

31 And: 'Throw down your staff!' وَأَنْ أَلْقِ عَصَاكَ
And when he saw it wriggling as if it were a snake, فَلَمَّا رَآهَا تَهْتَزُّ كَأَنَّهَا جَانٌّ

---

[1] Or 'it shall be no unfairness toward me.'

he turned his back to flee, without looking back.
'Moses! Come forward, and do not be afraid.
    You are indeed safe.'
32 'Insert your hand into your shirt.
    It will emerge bright, without any fault,
    and keep your arms drawn in awe to your sides.
These shall be two proofs from your Lord
    to Pharaoh and his elite.
They are indeed a transgressing lot.'
33 He said, 'My Lord! Indeed, I have killed one of their men,
    so I fear they will kill me.
34 Aaron, my brother
—he is more articulate than me in speech.
So send him with me as a helper to confirm me,
    for I fear that they will impugn me.'
35 He said, 'We will strengthen your arm
    by means of your brother,
and invest both of you with such authority
that they will not touch you.
With the help of Our signs, you two
and those who follow the two of you shall be the victors.'
36 When Moses brought them Our manifest signs,
    they said, 'This is nothing but concocted magic.
We never heard of such a thing among our forefathers.'
37 Moses said, 'My Lord knows best
    who brings guidance from Him
and in whose favour the outcome of that abode will be.
The wrongdoers do not prosper.'
38 Pharaoh said, 'O members of the elite!
I do not know of any god that you may have besides me.

Hāmān, light for me a fire over clay,[1]
and build me a tower
so that I may take a look at Moses' god,
and indeed I consider him to be a liar!'

39 He and his hosts acted arrogantly
in that land unduly
and thought they would not be brought back to Us.

40 So We seized him and his hosts,
and threw them into the sea.
So *observe* how was the fate of the wrongdoers!

41 We made them leaders who invite to the Fire,
and on the Day of Resurrection they will not receive any help.

42 We made a curse pursue them in this world,
and on the Day of Resurrection
they will be among the disfigured.

43 Certainly We gave Moses the Book,
after We had destroyed the former generations,
as a set of eye-openers for mankind,
and as guidance and mercy,
so that they may take admonition.

44 You were not on the western side[2]
when We revealed the commandments[3] to Moses,
nor were *you* among the witnesses.[4]

45 But We brought forth other generations
and time took its toll on them.
You did not dwell among the people of Midian

---

[1] That is, 'Light for me kilns for baking bricks of clay to build a tower from which I may take a look at the God of Moses.' Meant as a sarcasm aimed at Moses and the Israelites, many of whom were used as forced labour to make bricks.

[2] That is, on the western side of the mountain, or valley, of Sinai.

[3] Or 'the Law.'

[4] Or, 'nor were you among those present.'

reciting Our signs to them,
but it is We who are the senders of the apostles.

46 And you were not on the side of the Mount
when We called out [to Moses],
but [We have sent you as] a mercy from your Lord
that you may warn a people
to whom there did not come any warner before you,
so that they may take admonition.[1]

47 And lest—if an affliction were to befall them
because of what their hands have sent ahead[2]—
they should say, 'Our Lord!
Why did You not send us an apostle
so that we might have followed Your signs
and been among the faithful?'[3]

48 But when there came to them the truth from Us,
they said, 'Why has he not been given
the like of what Moses was given?'
Did they not disbelieve what Moses was given before
and said, 'Two magicians abetting each other,'
and said, 'We indeed disbelieve both of them'?

49 Say, 'Then bring some Book from God
better in guidance than both of them[4]
so that I may follow it,
if you are truthful.'

50 Then, if they do not respond to your summons,
know that they only follow their base desires,

---

[1] That is, 'The faithless imagine that this teaching is of your own contrivance. But it was We who sent Our revelations to Moses and gave him the scripture and the Law before you even came into the world, nor it was you who lived among the people of Midian to recite Our signs to them. It was We who have been sending the apostles before you, and it is We who have sent you as a mercy and guidance to mankind, after the passage of time had taken its toll and obscured the path of the prophets.'

[2] Or 'prepared,' or 'committed.'

[3] Cf. **20**:134.

[4] That is, better than the Qur'ān and the Book revealed to Moses.

and who is more astray

than him who follows his base desires

without any guidance from God?

Indeed, God does not guide the wrongdoing lot.

51 Certainly We have carried on this discourse[1] for them

so that they may take admonition.

52 Those to whom We gave the Book before it

are the ones who believe in it,

53 and when it is recited to them, they say, 'We believe in it.

It is indeed the truth from our Lord.

Indeed, we were *muslims* even before it came.'

54 Those will be given their reward two times

for their patience.

They repel evil conduct with good,

and spend out of what We have provided them,

55 and when they hear vain talk they avoid it and say,

'Our deeds belong to us and your deeds belong to you.

Peace be to you. We do not court the ignorant.'

56 You cannot guide whomever you wish,

but it is God who guides whomever He wishes,

and He knows best those who are guided.

57 They say, 'If we follow the guidance with you,

we will be driven out of our territory.'

Did We not establish a secure sanctuary[2] for them

where fruits of all kinds are brought

as a provision from Us?

But most of them do not know.

58 How many a town We have destroyed

that was proud of its lifestyle!

---

[1] That is, the Qur'ān.
[2] That is, the holy city of Makkah.

There lie their dwellings,
uninhabited after them except by a few,
and We were the sole inheritors.

59 Your Lord would not destroy the towns
until He had raised an apostle in their mother city
to recite Our signs to them.
We would never destroy the towns
except when their people were wrongdoers.

60 Whatever things you have been given
are only the wares of the life of this world and its glitter,
and what is with God is better and more lasting.
Will you not exercise your reason?

61 Is he to whom We have given a good promise,
which he will receive,
like him whom We have provided
the wares of the life of this world
but who will be arraigned on the Day of Resurrection?

62 The day He will call out to them
and ask, 'Where are My "partners"
that you used to claim?'

63 Those against whom the word had become due will say,
'Our Lord! These are the ones whom we have perverted.
We perverted them, as we were perverse ourselves.
We repudiate them in front of You:
it was not us that they worshiped.'

64 It will be said, 'Invoke your partners!'
So they will invoke them,
but they will not respond to them,
and they will sight the punishment,
wishing they had followed guidance.

65 The day He will call out to them وَيَوْمَ يُنَادِيهِمْ
and say, 'What response did you give to the apostles?' فَيَقُولُ مَاذَا أَجَبْتُمُ الْمُرْسَلِينَ ۝

66 That day all news will be withheld from them, فَعَمِيَتْ عَلَيْهِمُ الْأَنبَاءُ يَوْمَئِذٍ
so they will not question one another. فَهُمْ لَا يَتَسَاءَلُونَ ۝

67 As for him who repents and develops faith فَأَمَّا مَن تَابَ وَآمَنَ
and acts righteously, وَعَمِلَ صَالِحًا
maybe he will be among the felicitous. فَعَسَىٰ أَن يَكُونَ مِنَ الْمُفْلِحِينَ ۝

68 Your Lord creates whatever He wishes and chooses; وَرَبُّكَ يَخْلُقُ مَا يَشَاءُ وَيَخْتَارُ
they have no choice. مَا كَانَ لَهُمُ الْخِيَرَةُ
Immaculate is God and far above سُبْحَانَ اللَّهِ وَتَعَالَىٰ
having any partners that they ascribe to Him. عَمَّا يُشْرِكُونَ ۝

69 Your Lord knows whatever their breasts conceal وَرَبُّكَ يَعْلَمُ مَا تُكِنُّ صُدُورُهُمْ
and whatever they disclose. وَمَا يُعْلِنُونَ ۝

70 He is God, there is no god except Him. وَهُوَ اللَّهُ لَا إِلَٰهَ إِلَّا هُوَ
All praise belongs to Him in this world and the Hereafter. لَهُ الْحَمْدُ فِي الْأُولَىٰ وَالْآخِرَةِ
All judgement belongs to Him وَلَهُ الْحُكْمُ
and to Him you will be brought back. وَإِلَيْهِ تُرْجَعُونَ ۝

71 Say, 'Tell me, قُلْ أَرَأَيْتُمْ
if God were to make the night perpetual for you إِنْ جَعَلَ اللَّهُ عَلَيْكُمُ اللَّيْلَ سَرْمَدًا
until the Day of Resurrection, إِلَىٰ يَوْمِ الْقِيَامَةِ
what god other than God can bring you light? مَنْ إِلَٰهٌ غَيْرُ اللَّهِ يَأْتِيكُم بِضِيَاءٍ
Then, will you not listen?' أَفَلَا تَسْمَعُونَ ۝

72 Say, 'Tell me, قُلْ أَرَأَيْتُمْ
if God were to make the day إِنْ جَعَلَ اللَّهُ عَلَيْكُمُ النَّهَارَ
perpetual for you until the Day of Resurrection, سَرْمَدًا إِلَىٰ يَوْمِ الْقِيَامَةِ
what god other than God can bring you night مَنْ إِلَٰهٌ غَيْرُ اللَّهِ يَأْتِيكُم بِلَيْلٍ
wherein you can rest? تَسْكُنُونَ فِيهِ
Will you not see?' أَفَلَا تُبْصِرُونَ ۝

73 Out of His mercy He has made for you night and day, وَمِن رَّحْمَتِهِ جَعَلَ لَكُمُ اللَّيْلَ وَالنَّهَارَ

that you may rest therein
and that you may seek His bounty
and so that you may give thanks.

74 The day He will call out to them and say,
'Where are My "partners" that you used to claim?'

75 We shall draw from every nation a witness
and say, 'Produce your evidence.'
Then they will know that all reality belongs to God
and what they used to fabricate will forsake them.

76 Korah indeed belonged to the people of Moses,
but he bullied them.
We had given him so much treasures
that their chests indeed proved heavy
for a band of stalwarts.
When his people said to him, 'Do not boast!
Indeed, God does not like boasters.

77 Seek by the means that God has given you
the abode of the Hereafter,
while not forgetting your share of this world.
Be good to others just as God has been good to you,
and do not try to cause corruption in the land.
Indeed, God does not like the agents of corruption.'

78 He said, 'I have been given all this just
because of the knowledge that I have.'
Did he not know
that God had already destroyed before him
some of the generations who were more powerful than him
and greater in amassing wealth?[1]

---

[1] Or 'more numerous in strength.'

وَلَا يُسْأَلُ عَنْ ذُنُوبِهِمُ الْمُجْرِمُونَ ۝

The guilty will not be questioned about their sins.[1]

79 فَخَرَجَ عَلَىٰ قَوْمِهِ فِى زِينَتِهِ ۖ

79 Then he emerged before his people in his finery.

قَالَ الَّذِينَ يُرِيدُونَ الْحَيَاةَ الدُّنْيَا

Those who desired the life of the world said,

يَٰلَيْتَ لَنَا مِثْلَ مَآ أُوتِىَ قَٰرُونُ

'We wish we had like what Korah has been given!

إِنَّهُۥ لَذُو حَظٍّ عَظِيمٍ ۝

He is indeed greatly fortunate.'

80 وَقَالَ الَّذِينَ أُوتُوا الْعِلْمَ

80 Those who were given knowledge said to them,

وَيْلَكُمْ

'Woe to you!

ثَوَابُ اللَّهِ خَيْرٌ لِّمَنْ ءَامَنَ

God's reward is better for someone who has faith

وَعَمِلَ صَٰلِحًا

and acts righteously,

وَلَا يُلَقَّىٰهَآ إِلَّا الصَّٰبِرُونَ ۝

and no one will receive it except the patient.'

81 فَخَسَفْنَا بِهِۦ وَبِدَارِهِ الْأَرْضَ

81 So We caused the earth to swallow him and his house,

فَمَا كَانَ لَهُۥ مِن فِئَةٍ يَنصُرُونَهُۥ

and he had no party that might protect him

مِن دُونِ اللَّهِ

from God,

وَمَا كَانَ مِنَ الْمُنتَصِرِينَ ۝

nor could he rescue himself.

82 وَأَصْبَحَ الَّذِينَ تَمَنَّوْا مَكَانَهُۥ بِالْأَمْسِ

82 By dawn, those who longed to be in his place the day before

يَقُولُونَ وَيْكَأَنَّ اللَّهَ يَبْسُطُ الرِّزْقَ لِمَن يَشَآءُ مِنْ عِبَادِهِۦ وَيَقْدِرُ

were saying, 'Don't you see that God expands the provision and tightens it for whomever He wishes of His servants?

لَوْلَآ أَن مَّنَّ اللَّهُ عَلَيْنَا

Had God not shown us favour,

لَخَسَفَ بِنَا ۖ

He might have made the earth swallow us too.

وَيْكَأَنَّهُۥ لَا يُفْلِحُ الْكَٰفِرُونَ ۝

Don't you see that the faithless do not prosper.'

83 تِلْكَ الدَّارُ الْءَاخِرَةُ

83 This is the abode of the Hereafter

نَجْعَلُهَا لِلَّذِينَ

which We shall grant to those

لَا يُرِيدُونَ عُلُوًّا فِى الْأَرْضِ

who do not desire to domineer in the earth

وَلَا فَسَادًا ۚ

nor to cause corruption,

وَالْعَٰقِبَةُ لِلْمُتَّقِينَ ۝

and the outcome will be in favour of the Godwary.

84 مَن جَآءَ بِالْحَسَنَةِ

84 Whoever brings virtue

فَلَهُۥ خَيْرٌ مِّنْهَا ۖ

shall receive a reward better than it,

---

[1] Because 'the guilty shall be known by their mark.' Cf. 55:39-41.

but whoever brings vice
—those who commit misdeeds shall not be requited
except for what they used to do.

85 Indeed, He who has revealed to you the Qur'ān[1]
will surely restore you to the place of return.
Say, 'My Lord knows best him who brings guidance
and him who is in plain error.'

86 You did not expect
that the Book would be delivered to *you*,
but it was a mercy from *your* Lord.
So *do not be* ever an advocate of the faithless.

87 *Do not ever let* them bar *you* from God's signs
after they have been sent down to *you*.
Invite to *your* Lord
and never *be* one of the polytheists.

88 And *do not invoke* another god besides God;
there is no god except Him.
Everything is to perish except His Face.
All judgement belongs to Him
and to Him you will be brought back.

29. THE SPIDER[2]
al-'Ankabūt

In the Name of God,
the All-beneficent, the All-merciful.

1 *Alif, Lām, Mīm.*

2 Do the people suppose that they will be let off
because they say, 'We have faith,'
and they will not be tested?

---

[1] Or 'charged you with the Qur'ān.'
[2] This Makkī *sūrah* is named after verse 41 which mentions the spider (*'ankabūt*).

3 Certainly We tested those who were before them.
So God shall surely ascertain those who are truthful
and He shall surely ascertain the liars.

4 Do those who commit misdeeds suppose
that they can outmaneuver Us?
Evil is the judgement that they make.

5 Whoever expects to encounter God [should know]
that God's appointed time will indeed come,
and He is the All-hearing, the All-knowing.

6 Whoever strives, strives only for his own sake.[1]
God has indeed no need of the creatures.

7 As for those who have faith and do righteous deeds,
We will absolve them of their misdeeds
and We will surely reward them by the best
of hat they used to do.

8 We have enjoined man to be good to his parents.
But if they urge you to ascribe to Me as partner
that of which you have no knowledge,
then do not obey them.
To Me will be your return, whereat I will inform you
concerning what you used to do.

9 Those who have faith and do righteous deeds,
We will surely admit them among the righteous.

10 Among the people there are those who say,
'We have faith in God,'
but if such a one is tormented in God's cause,
he takes persecution by the people for God's punishment.
Yet if there comes any help[2] from your Lord,

---

[1] Or 'Whoever wages *jihād*, wages *jihād* only for his own sake.'
[2] Or 'victory.'

they will say, 'We were indeed with you.'
Does not God know best
what is in the breasts of the creatures?
11 God shall surely ascertain those who have faith
and He shall surely ascertain the hypocrites.

12 The faithless say to the faithful,
'Follow our way
and we will bear responsibility for your iniquities.'
They will not bear
anything of their iniquities.
They are indeed liars.

13 But they will carry their own burdens
and other burdens along with their own,
and they will surely be questioned
on the Day of Resurrection
concerning that which they used to fabricate.

14 Certainly We sent Noah to his people
and he remained with them
for a thousand-less-fifty years.
Then the flood overtook them while they were wrongdoers.

15 Then We delivered him and those who were in the Ark
and made it a sign for all the nations.

16 And Abraham, when he said to his people,
'Worship God and be wary of Him.
That is better for you,
should you know.

17 What you worship instead of God are mere idols,
and you invent a lie.

Indeed, those whom you worship besides God
have no control over your provision.
So seek all your provision from God
and worship Him and thank Him,
and to Him you shall be brought back.'[1]

18 If you impugn [the Apostle's teaching],
then other nations have impugned likewise before you,
and the Apostle's duty is only to communicate in clear terms.

19 Have they not regarded how God originates the creation?
Then He will bring it back.
That is indeed easy for God.

20 Say, 'Travel through the land and observe
how He has originated the creation.'
Then God will bring about the genesis of the Hereafter.
Indeed, God has power over all things.

21 He will punish whomever He wishes
and have mercy on whomever He wishes,
and to Him you will be returned.

22 You cannot frustrate Him on the earth
or in the heaven,
nor do you have besides God
any friend or helper.

23 Those who deny the signs of God
and the encounter with Him—
they have despaired of My mercy,
and for such there is a painful punishment.

24 But the only answer of his people was
that they said, 'Kill him, or burn him.'
Then God delivered him from the fire.

---

[1] The narrative of Abraham is resumed in verse 24 below.

There are indeed signs in that for people who have faith.

25 He said,
'You have taken idols for worship besides God just
for the sake of mutual affection amongst yourselves
in the life of the world.
Then on the Day of Resurrection
you will disown one another
and curse one another,[1]
and the Fire will be your abode
and you will not have any helpers.'

26 Thereupon Lot believed in him
and he said, 'I am indeed migrating toward my Lord.
Indeed, He is the All-mighty, the All-wise.'

27 And We gave him Isaac and Jacob
and We ordained among his descendants
prophethood and the Book
and We gave him his reward in this world,
and in the Hereafter he will indeed be
among the Righteous.

28 And Lot, when he said to his people,
'You indeed commit an indecency
not committed before you by any community!

29 What! Do you come to men and cut off the way,[2]
and commit outrages in your gatherings?'
But the only answer of his people was
that they said, 'Bring down on us God's punishment,
if you are truthful.'

30 He said, 'My Lord! Help me against this corruptive lot.'

---

[1] Cf. **43**:67.
[2] That is, the natural way of conjugal relations between the sexes.

وَلَمَّا جَاءَتْ رُسُلُنَا إِبْرَاهِيمَ 31 And when Our messengers[1] came to Abraham
بِالْبُشْرَىٰ with the good news,
قَالُوا they said,
إِنَّا مُهْلِكُو أَهْلِ هَـٰذِهِ الْقَرْيَةِ ۖ 'We are going to destroy the people of this town.
إِنَّ أَهْلَهَا كَانُوا ظَالِمِينَ ۝ Its people are indeed wrongdoers.'
قَالَ إِنَّ فِيهَا لُوطًا ۚ 32 He said, 'Lot is in it.'
قَالُوا نَحْنُ أَعْلَمُ بِمَن فِيهَا ۖ They said, 'We know better those who are in it.
لَنُنَجِّيَنَّهُ وَأَهْلَهُ إِلَّا امْرَأَتَهُ We will surely deliver him and his family, except his wife:
كَانَتْ مِنَ الْغَابِرِينَ ۝ she shall be one of those who remain behind.'
وَلَمَّا أَن جَاءَتْ رُسُلُنَا لُوطًا 33 And when Our messengers came to Lot,
سِيءَ بِهِمْ he was distressed on their account
وَضَاقَ بِهِمْ ذَرْعًا and in a predicament for their sake.
وَقَالُوا لَا تَخَفْ وَلَا تَحْزَنْ ۖ But they said, 'Do not be afraid, nor grieve!
إِنَّا مُنَجُّوكَ وَأَهْلَكَ إِلَّا امْرَأَتَكَ We shall deliver you and your family, except your wife:
كَانَتْ مِنَ الْغَابِرِينَ ۝ she will be one of those who remain behind.
إِنَّا مُنزِلُونَ 34 We are indeed going to bring down
عَلَىٰ أَهْلِ هَـٰذِهِ الْقَرْيَةِ upon the people of this town
رِجْزًا مِّنَ السَّمَاءِ a punishment from the sky
بِمَا كَانُوا يَفْسُقُونَ ۝ because of the transgressions they used to commit.'
وَلَقَد تَّرَكْنَا مِنْهَا آيَةً بَيِّنَةً 35 Certainly We have left of it a manifest sign
لِّقَوْمٍ يَعْقِلُونَ ۝ for a people who exercise their reason.

وَإِلَىٰ مَدْيَنَ أَخَاهُمْ شُعَيْبًا 36 And to Midian We sent Shu'ayb, their compatriot.
فَقَالَ يَا قَوْمِ اعْبُدُوا اللَّهَ He said, 'O my people! Worship God
وَارْجُوا الْيَوْمَ الْآخِرَ and expect to encounter the Last Day,
وَلَا تَعْثَوْا فِي الْأَرْضِ مُفْسِدِينَ ۝ and do not act wickedly on the earth causing corruption.'
فَكَذَّبُوهُ 37 But they impugned him,
فَأَخَذَتْهُمُ الرَّجْفَةُ whereupon the earthquake seized them
فَأَصْبَحُوا فِي دَارِهِمْ جَاثِمِينَ ۝ and they lay lifeless prostrate in their homes.

---

[1] That is, the angels sent to give the good news of Isaac's birth to Abraham and to destroy the people of Sodom.

38 And ʿĀd and Thamūd,
whose fate is evident to you from their habitations.
Satan made their deeds seem decorous to them,
thus he barred them from the way of God,
though they used to be perceptive.[1]

39 And Korah, Pharaoh, and Hāmān.
Certainly Moses brought them manifest proofs,
but they acted arrogantly in the land;
though they could not outmaneuver God.

40 So We seized each of them for his sin:
among them were those
upon whom We unleashed a rain of stones,
and among them were those who were seized by the Cry,
and among them were those
whom We caused the earth to swallow,
and among them were those whom We drowned.
It was not God who wronged them,
but it was they who used to wrong themselves.

41 The parable of those who take protectors instead of God,
is that of the spider that makes a home,
and indeed the frailest of homes is the home of a spider,
had they known!

42 God indeed knows
whatever thing they invoke besides Him,
and He is the All-mighty, the All-wise.

43 We draw these parables for mankind;
but no one grasps them
except those who have knowledge.

---

[1] That is, they let themselves be deceived by Satan despite their God-given ability to discern between good and evil.

44 God created the heavens and the earth
   with consummate wisdom.
   There is indeed a sign in that for the faithful.
45 *Recite* what has been revealed to you of the Book
   and *maintain* the prayer.
   Indeed, the prayer restrains
       from indecent and wrongful conduct,
   and the remembrance of God is surely greater.
   And God knows whatever deeds you do.

[PART 21]

46 Do not argue with the People of the Book
       except in a manner which is best,
       except such of them as are wrongdoers,
   and say, 'We believe in what has been sent down to us
       and has been sent down to you;
   our God and your God is one and the same
       and to Him do we submit.'

47 Thus have We sent down the Book to *you*;
   those to whom We have given the Book believe in it,
   and of these[1] there are some who believe in it,
   and none contests Our signs except the faithless.
48 You did not use to recite any scripture before it,
   nor did *you* write it with *your* right hand,
   for then the impugners would have been skeptical.
49 Indeed, it is present as manifest signs
   in the breasts of those who have been given knowledge,
   and none contests Our signs except wrongdoers.

---

[1] That is, of the people of Makkah.

50 They say, 'Why has not some sign[1] been sent down
to him from his Lord?'
Say, 'These signs are only from God,
and I am only a manifest warner.'

51 Does it not suffice them
that We have sent down to you the Book
which is recited to them?
There is indeed in that a mercy and admonition
for a people who have faith.

52 Say, 'God suffices as witness between me and you:
He knows whatever there is in the heavens and the earth.
Those who put faith in falsehood and defy God
—it is they who are the losers.'

53 They ask you to hasten the punishment.
Yet were it not for a specified time,
the punishment would have surely overtaken them.
Surely it will overtake them suddenly
while they are unaware.

54 They ask you to hasten the punishment,
and indeed hell will besiege the faithless

55 on the day when the punishment envelopes them
from above them and from under their feet,
and He will say, 'Taste what you used to do!'

56 O My servants who have faith!
My earth is indeed vast.
So worship only Me.

57 Every soul shall taste death.
Then you shall be brought back to Us.

58 Those who have faith and do righteous deeds,

---

[1] That is, a miracle.

لَنُبَوِّئَنَّهُم مِّنَ الْجَنَّةِ غُرَفًا We will settle them in the lofty abodes of paradise
تَجْرِى مِن تَحْتِهَا الْأَنْهَارُ with streams running in them,
خَالِدِينَ فِيهَا to remain in them.
نِعْمَ أَجْرُ الْعَامِلِينَ ۝ How excellent is the reward of the workers!
الَّذِينَ صَبَرُوا 59 —Those who are patient
وَعَلَىٰ رَبِّهِمْ يَتَوَكَّلُونَ ۝ and who put their trust in their Lord.

وَكَأَيِّن مِّن دَابَّةٍ 60 How many an animal there is
لَّا تَحْمِلُ رِزْقَهَا that does not carry its own provision.
اللَّهُ يَرْزُقُهَا وَإِيَّاكُمْ God provides them and you
وَهُوَ السَّمِيعُ الْعَلِيمُ ۝ and He is the All-hearing, the All-knowing.
وَلَئِن سَأَلْتَهُم مَّنْ خَلَقَ السَّمَاوَاتِ 61 If you ask them, 'Who created the heavens
وَالْأَرْضَ and the earth
وَسَخَّرَ الشَّمْسَ وَالْقَمَرَ and disposed the sun and the moon?'
لَيَقُولُنَّ اللَّهُ They will surely say, 'God.'
فَأَنَّىٰ يُؤْفَكُونَ ۝ Then where do they stray?
اللَّهُ يَبْسُطُ 62 God expands the provision
الرِّزْقَ لِمَن يَشَاءُ مِنْ عِبَادِهِ for whomever He wishes of His servants
وَيَقْدِرُ لَهُ and tightens it for him.
إِنَّ اللَّهَ بِكُلِّ شَيْءٍ عَلِيمٌ ۝ Indeed, God has knowledge of all things.
وَلَئِن سَأَلْتَهُم 63 And if you ask them,
مَّن نَّزَّلَ مِنَ السَّمَاءِ مَاءً 'Who sends down water from the sky,
فَأَحْيَا بِهِ الْأَرْضَ مِن بَعْدِ مَوْتِهَا with which He revives the earth after its death?'
لَيَقُولُنَّ اللَّهُ They will surely say, 'God.'
قُلِ الْحَمْدُ لِلَّهِ Say, 'All praise belongs to God!'
بَلْ أَكْثَرُهُمْ لَا يَعْقِلُونَ ۝ But most of them do not exercise their reason.
وَمَا هَٰذِهِ الْحَيَاةُ الدُّنْيَا 64 The life of this world is nothing
إِلَّا لَهْوٌ وَلَعِبٌ but diversion and play,
وَإِنَّ الدَّارَ الْآخِرَةَ لَهِيَ الْحَيَوَانُ but the abode of the Hereafter is indeed Life itself,
لَوْ كَانُوا يَعْلَمُونَ ۝ had they known!

65 When they board the ship, they invoke God
     putting exclusive faith in Him,
   but when He delivers them to land,
   behold, they ascribe partners to Him,
66 being ungrateful for what We have given them!
   So let them enjoy. Soon they will know!
67 Have they not seen
   that We have appointed a safe sanctuary,[1]
     while the people are despoiled all around them?
   Would they then believe in falsehood
   and be ungrateful toward the blessing of God?
68 Who is a greater wrongdoer than him
     who fabricates lies against God,
   or denies the truth when it comes to him?
   Is not the final abode of the faithless in hell?

69 As for those who strive in Us,
   We shall surely guide them in Our ways,
   and God is indeed with the virtuous.

30. The Byzantines[2]
al-Rūm

In the Name of God,
the All-beneficent, the All-merciful.

1 *Alif, Lām, Mīm.*
2 The Byzantines have been vanquished
3 in a nearby territory,
   but after their defeat they will be victorious
4 in a few years.

---

[1] That is, the city of Makkah.
[2] This late Makkī *sūrah* is named after verse 2 about the Byzantines (*al-Rūm*).

لِلَّهِ الْأَمْرُ مِن قَبْلُ وَمِن بَعْدُ
وَيَوْمَئِذٍ يَفْرَحُ الْمُؤْمِنُونَ ۝

All command belongs to God, before this and hereafter,
and on that day the faithful will rejoice
at God's help.

5 بِنَصْرِ اللَّهِ
يَنصُرُ مَن يَشَاءُ
وَهُوَ الْعَزِيزُ الرَّحِيمُ ۝

He helps whomever He wishes,
and He is the All-mighty, the All-merciful.

6 وَعْدَ اللَّهِ
لَا يُخْلِفُ اللَّهُ وَعْدَهُ
وَلَٰكِنَّ أَكْثَرَ النَّاسِ لَا يَعْلَمُونَ ۝

This is a promise of God:
God does not break His promise,
but most people do not know.

7 يَعْلَمُونَ ظَاهِرًا مِنَ الْحَيَاةِ الدُّنْيَا
وَهُمْ عَنِ الْآخِرَةِ هُمْ غَافِلُونَ ۝

They know just an outward aspect of the life of the world,
but they are oblivious of the Hereafter.

8 أَوَلَمْ يَتَفَكَّرُوا فِي أَنفُسِهِم
مَّا خَلَقَ اللَّهُ السَّمَاوَاتِ وَالْأَرْضَ
وَمَا بَيْنَهُمَا
إِلَّا بِالْحَقِّ
وَأَجَلٍ مُّسَمًّى
وَإِنَّ كَثِيرًا مِنَ النَّاسِ
بِلِقَاءِ رَبِّهِمْ لَكَافِرُونَ ۝

Have they not reflected in their own souls?
God did not create the heavens and the earth
and whatever is between them
except with consummate wisdom
and for a specified term.
Indeed, many of these people
disbelieve in the encounter with their Lord.

9 أَوَلَمْ يَسِيرُوا فِي الْأَرْضِ فَيَنظُرُوا
كَيْفَ كَانَ عَاقِبَةُ الَّذِينَ مِن قَبْلِهِمْ
كَانُوا أَشَدَّ مِنْهُمْ قُوَّةً
وَأَثَارُوا الْأَرْضَ
وَعَمَرُوهَا أَكْثَرَ مِمَّا عَمَرُوهَا
وَجَاءَتْهُمْ رُسُلُهُم بِالْبَيِّنَاتِ
فَمَا كَانَ اللَّهُ لِيَظْلِمَهُمْ
وَلَٰكِن كَانُوا أَنفُسَهُمْ يَظْلِمُونَ ۝

Have they not traveled through the land and observed
how was the fate of those who were before them?
They were more powerful than them,
and they plowed the earth
and developed it more than they have developed it.
Their apostles brought them manifest proofs.
So it was not God who wronged them,
but it was they who used to wrong themselves.

10 ثُمَّ كَانَ عَاقِبَةَ الَّذِينَ أَسَاءُوا السُّوأَىٰ
أَن كَذَّبُوا بِآيَاتِ اللَّهِ
وَكَانُوا بِهَا يَسْتَهْزِئُونَ ۝

Then the fate of those who committed misdeeds was
that they denied the signs of God
and they used to deride them.

11 اللَّهُ يَبْدَأُ الْخَلْقَ
ثُمَّ يُعِيدُهُ

God originates the creation,
then He will bring it back,

then you will be brought back to Him.

12 And when the Hour sets in,
    the guilty will despair.

13 None of those whom they ascribed as partners to God
    will intercede for them,
    and they will disavow their partners.[1]

14 The day the Hour sets in,
    they will be divided on that day in separate groups:

15 As for those who have faith and do righteous deeds,
    they shall be in a garden, rejoicing.

16 But as for those who were faithless
    and denied Our signs and the encounter of the Hereafter,
    they will be brought to the punishment.

17 So glorify God
    when you enter evening
    and when you rise at dawn.

18 To Him belongs all praise in the heavens and the earth,
    at nightfall and when you enter noontime.

19 He brings forth the living from the dead
    and brings forth the dead from the living,
    and revives the earth after its death.
    Likewise you too shall be raised from the dead.

20 Of His signs is that He created you from dust,
    then, behold, you are humans scattering all over!

21 And of His signs is that He created for you
    mates from your own selves
    that you may take comfort in them,
    and He ordained affection and mercy between you.
    There are indeed signs in that for a people who reflect.

---

[1] Or 'though they had been faithless for the sake of their partners [i.e. their false gods].'

وَمِنْ آيَاتِهِ خَلْقُ السَّمَاوَاتِ وَالْأَرْضِ وَاخْتِلَافُ أَلْسِنَتِكُمْ وَأَلْوَانِكُمْ ۚ إِنَّ فِي ذَٰلِكَ لَآيَاتٍ لِلْعَالِمِينَ ۝

22 Among His signs is the creation of the heavens and the earth and the difference of your languages and colours. There are indeed signs in that for those who know.

وَمِنْ آيَاتِهِ مَنَامُكُمْ بِاللَّيْلِ وَالنَّهَارِ وَابْتِغَاؤُكُمْ مِنْ فَضْلِهِ ۚ إِنَّ فِي ذَٰلِكَ لَآيَاتٍ لِقَوْمٍ يَسْمَعُونَ ۝

23 And of His signs is your sleep by night and day, and your pursuit of His bounty. There are indeed signs in that for a people who listen.

وَمِنْ آيَاتِهِ يُرِيكُمُ الْبَرْقَ خَوْفًا وَطَمَعًا وَيُنَزِّلُ مِنَ السَّمَاءِ مَاءً فَيُحْيِي بِهِ الْأَرْضَ بَعْدَ مَوْتِهَا ۚ إِنَّ فِي ذَٰلِكَ لَآيَاتٍ لِقَوْمٍ يَعْقِلُونَ ۝

24 And of His signs is that He shows you the lightning, arousing fear and hope, and He sends down water from the sky and with it revives the earth after its death. There are indeed signs in that for a people who exercise their reason.

وَمِنْ آيَاتِهِ أَنْ تَقُومَ السَّمَاءُ وَالْأَرْضُ بِأَمْرِهِ ۖ ثُمَّ إِذَا دَعَاكُمْ دَعْوَةً مِنَ الْأَرْضِ إِذَا أَنْتُمْ تَخْرُجُونَ ۝

25 And of His signs is that the heaven and the earth stand by His command, and then, when He calls you forth from the earth, behold, you will come forth.

وَلَهُ مَنْ فِي السَّمَاوَاتِ وَالْأَرْضِ ۖ كُلٌّ لَهُ قَانِتُونَ ۝

26 To Him belongs whoever is in the heavens and the earth. All are obedient to Him.

وَهُوَ الَّذِي يَبْدَأُ الْخَلْقَ ثُمَّ يُعِيدُهُ وَهُوَ أَهْوَنُ عَلَيْهِ ۚ وَلَهُ الْمَثَلُ الْأَعْلَىٰ فِي السَّمَاوَاتِ وَالْأَرْضِ ۚ وَهُوَ الْعَزِيزُ الْحَكِيمُ ۝

27 It is He who originates the creation, and then He will bring it back —and that is more simple for Him. His is the loftiest description in the heavens and the earth, and He is the All-mighty, the All-wise.

ضَرَبَ لَكُمْ مَثَلًا مِنْ أَنْفُسِكُمْ ۖ هَلْ لَكُمْ مِنْ مَا مَلَكَتْ أَيْمَانُكُمْ مِنْ شُرَكَاءَ فِي مَا رَزَقْنَاكُمْ فَأَنْتُمْ فِيهِ سَوَاءٌ

28 He draws for you an example from yourselves: Do you have among your slaves any partners who may share in what We have provided you, so that you are equal in its respect,

and you revere them as you revere one another?[1]
Thus do We elaborate[2] the signs
for a people who exercise their reason.
29 The wrongdoers indeed follow their base desires
without any knowledge.
So who will guide those whom God has led astray?
They will have no helpers.

30 So set your heart on this religion as a person of pure faith,
the original nature endowed by God
according to which He originated mankind
(There is no altering God's creation;
that is the upright religion,
but most people do not know.)
31 —turning to Him in penitence,
and be wary of Him, and maintain the prayer,
and do not be one of the polytheists
32 —those who split up their religion and became sects:
each faction rejoicing in what it possessed.

33 When distress befalls people, they supplicate their Lord,
turning to Him in penitence.
Then, when He lets them taste His mercy,
behold, a part of them ascribe partners to their Lord,
34 being ungrateful toward what We have given them.
So let them enjoy. Soon they will know!
35 Have We sent down to them any authority
which might assert what they associate with Him?
36 When We let people taste Our mercy,

---

[1] Or 'revere your own folks.'
[2] Or 'articulate.'

                                                                                they rejoice in it; فَرِحُوا بِهَا

but should an ill visit them وَإِنْ تُصِبْهُمْ سَيِّئَةٌ

because of what their hands have sent ahead, بِمَا قَدَّمَتْ أَيْدِيهِمْ

behold, they become despondent! إِذَا هُمْ يَقْنَطُونَ ۝

37 Do they not see that God expands the provision أَوَلَمْ يَرَوْا أَنَّ اللَّهَ يَبْسُطُ الرِّزْقَ

and tightens it for whomever He wishes? لِمَنْ يَشَاءُ وَيَقْدِرُ

There are indeed signs in that for people who have faith. إِنَّ فِي ذَٰلِكَ لَآيَاتٍ لِقَوْمٍ يُؤْمِنُونَ ۝

38 *Give* the relative his due, فَآتِ ذَا الْقُرْبَىٰ حَقَّهُ

and the needy and the traveler as well. وَالْمِسْكِينَ وَابْنَ السَّبِيلِ

That is better for those who seek God's pleasure, ذَٰلِكَ خَيْرٌ لِلَّذِينَ يُرِيدُونَ وَجْهَ اللَّهِ

and it is they who are the felicitous. وَأُولَٰئِكَ هُمُ الْمُفْلِحُونَ ۝

39 What you give in usury وَمَا آتَيْتُمْ مِنْ رِبًا

in order that it may increase people's wealth لِيَرْبُوَ فِي أَمْوَالِ النَّاسِ

does not increase with God. فَلَا يَرْبُو عِنْدَ اللَّهِ

But what you pay as *zakāt* seeking God's pleasure وَمَا آتَيْتُمْ مِنْ زَكَاةٍ تُرِيدُونَ وَجْهَ اللَّهِ

—it is they who will be given a manifold increase. فَأُولَٰئِكَ هُمُ الْمُضْعِفُونَ ۝

40 It is God who created you اللَّهُ الَّذِي خَلَقَكُمْ

and then He provided for you, ثُمَّ رَزَقَكُمْ

then He makes you die, then He will bring you to life. ثُمَّ يُمِيتُكُمْ ثُمَّ يُحْيِيكُمْ

Is there anyone among your 'partners' هَلْ مِنْ شُرَكَائِكُمْ

who does anything of that kind? مَنْ يَفْعَلُ مِنْ ذَٰلِكُمْ مِنْ شَيْءٍ

Immaculate is He and far above having سُبْحَانَهُ وَتَعَالَىٰ

any partners that they ascribe to Him! عَمَّا يُشْرِكُونَ ۝

41 Corruption has appeared in land and sea ظَهَرَ الْفَسَادُ فِي الْبَرِّ وَالْبَحْرِ

because of the doings of the people's hands, بِمَا كَسَبَتْ أَيْدِي النَّاسِ

that He may make them taste لِيُذِيقَهُمْ

some of what they have done, بَعْضَ الَّذِي عَمِلُوا

so that they may come back. لَعَلَّهُمْ يَرْجِعُونَ ۝

42 Say, 'Travel through the land and see
how was the fate of those who were before you,
most of whom were polytheists.'

43 So set your heart on the upright religion,
before there comes a day irrevocable from God.
On that day they shall be split into various groups.[1]

44 Whoever is faithless
shall face the consequences of his unfaith,
and those who act righteously
only prepare for their own souls,

45 so that He may reward those who have faith
and do righteous deeds
out of His grace.
Indeed, He does not like the faithless.

46 And of His signs is that He sends the winds
as bearers of good news
and to let you taste of His mercy,
and that the ships may sail by His command,
and that you may seek of His bounty,
and so that you may give Him thanks.

47 Certainly We sent apostles to their people before you
and they brought them manifest proofs.
Then We took vengeance upon those who were guilty,
and it was a must for Us to help the faithful.

48 It is God who sends the winds.
Then they generate a cloud,
then He spreads it as He wishes in the sky,
and forms it into fragments,
whereat you see the rain issuing from its midst.

---

[1] See **39**:71, 73; **56**:7-56.

فَإِذَا أَصَابَ بِهِ	Then, when He strikes with it
مَنْ يَشَاءُ مِنْ عِبَادِهِ	whomever of His servants He wishes,
إِذَا هُمْ يَسْتَبْشِرُونَ ۝	behold, they rejoice;
وَإِنْ كَانُوا مِنْ قَبْلِ أَنْ يُنَزَّلَ عَلَيْهِمْ	49 and, indeed, before it was sent down upon them,
مِنْ قَبْلِهِ لَمُبْلِسِينَ ۝	they had been despondent earlier.
فَانْظُرْ إِلَىٰ آثَارِ رَحْمَتِ اللَّهِ	50 So *observe* the effects of God's mercy:
كَيْفَ يُحْيِي الْأَرْضَ بَعْدَ مَوْتِهَا	how He revives the earth after its death!
إِنَّ ذَٰلِكَ لَمُحْيِي الْمَوْتَىٰ	He is indeed the reviver of the dead
وَهُوَ عَلَىٰ كُلِّ شَيْءٍ قَدِيرٌ ۝	and He has power over all things.
وَلَئِنْ أَرْسَلْنَا رِيحًا فَرَأَوْهُ مُصْفَرًّا	51 And if We send a wind and they see it[1] turn yellow,
لَظَلُّوا مِنْ بَعْدِهِ يَكْفُرُونَ ۝	they will surely become ungrateful after that.[2]
فَإِنَّكَ لَا تُسْمِعُ الْمَوْتَىٰ	52 Indeed, you cannot make the dead hear,
وَلَا تُسْمِعُ الصُّمَّ الدُّعَاءَ	nor can you make the deaf hear the call
إِذَا وَلَّوْا مُدْبِرِينَ ۝	when they turn their backs upon *you*,
وَمَا أَنْتَ بِهَادِ الْعُمْيِ عَنْ ضَلَالَتِهِمْ	53 nor can you lead the blind out of their error.
إِنْ تُسْمِعُ إِلَّا مَنْ	You can make hear only those
يُؤْمِنُ بِآيَاتِنَا فَهُمْ مُسْلِمُونَ ۝	who have faith in Our signs and have submitted.
اللَّهُ الَّذِي خَلَقَكُمْ مِنْ ضَعْفٍ	54 It is God who created you from a state of weakness,
ثُمَّ جَعَلَ مِنْ بَعْدِ ضَعْفٍ قُوَّةً	then He gave you power after weakness.
ثُمَّ جَعَلَ مِنْ بَعْدِ قُوَّةٍ ضَعْفًا وَشَيْبَةً	Then, after power, He ordained weakness and old age:
يَخْلُقُ مَا يَشَاءُ	He creates whatever He wishes
وَهُوَ الْعَلِيمُ الْقَدِيرُ ۝	and He is the All-knowing, the All-powerful.
وَيَوْمَ تَقُومُ السَّاعَةُ	55 On the day when the Hour sets in,
يُقْسِمُ الْمُجْرِمُونَ	the guilty will swear
مَا لَبِثُوا غَيْرَ سَاعَةٍ	that they had not remained except for an hour.
كَذَٰلِكَ كَانُوا يُؤْفَكُونَ ۝	That is how they were used to lying [in the world].
وَقَالَ الَّذِينَ أُوتُوا الْعِلْمَ وَالْإِيمَانَ	56 But those who were given knowledge and faith will say,
لَقَدْ لَبِثْتُمْ فِي كِتَابِ اللَّهِ	'Certainly you remained in God's Book[3]
إِلَىٰ يَوْمِ الْبَعْثِ	until the Day of Resurrection.

---

[1] That is, their farms and orchards.
[2] That is, after they have been joyous on God's reviving the dead earth and turning it green.
[3] That is, in the Preserved Tablet. Cf. 56:78.

This is the Day of Resurrection,
but you did not know.'

57 On that day,
the excuses of the wrongdoers will not benefit them,
nor will they be asked to propitiate God.

58 Certainly we have drawn for mankind in this Qur'ān
every kind of parable.
Indeed, if you bring them a sign,[1]
the faithless will surely say,
'You are nothing but fabricators!'

59 Thus does God seal the hearts
of those who do not know.

60 So *be patient!* God's promise is indeed true.
And do not let yourself to be demoralized
by those who have no conviction.

31. LUQMĀN[2]
Luqmān

In the Name of God,
the All-beneficent, the All-merciful.

1 *Alif, Lām, Mīm.*
2 These are the signs of the wise Book,
3 a guidance and mercy for the virtuous,
4 who maintain the prayer, pay the *zakāt*,
and are certain of the Hereafter.
5 Those follow their Lord's guidance,
and it is they who are the felicitous.
6 Among the people is he who buys diversionary talk
that he may lead astray from God's way

---

[1] That is, a miracle.
[2] A Makkī *sūrah*, named after Luqmān, whose account appears in verses 12-19.

بِغَيْرِ عِلْمٍ without any knowledge,

وَيَتَّخِذَهَا هُزُوًا and take it in derision.

أُولَٰئِكَ لَهُمْ عَذَابٌ مُهِينٌ ۝ For such there is a humiliating punishment.

7 وَإِذَا تُتْلَىٰ عَلَيْهِ آيَاتُنَا When Our signs are recited to him

وَلَّىٰ مُسْتَكْبِرًا he turns away disdainfully,

كَأَن لَّمْ يَسْمَعْهَا as if he had not heard them at all,

كَأَنَّ فِي أُذُنَيْهِ وَقْرًا as if there were a deafness in his ears.

فَبَشِّرْهُ بِعَذَابٍ أَلِيمٍ ۝ So *inform* him of a painful punishment.

8 إِنَّ الَّذِينَ آمَنُوا وَعَمِلُوا الصَّالِحَاتِ As for those who have faith and do righteous deeds,

لَهُمْ جَنَّاتُ النَّعِيمِ ۝ for them will be gardens of bliss,

9 خَالِدِينَ فِيهَا to remain in them

وَعْدَ اللَّهِ حَقًّا —a true promise of God,

وَهُوَ الْعَزِيزُ الْحَكِيمُ ۝ and He is the All-mighty, the All-wise.

10 خَلَقَ السَّمَاوَاتِ He created the heavens

بِغَيْرِ عَمَدٍ تَرَوْنَهَا without any pillars that you may see,

وَأَلْقَىٰ فِي الْأَرْضِ رَوَاسِيَ and cast firm mountains in the earth

أَن تَمِيدَ بِكُمْ lest it should shake with you,

وَبَثَّ فِيهَا مِن كُلِّ دَابَّةٍ and He has scattered in it every kind of animal.

وَأَنزَلْنَا مِنَ السَّمَاءِ مَاءً And We sent down water from the sky

فَأَنبَتْنَا فِيهَا مِن كُلِّ زَوْجٍ كَرِيمٍ ۝ and caused every splendid kind of plant to grow in it.

11 هَٰذَا خَلْقُ اللَّهِ This is the creation of God.

فَأَرُونِي مَاذَا خَلَقَ الَّذِينَ مِن دُونِهِ Now show Me what others besides Him have created.

بَلِ الظَّالِمُونَ فِي ضَلَالٍ مُبِينٍ ۝ The wrongdoers are indeed in plain error!

12 وَلَقَدْ آتَيْنَا لُقْمَانَ الْحِكْمَةَ Certainly We gave Luqman wisdom,

أَنِ اشْكُرْ لِلَّهِ saying, 'Give thanks to God;

وَمَن يَشْكُرْ فَإِنَّمَا and whoever gives thanks,

يَشْكُرُ لِنَفْسِهِ gives thanks only for his own sake.

وَمَن كَفَرَ And whoever is ungrateful, [let him know that]

فَإِنَّ اللَّهَ غَنِيٌّ حَمِيدٌ ۝ God is indeed all-sufficient, all-laudable.'

13 وَإِذْ قَالَ لُقْمَانُ لِابْنِهِ وَهُوَ يَعِظُهُ When Luqman said to his son, as he advised him:

يَا بُنَيَّ لَا تُشْرِكْ بِاللَّهِ   'O my son! Do not ascribe any partners to God.
إِنَّ الشِّرْكَ لَظُلْمٌ عَظِيمٌ ۝   Polytheism is indeed a great injustice.'

وَوَصَّيْنَا الْإِنْسَانَ بِوَالِدَيْهِ   14 We have enjoined man concerning his parents:
حَمَلَتْهُ أُمُّهُ وَهْنًا عَلَىٰ وَهْنٍ   His mother carried him through weakness upon weakness,
وَفِصَالُهُ فِي عَامَيْنِ   and his weaning takes two years.
أَنِ اشْكُرْ لِي وَلِوَالِدَيْكَ   Give thanks to Me and to your parents.
إِلَيَّ الْمَصِيرُ ۝   To Me is the return.

وَإِنْ جَاهَدَاكَ عَلَىٰ أَنْ تُشْرِكَ بِي   15 But if they urge you to ascribe to Me as partner
مَا لَيْسَ لَكَ بِهِ عِلْمٌ   that of which you have no knowledge,
فَلَا تُطِعْهُمَا   then do not obey them.
وَصَاحِبْهُمَا فِي الدُّنْيَا مَعْرُوفًا   Keep their company honourably in this world
وَاتَّبِعْ سَبِيلَ مَنْ أَنَابَ إِلَيَّ   and follow the way of those who turn to Me penitently.
ثُمَّ إِلَيَّ مَرْجِعُكُمْ   Then to Me will be your return,
فَأُنَبِّئُكُمْ بِمَا كُنْتُمْ تَعْمَلُونَ ۝   whereat I will inform you concerning what you used to do.

يَا بُنَيَّ   16 'O my son!
إِنَّهَا إِنْ تَكُ مِثْقَالَ حَبَّةٍ مِنْ خَرْدَلٍ   Even if it should be the weight of a mustard seed,
فَتَكُنْ فِي صَخْرَةٍ   and even though it should be in a rock,
أَوْ فِي السَّمَاوَاتِ أَوْ فِي الْأَرْضِ   or in the heavens, or in the earth,
يَأْتِ بِهَا اللَّهُ   God will produce it.
إِنَّ اللَّهَ لَطِيفٌ خَبِيرٌ ۝   God is indeed all-attentive, all-aware.

يَا بُنَيَّ أَقِمِ الصَّلَاةَ   17 O my son! Maintain the prayer
وَأْمُرْ بِالْمَعْرُوفِ وَانْهَ عَنِ الْمُنْكَرِ   and bid what is right and forbid what is wrong,
وَاصْبِرْ عَلَىٰ مَا أَصَابَكَ   and be patient through whatever may befall you.
إِنَّ ذَٰلِكَ مِنْ عَزْمِ الْأُمُورِ ۝   That is indeed the steadiest of courses.

وَلَا تُصَعِّرْ خَدَّكَ لِلنَّاسِ   18 Do not turn your cheek away disdainfully from the people,
وَلَا تَمْشِ فِي الْأَرْضِ مَرَحًا   and do not walk boastfully on the earth.
إِنَّ اللَّهَ لَا يُحِبُّ كُلَّ مُخْتَالٍ فَخُورٍ ۝   Indeed, God does not like any swaggering braggart.

وَاقْصِدْ فِي مَشْيِكَ   19 Be modest in your bearing,
وَاغْضُضْ مِنْ صَوْتِكَ   and lower your voice.
إِنَّ أَنْكَرَ الْأَصْوَاتِ لَصَوْتُ الْحَمِيرِ ۝   Indeed, the ungainliest of voices is the donkey's voice.'

20 Do you not see that God has disposed for you
whatever there is in the heavens
and whatever there is in the earth,
and He has showered upon you His blessings,
the outward and the inward?
Yet among the people are those
who dispute concerning God without any knowledge
or guidance or an illuminating scripture.

21 When they are told, 'Follow what God has sent down,'
they say,
'No, we will follow what we found our fathers following.'
What! Even if Satan be calling them
to the punishment of the Blaze?

22 Whoever surrenders his heart to God
and is virtuous,
has certainly held fast to the firmest handle,
and with God lies the outcome of all matters.

23 As for those who are faithless,
let their unfaith not grieve you.
To Us will be their return,
and We will inform them about what they have done.
Indeed, God knows best what is in the breasts.

24 We will provide for them for a short time,
then We will shove them toward a harsh punishment.

25 If you ask them,
'Who created the heavens and the earth?'
they will surely say, 'God.'
Say, 'All praise belongs to God!'
But most of them do not know.

26 To God belongs whatever is in the heavens and the earth.

Indeed, God is the All-sufficient, the All-laudable.

27 If all the trees on the earth were pens,
   and the sea replenished with seven more seas [were ink],
   the words of God would not be spent.
   God is indeed all-mighty, all-wise.

28 Your creation and your resurrection
   are not but as of a single soul.
   God is indeed all-hearing, all-seeing.

29 Have you not regarded that God
   makes the night pass into the day
   and makes the day pass into the night;
   and He has disposed the sun and the moon,
   each moving for a specified term,
   and that God is well aware of what you do?

30 That is because God is the Reality,[1]
   and whatever they invoke besides Him is nullity,[2]
   and because God is the All-exalted, the All-great.

31 Have you not regarded that the ships sail at sea
   with God's blessing,
   that He may show you some of His signs?
   There are indeed signs in that
   for every patient and grateful servant.

32 When waves cover them like awnings,
   they invoke God, putting exclusive faith in Him.
   But when He delivers them towards land,
   only some of them remain unswerving.
   No one will impugn Our signs
   except an ungrateful traitor.

33 O mankind! Be wary of your Lord

---

[1] Or 'That is because God is the Truth.'
[2] Or 'what they invoke besides Him is falsehood.'

and fear the day when a father will not atone for his child,
nor the child will atone for its father in any wise.
God's promise is indeed true.
So do not let the life of the world deceive you,
nor let the Deceiver[1] deceive you concerning God.

34 The knowledge of the Hour is indeed with God.
He sends down the rain,
and He knows what is in the wombs.
No soul knows what it will earn tomorrow,
and no soul knows in what land it will die.
God is indeed all-knowing, all-aware.

32. Prostration[2]
al-Sajdah

In the Name of God,
the All-beneficent, the All-merciful

1 *Alif, Lām, Mīm.*
2 The gradual sending down of the Book,
there is no doubt in it,
is from the Lord of all the worlds.
3 Do they say, 'He has fabricated it'?
Rather, it is the truth from *your* Lord,
that *you* may warn a people
to whom there did not come any warner before *you*,
so that they may be guided to the right path.
4 It is God who created the heavens and the earth
and whatever is between them in six days,[3]
then He settled on the Throne.

---

[1] That is, Satan, or anything that diverts a human being from the path of God.
[2] This Makkī *sūrah* is named after verse 15, which mentions prostration (*sajdah*).
[3] That is, in six periods of time. Cf. **57:4**.

You do not have any guardian or intercessor besides Him. Will you not then take admonition?

5 He directs the command[1] from the heaven to the earth; then it ascends toward Him in a day[2] whose span is a thousand years by your reckoning.

6 That is the Knower of the sensible and the Unseen, the All-mighty, the All-merciful,

7 who perfected everything that He created, and commenced man's creation from clay.

8 Then He made his progeny from an extract of a base fluid.

9 Then He proportioned him and breathed into him of His Spirit, and invested you with your hearing, sight and hearts. Little do you thank.

10 They say, 'When we have been lost in the dust,[3] shall we be indeed created anew?' Indeed, they disbelieve in the encounter with their Lord.

11 Say, 'You will be taken away by the angel of death, who has been charged with you. Then you will be brought back to your Lord.'

12 Were you to see when the guilty hang their heads before their Lord [confessing], 'Our Lord! We have seen and heard. Send us back so that we may act righteously.

---

[1] Cf. **10**:3, 31; **13**:2.
[2] That is, in a period of time.
[3] That is, 'Shall we be brought forth again after our bodies have decomposed and all traces of our physical remains have disappeared in the ground?'

Indeed, we are now convinced.'

13 Had We wished,
We would have given every soul its guidance,
but My word became due [against the faithless]:
'Surely, I will fill hell
with all the [guilty] jinn and humans.'[1]

14 So taste the punishment for your having forgotten
the encounter of this day of yours.
We too have forgotten you.
Taste the everlasting punishment
because of what you used to do.

15 Only those believe in Our signs who,
when they are reminded of them,
fall down in prostration
and celebrate the praise of their Lord,
and they are not arrogant.

16 Their sides vacate their beds[2]
to supplicate their Lord in fear and hope,
and they spend out of what We have provided them.

17 No one knows
what delights have been kept hidden for them
as a reward for what they used to do.

18 Is someone who is faithful
like someone who is a transgressor?
They are not equal.

19 As for those who have faith and do righteous deeds,
for them will be the gardens of the Abode
—a hospitality for what they used to do.

---

[1] Cf. 7:18; 11:119; 38:85.
[2] That is, they abandon their beds at night and forgo the pleasure of sleep to worship their Lord in a state of fear and hope.

20 وَأَمَّا الَّذِينَ فَسَقُوا   As for those who have transgressed,
فَمَأْوَاهُمُ النَّارُ   their refuge will be the Fire.
كُلَّمَا أَرَادُوا أَن يَخْرُجُوا مِنْهَا   Whenever they seek to leave it,
أُعِيدُوا فِيهَا   they will be turned back into it
وَقِيلَ لَهُمْ ذُوقُوا عَذَابَ النَّارِ   and told: 'Taste the punishment of this Fire
الَّذِي كُنتُم بِهِ تُكَذِّبُونَ ۝   which you used to deny.'
21 وَلَنُذِيقَنَّهُم مِّنَ الْعَذَابِ الْأَدْنَىٰ   We shall surely make them taste the nearer punishment
دُونَ الْعَذَابِ الْأَكْبَرِ   prior to the greater punishment,[1]
لَعَلَّهُمْ يَرْجِعُونَ ۝   so that they may come back.[2]
22 وَمَنْ أَظْلَمُ   Who is a greater wrongdoer
مِمَّن ذُكِّرَ بِآيَاتِ رَبِّهِ   than him who is reminded of his Lord's signs,
ثُمَّ أَعْرَضَ عَنْهَا   whereat he disregards them?
إِنَّا مِنَ الْمُجْرِمِينَ مُنتَقِمُونَ ۝   We shall indeed take vengeance upon the guilty.

23 وَلَقَدْ آتَيْنَا مُوسَى الْكِتَابَ   Certainly We gave Moses the Book, [declaring],
فَلَا تَكُن فِي مِرْيَةٍ مِّن لِّقَائِهِ   'Do not be in doubt about the encounter with Him,'
وَجَعَلْنَاهُ هُدًى   and We made it a source of guidance
لِّبَنِي إِسْرَائِيلَ ۝   for the Children of Israel.
24 وَجَعَلْنَا مِنْهُمْ أَئِمَّةً   We appointed amongst them *imams*
يَهْدُونَ بِأَمْرِنَا   to guide the people by Our command,
لَمَّا صَبَرُوا   when they had been patient
وَكَانُوا بِآيَاتِنَا يُوقِنُونَ ۝   and had conviction in Our signs.
25 إِنَّ رَبَّكَ هُوَ يَفْصِلُ بَيْنَهُمْ   Your Lord will indeed judge between them
يَوْمَ الْقِيَامَةِ   on the Day of Resurrection
فِيمَا كَانُوا فِيهِ يَخْتَلِفُونَ ۝   concerning that about which they used to differ.
26 أَوَلَمْ يَهْدِ لَهُمْ   Does it not dawn upon them
كَمْ أَهْلَكْنَا مِن قَبْلِهِم مِّنَ الْقُرُونِ   how many generations We have destroyed before them,
يَمْشُونَ فِي مَسَاكِنِهِمْ   amid [the ruins of] whose dwellings they walk?

---

[1] Or 'aside from the greater punishment.'
[2] By 'the nearer punishment' is meant the afflictions and hardships the faithless may be made to suffer in the world with the purpose of bringing them back to God and in order to save them from the greater punishment of the Hereafter.

There are indeed signs in that.
Will they not then listen?
27 Do they not see
    that We carry water to the parched earth
    and with it We bring forth crops
    from which they themselves and their cattle eat?
Will they not then see?
28 They say, 'When will this judgement be,
    if you are truthful?'
29 Say, 'On the day of judgement
    their [newly found] faith will not avail the faithless,
    nor will they be granted any respite.'
30 So *turn away* from them, and *wait*.
    They too are waiting.

33. THE CONFEDERATES[1]
al-Aḥzāb

In the Name of God,
the All-beneficent, the All-merciful

1 O Prophet! *Be wary* of God
    and *do not obey* the faithless and the hypocrites.
    God is indeed all-knowing, all-wise.
2 And *follow* that which is revealed to *you* from *your* Lord.
    God is indeed well aware of what *you* do.
3 And *put your* trust in God;
    God suffices as trustee.
4 God has not put two hearts within any man,
    nor has He made your wives

---

[1] This Madanī *sūrah* takes its name from verse 20 which refers to the campaign of the confederates (*aḥzāb*) against the Prophet (ṣ) during Dhū al-Qaʿdah 5 H.

whom you repudiate by *ẓihār*[1] your mothers,
nor has he made your adopted sons your actual sons.
These are mere utterances of your mouths.
But God speaks the truth
and He guides to the right way.

5 Call them after their fathers.
That is more just with God.
And if you do not know their fathers,
then they are your brethren in the faith and your kinsmen.
There will be no sin upon you
    for any mistake that you may make therein,
excepting what your hearts may intend deliberately.
And God is all-forgiving, all-merciful.

6 The Prophet is closer to the faithful than their own souls,[2]
    and his wives are their mothers.
The blood relatives
are more entitled to inherit from one another
in the Book of God[3]
than the other faithful and Emigrants,[4]
barring any favour you may do your kinsmen.[5]
This has been written in the Book.

7 [Recall] when We took a pledge from the prophets,
    and from *you* and from Noah and Abraham
    and Moses and Jesus son of Mary,

---

[1] A kind of repudiation of the marital relationship among pre-Islamic Arabs which took place on a husband's saying to his wife 'Be as my mother's back' (*ẓahr*; hence the derivative *ẓihār*). Concerning the revocation of such a divorce and the atonement prescribed, see 58:1-4.

[2] Or 'The Prophet has a greater right (or a greater authority) over the faithful than they have over their own selves.'

[3] That is, with respect to the right of inheritance.

[4] Or 'The blood relations have more right to inherit from one another than the rest of the faithful.'

[5] That is, by making a bequest in their favour.

and We took from them a solemn pledge, وَأَخَذْنَا مِنْهُمْ مِيثَاقًا غَلِيظًا ۝

8 so that He may question the truthful لِيَسْأَلَ الصَّادِقِينَ
touching their truthfulness. عَنْ صِدْقِهِمْ ۚ
And He has prepared for the faithless a painful punishment. وَأَعَدَّ لِلْكَافِرِينَ عَذَابًا أَلِيمًا ۝

9 O you who have faith! يَا أَيُّهَا الَّذِينَ آمَنُوا
Remember God's blessing upon you اذْكُرُوا نِعْمَةَ اللَّهِ عَلَيْكُمْ
when the hosts came at you, إِذْ جَاءَتْكُمْ جُنُودٌ
and We sent against them a gale فَأَرْسَلْنَا عَلَيْهِمْ رِيحًا
and hosts whom you did not see. وَجُنُودًا لَمْ تَرَوْهَا ۚ
And God sees best what you do. وَكَانَ اللَّهُ بِمَا تَعْمَلُونَ بَصِيرًا ۝

10 When they came at you from above إِذْ جَاءُوكُم مِّن فَوْقِكُمْ
and below you,[1] وَمِنْ أَسْفَلَ مِنكُمْ
and when the eyes rolled with fear وَإِذْ زَاغَتِ الْأَبْصَارُ
and the hearts leapt to the throats وَبَلَغَتِ الْقُلُوبُ الْحَنَاجِرَ
and you entertained misgivings about God, وَتَظُنُّونَ بِاللَّهِ الظُّنُونَا ۝

11 it was there that the faithful were tested هُنَالِكَ ابْتُلِيَ الْمُؤْمِنُونَ
and jolted with a severe agitation. وَزُلْزِلُوا زِلْزَالًا شَدِيدًا ۝

12 When the hypocrites were saying, وَإِذْ يَقُولُ الْمُنَافِقُونَ
as well as those in whose hearts is a sickness, وَالَّذِينَ فِي قُلُوبِهِم مَّرَضٌ
'God and His Apostle did not promise us مَا وَعَدَنَا اللَّهُ وَرَسُولُهُ
[anything] but delusion.' إِلَّا غُرُورًا ۝

13 And when a group of them said, 'O people of Yathrib! وَإِذْ قَالَتْ طَائِفَةٌ مِّنْهُمْ يَا أَهْلَ يَثْرِبَ
This is not a place for you to stand your ground, لَا مُقَامَ لَكُمْ
so go back!'[2] فَارْجِعُوا ۚ
And a group of them sought the Prophet's permission, وَيَسْتَأْذِنُ فَرِيقٌ مِّنْهُمُ النَّبِيَّ
saying, 'Our homes lie exposed[3] to the enemy,' يَقُولُونَ إِنَّ بُيُوتَنَا عَوْرَةٌ
although they were not exposed. وَمَا هِيَ بِعَوْرَةٍ ۖ

---

[1] That is, from the higher side of the valley, to the east of Madinah, and from the lower side of it towards the west.
[2] That is, return to your earlier creed, or go back to your homes.
[3] Or 'unprotected.'

They only sought to flee.

14 Had they been invaded from its flanks[1]
and had they been asked to apostatize,
they would have done so with only a mild hesitation,

15 though they had already pledged to God before
that they would not turn their backs to flee,
and pledges given to God are accountable.

16 Say, 'Flight will not avail you
should you flee from death, or from being killed,
and then you will be let to enjoy only for a little while.'

17 Say, 'Who is it that can protect you from God
if He desires to bring you harm,
or desire to grant you His mercy?'
They will not find for themselves
any friend or helper besides God.

18 God knows those of you who discourage others,
and those who say to their brethren, 'Come to us!'
and take little part in the battle,

19 grudging you their help.
So when there is panic,
you see them observing you,
their eyes rolling
like someone fainting at death.
Then, when the panic is over,
they scald you with their sharp tongues
in their greed for the spoils.
They never have had faith.
So God has made their works fail,
and that is easy for God.

---

[1] That is, of the city Madīnah.

يَحْسَبُونَ الْأَحْزَابَ لَمْ يَذْهَبُوا	20 They suppose the confederates have not left yet,
وَإِن يَأْتِ الْأَحْزَابُ	and were the confederates to come again,
يَوَدُّوا لَوْ أَنَّهُم بَادُونَ فِي الْأَعْرَابِ	they would wish they were in the desert with the Bedouins
يَسْأَلُونَ عَنْ أَنبَائِكُمْ ۖ	asking about your news,
وَلَوْ كَانُوا فِيكُم	and if they were with you
مَّا قَاتَلُوا إِلَّا قَلِيلًا ۝	they would fight but a little.
لَّقَدْ كَانَ لَكُمْ فِي رَسُولِ اللَّهِ	21 In the Apostle of God there is certainly for you
أُسْوَةٌ حَسَنَةٌ	a good exemplar,
لِّمَن كَانَ يَرْجُو اللَّهَ وَالْيَوْمَ الْآخِرَ	for those who look forward to God and the Last Day
وَذَكَرَ اللَّهَ كَثِيرًا ۝	and remember God much.
وَلَمَّا رَأَى الْمُؤْمِنُونَ الْأَحْزَابَ	22 But when the faithful saw the confederates,
قَالُوا	they said,
هَـٰذَا مَا وَعَدَنَا اللَّهُ وَرَسُولُهُ	'This is what God and His Apostle had promised us,
وَصَدَقَ اللَّهُ وَرَسُولُهُ ۚ	and God and His Apostle were true.'
وَمَا زَادَهُمْ إِلَّا إِيمَانًا وَتَسْلِيمًا ۝	And it only increased them in faith and submission.
مِّنَ الْمُؤْمِنِينَ رِجَالٌ	23 Among the faithful are men
صَدَقُوا مَا عَاهَدُوا اللَّهَ عَلَيْهِ ۖ	who are true to their pledge with God:
فَمِنْهُم مَّن قَضَىٰ نَحْبَهُ	some of them have fulfilled their pledge
وَمِنْهُم مَّن يَنتَظِرُ ۖ	and some of them still wait,
وَمَا بَدَّلُوا تَبْدِيلًا ۝	and they have not changed in the least,
لِّيَجْزِيَ اللَّهُ الصَّادِقِينَ بِصِدْقِهِمْ	24 that God may reward the true for their truthfulness
وَيُعَذِّبَ الْمُنَافِقِينَ إِن شَاءَ	and punish the hypocrites, if He wishes,
أَوْ يَتُوبَ عَلَيْهِمْ ۚ	or accept their repentance.
إِنَّ اللَّهَ كَانَ غَفُورًا رَّحِيمًا ۝	God is indeed all-forgiving, all-merciful.
وَرَدَّ اللَّهُ الَّذِينَ كَفَرُوا بِغَيْظِهِمْ	25 God sent back the faithless in their rage
لَمْ يَنَالُوا خَيْرًا ۚ	without their attaining any advantage,
وَكَفَى اللَّهُ الْمُؤْمِنِينَ الْقِتَالَ ۚ	and God spared the faithful of fighting,
وَكَانَ اللَّهُ قَوِيًّا عَزِيزًا ۝	and God is all-strong, all-mighty.
وَأَنزَلَ الَّذِينَ ظَاهَرُوهُم	26 And He dragged down those who had backed them

from among the People of the Book مِنْ أَهْلِ الْكِتَابِ
from their strongholds, مِن صَيَاصِيهِمْ
and He cast terror into their hearts, وَقَذَفَ فِي قُلُوبِهِمُ الرُّعْبَ
so that you killed a part of them, فَرِيقًا تَقْتُلُونَ
and took captive another part of them. وَتَأْسِرُونَ فَرِيقًا ۝

27 He bequeathed you their land, وَأَوْرَثَكُمْ أَرْضَهُمْ
their houses and their possessions وَدِيَارَهُمْ وَأَمْوَالَهُمْ
and a territory you had not trodden, وَأَرْضًا لَّمْ تَطَئُوهَا
and God has power over all things. وَكَانَ اللَّهُ عَلَىٰ كُلِّ شَيْءٍ قَدِيرًا ۝

28 O Prophet! *Say to your wives,* يَا أَيُّهَا النَّبِيُّ قُل لِّأَزْوَاجِكَ
'If you desire the life of the world and its glitter, إِن كُنتُنَّ تُرِدْنَ الْحَيَاةَ الدُّنْيَا وَزِينَتَهَا
come, I will provide for you فَتَعَالَيْنَ أُمَتِّعْكُنَّ
and release you in a graceful manner. وَأُسَرِّحْكُنَّ سَرَاحًا جَمِيلًا ۝

29 But if you desire God and His Apostle وَإِن كُنتُنَّ تُرِدْنَ اللَّهَ وَرَسُولَهُ
and the abode of the Hereafter, وَالدَّارَ الْآخِرَةَ
then God has indeed prepared فَإِنَّ اللَّهَ أَعَدَّ
a great reward for the virtuous among you.' لِلْمُحْسِنَاتِ مِنكُنَّ أَجْرًا عَظِيمًا ۝

30 O wives of the Prophet! يَا نِسَاءَ النَّبِيِّ
Whoever of you commits a gross indecency, مَن يَأْتِ مِنكُنَّ بِفَاحِشَةٍ مُّبَيِّنَةٍ
her punishment shall be doubled, يُضَاعَفْ لَهَا الْعَذَابُ ضِعْفَيْنِ
and that is easy for God. وَكَانَ ذَٰلِكَ عَلَى اللَّهِ يَسِيرًا ۝

[PART 22]

31 But whoever of you is obedient to God and His Apostle وَمَن يَقْنُتْ مِنكُنَّ لِلَّهِ وَرَسُولِهِ
and acts righteously, وَتَعْمَلْ صَالِحًا
We will give her a twofold reward, نُؤْتِهَا أَجْرَهَا مَرَّتَيْنِ
and hold for her in store a noble provision. وَأَعْتَدْنَا لَهَا رِزْقًا كَرِيمًا ۝

32 O wives of the Prophet! يَا نِسَاءَ النَّبِيِّ
You are not like other women: لَسْتُنَّ كَأَحَدٍ مِّنَ النِّسَاءِ
if you are Godwary, إِنِ اتَّقَيْتُنَّ

do not be complaisant in your speech,
lest he in whose heart is a sickness should aspire;
speak honourable words.

33 Stay in your houses and do not flaunt your finery
like the former days of pagan ignorance.
Maintain the prayer and pay the *zakāt*,
and obey God and His Apostle.

Indeed, God desires to repel all impurity from you,
O People of the Household,
and purify you with a thorough purification.

34 And remember what is recited in your homes
of the signs of God and wisdom.
God is indeed all-attentive, all-aware.

35 Indeed, the *muslim* men and the *muslim* women,
the faithful men and the faithful women,
the obedient men and the obedient women,
the truthful men and the truthful women,
the patient men and the patient women,
the humble[1] men and the humble women,
the charitable men and the charitable women,
the men who fast and the women who fast,
the men who guard their private parts
and the women who guard,
the men who remember God much
and the women who remember
—God holds in store for them forgiveness
and a great reward.

---

[1] That is, humble toward God.

36 A faithful man or woman may not,
 when God and His Apostle have decided on a matter,
  have any option in their matter,
 and whoever disobeys God and His Apostle
  has certainly strayed into manifest error.

37 When you said to him whom God had blessed,
  and whom you too had blessed,
  'Retain your wife for yourself, and be wary of God,'
  and you had hidden in your heart
  what God was to divulge,
  and you feared the people
  though God is worthier that you should fear Him,
  so when Zayd had got through with her,
  We wedded her to you,
  so that there may be no blame on the faithful
  in respect of the wives of their adopted sons,
  when the latter have got through with them,
  and God's command is bound to be fulfilled.

38 There is no blame on the Prophet
  in respect of that which God has made lawful for him:[1]
  God's precedent with those who passed away earlier
  —and God's commands are
  ordained by a precise ordaining—

39 such as deliver the messages of God
  and fear Him
  and fear no one except God,
  and God suffices as reckoner.

40 Muhammad is not the father of any man among you,

---

[1] Or 'prescribed for him.'

      but he is the Apostle of God and the Seal of the Prophets,
      and God has knowledge of all things.

41 O you who have faith!
    Remember God with frequent remembrance
42 and glorify Him morning and evening.
43 It is He who blesses you—and so do His angels—
    that He may bring you out from darkness into light,
    and He is most merciful to the faithful.
44 The day they encounter Him, their greeting will be, 'Peace,'
    and He holds in store for them a noble reward.

45 O Prophet! We have indeed sent *you* as a witness,
    as a bearer of good news and warner
46 and as a summoner to God by His permission,
    and as a radiant lamp.
47 *Announce* to the faithful the good news
    that there will be for them a great grace from God.
48 *Do not obey* the faithless and the hypocrites
    and *disregard* their torments, and *put your trust in God*,
    and God suffices as trustee.

49 O you who have faith!
    When you marry faithful women
    and then divorce them before you touch them,
    there shall be no period of waiting for you to reckon.
    But provide for them
    and release them in a graceful manner.
50 O Prophet! Indeed, We have made lawful to *you*

أَزْوَاجَكَ اللَّاتِي آتَيْتَ أُجُورَهُنَّ	your wives whom you have given their dowries,
وَمَا مَلَكَتْ يَمِينُكَ	and those whom your right hand owns,[1]
مِمَّا أَفَاءَ اللَّهُ عَلَيْكَ	of those whom God gave you as spoils of war,
وَبَنَاتِ عَمِّكَ	and the daughters of your paternal uncle,
وَبَنَاتِ عَمَّاتِكَ	and the daughters of your paternal aunts,
وَبَنَاتِ خَالِكَ	and the daughters of your maternal uncle,
وَبَنَاتِ خَالَاتِكَ	and the daughters of your maternal aunts
اللَّاتِي هَاجَرْنَ مَعَكَ	who migrated with you,
وَامْرَأَةً مُؤْمِنَةً إِنْ وَهَبَتْ نَفْسَهَا لِلنَّبِيِّ	and a faithful woman if she offers herself to the Prophet
إِنْ أَرَادَ النَّبِيُّ أَنْ يَسْتَنْكِحَهَا	and the Prophet desires to take her in marriage
خَالِصَةً لَكَ	(a privilege exclusively for you,
مِنْ دُونِ الْمُؤْمِنِينَ	not for the rest of the faithful;
قَدْ عَلِمْنَا مَا فَرَضْنَا عَلَيْهِمْ	We know what We have made lawful for them
فِي أَزْوَاجِهِمْ	with respect to their wives
وَمَا مَلَكَتْ أَيْمَانُهُمْ	and those whom their right hands own
لِكَيْلَا يَكُونَ عَلَيْكَ حَرَجٌ	so that there may be no blame on you),
وَكَانَ اللَّهُ غَفُورًا رَحِيمًا ۝	and God is all-forgiving, all-merciful.
تُرْجِي مَنْ تَشَاءُ مِنْهُنَّ	51 You may put off whichever of them you wish
وَتُؤْوِي إِلَيْكَ مَنْ تَشَاءُ	and consort with whichever of them you wish,
وَمَنِ ابْتَغَيْتَ	and as for any whom you may seek to consort with
مِمَّنْ عَزَلْتَ	from among those you have set aside earlier,
فَلَا جُنَاحَ عَلَيْكَ	there is no sin upon you [in receiving her again].
ذَٰلِكَ أَدْنَىٰ أَنْ تَقَرَّ أَعْيُنُهُنَّ	That makes it likelier that they will be comforted
وَلَا يَحْزَنَّ	and not feel unhappy,
وَيَرْضَيْنَ بِمَا آتَيْتَهُنَّ كُلُّهُنَّ	and all of them will be pleased with what you give them.
وَاللَّهُ يَعْلَمُ مَا فِي قُلُوبِكُمْ	God knows what is in your hearts,
وَكَانَ اللَّهُ عَلِيمًا حَلِيمًا ۝	and God is all-knowing, all-forbearing.
لَا يَحِلُّ لَكَ النِّسَاءُ مِنْ بَعْدُ	52 Beyond that, women are not lawful for you,
وَلَا أَنْ تَبَدَّلَ بِهِنَّ مِنْ أَزْوَاجٍ	nor that you should change them for other wives

---

[1] That is, slave women.

even though their beauty should impress you,
except those whom your right hand owns.
God is watchful over all things.

53 O you who have faith!
Do not enter the Prophet's houses
   for a meal until you are granted permission,
      without waiting for it to be readied.
But enter when you are invited,
   and disperse when you have taken your meal,
      without cozying up for chats.
Such conduct on your part offends the Prophet,
   and he is ashamed of asking you to leave;
but God is not ashamed of expressing the truth.
When you ask his womenfolk for something,
   do ask them from behind a curtain.
That is more chaste for your hearts and theirs.
You should not offend the Apostle of God,
   nor may you ever marry his wives after him.
That would indeed be a grave sin with God.

54 Whether you disclose anything or hide it,
      God indeed knows all things.

55 There is no sin on them[1] in socializing freely
   with their fathers, or their sons,
   or their brothers, or their brothers' sons,
   or the sons of their sisters,
   or their own womenfolk,[2]
   or what their right hands own.[3]
Be wary of God.

---

[1] That is, the Prophet's wives.
[2] That is, Muslim women.
[3] That is, their female slaves.

إِنَّ اللَّهَ كَانَ عَلَىٰ كُلِّ شَيْءٍ شَهِيدًا ۝ Indeed, God is witness to all things.

إِنَّ اللَّهَ وَمَلَائِكَتَهُ يُصَلُّونَ عَلَى النَّبِيِّ 56 Indeed, God and His angels bless the Prophet;
يَا أَيُّهَا الَّذِينَ آمَنُوا صَلُّوا عَلَيْهِ O you who have faith! Invoke blessings on him
وَسَلِّمُوا تَسْلِيمًا ۝ and invoke Peace upon him in a worthy manner.[1]

إِنَّ الَّذِينَ يُؤْذُونَ اللَّهَ وَرَسُولَهُ 57 Indeed, those who offend God and His Apostle
لَعَنَهُمُ اللَّهُ فِي الدُّنْيَا وَالْآخِرَةِ are cursed by God in the world and the Hereafter,
وَأَعَدَّ لَهُمْ عَذَابًا مُهِينًا ۝ and He has prepared a humiliating punishment for them.

وَالَّذِينَ يُؤْذُونَ الْمُؤْمِنِينَ وَالْمُؤْمِنَاتِ 58 Those who offend faithful men and women
بِغَيْرِ مَا اكْتَسَبُوا undeservedly,
فَقَدِ احْتَمَلُوا بُهْتَانًا وَإِثْمًا مُبِينًا ۝ certainly bear the guilt of slander and flagrant sin.

يَا أَيُّهَا النَّبِيُّ قُلْ لِأَزْوَاجِكَ وَبَنَاتِكَ 59 O Prophet! Tell your wives and your daughters
وَنِسَاءِ الْمُؤْمِنِينَ and the women of the faithful
يُدْنِينَ عَلَيْهِنَّ to draw closely over themselves their scarfs [when going out].
مِنْ جَلَابِيبِهِنَّ ذَٰلِكَ أَدْنَىٰ أَنْ يُعْرَفْنَ That makes it likely for them to be recognized
فَلَا يُؤْذَيْنَ and not be troubled,
وَكَانَ اللَّهُ غَفُورًا رَحِيمًا ۝ and God is all-forgiving, all-merciful.

لَئِنْ لَمْ يَنْتَهِ الْمُنَافِقُونَ 60 If the hypocrites do not desist,
وَالَّذِينَ فِي قُلُوبِهِمْ مَرَضٌ and also those in whose hearts is a sickness,
وَالْمُرْجِفُونَ فِي الْمَدِينَةِ and the rumour-mongers in the city do not give up,
لَنُغْرِيَنَّكَ بِهِمْ We will prompt *you* to take action against them;
ثُمَّ لَا يُجَاوِرُونَكَ فِيهَا إِلَّا قَلِيلًا ۝ then they will not be *your* neighbours in it except briefly.

مَلْعُونِينَ أَيْنَمَا ثُقِفُوا أُخِذُوا 61 Accursed, they will be seized wherever they are confronted
وَقُتِّلُوا تَقْتِيلًا ۝ and slain violently:

سُنَّةَ اللَّهِ فِي الَّذِينَ خَلَوْا مِنْ قَبْلُ 62 God's precedent with those who passed away before,
وَلَنْ تَجِدَ لِسُنَّةِ اللَّهِ تَبْدِيلًا ۝ and *you* will never find any change in God's precedent.

يَسْأَلُكَ النَّاسُ عَنِ السَّاعَةِ 63 The people question *you* concerning the Hour.
قُلْ إِنَّمَا عِلْمُهَا عِنْدَ اللَّهِ *Say,* 'Its knowledge is only with God.'
وَمَا يُدْرِيكَ What do *you* know,

---

[1] Or 'submit to him in complete submission.'

maybe the Hour is near.

64 Indeed, God has cursed the faithless
and prepared for them a blaze
65 in which they will remain forever
and will not find any friend or helper.
66 The day when their faces are turned about in the Fire,
they will say, 'We wish we had obeyed God
and obeyed the Apostle!'
67 They will say, 'Our Lord!
We obeyed our leaders and elders
and they led us astray from the way.'
68 Our Lord! Give them a double punishment
and curse them with a mighty curse.'
69 O you who have faith!
Do not be like those who offended Moses,
whereat God cleared him of what they alleged,
and he was distinguished in God's sight.
70 O you who have faith!
Be wary of God and speak upright words.
71 He will rectify your conduct for you
and forgive you your sins.
Whoever obeys God and His Apostle
will certainly achieve a great success.
72 Indeed, We presented the Trust to the heavens
and the earth and the mountains,
but they refused to undertake it,
and were apprehensive of it;
but the human being undertook it.
He is indeed most ignorant and unjust.

73 God will surely punish the hypocrites, men and women,
and the polytheists, men and women,
and God will turn clemently
to the faithful, men and women,
and God is all-forgiving, all-merciful.

34. Sheba[1]
Saba'

In the Name of God,
the All-beneficent, the All-merciful.

1 All praise belongs to God
to whom belongs whatever is in the heavens
and whatever is in the earth.
To Him belongs all praise in the Hereafter,
and He is the All-wise, the All-aware.

2 He knows whatever enters into the earth
and whatever emerges from it,
and whatever descends from the sky
and whatever ascends into it,
and He is the All-merciful, the All-forgiving.

3 The faithless say,
'The Hour will not overtake us.'
Say, Yes, it will surely overtake you, by my Lord,
the Knower of the Unseen,
not even an atom's weight escapes Him
in the heavens or in the earth,
nor is there anything smaller than that nor bigger,
but it is in a manifest Book,

---

[1] A Makkī *sūrah*, it is named after Sheba (*Saba'*) mentioned in verse 15.

4 that He may reward those who have faith
and do righteous deeds.
For such there will be forgiveness and a noble provision.
5 But those who contend with Our signs
seeking to frustrate their purpose,
for such is a painful punishment due to defilement.[1]
6 Those who have been given knowledge see
that what has been sent down to you from your Lord
is the truth
and that it guides to the path of the All-mighty,
the All-laudable.

7 The faithless say,
'Shall we show you a man who will inform you
that when you have been totally rent to pieces
you will indeed have a new creation?
8 Has he fabricated a lie against God,
or is there a madness in him?'
Indeed, those who do not believe in the Hereafter
languish in punishment and extreme error.
9 Have they not regarded that which is before them
and that which is behind them
of the heavens and the earth?
If We like, We can make the earth swallow them,
or let a fragment from the sky fall on them.
There is indeed a sign in that for every penitent servant.

10 Certainly We granted David a favour from Us [saying]:

---

[1] That is, owing to their inward defilement. According to an alternate reading which makes *alīm* the attribute of *rijz*, the translation will be: 'for such is the torment of a painful punishment.'

يَا جِبَالُ أَوِّبِي مَعَهُ وَالطَّيْرَ	'O mountains and birds, chime in with him!'[1]
وَأَلَنَّا لَهُ الْحَدِيدَ ۝	And We made iron soft for him,
أَنِ اعْمَلْ سَابِغَاتٍ	11 saying, 'Make easy coats of mail
وَقَدِّرْ فِي السَّرْدِ ۖ	and keep the measure in arranging the links,
وَاعْمَلُوا صَالِحًا ۖ	and act righteously.
إِنِّي بِمَا تَعْمَلُونَ بَصِيرٌ ۝	I indeed watch what you do.'
وَلِسُلَيْمَانَ الرِّيحَ	12 And for Solomon We subjected the wind:
غُدُوُّهَا شَهْرٌ	its morning course was a month's journey
وَرَوَاحُهَا شَهْرٌ ۖ	and its evening course was a month's journey.
وَأَسَلْنَا لَهُ عَيْنَ الْقِطْرِ ۖ	We made a fount of molten copper flow for him,
وَمِنَ الْجِنِّ	and [We placed at his service] some of the jinn
مَنْ يَعْمَلُ بَيْنَ يَدَيْهِ بِإِذْنِ رَبِّهِ ۖ	who would work for him by the permission of his Lord,
وَمَنْ يَزِغْ مِنْهُمْ عَنْ أَمْرِنَا	and if any of them swerved from Our command,
نُذِقْهُ مِنْ عَذَابِ السَّعِيرِ ۝	We would make him taste the punishment of the Blaze.
يَعْمَلُونَ لَهُ مَا يَشَاءُ مِنْ مَحَارِيبَ	13 They built for him as many temples as he wished,
وَتَمَاثِيلَ وَجِفَانٍ كَالْجَوَابِ	and figures, basins like cisterns,
وَقُدُورٍ رَاسِيَاتٍ ۚ	and caldrons fixed in the ground.
اعْمَلُوا آلَ دَاوُودَ شُكْرًا ۚ	'O House of David, work for God gratefully,
وَقَلِيلٌ مِنْ عِبَادِيَ الشَّكُورُ ۝	and few of My servants are grateful.'
فَلَمَّا قَضَيْنَا عَلَيْهِ الْمَوْتَ	14 When We decreed death for him,
مَا دَلَّهُمْ عَلَىٰ مَوْتِهِ	nothing apprised them of his death
إِلَّا دَابَّةُ الْأَرْضِ تَأْكُلُ مِنْسَأَتَهُ ۖ	except a worm which gnawed away at his staff.
فَلَمَّا خَرَّ	And when he fell down,
تَبَيَّنَتِ الْجِنُّ أَنْ لَوْ كَانُوا يَعْلَمُونَ	the humans realized that had the jinn known
الْغَيْبَ	the Unseen,
مَا لَبِثُوا فِي الْعَذَابِ الْمُهِينِ ۝	they would not have remained in a humiliating torment.
لَقَدْ كَانَ لِسَبَإٍ فِي مَسْكَنِهِمْ آيَةٌ ۖ	15 There was certainly a sign for Sheba in their habitation:
جَنَّتَانِ عَنْ يَمِينٍ وَشِمَالٍ ۖ	two gardens, to the right and to the left.
كُلُوا مِنْ رِزْقِ رَبِّكُمْ وَاشْكُرُوا لَهُ ۚ	'Eat of the provision of your Lord and give Him thanks:

---

[1] Cf. **38**:17-19.

a good land and an all-forgiving Lord!' بَلْدَةٌ طَيِّبَةٌ وَرَبٌّ غَفُورٌ ۝

16 But they disregarded [the path of God], فَأَعْرَضُوا
so We unleashed upon them a violent flood فَأَرْسَلْنَا عَلَيْهِمْ سَيْلَ الْعَرِمِ
and replaced their two gardens وَبَدَّلْنَاهُمْ بِجَنَّتَيْهِمْ
with two gardens bearing bitter fruit, جَنَّتَيْنِ ذَوَاتَىْ أُكُلٍ خَمْطٍ
tamarisk, and sparse lote trees. وَأَثْلٍ وَشَىْءٍ مِنْ سِدْرٍ قَلِيلٍ ۝

17 We requited them with that for their ingratitude. ذَٰلِكَ جَزَيْنَاهُمْ بِمَا كَفَرُوا
Do We thus requite anyone but ingrates? وَهَلْ نُجَازِى إِلَّا الْكَفُورَ ۝

18 We had placed between them وَجَعَلْنَا بَيْنَهُمْ
and the towns which We had blessed وَبَيْنَ الْقُرَى الَّتِى بَارَكْنَا فِيهَا
hamlets prominent [from the main route], قُرًى ظَاهِرَةً
and We had ordained the route through them: وَقَدَّرْنَا فِيهَا السَّيْرَ
'Travel through them in safety, night and day.' سِيرُوا فِيهَا لَيَالِىَ وَأَيَّامًا آمِنِينَ ۝

19 But they said, 'Our Lord! فَقَالُوا رَبَّنَا
Make the stages between our journeys far apart,' بَاعِدْ بَيْنَ أَسْفَارِنَا
and they wronged themselves. وَظَلَمُوا أَنْفُسَهُمْ
So We turned them into folktales فَجَعَلْنَاهُمْ أَحَادِيثَ
and caused them to disintegrate totally. وَمَزَّقْنَاهُمْ كُلَّ مُمَزَّقٍ
There are indeed signs in that إِنَّ فِى ذَٰلِكَ لَآيَاتٍ
for every patient and grateful servant. لِكُلِّ صَبَّارٍ شَكُورٍ ۝

20 Certainly Iblis had his conjecture come true about them. وَلَقَدْ صَدَّقَ عَلَيْهِمْ إِبْلِيسُ ظَنَّهُ
So they followed him—all except a part of the faithful. فَاتَّبَعُوهُ إِلَّا فَرِيقًا مِنَ الْمُؤْمِنِينَ ۝

21 He had no authority over them, وَمَا كَانَ لَهُ عَلَيْهِمْ مِنْ سُلْطَانٍ
but that We may ascertain those who believe in the Hereafter إِلَّا لِنَعْلَمَ مَنْ يُؤْمِنُ بِالْآخِرَةِ
from those who are in doubt about it, مِمَّنْ هُوَ مِنْهَا فِى شَكٍّ
and your Lord is watchful over all things. وَرَبُّكَ عَلَىٰ كُلِّ شَىْءٍ حَفِيظٌ ۝

22 Say, 'Invoke those whom you claim to be gods قُلِ ادْعُوا الَّذِينَ زَعَمْتُمْ
besides God! مِنْ دُونِ اللَّهِ
They do not control even an atom's weight لَا يَمْلِكُونَ مِثْقَالَ ذَرَّةٍ

    in the heavens or the earth,
    nor do they have any share in either of them,
    nor is any of them[1] His helper.'

23 Intercession is of no avail with Him
    except for those whom He permits.[2]
    When fear is lifted from their hearts,
    they say, 'What did your Lord say?'
    They say, 'The truth, and He is the All-exalted, the All-great.'

24 Say, 'Who provides for you from the heavens
    and the earth?'
    Say, 'God!
    Indeed, either we or you are rightly guided
    or in plain error.'

25 Say, 'You will not be questioned about our guilt,
    nor shall we be questioned about what you do.'

26 Say, 'Our Lord will bring us together,
    then He will judge between us with justice,
    and He is the All-knowing Judge.'[3]

27 Say, 'Show me those whom
    you associate with Him as partners.'
    No! [They can never show any such partner.
    Indeed, He is God, the All-mighty, the All-wise.

28 We did not send you except
    as a bearer of good news and warner to all mankind,
    but most people do not know.

29 They say, 'When will this promise be fulfilled,
    if you are truthful?'

30 Say, 'Your promised hour is a day

---

[1] That is, the gods worshiped by the polytheists.
[2] See Zamakhshari and Ṭabāṭabā'ī. Or 'except of those whom He permits.'
[3] Or, 'the Judge, the All-knowing.'

that you shall neither defer by an hour
    nor advance.'

31 The faithless say,
    'We will never believe in this Qur'ān,
    nor in what was revealed before it.'
But if you were to see
when the wrongdoers will be made to stop before their Lord
    casting the blame on one another.
Those who were abased will say
    to those who were arrogant,
'Had it not been for you, we would surely have been faithful.'

32 Those who were arrogant will say
    to those who were abased,
'Did we keep you from guidance
    after it had come to you?
No, you were guilty yourselves.'

33 Those who were abased will say
    to those who were arrogant,
'No, it was your night-and-day plotting,
    when you prompted us to forswear God
    and to set up equals to Him.'
They will hide their remorse when they sight the punishment,
    and We will put iron collars
    around the necks of the faithless.
Shall they be requited except for what they used to do?

34 We did not send a warner to any town
    without its affluent ones saying,
'We indeed disbelieve in what you have been sent with.'

35 They say, 'We have greater wealth and more children,
    and we will not be punished!'

36 Say, 'Indeed, my Lord expands the provision
and He tightens it for whomever He wishes,
but most people do not know.'

37 It is not your wealth, nor your children,
that will bring you close to Us in nearness,
excepting those who have faith and act righteously.
It is they for whom there will be a twofold reward
for what they did,
and they will be secure in lofty abodes.[1]

38 As for those who contend with Our signs
seeking to frustrate their purpose,
they will be brought to the punishment.

39 Say, 'Indeed, my Lord expands the provision
and tightens it for whomever of His servants He wishes.
and He will repay whatever you may spend,
and He is the best of providers.'

40 On the day He will gather them all together,
He will say to the angels,
'Was it you that these used to worship?'

41 They will say, 'Immaculate are You!
You are our friend, not they!
No, they used to worship the jinn;
most of them had faith in them.'

42 'Today
you have no power to benefit or harm one another,'
and We shall say to those who did wrong,
'Taste the punishment of the Fire
which you used to deny.'

43 When Our clear signs are recited to them,

---

[1] Cf. **29**:58; **39**:20.

they say, 'This is just a man who desires to keep you
from what your fathers used to worship.'
And they say, 'This is nothing but a fabricated lie.'
The faithless say of the truth when it comes to them:
'This is nothing but plain magic,'

44 though We did not give them[1] any scriptures
that they might have studied,
nor did We send them any warner before you.[2]

45 Those who were before them had denied likewise
—and these have not attained one-tenth[3]
of what We had given them—
and they impugned My apostles;
so how was My rebuttal![4]

46 Say, 'I give you just a single advice:
that you rise up for God's sake, in pairs or singly,
and then reflect:
there is no madness in your companion:
he is just a warner to you
before the befalling of a severe punishment.'

47 Say, 'Whatever reward I may have asked you
is for your own good.
My true reward lies only with God,
and He is witness to all things.'

48 Say, 'Indeed, my Lord hurls[5] the truth.
He is the knower of all that is Unseen.'

49 Say, 'The truth has come,
and falsehood neither originates anything

---

[1] That is, the pre-Islamic Arabs.
[2] Cf. **36**:6.
[3] Or 'a thousandth.'
[4] Or 'how was my requital.'
[5] Cf. **17**:81; **21**:18. Or 'casts the Truth;' i.e., into the hearts of His envoys.

nor restores [anything after its demise].'

50 Say, 'If I go astray,
my going astray is only to my own harm,
and if I am rightly guided
that is because of what my Lord has revealed to me.
He is indeed all-hearing and nearmost.'

51 Were you to see them when they will be terror stricken,
left without any escape,
and are seized from a close quarter.

52 They will say, 'We believe in it now.'
But how can they attain it from a far-off place,

53 when they denied it in the past
and drew conjectures about the Unseen from a far-off place?

54 A barrier will separate them from what they long for,
as was done earlier with their likes,
who had remained in grave doubt.

35. THE ORIGINATOR[1]
Fāṭir

In the Name of God,
the All-beneficent, the All-merciful.

1 All praise belongs to God, originator of the heavens
and the earth,
maker of the angels His messengers,
possessing wings, two, three or four of them.
He adds to the creation whatever He wishes.
Indeed, God has power over all things.

2 Whatever mercy God unfolds for the people,
no one can withhold it;

---

[1] This Makkī *sūrah* takes its name from the word *fāṭir* (originator), which occurs in verse 1.

وَمَا يُمْسِكْ فَلَا مُرْسِلَ لَهُ مِنْ بَعْدِهِ ۚ
وَهُوَ الْعَزِيزُ الْحَكِيمُ ۝

and whatever He withholds, no one can release except Him,[1]
and He is the All-mighty, the All-wise.

يَا أَيُّهَا النَّاسُ
اذْكُرُوا نِعْمَتَ اللَّهِ عَلَيْكُمْ ۚ
هَلْ مِنْ خَالِقٍ غَيْرُ اللَّهِ
يَرْزُقُكُم مِّنَ السَّمَاءِ وَالْأَرْضِ ۚ
لَا إِلَٰهَ إِلَّا هُوَ ۖ
فَأَنَّىٰ تُؤْفَكُونَ ۝

3 O mankind!
Remember God's blessing upon you!
Is there any creator other than God
who provides for you from the heaven and the earth?
There is no god except Him.
So where do you stray?

وَإِن يُكَذِّبُوكَ
فَقَدْ كُذِّبَتْ رُسُلٌ مِّن قَبْلِكَ ۚ
وَإِلَى اللَّهِ تُرْجَعُ الْأُمُورُ ۝

4 If they impugn you,
certainly many apostles were impugned before you,
and all matters are returned to God.

يَا أَيُّهَا النَّاسُ إِنَّ وَعْدَ اللَّهِ حَقٌّ ۖ
فَلَا تَغُرَّنَّكُمُ الْحَيَاةُ الدُّنْيَا ۖ
وَلَا يَغُرَّنَّكُم بِاللَّهِ الْغَرُورُ ۝

5 O mankind! God's promise is indeed true.
So do not let the life of the world deceive you,
nor let the Deceiver deceive you concerning God.[2]

إِنَّ الشَّيْطَانَ لَكُمْ عَدُوٌّ
فَاتَّخِذُوهُ عَدُوًّا ۚ
إِنَّمَا يَدْعُو حِزْبَهُ
لِيَكُونُوا مِنْ أَصْحَابِ السَّعِيرِ ۝

6 Satan is indeed your enemy,
so treat him as an enemy.
He only invites his confederates
so that they may be among the inmates of the Blaze.

الَّذِينَ كَفَرُوا لَهُمْ عَذَابٌ شَدِيدٌ ۖ
وَالَّذِينَ آمَنُوا وَعَمِلُوا الصَّالِحَاتِ
لَهُم مَّغْفِرَةٌ وَأَجْرٌ كَبِيرٌ ۝

7 There is a severe punishment for the faithless,
but for those who have faith and do righteous deeds
there will be forgiveness and a great reward.

أَفَمَن
زُيِّنَ لَهُ سُوءُ عَمَلِهِ
فَرَآهُ حَسَنًا ۖ
فَإِنَّ اللَّهَ يُضِلُّ مَن يَشَاءُ
وَيَهْدِي مَن يَشَاءُ ۖ
فَلَا تَذْهَبْ نَفْسُكَ عَلَيْهِمْ حَسَرَاتٍ ۚ
إِنَّ اللَّهَ عَلِيمٌ بِمَا يَصْنَعُونَ ۝

8 Is someone
the evil of whose conduct is presented as decorous to him,
so he regards it as good. . . .[3]
Indeed, God leads astray whomever He wishes
and guides whomever He wishes.
So do not fret *yourself* to death regretting for them.
Indeed, God knows best what they do.

---

[1] That is, after His withholding it. Or 'no one can release it except Him.'
[2] Cf. **31**:33.
[3] Ellipsis. The phrase omitted is 'like one who is truly virtuous?'

9 It is God who sends the winds and they raise a cloud;
then We drive it toward a dead land
and with it revive the earth after its death.
Likewise will be the resurrection of the dead.

10 Whoever seeks honour[1] [should know that]
honour entirely belongs to God.
To Him ascends the good word,
and He elevates righteous conduct;[2]
as for those who devise evil schemes,
there is a severe punishment for them
and their plotting shall come to naught.

11 God created you from dust,
then from a drop of seminal fluid,
then He made you mates.[3]
No female conceives or delivers
except with His knowledge,
and no elderly person advances in years,
nor is anything diminished of his life,
but it is recorded in a Book.
That is indeed easy for God.

12 Not alike are the two seas:[4]
this one sweet and agreeable, pleasant to drink,
and that one briny and bitter,
and from each you eat fresh meat
and obtain ornaments which you wear.
And you see the ships plowing through them,
that you may seek of His bounty,

---

[1] The word *'izzah* in Arabic has a composite meaning including the senses of honour, prestige, glory and might.
[2] Or 'righteous conduct elevates it.'
[3] That is, male and female.
[4] That is, the bodies of sweet water and fresh water. The word *bahr*, like *yamm* is used for a large river as well as for the sea (cf. 7:136, 20:78, 28:40, 51:40, where it is used for the Red Sea; and 20:39, 28:7, where it is used for the Nile).

and so that you may give thanks.

13 He makes the night pass into the day
and makes the day pass into the night,
and He has disposed the sun and the moon,
each moving for a specified term.
That is God, your Lord; to Him belongs all sovereignty.
As for those whom you invoke besides Him,
they do not control so much as the husk of a date stone.

14 If you invoke them they will not hear your invocation,
and even if they heard they cannot respond to you,
and on the Day of Resurrection
they will forswear your polytheism,
and none can inform you like the One who is all-aware.

15 O mankind! You are the ones who stand in need of God,
and God—He is the All-sufficient, the All-laudable.

16 If He wishes, He will take you away
and bring about a new creation,

17 and that is not a hard thing for God.

18 No bearer shall bear another's burden,
and should one heavily burdened call another to carry it,
nothing of it will be carried by anyone
even if he were a near relative.
You can only warn those who fear their Lord in secret
and maintain the prayer.
Whoever purifies himself, purifies only for his own sake,
and to God is the return.

19 The blind one and the seer are not equal,

20 nor darkness and light,

21 nor shade and torrid heat,

22 nor are the living equal to the dead.

إِنَّ ٱللَّهَ يُسْمِعُ مَن يَشَاءُ	Indeed, God makes whomever He wishes to hear,
وَمَا أَنتَ بِمُسْمِعٍ مَّن فِى ٱلْقُبُورِ ۝	and you cannot make those in the graves hear you.
إِنْ أَنتَ إِلَّا نَذِيرٌ ۝	23 You are just a warner.
إِنَّا أَرْسَلْنَـٰكَ بِٱلْحَقِّ	24 Indeed, We have sent you with the truth
بَشِيرًا وَنَذِيرًا	as a bearer of good news and warner,
وَإِن مِّنْ أُمَّةٍ إِلَّا خَلَا فِيهَا نَذِيرٌ ۝	and there is not a nation but a warner has passed in it.
وَإِن يُكَذِّبُوكَ	25 If they impugn you,
فَقَدْ كَذَّبَ ٱلَّذِينَ مِن قَبْلِهِمْ	those before them have impugned likewise:
جَاءَتْهُمْ رُسُلُهُم بِٱلْبَيِّنَـٰتِ	their apostles brought them manifest proofs,
وَبِٱلزُّبُرِ وَبِٱلْكِتَـٰبِ ٱلْمُنِيرِ ۝	holy writs, and illuminating scriptures.
ثُمَّ أَخَذْتُ ٱلَّذِينَ كَفَرُوا۟	26 Then I seized the faithless.
فَكَيْفَ كَانَ نَكِيرِ ۝	So how was My rebuttal!
أَلَمْ تَرَ	27 Have you not regarded
أَنَّ ٱللَّهَ أَنزَلَ مِنَ ٱلسَّمَاءِ مَاءً	that God sends down water from the sky,
فَأَخْرَجْنَا بِهِۦ ثَمَرَٰتٍ مُّخْتَلِفًا أَلْوَٰنُهَا	with which We produce fruits of diverse hues;
وَمِنَ ٱلْجِبَالِ جُدَدٌ	and in the mountains are stripes,
بِيضٌ وَحُمْرٌ مُّخْتَلِفٌ أَلْوَٰنُهَا	white and red, of diverse hues,
وَغَرَابِيبُ سُودٌ ۝	and others pitch black?
وَمِنَ ٱلنَّاسِ وَٱلدَّوَابِّ وَٱلْأَنْعَـٰمِ	28 And of humans and beasts and cattle
مُخْتَلِفٌ أَلْوَٰنُهُۥ كَذَٰلِكَ	there are likewise diverse hues.
إِنَّمَا يَخْشَى ٱللَّهَ مِنْ عِبَادِهِ ٱلْعُلَمَـٰٓؤُا۟	Only those of God's servants having knowledge fear Him.
إِنَّ ٱللَّهَ عَزِيزٌ غَفُورٌ ۝	God is indeed all-mighty, all-forgiving.
إِنَّ ٱلَّذِينَ يَتْلُونَ كِتَـٰبَ ٱللَّهِ	29 Indeed, those who recite the Book of God
وَأَقَامُوا۟ ٱلصَّلَوٰةَ	and maintain the prayer,
وَأَنفَقُوا۟ مِمَّا رَزَقْنَـٰهُمْ	and spend out of what We have provided them,
سِرًّا وَعَلَانِيَةً	secretly and openly,
يَرْجُونَ تِجَـٰرَةً لَّن تَبُورَ ۝	expect a commerce that will never go bankrupt,
لِيُوَفِّيَهُمْ أُجُورَهُمْ	30 so that He may pay them their full reward
وَيَزِيدَهُم مِّن فَضْلِهِۦٓ	and enhance them out of His bounty.
إِنَّهُۥ غَفُورٌ شَكُورٌ ۝	He is indeed all-forgiving, all-appreciative.

31 That which We have revealed to you of the Book
is the truth,
confirming what was revealed before it.
Indeed, God is aware and watchful of His servants.

32 Then We made heirs to the Book
those whom We chose from Our servants.
Yet some of them are those who wrong themselves,
and some of them are average,
and some of them are those
who take the lead in all the good works
by God's will.
That is the great grace of God!

33 Gardens of Eden, which they will enter,
adorned therein with bracelets of gold
and pearl,
and their garments therein will be of silk.

34 They will say, 'All praise belongs to God,
who has removed all grief from us.
Our Lord is indeed all-forgiving, all-appreciative,

35 who has settled us in the everlasting abode
by His grace.
In it we are untouched by toil
and untouched by fatigue.'

36 As for the faithless, there is for them the fire of hell:
they will neither be done away with so that they may die,
nor shall its punishment be lightened for them.
Thus do We requite every ingrate.

37 They will cry therein for help:
'Our Lord! Bring us out, so that we may act righteously
—differently from what we used to do!'

'Did We not give you a life long enough
    that one who is heedful might take admonition?
And moreover the warner had also come to you.
Now taste [the consequence of your deeds],
    for the wrongdoers have no helper.'

38 Indeed, God is the knower of the Unseen
    of the heavens and the earth.
He indeed knows well what is in the breasts.

39 It is He who made you successors on the earth.[1]
So whoever is faithless,
    his unfaith is to his own detriment.
The unfaith of the faithless does not increase them
    with their Lord in anything except disfavour,
and their unfaith increases the faithless in nothing
    except loss.

40 Say, 'Tell me about your 'partners'
    whom you invoke besides God?
Show me what part of the earth have they created.
Have they any share in the heavens?'
Have We given them a scripture
    so that they stand on a manifest proof from it?
No, the wrongdoers do not promise one another
    anything except delusion.

41 Indeed, God sustains the heavens and the earth
    lest they should fall apart,
and if they were to fall apart
there is none who can sustain them except Him.
He is indeed all-forbearing, all-forgiving.

42 They[2] had sworn by God with solemn oaths

---

[1] That is, of the former peoples.
[2] That is, the idolaters of Arabia.

that if a warner were to come to them,
they would be better guided than any of the nations.
But when a warner came to them,
it only increased their distance from the truth

43 due to their domineering conduct in the land
and their devising of evil schemes;
and evil schemes beset only their authors.
So do they await anything except
the precedent of the former peoples?
Yet you will never find any change in God's precedent,
and you will never find any revision in God's precedent.

44 Have they not traveled through the land
so that they may observe
how was the fate of those who were before them?
They were more powerful than them,
and God is not to be frustrated by anything
in the heavens or on the earth.
He is indeed all-knowing, all-powerful.

45 Were God to take humans to task
because of what they have earned,
He would not leave any living being on its back.[1]
But He respites them until a specified time,
and when their time comes, [He judges them],
for God has been watching His servants.

36. YA SIN[2]

Yā Sīn

In the Name of God,
the All-beneficent, the All-merciful.

---

[1] That is, on the surface of the earth.
[2] A Makkī *sūrah*. "Yā Sīn" (verse 1) is one of the names of the Prophet (ṣ).

يس ۝ 1 *Yā Sīn!*

وَالْقُرْآنِ الْحَكِيمِ ۝ 2 By the Wise[1] Qur'ān,

إِنَّكَ لَمِنَ الْمُرْسَلِينَ ۝ 3 you are indeed one of the apostles,

عَلَىٰ صِرَاطٍ مُسْتَقِيمٍ ۝ 4 on a straight path.

تَنزِيلَ 5 It is a scripture sent down gradually

الْعَزِيزِ الرَّحِيمِ ۝ from the All-mighty, the All-merciful

لِتُنذِرَ قَوْمًا مَا أُنذِرَ آبَاؤُهُمْ 6 that you may warn a people whose fathers were not warned,[2]

فَهُمْ غَافِلُونَ ۝ so they are oblivious.

لَقَدْ حَقَّ الْقَوْلُ عَلَىٰ أَكْثَرِهِمْ 7 The word has already become due against most of them,

فَهُمْ لَا يُؤْمِنُونَ ۝ so they will not have faith.

إِنَّا جَعَلْنَا فِي أَعْنَاقِهِمْ أَغْلَالًا 8 Indeed, We have put iron collars around their necks,

فَهِيَ إِلَى الْأَذْقَانِ which are up to the chins,

فَهُم مُّقْمَحُونَ ۝ so their heads are upturned.[3]

وَجَعَلْنَا مِن بَيْنِ أَيْدِيهِمْ سَدًّا 9 And We have put a barrier before them

وَمِنْ خَلْفِهِمْ سَدًّا and a barrier behind them,

فَأَغْشَيْنَاهُمْ فَهُمْ لَا يُبْصِرُونَ ۝ then We have blind-folded them, so they do not see.

وَسَوَاءٌ عَلَيْهِمْ 10 It is the same to them

أَأَنذَرْتَهُمْ أَمْ لَمْ تُنذِرْهُمْ whether you warn them or do not warn them,

لَا يُؤْمِنُونَ ۝ they will not have faith.

إِنَّمَا تُنذِرُ مَنِ اتَّبَعَ الذِّكْرَ 11 You can only warn someone who follows the Reminder[4]

وَخَشِيَ الرَّحْمَٰنَ بِالْغَيْبِ and fears the All-beneficent in secret;

فَبَشِّرْهُ بِمَغْفِرَةٍ so *give* him the good news of forgiveness

وَأَجْرٍ كَرِيمٍ ۝ and a noble reward.

إِنَّا نَحْنُ نُحْيِي الْمَوْتَىٰ 12 It is indeed We who revive the dead

وَنَكْتُبُ مَا قَدَّمُوا and write what they have sent ahead[5]

وَآثَارَهُمْ and their effects [which they left behind],[6]

---

[1] Or 'Definitive.'
[2] Cf. **28**:46; **32**:3; **34**:44.
[3] That is, they dwell in a state of blindness, defiance and arrogance in regard to the God-sent guidance and truth.
[4] That is, the Qur'ān.
[5] That is, the deeds they have done.
[6] That is, the good or evil legacy and imprint they leave behind in the society in which they have lived, and which outlive them.

and We have figured everything in a manifest *Imam*.[1]

13 Cite for them the example of the inhabitants of the town
when the apostles came to it.

14 When We sent to them two apostles,
they impugned both of them.
Then We reinforced them with a third,
and they said, 'We have indeed been sent to you.'

15 They said, 'You are nothing but humans like us,
and the All-beneficent has not sent down anything,
and you are only lying.'

16 They said, 'Our Lord knows
that we have indeed been sent to you,

17 and our duty is only to communicate in clear terms.'

18 They said, 'Indeed, we take you for a bad omen.
If you do not desist we will stone you,
and surely a painful punishment will visit you from us.'

19 They said, 'Your bad omens attend you.
What! If you are admonished . . . .[2]
You are indeed an unrestrained lot.'

20 There came a man from the city outskirts, hurrying.
He said, 'O my people! Follow the apostles!

21 Follow them who do not ask you any reward
and they are rightly guided.

22 Why should I not worship Him who has originated me,
and to whom you will be brought back?

23 Shall I take gods besides Him?
If the All-beneficent desired to cause me any distress,
their intercession will not avail me in any way,
nor will they rescue me.

---

[1] Or, in a manifest book.
[2] Ellipsis. The phrase omitted is 'do you take it for a bad omen?!'

24 إِنِّي إِذًا لَفِي ضَلَالٍ مُبِينٍ ۝ Indeed, then I would be in plain error.

25 إِنِّي آمَنْتُ بِرَبِّكُمْ فَاسْمَعُونِ ۝ Indeed, I have faith in your Lord, so listen to me.'

26 قِيلَ ادْخُلِ الْجَنَّةَ ۖ He was told, 'Enter paradise!'

قَالَ يَا لَيْتَ قَوْمِي يَعْلَمُونَ ۝ He said, 'Alas! Had my people only known

27 بِمَا غَفَرَ لِي رَبِّي for what my Lord forgave me

وَجَعَلَنِي مِنَ الْمُكْرَمِينَ ۝ and made me one of the honoured ones!'

[PART 23]

28 وَمَا أَنْزَلْنَا عَلَىٰ قَوْمِهِ مِنْ بَعْدِهِ After him We did not send down on his people

مِنْ جُنْدٍ مِنَ السَّمَاءِ a host from the heavens,

وَمَا كُنَّا مُنْزِلِينَ ۝ nor We would have sent down.[1]

29 إِنْ كَانَتْ إِلَّا صَيْحَةً وَاحِدَةً It was but a single Cry,

فَإِذَا هُمْ خَامِدُونَ ۝ and behold, they were stilled like burnt ashes!

30 يَا حَسْرَةً عَلَى الْعِبَادِ How regrettable of the servants!

مَا يَأْتِيهِمْ مِنْ رَسُولٍ There did not come to them any apostle

إِلَّا كَانُوا بِهِ يَسْتَهْزِئُونَ ۝ but that they used to deride him.

31 أَلَمْ يَرَوْا Have they not regarded

كَمْ أَهْلَكْنَا قَبْلَهُمْ مِنَ الْقُرُونِ how many generations We have destroyed before them

أَنَّهُمْ إِلَيْهِمْ لَا يَرْجِعُونَ ۝ who will not come back to them?

32 وَإِنْ كُلٌّ لَمَّا جَمِيعٌ لَدَيْنَا مُحْضَرُونَ ۝ And all of them will indeed be presented before Us.

33 وَآيَةٌ لَهُمُ الْأَرْضُ الْمَيْتَةُ أَحْيَيْنَاهَا A sign for them is the dead earth, which We revive

وَأَخْرَجْنَا مِنْهَا حَبًّا فَمِنْهُ يَأْكُلُونَ ۝ and bring forth grain out of it, so they eat of it.

34 وَجَعَلْنَا فِيهَا جَنَّاتٍ مِنْ نَخِيلٍ وَأَعْنَابٍ We make in it orchards of date palms and vines,

وَفَجَّرْنَا فِيهَا مِنَ الْعُيُونِ ۝ and We cause springs to gush forth in it,

35 لِيَأْكُلُوا مِنْ ثَمَرِهِ so that they may eat of its fruit

وَمَا عَمِلَتْهُ أَيْدِيهِمْ ۖ and what their hands have cultivated.[2]

أَفَلَا يَشْكُرُونَ ۝ Will they not then give thanks?

36 سُبْحَانَ الَّذِي خَلَقَ الْأَزْوَاجَ كُلَّهَا Immaculate is He who has created all the kinds[3]

مِمَّا تُنْبِتُ الْأَرْضُ وَمِنْ أَنْفُسِهِمْ of what the earth grows, and of themselves,

---

[1] Or 'and what We used to send down [before];' see Ṭabrisī, Fayḍ Kāshānī.
[2] Or 'and their hands did not cultivate it.' That is, it is We who produce the fruits, not their hands. Cf. **27**:60 and **56**:64.
[3] Or, 'all the pairs.'

and of what they do not know. وَمِمَّا لَا يَعْلَمُونَ ۝

37 A sign for them is the night, which We strip of daylight, وَآيَةٌ لَهُمُ اللَّيْلُ نَسْلَخُ مِنْهُ النَّهَارَ
   and behold, they find themselves in the dark! فَإِذَا هُم مُّظْلِمُونَ ۝

38 The sun runs on to its place of rest:[1] وَالشَّمْسُ تَجْرِي لِمُسْتَقَرٍّ لَّهَا
   That is the ordaining of the All-mighty, the All-knowing. ذَٰلِكَ تَقْدِيرُ الْعَزِيزِ الْعَلِيمِ ۝

39 As for the moon, We have ordained its phases, وَالْقَمَرَ قَدَّرْنَاهُ مَنَازِلَ
   until it becomes like an old palm leaf. حَتَّىٰ عَادَ كَالْعُرْجُونِ الْقَدِيمِ ۝

40 Neither it behooves the sun لَا الشَّمْسُ يَنبَغِي لَهَا
   to overtake the moon, أَن تُدْرِكَ الْقَمَرَ
   nor may the night outrun the day, وَلَا اللَّيْلُ سَابِقُ النَّهَارِ
   and each swims in an orbit. وَكُلٌّ فِي فَلَكٍ يَسْبَحُونَ ۝

41 A sign for them is that We carried their progeny وَآيَةٌ لَهُمْ أَنَّا حَمَلْنَا ذُرِّيَّتَهُمْ
   in the laden ship,[2] فِي الْفُلْكِ الْمَشْحُونِ ۝

42 and We have created for them what is similar to it, وَخَلَقْنَا لَهُم مِّن مِّثْلِهِ
   which they ride.[3] مَا يَرْكَبُونَ ۝

43 And if We like, We drown them, وَإِن نَّشَأْ نُغْرِقْهُمْ
   whereat they have no one to call for help, فَلَا صَرِيخَ لَهُمْ
   nor are they rescued وَلَا هُمْ يُنقَذُونَ ۝

44 —except by a mercy from Us إِلَّا رَحْمَةً مِّنَّا
   and for an enjoyment until some time. وَمَتَاعًا إِلَىٰ حِينٍ ۝

45 And when they are told, وَإِذَا قِيلَ لَهُمُ
   'Beware of that which is before you اتَّقُوا مَا بَيْنَ أَيْدِيكُمْ
   and that which is behind you,[4] وَمَا خَلْفَكُمْ
   so that you may receive His mercy.'[5] لَعَلَّكُمْ تُرْحَمُونَ ۝

46 There does not come to them any sign وَمَا تَأْتِيهِم مِّنْ آيَةٍ

---

[1] Or 'it has no place of rest.' This is in accordance with the alternate reading 'lā mustaqarra lahā.' Ṭabrisī in Majmaʿ al-Bayān narrates a tradition which ascribes the reading lā mustaqarra lahā to the Imams ʿAlī b. al-Ḥusayn, Muḥammad al-Bāqir, and Jaʿfar al-Ṣādiq, as well as to a number of the early exegetes such as Ibn ʿAbbās, Ibn Masʿūd, ʿIkrimah, and ʿAṭāʾ b. Abī Rabāḥ. See Muʿjam al-Qirāʾāt al-Qurʾāniyyah, v, 208, for further sources of this reading. The reading li mustaqarrin lahā seems to have been suggested and reinforced by the popular astronomical notions of the age.

[2] That is, in the ark of Noah.

[3] Or 'board,' that is, ships which are similar to their prototype, the ark of Noah; or, alternatively, the camel, which has been called 'the ship of the desert,' and other animals and means of transport.

[4] See 34:9.

[5] Ellipsis. The omitted clause is, 'they turn away arrogantly.'

مِنْ آيَاتِ رَبِّهِمْ
إِلَّا كَانُوا عَنْهَا مُعْرِضِينَ ۝

from among the signs of their Lord
but that they have been disregarding it.

وَإِذَا قِيلَ لَهُمْ
أَنْفِقُوا مِمَّا رَزَقَكُمُ اللَّهُ
قَالَ الَّذِينَ كَفَرُوا لِلَّذِينَ آمَنُوا
أَنُطْعِمُ
مَنْ لَوْ يَشَاءُ اللَّهُ أَطْعَمَهُ
إِنْ أَنْتُمْ إِلَّا فِي ضَلَالٍ مُبِينٍ ۝

47 When they are told,
'Spend out of what God has provided you,'
the faithless say to the faithful,
'Shall we feed someone
whom God would feed, if He wished?
You are only in plain error.'

وَيَقُولُونَ مَتَىٰ هَٰذَا الْوَعْدُ
إِنْ كُنْتُمْ صَادِقِينَ ۝

48 And they say, 'When will this promise be fulfilled,
if you are truthful?'

مَا يَنْظُرُونَ إِلَّا صَيْحَةً وَاحِدَةً
تَأْخُذُهُمْ وَهُمْ يَخِصِّمُونَ ۝

49 They do not await but a single Cry
that will seize them as they wrangle.

فَلَا يَسْتَطِيعُونَ تَوْصِيَةً
وَلَا إِلَىٰ أَهْلِهِمْ يَرْجِعُونَ ۝

50 Then they will not be able to make any will,
nor will they return to their folks.

وَنُفِخَ فِي الصُّورِ
فَإِذَا هُمْ
مِنَ الْأَجْدَاثِ إِلَىٰ رَبِّهِمْ يَنْسِلُونَ ۝

51 And when the Trumpet is blown,
behold, there they will be,
scrambling towards their Lord from their graves!

قَالُوا يَا وَيْلَنَا
مَنْ بَعَثَنَا مِنْ مَرْقَدِنَا
هَٰذَا مَا وَعَدَ الرَّحْمَٰنُ
وَصَدَقَ الْمُرْسَلُونَ ۝

52 They will say, 'Woe to us!
Who raised us from our place of sleep?'
'This is what the All-beneficent had promised
and the apostles had spoken the truth!'

إِنْ كَانَتْ إِلَّا صَيْحَةً وَاحِدَةً
فَإِذَا هُمْ جَمِيعٌ لَدَيْنَا مُحْضَرُونَ ۝

53 It will be but a single Cry,
and behold, they will all be presented before Us!

فَالْيَوْمَ لَا تُظْلَمُ نَفْسٌ شَيْئًا
وَلَا تُجْزَوْنَ إِلَّا مَا كُنْتُمْ تَعْمَلُونَ ۝

54 'Today no soul will be wronged in the least,
nor will you be requited except for what you used to do.'

إِنَّ أَصْحَابَ الْجَنَّةِ الْيَوْمَ
فِي شُغُلٍ فَاكِهُونَ ۝

55 Indeed, today the inhabitants of paradise
rejoice in their engagements

هُمْ وَأَزْوَاجُهُمْ
فِي ظِلَالٍ عَلَى الْأَرَائِكِ مُتَّكِئُونَ ۝

56 —they and their mates,
reclining on couches in the shades.

لَهُمْ فِيهَا فَاكِهَةٌ وَلَهُمْ مَا يَدَّعُونَ ۝

57 There they have fruits, and they have whatever they want.

سَلَامٌ قَوْلًا مِنْ رَبٍّ رَحِيمٍ ۝ 58	'Peace!'—a salutation from the all-merciful Lord.
وَامْتَازُوا الْيَوْمَ أَيُّهَا الْمُجْرِمُونَ ۝ 59	And 'Get apart today, you guilty ones!'
أَلَمْ أَعْهَدْ إِلَيْكُمْ يَا بَنِي آدَمَ 60	'Did I not exhort you, O children of Adam,
أَنْ لَا تَعْبُدُوا الشَّيْطَانَ	saying, "Do not worship Satan.
إِنَّهُ لَكُمْ عَدُوٌّ مُبِينٌ ۝	He is indeed your manifest enemy.
وَأَنِ اعْبُدُونِي هَٰذَا صِرَاطٌ مُسْتَقِيمٌ ۝ 61	Worship Me. That is a straight path"?
وَلَقَدْ أَضَلَّ مِنْكُمْ جِبِلًّا كَثِيرًا 62	He has already led astray many of your generations.
أَفَلَمْ تَكُونُوا تَعْقِلُونَ ۝	Did you not exercise your reason?
هَٰذِهِ جَهَنَّمُ الَّتِي كُنْتُمْ تُوعَدُونَ ۝ 63	This is the hell you had been promised!
اصْلَوْهَا الْيَوْمَ بِمَا كُنْتُمْ تَكْفُرُونَ ۝ 64	Enter it today, because of what you used to deny.
الْيَوْمَ نَخْتِمُ عَلَىٰ أَفْوَاهِهِمْ 65	Today We shall seal their mouths,
وَتُكَلِّمُنَا أَيْدِيهِمْ	and their hands will speak to Us,
وَتَشْهَدُ أَرْجُلُهُمْ	and their feet will bear witness
بِمَا كَانُوا يَكْسِبُونَ ۝	concerning what they used to earn.'
وَلَوْ نَشَاءُ لَطَمَسْنَا عَلَىٰ أَعْيُنِهِمْ 66	Had We wished We would have blotted out their eyes;[1]
فَاسْتَبَقُوا الصِّرَاطَ	then, were they to advance towards the path,
فَأَنَّىٰ يُبْصِرُونَ ۝	how would have they seen?
وَلَوْ نَشَاءُ 67	Had We wished
لَمَسَخْنَاهُمْ عَلَىٰ مَكَانَتِهِمْ	We would have deformed them in their place;[2]
فَمَا اسْتَطَاعُوا مُضِيًّا	then, they would neither have been able to move ahead,
وَلَا يَرْجِعُونَ ۝	nor to return.[3]
وَمَنْ نُعَمِّرْهُ 68	And whomever We give a long life,
نُنَكِّسْهُ فِي الْخَلْقِ	We cause him to regress in creation.
أَفَلَا يَعْقِلُونَ ۝	Then, will they not exercise their reason?
وَمَا عَلَّمْنَاهُ الشِّعْرَ وَمَا يَنْبَغِي لَهُ 69	We did not teach *him* poetry, nor does it behoove *him*.
إِنْ هُوَ إِلَّا ذِكْرٌ وَقُرْآنٌ مُبِينٌ ۝	This is just a reminder and a manifest Qur'ān,
لِيُنْذِرَ مَنْ كَانَ حَيًّا 70	so that anyone who is alive may be warned
وَيَحِقَّ الْقَوْلُ عَلَى الْكَافِرِينَ ۝	and that the word may come due against the faithless.

---

[1] That is, the insight to see the course of true human felicity.
[2] That is, brought them to a standstill with their deformed inner state.
[3] That is, they would have neither been able to move ahead to make spiritual progress, nor to return to their original state of unsullied God-given nature.

71 أَوَلَمْ يَرَوْا أَنَّا خَلَقْنَا لَهُم مِّمَّا عَمِلَتْ أَيْدِينَا أَنْعَامًا فَهُمْ لَهَا مَالِكُونَ ۝

71 Have they not seen that We have created for them, of what Our hands have worked, cattle, so they have become their masters?

72 وَذَلَّلْنَاهَا لَهُمْ فَمِنْهَا رَكُوبُهُمْ وَمِنْهَا يَأْكُلُونَ ۝

72 And We made them tractable for them, so some of them make their mounts and some of them they eat.

73 وَلَهُمْ فِيهَا مَنَافِعُ وَمَشَارِبُ أَفَلَا يَشْكُرُونَ ۝

73 There are other benefits for them therein, and drinks.[1] Will they not then give thanks?

74 وَاتَّخَذُوا مِن دُونِ اللَّهِ آلِهَةً لَّعَلَّهُمْ يُنصَرُونَ ۝

74 They have taken gods besides God, hoping that they might be helped.

75 لَا يَسْتَطِيعُونَ نَصْرَهُمْ وَهُمْ لَهُمْ جُندٌ مُّحْضَرُونَ ۝

75 But they cannot help them, while they are an army mobilized for their defence.[2]

76 فَلَا يَحْزُنكَ قَوْلُهُمْ إِنَّا نَعْلَمُ مَا يُسِرُّونَ وَمَا يُعْلِنُونَ ۝

76 So do not let their remarks grieve you. We indeed know whatever they hide and whatever they disclose.

77 أَوَلَمْ يَرَ الْإِنسَانُ أَنَّا خَلَقْنَاهُ مِن نُّطْفَةٍ فَإِذَا هُوَ خَصِيمٌ مُّبِينٌ ۝

77 Does not man see that We created him from a drop of seminal fluid, and behold, he is an open contender!?

78 وَضَرَبَ لَنَا مَثَلًا وَنَسِيَ خَلْقَهُ قَالَ مَن يُحْيِي الْعِظَامَ وَهِيَ رَمِيمٌ ۝

78 He draws comparisons for Us, and forgets his own creation. He says, 'Who will revive the bones when they have decayed?'

79 قُلْ يُحْيِيهَا الَّذِي أَنشَأَهَا أَوَّلَ مَرَّةٍ وَهُوَ بِكُلِّ خَلْقٍ عَلِيمٌ ۝

79 Say, 'He will revive them who produced them the first time, and He has knowledge of all creation.

80 الَّذِي جَعَلَ لَكُم مِّنَ الشَّجَرِ الْأَخْضَرِ نَارًا فَإِذَا أَنتُم مِّنْهُ تُوقِدُونَ ۝

80 —He, who made for you fire out of the green tree, and behold, you light fire from it!

---

[1] That is, milk and other drinks derived from it.
[2] That is, while the idols are unable to offer the idolaters any kind of assistance, the idolaters are ready to fight for them and defend them.

81 Is not He who created the heavens and the earth أَوَلَيْسَ الَّذِى خَلَقَ السَّمَاوَاتِ وَالْأَرْضَ
able to create the like of them? بِقَادِرٍ عَلَىٰ أَنْ يَخْلُقَ مِثْلَهُمْ
Yes indeed! He is the All-creator, the All-knowing. بَلَىٰ وَهُوَ الْخَلَّاقُ الْعَلِيمُ ۝

82 All His command, when He wills something, إِنَّمَا أَمْرُهُ إِذَا أَرَادَ شَيْئًا
is to say to it 'Be,' and it is. أَنْ يَقُولَ لَهُ كُنْ فَيَكُونُ ۝

83 So immaculate is He فَسُبْحَانَ الَّذِى
in whose hand is the dominion of all things بِيَدِهِ مَلَكُوتُ كُلِّ شَىْءٍ
and to whom you shall be brought back. وَإِلَيْهِ تُرْجَعُونَ ۝

37. THE RANGED ONES[1]
al-Ṣāffāt

In the Name of God,
the All-beneficent, the All-merciful.

1 By the angels ranged in ranks, وَالصَّافَّاتِ صَفًّا ۝
2 by the ones who drive vigorously,[2] فَالزَّاجِرَاتِ زَجْرًا ۝
3 by the ones who recite the reminder:[3] فَالتَّالِيَاتِ ذِكْرًا ۝
4 indeed your God is certainly One, إِنَّ إِلَٰهَكُمْ لَوَاحِدٌ ۝
5 the Lord of the heavens and the earth رَبُّ السَّمَاوَاتِ وَالْأَرْضِ
and whatever is between them, وَمَا بَيْنَهُمَا
and the Lord of the easts.[4] وَرَبُّ الْمَشَارِقِ ۝
6 We have indeed adorned the lowest heaven[5] إِنَّا زَيَّنَّا السَّمَاءَ الدُّنْيَا
with the finery of the stars[6] بِزِينَةٍ الْكَوَاكِبِ ۝
7 and to guard from every froward devil. وَحِفْظًا مِنْ كُلِّ شَيْطَانٍ مَارِدٍ ۝
8 They do not eavesdrop on the Supernal Elite لَا يَسَّمَّعُونَ إِلَى الْمَلَإِ الْأَعْلَىٰ
—they are shot at from every side, وَيُقْذَفُونَ مِنْ كُلِّ جَانِبٍ ۝
9 to drive them away, دُحُورًا

---

[1] This Makkī *sūrah* takes its name from verse 1, which refers to a group of angels as 'those ranged in ranks' (*ṣāffāt*). Also see verses 164–166 below.
[2] Or 'by those who restrain in order to deter (or prevent).' May refer to the angels who drive the clouds, or drive away the eavesdropping devils, or to angels (or verses of the Qur'ān) that restrain people from sins.
[3] That is, the faithful, or the angels, who recite the Qur'ān or the scriptures.
[4] I. e., points of sunrise at the winter and summer solstices. Or 'the first beginnings.' Cf. 7:137; **55:**17; **70:**40.
[5] Or 'the heaven of the earth,' or 'the nearest heaven.'
[6] Or 'We have adorned the nearest heaven with an adornment, the stars.'

وَلَهُمْ عَذَابٌ وَاصِبٌ ۝		and there is a perpetual punishment for them—
إِلَّا مَنْ خَطِفَ الْخَطْفَةَ	10	except any who snatches a snatch,[1]
فَأَتْبَعَهُ شِهَابٌ ثَاقِبٌ ۝		whereat a piercing flame pursues him.[2]
فَاسْتَفْتِهِمْ أَهُمْ أَشَدُّ خَلْقًا	11	Ask them, is their creation more prodigious[3]
أَمْ مَنْ خَلَقْنَا		or that of other creatures that We have created?
إِنَّا خَلَقْنَاهُمْ مِنْ طِينٍ لَازِبٍ ۝		Indeed, We created them from a viscous clay.
بَلْ عَجِبْتَ وَيَسْخَرُونَ ۝	12	Indeed, you wonder, while they engage in ridicule,
وَإِذَا ذُكِّرُوا لَا يَذْكُرُونَ ۝	13	and even when admonished do not take admonition,
وَإِذَا رَأَوْا آيَةً	14	and when they see a sign,
يَسْتَسْخِرُونَ ۝		they make it an object of ridicule
وَقَالُوا إِنْ هَذَا إِلَّا سِحْرٌ مُبِينٌ ۝	15	and say, 'This is nothing but plain magic!'
أَإِذَا مِتْنَا	16	'What! When we are dead
وَكُنَّا تُرَابًا وَعِظَامًا		and become dust and bones,
أَإِنَّا لَمَبْعُوثُونَ ۝		shall we be indeed resurrected?
أَوَآبَاؤُنَا الْأَوَّلُونَ ۝	17	And our forefathers, too?!'
قُلْ نَعَمْ وَأَنْتُمْ دَاخِرُونَ ۝	18	Say, 'Yes! And you will be utterly humble.'
فَإِنَّمَا هِيَ زَجْرَةٌ وَاحِدَةٌ	19	It will be only a single shout
فَإِذَا هُمْ يَنْظُرُونَ ۝		and behold, they will look on
وَقَالُوا يَا وَيْلَنَا هَذَا يَوْمُ الدِّينِ ۝	20	and say, 'Woe to us! This is the Day of Retribution!'
هَذَا يَوْمُ الْفَصْلِ	21	'This is the Day of Judgement
الَّذِي كُنْتُمْ بِهِ تُكَذِّبُونَ ۝		that you used to deny!'
احْشُرُوا الَّذِينَ ظَلَمُوا وَأَزْوَاجَهُمْ	22	'Gather the wrongdoers and their mates[4]
وَمَا كَانُوا يَعْبُدُونَ ۝		and what they used to worship
مِنْ دُونِ اللَّهِ	23	besides God,
فَاهْدُوهُمْ إِلَى صِرَاطِ الْجَحِيمِ ۝		and show them the way to hell!
وَقِفُوهُمْ إِنَّهُمْ مَسْئُولُونَ ۝	24	But first stop them! For they must be questioned.'
مَا لَكُمْ لَا تَنَاصَرُونَ ۝	25	'Why is it that you do not support[5] one another today?'

---

[1] That is, of celestial intelligence. See Ṭabarī for several related traditions from the Prophet (ṣ).
[2] Cf. **15:17-18**.
[3] Or 'stronger,' or 'more difficult.' Cf. **79:27**.
[4] Or 'their kind,' or 'their counterparts.'
[5] Or 'help.'

بَلْ هُمُ الْيَوْمَ مُسْتَسْلِمُونَ ۝	26	They are indeed meek and submissive today!
وَأَقْبَلَ بَعْضُهُمْ عَلَىٰ بَعْضٍ يَتَسَاءَلُونَ ۝	27	Some of them will turn to others, questioning each other.
قَالُوا إِنَّكُمْ كُنتُمْ تَأْتُونَنَا عَنِ الْيَمِينِ ۝	28	They will say, 'Indeed, you used to accost us peremptorily.'[1]
قَالُوا بَل لَّمْ تَكُونُوا مُؤْمِنِينَ ۝	29	They will answer, 'No, you yourselves had no faith.
وَمَا كَانَ لَنَا عَلَيْكُم مِّن سُلْطَانٍ ۖ بَلْ كُنتُمْ قَوْمًا طَاغِينَ ۝	30	We had no authority over you. No, you yourselves were a rebellious lot.
فَحَقَّ عَلَيْنَا قَوْلُ رَبِّنَا ۖ إِنَّا لَذَائِقُونَ ۝	31	So our Lord's word became due against us that we shall indeed taste the punishment.
فَأَغْوَيْنَاكُمْ إِنَّا كُنَّا غَاوِينَ ۝	32	We perverted you, for we were perverse ourselves.'
فَإِنَّهُمْ يَوْمَئِذٍ فِي الْعَذَابِ مُشْتَرِكُونَ ۝	33	So that day they will share the punishment.
إِنَّا كَذَٰلِكَ نَفْعَلُ بِالْمُجْرِمِينَ ۝	34	Indeed, that is how We deal with the guilty.
إِنَّهُمْ كَانُوا إِذَا قِيلَ لَهُمْ لَا إِلَٰهَ إِلَّا اللَّهُ يَسْتَكْبِرُونَ ۝	35	Indeed, it was they who, when they were told, 'There is no god except God,' used to be disdainful,
وَيَقُولُونَ أَئِنَّا لَتَارِكُو آلِهَتِنَا لِشَاعِرٍ مَّجْنُونٍ ۝	36	and they would say, 'Shall we abandon our gods for a crazy poet?'
بَلْ جَاءَ بِالْحَقِّ وَصَدَّقَ الْمُرْسَلِينَ ۝	37	He has indeed brought them the truth, and confirmed the former apostles.
إِنَّكُمْ لَذَائِقُو الْعَذَابِ الْأَلِيمِ ۝	38	You will indeed taste the painful punishment
وَمَا تُجْزَوْنَ إِلَّا مَا كُنتُمْ تَعْمَلُونَ ۝	39	and you will be requited only for what you used to do
إِلَّا عِبَادَ اللَّهِ الْمُخْلَصِينَ ۝	40	—all except God's exclusive servants.
أُولَٰئِكَ لَهُمْ رِزْقٌ مَّعْلُومٌ ۝	41	For such there is a known[2] provision
فَوَاكِهُ ۖ وَهُم مُّكْرَمُونَ ۝	42	—fruits—and they will be held in honour
فِي جَنَّاتِ النَّعِيمِ ۝	43	in the gardens of bliss,
عَلَىٰ سُرُرٍ مُّتَقَابِلِينَ ۝	44	reclining on couches, facing one another,
يُطَافُ عَلَيْهِم بِكَأْسٍ مِّن مَّعِينٍ ۝	45	served around with a cup from a clear fountain,
بَيْضَاءَ لَذَّةٍ لِّلشَّارِبِينَ ۝	46	snow-white, delicious to the drinkers,

[1] Or 'obligingly.'
[2] That is, distinct and special.

47 wherein there will be neither headache
   nor will it cause them stupefaction,
48 and with them will be maidens of restrained glances
   with big beautiful eyes,
49 as if they were hidden[1] ostrich eggs.
50 Some of them will turn to others,
   questioning each other.
51 One of them will say, 'I had indeed a companion
52 who used to say,
   "Are you really among those who affirm
53 that when we have died and become dust and bones,
   we will indeed be brought to retribution?"'
54 He[2] will say, 'Will you have a look?'
55 Then he will take a look
   and sight him in the middle of hell.
56 He will say, 'By God, you had almost ruined me!
57 Had it not been for my Lord's blessing,
   I too would have been among the arraigned!'
58 'Is it true that we will not die anymore,
59 aside from our earlier death,
   and that we will not be punished?
60 This is indeed a mighty triumph!
61 Let all workers work for the like of this!'
62 Is this a better reception, or the Zaqqūm tree?
63 Indeed, We have made it a punishment
   for the wrongdoers.
64 It is a tree that rises from the depths of hell.
65 Its blossoms are as if they were devils' heads.[3]

---

[1] That is, well reserved.
[2] That is, one of his companions in paradise.
[3] 'The devil's head' is either a purely imaginative metaphor, or a simile that likens the blossoms of the *Zaqqūm* tree to that of an Arabian plant by this name, or to certain rocks found around the city of Makkah which were called 'the devils' heads' because of their hideous appearance.

66	They will eat from it فَإِنَّهُمْ لَآكِلُونَ مِنْهَا
	and gorge with it their bellies. فَمَالِئُونَ مِنْهَا الْبُطُونَ ۝
67	On top of that they will take ثُمَّ إِنَّ لَهُمْ عَلَيْهَا
	a solution of scalding water. لَشَوْبًا مِنْ حَمِيمٍ ۝
68	Then their retreat will be toward hell. ثُمَّ إِنَّ مَرْجِعَهُمْ لَإِلَى الْجَحِيمِ ۝
69	They had found their fathers astray, إِنَّهُمْ أَلْفَوْا آبَاءَهُمْ ضَالِّينَ ۝
70	yet they press onwards in their footsteps. فَهُمْ عَلَىٰ آثَارِهِمْ يُهْرَعُونَ ۝
71	Most of the former peoples went astray before them, وَلَقَدْ ضَلَّ قَبْلَهُمْ أَكْثَرُ الْأَوَّلِينَ ۝
72	and We had certainly sent warners among them. وَلَقَدْ أَرْسَلْنَا فِيهِمْ مُنْذِرِينَ ۝
73	So *observe* how was the fate of those who were warned فَانْظُرْ كَيْفَ كَانَ عَاقِبَةُ الْمُنْذَرِينَ ۝
74	—all except God's exclusive servants! إِلَّا عِبَادَ اللَّهِ الْمُخْلَصِينَ ۝

75	Certainly Noah called out to Us وَلَقَدْ نَادَانَا نُوحٌ
	and how well did We respond! فَلَنِعْمَ الْمُجِيبُونَ ۝
76	We delivered him and his family وَنَجَّيْنَاهُ وَأَهْلَهُ
	from their great distress, مِنَ الْكَرْبِ الْعَظِيمِ ۝
77	and made his descendants the survivors, وَجَعَلْنَا ذُرِّيَّتَهُ هُمُ الْبَاقِينَ ۝
78	and left for him a good name among posterity: وَتَرَكْنَا عَلَيْهِ فِي الْآخِرِينَ ۝
79	'Peace to Noah, throughout the nations!' سَلَامٌ عَلَىٰ نُوحٍ فِي الْعَالَمِينَ ۝
80	Thus do We reward the virtuous. إِنَّا كَذَٰلِكَ نَجْزِي الْمُحْسِنِينَ ۝
81	He is indeed one of Our faithful servants. إِنَّهُ مِنْ عِبَادِنَا الْمُؤْمِنِينَ ۝
82	Then We drowned the rest. ثُمَّ أَغْرَقْنَا الْآخَرِينَ ۝

83	Abraham was indeed among his followers, وَإِنَّ مِنْ شِيعَتِهِ لَإِبْرَاهِيمَ ۝
84	when he came to his Lord with a sound heart,[1] إِذْ جَاءَ رَبَّهُ بِقَلْبٍ سَلِيمٍ ۝
85	when he said to his father and his people, إِذْ قَالَ لِأَبِيهِ وَقَوْمِهِ
	'What is it that you are worshiping? مَاذَا تَعْبُدُونَ ۝
86	Is it a lie, gods other than God, that you desire? أَئِفْكًا آلِهَةً دُونَ اللَّهِ تُرِيدُونَ ۝
87	Then what is your idea فَمَا ظَنُّكُمْ
	about the Lord of all the worlds?' بِرَبِّ الْعَالَمِينَ ۝

---

[1] Cf. 26:89.

88 فَنَظَرَ نَظْرَةً فِي النُّجُومِ ۝ Then he made an observation of the stars[1]

89 فَقَالَ إِنِّي سَقِيمٌ ۝ and said, 'I am indeed sick!'

90 فَتَوَلَّوْا عَنْهُ مُدْبِرِينَ ۝ So they went away leaving him behind.

91 فَرَاغَ إِلَىٰ آلِهَتِهِمْ Then he stole away to their gods
فَقَالَ أَلَا تَأْكُلُونَ ۝ and said, 'Will you not eat?

92 مَا لَكُمْ لَا تَنْطِقُونَ ۝ Why do you not speak?'

93 فَرَاغَ عَلَيْهِمْ ضَرْبًا بِالْيَمِينِ ۝ Then he attacked them, striking forcefully.

94 فَأَقْبَلُوا إِلَيْهِ يَزِفُّونَ ۝ They came running towards him.

95 قَالَ أَتَعْبُدُونَ He said, 'Do you worship
مَا تَنْحِتُونَ ۝ what you have carved yourselves,

96 وَاللَّهُ خَلَقَكُمْ when God has created you
وَمَا تَعْمَلُونَ ۝ and whatever you make?'

97 قَالُوا ابْنُوا لَهُ بُنْيَانًا They said, 'Build a structure for him
فَأَلْقُوهُ فِي الْجَحِيمِ ۝ and cast him into a huge fire.'

98 فَأَرَادُوا بِهِ كَيْدًا So they sought to outwit him,
فَجَعَلْنَاهُمُ الْأَسْفَلِينَ ۝ but We made them the lowermost.

99 وَقَالَ إِنِّي ذَاهِبٌ إِلَىٰ رَبِّي He said, 'Indeed, I am going toward my Lord,
سَيَهْدِينِ ۝ who will guide me.'

100 رَبِّ هَبْ لِي مِنَ الصَّالِحِينَ ۝ 'My Lord! Give me an heir, one of the righteous.'

101 فَبَشَّرْنَاهُ بِغُلَامٍ حَلِيمٍ ۝ So We gave him the good news of a forbearing son.[2]

102 فَلَمَّا بَلَغَ مَعَهُ السَّعْيَ When he was old enough to assist in his endeavour,
قَالَ يَا بُنَيَّ he said, 'My son!
إِنِّي أَرَىٰ فِي الْمَنَامِ أَنِّي أَذْبَحُكَ I see in dreams that I am sacrificing you.
فَانْظُرْ مَاذَا تَرَىٰ See what you think.'
قَالَ يَا أَبَتِ He said, 'Father!
افْعَلْ مَا تُؤْمَرُ Do whatever you have been commanded.
سَتَجِدُنِي إِنْ شَاءَ اللَّهُ If God wishes, you will find me
مِنَ الصَّابِرِينَ ۝ to be patient.'

---

[1] Or 'cast a glance at the stars.'
[2] That is, Ishmael, who was Abraham's first born. That it was Ishmael to whom the following episode of the sacrifice pertains is also supported by the fact that verses pertaining to the birth of Isaac follow the account of Ishmael's sacrifice.

فَلَمَّا أَسْلَمَا وَتَلَّهُ لِلْجَبِينِ ۝	103 So when they had both surrendered to God's will and he had laid him down on his temple,
وَنَادَيْنَاهُ أَنْ يَا إِبْرَاهِيمُ ۝	104 We called out to him, 'O Abraham!
قَدْ صَدَّقْتَ الرُّؤْيَا	105 You have indeed fulfilled your vision![1]
إِنَّا كَذَٰلِكَ نَجْزِي الْمُحْسِنِينَ ۝	Thus indeed do We reward the virtuous!
إِنَّ هَٰذَا لَهُوَ الْبَلَاءُ الْمُبِينُ ۝	106 This was indeed a manifest test.'
وَفَدَيْنَاهُ بِذِبْحٍ عَظِيمٍ ۝	107 Then We ransomed him with a great sacrifice,
وَتَرَكْنَا عَلَيْهِ فِي الْآخِرِينَ ۝	108 and left for him a good name in posterity:
سَلَامٌ عَلَىٰ إِبْرَاهِيمَ ۝	109 'Peace be to Abraham!'
كَذَٰلِكَ نَجْزِي الْمُحْسِنِينَ ۝	110 Thus do We reward the virtuous.
إِنَّهُ مِنْ عِبَادِنَا الْمُؤْمِنِينَ ۝	111 He is indeed one of Our faithful servants.
وَبَشَّرْنَاهُ بِإِسْحَاقَ نَبِيًّا مِنَ الصَّالِحِينَ ۝	112 We gave him the good news of the birth of Isaac, a prophet, one of the righteous.
وَبَارَكْنَا عَلَيْهِ وَعَلَىٰ إِسْحَاقَ وَمِنْ ذُرِّيَّتِهِمَا مُحْسِنٌ وَظَالِمٌ لِنَفْسِهِ مُبِينٌ ۝	113 And We blessed him and Isaac. Among their descendants some are virtuous, and some who manifestly wrong themselves.
وَلَقَدْ مَنَنَّا عَلَىٰ مُوسَىٰ وَهَارُونَ ۝	114 Certainly We favoured Moses and Aaron
وَنَجَّيْنَاهُمَا وَقَوْمَهُمَا مِنَ الْكَرْبِ الْعَظِيمِ ۝	115 and delivered them and their people from their great distress,
وَنَصَرْنَاهُمْ فَكَانُوا هُمُ الْغَالِبِينَ ۝	116 and We helped them, so they became the victors.
وَآتَيْنَاهُمَا الْكِتَابَ الْمُسْتَبِينَ ۝	117 We gave them the illuminating scripture
وَهَدَيْنَاهُمَا الصِّرَاطَ الْمُسْتَقِيمَ ۝	118 and guided them to the straight path
وَتَرَكْنَا عَلَيْهِمَا فِي الْآخِرِينَ ۝	119 and left for them a good name in posterity.
سَلَامٌ عَلَىٰ مُوسَىٰ وَهَارُونَ ۝	120 'Peace be to Moses and Aaron!'
إِنَّا كَذَٰلِكَ نَجْزِي الْمُحْسِنِينَ ۝	121 Thus indeed do We reward the virtuous.
إِنَّهُمَا مِنْ عِبَادِنَا الْمُؤْمِنِينَ ۝	122 They are indeed among Our faithful servants.
وَإِنَّ إِلْيَاسَ لَمِنَ الْمُرْسَلِينَ ۝	123 Indeed, Ilyās was one of the apostles.

[1] Or 'dream.'

إِذْ قَالَ لِقَوْمِهِ أَلَا تَتَّقُونَ ۝	124	When he said to his people, 'Will you not be Godwary?
أَتَدْعُونَ بَعْلًا	125	Do you invoke Baal
وَتَذَرُونَ أَحْسَنَ الْخَالِقِينَ ۝		and abandon the best of creators,
اللَّهَ رَبَّكُمْ	126	God, your Lord
وَرَبَّ آبَائِكُمُ الْأَوَّلِينَ ۝		and Lord of your forefathers?,'
فَكَذَّبُوهُ	127	they impugned him.
فَإِنَّهُمْ لَمُحْضَرُونَ ۝		So they will indeed be arraigned
إِلَّا عِبَادَ اللَّهِ الْمُخْلَصِينَ ۝	128	—all except God's exclusive servants.
وَتَرَكْنَا عَلَيْهِ فِي الْآخِرِينَ ۝	129	We left for him a good name in posterity.
سَلَامٌ عَلَىٰ إِلْ يَاسِينَ ۝	130	'Peace be to Ilyās!'[1]
إِنَّا كَذَٰلِكَ نَجْزِي الْمُحْسِنِينَ ۝	131	Thus indeed do We reward the virtuous.
إِنَّهُ مِنْ عِبَادِنَا الْمُؤْمِنِينَ ۝	132	He is indeed one of Our faithful servants.
وَإِنَّ لُوطًا لَمِنَ الْمُرْسَلِينَ ۝	133	Indeed, Lot was one of the apostles.
إِذْ نَجَّيْنَاهُ وَأَهْلَهُ أَجْمَعِينَ ۝	134	When We delivered him and all his family,
إِلَّا عَجُوزًا	135	excepting an old woman
فِي الْغَابِرِينَ ۝		among those who remained behind.
ثُمَّ دَمَّرْنَا الْآخَرِينَ ۝	136	Then We destroyed the rest.
وَإِنَّكُمْ لَتَمُرُّونَ عَلَيْهِمْ مُصْبِحِينَ ۝	137	Indeed, you pass by them at morning
وَبِاللَّيْلِ	138	and evening [on the Syrian route of your caravans].
أَفَلَا تَعْقِلُونَ ۝		So do you not exercise your reason?
وَإِنَّ يُونُسَ لَمِنَ الْمُرْسَلِينَ ۝	139	Jonah was indeed one of the apostles.
إِذْ أَبَقَ إِلَى الْفُلْكِ الْمَشْحُونِ ۝	140	When he absconded toward the laden ship,
فَسَاهَمَ	141	he drew lots with them
فَكَانَ مِنَ الْمُدْحَضِينَ ۝		and was the one to be refuted and thrown overboard.
فَالْتَقَمَهُ الْحُوتُ	142	Then the fish swallowed him,

---

[1] In accordance with an alternate reading (*salāmun 'alā Āl-i Yā Sīn*), narrated from Nāfi', Ibn 'Āmir, Ya'qūb, Ruways, al-A'raj, Shaybah, Zayd ibn 'Alī and others (see *Mu'jam al-Qirā'āt al-Qur'āniyyah*, vol. 5, p. 246), the translation will be 'Peace be upon the progeny of Yā Sīn' (i.e. the Prophet, who is referred to as *Yā Sīn* in **36:1**). Traditions narrated from Ibn 'Abbās (*al-Durr al-Manthūr*, vol. 5, p. 286), Imam Ja'far al-Ṣādiq (*Ma'ānī al-Akhbār*, p. 122) and Imam 'Alī ibn Mūsā al-Riḍā ('*Uyūn Akhbār al-Riḍā*, vol. 1, p.237) also support this reading.

وَهُوَ مُلِيمٌ ۝ while he was blameworthy.

فَلَوْلَا أَنَّهُ كَانَ مِنَ الْمُسَبِّحِينَ ۝ 143 Had he not been one of those who celebrate God's glory,

لَلَبِثَ فِي بَطْنِهِ إِلَىٰ يَوْمِ يُبْعَثُونَ ۞ ۝ 144 he would have surely remained in its belly till the day they will be resurrected.

فَنَبَذْنَاهُ بِالْعَرَاءِ وَهُوَ سَقِيمٌ ۝ 145 Then We cast him on a bare shore, and he was sick.

وَأَنْبَتْنَا عَلَيْهِ شَجَرَةً مِنْ يَقْطِينٍ ۝ 146 So We made a gourd plant grow above him.

وَأَرْسَلْنَاهُ إِلَىٰ مِائَةِ أَلْفٍ أَوْ يَزِيدُونَ ۝ 147 We sent him to a community of hundred thousand or more,

فَآمَنُوا فَمَتَّعْنَاهُمْ إِلَىٰ حِينٍ ۝ 148 and they believed in him. So We provided for them for a while.

فَاسْتَفْتِهِمْ أَلِرَبِّكَ الْبَنَاتُ وَلَهُمُ الْبَنُونَ ۝ 149 Ask them, are daughters to be for your Lord while sons are to be for them?[1]

أَمْ خَلَقْنَا الْمَلَائِكَةَ إِنَاثًا وَهُمْ شَاهِدُونَ ۝ 150 Did We create the angels females while they were present?[2]

أَلَا إِنَّهُمْ مِنْ إِفْكِهِمْ لَيَقُولُونَ ۝ 151 Be aware that it is out of their mendacity that they say,

وَلَدَ اللَّهُ وَإِنَّهُمْ لَكَاذِبُونَ ۝ 152 'God has begotten offspring,' and they indeed speak a falsehood.

أَصْطَفَى الْبَنَاتِ عَلَى الْبَنِينَ ۝ 153 Has He preferred daughters to sons?

مَا لَكُمْ كَيْفَ تَحْكُمُونَ ۝ 154 What is the matter with you? How do you judge?

أَفَلَا تَذَكَّرُونَ ۝ 155 Will you not then take admonition?

أَمْ لَكُمْ سُلْطَانٌ مُبِينٌ ۝ 156 Do you have a manifest authority?[3]

فَأْتُوا بِكِتَابِكُمْ إِنْ كُنْتُمْ صَادِقِينَ ۝ 157 Then produce your scripture, should you be truthful.

وَجَعَلُوا بَيْنَهُ وَبَيْنَ الْجِنَّةِ نَسَبًا وَلَقَدْ عَلِمَتِ الْجِنَّةُ إِنَّهُمْ لَمُحْضَرُونَ ۝ 158 And they have set up a kinship between Him and the jinn, while the jinn certainly know that they will be presented before Him.

---

[1] Cf. **6:**100; **16:**57; **17:**40; **43:**16; **52:**39.
[2] Or 'while they were witnesses.'
[3] That is, in support of what they assert.

سُبْحَانَ اللَّهِ عَمَّا يَصِفُونَ ۝	159	Clear is God of whatever they allege about Him
إِلَّا عِبَادَ اللَّهِ الْمُخْلَصِينَ ۝	160	—all except God's exclusive servants.
فَإِنَّكُمْ وَمَا تَعْبُدُونَ ۝	161	Indeed, you and what you worship
مَا أَنتُمْ عَلَيْهِ بِفَاتِنِينَ ۝	162	cannot mislead anyone about Him,
إِلَّا مَنْ هُوَ صَالِ الْجَحِيمِ ۝	163	except someone who is bound for hell.
وَمَا مِنَّا إِلَّا لَهُ مَقَامٌ مَّعْلُومٌ ۝	164	'There is none among us but has a known place.[1]
وَإِنَّا لَنَحْنُ الصَّافُّونَ ۝	165	We are indeed the ranged ones.
وَإِنَّا لَنَحْنُ الْمُسَبِّحُونَ ۝	166	Indeed, we celebrate God's glory.'
وَإِن كَانُوا لَيَقُولُونَ ۝	167	Indeed, they[2] used to say,
لَوْ أَنَّ عِندَنَا ذِكْرًا مِّنَ الْأَوَّلِينَ ۝	168	'Had we possessed a reminder from our predecessors,
لَكُنَّا عِبَادَ اللَّهِ الْمُخْلَصِينَ ۝	169	we would have surely been God's exclusive servants.'
فَكَفَرُوا بِهِ	170	But they denied it [when it came to them].
فَسَوْفَ يَعْلَمُونَ ۝		Soon they will know!
وَلَقَدْ سَبَقَتْ كَلِمَتُنَا	171	Certainly Our decree has gone beforehand
لِعِبَادِنَا الْمُرْسَلِينَ ۝		in favour of Our servants, the apostles,
إِنَّهُمْ لَهُمُ الْمَنصُورُونَ ۝	172	that they will indeed receive God's help,
وَإِنَّ جُندَنَا لَهُمُ الْغَالِبُونَ ۝	173	and indeed Our hosts will be the victors.
فَتَوَلَّ عَنْهُمْ حَتَّىٰ حِينٍ ۝	174	So *leave* them alone for a while,
وَأَبْصِرْهُمْ	175	and *watch* them;
فَسَوْفَ يُبْصِرُونَ ۝		soon they will see [the truth of the matter]!
أَفَبِعَذَابِنَا يَسْتَعْجِلُونَ ۝	176	Do they seek to hasten Our punishment?
فَإِذَا نَزَلَ بِسَاحَتِهِمْ	177	But when it descends in their courtyard
فَسَاءَ صَبَاحُ الْمُنذَرِينَ ۝		it will be a dismal dawn for those who had been warned.
وَتَوَلَّ عَنْهُمْ حَتَّىٰ حِينٍ ۝	178	So *leave* them alone for a while,
وَأَبْصِرْ فَسَوْفَ يُبْصِرُونَ ۝	179	and *watch*; soon they will see!
سُبْحَانَ رَبِّكَ رَبِّ الْعِزَّةِ	180	Clear is *your* Lord, the Lord of Might,
عَمَّا يَصِفُونَ ۝		of whatever they allege concerning Him.

---

[1] Verses 164-166 quote the words of the angels referred to in verse 1.
[2] That is, the pagans of Makkah.

وَسَلَامٌ عَلَى الْمُرْسَلِينَ ۝ 181 Peace be to the apostles!

وَالْحَمْدُ لِلَّهِ رَبِّ الْعَالَمِينَ ۝ 182 All praise belongs to God, Lord of all the worlds.

38. Ṣād[1]

Ṣād

بِسْمِ اللَّهِ
الرَّحْمَٰنِ الرَّحِيمِ

In the Name of God,
the All-beneficent, the All-merciful.

ص وَالْقُرْآنِ ذِي الذِّكْرِ ۝ 1 Ṣād. By the Qur'ān bearing the Reminder.[2]

بَلِ الَّذِينَ كَفَرُوا 2 The faithless indeed

فِي عِزَّةٍ وَشِقَاقٍ ۝ dwell in conceit and defiance.

كَمْ أَهْلَكْنَا مِنْ قَبْلِهِمْ مِنْ قَرْنٍ 3 How many a generation We have destroyed before them!

فَنَادَوْا وَلَاتَ حِينَ مَنَاصٍ ۝ They cried out for help, but gone was the time for escape.

وَعَجِبُوا أَنْ جَاءَهُمْ 4 They consider it odd that there should come to them

مُنْذِرٌ مِنْهُمْ a warner from among themselves,

وَقَالَ الْكَافِرُونَ and the faithless say,

هَٰذَا سَاحِرٌ كَذَّابٌ ۝ 'This is a magician, a mendacious liar.'

أَجَعَلَ الْآلِهَةَ إِلَٰهًا وَاحِدًا 5 'Has he reduced the gods to one god?

إِنَّ هَٰذَا لَشَيْءٌ عُجَابٌ ۝ This is indeed an odd thing!'

وَانْطَلَقَ الْمَلَأُ مِنْهُمْ 6 Their elite go about [urging others]:

أَنِ امْشُوا وَاصْبِرُوا عَلَىٰ آلِهَتِكُمْ 'Go and stand by your gods!

إِنَّ هَٰذَا لَشَيْءٌ يُرَادُ ۝ This is indeed the desirable thing to do.

مَا سَمِعْنَا بِهَٰذَا فِي الْمِلَّةِ الْآخِرَةِ 7 We did not hear of this in the latter-day creed.[3]

إِنْ هَٰذَا إِلَّا اخْتِلَاقٌ ۝ This is nothing but a fabrication.

أَأُنْزِلَ عَلَيْهِ الذِّكْرُ مِنْ بَيْنِنَا 8 Has the reminder been sent down to him out of all of us?'

بَلْ هُمْ فِي شَكٍّ مِنْ ذِكْرِي They are indeed in doubt concerning My Reminder.

بَلْ لَمَّا يَذُوقُوا عَذَابِ ۝ Rather they have not yet tasted My punishment.

أَمْ عِنْدَهُمْ خَزَائِنُ رَحْمَةِ رَبِّكَ 9 Do they possess the treasuries of the mercy of your Lord,

الْعَزِيزِ الْوَهَّابِ ۝ the All-mighty, the All-munificent?

---

[1] This Makkī *sūrah* is named after the letter Ṣād, in verse 1.
[2] Ellipsis: the omitted phrase is 'you are indeed one of the apostles, on a straight path.' Cf. **36**:3.
[3] That is, in the polytheistic creed prevalent in pre-Islamic Arabia.

10 Do they own the kingdom of the heavens and the earth
and whatever is between them?
If so, let them ascend [to the higher spheres]
by the means[1] of ascension.

11 They are but a host routed out there
of the factions.[2]

12 Before them Noah's people impugned their apostle
and so did the people of 'Ād, and Pharaoh, the Impaler,[3]

13 and Thamūd, and the people of Lot,
and the inhabitants of Aykah:[4]
those were the factions.

14 Each of them did not but impugn the apostles;
so My retribution became due against them.

15 These[5] too do not await but a single Cry
which will not grant them any respite.

16 They say, 'Our Lord! Hasten on for us our share[6]
before the Day of Reckoning.'

17 *Be patient* over what they say,
and *remember* Our servant, David, the man of strength.
He was indeed a penitent soul.

18 We disposed the mountains to glorify God with him
at evening and dawn,

---

[1] Or 'let them ascend by the contrivances.' Or 'let them ascend by the ladder,' or 'let them ascend into the heavens.'

[2] A prophesy of the defeat of the Makkan army at Badr (see Ṭabarī and Ṭabrisī). Or 'from among the confederates,' that is, of Satan (cf. **35**:6, **58**:19).

[3] Lit.: 'the one of stakes.' According to several traditions, Pharaoh used to torture and execute his victims by piercing their bodies with stakes, or *awtād* (see *Biḥār al-anwār*, vol. 13, p. 136, from *'Ilal al-Sharāyi'*, p. 161; vol. 71, p. 13; vol. 75, p. 403). Hence the epithet *'dhi'l-awtād,'* which occurs twice in the Qur'ān with reference to Pharaoh, refers to him as one who used to impale his victims. Other alternate explanations suggested for this epithet by the commentators are not convincing.

[4] Cf. **15**:78.

[5] That is, the pagans of Makkah.

[6] That is, 'our share of punishment,' said mockingly.

19 and the birds as well, gathered in flocks,
     all echoing him in a chorus.
20 We consolidated his kingdom
     and gave him wisdom and conclusive speech.
21 Has there not come to you the account of the contenders
     when they scaled the wall into the sanctuary?[1]
22 When they entered into the presence of David,
     he was alarmed by them.
   They said, 'Do not be afraid. We are only two contenders:
     one of us has bullied the other.
   So judge justly between us
     and do not exceed the bounds of justice,
     and show us the right path.'
23 'This brother of mine has ninety-nine ewes,
     while I have only a single ewe,
     and yet he says, 'Commit it to my care,'
     and he browbeats me in speech.'
24 He said, 'He has certainly wronged you
     by asking your ewe in addition to his own ewes,
     and indeed many partners
     bully one another,
     except such as have faith and do righteous deeds,
     and few are they.'
   Then David knew that We had tested him,
     whereat he pleaded with his Lord for forgiveness,
     and fell down in prostration and repented.
25 So We forgave him that,
     and he has indeed a station of nearness with Us
     and a good destination.

---

[1] Or 'sanctum.'

26 'O David! We have indeed made you a vicegerent
       on the earth.
    So judge between people with justice,
       and do not follow your base desire,
          or it will lead you astray from the way of God.
    Those who stray from the way of God
       —there is a severe punishment for them
       because of their forgetting the Day of Reckoning.'
27 We did not create the heaven and the earth
       and whatever is between them in vain.
    That is a conjecture of the faithless.
    So woe to the faithless for the Fire!
28 Shall We treat those who have faith
       and do righteous deeds
          like those who cause corruption on the earth?
    Shall We treat the Godwary like the vicious?
29 This is a blessed Book that We have sent down to you,
       so that they may contemplate its signs
    and that those who possess intellect may take admonition.

30 And to David We gave Solomon
       —what an excellent servant he was!
    He was indeed a penitent soul.
31 One evening when there were displayed before him
       prancing steeds,
32 he said,
    'I have indeed preferred the love of worldly niceties
       to the remembrance of my Lord
    until the sun disappeared behind the night's veil.'

33 'Bring it[1] back for me!'
   Then he [and others] began to wipe their legs and necks. ﴿٣٣﴾

34 Certainly We tried Solomon,
   and cast a lifeless body on his throne.
   Thereupon he was penitent. ﴿٣٤﴾

35 He said, 'My Lord! Forgive me,
   and grant me a kingdom
   that will not befit anyone except me,[2]
   Indeed, You are the All-munificent.' ﴿٣٥﴾

36 So We disposed the wind for him,
   blowing softly by his command wherever he intended, ﴿٣٦﴾

37 and every builder and diver from the demons, ﴿٣٧﴾

38 and others, too, bound together in chains. ﴿٣٨﴾

39 'This is Our bounty:
   so withhold or bestow from it without any reckoning.' ﴿٣٩﴾

40 He has indeed a station of nearness with Us
   and a good destination. ﴿٤٠﴾

41 And *mention* Our servant Job [in the Qur'ān].
   When he called out to his Lord,
   'The devil has visited on me
   hardship and torment,' ﴿٤١﴾

42 [We told him:] 'Stamp your foot on the ground;
   this ensuing spring will be a cooling bath and drink.' ﴿٤٢﴾

43 We gave him back his family, along with others like them,
   as a mercy from Us

---

[1] Or 'them.' The pronoun may be taken as referring to the sun or to the horses. However, most exegetes have taken it as referring to the sun and its setting. While Solomon was engaged in viewing the horses, the sun set, and the time of the afternoon prayer (supererogatory or obligatory) elapsed. According to a tradition narrated from al-Imām al-Ṣādiq ('a), when Solomon noticed that the sun had set, he called out to the angels to bring it back so that he could offer the afternoon prayer. Also, according to this tradition, the wiping of legs and necks mentioned in the verse refers to the performance of ablution (*wuḍū*') before the prayer by Solomon and his men as prescribed in their Law. (*Biḥār*, vol. 14, p. 101; vol. 82, p. 341)

[2] Cf. **35**:41. Or 'a kingdom that will not befit anyone after me.'

وَذِكْرَىٰ لِأُولِي الْأَلْبَابِ ۝ and an admonition for those who possess intellect.

وَخُذْ بِيَدِكَ ضِغْثًا 44 [We told him:] 'Take a faggot in your hand
فَاضْرِب بِّهِ and then strike [your wife] with it,
وَلَا تَحْنَثْ ۗ but break not your oath.'
إِنَّا وَجَدْنَاهُ صَابِرًا ۚ Indeed, We found him to be patient.
نِّعْمَ الْعَبْدُ ۖ What an excellent servant!
إِنَّهُ أَوَّابٌ ۝ He was indeed a penitent soul.

وَاذْكُرْ عِبَادَنَا إِبْرَاهِيمَ 45 And *mention* Our servants Abraham,
وَإِسْحَاقَ وَيَعْقُوبَ Isaac and Jacob,
أُولِي الْأَيْدِي وَالْأَبْصَارِ ۝ men of strength and insight.
إِنَّا أَخْلَصْنَاهُم بِخَالِصَةٍ 46 We indeed purified them with exclusive
ذِكْرَى الدَّارِ ۝ remembrance of the abode of the Hereafter.
وَإِنَّهُمْ عِندَنَا 47 Indeed, they are with Us
لَمِنَ الْمُصْطَفَيْنَ الْأَخْيَارِ ۝ among the elect of the best.
وَاذْكُرْ إِسْمَاعِيلَ وَالْيَسَعَ وَذَا الْكِفْلِ ۖ 48 And *mention* Ishmael, Elisha and Dhu'l-Kifl
وَكُلٌّ مِّنَ الْأَخْيَارِ ۝ —each of whom was among the elect.
هَـٰذَا ذِكْرٌ ۚ 49 This is a reminder,
وَإِنَّ لِلْمُتَّقِينَ لَحُسْنَ مَآبٍ ۝ and indeed the Godwary have a good destination:
جَنَّاتِ عَدْنٍ 50 the Gardens of Eden,
مُّفَتَّحَةً لَّهُمُ الْأَبْوَابُ ۝ whose gates will be flung open for them.
مُتَّكِئِينَ فِيهَا 51 Reclining therein on couches,
يَدْعُونَ فِيهَا بِفَاكِهَةٍ كَثِيرَةٍ they will call for abundant fruits
وَشَرَابٍ ۝ and drinks,
وَعِندَهُمْ قَاصِرَاتُ الطَّرْفِ 52 and there will be with them maidens of restrained glances,
أَتْرَابٌ ۝ of a like age.
هَـٰذَا مَا تُوعَدُونَ لِيَوْمِ الْحِسَابِ ۝ 53 This is what you are promised on the Day of Reckoning.
إِنَّ هَـٰذَا لَرِزْقُنَا مَا لَهُ مِن نَّفَادٍ ۝ 54 This is Our provision, which will never be exhausted.
هَـٰذَا ۚ 55 This [will be for the righteous],
وَإِنَّ لِلطَّاغِينَ and as for the rebellious

لَشَرَّ مَآبٍ ۝		there will surely be a bad destination:
جَهَنَّمَ يَصْلَوْنَهَا فَبِئْسَ الْمِهَادُ ۝	56	hell, which they shall enter, an evil resting place.
هَٰذَا فَلْيَذُوقُوهُ حَمِيمٌ وَغَسَّاقٌ ۝	57	This is scalding water and pus; let them taste it,
وَآخَرُ مِنْ شَكْلِهِ أَزْوَاجٌ ۝	58	and other kinds of torments resembling it.
هَٰذَا فَوْجٌ مُقْتَحِمٌ مَعَكُمْ	59	'This is a group plunging into hell along with you.'[1]
لَا مَرْحَبًا بِهِمْ		[They will respond,] 'May wretchedness be their lot!
إِنَّهُمْ صَالُو النَّارِ ۝		For they will enter the Fire.'[2]
قَالُوا بَلْ أَنْتُمْ لَا مَرْحَبًا بِكُمْ	60	They[3] will say, 'No, may wretchedness be your lot!
أَنْتُمْ قَدَّمْتُمُوهُ لَنَا		You prepared this hell for us.
فَبِئْسَ الْقَرَارُ ۝		What an evil abode!'
قَالُوا	61	They will say,
رَبَّنَا مَنْ قَدَّمَ لَنَا هَٰذَا		'Our Lord! Whoever has prepared this for us,
فَزِدْهُ عَذَابًا ضِعْفًا فِي النَّارِ ۝		double his punishment in the Fire!'
وَقَالُوا مَا لَنَا لَا نَرَىٰ رِجَالًا	62	And they will say, 'Why is it that we do not see here men
كُنَّا نَعُدُّهُمْ مِنَ الْأَشْرَارِ ۝		whom we used to count among the bad ones,
أَتَّخَذْنَاهُمْ سِخْرِيًّا	63	ridiculing them,
أَمْ زَاغَتْ عَنْهُمُ الْأَبْصَارُ ۝		or do our eyes miss them here?'
إِنَّ ذَٰلِكَ لَحَقٌّ	64	That is indeed a true account
تَخَاصُمُ أَهْلِ النَّارِ ۝		of the contentions of the inmates of the Fire.
قُلْ إِنَّمَا أَنَا مُنْذِرٌ	65	Say, 'I am just a warner,
وَمَا مِنْ إِلَٰهٍ إِلَّا اللَّهُ		and there is no god except God,
الْوَاحِدُ الْقَهَّارُ ۝		the One, the All-paramount,
رَبُّ السَّمَاوَاتِ وَالْأَرْضِ	66	the Lord of the heavens and the earth
وَمَا بَيْنَهُمَا		and whatever is between them,
الْعَزِيزُ الْغَفَّارُ ۝		the All-mighty, the All-forgiving.'
قُلْ هُوَ نَبَأٌ عَظِيمٌ ۝	67	Say, 'It is a great prophesy
أَنْتُمْ عَنْهُ مُعْرِضُونَ ۝	68	of which you are disregardful.
مَا كَانَ لِيَ مِنْ عِلْمٍ بِالْمَلَإِ الْأَعْلَىٰ	69	I have no knowledge of the Supernal Elite

[1] Said by the angels to leaders of the faithless concerning their followers.
[2] Said by the leaders of the faithless concerning their followers.
[3] That is, the followers, who respond to the unfriendly welcome of their leaders.

when they contend.

70 All that is revealed to me is that I am just a manifest warner.'

71 When your Lord said to the angels, 'Indeed, I am about to create a human being out of clay.

72 So when I have proportioned him and breathed into him of My spirit, fall down in prostration before him.'

73 Thereat the angels prostrated, all of them together,

74 but not Iblis; he acted arrogantly and he was one of the faithless.

75 He said, 'O Iblis! What kept you from prostrating before what I have created with My own two hands? Are you arrogant, or are you one of the exalted ones?'

76 'I am better than him,' he said. 'You created me from fire, and You created him from clay.'

77 He said, 'Begone hence, for you are indeed an outcast,

78 and indeed My curse will be on you till the Day of Retribution.'

79 He said, 'My Lord! Respite me till the day they will be resurrected.'

80 Said He, 'You are indeed among the reprieved

81 until the day of the known time.'

82 He said, 'By Your might, I will surely pervert them all,

83 except Your exclusive servants among them.'

84 Said He, 'The truth is that—and I speak the truth—

85 I will surely fill hell with you and all of those who follow you.'[1]

---

[1] Cf. **7:18**; **11:119**; **32:13**.

86 Say, 'I do not ask you any reward for it,
and I am no impostor.[1]

87 It is just a reminder for all the nations,

88 and you will surely learn its tidings in due time.'

39. THRONGS[2]
al-Zumar

In the Name of God,
the All-beneficent, the All-merciful.

1 The gradual sending down of the Book is from God,
the All-mighty, the All-wise.

2 We have indeed sent down the Book to you with the truth;
so worship God, putting exclusive faith[3] in Him.

3 Indeed, only exclusive faith is worthy of God,
and those who take others as masters besides Him
[claiming,] 'We only worship them
so that they may bring us near to God,'
God will judge between them
concerning that about which they differ.
Indeed, God does not guide
someone who is a liar and an ingrate.

4 Had God intended to take an offspring,
He could have chosen from those He has created
whatever He wished.
Immaculate is He!
He is God, the One, the All-paramount.

5 He created the heavens and the earth
with consummate wisdom.

---

[1] Or 'nor am I one of those who impose themselves [upon others].'
[2] This Makkī *sūrah* takes its name from verses 71 & 73 in which the word *zumar* (throngs) occurs.
[3] Or 'pure faith.'

He winds the night over the day,
    and winds the day over the night,
and He has disposed the sun and the moon,
    each moving for a specified term.[1]
Indeed, He is the All-mighty, the All-forgiving!

6 He created you from a single soul,
    then made from it its mate,
and He has sent down for you
    eight pairs of the cattle.[2]
He creates you in the wombs of your mothers,
    creation after creation,
in a threefold darkness.
That is God, your Lord!
To Him belongs all sovereignty. There is no god except Him.
    Then, where are you being led away?

7 If you are ungrateful, God has indeed no need of you,
though He does not approve ingratitude for His servants;
    and if you give thanks, He approves that for you.
No bearer shall bear another's burden;
    then your return will be to your Lord,
whereat He will inform you concerning what you used to do.
    Indeed, He knows best what is in the breasts.

8 When distress befalls man, he supplicates his Lord,
    turning to Him penitently.
Then, when He grants him a blessing from Himself,
he forgets that for which he had supplicated Him earlier,[3]
    and sets up equals to God,

---

[1] Or 'until a specified time.'
[2] Cf. **6:143**.
[3] Cf. **6:41**.

that he may lead people astray from His way.
Say, 'Revel in your ingratitude[1] for a while.
You are indeed among the inmates of the Fire.'
9 Is he who supplicates[2] in the watches of the night,
    prostrating and standing,
    being apprehensive of the Hereafter
    and expecting the mercy of his Lord . . . ?[3]
Say, 'Are those who know equal
    to those who do not know?'
Only those who possess intellect take admonition.
10 Say, '[God declares:] "O My servants who have faith!
    Be wary of your Lord.
For those who do good in this world
    there will be a good reward,
    and God's earth is vast.
Indeed, the patient will be paid in full their reward
    without any reckoning." '
11 Say, 'I have been commanded to worship God
    with exclusive faith in Him,
12 and I have been commanded
    to be the foremost of those who submit to Him.'
13 Say, 'Indeed, should I disobey my Lord, I fear
    the punishment of a tremendous day.'
14 Say, 'I worship only God,
    putting my exclusive faith in Him.
15 You worship whatever you wish besides Him.'
Say, 'The losers are those
    who ruin themselves and their families

---

[1] Or 'faithlessness.'
[2] Or 'is obedient.'
[3] Ellipsis. The omitted phrase is, 'like someone who is not such?'

    on the Day of Resurrection.'
Behold! That is indeed a manifest loss!

16 There will be canopies of fire above them,
    and similar canopies beneath them.
    With that God deters His servants.
    So, My servants, be wary of Me!

17 As for those who stay clear
    of the worship of satanic entities
    and turn penitently to God,
    there is good news for them.
    So *give* good news to My servants

18 who listen to the word of God
    and follow the best interpretation of it.[1]
    They are the ones whom God has guided
    and it is they who possess intellect.

19 Can he
    against whom the word of punishment has become due?[2]
    Can you rescue someone who is in the Fire?

20 But as for those who are wary of their Lord,
    for them there will be lofty abodes
    with other lofty abodes built above them,
    with streams running beneath them
    —a promise of God.
    God does not break His promise.

21 Have you not seen that God sends down
    water from the sky,
    then He conducts it through the ground as springs.
    Then He brings forth with it crops of diverse hues.
    Then they wither and you see them turn yellow.

---

[1] Or 'who listen to all points of view and follow the best of them.'
[2] Ellipsis; the omitted phrase is, 'escape his punishment?'

Then He turns them into chaff. ثُمَّ يَجْعَلُهُ حُطَامًا
There is indeed a lesson in that إِنَّ فِي ذَٰلِكَ لَذِكْرَىٰ
for those who possess intellect. لِأُولِي الْأَلْبَابِ ۩

22 Is someone whose breast God has opened to Islam أَفَمَن شَرَحَ اللَّهُ صَدْرَهُ لِلْإِسْلَامِ
so that he walks in a light from His Lord?[1] فَهُوَ عَلَىٰ نُورٍ مِّن رَّبِّهِ
So woe to those whose hearts have been hardened فَوَيْلٌ لِّلْقَاسِيَةِ قُلُوبُهُم
to the remembrance of God! مِّن ذِكْرِ اللَّهِ
They are in plain error. أُولَٰئِكَ فِي ضَلَالٍ مُّبِينٍ ۩

23 God has sent down the best of discourses, اللَّهُ نَزَّلَ أَحْسَنَ الْحَدِيثِ
a scripture composed of similar[2] motifs, كِتَابًا مُّتَشَابِهًا مَّثَانِيَ
whereat shiver تَقْشَعِرُّ مِنْهُ
the skins of those who fear their Lord, جُلُودُ الَّذِينَ يَخْشَوْنَ رَبَّهُمْ
then their skins and hearts relax ثُمَّ تَلِينُ جُلُودُهُمْ وَقُلُوبُهُمْ
at the remembrance of God. إِلَىٰ ذِكْرِ اللَّهِ
That is God's guidance, ذَٰلِكَ هُدَى اللَّهِ
by which He guides whomever He wishes; يَهْدِي بِهِ مَن يَشَاءُ
and whomever God leads astray has no guide. وَمَن يُضْلِلِ اللَّهُ فَمَا لَهُ مِنْ هَادٍ ۩

24 What! Is someone who fends off with his face أَفَمَن يَتَّقِي بِوَجْهِهِ
the terrible punishment on the Day of Resurrection?[3] سُوءَ الْعَذَابِ يَوْمَ الْقِيَامَةِ
And the wrongdoers will be told, وَقِيلَ لِلظَّالِمِينَ
'Taste what you used to earn.' ذُوقُوا مَا كُنتُمْ تَكْسِبُونَ ۩

25 Those who were before them impugned the apostles, كَذَّبَ الَّذِينَ مِن قَبْلِهِمْ
whereat the punishment overtook them فَأَتَاهُمُ الْعَذَابُ
whence they were not aware. مِنْ حَيْثُ لَا يَشْعُرُونَ ۩

26 So God made them taste disgrace in the life of the world, فَأَذَاقَهُمُ اللَّهُ الْخِزْيَ فِي الْحَيَاةِ الدُّنْيَا
and the punishment of the Hereafter will surely be greater, وَلَعَذَابُ الْآخِرَةِ أَكْبَرُ
if they knew. لَوْ كَانُوا يَعْلَمُونَ ۩

27 We have drawn for mankind in this Qur'ān وَلَقَدْ ضَرَبْنَا لِلنَّاسِ فِي هَٰذَا الْقُرْآنِ

---

[1] Ellipsis. The omitted phrase is, 'like someone who is not such?'
[2] Or 'parallel motifs.'
[3] Ellipsis. The omitted phrase is, 'like someone who is secure from any kind of punishment?'

every kind of example,
so that they may take admonition:

28 an Arabic Qur'ān, without any deviousness,
so that they may be Godwary.

29 God draws an example:
a man jointly owned by several contending masters,
and a man belonging entirely to one man:
are the two equal in comparison?[1]
All praise belongs to God!
But most of them do not know.

30 You will die, and they too will die.

31 Then on the Day of Resurrection you will contend before your Lord.

[PART 24]

32 So who is a greater wrongdoer
than him who attributes falsehoods to God,
and denies the truth when it reaches him?
Is not the final abode of the faithless in hell?

33 He who brings the truth and he who confirms it
—it is they who are the Godwary.

34 They will have what they wish near their Lord
—that is the reward of the virtuous—

35 that God may absolve them of
the worst of what they did,
and pay them their reward
by the best of what they used to do.

36 Does not God suffice to defend His servant?
They[2] would frighten you of others than Him.

---

[1] The parable compares the polytheist with the monotheist. The worshiper of multiple deities is likened to a slave trying to please several masters.

[2] That is, the idolaters, who threatened the Prophet with the vengeance of their gods.

وَمَنْ يُضْلِلِ اللَّهُ فَمَا لَهُ مِنْ هَادٍ ۩

Yet whomever God leads astray has no guide,

وَمَنْ يَهْدِ اللَّهُ 37

and whomever God guides,

فَمَا لَهُ مِنْ مُضِلٍّ

there is no one who can lead him astray.

أَلَيْسَ اللَّهُ بِعَزِيزٍ ذِي انتِقَامٍ ۩

Is not God an all-mighty avenger?

وَلَئِنْ سَأَلْتَهُمْ 38

If you ask them,

مَنْ خَلَقَ السَّمَاوَاتِ وَالْأَرْضَ

'Who created the heavens and the earth?'

لَيَقُولُنَّ اللَّهُ

they will surely say, 'God.'

قُلْ أَفَرَأَيْتُمْ مَا تَدْعُونَ مِنْ دُونِ اللَّهِ

Say, 'Have you considered what you invoke besides God?

إِنْ أَرَادَنِيَ اللَّهُ بِضُرٍّ

Should God desire some distress for me,

هَلْ هُنَّ كَاشِفَاتُ ضُرِّهِ

can they remove the distress visited by Him?

أَوْ أَرَادَنِي بِرَحْمَةٍ

Or should He desire some mercy for me,

هَلْ هُنَّ مُمْسِكَاتُ رَحْمَتِهِ

can they withhold His mercy?'

قُلْ حَسْبِيَ اللَّهُ

Say, 'God is sufficient for me.

عَلَيْهِ يَتَوَكَّلُ الْمُتَوَكِّلُونَ ۩

In Him alone let all the trusting put their trust.'

قُلْ يَا قَوْمِ اعْمَلُوا عَلَىٰ مَكَانَتِكُمْ 39

Say, 'O my people! Act according to your ability.

إِنِّي عَامِلٌ

I too am acting.

فَسَوْفَ تَعْلَمُونَ ۩

Soon you will know

مَنْ يَأْتِيهِ عَذَابٌ 40

who will be overtaken by a punishment

يُخْزِيهِ

that will disgrace him,

وَيَحِلُّ عَلَيْهِ عَذَابٌ مُقِيمٌ ۩

and on whom a lasting punishment will descend.'

إِنَّا أَنزَلْنَا عَلَيْكَ الْكِتَابَ 41

Indeed, We have sent down to you the Book

لِلنَّاسِ بِالْحَقِّ

with the truth for the deliverance of mankind.

فَمَنِ اهْتَدَىٰ فَلِنَفْسِهِ

So whoever is guided is guided for his own sake,

وَمَنْ ضَلَّ فَإِنَّمَا يَضِلُّ عَلَيْهَا

and whoever goes astray, goes astray to his own detriment,

وَمَا أَنتَ عَلَيْهِمْ بِوَكِيلٍ ۩

and it is not *your* duty to watch over them.

اللَّهُ يَتَوَفَّى الْأَنفُسَ حِينَ مَوْتِهَا 42

God takes the souls at the time of their death,

وَالَّتِي لَمْ تَمُتْ فِي مَنَامِهَا

and those who have not died, in their sleep.

فَيُمْسِكُ الَّتِي قَضَىٰ عَلَيْهَا الْمَوْتَ

Then He retains those for whom He has ordained death

وَيُرْسِلُ الْأُخْرَىٰ إِلَىٰ أَجَلٍ مُسَمًّى

and releases the others until a specified time.

There are indeed signs in that for people who reflect.

43 Have they taken intercessors besides God?
Say, 'What! Even though they do not control anything
and cannot reason?!'

44 Say, 'All intercession rests with God.
To Him belongs the kingdom of the heavens
and the earth;
then you will be brought back to Him.'

45 When God is mentioned alone,
thereat shrink away the hearts of those
who do not believe in the Hereafter,
but when others are mentioned besides Him,
behold, they rejoice!

46 Say, 'O God! Originator of the heavens and the earth,
Knower of the sensible and the Unseen,
You will judge between Your servants
concerning that about which they used to differ.'

47 Even if the wrongdoers possessed
all that is on the earth, and as much of it besides,
they would offer it to redeem themselves with it
from a terrible punishment on the Day of Resurrection,
and there will appear to them from God
what they had never reckoned.

48 The evils of what they had earned will appear to them,
and they will be besieged by what they used to deride.

49 When distress befalls man, he supplicates Us.
Then, when We grant him a blessing from Us,
he says, 'I was given it by virtue of my knowledge.'
It is indeed a test,
but most of them do not know.

50 قَدْ قَالَهَا الَّذِينَ مِن قَبْلِهِمْ فَمَا أَغْنَىٰ عَنْهُم مَّا كَانُوا يَكْسِبُونَ ۝

Those who were before them also said that,
but what they used to earn did not avail them.

51 فَأَصَابَهُمْ سَيِّئَاتُ مَا كَسَبُوا ۚ وَالَّذِينَ ظَلَمُوا مِنْ هَٰؤُلَاءِ سَيُصِيبُهُمْ سَيِّئَاتُ مَا كَسَبُوا وَمَا هُم بِمُعْجِزِينَ ۝

So the evils of what they had earned visited them,
and as for the wrongdoers among these,
the evils of what they earn shall be visited on them
and they will not frustrate God's might.

52 أَوَلَمْ يَعْلَمُوا أَنَّ اللَّهَ يَبْسُطُ الرِّزْقَ لِمَن يَشَاءُ وَيَقْدِرُ ۚ إِنَّ فِي ذَٰلِكَ لَآيَاتٍ لِّقَوْمٍ يُؤْمِنُونَ ۝

Do they not know that God expands the provision
and tightens it for whomever He wishes?
There are indeed signs in that for a people who have faith.

53 قُلْ يَا عِبَادِيَ الَّذِينَ أَسْرَفُوا عَلَىٰ أَنفُسِهِمْ لَا تَقْنَطُوا مِن رَّحْمَةِ اللَّهِ ۚ إِنَّ اللَّهَ يَغْفِرُ الذُّنُوبَ جَمِيعًا ۚ إِنَّهُ هُوَ الْغَفُورُ الرَّحِيمُ ۝

Say [that God declares,] 'O My servants
who have committed excesses against their own souls,
do not despair of the mercy of God.
God will indeed forgive all sins.
Indeed, He is the All-forgiving, the All-merciful.

54 وَأَنِيبُوا إِلَىٰ رَبِّكُمْ وَأَسْلِمُوا لَهُ مِن قَبْلِ أَن يَأْتِيَكُمُ الْعَذَابُ ثُمَّ لَا تُنصَرُونَ ۝

Turn penitently to Him and submit to Him
before the punishment overtakes you,
whereupon you will not be helped.

55 وَاتَّبِعُوا أَحْسَنَ مَا أُنزِلَ إِلَيْكُم مِّن رَّبِّكُم مِّن قَبْلِ أَن يَأْتِيَكُمُ الْعَذَابُ بَغْتَةً وَأَنتُمْ لَا تَشْعُرُونَ ۝

And follow the best of what has been sent down to you
from your Lord,
before the punishment overtakes you suddenly
while you are unaware.'

56 أَن تَقُولَ نَفْسٌ يَا حَسْرَتَا عَلَىٰ مَا فَرَّطتُ فِي جَنبِ اللَّهِ وَإِن كُنتُ لَمِنَ السَّاخِرِينَ ۝

Lest anyone should say,
'Alas for my negligence in the vicinage of God!
I was indeed among those who ridiculed.'

57 أَوْ تَقُولَ لَوْ أَنَّ اللَّهَ هَدَانِي لَكُنتُ مِنَ الْمُتَّقِينَ ۝

Or say, 'Had God guided me,
I would have surely been among the Godwary!'

58 أَوْ تَقُولَ حِينَ تَرَى الْعَذَابَ لَوْ أَنَّ لِي كَرَّةً فَأَكُونَ مِنَ الْمُحْسِنِينَ ۝

Or say, when he sights the punishment,
'If only there were a second chance for me
I would be among the virtuous!'

59 [They will be told,] 'Yes, My signs did come to you,
   but you denied them and acted arrogantly
   and you were among the faithless.'

60 On the Day of Resurrection you will see
   those who attributed lies to God
   with their faces blackened.
   Is not the final abode of the arrogant in hell?

61 God will deliver
   those who were Godwary with their salvation.
   No ill shall touch them, nor will they grieve.

62 God is creator of all things,
   and He watches over all things.

63 To Him belong the keys of the heavens and the earth,
   and those who disbelieve in the signs of God
   —it is they who are the losers.

64 Say, 'Will you, then, bid me to worship other than God,
   O you ignorant ones?!'

65 Certainly it has been revealed to you
   and to those who have been before you:
   'If you ascribe a partner to God your works shall fail
   and you shall surely be among the losers.

66 Rather, worship God and be among the grateful!'

67 They do not regard God with the regard due to Him,
   yet the entire earth will be in His fist
      on the Day of Resurrection,
   and the heavens, scrolled, in His right hand.
   Immaculate is He and far above having
   any partners that they ascribe to Him.

68 وَنُفِخَ فِي الصُّورِ And the Trumpet will be blown,
فَصَعِقَ مَنْ فِي السَّمَاوَاتِ and whoever is in the heavens will swoon
وَمَنْ فِي الْأَرْضِ and whoever is on the earth,
إِلَّا مَنْ شَاءَ اللَّهُ except whomever God wishes.
ثُمَّ نُفِخَ فِيهِ أُخْرَىٰ Then it will be blown a second time,
فَإِذَا هُمْ قِيَامٌ يَنْظُرُونَ ۝ and behold, they will rise up, looking on!

69 وَأَشْرَقَتِ الْأَرْضُ بِنُورِ رَبِّهَا The earth will glow with the light of her Lord
وَوُضِعَ الْكِتَابُ and the Book[1] will be set up,
وَجِيءَ بِالنَّبِيِّينَ وَالشُّهَدَاءِ and the prophets and the martyrs[2] will be brought,
وَقُضِيَ بَيْنَهُمْ بِالْحَقِّ and judgment will be made between them with justice
وَهُمْ لَا يُظْلَمُونَ ۝ and they will not be wronged.

70 وَوُفِّيَتْ كُلُّ نَفْسٍ Every soul will be recompensed fully
مَا عَمِلَتْ for what it has done,
وَهُوَ أَعْلَمُ بِمَا يَفْعَلُونَ ۝ and He is best aware of what they do.

71 وَسِيقَ الَّذِينَ كَفَرُوا إِلَىٰ جَهَنَّمَ زُمَرًا The faithless will be driven to hell in throngs.
حَتَّىٰ إِذَا جَاءُوهَا فُتِحَتْ أَبْوَابُهَا When they reach it, and its gates are opened,
وَقَالَ لَهُمْ خَزَنَتُهَا its keepers will say to them,
أَلَمْ يَأْتِكُمْ رُسُلٌ 'Did there not come to you any apostles
مِنْكُمْ from among yourselves,
يَتْلُونَ عَلَيْكُمْ آيَاتِ رَبِّكُمْ reciting to you the signs of your Lord
وَيُنْذِرُونَكُمْ and warning you
لِقَاءَ يَوْمِكُمْ هَٰذَا of the encounter of this day of yours?'
قَالُوا They will say,
بَلَىٰ وَلَٰكِنْ حَقَّتْ كَلِمَةُ الْعَذَابِ 'Yes, but the word of punishment became due
عَلَى الْكَافِرِينَ ۝ against the faithless.'

72 قِيلَ ادْخُلُوا أَبْوَابَ جَهَنَّمَ It will be said, 'Enter the gates of hell
خَالِدِينَ فِيهَا to remain in it.
فَبِئْسَ مَثْوَى الْمُتَكَبِّرِينَ ۝ Evil is the ultimate abode of the arrogant.'

73 وَسِيقَ الَّذِينَ اتَّقَوْا رَبَّهُمْ إِلَى الْجَنَّةِ Those who are wary of their Lord will be led to paradise

---

[1] That is, the record of the people's deeds.
[2] Or 'the witnesses.'

in throngs.
When they reach it and its gates are opened,
its keepers will say to them, 'Peace be to you!
You are welcome![1] Enter it to remain.'

74 They will say, 'All praise belongs to God,
who has fulfilled His promise to us
and made us inheritors of the earth,
that we may settle in paradise wherever we may wish!'
How excellent is the reward of the workers.

75 And you will see the angels
surrounding the Throne,
celebrating the praise of their Lord,
and judgment will be made between them with justice,
and it will be said, 'All praise belongs to God,
the Lord of all the worlds!'

40. THE FORGIVER[2]
Ghāfir

In the Name of God,
the All-beneficent, the All-merciful.

1 Ḥā, Mīm:

2 The gradual sending down of the Book is from God,
the All-mighty, the All-knowing,

3 forgiver of sins and acceptor of repentance,
severe in retribution, yet all-bountiful;
there is no god except Him
and toward Him is the destination.

4 No one disputes the signs of God
except the faithless.

---

[1] Or 'You are excellent!' Or 'You have been pure.'
[2] This Makkī *sūrah* takes its name from the phrase *"ghāfir al-dhanb"* (forgiver of sins) which occurs in verse 3.

So do not be misled by their bustle in the towns.

5 The people of Noah denied before them
    and the [heathen] factions who came after them.
    Every nation attempted to lay hands on their apostle
    and disputed erroneously to refute the truth.
    Then I seized them; so how was My retribution?!

6 That is how the word of *your* Lord became due
    concerning the faithless,
    that they shall be inmates of the Fire.

7 Those who bear the Throne and those who are around it
    celebrate the praise of their Lord and have faith in Him,
    and they plead for forgiveness for the faithful:
    'Our Lord!
    You embrace all things in Your mercy and knowledge.
    So forgive those who repent and follow Your way
    and save them from the punishment of hell.

8 Our Lord! Admit them into the Gardens of Eden,
    which You have promised them,
    along with whoever is righteous among their forebears,
    their spouses and their descendants.[1]
    Indeed, You are the All-mighty, the All-wise.

9 Save them from the ills [of the Day of Resurrection];
    and whomever You save from the ills that day,[2]
    You will have had mercy upon him,
    and that is a mighty triumph.'

10 It will be proclaimed to the faithless:
    'Surely God's outrage towards you is greater
    than your outrage towards yourselves,
    as you were invited to faith, but you disbelieved.'

---

[1] Cf. **13:23**.
[2] That is, the day of judgement.

11 They will say, 'Our Lord!
Twice did You make us die and twice did You give us life.
We admit our sins.
Is there any way out from this plight?'

12 [They will be told,] 'This plight of yours is because,
when God was invoked alone, you would disbelieve,
but would believe if partners were ascribed to Him.
So the judgment belongs to God,
the All-exalted, the All-great.'

13 It is He who shows you His signs
and sends down provision for you from the sky.
Yet no one takes admonition
except those who return penitently to God.

14 So supplicate God putting exclusive faith in Him,
though the faithless should be averse.

15 Raiser of ranks, Lord of the Throne,
He casts the Spirit of His command
upon whomever of His servants that He wishes,
that he may warn people of the Day of Encounter.

16 The day when they will emerge from their graves,
nothing about them will be hidden from God.
'To whom does the sovereignty belong today?'
'To God, the One, the All-paramount!'

17 'Today every soul shall be requited for what it has earned.
There will be no injustice today.
God is indeed swift at reckoning.'

18 Warn them of the Approaching Day[1]
when the hearts will be at the throats,

---

[1] Cf. 'the Imminent [Hour]' (**53**:57).

choking with suppressed agony, كَاظِمِينَ

and the wrongdoers will have no sympathizer, مَا لِلظَّالِمِينَ مِنْ حَمِيمٍ

nor any intercessor who might be heard. وَلَا شَفِيعٍ يُطَاعُ ۞

19 He knows the treachery of the eyes[1] يَعْلَمُ خَائِنَةَ الْأَعْيُنِ

and what the breasts hide. وَمَا تُخْفِي الصُّدُورُ ۞

20 God judges with justice, وَاللَّهُ يَقْضِي بِالْحَقِّ

while those whom they invoke besides Him وَالَّذِينَ يَدْعُونَ مِنْ دُونِهِ

do not judge by anything. لَا يَقْضُونَ بِشَيْءٍ

Indeed, it is God who is the All-hearing, the All-seeing. إِنَّ اللَّهَ هُوَ السَّمِيعُ الْبَصِيرُ ۞

21 Have they not traveled through the land أَوَلَمْ يَسِيرُوا فِي الْأَرْضِ

to see how was the fate of those فَيَنْظُرُوا كَيْفَ كَانَ عَاقِبَةُ الَّذِينَ

who were before them? كَانُوا مِنْ قَبْلِهِمْ

They were greater than them in might كَانُوا هُمْ أَشَدَّ مِنْهُمْ قُوَّةً

and with respect to the effects they left in the land. وَآثَارًا فِي الْأَرْضِ

But then God seized them for their sins, فَأَخَذَهُمُ اللَّهُ بِذُنُوبِهِمْ

and they had no defender against God's punishment. وَمَا كَانَ لَهُمْ مِنَ اللَّهِ مِنْ وَاقٍ ۞

22 That was because their apostles used to bring them ذَلِكَ بِأَنَّهُمْ كَانَتْ تَأْتِيهِمْ رُسُلُهُمْ

manifest proofs, بِالْبَيِّنَاتِ

but they defied them. فَكَفَرُوا

So God seized them. فَأَخَذَهُمُ اللَّهُ

He is indeed all-strong, severe in retribution. إِنَّهُ قَوِيٌّ شَدِيدُ الْعِقَابِ ۞

23 Certainly We sent Moses with Our signs وَلَقَدْ أَرْسَلْنَا مُوسَى بِآيَاتِنَا

and a clear authority وَسُلْطَانٍ مُبِينٍ ۞

24 to Pharaoh, Hāmān and Korah, إِلَى فِرْعَوْنَ وَهَامَانَ وَقَارُونَ

but they said, 'A magician and a mendacious liar.' فَقَالُوا سَاحِرٌ كَذَّابٌ ۞

25 So when he brought them the truth from Us, فَلَمَّا جَاءَهُمْ بِالْحَقِّ مِنْ عِنْدِنَا

they said, 'Kill the sons of the faithful who are with him, قَالُوا اقْتُلُوا أَبْنَاءَ الَّذِينَ آمَنُوا مَعَهُ

and spare their women.' وَاسْتَحْيُوا نِسَاءَهُمْ

---

[1] That is, the sins committed with the eyes.

But the stratagems[1] of the faithless only go awry.

26 And Pharaoh said, 'Let me kill Moses,
    and let him invoke his Lord.
Indeed, I fear that he will change your religion,
    or bring forth corruption in our land.'

27 Moses said,
'I seek the protection of my Lord and your Lord
    from every arrogant one
    who does not believe in the Day of Reckoning.'

28 Said a man of faith from Pharaoh's clan,
    who concealed his faith,
'Will you kill a man for saying, "My Lord is God,"
while he has already brought you clear proofs
    from your Lord?
Should he be lying,
    his falsehood will be to his own detriment;
but if he is truthful,
    there shall visit you some of what he promises you.
Indeed, God does not guide
    someone who is a transgressor and liar.

29 O my people! Today sovereignty belongs to you[2]
    and you are dominant in the land.
But who will save us from God's punishment
    should it overtake us?'
Pharaoh said, 'I just point out to you
    what I see to be advisable for you,
and I guide you only to the way of rectitude.'

30 He who had faith said, 'O my people!
Indeed, I fear for you a day

---

[1] Or 'the guile of the faithless.'
[2] Or 'Today the kingdom is yours.'

    like the day of the heathen factions,

31 like the case of the people of Noah, of ʿĀd and Thamūd,
    and those who came after them,
    and God does not desire any wrong for His servants.

32 O my people!
    I fear for you a day of mutual distress calls,

33 a day when you will turn back to flee,
    not having anyone to protect you from God,
    and whomever God leads astray has no guide.

34 Certainly Joseph brought you
    clear proofs earlier,
    but you continued to remain in doubt
    concerning what he had brought you.
    When he died, you said,
    "God will never send any apostle after him."
    That is how God leads astray
    those who are unrestrained and skeptical.

35 Those who dispute the signs of God
    without any authority that may have come to them
    —that is greatly outrageous to God
    and to those who have faith.
    That is how God seals
    the heart of every arrogant tyrant.'

36 Pharaoh said, 'O Hāmān! Build me a tower
    so that I may reach the routes

37 —the routes[1] of the heavens—
    and take a look at the God of Moses,
    and indeed I consider him a liar.'
    To Pharaoh was thus presented as decorous

---

[1] Or 'the means.'

the evil of his conduct, سُوءُ عَمَلِهِ

and he was kept from the way of God. وَصُدَّ عَنِ السَّبِيلِ

Pharaoh's stratagems[1] only led him into ruin. وَمَا كَيْدُ فِرْعَوْنَ إِلَّا فِي تَبَابٍ ۝

38 And he who had faith said, 'O my people! وَقَالَ الَّذِي آمَنَ يَا قَوْمِ

Follow me, I will guide you to the way of rectitude. اتَّبِعُونِ أَهْدِكُمْ سَبِيلَ الرَّشَادِ ۝

39 O my people! يَا قَوْمِ

This life of the world is only a passing enjoyment, إِنَّمَا هَذِهِ الْحَيَاةُ الدُّنْيَا مَتَاعٌ

and indeed the Hereafter is the abiding home. وَإِنَّ الْآخِرَةَ هِيَ دَارُ الْقَرَارِ ۝

40 Whoever commits a misdeed مَنْ عَمِلَ سَيِّئَةً

shall not be requited except with its like, فَلَا يُجْزَى إِلَّا مِثْلَهَا

but whoever acts righteously, whether male or female, وَمَنْ عَمِلَ صَالِحًا مِنْ ذَكَرٍ أَوْ أُنْثَى

should he be faithful وَهُوَ مُؤْمِنٌ

—such will enter paradise فَأُولَٰئِكَ يَدْخُلُونَ الْجَنَّةَ

and will be provided therein without any reckoning. يُرْزَقُونَ فِيهَا بِغَيْرِ حِسَابٍ ۝

41 O my people! وَيَا قَوْمِ

Think, what makes me invite you to deliverance, مَا لِي أَدْعُوكُمْ إِلَى النَّجَاةِ

while you invite me toward the Fire? وَتَدْعُونَنِي إِلَى النَّارِ ۝

42 You invite me to defy God and to ascribe to Him partners تَدْعُونَنِي لِأَكْفُرَ بِاللَّهِ وَأُشْرِكَ بِهِ

of which I have no knowledge, مَا لَيْسَ لِي بِهِ عِلْمٌ

while I call you to the All-mighty, the All-forgiving. وَأَنَا أَدْعُوكُمْ إِلَى الْعَزِيزِ الْغَفَّارِ ۝

43 Undoubtedly, that to which you invite me لَا جَرَمَ أَنَّمَا تَدْعُونَنِي إِلَيْهِ

has no invitation in the world لَيْسَ لَهُ دَعْوَةٌ فِي الدُّنْيَا

nor in the Hereafter, وَلَا فِي الْآخِرَةِ

and indeed our return will be to God, وَأَنَّ مَرَدَّنَا إِلَى اللَّهِ

and indeed it is the transgressors who will be وَأَنَّ الْمُسْرِفِينَ هُمْ

inmates of the Fire. أَصْحَابُ النَّارِ ۝

44 Soon you will remember what I tell you, فَسَتَذْكُرُونَ مَا أَقُولُ لَكُمْ

and I entrust my affair to God. وَأُفَوِّضُ أَمْرِي إِلَى اللَّهِ

God indeed watches His servants.' إِنَّ اللَّهَ بَصِيرٌ بِالْعِبَادِ ۝

---

[1] Or 'Pharaoh's guile.'

45 Then God saved him from their evil schemes,
while a terrible punishment besieged Pharaoh's clan:
46 the Fire, to which they are exposed morning and evening.
On the day when the Hour sets in,
Pharaoh's clan will enter the severest punishment.
47 When they argue in the Fire,
the oppressed will say to the oppressors,
'We used to follow you;
will you avail us against
a portion of the Fire?'
48 The oppressors will say, 'We are all in it together.
Indeed, God has judged between His servants.'
49 Those who are in the Fire will say to the keepers of hell,
'Invoke your Lord to lighten for us
at least a day's punishment.'
50 They will say,
'Did not your apostles bring you clear proofs?'
They will say, 'Yes.'
They will say, 'Then invoke Him yourselves.'
But the invocations of the faithless only go awry.
51 We shall indeed help Our apostles
and those who have faith
in the life of the world
and on the day when the witnesses rise up,
52 the day
when the excuses of the wrongdoers will not benefit them,
the curse will lie on them,
and for them will be the ills of the ultimate abode.
53 Certainly We gave guidance to Moses
and gave the Book as a legacy to the Children of Israel,

54 as guidance and admonition
   for those who possess intellect.
55 So *be patient!* God's promise is indeed true.
   Plead to God for forgiveness of *your* sin,
      and *celebrate* the praise of *your* Lord,
         morning and evening.
56 Indeed, those who dispute the signs of God
   without any authority that may have come to them
   —there is only vanity in their breasts,
      which they will never satisfy.
   So *seek* the protection of God;
      indeed, He is the All-hearing, the All-seeing.

57 The creation of the heavens and the earth is surely
   more prodigious than the creation of mankind,[1]
   but most people do not know.
58 The blind one and the seer are not equal,
   neither are those who have faith
      and do righteous deeds
      and those who work evil.
   Little is the admonition that you take!
59 The Hour is indeed bound to come;
   there is no doubt in it.
   But most people do not believe.
60 Your Lord has said, 'Call Me and I will hear you!'
   Indeed, those who are disdainful of My worship
      will enter hell in utter humiliation.
61 It is God who made the night for you,
   that you may rest in it,

---

[1] Cf. **37**:11, **79**:27.

وَالنَّهَارَ مُبْصِرًا ۚ	and the day to provide visibility.
إِنَّ اللَّهَ لَذُو فَضْلٍ عَلَى النَّاسِ	God is indeed gracious to mankind,
وَلَٰكِنَّ أَكْثَرَ النَّاسِ لَا يَشْكُرُونَ ۝	but most people do not give thanks.
ذَٰلِكُمُ اللَّهُ رَبُّكُمْ خَالِقُ كُلِّ شَيْءٍ	62 That is God, your Lord, the creator of all things,
لَّا إِلَٰهَ إِلَّا هُوَ ۖ	there is no god except Him.
فَأَنَّىٰ تُؤْفَكُونَ ۝	Then where do you stray?
كَذَٰلِكَ يُؤْفَكُ	63 Thus are made to stray
الَّذِينَ كَانُوا بِآيَاتِ اللَّهِ يَجْحَدُونَ ۝	those who were used to impugning the signs of God.
اللَّهُ الَّذِي جَعَلَ لَكُمُ الْأَرْضَ قَرَارًا	64 It is God who made for you the earth an abode,
وَالسَّمَاءَ بِنَاءً	and the sky a canopy.
وَصَوَّرَكُمْ فَأَحْسَنَ صُوَرَكُمْ	He formed you and perfected your forms,
وَرَزَقَكُم مِّنَ الطَّيِّبَاتِ ۚ	and provided you with all the good things.
ذَٰلِكُمُ اللَّهُ رَبُّكُمْ ۖ	That is God, your Lord!
فَتَبَارَكَ اللَّهُ رَبُّ الْعَالَمِينَ ۝	Blessed is God, Lord of all the worlds!
هُوَ الْحَيُّ لَا إِلَٰهَ إِلَّا هُوَ	65 He is the Living One, there is no god except Him.
فَادْعُوهُ مُخْلِصِينَ لَهُ الدِّينَ ۗ	So supplicate Him, putting exclusive faith in Him.
الْحَمْدُ لِلَّهِ رَبِّ الْعَالَمِينَ ۝	All praise belongs to God, Lord of all the worlds.
قُلْ إِنِّي نُهِيتُ أَنْ أَعْبُدَ	66 Say, 'I have been forbidden to worship
الَّذِينَ تَدْعُونَ مِن دُونِ اللَّهِ	those whom you invoke besides God,
لَمَّا جَاءَنِيَ الْبَيِّنَاتُ مِن رَّبِّي	as clear proofs have come to me from my Lord,
وَأُمِرْتُ أَنْ أُسْلِمَ	and I have been commanded to submit
لِرَبِّ الْعَالَمِينَ ۝	to the Lord of all the worlds.
هُوَ الَّذِي خَلَقَكُم مِّن تُرَابٍ	67 It is He who created you from dust,
ثُمَّ مِن نُّطْفَةٍ	then from a drop of seminal fluid,
ثُمَّ مِنْ عَلَقَةٍ	then from a clinging tissue,
ثُمَّ يُخْرِجُكُمْ طِفْلًا	then He brings you forth as infants,
ثُمَّ لِتَبْلُغُوا أَشُدَّكُمْ	then He nurtures you so that you may come of age,
ثُمَّ لِتَكُونُوا شُيُوخًا ۚ	and then that you may become aged
وَمِنكُم مَّن يُتَوَفَّىٰ مِن قَبْلُ ۖ	—though there are some of you who die earlier—
وَلِتَبْلُغُوا أَجَلًا مُّسَمًّى	and complete a specified term,

    and so that you may exercise your reason.

68 It is He who gives life and brings death.
    When He decides on a matter,
    He just says to it, 'Be!' and it is.

69 Have you not regarded those
    who dispute the signs of God,
    where they are being led away from God's way?

70 —Those who deny the Book
    and what we have sent with Our apostles.
    Soon they will know

71 when, with iron collars around their necks
    and chains,
    they are dragged

72 into scalding waters, and then set aflame in the Fire.

73 Then they will be told,
    'Where are those whom you used to take as 'partners'

74 besides God?'
    They will say, 'They have forsaken us.
    Indeed, we did not invoke anything before.'
    That is how God leads the faithless astray.

75 'That punishment is because you used to boast
    unduly on the earth
    and because you used to strut.'

76 Enter the gates of hell, to remain in it.'
    Evil is the final abode of the arrogant.

77 So *be patient!* God's promise is indeed true.
    Whether We show *you* a part of what We promise them,
    or take *you* away before that,
    in any case they will be brought back to Us.

78 Certainly We have sent apostles before you.

Of them are those We have recounted to you, مِنْهُمْ مَنْ قَصَصْنَا عَلَيْكَ
and of them are those We have not recounted to you. وَمِنْهُمْ مَنْ لَمْ نَقْصُصْ عَلَيْكَ
An apostle may not bring any sign وَمَا كَانَ لِرَسُولٍ أَنْ يَأْتِيَ بِآيَةٍ
except by God's permission. إِلَّا بِإِذْنِ اللَّهِ
Hence when God's edict comes, فَإِذَا جَاءَ أَمْرُ اللَّهِ
judgment is made with justice, قُضِيَ بِالْحَقِّ
and it is thence that the falsifiers become losers. وَخَسِرَ هُنَالِكَ الْمُبْطِلُونَ ۝

79 It is God who created the cattle for you اللَّهُ الَّذِي جَعَلَ لَكُمُ الْأَنْعَامَ
that you may ride some of them, لِتَرْكَبُوا مِنْهَا
and some of them you eat; وَمِنْهَا تَأْكُلُونَ ۝

80 and there are numerous uses in them for you, وَلَكُمْ فِيهَا مَنَافِعُ
and that over them[1] you may satisfy وَلِتَبْلُغُوا عَلَيْهَا
any need that is in your breasts, حَاجَةً فِي صُدُورِكُمْ
and you are carried on them and on ships. وَعَلَيْهَا وَعَلَى الْفُلْكِ تُحْمَلُونَ ۝

81 He shows you His signs. وَيُرِيكُمْ آيَاتِهِ
So which of the signs of God do you deny? فَأَيَّ آيَاتِ اللَّهِ تُنْكِرُونَ ۝

82 Have they not traveled through the land أَفَلَمْ يَسِيرُوا فِي الْأَرْضِ
so that they may observe فَيَنْظُرُوا
how was the fate of those who were before them? كَيْفَ كَانَ عَاقِبَةُ الَّذِينَ مِنْ قَبْلِهِمْ
They were more numerous than them كَانُوا أَكْثَرَ مِنْهُمْ
and were greater in power وَأَشَدَّ قُوَّةً
and with respect to the effects they left in the land. وَآثَارًا فِي الْأَرْضِ
But what they used to earn did not avail them. فَمَا أَغْنَى عَنْهُمْ مَا كَانُوا يَكْسِبُونَ ۝

83 When their apostles brought them clear proofs, فَلَمَّا جَاءَتْهُمْ رُسُلُهُمْ بِالْبَيِّنَاتِ
they boasted about the knowledge they possessed, فَرِحُوا بِمَا عِنْدَهُمْ مِنَ الْعِلْمِ
and they were besieged by what they used to deride. وَحَاقَ بِهِمْ مَا كَانُوا بِهِ يَسْتَهْزِئُونَ ۝

84 Then, when they sighted Our punishment, فَلَمَّا رَأَوْا بَأْسَنَا
they said, 'We believe in God alone قَالُوا آمَنَّا بِاللَّهِ وَحْدَهُ
and disavow what we used to take as His partners.' وَكَفَرْنَا بِمَا كُنَّا بِهِ مُشْرِكِينَ ۝

---

[1] That is, by riding them or by using them as beasts of burden.

85 But their faith was of no benefit to them
when they sighted Our punishment
—God's precedent
which has already passed among His servants,
and it is thence that the faithless will be losers.

41. ELABORATED[1]
Fuṣṣilat

In the Name of God,
the All-beneficent, the All-merciful.

1 Hā, Mīm.
2 A gradually sent down revelation
from the All-beneficent, the All-merciful,
3 this is a Book whose signs have been elaborated
for a people who have knowledge, an Arabic Qur'ān,
4 a bearer of good news and warner.
But most of them turn away from it,
and so they do not listen.
5 They say, 'Our hearts are in veils
which shut them off from what you invite us to,
and there is a deafness in our ears,
and there is a curtain between us and you.
So act [as your faith requires];
we too are acting [according to our own].'
6 Say, 'I am just a human being like you.
It has been revealed to me that your God is the One God.
So worship Him single-mindedly
and plead to Him for forgiveness.'
And woe to the polytheists

---

[1] This Makkī *surah* is named after the word *fuṣṣilat* (elaborated) in verse 3.

7 ﴿الَّذِينَ لَا يُؤْتُونَ الزَّكَاةَ
وَهُم بِالْآخِرَةِ هُمْ كَافِرُونَ ۝﴾ —those who do not pay the *zakāt*
and disbelieve in the Hereafter.

8 ﴿إِنَّ الَّذِينَ آمَنُوا وَعَمِلُوا الصَّالِحَاتِ
لَهُمْ أَجْرٌ غَيْرُ مَمْنُونٍ ۝﴾ As for those who have faith and do righteous deeds,
there will be an everlasting reward for them.

9 ﴿قُلْ أَئِنَّكُمْ لَتَكْفُرُونَ بِالَّذِي
خَلَقَ الْأَرْضَ فِي يَوْمَيْنِ
وَتَجْعَلُونَ لَهُ أَندَادًا
ذَٰلِكَ رَبُّ الْعَالَمِينَ ۝﴾ *Say,* 'Do you really disbelieve in Him who
created the earth in two days,[1]
and ascribe partners to Him?
That is the Lord of all the worlds!'

10 ﴿وَجَعَلَ فِيهَا رَوَاسِيَ مِن فَوْقِهَا
وَبَارَكَ فِيهَا وَقَدَّرَ فِيهَا
أَقْوَاتَهَا فِي أَرْبَعَةِ أَيَّامٍ
سَوَاءً لِّلسَّائِلِينَ ۝﴾ He set in it firm mountains rising above it,
and blessed it, and ordained in it
its various means of sustenance, in four days,
equally for all the seekers.

11 ﴿ثُمَّ اسْتَوَىٰ إِلَى السَّمَاءِ وَهِيَ دُخَانٌ
فَقَالَ لَهَا وَلِلْأَرْضِ
ائْتِيَا طَوْعًا أَوْ كَرْهًا
قَالَتَا أَتَيْنَا طَائِعِينَ ۝﴾ Then He turned to the heaven, and it was smoke,
and He said to it and to the earth,
'Come! Willingly or unwillingly!'
They said, 'We come obediently.'

12 ﴿فَقَضَاهُنَّ سَبْعَ سَمَاوَاتٍ فِي يَوْمَيْنِ
وَأَوْحَىٰ فِي كُلِّ سَمَاءٍ أَمْرَهَا
وَزَيَّنَّا السَّمَاءَ الدُّنْيَا بِمَصَابِيحَ
وَحِفْظًا
ذَٰلِكَ تَقْدِيرُ الْعَزِيزِ الْعَلِيمِ ۝﴾ Then He set them up as seven heavens in two days,
and revealed [to the angels] in each heaven its ordinance.
We have adorned the lowest heaven with lamps
and guarded them.[2]
That is the ordaining of the All-mighty, the All-knowing.

13 ﴿فَإِنْ أَعْرَضُوا فَقُلْ أَنذَرْتُكُمْ صَاعِقَةً
مِّثْلَ صَاعِقَةِ عَادٍ وَثَمُودَ ۝﴾ But if they turn away, *say,* 'I warn you of a thunderbolt,
like the thunderbolt of 'Ād and Thamūd.'

14 ﴿إِذْ جَاءَتْهُمُ الرُّسُلُ
مِن بَيْنِ أَيْدِيهِمْ وَمِنْ خَلْفِهِمْ
أَلَّا تَعْبُدُوا إِلَّا اللَّهَ
قَالُوا لَوْ شَاءَ رَبُّنَا
لَأَنزَلَ مَلَائِكَةً﴾ When the apostles came to them,
before them and in their own time,[3]
saying, 'Worship no one except God!'
They said, 'Had our Lord wished,
He would have sent down angels to us.

---

[1] That is, in two epochs of time.
[2] Cf. **37**:6-7; **67**:5.
[3] That is, in a previous era and in their own time. Or 'from their front and rear,' that is, from all sides.

We indeed disbelieve in what you have been sent with.' فَإِنَّا بِمَا أُرْسِلْتُم بِهِ كَافِرُونَ ۝

15 As for ʿĀd, فَأَمَّا عَادٌ

    they acted arrogantly in the land unduly, فَاسْتَكْبَرُوا فِي الْأَرْضِ بِغَيْرِ الْحَقِّ

    and they said, 'Who is more powerful than us?' وَقَالُوا مَنْ أَشَدُّ مِنَّا قُوَّةً

Did they not see that God, who created them, أَوَلَمْ يَرَوْا أَنَّ اللَّهَ الَّذِي خَلَقَهُمْ

    is more powerful than them? هُوَ أَشَدُّ مِنْهُمْ قُوَّةً

They used to impugn Our signs; وَكَانُوا بِآيَاتِنَا يَجْحَدُونَ ۝

16 so We unleashed upon them an icy gale فَأَرْسَلْنَا عَلَيْهِمْ رِيحًا صَرْصَرًا

    during ill-fated days, فِي أَيَّامٍ نَحِسَاتٍ

    in order that We might make them taste لِنُذِيقَهُمْ

a humiliating punishment in the life of the world. عَذَابَ الْخِزْيِ فِي الْحَيَاةِ الدُّنْيَا

Yet the punishment of the Hereafter will surely be وَلَعَذَابُ الْآخِرَةِ

    more disgraceful, أَخْزَىٰ

    and they will not be helped. وَهُمْ لَا يُنصَرُونَ ۝

17 As for the people of Thamūd, We guided them, وَأَمَّا ثَمُودُ فَهَدَيْنَاهُمْ

    but they preferred blindness to guidance. فَاسْتَحَبُّوا الْعَمَىٰ عَلَى الْهُدَىٰ

    So the bolt of a humiliating punishment seized them فَأَخَذَتْهُمْ صَاعِقَةُ الْعَذَابِ الْهُونِ

    because of what they used to earn. بِمَا كَانُوا يَكْسِبُونَ ۝

18 And We delivered those who had faith and were Godwary. وَنَجَّيْنَا الَّذِينَ آمَنُوا وَكَانُوا يَتَّقُونَ ۝

19 The day the enemies of God are gathered toward the Fire, وَيَوْمَ يُحْشَرُ أَعْدَاءُ اللَّهِ إِلَى النَّارِ

    while they are held in check. فَهُمْ يُوزَعُونَ ۝

20 when they come to it, حَتَّىٰ إِذَا مَا جَاءُوهَا

    their hearing will bear witness against them شَهِدَ عَلَيْهِمْ سَمْعُهُمْ

    and their eyes and skins وَأَبْصَارُهُمْ وَجُلُودُهُم

    concerning what they used to do. بِمَا كَانُوا يَعْمَلُونَ ۝

21 They will say to their skins, وَقَالُوا لِجُلُودِهِمْ

    'Why did you bear witness against us?' لِمَ شَهِدتُّمْ عَلَيْنَا

They will say, 'We were given speech by God, قَالُوا أَنطَقَنَا اللَّهُ

    who gave speech to all things. الَّذِي أَنطَقَ كُلَّ شَيْءٍ

He created you the first time
and you are being brought back to Him.

22 You could not hide [while perpetrating sinful acts
lest your hearing should bear witness against you,
or for that matter your eyes, or your skin,
but you thought that God did not know
most of what you did.

23 That misconception which you entertained
about your Lord ruined you.
So you became losers.'

24 Should they be patient, the Fire is their abode;
and should they seek to propitiate God,
they will not be redeemed.

25 We have assigned them companions
who make to seem decorous to them
their present and their past conduct,[1]
and the word became due against them,[2]
along with the nations that passed away before them
of jinn and humans.
They were indeed losers.

26 The faithless say,
'Do not listen to this Qur'ān and hoot it down
so that you may prevail over the Apostle.'

27 We will surely make the faithless taste
a severe punishment,
and We will surely requite them
by the worst of what they used to do.

28 That is the requital of the enemies of God—the Fire!
In it they will have an everlasting abode,

---

[1] Lit., 'whatever is before them and whatever is behind them.'
[2] Cf. 7:18; 11:119; 17:16; 23:27; 27:82; 28:63; 32:13; 36:7, 70; 38:85; 41:25; 46:18.

                                              as a requital for their impugning Our signs.

29 The faithless will say, 'Our Lord!
    Show us those who led us astray
    from among jinn and humans
        so that we may trample them under our feet,
        so that they may be among the lowermost!'
30 Indeed, those who say, 'Our Lord is God!'
    and then remain steadfast,
    the angels descend upon them,
    saying, 'Do not fear, nor be grieved!
    Receive the good news of the paradise
    which you have been promised.
31 We are your friends in the life of this world
    and in the Hereafter,
    and you will have in it whatever your souls desire,
    and you will have in it whatever you ask for,
32 as a hospitality from One all-forgiving, all-merciful.'
33 Who has a better call than him
    who summons to God and acts righteously
    and says, 'I am indeed one of the *muslims*'?
34 Good and evil conduct are not equal.[1]
    Repel evil with what is best.
    If you do so, he, between whom and you was enmity,
    will be as though he were a sympathetic friend.
35 But none is granted it except those who are patient,
    and none is granted it except the greatly endowed.
36 Should an incitement from Satan prompt you,
    seek the protection of God.
    Indeed, He is the All-hearing, the All-knowing.

---

[1] Or 'virtue and vice are not equal.'

Fuṣṣilat

37 وَمِنْ آيَاتِهِ اللَّيْلُ وَالنَّهَارُ وَالشَّمْسُ وَالْقَمَرُ ۚ لَا تَسْجُدُوا لِلشَّمْسِ وَلَا لِلْقَمَرِ وَاسْجُدُوا لِلَّهِ الَّذِي خَلَقَهُنَّ إِنْ كُنْتُمْ إِيَّاهُ تَعْبُدُونَ ۝

37 Among His signs are night and day
and the sun and the moon.
Do not prostrate to the sun, nor to the moon,
but prostrate to God who created them,
if it is Him that you worship.

38 فَإِنِ اسْتَكْبَرُوا فَالَّذِينَ عِنْدَ رَبِّكَ يُسَبِّحُونَ لَهُ بِاللَّيْلِ وَالنَّهَارِ وَهُمْ لَا يَسْأَمُونَ ۩ ۝

38 But if they disdain [the worship of God],
those who are near your Lord glorify Him
night and day
and they are not wearied.

39 وَمِنْ آيَاتِهِ أَنَّكَ تَرَى الْأَرْضَ خَاشِعَةً فَإِذَا أَنْزَلْنَا عَلَيْهَا الْمَاءَ اهْتَزَّتْ وَرَبَتْ ۚ إِنَّ الَّذِي أَحْيَاهَا لَمُحْيِي الْمَوْتَىٰ ۚ إِنَّهُ عَلَىٰ كُلِّ شَيْءٍ قَدِيرٌ ۝

39 Among His signs is that you see the earth desolate;
but when We send down water upon it,
it stirs and swells.
Indeed, He who revives it will also revive the dead.
Indeed, He has power over all things.

40 إِنَّ الَّذِينَ يُلْحِدُونَ فِي آيَاتِنَا لَا يَخْفَوْنَ عَلَيْنَا ۗ أَفَمَنْ يُلْقَىٰ فِي النَّارِ خَيْرٌ أَمْ مَنْ يَأْتِي آمِنًا يَوْمَ الْقِيَامَةِ ۚ اعْمَلُوا مَا شِئْتُمْ ۖ إِنَّهُ بِمَا تَعْمَلُونَ بَصِيرٌ ۝

40 Those who abuse Our signs
are not hidden from Us.
Is someone who is cast in the Fire better off,
or someone who arrives safely on the Day of Resurrection?
Act as you wish;
indeed He watches what you do.

41 إِنَّ الَّذِينَ كَفَرُوا بِالذِّكْرِ لَمَّا جَاءَهُمْ ۖ وَإِنَّهُ لَكِتَابٌ عَزِيزٌ ۝

41 Those who deny the Reminder,
when it comes to them.... [1]
It is indeed an august Book:

42 لَا يَأْتِيهِ الْبَاطِلُ مِنْ بَيْنِ يَدَيْهِ وَلَا مِنْ خَلْفِهِ ۖ تَنْزِيلٌ مِنْ حَكِيمٍ حَمِيدٍ ۝

42 falsehood cannot approach it,
at present or in future,
a revelation sent down from One all-wise, all-laudable.

43 مَا يُقَالُ لَكَ إِلَّا مَا قَدْ قِيلَ لِلرُّسُلِ مِنْ قَبْلِكَ ۚ إِنَّ رَبَّكَ لَذُو مَغْفِرَةٍ

43 Nothing is said to you except
what has already been said to the apostles before you.
Indeed, your Lord is One who forgives

---

[1] Ellipsis. The phrase omitted, considering the context, is, 'will face a severe punishment.'

and One who metes out a painful retribution.

44 Had We made it a non-Arabic[1] Qur'ān,
they[2] would have said,
'Why have not its signs been articulated?'
'What! A non-Arabian scripture[3]
and an Arabian prophet!?'
Say, 'It is guidance and healing for those who have faith,
As for those who are faithless,
there is deafness in their ears and it is lost to their sight:
to them it is as if they were called from a distant place.'

45 Certainly We gave Moses the Book,
but differences arose about it;
and were it not for a prior decree of your Lord,
judgement would have been made between them,
for they are in grave doubt concerning it.

46 Whoever acts righteously, it is for his own soul,
and whoever does evil, it is to its detriment,
and your Lord is not tyrannical to His servants.

[PART 25]

47 On Him devolves the knowledge of the Hour,
and no fruit emerges from its covering
and no female conceives or delivers
except with His knowledge.
On the day when He will call out to them,
'Where are My "partners"?'
They will say, 'We have informed You
that there is no witness amongst us.'

48 What they used to invoke before has forsaken them,

---

[1] Or 'a barbaric Qur'ān;' that is, in a language other than articulate literary Arabic.
[2] That is, the Arabs.
[3] Or 'a barbaric scripture.'

and they know there is no escape for them. وَظَنُّوا مَا لَهُم مِّن مَّحِيصٍ ۝

49 Man is never wearied of supplicating for good, لَا يَسْأَمُ الْإِنسَانُ مِن دُعَاءِ الْخَيْرِ

and should any ill befall him, وَإِن مَّسَّهُ الشَّرُّ

he becomes hopeless and despondent. فَيَئُوسٌ قَنُوطٌ ۝

50 If We let him have a taste of Our mercy وَلَئِنْ أَذَقْنَاهُ رَحْمَةً مِّنَّا

after distress has befallen him, مِن بَعْدِ ضَرَّاءَ مَسَّتْهُ

he will surely say, 'This is my due! لَيَقُولَنَّ هَٰذَا لِي

I do not think the Hour will ever come, وَمَا أَظُنُّ السَّاعَةَ قَائِمَةً

and in case I am returned to my Lord, وَلَئِن رُّجِعْتُ إِلَىٰ رَبِّي

I will indeed have the best reward with Him.' إِنَّ لِي عِندَهُ لَلْحُسْنَىٰ

So We will surely inform the faithless فَلَنُنَبِّئَنَّ الَّذِينَ كَفَرُوا

about what they have done, بِمَا عَمِلُوا

and will surely make them taste a harsh punishment. وَلَنُذِيقَنَّهُم مِّنْ عَذَابٍ غَلِيظٍ ۝

51 When We bless the human being, وَإِذَا أَنْعَمْنَا عَلَى الْإِنسَانِ

he is disregardful and turns aside; أَعْرَضَ وَنَأَىٰ بِجَانِبِهِ

but when an ill befalls him, وَإِذَا مَسَّهُ الشَّرُّ

he makes protracted supplications. فَذُو دُعَاءٍ عَرِيضٍ ۝

52 Say, 'Tell me, if it is from God قُلْ أَرَأَيْتُمْ إِن كَانَ مِنْ عِندِ اللَّهِ

and you disbelieve it, ثُمَّ كَفَرْتُم بِهِ

who will be more astray than those who are مَنْ أَضَلُّ مِمَّنْ هُوَ

in extreme defiance.' فِي شِقَاقٍ بَعِيدٍ ۝

53 Soon We will show them Our signs سَنُرِيهِمْ آيَاتِنَا

in the horizons and in their own souls فِي الْآفَاقِ وَفِي أَنفُسِهِمْ

until it becomes clear to them that He is the Real.[1] حَتَّىٰ يَتَبَيَّنَ لَهُمْ أَنَّهُ الْحَقُّ

Is it not sufficient that *your* Lord أَوَلَمْ يَكْفِ بِرَبِّكَ أَنَّهُ

is witness to all things? عَلَىٰ كُلِّ شَيْءٍ شَهِيدٌ ۝

54 Behold, they are indeed in doubt أَلَا إِنَّهُمْ فِي مِرْيَةٍ

about the encounter with their Lord! مِّن لِّقَاءِ رَبِّهِمْ

Behold! He embraces all things! أَلَا إِنَّهُ بِكُلِّ شَيْءٍ مُّحِيطٌ ۝

---

[1] Or 'until it becomes clear to them that it [i.e. the Qur'ān, or Islam] (or he) [i.e. the Apostle] is the truth.'

42. Counsel[1]
al-Shūrā

In the Name of God,
the All-beneficent, the All-merciful.

1 *Ḥā, Mīm,*

2 *ʿAyn, Sīn, Qāf.*

3 Thus does He reveal to you
and to those who were before you,
God, the All-mighty and the All-wise:

4 to Him belongs whatever is in the heavens
and whatever is in the earth,
and He is the All-exalted, the All-supreme.

5 The heavens are about to be rent apart
from above them,
while the angels celebrate the praise of their Lord
and plead for forgiveness for those who are on the earth.
Indeed, God is the All-forgiving, the All-merciful!

6 As for those who have taken masters besides Him,
God is watchful over them,
and you are not their keeper.

7 Thus have We revealed to you an Arabic Qurʾān
that you may warn
the people of the Mother of the Towns[2]
and those around it,
and warn them of the Day of Gathering,[3]
in which there is no doubt,

---

[1] This Makkī *sūrah* takes its name from verse 38 concerning *shūrā* (counsel).
[2] That is, the city of Makkah.
[3] Cf. **64:**9.

فَرِيقٌ فِي الْجَنَّةِ	whereupon a part of mankind will be in paradise
وَفَرِيقٌ فِي السَّعِيرِ ۝	and a part will be in the Blaze.
8 وَلَوْ شَاءَ اللَّهُ	8 Had God wished,
لَجَعَلَهُمْ أُمَّةً وَاحِدَةً	He would have surely made them one community;
وَلَٰكِن يُدْخِلُ مَن يَشَاءُ فِي رَحْمَتِهِ	but He admits whomever He wishes into His mercy,
وَالظَّالِمُونَ مَا لَهُم مِّن وَلِيٍّ وَلَا نَصِيرٍ ۝	and the wrongdoers do not have any friend or helper.
9 أَمِ اتَّخَذُوا مِن دُونِهِ أَوْلِيَاءَ	9 Have they taken masters besides Him?
فَاللَّهُ هُوَ الْوَلِيُّ	[Say,] 'It is God who is the true Master,
وَهُوَ يُحْيِي الْمَوْتَىٰ	and He revives the dead,
وَهُوَ عَلَىٰ كُلِّ شَيْءٍ قَدِيرٌ ۝	and He has power over all things.
10 وَمَا اخْتَلَفْتُمْ فِيهِ مِن شَيْءٍ	10 Whatever thing you may differ about,
فَحُكْمُهُ إِلَى اللَّهِ	its judgement is with God.
ذَٰلِكُمُ اللَّهُ رَبِّي	That is God, my Lord:
عَلَيْهِ تَوَكَّلْتُ	in Him alone I have put my trust,
وَإِلَيْهِ أُنِيبُ ۝	and to Him alone do I turn penitently.
11 فَاطِرُ السَّمَاوَاتِ وَالْأَرْضِ	11 The originator of the heavens and the earth,
جَعَلَ لَكُم مِّنْ أَنفُسِكُمْ أَزْوَاجًا	He made for you mates from your own selves,
وَمِنَ الْأَنْعَامِ أَزْوَاجًا	and pairs of the cattle,
يَذْرَؤُكُمْ فِيهِ	by which means He multiplies you.
لَيْسَ كَمِثْلِهِ شَيْءٌ	Nothing is like Him[1]
وَهُوَ السَّمِيعُ الْبَصِيرُ ۝	and He is the All-hearing, the All-seeing.
12 لَهُ مَقَالِيدُ السَّمَاوَاتِ وَالْأَرْضِ	12 To Him belong the keys of the heavens and the earth:
يَبْسُطُ الرِّزْقَ	He expands the provision
لِمَن يَشَاءُ وَيَقْدِرُ	and tightens it for whomever He wishes.
إِنَّهُ بِكُلِّ شَيْءٍ عَلِيمٌ ۝	Indeed, He has knowledge of all things.'
13 شَرَعَ لَكُم مِّنَ الدِّينِ	13 He has prescribed for you the religion
مَا وَصَّىٰ بِهِ نُوحًا	which He had enjoined upon Noah
وَالَّذِي أَوْحَيْنَا إِلَيْكَ	and which We have also revealed to *you*,

---

[1] In case the *kāf* in *ka-mithlihī* is not taken as redundant, the meaning will be, 'There is nothing like His likeness.'

and which We had enjoined upon Abraham,
   Moses and Jesus,
declaring, 'Maintain the religion,
   and do not be divided in it.'
Hard on the polytheists is that to which you summon them.
   God chooses for it[1] whomever He wishes
   and He guides to it[2] whomever returns penitently.

14 They did not divide into sects
   except after the knowledge had come to them,
   out of envy among themselves;
   and were it not for a prior decree of your Lord
      [granting them reprieve] until a specified time,
   decision would have been made between them.
   Indeed, those who were made heirs to the Book
      after them
   are in grave doubt concerning it.

15 So *summon* to this [unity of religion],
   and *be* steadfast, just as *you* have been commanded,
   and *do not follow* their base desires,
   and *say*, 'I believe in whatever Book God has sent down.
   I have been commanded to do justice among you.
   God is our Lord and your Lord.
   Our deeds belong to us and your deeds belong to you.
   There is no quarrel between us and you.
   God will bring us together
      and toward Him is the destination.'

16 Those who argue concerning God,
   after His call has been answered,
   their argument stands refuted with their Lord,

---

[1] Or 'for Himself.'
[2] Or 'to Himself.'

      and upon them shall be His wrath,
      and there is a severe punishment for them.

17 It is God who has sent down the Book with the truth and the Balance.
      What do you know—maybe the Hour is near!

18 Those who do not believe in it ask you to hasten it,
      but those who have faith are apprehensive of it,
      and know that it is true.
      Indeed, those who are in doubt about the Hour[1]
      are in extreme error!

19 God is all-attentive to His servants.
      He provides for whomever He wishes
      and He is the All-strong, the All-mighty.

20 Whoever desires the tillage of the Hereafter,
      We will enhance for him his tillage,
      and whoever desires the tillage of the world,
      We will give to him some of it,
      but he will have no share in the Hereafter.

21 Do they have 'partners' besides God
      who have ordained for them a religion
      which has not been permitted by God?
      Were it not for a prior conclusive word,[2]
      judgement would have been made between them,
      and there awaits the wrongdoers a painful punishment.

22 You will see the wrongdoers
      fearful because of what they have earned,
      when it is about to befall them;
      but those who have faith and do righteous deeds

---

[1] Or 'dispute the Hour.'
[2] That is, God's promise to provide the faithless and to grant them a respite before retribution. See **2**:36, 126; **9**:68-69; **15**:3; **31**:23-24.

will be in the gardens of paradise:
they will have whatever they wish near their Lord.
That is the great grace.

23 That is the good news that God gives to His servants
who have faith
and do righteous deeds!
Say, 'I do not ask you any reward for it
except the love of my relatives.'
Whoever performs a good deed,
We shall enhance its goodness for him.
God is indeed all-forgiving, all-appreciative.

24 Do they say, 'He has fabricated a lie against God'?
If so, should God wish, He would set a seal on *your* heart,
and God will efface the falsehood
and confirm the truth with His words.
Indeed, He knows well what is in the breasts.

25 It is He who accepts the repentance of His servants,
and excuses their misdeeds and knows what you do.

26 He answers the supplications of those who have faith
and do righteous deeds
and enhances them out of His grace.
But as for the faithless,
there is a severe punishment for them.

27 Were God to expand the provision for all His servants,
they would surely create havoc on the earth.
But He sends down in a precise measure
whatever He wishes.
He is indeed aware and watchful of His servants.

28 It is He who sends down the rain
after they have been despondent,

al-Shūrā

and unfolds His mercy,

and He is the Guardian, the All-laudable.

29 Among His signs is the creation of the heavens
 and the earth
 and whatever creatures He has scattered in them,
 and He is able to gather them whenever He wishes.

30 Whatever affliction that may visit you
 is because of what your hands have earned,
 and He excuses many an offense of yours.

31 You cannot frustrate God on the earth,
 and you do not have besides God any friend
 or helper.

32 Among His signs are the ships that run on the sea
 appearing like landmarks.

33 If He wishes He stills the wind,
 whereat they remain standstill on its surface.
 There are indeed signs in that
 for every patient and grateful servant.

34 Or He wrecks them because of what they[1] have earned,
 and He excuses many an offense.

35 Let those who dispute Our signs know
 that there is no escape for them.

36 Whatever you have been given
 are the wares of the life of this world,
 but what is with God is better and more lasting
 for those who have faith
 and who put their trust in their Lord.

37 —Those who avoid major sins and indecencies
 and forgive when angered;

---

[1] That is, those who are on the ships.

38 those who answer their Lord, maintain the prayer,
and their affairs are by counsel among themselves,
and they spend out of what We have provided them;

39 those who, when afflicted by aggression,
defend themselves.

40 The requital of evil is an evil like it.
So whoever excuses and conciliates,
his reward lies with God.
Indeed, He does not like the wrongdoers.

41 As for those who retaliate after being wronged,
there is no ground for action against them.

42 The ground for action is only against those
who oppress the people
and commit tyranny in the land in violation of justice.
For such there shall be a painful punishment.

43 As for those who endure patiently and forgive
—that is indeed the steadiest of courses.

44 Those whom God leads astray
have no friend apart from Him.
You will see the wrongdoers,
when they sight the punishment,
saying, 'Is there any way for a retreat?'

45 You will see them being exposed to it,
humbled by abasement,
furtively looking askance.
The faithful will say,
'The losers are indeed those
who have ruined themselves and their families
on the Day of Resurrection.
Behold, the wrongdoers will indeed abide

في عَذابٍ مُقيمٍ ۝

46 They have no protectors to help them besides God.

وَما كانَ لَهُم مِن أَولِياءَ يَنصُرونَهُم مِن دونِ اللَّهِ ۗ

For those whom God leads astray, there is no way out.'

وَمَن يُضلِلِ اللَّهُ فَما لَهُ مِن سَبيلٍ ۝

47 Respond to your Lord before there comes a day for which there will be no revoking from God. On that day you will have no refuge, nor will you have any chance of denial [of your sins].

اسْتَجيبوا لِرَبِّكُم مِن قَبلِ أَن يَأتِيَ يَومٌ لا مَرَدَّ لَهُ مِنَ اللَّهِ ۚ ما لَكُم مِن مَلجَإٍ يَومَئِذٍ وَما لَكُم مِن نَكيرٍ ۝

48 But if they disregard [your warnings], [remember that] We have not sent you as their keeper. Your duty is only to communicate. Indeed, when We let man taste Our mercy, he rejoices in it; but should an ill visit them because of what their hands have sent ahead, then man is very ungrateful.

فَإِن أَعرَضوا فَما أَرسَلناكَ عَلَيهِم حَفيظًا ۖ إِن عَلَيكَ إِلَّا البَلاغُ ۗ وَإِنّا إِذا أَذَقنَا الإِنسانَ مِنّا رَحمَةً فَرِحَ بِها ۖ وَإِن تُصِبهُم سَيِّئَةٌ بِما قَدَّمَت أَيديهِم فَإِنَّ الإِنسانَ كَفورٌ ۝

49 To God belongs the kingdom of the heavens and the earth. He creates whatever He wishes; He gives females to whomever He wishes, and gives males to whomever He wishes,

لِلَّهِ مُلكُ السَّماواتِ وَالأَرضِ ۚ يَخلُقُ ما يَشاءُ ۚ يَهَبُ لِمَن يَشاءُ إِناثًا وَيَهَبُ لِمَن يَشاءُ الذُّكورَ ۝

50 or He combines them males and females, and makes sterile whomever He wishes. He is indeed all-knowing, all-powerful.

أَو يُزَوِّجُهُم ذُكرانًا وَإِناثًا ۖ وَيَجعَلُ مَن يَشاءُ عَقيمًا ۚ إِنَّهُ عَليمٌ قَديرٌ ۝

51 It is not possible for any human that God should speak to him, except through revelation or from behind a veil,[1] or send a messenger who reveals by His permission

وَما كانَ لِبَشَرٍ أَن يُكَلِّمَهُ اللَّهُ إِلّا وَحيًا أَو مِن وَراءِ حِجابٍ أَو يُرسِلَ رَسولًا فَيوحِيَ بِإِذنِهِ

---

[1] As from a tree, as in the case of Moses ('a).

مَا يَشَاءُ ۚ whatever He wishes.

إِنَّهُ عَلِيٌّ حَكِيمٌ ۝ He is indeed all-exalted, all-wise.

وَكَذَٰلِكَ أَوْحَيْنَا إِلَيْكَ 52 Thus have We imbued you

رُوحًا مِنْ أَمْرِنَا ۚ with a Spirit of Our command.[1]

مَا كُنْتَ تَدْرِى مَا الْكِتَابُ وَلَا الْإِيمَانُ You did not know what the Book is, nor what is faith;

وَلَٰكِنْ جَعَلْنَاهُ نُورًا نَهْدِى بِهِ but We made it a light that We may guide by its means

مَنْ نَشَاءُ مِنْ عِبَادِنَا ۚ whomever We wish of Our servants.

وَإِنَّكَ لَتَهْدِى إِلَىٰ صِرَاطٍ مُسْتَقِيمٍ ۝ You indeed guide to a straight path,

صِرَاطِ اللَّهِ الَّذِى لَهُ 53 the path of God, to whom belongs

مَا فِى السَّمَاوَاتِ وَمَا فِى الْأَرْضِ ۗ whatever is in the heavens and whatever is in the earth.

أَلَا إِلَى اللَّهِ تَصِيرُ الْأُمُورُ ۝ Behold, all matters return to God!

سُورَةُ الزُّخْرُفِ 43. ORNAMENTS[2]
al-Zukhruf

بِسْمِ اللَّهِ In the Name of God,
الرَّحْمَٰنِ الرَّحِيمِ the All-beneficent, the All-merciful.

حم ۝ 1 Ḥā, Mīm.

وَالْكِتَابِ الْمُبِينِ ۝ 2 By the Manifest Book,

إِنَّا جَعَلْنَاهُ قُرْآنًا عَرَبِيًّا 3 We have made it an Arabic Qurʾān

لَعَلَّكُمْ تَعْقِلُونَ ۝ so that you may exercise your reason,

وَإِنَّهُ فِى أُمِّ الْكِتَابِ 4 and it is in the Mother Book,

لَدَيْنَا لَعَلِىٌّ حَكِيمٌ ۝ sublime and wise with Us.

أَفَنَضْرِبُ عَنْكُمُ الذِّكْرَ 5 Shall We keep back the Reminder from you

صَفْحًا أَنْ كُنْتُمْ قَوْمًا مُسْرِفِينَ ۝ and disregard you because you are an unrestrained lot?

وَكَمْ أَرْسَلْنَا مِنْ نَبِىٍّ فِى الْأَوَّلِينَ ۝ 6 How many a prophet We have sent to the former peoples!

وَمَا يَأْتِيهِمْ مِنْ نَبِىٍّ 7 There did not come to them any prophet

إِلَّا كَانُوا بِهِ يَسْتَهْزِئُونَ ۝ but that they used to deride him.

فَأَهْلَكْنَا أَشَدَّ مِنْهُمْ بَطْشًا 8 So We destroyed those who were stronger than these,[3]

---

[1] A report of *al-Kāfī* (i, 214) from Imam Jaʿfar al-Ṣādiq (ʿa) explains the 'Spirit' as a 'creature of God greater than Gabriel and Michael who accompanied the Prophet (ṣ), and accompanies the Imams of his Family after him.'
[2] This Makkī *sūrah* takes its name from the word *zukhruf* in verse 35.
[3] That is, the Arab polytheists.

and the example of the former peoples has come to pass.

9 If you ask them, 'Who created the heavens and the earth?'
they will surely say,
'The All-mighty and the All-knowing created them.'

10 He, who made the earth a cradle for you
and made for you in it ways
so that you may be guided to your destinations,

11 and who sent down water from the sky
in a measured manner,
and We revived with it a dead country.
(Likewise you shall be raised from the dead.)

12 He, who created all the kinds[1]
and made for you the ships and the cattle,
which you ride,

13 that you may sit on their backs,
then remember the blessing of your Lord
when you are settled on them, and say,
'Immaculate is He who has disposed this for us,
and we by ourselves were no match for it.

14 Indeed, we shall return to our Lord.'

15 They ascribe to Him offspring[2] from among His servants!
The human being is indeed a manifest ingrate.

16 Did He adopt daughters from what He creates
while He preferred you with sons?

17 When one of them is brought the news
of what he ascribes to the All-beneficent,
his face becomes darkened[3]

---

[1] Or, 'all the pairs.'
[2] Lit.: 'They assign to Him a portion from among His servants.'
[3] That is, when he is brought the news of the birth of a daughter.

and he chokes with suppressed rage, [and says]

18 'What! One who is brought up amid ornaments
and is inconspicuous in contests?'

19 They have made the angels
—who are servants of the All-beneficent—females.
Were they witness to their creation?
Their testimony will be written down
and they shall be questioned.

20 They say, 'Had the All-beneficent wished,
we would not have worshiped them.'[1]
They do not have any knowledge of that
and they do nothing but surmise.

21 Did We give them a Book before this,
so that they are holding fast to it?

22 No, they said, 'We found our fathers following a creed,
and we are indeed guided in their footsteps.'

23 So it has been that We did not send
any warner to a town before you,
without its affluent ones saying,
'We found our fathers following a creed
and we are indeed following in their footsteps.'

24 He would say, 'What! Even if I bring you
a better guidance than what you found your fathers following?!'
They would say,
'We indeed disbelieve in what you are sent with.'

25 Thereupon We took vengeance on them;
so *observe* how was the fate of the deniers.

26 When Abraham said to his father and his people,

---

[1] That is, the gods worshiped by the polytheists. Cf. **16**:35.

'I repudiate what you worship, إِنَّنِي بَرَاءٌ مِمَّا تَعْبُدُونَ ۝
27 excepting Him who originated me; إِلَّا الَّذِي فَطَرَنِي
    indeed He will guide me.' فَإِنَّهُ سَيَهْدِينِ ۝
28 He made it[1] a lasting word among his posterity وَجَعَلَهَا كَلِمَةً بَاقِيَةً فِي عَقِبِهِ
    so that they may come back to the right path. لَعَلَّهُمْ يَرْجِعُونَ ۝
29 Indeed, I provided for these[2] and their fathers بَلْ مَتَّعْتُ هَٰؤُلَاءِ وَآبَاءَهُمْ
    until there came to them the truth and a manifest apostle. حَتَّىٰ جَاءَهُمُ الْحَقُّ وَرَسُولٌ مُبِينٌ ۝
30 But when the truth came to them, they said, وَلَمَّا جَاءَهُمُ الْحَقُّ قَالُوا
    'This is magic, and we indeed disbelieve in it.' هَٰذَا سِحْرٌ وَإِنَّا بِهِ كَافِرُونَ ۝
31 And they said, 'Why was not this Qur'ān sent down وَقَالُوا لَوْلَا نُزِّلَ هَٰذَا الْقُرْآنُ
    to some great man from the two cities?'[3] عَلَىٰ رَجُلٍ مِنَ الْقَرْيَتَيْنِ عَظِيمٍ ۝
32 Is it they who dispense the mercy of your Lord? أَهُمْ يَقْسِمُونَ رَحْمَتَ رَبِّكَ
    It is We who have dispensed among them نَحْنُ قَسَمْنَا بَيْنَهُمْ
        their livelihood in the present life, مَعِيشَتَهُمْ فِي الْحَيَاةِ الدُّنْيَا
      and raised some of them above others in rank, وَرَفَعْنَا بَعْضَهُمْ فَوْقَ بَعْضٍ دَرَجَاتٍ
        so that some may take others into service, لِيَتَّخِذَ بَعْضُهُمْ بَعْضًا سُخْرِيًّا
    and your Lord's mercy is better than what they amass. وَرَحْمَتُ رَبِّكَ خَيْرٌ مِمَّا يَجْمَعُونَ ۝
33 Were it not [for the danger] that mankind would be وَلَوْلَا أَنْ يَكُونَ النَّاسُ
    one community,[4] أُمَّةً وَاحِدَةً
    We would have made for those who defy the All-beneficent, لَجَعَلْنَا لِمَنْ يَكْفُرُ بِالرَّحْمَٰنِ
        silver roofs for their houses لِبُيُوتِهِمْ سُقُفًا مِنْ فِضَّةٍ
      and silver stairways by which they ascend; وَمَعَارِجَ عَلَيْهَا يَظْهَرُونَ ۝
34 and silver doors for their houses وَلِبُيُوتِهِمْ أَبْوَابًا
      and silver couches on which they recline; وَسُرُرًا عَلَيْهَا يَتَّكِئُونَ ۝
35 and ornaments of gold;[5] وَزُخْرُفًا
      yet all that would be nothing but وَإِنْ كُلُّ ذَٰلِكَ لَمَّا

---

[1] That is, the word of *tawḥīd*, 'There is no god except God,' the monotheistic creed of Abraham, or, in accordance with the traditions of the Imams Muḥammad al-Bāqir and Jaʿfar al-Ṣādiq (ʿa) Abraham's imamate (cf. 2:124; *Tafsīr al-Ṣāfī, Majmaʿ al-Bayān*).

[2] That is, the Arabs.

[3] That is, Makkah and Madinah, which were the two major towns of Arabia at that time.

[4] That is, a monolithic community of people without faith.

[5] Or 'houses embellished with gold.'

the wares of the life of this world,
and the Hereafter near *your* Lord is for the Godwary.

36 Whoever turns a blind eye to[1]
the remembrance of the All-beneficent,
We assign him a devil to be his companion.

37 They[2] indeed bar them from the way of God
while they suppose that they are rightly guided.

38 When he comes to Us, he will say,
'I wish there had been between me and you
the distance between the east and the west!
What an evil companion you are!'

39 'That[3] will be of no avail to you today.
As you did wrong,
so will you share in the punishment.'

40 Can *you*, then, make the deaf hear or guide the blind
and those who are in plain error?

41 We will take vengeance on them, whether We take *you* away

42 or show *you* what We have promised them,
for indeed We hold them in Our power.

43 So *hold fast* to what has been revealed to *you*.
You are indeed on a straight path.

44 It is indeed a reminder for *you* and for *your* people,
and soon you will be questioned.

45 Ask those of Our apostles We have sent before *you*:[4]
Did We set up besides the All-beneficent
any gods to be worshiped?

46 Certainly We sent Moses with Our signs

---

[1] Or 'whoever shuns.'
[2] That is, the devils thus assigned.
[3] That is, 'your desire to keep away from your evil companion.'
[4] That is, during the cosmic journey of the Prophet (see **17:1**, **53:8-18**).

إِلَىٰ فِرْعَوْنَ وَمَلَئِهِ	to Pharaoh and his elite.
فَقَالَ إِنِّي رَسُولُ	He said, 'I am indeed an apostle
رَبِّ الْعَالَمِينَ ۝	of the Lord of all the worlds.'
فَلَمَّا جَاءَهُم بِآيَاتِنَا	47 But when he brought them Our signs,
إِذَا هُم مِّنْهَا يَضْحَكُونَ ۝	behold, they laughed at them.
وَمَا نُرِيهِم مِّنْ آيَةٍ	48 We did not show them any sign
إِلَّا هِيَ أَكْبَرُ مِنْ أُخْتِهَا	but it was greater than the other,
وَأَخَذْنَاهُم بِالْعَذَابِ	and We visited on them punishment
لَعَلَّهُمْ يَرْجِعُونَ ۝	so that they might come back.
وَقَالُوا يَا أَيُّهَ السَّاحِرُ	49 They would say, 'O magician!
ادْعُ لَنَا رَبَّكَ	Invoke your Lord for us
بِمَا عَهِدَ عِندَكَ	by the covenant He has made with you.
إِنَّنَا لَمُهْتَدُونَ ۝	We will indeed be guided [when the scourge is removed.'
فَلَمَّا كَشَفْنَا عَنْهُمُ الْعَذَابَ	50 But when We lifted the punishment from them,
إِذَا هُمْ يَنكُثُونَ ۝	behold, they would break their pledge.
وَنَادَىٰ فِرْعَوْنُ فِي قَوْمِهِ	51 And Pharaoh proclaimed to his people,
قَالَ يَا قَوْمِ	saying, 'O my people!
أَلَيْسَ لِي مُلْكُ مِصْرَ	Do not the kingdom of Egypt belong to me
وَهَٰذِهِ الْأَنْهَارُ تَجْرِي مِن تَحْتِي	and these rivers that run at my feet?
أَفَلَا تُبْصِرُونَ ۝	Do you not see?
أَمْ أَنَا خَيْرٌ مِّنْ هَٰذَا الَّذِي هُوَ مَهِينٌ	52 Am I not better than this wretch
وَلَا يَكَادُ يُبِينُ ۝	who cannot even speak clearly?
فَلَوْلَا أُلْقِيَ عَلَيْهِ أَسْوِرَةٌ مِّن ذَهَبٍ	53 Why no bracelets of gold have been cast upon him,
أَوْ جَاءَ مَعَهُ الْمَلَائِكَةُ مُقْتَرِنِينَ ۝	nor any angels accompany him as escorts?'
فَاسْتَخَفَّ قَوْمَهُ فَأَطَاعُوهُ	54 Thus did he misled his people and they obeyed him.
إِنَّهُمْ كَانُوا قَوْمًا فَاسِقِينَ ۝	They were indeed a transgressing lot.
فَلَمَّا آسَفُونَا	55 So when they roused Our wrath,
انتَقَمْنَا مِنْهُمْ فَأَغْرَقْنَاهُمْ أَجْمَعِينَ ۝	We took vengeance on them and drowned them all.
فَجَعَلْنَاهُمْ سَلَفًا	56 Thus We made them the vanguard[1]

[1] That is, of those who enter hell.

and an example for posterity.

57 When the Son of Mary was cited as an example,
behold, *your* people raise an outcry.[1]
58 They say, 'Are our gods better or he?'
They cite him to you only for the sake of contention.
They are indeed a contentious lot.
59 He was just a servant whom We had blessed
and made an exemplar for the Children of Israel.
60 Had We wished We would have set angels in your stead
to be your successors on the earth.
61 [Say,] 'He[2] is indeed a portent of the Hour;
so do not doubt it and follow Me.
This is a straight path.
62 Do not let Satan bar you from the way of God.
He is indeed your manifest enemy.
63 When Jesus brought those clear proofs,
he said, 'I have certainly brought you wisdom,
and I have come to make clear to you
some of the things that you differ about.
So be wary of God and obey me.
64 God is indeed my Lord and your Lord; so worship Him.
This is a straight path.'
65 But the factions differed among themselves.
So woe to the wrongdoers for the punishment
of a painful day.
66 Do they await anything but that the Hour
should overtake them suddenly while they are unaware?

---

[1] Or 'laughed at it.' (*Ma'ānī al-akhbār*, p. 220) Or 'turn away,' in accordance with an alternate reading (*yaṣuddūn* instead of *yaṣiddūn*) narrated from many authorities. (*Mu'jam al-Qirā'āt al-Qur'āniyyah*, vol. 6, p. 121)

[2] That is, Jesus ('a), or 'Alī ibn Abī Ṭālib ('a), in accordance with traditions narrated from the Prophet (ṣ) and Imam Ja'far al-Ṣādiq ('a). (*Tafsīr al-Burhān*).

67 الْأَخِلَّاءُ يَوْمَئِذٍ بَعْضُهُمْ لِبَعْضٍ عَدُوٌّ إِلَّا الْمُتَّقِينَ ۝ On that day, friends will be one another's enemies,
except for the Godwary.

68 يَا عِبَادِ [They will be told,] 'O My servants!
لَا خَوْفٌ عَلَيْكُمُ الْيَوْمَ Today you will have no fear,
وَلَا أَنْتُمْ تَحْزَنُونَ ۝ nor will you grieve

69 الَّذِينَ آمَنُوا بِآيَاتِنَا —those who believed in Our signs
وَكَانُوا مُسْلِمِينَ ۝ and had been *muslims*.

70 ادْخُلُوا الْجَنَّةَ Enter paradise,
أَنْتُمْ وَأَزْوَاجُكُمْ تُحْبَرُونَ ۝ you and your spouses, rejoicing.'

71 يُطَافُ عَلَيْهِمْ بِصِحَافٍ مِنْ ذَهَبٍ وَأَكْوَابٍ They will be served around with golden dishes
and goblets,
وَفِيهَا مَا تَشْتَهِيهِ الْأَنْفُسُ وَتَلَذُّ الْأَعْيُنُ and therein[1] will be whatever the souls desire
and eyes delight in.
وَأَنْتُمْ فِيهَا خَالِدُونَ ۝ 'You will remain in it.

72 وَتِلْكَ الْجَنَّةُ الَّتِي أُورِثْتُمُوهَا That is the paradise you have been given to inherit
بِمَا كُنْتُمْ تَعْمَلُونَ ۝ for what you used to do.

73 لَكُمْ فِيهَا فَاكِهَةٌ كَثِيرَةٌ There are abundant fruits for you in it,
مِنْهَا تَأْكُلُونَ ۝ from which you will eat.'

74 إِنَّ الْمُجْرِمِينَ The guilty will indeed
فِي عَذَابِ جَهَنَّمَ خَالِدُونَ ۝ remain in the punishment of hell.

75 لَا يُفَتَّرُ عَنْهُمْ It will not be lightened for them
وَهُمْ فِيهِ مُبْلِسُونَ ۝ and they will be despondent in it.

76 وَمَا ظَلَمْنَاهُمْ We did not wrong them,
وَلَكِنْ كَانُوا هُمُ الظَّالِمِينَ ۝ but they themselves were wrongdoers.

77 وَنَادَوْا They will call out,
يَا مَالِكُ لِيَقْضِ عَلَيْنَا رَبُّكَ 'O Mālik![2] Let your Lord finish us off!'
قَالَ إِنَّكُمْ مَاكِثُونَ ۝ He will say, 'You will indeed stay on.'

78 لَقَدْ جِئْنَاكُمْ بِالْحَقِّ 'We certainly brought you the truth,
وَلَكِنَّ أَكْثَرَكُمْ لِلْحَقِّ كَارِهُونَ ۝ but most of you were averse to the truth.'

---

[1] That is, in paradise.
[2] The name of the angel in charge of hell.

79 Have they settled on some [devious] plan? أَمْ أَبْرَمُوا أَمْرًا
   Indeed, We, too, are settling on Our plans. فَإِنَّا مُبْرِمُونَ ۝

80 Do they suppose that We do not hear أَمْ يَحْسَبُونَ أَنَّا لَا نَسْمَعُ
   their secret thoughts and their secret talks? سِرَّهُمْ وَنَجْوَاهُم
   Of course! Our messengers are with them, بَلَىٰ وَرُسُلُنَا لَدَيْهِمْ
   recording [everything]. يَكْتُبُونَ ۝

81 Say, 'If the All-beneficent had an offspring, قُلْ إِنْ كَانَ لِلرَّحْمَـٰنِ وَلَدٌ
   I would have been the first to worship him.' فَأَنَا أَوَّلُ الْعَابِدِينَ ۝

82 Clear is the Lord of the heavens and the earth, سُبْحَانَ رَبِّ السَّمَاوَاتِ وَالْأَرْضِ
   the Lord of the Throne, رَبِّ الْعَرْشِ
   of whatever they allege concerning Him! عَمَّا يَصِفُونَ ۝

83 So leave them to gossip and play فَذَرْهُمْ يَخُوضُوا وَيَلْعَبُوا
   until they encounter the day they are promised. حَتَّىٰ يُلَاقُوا يَوْمَهُمُ الَّذِي يُوعَدُونَ ۝

84 It is He who is God in the heaven and God on the earth; وَهُوَ الَّذِي فِي السَّمَاءِ إِلَـٰهٌ وَفِي الْأَرْضِ إِلَـٰهٌ
   and He is the All-Wise, the All-Knowing. وَهُوَ الْحَكِيمُ الْعَلِيمُ ۝

85 Blessed is He to whom belongs the kingdom وَتَبَارَكَ الَّذِي
   of the heavens and the earth, لَهُ مُلْكُ السَّمَاوَاتِ وَالْأَرْضِ
   and whatever is between them, وَمَا بَيْنَهُمَا
   and with Him is the knowledge of the Hour, وَعِنْدَهُ عِلْمُ السَّاعَةِ
   and to Him you will be brought back. وَإِلَيْهِ تُرْجَعُونَ ۝

86 Those whom they invoke besides Him have no power وَلَا يَمْلِكُ الَّذِينَ يَدْعُونَ مِنْ دُونِهِ
   of intercession, الشَّفَاعَةَ
   except those who are witness to the truth إِلَّا مَنْ شَهِدَ بِالْحَقِّ
   and who know for whom to intercede. وَهُمْ يَعْلَمُونَ ۝

87 If you ask them, 'Who created them?' وَلَئِنْ سَأَلْتَهُمْ مَنْ خَلَقَهُمْ
   they will surely say, 'God.' لَيَقُولُنَّ اللَّهُ
   Then where do they stray? فَأَنَّىٰ يُؤْفَكُونَ ۝

88 And his[1] plaint: 'My Lord! وَقِيلِهِ يَا رَبِّ

---

[1] That is, of the Apostle of God (ṣ).

إِنَّ هَٰؤُلَاءِ قَوْمٌ لَا يُؤْمِنُونَ ۝ These are indeed a people who will not have faith!'

فَاصْفَحْ عَنْهُمْ وَقُلْ سَلَامٌ 89 So *disregard* them, and say, 'Peace!'

فَسَوْفَ يَعْلَمُونَ ۝ Soon they will know.

44 SMOKE[1]
al-Dukhān

بِسْمِ اللَّهِ الرَّحْمَٰنِ الرَّحِيمِ

In the Name of God,
the All-beneficent, the All-merciful.

حم ۝ 1 Ḥā, Mīm.

وَالْكِتَابِ الْمُبِينِ ۝ 2 By the Manifest Book!

إِنَّا أَنزَلْنَاهُ فِي لَيْلَةٍ مُّبَارَكَةٍ 3 We sent it down on a blessed night

إِنَّا كُنَّا مُنذِرِينَ ۝ and We have indeed been warning mankind.

فِيهَا يُفْرَقُ كُلُّ أَمْرٍ حَكِيمٍ ۝ 4 Every definitive matter is resolved on it,[2]

أَمْرًا مِّنْ عِندِنَا 5 as an ordinance[3] from Us.

إِنَّا كُنَّا مُرْسِلِينَ ۝ We have been sending apostles,

رَحْمَةً مِّن رَّبِّكَ 6 as a mercy from *your* Lord

إِنَّهُ هُوَ السَّمِيعُ الْعَلِيمُ ۝ —indeed, He is the All-hearing, the All-knowing—

رَبِّ السَّمَاوَاتِ وَالْأَرْضِ 7 the Lord of the heavens and the earth,

وَمَا بَيْنَهُمَا and whatever is between them,

إِن كُنتُم مُّوقِنِينَ ۝ should you have conviction.

لَا إِلَٰهَ إِلَّا هُوَ 8 There is no god except Him:

يُحْيِي وَيُمِيتُ He gives life and brings death,

رَبُّكُمْ وَرَبُّ آبَائِكُمُ الْأَوَّلِينَ ۝ your Lord and the Lord of your forefathers.

بَلْ هُمْ فِي شَكٍّ يَلْعَبُونَ ۝ 9 But they play around in doubt.

فَارْتَقِبْ يَوْمَ 10 So *watch out* for the day when

تَأْتِي السَّمَاءُ بِدُخَانٍ مُّبِينٍ ۝ the sky brings on a manifest smoke

يَغْشَى النَّاسَ 11 enveloping the people.

هَٰذَا عَذَابٌ أَلِيمٌ ۝ [They will cry out:] 'This is a painful punishment.

---

[1] This Makkī *sūrah* is named after 'the smoke' mentioned in verse 10.
[2] That is, on the Night of Ordainment. See **97**:1-5.
[3] Or 'edict.'

12 Our Lord! Remove this punishment from us. رَبَّنَا اكْشِفْ عَنَّا الْعَذَابَ
    We have indeed believed!' إِنَّا مُؤْمِنُونَ ۞

13 What will the admonition avail them, أَنَّىٰ لَهُمُ الذِّكْرَىٰ
    when a manifest apostle had already come to them, وَقَدْ جَاءَهُمْ رَسُولٌ مُبِينٌ ۞

14 but they turned away from him ثُمَّ تَوَلَّوْا عَنْهُ
    and said, 'A tutored madman?' وَقَالُوا مُعَلَّمٌ مَجْنُونٌ ۞

15 Indeed, We will withdraw the punishment a little; إِنَّا كَاشِفُو الْعَذَابِ قَلِيلًا
    but you will revert to your earlier ways. إِنَّكُمْ عَائِدُونَ ۞

16 The day We shall strike with the most terrible striking, يَوْمَ نَبْطِشُ الْبَطْشَةَ الْكُبْرَىٰ
    We will indeed take vengeance on them. إِنَّا مُنْتَقِمُونَ ۞

17 Certainly We tried the people of Pharaoh before them, وَلَقَدْ فَتَنَّا قَبْلَهُمْ قَوْمَ فِرْعَوْنَ
    when a noble apostle came to them, وَجَاءَهُمْ رَسُولٌ كَرِيمٌ ۞

18 saying, 'Give over the servants of God[1] to me; أَنْ أَدُّوا إِلَيَّ عِبَادَ اللَّهِ
    indeed I am a trusted apostle sent to you. إِنِّي لَكُمْ رَسُولٌ أَمِينٌ ۞

19 Do not defy God. وَأَنْ لَا تَعْلُوا عَلَى اللَّهِ
    I indeed bring you a clear authority. إِنِّي آتِيكُمْ بِسُلْطَانٍ مُبِينٍ ۞

20 I seek the protection of my Lord and your Lord, وَإِنِّي عُذْتُ بِرَبِّي وَرَبِّكُمْ
    lest you should stone me. أَنْ تَرْجُمُونِ ۞

21 And if you do not believe me, keep out of my way.' وَإِنْ لَمْ تُؤْمِنُوا لِي فَاعْتَزِلُونِ ۞

22 Then he invoked his Lord, 'These are indeed a guilty lot.' فَدَعَا رَبَّهُ أَنَّ هَٰؤُلَاءِ قَوْمٌ مُجْرِمُونَ ۞

23 [God told him,] 'Set out with My servants by night, فَأَسْرِ بِعِبَادِي لَيْلًا
    for you will be pursued. إِنَّكُمْ مُتَّبَعُونَ ۞

24 Leave behind the sea unmoved [and parted, وَاتْرُكِ الْبَحْرَ رَهْوًا
    for they will be a drowned host.' إِنَّهُمْ جُنْدٌ مُغْرَقُونَ ۞

25 How many gardens and springs did they leave behind! كَمْ تَرَكُوا مِنْ جَنَّاتٍ وَعُيُونٍ ۞

26 Fields and splendid places, وَزُرُوعٍ وَمَقَامٍ كَرِيمٍ ۞

27 and the affluence wherein they rejoiced! وَنَعْمَةٍ كَانُوا فِيهَا فَاكِهِينَ ۞

28 So it was; and We bequeathed them to another people. كَذَٰلِكَ وَأَوْرَثْنَاهَا قَوْمًا آخَرِينَ ۞

---

[1] That is, the Israelites.

29 فَمَا بَكَتْ عَلَيْهِمُ السَّمَاءُ وَالْأَرْضُ وَمَا كَانُوا مُنْظَرِينَ ۝ So neither the heaven wept for them, nor the earth,
      nor were they granted any respite.
30 وَلَقَدْ نَجَّيْنَا بَنِي إِسْرَائِيلَ مِنَ الْعَذَابِ الْمُهِينِ ۝ Certainly We delivered the Children of Israel
      from the humiliating torment,
31 مِنْ فِرْعَوْنَ إِنَّهُ كَانَ عَالِيًا مِنَ الْمُسْرِفِينَ ۝ of Pharaoh.
      He was indeed a tyrant among the transgressors.
32 وَلَقَدِ اخْتَرْنَاهُمْ عَلَىٰ عِلْمٍ عَلَى الْعَالَمِينَ ۝ Certainly We chose them knowingly above all the nations.
33 وَآتَيْنَاهُمْ مِنَ الْآيَاتِ مَا فِيهِ بَلَاءٌ مُبِينٌ ۝ And We gave them some signs
      in which there was a manifest test.

34 إِنَّ هَٰؤُلَاءِ لَيَقُولُونَ ۝ These ones say,
35 إِنْ هِيَ إِلَّا مَوْتَتُنَا الْأُولَىٰ وَمَا نَحْنُ بِمُنْشَرِينَ ۝ 'It will be only our first death,
      and we will not be resurrected.
36 فَأْتُوا بِآبَائِنَا إِنْ كُنْتُمْ صَادِقِينَ ۝ Bring our fathers back to life, if you are truthful.'
37 أَهُمْ خَيْرٌ أَمْ قَوْمُ تُبَّعٍ وَالَّذِينَ مِنْ قَبْلِهِمْ أَهْلَكْنَاهُمْ إِنَّهُمْ كَانُوا مُجْرِمِينَ ۝ Are they better, or the people of Tubba',[1]
      and those who were before them?
      We destroyed them; indeed they were guilty.
38 وَمَا خَلَقْنَا السَّمَاوَاتِ وَالْأَرْضَ وَمَا بَيْنَهُمَا لَاعِبِينَ ۝ We did not create the heavens and the earth
      and whatever is between them for play.
39 مَا خَلَقْنَاهُمَا إِلَّا بِالْحَقِّ وَلَٰكِنَّ أَكْثَرَهُمْ لَا يَعْلَمُونَ ۝ We did not create them
      except with consummate wisdom;
      but most of them do not know.
40 إِنَّ يَوْمَ الْفَصْلِ مِيقَاتُهُمْ أَجْمَعِينَ ۝ The Day of Judgement is indeed the tryst for them all,
41 يَوْمَ لَا يُغْنِي مَوْلًى عَنْ مَوْلًى شَيْئًا وَلَا هُمْ يُنْصَرُونَ ۝ the day when a friend will not avail a friend in any way,
      nor will they be helped,
42 إِلَّا مَنْ رَحِمَ اللَّهُ إِنَّهُ هُوَ الْعَزِيزُ الرَّحِيمُ ۝ except for him on whom God has mercy.
      Indeed, He is the All-mighty, the All-merciful.
43 إِنَّ شَجَرَتَ الزَّقُّومِ ۝ Indeed, the tree of Zaqqūm
44 طَعَامُ الْأَثِيمِ ۝ will be the food of the sinful.

---

[1] Name of a Yemenite king. Tubba' is said to be the title of a dynasty of Yemenite kings (like pharaoh, caesar and khaqan).

45 Like molten copper it will boil in their bellies,
46 seething like boiling water.
47 [The keepers of hell will be told,] 'Seize him
    and drag him to the middle of hell,
48 then pour over his head
    boiling water as punishment,
49 [and tell him]' "Taste this!
    You are indeed the [self-styled] mighty and noble!
50 This is what you used to doubt!" '
51 The Godwary will indeed be in a safe place,
52 amid gardens and springs,
53 dressed in fine and heavy silk,
    sitting face to face.
54 So shall it be, and We shall wed them to big-eyed houris.
55 Secure, there they will call for every kind of fruit they wish.
56 There they will not taste death
    other than the first death,
    and He will save them from the punishment of hell
57 —a grace from *your* Lord.
    That is a great success.

58 We have indeed made it simple in *your* language,
    so that they may take admonition.
59 So *wait!* They too are waiting.

45. FALLEN ON KNEES[1]
al-Jāthiyah

In the Name of God,
the All-beneficent, the All-merciful.

---

[1] This Makkī *sūrah* is named after the word *jāthiyah* (kneeling) in verse 28.

al-Jāthiyah

1 *Hā, Mīm.*

2 The gradual sending down of the Book is from God,
    the All-mighty, the All-wise.

3 In the heavens and the earth there are indeed signs
    for the faithful.

4 And in your own creation,
    and whatever animals that He scatters abroad,
    there are signs for a people who have certainty.

5 And in the alternation of night and day
    and what God sends down from the sky of His provision
    with which He revives the earth after its death,
    and in the changing of the winds
    there are signs for a people who exercise their reason.

6 These are the signs of God that We recite for you in truth.
    So what discourse
    will they believe after God and His signs?

7 Woe to every sinful liar,

8 who hears the signs of God being recited to him,
    yet persists arrogantly, as if he had not heard them.
    So *inform* him of a painful punishment.

9 When he learns anything about Our signs,
    he takes them in derision.
    For such there is a humiliating punishment.

10 Ahead of them is hell;
    neither what they have earned will avail them in any way,
    nor what they had taken as protectors besides God,
    and there is a great punishment for them.

11 This is true guidance;
    as for those who deny the signs of their Lord,

there is a painful punishment for them due to defilement.[1]

12 It is God who disposed the sea for your benefit
　　so that the ships may sail in it by His command,
　　that you may seek of His bounty,
　　and that you may give thanks.

13 He has disposed for your benefit
　　whatever is in the heavens and whatever is on the earth;
　　　all is from Him.
　　There are indeed signs in that for people who reflect.

14 *Say to the faithful*
　　to forgive those who do not expect God's days,
　　that He may Himself requite every people
　　　for what they used to earn.

15 Whoever acts righteously, it is for his own soul,
　　and whoever does evil, it is to its own detriment,
　　then you will be brought back to your Lord.

16 Certainly We gave the Children of Israel the Book,
　　　judgement and prophethood,
　　and We provided them with all the good things,
　　and We gave them an advantage over all the nations,

17 and We gave them clear precepts.
　　But they did not differ
　　　except after knowledge had come to them,
　　　out of envy among themselves.
　　Your Lord will indeed judge between them
　　　on the Day of Resurrection
　　concerning that about which they used to differ.

18 Then We set *you* upon a clear course of the Law;

---

[1] Or 'There is the torment of a dreadfully painful punishment.' Cf. 34:5.

فَاتَّبِعْهَا وَلَا تَتَّبِعْ so *follow it*, and *do not follow*
أَهْوَاءَ الَّذِينَ لَا يَعْلَمُونَ ۝ the base desires of those who do not know.

19 إِنَّهُمْ لَنْ يُغْنُوا عَنْكَ مِنَ اللَّهِ شَيْئًا They will indeed not avail *you* in any way against God.
وَإِنَّ الظَّالِمِينَ بَعْضُهُمْ أَوْلِيَاءُ بَعْضٍ Indeed, the wrongdoers are friends of one another,
وَاللَّهُ وَلِيُّ الْمُتَّقِينَ ۝ but God is the friend of the Godwary.

20 هَٰذَا بَصَائِرُ لِلنَّاسِ These are eye-openers for mankind,
وَهُدًى وَرَحْمَةٌ لِقَوْمٍ يُوقِنُونَ ۝ and guidance and mercy for a people who have certainty.

21 أَمْ حَسِبَ الَّذِينَ اجْتَرَحُوا السَّيِّئَاتِ Do those who have perpetrated misdeeds suppose
أَنْ نَجْعَلَهُمْ كَالَّذِينَ آمَنُوا that We shall treat them as those who have faith
وَعَمِلُوا الصَّالِحَاتِ and do righteous deeds,
سَوَاءً مَحْيَاهُمْ وَمَمَاتُهُمْ their life and death being equal?
سَاءَ مَا يَحْكُمُونَ ۝ Evil is the judgement that they make!

22 وَخَلَقَ اللَّهُ السَّمَاوَاتِ God created the heavens and the earth
وَالْأَرْضَ بِالْحَقِّ with consummate wisdom,
وَلِتُجْزَىٰ كُلُّ نَفْسٍ بِمَا كَسَبَتْ so that every soul may be requited for what it has earned
وَهُمْ لَا يُظْلَمُونَ ۝ and they will not be wronged.

23 أَفَرَأَيْتَ مَنِ اتَّخَذَ إِلَٰهَهُ هَوَاهُ Have *you* seen him who has taken his base desire to be his god
وَأَضَلَّهُ اللَّهُ عَلَىٰ عِلْمٍ and whom God has led astray knowingly,
وَخَتَمَ عَلَىٰ سَمْعِهِ وَقَلْبِهِ set a seal upon his hearing and his heart,
وَجَعَلَ عَلَىٰ بَصَرِهِ غِشَاوَةً and put a blindfold on his sight?
فَمَنْ يَهْدِيهِ مِنْ بَعْدِ اللَّهِ So who will guide him after God has given him up?
أَفَلَا تَذَكَّرُونَ ۝ Will you not then take admonition?

24 وَقَالُوا مَا هِيَ إِلَّا حَيَاتُنَا الدُّنْيَا They say, 'There is nothing but the life of this world:
نَمُوتُ وَنَحْيَا وَمَا يُهْلِكُنَا إِلَّا الدَّهْرُ we live and we die, and nothing destroys us but time.'
وَمَا لَهُمْ بِذَٰلِكَ مِنْ عِلْمٍ But they do not have any knowledge of that
إِنْ هُمْ إِلَّا يَظُنُّونَ ۝ and they only make conjectures.

25 وَإِذَا تُتْلَىٰ عَلَيْهِمْ آيَاتُنَا بَيِّنَاتٍ When Our clear signs are recited to them,
مَا كَانَ حُجَّتَهُمْ إِلَّا أَنْ قَالُوا their only argument is to say,
ائْتُوا بِآبَائِنَا إِنْ كُنْتُمْ صَادِقِينَ ۝ 'Bring our fathers back to life, if you are truthful.'

26 Say, 'It is God who gives you life, then He makes you die.
Then He will gather you on the Day of Resurrection,
in which there is no doubt.
But most people do not know.'

27 To God belongs the kingdom of the heavens
and the earth,
and when the Hour sets in,
the falsifiers will be losers on that day.

28 And you will see every nation fallen on its knees.
Every nation will be summoned to its book:
'Today you will be requited for what you used to do.

29 This is Our book which speaks truly against you.
Indeed, We used to record what you used to do.'

30 As for those who have faith and do righteous deeds,
their Lord will admit them into His mercy.
That is a manifest triumph!

31 But as for the faithless, [they will be asked,]
'Were not My signs recited to you?
But you were disdainful and you were a guilty lot.

32 When it was said, "God's promise is indeed true
and there is no doubt about the Hour,"
you said, "We do not know what the Hour is.
We know nothing beyond conjectures
and we do not possess any certainty."'

33 The evils of what they had done will appear to them,
and they will be besieged by what they used to deride.

34 And it will be said, 'Today We will forget you,
just as you forgot the encounter of this day of yours.
The Fire will be your abode,
and you will not have any helpers.

35 That is because you took the signs of God
in derision,
and the life of the world had deceived you.'
So today they will not be brought out of it,
nor will they be asked to propitiate God.

36 So all praise belongs to God,
the Lord of the heavens and the Lord of the earth,
the Lord of all the worlds.

37 To Him belongs all supremacy in the heavens
and the earth,
and He is the All-mighty, the All-wise.

[PART 26]

46. AHQAF[1]

al-Aḥqāf

In the Name of God,
the All-beneficent, the All-merciful.

1 *Ḥā, Mīm.*

2 The gradual sending down of the Book is from God,
the All-mighty, the All-wise.

3 We did not create the heavens and the earth
and whatever is between them
except with consummate wisdom and for a specified term.
Yet the faithless
are disregardful of what they are warned.

4 *Say,* 'Tell me about those whom you invoke besides God.
Show me, what part of the earth have they created.
Do they have any share in the heavens?
Bring me a scripture revealed before this,
or some vestige of divine knowledge,

---

[1] This Makkī *sūrah* takes its name from verse 21, where *Aḥqāf* is mentioned.

إِنْ كُنْتُمْ صَادِقِينَ ۝   if you are truthful.'

5 Who is more astray than him who invokes besides God   وَمَنْ أَضَلُّ مِمَّنْ يَدْعُو مِنْ دُونِ اللَّهِ
     such as would not respond to him   مَنْ لَا يَسْتَجِيبُ لَهُ
     till the Day of Resurrection   إِلَىٰ يَوْمِ الْقِيَامَةِ
     and who are oblivious of their invocation?   وَهُمْ عَنْ دُعَائِهِمْ غَافِلُونَ ۝

6 When mankind are gathered on Judgement's Day   وَإِذَا حُشِرَ النَّاسُ
     they will be their enemies   كَانُوا لَهُمْ أَعْدَاءً
     and they will disavow their worship.   وَكَانُوا بِعِبَادَتِهِمْ كَافِرِينَ ۝

7 When Our clear signs are recited to them,   وَإِذَا تُتْلَىٰ عَلَيْهِمْ آيَاتُنَا بَيِّنَاتٍ
     the faithless say of the truth when it comes to them: قَالَ الَّذِينَ كَفَرُوا لِلْحَقِّ لَمَّا جَاءَهُمْ
     'This is plain magic.'   هَٰذَا سِحْرٌ مُبِينٌ ۝

8 Or do they say, 'He has fabricated it?'   أَمْ يَقُولُونَ افْتَرَاهُ
     Say, 'Should I have fabricated it,   قُلْ إِنِ افْتَرَيْتُهُ
     you would not avail me anything against God.   فَلَا تَمْلِكُونَ لِي مِنَ اللَّهِ شَيْئًا
     He best knows what you gossip concerning it.   هُوَ أَعْلَمُ بِمَا تُفِيضُونَ فِيهِ
     He suffices as witness between me and you,   كَفَىٰ بِهِ شَهِيدًا بَيْنِي وَبَيْنَكُمْ
     and He is the All-forgiving, the All-merciful.'   وَهُوَ الْغَفُورُ الرَّحِيمُ ۝

9 Say, 'I am not a novelty among the apostles,   قُلْ مَا كُنْتُ بِدْعًا مِنَ الرُّسُلِ
     nor do I know what will be done with me or with you.   وَمَا أَدْرِي مَا يُفْعَلُ بِي وَلَا بِكُمْ
     I just follow whatever is revealed to me,   إِنْ أَتَّبِعُ إِلَّا مَا يُوحَىٰ إِلَيَّ
     and I am just a manifest warner.'   وَمَا أَنَا إِلَّا نَذِيرٌ مُبِينٌ ۝

10 Say, 'Tell me, if it is from God   قُلْ أَرَأَيْتُمْ إِنْ كَانَ مِنْ عِنْدِ اللَّهِ
     and you disbelieve in it,   وَكَفَرْتُمْ بِهِ
     and a witness from the Children of Israel has testified   وَشَهِدَ شَاهِدٌ مِنْ بَنِي إِسْرَائِيلَ
     to its like   عَلَىٰ مِثْلِهِ
     and believed in it, while you are disdainful of it?'[1]   فَآمَنَ وَاسْتَكْبَرْتُمْ
     Indeed, God does not guide the wrongdoing lot.   إِنَّ اللَّهَ لَا يَهْدِي الْقَوْمَ الظَّالِمِينَ ۝

11 The faithless say about the faithful,   وَقَالَ الَّذِينَ كَفَرُوا لِلَّذِينَ آمَنُوا
     'Had it been something good,   لَوْ كَانَ خَيْرًا

---

[1] Ellipsis; the omitted phrase is, 'who will be more astray than him who is in extreme defiance.' See **41:52**.

they would not have taken the lead over us in accepting it.'
And since they could not find the way to it,
they will say, 'It is an ancient lie.'

12 Yet before it the Book of Moses was a guide and mercy,
and this is a Book in the Arabic language which confirms it,
sent to warn the wrongdoers,
and as a bearer of good news for the virtuous.

13 Those who say, 'Our Lord is God,' and remain steadfast,
they will have no fear, nor will they grieve.

14 They shall be the inhabitants of paradise,
to abide in it
—a reward for what they used to do.

15 We have enjoined man to be kind to his parents.
His mother has carried him in travail
and bore him in travail,
and his gestation and weaning take thirty months.
When he comes of age
and reaches forty years,
he says, 'My Lord!
Inspire me to give thanks for Your blessing
with which You have blessed me and my parents,
and that I may do righteous deeds which please You,
and invest my descendants with righteousness.
I have indeed turned to you in penitence,
and I am one of the *muslims*.'

16 Such are the ones from whom We accept
the best of what they do
and overlook their misdeeds,
who will be among the inhabitants of paradise

—a true promise which they had been given.

17 As for him who says to his parents, 'Fie on you!
Do you promise me that I shall be raised from the dead
when generations have passed away before me?'
And they invoke God's help, [and say]:
'Woe to you! Believe! God's promise is indeed true.'
But he says,
'These are nothing but myths of the ancients.'

18 Such are the ones against whom the word became due,
along with the nations that have passed away before them
of jinn and humans.
They were indeed the losers.

19 For everyone there are degrees of merit
pertaining to what they have done,
so that He may recompense them fully for their works
and they will not be wronged.

20 The day when the faithless are exposed to the Fire,
[they will be told,] 'You have exhausted your good things
in the life of the world and enjoyed them.
So today you will be requited with a humiliating punishment
for your acting arrogantly on the earth
unduly,
and for the transgressions you used to commit.'

21 And mention [Hūd] the compatriot of ʿĀd,
when he warned his people at Aḥqāf
—and warners have passed
before and after him—
saying, 'Do not worship anyone but God.
I indeed fear for you the punishment
of a tremendous day.'

22 قَالُوا أَجِئْتَنَا لِتَأْفِكَنَا عَنْ آلِهَتِنَا They said, 'Have you come to turn us away from our gods?
فَأْتِنَا بِمَا تَعِدُنَا Then bring us what you threaten us with,
إِنْ كُنتَ مِنَ الصَّادِقِينَ ۝ if you are truthful.'

23 قَالَ إِنَّمَا الْعِلْمُ عِندَ اللَّهِ He said, 'Its knowledge is with God alone,
وَأُبَلِّغُكُم مَّا أُرْسِلْتُ بِهِ and I communicate to you what I have been sent with.
وَلَٰكِنِّي أَرَاكُمْ قَوْمًا تَجْهَلُونَ ۝ But I see that you are an ignorant lot.'

24 فَلَمَّا رَأَوْهُ عَارِضًا مُّسْتَقْبِلَ أَوْدِيَتِهِمْ When they saw it as a cloud advancing toward their valleys,
قَالُوا هَٰذَا عَارِضٌ مُّمْطِرُنَا they said, 'This cloud brings us rain.'
بَلْ هُوَ مَا اسْتَعْجَلْتُم بِهِ 'No, it is what you sought to hasten:
رِيحٌ فِيهَا عَذَابٌ أَلِيمٌ ۝ a hurricane carrying a painful punishment,

25 تُدَمِّرُ كُلَّ شَيْءٍ بِأَمْرِ رَبِّهَا destroying everything by its Lord's command.'
فَأَصْبَحُوا لَا يُرَىٰ So they became such that nothing could be seen
إِلَّا مَسَاكِنُهُمْ except their dwellings.
كَذَٰلِكَ نَجْزِي الْقَوْمَ الْمُجْرِمِينَ ۝ Thus do We requite the guilty lot.

26 وَلَقَدْ مَكَّنَّاهُمْ Certainly We had granted them power
فِيمَا إِن مَّكَّنَّاكُمْ فِيهِ in respects that We have not granted you,
وَجَعَلْنَا لَهُمْ سَمْعًا وَأَبْصَارًا وَأَفْئِدَةً and We had vested them with hearing, sight and hearts.
فَمَا أَغْنَىٰ عَنْهُمْ سَمْعُهُمْ But neither did their hearing avail them
وَلَا أَبْصَارُهُمْ وَلَا أَفْئِدَتُهُم مِّن شَيْءٍ in any way, nor their sight, nor their hearts,
إِذْ كَانُوا يَجْحَدُونَ بِآيَاتِ اللَّهِ when they had been impugning the signs of God.
وَحَاقَ بِهِم مَّا كَانُوا بِهِ يَسْتَهْزِئُونَ ۝ So they were besieged by what they used to deride.

27 وَلَقَدْ أَهْلَكْنَا Certainly We have destroyed
مَا حَوْلَكُم مِّنَ الْقُرَىٰ the towns that were around you,
وَصَرَّفْنَا الْآيَاتِ and We have paraphrased the signs variously
لَعَلَّهُمْ يَرْجِعُونَ ۝ so that they may come back.

28 فَلَوْلَا نَصَرَهُمُ الَّذِينَ So why did not those [fake deities] help them
اتَّخَذُوا مِن دُونِ اللَّهِ whom they had taken, besides God,
قُرْبَانًا آلِهَةً as gods, as a means of nearness to Him?
بَلْ ضَلُّوا عَنْهُمْ Indeed, they forsook them;
وَذَٰلِكَ إِفْكُهُمْ وَمَا كَانُوا يَفْتَرُونَ ۝ that was their lie and what they used to fabricate.

29 وَإِذْ صَرَفْنَا إِلَيْكَ نَفَرًا مِنَ الْجِنِّ When We dispatched toward you a team of jinn
يَسْتَمِعُونَ الْقُرْآنَ listening to the Qur'ān,
فَلَمَّا حَضَرُوهُ قَالُوا أَنْصِتُوا when they were in its presence, they said, 'Listen quietly!'
فَلَمَّا قُضِيَ When it was finished,
وَلَّوْا إِلَىٰ قَوْمِهِمْ مُنْذِرِينَ ۝ they went back to their people as warners.

30 قَالُوا يَا قَوْمَنَا إِنَّا سَمِعْنَا كِتَابًا They said, 'O our people! We have indeed heard a Book
أُنْزِلَ مِنْ بَعْدِ مُوسَىٰ which has been sent down after Moses,
مُصَدِّقًا لِمَا بَيْنَ يَدَيْهِ confirming what was before it.
يَهْدِي إِلَى الْحَقِّ It guides to the truth
وَإِلَىٰ طَرِيقٍ مُسْتَقِيمٍ ۝ and to a straight path.

31 يَا قَوْمَنَا أَجِيبُوا دَاعِيَ اللَّهِ O our people! Respond to God's summoner
وَآمِنُوا بِهِ and have faith in Him.
يَغْفِرْ لَكُمْ مِنْ ذُنُوبِكُمْ He will forgive you some of your sins
وَيُجِرْكُمْ مِنْ عَذَابٍ أَلِيمٍ ۝ and deliver you from a painful punishment.'

32 وَمَنْ لَا يُجِبْ دَاعِيَ اللَّهِ Those who do not respond to God's summoner
فَلَيْسَ بِمُعْجِزٍ فِي الْأَرْضِ cannot frustrate God on the earth,
وَلَيْسَ لَهُ مِنْ دُونِهِ أَوْلِيَاءُ and they will not find any friends besides Him.
أُولَٰئِكَ فِي ضَلَالٍ مُبِينٍ ۝ They are in manifest error.

33 أَوَلَمْ يَرَوْا أَنَّ اللَّهَ Do they not see that God,
الَّذِي خَلَقَ السَّمَاوَاتِ وَالْأَرْضَ who created the heavens and the earth
وَلَمْ يَعْيَ بِخَلْقِهِنَّ and who was not exhausted by their creation,
بِقَادِرٍ عَلَىٰ أَنْ يُحْيِيَ الْمَوْتَىٰ is able to revive the dead?
بَلَىٰ إِنَّهُ عَلَىٰ كُلِّ شَيْءٍ قَدِيرٌ ۝ Yes, indeed He has power over all things.

34 وَيَوْمَ يُعْرَضُ الَّذِينَ كَفَرُوا The day when the faithless are exposed
عَلَى النَّارِ to the Fire,
أَلَيْسَ هَٰذَا بِالْحَقِّ [He will say,] 'Is this not a fact?'
قَالُوا بَلَىٰ وَرَبِّنَا They will say, 'Yes, by our Lord!'
قَالَ فَذُوقُوا الْعَذَابَ He will say, 'So taste the punishment
بِمَا كُنْتُمْ تَكْفُرُونَ ۝ because of what you used to disbelieve.'

35 *So be patient,*
just as the resolute among the apostles were patient,
and *do not seek* to hasten the punishment for them.
The day when they see what they are promised, it will be as if they had remained in the world just an hour of a day.
This is a proclamation.
Will anyone be destroyed except the transgressing lot?

47. Muḥammad[1]
Muḥammad

In the Name of God,
the All-beneficent, the All-merciful.

1 Those who are themselves faithless
and bar others from the way of God
—He will make their works go to waste.

2 But those who have faith and do righteous deeds
and believe in what has been sent down to Muḥammad
—and it is the truth from their Lord—
He shall absolve them of their misdeeds
and set right their affairs.

3 That is because the faithless
follow falsehood
and those who have faith follow the truth
from their Lord.
That is how God draws comparisons for mankind.

4 When you meet the faithless in battle,
strike their necks.
When you have thoroughly decimated them,

---

[1] This Madanī *sūrah* is named after verse 2, which mentions the Prophet's name.

فَشُدُّوا الْوَثَاقَ   bind the captives firmly.

فَإِمَّا مَنًّا بَعْدُ   Thereafter, either oblige them [by setting them free],

وَإِمَّا فِدَاءً   or take ransom,

حَتَّىٰ تَضَعَ الْحَرْبُ أَوْزَارَهَا   until the war lays down its burdens.

ذَٰلِكَ   That [is God's ordinance].

وَلَوْ يَشَاءُ اللَّهُ   Had God wished

لَانْتَصَرَ مِنْهُمْ   He could have taken vengeance on them,[1]

وَلَٰكِنْ لِيَبْلُوَ بَعْضَكُمْ بِبَعْضٍ   but that He may test some of you by means of others.

وَالَّذِينَ قُتِلُوا فِي سَبِيلِ اللَّهِ   As for those who were slain in the way of God,

فَلَنْ يُضِلَّ أَعْمَالَهُمْ ۞   He will not let their works go to waste.

سَيَهْدِيهِمْ وَيُصْلِحُ بَالَهُمْ ۞   5 He will guide them and set right their affairs

وَيُدْخِلُهُمُ الْجَنَّةَ   6 and admit them into paradise

عَرَّفَهَا لَهُمْ ۞   with which He has acquainted them.

يَا أَيُّهَا الَّذِينَ آمَنُوا   7 O you who have faith!

إِنْ تَنْصُرُوا اللَّهَ يَنْصُرْكُمْ   If you help God, He will help you

وَيُثَبِّتْ أَقْدَامَكُمْ ۞   and make your feet steady.

وَالَّذِينَ كَفَرُوا فَتَعْسًا لَهُمْ   8 As for the faithless, their lot will be to fall into ruin,[2]

وَأَضَلَّ أَعْمَالَهُمْ ۞   and He will make their works go to waste.

ذَٰلِكَ بِأَنَّهُمْ كَرِهُوا مَا أَنْزَلَ اللَّهُ   9 That is because they loathed what God has sent down,

فَأَحْبَطَ أَعْمَالَهُمْ ۞   so He made their works fail.

أَفَلَمْ يَسِيرُوا فِي الْأَرْضِ فَيَنْظُرُوا   10 Have they not traveled through the land to observe

كَيْفَ كَانَ عَاقِبَةُ الَّذِينَ مِنْ قَبْلِهِمْ   how was the fate of those who were before them?

دَمَّرَ اللَّهُ عَلَيْهِمْ وَلِلْكَافِرِينَ أَمْثَالُهَا ۞   God destroyed them and a similar fate awaits these faithless.

ذَٰلِكَ بِأَنَّ اللَّهَ مَوْلَى الَّذِينَ آمَنُوا   11 That is because God is the protector of the faithful,

وَأَنَّ الْكَافِرِينَ لَا مَوْلَى لَهُمْ ۞   and because the faithless have no protector.

إِنَّ اللَّهَ يُدْخِلُ الَّذِينَ آمَنُوا   12 God will indeed admit those who have faith

وَعَمِلُوا الصَّالِحَاتِ   and do righteous deeds

جَنَّاتٍ تَجْرِي مِنْ تَحْتِهَا الْأَنْهَارُ   into gardens with streams running in them.

وَالَّذِينَ كَفَرُوا يَتَمَتَّعُونَ وَيَأْكُلُونَ   As for the faithless, they enjoy and eat

---

[1] That is, without your mediation.
[2] Or 'their lot will be wretchedness.'

like the cattle do كَمَا تَأْكُلُ الْأَنْعَامُ
and the Fire will be their final abode. وَالنَّارُ مَثْوًى لَهُمْ ۝

13 How many a town there has been وَكَأَيِّنْ مِنْ قَرْيَةٍ
which was more powerful هِيَ أَشَدُّ قُوَّةً
than *your* town which expelled *you*, مِنْ قَرْيَتِكَ الَّتِي أَخْرَجَتْكَ
which We have destroyed, and they had no helper. أَهْلَكْنَاهُمْ فَلَا نَاصِرَ لَهُمْ ۝

14 Is he who stands on a clear proof from his Lord أَفَمَنْ كَانَ عَلَى بَيِّنَةٍ مِنْ رَبِّهِ
like those كَمَنْ
to whom the evil of their conduct is made to seem decorous زُيِّنَ لَهُ سُوءُ عَمَلِهِ
and who follow their base desires? وَاتَّبَعُوا أَهْوَاءَهُمْ ۝

15 A description of the paradise promised to the Godwary: مَثَلُ الْجَنَّةِ الَّتِي وُعِدَ الْمُتَّقُونَ
therein are streams of unstaling water فِيهَا أَنْهَارٌ مِنْ مَاءٍ غَيْرِ آسِنٍ
and streams of milk unchanging in flavour, وَأَنْهَارٌ مِنْ لَبَنٍ لَمْ يَتَغَيَّرْ طَعْمُهُ
and streams of wine delicious to the drinkers, وَأَنْهَارٌ مِنْ خَمْرٍ لَذَّةٍ لِلشَّارِبِينَ
and streams of purified honey; وَأَنْهَارٌ مِنْ عَسَلٍ مُصَفًّى
there will be every kind of fruit for them in it, وَلَهُمْ فِيهَا مِنْ كُلِّ الثَّمَرَاتِ
and forgiveness from their Lord. وَمَغْفِرَةٌ مِنْ رَبِّهِمْ
Are such ones like those who abide in the Fire كَمَنْ هُوَ خَالِدٌ فِي النَّارِ
and are given to drink boiling water وَسُقُوا مَاءً حَمِيمًا
which cuts up their bowels? فَقَطَّعَ أَمْعَاءَهُمْ ۝

16 There are some among them who prick up their ears at *you*. وَمِنْهُمْ مَنْ يَسْتَمِعُ إِلَيْكَ
But when they go out from *your* presence, حَتَّى إِذَا خَرَجُوا مِنْ عِنْدِكَ
they say to those who have been given knowledge, قَالُوا لِلَّذِينَ أُوتُوا الْعِلْمَ
'What did he say just now?' مَاذَا قَالَ آنِفًا
They are the ones on whose hearts God has set a seal أُولَئِكَ الَّذِينَ طَبَعَ اللَّهُ عَلَى قُلُوبِهِمْ
and they follow their base desires. وَاتَّبَعُوا أَهْوَاءَهُمْ ۝

17 As for those who are rightly guided, وَالَّذِينَ اهْتَدَوْا
He enhances their guidance, زَادَهُمْ هُدًى
and invests them with their Godwariness. وَآتَاهُمْ تَقْوَاهُمْ ۝

18 Do they await anything except that the Hour فَهَلْ يَنْظُرُونَ إِلَّا السَّاعَةَ

should overtake them suddenly?
Its portents have already come.
Of what avail to them
will their admonition be when it overtakes them?

19 *Know* that there is no god except God,
and *plead* to God for forgiveness of *your* sin
and for the faithful, men and women.
God knows your itinerary and your final abode.

20 The faithful say, 'If only a *sūrah* were sent down!'
But when a conclusive *sūrah* is sent down
and warfare is mentioned in it,
you see those in whose hearts is sickness[1]
looking upon *you*
with the look of someone fainting at death.
So woe to them!

21 Obedience and upright speech . . . .[2]
So when the matter has been resolved upon,
if they remain true to God,
that will surely be better for them.

22 May it not be that if you were to wield authority
you would cause corruption in the land
and ill-treat your blood relations?

23 They are the ones whom God has cursed,
so He made them deaf and blinded their sight.

24 Do they not contemplate the Qur'ān,
or are there locks on their hearts?

25 Indeed, those who turned their backs
after the guidance had become clear to them,
it was Satan who had seduced them

---

[1] That is, the hypocrites.
[2] Ellipsis; the omitted phrase is 'are all that is expected of you.'

وَأَمْلَىٰ لَهُمْ ۝ and he had given them [far-flung] hopes.[1]

ذَٰلِكَ بِأَنَّهُمْ قَالُوا 26 That is because they said

لِلَّذِينَ كَرِهُوا مَا نَزَّلَ اللَّهُ to those who loathed what God had sent down:

سَنُطِيعُكُمْ فِي بَعْضِ الْأَمْرِ ۖ 'We will obey you in some matters,'

وَاللَّهُ يَعْلَمُ إِسْرَارَهُمْ ۝ and God knows their secret dealings.

فَكَيْفَ إِذَا تَوَفَّتْهُمُ الْمَلَائِكَةُ 27 But how will it be when the angels take them away,

يَضْرِبُونَ وُجُوهَهُمْ وَأَدْبَارَهُمْ ۝ striking their faces and their backs?!

ذَٰلِكَ بِأَنَّهُمُ اتَّبَعُوا مَا أَسْخَطَ اللَّهَ 28 That, because they pursued what displeased God

وَكَرِهُوا رِضْوَانَهُ and loathed His pleasure.

فَأَحْبَطَ أَعْمَالَهُمْ ۝ So He has made their works fail.

أَمْ حَسِبَ الَّذِينَ فِي قُلُوبِهِمْ مَرَضٌ 29 Do those in whose hearts is sickness suppose

أَنْ لَنْ يُخْرِجَ اللَّهُ أَضْغَانَهُمْ ۝ that God will not expose their spite?

وَلَوْ نَشَاءُ لَأَرَيْنَاكَهُمْ 30 If We wish, We will show them[2] to you

فَلَعَرَفْتَهُمْ بِسِيمَاهُمْ ۚ so that you recognize them by their mark.

وَلَتَعْرِفَنَّهُمْ فِي لَحْنِ الْقَوْلِ ۚ Yet you will recognize them by their tone of speech,

وَاللَّهُ يَعْلَمُ أَعْمَالَكُمْ ۝ and God knows your deeds.

وَلَنَبْلُوَنَّكُمْ 31 We will surely test you

حَتَّىٰ نَعْلَمَ الْمُجَاهِدِينَ مِنْكُمْ until We ascertain those of you who wage *jihād*

وَالصَّابِرِينَ and those who are steadfast,

وَنَبْلُوَ أَخْبَارَكُمْ ۝ and We shall appraise your record.

إِنَّ الَّذِينَ كَفَرُوا 32 Indeed, those who are faithless

وَصَدُّوا عَنْ سَبِيلِ اللَّهِ وَشَاقُّوا الرَّسُولَ and bar from the way of God and defy the Apostle

مِنْ بَعْدِ مَا تَبَيَّنَ لَهُمُ الْهُدَىٰ after guidance has become clear to them,

لَنْ يَضُرُّوا اللَّهَ شَيْئًا they will not hurt God in the least

وَسَيُحْبِطُ أَعْمَالَهُمْ ۝ and He shall make their works fail.

يَا أَيُّهَا الَّذِينَ آمَنُوا أَطِيعُوا اللَّهَ 33 O you who have faith! Obey God

وَأَطِيعُوا الرَّسُولَ and obey the Apostle,

وَلَا تُبْطِلُوا أَعْمَالَكُمْ ۝ and do not render your works void.

إِنَّ الَّذِينَ كَفَرُوا 34 Indeed, those who are faithless

---

[1] Or 'and He [i.e. God] gave them respite.'
[2] That is, the hypocrites.

                      and bar from the way of God
                      and then die faithless,
                      God will never forgive them.

35 So do not slacken and do not call for peace
    when you have the upper hand and God is with you,
    and He will not stint the reward of your works.

36 The life of the world is just play and diversion,
    but if you are faithful and Godwary,
    He will give you your rewards,
    and will not ask your wealth in return from you.

37 Should He ask it from you, and press you,
    you will be stingy, and He will expose your spite.

38 Ah! There you are,
    being invited to spend in the way of God;
    yet among you there are those who are stingy;
    and whoever is stingy is stingy only to himself.
    God is the All-sufficient, and you are all-needy,
    and if you turn away
    He will replace you with another people,
    and they will not be like you.

48. VICTORY[1]
al-Fatḥ

In the Name of God,
the All-beneficent, the All-merciful.

1 We have indeed inaugurated for you a clear victory,[2]
2 that God may forgive you
    what is past of *your* sin and what is to come,

---

[1] A Madanī *sūrah* revealed during the Prophet's return journey from Ḥudaybiyyah in Dhū al-Qaʿadah 6 H. Named after verse 1 where victory (*fatḥ*) is mentioned.

[2] Or 'We have indeed initiated for you a clear breakthrough.'

and that He may perfect His blessing upon you
and guide you on a straight path,
3 and God will help you with a mighty help.
4 It is He who sent down composure
into the hearts of the faithful
that they might enhance in their faith.
To God belong the hosts of the heavens and the earth,
and God is all-knowing, all-wise.
5 That He may admit the faithful, men and women,
into gardens with streams running in them,
to remain in them,
and that He may absolve them of their misdeeds.
That is a great triumph with God.
6 That He may punish the hypocrites, men and women,
and the polytheists, men and women,
who entertain a bad opinion of God.
For them shall be an adverse turn of fortune:
God is wrathful with them and He has cursed them,
and prepared hell for them, and it is an evil destination.
7 To God belong the hosts of the heavens and the earth,
and God is all-mighty, all-wise.
8 We have indeed sent you as a witness,
and as a bearer of good news and warner,
9 that you may have faith in God and His Apostle,
and that you may support him and revere him,
and that you may glorify Him morning and evening.

10 Indeed, those who swear allegiance to you,
swear allegiance only to God:
the hand of God is above their hands.

فَمَنْ نَكَثَ

Then whosoever breaks his oath,

فَإِنَّمَا يَنْكُثُ عَلَىٰ نَفْسِهِ

breaks it only to his own detriment,

وَمَنْ أَوْفَىٰ بِمَا عَاهَدَ عَلَيْهُ اللَّهَ

and whoever fulfills the covenant he has made with God,

فَسَيُؤْتِيهِ أَجْرًا عَظِيمًا ۝

He will give him a great reward.

سَيَقُولُ لَكَ الْمُخَلَّفُونَ مِنَ الْأَعْرَابِ

11 The Bedouins who had stayed back will tell you,

شَغَلَتْنَا أَمْوَالُنَا وَأَهْلُونَا

'Our possessions and families kept us occupied.

فَاسْتَغْفِرْ لَنَا

So plead to God for our forgiveness!'

يَقُولُونَ بِأَلْسِنَتِهِمْ مَا لَيْسَ فِي قُلُوبِهِمْ

They will say with their tongues what is not in their hearts.

قُلْ فَمَنْ يَمْلِكُ لَكُمْ مِنَ اللَّهِ شَيْئًا

Say, 'Who can be of any avail to you against God,

إِنْ أَرَادَ بِكُمْ ضَرًّا

should He desire to cause you harm,

أَوْ أَرَادَ بِكُمْ نَفْعًا

or desire to bring you benefit?

بَلْ كَانَ اللَّهُ بِمَا تَعْمَلُونَ خَبِيرًا ۝

God is indeed well aware of what you do.'

بَلْ ظَنَنْتُمْ

12 Rather, you thought

أَنْ لَنْ يَنْقَلِبَ الرَّسُولُ وَالْمُؤْمِنُونَ

that the Apostle and the faithful will not return

إِلَىٰ أَهْلِيهِمْ أَبَدًا

to their folk ever

وَزُيِّنَ ذَٰلِكَ فِي قُلُوبِكُمْ

and that was made to seem decorous to your hearts,

وَظَنَنْتُمْ ظَنَّ السَّوْءِ

and you entertained evil thoughts

وَكُنْتُمْ قَوْمًا بُورًا ۝

and you were a ruined lot.

وَمَنْ لَمْ يُؤْمِنْ بِاللَّهِ وَرَسُولِهِ

13 Those who have no faith in God and His Apostle [should

فَإِنَّا أَعْتَدْنَا لِلْكَافِرِينَ سَعِيرًا ۝

know that We have prepared a blaze for the faithless.

وَلِلَّهِ مُلْكُ السَّمَاوَاتِ

14 To God belongs the kingdom of the heavens

وَالْأَرْضِ

and the earth:

يَغْفِرُ لِمَنْ يَشَاءُ

He forgives whomever He wishes

وَيُعَذِّبُ مَنْ يَشَاءُ

and punishes whomever He wishes,

وَكَانَ اللَّهُ غَفُورًا رَحِيمًا ۝

and God is all-forgiving, all-merciful.

سَيَقُولُ الْمُخَلَّفُونَ

15 Those who stayed behind [in this journey] will say,

إِذَا انْطَلَقْتُمْ إِلَىٰ مَغَانِمَ لِتَأْخُذُوهَا

when you set out to capture booty [in the near future]:

ذَرُونَا نَتَّبِعْكُمْ

'Let us follow you.'

يُرِيدُونَ أَنْ يُبَدِّلُوا كَلَامَ اللَّهِ

They desire to change the word of God.

قُلْ لَنْ تَتَّبِعُونَا

Say, 'You will not follow us!

God has said this beforehand.'
Then they will say, 'You are envious of us.'
Indeed, they do not understand but a little!

16 Say to the Bedouins who stayed behind,
'Later on, you will be called against a people of great might:
they will either embrace Islam, or you will fight them.
So if you obey, God will give you a good reward;
but if you turn away like you turned away before,
He will punish you with a painful punishment.'

17 There is no blame on the blind,
nor is there any blame on the lame,
nor is there blame on the sick [if they stay back];
and whoever obeys God and His Apostle,
He will admit him into gardens
with streams running in them,
and whoever turns away,
He will punish him with a painful punishment.

18 God was certainly pleased with the faithful
when they swore allegiance to you under the tree.
He knew what was in their hearts,
so He sent down composure on them,
and requited them with a victory near at hand

19 and abundant spoils that they will capture,
and God is all-mighty, all-wise.

20 God has promised you abundant spoils
which you will capture.
He has expedited this one for you
and withheld men's hands from you,
so that it may be a sign for the faithful
and that He may guide you to a straight path.

21 And other spoils as well which you have not yet captured:
God has comprehended them
and God has power over all things.
22 If the faithless fight you, they will turn their backs to flee.
Then they will not find any friend or helper.
23 It is God's precedent that has passed before,
and you will never find any change in God's precedents.
24 It is He who withheld their hands from you
and your hands from them
in the valley of Makkah
after He had given you victory over them,
and God sees best what you do.
25 They are the ones who disbelieved
and barred you from the Sacred Mosque,
and kept the offering from reaching its destination.
And were it not for certain faithful men
and faithful women,
whom you did not know
—lest you should trample them
and thus the blame for killing them should fall on you
unawares— . . .;[1] [He held you back]
so that God may admit into His mercy
whomever He wishes.
Had they been separate,
We would have surely punished the faithless among them
with a painful punishment.
26 When the faithless nourished
bigotry in their hearts,
the bigotry of pagan ignorance,

---

[1] Ellipsis; the omitted phrase is 'We would have given you a free hand against them.'

فَأَنزَلَ اللَّهُ سَكِينَتَهُ عَلَىٰ رَسُولِهِ وَعَلَى الْمُؤْمِنِينَ وَأَلْزَمَهُمْ كَلِمَةَ التَّقْوَىٰ وَكَانُوا أَحَقَّ بِهَا وَأَهْلَهَا ۚ وَكَانَ اللَّهُ بِكُلِّ شَيْءٍ عَلِيمًا ۝

God sent down His composure upon His Apostle and the faithful,
and made them abide by the word of Godwariness,
for they were the worthiest of it and deserved it,
and God has knowledge of all things.

27 لَّقَدْ صَدَقَ اللَّهُ رَسُولَهُ الرُّؤْيَا بِالْحَقِّ ۖ لَتَدْخُلُنَّ الْمَسْجِدَ الْحَرَامَ إِن شَاءَ اللَّهُ آمِنِينَ مُحَلِّقِينَ رُءُوسَكُمْ وَمُقَصِّرِينَ لَا تَخَافُونَ ۖ فَعَلِمَ مَا لَمْ تَعْلَمُوا فَجَعَلَ مِن دُونِ ذَٰلِكَ فَتْحًا قَرِيبًا ۝

27 Certainly God has fulfilled His Apostle's vision in all truth:
God willing, you will surely enter the Sacred Mosque, in safety,
with your heads shaven or hair cropped, without any fear.
So He knew what you did not know,
and He assigned you besides that a victory near at hand.

28 هُوَ الَّذِي أَرْسَلَ رَسُولَهُ بِالْهُدَىٰ وَدِينِ الْحَقِّ لِيُظْهِرَهُ عَلَى الدِّينِ كُلِّهِ ۚ وَكَفَىٰ بِاللَّهِ شَهِيدًا ۝

28 It is He who has sent His Apostle with guidance and the true religion
that He may make it prevail over all religions,
and God suffices as witness.

29 مُّحَمَّدٌ رَّسُولُ اللَّهِ ۚ وَالَّذِينَ مَعَهُ أَشِدَّاءُ عَلَى الْكُفَّارِ رُحَمَاءُ بَيْنَهُمْ ۖ تَرَاهُمْ رُكَّعًا سُجَّدًا يَبْتَغُونَ فَضْلًا مِّنَ اللَّهِ وَرِضْوَانًا ۖ سِيمَاهُمْ فِي وُجُوهِهِم مِّنْ أَثَرِ السُّجُودِ ۚ ذَٰلِكَ مَثَلُهُمْ فِي التَّوْرَاةِ ۚ وَمَثَلُهُمْ فِي الْإِنجِيلِ كَزَرْعٍ أَخْرَجَ شَطْأَهُ فَآزَرَهُ فَاسْتَغْلَظَ فَاسْتَوَىٰ عَلَىٰ سُوقِهِ يُعْجِبُ الزُّرَّاعَ

29 Muḥammad, the Apostle of God,
and those who are with him
are hard against the faithless
and merciful amongst themselves.
You see them bowing and prostrating in worship,
seeking God's grace and His pleasure.
Their mark is visible on their faces,
from the effect of prostration.
Such is their description in the Torah
and their description in the Evangel:
like a tillage that sends out its shoots and builds them up,
and they grow stout and settle on their stalks,
impressing the sowers,

so that He may enrage the faithless by them.
God has promised those
of them who have faith and do righteous deeds
forgiveness and a great reward.

49. Apartments[1]
al-Ḥujurāt

In the Name of God,
the All-beneficent, the All-merciful.

1 O you who have faith!
Do not venture ahead of God and His Apostle,
and be wary of God.
God is indeed all-hearing, all-knowing.

2 O you who have faith!
Do not raise your voices above the voice of the Prophet,
and do not speak aloud to him
like you shout to one another,
lest your works should fail
without your being aware.

3 Indeed, those who lower their voices
in the presence of the Apostle of God
—they are the ones
whose hearts God has tested for Godwariness.
For them will be forgiveness and a great reward.

4 Indeed, those who call you from behind the apartments,
most of them do not exercise their reason.

5 Had they been patient until you came out for them,
it would have been better for them,
and God is all-forgiving, all-merciful.

6 O you who have faith!

---
[1] This Madanī *sūrah* takes its name from the word *ḥujurāt* (apartments) in verse 4.

If a vicious character brings you some news, verify it,
    lest you should harm some people out of ignorance,
    and then become regretful for what you have done.

7 Know that the Apostle of God is among you.
Should he comply with you in many matters,
    you would surely suffer.
But God has endeared faith to you
    and made it appealing in your hearts,
and He has made hateful to you
    faithlessness, transgression and disobedience.
It is such who are the right-minded
8 —a grace and blessing from God,
    and God is all-knowing, all-wise.

9 If two groups of the faithful fight one another,
    make peace between them.
But if one party of them aggresses against the other,
    fight the one which aggresses until it returns
    to God's ordinance.
Then, if it returns, make peace between them fairly,
    and do justice.
God indeed loves the just.

10 The faithful are indeed brothers.
    Therefore, make peace between your brothers
and be wary of God, so that you may receive His mercy.

11 O you who have faith!
Let not any people ridicule another people:
    it may be that they are better than they are;
nor let women ridicule women:
    it may be that they are better than they are.
And do not defame one another,

وَلَا تَنَابَزُوا بِالْأَلْقَابِ ۖ nor insult one another by calling nicknames.
بِئْسَ الِاسْمُ الْفُسُوقُ بَعْدَ الْإِيمَانِ ۚ How evil are profane names subsequent to faith!
وَمَن لَّمْ يَتُبْ As for those who are not penitent of their past conduct
فَأُولَٰئِكَ هُمُ الظَّالِمُونَ ۝ —they are the wrongdoers.

يَا أَيُّهَا الَّذِينَ آمَنُوا 12 O you who have faith!
اجْتَنِبُوا كَثِيرًا مِنَ الظَّنِّ Avoid much suspicion.
إِنَّ بَعْضَ الظَّنِّ إِثْمٌ ۖ Some suspicions are indeed sins.
وَلَا تَجَسَّسُوا وَلَا يَغْتَب بَّعْضُكُم بَعْضًا ۚ And do not spy on or backbite one another.
أَيُحِبُّ أَحَدُكُمْ أَن يَأْكُلَ لَحْمَ أَخِيهِ مَيْتًا Will any of you love to eat the flesh of his dead brother?
فَكَرِهْتُمُوهُ ۚ You would hate it.
وَاتَّقُوا اللَّهَ ۚ إِنَّ اللَّهَ تَوَّابٌ رَّحِيمٌ ۝ Be wary of God; God is indeed all-clement, all-merciful.

يَا أَيُّهَا النَّاسُ 13 O mankind!
إِنَّا خَلَقْنَاكُم مِّن ذَكَرٍ وَأُنثَىٰ Indeed, We created you from a male and a female
وَجَعَلْنَاكُمْ شُعُوبًا وَقَبَائِلَ and made you nations and tribes
لِتَعَارَفُوا ۚ that you may be well acquainted with one another.[1]
إِنَّ أَكْرَمَكُمْ عِندَ اللَّهِ The noblest[2] of you in the sight of God is indeed
أَتْقَاكُمْ ۚ the one most Godwary among you.
إِنَّ اللَّهَ عَلِيمٌ خَبِيرٌ ۝ God is indeed all-knowing, all-aware.

قَالَتِ الْأَعْرَابُ آمَنَّا ۖ 14 The Bedouins say, 'We have faith.'
قُل لَّمْ تُؤْمِنُوا Say, 'You do not have faith yet;
وَلَٰكِن قُولُوا أَسْلَمْنَا rather say, "We have embraced Islam,"[3]
وَلَمَّا يَدْخُلِ الْإِيمَانُ فِي قُلُوبِكُمْ ۖ for faith has not yet entered into your hearts.
وَإِن تُطِيعُوا اللَّهَ وَرَسُولَهُ Yet if you obey God and His Apostle,
لَا يَلِتْكُم مِّنْ أَعْمَالِكُمْ شَيْئًا ۚ He will not stint anything of the reward of your works.
إِنَّ اللَّهَ غَفُورٌ رَّحِيمٌ ۝ God is indeed all-forgiving, all-merciful.'

إِنَّمَا الْمُؤْمِنُونَ الَّذِينَ آمَنُوا 15 The faithful are only those who have attained faith
بِاللَّهِ وَرَسُولِهِ in God and His Apostle
ثُمَّ لَمْ يَرْتَابُوا and then have never doubted,

---

[1] That is, by virtue of the ties of filiation, kinship, cognation and ancestry.
[2] Or 'the most honoured.'
[3] Or 'We have submitted.'

and who wage *jihād* with their possessions and persons
in the way of God.
It is they who are the truthful.[1]

16 Say, 'Will you inform God about your faith
while God knows whatever there is in the heavens
and whatever there is in the earth,
and God has knowledge of all things?'

17 They count it as a favour to you
that they have embraced Islam.
Say, 'Do not count your embracing of Islam as a favour to me.
Rather, it is God who has done you a favour
in that He has guided you to faith,
if you are truthful.[2]

18 God indeed knows
the Unseen of the heavens and the earth,
and God watches what you do.'

50. QAF[3]
Qāf

In the Name of God,
the All-beneficent, the All-merciful.

1 *Qāf*. By the glorious Qur'ān.
2 They consider it indeed odd
that a warner should have come to them
from among themselves.
So the faithless say,
'This is an odd thing.
3 What! When we are dead

---

[1] Or 'the sincere.'
[2] That is, if you are sincere in your claim of having embraced Islam.
[3] This Makkī *sūrah* takes its name from the letter *qāf* in verse 1.

and have become dust [shall we be raised again]?
That is a far-fetched return!'

4 We know what the earth diminishes from them,[1]
and with Us is a preserving Book.

5 They indeed denied the truth when it came to them;
so they are now in a perplexed state of affairs.

6 Have they not then considered the heaven above them,
how We have built it and adorned it,
and that there are no cracks in it?

7 And We spread out the earth,
and cast in it firm mountains,
and caused every delightful kind of plant to grow in it.

8 In this there is an insight and admonition
for every penitent servant.

9 We send down from the sky salubrious water,
with which We grow gardens
and the grain which is harvested,

10 and tall date palms with regularly arranged blossoms,

11 as a provision for Our servants;
and with it We revive a dead country.
Likewise will be the rising from the dead.

12 The people of Noah denied before them,
and so did the inhabitants of Rass[2] and Thamūd,

13 and 'Ād, Pharaoh and the compatriots of Lot,

14 and the inhabitants of Aykah and the people of Tubba'.[3]
Each of them impugned the apostles
and so My threat became due against them.

---

[1] That is, from their bodies when they disintegrate after death.
[2] See **25:38**.
[3] Cf. **44:37**.

أَفَعَيِينَا بِالْخَلْقِ الْأَوَّلِ	15 Have We been exhausted by the first creation?
بَلْ هُمْ فِي لَبْسٍ مِنْ خَلْقٍ جَدِيدٍ ۝	No, they are in doubt about a new creation.
وَلَقَدْ خَلَقْنَا الْإِنْسَانَ	16 Certainly We have created the human being
وَنَعْلَمُ مَا تُوَسْوِسُ بِهِ نَفْسُهُ	and We know to what his soul tempts him,
وَنَحْنُ أَقْرَبُ إِلَيْهِ مِنْ حَبْلِ الْوَرِيدِ ۝	and We are nearer to him than his jugular vein.
إِذْ يَتَلَقَّى الْمُتَلَقِّيَانِ	17 When the twin recorders record his deeds,
عَنِ الْيَمِينِ وَعَنِ الشِّمَالِ قَعِيدٌ ۝	seated on the right hand and on the left:
مَا يَلْفِظُ مِنْ قَوْلٍ	18 he says no word
إِلَّا لَدَيْهِ رَقِيبٌ عَتِيدٌ ۝	but that there is a ready observer beside him.
وَجَاءَتْ سَكْرَةُ الْمَوْتِ بِالْحَقِّ	19 The throes of death bring the truth:[1]
ذَلِكَ مَا كُنْتَ مِنْهُ تَحِيدُ ۝	'This is what you used to shun!'
وَنُفِخَ فِي الصُّورِ ذَلِكَ يَوْمُ الْوَعِيدِ ۝	20 And the Trumpet will be blown: 'This is the promised day.'
وَجَاءَتْ كُلُّ نَفْسٍ	21 Every soul will come
مَعَهَا سَائِقٌ وَشَهِيدٌ ۝	accompanied by two angels, a driver and a witness:
لَقَدْ كُنْتَ فِي غَفْلَةٍ مِنْ هَذَا	22 [It will be told,] 'You were certainly oblivious of this!
فَكَشَفْنَا عَنْكَ غِطَاءَكَ	We have removed your veil from you,
فَبَصَرُكَ الْيَوْمَ حَدِيدٌ ۝	so today your eyesight is acute.'
وَقَالَ قَرِينُهُ	23 Then his companion angel will say,
هَذَا مَا لَدَيَّ عَتِيدٌ ۝	'This is what is ready with me [of his record of deeds].'
أَلْقِيَا فِي جَهَنَّمَ كُلَّ كَفَّارٍ عَنِيدٍ ۝	24 'The two of you cast every stubborn ingrate into hell,
مَنَّاعٍ لِلْخَيْرِ مُعْتَدٍ مُرِيبٍ ۝	25 every hinderer of good,[2] transgressor and skeptic,
الَّذِي جَعَلَ مَعَ اللَّهِ إِلَهًا آخَرَ	26 who had set up another god along with God,
فَأَلْقِيَاهُ فِي الْعَذَابِ الشَّدِيدِ ۝	and cast him into the severe punishment.'
قَالَ قَرِينُهُ	27 His companion[3] will say,
رَبَّنَا مَا أَطْغَيْتُهُ	'Our Lord! I did not incite him to rebel,
وَلَكِنْ كَانَ فِي ضَلَالٍ بَعِيدٍ ۝	but he was himself in extreme error.'
قَالَ لَا تَخْتَصِمُوا لَدَيَّ	28 He will say, 'Do not wrangle in My presence,
وَقَدْ قَدَّمْتُ إِلَيْكُمْ بِالْوَعِيدِ ۝	for I had already warned you in advance.

---

[1] Or 'The throes/swoons of death arrive with the truth.'
[2] Or 'grudging giver.'
[3] That is, Satan.

29 مَا يُبَدَّلُ الْقَوْلُ لَدَيَّ The word of judgement is unalterable with Me,
وَمَا أَنَا بِظَلَّامٍ لِّلْعَبِيدِ ۝ and I am not tyrannical to My servants.'

30 يَوْمَ نَقُولُ لِجَهَنَّمَ هَلِ امْتَلَأْتِ The day when We shall say to hell, 'Are you full?'
وَتَقُولُ هَلْ مِن مَّزِيدٍ ۝ It will say, 'Is there any more?'

31 وَأُزْلِفَتِ الْجَنَّةُ لِلْمُتَّقِينَ And paradise will be brought near for the Godwary,
غَيْرَ بَعِيدٍ ۝ it will not be distant any more:

32 هَٰذَا مَا تُوعَدُونَ 'This is what you were promised.
لِكُلِّ أَوَّابٍ حَفِيظٍ ۝ It is for every penitent and dutiful servant

33 مَّنْ خَشِيَ الرَّحْمَٰنَ بِالْغَيْبِ who fears the All-beneficent in secret
وَجَاءَ بِقَلْبٍ مُّنِيبٍ ۝ and comes with a penitent heart.

34 ادْخُلُوهَا بِسَلَامٍ ۖ ذَٰلِكَ يَوْمُ الْخُلُودِ ۝ Enter it in peace! This is the day of immortality.'

35 لَهُم مَّا يَشَاءُونَ فِيهَا There they will have whatever they wish,
وَلَدَيْنَا مَزِيدٌ ۝ and with Us there is yet more.

36 وَكَمْ أَهْلَكْنَا قَبْلَهُم مِّن قَرْنٍ How many generations We have destroyed before them,
هُمْ أَشَدُّ مِنْهُم بَطْشًا who were stronger than these,
فَنَقَّبُوا فِي الْبِلَادِ insomuch that they ransacked the towns?!
هَلْ مِن مَّحِيصٍ ۝ Is there any escape [from God's punishment]?

37 إِنَّ فِي ذَٰلِكَ لَذِكْرَىٰ There is indeed an admonition in that
لِمَن كَانَ لَهُ قَلْبٌ for one who has a heart,
أَوْ أَلْقَى السَّمْعَ وَهُوَ شَهِيدٌ ۝ or gives ear, being attentive.

38 وَلَقَدْ خَلَقْنَا السَّمَاوَاتِ وَالْأَرْضَ Certainly We created the heavens and the earth,
وَمَا بَيْنَهُمَا فِي سِتَّةِ أَيَّامٍ and whatever is between them, in six days,
وَمَا مَسَّنَا مِن لُّغُوبٍ ۝ and any fatigue did not touch Us.

39 فَاصْبِرْ عَلَىٰ مَا يَقُولُونَ So *be patient* at what they say
وَسَبِّحْ بِحَمْدِ رَبِّكَ and *celebrate* the praise of *your* Lord
قَبْلَ طُلُوعِ الشَّمْسِ وَقَبْلَ الْغُرُوبِ ۝ before the rising of the sun and before the sunset,

40 وَمِنَ اللَّيْلِ فَسَبِّحْهُ and *glorify* Him through part of the night
وَأَدْبَارَ السُّجُودِ ۝ and after the prostrations.

41 وَاسْتَمِعْ يَوْمَ And *be on the alert* for the day

يُنَادِ الْمُنَادِ مِنْ مَكَانٍ قَرِيبٍ ۝ when the caller calls from a close quarter,
يَوْمَ يَسْمَعُونَ الصَّيْحَةَ بِالْحَقِّ ۚ 42 the day when they hear the Cry in all truth.
ذَٰلِكَ يَوْمُ الْخُرُوجِ ۝ That is the day of rising from the dead.
إِنَّا نَحْنُ نُحْيِي وَنُمِيتُ 43 It is indeed We who give life and bring death,
وَإِلَيْنَا الْمَصِيرُ ۝ and toward Us is the final destination.
يَوْمَ تَشَقَّقُ الْأَرْضُ عَنْهُمْ 44 The day the earth is split open for disentombing them,
سِرَاعًا ۚ they will come out hastening.
ذَٰلِكَ حَشْرٌ عَلَيْنَا يَسِيرٌ ۝ That gathering[1] is easy for Us to carry out.
نَحْنُ أَعْلَمُ بِمَا يَقُولُونَ ۖ 45 We know well what they say,
وَمَا أَنْتَ عَلَيْهِمْ بِجَبَّارٍ ۖ and *you* are not there to compel them.
فَذَكِّرْ بِالْقُرْآنِ مَنْ يَخَافُ وَعِيدِ ۝ So *admonish* by the Qur'ān him who fears My threat.

51. THE SCATTERERS[2]
al-Dhāriyāt

بِسْمِ اللَّهِ
الرَّحْمَٰنِ الرَّحِيمِ

In the Name of God,
the All-beneficent, the All-merciful.

وَالذَّارِيَاتِ ذَرْوًا ۝ 1 By the scattering winds that disperse the clouds;
فَالْحَامِلَاتِ وِقْرًا ۝ 2 by the rain bearing clouds laden with water;
فَالْجَارِيَاتِ يُسْرًا ۝ 3 by the ships which move gently on the sea;
فَالْمُقَسِّمَاتِ أَمْرًا ۝ 4 by the angels who dispense livelihood by His command:
إِنَّمَا تُوعَدُونَ لَصَادِقٌ ۝ 5 what you are promised is indeed true,
وَإِنَّ الدِّينَ لَوَاقِعٌ ۝ 6 and indeed, the retribution[3] will surely come to pass!
وَالسَّمَاءِ ذَاتِ الْحُبُكِ ۝ 7 By the heaven full of adornment with stars,[4]
إِنَّكُمْ لَفِي قَوْلٍ مُخْتَلِفٍ ۝ 8 you are indeed of different opinions!
يُؤْفَكُ عَنْهُ 9 He is turned away from it[5]
مَنْ أُفِكَ ۝ who has been turned away from the truth.
قُتِلَ الْخَرَّاصُونَ ۝ 10 Perish the liars,

---

[1] Or 'resurrection.'
[2] A Makkī *sūrah*, it is named after 'the scatterers' (*dhāriyāt*) mentioned in verse 1.
[3] Or 'judgement.'
[4] Or, 'By the heaven full of tracks' (or pathways).
[5] That is, from the Qur'ān. Or 'from him,' that is, from the Apostle of God.

11 الَّذِينَ هُمْ فِي غَمْرَةٍ سَاهُونَ ۝ who are heedless in a stupor!

12 يَسْأَلُونَ أَيَّانَ يَوْمُ الدِّينِ ۝ They ask, 'When will be the Day of Retribution?'

13 يَوْمَ هُمْ عَلَى النَّارِ يُفْتَنُونَ ۝ It is the day when they will be tormented in the Fire,

14 ذُوقُوا فِتْنَتَكُمْ [and told]: 'Taste your torment.

هَذَا الَّذِي كُنْتُمْ بِهِ تَسْتَعْجِلُونَ ۝ This is what you used to hasten.'

15 إِنَّ الْمُتَّقِينَ فِي جَنَّاتٍ وَعُيُونٍ ۝ Indeed, the Godwary will be amid gardens and springs,

16 آخِذِينَ مَا آتَاهُمْ رَبُّهُمْ receiving what their Lord has given them,

إِنَّهُمْ كَانُوا قَبْلَ ذَلِكَ مُحْسِنِينَ ۝ for they had been virtuous hitherto.

17 كَانُوا قَلِيلًا مِنَ اللَّيْلِ مَا يَهْجَعُونَ ۝ They used to sleep a little during the night,

18 وَبِالْأَسْحَارِ هُمْ يَسْتَغْفِرُونَ ۝ and at dawns they would plead for forgiveness,

19 وَفِي أَمْوَالِهِمْ حَقٌّ and there was a share in their wealth

لِلسَّائِلِ وَالْمَحْرُومِ ۝ for the beggar and the deprived.

20 وَفِي الْأَرْضِ آيَاتٌ لِلْمُوقِنِينَ ۝ In the earth are signs for those who have conviction,

21 وَفِي أَنْفُسِكُمْ and in your souls as well.

أَفَلَا تُبْصِرُونَ ۝ Will you not then perceive?

22 وَفِي السَّمَاءِ رِزْقُكُمْ And in the heaven is your provision

وَمَا تُوعَدُونَ ۝ and what you are promised.

23 فَوَرَبِّ السَّمَاءِ وَالْأَرْضِ By the Lord of the heaven and the earth,

إِنَّهُ لَحَقٌّ مِثْلَ مَا أَنَّكُمْ تَنْطِقُونَ ۝ it is indeed the truth, just as it is a fact that you speak.

24 هَلْ أَتَاكَ حَدِيثُ Did you receive the story of

ضَيْفِ إِبْرَاهِيمَ الْمُكْرَمِينَ ۝ Abraham's honoured guests?

25 إِذْ دَخَلُوا عَلَيْهِ فَقَالُوا سَلَامًا When they entered into his presence they said, 'Peace!'

قَالَ سَلَامٌ قَوْمٌ مُنْكَرُونَ ۝ 'Peace!' He answered, 'You are an unfamiliar folk.'[1]

26 فَرَاغَ إِلَى أَهْلِهِ Then he retired to his family

فَجَاءَ بِعِجْلٍ سَمِينٍ ۝ and brought a fat roasted calf

27 فَقَرَّبَهُ إِلَيْهِمْ and put it near them.

قَالَ أَلَا تَأْكُلُونَ ۝ He said, 'Will you not eat?'

28 فَأَوْجَسَ مِنْهُمْ خِيفَةً Then he felt a fear of them.

قَالُوا لَا تَخَفْ They said, 'Do not be afraid!'

---

[1] Cf. **15**:62.

	and they gave him the good news of a wise son.[1]	وَبَشَّرُوهُ بِغُلَامٍ عَلِيمٍ ۝
29	Then his wife came forward crying with joy.	فَأَقْبَلَتِ امْرَأَتُهُ فِي صَرَّةٍ
	She beat her face and said,	فَصَكَّتْ وَجْهَهَا وَقَالَتْ
	'A barren old woman!'	عَجُوزٌ عَقِيمٌ ۝
30	They said, 'So has your Lord said.	قَالُوا كَذَٰلِكِ قَالَ رَبُّكِ
	Indeed, He is the All-wise, the All-knowing.'	إِنَّهُ هُوَ الْحَكِيمُ الْعَلِيمُ ۝

[PART 27]

31	He said, 'O messengers, what is now your errand?'	قَالَ فَمَا خَطْبُكُمْ أَيُّهَا الْمُرْسَلُونَ ۝
32	They said, 'We have been sent toward a guilty people	قَالُوا إِنَّا أُرْسِلْنَا إِلَىٰ قَوْمٍ مُجْرِمِينَ ۝
33	that We may rain upon them stones of clay,	لِنُرْسِلَ عَلَيْهِمْ حِجَارَةً مِنْ طِينٍ ۝
34	sent for the transgressors from your Lord.	مُسَوَّمَةً عِنْدَ رَبِّكَ لِلْمُسْرِفِينَ ۝
35	So We picked out those who were faithful in it,	فَأَخْرَجْنَا مَنْ كَانَ فِيهَا مِنَ الْمُؤْمِنِينَ ۝
36	but did not find there	فَمَا وَجَدْنَا فِيهَا
	other than one house of *muslims*,	غَيْرَ بَيْتٍ مِنَ الْمُسْلِمِينَ ۝
37	and We have left therein a sign	وَتَرَكْنَا فِيهَا آيَةً
	for those who fear a painful punishment.'	لِلَّذِينَ يَخَافُونَ الْعَذَابَ الْأَلِيمَ ۝
38	And in Moses, [too, there is a sign]	وَفِي مُوسَىٰ
	when We sent him to Pharaoh with a manifest authority.	إِذْ أَرْسَلْنَاهُ إِلَىٰ فِرْعَوْنَ بِسُلْطَانٍ مُبِينٍ ۝
39	But he turned away assured of his might,	فَتَوَلَّىٰ بِرُكْنِهِ
	and said, 'A magician, or a crazy man!'	وَقَالَ سَاحِرٌ أَوْ مَجْنُونٌ ۝
40	So We seized him and his hosts	فَأَخَذْنَاهُ وَجُنُودَهُ
	and cast them into the sea,	فَنَبَذْنَاهُمْ فِي الْيَمِّ
	while he was blameworthy.	وَهُوَ مُلِيمٌ ۝
41	And in 'Ād when We unleashed upon them	وَفِي عَادٍ إِذْ أَرْسَلْنَا عَلَيْهِمُ
	a barren wind.	الرِّيحَ الْعَقِيمَ ۝
42	It left nothing that it came upon	مَا تَذَرُ مِنْ شَيْءٍ أَتَتْ عَلَيْهِ
	without making it like decayed bones.	إِلَّا جَعَلَتْهُ كَالرَّمِيمِ ۝
43	And in Thamūd, when they were told,	وَفِي ثَمُودَ إِذْ قِيلَ لَهُمْ
	'Enjoy for a while.'	تَمَتَّعُوا حَتَّىٰ حِينٍ ۝

---

[1] See 11:69–73 and 15:51–60 for parallel descriptions of the episode of Abraham's guests.

44 Then they defied the command of their Lord,
     so the thunderbolt seized them as they looked on.
45 So they were neither able to rise up,
     nor to come to one another's aid.[1]
46 And the people of Noah formerly.
     They were indeed a transgressing lot.

47 We have built the heaven with might,
     and We are indeed its expanders.[2]
48 We have spread out the earth
     and how excellent spreaders We have been!
49 In all things We have created pairs
     so that you may take admonition.
50 [Say,] 'So flee toward God.
     I am indeed a manifest warner from Him to you.
51 Do not set up another god besides God.
     I am indeed a manifest warner from Him to you.'
52 So it was, that there did not come
     to those who were before them any apostle,
     but they said, 'A magician,' or 'A crazy man!'
53 Did they enjoin this upon one another?!
     Rather they were a rebellious lot.
54 So *turn away* from them,
     as you will not be blameworthy.
55 And *admonish*,
     for admonition indeed benefits the faithful.
56 I did not create the jinn and the humans
     except that they may worship Me.
57 I desire no provision from them,

---

[1] Or 'nor to guard themselves (from the punishment).'
[2] Or 'indeed We are expanding it.'

وَمَا أُرِيدُ أَن يُطْعِمُونِ ۝ nor do I desire that they should feed Me.

58 إِنَّ اللَّهَ هُوَ الرَّزَّاقُ It is God who is indeed the all-provider,
ذُو الْقُوَّةِ الْمَتِينُ ۝ powerful and all-strong.

59 فَإِنَّ لِلَّذِينَ ظَلَمُوا ذَنُوبًا The lot of those who do wrong now will indeed
مِثْلَ ذَنُوبِ أَصْحَابِهِمْ be like the lot of their earlier counterparts.
فَلَا يَسْتَعْجِلُونِ ۝ So let them not ask Me to hasten on that fate.

60 فَوَيْلٌ لِّلَّذِينَ كَفَرُوا Woe to the faithless
مِنْ يَوْمِهِمُ الَّذِي يُوعَدُونَ ۝ for the day they are promised!

52. THE MOUNT[1]
al-Ṭūr

In the Name of God,
the All-beneficent, the All-merciful.

1 وَالطُّورِ ۝ By the Mount [Sinai],
2 وَكِتَابٍ مَّسْطُورٍ ۝ by the Book inscribed
3 فِي رَقٍّ مَّنشُورٍ ۝ on an unrolled parchment,
4 وَالْبَيْتِ الْمَعْمُورِ ۝ by the House greatly frequented,[2]
5 وَالسَّقْفِ الْمَرْفُوعِ ۝ by the vault raised high,
6 وَالْبَحْرِ الْمَسْجُورِ ۝ by the surging sea:[3]
7 إِنَّ عَذَابَ رَبِّكَ لَوَاقِعٌ ۝ indeed your Lord's punishment will surely befall.
8 مَّا لَهُ مِن دَافِعٍ ۝ There is none who can avert it.
9 يَوْمَ تَمُورُ السَّمَاءُ مَوْرًا ۝ On the day when the heaven whirls violently
10 وَتَسِيرُ الْجِبَالُ سَيْرًا ۝ and the mountains move with an awful motion:
11 فَوَيْلٌ يَوْمَئِذٍ لِّلْمُكَذِّبِينَ ۝ woe to the deniers on that day
12 الَّذِينَ هُمْ فِي خَوْضٍ يَلْعَبُونَ ۝ —those who play around in vain talk,
13 يَوْمَ the day when
يُدَعُّونَ إِلَىٰ نَارِ جَهَنَّمَ دَعًّا ۝ they will be shoved forcibly toward the fire of hell
14 هَٰذِهِ النَّارُ الَّتِي [and told:] 'This is the Fire

---

[1] This Makkī *sūrah* takes its name from "the mount" (*ṭūr*) mentioned in verse 1.
[2] The Holy Kaʿbah, or its counterpart in the fourth (or the seventh) heaven, frequented by the angels.
[3] Or 'the sea set afire.'

which you used to deny!'

15 Is this, then, also magic,
or is it you who do not perceive?

16 'Enter it,
and whether you are patient or impatient
it will be the same for you.
You are only being requited for what you used to do.'

17 The Godwary will indeed be amid gardens and bliss,

18 rejoicing because of what their Lord has given them
and that their Lord has saved them
from the punishment of hell.

19 [They will be told:] 'Enjoy your food and drink
as a reward for what you used to do.'

20 They will be reclining on arrayed couches,
and We will wed them to big-eyed houris.

21 The faithful
and their descendants who followed them in faith
—We will make their descendants join them
and We will not stint anything from their deeds.
Every person is hostage to what he has earned.

22 We will provide them with fruits and meat,
such as they desire.

23 There they will pass from hand to hand a cup
wherein there will be neither any vain talk
nor sinful speech.

24 They will be waited upon by their youths,
as if they were guarded pearls.

25 They will turn to one another,
questioning each other.

26 They will say, 'Indeed, formerly, we used to be

                           apprehensive about our families.

27 But God showed us favour and He saved us
       from the punishment of the [infernal] miasma.

28 We used to supplicate Him in anticipation.
       Indeed, He is the All-benign, the All-merciful.'

29 So *admonish*.
       By your Lord's blessing, you are not
          a soothsayer, nor mad.

30 Do they say, 'He is a poet,
       for whom we await a fatal accident'?

31 Say, 'Wait! I too am waiting along with you.'

32 Is it their intellects which prompt them to say this,
       or are they a rebellious lot?

33 Do they say, 'He has improvised it himself?'
       Rather they have no faith!

34 Let them bring a discourse like it, if they are truthful.

35 Were they created from nothing?
       Or are they their own creators?

36 Did they create the heavens and the earth?
       Rather they have no certainty!

37 Do they possess the treasuries of *your* Lord?
       Or do they control them?

38 Do they have a ladder [leading up to the heaven]
       whereby they eavesdrop?[1]
       If so, let their eavesdropper produce a manifest authority.

39 Does He have daughters while you have sons?[2]

40 Do you ask them for a reward,
       so that they are wary of being weighed down with debt?

41 Do they have access to the Unseen,

---

[1] That is, on the conversation of the angels.
[2] Cf. **4**:117; **16**:57-59; **17**:40; **37**:149-154; **43**:16-19; **53**:21-23, 27.

42 Do they seek to outmaneuver God?
But it is the faithless who are the outmaneuvered ones!

43 Do they have any god other than God?
Clear is God of any partners that they ascribe to Him!

44 Were they to see a fragment falling from the sky,
they would say, 'A cumulous cloud.'

45 So leave them until they encounter the day
when they will drop down dead;

46 the day when their guile will not avail them in any way,
nor will they be helped.

47 For those who do wrong,
there is indeed a punishment besides that,
but most of them do not know.

48 So *submit patiently* to the judgement of *your* Lord,
for indeed *you* fare before Our eyes.
And *celebrate* the praise of *your* Lord when *you* rise at dawn,

49 and also *glorify* Him during the night
and at the receding of the stars.

53. THE STAR[1]
al-Najm

In the Name of God,
the All-beneficent, the All-merciful.

1 By the star when it sets:[2]

2 your companion[3] has neither gone astray, nor amiss.

3 Nor does he speak out of any base desire:

4 it is just a revelation that is revealed to him,

---

[1] This Makkī *sūrah* takes its name from verse 1, which mentions 'the star' (*najm*).
[2] Or 'falls.'
[3] That is, the Apostle of God.

5 taught him by One of great powers, عَلَّمَهُ شَدِيدُ الْقُوَىٰ ۝
6 possessed of sound judgement.[1] ذُو مِرَّةٍ
He[2] settled,[3] فَاسْتَوَىٰ ۝
7 while he was on the highest horizon. وَهُوَ بِالْأُفُقِ الْأَعْلَىٰ ۝
8 Then he drew nearer and nearer ثُمَّ دَنَا فَتَدَلَّىٰ ۝
9 until he was within two bows' length or even nearer, فَكَانَ قَابَ قَوْسَيْنِ أَوْ أَدْنَىٰ ۝
10 whereat He revealed to His servant whatever He revealed. فَأَوْحَىٰ إِلَىٰ عَبْدِهِ مَا أَوْحَىٰ ۝
11 His heart did not deny what he saw. مَا كَذَبَ الْفُؤَادُ مَا رَأَىٰ ۝
12 Will you then dispute with him about what he saw?! أَفَتُمَارُونَهُ عَلَىٰ مَا يَرَىٰ ۝
13 Certainly he saw it[4] yet another time, وَلَقَدْ رَآهُ نَزْلَةً أُخْرَىٰ ۝
14 by the Lote Tree of the Ultimate Boundary, عِنْدَ سِدْرَةِ الْمُنْتَهَىٰ ۝
15 near which is the Garden of the Abode, عِنْدَهَا جَنَّةُ الْمَأْوَىٰ ۝
16 when there covered the Lote Tree what covered it. إِذْ يَغْشَى السِّدْرَةَ مَا يَغْشَىٰ ۝
17 His gaze did not swerve, nor did it overstep the bounds. مَا زَاغَ الْبَصَرُ وَمَا طَغَىٰ ۝
18 Certainly he saw some of the greatest signs of his Lord. لَقَدْ رَأَىٰ مِنْ آيَاتِ رَبِّهِ الْكُبْرَىٰ ۝

19 Have you considered Lāt and 'Uzzā? أَفَرَأَيْتُمُ اللَّاتَ وَالْعُزَّىٰ ۝
20 and Manāt, the third one? وَمَنَاةَ الثَّالِثَةَ الْأُخْرَىٰ ۝
21 Are you to have males and He females? أَلَكُمُ الذَّكَرُ وَلَهُ الْأُنْثَىٰ ۝
22 That, then, will be an unfair division! تِلْكَ إِذًا قِسْمَةٌ ضِيزَىٰ ۝
23 These are but names which you have coined إِنْ هِيَ إِلَّا أَسْمَاءٌ سَمَّيْتُمُوهَا
—you and your fathers— أَنْتُمْ وَآبَاؤُكُمْ
for which God has not sent down any authority. مَا أَنْزَلَ اللَّهُ بِهَا مِنْ سُلْطَانٍ
They follow nothing but conjectures إِنْ يَتَّبِعُونَ إِلَّا الظَّنَّ
and the desires of the [lower] soul, وَمَا تَهْوَى الْأَنْفُسُ
while there has already come to them وَلَقَدْ جَاءَهُمْ
the guidance from their Lord. مِنْ رَبِّهِمُ الْهُدَىٰ ۝

---

[1] Or 'possessed of strength.'
[2] That is, the Apostle of God (ṣ); or the Angel Gabriel, according to some commentators.
[3] Or 'stood upright.'
[4] Or 'them.' To explain, the object of the pronoun *hū* is specified in verse 18, 'Certainly he saw some of the greatest signs of his Lord.' This interpretation is also supported by a tradition of Imam 'Ali b. Mūsā al-Riḍā ('a) cited in the *Uṣūl al-Kāfī*, vol. 1, p. 95, ḥadīth 2.

24 أَمْ لِلْإِنسَانِ مَا تَمَنَّىٰ ۝

24 Shall the human being have whatever he yearns for?

25 فَلِلَّهِ الْآخِرَةُ وَالْأُولَىٰ ۝

25 Yet to God belong this world and the Hereafter.

26 وَكَم مِّن مَّلَكٍ فِي السَّمَاوَاتِ لَا تُغْنِي شَفَاعَتُهُمْ شَيْئًا إِلَّا مِن بَعْدِ أَن يَأْذَنَ اللَّهُ لِمَن يَشَاءُ وَيَرْضَىٰ ۝

26 How many an angel there is in the heavens
    whose intercession is not of any avail,
    except after God permits
    whomever He wishes and approves of!

27 إِنَّ الَّذِينَ لَا يُؤْمِنُونَ بِالْآخِرَةِ لَيُسَمُّونَ الْمَلَائِكَةَ تَسْمِيَةَ الْأُنثَىٰ ۝

27 Indeed, those who do not believe in the Hereafter
    give female names to the angels.

28 وَمَا لَهُم بِهِ مِنْ عِلْمٍ ۖ إِن يَتَّبِعُونَ إِلَّا الظَّنَّ ۖ وَإِنَّ الظَّنَّ لَا يُغْنِي مِنَ الْحَقِّ شَيْئًا ۝

28 They do not have any knowledge of that.
    They follow nothing but conjectures,
    and conjecture is no substitute for the truth.

29 فَأَعْرِضْ عَن مَّن تَوَلَّىٰ عَن ذِكْرِنَا وَلَمْ يُرِدْ إِلَّا الْحَيَاةَ الدُّنْيَا ۝

29 So *disregard* those who turn away from Our remembrance
    and desire nothing but the life of the world.

30 ذَٰلِكَ مَبْلَغُهُم مِّنَ الْعِلْمِ ۚ إِنَّ رَبَّكَ هُوَ أَعْلَمُ بِمَن ضَلَّ عَن سَبِيلِهِ وَهُوَ أَعْلَمُ بِمَنِ اهْتَدَىٰ ۝

30 That is the ultimate reach of their knowledge.
    Indeed, your Lord knows best
    those who stray from His way,
    and He knows best those who are rightly guided.

31 وَلِلَّهِ مَا فِي السَّمَاوَاتِ وَمَا فِي الْأَرْضِ لِيَجْزِيَ الَّذِينَ أَسَاءُوا بِمَا عَمِلُوا وَيَجْزِيَ الَّذِينَ أَحْسَنُوا بِالْحُسْنَى ۝

31 To God belongs whatever is in the heavens
    and whatever is in the earth,
    that He may requite those who do evil
    for what they have done,
    and reward those who do good with the best of rewards.

32 الَّذِينَ يَجْتَنِبُونَ كَبَائِرَ الْإِثْمِ وَالْفَوَاحِشَ إِلَّا اللَّمَمَ ۚ إِنَّ رَبَّكَ وَاسِعُ الْمَغْفِرَةِ ۚ هُوَ أَعْلَمُ بِكُمْ إِذْ أَنشَأَكُم مِّنَ الْأَرْضِ وَإِذْ أَنتُمْ أَجِنَّةٌ فِي بُطُونِ أُمَّهَاتِكُمْ ۖ فَلَا تُزَكُّوا أَنفُسَكُمْ ۖ

32 Those who avoid major sins and indecencies,
    apart from minor and occasional lapses.
    Your Lord is indeed expansive in His forgiveness.
    He knows you best
    since the time He produced you from the earth,
    and since you were fetuses in the bellies of your mothers.
    So do not flaunt your piety:

He knows best those who are Godwary.

33 Did you see him who turned away,
34 gave a little and held off?
35 Does he have the knowledge of the Unseen, so that he sees?
36 Has he not been informed of what is in the scriptures of Moses,
37 and of Abraham, who fulfilled his summons:
38 that no bearer shall bear another's burden,
39 that nothing belongs to man except what he strives for,
40 and that he will soon be shown his endeavour,
41 then he will be requited for it with the fullest requital;
42 that the terminus is toward your Lord,
43 that it is He who makes men laugh and weep,
44 that it is He who brings death and gives life,
45 that it is He who created the mates,[1] the male and the female,
46 from a drop of seminal fluid when emitted;
47 that with Him lies the second genesis,
48 that it is He who enriches and grants possessions,
49 that it is He who is the Lord of Sirius;
50 that it is He who destroyed the former 'Ād,
51 and Thamud, sparing none of them,
52 and the people of Noah before that; indeed they were more unjust and rebellious;
53 and He overthrew the town that was overturned,[2]
54 covering it with what covered it.
55 Then which of the bounties of your Lord will you dispute?
56 This is a warner, in the tradition of the warners of old.

---

[1] Or 'the sexes.'
[2] That is, Sodom. Elsewhere mentioned as plural; see 9:70, 69:9.

57 The Imminent Hour is near at hand.

58 There is none who may unveil it besides God.

59 Do you then wonder at this discourse,

60 and laugh, and not weep,

61 while you remain heedless?!

62 So prostrate yourselves to God and worship Him!

54. THE MOON[1]
al-Qamar

In the Name of God,
the All-beneficent, the All-merciful.

1 The Hour has drawn near and the moon is split.

2 If they see a sign, they turn away
and say, 'An incessant[2] magic!'

3 They denied, and followed their base desires,
and every matter has its denouement appropriate to it.

4 There have already come to them reports
containing admonishment

5 and representing far-reaching wisdom;
but warnings are of no avail!

6 So *turn away* from them!
The day when the Caller calls to a dire thing,

7 with a humbled look in their eyes,
they will emerge from the graves
like scattered locusts,

8 scrambling toward the summoner.
The faithless will say, 'This is a hard day!'

9 The people of Noah impugned before them.
So they impugned Our servant and said,

---

[1] This Makkī *sūrah* is named after verse 1, which mentions the moon (*qamar*).
[2] Or 'powerful.'

مَجْنُونٌ وَٱزْدُجِرَ ۞	'A crazy man,' and he was reviled.[1]
فَدَعَا رَبَّهُ 10	Thereat he invoked his Lord,
أَنِّى مَغْلُوبٌ فَٱنتَصِرْ ۞	[saying,] 'I have been overcome, so help me.'
فَفَتَحْنَآ أَبْوَٰبَ ٱلسَّمَآءِ 11	Then We opened the gates of the heaven
بِمَآءٍ مُّنْهَمِرٍ ۞	with pouring waters
وَفَجَّرْنَا ٱلْأَرْضَ عُيُونًا 12	and We made the ground burst forth with springs,
فَٱلْتَقَى ٱلْمَآءُ عَلَىٰٓ أَمْرٍ قَدْ قُدِرَ ۞	and the waters met for a preordained purpose.
وَحَمَلْنَٰهُ عَلَىٰ ذَاتِ أَلْوَٰحٍ وَدُسُرٍ ۞ 13	We bore him on a vessel made of planks and nails,
تَجْرِى بِأَعْيُنِنَا 14	which sailed [over the flood waters] in Our sight,
جَزَآءً لِّمَن كَانَ كُفِرَ ۞	as a retribution for him who was met with disbelief.
وَلَقَد تَّرَكْنَٰهَآ ءَايَةً 15	Certainly We have left it as a sign;
فَهَلْ مِن مُّدَّكِرٍ ۞	so is there anyone who will be admonished?
فَكَيْفَ كَانَ عَذَابِى وَنُذُرِ ۞ 16	So how were My punishment and warnings?
وَلَقَدْ يَسَّرْنَا ٱلْقُرْءَانَ 17	Certainly We have made the Qur'ān simple
لِلذِّكْرِ	for the sake of admonishment.
فَهَلْ مِن مُّدَّكِرٍ ۞	So is there anyone who will be admonished?
كَذَّبَتْ عَادٌ 18	The people of 'Ād impugned their apostle.
فَكَيْفَ كَانَ عَذَابِى وَنُذُرِ ۞	So how were My punishment and warnings?
إِنَّآ أَرْسَلْنَا عَلَيْهِمْ رِيحًا صَرْصَرًا 19	Indeed, We unleashed upon them an icy gale
فِى يَوْمِ نَحْسٍ مُّسْتَمِرٍّ ۞	on an incessantly ill-fated day,
تَنزِعُ ٱلنَّاسَ 20	knocking down people
كَأَنَّهُمْ أَعْجَازُ نَخْلٍ مُّنقَعِرٍ ۞	like trunks of uprooted palm trees.
فَكَيْفَ كَانَ عَذَابِى وَنُذُرِ ۞ 21	So how were My punishment and warnings?!
وَلَقَدْ يَسَّرْنَا ٱلْقُرْءَانَ 22	Certainly We have made the Qur'ān simple
لِلذِّكْرِ	for the sake of admonishment.
فَهَلْ مِن مُّدَّكِرٍ ۞	So is there anyone who will be admonished?
كَذَّبَتْ ثَمُودُ بِٱلنُّذُرِ ۞ 23	The people of Thamūd denied the warnings,
فَقَالُوٓا۟ 24	and they said,
أَبَشَرًا مِّنَّا وَٰحِدًا نَّتَّبِعُهُۥٓ	'Are we to follow a lone human from ourselves?!

---

[1] Or 'he was proscribed,' or 'he was ostracized.'

إِنَّا إِذًا لَفِى ضَلَالٍ وَسُعُرٍ ۝

Then we would indeed be in error and madness.'

25 أَأُلْقِىَ الذِّكْرُ عَلَيْهِ مِنْ بَيْنِنَا 'Has the Reminder been cast upon him from among us?

بَلْ هُوَ كَذَّابٌ أَشِرٌ ۝ No, he is a self-conceited[1] liar.'

26 سَيَعْلَمُونَ غَدًا مَنِ الْكَذَّابُ الْأَشِرُ ۝ 'Tomorrow they will know who is a self-conceited liar.

27 إِنَّا مُرْسِلُو النَّاقَةِ فِتْنَةً لَهُمْ We are sending the She-camel as a test for them;

فَارْتَقِبْهُمْ وَاصْطَبِرْ ۝ so watch them and be steadfast.

28 وَنَبِّئْهُمْ أَنَّ الْمَاءَ قِسْمَةٌ بَيْنَهُمْ Inform them that the water is to be shared between them;

كُلُّ شِرْبٍ مُحْتَضَرٌ ۝ each of them showing up at his turn.'

29 فَنَادَوْا صَاحِبَهُمْ But they called their companion,

فَتَعَاطَى فَعَقَرَ ۝ and he took a knife and hamstrung her.

30 فَكَيْفَ كَانَ عَذَابِى وَنُذُرِ ۝ So how were My punishment and warnings?!

31 إِنَّا أَرْسَلْنَا عَلَيْهِمْ صَيْحَةً وَاحِدَةً We sent against them a single Cry,

فَكَانُوا كَهَشِيمِ الْمُحْتَظِرِ ۝ and they became like the dry sticks of a corral builder.

32 وَلَقَدْ يَسَّرْنَا الْقُرْآنَ Certainly We have made the Qur'ān simple

لِلذِّكْرِ for the sake of admonishment.

فَهَلْ مِنْ مُدَّكِرٍ ۝ So is there anyone who will be admonished?

33 كَذَّبَتْ قَوْمُ لُوطٍ بِالنُّذُرِ ۝ And the people of Lot denied the warnings.

34 إِنَّا أَرْسَلْنَا عَلَيْهِمْ حَاصِبًا We unleashed a rain of stones upon them,

إِلَّا آلَ لُوطٍ نَجَّيْنَاهُمْ بِسَحَرٍ ۝ excepting the family of Lot, whom We delivered at dawn

35 نِعْمَةً مِنْ عِنْدِنَا as a blessing from Us.

كَذَلِكَ نَجْزِى مَنْ شَكَرَ ۝ Thus do We reward those who give thanks.

36 وَلَقَدْ أَنْذَرَهُمْ بَطْشَتَنَا He had already warned them of Our punishment,

فَتَمَارَوْا بِالنُّذُرِ ۝ but they disputed the warnings.

37 وَلَقَدْ رَاوَدُوهُ عَنْ ضَيْفِهِ They even solicited of him his guests,

فَطَمَسْنَا أَعْيُنَهُمْ whereat We blotted out their eyes, [saying,]

فَذُوقُوا عَذَابِى وَنُذُرِ ۝ 'Taste My punishment and warnings!'

38 وَلَقَدْ صَبَّحَهُمْ بُكْرَةً Early at dawn there visited them

عَذَابٌ مُسْتَقِرٌّ ۝ an abiding punishment:

39 فَذُوقُوا عَذَابِى وَنُذُرِ ۝ 'Taste My punishment and warnings!'

---

[1] Or 'insolent.'

40 وَلَقَدْ يَسَّرْنَا الْقُرْآنَ لِلذِّكْرِ Certainly We have made the Qur'ān simple for the sake of admonishment.
فَهَلْ مِنْ مُدَّكِرٍ So is there anyone who will be admonished?
41 وَلَقَدْ جَاءَ آلَ فِرْعَوْنَ النُّذُرُ Certainly Our warnings did come to Pharaoh's clan
42 كَذَّبُوا بِآيَاتِنَا كُلِّهَا who denied all of Our signs.
فَأَخَذْنَاهُمْ أَخْذَ عَزِيزٍ مُقْتَدِرٍ So We seized them with the seizing of One all-mighty, Omnipotent.
43 أَكُفَّارُكُمْ خَيْرٌ مِنْ أُولَٰئِكُمْ Are your faithless better than those?
أَمْ لَكُمْ بَرَاءَةٌ فِي الزُّبُرِ Have you some sort of immunity in the scriptures?
44 أَمْ يَقُولُونَ نَحْنُ جَمِيعٌ مُنْتَصِرٌ Do they say, 'We are a confederate league'?
45 سَيُهْزَمُ الْجَمْعُ وَيُوَلُّونَ الدُّبُرَ The league will be routed and turn its back to flee.
46 بَلِ السَّاعَةُ مَوْعِدُهُمْ Indeed, the Hour is their tryst,
وَالسَّاعَةُ أَدْهَىٰ وَأَمَرُّ and the Hour will be most calamitous and bitter.
47 إِنَّ الْمُجْرِمِينَ فِي ضَلَالٍ وَسُعُرٍ The guilty are indeed steeped in error and madness.
48 يَوْمَ يُسْحَبُونَ فِي النَّارِ عَلَىٰ وُجُوهِهِمْ The day when they are dragged into the Fire on their faces,
ذُوقُوا مَسَّ سَقَرَ [it will be said to them,] 'Taste the touch of hell!'
49 إِنَّا كُلَّ شَيْءٍ خَلَقْنَاهُ بِقَدَرٍ Indeed, We have created everything in a measure
50 وَمَا أَمْرُنَا إِلَّا وَاحِدَةٌ and Our command is but a single word,
كَلَمْحٍ بِالْبَصَرِ like the twinkling of an eye.
51 وَلَقَدْ أَهْلَكْنَا أَشْيَاعَكُمْ Certainly We have destroyed your likes.
فَهَلْ مِنْ مُدَّكِرٍ So is there anyone who will be admonished?
52 وَكُلُّ شَيْءٍ فَعَلُوهُ فِي الزُّبُرِ Everything they have done is in the books,
53 وَكُلُّ صَغِيرٍ وَكَبِيرٍ مُسْتَطَرٌ and everything big and small, is committed to writing.
54 إِنَّ الْمُتَّقِينَ فِي جَنَّاتٍ وَنَهَرٍ The Godwary will indeed be amid gardens and streams,
55 فِي مَقْعَدِ صِدْقٍ in the abode of truthfulness[1]
عِنْدَ مَلِيكٍ مُقْتَدِرٍ with an omnipotent King.

---

[1] Or 'in a worthy abode.'

55. The All-Beneficent[1]
al-Raḥmān

In the Name of God,
the All-beneficent, the All-merciful.

1 The All-beneficent
2 has taught the Qur'ān.
3 He created the human being,
4 and taught him articulate speech.
5 The sun and the moon are disposed calculatedly,
6 and the herb and the tree prostrate to God.
7 He raised the heaven high and set up the balance,
8 declaring, 'Do not infringe the balance!
9 Maintain the weights with justice,
and do not shorten the balance!'
10 And the earth—He laid it out for mankind.
11 In it are fruits and date-palms with sheaths,
12 grain with husk, and fragrant herbs.
13 So which of your Lord's bounties will you both[2] deny?
14 He created man out of dry clay,[3] like the potter's,
15 and created the jinn out of a flame of a fire.
16 So which of your Lord's bounties will you both deny?
17 Lord of the two easts and Lord of the two wests![4]
18 So which of your Lord's bounties will you both deny?
19 He merged the two seas,[5] meeting each other.
20 There is a barrier between them
which they do not overstep.

---

[1] This Makkī *sūrah* takes its name from verse 1, which mentions "the All-beneficent" (*al-raḥmān*).
[2] That is, the jinn and humans. The pronoun 'you' and the adjective 'your' are both dual in the Arabic.
[3] Cf. **15:**26, 28, 33.
[4] That is, the points of sunrise and sunset at the winter and summer solstices.
[5] See the footnote at **35:**12.

21 So which of your Lord's bounties will you both deny?

فَبِأَيِّ آلَاءِ رَبِّكُمَا تُكَذِّبَانِ

22 From them emerge the pearl and the coral.

يَخْرُجُ مِنْهُمَا اللُّؤْلُؤُ وَالْمَرْجَانُ

23 So which of your Lord's bounties will you both deny?

24 His are the sailing ships[1] on the sea appearing like landmarks.

وَلَهُ الْجَوَارِ الْمُنْشَآتُ فِي الْبَحْرِ كَالْأَعْلَامِ

25 So which of your Lord's bounties will you both deny?

26 Everyone on it[2] is ephemeral,

كُلُّ مَنْ عَلَيْهَا فَانٍ

27 yet lasting is the Face of your Lord, majestic and munificent.[3]

وَيَبْقَى وَجْهُ رَبِّكَ ذُو الْجَلَالِ وَالْإِكْرَامِ

28 So which of your Lord's bounties will you both deny?

29 Everyone in the heavens and the earth asks Him. Every day He is engaged in some work.

يَسْأَلُهُ مَنْ فِي السَّمَاوَاتِ وَالْأَرْضِ كُلَّ يَوْمٍ هُوَ فِي شَأْنٍ

30 So which of your Lord's bounties will you both deny?

31 Soon We shall make Ourselves unoccupied for you, O you notable two![4]

سَنَفْرُغُ لَكُمْ أَيُّهَ الثَّقَلَانِ

32 So which of your Lord's bounties will you both deny?

33 O community of the jinn and humans! If you can pass through the confines of the heavens and the earth, then do pass through. But you will not pass through except by an authority.

يَا مَعْشَرَ الْجِنِّ وَالْإِنْسِ إِنِ اسْتَطَعْتُمْ أَنْ تَنْفُذُوا مِنْ أَقْطَارِ السَّمَاوَاتِ وَالْأَرْضِ فَانْفُذُوا لَا تَنْفُذُونَ إِلَّا بِسُلْطَانٍ

34 So which of your Lord's bounties will you both deny?

35 There will be unleashed upon you a flash of fire and a smoke; then you will not be able to help one another.

يُرْسَلُ عَلَيْكُمَا شُوَاظٌ مِنْ نَارٍ وَنُحَاسٌ فَلَا تَنْتَصِرَانِ

---

[1] Or 'the watercrafts.'
[2] That is, on the earth.
[3] The adjectives 'majestic' and 'munificent' pertain to the Face.
[4] That is, the jinn and humans, or the Qur'ān and the Prophet's Family, referred to as *'thaqalayn'* in a famous tradition cited in Sunnī and Shīʿī sources.

36 فَبِأَيِّ آلَاءِ رَبِّكُمَا تُكَذِّبَانِ ۝ So which of your Lord's bounties will you both deny?

37 فَإِذَا انْشَقَّتِ السَّمَاءُ When the sky is split open,
فَكَانَتْ وَرْدَةً كَالدِّهَانِ ۝ and turns crimson like tanned leather.

38 فَبِأَيِّ آلَاءِ رَبِّكُمَا تُكَذِّبَانِ ۝ So which of your Lord's bounties will you both deny?

39 فَيَوْمَئِذٍ On that day
لَا يُسْأَلُ عَنْ ذَنْبِهِ إِنْسٌ neither humans will be questioned about their sins,
وَلَا جَانٌّ ۝ nor jinn.[1]

40 فَبِأَيِّ آلَاءِ رَبِّكُمَا تُكَذِّبَانِ ۝ So which of your Lord's bounties will you both deny?

41 يُعْرَفُ الْمُجْرِمُونَ بِسِيمَاهُمْ The guilty will be recognized by their mark;
فَيُؤْخَذُ بِالنَّوَاصِي وَالْأَقْدَامِ ۝ so they will be seized by their forelocks and feet.

42 فَبِأَيِّ آلَاءِ رَبِّكُمَا تُكَذِّبَانِ ۝ So which of your Lord's bounties will you both deny?

43 هَذِهِ جَهَنَّمُ 'This is the hell
الَّتِي يُكَذِّبُ بِهَا الْمُجْرِمُونَ ۝ which the guilty would deny!'

44 يَطُوفُونَ بَيْنَهَا وَبَيْنَ حَمِيمٍ آنٍ ۝ They shall circuit between it and boiling hot water.

45 فَبِأَيِّ آلَاءِ رَبِّكُمَا تُكَذِّبَانِ ۝ So which of your Lord's bounties will you both deny?

46 وَلِمَنْ خَافَ مَقَامَ رَبِّهِ جَنَّتَانِ ۝ For him who stands in awe of his Lord will be two gardens.

47 فَبِأَيِّ آلَاءِ رَبِّكُمَا تُكَذِّبَانِ ۝ So which of your Lord's bounties will you both deny?

48 ذَوَاتَا أَفْنَانٍ ۝ Both abounding in branches.[2]

49 فَبِأَيِّ آلَاءِ رَبِّكُمَا تُكَذِّبَانِ ۝ So which of your Lord's bounties will you both deny?

50 فِيهِمَا عَيْنَانِ تَجْرِيَانِ ۝ In both of them will be two flowing springs.

51 فَبِأَيِّ آلَاءِ رَبِّكُمَا تُكَذِّبَانِ ۝ So which of your Lord's bounties will you both deny?

52 فِيهِمَا مِنْ كُلِّ فَاكِهَةٍ زَوْجَانِ ۝ In both of them will be two kinds of every fruit.

53 فَبِأَيِّ آلَاءِ رَبِّكُمَا تُكَذِّبَانِ ۝ So which of your Lord's bounties will you both deny?

54 مُتَّكِئِينَ عَلَىٰ فُرُشٍ They will be reclining on beds
بَطَائِنُهَا مِنْ إِسْتَبْرَقٍ lined with heavy silk.
وَجَنَى الْجَنَّتَيْنِ دَانٍ ۝ And the fruit of the two gardens will be near at hand.

55 فَبِأَيِّ آلَاءِ رَبِّكُمَا تُكَذِّبَانِ ۝ So which of your Lord's bounties will you both deny?

---

[1] Cf. **28**:78.
[2] Or 'Both full of variety;' that is, of fruits.

56 فِيهِنَّ قَاصِرَاتُ الطَّرْفِ لَمْ يَطْمِثْهُنَّ إِنسٌ قَبْلَهُمْ وَلَا جَانٌّ ۝ In them are maidens of restrained glances, whom no human has touched before, nor jinn.

57 فَبِأَيِّ آلَاءِ رَبِّكُمَا تُكَذِّبَانِ ۝ So which of your Lord's bounties will you both deny?

58 كَأَنَّهُنَّ الْيَاقُوتُ وَالْمَرْجَانُ ۝ As though they were rubies and corals.

59 فَبِأَيِّ آلَاءِ رَبِّكُمَا تُكَذِّبَانِ ۝ So which of your Lord's bounties will you both deny?

60 هَلْ جَزَاءُ الْإِحْسَانِ إِلَّا الْإِحْسَانُ ۝ Is the requital of goodness anything but goodness?

61 فَبِأَيِّ آلَاءِ رَبِّكُمَا تُكَذِّبَانِ ۝ So which of your Lord's bounties will you both deny?

62 وَمِن دُونِهِمَا جَنَّتَانِ ۝ Beside these two, there will be two other gardens.

63 فَبِأَيِّ آلَاءِ رَبِّكُمَا تُكَذِّبَانِ ۝ So which of your Lord's bounties will you both deny?

64 مُدْهَامَّتَانِ ۝ Dark green.

65 فَبِأَيِّ آلَاءِ رَبِّكُمَا تُكَذِّبَانِ ۝ So which of your Lord's bounties will you both deny?

66 فِيهِمَا عَيْنَانِ نَضَّاخَتَانِ ۝ In both of them will be two gushing springs.

67 فَبِأَيِّ آلَاءِ رَبِّكُمَا تُكَذِّبَانِ ۝ So which of your Lord's bounties will you both deny?

68 فِيهِمَا فَاكِهَةٌ وَنَخْلٌ وَرُمَّانٌ ۝ In both of them will be fruits, date-palms and pomegranates.

69 فَبِأَيِّ آلَاءِ رَبِّكُمَا تُكَذِّبَانِ ۝ So which of your Lord's bounties will you both deny?

70 فِيهِنَّ خَيْرَاتٌ حِسَانٌ ۝ In them are maidens good and lovely.

71 فَبِأَيِّ آلَاءِ رَبِّكُمَا تُكَذِّبَانِ ۝ So which of your Lord's bounties will you both deny?

72 حُورٌ مَقْصُورَاتٌ فِي الْخِيَامِ ۝ Houris secluded in pavilions.

73 فَبِأَيِّ آلَاءِ رَبِّكُمَا تُكَذِّبَانِ ۝ So which of your Lord's bounties will you both deny?

74 لَمْ يَطْمِثْهُنَّ إِنسٌ قَبْلَهُمْ وَلَا جَانٌّ ۝ Whom no human has touched before, nor jinn.

75 فَبِأَيِّ آلَاءِ رَبِّكُمَا تُكَذِّبَانِ ۝ So which of your Lord's bounties will you both deny?

76 مُتَّكِئِينَ عَلَىٰ رَفْرَفٍ خُضْرٍ وَعَبْقَرِيٍّ حِسَانٍ ۝ Reclining on green cushions and lovely carpets.

77 فَبِأَيِّ آلَاءِ رَبِّكُمَا تُكَذِّبَانِ ۝ So which of your Lord's bounties will you both deny?

78 تَبَارَكَ اسْمُ رَبِّكَ ذِي الْجَلَالِ وَالْإِكْرَامِ ۝ Blessed is the Name of your Lord, the Majestic and the Munificent!

56. THE IMMINENT HOUR[1]
al-Wāqi'ah

بِسْمِ اللَّهِ الرَّحْمَٰنِ الرَّحِيمِ

In the Name of God,
the All-beneficent, the All-merciful.

1 When the Imminent[2] Hour befalls

2 —there is no denying that it will befall—

3 it will be lowering and exalting.[3]

4 When the earth is shaken violently,

5 and the mountains are shattered into bits

6 and become scattered dust,

7 you will be three groups:

8 The People of the Right Hand
—and what are the People of the Right Hand?

9 And the People of the Left Hand
—and what are the People of the Left Hand?

10 And the Foremost Ones are the foremost ones:[4]

11 they are the ones brought near to God,

12 who will reside in the gardens of bliss.

13 A multitude from the former peoples[5]

14 and a few from the latter ones.

15 On brocaded couches,

16 reclining on them, face to face.

17 They will be waited upon by immortal youths,

18 with goblets and ewers and a cup of a clear wine,[6]

19 which causes them neither headache nor stupefaction,

---

[1] This Makkī sūrah takes its name from verse 1, which mentions al-wāqi'ah (the Imminent Hour, i.e., the Day of Resurrection).
[2] That is, the Day of Resurrection and Judgement.
[3] That is, abasing the faithless and raising the faithful in station.
[4] Cf. 2:148, 5:48, 23:61, 35:32, 57:21.
[5] That is, from the communities of the former prophets.
[6] Or 'flowing wine.'

وَفَاكِهَةٍ مِمَّا يَتَخَيَّرُونَ ۝	20	and such fruits as they prefer
وَلَحْمِ طَيْرٍ مِمَّا يَشْتَهُونَ ۝	21	and such flesh of fowls as they desire,
وَحُورٌ عِينٌ ۝	22	and big-eyed houris
كَأَمْثَالِ اللُّؤْلُؤِ الْمَكْنُونِ ۝	23	like guarded pearls,
جَزَاءً بِمَا كَانُوا يَعْمَلُونَ ۝	24	a reward for what they used to do.
لَا يَسْمَعُونَ فِيهَا لَغْوًا وَلَا تَأْثِيمًا ۝	25	They will not hear therein any vain talk or sinful speech,
إِلَّا قِيلًا سَلَامًا سَلَامًا ۝	26	but only the watchword, 'Peace!' 'Peace!'
وَأَصْحَابُ الْيَمِينِ	27	And the People of the Right Hand
مَا أَصْحَابُ الْيَمِينِ ۝		—what are the People of the Right Hand?!
فِي سِدْرٍ مَخْضُودٍ ۝	28	Amid thornless lote trees
وَطَلْحٍ مَنْضُودٍ ۝	29	and bananas regularly set in clusters,[1]
وَظِلٍّ مَمْدُودٍ ۝	30	and extended shade,[2]
وَمَاءٍ مَسْكُوبٍ ۝	31	and ever-flowing water
وَفَاكِهَةٍ كَثِيرَةٍ ۝	32	and abundant fruits,
لَا مَقْطُوعَةٍ وَلَا مَمْنُوعَةٍ ۝	33	neither inaccessible, nor forbidden,
وَفُرُشٍ مَرْفُوعَةٍ ۝	34	and noble spouses.
إِنَّا أَنْشَأْنَاهُنَّ إِنْشَاءً ۝	35	We have created them with a special creation,
فَجَعَلْنَاهُنَّ أَبْكَارًا ۝	36	and made them virgins,
عُرُبًا أَتْرَابًا ۝	37	loving, of a like age,
لِأَصْحَابِ الْيَمِينِ ۝	38	for the People of the Right Hand.
ثُلَّةٌ مِنَ الْأَوَّلِينَ ۝	39	A multitude from the former peoples
وَثُلَّةٌ مِنَ الْآخِرِينَ ۝	40	and a multitude from the latter ones.
وَأَصْحَابُ الشِّمَالِ	41	And the People of the Left Hand
مَا أَصْحَابُ الشِّمَالِ ۝		—what are the People of the Left Hand?!
فِي سَمُومٍ وَحَمِيمٍ ۝	42	Amid infernal miasma and boiling water
وَظِلٍّ مِنْ يَحْمُومٍ ۝	43	and the shadow of a dense black smoke,
لَا بَارِدٍ وَلَا كَرِيمٍ ۝	44	neither cool nor beneficial.[3]

---

[1] This is according to the reading *wa ṭalḥ'in manḍūd*. According to an alternate reading, *wa ṭal'in manḍūd*, narrated from Imam ʿAlī, Imam Jaʿfar al-Ṣādiq and Ibn ʿAbbās it would mean 'regularly arranged blossoms [in clusters]. (*Muʿjam, al-Kashshāf*)

[2] Or 'twilight;' see the note at **25:45**.

[3] Cf. **77:30-31**.

45 إِنَّهُمْ كَانُوا قَبْلَ ذَٰلِكَ مُتْرَفِينَ ۝ They had indeed been affluent before this,

46 وَكَانُوا يُصِرُّونَ عَلَى الْحِنثِ الْعَظِيمِ ۝ and they used to persist in the great sin.[1]

47 وَكَانُوا يَقُولُونَ And they used to say,

أَئِذَا مِتْنَا وَكُنَّا تُرَابًا وَعِظَامًا 'What! When we are dead and become dust and bones,

أَئِنَّا لَمَبْعُوثُونَ ۝ shall we be resurrected?

48 أَوَآبَاؤُنَا الْأَوَّلُونَ ۝ And our forefathers, too?'

49 قُلْ إِنَّ الْأَوَّلِينَ وَالْآخِرِينَ ۝ Say, 'The former and the latter peoples

50 لَمَجْمُوعُونَ إِلَىٰ مِيقَاتِ يَوْمٍ مَعْلُومٍ ۝ will indeed be gathered for the tryst of a known day.

51 ثُمَّ إِنَّكُمْ أَيُّهَا الضَّالُّونَ الْمُكَذِّبُونَ ۝ Then indeed, you, astray deniers,

52 لَآكِلُونَ مِنْ شَجَرٍ مِنْ زَقُّومٍ ۝ will surely eat from the Zaqqūm tree

53 فَمَالِئُونَ مِنْهَا الْبُطُونَ ۝ and stuff your bellies with it,

54 فَشَارِبُونَ عَلَيْهِ مِنَ الْحَمِيمِ ۝ and drink boiling water on top of it,

55 فَشَارِبُونَ شُرْبَ الْهِيمِ ۝ drinking like thirsty camels.'

56 هَـٰذَا نُزُلُهُمْ Such will be the hospitality they receive

يَوْمَ الدِّينِ ۝ on the Day of Retribution.[2]

57 نَحْنُ خَلَقْنَاكُمْ فَلَوْلَا تُصَدِّقُونَ ۝ We created you. Then why do you not acknowledge it?

58 أَفَرَأَيْتُم مَّا تُمْنُونَ ۝ Have you considered the sperm that you emit?

59 أَأَنتُمْ تَخْلُقُونَهُ أَمْ نَحْنُ الْخَالِقُونَ ۝ Is it you who create it, or are We the creator?

60 نَحْنُ قَدَّرْنَا بَيْنَكُمُ الْمَوْتَ We have ordained death among you,

وَمَا نَحْنُ بِمَسْبُوقِينَ ۝ and We are not to be outmaneuvered

61 عَلَىٰ أَن نُّبَدِّلَ أَمْثَالَكُمْ from replacing you with your likes

وَنُنشِئَكُمْ فِي مَا لَا تَعْلَمُونَ ۝ and recreating you in a realm you do not know.

62 وَلَقَدْ عَلِمْتُمُ النَّشْأَةَ الْأُولَىٰ Certainly you have known the first genesis,

فَلَوْلَا تَذَكَّرُونَ ۝ then why do you not take admonition?

63 أَفَرَأَيْتُم مَّا تَحْرُثُونَ ۝ Have you considered what you sow?

64 أَأَنتُمْ تَزْرَعُونَهُ أَمْ نَحْنُ الزَّارِعُونَ ۝ Is it you who make it grow, or are We the grower?

65 لَوْ نَشَاءُ لَجَعَلْنَاهُ حُطَامًا If We wish, We turn it into chaff,

---

[1] That is, *shirk*. Cf. **31**:13.
[2] Or 'the Day of Judgement.'

فَظَلْتُمْ تَفَكَّهُونَ ۝		whereat you are left stunned[1] [saying to yourselves,]
إِنَّا لَمُغْرَمُونَ ۝	66	'We have indeed suffered loss!
بَلْ نَحْنُ مَحْرُومُونَ ۝	67	Rather, we are totally deprived!'
أَفَرَأَيْتُمُ الْمَاءَ الَّذِي تَشْرَبُونَ ۝	68	Have you considered the water that you drink?
أَأَنْتُمْ أَنْزَلْتُمُوهُ مِنَ الْمُزْنِ	69	Is it you who bring it down from the rain cloud,
أَمْ نَحْنُ الْمُنْزِلُونَ ۝		or is it We who bring it down?
لَوْ نَشَاءُ جَعَلْنَاهُ أُجَاجًا	70	If We wish We can make it bitter.
فَلَوْلَا تَشْكُرُونَ ۝		Then why do you not give thanks?
أَفَرَأَيْتُمُ النَّارَ الَّتِي تُورُونَ ۝	71	Have you considered the fire that you kindle?
أَأَنْتُمْ أَنْشَأْتُمْ شَجَرَتَهَا	72	Was it you who caused its tree to grow,
أَمْ نَحْنُ الْمُنْشِئُونَ ۝		or were We the grower?
نَحْنُ جَعَلْنَاهَا تَذْكِرَةً	73	It was We who made it a reminder
وَمَتَاعًا لِلْمُقْوِينَ ۝		and a boon for the desert-dwellers.
فَسَبِّحْ بِاسْمِ رَبِّكَ الْعَظِيمِ ۝	74	So *celebrate* the Name of *your* Lord, the All-supreme.
فَلَا أُقْسِمُ بِمَوَاقِعِ النُّجُومِ ۝	75	I swear by the places where[2] the stars set![3]
وَإِنَّهُ لَقَسَمٌ لَوْ تَعْلَمُونَ عَظِيمٌ ۝	76	And indeed it is a great oath, should you know.
إِنَّهُ لَقُرْآنٌ كَرِيمٌ ۝	77	This is indeed a noble Qur'ān,
فِي كِتَابٍ مَكْنُونٍ ۝	78	in a guarded Book,[4]
لَا يَمَسُّهُ إِلَّا الْمُطَهَّرُونَ ۝	79	—no one touches it except the pure ones—
تَنْزِيلٌ مِنْ رَبِّ الْعَالَمِينَ ۝	80	sent down gradually from the Lord of all the worlds.
أَفَبِهَذَا الْحَدِيثِ أَنْتُمْ مُدْهِنُونَ ۝	81	What! Do you take lightly this discourse?
وَتَجْعَلُونَ رِزْقَكُمْ أَنَّكُمْ تُكَذِّبُونَ ۝	82	And make your denial of it your vocation?[5]
فَلَوْلَا إِذَا بَلَغَتِ الْحُلْقُومَ ۝	83	So when it[6] reaches the throat of the dying person
وَأَنْتُمْ حِينَئِذٍ تَنْظُرُونَ ۝	84	and at that moment you are looking on

---

[1] Or 'regretful.'
[2] Or 'by the times when.'
[3] Or 'by the places where the stars fall.' Or 'I swear by the orbits of the stars.'
[4] That is, the Preserved Tablet.
[5] Or 'livelihood.' According to the reading *taj'alūna shukrakum*, narrated from Imam 'Alī ibn Abī Ṭālib and Imam al-Ṣādiq in *al-Tafsīr al-Qummī* under this verse, the translation will be 'You make your denial of it your thanksgiving.' That is, instead of being grateful for it, you deny it.
[6] That is, the soul, while leaving the body during the death-throes.

85 —and We are nearer to him[1] than you are,
    though you do not perceive—
86 then why do you not, if you are not subject[2]
87 [to Divine dispensation], restore it, if you are truthful?
88 Then, if he be of those brought near,[3]
89 then ease, abundance, and a garden of bliss.
90 And if he be of the People of the Right Hand,
91 he will be told, 'Peace be to you,
    of the People of the Right Hand!'
92 But if he be of the impugners, the astray ones,
93 then a treat of boiling water
94 and entry into hell.[4]
95 This is indeed certain truth.
96 So *celebrate* the Name of *your* Lord, the All-supreme!

57. IRON[5]
al-Ḥadīd

In the Name of God,
the All-beneficent, the All-merciful.

1 Whatever there is in the heavens and the earth glorifies God,
    and He is the All-mighty, the All-wise.
2 To Him belongs the kingdom of the heavens and the earth:
    He gives life and brings death,
    and has power over all things.
3 He is the First and the Last,
    the Manifest and the Hidden,
    and He has knowledge of all things.

---

[1] That is, to the dying person.
[2] Or 'if you are not liable to retribution.'
[3] That is, of 'the foremost ones' mentioned in verses 10–11.
[4] Or 'roasting in hell.'
[5] This Madanī *sūrah* takes its name from verse 25, which mentions iron (*ḥadīd*).

4 It is He who created the heavens and the earth
in six days;
then settled on the Throne.
He knows whatever enters the earth
and whatever emerges from it
and whatever descends from the heaven
and whatever ascends to it,
and He is with you wherever you may be,
and God watches what you do.

5 To Him belongs the kingdom of the heavens and the earth,
and to God all matters are returned.[1]

6 He makes the night pass into the day
and makes the day pass into the night,
and He knows best what is in the breasts.

7 Have faith in God and His Apostle,
and spend out of that to which He has made you heirs.[2]
Those of you who have faith and spend in God's way
—there is a great reward for them.

8 Why should you not have faith in God
when the Apostle invites you to have faith in your Lord
and He has certainly made a covenant with you,
if you are genuinely faithful?

9 It is He who sends down manifest signs to His servant
that He may bring you out of darkness into light,
and indeed God is most kind and merciful to you.

10 Why should you not spend in the way of God,
when to God belongs the heritage of the heavens
and the earth?
Not equal to others are those of you

---

[1] Cf. 2:210, 3:109, 8:44, 11:123, 19:40, 22:76, 30:11, 96:8.
[2] That is, of the past generations.

    who spent their means and fought before the victory.[1]
    They are greater in rank
        than those who have spent and fought afterwards.
    Yet God has promised the best reward to each
    and God is well aware of what you do.

11 Who is it that will lend God a good loan,
    that He may multiply it for him
    and that there may be a noble reward for him?

12 The day you will see the faithful, men and women,
    with their light moving swiftly in front of them
    and on their right, [being greeted with the words:]
    'There is good news for you today!
    Gardens with streams running in them,
        to remain in them.
    That is a mighty triumph.'

13 The day the hypocrites, men and women, will say
    to the faithful,
    'Please wait, that we may glean something from your light!'
    They will be told: 'Go back and grope for light!'[2]
    Then there will be set up between them a wall
    with a gate, with mercy within
    and punishment without.

14 They will call out to them,
    'Did we not use to be with you?'
    They will say, 'Yes! But you cast yourselves into perdition.
    You awaited[3] and were skeptical,
    and [false] hopes deceived you until God's edict[4] came,
    and the Deceiver deceived you concerning God.

---

[1] That is, the Prophet's triumphant return to Makkah.
[2] That is, go back into the world. Said mockingly to the hypocrites. Cf. 2:15, 11:38.
[3] That is, waited for a reverse of fortune for Muslims. See 4:141, 9:50-52, 98, 23:25, 52:30-31.
[4] That is, death.

al-Ḥadīd

15 Today, no ransom shall be accepted from you,
nor from the faithless.
The Fire will be your abode:
it is your ultimate refuge and an evil destination it is.'

16 Is it not time yet for those who have faith
that their hearts should be humbled for God's remembrance
and toward the truth which has come down to them,
not being like those who were given the Book before?[1]
Time took its toll on them
and so their hearts were hardened,
and many of them are transgressors.

17 Know that God revives the earth
after its death.
We have certainly made the signs clear for you,
so that you may exercise your reason.

18 Indeed, the charitable men and women
and those who lend God a good loan
—it shall be multiplied for them,
and there will be a noble reward for them.

19 Those who have faith in God and His apostles
—it is they who are the truthful
and the witnesses with their Lord;
they shall have their reward and their light.
But as for those who are faithless and deny Our signs,
they shall be the inmates of hell.

20 Know that the life of this world[2] is mere
diversion and play,
glamour and mutual vainglory among you

---

[1] That is, the Jews.
[2] The expression *al-ḥayāt al-dunyā* may be also be translated as 'the present life,' 'the nearer life,' or 'the lower life.'

وَتَكَاثُرٌ فِي الْأَمْوَالِ وَالْأَوْلَادِ   and rivalry for wealth and children
كَمَثَلِ غَيْثٍ أَعْجَبَ الْكُفَّارَ نَبَاتُهُ   —like the rain whose vegetation impresses the farmer;
ثُمَّ يَهِيجُ فَتَرَاهُ مُصْفَرًّا   then it withers and you see it turn yellow,
ثُمَّ يَكُونُ حُطَامًا   then it becomes chaff.
وَفِي الْآخِرَةِ عَذَابٌ شَدِيدٌ   Whereas in the Hereafter there is a severe punishment
وَمَغْفِرَةٌ مِنَ اللَّهِ وَرِضْوَانٌ   and forgiveness from God and His approval.
وَمَا الْحَيَاةُ الدُّنْيَا إِلَّا مَتَاعُ الْغُرُورِ ۲۰   The life of this world is nothing but the wares of delusion.
سَابِقُوا إِلَىٰ مَغْفِرَةٍ مِنْ رَبِّكُمْ   21 Take the lead towards forgiveness from your Lord
وَجَنَّةٍ عَرْضُهَا كَعَرْضِ السَّمَاءِ وَالْأَرْضِ   and a paradise as vast as the heavens and the earth,
أُعِدَّتْ لِلَّذِينَ آمَنُوا بِاللَّهِ وَرُسُلِهِ   prepared for those who have faith in God and His apostles.
ذَٰلِكَ فَضْلُ اللَّهِ   That is God's grace,
يُؤْتِيهِ مَنْ يَشَاءُ   which He grants to whomever He wishes,
وَاللَّهُ ذُو الْفَضْلِ الْعَظِيمِ ۲۱   and God is dispenser of a mighty grace.
مَا أَصَابَ مِنْ مُصِيبَةٍ فِي الْأَرْضِ   22 No affliction visits the land,
وَلَا فِي أَنْفُسِكُمْ   or yourselves,
إِلَّا فِي كِتَابٍ مِنْ قَبْلِ أَنْ نَبْرَأَهَا   but it is in a Book before We bring it about
إِنَّ ذَٰلِكَ عَلَى اللَّهِ يَسِيرٌ ۲۲   —that is indeed easy for God—
لِكَيْلَا تَأْسَوْا عَلَىٰ مَا فَاتَكُمْ   23 so that you may not grieve for what escapes you,
وَلَا تَفْرَحُوا بِمَا آتَاكُمْ   nor rejoice for what comes your way,
وَاللَّهُ لَا يُحِبُّ كُلَّ مُخْتَالٍ فَخُورٍ ۲۳   and God does not like any arrogant braggart.
الَّذِينَ يَبْخَلُونَ   24 Such as are themselves stingy
وَيَأْمُرُونَ النَّاسَ بِالْبُخْلِ   and bid other people to be stingy.
وَمَنْ يَتَوَلَّ   And whoever turns away [should know that]
فَإِنَّ اللَّهَ هُوَ الْغَنِيُّ الْحَمِيدُ ۲٤   indeed God is the All-sufficient, the All-laudable.
لَقَدْ أَرْسَلْنَا رُسُلَنَا بِالْبَيِّنَاتِ   25 Certainly We sent Our apostles with clear proofs,
وَأَنْزَلْنَا مَعَهُمُ الْكِتَابَ وَالْمِيزَانَ   and We sent down with them the Book and the Balance,
لِيَقُومَ النَّاسُ بِالْقِسْطِ   so that mankind may maintain justice;
وَأَنْزَلْنَا الْحَدِيدَ   and We sent down[1] iron,
فِيهِ بَأْسٌ شَدِيدٌ وَمَنَافِعُ لِلنَّاسِ   in which there is great might and uses for mankind,

---

[1] That is, created.

and so that God may know those who help Him
and His apostles with faith in the Unseen.
God is indeed all-strong, all-mighty.

26 Certainly We sent Noah and Abraham
and We ordained among their descendants
prophethood and the Book.
Some of them are rightly guided,
and many of them are transgressors.

27 Then We followed them up with Our apostles
and We followed them with Jesus son of Mary
and We gave him the Evangel,
and We put into the hearts of those who followed him
kindness and mercy.
But as for monasticism, they innovated it
—We had not prescribed it for them—
only seeking God's pleasure.
Yet they did not observe it with due observance.
So We gave to the faithful among them their due reward,
but many of them are transgressors.

28 O you who have faith!
Be wary of God and have faith in His Apostle.
He will grant you a double share of His mercy
and give you a light to walk by,
and He will forgive you,
and God is all-forgiving, all-merciful;

29 so that the People of the Book may know
that they have no power over anything of God's grace,
and that all grace is in God's hand
which He grants to whomever He wishes
and God is dispenser of a mighty grace.

[PART 28]

58. THE PLEADER[1]
al-Mujādilah

In the Name of God,
the All-beneficent, the All-merciful.

1 God has certainly heard the speech of her
who pleads with you about her husband
and complains to God.
God hears the conversation between the two of you.
God is indeed all-hearing, all-seeing.

2 As for those of you who repudiate their wives by *ẓihār*,[2]
they are not their mothers;
their mothers are only those who bore them,
and indeed they utter an outrage and lie.
God is indeed all-excusing, all-forgiving.

3 Those who repudiate their wives by *ẓihār*
and then retract what they have said,
shall set free a slave before they may touch each other.
This you are advised to carry out,
and God is well aware of what you do.

4 He who can not afford to free a slave
shall fast for two successive months
before they may touch each other.
If he cannot do so, he shall feed sixty needy persons.
This, that you may have faith in God and His Apostle.
These are God's bounds,
and there is a painful punishment for the faithless.

---

[1] This Madanī *sūrah* is named after the phrase *tujādiluka*, "she pleads with you" in verse 1.
[2] A kind of repudiation of the marital relationship among pre-Islamic Arabs which took place on a husband's saying to his wife 'Be as my mother's back' (*ẓahr*; hence the derivative *ẓihār*).

5 إِنَّ الَّذِينَ يُحَادُّونَ اللَّهَ وَرَسُولَهُ كُبِتُوا
كَمَا كُبِتَ الَّذِينَ مِن قَبْلِهِمْ
وَقَدْ أَنزَلْنَا آيَاتٍ بَيِّنَاتٍ
وَلِلْكَافِرِينَ عَذَابٌ مُّهِينٌ ۝

5 Those who oppose God and His Apostle will indeed be subdued,
just as those who passed before them were subdued.
We have certainly sent down manifest signs,
and there is a humiliating punishment for the faithless.

6 يَوْمَ يَبْعَثُهُمُ اللَّهُ جَمِيعًا
فَيُنَبِّئُهُم بِمَا عَمِلُوا
أَحْصَاهُ اللَّهُ وَنَسُوهُ
وَاللَّهُ عَلَىٰ كُلِّ شَيْءٍ شَهِيدٌ ۝

6 The day when God will raise them all together,
He will inform them about what they have done.
God has kept account of it, while they have forgotten it,
and God is witness to all things.

7 أَلَمْ تَرَ أَنَّ اللَّهَ يَعْلَمُ
مَا فِي السَّمَاوَاتِ
وَمَا فِي الْأَرْضِ
مَا يَكُونُ مِن نَّجْوَىٰ ثَلَاثَةٍ
إِلَّا هُوَ رَابِعُهُمْ
وَلَا خَمْسَةٍ إِلَّا هُوَ سَادِسُهُمْ
وَلَا أَدْنَىٰ مِن ذَٰلِكَ وَلَا أَكْثَرَ
إِلَّا هُوَ مَعَهُمْ أَيْنَ مَا كَانُوا
ثُمَّ يُنَبِّئُهُم بِمَا عَمِلُوا
يَوْمَ الْقِيَامَةِ
إِنَّ اللَّهَ بِكُلِّ شَيْءٍ عَلِيمٌ ۝

7 Have you not regarded that God knows
whatever there is in the heavens
and whatever there is in the earth?
There does not take place any secret talk among three,
but He is their fourth companion,
nor among five but He is their sixth,
nor when they are less than that or more,
but He is with them wherever they may be.
Then He will inform them about what they have done
on the Day of Resurrection.
Indeed, God has knowledge of all things.

8 أَلَمْ تَرَ إِلَى الَّذِينَ
نُهُوا عَنِ النَّجْوَىٰ
ثُمَّ يَعُودُونَ لِمَا نُهُوا عَنْهُ
وَيَتَنَاجَوْنَ بِالْإِثْمِ وَالْعُدْوَانِ
وَمَعْصِيَتِ الرَّسُولِ
وَإِذَا جَاءُوكَ حَيَّوْكَ بِمَا
لَمْ يُحَيِّكَ بِهِ اللَّهُ

8 Have you not regarded those
who were forbidden from secret talks[1]
but again resumed what they had been forbidden from,
and hold secret talks imbued with sin and transgression
and disobedience to the Apostle?
And when they[2] come to *you*, they greet *you* with words
with which God never greeted *you*,

---

[1] That is, the Jews and the hypocrites.
[2] That is, the Jews and the hypocrites who, instead of the words of greeting *as-salāmu 'alaykum* (peace be on you), would greet the Prophet (ṣ) with such words as *as-sāmu 'alaykum* (death to you). They told themselves that if the Prophet (ṣ) were really from God, He would punish them for it.

and they say to themselves,[1]
'Why does not God punish us for what we say?!'
Let hell suffice them: they shall enter it,
and it is an evil destination!

9 O you who have faith! When you converse privately,
do not hold private conversations imbued
with sin and aggression against other's rights
and disobedience to the Apostle,
but converse privately in a spirit of piety and Godfearing,
and be wary of God
toward whom you will be gathered.

10 Malicious secret talks are indeed from Satan,
that he may upset the faithful,
but he cannot harm them in any way except by God's leave,
and in God alone let all the faithful put their trust.

11 O you who have faith!
When you are told, 'Make room,' in sittings,
then do make room; God will make room for you.
And when you are told, 'Rise up!' Do rise up.
God will raise those of you who have faith
and those who have been given knowledge in rank,
and God is well aware of what you do.

12 O you who have faith!
When you converse privately with the Apostle,
offer a charity before your private talk.
That is better for you and purer.
But if you cannot afford to make the offering,
then God is indeed all-forgiving, all-merciful.

13 Were you dismayed at offering

---

[1] Or 'in their hearts.'

charity before your private talks?
Since you did not do it,
and God has excused you [for your failure to comply],
now maintain the prayer and pay the zakāt,
and obey God and His Apostle.
God is well aware of what you do.

14 Have you not regarded those who befriend
people[1] at whom God is wrathful?
They neither belong to you, nor to them,
and they swear false oaths [that they are with you]
and they know.

15 God has prepared a severe punishment for them.
Evil indeed is what they used to do.

16 They make a shield of their oaths
and bar people from the way of God;
so there is a humiliating punishment for them.

17 Their possessions and children will not avail them
in any way against God.
They shall be the inmates of the Fire
and they shall remain in it.

18 The day when God will raise them all together,
they will swear to Him just like they swear to you now,
supposing that they stand on something.
Behold, they are indeed liars!

19 Satan has prevailed upon them,
so he has caused them to forget the remembrance of God.
They are Satan's confederates.
Behold,
it is Satan's confederates who are indeed the losers!

---

[1] That is, the Jews, with whom the hypocrites amongst Muslims were on intimate terms.

20 Indeed, those who oppose God and His Apostle
—they will be among the most abased.

21 God has ordained:
'I shall surely prevail, I and My apostles.'
God is indeed all-strong, all-mighty.

22 You will not find a people believing in God
and the Last Day
endearing those who oppose God and His Apostle,
even though they be their own parents, or children,
or brothers, or kinsfolk.
For such, He has written faith into their hearts
and strengthened them with a spirit from Him.
He will admit them into gardens
with streams running in them,
to remain in them:
God is pleased with them, and they are pleased with Him.
They are God's confederates.
Behold, the confederates of God are indeed felicitous!

59. The Banishment[1]
al-Ḥashr

In the Name of God,
the All-beneficent, the All-merciful.

1 Whatever there is in the heavens glorifies God
and whatever there is in the earth,
and He is the All-mighty, the All-wise

2 It is He who expelled the faithless
belonging to the People of the Book

---

[1] This Madanī *sūrah* takes its name from the banishment (*ḥashr*) of a Jewish tribe from Madīnah, which occurred on the 4th of Rabīʿ I in 4 H., about four months after the Battle of Uḥud. The *sūrah* was apparently revealed soon after the event.

مِنْ دِيَارِهِمْ	from their homes
لِأَوَّلِ الْحَشْرِ	at the outset of their en masse banishment.
مَا ظَنَنْتُمْ أَنْ يَخْرُجُوا	You did not think that they would go out,
وَظَنُّوا أَنَّهُمْ مَانِعَتُهُمْ حُصُونُهُمْ	and they thought their fortresses would protect them
مِنَ اللَّهِ	from God.
فَأَتَاهُمُ اللَّهُ مِنْ حَيْثُ لَمْ يَحْتَسِبُوا	But God came at them from whence they did not suppose,
وَقَذَفَ فِي قُلُوبِهِمُ الرُّعْبَ	and He cast terror into their hearts.
يُخْرِبُونَ بُيُوتَهُمْ بِأَيْدِيهِمْ	They demolish their houses with their own hands
وَأَيْدِي الْمُؤْمِنِينَ	and the hands of the faithful.
فَاعْتَبِرُوا يَا أُولِي الْأَبْصَارِ ۝	So take lesson, O you who have insight!
٣ وَلَوْلَا أَنْ كَتَبَ اللَّهُ عَلَيْهِمُ الْجَلَاءَ	3 If God had not ordained banishment for them,
لَعَذَّبَهُمْ فِي الدُّنْيَا	He would have surely punished them in this world,
وَلَهُمْ فِي الْآخِرَةِ	and in the Hereafter there is for them
عَذَابُ النَّارِ ۝	the punishment of the Fire.
٤ ذَٰلِكَ بِأَنَّهُمْ شَاقُّوا اللَّهَ وَرَسُولَهُ	4 That is because they defied God and His Apostle;
وَمَنْ يُشَاقِّ اللَّهَ	and whoever defies God,
فَإِنَّ اللَّهَ شَدِيدُ الْعِقَابِ ۝	God is indeed severe in retribution.
٥ مَا قَطَعْتُمْ مِنْ لِينَةٍ	5 Whatever palm trees you cut down
أَوْ تَرَكْتُمُوهَا قَائِمَةً عَلَىٰ أُصُولِهَا	or left standing on their roots,
فَبِإِذْنِ اللَّهِ	it was by God's will
وَلِيُخْزِيَ الْفَاسِقِينَ ۝	and in order that He may disgrace the transgressors.
٦ وَمَا أَفَاءَ اللَّهُ عَلَىٰ رَسُولِهِ مِنْهُمْ	6 The spoils that God gave to His Apostle from them,
فَمَا أَوْجَفْتُمْ عَلَيْهِ مِنْ خَيْلٍ	you did not spur any horse for its sake,
وَلَا رِكَابٍ	nor any riding camel,
وَلَٰكِنَّ اللَّهَ يُسَلِّطُ رُسُلَهُ	but God makes His apostles prevail
عَلَىٰ مَنْ يَشَاءُ	over whomever He wishes,
وَاللَّهُ عَلَىٰ كُلِّ شَيْءٍ قَدِيرٌ ۝	and God has power over all things.
٧ مَا أَفَاءَ اللَّهُ عَلَىٰ رَسُولِهِ	7 The spoils that God gave to His Apostle
مِنْ أَهْلِ الْقُرَىٰ	from the people of the townships,
فَلِلَّهِ وَلِلرَّسُولِ	are for God and the Apostle,

the relatives[1] and the orphans,
the needy and the traveler,
so that they do not circulate among the rich among you.
Take whatever the Apostle gives you,
 and refrain from whatever he forbids you,
 and be wary of God.
God is indeed severe in retribution.

8 They are also for the poor Emigrants
 who have been expelled from their homes
 and wrested of their possessions,
 who seek grace from God and His pleasure
 and help God and His Apostle.
 It is they who are the truthful.[2]

9 They are as well for those who were settled in the land[3]
 and abided in faith before them,
 who love those who migrate toward them,
 and do not find in their breasts any need
 for that which is given to them,[4]
 but prefer [the Immigrants] to themselves,
 though poverty be their own lot.
 Those who are saved from their own greed
 —it is they who are the felicitous.

10 And also for those who came in after them,
 who say, 'Our Lord, forgive us and our brethren
 who were our forerunners in the faith,
 and do not put any rancour in our hearts
 toward the faithful.
 Our Lord, You are indeed most kind and merciful.'

---

[1] That is, of the Prophet (ṣ), the Banū Hāshim.
[2] That is, true and loyal to their covenant with God and His Apostle.
[3] That is, Madīnah, to which the early Muslims migrated with the Prophet (ṣ).
[4] That is, to the Immigrants.

11 Have you not regarded the hypocrites
who say to their brethren,
the faithless from among the People of the Book:
'If you are expelled, we will surely go out with you,
and we will never obey anyone against you,
and if you are fought against, we will surely help you,'
and God bears witness that they are indeed liars.

12 Surely, if they are expelled, they will not go out with them,
and if they are fought against, they will not help them,
and were they to help them,
they will turn their backs to flee
and eventually they[1] will not be helped.

13 They have indeed a greater awe of you in their hearts
than of God.
That is because they are a lot who do not understand.

14 They will not fight against you even when united,
except in fortified townships
or from behind walls.
Their strength is great only amongst themselves.
You suppose them to be united,
but their hearts are divided.
That is because they are a lot who do not exercise their reason

15 —just like those who, recently before them,
tasted the evil consequence of their conduct,[2]
and there is a painful punishment for them.

16 [The hypocrites are] like Satan
when he tells man to disbelieve,
but when he disbelieves, he says, 'I am absolved of you.

---

[1] That is, the faithless from among the People of the Book.
[2] This refers to Banū Qaynuqāʿ, another Jewish tribe which was expelled earlier from Madīnah a month after Badr for violating their treaty with the Prophet (ṣ).

إِنِّي أَخَافُ اللَّهَ رَبَّ الْعَالَمِينَ ۞

Indeed, I fear God, the Lord of all the worlds.'

17 فَكَانَ عَاقِبَتَهُمَا أَنَّهُمَا فِي النَّارِ خَالِدَيْنِ فِيهَا

17 So the fate of both is that they will be in the Fire, to remain in it.

وَذَٰلِكَ جَزَاءُ الظَّالِمِينَ ۞

Such is the requital of the wrongdoers.

18 يَا أَيُّهَا الَّذِينَ آمَنُوا اتَّقُوا اللَّهَ وَلْتَنظُرْ نَفْسٌ مَّا قَدَّمَتْ لِغَدٍ ۖ وَاتَّقُوا اللَّهَ

18 O you who have faith! Be wary of God and let every soul consider what it sends ahead[1] for tomorrow, and be wary of God.

إِنَّ اللَّهَ خَبِيرٌ بِمَا تَعْمَلُونَ ۞

God is indeed well aware of what you do

19 وَلَا تَكُونُوا كَالَّذِينَ نَسُوا اللَّهَ فَأَنسَاهُمْ أَنفُسَهُمْ ۚ

19 Do not be like those who forget God, so He makes them forget their own souls.

أُولَٰئِكَ هُمُ الْفَاسِقُونَ ۞

It is they who are the transgressors.

20 لَا يَسْتَوِي أَصْحَابُ النَّارِ وَأَصْحَابُ الْجَنَّةِ ۚ

20 Not equal are the inmates of the Fire and the inhabitants of paradise.

أَصْحَابُ الْجَنَّةِ هُمُ الْفَائِزُونَ ۞

It is the inhabitants of paradise who are the successful ones.

21 لَوْ أَنزَلْنَا هَٰذَا الْقُرْآنَ عَلَىٰ جَبَلٍ لَّرَأَيْتَهُ خَاشِعًا مُّتَصَدِّعًا مِّنْ خَشْيَةِ اللَّهِ ۚ وَتِلْكَ الْأَمْثَالُ نَضْرِبُهَا لِلنَّاسِ لَعَلَّهُمْ يَتَفَكَّرُونَ ۞

21 Had We sent down this Qur'ān upon a mountain, you would have seen it humbled and go to pieces with the fear of God. We draw such comparisons for mankind so that they may reflect.

22 هُوَ اللَّهُ الَّذِي لَا إِلَٰهَ إِلَّا هُوَ ۖ عَالِمُ الْغَيْبِ وَالشَّهَادَةِ ۖ هُوَ الرَّحْمَٰنُ الرَّحِيمُ ۞

22 He is God—there is no god except Him— Knower of the sensible and the Unseen, He is the All-beneficent, the All-merciful.

23 هُوَ اللَّهُ الَّذِي لَا إِلَٰهَ إِلَّا هُوَ الْمَلِكُ الْقُدُّوسُ السَّلَامُ الْمُؤْمِنُ الْمُهَيْمِنُ الْعَزِيزُ الْجَبَّارُ الْمُتَكَبِّرُ ۚ سُبْحَانَ اللَّهِ عَمَّا يُشْرِكُونَ ۞

23 He is God—there is no god except Him— the Sovereign, the All-holy, the All-benign,[2] the Securer, the All-conserver, the All-mighty, the All-compeller and the All-magnanimous. Clear is God of any partners that they may ascribe to Him!

24 هُوَ اللَّهُ الْخَالِقُ الْبَارِئُ الْمُصَوِّرُ ۖ

24 He is God, the Creator, the Maker and the Former.

---

[1] Or 'prepares,' or 'makes ready.'
[2] Or 'the Impeccable.'

To Him belong the Best Names.
Whatever there is in the heavens and the earth glorifies Him,
and He is the All-mighty, the All-wise.

60. THE WOMAN TESTED[1]
al-Mumtaḥanah

In the Name of God,
the All-beneficent, the All-merciful.

1 O you who have faith!
Do not take My enemy and your enemy
   for allies,
[secretly] offering them affection
(for they have certainly denied
   what has come to you of the truth,
   expelling the Apostle and you,
   because you have faith in God, your Lord)
if you have set out for *jihād* in My way
   and to seek My pleasure.
You secretly nourish affection for them,
   while I know well whatever you hide
   and whatever you disclose,
and whoever among you does that
   has certainly strayed from the right way.
2 If they were to confront you
   they would be your enemies,
and would stretch out against you their hands
   and unleash their tongues with evil intentions,
   and they are eager that you too should be faithless.
3 Your relatives and children will not avail you

---

[1] This Madanī *sūrah* takes its name from verse 10 concerning the testing (*imtiḥān*) of new female converts to Islam.

on the Day of Resurrection:
He will separate you from one another,
and God watches what you do.

4 There is certainly a good exemplar for you in Abraham
and those who were with him,
when they said to their own people,
'We indeed repudiate you
and whatever you worship besides God.
We disown you,
and between you and us there have appeared
enmity and hate for ever,
unless you come to have faith in God alone,'
apart from Abraham's saying to his father,
'I will surely plead forgiveness for you,
though I cannot avail you anything against God.'
[They prayed,] 'Our Lord! In You do we put our trust,
to You do we turn penitently,
and toward You is the destination.

5 Our Lord! Do not make us a test for the faithless,
and forgive us.
Our Lord! Indeed, You are the All-mighty, the All-wise.'

6 There is certainly a good exemplar for you in them
—for those who look forward to God and the Last Day—
and whoever turns away [should know that]
God is indeed the All-sufficient, the All-laudable.

7 It may be that God will bring about
between you and those with whom you are at enmity
comity,
and God is all-powerful,
and God is all-forgiving, all-merciful.

8 God does not forbid you in regard to those
   who did not make war against you on account of religion
   and did not expel you from your homes,
   that you deal with them with kindness and justice.
   God indeed loves the just.

9 God forbids you only in regard to those
   who made war against you on account of religion
   and expelled you from your homes
   and supported [the Makkans] in your expulsion,
   that you make friends with them,
   and whoever makes friends with them
   —it is they who are the wrongdoers.

10 O you who have faith! When there come to you
   faithful women as immigrants, test them.
   God knows best the state of their faith.
   Then, if you ascertain them to be genuinely faithful,
   do not send them back to the faithless.
   They[1] are not lawful for them,[2]
   nor are they[3] lawful for them,[4]
   but give them[5] what they have spent [for dowry].
   There is no sin upon you in marrying them
   when you have given them their dowries.
   Do not hold on to conjugal ties with faithless women.
   Demand [from the infidels]
   what you have spent [for dowry]
   and let them demand from you what they have spent.[6]
   That is God's judgment; He judges between you,

---

[1] That is, faithful women.
[2] That is, for infidel men.
[3] That is, infidel men.
[4] That is, for faithful women.
[5] The infidel men who were their husbands before.
[6] That is, the dowry given to the women who were formerly their wives.

and God is all-knowing, all-wise.

11 If anything pertaining to your wives[1] is not reclaimed from the faithless[2] and then you have your turn, then give to those whose wives have left the like of what they have spent, and be wary of God in whom you have faith.

12 O Prophet! If faithful women come to you to take the oath of allegiance to you, pledging that they shall not ascribe any partners to God, that they shall not steal, nor commit adultery, nor kill their children, nor produce a lie that they may have hatched between their hands and feet, nor disobey you in what is right, then accept their allegiance and plead for them to God for forgiveness. God is indeed all-forgiving, all-merciful

13 O you who have faith! Do not befriend a people at whom God is wrathful: they have despaired of the Hereafter just as the faithless have despaired of the occupants of the graves.

61. Ranks[3]
al-Ṣaff

In the Name of God,
the All-beneficent, the All-merciful.

1 Whatever there is in the heavens glorifies God

---

[1] That is, the dowries you had paid to your former wives.
[2] That is, if their dowry is not paid by the infidels. Or 'If any of your wives goes away toward the infidels.'
[3] This Madanī *sūrah* is named after verse 4, in which the word *ṣaff* (ranks) occurs.

وَمَا فِى الْأَرْضِ	and whatever there is in the earth,
وَهُوَ الْعَزِيزُ الْحَكِيمُ ۝	and He is the All-mighty, the All-wise

2 يَا أَيُّهَا الَّذِينَ آمَنُوا O you who have faith!
لِمَ تَقُولُونَ مَا لَا تَفْعَلُونَ ۝ Why do you say what you do not do?

3 كَبُرَ مَقْتًا عِندَ اللَّهِ It is greatly outrageous to God
أَن تَقُولُوا مَا لَا تَفْعَلُونَ ۝ that you should say what you do not do.

4 إِنَّ اللَّهَ يُحِبُّ الَّذِينَ God indeed loves those who
يُقَاتِلُونَ فِى سَبِيلِهِ صَفًّا fight in His way in ranks,
كَأَنَّهُم بُنْيَانٌ مَّرْصُوصٌ ۝ as if they were a compact structure.

5 وَإِذْ قَالَ مُوسَىٰ لِقَوْمِهِ When Moses said to his people,
يَا قَوْمِ لِمَ تُؤْذُونَنِى 'O my people! Why do you torment me,
وَقَد تَّعْلَمُونَ when you certainly know
أَنِّى رَسُولُ اللَّهِ إِلَيْكُمْ that I am God's apostle to you?'
فَلَمَّا زَاغُوا So when they swerved from the right path,
أَزَاغَ اللَّهُ قُلُوبَهُمْ God made their hearts swerve,
وَاللَّهُ لَا يَهْدِى الْقَوْمَ الْفَاسِقِينَ ۝ and God does not guide the transgressing lot.

6 وَإِذْ قَالَ عِيسَى ابْنُ مَرْيَمَ And when Jesus son of Mary said,
يَا بَنِى إِسْرَائِيلَ 'O Children of Israel!
إِنِّى رَسُولُ اللَّهِ إِلَيْكُم I am indeed the apostle of God to you,
مُّصَدِّقًا لِّمَا بَيْنَ يَدَىَّ مِنَ التَّوْرَاةِ to confirm what is before me of the Torah
وَمُبَشِّرًا بِرَسُولٍ and to give good news of an apostle
يَأْتِى مِن بَعْدِى اسْمُهُ أَحْمَدُ who will come after me, whose name is Aḥmad.'
فَلَمَّا جَاءَهُم بِالْبَيِّنَاتِ But when he brought them clear proofs,
قَالُوا هَـٰذَا سِحْرٌ مُّبِينٌ ۝ they said, 'This is plain magic.'

7 وَمَنْ أَظْلَمُ مِمَّنِ Who is a greater wrongdoer than him
افْتَرَىٰ عَلَى اللَّهِ الْكَذِبَ who fabricates falsehoods against God
وَهُوَ يُدْعَىٰ إِلَى الْإِسْلَامِ while he is being summoned to Islam?
وَاللَّهُ لَا يَهْدِى الْقَوْمَ الظَّالِمِينَ ۝ And God does not guide the wrongdoing lot.

8 يُرِيدُونَ لِيُطْفِئُوا نُورَ اللَّهِ They desire to put out the light of God
بِأَفْوَاهِهِمْ with their mouths,

      but God will perfect His light,
      though the faithless should be averse.

9 It is He who has sent His Apostle
    with guidance and the true religion
    that He may make it prevail over all religions
    though the polytheists should be averse.

10 O you who have faith!
    Shall I show you a deal
    that will deliver you from a painful punishment?

11 Have faith in God and His Apostle
    and wage *jihād* in the way of God
      with your persons and possessions.
    That is better for you, should you know.

12 He will forgive your sins
    and admit you into gardens
      with streams running in them,
    and into good dwellings in the Gardens of Eden.
    That is the great success.

13 And other [blessings] besides which you cherish:
    help from God and a victory near at hand,
    and *give* good news to the faithful.

14 O you who have faith! Be God's helpers,
    just as Jesus son of Mary said to his disciples,
    'Who will be my helpers for God's sake?'
    The Disciples said, 'We will be God's helpers!'
    So a group of the Children of Israel believed,
      and a group disbelieved.
    Then We strengthened the faithful against their enemies
    and they came to prevail over them.

62. Friday[1]
al-Jumu'ah

In the Name of God,
the All-beneficent, the All-merciful.

1 Whatever there is in the heavens glorifies God
and whatever there is in the earth,
the Sovereign, the All-holy, the All-mighty, the All-wise.

2 It is He who sent to the unlettered people
an apostle from among themselves,
to recite to them His signs, to purify them,
and to teach them the Book and wisdom,
and earlier they had indeed been in manifest error.

3 And to others from among them as well
who have not yet joined them,
and He is the All-mighty, the All-wise.

4 That is God's grace
which He grants to whomever He wishes,
and God is dispenser of a mighty grace.

5 The example of those who were charged with the Torah,
then failed to carry it,
is that of an ass carrying books.
Evil is the example of the people who deny God's signs,
and God does not guide the wrongdoing lot.

6 Say, 'O Jews!
If you claim that you are God's favourites
to the exclusion of other people,
then long for death, if you are truthful.'

7 Yet they will never long for it,

---

[1] This Madanī sūrah in named after *Jumu'ah* (Friday) prayer mentioned in verse 9.

        because of what their hands have sent ahead,
        and God knows best the wrongdoers.

8 Say, 'The death that you flee
    will indeed encounter you.
    Then you will be returned
    to the Knower of the sensible and the Unseen
    and He will inform you about what you used to do.'

9 O you who have faith!
    When the call is made for prayer on Friday,
    hurry to the remembrance of God and leave all business.
    That is better for you, should you know.

10 And when the prayer is finished
     disperse through the land and seek God's grace,
     and remember God much so that you may be felicitous.

11 When they sight a deal or a diversion,
     they scatter off towards it and leave you standing!
     Say, 'What is with God is better than
     diversion and dealing,
     and God is the best of providers.'

63. THE HYPOCRITES[1]
al-Munāfiqūn

In the Name of God,
the All-beneficent, the All-merciful.

1 When the hypocrites come to you
   they say, 'We bear witness
   that *you* are indeed the apostle of God.'
   God knows that *you* are indeed His Apostle,
   and God bears witness that the hypocrites are indeed liars.

---

[1] This Madanī *sūrah* is named after its main topic, the hypocrites (*munāfiqūn*).

2 They make a shield of their oaths
    and bar from the way of God.
    Evil indeed is what they have been doing.
3 That is because they believed and then disbelieved,
    so their hearts were sealed.
    Hence they do not understand.
4 When you see them, their bodies impress you,
    and if they speak, you listen to their speech.
    Yet they are like dry logs set reclining against a wall.
    They suppose every cry is directed against them.
    They are the enemy, so beware of them.
    May God assail them, where do they stray?!
5 When they are told, 'Come,
    that God's Apostle may plead for forgiveness for you,'
    they twist their heads
    and you see them turn away disdainfully.
6 It is the same for them
    whether you plead for forgiveness for them,
    or do not plead for forgiveness for them:
    God will never forgive them.
    Indeed, God does not guide the transgressing lot.
7 They are the ones who say, 'Do not spend
    on those who are with the Apostle of God
    until they scatter off from around him.'
    Yet to God belong the treasuries of the heavens
    and the earth,
    but the hypocrites do not understand.
8 They say, 'When we return to the city,
    the mighty will surely expel the weak from it.'
    Yet all might belongs to God and His Apostle,

and the faithful,
but the hypocrites do not know.

9 O you who have faith!
Do not let your possessions and children distract you
    from the remembrance of God,
and whoever does that
    —it is they who are the losers.

10 Spend out of what We have provided you
    before death comes to any of you,
    whereat he might say, 'My Lord,
    why did You not respite me for a short time
    so that I could have given charity
    and become one of the righteous!'

11 But God will never respite anyone
    when his time has come,
    and God is well aware of what you do.

64. PRIVATION[1]
al-Taghābun

In the Name of God,
    the All-beneficent, the All-merciful.

1 Whatever there is in the heavens glorifies God
    and whatever there is in the earth.
To Him belongs all sovereignty and to Him belongs all praise,
    and He has power over all things.

2 It is He who created you.
Then some of you are faithless and some of you are faithful,
    and God watches what you do.

---

[1] This Madanī *sūrah* takes its name from "the day of privation (or dispossession)" (*yawm al-taghābun*) mentioned in verse 9.

3 He created the heavens and the earth
    with consummate wisdom,
  and He formed you and perfected your forms,
  and toward Him is your destination.
4 He knows whatever there is in the heavens
    and the earth,
  and He knows whatever you hide and whatever you disclose,
  and God knows best what is in your breasts.
5 Has there not come to you the account
    of those who were faithless before?
  They tasted the evil consequence of their conduct,
  and there is a painful punishment for them.
6 That was because their apostles would bring them
    clear proofs,
  but they said, 'Will humans be our guides?!'
  So they disbelieved and turned away,
    and God had no need [of their faith]
  and God is all-sufficient, all-laudable.
7 The faithless claim that they will not be resurrected.
  Say, 'Yes, by my Lord, you will surely be resurrected;
    then you will surely be informed of what you did,
  and that is easy for God.'
8 So have faith in God and His Apostle
    and the light which We have sent down,
  and God is well aware of what you do.
9 When He will bring you together for the Day of Gathering,
    it will be a day of privation [and regret].[1]
  As for those who have faith in God and act righteously,

---

[1] The explanation given by the commentators is that the faithless will find themselves dispossessed of their place in paradise and that their pursuit of ephemeral gains has landed them in hell. The faithful will appropriate their places in paradise, happy to have been saved from occupying what would have been their place in hell if they did not have faith in God and had not performed righteous deeds.

He will absolve them of their misdeeds
and admit them into gardens
with streams running in them,
to remain in them forever.
That is a mighty triumph.

10 But as for those who are faithless and deny Our signs,
—they will be the inmates of the Fire, to remain in it,
and it is an evil destination.

11 No affliction visits anyone except by God's leave.
Whoever has faith in God, He guides his heart,
and God has knowledge of all things.

12 Obey God and obey the Apostle;
but if you turn away,
Our Apostle's duty is only to communicate in clear terms.

13 God—there is no god except Him—
in God alone let all the faithful put their trust.

14 O you who have faith!
You have indeed enemies among your spouses and children,
so beware of them.
Yet if you excuse, forbear and forgive,
then God is indeed all-forgiving, all-merciful.

15 Your possessions and children are only a test,
and God—with Him is a great reward!

16 So be wary of God as much as you can,
and listen and obey, and spend in the way of God;
that is better for yourselves.
Those who are saved from their own greed
—it is they who are the felicitous.

17 If you lend God a good loan,

He shall multiply it for you and forgive you,
and God is all-appreciative, all-forbearing,
18 Knower of the sensible and the Unseen,
the All-mighty, the All-wise.

65. DIVORCE[1]
al-Ṭalāq

In the Name of God,
the All-beneficent, the All-merciful.

1 O Prophet! When you[2] divorce women,
divorce them at the conclusion of their term[3]
and calculate the term,
and be wary of God, your Lord.
Do not turn them out from their homes,
nor shall they go out,
unless they commit a gross[4] indecency.[5]
These are God's bounds,
and whoever transgresses the bounds of God
certainly wrongs himself.
You never know,
maybe God will bring off something new later on.
2 Then, when they have completed their term,
either retain them honourably
or separate from them honourably,
and take the witness
of two honest men from among yourselves,
and bear witness for the sake of God.

---

[1] This Madanī *sūrah* takes its name from verse 1 concerning divorce (*ṭalāq*).
[2] That is, Muslim men.
[3] See 2:227-233, 33:49.
[4] Or 'proven,' according to an alternative reading (*mubayyanah* instead of *mubayyinah*).
[5] That is, adultery, lesbianism, theft or revilement of the husband and his family. (See *Tafsīr al-Ṣāfī*, Ṭabarī)

To comply with this is advised
    whoever believes in God and the Last Day.
Whoever is wary of God, He shall make a way out for him,
and provide for him from whence he does not count upon.
Whoever puts his trust in God, He will suffice him.
Indeed, God carries through His commands.
Certainly God has ordained a measure for everything.

4 As for those of your wives who have ceased having menses
—or if you have any doubts [concerning its cause]—
    their term of waiting shall be three months,
    and of those as well who have not yet had menses.
As for those who are pregnant,
    their term shall be until they deliver.
And whoever is wary of God,
    He shall grant him ease in his affairs.

5 That is God's ordinance which He has sent down to you,
    and whoever is wary of God,
    He shall absolve him of his misdeeds
    and give him a great reward.

6 House them[1] where you live,
    in accordance with your means,
    and do not harass them to put them in straits,
    and should they be pregnant,
    maintain them until they deliver.
If they suckle the baby for you, give them their wages,
    and consult together honourably.
But if you make things difficult for each other,
    then another woman will suckle the baby for him.[2]

7 Let the affluent man spend out of his affluence,

---

[1] That is, the divorcée in her waiting period (*'iddah*).
[2] That is, the father will arrange for a wet nurse to suckle the infant.

and let he whose provision has been tightened
spend out of what God has given him.
God does not task any soul
except according to what He has given it.
God will bring about ease after hardship.

8 How many a town defied the command of its Lord and His apostles,
then We called it to a severe account
and punished it with a dire punishment.

9 So it tasted the evil consequences of its conduct,
and the outcome of its conduct was ruin.

10 God has prepared for them a severe punishment.
So be wary of God,
O you who possess intellect and have faith!
God has already sent down to you a reminder,

11 an apostle reciting to you the manifest signs of God,
that He may bring out those who have faith
and do righteous deeds
from darkness into light.
And whoever has faith in God and does righteous deeds,
He shall admit him into gardens
with streams running in them,
to remain in them forever.
God has certainly granted him an excellent provision.

12 It is God who has created seven heavens,
and of the earth a number similar to them.
The command gradually descends through them,
that you may know that God has power over all things,
and that God comprehends all things in knowledge.

66. The Disallowing
al-Taḥrīm

In the Name of God,
the All-beneficent, the All-merciful.

1 O Prophet! Why do you disallow yourself
what God has made lawful for you,
seeking to please your wives?
And God is all-forgiving, all-merciful.

2 God has certainly made lawful for you
the dissolution of your oaths,[2]
and God is your Master
and He is the All-knowing, the All-wise.

3 When the Prophet confided a matter to one of his wives,
but when she divulged it [instead of keeping the secret]
and God disclosed that to him,
he apprised her of part of the matter
and ignored part of it.
So when he told her about it,
she said, 'Who informed you about it?'
He said,
'The All-knowing and the All-aware has informed me.'

4 If the two of you[3] repent to God ...[4]
for your hearts have certainly swerved,
and if you back each other against him,
then know that God is indeed his protector,
and Gabriel, the righteous among the faithful,
and, thereafter, the angels are his supporters.

---

[1] Named 'Taḥrīm' after the phrase li mā tuḥarrimu ("why do you disallow") in verse 1.
[2] See 2:225, 5:89. Concerning emphasis on keeping oaths, see 16:91-94.
[3] That is, Ḥafṣah and 'Āyishah, two of the Prophet's wives.
[4] Ellipsis. The omitted phrase is, 'it will be better for you.'

5 It may be that if he divorces you
his Lord will give him, in your stead, wives better than you:
such as are *muslim*, faithful, obedient,
penitent, devout and given to fasting,
virgins and non-virgins.

6 O you who have faith!
Save yourselves and your families from a Fire
whose fuel will be people and stones,
over which are assigned severe and mighty angels,
who do not disobey whatever God commands them
and carry out what they are commanded.

7 [They will call out to the faithless:] 'O faithless ones!
Do not make any excuses today.
You are being requited only for what you used to do.'

8 O you who have faith!
Repent to God with sincere repentance!
Maybe your Lord
will absolve you of your misdeeds
and admit you into gardens
with streams running in them,
on the day when God will not let down the Prophet
and the faithful who are with him.
Their light will move swiftly before them
and on their right.
They will say, 'Our Lord!
Perfect our light for us and forgive us!
Indeed, You have power over all things.'

9 O Prophet! Wage *jihād* against the faithless
and the hypocrites

and be severe with them.
Their refuge will be hell, and it is an evil destination.

10 God cites an example of the faithless:
the wife of Noah and the wife of Lot.
They were under two of our righteous servants,
yet they betrayed them.
So they[1] did not avail them[2] in any way against God,
and it was said to them,
'Enter the Fire, along with those who enter it.'

11 God cites an example of the faithful:
the wife of Pharaoh, when she said,
'My Lord! Build me a home near You in paradise,
and deliver me from Pharaoh and his conduct,
and deliver me from the wrongdoing lot.'

12 And Mary, daughter of Imran,
who guarded the chastity of her womb,
so We breathed into it of Our spirit.
She confirmed the words of her Lord and His Books,
and she was one of the obedient.

[PART 29]

67. SOVEREIGNTY[3]

al-Mulk

In the Name of God,
the All-beneficent, the All-merciful.

1 Blessed is He in whose hands is all sovereignty
and He has power over all things.

2 He, who created death and life
that He may test you

---

[1] That is, Noah and Lot.
[2] That is, the wives.
[3] This Makkī *sūrah* is named after 'Divine sovereignty' (*mulk*) mentioned in verse 1.

أَيُّكُمْ أَحْسَنُ عَمَلًا	to see which of you is best in conduct.
وَهُوَ الْعَزِيزُ الْغَفُورُ ۝	And He is the All-mighty, the All-forgiving.
الَّذِي خَلَقَ سَبْعَ سَمَاوَاتٍ طِبَاقًا	3 He created seven heavens in layers.
مَا تَرَىٰ	You do not see
فِي خَلْقِ الرَّحْمَـٰنِ مِن تَفَاوُتٍ	any discordance in the creation of the All-beneficent.
فَارْجِعِ الْبَصَرَ هَلْ تَرَىٰ مِن فُطُورٍ ۝	Look again! Do you see any flaw?
ثُمَّ ارْجِعِ الْبَصَرَ كَرَّتَيْنِ	4 Look again once more.
يَنقَلِبْ إِلَيْكَ الْبَصَرُ خَاسِئًا وَهُوَ حَسِيرٌ ۝	Your look will return to you, humbled and weary.
وَلَقَدْ زَيَّنَّا السَّمَاءَ الدُّنْيَا بِمَصَابِيحَ	5 We have certainly adorned the lowest heaven with lamps,
وَجَعَلْنَاهَا	and made them
رُجُومًا لِّلشَّيَاطِينِ	the means of pelting missiles[1] against the devils,
وَأَعْتَدْنَا لَهُمْ عَذَابَ السَّعِيرِ ۝	and We have prepared for them punishment of the Blaze.
وَلِلَّذِينَ كَفَرُوا بِرَبِّهِمْ	6 For those who defy their Lord
عَذَابُ جَهَنَّمَ ۖ وَبِئْسَ الْمَصِيرُ ۝	is the punishment of hell, and it is an evil destination.
إِذَا أُلْقُوا فِيهَا	7 When they are thrown in it
سَمِعُوا لَهَا شَهِيقًا وَهِيَ تَفُورُ ۝	they hear it blaring, as it seethes,
تَكَادُ تَمَيَّزُ مِنَ الْغَيْظِ	8 almost exploding with rage.
كُلَّمَا أُلْقِيَ فِيهَا فَوْجٌ	Whenever a group is thrown in it,
سَأَلَهُمْ خَزَنَتُهَا	its keepers will ask them,
أَلَمْ يَأْتِكُمْ نَذِيرٌ ۝	'Did not any warner come to you?'
قَالُوا بَلَىٰ قَدْ جَاءَنَا نَذِيرٌ	9 They will say, 'Yes, a warner did come to us,
فَكَذَّبْنَا وَقُلْنَا	but we impugned him and said,
مَا نَزَّلَ اللَّهُ مِن شَيْءٍ	'God did not send down anything;
إِنْ أَنتُمْ إِلَّا فِي ضَلَالٍ كَبِيرٍ ۝	you are only in great error.'
وَقَالُوا لَوْ كُنَّا نَسْمَعُ أَوْ نَعْقِلُ	10 They will say, 'Had we listened or exercised our reason,
مَا كُنَّا فِي أَصْحَابِ السَّعِيرِ ۝	we would not have been among inmates of the Blaze.'
فَاعْتَرَفُوا بِذَنبِهِمْ	11 Thus they will admit their sin.
فَسُحْقًا لِّأَصْحَابِ السَّعِيرِ ۝	So away with the inmates of the Blaze!
إِنَّ الَّذِينَ يَخْشَوْنَ رَبَّهُم بِالْغَيْبِ	12 Indeed, for those who fear their Lord in secret

---

[1] Or 'made them the [alleged] cause for the conjectures of the devils,' i.e. the astrologers from humans and jinn (*Tafsīr al-Ṣāfī*).

there will be forgiveness and a great reward.
13 Speak secretly, or do so openly,
   indeed He knows well what is in the breasts.
14 Would He who has created not know?
   And He is the All-attentive, the All-aware.
15 It is He who made the earth tractable for you;
   so walk on its flanks and eat of His provision,
   and towards Him is the resurrection.
16 Are you secure that He who is in the heaven
   will not make the earth swallow you while it quakes?
17 Are you secure that He who is in the heaven
   will not unleash upon you a rain of stones?
   Soon you will know how My warning has been!
18 Certainly those who were before them had impugned;
   but then how was My rebuttal![1]
19 Have they not regarded the birds above them,
   spreading and closing their wings?
   No one sustains them except the All-beneficent.
   He indeed watches all things.
20 Who is it that is your host
   who may help you, besides the All-beneficent?
   The faithless only dwell in delusion.
21 Who is it that may provide for you
   if He withholds His provision?
   Indeed, they persist in defiance and aversion.
22 Is he who walks prone on his face better guided,
   or he who walks upright on a straight path?
23 Say, 'It is He who created you
   and invested you with hearing, sight, and the hearts.

---

[1] Or, 'how was My requital.'

Little do you thank.'

24 Say, 'It is He who created you on the earth,
and toward Him you will be gathered.'

25 They say, 'When will this promise be fulfilled,
if you are truthful?'

26 Say, 'Its knowledge is only with God;
I am only a manifest warner.'

27 When they see it brought near,
the countenances of the faithless will be contorted,
and they will be told,
'This is what you had been asking for!'

28 Say, 'Tell me, irrespective of whether God destroys me
and those who are with me, or He has mercy on us,
who will shelter the faithless from a painful punishment?'

29 Say, 'He is the All-beneficent;
we have faith in Him, and in Him do we trust.
Soon you will know who is in plain error.'

30 Say, 'Tell me,
should your water sink down into the ground,
who will bring you running water?'

68. THE PEN[1]
al-Qalam

In the Name of God,
the All-beneficent, the All-merciful.

1 *Nūn.* By the Pen and what they write:
2 by your Lord's blessing, you are not crazy,[2]
3 and yours indeed will be an everlasting reward,
4 and indeed you possess a great character.

---

[1] This Makkī *sūrah* takes its name from "the Pen" (*al-qalam*) mentioned in verse 1.
[2] Or 'possessed by a demon' (*jinn*).

5 You will see and they will see, فَسَتُبْصِرُ وَيُبْصِرُونَ ۝

6 which one of you is crazy. بِأَييِّكُمُ الْمَفْتُونُ ۝

7 Indeed, *your* Lord knows best إِنَّ رَبَّكَ هُوَ أَعْلَمُ
   those who stray from His way, بِمَن ضَلَّ عَن سَبِيلِهِ
   and He knows best those who are guided. وَهُوَ أَعْلَمُ بِالْمُهْتَدِينَ ۝

8 So *do not obey* the deniers, فَلَا تُطِعِ الْمُكَذِّبِينَ ۝

9 who are eager that *you* should be undemanding, وَدُّوا لَوْ تُدْهِنُ
   so that they may be undemanding towards *you*. فَيُدْهِنُونَ ۝

10 And *do not obey* any vile swearer, وَلَا تُطِعْ كُلَّ حَلَّافٍ مَّهِينٍ ۝

11 scandal-monger, talebearer, هَمَّازٍ مَّشَّاءٍ بِنَمِيمٍ ۝

12 hinderer of all good, sinful transgressor, مَّنَّاعٍ لِّلْخَيْرِ مُعْتَدٍ أَثِيمٍ ۝

13 callous and, on top of that, baseborn [who behaves عُتُلٍّ بَعْدَ ذَٰلِكَ زَنِيمٍ ۝

14 thus only because he has wealth and children. أَن كَانَ ذَا مَالٍ وَبَنِينَ ۝

15 When Our signs are recited to him, إِذَا تُتْلَىٰ عَلَيْهِ آيَاتُنَا
   he says, 'Myths of the ancients!' قَالَ أَسَاطِيرُ الْأَوَّلِينَ ۝

16 Soon We shall brand him on his snout. سَنَسِمُهُ عَلَى الْخُرْطُومِ ۝

17 We have indeed tested them[1] إِنَّا بَلَوْنَاهُمْ
   just as We tested the People of the Garden كَمَا بَلَوْنَا أَصْحَابَ الْجَنَّةِ
   when they vowed they would gather its fruit at dawn, إِذْ أَقْسَمُوا لَيَصْرِمُنَّهَا مُصْبِحِينَ ۝

18 and they did not make any exception.[2] وَلَا يَسْتَثْنُونَ ۝

19 Then a visitation from your Lord visited it[3] فَطَافَ عَلَيْهَا طَائِفٌ مِّن رَّبِّكَ
   while they were asleep. وَهُمْ نَائِمُونَ ۝

20 So by dawn it was like a harvested field.[4] فَأَصْبَحَتْ كَالصَّرِيمِ ۝

21 At dawn they called out to one another, فَتَنَادَوْا مُصْبِحِينَ ۝

22 'Get off early to your field أَنِ اغْدُوا عَلَىٰ حَرْثِكُمْ
   if you have to gather the fruits.' إِن كُنتُمْ صَارِمِينَ ۝

23 So off they went, whispering to one another: فَانطَلَقُوا وَهُمْ يَتَخَافَتُونَ ۝

24 'Today no needy man shall come to you in it.' أَن لَّا يَدْخُلَنَّهَا الْيَوْمَ عَلَيْكُم مِّسْكِينٌ ۝

---

[1] That is, the people of Makkah, through famine and hunger.
[2] That is, for God's will, by saying, for instance, 'God willing.' See **18:24**
[3] That is, the garden.
[4] Or 'like a sand dune,' or 'like a gloomy night,' or 'like black ashes.'

25 They set out early morning considering themselves able to deprive [the poor of its fruit].

26 But when they saw it, they said, 'We have indeed lost our way!'

27 'No, it is we who have been deprived!'

28 The most upright among them said, 'Did I not tell you, "Why do you not glorify God?"'

29 They said, 'Immaculate is our Lord! We have indeed been wrongdoers!'

30 Then they turned to one another, blaming each other.

31 They said, 'Woe to us! Indeed, we have been rebellious.

32 Maybe our Lord will give us a better one in its place. Indeed, we earnestly beseech our Lord.'

33 Such was their punishment; and the punishment of the Hereafter is surely greater, had they known.

34 For the Godwary, there will indeed be gardens of bliss near their Lord.

35 Shall We treat those who submit to Us like We treat the guilty?

36 What is the matter with you? How do you judge!

37 Do you possess a scripture in which you read

38 that you shall have in it[1] whatever you choose?

39 Do you have a pledge binding on Us until the Day of Resurrection that you shall indeed have whatever you decide?

40 Ask them, which of them will aver any of that!

41 Do they have any 'partners' [that they claim for God]? Then let them produce their partners, if they are truthful.

---

[1] That is, in the next world.

42 The day when the catastrophe occurs[1]
and they are called to prostrate themselves,
they will not be able to do it.
43 With a humbled look, they will be overcast by abasement.
Certainly, they were called to prostrate themselves
while they were yet sound.
44 So leave Me with those who deny this discourse.
We will draw them imperceptibly into ruin
whence they do not know.
45 I will grant them respite,
for My devising is indeed sure.
46 Do you ask them for a reward,
so that they are weighed down with debt?
47 Do they possess access to the Unseen
so that they write it down?
48 So *submit patiently* to the judgement of your Lord,
and do not be like the Man of the Fish[2]
who called out as he choked with grief.
49 Had it not been for a blessing that came to his rescue
from his Lord,
he would surely have been cast on the bare shore,
being blameworthy.
50 So his Lord chose him
and made him one of the righteous.
51 Indeed, the faithless almost devour you
with their eyes
when they hear this Reminder,
and they say, 'He is indeed crazy.'
52 Yet it is just a reminder for all the nations.

---

[1] Literally, 'when the shank is uncovered,' an idiom implying the occurrence of a calamity, or a disclosure and denouement.
[2] That is, Jonah, elsewhere referred to as *'Dhun Nūn.'* See 21:87.

69. The Besieger[1]
al-Ḥāqqah

In the Name of God,
the All-beneficent, the All-merciful.

1 The Besieger![2]
2 What is the Besieger?!
3 What will show you what is the Besieger?!
4 Thamūd and ʿĀd denied the Cataclysm.
5 As for Thamūd, they were destroyed by the Cry.
6 And as for ʿĀd,
    they were destroyed by a fierce icy gale,
7 which He clamped upon them
    for seven grueling[3] nights and eight days,
    so that you could see the people there lying about prostrate,
    as if they were hollow trunks of palm trees.
8 So do you see any remaining trace of them?
9 Then Pharaoh and those who were before him
    and the towns that were overturned
    brought about iniquity.
10 They disobeyed the apostle of their Lord,
    so He seized them with a terrible seizing.
11 Indeed, when the Flood rose high,
    We carried you in a floating ark,
12 that We might make it a reminder for you
    and that receptive ears might remember it.
13 When the Trumpet is blown with a single blast

---

[1] This Makkī sūrah takes its name from *"al-Ḥāqqah"* (the Besieger) mentioned in verse 1.
[2] Or 'the Inevitable.' That is, the Day of Resurrection.
[3] Or 'successive.'

وَحُمِلَتِ الْأَرْضُ وَالْجِبَالُ	14	and the earth and the mountains are lifted
فَدُكَّتَا دَكَّةً وَاحِدَةً ۝		and levelled with a single leveling,[1]
فَيَوْمَئِذٍ وَقَعَتِ الْوَاقِعَةُ ۝	15	then, on that day, will the Imminent Hour befall[2]
وَانْشَقَّتِ السَّمَاءُ	16	and the heaven will be split open
فَهِيَ يَوْمَئِذٍ وَاهِيَةٌ ۝		—for it will be frail on that day—
وَالْمَلَكُ عَلَىٰ أَرْجَائِهَا	17	with the angels all over it,
وَيَحْمِلُ عَرْشَ رَبِّكَ فَوْقَهُمْ		and the Throne of your Lord will be borne
يَوْمَئِذٍ ثَمَانِيَةٌ ۝		that day by eight angels.
يَوْمَئِذٍ تُعْرَضُونَ	18	That day you will be presented before your Lord:
لَا تَخْفَىٰ مِنْكُمْ خَافِيَةٌ ۝		none of your secrets will remain hidden.
فَأَمَّا مَنْ أُوتِيَ كِتَابَهُ بِيَمِينِهِ	19	As for him who is given his book in his right hand,
فَيَقُولُ هَاؤُمُ اقْرَءُوا كِتَابِيَهْ ۝		he will say, 'Here, take and read my book!
إِنِّي ظَنَنْتُ أَنِّي مُلَاقٍ حِسَابِيَهْ ۝	20	I indeed knew that I will encounter my account.'
فَهُوَ فِي عِيشَةٍ رَاضِيَةٍ ۝	21	So he will have a pleasant life,
فِي جَنَّةٍ عَالِيَةٍ ۝	22	in an elevated garden,
قُطُوفُهَا دَانِيَةٌ ۝	23	whose clusters of fruits will be within easy reach.
كُلُوا وَاشْرَبُوا هَنِيئًا	24	[He will be told]: 'Enjoy your food and drink,
بِمَا أَسْلَفْتُمْ فِي الْأَيَّامِ الْخَالِيَةِ ۝		for what you had sent in advance in past days.'
وَأَمَّا مَنْ أُوتِيَ كِتَابَهُ بِشِمَالِهِ	25	But as for him who is given his book in his left hand,
فَيَقُولُ يَا لَيْتَنِي لَمْ أُوتَ كِتَابِيَهْ ۝		he will say, 'I wish I had not been given my book,
وَلَمْ أَدْرِ مَا حِسَابِيَهْ ۝	26	nor had I ever known what my account is!
يَا لَيْتَهَا كَانَتِ الْقَاضِيَةَ ۝	27	I wish death had been the end of it all!
مَا أَغْنَىٰ عَنِّي مَالِيَهْ ۝	28	My wealth did not avail me.
هَلَكَ عَنِّي سُلْطَانِيَهْ ۝	29	My authority has left me.'
خُذُوهُ فَغُلُّوهُ ۝	30	[The angels will be told:] 'Seize him and fetter him!
ثُمَّ الْجَحِيمَ صَلُّوهُ ۝	31	Then put him into hell.
ثُمَّ فِي سِلْسِلَةٍ ذَرْعُهَا سَبْعُونَ ذِرَاعًا	32	Then, in a chain whose length is seventy cubits,
فَاسْلُكُوهُ ۝		string him.
إِنَّهُ كَانَ لَا يُؤْمِنُ بِاللَّهِ الْعَظِيمِ ۝	33	Indeed, he had no faith in God, the All-supreme,

---

[1] Or 'crumbled with a single crumbling.'
[2] 56:1-6

34 وَلَا يَحُضُّ عَلَىٰ طَعَامِ الْمِسْكِينِ ۝ and he did not urge the feeding of the needy,

35 فَلَيْسَ لَهُ الْيَوْمَ هَاهُنَا حَمِيمٌ ۝ so he has no friend here today,

36 وَلَا طَعَامٌ إِلَّا مِنْ غِسْلِينٍ ۝ nor any food except pus,

37 لَا يَأْكُلُهُ إِلَّا الْخَاطِئُونَ ۝ which no one shall eat except the iniquitous.'

38 فَلَا أُقْسِمُ بِمَا تُبْصِرُونَ ۝ I swear by what you see

39 وَمَا لَا تُبْصِرُونَ ۝ and what you do not see:

40 إِنَّهُ لَقَوْلُ رَسُولٍ كَرِيمٍ ۝ it is indeed the speech of a noble apostle,

41 وَمَا هُوَ بِقَوْلِ شَاعِرٍ ۝ and it is not the speech of a poet.

قَلِيلًا مَا تُؤْمِنُونَ ۝ Little is the faith that you have!

42 وَلَا بِقَوْلِ كَاهِنٍ ۝ Nor is it the speech of a soothsayer

قَلِيلًا مَا تَذَكَّرُونَ ۝ —little is the admonition that you take!—

43 تَنْزِيلٌ مِنْ رَبِّ الْعَالَمِينَ ۝ gradually sent down from the Lord of all the worlds.

44 وَلَوْ تَقَوَّلَ عَلَيْنَا بَعْضَ الْأَقَاوِيلِ ۝ Had he faked any sayings in Our name,

45 لَأَخَذْنَا مِنْهُ بِالْيَمِينِ ۝ We would have surely seized him by the right hand

46 ثُمَّ لَقَطَعْنَا مِنْهُ الْوَتِينَ ۝ and then cut off his aorta,

47 فَمَا مِنْكُمْ مِنْ أَحَدٍ عَنْهُ حَاجِزِينَ ۝ and none of you could have held Us off from him.

48 وَإِنَّهُ لَتَذْكِرَةٌ لِلْمُتَّقِينَ ۝ It is indeed a reminder for the Godwary.

49 وَإِنَّا لَنَعْلَمُ ۝ We indeed know

أَنَّ مِنْكُمْ مُكَذِّبِينَ ۝ that there are some among you who deny it.

50 وَإِنَّهُ لَحَسْرَةٌ عَلَى الْكَافِرِينَ ۝ And it will indeed be a matter of regret for the faithless.

51 وَإِنَّهُ لَحَقُّ الْيَقِينِ ۝ It is indeed certain truth.

52 فَسَبِّحْ بِاسْمِ رَبِّكَ الْعَظِيمِ ۝ So *celebrate* the Name of *your* Lord, the All-supreme.

70. LOFTY STATIONS[1]
al-Ma'ārij

بِسْمِ اللَّهِ الرَّحْمَٰنِ الرَّحِيمِ

In the Name of God,
the All-beneficent, the All-merciful.

1 سَأَلَ سَائِلٌ بِعَذَابٍ وَاقِعٍ ۝ An asker asked for a punishment sure to befall

2 لِلْكَافِرِينَ لَيْسَ لَهُ دَافِعٌ ۝ —which none can avert from the faithless—

---
[1] This Madanī *sūrah* is named after the phrase *dhil ma'ārij* (of lofty stations) in verse 3.

3 مِنَ اللَّهِ ذِي الْمَعَارِجِ ۝ from God, Lord of the lofty stations.

4 تَعْرُجُ الْمَلَائِكَةُ وَالرُّوحُ إِلَيْهِ The angels and the Spirit ascend to Him
فِي يَوْمٍ كَانَ مِقْدَارُهُ خَمْسِينَ أَلْفَ سَنَةٍ ۝ in a day whose span is fifty thousand years.

5 فَاصْبِرْ صَبْرًا جَمِيلًا ۝ So *be patient*, with a patience that is graceful.

6 إِنَّهُمْ يَرَوْنَهُ بَعِيدًا ۝ They indeed see it to be far off,

7 وَنَرَاهُ قَرِيبًا ۝ and We see it to be near.

8 يَوْمَ تَكُونُ السَّمَاءُ كَالْمُهْلِ ۝ The day when the sky will be like molten copper,

9 وَتَكُونُ الْجِبَالُ كَالْعِهْنِ ۝ and the mountains like tufts of dyed wool,

10 وَلَا يَسْأَلُ حَمِيمٌ حَمِيمًا ۝ and no friend will inquire about friend,

11 يُبَصَّرُونَهُمْ though they will be placed within each other's sight.
يَوَدُّ الْمُجْرِمُ لَوْ يَفْتَدِي The guilty one will wish he could ransom himself
مِنْ عَذَابِ يَوْمِئِذٍ from the punishment of that day
بِبَنِيهِ ۝ at the price of his children,

12 وَصَاحِبَتِهِ وَأَخِيهِ ۝ his spouse and his brother,

13 وَفَصِيلَتِهِ الَّتِي تُؤْوِيهِ ۝ his kin which had sheltered him

14 وَمَنْ فِي الْأَرْضِ جَمِيعًا and all those who are upon the earth,
ثُمَّ يُنْجِيهِ ۝ if that might deliver him.

15 كَلَّا إِنَّهَا لَظَىٰ ۝ Never! It is indeed a blazing fire,

16 نَزَّاعَةً لِلشَّوَىٰ ۝ which strips away the scalp.

17 تَدْعُو مَنْ أَدْبَرَ It invites him who has turned his back on the truth
وَتَوَلَّىٰ ۝ and forsaken it,

18 وَجَمَعَ فَأَوْعَىٰ ۝ amassing wealth and hoarding it.

19 إِنَّ الْإِنْسَانَ خُلِقَ هَلُوعًا ۝ The human being has indeed been created covetous:

20 إِذَا مَسَّهُ الشَّرُّ جَزُوعًا ۝ anxious when an ill befalls him

21 وَإِذَا مَسَّهُ الْخَيْرُ مَنُوعًا ۝ and grudging charity when good comes his way

22 إِلَّا الْمُصَلِّينَ ۝ —[all are such] except the prayerful,

23 الَّذِينَ هُمْ عَلَىٰ صَلَاتِهِمْ دَائِمُونَ ۝ those who persevere in their prayers

24 وَالَّذِينَ فِي أَمْوَالِهِمْ حَقٌّ مَعْلُومٌ ۝ and there is a known share in whose wealth

25 لِلسَّائِلِ وَالْمَحْرُومِ ۝ for the beggar and the deprived,

26 وَالَّذِينَ يُصَدِّقُونَ بِيَوْمِ الدِّينِ ۝ and who affirm the Day of Retribution,

27 وَالَّذِينَ هُمْ مِنْ عَذَابِ رَبِّهِم مُّشْفِقُونَ ۝

27 and those who are apprehensive of the punishment of their Lord

28 إِنَّ عَذَابَ رَبِّهِمْ غَيْرُ مَأْمُونٍ ۝

28 (there is indeed no security from the punishment of their Lord)

29 وَالَّذِينَ هُمْ لِفُرُوجِهِمْ حَافِظُونَ ۝

29 and those who guard their private parts

30 إِلَّا عَلَىٰ أَزْوَاجِهِمْ أَوْ مَا مَلَكَتْ أَيْمَانُهُمْ فَإِنَّهُمْ غَيْرُ مَلُومِينَ ۝

30 (except from their spouses and their slave women, for then they are not blameworthy;

31 فَمَنِ ابْتَغَىٰ وَرَاءَ ذَٰلِكَ فَأُولَٰئِكَ هُمُ الْعَادُونَ ۝

31 but whoever seeks beyond that —it is they who are the transgressors)

32 وَالَّذِينَ هُمْ لِأَمَانَاتِهِمْ وَعَهْدِهِمْ رَاعُونَ ۝

32 and those who keep their trusts and covenants,

33 وَالَّذِينَ هُم بِشَهَادَاتِهِمْ قَائِمُونَ ۝

33 and those who are conscientious in their testimonies,

34 وَالَّذِينَ هُمْ عَلَىٰ صَلَاتِهِمْ يُحَافِظُونَ ۝

34 and those who are watchful of their prayers.

35 أُولَٰئِكَ فِي جَنَّاتٍ مُّكْرَمُونَ ۝

35 They will be in gardens, held in honour.

36 فَمَالِ الَّذِينَ كَفَرُوا قِبَلَكَ مُهْطِعِينَ ۝

36 What is the matter with the faithless[1] that they scramble toward you

37 عَنِ الْيَمِينِ وَعَنِ الشِّمَالِ عِزِينَ ۝

37 from left and right in groups?

38 أَيَطْمَعُ كُلُّ امْرِئٍ مِّنْهُمْ أَن يُدْخَلَ جَنَّةَ نَعِيمٍ ۝

38 Does each man among them hope to enter the garden of bliss?

39 كَلَّا

39 Never!

إِنَّا خَلَقْنَاهُم مِّمَّا يَعْلَمُونَ ۝

Indeed, We created them from what they know.[2]

40 فَلَا أُقْسِمُ بِرَبِّ الْمَشَارِقِ وَالْمَغَارِبِ إِنَّا لَقَادِرُونَ ۝

40 So I swear by the Lord of the easts and the wests that We are able

41 عَلَىٰ أَن نُّبَدِّلَ خَيْرًا مِّنْهُمْ وَمَا نَحْنُ بِمَسْبُوقِينَ ۝

41 to replace them with others better than them and We are not to be outmaneuvered.

42 فَذَرْهُمْ يَخُوضُوا وَيَلْعَبُوا حَتَّىٰ يُلَاقُوا يَوْمَهُمُ الَّذِي يُوعَدُونَ ۝

42 So leave them to gossip and play till they encounter the day they are promised:

43 يَوْمَ يَخْرُجُونَ مِنَ الْأَجْدَاثِ سِرَاعًا كَأَنَّهُمْ إِلَىٰ نُصُبٍ يُوفِضُونَ ۝

43 the day when they emerge from the graves, hastening, as if racing toward a target,

44 خَاشِعَةً أَبْصَارُهُمْ

44 with a humbled look in their eyes,

---

[1] That is, the hypocrites.
[2] That is, from a drop of sperm.

overcast by abasement.
That is the day they had been promised.

71. NOAH[1]
Nūḥ

In the Name of God,
the All-beneficent, the All-merciful.

1 Indeed, We sent Noah to his people,
saying, 'Warn your people
before a painful punishment overtakes them.'

2 He said, 'O my people!
I am indeed a manifest warner to you.

3 Worship God and be wary of Him,
and obey me,

4 that He may forgive you some of your sins
and respite you until a specified time.
When God's appointed time indeed comes,
it cannot be deferred, if you know.'

5 He said, 'My Lord!
I have indeed summoned my people day and night

6 but my summons only increases their evasion.

7 Indeed, whenever I have summoned them
so that You might forgive them,
they would put their fingers into their ears
and draw their cloaks over their heads,
and they were persistent in their unfaith
and disdainful in their arrogance.

8 Again I summoned them aloud,

9 and again appealed to them publicly

---

[1] This Makkī *sūrah* is named after Noah ('a), whose account is related in it.

	and confided with them privately,
10	telling them: "Plead to your Lord for forgiveness.
	He is indeed all-forgiving.
11	He will send for you abundant rains from the heaven
12	and aid you with wealth and children,
	and provide you with gardens
	and provide you with streams.
13	What is the matter with you
	that you do not look upon God with veneration,
14	though He has created you in various stages?
15	Have you not seen how God has created
	the seven heavens in layers
16	and made therein the moon for a light,
	and the sun for a lamp?
17	God made you grow from the earth,
	with a vegetable growth.
18	Then He makes you return to it,
	and He will bring you forth without fail.
19	God has made the earth a vast expanse for you
20	so that you may travel over its spacious ways."'
21	Noah said, 'My Lord! They have disobeyed me,
	following those
	whose wealth and children only add to their loss,
22	and they have devised an outrageous plot.
23	They say, "Do not abandon your gods.
	Do not abandon Wadd, nor Suwā,
	nor Yaghūth, Ya'ūq and Nasr,"[1]
24	and already they have led many astray.
	Do not increase the wrongdoers in anything but error.'

---

[1] Names of Babylonian gods worshiped by the polytheists.

25 They were drowned because of their iniquities,
then made to enter a Fire,
and they did not find for themselves
any helpers besides God.

26 And Noah said, 'My Lord! Do not leave on the earth
any inhabitant from among the faithless.

27 If You leave them, they will lead astray Your servants,
and will beget none except vicious ingrates.

28 My Lord! Forgive me and my parents,
and whoever enters my house in faith,
and the faithful men and women,
and do not increase the wrongdoers in anything but ruin.'

72. THE JINN[1]
al-Jinn

In the Name of God,
the All-beneficent, the All-merciful.

1 *Say,* 'It has been revealed to me
that a team of the jinn listened [to the Qur'ān],
and they said, "We have indeed heard a wonderful *qur'ān*,

2 which guides to rectitude.
Hence we have believed in it
and we will never ascribe any partner to our Lord.

3 Exalted be the majesty of our Lord,
He has taken neither any spouse nor offspring.

4 The foolish ones among us used to speak
atrocious lies concerning God.

5 We thought that humans and jinn would never utter
any falsehood concerning God.

---

[1] This Makkī *sūrah* is named after the jinn, whose account is given in its first part.

6 Indeed, some persons from the humans
would seek the protection of some persons from the jinn,
thus only adding to their rebellion.

7 They[1] thought, just as you think,
that God will not raise anyone from the dead.

8 Indeed, we made for the heaven and found it
full of mighty sentries and flames.[2]

9 We used to sit in its positions to eavesdrop,
but anyone listening now
finds a flame waiting for him.

10 We do not know whether ill is intended
for those who are on the earth,
or whether their Lord intends good for them.

11 Among us some are righteous and some are otherwise:
we are various sects.

12 We know that we cannot frustrate God on the earth,
nor can we frustrate Him by fleeing.

13 When we heard the message of guidance,
we believed in it.
Whoever that has faith in his Lord
will fear neither privation nor oppression.

14 Among us some are *muslims* and some of us are perverse."'[3]
Those who submit—it is they who pursue rectitude.

15 As for the perverse, they will be firewood for hell.

16 If they are steadfast on the path of God,
We shall provide them with abundant water,

17 so that We may test them therein,
and whoever turns away from the remembrance of his Lord,

---

[1] That is, the humans who invoked protection of the jinn.
[2] Or 'meteors.'
[3] Or 'unjust.'

He will let him into an escalating punishment.

18 The places of worship belong to God,
so do not invoke anyone along with God.

19 When the servant of God[1] rose to pray to Him,
they almost crowded around him.

20 Say, 'I pray only to my Lord
and I do not ascribe any partner to Him.'

21 Say, 'I have no power to bring you any harm
or good [of my own accord].'

22 Say, 'Neither can anyone shelter me from God,
nor can I find any refuge besides Him.

23 [I have no duty] except to transmit from God,
and to communicate His messages;
and whoever disobeys God and His apostle,
there will indeed be for him the fire of hell,
to remain in it forever.'

24 When they see what they are promised,
they will know who is weaker in supporters
and fewer in numbers.

25 Say, 'I do not know if what you are promised is near,
or if my Lord has set a long term for it.'

26 Knower of the Unseen,
He does not disclose His [knowledge of the] Unseen to anyone

27 except an apostle that He approves of.
Then He dispatches before
and behind him a sentinel

28 so that He may ascertain
that they have delivered the messages of their Lord,
and He encompasses all that is with them,

---

[1] That is, the Prophet.

وَأَحْصَىٰ كُلَّ شَيْءٍ عَدَدًا ۝ and He keeps a count of all things.

73. ENWRAPPED[1]
al- Muzzammil

بِسْمِ اللَّهِ
الرَّحْمَٰنِ الرَّحِيمِ

In the Name of God,
the All-beneficent, the All-merciful.

1 يَا أَيُّهَا الْمُزَّمِّلُ ۝ 1 O you wrapped up in your mantle!

قُمِ اللَّيْلَ إِلَّا قَلِيلًا ۝ 2 *Stand vigil* through the night, except for a little of it,

نِصْفَهُ أَوِ انْقُصْ مِنْهُ قَلِيلًا ۝ 3 a half, or *reduce* a little from that

أَوْ زِدْ عَلَيْهِ 4 or *add* to it,

وَرَتِّلِ الْقُرْآنَ تَرْتِيلًا ۝ and *recite* the Qur'ān in a measured tone.

إِنَّا سَنُلْقِي عَلَيْكَ قَوْلًا ثَقِيلًا ۝ 5 Indeed, soon We will cast on you a weighty discourse.

إِنَّ نَاشِئَةَ اللَّيْلِ هِيَ أَشَدُّ وَطْئًا 6 The watch of the night is indeed firmer in tread

وَأَقْوَمُ قِيلًا ۝ and more upright in respect to speech,

إِنَّ لَكَ فِي النَّهَارِ سَبْحًا طَوِيلًا ۝ 7 for during the day *you* have drawn-out engagements.

وَاذْكُرِ اسْمَ رَبِّكَ 8 So *celebrate* the Name of your Lord

وَتَبَتَّلْ إِلَيْهِ تَبْتِيلًا ۝ and dedicate yourself to Him with total dedication.[2]

رَبُّ الْمَشْرِقِ وَالْمَغْرِبِ 9 Lord of the east and the west,

لَا إِلَٰهَ إِلَّا هُوَ there is no god except Him,

فَاتَّخِذْهُ وَكِيلًا ۝ so take Him for your trustee,

وَاصْبِرْ عَلَىٰ مَا يَقُولُونَ 10 and *be patient* over what they say,

وَاهْجُرْهُمْ هَجْرًا جَمِيلًا ۝ and *distance yourself* from them in a graceful manner.

وَذَرْنِي وَالْمُكَذِّبِينَ أُولِي النَّعْمَةِ 11 Leave Me to deal with the deniers, the opulent,

وَمَهِّلْهُمْ قَلِيلًا ۝ and *give* them a little respite.

إِنَّ لَدَيْنَا أَنْكَالًا وَجَحِيمًا ۝ 12 With Us indeed are heavy fetters and a fierce fire,

وَطَعَامًا ذَا غُصَّةٍ 13 and a food that chokes those who eat it,

وَعَذَابًا أَلِيمًا ۝ and a painful punishment prepared for

يَوْمَ تَرْجُفُ الْأَرْضُ وَالْجِبَالُ 14 the day when the earth and the mountains will quake,

---

[1] This early Makkī *sūrah* takes its name from the word *"muzzammil"* (wrapped in mantle) in verse 1.
[2] Or 'supplicate with your forefinger pointed towards heaven' (see *al-Tafsīr al-Burhān* for traditions relating to *tabattul*).

and the mountains will be like dunes of shifting sand.
15 We have indeed sent to you an apostle
    to be a witness to you,
    just as We sent an apostle to Pharaoh.
16 But Pharaoh disobeyed the apostle,
    so We seized him with a terrible seizing.
17 So if you disbelieve, how will you avoid the day
    which will make children white-headed,
18 and wherein the heaven will be rent apart?
    His promise is bound to be fulfilled.
19 This is indeed a reminder.
    So let anyone who wishes take the way toward his Lord.
20 Your Lord indeed knows
    that you stand vigil for nearly two thirds of the night
    —or at times a half or a third of it—
    along with a group of those who are with you.
    God measures the night and the day.
    He knows that you cannot calculate it exactly
    and so He was lenient toward you.
    So recite as much of the Qur'ān as is feasible.
    He knows that some of you will be sick,
    while others will travel in the land
        seeking God's bounty,
    and yet others will fight in the way of God.
    So recite as much of it as is feasible,
        and maintain the prayer and pay the *zakāt*
        and lend God a good loan.
    Whatever good you send ahead for your souls
        you will find it with God in a form
        that is better and greater with respect to reward.

وَاسْتَغْفِرُوا اللَّهَ ۖ And plead to God for forgiveness;
إِنَّ اللَّهَ غَفُورٌ رَحِيمٌ ۝ indeed God is all-forgiving, all-merciful.

74. SHROUDED[1]
al-Muddaththir

بِسْمِ اللَّهِ
الرَّحْمَـٰنِ الرَّحِيمِ

In the Name of God,
the All-beneficent, the All-merciful.

1 يَا أَيُّهَا الْمُدَّثِّرُ ۝ O you wrapped up in your mantle!
2 قُمْ فَأَنذِرْ ۝ Rise up and warn!
3 وَرَبَّكَ فَكَبِّرْ ۝ Magnify your Lord,
4 وَثِيَابَكَ فَطَهِّرْ ۝ purify *your* clothes
5 وَالرُّجْزَ فَاهْجُرْ ۝ and *keep away* from all impurity!
6 وَلَا تَمْنُن تَسْتَكْثِرُ ۝ *Do not grant* a favour seeking a greater gain,
7 وَلِرَبِّكَ فَاصْبِرْ ۝ and *be patient* for the sake of your Lord.
8 فَإِذَا نُقِرَ فِي النَّاقُورِ ۝ When the Trumpet will be sounded,
9 فَذَٰلِكَ يَوْمَئِذٍ يَوْمٌ عَسِيرٌ ۝ that day will be a day of hardship,
10 عَلَى الْكَافِرِينَ غَيْرُ يَسِيرٍ ۝ not at all easy for the faithless.
11 ذَرْنِي وَمَنْ خَلَقْتُ وَحِيدًا ۝ Leave Me to deal with him whom I created alone
12 وَجَعَلْتُ لَهُ مَالًا مَّمْدُودًا ۝ and furnished him with extensive means,
13 وَبَنِينَ شُهُودًا ۝ and gave him sons to be at his side,
14 وَمَهَّدتُّ لَهُ تَمْهِيدًا ۝ and facilitated all matters for him.
15 ثُمَّ يَطْمَعُ أَنْ أَزِيدَ ۝ Still he is eager that I should give him more.
16 كَلَّا ۖ إِنَّهُ كَانَ لِآيَاتِنَا عَنِيدًا ۝ No indeed! He is an obstinate opponent of Our signs.
17 سَأُرْهِقُهُ صَعُودًا ۝ Soon I will overwhelm him with hardship.
18 إِنَّهُ فَكَّرَ وَقَدَّرَ ۝ Indeed, he reflected and decided.
19 فَقُتِلَ كَيْفَ قَدَّرَ ۝ Perish he, how he decided!
20 ثُمَّ قُتِلَ كَيْفَ قَدَّرَ ۝ Again, perish he, how he decided!
21 ثُمَّ نَظَرَ ۝ Then he looked;
22 ثُمَّ عَبَسَ وَبَسَرَ ۝ then he frowned and scowled,.

---

[1] This early Makkī *sūrah* takes its name from the word "*muddaththir*" (wrapped in mantle) in verse 1.

ثُمَّ أَدْبَرَ وَاسْتَكْبَرَ ۝	23 and turned away disdainfully,
فَقَالَ إِنْ هَذَا إِلَّا سِحْرٌ يُؤْثَرُ ۝	24 saying, 'It[1] is nothing but traditional sorcery.
إِنْ هَذَا إِلَّا قَوْلُ الْبَشَرِ ۝	25 It is nothing but the speech of a human.'
سَأُصْلِيهِ سَقَرَ ۝	26 Soon I will cast him into *Saqar*.[2]
وَمَا أَدْرَاكَ مَا سَقَرُ ۝	27 And what will show you what is *Saqar*?
لَا تُبْقِي وَلَا تَذَرُ ۝	28 It neither spares nor leaves anything.
لَوَّاحَةٌ لِلْبَشَرِ ۝	29 It burns the skin.
عَلَيْهَا تِسْعَةَ عَشَرَ ۝	30 There are nineteen keepers over it.
وَمَا جَعَلْنَا أَصْحَابَ النَّارِ إِلَّا مَلَائِكَةً	31 We have assigned only angels as keepers of the Fire,
وَمَا جَعَلْنَا عِدَّتَهُمْ	and We have made their number
إِلَّا فِتْنَةً لِلَّذِينَ كَفَرُوا	merely a stumbling block for the faithless,
لِيَسْتَيْقِنَ الَّذِينَ أُوتُوا الْكِتَابَ	so that those who were given the Book may be reassured
وَيَزْدَادَ الَّذِينَ آمَنُوا إِيمَانًا	and the faithful may increase in their faith,
وَلَا يَرْتَابَ الَّذِينَ أُوتُوا الْكِتَابَ	and so that those given the Book may not be in doubt,
وَالْمُؤْمِنُونَ	along with the faithful,
وَلِيَقُولَ الَّذِينَ فِي قُلُوبِهِمْ مَرَضٌ	and so that those in whose hearts is sickness may say,
وَالْكَافِرُونَ	along with the faithless,
مَاذَا أَرَادَ اللَّهُ بِهَذَا مَثَلًا	'What did God mean by this description?'
كَذَلِكَ يُضِلُّ اللَّهُ مَنْ يَشَاءُ	Thus does God lead astray whomever He wishes
وَيَهْدِي مَنْ يَشَاءُ	and guides whomever He wishes.
وَمَا يَعْلَمُ جُنُودَ رَبِّكَ إِلَّا هُوَ	No one knows the hosts of *your* Lord except Him,
وَمَا هِيَ إِلَّا ذِكْرَى لِلْبَشَرِ ۝	and it[3] is just an admonition for all humans.
كَلَّا وَالْقَمَرِ ۝	32 No indeed! By the Moon!
وَاللَّيْلِ إِذْ أَدْبَرَ ۝	33 By the night when it recedes!
وَالصُّبْحِ إِذَا أَسْفَرَ ۝	34 By the dawn when it brightens!
إِنَّهَا لَإِحْدَى الْكُبَرِ ۝	35 They[4] are indeed one of the greatest signs
نَذِيرًا لِلْبَشَرِ ۝	36 —a warner to all humans,
لِمَنْ شَاءَ مِنْكُمْ أَنْ يَتَقَدَّمَ	37 alike for those of you who like to advance ahead

---

[1] That is, the Qur'ān.
[2] *Saqar* is another name for hell or a part of it.
[3] That is, the statement that there are nineteen wardens in charge of hell.
[4] That is, the verses of the Qur'ān.

and those who would remain behind. أَوْ يَتَأَخَّرَ ۝

38 Every soul is hostage to what it has earned, كُلُّ نَفْسٍ بِمَا كَسَبَتْ رَهِينَةٌ ۝

39 except the People of the Right Hand. إِلَّا أَصْحَابَ الْيَمِينِ ۝

40 They will be in gardens, questioning فِي جَنَّاتٍ يَتَسَاءَلُونَ ۝

41 the guilty: عَنِ الْمُجْرِمِينَ ۝

42 'What drew you into Hell?' مَا سَلَكَكُمْ فِي سَقَرَ ۝

43 They will answer, قَالُوا

'We were not among those who prayed.[1] لَمْ نَكُ مِنَ الْمُصَلِّينَ ۝

44 Nor did we feed the poor. وَلَمْ نَكُ نُطْعِمُ الْمِسْكِينَ ۝

45 We used to indulge in profane gossip وَكُنَّا نَخُوضُ

with the gossipers, مَعَ الْخَائِضِينَ ۝

46 and we used to deny the Day of Retribution,[2] وَكُنَّا نُكَذِّبُ بِيَوْمِ الدِّينِ ۝

47 until death came to us.' حَتَّىٰ أَتَانَا الْيَقِينُ ۝

48 So the intercession of the intercessors will not avail them. فَمَا تَنْفَعُهُمْ شَفَاعَةُ الشَّافِعِينَ ۝

49 What is the matter with them that they evade the Reminder فَمَا لَهُمْ عَنِ التَّذْكِرَةِ مُعْرِضِينَ ۝

50 as if they were terrified asses كَأَنَّهُمْ حُمُرٌ مُسْتَنْفِرَةٌ ۝

51 fleeing from a lion? فَرَّتْ مِنْ قَسْوَرَةٍ ۝

52 But everyone of them desires بَلْ يُرِيدُ كُلُّ امْرِئٍ مِنْهُمْ

to be given unrolled scriptures [from God]. أَنْ يُؤْتَىٰ صُحُفًا مُنَشَّرَةً ۝

53 No! Indeed, they do not fear the Hereafter. كَلَّا ۖ بَلْ لَا يَخَافُونَ الْآخِرَةَ ۝

54 No! It is indeed a reminder. كَلَّا إِنَّهُ تَذْكِرَةٌ ۝

55 So let anyone who wishes be mindful of it. فَمَنْ شَاءَ ذَكَرَهُ ۝

56 And they will not be mindful unless God wishes. وَمَا يَذْكُرُونَ إِلَّا أَنْ يَشَاءَ اللَّهُ

He is worthy of your being wary of Him هُوَ أَهْلُ التَّقْوَىٰ

and He is worthy to forgive. وَأَهْلُ الْمَغْفِرَةِ ۝

---

[1] Or 'We were not among followers of the leaders (or forerunners, mentioned in 56:10).' (See *Tafsīr al-Qummī*, *Tafsīr Furāt al-Kūfī*, *al-Kāfī*, i, 484, "Kitāb al-Ḥujjah," bāb 108 (bāb fīhi nukat wa nutaf min al-tanzīl fī al-wilāyah), no. 38.

[2] Or 'the Day of Judgement.'

75. Resurrection[1]
al-Qiyāmah

In the Name of God,
the All-beneficent, the All-merciful.

1 I swear by the Day of Resurrection!

2 And I swear by the self-critical soul!

3 Does the human being suppose that We will not put together his bones at resurrection?

4 Of course, We are able to reshape even his fingertips!

5 The human being indeed desires to go on living viciously.

6 He asks, 'When will this "day of resurrection" be?!'

7 But when the eyes are dazzled,

8 the moon is eclipsed,

9 and the sun and the moon are brought together,

10 that day the human being will say, 'Where is the escape [from this day]?'

11 No indeed! There will be no refuge!

12 That day the final goal will be toward *your* Lord.

13 On that day the human being will be informed about what works he had sent ahead and the legacy he had left behind.

14 Rather the human being is witness to his own self,

15 though he should offer his excuses to justify his faults.

16 *Do not move your tongue with it to hasten it.*

17 *It is indeed up to Us to put it together and to recite it.*

18 *And when We have recited it, follow its recitation.*

19 *Then, its exposition also lies with Us.*

20 No! Indeed, you love this transitory life

---

[1] This Makkī *sūrah* takes its name from verse 1, which mentions the Day of Resurrection.

وَتَذَرُونَ الْآخِرَةَ ۝	21	and forsake the Hereafter.
وُجُوهٌ يَوْمَئِذٍ نَاضِرَةٌ ۝	22	Some faces will be fresh on that day,
إِلَىٰ رَبِّهَا نَاظِرَةٌ ۝	23	looking to their Lord,
وَوُجُوهٌ يَوْمَئِذٍ بَاسِرَةٌ ۝	24	and some faces will be scowling on that day,
تَظُنُّ أَن يُفْعَلَ بِهَا فَاقِرَةٌ ۝	25	knowing that they will be dealt out a punishment breaking the spine.
كَلَّا إِذَا بَلَغَتِ التَّرَاقِيَ ۝	26	No indeed! When the soul reaches the collar bones,
وَقِيلَ مَنْ ۜ رَاقٍ ۝	27	and it is said, 'Who will take him up?'[1]
وَظَنَّ أَنَّهُ الْفِرَاقُ ۝	28	and he knows that it is the time of parting,
وَالْتَفَّتِ السَّاقُ بِالسَّاقِ ۝	29	and each shank clasps the other shank,[2]
إِلَىٰ رَبِّكَ يَوْمَئِذٍ الْمَسَاقُ ۝	30	that day he shall be driven toward *your* Lord.
فَلَا صَدَّقَ وَلَا صَلَّىٰ ۝	31	He neither confirmed God's messages, nor did he pray,
وَلَٰكِن كَذَّبَ وَتَوَلَّىٰ ۝	32	but denied them and turned away,
ثُمَّ ذَهَبَ إِلَىٰ أَهْلِهِ يَتَمَطَّىٰ ۝	33	and went away swaggering to his family.
أَوْلَىٰ لَكَ فَأَوْلَىٰ ۝	34	So woe to you! Woe to you!
ثُمَّ أَوْلَىٰ لَكَ فَأَوْلَىٰ ۝	35	Again, woe to you! Woe to you!
أَيَحْسَبُ الْإِنسَانُ أَن يُتْرَكَ سُدًى ۝	36	Does the human being suppose that he has been abandoned to futility?
أَلَمْ يَكُ نُطْفَةً مِّن مَّنِيٍّ يُمْنَىٰ ۝	37	Was he not a drop of emitted semen
ثُمَّ كَانَ عَلَقَةً ۝	38	and then a clinging tissue?
فَخَلَقَ فَسَوَّىٰ ۝		Whereat He created and proportioned him,
فَجَعَلَ مِنْهُ الزَّوْجَيْنِ الذَّكَرَ وَالْأُنثَىٰ ۝	39	and made of him the two sexes, male and female.
أَلَيْسَ ذَٰلِكَ بِقَادِرٍ عَلَىٰ أَن يُحْيِيَ الْمَوْتَىٰ ۝	40	Is not someone like that able to revive the dead?

---

[1] Said by the angels of mercy and the angels of wrath present at the side of the dying person, as to which of them will take charge of him. Or those who are present by the side of the dying person say, 'Where is the medicine man?'

[2] An idiom suggesting a time of great hardship, or, metaphorically, death throes.

76. The Human Being
al-Insān

بِسْمِ اللَّهِ الرَّحْمَٰنِ الرَّحِيمِ

In the Name of God,
the All-beneficent, the All-merciful.

1 Has there been a period of time for the human being when he was not anything worthy of mention?

2 We have indeed created the human being from the drop of a mixed fluid[2] so that We may put him to test, so We endowed him with hearing and sight.

3 We have indeed guided him to the way, be he grateful or ungrateful.

4 We have indeed prepared for the faithless chains, iron collars and a blaze.

5 Indeed, the pious will drink from a cup seasoned with *Kāfūr*,[3]

6 a spring where God's servants will drink, making it gush forth as they please.

7 They fulfill their vows and fear a day whose ill will be widespread.

8 For the love of Him they feed the needy, the orphan and the prisoner,

9 [saying,] 'We feed you only for the sake of God. We desire no reward from you, nor thanks.

10 We indeed fear from our Lord a frowning and fateful day.'

11 So God saved them from that day's ills

---

[1] This Madanī *sūrah* takes its name from the word "man" (*al-insān*) mentioned in verse 1.
[2] That is, from the mixing of sperm and ovum.
[3] Lit., camphor.

وَلَقَّاهُمْ نَضْرَةً وَسُرُورًا ⑪	and graced them with freshness and joy.
12 وَجَزَاهُم بِمَا صَبَرُوا	He rewarded them for their patience
جَنَّةً وَحَرِيرًا ⑫	with a garden and garments of silk,
13 مُّتَّكِئِينَ فِيهَا عَلَى الْأَرَائِكِ	reclining therein on couches,
لَا يَرَوْنَ فِيهَا شَمْسًا	without facing therein any scorching sun,
وَلَا زَمْهَرِيرًا ⑬	or biting cold.
14 وَدَانِيَةً عَلَيْهِمْ ظِلَالُهَا	Its shades will be close over them
وَذُلِّلَتْ قُطُوفُهَا تَذْلِيلًا ⑭	and its clusters of fruits will be hanging low.
15 وَيُطَافُ عَلَيْهِم بِآنِيَةٍ مِّن فِضَّةٍ	They will be served around with vessels of silver
وَأَكْوَابٍ كَانَتْ قَوَارِيرَا۠ ⑮	and goblets of crystal
16 قَوَارِيرَ مِن فِضَّةٍ	—crystal of silver—[1]
قَدَّرُوهَا تَقْدِيرًا ⑯	from which they will dispense in a precise measure.
17 وَيُسْقَوْنَ فِيهَا كَأْسًا	They will be served therein with a cup of a drink
كَانَ مِزَاجُهَا زَنجَبِيلًا ⑰	seasoned with *Zanjabīl*,[2]
18 عَيْنًا فِيهَا تُسَمَّىٰ سَلْسَبِيلًا ⑱	from a spring in it named *Salsabīl*.
19 وَيَطُوفُ عَلَيْهِمْ وِلْدَانٌ مُّخَلَّدُونَ	They will be waited upon by immortal youths,
إِذَا رَأَيْتَهُمْ	whom, were you to see them,
حَسِبْتَهُمْ لُؤْلُؤًا مَّنثُورًا ⑲	you will suppose them to be scattered pearls.
20 وَإِذَا رَأَيْتَ	As you look on,
ثَمَّ رَأَيْتَ نَعِيمًا وَمُلْكًا كَبِيرًا ⑳	you will see there bliss and a great kingdom.
21 عَالِيَهُمْ ثِيَابُ سُندُسٍ خُضْرٌ وَإِسْتَبْرَقٌ	Upon them will be green garments of fine and heavy silk,
وَحُلُّوا أَسَاوِرَ مِن فِضَّةٍ	and they will be adorned with bracelets of silver.
وَسَقَاهُمْ رَبُّهُمْ شَرَابًا طَهُورًا ㉑	Their Lord will give them to drink a pure drink.
22 إِنَّ هَٰذَا كَانَ لَكُمْ جَزَاءً	[They will be told]: 'This is your reward,
وَكَانَ سَعْيُكُم مَّشْكُورًا ㉒	and your efforts have been well-appreciated.'
23 إِنَّا نَحْنُ نَزَّلْنَا عَلَيْكَ الْقُرْآنَ	We have indeed sent down the Qur'ān to you
تَنزِيلًا ㉓	in a gradual descent.
24 فَاصْبِرْ لِحُكْمِ رَبِّكَ	So *submit patiently* to the judgement of *your Lord*
وَلَا تُطِعْ مِنْهُمْ آثِمًا أَوْ كَفُورًا ㉔	and *do not obey any sinner or ingrate from among them,*

---

[1] According to *Tafsīr al-Qummī*, vol. 2, p. 399, the silver will be transparent.
[2] Lit., ginger.

	25 and *celebrate* the Name of *your* Lord morning and evening,
وَاذْكُرِ اسْمَ رَبِّكَ بُكْرَةً وَأَصِيلًا ٢٥	
وَمِنَ اللَّيْلِ فَاسْجُدْ لَهُ	26 and *worship* Him for a watch of the night
وَسَبِّحْهُ لَيْلًا طَوِيلًا ٢٦	and *glorify* Him the night long.
إِنَّ هَٰؤُلَاءِ يُحِبُّونَ الْعَاجِلَةَ	27 They indeed love this transitory life
وَيَذَرُونَ وَرَاءَهُمْ يَوْمًا ثَقِيلًا ٢٧	and disregard a heavy day that is ahead of them.
نَحْنُ خَلَقْنَاهُمْ وَشَدَدْنَا أَسْرَهُمْ	28 We created them and strengthened their joints,
وَإِذَا شِئْنَا	and whenever We like
بَدَّلْنَا أَمْثَالَهُمْ تَبْدِيلًا ٢٨	We will replace them with others like them.
إِنَّ هَٰذِهِ تَذْكِرَةٌ	29 This is indeed a reminder.
فَمَنْ شَاءَ اتَّخَذَ إِلَىٰ رَبِّهِ سَبِيلًا ٢٩	So let anyone who wishes take the way toward his Lord.
وَمَا تَشَاءُونَ إِلَّا أَنْ يَشَاءَ اللَّهُ	30 But you will not wish unless it is willed by God.
إِنَّ اللَّهَ كَانَ عَلِيمًا حَكِيمًا ٣٠	God is indeed all-knowing, all-wise.
يُدْخِلُ مَنْ يَشَاءُ فِي رَحْمَتِهِ	31 He admits whomever He wishes into His mercy,
وَالظَّالِمِينَ أَعَدَّ لَهُمْ	and for the wrongdoers He has prepared
عَذَابًا أَلِيمًا ٣١	a painful punishment.

77. THE EMISSARIES[1]
al-Mursalāt

بِسْمِ اللَّهِ الرَّحْمَٰنِ الرَّحِيمِ

In the Name of God,
the All-beneficent, the All-merciful.

وَالْمُرْسَلَاتِ عُرْفًا ١	1 By the angelic emissaries sent successively,[2]
فَالْعَاصِفَاتِ عَصْفًا ٢	2 by those who sweep along like a gale,
وَالنَّاشِرَاتِ نَشْرًا ٣	3 by those who publish [the Divine messages] far and wide,
فَالْفَارِقَاتِ فَرْقًا ٤	4 by those who separate the truth from falsehood distinctly,
فَالْمُلْقِيَاتِ ذِكْرًا ٥	5 by those who inspire God's remembrance,
عُذْرًا أَوْ نُذْرًا ٦	6 as exemption or warning:
إِنَّمَا تُوعَدُونَ لَوَاقِعٌ ٧	7 what you are promised will surely befall.
فَإِذَا النُّجُومُ طُمِسَتْ ٨	8 When the stars are blotted out,
وَإِذَا السَّمَاءُ فُرِجَتْ ٩	9 and the heaven is cleft,

---

[1] This Makkī *sūrah* is named after the "emissaries" (*mursalāt*) mentioned in verse 1.
[2] Or 'By the benign emissaries.'

وَإِذَا الْجِبَالُ نُسِفَتْ ۝	10	when the mountains are scattered[1] like dust,
وَإِذَا الرُّسُلُ أُقِّتَتْ ۝	11	and the time is set for the apostles [to bear witness]
لِأَيِّ يَوْمٍ أُجِّلَتْ ۝	12	—for what day has all that been set to occur?
لِيَوْمِ الْفَصْلِ ۝	13	For the Day of Judgement!
وَمَا أَدْرَاكَ مَا يَوْمُ الْفَصْلِ ۝	14	And what will show you what is the Day of Judgement!?
وَيْلٌ يَوْمَئِذٍ لِلْمُكَذِّبِينَ ۝	15	Woe to the deniers on that day!
أَلَمْ نُهْلِكِ الْأَوَّلِينَ ۝	16	Did We not destroy the former peoples,
ثُمَّ نُتْبِعُهُمُ الْآخِرِينَ ۝	17	and then made the latter ones follow them?
كَذَلِكَ نَفْعَلُ بِالْمُجْرِمِينَ ۝	18	That is how We deal with the guilty.
وَيْلٌ يَوْمَئِذٍ لِلْمُكَذِّبِينَ ۝	19	Woe to the deniers on that day!
أَلَمْ نَخْلُقْكُمْ مِنْ مَاءٍ مَهِينٍ ۝	20	Have We not created you from a base fluid,
فَجَعَلْنَاهُ فِي قَرَارٍ مَكِينٍ ۝	21	and then lodged it in a secure abode
إِلَى قَدَرٍ مَعْلُومٍ ۝	22	until a known span of time?
فَقَدَرْنَا ۝	23	Then We determined,
فَنِعْمَ الْقَادِرُونَ ۝		and how excellent determiners We are!
وَيْلٌ يَوْمَئِذٍ لِلْمُكَذِّبِينَ ۝	24	Woe to the deniers on that day!
أَلَمْ نَجْعَلِ الْأَرْضَ كِفَاتًا ۝	25	Have We not made the earth a receptacle
أَحْيَاءً وَأَمْوَاتًا ۝	26	for the living and the dead,
وَجَعَلْنَا فِيهَا رَوَاسِيَ شَامِخَاتٍ	27	and set in it lofty and firm mountains,
وَأَسْقَيْنَاكُمْ مَاءً فُرَاتًا ۝		and given you agreeable water to drink?
وَيْلٌ يَوْمَئِذٍ لِلْمُكَذِّبِينَ ۝	28	Woe to the deniers on that day!
انْطَلِقُوا	29	[The faithless will be told:] 'Proceed
إِلَى مَا كُنْتُمْ بِهِ تُكَذِّبُونَ ۝		toward what you used to deny!
انْطَلِقُوا إِلَى ظِلٍّ ذِي ثَلَاثِ شُعَبٍ ۝	30	Proceed toward the triple-forked shadow,
لَا ظَلِيلٍ وَلَا يُغْنِي مِنَ اللَّهَبِ ۝	31	neither shady nor of any avail against the flames.

---

[1] Or 'blown away.'

إِنَّهَا تَرْمِي بِشَرَرٍ كَالْقَصْرِ ۝ 32 Indeed, it throws up giant sparks like castles,[1]

كَأَنَّهُ جِمَالَتٌ صُفْرٌ ۝ 33 bright like yellow camels.

وَيْلٌ يَوْمَئِذٍ لِلْمُكَذِّبِينَ ۝ 34 Woe to the deniers on that day!

هَٰذَا يَوْمُ لَا يَنطِقُونَ ۝ 35 This is a day wherein they will not speak,

وَلَا يُؤْذَنُ لَهُمْ فَيَعْتَذِرُونَ ۝ 36 nor will they be permitted to offer excuses.

وَيْلٌ يَوْمَئِذٍ لِلْمُكَذِّبِينَ ۝ 37 Woe to the deniers on that day!

هَٰذَا يَوْمُ الْفَصْلِ 38 'This is the Day of Judgement.

جَمَعْنَاكُمْ وَالْأَوَّلِينَ ۝ We have brought you together with the former peoples.

فَإِن كَانَ لَكُمْ كَيْدٌ فَكِيدُونِ ۝ 39 If you have any stratagems, now try them out against Me!'

وَيْلٌ يَوْمَئِذٍ لِلْمُكَذِّبِينَ ۝ 40 Woe to the deniers on that day!

إِنَّ الْمُتَّقِينَ فِي ظِلَالٍ وَعُيُونٍ ۝ 41 Indeed, the Godwary will be amid shades and springs,

وَفَوَاكِهَ مِمَّا يَشْتَهُونَ ۝ 42 and enjoying such fruits as they desire.

كُلُوا وَاشْرَبُوا هَنِيئًا 43 [They will be told:] 'Enjoy your food and drink,

بِمَا كُنتُمْ تَعْمَلُونَ ۝ a reward for what you used to do.'

إِنَّا كَذَٰلِكَ نَجْزِي الْمُحْسِنِينَ ۝ 44 Thus indeed do We reward the virtuous.

وَيْلٌ يَوْمَئِذٍ لِلْمُكَذِّبِينَ ۝ 45 Woe to the deniers on that day!

كُلُوا وَتَمَتَّعُوا قَلِيلًا 46 [Let them be told:] 'Eat and enjoy a little!

إِنَّكُم مُّجْرِمُونَ ۝ You are indeed guilty.'

وَيْلٌ يَوْمَئِذٍ لِلْمُكَذِّبِينَ ۝ 47 Woe to the deniers on that day!

وَإِذَا قِيلَ 48 When they are told,

لَهُمُ ارْكَعُوا لَا يَرْكَعُونَ ۝ 'Bow down in prayer,' they do not bow down!

وَيْلٌ يَوْمَئِذٍ لِلْمُكَذِّبِينَ ۝ 49 Woe to the deniers on that day!

فَبِأَيِّ حَدِيثٍ بَعْدَهُ يُؤْمِنُونَ ۝ 50 So what discourse will they believe after this?

---

[1] Or 'like the trunks (of huge trees).'

[PART 30]

78. THE TIDING[1]
al-Naba'

بِسْمِ اللَّهِ الرَّحْمَٰنِ الرَّحِيمِ

In the Name of God,
the All-beneficent, the All-merciful.

1. What is it about which they are questioning each other?!
2. Is it about the Great Tiding,
3. the one about which they differ?
4. No indeed! Soon they will know!
5. Once again, no indeed! Soon they will know!
6. Did We not make the earth a resting place?
7. and the mountains stakes?
8. and create you in pairs?
9. and make your sleep for rest?
10. and make the night a covering?
11. and make the day for livelihood?
12. and build above you the seven mighty heavens?
13. and make the sun for a radiant lamp?
14. and send down water pouring from the rain-clouds,
15. that We may bring forth with it grains and plants,
16. and luxuriant gardens?
17. The Day of Judgement is indeed the tryst,
18. the day the Trumpet will be blown, and you will come in groups,
19. and the heaven will be opened and become gates,
20. and the mountains will be set moving, becoming a mirage.
21. Hell is indeed in ambush,
22. a resort for the rebels,

---

[1] This Makkī *sūrah* takes its name from the expression *al-naba' al-'aẓīm* (the great tiding) in verse 2.

23	to reside therein for ages,	لَابِثِينَ فِيهَا أَحْقَابًا ۝
24	tasting in it neither any coolness nor drink,	لَّا يَذُوقُونَ فِيهَا بَرْدًا وَلَا شَرَابًا ۝
25	except boiling water and pus,	إِلَّا حَمِيمًا وَغَسَّاقًا ۝
26	a fitting requital.	جَزَاءً وِفَاقًا ۝
27	They did not indeed expect any reckoning,	إِنَّهُمْ كَانُوا لَا يَرْجُونَ حِسَابًا ۝
28	and they denied Our signs mendaciously,	وَكَذَّبُوا بِآيَاتِنَا كِذَّابًا ۝
29	and We have figured everything in a Book.	وَكُلَّ شَيْءٍ أَحْصَيْنَاهُ كِتَابًا ۝
30	Now taste! We shall increase you in nothing but punishment!	فَذُوقُوا فَلَن نَّزِيدَكُمْ إِلَّا عَذَابًا ۝
31	Deliverance and triumph indeed await the Godwary:	إِنَّ لِلْمُتَّقِينَ مَفَازًا ۝
32	gardens and vineyards,	حَدَائِقَ وَأَعْنَابًا ۝
33	and buxom maidens of a like age,	وَكَوَاعِبَ أَتْرَابًا ۝
34	and brimming cups.	وَكَأْسًا دِهَاقًا ۝
35	Therein they will hear neither vain talk nor lies	لَّا يَسْمَعُونَ فِيهَا لَغْوًا وَلَا كِذَّابًا ۝
36	—a reward and sufficing[1] bounty from *your* Lord,	جَزَاءً مِّن رَّبِّكَ عَطَاءً حِسَابًا ۝
37	the Lord of the heavens and the earth and whatever is between them, the All-beneficent, whom they will not be able to address	رَّبِّ السَّمَاوَاتِ وَالْأَرْضِ وَمَا بَيْنَهُمَا الرَّحْمَٰنِ ۖ لَا يَمْلِكُونَ مِنْهُ خِطَابًا ۝
38	on the day when the Spirit and the angels stand in an array. None shall speak except whom the All-beneficent permits and who says what is right.	يَوْمَ يَقُومُ الرُّوحُ وَالْمَلَائِكَةُ صَفًّا ۖ لَّا يَتَكَلَّمُونَ إِلَّا مَنْ أَذِنَ لَهُ الرَّحْمَٰنُ وَقَالَ صَوَابًا ۝
39	That day is true for certain. So let anyone who wishes take resort with his Lord.	ذَٰلِكَ الْيَوْمُ الْحَقُّ ۖ فَمَن شَاءَ اتَّخَذَ إِلَىٰ رَبِّهِ مَآبًا ۝
40	We have indeed warned you of a punishment near at hand —the day when a person will observe[2] what his hands have sent ahead, and the faithless one will say, 'I wish I were dust!'	إِنَّا أَنذَرْنَاكُمْ عَذَابًا قَرِيبًا يَوْمَ يَنظُرُ الْمَرْءُ مَا قَدَّمَتْ يَدَاهُ وَيَقُولُ الْكَافِرُ يَا لَيْتَنِي كُنتُ تُرَابًا ۝

---

[1] Or 'abounding,' or 'well-deserved.'
[2] Or 'consider.'

79. THE WRESTERS[1]
al-Nāzi'āt

بِسْمِ اللَّهِ الرَّحْمَٰنِ الرَّحِيمِ

In the Name of God,
the All-beneficent, the All-merciful.

1 وَالنَّازِعَاتِ غَرْقًا ۝ By those angels who wrest the soul violently,

2 وَالنَّاشِطَاتِ نَشْطًا ۝ by those who draw it out gently,

3 وَالسَّابِحَاتِ سَبْحًا ۝ by those who swim smoothly,

4 فَالسَّابِقَاتِ سَبْقًا ۝ by those who, racing, take the lead,

5 فَالْمُدَبِّرَاتِ أَمْرًا ۝ by those who direct the affairs of creatures:

6 يَوْمَ تَرْجُفُ الرَّاجِفَةُ ۝ the day when the Quaker quakes

7 تَتْبَعُهَا الرَّادِفَةُ ۝ and is followed by its Successor,[2]

8 قُلُوبٌ يَوْمَئِذٍ وَاجِفَةٌ ۝ hearts will be trembling on that day,

9 أَبْصَارُهَا خَاشِعَةٌ ۝ bearing a humbled look.

10 يَقُولُونَ أَإِنَّا لَمَرْدُودُونَ فِي الْحَافِرَةِ ۝ They will say, 'Are we being returned to our earlier state?

11 أَإِذَا كُنَّا عِظَامًا نَخِرَةً ۝ What, even after we have been decayed bones?!'

12 قَالُوا تِلْكَ إِذًا كَرَّةٌ خَاسِرَةٌ ۝ They will say, 'This is, then, a ruinous return!'

13 فَإِنَّمَا هِيَ زَجْرَةٌ وَاحِدَةٌ ۝ Yet it will be only a single shout,

14 فَإِذَا هُمْ بِالسَّاهِرَةِ ۝ and behold, they will be awake.

15 هَلْ أَتَاكَ حَدِيثُ مُوسَىٰ ۝ Did you receive the story of Moses,

16 إِذْ نَادَاهُ رَبُّهُ when his Lord called out to him

بِالْوَادِ الْمُقَدَّسِ طُوًى ۝ in the holy valley of Ṭuwā?

17 اذْهَبْ إِلَىٰ فِرْعَوْنَ إِنَّهُ طَغَىٰ ۝ And said, 'Go to Pharaoh, for he has indeed rebelled,

18 فَقُلْ هَلْ لَكَ إِلَىٰ أَنْ تَزَكَّىٰ ۝ and say, "Would you purify yourself?

19 وَأَهْدِيَكَ إِلَىٰ رَبِّكَ فَتَخْشَىٰ ۝ I will guide you to your Lord, that you may fear Him?"'

20 فَأَرَاهُ الْآيَةَ الْكُبْرَىٰ ۝ Then he showed him the greatest sign.

21 فَكَذَّبَ وَعَصَىٰ ۝ But he denied and disobeyed.

22 ثُمَّ أَدْبَرَ يَسْعَىٰ ۝ Then he turned back, walking swiftly,

---

[1] This Makkī *sūrah* takes its name from "the wresters" (*al-nāzi'āt*) mentioned in verse 1.
[2] Apparently, 'the Quaker' and 'the Successor' refer to the first and the second blasts of the Trumpet sounded by the Angel Isrāfīl on the Day of Resurrection. Cf. **39**:68; **73**:14.

23	and gathered the people and proclaimed,
فَحَشَرَ فَنَادَىٰ ۝	
24	saying, 'I am your exalted lord!'
فَقَالَ أَنَا رَبُّكُمُ الْأَعْلَىٰ ۝	
25	So God seized him with the punishment
فَأَخَذَهُ اللَّهُ	of this life and the Hereafter.
نَكَالَ الْآخِرَةِ وَالْأُولَىٰ ۝	
26	There is indeed a moral in that for those who fear!
إِنَّ فِي ذَٰلِكَ لَعِبْرَةً لِّمَن يَخْشَىٰ ۝	
27	Is your creation more prodigious
أَأَنتُمْ أَشَدُّ خَلْقًا	
أَمِ السَّمَاءُ ۚ بَنَاهَا ۝	or that of the heaven He has built?
28	He raised its vault and fashioned it,
رَفَعَ سَمْكَهَا فَسَوَّاهَا ۝	
29	and darkened its night, and brought forth its daylight,
وَأَغْطَشَ لَيْلَهَا وَأَخْرَجَ ضُحَاهَا ۝	
30	Thereafter He spread out the earth,
وَالْأَرْضَ بَعْدَ ذَٰلِكَ دَحَاهَا ۝	
31	bringing forth from it its water and pastures
أَخْرَجَ مِنْهَا مَاءَهَا وَمَرْعَاهَا ۝	
32	and setting firmly its mountains,
وَالْجِبَالَ أَرْسَاهَا ۝	
33	as a place of sustenance for you and your livestock.
مَتَاعًا لَّكُمْ وَلِأَنْعَامِكُمْ ۝	
34	When the Greatest Catastrophe befalls
فَإِذَا جَاءَتِ الطَّامَّةُ الْكُبْرَىٰ ۝	
35	—the day when man will remember his endeavours,
يَوْمَ يَتَذَكَّرُ الْإِنسَانُ مَا سَعَىٰ ۝	
36	and hell is brought into view for those who can see—
وَبُرِّزَتِ الْجَحِيمُ لِمَن يَرَىٰ ۝	
37	as for him who has been rebellious
فَأَمَّا مَن طَغَىٰ ۝	
38	and who preferred the life of this world,
وَآثَرَ الْحَيَاةَ الدُّنْيَا ۝	
39	his refuge will indeed be hell.
فَإِنَّ الْجَحِيمَ هِيَ الْمَأْوَىٰ ۝	
40	But as for him who is awed to stand before his Lord
وَأَمَّا مَنْ خَافَ مَقَامَ رَبِّهِ	
وَنَهَى النَّفْسَ عَنِ الْهَوَىٰ ۝	and restrains his soul from following base desires,
41	his refuge will indeed be paradise.
فَإِنَّ الْجَنَّةَ هِيَ الْمَأْوَىٰ ۝	
42	They ask you concerning the Hour,
يَسْأَلُونَكَ عَنِ السَّاعَةِ	
أَيَّانَ مُرْسَاهَا ۝	"When will it set in,
43	considering your frequent mention of it?"
فِيمَ أَنتَ مِن ذِكْرَاهَا ۝	
44	Its outcome is with your Lord.
إِلَىٰ رَبِّكَ مُنتَهَاهَا ۝	
45	You are only a warner for those who are afraid of it.
إِنَّمَا أَنتَ مُنذِرُ مَن يَخْشَاهَا ۝	
46	The day they see it, it shall be as if
كَأَنَّهُمْ يَوْمَ يَرَوْنَهَا	
لَمْ يَلْبَثُوا	they had not stayed in the world
إِلَّا عَشِيَّةً أَوْ ضُحَاهَا ۝	except for an evening or forenoon.

80. HE FROWNED[1]
'Abasa

بِسْمِ اللَّهِ الرَّحْمَٰنِ الرَّحِيمِ

In the Name of God,
the All-beneficent, the All-merciful.

1 عَبَسَ وَتَوَلَّىٰ ۝ He frowned and turned away

2 أَن جَاءَهُ الْأَعْمَىٰ ۝ when the blind man approached him.

3 وَمَا يُدْرِيكَ لَعَلَّهُ يَزَّكَّىٰ ۝ And how do you know, maybe he would purify himself,

4 أَوْ يَذَّكَّرُ فَتَنفَعَهُ الذِّكْرَىٰ ۝ or take admonition and the admonition would benefit him!

5 أَمَّا مَنِ اسْتَغْنَىٰ ۝ But as for someone who is wealthy,[2]

6 فَأَنتَ لَهُ تَصَدَّىٰ ۝ you attend to him,

7 وَمَا عَلَيْكَ أَلَّا يَزَّكَّىٰ ۝ though you are not liable if he does not purify himself.

8 وَأَمَّا مَن جَاءَكَ يَسْعَىٰ ۝ But as for someone who comes hurrying to you,

9 وَهُوَ يَخْشَىٰ ۝ while he fears God,

10 فَأَنتَ عَنْهُ تَلَهَّىٰ ۝ you are neglectful of him.

11 كَلَّا إِنَّهَا تَذْكِرَةٌ ۝ No indeed! These [verses of the Qur'ān] are a reminder

12 فَمَن شَاءَ ذَكَرَهُ ۝ —so let anyone who wishes remember it—

13 فِي صُحُفٍ مُّكَرَّمَةٍ ۝ in honoured scriptures,

14 مَّرْفُوعَةٍ مُّطَهَّرَةٍ ۝ exalted and purified,

15 بِأَيْدِي سَفَرَةٍ ۝ in the hands of envoys,[3]

16 كِرَامٍ بَرَرَةٍ ۝ noble and pious.

17 قُتِلَ الْإِنسَانُ مَا أَكْفَرَهُ ۝ Perish man! How ungrateful is he!

18 مِنْ أَيِّ شَيْءٍ خَلَقَهُ ۝ From what did He create him?

19 مِن نُّطْفَةٍ خَلَقَهُ فَقَدَّرَهُ ۝ He created him from a drop of fluid; then proportioned him.

20 ثُمَّ السَّبِيلَ يَسَّرَهُ ۝ Then He made the way easy for him;

21 ثُمَّ أَمَاتَهُ فَأَقْبَرَهُ ۝ then He made him die and buried him;

22 ثُمَّ إِذَا شَاءَ أَنشَرَهُ ۝ and then, when He wished, resurrected him.

23 كَلَّا No indeed!

---

[1] This Makkī sūrah takes its name from the word 'abasa (he frowned) in verse 1.
[2] Or 'self-complacent.'
[3] Or 'scribes.'

	لَمَّا يَقْضِ مَا أَمَرَهُ ۝	He has not yet carried out what He has commanded him.
24	فَلْيَنظُرِ الْإِنسَانُ إِلَىٰ طَعَامِهِ ۝	Let the human being consider his food:
25	أَنَّا صَبَبْنَا الْمَاءَ صَبًّا ۝	We pour down plenteous water from the sky,
26	ثُمَّ شَقَقْنَا الْأَرْضَ شَقًّا ۝	then We split the earth, making fissures in it
27	فَأَنبَتْنَا فِيهَا حَبًّا ۝	and make the grain grow in it,
28	وَعِنَبًا وَقَضْبًا ۝	as well as vines and vegetables,
29	وَزَيْتُونًا وَنَخْلًا ۝	olives and date palms,
30	وَحَدَائِقَ غُلْبًا ۝	and densely-planted gardens,
31	وَفَاكِهَةً وَأَبًّا ۝	fruits and pastures,
32	مَتَاعًا لَّكُمْ وَلِأَنْعَامِكُمْ ۝	as a sustenance for you and your livestock.
33	فَإِذَا جَاءَتِ الصَّاخَّةُ ۝	So when the deafening Cry comes
34	يَوْمَ يَفِرُّ الْمَرْءُ مِنْ أَخِيهِ ۝	—the day when a man will evade his brother,
35	وَأُمِّهِ وَأَبِيهِ ۝	his mother and his father,
36	وَصَاحِبَتِهِ وَبَنِيهِ ۝	his spouse and his sons—
37	لِكُلِّ امْرِئٍ مِّنْهُمْ يَوْمَئِذٍ شَأْنٌ يُغْنِيهِ ۝	that day each of them will have a task to keep him preoccupied.
38	وُجُوهٌ يَوْمَئِذٍ مُّسْفِرَةٌ ۝	Some faces will be bright on that day,
39	ضَاحِكَةٌ مُّسْتَبْشِرَةٌ ۝	laughing and joyous,
40	وَوُجُوهٌ يَوْمَئِذٍ عَلَيْهَا غَبَرَةٌ ۝	and some faces on that day will be covered with dust,
41	تَرْهَقُهَا قَتَرَةٌ ۝	overcast with gloom.
42	أُولَٰئِكَ هُمُ الْكَفَرَةُ الْفَجَرَةُ ۝	It is they who are the faithless, the vicious.[1]

81. THE WINDING UP[2]
al-Takwīr

In the Name of God,
the All-beneficent, the All-merciful.

1	إِذَا الشَّمْسُ كُوِّرَتْ ۝	When the sun is wound up,[3]
2	وَإِذَا النُّجُومُ انكَدَرَتْ ۝	when the stars scatter,[4]

---

[1] Or 'vicious ingrates.'
[2] This Makkī *sūrah* is named after "the winding up" or "the darkening" (*takwīr*) of the sun mentioned in verse 1.
[3] Or 'turns dark.'
[4] Or 'fall down.'

3	وَإِذَا الْجِبَالُ سُيِّرَتْ ۝	when the mountains are set moving,
4	وَإِذَا الْعِشَارُ عُطِّلَتْ ۝	when the pregnant camels are neglected,
5	وَإِذَا الْوُحُوشُ حُشِرَتْ ۝	when the wild beasts are gathered,
6	وَإِذَا الْبِحَارُ سُجِّرَتْ ۝	when the seas are set afire,
7	وَإِذَا النُّفُوسُ زُوِّجَتْ ۝	when the souls are assorted,[1]
8	وَإِذَا الْمَوْءُودَةُ سُئِلَتْ ۝	when the girl buried-alive will be asked
9	بِأَيِّ ذَنْبٍ قُتِلَتْ ۝	for what sin she was killed.
10	وَإِذَا الصُّحُفُ نُشِرَتْ ۝	When the records of deeds are unfolded,
11	وَإِذَا السَّمَاءُ كُشِطَتْ ۝	when the sky is stripped off,
12	وَإِذَا الْجَحِيمُ سُعِّرَتْ ۝	when hell is set ablaze,
13	وَإِذَا الْجَنَّةُ أُزْلِفَتْ ۝	when paradise is brought near,
14	عَلِمَتْ نَفْسٌ مَا أَحْضَرَتْ ۝	then a soul shall know what it has readied for itself.
15	فَلَا أُقْسِمُ بِالْخُنَّسِ ۝	So I swear by the stars that return,
16	الْجَوَارِ الْكُنَّسِ ۝	the comets,[2]
17	وَاللَّيْلِ إِذَا عَسْعَسَ ۝	by the night as it approaches,
18	وَالصُّبْحِ إِذَا تَنَفَّسَ ۝	by the dawn as it breathes,
19	إِنَّهُ لَقَوْلُ رَسُولٍ كَرِيمٍ ۝	it is indeed the speech of a noble apostle,[3]
20	ذِي قُوَّةٍ عِنْدَ ذِي الْعَرْشِ مَكِينٍ ۝	powerful and eminent with the Lord of the Throne,
21	مُطَاعٍ ثَمَّ أَمِينٍ ۝	one who is obeyed and trustworthy as well.
22	وَمَا صَاحِبُكُمْ بِمَجْنُونٍ ۝	Your companion is not crazy:
23	وَلَقَدْ رَآهُ بِالْأُفُقِ الْمُبِينِ ۝	certainly *he* saw him on the manifest horizon,
24	وَمَا هُوَ عَلَى الْغَيْبِ بِضَنِينٍ ۝	and *he* is not miserly concerning the Unseen.
25	وَمَا هُوَ بِقَوْلِ شَيْطَانٍ رَجِيمٍ ۝	And it is not the speech of an outcast Satan.
26	فَأَيْنَ تَذْهَبُونَ ۝	So where are you going?
27	إِنْ هُوَ إِلَّا ذِكْرٌ لِلْعَالَمِينَ ۝	It is just a reminder for all the nations,
28	لِمَنْ شَاءَ مِنْكُمْ أَنْ يَسْتَقِيمَ ۝	for those of you who wish to walk straight;[4]
29	وَمَا تَشَاءُونَ إِلَّا أَنْ يَشَاءَ اللَّهُ رَبُّ الْعَالَمِينَ ۝	but you will not wish unless it is wished by God, the Lord of all the worlds.

[1] That is, separated into different groups according to their character; cf. **56**:7; **37**:22. Or 'mated;' cf. **52**:20.
[2] Lit. 'the brooming planets,' which apparently refers to the comets, called 'broom stars' in some cultures.
[3] Cf. **69**:40.
[4] Or 'for those of you who wish to be steadfast.'

82. The Rending[1]
al-Infiṭār

In the Name of God,
the All-beneficent, the All-merciful.

1 When the sky is rent apart,
2 when the stars are scattered,
3 when the seas are merged,
4 when the graves are overturned,
5 then a soul shall know what it has sent ahead and left behind.
6 O human being! What has deceived you about your generous[2] Lord,
7 who created you and proportioned you, and gave you an upright nature,
8 and composed you in any form that He wished?
9 No indeed! You rather deny the Retribution.
10 There are indeed watchers over you,
11 noble writers
12 who know whatever you do.
13 The pious shall indeed be amid bliss,
14 and the vicious shall indeed be in hell
15 entering it on the Day of Retribution,[3]
16 and they shall not be absent from it.
17 And what will show you what is the Day of Retribution?
18 Again, what will show you what is the Day of Retribution?
19 It is a day when no soul will be of any avail to another soul and all command that day will belong to God.

---

[1] This Makkī *sūrah* takes its name from "the renting apart" (*infiṭār*) of the sky mentioned in verse 1.
[2] Or 'noble.'
[3] Or 'the Day of Judgement.'

83. The Defrauders[1]
al-Muṭaffifīn

In the Name of God,
the All-beneficent, the All-merciful.

1. Woe to the defrauders who use short measures,
2. who, when they measure [a commodity bought] from the people, take the full measure,
3. but diminish when they measure or weigh for them.
4. Do they not know that they will be resurrected
5. on a tremendous day,
6. a day when mankind will stand before the Lord of all the worlds?
7. Indeed, the record of the vicious is in *Sijjīn*.
8. And what will show you what is *Sijjīn*?
9. It is a written record.
10. Woe to the deniers on that day,
11. who deny the Day of Retribution;
12. and none denies it except every sinful transgressor.
13. When Our signs are recited to him, he says, 'Myths of the ancients!'
14. No! Rather their hearts have been sullied[2] by what they have been earning.
15. Indeed, they will be alienated from their Lord on that day.
16. Then they will enter hell
17. and be told, 'This is what you used to deny!'

---

[1] This Madanī *sūrah* takes its name from verse 1, which condemns the tradesmen who cheat customers by using short weights and measures (*muṭaffifūn*).
[2] Or 'overcast.'

18 Indeed, the record of the pious is in *Illiyūn*.

19 And what will show you what is *Illiyūn*?

20 It is a written record,

21 witnessed by those brought near to God.

22 The pious will be amid bliss,

23 observing as they recline on couches.

24 You will perceive in their faces the freshness of bliss.

25 They will be served with a sealed pure wine,

26 whose seal is musk
—for such let the viers vie—

27 and whose seasoning is from *Tasnīm*,
a spring where those brought near to God drink.

29 Indeed, the guilty
used to laugh at the faithful,

30 and when they passed them by
they would wink at each other,

31 and when they returned to their folks,
they would return amused,

32 and when they saw them they would say,
'These are indeed astray!'

33 Though they were not sent to watch over them.

34 So today
the faithful will laugh at the faithless,

35 observing from their couches:

36 Have the faithless been requited
for what they used to do?

84. The Splitting[1]
al-Inshiqāq

In the Name of God,
the All-beneficent, the All-merciful.

1 When the heaven is split open
2 and gives ear to its Lord as it should.
3 When the earth is spread out
4 and throws out what is in it, emptying itself,
5 and gives ear to its Lord as it should.
6 O human being! You are labouring toward your Lord, laboriously, and you will encounter Him.
7 As for him who is given his record in his right hand,
8 he will receive an easy reckoning,
9 and he will return to his folks joyfully.
10 But as for him who is given his record from behind his back,
11 he will pray for annihilation,[2]
12 and enter the Blaze.
13 Indeed, he used to be joyful among his folk,
14 and he thought that he would never return.
15 Yes, his Lord had been watching him.
16 I swear by the evening glow,
17 by the night and what it is fraught with,
18 by the moon when it blooms full:
19 you will surely fare from stage to stage.
20 What is the matter with them that they will not believe,
21 and when the Qur'ān is recited to them

---

[1] This Makkī *sūrah* is named after the 'splitting open' (*inshiqāq*) of the heaven mentioned in verse 1.
[2] Cf. **25:13-14, 78:**40.

                                      will not prostrate?

22 Indeed, the faithless impugn the Apostle,
23   and God knows best what they keep to themselves.
24 So *inform* them of a painful punishment,
25 excepting such as are faithful and do righteous deeds:
    for them there will be an everlasting reward.

85. THE HOUSES
al-Burūj

In the Name of God,
the All-beneficent, the All-merciful.

1 By the heaven with its houses,
2 by the Promised Day,
3 by the Witness[2] and the Witnessed:[3]
4 perish the People of the Ditch!
5 The fire, abounding in fuel,
6 above which they sat
7 and were themselves
   witness to what they did to the faithful.
8 They were vindictive towards them only
   because they had faith in God,
   the All-mighty and the All-laudable,
9 to whom belongs the kingdom of the heavens
   and the earth,
   and God is witness to all things.
10 Indeed, those who persecute the faithful men and women
   and do not repent thereafter,
   there is for them the punishment of hell

---

[1] This Makkī *sūrah* takes its name from 'the houses' (*burūj*) mentioned in verse 1.
[2] That is the Prophet (ṣ); cf. 2:143; 4:41; 16:89; 33:45.
[3] That is, the Day of Judgement; cf. 11:103

and the punishment of burning.
11 Indeed, those who have faith and do righteous deeds,
—for them will be gardens with streams running in them.
That is the supreme triumph.
12 Your Lord's seizing is indeed severe.
13 It is He who initiates the creation and brings it back,
14 and He is the All-forgiving, the All-affectionate,
15 Lord of the Throne, the All-glorious,[1]
16 doer of what He desires.
17 Did you receive the story of the hosts
18 of Pharaoh and Thamūd?
19 The faithless indeed dwell in denial
20 and God besieges them from all around.
21 It is indeed a glorious Qur'ān,
22 in a preserved tablet.

86. THE NIGHTLY VISITOR[2]
al-Ṭāriq

In the Name of God,
the All-beneficent, the All-merciful.

1 By the heaven and the nightly visitor,
2 (and what will show you what is the nightly visitor?
3 It is the brilliant star):
4 there is a guard[3] over every soul.
5 So let man consider from what he was created.
6 He was created from an effusing fluid
7 which issues from between the loins and the breast-bones.
8 He is indeed able to bring him back after death,

---

[1] Or 'Lord of the Glorious Throne,' in accordance with an alternate reading.
[2] This Makkī *sūrah* is named after 'the nightly visitor' (*ṭāriq*) mentioned in verse 1.
[3] Or 'watcher.'

9 on the day when the secrets are examined, يَوْمَ تُبْلَى السَّرَائِرُ ۝

10 and he shall have neither power nor helper. فَمَا لَهُ مِن قُوَّةٍ وَلَا نَاصِرٍ ۝

11 By the resurgent heaven,[1] وَالسَّمَاءِ ذَاتِ الرَّجْعِ ۝

12 and by the furrowed earth:[2] وَالْأَرْضِ ذَاتِ الصَّدْعِ ۝

13 it[3] is indeed a conclusive discourse إِنَّهُ لَقَوْلٌ فَصْلٌ ۝

14 and not a jest. وَمَا هُوَ بِالْهَزْلِ ۝

15 They are indeed devising a stratagem, إِنَّهُمْ يَكِيدُونَ كَيْدًا ۝

16 and I, too, am devising a plan. وَأَكِيدُ كَيْدًا ۝

17 So *respite* the faithless; *give* them a gentle respite. فَمَهِّلِ الْكَافِرِينَ أَمْهِلْهُمْ رُوَيْدًا ۝

87. THE MOST EXALTED[4]
al-Aʿlā

In the Name of God,
the All-beneficent, the All-merciful.

1 *Celebrate* the Name of *your* Lord, the Most Exalted,

2 who created and proportioned,

3 who determined and guided,

4 who brought forth the pasture,

5 and then turned it into a black scum.

6 We shall have *you* recite, then *you* will not forget any of it

7 except what God may wish.

Indeed, He knows what is open to view and hidden.

8 We shall smooth *your* way to [preach] the easiest [canon].

9 So *admonish*, for admonition is indeed beneficial:[5]

10 he who fears will take admonition,

11 and the most wretched will shun it

12 —he who will enter the Great Fire,

---

[1] Or 'the heaven of the returning rains.'
[2] Or 'the earth splitting [with verdure].'
[3] That is, the Qurʾān.
[4] This Makkī *sūrah* is named after the phrase 'the Most Exalted' (*al-aʿlā*) in verse 1.
[5] Or 'Admonish, if admonition be useful.'

13 then he will neither live in it, nor die.
14 Felicitous is he who purifies himself,
15 celebrates the Name of his Lord, and prays.
16 Rather you prefer the life of this world,
17 while the Hereafter is better and more lasting.
18 This is indeed in the former scriptures,
19 the scriptures of Abraham and Moses.

88. THE ENVELOPER[1]
al-Ghāshiyah

In the Name of God,
the All-beneficent, the All-merciful.

1 Did you receive the account of the Enveloper?
2 Some faces on that day will be humbled,
3 wrought-up and weary:
4 they will enter a scorching fire,
5 and made to drink from a boiling spring.
6 They will have no food except cactus,
7 neither nourishing, nor of avail against hunger.
8 Some faces on that day will be joyous,
9 pleased with their endeavour;
10 in a lofty garden,
11 where they will not hear any vain talk.
12 In it there is a flowing spring
13 and raised couches,
14 with goblets set,
15 and cushions laid out in an array,
16 and carpets spread out.
17 Do they not consider the camel,

---

[1] A Makkī *sūrah*, it is named after 'the Enveloper' (*al-ghāshiyah*), mentioned in verse 1.

17 to see how it has been created? كَيْفَ خُلِقَتْ ۝

18 and the heaven, how it has been raised? وَإِلَى السَّمَاءِ كَيْفَ رُفِعَتْ ۝

19 and the mountains, how they have been set? وَإِلَى الْجِبَالِ كَيْفَ نُصِبَتْ ۝

20 and the earth, how it has been surfaced? وَإِلَى الْأَرْضِ كَيْفَ سُطِحَتْ ۝

21 So *admonish*—for you are only an admonisher, فَذَكِّرْ إِنَّمَا أَنْتَ مُذَكِّرٌ ۝

22 not a taskmaster over them— لَسْتَ عَلَيْهِمْ بِمُصَيْطِرٍ ۝

23 except him who turns away and disbelieves. إِلَّا مَنْ تَوَلَّى وَكَفَرَ ۝

24 Him God will punish with the greatest punishment. فَيُعَذِّبُهُ اللَّهُ الْعَذَابَ الْأَكْبَرَ ۝

25 To Us indeed will be their return. إِنَّ إِلَيْنَا إِيَابَهُمْ ۝

26 Then, indeed, their reckoning will lie with Us. ثُمَّ إِنَّ عَلَيْنَا حِسَابَهُمْ ۝

89. THE DAWN[1]
al-Fajr

سُورَةُ الْفَجْرِ

In the Name of God,
the All-beneficent, the All-merciful.

بِسْمِ اللَّهِ
الرَّحْمَنِ الرَّحِيمِ

1 By the Dawn,[2] وَالْفَجْرِ ۝

2 by the ten nights, وَلَيَالٍ عَشْرٍ ۝

3 by the Even and the Odd, وَالشَّفْعِ وَالْوَتْرِ ۝

4 by the night when it departs! وَاللَّيْلِ إِذَا يَسْرِ ۝

5 Is there an oath in that for one possessing intellect? هَلْ فِي ذَلِكَ قَسَمٌ لِذِي حِجْرٍ ۝

6 Have you not regarded أَلَمْ تَرَ

how *your* Lord dealt with the people of 'Ād, كَيْفَ فَعَلَ رَبُّكَ بِعَادٍ ۝

7 and Iram, the city of pillars, إِرَمَ ذَاتِ الْعِمَادِ ۝

8 the like of which was not created among cities, الَّتِي لَمْ يُخْلَقْ مِثْلُهَا فِي الْبِلَادِ ۝

9 and the people of Thamūd, وَثَمُودَ

who hollowed out the rocks in the valley, الَّذِينَ جَابُوا الصَّخْرَ بِالْوَادِ ۝

10 and Pharaoh, the impaler,[3] وَفِرْعَوْنَ ذِي الْأَوْتَادِ ۝

11 —those who rebelled against God in their cities الَّذِينَ طَغَوْا فِي الْبِلَادِ ۝

---

[1] This Makkī *sūrah* is named after 'the Dawn' (*al-fajr*) mentioned in verse 1.
[2] Interpreted as the month of Muḥarram, which marks the beginning of the year. (Ṭabarī, *Ta'rīkh*, ii, 390, from Ibn 'Abbās)
[3] See the note at **38:12**.

12 and caused much corruption in them, فَأَكْثَرُوا فِيهَا الْفَسَادَ ۝

13 so *your* Lord poured on them lashes of punishment. فَصَبَّ عَلَيْهِمْ رَبُّكَ سَوْطَ عَذَابٍ ۝

14 Your Lord is indeed in ambush. إِنَّ رَبَّكَ لَبِالْمِرْصَادِ ۝

15 As for man, whenever his Lord tests him فَأَمَّا الْإِنْسَانُ إِذَا مَا ابْتَلَاهُ رَبُّهُ
    and grants him honour and blesses him, فَأَكْرَمَهُ وَنَعَّمَهُ
    he says, 'My Lord has honoured me.' فَيَقُولُ رَبِّي أَكْرَمَنِ ۝

16 But when He tests him وَأَمَّا إِذَا مَا ابْتَلَاهُ
    and tightens for him his provision, فَقَدَرَ عَلَيْهِ رِزْقَهُ
    he says, 'My Lord has humiliated me.' فَيَقُولُ رَبِّي أَهَانَنِ ۝

17 No indeed! No, you do not honour the orphan كَلَّا ۖ بَل لَّا تُكْرِمُونَ الْيَتِيمَ ۝

18 and do not urge the feeding of the needy. وَلَا تَحَاضُّونَ عَلَىٰ طَعَامِ الْمِسْكِينِ ۝

19 You eat your inheritance rapaciously وَتَأْكُلُونَ التُّرَاثَ أَكْلًا لَّمًّا ۝

20 and love wealth with much fondness. وَتُحِبُّونَ الْمَالَ حُبًّا جَمًّا ۝

21 No indeed! When the earth is levelled[1] to a plain, كَلَّا إِذَا دُكَّتِ الْأَرْضُ دَكًّا دَكًّا ۝

22 and *your* Lord's edict arrives with the angels in ranks, وَجَاءَ رَبُّكَ وَالْمَلَكُ صَفًّا صَفًّا ۝

23 the day when hell is brought near, وَجِيءَ يَوْمَئِذٍ بِجَهَنَّمَ
    man will take admonition on that day, يَوْمَئِذٍ يَتَذَكَّرُ الْإِنْسَانُ
    but what will the admonition avail him? وَأَنَّىٰ لَهُ الذِّكْرَىٰ ۝

24 He will say, 'Alas, had I sent ahead for my life!' يَقُولُ يَا لَيْتَنِي قَدَّمْتُ لِحَيَاتِي ۝

25 On that day none shall punish as He punishes, فَيَوْمَئِذٍ لَّا يُعَذِّبُ عَذَابَهُ أَحَدٌ ۝

26 and none shall bind as He binds. وَلَا يُوثِقُ وَثَاقَهُ أَحَدٌ ۝

27 'O soul at peace! يَا أَيَّتُهَا النَّفْسُ الْمُطْمَئِنَّةُ ۝

28 Return to your Lord, pleased and pleasing! ارْجِعِي إِلَىٰ رَبِّكِ رَاضِيَةً مَّرْضِيَّةً ۝

29 Then enter among My servants, فَادْخُلِي فِي عِبَادِي ۝

30 and enter My paradise!' وَادْخُلِي جَنَّتِي ۝

---

[1] Or 'crumbled into fragments.'

90. THE TOWN[1]
al-Balad

In the Name of God,
the All-beneficent, the All-merciful.

1 I swear by this town,
2 as you reside in this town,
3 and by the father and him whom he begot:
4 certainly We created man in travail.
5 Does he suppose that no one will ever have power over him?
6 He says, 'I have squandered immense wealth.'
7 Does he suppose that no one sees him?
8 Have We not made for him two eyes,
9 a tongue, and two lips,
10 and shown him the two paths of good and evil?
11 Yet he has not embarked upon the uphill task.
12 And what will show you what is the uphill task?
13 It is the freeing of a slave,
14 or feeding during days of general starvation
15 an orphan among relatives,
16 or a needy person in desolation,
17 while being one of those who have faith
and enjoin one another to patience
and enjoin one another to compassion.
18 They are the People of the Right Hand.
19 But those who deny Our signs,
they are the People of the Left Hand.
20 A closed Fire will be imposed upon them.

---

[1] This Makkī *sūrah* is named after the 'town' (*balad*) mentioned in verse 1.

91. The Sun[1]
al-Shams

بِسْمِ اللَّهِ الرَّحْمَٰنِ الرَّحِيمِ

In the Name of God,
the All-beneficent, the All-merciful.

1 By the sun and her forenoon splendour,
2 by the moon when he follows her,
3 by the day when it reveals her,
4 by the night when it covers her,
5 by the heaven and Him who built it,
6 by the earth and Him who spread it,
7 by the soul and Him who fashioned it,
8 and inspired it with [discernment between] its virtues and vices:
9 one who purifies it is felicitous
10 and one who betrays it fails.
11 The people of Thamūd denied [God's signs] out of their rebellion,
12 when the most wretched of them rose up.
13 The apostle of God had told them, 'This is God's she-camel, let her drink!'
14 But they impugned him and hamstrung her. So their Lord brought down His punishment upon them[2] because of their sin, and levelled it,[3]
15 and He does not fear its outcome.

---

[1] This Makkī sūrah is named after 'the sun' (al-shams), mentioned in verse 1.
[2] Or 'destroyed them,' or 'crushed them.'
[3] That is, razed their city to the ground.

92. The Night
al-Layl

سُورَةُ اللَّيْلِ

بِسْمِ اللَّهِ الرَّحْمَٰنِ الرَّحِيمِ

In the Name of God,
the All-beneficent, the All-merciful.

1 By the night when it envelops, وَاللَّيْلِ إِذَا يَغْشَىٰ ۝

2 by the day when it brightens, وَالنَّهَارِ إِذَا تَجَلَّىٰ ۝

3 by Him who created the male and the female: وَمَا خَلَقَ الذَّكَرَ وَالْأُنثَىٰ ۝

4 your endeavours are indeed diverse. إِنَّ سَعْيَكُمْ لَشَتَّىٰ ۝

5 As for him who gives and is Godwary فَأَمَّا مَنْ أَعْطَىٰ وَاتَّقَىٰ ۝

6 and confirms the best promise, وَصَدَّقَ بِالْحُسْنَىٰ ۝

7 We will ease him toward facility. فَسَنُيَسِّرُهُ لِلْيُسْرَىٰ ۝

8 But as for him who is stingy and self-complacent, وَأَمَّا مَن بَخِلَ وَاسْتَغْنَىٰ ۝

9 and denies the best promise, وَكَذَّبَ بِالْحُسْنَىٰ ۝

10 We will ease him toward hardship. فَسَنُيَسِّرُهُ لِلْعُسْرَىٰ ۝

11 His wealth shall not avail him when he perishes. وَمَا يُغْنِي عَنْهُ مَالُهُ إِذَا تَرَدَّىٰ ۝

12 Guidance indeed rests with Us إِنَّ عَلَيْنَا لَلْهُدَىٰ ۝

13 and to Us belong the world and the Hereafter. وَإِنَّ لَنَا لَلْآخِرَةَ وَالْأُولَىٰ ۝

14 So I warn you of a blazing fire, فَأَنذَرْتُكُمْ نَارًا تَلَظَّىٰ ۝

15 which none shall enter except the most wretched, لَا يَصْلَاهَا إِلَّا الْأَشْقَى ۝

16 he who impugns God's prophets and turns his back. الَّذِي كَذَّبَ وَتَوَلَّىٰ ۝

17 The Godwary will be spared that وَسَيُجَنَّبُهَا الْأَتْقَى ۝

18 —those who give their wealth to purify themselves الَّذِي يُؤْتِي مَالَهُ يَتَزَكَّىٰ ۝

19 and do not expect any reward from anyone, وَمَا لِأَحَدٍ عِندَهُ مِن نِّعْمَةٍ تُجْزَىٰ ۝

20 but seek only the pleasure of their Lord, the Most Exalted, إِلَّا ابْتِغَاءَ وَجْهِ رَبِّهِ الْأَعْلَىٰ ۝

21 and soon they will be well-pleased. وَلَسَوْفَ يَرْضَىٰ ۝

---

[1] This Makkī *sūrah* is named after 'the night' (*al-layl*), mentioned in verse 1.

93. THE MORNING BRIGHTNESS[1]
al-Ḍuḥā

سُورَةُ الضُّحَى

بِسْمِ اللَّهِ الرَّحْمَٰنِ الرَّحِيمِ

In the Name of God,
the All-beneficent, the All-merciful.

1 By the morning brightness, وَالضُّحَىٰ

2 by the night when it is calm! وَاللَّيْلِ إِذَا سَجَىٰ

3 Your Lord has neither forsaken you, nor is He displeased with you, مَا وَدَّعَكَ رَبُّكَ وَمَا قَلَىٰ

4 and the Hereafter shall be better for you than the world. وَلَلْآخِرَةُ خَيْرٌ لَكَ مِنَ الْأُولَىٰ

5 Soon your Lord will give you that with which you will be pleased. وَلَسَوْفَ يُعْطِيكَ رَبُّكَ فَتَرْضَىٰ

6 Did He not find you an orphan and shelter you? أَلَمْ يَجِدْكَ يَتِيمًا فَآوَىٰ

7 Did He not find you astray and guide you? وَوَجَدَكَ ضَالًّا فَهَدَىٰ

8 Did He not find you needy and enrich you? وَوَجَدَكَ عَائِلًا فَأَغْنَىٰ

9 So, as for the orphan, do not oppress him; فَأَمَّا الْيَتِيمَ فَلَا تَقْهَرْ

10 and as for the beggar, do not chide him; وَأَمَّا السَّائِلَ فَلَا تَنْهَرْ

11 and as for your Lord's blessing, proclaim it! وَأَمَّا بِنِعْمَةِ رَبِّكَ فَحَدِّثْ

94. OPENING[2]
al-Sharḥ

سُورَةُ الشَّرْحِ

بِسْمِ اللَّهِ الرَّحْمَٰنِ الرَّحِيمِ

In the Name of God,
the All-beneficent, the All-merciful.

1 Did We not open your breast for you أَلَمْ نَشْرَحْ لَكَ صَدْرَكَ

2 and relieve you of your burden وَوَضَعْنَا عَنْكَ وِزْرَكَ

3 which almost broke your back? الَّذِي أَنْقَضَ ظَهْرَكَ

4 Did We not exalt your name? وَرَفَعْنَا لَكَ ذِكْرَكَ

5 Ease indeed accompanies hardship. فَإِنَّ مَعَ الْعُسْرِ يُسْرًا

---

[1] Probably a Madanī sūrah like the one following it, it is named after 'the morning brightness' (ḍuḥā) mentioned in verse 1.
[2] Named after the phrase "Did We not open" (a lam nashraḥ) in verse 1.

6 إِنَّ مَعَ الْعُسْرِ يُسْرًا ۝ Ease indeed accompanies hardship.
7 فَإِذَا فَرَغْتَ فَانْصَبْ ۝ So when you are done, *appoint*,[1]
8 وَإِلَىٰ رَبِّكَ فَارْغَبْ ۝ and *supplicate your Lord*.

95. THE FIG[2]
al-Tīn

سُورَةُ التِّين

بِسْمِ اللَّهِ
الرَّحْمَٰنِ الرَّحِيمِ

In the Name of God,
the All-beneficent, the All-merciful.

1 وَالتِّينِ وَالزَّيْتُونِ ۝ By the fig and the olive,
2 وَطُورِ سِينِينَ ۝ by Mount Sinai,
3 وَهَٰذَا الْبَلَدِ الْأَمِينِ ۝ and by this secure town;[3]
4 لَقَدْ خَلَقْنَا الْإِنْسَانَ فِي أَحْسَنِ تَقْوِيمٍ ۝ We certainly created man in the best of forms;
5 ثُمَّ رَدَدْنَاهُ أَسْفَلَ سَافِلِينَ ۝ then We relegated him to the lowest of the low,
6 إِلَّا الَّذِينَ آمَنُوا وَعَمِلُوا الصَّالِحَاتِ فَلَهُمْ أَجْرٌ غَيْرُ مَمْنُونٍ ۝ except those who have faith and do righteous deeds. There will be an everlasting reward for them.
7 فَمَا يُكَذِّبُكَ بَعْدُ بِالدِّينِ ۝ So what makes you deny the Retribution?
8 أَلَيْسَ اللَّهُ بِأَحْكَمِ الْحَاكِمِينَ ۝ Is not God the fairest of all judges?

96. THE CLINGING TISSUE[4]
al-'Alaq

سُورَةُ الْعَلَق

بِسْمِ اللَّهِ
الرَّحْمَٰنِ الرَّحِيمِ

In the Name of God,
the All-beneficent, the All-merciful.

1 اقْرَأْ بِاسْمِ رَبِّكَ الَّذِي خَلَقَ ۝ *Read in the Name of your Lord who created*;
2 خَلَقَ الْإِنْسَانَ مِنْ عَلَقٍ ۝ created the human being from a clinging tissue.
3 اقْرَأْ وَرَبُّكَ الْأَكْرَمُ ۝ *Read, and your Lord is the most generous*,
4 الَّذِي عَلَّمَ بِالْقَلَمِ ۝ who taught by the pen,
5 عَلَّمَ الْإِنْسَانَ مَا لَمْ يَعْلَمْ ۝ taught the human being what he did not know.
6 كَلَّا إِنَّ الْإِنْسَانَ لَيَطْغَىٰ ۝ The human being indeed becomes rebellious

---

[1] Or 'when you are finished [with prayer], exert yourself [in supplicating to God].'
[2] A Makkī *sūrah*. Named after 'the fig' (*tīn*) mentioned in verse 1.
[3] That is, the holy city of Makkah.
[4] A Makkī *sūrah*. Named after 'the clinging mass' (*'alaq*) mentioned in verse 2.

7 when he considers himself without need.

8 To your Lord is indeed the return.

9 Tell me, he who forbids

10 a servant when he prays,

11 tell me, should he be on true guidance,

12 or bid others to Godwariness,

13 tell me, should he call him a liar and turn away

14 —does he not know that God sees him?

15 No indeed! If he does not stop,
We shall seize him by the forelock,

16 a lying, sinful forelock!

17 Then let him call out his gang!

18 We too shall call the keepers of hell.

19 No indeed! Do not obey him,
but prostrate and draw near to God!

97. The Ordainment[1]
al-Qadr

In the Name of God,
the All-beneficent, the All-merciful.

1 Indeed, We sent it[2] down on the Night of Ordainment.

2 And what will show you what is the Night of Ordainment?

3 The Night of Ordainment is better than a thousand months.

4 In it, the angels and the Spirit descend
by the leave of their Lord with every command.

5 It is peaceful until the rising of the dawn.

---

[1] A Makkī *sūrah*. Named after the phrase 'the night of ordainment' (*laylat al-qadr*) in verses 1-3.
[2] That is, the Qur'ān. See 44:2-5.

98. The Proof[1]
al-Bayyinah

In the Name of God,
the All-beneficent, the All-merciful.

1 The faithless from among the People of the Book and the polytheists were not set apart until the proof had come to them:

2 an apostle from God reciting impeccable scriptures,

3 wherein are upright writings.

4 Those who were given the Book did not divide except after the proof had come to them,

5 though all they were told was to worship God, dedicating their faith to Him as men of pure faith, and to maintain the prayer and pay the *zakāt*, and that is the upright religion.

6 Indeed, the faithless from among the People of the Book and the polytheists will be in the fire of hell, to remain in it. It is they who are the worst of creatures.

7 Indeed, those who have faith and do righteous deeds —it is they who are the best of creatures.

8 Their reward, near their Lord, is the Gardens of Eden, with streams running in them, to remain in them forever. God is pleased with them, and they are pleased with Him. That is for those who fear their Lord.

---

[1] A Madanī *sūrah*. Named after 'the proof' (*al-bayyinah*) mentioned in verses 1, 4.

99. THE QUAKE[1]
al-Zalzalah

بِسْمِ اللَّهِ الرَّحْمَٰنِ الرَّحِيمِ

In the Name of God,
the All-beneficent, the All-merciful.

1 إِذَا زُلْزِلَتِ الْأَرْضُ زِلْزَالَهَا ۝ When the earth is rocked with a terrible quake

2 وَأَخْرَجَتِ الْأَرْضُ أَثْقَالَهَا ۝ and discharges her burdens,

3 وَقَالَ الْإِنسَانُ مَا لَهَا ۝ and man says, 'What is the matter with her?'

4 يَوْمَئِذٍ تُحَدِّثُ أَخْبَارَهَا ۝ On that day she will relate her chronicles

5 بِأَنَّ رَبَّكَ أَوْحَىٰ لَهَا ۝ for her Lord will have inspired her.

6 يَوْمَئِذٍ يَصْدُرُ النَّاسُ أَشْتَاتًا لِّيُرَوْا أَعْمَالَهُمْ ۝ On that day, mankind will issue forth in various groups[2] to be shown their deeds.

7 فَمَن يَعْمَلْ مِثْقَالَ ذَرَّةٍ خَيْرًا يَرَهُ ۝ So whoever does an atom's weight of good will see it,

8 وَمَن يَعْمَلْ مِثْقَالَ ذَرَّةٍ شَرًّا يَرَهُ ۝ and whoever does an atom's weight of evil will see it.

100. THE CHARGERS[3]
al-'Ādiyāt

بِسْمِ اللَّهِ الرَّحْمَٰنِ الرَّحِيمِ

In the Name of God,
the All-beneficent, the All-merciful.

1 وَالْعَادِيَاتِ ضَبْحًا ۝ By the snorting chargers,

2 فَالْمُورِيَاتِ قَدْحًا ۝ by the strikers of sparks [with their hoofs],

3 فَالْمُغِيرَاتِ صُبْحًا ۝ by the raiders at dawn,

4 فَأَثَرْنَ بِهِ نَقْعًا ۝ raising therein a trail of dust,

5 فَوَسَطْنَ بِهِ جَمْعًا ۝ and cleaving therein a host!

6 إِنَّ الْإِنسَانَ لِرَبِّهِ لَكَنُودٌ ۝ The human being is indeed ungrateful to his Lord,

7 وَإِنَّهُ عَلَىٰ ذَٰلِكَ لَشَهِيدٌ ۝ and indeed he is himself witness to that,

8 وَإِنَّهُ لِحُبِّ الْخَيْرِ لَشَدِيدٌ ۝ and he is indeed an avid lover of wealth.

9 أَفَلَا يَعْلَمُ Does he not know

---

[1] A Makkī *sūrah*, it takes its name, meaning 'the quake' (*zalzalah*) from verse 1.
[2] Or 'separate groups.'
[3] A Makkī *sūrah*, it takes its name from 'the chargers' (*al-'ādiyāt*) mentioned in verse 1.

إِذَا بُعْثِرَ مَا فِي الْقُبُورِ ۝ that when what is buried in the graves is turned over,[1]

وَحُصِّلَ مَا فِي الصُّدُورِ ۝ 10 and what is concealed in the breasts is divulged,

إِنَّ رَبَّهُم بِهِمْ يَوْمَئِذٍ لَّخَبِيرٌ ۝ 11 their Lord will be well-informed about them on that day?

101. THE CATASTROPHE[2]
al-Qāri'ah

In the Name of God,
the All-beneficent, the All-merciful.

الْقَارِعَةُ ۝ 1 The Catastrophe!

مَا الْقَارِعَةُ ۝ 2 What is the Catastrophe?

وَمَا أَدْرَاكَ مَا الْقَارِعَةُ ۝ 3 What will show you what is the Catastrophe?

يَوْمَ يَكُونُ النَّاسُ 4 It is the day when humankind will be

كَالْفَرَاشِ الْمَبْثُوثِ ۝   like scattered moths

وَتَكُونُ الْجِبَالُ 5 and the mountains will be

كَالْعِهْنِ الْمَنفُوشِ ۝   like carded tufts of dyed wool.

فَأَمَّا مَن ثَقُلَتْ مَوَازِينُهُ ۝ 6 As for him whose deeds weigh heavy in the scales,

فَهُوَ فِي عِيشَةٍ رَّاضِيَةٍ ۝ 7 he will have a pleasing life.

وَأَمَّا مَنْ خَفَّتْ مَوَازِينُهُ ۝ 8 But as for him whose deeds weigh light in the scales,

فَأُمُّهُ هَاوِيَةٌ ۝ 9 his home will be the Abyss.

وَمَا أَدْرَاكَ مَا هِيَهْ ۝ 10 And what will show you what it is?

نَارٌ حَامِيَةٌ ۝ 11 It is a scorching fire!

102. RIVALRY[3]
al-Takāthur

In the Name of God,
the All-beneficent, the All-merciful.

أَلْهَاكُمُ التَّكَاثُرُ ۝ 1 Rivalry [and vainglory] distracted you

حَتَّىٰ زُرْتُمُ الْمَقَابِرَ ۝ 2 until you visited even the graves.

---

[1] Or 'uncovered,' or 'disinterred.'
[2] A Makkī *sūrah*, it takes its name from 'the catastrophe'(*qāri'ah*) mentioned in verses 1-3.
[3] A Makkī *sūrah*, it is named after the 'rivalry' (*takāthur*) mentioned in verses 1-3.

3 كَلَّا سَوْفَ تَعْلَمُونَ ۝ No indeed! Soon you will know!

4 ثُمَّ كَلَّا سَوْفَ تَعْلَمُونَ ۝ Once again, no indeed! Soon you will know!

5 كَلَّا لَوْ تَعْلَمُونَ عِلْمَ الْيَقِينِ ۝ No indeed! Were you to know with certain knowledge,

6 لَتَرَوُنَّ الْجَحِيمَ ۝ you would have surely seen hell [in this very life].

7 ثُمَّ لَتَرَوُنَّهَا عَيْنَ الْيَقِينِ ۝ Afterwards you will surely see it with the eye of certainty.

8 ثُمَّ لَتُسْأَلُنَّ يَوْمَئِذٍ عَنِ النَّعِيمِ ۝ Then, on that day, you will surely be questioned concerning the Blessing.[1]

103. TIME[2]
al-ʿAṣr

سورة العصر

بِسْمِ اللَّهِ الرَّحْمَنِ الرَّحِيمِ

In the Name of God, the All-beneficent, the All-merciful.

1 وَالْعَصْرِ ۝ By Time!

2 إِنَّ الْإِنسَانَ لَفِي خُسْرٍ ۝ The human being is indeed in loss,

3 إِلَّا الَّذِينَ آمَنُوا وَعَمِلُوا الصَّالِحَاتِ وَتَوَاصَوْا بِالْحَقِّ وَتَوَاصَوْا بِالصَّبْرِ ۝ except those who have faith and do righteous deeds, and enjoin one another to follow the truth, and enjoin one another to patience and fortitude.

104. THE SCANDAL-MONGER[3]
al-Humazah

سورة الهمزة

بِسْمِ اللَّهِ الرَّحْمَنِ الرَّحِيمِ

In the Name of God, the All-beneficent, the All-merciful.

1 وَيْلٌ لِّكُلِّ هُمَزَةٍ لُّمَزَةٍ ۝ Woe to every scandal-monger and slanderer,

2 الَّذِي جَمَعَ مَالًا وَعَدَّدَهُ ۝ who amasses wealth and counts it over.

3 يَحْسَبُ أَنَّ مَالَهُ أَخْلَدَهُ ۝ He supposes his wealth will make him immortal!

4 كَلَّا لَيُنبَذَنَّ فِي الْحُطَمَةِ ۝ No indeed! He will surely be cast into the Crusher.

5 وَمَا أَدْرَاكَ مَا الْحُطَمَةُ ۝ And what will show you what is the Crusher?

6 نَارُ اللَّهِ الْمُوقَدَةُ ۝ It is the fire of God, set ablaze,

---

[1] In a report, Imam ʿAlī b. Mūsā al-Riḍā (ʿa) interprets the 'Blessing' as the teaching relating to *tawḥīd*, prophethood and the *walāyah* of the Prophet (ṣ) and the Imams of his family. *ʿUyūn Akhbār al-Riḍā* (ii, 129)

[2] A Makkī *sūrah*, it is named after the phrase 'By Time' (*wal ʿaṣr*) in verse 1.

[3] A Makkī *sūrah*, it is named after 'the slanderer' (*humazah*) from verse 1.

7 اَلَّتِي تَطَّلِعُ عَلَى الْأَفْئِدَةِ ۝ which will overspread the hearts.
8 إِنَّهَا عَلَيْهِمْ مُؤْصَدَةٌ ۝ Indeed, it will close in upon them
9 فِي عَمَدٍ مُمَدَّدَةٍ ۝ in outstretched columns.

105. THE ELEPHANT[1]
al-Fīl

سُورَةُ الْفِيلِ

بِسْمِ اللَّهِ
الرَّحْمَٰنِ الرَّحِيمِ

In the Name of God,
the All-beneficent, the All-merciful.

1 أَلَمْ تَرَ كَيْفَ فَعَلَ رَبُّكَ بِأَصْحَابِ الْفِيلِ ۝ Have you not regarded how *your* Lord dealt with the army of the elephants?
2 أَلَمْ يَجْعَلْ كَيْدَهُمْ فِي تَضْلِيلٍ ۝ Did He not make their stratagems go awry,
3 وَأَرْسَلَ عَلَيْهِمْ طَيْرًا أَبَابِيلَ ۝ and send against them flocks of birds
4 تَرْمِيهِمْ بِحِجَارَةٍ مِنْ سِجِّيلٍ ۝ pelting them with stones of shale,
5 فَجَعَلَهُمْ كَعَصْفٍ مَأْكُولٍ ۝ thus making them like chewed-up straw?

106. QURAYSH[2]
Quraysh

سُورَةُ قُرَيْشٍ

بِسْمِ اللَّهِ
الرَّحْمَٰنِ الرَّحِيمِ

In the Name of God,
the All-beneficent, the All-merciful.

1 لِإِيلَافِ قُرَيْشٍ ۝ In gratitude for solidarity[3] among the Quraysh,
2 إِيلَافِهِمْ رِحْلَةَ الشِّتَاءِ وَالصَّيْفِ ۝ their solidarity during winter and summer journeys,
3 فَلْيَعْبُدُوا رَبَّ هَٰذَا الْبَيْتِ ۝ let them worship the Lord of this House,
4 الَّذِي أَطْعَمَهُمْ مِنْ جُوعٍ who has fed them and saved them from hunger,
وَآمَنَهُمْ مِنْ خَوْفٍ ۝ and secured them from fear.

---

[1] A Makkī *sūrah*, it is named after 'the Elephant' (*al-fīl*) mentioned in verse 2, which refers to the force dispatched by Abrahah to Makkah with the aim of destroying the Ka'bah as *aṣḥāb al-fīl* ('the Army of the Elephant').

[2] This Makkī *sūrah* takes its name from verse 1, which mentions the Quraysh, the Makkan tribe to which the Prophet (ṣ) belonged.

[3] That is, the team spirit amongst the clans of Quraysh, who conducted the trade caravans between Yemen and Syria in summer and winter.

107. VITAL AID[1]
AL-MĀ'ŪN

سُورَةُ الْمَاعُون

بِسْمِ اللَّهِ الرَّحْمَـٰنِ الرَّحِيمِ

In the Name of God,
the All-beneficent, the All-merciful.

1 Did you see him who denies the Retribution? أَرَأَيْتَ الَّذِى يُكَذِّبُ بِالدِّينِ

2 That is the one who drives away the orphan, فَذَٰلِكَ الَّذِى يَدُعُّ الْيَتِيمَ

3 and does not urge the feeding of the needy. وَلَا يَحُضُّ عَلَىٰ طَعَامِ الْمِسْكِينِ

4 Woe to those who pray, فَوَيْلٌ لِّلْمُصَلِّينَ

5 but are heedless of their prayers, الَّذِينَ هُمْ عَن صَلَاتِهِمْ سَاهُونَ

6 who show off الَّذِينَ هُمْ يُرَاءُونَ

7 but deny vital aid. وَيَمْنَعُونَ الْمَاعُونَ

108. ABUNDANCE[2]
al-Kawthar

سُورَةُ الْكَوْثَر

بِسْمِ اللَّهِ الرَّحْمَـٰنِ الرَّحِيمِ

In the Name of God,
the All-beneficent, the All-merciful.

1 We have indeed given you abundance. إِنَّا أَعْطَيْنَاكَ الْكَوْثَرَ

2 So pray to your Lord, and sacrifice the sacrificial camel.[3] فَصَلِّ لِرَبِّكَ وَانْحَرْ

3 It is indeed your enemy who is without posterity. إِنَّ شَانِئَكَ هُوَ الْأَبْتَرُ

109. THE FAITHLESS[4]
al-Kāfirūn

سُورَةُ الْكَافِرُون

بِسْمِ اللَّهِ الرَّحْمَـٰنِ الرَّحِيمِ

In the Name of God,
the All-beneficent, the All-merciful.

1 Say, 'O faithless ones! قُلْ يَا أَيُّهَا الْكَافِرُونَ

2 I do not worship what you worship, لَا أَعْبُدُ مَا تَعْبُدُونَ

---

[1] This Makkī sūrah takes its name from verse 7, in which word *al-mā'ūn* (meaning 'the aid') occurs.
[2] This Makkī sūrah takes its name from 'the abundance' (*al-kawthar*) mentioned in verse 1.
[3] Or 'raise your hands.' As according to this interpretation, the phrase refers to the practice of raising the hands to the ears during prayers.
[4] This Makkī sūrah takes its name from the expression 'the faithless' (*al-kāfirūn*), mentioned in verse 1.

3 nor do you worship what I worship;
4 nor will I worship what you have worshiped
5 nor will you worship what I worship.
6 To you your religion, and to me my religion.'

110. Help[1]
al-Naṣr

In the Name of God,
the All-beneficent, the All-merciful.

1 When God's help comes with victory
2 and you see the people entering God's religion in throngs,
3 *celebrate* the praise of your Lord, and *plead* to Him for forgiveness. He is indeed all-clement.

111. Palm Fibre[2]
al-Masad

In the Name of God,
the All-beneficent, the All-merciful.

1 Perish the hands of Abu Lahab and perish he!
2 Neither his wealth availed him, nor what he had earned.
3 Soon he will enter the blazing fire,
4 and his wife, too, the firewood carrier,[3]
5 with a rope of palm fibre around her neck.

---

[1] This late Madanī *sūrah* takes its name from verse 1, in which phrase *naṣrullāh* (meaning 'God's help') occurs.

[2] This Makkī *sūrah* takes its name from verse 5 in which the phrase *ḥablun min masad* (meaning 'a rope of palm fibre') occurs.

[3] Or 'the informer.'

112. PURE MONOTHEISM[1]
al-Ikhlāṣ

بِسْمِ اللَّهِ الرَّحْمَٰنِ الرَّحِيمِ

In the Name of God,
the All-beneficent, the All-merciful.

1 Say, 'He is God, the One.

2 God is the All-embracing.

3 He neither bore, nor was born,

4 nor has He any equal.'

113. DAYBREAK[2]
al-Falaq

بِسْمِ اللَّهِ الرَّحْمَٰنِ الرَّحِيمِ

In the Name of God,
the All-beneficent, the All-merciful.

1 Say, 'I seek the protection of the Lord of daybreak[3]

2 from the evil of what He has created,

3 and from the evil of the dark night when it falls,

4 and from the evil of the witches who blow on knots,

5 and from the evil of the envious one when he envies.'

114. HUMANS[4]
al-Nās

بِسْمِ اللَّهِ الرَّحْمَٰنِ الرَّحِيمِ

In the Name of God,
the All-beneficent, the All-merciful.

1 Say, 'I seek the protection of the Lord of humans,

2 Sovereign of humans,

3 God of humans,

---

[1] This Makkī *sūrah*—also called *Sūrat al-Tawḥīd*—is a statement of pure monotheism, or *tawḥīd*. It is also called 'the *Sūrah* of Ikhlāṣ,' as it negates many deviant notions concerning God and posits *tawḥīd* in its exclusive purity.

[2] This Makkī *sūrah* takes its name from 'the daybreak' (*al-falaq*) mentioned in verse 1.

[3] Or 'the Lord of *Falaq*.' '*Falaq*' is said to be the name of a pit in hell.

[4] This Makkī *sūrah* takes its name from the word 'humans' (*al-nās*) which recurs throughout the *sūrah*.

4 مِنْ شَرِّ الْوَسْوَاسِ الْخَنَّاسِ ۞   from the evil of the sneaky tempter

5 الَّذِى يُوَسْوِسُ فِى صُدُورِ النَّاسِ ۞   who puts temptations into the breasts of humans,

6 مِنَ الْجِنَّةِ وَالنَّاسِ ۞   from among the jinn and humans.'

Sources Consulted

A Translation of the Qur'ān (English). The first 30 *sūrahs*; unpublished. By a team of translators working under the auspices of Al-Balāgh Foundation, Tehran.

Ali, Abdullah Yusuf, *The Meaning of the Holy Qur'ān*. Brentwood: Amana, 1995.

Ali, S. V. Mir Ahmed. *The Holy Qur'an*. Elmhurst: Tahrike Tarsile Qur'an, 1988.

Arberry, Arthur J. *The Koran Interpreted*. London: Oxford University Press, 1964.

Al-'Askarī, al-Imām Abū Muḥammad al-Ḥasan b. 'Alī. *al-Tafsīr al-Mansūb ilā al-Imām Abī Muḥammad al-Ḥasan b. 'Alī al-'Askarī ('a)*. 1st ed. Qum: Mu'assasat al-Imām al-Mahdī, 1409 H.

Al-Astarābādī, al-Sayyid Sharaf al-Dīn 'Alī al-Ḥusaynī al-Gharawī. *Ta'wīl al-Āyāt al-Ẓāhirah fī Faḍā'il al-'Itrat al-Ṭāhirah*. 3rd ed. Qum: Mu'assasat al-Nashr al-Islāmī al-Tābi'ah li Jamā'at al-Mudarrisīn, 1421 H. Sh.

Al-'Ayyāshī, Abū Naṣr Muḥammad b. Mas'ūd b. 'Ayyāsh al-Sulamī al-Samarqandī. *Kitāb al-Tafsīr*, edited by Sayyid Hāshim al-Rasūlī al-Maḥallātī. Tehran: al-Maktabat al-'Ilmiyyah al-Islāmiyyah, n.d.

Al-Baḥrānī, al-Sayyid Hāshim al-Ḥusaynī. *al-Burhān fī Tafsīr al-Qur'ān*. 1st ed. Tehran: Bunyād-e Bi'that, 1415 H.

Barakāt, Muḥammad Fāris. *al-Jāmi' li Mawāḍi' Āyāt al-Qur'ān al-Karīm*. Qum: Dār al-Hijrah, 1404 H.

Bargnaysī, Kāẓim. "Reflections on a Qur'ānic Metaphor: The Meaning of '*khatf al-ṭayr*' in Verse 31 of Sūrat al-Ḥajj." Trans. A. Q. Qarā'ī, *al-Tawḥīd*, 13, no. 4 (1996): 5-35.

Bayḍāwī, Nāṣir al-Dīn Abū Sa'īd 'Abd Allāh b. 'Umar b. Muḥammad al-Shīrāzī. *Tafsīr al-Bayḍāwī*. 1st ed. Beirut: Mu'assasat al-A'lamī lil-Maṭbū'āt, 1410 H./1990.

Dehlawī, Shāh Walī Allāh. *al-Qur'ān al-Ḥakīm* (Persian Translation). Peshawar: Nūrānī Kutub-khānah, n.d.

Fānī, K., and B. Khorramshāhī. *Farhang-e Mawḍū'ī-ye Qur'ān-e Majīd* (A Subject Index to the Glorious Qur'ān). 2nd ed. Tehran: Intishārāt-e al-Hudā, 1369 H. Sh.

Al-Kāshānī, al-Mawlā Muḥsin al-Fayḍ. *Tafsīr al-Ṣāfī (al-Ṣāfī fī Tafsīr Kalām Allāh)*. 2nd ed. Mashhad: Dār al-Murtaḍā lil-Nashr, 1402 H./1982.

Al-Kūfī, Abū al-Qāsim Furāt b. Ibrāhīm b. Furāt. *Tafsīr Furāt al-Kūfī*, edited by Muḥammad al-Kāẓim. 1st ed. Tehran: Mu'assasat al-Ṭab' wal-Nashr al-Tābi'ah li Wizārat al-Thaqāfah wal-Irshād al-Islāmī, 1410 H./1990.

Al-Ḥaskānī, al-Ḥākim 'Ubayd Allāh b. 'Abd Allāh b. Aḥmad. *Shawāhid al-Tanzīl*, edited by al-Shaykh Muḥammad Bāqir al-Maḥmūdī. Tehran: Mu'assasat al-Ṭab' wal-Nashr al-Tābi'ah li Wizārat al-Thaqāfah wal-Irshād al-Islāmī, 1411 H./1990.

Al-Ḥuwayzi, al-Shaykh 'Abd 'Alī b. Jumu'ah al-'Arūsī. *Tafsīr Nūr al-Thaqalayn*, 2nd ed. Qum: al-Maṭba'ah al-'Ilmiyyah, n.d.

Ibn Kathīr, Abū al-Fidā' Ismā'īl al-Qurashī al-Dimashqī. *Tafsīr al-Qur'ān al-'Aẓīm*, 2nd ed. Beirut: Dār al-Ma'rifah, 1308 H./1988.

Izutsu, Toshihiko. *Ethico-Religious Concepts in the Qur'ān*. Montreal: McGill University Press, 1966.

Jeffery, Arthur. *The Foreign Vocabulary of the Qur'ān*. Baroda: Oriental Institute, 1938.

Al-Kulaynī. *Uṣūl al-Kāfī*, edited by al-Shaykh Muḥammad Jawād al-Faqīh. Beirut: Dār al-Aḍwā' lil-Ṭabā'ah wal-Nashr wal-Tawzī', 1413 H./1992.

Al-Majlisī, al-Shaykh Muḥammad Bāqir. *Biḥār*

al-Anwār al-Jāmi'ah li-Durar Akbār al-A'immat al-Aṭhār. 3rd ed. Beirut: Dār Iḥyā' al-Turāth al-'Arabī, 1402 H./ 1983.

Marzūq, 'Abd al-Ṣabūr. *Mu'jam al-A'lām wa al-Mawḍū'āt fī al-Qur'ān al-Karīm*, 1st ed. Cairo: Dār al-Shurūq, 1415 H./1995.

Al-Mashhadī, al-Shaykh Muḥammad b. Muḥammad Riḍā al-Qummī. *Tafsīr Kanz al-Daqā'iq wa Baḥr al-Gharā'ib*. 1st ed. Tehran: Mu'assasat al-Ṭab' wal-Nashr al-Tābi'ah li Wizārat al-Thaqāfah wal-Irshād al-Islāmī, 1366 H. Sh.

Mujtabawī, Sayyid Jalāl al-Dīn. *al-Qur'ān al-Ḥakīm* (Persian Translation). 1st ed. Tehran: Intishārāt-e Ḥikmat, 1313 H./1371 H. Sh.

Narm Afzār-e Tarjume wa Tafsīr-e Qur'ānī-ye Jāmi'. Ver. 4.1. CD-ROM. Tehran: Nashr-e Ḥadīth-e Ahl al-Bayt Institute, n.d. This software, which has been of invaluable help to this translator in the course of his work, consisted of 18 Persian translations of the Qur'ān and 51, mostly Shī'ī, commentaries.

Nida, Eugene A. *Toward a Science of Translating, with Special Reference to Principles and Procedures Involved in Bible Translation*. Leiden: Brill, 1964.

—, and Charles R. Taber. *The Theory and Practice of Translation*. Leiden: E. J. Brill, 1984.

Pickthall, Marmaduke. *The Glorious Qur'an*. 3rd ed. New York: Mustazafin Foundation of New York, 1987.

Qarā'ī, Sayyid 'Alī Qulī, "Dilhā-ye Nāpāk: Taḥqīqī dar bāreh-ye 'Ibārat-e qulūbunā ghulf." *Tarjumān-e Waḥy* 5, no. 1 (2002): 4-31; 5, no. 2 (2002): 4-25.

Al-Qummī, Abū al-Ḥasan 'Alī b. Ibrāhīm. *Tafsīr al-Qummī*, edited by al-Sayyid al-Ṭayyib al-Mūsawī al-Jazā'irī. 3rd ed. Qum: Mu'assasah Dār al-Kitāb lil-Ṭabā'ah wal-Nashr, 1404 H.

Qumsheh'ī, Mahdī Ilāhī. *Qur'ān-e Karīm* (Persian Translation). 1st ed. Tehran: Bunyād-e Nashr-e Qur'ān, 1367 H. Sh.

Al-Rāzī, Abū al-Futūḥ Ḥusayn b. 'Alī b. Muḥammad al-Khuzā'ī al-Nayshābūrī. *Rawḍ al-Jinān wa Rawḥ al-Janān*. Bunyād-e Pazhohishhā-ye Islāmī-ye Āstān-e Quds-e Raḍawī, 1366-1374 H. Sh.

Al-Rāzī, al-Fakhr. *al-Tafsīr al-Kabīr*. 1st ed. Beirut: Dār Iḥyā' al-Turāth al-'Arabī, 1415/1995.

Al-Ṣadūq, al-Shaykh Abū Ja'far Muḥammad b. 'Alī b. al-Ḥusayn b. Bābwayh al-Qummī. *Ma'ānī al-Akhbār*, edited by 'Alī Akbar al-Ghaffārī. Tehran: Maktabat al-Ṣadūq, 1379 H./1338 H. Sh.

—, *'Uyūn Akhbār al-Riḍā ('a)*, edited by al-Sayyid Mahdī al-Ḥusaynī al-Lājiwardī. Tehran: Intishārāt-e Jahān, n.d.

Sha'rānī, Ḥājj Mīrzā Abū al-Ḥasan. *al-Qur'ān al-Karīm* (Persian Translation). 2nd ed. Tehran: Kitābfurūshī-ye Islāmiyyah, 1374 H. Sh.

Shīrāzī, Āyatullāh Nāṣir Makārim. *Qur'ān-e Majīd* (Persian Translation), 1st ed. Qum: Dār al-Qur'ān al-Karīm, 1373 H. Sh.

Al-Suyūṭī, Jalāl al-Dīn 'Abd al-Raḥmān. *Durr al-Manthūr fī al-Tafsīr bil-Ma'thūr*. Qum: Manshūrāt Maktabah Āyatullāh Mar'ashī, 1404 H.

Al-Ṭabarī, Abū Ja'far Muḥammad b. Jarīr. *Jāmi' al-Bayān 'an Ta'wīl Āy al-Qur'ān*, edited by Ṣidqī Jamīl al-'Aṭṭār. Beirut: Dār al-Fikr, 1415 H./1995.

—, *Ta'rīkh al-Ṭabarī*, edited by Muḥammad Abū al-Faḍl Ibrāhīm. 6th ed. Cairo: Dār al-Ma'ārif, n.d.

Al-Ṭabāṭabā'ī, al-Sayyid Muḥammad Ḥusayn. *al-Mīzān fī Tafsīr al-Qur'ān*. 3rd ed. Tehran: Dār al-Kutub al-Islāmiyyah, 1397 H.,

Al-Ṭabrisī, Amīn al-Dīn Abū 'Alī al-Faḍl b. al-Ḥasan al-Ṭūsī. *Majma' al-Bayān fī Tafsīr al-Qur'ān*. Beirut: Dār Iḥyā' al-Turāth al-'Arabī, 1379 H.

Al-Ṭūsī, Abū Ja'far Muḥammad b. al-Ḥasan. *al-Tibyān fī Tafsīr al-Qur'ān*, edited by Aḥmad Ḥabīb al-Qaṣīr al-'Āmilī. Qum: Maktab al-I'lām al-Islāmī, 1409 H.

'Umar, Aḥmad Mukhtār, and 'Abd al-'Āl Sālim Mukarram. *Mu'jam al-Qirā'āt al-Qur'āniyyah*. Qum: Intishārāt-e Usweh, 1412 H./1991.

Al-Zamakhsharī, Jār Allāh Maḥmūd b. 'Umar. *al-Kashshāf 'an Ḥaqā'iq Ghawāmiḍ al-Tanzīl wa 'Uyūn al-Aqāwīl fī Wujūh al-Ta'wīl*. n.p.: Nashr Adab al-Ḥawzah, n.d.

An Abridged Index of Subjects, Names & Terms

Aaron (*'a*), 4:163, 6:84, 7:122, 7:142, 7:150, 7:172, 10:75, 19:53, 20:30, 20:40, 20:90, 20:92, 21:48, 23:45, 25:35, 26:12, 26:48, 28:34, 37:114-120; House of, 2:248

Abel & Cain 5:27-31

Abraham (*'a*) 2:124-132, 2:135, 136, 140, 258, 260, 3:65, 67-68, 84, 95, 97, 4:54-55, 4:125, 163, 6:74-83, 6:161, 9:70, 114, 11:69-76, 12:6, 38, 14:35, 15:51-56, 16:120, 123, 19:41-49, 19:58, 21:51-73, 22:26, 22:43, 22:78, 26:69, 29:16, 29:25, 29:31, 33:7, 37:83-109, 38:45, 42:13, 43:26, 51:24-34, 53:37, 57:26, 60:4-5, 87:19; Ka'bah and *ḥajj* 2:125-127; 3:96-7; 22:26-27; imamate 2:124; Nimrod, argument with 2:258; renunciation of pagan gods 19:46; 37:84-85; raising of the dead 2:260; shown the dominions of the heavens and the earth 6:75; supplications of 2:127-129; 14:35-41; 19:48; 26:83 -89; 37:100; 60:4-5; visions 37:102-105

Abrogation (*naskh*) 2:106; 13:39; 16:101; legitimacy of 2:142

Abū Lahab ('Abd al-'Uzzā) 111:1-3

'Ād 7:65-72, 74; 9:70; 11:50-60; 14:9; punishment of 7:71-72; 23:40-41; 26:139; 29:38; 41:16; 46:25-26; 51:41-42; 54:18-21

Adam (*'a*) 2:31-38; 3:33, 59; 5:27; 7:11, 19-25; 17:61, 70; 18:50; 19:58; 20:115-123; 38:71-76;; and Satan 2:36; 7:20-22; 20:120; chosen by God 20:122; creation of 3:59; 4:1; 7:189; 17:61; 39:6; prostration before 2:34; 7:11; 15:30-33; 17:61; 18:50; 20:116; repentance 2:37; 7:23; taught the Names 2:31-33, 37

Adornment (women) 24:31, 60; 33:33

Advice (*maw'iẓah*) 2:66, 231-232, 275; 3:138; 4:34, 58, 63, 66; 5:46; 7:110, 145, 164; 10:57; 11:46, 120; 16:90, 125; 20:94; 24:17, 34; 25:77; 26:35, 136; 31:13; 34:46; 58:3; 65:2

Affluent 2:273; 4:6; 9:93; 11:116; 16:92; 17:16; 18:32-44; 21:13; 23:33, 64; 24:22; 26:146-152; 34:34-37; 65:7; 73:11-13; (*mūsi'*) 2:236; denial of the apostles 34:34; 43:23

Afreet 27:39

Aggression/Reprisal (*'udwān*) 2:85, 173, 193-194; 4:30; 5:2, 62, 87; 6:145; 7:33; 10:90; 16:90, 115; 22:60; 8:28; 42:39, 42; 49:9; 58:9

Agreements (*'uqūd*) 2:282; 5:1; loyalty to agreements & commitments 2:27, 40, 100, 177; 3:76-77; 5:1, 8; 6:152; 13:20-21, 25; 16:91-95; 17:34; 23:8

*****Ahl al-Bayt** (*'a*) 2:143; 3:104, 110; 7:181; 14:24-25, 37; 19:58; 21:101; 22:77-78; 24:36-37; 27:59; 28:5; 29:47, 49, 69; 33:33, 56; 35:32; 37:130, 165-166; 38:75; 42:23; 55:31; 59:7; 102:8

Aḥmad 61:6

Aḥqāf 46:21

*****'Alī b. Abī Ṭālib** (*'a*) 2:156, 207, 274; 3:172-174, 191-195; 4:83; 5:3, 55, 67; 8: 64; 9:3, 16, 19-20; 11:12, 17; 12:108; 13:19-21, 43; 16:91-94; 17:73-4; 21:24; 24:55; 25:74; 26:214; 29:2; 33:23, 25; 39:9; 43:4, 43; 47:9, 25-26; 48:26; 53:1-4; 56:10-11; 58:12; 66:4; 70:1-2; 76:5-22; 94:7; 100:1-5

Angel(s) (*malā'ikah*) 2:177, 285; administer death 4:97; 6:61, 93; 7:36; 8:51; 16:28, 32; 32:11; bless the faithful 33:43; descend upon the faithful 41:30; guard humans 6:61; 13:11; 72:27; 82:10; 86:4; plead forgiveness for earth's denizens 42:5; record deeds 10:21; 43:80; 50:17-18; 82:11-12; warners 16:2

Angel of Death 32:11

Ant(s) 27:18

Aorta 69:46

Ape(s) 2:65; 5:60; 7:166

Apostles (*mursalūn, rusul*) accused of sorcery 7:109; 10:2, 77; 20:63; 26:34; 38:4; 40:24; 43:49; 51:39, 52; derided 13:32; 15:11; 18:106; 21:41; 36:30; maintenance of justice 57:25; obligation to follow them 14:44; 20:134; relative merit 2:253; tormented 6:34; 14:12; ultimate victory 58:21; warners 2:119, 213; 4:165; 5:19; 6:48, 130; 7:184, 188; 11:2, 12, 25; 13:7; 15:89;

Arabic 12:2; 13:37; 16:103; 20:113; 26:195; 39:28; 41:3, 44; 42:7; 43:3; 46:12

Arabic Qur'ān 12:2; 20:113; 39:28; 41:3; 42:7; 43:3

'Arafāt 2:198-9

Arrogance/disdain (*istikbār*) 2:34, 87; 4:172, 173;

761

5:82;
Ass 2:259; 16:8; 31:19; 62:5; 74:50
Asylum/shelter 3:112; 9:6; 23:88; 67:28; 72:22
Atonement(s) (*kaffārah*) 2:184, 196, 271; fasting 2: 184, 196; 5:95; fasting for 2 months 4:92; 58:4; fasting for 3 days 2:196; 5:89; fasting for 7 days 2:196; feeding 10 needy persons 5:89; feeding 60 needy persons 58:4; feeding a needy person 2:184; 5:95; for hunting 5:95; for manslaughter 4:92; for not fasting 2:184; for unfulfilled vows and oaths 5:89; 58:3-4; freeing a slave 4:92; 5:89; 58:3; *ḥajj* 2:196; oath 5:89; sacrificial offering 5:95; *ẓihār* 58:3-4
Āyat al-kursī 2:255-257
Āyat al-mubāhalah 3:61
Āyat al-taṭhīr 33:33

Bachelorhood 4:25; 24:33
Backbiting 49:12
*****Banū Naḍīr** 3:178; 59:2-6
*****Banū Qurayḍah** 8:55-58; 33:26-27
*****Banū Umayyah** 17:60; 24:40; 26:205-7; 47:22-23; 77:17-8; 91:4; 92:1; 97:1-5
Barzakh 23:100; 25:53; 55:20
Bedouins 9:90, 97-9, 101, 120; 33:20; 48:11, 16; 49:14
*****Benjamin** 12:8, 59, 63, 69, 76-83, 87, 89, 90
Bidding what is right 2:40; 3:104, 110, 114; 7:157, 200; 9:71, 112; 22:41; 31:17
Bird(s) 2:260; 3:49; 5:110; 6:38; 12:36; 16:79; 21:78; 24:41; 27:16, 17; 34:10; 38:19; 67:19; 105:3; crow 5:31; flocks of ~105:3-4
Blind (*a'mā*) 2:18, 171; 5:71; 6:50, 104; 7:64; 10:43; (*akmah*) 3:49; 5:110
Blind imitation 2:170; 5:104; 7:28; 10:78; 26:74; 31:21; 34:43; 37:69-70; 43:22-25
Blindness 6:114; 17:72; 25:73
Blood 2:30, 84, 173; 5:3; 6:145; 7:133; 12:18; 16:66, 115; 22:37
Blood money (*diyah*) 2:178; 4:92
Blood relatives 2:180, 215; 4:1, 7, 33, 35-6, 135; 47:22; 60:3; 90:15; (*ulu al-arḥām*) 8:75; 13:21; 33:6; 47:22; (*ulu al-qurbā*) 4:8; 9:113; 24:22; (*dhawi al-qurbā*) 2:27, 83, 177; kindness to 2:27; 4:36; 13:21, 25; 16:90; 90:15; rights of 17:26; 30:38; 33:6; severing ties of kinship with 13:21, 25; 47:22
Bracelets 18:31; 22:23; 35:33; 43:53; 76:21
Breach of trust 3:161
Breast feeding 2:233; 46:15; 65:6; wet-nursing

2:233; 65:6
Brotherhood 2:220; 3:103, 9:11; 49:10, 13
Burning at stakes 21:68; 29:24
Byzantium (*Rūm*) 30:2- 4

Calumny (*buhtān*) 3:55; 4:21, 112, 156; 24:11-12, 16; 33:58; 60:12; 104:1
Campaigns of the Prophet (ṣ); Badr *2:214; 3:123-128, *140, *165, *173-174; *8:5-18, *39-48; 9:25; *Banū al-Naḍīr 59:2-6, 11-14; *Banū Nakhlah 5:11; *Dhāt al-Salāsil 100:1-5; *Ḥamrā' al-Asad 3:172-175; Ḥunayn 9:25-27; *Khandaq (Ditch) 2:214; 33:9-27; *Khaybar 48:16, 19; *Makkah 48:1-27; 57:10; 61:13; *Tabūk 9:38-59, 117-118; *Uḥud 3:121-127, 139-140, 151-172; 4:104
Captive(s) 2:85, 177; 8:30, 67, 70-1; 47:4; 76:8
Caravan 5:96; 8:42; 12:10, 19, 70, 82, 94
Carrion (*maytah*) 2:173; 5:3; 6:139, 145; 16:115
Cattle (*an'ām*) 3:14; 4:119; 5:95; 6:136, 138-9, 142, 179;
Charity (*infāq, ṣadaqah*) 2:3, 177, 195-6, 215, 219, 245, 254, 261-268, 270-274, 276, 280; 3:92, 117, 134; 4:34, 36-8, 92, 114;
Chastity 2:25; 3:15, 39; 4:25, 57; 5:5; 19:20, 28; 21:91; 24:33; 33:53; 66:12
Cheek 31:18
Child-bearing 3:36; 11:72; 19:22-3; 22:2; 35:11; 41:47; 46:15; 65:4
Christians (*naṣārā*) 2:62, 111, 120, 135, 140; 3:19, 61, 70, 79-80, 110, 113, 115; 5:15, 18, 74, 77, 83-85, 114; 57:27; alliance with 5:51; argue with the Prophet (ṣ) 3:61; Christ's sonship 2:116; 5:73; 9:30; 10:68; 18:4-5; 19:88-93; 21:26; 25:2; 39:4; 72:3; covenant 5:14; fabricate lies about God 9:30; 18:5; faith 2:137; 3:113-4; 5:69, 83-5; 57:27; faithlessness 5:17, 72, 73, 86; false doctrines 2:116; 5:75; 9:30; 10:68; 18:4-5; 19:88-9, 91-3; 21:26; 25:2; 39:4; 72:3; forgot part of their teachings 5:14; hatred and enmity among them 5:14; kindly character 57:27; monasticism 57:27; many transgressors 57:27; *mubāhalah* 3:61; nearest in affection to the faithful 5:82; polytheism 5:72-77; 9:31; salvation of 3:113-5; 5:69; 57:27
Churches 22:40
Clothing (*kiswah*) 2:233, 259; 4:5; 5:89; 23:14
Clothes 2:187; 7:26; 11:5; 14:50; 18:31; 22:19; 24:58, 60; 35:33; 71:7; 74:4; 76:12, 21; cloaks of fire 22:19
Coats of mail 16:81; 21:80; 34:11
Coming of age 6:152; 12:22; 17:34; 18:82; 22:5; 28:14; 40:67; 46:15

Commanding what is right & forbidding what is wrong 2:44; 3:104, 110; 4:114; 7:157, 164, 199; 9:67, 71, 112; 11:117; 22:41; 31:17

Companion 4:36; 26:61; 58:7; (*qarīn*) 4:38; 37:51; 50:23, 27; (*ṣāḥib*) 6:71; 7:184; 9:40; 18:9, 34, 37; 34:46; 53:2; 54:29; 81:22; evil companion 22:13; 37:51; 41:25; 43:36, 38; excellent companions (*rafīq*) 4:69

Companions of the Cave 18:9-26

Company 4:72; 11:12; 17:104; 18:28, 76; 19:73; 25:35; (*musāḥabah*) 31:15; company of polytheists and those who mock God's signs 4:140; 6:68, 70, 106; 7:199; 15:94; 53:29

Compulsion (*iḍṭirār*) 2:126, 173; 5:3; 6:119, 145; (*ikrāh*) 2:256; 4:19; 7:88; 8:5; 16:106; 20:73; 24:33

Concealment; of faith 40:28; of good deeds 4:149; of knowledge & testimony 2:146, 159-160, 174, 283; 3:187; 4:37, 42; 5:15, 106; 6:91

Conceit (*'izzah*) 2:206; 38:2; 54:25-6

Conciliation 4:114, 129; 9:8, 62; 42:40

Confession (*i'tirāf*) 9:102; 32:12; 40:11; 67:10-11

Conjecture (*ẓann*) 2:78; 3:154; no a substitute for truth 10:36; 53:28

Constellations (*burūj*) 15:16; 25:61; 85:1

Contentment (*qinā'ah*) 7:31; 9:59

Cooperation 5:2; 8:74; 9:71

Copper (*qiṭr*) 18:96; 34:12; molten copper (*muhl*) 18:29; 44:45; 70:8

Corpse 5:31; 38:34

Corruption (*fasād*) 2:11, 12, 27, 30, 60, 205; — corruption on earth 2:205, 251; 5:32, 33, 64; corruption of land and sea 30:41; corruption of the heavens and the earth 21:22; 23:71

Corruption, agents of (*mufsidūn*) 2:11, 12, 30, 220; 3:63; 5:64; 7:86, 103, 142; 10:40, 81, 91; 11:85; 27:14; 28:4, 77; 29:30; fate of 7:86, 103; 27:14; punishment of 5:32, 33

Corruption of scriptures (*taḥrīf*) 2:75, 79; 3:78; 5:13

Covenant/promise/treaty (*'ahd, iṣr, mīthāq*) 2:27, 40, 80, 83-4, 93, 124, 177; breaking of 2:27, 83, 100; 4:155; 5:13; 7:102; 8:58; 13:20, 25; 16:91-2, 94-5; loyalty to covenants 2:80, 177; 3:76-7; 5:1, 7; 6:152; 9:4, 7, 111; 13:20, 25; 16:91, 95; 17:34; 21:9; 23:8; 33:23; 48:10; 70:32; 76:7; primordial covenant 7:172; 57:8

Covetousness 9:34; 57:20; 102:1

Creation of the Jinn 6:100; 7:12, 179; 15:27; 38:77; 51:56; 55:15

Creation of man 2:21, 228; 3:59; created for mankind 2:29; 16:5-8, 13; 36:42, 71; 40:79

Creation of the heavens and the earth 2:164; 3:190-1;

Crucifixion 4:157; 5:33; 7:124; 12:41; 20:71; 26:49

Cure (*shifā'*) 10:57; 16:69; 17:82; 26:80

Curse (*la'nah*) 2:159-162; 3:61, 87; 7:38; 11:60, 99; 13:25; 15:35; 24:23; 28:42; 29:25; 33:68; 40:52; 48:6

Custody 12:66; (*kifālah*) 20:40; 28:12

Daughter(s) 2:221; 4:23; 11:78-9; 15:71; 16:58-9; 28:27; 43:17; 66:12; attributed to God 16:57, 100; 37:149, 153; 43:16; 52:39; infanticide 16:58-9

David (*'a*) 2:251; 4:163; 5:78; 6:84; 17:55; 21:78-80; 27:15-6; 34:10-11, 13; 38:17-26

Day of Resurrection (*yawm al-qiyāmah*) 2:85, 113, 174, 212, 3:55, 77, 161, 180, 185, 194; day every nation will be summoned to its book and requited for what its conduct 45:28; day every soul will be rewarded for what it has earned 40:17; day every soul will find what it has done 3:30; 78:40; day in which hearts and sights will be transformed 24:37; day mankind will issue forth in groups 99:6; day no soul shall compensate for another 2:48, 123; day of judgement (*~al-faṣl*) 37:21; 44:40; 60:3; 77:13-4, 38; 78:17; day of retribution 1:4; 15:35; 26:82; 37:20; 38:78; 51:12; 56:56; 70:26; 74:46; 82:15-19; 83:11; day secrets will be divulged 69:18; 86:9; day the earth and the heavens will be transformed 14:48; day God shall raise a witness from every nation 27:83; day when the hearts will be at the throats 40:18; day when the Spirit and the angels stand in an array 78:38; day when tongues, hands and feet will give witness 24:24; day that will make children white-headed 73:17; frowning and fateful day 76:10, 11

Days of God 14:5; 45:14; 55:29

Dead (*amwāt*) 2:28, 73, 154; 3:169; 6:111; 16:21; 35:22; 77:26; (*mawtā*) 2:73, 260; 3:49; 5:110; 6:36, 111; 7:57; 13:31; 27:80; 30:52; (*mayyit*) 3:27; 10:31; 14:17; 30:19; 39:30; 49:12

Dead (of the heart) 6:36, 122; 27:80

Deaf/deafness (*ṣumm*) 2:18, 171; 5:71; 6:25, 39; 8:22; 10:42; 11:24; 17:46, 97; 18:57; 21:45; 25:73; 27:80; 30:52; 31:7; 41:5, 44; 43:40; 47:23; 80:33

Death (*mawt*) in a state of purity 16:32; in faithlessness 2:162; 4:18; 9:55, 85, 125; 47:34; in the state of evil-doing 9:84; in the state of Islam 2:132 3:102; 7:126; 12:101; repentance at 4:18; 23:99-100; taste of death 3:185; 21:35; 29:57

Deeds; lasting righteous deeds 19:76; rectification of 33:71; recording of deeds 10:21; 43:80; 50:17-8, 21; 82:10-12; righteous deeds 2:25, 62, 82, 277; unrighteous deeds 11:46

Denial (*takdhīb*) 6:148; 7:96, 101; 10:45; 20:48, 56; 26:6; 29:18; 34:45; 54:3; 55:13-78; 67:18; 75:32; 92:9, 16; 96:13; >Deniers

Deniers 3:137; 5:10, 70; 6:5, 11, 21, 148; 7:64, 92

Deprived (*maḥrūm*) 51:19; 56:67; 68:27; 70:25

Desire(s) (*hawā*) 2:87, 120, 145; (*shahawāt*) 3:14; 4:27; 7:81; 9:24; 16:57; 41:31; 43:71; cause of injustice 4:135; pursuit of 4:27; 18:28; 19:59; 20:16; 28:50; 30:29; 38:26; 45:18, 23; 47:14, 16; 53:23; 54:3; 79:40; sexual desire 7:81; 27:55

Deviance 2:182; 9:117; 23:74; (*zaygh*) 3:7; 34:12; 38:63; 53:17; 61:5; 66:4

Dhu'l-Kifl ('a) 21:85; 38:48

Dhu'l-Qarnayn 18:83-98

Dīnār 3:75

Dirham 12:20

Disciples of Jesus ('a) 3:52-3; 5:111-5; 61:14

Disobedience ('*iṣyān*) 2:61, 93; 3:112, 152; 4:14, 42, 46; (*ma'ṣiyah*) 58:8, 9

Disobedient 10:91; 19:14, 44

Dispute (*jidāl, jadal, mujādalah*) 2:197; 4:65; 6:25,; (*tanāzu'*) 3:152; 4:59; 8:43, 46; 18:21-2; 20:62; concerning God 13:13; 22:3, 8, 19; 31:20; 40:4-5, 35, 56, 69; 42:39; disputing without knowledge 22:3, 8; 31:20;

Distress ('*anat*) 3:118; 9:128; 49:7; (*ḍarrā'*) 2:177, 214; 3:134; 6:17, 42; 7:94-95; 10:12, 21, 107;

Disunity 3:103; 6:153, 159; 30:14; 42:13-14; among Muslims 9:107

Divorce (*ṭalāq*) 2:226-233, 236-7, 241; 4:19-21, 130; 33:49; 65:1-7

Doubt (*rayb, miryah, shakk*) 2:2, 23, 147, 282; (*labs*) 50:15; avoidance of 2:282; 11:17, 110; grave doubt 11:62, 110; 14:9; 34:54; 41:45; 42:14

Dowry (*mahr*) 2:229, 236-7; 4:4, 19-21, 24-5; 5:5; 33:50; 60:10; 65:6

Dream 8:43; 12:4-6, 36, 43, 100-1; 17:60; 37:102, 105; 48:27; interpretation of 12:6, 21, 43, 44

Drunkenness 4:43; 15:72; 22:2

Duty 2:20, 233; 3:97; 5:92, 99; everyone's according to his means 65:7; not beyond capacity 2:286; 6:152; 7:42; 23:62

Dwelling(s) (*masākin*) 9:24, 72; 14:45; 15:82; 20:128; 21:13; 27:18; 28:58; 32:26; 46:25; 61:12;; good dwellings 61:12

Ear(s) 2:19; 4:119; 5:45; 6:25; 7:179, 195; receptive 69:11

Earthquake (*rajfah*) 7:78, 91, 155; 11:67, 94; 29:37; 73:14; 99:1-4

Ease (*mirfaq*) 18:16; (*rawḥ*) 56:89; (*usr*) 3:134; 7:95; (*yusr*) 2:185; 18:88; 65:2, 7; 87:8; 94:5-6; time of ease 2:280

Eavesdropper(s) 5:41, 42; 9:47; 15:18; 26:223; 37:8; 52:38; 72:9

Education 2:31-2, 102, 129, 151, 239, 251, 282; 3:48, 79, 164; 4:113; 5:4, 110; 6:91; 12:6, 21, 37, 68, 101; 18:65-6; 20:71; 21:80; 27:16; 36:69; 53:5; 55:2, 4; 62:2; 96:4-5; religious education 9:122

Egypt 12:21, 99; king of Egypt 12:43, 50, 54, 72, 76; kingdom of Egypt 43:51

Elect (*akhyār*) 38:47, 48

Elect of God 2:130, 247; 3:33-4, 42, 179; 6:87; 7:144; 12:6; 16:121; 19:58; 20:13, 41, 122; 22:75, 78; 27:59; 35:32-35; 38:45-8; 39:4; 42:13; 44:32; 68:50

Elite (*mala'*) 2:246; 7:60, 66, 75, 88, 90, 103, 107, 127; 10:75, 83, 88; 11:27, 97; 23:24, 33, 46; 26:34; 27:29, 32, 38; 28:20, 32, 38; 37:8; 38:6, 69; 43:46

Eloquence 6:112; 28:34; 55:1-4

Emancipation (of slaves/captives) 2:177; 4:92; 5:89; 9:60; 24:33; 47:4; 58:3; 90:13

Emigrants (*muhājirūn*) 2:218; 3:195; 4:97-100; 8:72-75; 9:20, 100, 117; 16:41, 110; 22:58-9; 24:22; 33:6; 59:8-9; 60:10

Encounter with God (*liqā' Allah*) 2:46, 223, 249; 6:154; 9:77; 11:29; 13:2; 32:23; 33:44; 41:54; 84:6; denial of 6:31; 10:7, 11, 15, 45; 18:105; 25:21; 29:23; 30:8; 32:10; expectation of 10:7, 11, 15; 13:2; 18:110; 25:21; 29:5

Endeavour (*sa'y*) 17:19; 18:104; 21:94; 37:102; 53:39-41; 76:22; 79:35; 88:9; 92:4; miscarried efforts 18:104

Enemy ('*adū*) 2:36, 97-8, 168, 204, 208; 3:103; 4:45, 101; (*khiṣām*) 2:204

Error/being astray 1:7; 2:16, 175; 4:44; 7:61

Error/perversity (*ghayy*) 2:256; 7:30, 146, 202; 28:63; 37:32

Eve 2:35-38; 4:1; 7:19-25, 189; 20:117-123

Evidence /testimony /proof (*bayyinah, shahādah*)

2:87, 92, 140, 156, 185, 209, 213, 253, 282-3; (*burhān*) 2:111; 4:174; 12:24; 21:24; 23:117; 27:64; 28:32, 75

Evil 2:102, 126, 206; 3:12, 151, 162, 187, 197;

Expulsion from paradise 2:36; 7:13, 18, 27; 15:34, 48; 20:117; 38:77

Expulsion (*ikhrāj*) 2:36, 84-5, 191, 217, 240, 246; 3:195; 7:13, 18, 27, 82, 88, 110, 123; 8:30; 9:13, 40; 14:13; 15:34, 48; 17:76; 20:57, 63, 117; 22:40; 26:35, 57, 167; 27:37, 56; 38:77; 47:13; 59:2, 8, 11-2; 60:1, 8-9; 63:8; 65:1

Fabrication (*iftirā'*) 3:24; 4:112; 6:24, 112, 137-8; (*ikhtilāq*) 38:7

Fabrication of lies against God 2:79; 3:78, 94;

Fabricators 7:152; 11:50; 16:101, 116; 30:58

Faith/belief (*īmān*); belief in the Hereafter 2:4, 177, 232; 6:92; 9:99; 12:37; 16:22, 60; 17:10, 45; 23:74; 27:3-4; 34:21;; belief in the Scriptures 2:4, 21, 136, 177, 285; 3:84, 119, 199; 4:136; 5:59; 8:41; 11:71; 29:46;; belief in Resurrection 2:260; 40:27; 70:26; belief in the Unseen 2:3; benefit of last-minute faith 32:29; 34:52; 40:85; 44:12; enhancement of 9:124; 33:22; 47:17; 48:4; 74:31; exclusive faith 7:29; 10:22; 29:65; 31:32; 39:2-3, 11, 14; 40:14, 65; faith in falsehood 16:72; 29:52, 67; faith in the jinn 34:41; faith, in God, His angels and apostles 2:177, 186, 256, 285; 3:52, 84, 110, 179, 193; faith in God and the Last Day 2:8, 62, 126, 177, 228, 264; 3:114; 4:59, 162; 5:69; 9:18-9, 29;; faith in God's signs 6:54; 27:82; 30:53; faith in God's words 7:158

Faithful (*mu'minūn*); adornments 7:32; advice and admonition 7:2; 10:57; 11:120; 51:55; God defends them 22:38; 33:25; God has bought their souls and possessions 9:111; God's help for 3:123-127; 30:47; 40:51; 47:7; 48:18-20; allegiance to God and the Apostle 48:10, 18; alliances/friendship with the faithless 3:28, 100; 60:7-9; apostasy 3:144, 149; apprehensive of the Hour 42:18; avoid major sins 42:37; avoid vain talk 23:3; best of creatures 98:7; bid what is right 9:71; bless the Prophet (ṣ) 33:56; blessed by God and the angels 33:43; brotherhood 3:103; 49:10; civil war 49:9; conduct towards the Prophet (ṣ) 49:1-5; contrasted with the faithless 3:162; 22:19-25; 28:61; 30:14-16; 32:18-21; 35:8; 38:28; 39:9, 22, 24; 40:58; 41:40; 45:21; 47:14; 59:20; 67:22; 68:35-36; cure and mercy for 17:82; definition of 8:74; 46:23:1-11; 36-43; 49:15; deliverance 10:103; 21:88; 27:53; 41:18; 61:10-13;

deliverance from Fire 66:6; demand of help 8:72; derided 23:110; 83:29; distancing from wrongdoers 11:113; doubt 49:15; endeavour 17:19; enemy 60:1; eternal felicity 16:97; 20:75-6; 57:28; exemplar for 33:21; 60:4, 6; faith 2:285; 8:2; 10:9; 48:4; 49:15; 58:22; 74:31; fear of God 3:175; follow the revelation/truth 7:3; 47:3; following/ friendship forbidden 2:208; 3:100-1, 118, 149, 156; 4:89, 144; 5:49, 51, 57; 7:3; 60:12; 9:16, 23; 24:21; 25:52; 60:1-3; 64:14-5; 68:8; 76:24; 96:19; forbid what is wrong 3:110, 114; 9:71, 112; forbidden ridicule & defamation 49:11; forgiveness of sins 8:4, 74; 33:73; 40:7; 47:19; 48:29; 71:28; fortified by God 14:27; 16:102; free of rancour towards the faithful 59:10; fulfil their pledges and trusts 23:8; 33: 23; given good news 2:223; 4:122; 9:112, 124; 10:2; 17:9; 18:2; 27:2; 33:47; 42:23; 57:12; 61:13; good standing with God 10:2; guardianship 5:55-56; guidance 10:9; 27:2; 22:54; 27:77; 48:20; 64:11; healing of hearts 9:14; hearts 9:14-15; 57:16; 58:22; 64:11; hearts tremble when God is mentioned 8:2; heirdom 5:55, 56; 8:72; helping one another 8:72, 74; hold fast to God 4:175; humble hearts 57:16; humble in prayers 23:2; incredulous of dubious reports 49:6; inheritance 8:72; *jihād* 8:72, 74; 49:15; keep looks downcast 24:30-31; light 57:12, 13, 19, 28; 66:8; lose courage 3:122; maintenance of mosques 9:18; mark 48:29; merciful to one another 48:29; mercy 27:77; migration 2:218; 33:195; 4:97-100; 8:72-75; modesty 23:5; noblest of them 49:13; obedience 9:71; 24:51; 64:16; parable of 11:24; 48:29; peacemaking with justice 49:10; plead forgiveness 9:113; prayers answered by God 42:26; promised victory 61:13; rage of their hearts 9:15; raised in rank 58:11; ranks with God 3:163; 8:4; reconciliation 49:9-10; rejoice 3:171; 9:111, 124; 10:58; 13:36; 30:4; 36:55; remembrance of God 2:152, 198, 200, 231; reward 2:25, 281; 3:15, 107, 136, 198; severe towards the faithless 9:123; 48:29; shaken 2:214; 3:122, 155-6; 33:11; shelter and help 8:72, 74; signs for 15:75, 77; 29:44; 45:3; 48:20; sorrow 3:139; 58:10; speech 33:70; steadfastness 2:177; 8:15-6, 45; 33:23; 41:30; 46:13; 47:7; successors on the earth 24:55; superior strength 8:65-6; tested (*ibtilā'*) 2:49, 155, 214; tormented 33:58; 85:10; 89:15; tranquillity 9:26; 48:4, 18, 26; truthfulness 33:23; 49:15; unity 3:103, 105; 42:13, 14; upper hand 3:139; warned 2:195,

208, 231, 264, 267, 279, 283; 3:103, 118; warned from obeying Jews and Christians 3:100; watchful of their prayers 6:92; 23:9; will have no fear or grief 2:38, 62, 112, 262, 274, 277; 3:170; 5:69; 6:48; 7:35, 49; 10:62; 20:112; 24:55; 39:61; 46:13; 72:13; *zakāt* 23:4

Faithful women (*mu'mināt*) 2:221; 5:5; 9:71-2; 24:12, 23, 31; 33:35, 49, 58, 73; 47:19; 48:5, 25; 57:12; 60:10, 12; 66:5; 71:28; 85:10;; bid what is right 9:71; cast down their eyes 24:31; forbid what is wrong 9:71; immigrant faithful women 60:10; marriage 2:221; 33:49; oath of allegiance 60:12; repentance accepted 33:73; reward 9:72; 33:35; 48:5; tormenting of 33:58; 85:10

Faithless (*kāfirūn*) 2:6-7, 19, 24, 26, 34, 39, 89, 90, 98, 102, 104-5, 126, 161-2, 171, 191, 212, 217, 250, 253, 254, 258, 264, 286;

—and hypocrites 4:141
—and the People of the Book 5:80-1
—and the Faithful 4:141, 144; 19:73; 22:19-24; 29:12; 36:47
—arguments/disputations 2:118; 4:152; 6:8, 25; 7:66; 13:5, 13; 17:90-96; 18:56; 25:7-9, 21; 40:4; 42:16; 43:31; 45:25; 46:7; 64:6
—arrogance 45:31; 46:10, 20; 64:6
—at death 8:50-1; 16:28
—bigotry 48:26
—blind and deaf hearts 2:7; 6:25; 17:46; 18:57; 41:5, 44
—conceit and defiance 38:2
—confessions 6:31; 67:9-11
—consequences of their conduct 64:5
—cursed by Allāh 2:89, 161-2; 9:68; 23:44; 33:64
—denial of resurrection 6:29; 11:7; 13:5; 16:38-9;
—derision 5:57; 6:5, 10; 11:8; 16:34; 18:106;
—desires 6:56, 119; 15:3
—despair of 5:3; 12:87; 60:13
—devils unleashed upon them 19:83
—disgraced on the Day of Resurrection 16:27
—disregard for the signs of Allāh 6:4, 46; 12:105;
—eager to see the faithful in distress 3:118;
—fabrications of 6:112; 7:53; 11:21; 19:88-9
—fate 3:137; 6:11; 7:84, 86, 103;
—follow falsehood 47:3
—friendship of 4:89, 139, 144; 5:57, 80; 9:23; 60:1, 8-9, 13
—futility of last-minute faith 6:158; 10:50-51; 32:29;
—futility of their works 2:217; 3:21, 117; 5:53; 7:147;

—have no protector 47:11
—hostility towards the faithful 2:105, 109; 3:118-20; 4:101; 5:13; 9:120; 40:10; 60:1-2
—hostility towards Allāh, His angels and apostles 2:98
—ignorance 6:37; 21:24; 27:66; 30:7
—indifference to advice 26:136
—invocations of 13:14; 40:50
—liars 6:28; 16:39; 25:4
—losers 2:264; 6:31; 7:53; 8:37; 11:21-2; 14:18; 29:52; 35:39; 39:63; 40:85
—metaphors of 2:7, 18; 6:36, 39, 50, 104, 122; 7:176-7; 8:22, 55; 10:42-43; 11:24; 13:16, 19; 17:72; 18:57; 21:45; 22:46; 25:44, 73; 27:80-81; 30:52-53; 31:7;
—no respite on sighting punishment 36:49-50
—not to be obeyed 11:114; 25:52; 33:1, 48; 42:15; 45:17; 68:8-9; 76:24; 96:19
—not to be taken as allies or friends 3:28, 118-120, 149; 4:144; 5:54, 82; 9:16, 23; 58:14-19, 22; 60:1-9, 13
—obstinacy 2:6; 6:7, 28, 37, 109, 111; 7:193; 10:96-7;
—obstruct the way of Allāh 4:167; 8:36; 11:19;
—parables of 11:24; 14:18; 24:39-40; 25:44
—punishment of 2:7, 10, 90, 104, 114, 126, 162, 165-6;
—respited 3:178; 13:32; 15:3; 22:44; 73:11; 86:17
—Satan, their master 2:257; 4:76
—spend their wealth to bar from the way of Allāh 8:36
—spiritual defilement 6:125
—take guardians others than Allāh 6:14; 13:16
—to be treated severely 9:123; 47:4; 48:29; 66:9; 71:26-7; 96:15-6
—treaty with 4:90
—warfare with 4:90-1; 48:22
—wish to return to the world 23:99-100

Faithlessness/unbelief (*kufr*) 2:6, 28, 39, 88, 93, 102, 108, 217; 3:52, 80, 90, 106, 167, 176-7; (fitnah) 2:191, 193, 217; 4:101; 8:39; 9:49; 33:14
—faith changed for unfaith 2:108, 175
—increase in 3:90; 4:137; 35:39
—leaders of unfaith 9:12
—made hateful to the faithful 49:7
—partial disbelief 4:150
—zealous in unfaith 5:41;

Falsehood/nullity/wrong/vanity (*bāṭil*) 2:42, 188; (*kidhb*) 2:10, 79; 4:50; 5:41-2; 16:62, 105; 18:5; 29:67; 37:152; 39:32; 40:28; 58:14; 61:2-3, 7;

72:4-5; attributed to God 3:75, 78, 94; 4:50; 5:103; atrocious lie(s) 18:14; 72:4; false attribution to God 2:170; 4:171; 6:93; 7:28, 33, 169; 10:68; 19:88-9; false speech 22:30; 25:4, 72; 58:2; false testimony 25:72

Family/relatives 2:215; (*ahl*) 5:89; 12:25, 65, 88, 93; 39:15; 48:11-2; 52:26; 75:33; 83:31; 84:9, 13; husband and wife 2:102, 223; 4:25, 34-5, 129; 30:21; kin (*faṣīlah*) 70:13; kinsfolk (*'ashīrah*) 9:24; 26:214; 24:8; 33:5; 37:158; 58:22; parents and children 2:83, 180, 215; 4:7, 11, 33, 36, 135; 6:151; 12:99-100; 14:41; 17:23; 18:80; 19:14; 27:19; 29:8; 31:13-9; 46:15-18; 58:22; 71:28

Family (Progeny) of Abraham 3:33; 4:54; 6:84-87;; chosen by God 3:33; given scriptures & wisdom 4:54; 6:89; given judgement (*ḥukm*) 6:89; given sovereignty (kingdom) 4:54

Family of David 34:13

Family of 'Imrān 3:33

Family of Jacob 12:6; 19:6;

Fasting (*ṣawm*) 2:183-185, 187; 5:89; 19:26; 33:35; 58:4; atonement for oaths 5:89; atonement for missed fasts of Ramaḍān 2:184, 185; days of 2:184; recourse in 2:45; sickness 2:184, 185; travelling 2:184, 185

*****Fāṭimah** ('a) 3:61; 30:38; 44:3; 55:19-20; 58:1; 59:9; 76:8-11; descendants of 35:32; *tasbīḥ* of 33:41-42

Fear of God 2:74, 150; 4:77; 5:3, 23, 28, 44;

Feeding (*iṭ'ām*) 51:57; feeding the needy (*iṭ'ām al-miskīn*) 2:184; 5:89; 22:28, 36; 36:47; 69:34; 74:44; 76:8-9; 89:18; 90:14; 107:3

Felicitous (*mufliḥūn*)/**Felicity** (*falāḥ*) 2:5, 189; 3:104, 130, 200;

Fire (hell) (*al-nār*) 2:17, 24, 39, 80-1, 126, 167, 174-5, 201, 217, 221, 257, 275; fuel of 2:24; 3:10; 66:6; prepared for the faithless 2:24; 3:131; 5:37; 10:8; 11:17; 13:35; 16:62; 17:8; 35:36; 46:20, 34; 48:13; 57:15;

Follower 2:166-7; 3:175; 14:21; (*shī'ah*) 28:15; 37:83

Food 2:61, 169, 172, 259; 3:93; 5:3, 5-6, 75, 90-91, 95-6; 12:37;

Food and drink 2:59-60, 169, 173, 187; 5:93; 6:142-146; 16:66; 20:53-4; 23:19-21; 36:73

Fool(s)/feeble-minded 2:13, 142, 282; 4:5; 7:155; 72:4; management of their affairs 4:5, 282; property of 4:5

Foolishness 2:13, 130, 142; 6:140; 7:66-7

Forgiveness (*maghfirah*); pleading for (*istighfār*) 2:199; 3:17, 135, 159, 193; promptness in pleading forgiveness 4:17

Fornication 4:25; 17:32; 25:68

Fornicator 24:2-3, 26

Friday prayer 62:9-11

Friend(s)/ally/guardian (*walī*) 2:254; 4:89, 123; 5:51, 57; 9:74; 13:37; 17:111; 18:17; 19:45; 24:61; 33:65; 41:34; 42:8, 31; 43:67; 48:22; 69:35; 70:10; confidant 3:118; 9:16; friends of Satan 4:76; 6:121, 128; 7:27; 16:100; 22:4; friends of angels 41:31; sympathizer (*ḥamīm*) 26:101; 40:18; 41:34; 69:35; 70:10

Friends of God 62:6; 10:62-3; dedicated friend (*khalīl*) 4:125;

Friendship 2:254; 4:89, 144; 5:51, 57; 6:129; 9:23, 71; 11:113; 14:31; 17:73; 25:28; 43:67; 44:41; 58:14; 60:9, 13

Gabriel 2:97-8; *3:39, 42, 45; 20:96; *53:5; 66:4; 69:40; 81:19-21; Trusted Spirit (*rūḥ al-amīn*) 26:193

Gambling (*maysir*) 2:219; 4:29; 5:90-1

Game of land and sea 5:96; 7:163-164; 16:14

Garment(s) (*libās*) 2:187; 7:26-7; 22:23; 25:47; 35:33; 78:10; >Clothes

Generation(s) (*qarn*) 2:66; 6:6; 10:13; 11:116; destruction of 6:6; 10:13; 17:17; 19:98; 20:128; 28:43, 78; 32:26; 36:31; 38:3; 50:36; former generations 20:51; 28:43; 56:13, 39; latter generations 56:14, 40, 49; 77:17

Genocide 2:49; 7:127, 141; 14:6; 40:25

Glorification of God (*tasbīḥ*) 2:30, 116;

God, allegations about Him 6:100, 129; 21:18, 22; 23:91; 37:159, 180; 43:82; 10:3, 31; 13:2; 32:5; and the faithful 2:137; 3:141, 154, 171, 173, 195; 4:28, 132, 171; 7:170; 8:62, 66; 9:59, 120, 129; 11:115; 12:56, 90; 15:95; 17:65; 18:30; 22:38, 78; 25:31; 33:3, 43, 48; 39:36, 38; 47:35; 65:3;; and the faithless 2:264; 3:32; 5:67; 6:107; 8:12; 9:37; 17:59; 30:45; 33:25; 39:16; 59:2; 60:1, 9; 83:15; 92:14; buys the souls and possessions of the faithful 2:207; 9:111; covenant/promise of (*'ahd*) 2:27, 80, 124; 3:77, 81; 6:152; 9:7; 13:20, 25; 27:91, 95; 19:78, 87; 33:15, 23; 36:60; 43:39; 48:10; discloses Himself (*tajallā*) 7:143; dislikes the faithless, agents of corruption, braggarts, traitors, transgressors and wrongdoers 3:32, 57, 140; 4:107; 5:64, 87; 7:55; 22:38; 28:76, 77; 30:45; 42:40; falsehood: abolishes falsehood 8:8; 21:18; 42:24; fear of God 3:175; 5:94; 8:48;

13:13; 14:14; 16:50-51; 17:57; 32:16; 33:26; 55:46; 59:13, 16; 70:27; 76:10; 79:40; hearts 2:7; 4:155; 6: 46, 110; 7:100, 101; 8:11, 24; helpers of God 3:52; 59:8; 61:14; hosts of God (*junūd*) 9:26, 40; 33:9; 37:173; 48:4, 7; 74:31; Inheritor 19:40, 80; 28:58; 57:10; intercession rests with Him 39:44; justice: loves the just 5:42; 60:8; justice: not tyrannical to the servants 3:182; 8:51; 22:10; 41:46; justice: not unjust 2:272, 286; 3:25, 108, 117, 182; light of 9:32; 24:35, 40; 39:69; 61:8; love of God 2:165, 176; 3:31; 5:54; 9:24; 19:95; 20:39; 58:22; 76:8; loves the Godwary 3:76; 9:4, 7; loves the just 5:42; 49:9; 60:8; loves the patient 3:146; loves the penitent 2:222; loves the virtuous 2:195; 3:134, 148; 5:13, 93; loves those who fight in His way 61:4; loves those who follow the Prophet 3:31; loves those who keep pure 2:222; 9:108; loves those who trust Him 3:159; made every thing faultless 32:7; 40:64; 64:3; 95:4; messages of God 7:62, 68, 93, 144; 14:4; 33:39; 72:23, 28; monotheism: nothing is like Him 42:11; nearness to Him 17:57; 34:37; 39:3; 96:19; needy: resort of the needy 55:29; power: irresistible 2:255; 6:134; 8:59; 9:2, 3; 10:53; promise: true to His promise 2:80; 3:9; 13:31; 14:47; provider: 2:245; 13:26; 17:30; 28:82; 29:62; 30:37; reckoning lies with Him 2:284; 13:40; 21:47; 23:117; 26:113; 33:39; 65:8; 88:26; signs of His Existence 41:53; 6:75-79; 6:95-99; 16:10-18; 30:20-25; 35:27-28; 55:5-30; speaks 2:118, 174, 253; 3:77; 4:164; 7:143; 20:12-25, 36-46; 42:51; *sunnah* of God 17:77; 33:38, 62; 35:43; 40:85; 48:23; Throne of 7:54; 9:129; 10:3; 11:7; 17:42; 21:22; 23:86, 116; 39:75; 40:7, 15; 43:82; 69:17; 81:20; 85:15; transgressors 2:26, 190; 5:87, 108; 6:119; 7:55; treasuries of God 6:50, 59; 11:31; 15:21; 16:96; 17:100; 38:9; 52:37; 63:7;

god(s) (*ilāh*) 2:163; 6:74; 7:127, 138, 140;

Godfearing (*khashiyah*) 2:74, 150; 3:175; 4:8, 77;

Godwary (*muttaqūn*) 2:2, 66; 3: 15-16, 76, 134, 138; supplication of 3:16

Good news 2:25, 97, 119, 155, 223; 3:39, 45, 126; 8:10;

Governance, principles of 2:83, 173, 185, 251; 3:28, 79, 159; 4:74-6, 139; 5:52; 6:14, 164; 8:65; 10:47-49; 12:40; 14:9-15; 22:78; 29:41; 40:21-22; 42:10, 38; 49:13; 61:6; 89:6-14;; commitment to agreements 5:1; 16:91; criterion of relative merit 16:76; 49:13; defence and deterrence 2:251; 8:60; dignity of the human being 17:70; gender relations 2:228; 3:195; 16:97; 30:21; divine law 3:23; 4:58, 65, 105; 5:43, 44-5, 47, 48-50; 6:57, 62, 114; 10:35; 13:41; 18:26; 24:48, 51; 28:70; 38:26; 45:16; 52:48; 68:48; 76:24; influence of non-Muslim powers 4:141; judiciary 2:188, 229; 4:58, 65, 105; 5:42, 48, 50; 6:57; 42:10; justice 3:18, 21; 4:30, 135; 5:8; 6:152; 7:29; 10:4, 54; 21:47; 34:26; 36:54; 38:26; 40:17, 78; 42:15; 49:9; 55:9; 57:25; leadership: prerequisites 2:73, 124, 247; 10:35; 14:21; 24:55; 32:24; 39:9; legislation 2:229; 4:59; 5:44-5, 47; 6:57; 30:30; 33:36; maintenance of the moral and social order 3:104; 9:71; negation of disruptive influences —principles of economy 2:29, 188, 275-6, 278, 168; 3:14, 130; 4:5, 29, 161; 5:66; 6:141; 7:31, 96, 128; 8:1; 9:34; 17:26-7; 25:67; 30:39; 59:7; 96:6-7; respect for legitimate government 4:59, 83; relations with non-Muslims 3:64; 16:90; 60:8

Grace (*faḍl*) 2:64, 90, 105, 198, 243, 251, 268; 3:73-4, 170-1, 174, 180;

Guardianship of God (*walāyah*) 2:257; 3:68, 122, 150;

Guest 11:78; 15:51, 68; 18:77; 51:24; 54:37

Guide (*hādī*) 7:181; 13:7, 33; 39:23, 36; 40:33; (*murshid*) 18:17

Guided (*muhtadūn*) 2:16, 70, 157, 170; better guided 4:51; 17:84; 28:49; 35:42; 43:24; 67:22

Guilty (*mujrimūn*) 2:54; 4:112; 5:107; 6:55, 124, 147; aversion of 8:8; 10:82; confession of 32:12; deny existence of hell 55:43; despair of 30:12; entreaties of 32:12; error and madness 54:47; fate of 27:69; 32:12; 37:34; fear of 18:49; hearts of 15:12; 26:200; lead astray 26:99; major criminals (*akābir*) 6:123; not questioned for their sins 28:78; ransom 70:11-14; recognized by their mark 55:41; retribution 10:13; 12:110; 14:49; 18:53; 19:86; 20:74; 25:22; 30:47; 32:22; 43:74-78; 46:25; 54:47-8; 55:41; 77:18; 83:29-36; ridicule the faithful 83:29-31; set apart from others 36:59; support of 28:17; swear 30:55

Ḥajj & ʿUmrah 2:125, 128, 158, 189, 196-203; 3:96-7; 5:1-2; 95-7; 9:3, 19; 22:26-37; 27:91; 28:57; 29:67; 42:7; 90:1-2; 95:3; 106:3; 108:2; ability (*istiṭāʿah*) 3:97; atonements (*kaffārāt*) 2:196; 5:95; disputing, vicious talk, and sex prohibited during *ḥajj* 2:197; greater *ḥajj* (*al-ḥajj al-akbar*) 9:3; *ḥajj tamattuʿ* 2:196; *ḥalq & taqṣīr* 2:196; 22:29; 48:27; hunting prohibited 5:95- 96; *iḥrām* 5:1, 95-6; maintenance of the sanctity of its sacraments 5:1-2; months of 2:197; necklaces 5:2, 97; *ramy al-jamarāt* 2:200;

rites 2:196, 199-200, 203; 3:97; 22:28-9, 34, 36; sacrificial offering (*hady*) 2:196; 5:2, 95, 97; 22:28, 33, 36; *ṭawāf* 2:158, 200; 22:26; water supply 9:19

Ḥanīf 2:135; 3:67, 95, 125; 6:79, 161; 10:105; 16:120, 123; 30:30; 98:5

Hārūt & Mārūt 2:102

Healing 3:49; 5:110; 10:57; 16:69; 17:82; 26:80; 41:44; healing of the hearts 9:14; 10:57; 17:82

Heavens (*samāwāt*) 2:29, 33, 107, 116-7, 164, 255, 284;

Heir(s) 2:182, 233; 4:11, 33; 5:106-7; 7:137; 8:72-3; 15:23-4; 17:33; 19:5; 21:89; 23:10; 26:85; 27:49; 28:5, 58; 35:32 37:100; 39:74; 40:53; 42:14; inheritors of the earth/land 7:100, 128; 21:105

Hell (*Jahannam*) 2:206; 3:12, 162, 197; 4:55, 93, 97, 115, 121, 140, 169;

*History; invitation to study of past nations 3:137; 6:11; 7:34; 12:109, 111; 16:36; 22:46; 27:69; 29:20; 30:9-10, 42; 35:44; 40:21-22, 82, 47:10; lessons of history 6:6, 42-45; 7:4-5, 59ff, 84, 86, 93-102, 103; 8:52-54; 9:69, 70; 10:13, 39, 73, 102;

Holy Land 5:21

Holy Mosque 2:144, 149-150, 191, 196, 217; 5:2; 8:34; 9:7, 19; 17:1; 29:67; 48:25-7; entry into 48:27; expulsion of its people 2:217; guardians 8:34; maintenance of 9:19; natives and visitors 22:25; obstruction 5:2; 8:34; 22:25; 48:25; polytheists forbidden entry 9:28; warfare 2:217

Holy Spirit 2:87, 253; 5:110; 16:102; 19:17-21, *24

Homosexuality 7:80-4; 11:77-80; 15:66-75; 21:74; 26:160-173; 27:54-8; 29:28-35; 37:136-7; 54:33-9

Hoopoe 27:20-28

Horizon(s) 41:53; Highest Horizon (*al-ufuq al-a'lā*) 53:7; Manifest Horizon (*al-ufuq al-mubīn*) 81:23

Hosts/troops 2:249; 3:13, 155, 166; 7:27; 8:41, 45, 48; 19:75; 20:78; 26:61, 95; 27:17-8, 37; 28:6, 8, 39-40; 33:9; 38:11; 44:24; 51:40; 67:20; 85:17-8; 100:5; divine 9:26, 40; 33:9; 36:28; 37:173; 48:4, 7; 74:31; hosts of Iblis 26:95

Hūd ('a) 7:65-72; 11:50-60, 89; 23:31-41; 26:124-140; 46:21-26; 51:41-2; 54:18-21

Human dignity 17:70.

Human diversity 5:48; 14:4; 22:34, 67; 30:22 49:13

Humans (ins) 6:128, 130; 7:38, 179; 10:24; 11:119; 14:10; 17:88, 95; 23:47; 25:49; 27:17; 30:20; 32:13; 35:28; 36:15; 41:25, 29; 46:18; 51:56; 55:33-35, 39, 56, 74; 67:6; 72:5-6; 74:31, 36; 114:1-6;

Humility 2:45; 3:199; 5:54; 7:206; 11:23; 15:88; heads bowed in humility 26:4; lowering one's wings 15:88; 17:24; 26:215; utter humility 16:48; 27:87; 37:18; 40:60

Hunting 5:2, 4, 94-96; hunting dogs 5:4; purification of the game caught 5:3

Hypocrites (*munāfiqūn*) 2:8-20, 204-206; 3:72, 118-120, 167; 4:60-68, 72-73, 77-85, 88, 138-147; and the faithful 4:141, 146; and the Jews 59:11; bad opinion of God 3:154; 33:10; bar the way of God 8:48; 58:16; 63:2; children 58:17; contentions 3:154; corruption, cause 2:11-12; cowardice 63:4; cursed by God 9:68; 47:23; 48:6; 63:4; deaf and blind 47:23; deception 57:14; deride the faithful 2:14-5; 4:140; 9:64-5, 79; devils 2:14; devoid of understanding 59:13; 63:3, 7; bewaring them 4:140; 63:4; disregardful 4:61; 24:48; dissimulation 5:61; doubts 57:14; dry logs set reclining (metaphor) 63:4; enjoin what is wrong 9:67; enmity 3:119-120; 5:62; 63:4; entreat the faithful for light 57:13; error, bought for guidance 2:16; evade *jihād* 3:154-5, 167; 4:72-3, 77-83; 5:52; 9:81-3; 24:53; 33:12-20; evil conduct 63:2; excuses 9:66; failure of their works 5:53; 47:28; faithlessness 4:88-9; 5:61; 9:55, 74, 80, 85, 126; 33:14, 19; 57:14; 63:3; fear 9:56, 64; 33:19; 47:20; 59:13; flight 33:15-16; follow desires 47:16; foolishness 2:13; forbid charity 63:7; forbid what is right 9:67; forgiveness 9:66, 80; 47:34; 63:6; friendships 4:89, 139; 9:73; friendship of the Jews 58:14; furtiveness 11:5; grace of God 9:74-76; grudging givers 9:53-4, 67; guile 3:120; 4:142; 5:53; have no helpers 4:145; 9:74; hearts sealed 47:16; hell will be their abode 4:140; 9:73; 57:15; 66:9; killing of 4:89-91; 33:61; liars 9:77, 107; 58:14, 16; 59:11-2; 63:1; losers 5:53; migration 4:89; opportunists 4:141; 5:52; ostentation 4:142; 107:4-7; parable 2:17-20; 63:4; pleading forgiveness for them 9:80; 63:6; pledges 9:75; 33:15; prayer 4:142; 107:4-5; profane gossip 9:69; promise 59:11-14; punishment 4:138, 145; 9:55, 66, 68, 74, 79, 85; 33:24, 73; 48:6; 58:16-17; 66:9; rebellion 2:15; regrets 5:52; repentance 4:146; 9:74, 126; requital of 9:82; 66:10; secret dealings 47:26; secret thoughts and consultations 9:78; severity towards 66:9; share of worldly enjoyment 9:69; sharp tongues 33:19; sick hearts 2:10; 5:52; 8:49; 9:129; 22:53; 24:50; 33:12, 60; 47:20, 29; 74:31; stinginess 9:76; swear 24:53; threatened 33:60; 63:8; tone of speech 47:30; torments of 33:48; transgressions 9:24, 53,

67, 80; wavering character 4:143; 9:45; wealth 9:55, 85; 58:17; wealth of no avail 58:17; wrath of God upon them 48:6

Iblīs 2:34; 7:11; 15:31-40; 17:61-65; 18:50; 20:116; 26:95; 34:20; 38:74-5; *74:11-16, *18-29;

Idols (*aṣnām*) 6:74; 7:138, 191-198; 14:35; 21:57, 98; 26:71; (*anṣāb*) 5:90; (*awthān*) 22:12, 30; 29:17, 25; (*jibt*) 4:51; (*nuṣub*) 5:3, 90; Baal 37:125; biggest of idols 21:58, 63; eschewal of 14:35; Lāt 53:19; lifeless 16:21; 37:91-92; Manāt 53:20; misguidance 14:36; 25:17; Nasr 71:23; powerless 16:20, 73; 17:56-7; 21:43; 22:73; 26:72-3; 29:17; 34:22; 35:13-4; 36:75; 37:91, 92; 39:43; 46:4-5, 28; Suwā' 71:23; unable to cause harm or bring benefit 10:18, 106; 22:12; 25:3, 55; 26:73, 93; 'Uzzā 53:19; Wadd 71:23; worship of 7:71, 138-140; 16:20-1, 56; 21:66-7; 26:71-3; 29:16-17; 46:6; Ya'ūq 71:23; Yaghūth 71:23

Idrīs ('a) 19:56-7; 21:85-86; 37:129

Iḥrām 5:1-2, 95-6

'Illīyyūn 83:18-21

Ilyās ('a) 6:85; 37:123-132

Ilyāsīn 37:130

Imām(s) 2:124; 17:71; 21:73; 25:74; 28:5; 32:24; 36:12

*al-Imam al-Mahdī ('a) 5:54; 6:158; 7:128; 11:8; 16:1, 38; 17:33; 21:12, 73, 105; 22:39; 24:55; 26:4; 27:62; 30:2-3; 32:28-30; 38:79-81, 88; 40:84; 41:53; 42:2, 41; 43:61; 45:14; 51:23; 55:41; 57:16-17; 61:9; 67:30; 70:43-44; 74:8-10; 89:1

Immortality 21:34, 120; 26:129; 50:34

Indecent act(s) (*fāḥishah*) 2:169, 268; 3:135; 4:15, 19, 22, 25; 6:151; 7:28, 33; 12:24; 16:90; 17:32; 24:19, 21; 27:54; 29:28, 45; 33:30; 42:37; 53:32; 65:1; inward and outward sins/indecencies 6:120, 151; 7:33; 16:90; propagation of 24:19

Inequality 3:113; 4:95; 5:100; 6:50, 165; 9:19;

Infanticide 2:49; 6:137, 140, 151; 7:141; 14:6; 16:58-59; 17:31; 28:4; 40:25; 43:17; 60:12; 81:8-9

Ingratitude (*kufrān, kufūr*) 2:152, 243; 7:17; 10:12, 60; 11:9; 12:38; 14:7, 28, 34;; not approved by God 39:7

Inheritance (*irth*) 4:7-12, 19, 33, 176; 8:72-3, 75; 17:33; 19:6; 21:89; 33:6; brother(s) 4:11-2, 176; children 4:11-2; husband 4:12; men 4:7, 11, 176; mother 4:11; needy (*masākīn*) 4:8; orphans 4:8, 127; parents 4:7, 11, 33, 127; pledge of brotherhood 4:33; relatives 4:7-8, 33; 33:6; siblings (*kalālah*) 4:12, 176; sister 4:176; unlawful consumption 89:19; wife 4:12, 176; women 4:7, 11-12, 127, 176

Inheritance of the prophets 19:5-6; 21:89-90; 27:16; 37:100

Inheritance of the Book 7:169; 35:32; 40:53; 42:14

Inheritance of the earth/land 7:100, 128, 137; 15:23; 19:40; 21:105-6; 22:40-41; 24:55; 28:5, 58; 37:171-173; 39:74; 40:51

Injustice 4:30, 155; 6:131; 11:117; 22:40; 24:50; 26:209; 31:13; 36:54; 40:17; negation of injustice & oppression 2:272, 281, 286; 3:25, 108, 117, 161, 181-2; 4:40, 49, 124; 6::131, 152, 161;

Intellect 52:32

Intellect, possessors of 2:179, 197, 269; 3:7, 190; 5:100; 12:111; 13:19; 14:52; 38:29, 43; 39:9, 18, 21; 40:54; 65:10; 89:5; >Reason

Intercession (*shafā'ah*) 2:48, 123, 254-5; 6:51, 70, 94; 7:53; 10:3, 18; 19:87; 20:109; 21:28; 26:100;

Intercessor(s) 6:51, 69, 94; 7:53; 10:3, 18; 26:100; 30:13; 32:4; 39:43; 40:18; 74:48; intercessors other than God 39:43

Iram of Pillars 89:7-8

Iron 13:5; 17:50; 18:96; 22:21; 34:10, 33; 36:8; 40:71; 57:25; 76:4

Isaac ('a) 2:132-133, 136, 140; 3:84; 4:163; 6:84; 11:71; 12:6, 38; 14:39; 19:49; 21:72; 29:27; 37:112-113; 38:45-47

Ishmael ('a) 2:125-129, 133, 136, 140; 3:84; 4:163; 6:86; 14:35, 37, 39; 19:54; 21:85-86; 37:101-107; 38:48

Islam (submission to God) 2:112, 131, 133, 136, 208; 3:20, 83-4, 102; 4:65, 125; 5:44, 111;

Islām (al-) 2:132; 3:19, 52, 64, 67, 80, 85, 102; 5:3, 111; 6:125; 7:126; 9:33, 74; 15:2; 16:89, 102; 22:78; 28:53; 33:35; 39:22; 41:33; 42:13; 43:69; 46:15; 48:16, 28; 49:14, 17; 51:36; 61:7, 9; 66:5; 72:14; best religion 4:125; sole religion 3:85; upright religion 98:5

Isrāfīl* 50:41; 54:6

Jacob ('a) 2:132-3, 136, 140; 3:84, 93; 4:163; 6:84; 11:71; 12:6, 38, 68; 19:6, 49, 58; 21:72; 29:27; 38:45-47

Jesus ('a) 2:87, 136, 253; 3:39-62, 84; 4:157-159, 163, 171-2; a sign for all the nations 21:91; 23:50; apostleship 3:49; 4:171; 5:46, 75; 19:30; 42:13; 43:63; 57:27; 61:6; birth 19:22-27; 33; confirmed the

Torah 3:50; 5:46; 61:6; covenant of 33:7; creaturehood 3:59; 4:172; 5:17; crucifixion 4:157; cursed the faithless Israelites 5:78; deification of 5:17, 72-78, 116-7; 9:30-1; Disciples 3:52-3; 5:111-5; 61:14; foretold 3:39, 45; foretells the advent of Prophet Muḥammad (ṣ) 61:6; made some things lawful 3:50; miracles 2:253; 3:46, 49-50; 5:110; 43:63; prayer and zakāt 19:31; raised to the heaven 3:55; 4:158; servant of God 4:172; 5:72-5, 116-117; 19:30; 43:59; spoke as infant 3:46; 5:110; 19:24, 29-33; strengthened with the Holy Spirit 2:87, 253; 5:110; table is sent down for him 5:112-115; teaches wisdom 43:63; Word of God 3:45; 19:34

Jews 2:62, 94, 113, 120, 135, 140; 3:67; 4:160-161; 5:41, 44, 64, 69; 6:146; 9:30; 16:118; 22:17; 59:14; 62:6-8; alliances with them proscribed 5:51; attitude towards non-Jews 3:75; claim to be God's chosen people 5:18; 62:6; claims of exclusive salvation 2:111; faithful and righteous among them 3:113, 199; 5:69; 7:159; hostility toward Muslims 5:82; misinterpretation of scriptures 4:46; practice of usury 4:161; warmongering 5:64

Jihād, evading 2:246; 3:155-6, 167-8; 4:72; 9:38, 42-57, 80-8, 90, 93; 33:13; 47:20; 48:11-2, 15-6; exemption from 9:91-2; 48:17; merits of 2:216, 218; 4:95; 9:111, 121; 57:10; obligation of 2:216; pursuit of the infidels 4:104; summons to 2:190-1, 216-8, 244; 3:139, 142, 146, 156-8, 200; with possessions (amwāl) 4:95; 8:72; 9:20, 41, 44, 81, 88, 111; 49:15; 61:11

Jihād, performers of (mujāhidūn) 2:154-7; 3:142; 8:72, 74-5; 9:16, 19- 20; 47:4-6, 31; God loves them 61:4; helped 22:39; merit of 2:154, 218; 4:74, 95; 9:20, 120-1; 57:10; reward of 4:74, 95; 9:21, 89, 121; 16:110; 47:5-6; those who wage jihād with their persons and possessions 4:95; 8:72; 9:20, 41, 44, 81, 88; 49:15; 61:11

Jinn 6:100, 112, 128, 130; 7:38, 179; 11:119; 15:27; 17:88; 18:50; 27:17, 39; 32:13; 34:12, 14, 41; 37:158; 41:25, 29; 46:18, 29-31; 51:56; 55:15, 33, 39, 56, 74; 72:1-13; 114:6

Job ('a) 4:163; 6:84; 21:83-88; 38:41-44

John ('a) 3:39-41; 6:85; 19:7, 12-15; 21:90

Jonah ('a) 4:163; 6:86; 10:98; 21:87-88; 37:139-148; 68:48-50

Joseph ('a) 6:84; 12:1-101; 40:34

*Joshua 5:23; 18:60-65

Judgement (fatḥ) 7:89; 34:26; (ḥukm) 2:113; 3:23, 55, 79; 4:58, 65, 141; 5:42-5, 47-50, 95; 6:57, 62, 89, 114,

136; conformity with revelation 5:44-50; prophets & scriptures, as judges 2:213; 3:23; 4:65, 105; 5:42, 44-5, 47-9; 16:64; 24:48, 51; 57:25

Judges 2:188

Jūdī, Mount 11:44

Jugular vein 50:16

Justice ('adl, qisṭ) 2:282; 3:18, 21; 4:3, 49, 58, 124, 127, 129, 135; 5:8, 42, 106; 6:115, 152; 7:29, 89, 159, 181; cosmic Justice 3:18; 39:47-48; 99:6-8; judgement 4:58; 5:42, 95; 6:152; 7:29, 89; 10:47, 54; 21:112; 34:26; 38:22, 26; 39:69, 75; 40:78; 49:9; maintenance of 3:18; 4:58, 135; 55:9; 57:25; prophets and scriptures for justice 57:25

Ka'bah 2:125, 127, 158; 3:96; 5:2, 97; 8:35; 14:37; 22:26, 29, 33; 29:67; 106:3

*Khiḍr 18:65-82

King(s) (malik) 2:246-247; 5:20; 18:79; 27:34; 54:55; omnipotent king 54:55

King of Egypt 12:43, 50-54, 72; his law 12:76

Korah (Qārūn) 28:76-82; 29:39-40; 40:24

Lamp(s) (miṣbāḥ, sirāj) 24:35; 25:61; 33:46; 41:12; 67:5; 71:16; 78:13

Last Day 2:8, 62, 126, 177, 228, 232, 264; 3:114; 29:36; 60:6; belief in 2:62, 177, 228, 232, 264; 3:114; 4:38-9, 59, 162; 5:69; 9:18-9, 29, 44-5, 99; 24:2; 33:21; 58:22; 65:2; >Day of Resurrection; Hereafter; disbelief in 4:136

Laws; fabrication & alteration 5:87, 103; 6:140; 9:37; 10:15, 64; 13:41; 16:101; 33:62; 35:43; The Decalogue 6:151-53; uninformed opinion on matters of law 16:116-117

Learning 2:102, 129, 151; 3:48, 79, 146-8, 164; 5:4; 9:122; 12:6, 21; 18:66; 33:21; 36:69; 38:88; 45:9; 62:2;; knowledge and practice 61:2-3;

Lesson/moral 3:13, 137; 7:86; 10:101; 12:105, 109, 111; 14:5; 16:65-6; 22:46; 23:21; 24:44;

Life of the world 2:85-86, 204, 212; 3:14, 117, 185; 4:74, 94, 109; 6:29, 32, 70, 130; 7:32, 51, 152;

Light (nūr) 2:17, 257; 4:174; 5:15, 16, 44, 46; 6:1, 91, 122; 7:157; 10:5; 13:16; 14:1, 5; 21:48; 24:35, 40; 28:71; 33:43; 35:20; 39:22, 69; 42:52; 57:9, 12, 13, 19, 28; 61:8; 64:8; 65:11; 66:8; 71:16

Light of God 9:32; 24:35; 39:69; 61:8; effort to put it out 9:32; 61:8

Loser(s) 2:27, 64, 121; 3:85, 149; biggest losers 11:22; 18:103; 21:70; 27:5

Lot (*'a*) 6:86; 7:80-84; 11:71, 77-83, 89; 15:57-77; 21:71, 74-5; 22:43; 26:160-74; 27:54-58; 29:26, 28-35; 37:133-138; 38:13; 50:13; 51:32-7; 54:33-39

Lote tree 34:16; 53:14, 16; 56:28

Love 2:93, 165, 177, 195, 216, 222; 3:14, 31, 76, 92, 119, 134, 146, 148, 152, 159, 188; 4:73; 5:13, 18, 42, 54, 93; 9:4, 7, 24, 108; 12:8, 9, 30; 19:96; 20:39; 24:22; 30:21; 38:32; 42:23; 48:9; 49:7, 9; 58:22; 59:9; 60:8; 61:4, 13; 75:20; 76:8, 27; 89:20; 100:8

Love of God 2:166, 186; 3:31; 5:54; 9:24; 58:22; 76:8-9

Luqmān 31:12-3, 16-19

Madīnah 33:13, 60; 59:9; 63:8

Madness (*jinnah*) 7:184; 23:25, 70; 34:8, 46; (*su'ur*) 54:24, 47

Magic 2:102; 5:110; 6:7; 7:116; 10:76-7, 81; 11:7; teaching of 2:102; 20:71; traditional magic 74:24

Magician(s) 7:109, 112-3, 120; 10:2, 77, 79-80; 20:63, 69-70; 26:34, 37-8, 40-1, 46; 38:4; 40:24; 43:49; 51:39, 52; find faith 20:70-3; 26:46-51; witches who blow on knots 113:4

Maintenance (*nafaqah*) 2:233, 236, 240, 241; 4:5, 34, 129; 9:121; 33:49; 60:10-11; 65:6-7

Makkah 2:126; 3:96-7; 4:5, 75; 6:92; 8:34-5; 14:35; 16:112; 27:91; 28:57, 85; 29:67; 42:7; 43:31; 47:13; 48:24

Mankind (*nās*) 2:13, 165, 187; 3:138; 10:11, 21, 99; 11:7; a single nation 2:213; 10:19; 11:118; brought out of darkness into light 14:1; creation 40:57, 64; 64:3; curse 2:161; 3:87; divergent beliefs 2:113, 214, 253; 3:19, 55, 105; 5:48; 6:65, 164; 7:24; 10:19; 11:118-119; 16:39, 64, 124; 19:37; 21:93; 22:69; 23:53; 27:76;; 30:6-7; 32:25; 39:3, 46; 41:45; 42:10; 43:63, 65; 45:17; 49:13; 110:2; diversity 30:22; 35:28; diversity of means 6:165; 16:71, 75; 43:32; divine spirit 15:29; follow conjectures 6:116; guidance 10:108; haste 10:11; 16:1; 21:27; ignorance and weakness at birth 4:27; 16:78; inborn goodness 30:30;; inequality 6:165; 16:71, 75; 17:21; 43:21; many of them are transgressors 57:26; most Godwary of them 49:13; most of them are ungrateful 25:50; most of them are astray 6:116; most of them detest the truth 43:78; most of them do not apply reason 29:63; most of them do not give thanks to God 12:38; 23:78; 27:73; 32:9; 34:13; 40:61; 67:23; most of them do not have faith 11:17; 12:103, 106; most of them do not know 12:21, 40, 68; nations and tribes 49:13

Manna and quails 2:57; 7:160; 20:80

Manners; harsh manners 3:159

Manslaughter (*qatl*) 2:30, 54, 72, 85, 178; 3:21; 4:29, 66; 5:28-30, 32-3, 45; 6:151; 17:31, 33; 25:68; 28:15, 19; blood money (*diyah*) 4:92; deliberate murder 4:93; punishment for 2:178; 4:92-3; 5:45; retaliation (*qiṣāṣ*) 2:178; 5:45; unintentional 4:92

Marriage (*nikāḥ*) 2:221, 223, 228, 230, 232, 235-237; 4:3-4, 19-25, 127; 5:5; 16:72; 23:6-7; 24:26, 32-3, 60; 25:54; 30:21; 33:37, 49-50; 44:54; 52:20; 60:10; intermarriage with idolaters 2:221; marrying off single persons 24:32; prohibitions pertaining to marriage 4:22-25; 5:5; 24:3; 33:6, 53; desirability of remarriage 2:232; restoration of marital relations 2:228, 230; separation 2:229, 231; 33:49; 65:2; slave women 4:3, 24-25; 24:32; 33:50; temporary marriage (*mut'ah*) 4:24

Martyr/witness (*shahīd*) 2:155; 3:140, 157-8, 169-171, 195; 4:69, 74; 9:111; 22:58; 47:4-6; 57:19

Mary (*'a*) 3:33-37, 42-47; 4:156, 171; 5:17, 75; 19:16-34; 66:12; >Jesus; a sign for all the nations 23:50; Aaronic lineage 19:28; slandered by the Jews 4:156; 19:28; virginity 3:47; 19:20

Mash'ar al-Ḥarām 2:198

Measure 6:152; 7:85; 11:84-5; 12:59, 63, 88; 13:8; 15:21; 17:35; 23:18; 25:2; 26:181; 34:11; 42:27; 43:11; 54:49; 65:3; 73:20; 76:16; 83:1-3; observance of right weights and measures 6:152; 7:85; 12:59, 88; 17:35; 26:181; 81:1-3

Mercy (*raḥmah*); God's all-inclusive mercy 6:147; 7:156; 15:56; 39:53; 40:7; effects of God's mercy 30:50

Midian, people of 7:85; 9:70; 11:84-95; 15:78-9; 20:40; 22:44; 26:176-191; 28:22, 23, 45; 29:36-7;

Milk 16:66; 47:15

Miracles 2:60, 73, 260; 3:49; 5:110; 6:111; 7:107, 117, 160; 12:93, 96; 20:19-23, 69; 26:32, 45, 63; 27:10, 16, 40; 28:31; 34:10; 38:18-8; 54:1; 105:3

Misdeed(s) (*sayyi'ah*) 2:81, 271; 3:193, 195; 4:18, 32; absolved 3:193, 195; 4:31; 5:12, 65; 8:29; 10:41; 11:35; 29:7; 39:35; 47:2; 48:5; 64:9; 65:5; 66:8; changed to good deeds 25:70; consequences of 5:95; 59:15; 64:5; 65:9; effaced by good deeds 11:114; returning with good deeds 23:96; 41:34; reward of 6:160; 17:7; 27:90; 28:84; 40:40; 42:40

Monasteries 22:40

Monasticism (*rahbāniyyah*) 57:27

Money 12:62, 65; (*wariq*) 18:19

Monks 5:82; >Monasticism; bar the way of God 9:34; taken as Lords apart from God 9:31; unlawfully eat up people's wealth 9:34

Monogamy & polygamy 4:3

Moses (ʻa); God's chosen 7:144; 20:13, 41; and Khiḍr* 18:65-82; and Pharaoh 7:103-141; 10:75-92; 17:101-104; 20:24, 43-60, 77-79; 23:45-48; 26:11-66; 27:12-4; 40:23-45; 43:46-56; 44:17-31; 79:17-26; and Shuʻayb* 28:23-28; and the burning bush 20:10-11; 27:7-8; 28:29-30; and the magicians 7:113-126; 10:80-81; 20:64-73; 26:38-51; and the Torah 2:87, 136; 6:91, 154; 23:49; annoyed with Aaron 7:150; apostleship 7:103-4, 144; appoints Aaron as successor 7:142; at Midian 20:40; 28:22-29; at the Mount 7:143; 19:52; 28:29; Book of 11:17; 46:12; 53:36; breastfed 28:12-13; brings his people out of darkness into light 14:5; called bewitched 17:101; called by God 19:52; 20:11; 26:10; covenant 33:7; 43:49; dedicated to God 19:51; deliverance of his people 26:65; 37:115; derided 43:47; desires to see God 7:143; distinguished in God's sight 33:69; flees Egypt 26:21; 28:21-2; gives good news to the faithful 10:87; granted judgement and knowledge 28:14; gratitude 7:144; hitch in his tongue 20:27; 26:13; 43:52; house of 2:248; impugned 22:44; 23:46-7; 26:12; 28:36; 40:24, 37; in the valley of Ṭuwā 20:11; 79:16; infancy 26:18; 28:7-13; miracles 2:50, 56, 60; 7:107-8, 117, 133, 160; 20:20-2; 26:32-3, 63; 27:10, 12; 28:31-2, 36; 40:23; 79:20; mother 20:38-9; 28:7, 10-13; parting of the sea 26:63; people of 7:148, 159; 10:83; 28:76; 32:23; prayer and its maintenance 10:87; 20:14; prayer answered 10:89; 20:36; prayer for water 2:60; 7:160; prays against Pharaoh and his people 10:88; reared under God's care 20:39; rebukes the Israelites concerning idol worship 7:140, 20:86; repentance 7:143; 27:11; 28:16; revealed to 7:117, 160; 10:87; 11:110; 20:13, 77; 25:35; 26:52, 63; 28:43; 32:23; selects seventy men 7:155; sister of 20:40; 28:11; spoken to by God 4:164; 7:143; 20:12-46; 27:8-12; steadfastness 10:89; supplications 5:25; 7:151, 155-6; 10:88; 20:25-35; 26:12; 28:16-7, 21-2, 24, 33-4; 44:22; tablets 7:145, 150, 154; tested with ordeals 20:40; tormented by the Israelites 33:69; 61:5; miracle of bright hand 7:108; 20:22-3; 26:33; 27:12; 28:32; wife 28:23-29.

Moses and Aaron 20:29-34, 42-48, 92-94; 23:45-49; 26:13; 37:115-120; 28:34; apostleship 23:45; 25:35-6; 26:15-17; 28:34; 37:117-120;

Mosque(s) 2:114; 4:43; 9:107; 18:21; 22:40; 24:36-7; 72:18; adornment 7:31; barring access to 2:114; built for defiance and disunity among Muslims 9:107; built for sabotage 9:107-109; confinement (iʻtikāf) 2:187; founded on Godwariness 9:108-9; Holy Mosque 2:144, 149-150, 191, 196, 217; 5:2; 8:34; 9:7, 17-9, 28; 17:1; 22:25; 48:25, 27; maintenance of 9:17-8; al-Masjid al-Aqṣā 17:1; Masjid al-Dirār 9:107; Masjid Qubā* 9:107-109; retreats (for iʻtikāf) 2:187; ruination of 2:114; 22:40

Moths, scattered 101:4

Mother(s) (umm) 4:23; 16:78; 24:61; 31:14; 33:4, 6; 39:6; 46:15; 53:32; 58:2; 80:35; (wālidah) 2:233; 19:32; motherhood through fosterage 4:23; mother of Jesus 5:17, 75, 110, 116; 23:50; mother of Moses 20:38-9; 20:94; 28:7, 9, 13; mother's share in inheritance 4:11; wife's mother 4:23

Mountain(s) (aʻlām) 42:32; 55:24; (jibāl) 2:260; 7:74, 143, 171; (rawāsī) 13:3; 15:19; 16:15; 21:31; 27:61; 31:10; 41:10; 50:7; 77:27; 79:32; (ṭawd) 26:63

Muḥammad (ṣ) (Apostle of God); admonisher 6:70; 50:45; 51:55; 52:29; 87:9; 88:21; allegiance sworn to him 48:10, 18; 60:12; and Abraham 3:68; and Gabriel 2:97; 53:5-10; 66:4; and the faithless 15:2-3, 6-8; 17:45-52; 73:10; 109:1-6; and the Jews 3:183-4; 5:41-3; and the Jinn 72:1-15; and the People of the Book 2:120; 3:20; 4:153; 5:15, 19, 48-9; 6:20; 42:14-5; and the polytheists 3:20; 13:36; 17:73-6; and the poor 6:52; apostleship 3:144, 164; 4:79; 7:158; 9:33; argument with the Christians 3:61; ascension to heaven (miʻrāj) 17:1; bearer of good news 10:2; 11:2; 19:97; 36:11; 39:17; 61:13; bids what is right 7:157, 199; blessings to be invoked for him 33:56; brings people out of darkness into light 14:1; 57:9; 65:11; brought the truth 37:37; called a madman 7:184; 15:6; 23:70; 34:8, 46; 37:36; 44:14; 51:52; 52:29; 68:51; called a magician 21:3; 34:43; 38:4; 51:52; 52:29; 61:6; called a poet 21:5; 37:36; 52:30; called a bewitched man 17:47; 25:8; character & conduct 3:159; 4:36, 113; 7:156-7; 8:33; 9:128; 21:107; 22:67; 26:218-9; 27:79; 33:6, 50-52; 42:52; 43:43; 48:1-2; 52:29, 48; 53:2; 68:2-6; 81:24; 87:6-9; 90:1-2; 93:3-10; 94:1-4; 108:1-3; charged with fabrication 10:38; 11:35; 16:101, 103; 21:5; 25:4-5; 32:3; 34:8; 42:24; 46:8; 52:33; close relatives 26:214; 30:38; 33:6; 42:23; 59:7; communicator 5:67; 22:67; 26:214; 87:9;

companions 6:52; 18:28; 48:18, 29; 58:7-13; 63:7; 73:20; compassion for the faithful 9:128; 15:88; 26:215; 48:29; confirms former apostles 37:37; confirms former scriptures 2:101; 3:81; 6:89-90; daughters 33:59; death 3:144; 10:46; 13:40; 15:99; 21:34; 39:30; demands made of him 2:108; 4:153; 6:37; 7:203; 8:32; 10:15, 20; 11:12; 13:27; 15:7; 17:90-94; 20:133; 21:5; 25:7-8; 47:20; denial of his apostleship 13:43; 48:13; derided 4:140; 6:10; 9:65; 13:32; 15:11, 95; 21:36, 41; 25:41; 37:14; 58:8; descent of the Book on his heart 26:194; disobedience to him 4:42; 24:63; 58:8-9; disputed with 6:25; 8:6; 22:67-8; 58:1; does not speak out of his own desire 53:3; dream/vision 17:60; 48:27; duty to communicate and warn 3:20; 4:79-80; 5:92, 99; 6:48, 66, 107; 10:46; 13:40; 16:35, 82; 17:54; 21:108-9; 22:49; 24:54; 27:80-1, 92; 29:18; 33:39; 40:77; 42:6, 48; 43:40-4; 50:45; 64:12; 72:23; 88:21-2; eagerness to convert and concern for the faithful 9:128; 10:99; 12:103; 16:37; 18:6; 26:3; 27:70; 28:56; 35:8; ease 87:8; etiquette of Muslims toward him 24:62-3; 33:53; 48:9; 49:1-5, 7; exemplar for all Muslims 33:21; faith in him 4:55, 136, 170; 5:104; 7:158; 24:47, 62; 46:31; 48:9, 13; 49:15; 57:7, 28; 58:4; 61:11; 64:8; faith of 2:285; 7:158; 10:104; 12:108; 42:15; 109:1-6; follows what is revealed to him 6:50, 106; 10:15, 109; 13:37; 19:65; 33:2; 45:18; 46:9; forbids what is wrong 7:157; 9:29; 96:19; foretold in Torah and the Evangel 2:76; 7:157; 61:6; grieves for the faithless 18:6; guardian of the faithful 5:55-6; 9:16; 33:6; hard against the faithless 48:28; human nature 17:93-4; 18:110; 21:3, 7-8; 25:7; 39:30; 41:6; 63:4; impugned 3:184; 6:33, 66, 147; 10:2, 41; 22:42; 23:69; 25:41; 28:48-50; 29:18; 34:43, 45; 35:4, 25, 42-3; 48:13; 54:3; invocations of God's protection 7:200; 16:98; 23:97-8; 40:56; 41:36; 68:51; *jihād* 4:84; 9:73, 88; 66:9; judgement 4:65, 83; 4:105; 5:42-3, 48, 50; knowledge 2:120, 145; 3:61; 13:37; 20:114; 33:63; 67:26; knowledge of the Unseen 6:50; 7:187-8; 11:49; 12:102; 21:109, 111; 38:69-70; 46:9; 67:26; 72:25-8; makes lawful all good things 7:157; mercy of God 17:87; 28:86; 94:1-4; messenger of universal mercy 21:107; migration from Makkah 8:5; 9:13, 40; 47:13; 60:1; name exalted 94:4; nearest to Abraham 3:68; 16:123; nightly devotions 73:1-7, 20; 76:26; not a poet 36:69; 69:41; not a soothsayer 52:29; 69:42; not a tyrant 50:45; not an angel 6:50; not an impostor 38:86; not his duty to watch over 6:66, 104, 107; 10:108; 17:54; 25:43; 39:41; 42:6, 48; 88:22; not mad/ demon-possessed (*majnūn*) 7:184; 52:29; 68:2; 81:22; obedience to him 3:31-2, 132; 4:13, 59, 64-5, 69, 80; 5:7, 92; 8:1, 20, 46; 9:71, 120; 24:47, 51-4, 56; 33:33, 66, 71; 47:21, 33; 48:17; 49:14; 59:7; 58:13; 64:12, 16; path of 12:108; 36:4; 43:43; patience 10:109; 11:49, 115; 16:127; 19:65; 20:130; 30:60; 38:17; 40:55, 77; 46:35; 50:39; 52:48; 68:48; 70:5; 73:10; 74:7; 76:24; peacemaking 8:61; 43:89; pleads forgiveness 3:159; 4:64, 106; 9:80, 113; 24:62; 40:55; 47:19; 48:11; 60:12; 63:5-6; 110:3; praise of God 15:98; 17:111; 25:58; 27:59; praiseworthy station 17:79; prayer 6:162; 9:108; 17:78-9, 110; 26:219; 52:48-9; 73:2-8; 96:9-10; 108:2; progeny 108:1; purifies the faithful 2:151; 3:164; 9:103; 62:2; reliance on revelation 43:43; repentance 9:117; repudiates faithlessness and polytheism 25:52; 28:86, 87; 72:20; 109:1-6; resigned to Divine will 3:128; 7:188; 8:64; 10:49; 72:21; ruling sought 4:127, 176; 5:4; 8:1; 20:105; sees Gabriel 53:5-18; 81:23; sees the signs of God 17:1; 53:18; stands on a manifest proof 6:57; steadfastness 10:104, 109; 11:112; 36:4; 42:15; strengthened with God's help 3:13; 8:26, 62; 9:40; 11:120; 25:32; submission to God 6:14, 71, 163; 22:34; 27:91; 40:66; summoner 12:108; 13:36; 16:125; 21:108-9; 22:67; 23:73; 24:63; 28:50, 87; 33:46; 41:33; 42:13, 15; 46:31-2; supplications 17:80, 111; 18:24; 20:114; 21:112; 23:93-4, 97-8, 118; 43:88; sworn by 15:72; 90:3; taught the Qur'ān 55:2; teaches the Book and wisdom 3:164; 62:2; tormented 9:61; 33:53, 57; tranquillity 9:26, 40; 48:26; treaties 8:56, 58; 9:1, 7, 12-3; trust in God 3:159; 4:81; 8:61; truthfulness 27:79; turns penitently to God 42:10; urges the faithful to *jihād* 4:84; 8:65; warns 6:19, 51, 92; 7:2, 69; 10:2; 14:44; 18:4; 19:39, 97; 21:45; 26:214; 27:92; 28:46; 32:3; 35:18; 36:6, 10-11; 39:39; 41:13; 42:7; 74:2; witness over his ummah 2:143; 4:41; 16:89; 22:78; 73:15; wives & daughters 33:6, 28-34, 50, 52, 59; 66:1-5

Muḥammad (ṣ), names and attributes; admonisher (*mudhakkir*) 88:21; Aḥmad 61:6; Apostle of God 7:158; 9:61, 81, 120; Arabian 41:44; bearer of good news (*bashīr, mubashshir*) 2:25, 97, 119, 155, 223; first of worshippers 43:81; first to submit 6:163; 39:12; good exemplar 33:21; guardian 5:55; light 5:15; manifest apostle 43:29; 44:13; mercy for all the worlds 8:33; 9:61; 21:107; most kind and merciful to the faithful 9:128; orphan 93:6; proof (*burhān*) 4:174; Prophet 5:81; 8:64, 65, 70, 9:61,

73, 113, 117; radiant lamp 33:46; reminder (*dhikr*) 65:10-11; Seal of the Prophets 33:40; servant of God (*'abd Allah*) 72:19; summoner to God 33:46; 46:31, 32; uninstructed prophet (*ummī*) 7:157; 16:103; 29:48; warner (*mundhir*) 13:7; 26:194; 27:92; 38:65; 50:2; 79:45; (*nadhīr*) 2:119; 5:19; witness (*shāhid*) 33:45; 48:8; 73:15

Muḥkam & mutashābih (*verses*) 3:7

Muslim(s) 2:112, 128, 131-3, 136, 208; 3:20, 52, 64, 67, 80, 83-4, 102; 4:65, 125; 5:44, 111; 6:14, 71, 163; 7:126; 10:72, 84, 90; 11:14; 12:101; 15:2; 16:28, 81, 87, 89, 102; 21:101, 108; 22:34, 78; 27:31, 38, 42, 44, 81, 91; 28:53; 29:46; 30:53; 33:22, 35; 37:26, 103; 39:12, 54; 40:66; 41:33; 43:69; 46:15; 51:36; 52:48; 68:5, 35, 48; 72:14; 76:24; enemies of 4:45; reward of 33:35, 71, 73; witnesses to mankind 22:78

Myths of the ancients 6:25; 8:31; 16:24; 23:83; 25:5; 27:68; 46:17; 68:15; 83:13

Nation(s) (*shu'ūb*) 6:123; (*umam*) 2:128, 134, 141; 3:104; 6:42-45; 7:38, 160; 11:48; 13:30; 16:93; 45:28; 35:24; 46:18; a specified term for every nation 7:34; 10:49; 15:5; 16:61; 17:58; 23:43; 34:29; 35:45; 36:44; 71:4; an apostle and warner for every nation 10:47; 13:30; 16:36; 23:44; 35:24; best, upright nation 3:110, 113; 5:66; book of its deeds 45:28; every nation appointed a rite 22:34, 67; mankind were one nation 2:213; 5:48; 10:19; 11:118; 16:93; 21:92; 23:52; 42:8; 43:33; middle nation 2:143; 3:104, 110; nation submissive to God 2:128; witness from every nation 4:41; 16:84, 89; 28:75

Near to God (*muqarrabūn*) 3:21; 5:42; 49:9; 60:8

Needy (*masākīn*) 2:83, 177,184, 215; 4:8, 36; 5:89, 95; 8:41; 9:60; 17:26; 18:79; 24:22; 30:38; 58:4; 59:7; 68:24; 69:34; 76:8; 89:18; 90:16; 107:3; kindness to 4:36; 24:22; one-fifth of the *anfāl* 8:41; 59:7; rights of 17:26; 30:38

Night journey 11:81; 17:1; 20:77; 26:52; 44:23

Night of Ordainment (*laylat al-qadr*) 97:1-5

Noah (*'a*) 4:163; 7: 59-64; 9:70; 10:71-73; 11:25-48, 89; 14:9; 17:3; 21:76-77; 22:42; 23:23-31; 25:37; 26:66, 105-120; 29:14-15; 36:41; 37:75-83; 38:12; 40:5, 31; 42:13; 50:12; 51:46; 53:52; 54:9, 11-15; 57:26; 69:11; 71:1-28; chosen 3:33; covenant 33:7; prays against the faithless 71:26-27; supplications 11:45-46; 23:26, 29; 26:117, 118; 54:10; 71:5, 6, 26-28; wife of 66:10

Nocturnal consultations 4:81, 108; 27:49

Oath(s) (*yamīn*) 2:224, 225; 3:77; 5:53, 89, 108; 6:109; 9:12-13; 16:38, 91, 92, 94; 24:53; 35:42; 58:16; 63:2; 68:39; frivolous oaths 5:89; mutual oath-taking (*li'ān*) 24:6-9

Obedience (*ṭā'ah*) 2:285; 3:32, 132; 71:3; (*qunūt*) 2:238; 3:43; 33:31

Obedient (*qānit*) 2:116, 238; 3:17; 16:120; 30:26; 39:9; 66:12; reward of 33:35

Offering (*qurbān*) 3:183; 5:27; 46:28 (*hadi*) 2:196; 5:2, 95, 97; 48:25

Old age 14:39; 15:54; 17:23;19:4, 8; 30:54; 40:67

Old man (*shaykh*) 11:72; 12:78; 28:23; very old man 12:78

Old woman (*'ajūz*) 11:72; 26:171; 37:135; 51:29

Olive 6:99, 141; 16:11; 23:20; 24:35; 80:29; 95:1; sworn by 95:1

Omen; bad omen 7:131; 27:47; 36:18, 19

Orphan(s) (*yatīm, yatāmā*) 2:215, 220; 4:8, 10; 6:152; 17:34; 18:82; 89:17; 93:6, 9; 107:2

Parable /example/ description (*mathal*) 2:17, 26, 171, 214, 261, 264, 265; 3:59, 117

Paradise 2:111; 3:133, 185; 4:124; 7:40, 46, 49; Adam's expulsion from 2:36, 38; 7:24; everlasting abode 2:25, 82; 3:15, 107, 136, 198; 4:13, 122; wine of 37:45, 47; 52:23, 24; 56:18, 19; 76:5, 17, 19, 21; 78:34; abode of peace 6:217; 10:25; abode of the Godwary 16:30; *Firdaws* 18:17; 23:11; Gardens of Eden 9:72; 13:23; 16:31; 18:31; 19:61; 20:76; 35:33; 38:50; 40:8; 61:12; 98:8; *Tūbā* 13:29; vast expanse 3:133; 57:21

Paradise, Inhabitants of (*aṣḥāb al-jannah*) 7:42-46, 50; 10:10; 13:13; 14:23; 15:46; bliss 37:45-50; descriptions of 15:45-48; 21:101-103; 22:24-25; 25:16; 30:16; 34:37; 35:35; 36:56-57; 37:24-50; 38:50-54; food & drink 37:40-47; 52:19, 22, 23; 56:18-23, 32-33; 69:24; 76:5, 14-19; 77:42-43; 78:34; 83:25-28; 40:8; freedom from fear & grief 21:103; 43:68; immortality 44:56; freshness of their faces 75:22; 83:24; 88:8-9; supplication of 10:10

Paramour(s) 4:25; 5:5

Patience & the Patient 2:45, 153-157, 177, 249-250; reward of 23:111; 28:54

Peace 13:28; 89:27-30; 48:4; 49:9; (*salām*) 2:94; 4:16; 6:54; 7:46; (*silm*) 2:208; 4:90, 91, 94; 8:61; peace-making 2:208; 4:113, 127; 8:1; 49:9-10

Pearl (*lu'lu'*) 22:23; 35:33; 52:24; 55:22; 56:23

Pen(s) (*qalam, aqlām*) 3:44; 31:27; 68:1; 96:4
Penitence (*inābah*) 13:27; 29:15; 40:13; 42:10; 60:4
Penitent (*awwāb*) 17:25; 38:17, 19; 50:33; (*munīb*) 11:75; 30:31, 33; 34:9; 39:8; 50:9, 34
Penury (*imlāq*) 6:151; 17:31
People of the Book 2:100, 105, 109, 120, 135-140, 145, 146; 3:64-89, 186-188; 4:49-53, 131, 153; 5:59, 69; 6:155-156; 33:26; 57:29; 98:1-7
Pharaoh 2:49; 7:103, 104, 106, 109-113; 17:101-103; 20:24, 43-79; 26:11-53; 27:12; 28:3-43; 40:23-52; 43:46-56; 44:17-31; 54:40-42; 69:8, 10; 73:15, 16; 80:18
Pharaoh's clan (*āl-i Firʿawn*) 2:49-50; 3:11; 7:130, 141; 8:52, 54; 10:75-95; 14:6; 26:11
Piety (*birr*) 2:44, 177, 189; 3:92; 5:2
Pious (*abrār*) 3:193, 198; 76:5; 82:13; 83:18, 22
Pity 24:2; 57:27
Play (*laʿb*) 5:57, 58; 6:32, 70, 91; 7:51, 98; 9:65; 12:12; 21:2, 16, 55; 29:64; 43:83; 44:9; 47:36; 52:12; 57:20; 70:42
Poet(s) 21:5; 26:224-227; 37:36; 52:30; 69:41
Poetry 36:69; 37:36-37; 69:40-41
Polytheism (*shirk*) 2:22; 4:36, 171; 10:104-6; 12:40; 16:51; 17:22, 39; 18:110; 22:26, 30; 24:55; 26:213; 28:88; 29:8; 30:31; 31:15; 46:21; 51:51
Polytheist(s) (*mushrikūn*) 2:105-135, 221; 3:67, 95, 186; 5:82; 6:14, 22, 23, 79, 106, 121, 136, 140; 12:106; 22:17; 24:2, 3; 30:31; 41:6; 42:13
Poor (*fuqarāʾ*) 2:177, 271, 273; 4:6, 135; 6:52; 9:60, 91; 18:28; 22:28, 46; 24:32; 28:25; 47:38; 59:7, 8; those in need of God (*fuqarāʾ ila God*) 35:15
Pork 2:174; 5:3; 6:145; 16:115
Possessions (*amwāl*) 2:156, 188, 261-262; 3:10; 4:20, 24; Property; a test 8:28; 9:24, 55, 69, 85; 18:33; 19:77; 28:78; 34:35-37; 57:20; 58:17; 23:9; 69:28; 64:15; 71:21; 74:12; 90:6; 92:11; 104:2-3
Praise (*ḥamd*) 1:2; 2:30; 3:188; 6:1, 45; 7:43
Prayer (*ṣalāt*) 2:43, 45, 115, 125 238; 3:43, 113; fivefold prayers 11:114; 17:78; 20:130; 40:55; 50:41, 42; Friday prayer 62:9-10; group prayer 2:43; 4:101-102; 7:204; 15:24; night prayer 24:58; non-performance of 74:43; 75:31; 77:48; 96:10; prayer during journey 4:43, 101; 5:5; prayer for rain 2:60; shortening (*qaṣr*) of in prayer 4:100-101; *qiblah* 2:116, 143-145, 148-150; watchfulness over 2:238; 6:92; 23:9; 70:23, 33
Preaching (*tablīgh*) 3:104; 10:41; 16:125; 20:43; 21:109; 22:67-68

Precedent(s) (*sunnah*) 3:137; 4:26; 8:38, 52, 54; 15:13; 17:59, 77; 18:55; 33:38, 62; 35:43; 40:85; 43:8; 48:23
Pregnancy 2:228; 3:47; 7:189; 13:8; 19:22-23; 22:2; 31:14; 35:11; 41:47; 46:15; 65:5-6
Prejudice 5:104; 7:28; 9:114; 10:78; 14:10; 31:21; 43:22; 48:26
Preserved Tablet 56:78; >Book
Prison 12:25, 32, 33, 35, 42, 100; 17:8
Prisoners 76:8; of war 8:67-70
Private parts 7:22, 26; 21:91; 23:5; 24:30, 31; 33:35; 66:12; 70:29-31; covering private parts; guarding
Priest (*qissīs*) 74:51
Promise (*mīʿād*) 3:9; 8:42; 34:30; (*waʿd*) 3:152; 11:65; 17:5, 7; 21:9; good promise 28:62; loyalty to promises 2:80, 177; 3:76; 5:7; 6:152; 9:4, 7, 111; 13:20; 16:91, 94, 95; 17:34; 21:9; 23:8; 48:10; 70:32; 76:7; other promise 17:6, 104; promise of the Hereafter 34:29; true promise 21:97; 46:16
Proof(s) (*bayyinah*) >Evidence; manifest proofs (*bayyināt*) 2:87, 92, 99, 105, 159, 185, 209, 213, 253
Property (*khayr*) 2:180, 273; 33:20; >Possessions; >Wealth
Prostration (*sujūd*) 2:125; 3:43, 113; 4:102, 154
Punishments (*ḥudūd*); >Bounds of God; adultery, for 4:15, 25; 24: 2; averting of 24:8; slander, for 24:4; sodomy, for 4:16; theft, for 5:38; war against God and His Apostle, for 5:33
Purification 2:125, 129, 175; 3:77, 164; 4:49; 9:108; 24:21; 33:33; 53:32; 62:2; 74:4; 80:3, 7; 91:9; self-purification 20:76; 35:18; 79:18; 87:14; 91:9; 92:18; those who keep pure 9:108; 56:79
Purity 2:124, 222; 3:42; 4:43; 5:6; 9:108; 56:79; 74:4

Qur'ān 2: 23-24, 41, 89, 44, 101, 121, 219, 152; 3: 58, 70, 72, 101, 108,164; 4:1; 5:15; admonishment 54:17, 22, 32, 40; 74:55; basis of judgement 4:105; belief in it 2:99, 121; 4:47, 105, 136; 7:185; 10:40; 11:17; 17:107; 28:52; 47:2; beyond doubt 2:2; 10:37; 32:2; challenges 2:23, 24; 8:31; 10:38; 11:13; 13:31; 17:88; 28:49; 52:33-34; confirms earlier scriptures 2:89, 91, 97; 3:3; 4:47; 5:48; 6:92; 10:37; 12:111; 27:76; 35:31; 46:12, 30; contemplation 23:68; 38:29; 47:24; elaboration of all things 12:111; etiquette of its recitation 16:98; falsehood does not approach it 41:42; freedom from discrepancy 4:82; jinn's belief in 72:1, 2; listening etiquette 7:204; 9:6; 46:29, 30; 72:1; made easy 54:17, 22, 32, 40; 39:23; none except the pure touch it 56:79; 86:14; partial belief in it 15:90-93; reading of 7:204; 17:106; 20:114; 22:52; 73:20; 75:17-19; 84:21; 87:6; 96:1, 3; revealed on the Night of Ordainment (*laylat al-qadr*) 44:1-5; 97:1-5; secure from corruption & forgery 69:44-47; truthfulness of 12:111; 69:40-47; 81:19-21, 25; 98:3

Quraysh 9:7; 106:1-4

Rabbi 5:44, 64
Ramaḍān 2:185
Ransom (*'adl, fidyah*) 2:48, 85, 123, 229; 3:91; 5:36; 6:70; 10:54; 13:18; 37:107; 39:47; 41:24; 45:6; 47:4; 57:15; 70:11-14; ransom of captives 2:85
Reason/intellect (*'aql*) 2:44, 73, 75, 76, 164, 170, 171, 242; 3:65, 118; 5:58-9, 103; 6:32, 151; irrational humans 2:170-1; 5:58, 103; 8:22; 10:100; 25:44; 29:63; 49:4; 59:14; 67:10; rational persons 2:164, 269; 16:12, 67; 13:4; 16:12, 67; 20:128; 29:35; 30:24, 28; 45:5; reasoning 2:73, 242; 3:118; 5:151; 6:32; 12:2; 21:67; 22:46; 24:61; 26:28; 36:62; 40:67; 43:3; 57:17
Rebellion (*ṭughyān*) 2:15; 5:64, 68; 6:110; 7:186; 17:60; 18:80; 23:75; 53:17; 69:11; 79:17, 37-40; 91:11; 96:6; (*'ulū*) 17:4; 23:91; 27:14; great rebellion 17:60
Reckoning (*ḥisāb*) 2:202, 212, 284; 3:9, 27, 37, 199; adverse reckoning 13:18, 21; easy reckoning 84:8; self-reckoning sufficient 17:14
Rectitude (*rushd, rashd, rishād*) 2:186, 256; 4:6; 7:146; 18:10, 24; 21:51; 40:29, 38; 72:2, 10, 14, 21
Reflection (*tafakkur*) 2:219, 266; 3:191; 6:51; 7:184; 16:44; 30:8; 57:21; 74:18
Reform (*iṣlāḥ*) 2:11, 161, 182, 220; 3:89; 4:16, 114; 6:48, 54; 7:35, 56, 142; 8:1; 11:88; 24:5; 42:40; 49:9, 10
Reformers (*muṣliḥūn*) 2:11, 22; 7:35, 170; 11:117; 28:19
Refuge (*malja'*) 9:57, 118; 42:47; (*maw'il*) 18:58; (*mawlā*) 57:15; (*multaḥad*) 18:27; 72:22; (*wazar*) 75:11
Religion (*dīn*) 3:19; 6:70; 7:19; 8:72; 9:11, 122; absence of compulsion and impediment 2:256; 10:99; 18:29; 22:78; change of 40:26; exceeding the proper bounds in religion (*ghuluww*) 4:171; 5:77; made a plaything 7:51; maintenance of 42:13; religion exclusively for God 2:193; 3:83, 85; 8:39; 16:52; 39:3, 11, 14; 40:14, 65; religion of God 24:2; 110:2; ~ of truth 9:29, 33; 48:28; 61:9; schism 6:159; 30, 32; 28:4; upright religion 6:171; 9:36; 12:40; 30:30, 43; 98:5
Remembrance (*dhikrā*); remembrance of God 2:152, 198, 200, 203, 239; 3:41, 135, 191; 4:103, 142; remembrance of God's blessings 2:40, 47, 122, 125, 231; 3:103; 5:7, 11, 20, 110; 7:69, 74, 86; 8:26; 14:6; 19:67; 33:9; 35:3; 43:13;; remembrance of revealed teaching 2:63; 7:171; 20:113; 33:34; 74:55; 80:12; evasion of 74:49-51; new reminder 26:5; People of the Reminder16:43; 21:7
Responsibility 2:134, 139, 141, 143; 5:105; 6:52, 69, 70, 104, 164; 7:173; 10:41; decision 7:158; 90:8-17; 43:22-25; 39:29; 2:256;; duty 37:164-65; 6:165;; individual responsibility 5:105; 41:46; 4:79-80; 53:36-42;; none will bear another's burden 6:164; 17:15; 35:18; 39:7; 53:38; predestination 29:62; 9:51; 36:7-10;; synergy 2:152; 13:11; 65:7; 76:29-31; 64:11
Resurrection (*ba'th*); denial of 6:29; 11:7; 16:38; differences regard it 78:3; disavowal of one's deeds on 3:30; dissolution of ties of kinship 23:101; faith in 2:62, 121; 70:26; fear of it 79:45; imminent 53:57; 56:1, 15; inevitable & certain 2:223; 3:9; 6:134; 10:53; 13:2; 15:85; intercession 2:48, 123; sky frail on that day 69:16; suddenness 21:40; terrors of 43:67; 68:42, 43; undeniable 56:2; unveiling of 53:58
Retribution/requital 2:85, 191; 3:87, 153; 4:93; 5:29, 33, 38, 60, 85; 6:138-9, 146, 157; (*dīn*) 1:4; 51:5; 82:9; 95:7; (*'iqāb*) 2:196, 211; 3:11; 5:2; 13, 32; 38:14; 40:5; inevitable 51:5-6; those subject to (*madīnūn*) 37:53
Revelation (*waḥy*) 2:76, 97; 3:2, 44; 4:163; concealment of 2:175; 47:9, 26; denial of 6:91; faith in 2:91, 136, 171; 3:53, 84; 4:60-61, 162; 5:59, 66, 104; 7:3; 31:21; 39:55; 42:15; observance of 5:66, 68; scriptures >Scripture(s)
Reward (*ajr, jazā', thawāb*); ~ in the world and the Hereafter 3:145; 4:133; 11:15-16; 17:18-21; 42:20; ~ of the Hereafter 3:145, 152; 4:134; ~ of the world 3:145, 152; 4:134; twofold reward 34:37; 33:30
Ridicule (*istihzā'*) 2:14-15, 67, 212, 231; 5:57, 58
Righteous (*ṣāliḥūn*) 2:130; 3:46, 114; 4:69; 5:84; 6:85
Ritual impurity (*janābah*) 4:43; 5:6
Ritual purity (*ṭahārah*), 4:42; 5:7; 9:108; 74:3

Sabbath 2:65; 4:47; 7:163; 16:124
Sabbath-breakers (*aṣḥāb al-sabt*) 4:47
Sacraments (*sha'ā'ir*) 2:158; 5:2; 22:30, 32, 36; non-violation 5:2
Sacrifice (*naḥr*) 108:2; (*nusuk*) 2:196; 6:142; great sacrifice (*al-dhibḥ al-'aẓīm*) 37:107
Sacrificial offering (*hady*) 2:196; 5:2, 95, 97; 22:28,

36, 37; 48:25
Ṣāliḥ ('a) 7:73-79; 11:61-68; 15:80-84; 17:59; 26:142-159; 27:45-53; 51:43-45; 54:23-31; 89:9; 91:11-14
Sāmirī 20:85, 87-8, 95-6
Satan 2:275; 3:36, 155, 175; 4:60, 76, 117-119; arrogance 2:34; authority (sulṭān) 16:99, 100; 17:65; 34:21; bars from God's way 27:24; 29:38; 43:37, 62; befriending 16:100; 18:50; 22:4; caused the fall of Adam & Eve 2:36; consigned to perversity 7:16; 38:82; cursed 4:118; deceiver 7:22; 31:33; 35:5; 57:14; enemy of man 2:169, 208; 6:142; 12:5; 17:53; 28:15; 35:6; 36:60; 43:62; evil companion 43:38; fate of 59:17; followed 2:168-169, 208; 4:38, 83, 119; 6:113; 7:18, 175; 22:3; 24:21; 34:20; 36:60; 38:85; 58:19; friends of 3:175; 4:76, 119-120; gives false hopes 4:119-120; 8:48; 14:22; 17:64; 47:25; infantry and cavalry of 17:64; invocation of protection against 3:36; 7:200; 16:98; makes evil deeds seem decorous 6:43; 8:48; 16:63; 27:24; 29:38; party of 35:6; 58:19; promises 4:120;; prompts evil, rebellion and unfaith 2:169, 268; 4:118-119; 24:21; 29:38; 50:27; share in property and children 17:64; temptation 7:20, 27, 200; 12:100; 14:22; 20:120; 41:36; 59:16; 114:4-5
Satans 2:14, 102; 6:71; 7:27; 19:68-72; 26:210-212; 37:65; eavesdroppers 26:223; 37:8-10; friends of 6:121, 128; 7:30; in Solomon's service 21:82; 38:37; inspire 6:112, 121; 26:210, 212, 221, 222; liars 26:223; obedience to 6:121; obeyed 6:121, 128; protection from their promptings 23:97; punishment 37:9; 67:5; shot at with missiles 67:5; unleashed at the faithless 19:83; urge the faithless 19:83
Satans, from humans 6:112; friends of jinn 6:128
Satans, from jinn 6:112; claim many humans 6:128
Saul (Ṭālūt) 2:247-251
Scribes, Jewish (aḥbār) 5:44, 63; 9:31-35; bar the way of God 9:34-35; eat up people's wealth wrongfully 9:34; taken as lords 9:31
Scripture(s) (kutub, zubur, ṣuḥuf) 2:4, 38, 97, 231, 285; 3:23, 184; belief in 2:177, 285; 3:84; 4:136; concealment of 2:159, 174; confirmation of 2:41, 89, 98, 101, 136; 3:3, 50; 4:47; 5:46, 48; 6:92; 10:37; 12:111; 35:31; 46:12, 30; 61:6; corruption of 2:79-81; 3:78; 4:46, 50; denial of 10:39; differences about them 2:176, 213; disbelief in 4:136; former scriptures 20:133; 87:18; guidance and good news 2:97; 16:89, 102; 27:2; parables 17:89; 30:58; 39:27

Seal (ṭab') 4:155; 7:100, 101; 9:87, 93; 10:74; 16:108; 30:59; 40:35; 47:16; 63:3; (khatm) 2:7; 6:46; 36:65; 42:24; 45:23; 83:25, 26
Secret talks (najwā) 4:114; 9:78; 12:80; 17:47; 20:62; 21:3; 43:80; 58:7-13
Self-cultivation and Spiritual Growth; cultivate the good 91:7-10;; perseverance and patience 2:153-57; 18:65-82; 40:55; 57:22; >Patience; preparing the start 17:14; purity 2:168; 4:49; 9:108; 16:32; 18:19; 19:19; 20:76; 22:24, 31; 24:21; 30:30; 56:79; 58:12; 76:21; 98:5; self-control 3:134; 24:21, 22 >Abstemiousness; sincerity 9:91; 66:8; spiritual growth 2:58, 247, 261; 4:173; 7:161; 10:25; 14:7; 18:13; 19:76; 24:37-8; 35:29-30; 42:20, 23, 26; 47:4-7, 15, 17; 48:4, 29; vigilance 3:190-91; 11:93
Self-Denial and Renunciation; asceticism and monasticism 2:183-85; 57:27;; control anger 3:134; humility 18:23-24; 23:1-5 >Humility; renunciation of wealth 3:14-15; 47:38; 104:1-3; 62:11; repentance 2:222; 4:17-18; 25:71; 39:53-58 >Repentance; restraint and moderation 6:120; 18:8; self-denial; separation from family 4:100; 9:23-24; 29:8; 64:14-15; separation from the world 6:32; 7:51; 6:107; 18:46; 23:33; 28:79; 29:25; 30:7; 31:33; 33:28; 35:5; 40:39; 45:35; 47:36; 53:29; subdue desires and passions 23:5-11; 47:14
Self-defence 2:178-9, 194; 5:48; 42:39-43
Sexual intercourse 2:187, 197, 222, 223; 4:43; 5:6; 7:189; 26:166; 27:55
Shame 2:26; 28:25; 33:53
Sharī'ah 42:13; 45:18; easy and practical sharī'ah 2:178-185, 196, 233, 256, 282; 4:28, 97-99, 101-102; 5:6; 9:91; 10:99; 16:114-116; 22:78; 24:60-61; 33:37; 47:17; 73:20
Shu'ayb ('a) 7:85-93; 11:84-95; 15:78-79; 26:177, 186-191; 29:36-37
Sign (āyah), as miracle 2:73, 118, 211, 248, 259
Sign(s) (āyah) 3:41; 11:103; 15:76, 77
Sijjīn 83:7, 8
Sin(s) (dhanb) 3:11, 16, 31, 135, 147, 193;(ithm) 2:35-38, 85, 174, 181, 182, 188, 203, 219; (junāḥ) 2:158, 198, 230, 231, 233, 235, 236, 240, 282; 4:24, 101, 102; 24:29, 59, 60, 61; 33:5:51; admission of 40:11; 67:9, 11; atonement and forgiveness of sins 3:31; 39:53;; inward sin 6:120; major sins 4:30; 42:37; 53:31-32; great sin (ḥinth) 56:46; (ḥūb) 4:2; outward sin 6:120; penchant for sin 5:62; the refining fire 21:35; 29:2-3

Sins, the Major; addiction 5:90-91; adultery 17:32; 24:30-32, 33; 25:68-69; 29:28-29; hypocrisy 2:8-12, 264; 41:51; 107:4-7; lying and deceit 61:2-3; murder 4:92; 5:27-32; 17:31, 33; slander and foul speech 4:112; 49:6-12;; theft 3:130; 4:10; 5:38; 83:1-3

Sirius 49:13

Slander 24:4-17, 23-24; 33:58; 60:12; 104:1; punishment for 24:4-5, 23-24

Slaughtering (*dhibḥ*) 2:49, 67, 71, 221; 5:32; 6:118, 119, 121, 142; 7: 141; 14:6; 27:21; 28:4; 37:102

Slave 2:221; 4:3, 24; 16:71, 75; 23:6; 24:31, 32, 33, 58; 30:28; 33:50; 39:29; 70:30; believing slave 2:221; emancipation deal (*mukātabah*) 24:33; 58:3; 90:12-13; female slaves 2:221; 4:25; 24:32, 33; kindness towards 4:36; manumission of 2:177; 4:91; 5:92; marriage 4:3, 24, 25; 24:32

Sleep 2:225; 6:60; 7:4, 97; 18:11, 18; 25:47; 30:23; 36:52; 37:102; 39:42; 68:19; 78:9

Sodom 11:82; 15:74

Sodomy 26:165

Solomon ('a) 2:102; 4:163; 6:84; 21:78-84; 27:15-44; 34:12-21; 38:30-40; and the ant 27:18-19; and the Hoopoe 27:20-28; excellent servant 38:30; hosts 27:17, 18; language of the birds 27:16; nearness to God 38:40; supplication of 27:19; 38:35; tested 38:34; winds subject to him 21:81; 34:12; 38:36; wisdom and knowledge 21:79; 27:15

Speech (*nuṭq*) 21:63, 65; 23:67; 31:6; 37:92; 38:20, 23; 45:25; 51:23; 78:38; articulate speech 55:4; conformity with deeds 2:44; 61:2; tone of 47:30

Speech of the birds 27:16

Sperm (*manī*) 32:8; 75:37; 77:20; 76:2; 86:6, 7; drop of (*nuṭfah*) 16:4; 18:37; 22:5; 23:13, 14; 35:11; 36:77; 40:67; 53:46; 56:58, 59; 75:37; 80:19

Spider 29:41

Spirit (*rūḥ*) 4:171; 15:29; 17:85; 70:4; 78:38; 97:4; Trustworthy Spirit 26:193; Holy Spirit 2:87, 253; 3:39, 42, 45; 5:110; 16:2, 102; 19:17, 21, 24

Spouses (*zawjayn*) 4:35, 128; duties of 2:187, 234, 235, 240; 4:35- 36, 128

Star(s) 67:5; 72:8-9; (*kawkab*) 6:76; 12:4; 24:35; 37:6, 7; 82:2; (*najm*) 6:97; 7:54; 16:12, 16; 22:18; 37:88; 52:49; 53:1; 55:6; 56:75; 77:8; 81:2; 86:3

Steadfastness 2:250; 3:139, 140, 146, 152, 173, 187; 8:12, 15, 46; 9:7; 10:89; 11:112; 14:13; 16:94, 103; 41:30; 42:15; 46:12; 47:7, 35; 58:22; 72:16; 81:28; (*iṣṭibār*) 19:65; 20:132; 54:27

Steadiest of courses 3:186; 31:17; 42:43

Stinginess 3:180; 9:34, 76; 17:100; 25:67; 47:37, 38; 57:24; 92:8

Stoning (*rajm*) 18:20; 26:116; 36:18; 44:20

Submission (*islām, taslīm*) 2:112, 131; 3:20, 83; 4:94, 125; 5:44; 6:14, 71, 79; 10:105; 16:28, 81, 87; 20:111; 27:31; 30:30, 43; 31:22; 40:66; >Muslims

Submission to God 2:157; 4:65; 33:22

Sun 6:78; 18:17, 18; 20:130; 17:78; 18:86, 90; 36:38; 38:32-33; 50:39; 91:1; prostrates before God 22:18; prostration to 27:24; 41:37; sun & moon brought together 75:9; sworn by 91:1; winding up of 81:1

Suicide 2:195; 4:29-30

Supernal Elite (*al-malā al-a'lā*) 37:8; 38:69

Superstitious customs & notions 5:106; 6:21, 93-94, 137-140, 143-4, 157; 7:32, 35, 36, 173-6, 182; 8:31, 54; 10:18, 39, 59-60, 69-70, 95; 11:18-22; 16:116-7; 18:15; 27:83-85; 29:68; 39:32, 59, 60; 40:35, 56, 63, 69-76; 41:40; 42:35; 45:6-9; 61:7-8; 62:5; 68:15-16

Supplications, Qur'ānic 1:5-7; 2:127-129, 201, 250, 285, 286; 3:8, 9, 16, 35-6, 38, 53, 147, 173, 191-194; 4:75; 5:114; 7:23, 47, 126, 151, 155-156; 10:85-86; 12:101; 14:35-41; 17:24, 80; 18:10; 20:25-35, 114; 21:83-4, 87-9; 23:28-9, 97-98, 109, 118; 25:65, 74; 26:83-9; 27:19; 28:16-7, 21-2, 24; 40:7-9, 44; 44:12; 46:15; 59:10; 60:4-5; 66:8, 11; 71:28; 113:1-5; 114:1-6

Suspicion 49:12

Swearing 4:62; 5:53, 89, 106-107; 6:109; 7:49; 9:42, 56, 62, 74, 95-96; 14:44; 16:38; 24:53; 35:42; 58:14, 18; 68:10, 17; false oaths 58:14

Synagogue (*ṣalawāt*) 22:40

Tasnīm 83:27

Ṭawāf 2:159, 200; 22:26, 29; 37:45; 43:71; 52:24; 55:44; 68:19; 76:17, 19; performers of ṭawāf 24:58

Tayammum 4:43; 5:6

Teaching 2:31-32; 20:71; 26:49; 62:2; 96:4; of the Book and wisdom 2:129, 152; without expecting a reward 6:90; 23:73; 25:57; 26:109, 127, 145, 164, 180; 34:47; 36:21; 38:86; 42:23; 52:40.

Temptation (*fitnah*) 2:102; 5:41; 6:53; 8:25, 28, 39, 73; (*nazgh*) 7:200; 12:10; 41:36; (*ṭā'if*) 7:201; (*waswasah*) 2:35-36; 7:20-22; 20:120; 50:16; 114:4-5; courting of 3:7; 9:47, 48

Testimony (*shahādah*) 2:42, 84, 140, 181, 282; 3:18, 52, 64, 86; distortion of 4:135; false witness 22:30; 25:72; hearing, sight & limbs as witnesses 24:24;

36:65; 41:20-22.; hiding 2:140, 175, 283; 3:71; 5:106; rejection of 24:4; testimony against oneself 6:130; 7:37; 9:17; 24:6-9; 26:20; witness to the truth 43:86; women's testimony 2:282

Thamūd, people of 7:73-79; 9:70; 11:61-68; 15:80-84; 23:31; 25:38; 26:141-159; 27:45-53; 40:31; 51:43-45; 54:23-32; 85:17; 89:9

Theft 4:38; 12:70, 73, 77; 60:12; punishment for theft 4:38

Throne 12:100; 27:23, 38, 41, 42

Throne, Divine (*'arsh*) 7:54; 10:3; 11:7; 13:2; 17:42; 18:5; 20:5; 23:86, 116; 25:59; 32:4; 39:68, 75; 40:7; 57:4; 69:17; bearers of 40:7; 69:17

Time (*'aṣr*) 73:1; (*dahr*) 45:24; 76:1; (*waqt*) 7:187; 15:38; God's appointed time 29:5; 71:4; divine 22:47; 32:5; 70:4; long time (*malī*) 19:46; takes its toll upon peoples 57:16; time-keeping signs (*mawāqīt*) 2:189

Tongue(s)/language (*lisān, alsinah*) 3:78; 4:46; 16:62, 116; 20:27; 24:15; 28:34; 33:19; 48:11; 60:2; 75:16; 90:9; diversity of 30:22; witness of 24:24

Torah 2:4, 41, 53, 64, 87, 101; 3:3, 4, 48, 50, 65, 78, 93; affirms the Prophet's genuineness 7:157; bearers of 62:5; corruption of 2:75; 3:78; criterion (*furqān*) 2:53; 21:48; elaboration of all things 6:154; 7:145; foretells the Prophet's ministry 2:76; guidance & mercy 6:154; 7:154; 17:2; 28:43; 32:23; 40:54; illuminating scripture 37:117; Jews' disbelief of it 28:48; Jews' ignorance about it 2:79; 5:43; leader & mercy 11:17; 46:12; light 21:48; observance of 5:68; recitation of 3:93; reminder 21:48

Tradition (*ṭarīqah*) 20:63, 104; 72:16

Trade 2:16, 282; 4:29; 9:24; 24:37; 35:29; 61:10; 62:11; zakāt 2:267

Tranquility (*sakīnah*) 2:248; 9:26

Transgression (*fisq, fusūq*) 2:26, 59, 197, 282; 5:3; 6:49, 121, 145; 17:16; 18:50; 46:20; 49:7, 11; (*i'tidā'*) 2:61, 85, 178, 190, 193-194, 231; 3:112; 5:2, 87, 94, 107

Transgressor(s) (*fasiqūn*) 2:26, 99; 3:82, 110; 5:25, 26, 47, 49, 59, 81; (*'ādūn*) 23:7; 70:31; (*mu'tadūn*) 2:190; 5:87; 6:119; 7:55; 9:10; 10:74; 50:26; 68:12; 83:12, 13; reports brought by 49:6

Traveller 2:177, 184, 185, 215, 283; 5:6; 9:60; kindness to 4:36; rights of 17:26; 30:38; share in the one-fifth (*khums*) 8:41; 59:7

Tribes, the Twelve 2:136, 140; 3:84; 4:163; 7:160

Trinity 4:171; 5:73, 116

Trumpet (*ṣūr*) 6:73; 18:99, 99; 20:102; 23:101; 27:87; 36:49, 51; 39:68; 50:21; 69:13; 78:18; (*nāqūr*) 74:8

Trust (*amānah*) 2:283; 3:75; 4:58; 8:27; 12:54; 23:8; 33:72; 70:32; willingness to trust 9:61

Truth/Real (*al-Ḥaqq*); a nation that guides by the truth 7:159, 181; advent of 17:81; 5:84; 10:76, 94, 108; God is not ashamed of declaring it 33:53; annihilates falsehood, 17:81; 21:18; 34:48; 42:24; 61:8-9; aversion to 43:78; 23:70; basis of judgement 38:22, 26; 39:69, 75; 40:20, 78; belongs to God 28:75; certain truth 56:95; 69:51; comparison between truth and falsehood 13:17; concealment of 2:42, 146, 160, 175; 3:71; confirmed by God with His words 8:7, 8; 42:24; conjecture no substitute for truth 53:28; denial of 6:5, 66; 23:90; 29:68; 34:43; 40:5; 46:7; 50:5; destroys falsehood 21:18; 42:24; difference concerning 2:213; 8:6; disbelief in 2:91; 60:1; disputing the truth 18:56; 40:5; enjoinment of 103:3; eternal truth 10:64; 16:3; followed by the faithful 47:3; guidance to truth 10:35; hurled at falsehood 21:18; 34:48; manifestation of 2:109; mixing with falsehood (*iltibās*) 2:42; 3:71; religion of truth 9:32; 48:28; 61:9; were the truth to follow people's desires 23:71

Truthful (*ṣādiqūn*) 2:111; 3:17; 4:119; 6:143, 146

Truthful One(s) (*ṣiddīq*) 4:69; 19:41, 56; 24:61; 26:101; 57:19

Truthfulness (*ṣidq*) 2:31, 177; 6:115; 10:2; 17:80; 19:50; 21:9; 33:8, 22-24; 39:32-33; 46:16; 47:21

Ṭūbā 13:29

Tubba' 44:37

Ṭuwā, valley of 20:12; 79:16

Twelve chiefs 5:12

Uḥud, Battle of 3:121-122, 138-147, 151-172

Ulu al-'azm, of the apostles 46:35

'Umrah 2:159, 196

Uncircumcised (*ghulf*) 2:88; 4:155

Unfair (*ẓalūm*) 14:34; 33:72

Ungrateful (*kafūr*) 11:9; 17:67; 22:38, 66; 4:16; 35:36; 42:48; 43:15; 76:3, 24

Unity of God (*tawḥīd*) 1:5; 2:22, 133, 164; 3:2, 64; arguments in favour of 2:115, 117; 17:42; 21:22; 22:73; 23:91; 29:61-63; 31:25; 39:38; 40:28; 43:9, 87; 46:4; 52:35-43; 56:57-73

Unlawful 2:174; 4:19; 6:119, 121, 138, 145; 10:59; 16:116; 21:95; making s.th. unlawful 2:174; 3:93; 5:1, 3, 87, 96; 6:119, 121, 138, 139, 140, 143-146,

148, 150, 151; 7:33, 50, 157
Unlawful income (*suḥt*) 5:42, 62, 63
Unseen (*ghayb*) 2:3, 33; 3:44, 179; 5:94; 6:50, 73; known to God and whoever He likes 72:26-27; news of 3:44; 11:49; 12:102; treasures of 6:59
Usury 2:275, 276, 278-280; 3:130; 4:161; 30:39; brought to naught 2:276; derangement of those who take usury 2:275; forbidden 4:161

Vanity (*kibr*) 40:56
Vegetation 6:99; 7:58; 10:24; 18:45; 20:53; 26:7; 48:29; 57:20; 71:17; 78:15;; diversity of 6:141; 13:4; 16:13; 35:27; 39:21
Vicegerent/viceroy/successor (*khalīfah*) 2:30; 6:165; 7:69, 75, 129, 142; 10:14, 73; 15:24; 24:55; 27:62; 35:39; 38:26; 43:60; 57:7; 79:7
Victory/breakthrough (*fatḥ*) 2:89; 3:126; 4:141; 5:52; 8:10; 14:15; 32:28-9; 48:1, 18, 24, 27; 57:10; 61:13; 78:31; 110:1; from God 2:249; 3:13, 126, 160; 8:10, 63; 9:25-6; 10:103; 30:4, 47; victor(s) 5:23, 56
Violence 6:65; 16:81; 17:5; 21:80; 59:14
Virtuous (*muḥsinūn*) 2:58, 112, 195, 236; 3:134; God's love for 2:195; 3:134, 148; 5:13, 93; 16:128; 29:69; blameless 9:91; close to God's mercy 7:56; enhanced 7:161; given good news 22:37; 46:12; reward of 2:112, 195; 3:148, 172; 5:85; 6:84, 154; 9:120; 10:26; 11:115; 12:22, 56, 90; 16:30-2; 18:30; 28:14; 33:29; 37:80, 105, 110, 121, 131; 39:10, 34; 77:44; virtuous women and their reward 33:29
Vow(s) (*nadhr*) 2:270; 3:35; 5:89, 106; 16:91; 19:26; 22:29; 24:22; 68:17; 76:7

Waiting period (*'iddah*) 2:234
War, against God and His Apostle 2:279; 5:33-34; 9:107; punishment 5:33
Warfare 2:279; 4:83; 9:13-4; 47:4, 20; 60:8-9; civil war 49:9-10; spoils (*fay', ghanīmah*) 8:41, 69; 48:15, 19-21; 59:6-10; war secrets 4:83
Warner(s) (*nadhīr, mundhir*) 2:119, 213; Warning 2:6, 35, 48, 123, 235, 281; fate of those who were warned 10:73; 27:58; 37:73
Waste (*farth*) 16:66
Wastefulness 6:141; 7:31; 17:26-7, 29; 25:67; wasteful, brothers of satans 17:27
Wastage 2:143; 3:171, 195; 7:170; 9:120; 11:115; 12:56, 90; 18:30
Water 11:7; 23:18, 50; 25:53; 35:12; 47:15; boiling water (*ḥamīm*) 6:70; 10:4; 18:29; 22:19; 37:67; 38:57; 40:72; 44:46, 48; 47:15; 55:44; 56:42, 54, 93; 78:25; maintenance of its sources 15:22; prayer for (*istisqā'*) 2:60; 7:160; purifying water 8:11; 25:48; revival of the earth with 29:63; 30:24; 43:11; 50:11; sinking of the water table 67:30; source of life 16:65; 21:30; 25:48-9; 29:63; 35:9; 41:39; 45:5
Way of God (*sabīl Allah*) 2:154, 190, 218, 244, 246; 3:157, 168-9, 173-4, 195; 4: 54, 75-6, 95, 100; attempts to make it crooked 7:45, 86; 11:19; 14:3; death in the way of 2:154; 3:157, 169, 195; 22:58; 47:4; hurt suffered in 3:195; 9:120; 29:10; obstruction of 2:217; 3:99; 4:160, 167; pursuit of 40:7; 73:19; 76:29; spending in the way of God 2:195, 261-2, 265; 8:60; 9:34, 60; 47:38; 57:7, 10; ways of the Lord 16:69
Wayfarers 9:112
Wealth/property (*māl*); and children 8:28; 9:55, 69; 17:6, 64; 18:46; amassing of 9:34-35; 28:78; 70:18; 104:2; love of 89:20; 100:8; spending in the way of God 2:3, 195, 215, 219, 254, 261-2, 264-8, 272-4; 3:92, 117, 134; 4:33, 38; used to bar people from God's way 8:36; wrongful consumption of 9:34
Wealthy 2:236; 273; 3:181; 4:6, 135; 9:86, 93; 11:116; 16:92; 17:16; 23:33, 64; 24:22; 34:34; 43:23; 56:45; 59:7; 65:7
Weaning 2:233; 31:14; 46:15
Weapons 4:102
Weights & measures 6:152; 7:85; 12:59, 63, 65, 88; 17:35; 26:181
Widows(s) 2:235, 240
Wife/spouse 2:102, 187, 222, 226, 228, 234, 240; 3:40; Abraham's 11:71; 51:29; Abu Lahab's 111:4-5; accusation of adultery 24:6; adopted son's 33:37; chieftain's wife 12:21, 25, 30, 51; fairness between wives 4:129; Imran's 3:35; Job's 38:44; Lot's wife 7:83; 11:81; 15:60; 27:57; 29:32-3; 66:10; Noah's 66:10; noble spouses 56:34; Pharaoh's wife 28:9; 66:11; Prophet's wives >Wives of the Prophet (ṣ); rights of 2:228; son's wife 4:23; Zayd's 33:37; Zechariah's 3:40; 19:5, 8; 21:90
Wine 2:219; 4:43; 5:90-1; 12:41; 16:67; 47:15; 56:18; 83:25-8; wine & gambling 2:219; 5:90-1
Wisdom (*ḥikmah*) 4:129, 151, 231, 251, 269; 3:48, 81, 164; 4:54, 113; 5:110; 16:125; 17:39; 31:12; 33:34; 38:20; 43:63; 62:2; far-reaching wisdom 54:5
Wise (*ulu al-nuhā*) 20:54, 128; (*dhū ḥijr*) 89:5; > Intellect, possessors of; possessors of insight 3:13; 24:44; 59:2; remnant of the wise (*ulu al-baqiyyah*)

11:116; right-minded (*al-rāshidūn*) 49:7

Witness(es) (*ashhād, shuhadā'*) 2:133, 143, 282; 3:53, 81, 98-9, 140; 4:15, 33, 79, 41, 135, 159, 161; integrity of 65:2; taking witness 2:204, 282; 4:6, 15; 11:54; 16:91; 18:51; 65:2

Witnessing 11:103; 22:28; 24:2; 27:49; 83:21; bearing witness 3:18, 52, 64, 81, 86; 4:166; 5:111; 6:19; 7:172; 9:107; 21:61; 24:24; 36:65; 41:20-2; 43:19; 59:11; 63:1; 65:2

Wives of the Prophet (ṣ) 4:129; 24:11-7; 33:6, 28-34, 37, 50-53, 55, 59; 66:1-5; forbidden to remarry 33:53; mothers of the faithful 33:6; superior station 33:32

Women (*nisā'*) 2:49, 178, 187, 221, 23, 231, 235; 3:14, 42, 61; chaste women 4:24-5; 5:5; 24:4, 23; 33:35; child-bearing 65:3, 6; detention (on charge of adultery) 4:15; desertion by husband 4:128; divorce 2:226-233, 236-7, 241; 4:130; 65:1-7; dowry 4:4; dress 24:31, 60; 24:31; 33:53, 55, 59; *īlā* 2:226; inheritance 2:240; 4:7, 11-2, 19, 127, 176; *maḥārim* 24:31; 33:55; maintenance 2:233; 65:6-7; marital discord 2:229; 4:35, 128-9; marriage 2:221, 232, 235; 4:3-4, 22-25, 127; 33:49; men, managers of their affairs 4:34; menses 2:222, 228; 65:4; misconduct 4:34; modesty 24:31; 33:35; period of waiting (*'iddah*) 2:226, 228, 231-2; 33:49; 65:1-2, 4, 6; pregnancy 2:228; 3:47; 7:189; 31:14; 46:15; 65:4, 6; proposing to widows 2:235; socializing, rules of proper conduct 24:31, 60; 33:55; suckling 2:233; 4:23; 65:6; temporary marriage (*mut'ah*) 4:24; testimony of 2:282

Word(s) **of God** (*kalām, kalimah, qawl*) 2:75; 3:39, 45; 4:171; confirm the truth 10:82; 42:24; belief in them 7:158; inexhaustible 18:109; 31:27; unchanging 6:34, 115; 10:64; 18:27; 48:15; 50:29

Works; failed works 2:217, 264, 266; 3:22; gone awry 47:1, 4, 8; 18:104; good works 21:73, 90

World (*dunyā*) 2:114, 130, 200-1, 220; 3:152, 185; deceptions of 6:130; 7:51; 10:70; 31:33; 35:5; 45:35; 57:20; life of this world 2:85, 204, 212; love of 3:14; 9:24; 11:15-6; 13:26; 17:18; 28:79; 38:32; 53:29; 75:20; 76:27; 89:20; parables of 3:117; 10:24; 18:45; 57:20; wares of delusion 3:185; 9:38; 57:20; world and the Hereafter 2:217, 220; 3:14-15, 22, 45, 56, 185; 4:74, 77, 134

Worship (*'ibādah*) 2:114; 4:172; 7:206; 21:19-20; 22:11; 34:40; 40:60; 96:10-6; jinn, worship of 34:41; nocturnal devotions 3:113; 17:79; 25:64; 32:16; 50:40; 51:17-8; 52:49; 73:1-9; 76:26; worship, a divine prerogative 1:5; 2:21; 7:29, 70; 10:104; worship of Satan 19:44; 36:60; 39:17

Writing 2:79, 282; 3:52; 5:83; 7:157; 9:120-1; 10:21; 17:58; 19:79; 21:94, 104; 29:48; 33:12; 43:19, 80; 52:41; 54:53; 58:22; 68:1, 47; 83:9, 20; taking down (*iktitāb*) 25:5

Wrongdoer(s) (*ẓālimūn*); God does not guide them 5:51; 6:144; 9:19, 109; 28:50; 46:10; 61:7; 62:5; allies of one another 45:19; beyond redemption 10:54; 39:47; cursed 7:44; 11:18, 44; 40:52; 23:41; 71:28; deny God's signs 6:33; 29:49; deprived of felicity 6:135; 12:23; 28:37; deprived of intercession 23:27; 40:18; destruction 6:45, 47; 14:13; 15:78-9; 18:59; friends of one another 6:129; 45:19; punishment of 3:117; 7:165; 10:52; 11:67, 83, 94; 14:22; respite given 14:42, 44; retribution 5:29; 7:41; 12:75; 21:29; 39:51; 59:17; Satan and his offspring their guardians 18:49

Wrongdoing (*ẓulm*); wrong done to oneself 2:57, 231; 3:117, 135; 4:64, 97, 110; 7:23, 160, 177; 9:36, 70; 10:44, 54; 11:101; 14:45; 16:28, 33, 90, 118; 18:35; 27:44; 28:16; 29:40; 30:9; 34:19; 35:32; 37:113; 65;1

Wuḍu 4:43; 5:6

Yathrib 33:13

Youth 10:83; 12:36, 62; 18:10, 13, 60, 62; 21:60; youths of paradise (*ghilmān*) 52:24; 56:17; 76:19

Zakāt 2:34, 43, 83, 110, 177, 215, 264, 277; non-payment of 9:34; 107:7

Zanjabīl 76:17

Zaqqūm, tree of 37:62-66; 44:43-46; 56:52-56

Zayd b. Ḥārithah 33:5, 37-38, 40

Zechariah ('a) 3:37-41; 6:85; 19:2-11; 21:89-90; supplication of 3:38; 19:3-6; 21:89, 90

Zygote (*'alaq, 'alaqah*) 22:5; 96:2

Printed in the USA
CPSIA information can be obtained
at www.ICGtesting.com
LVHW082329030424
776388LV00010B/328

9 781955 725293